基于域外文献的
南方汉语研究论集

国家社科基金重大项目『海外珍藏汉语文献与南方明清汉语研究』成果

JIYU YUWAI WENXIAN DE
NANFANG HANYU YANJIU LUNJI

李　炜　庄初升　主编

 商务印书馆
创于1897　The Commercial Press

2019 年 · 北京

图书在版编目（CIP）数据

基于域外文献的南方汉语研究论集/李炜,庄初升
主编.—北京:商务印书馆,2019
ISBN 978-7-100-16961-5

Ⅰ.①基… Ⅱ.①李…②庄… Ⅲ.①汉语方言—
文集 Ⅳ.①H17-53

中国版本图书馆 CIP 数据核字(2018)第 296883 号

基于域外文献的南方汉语研究论集
李 炜 庄初升 主编

商 务 印 书 馆 出 版
(北京王府井大街 36 号 邮政编码 100710)
商 务 印 书 馆 发 行
北京新华印刷有限公司印刷
ISBN 978-7-100-16961-5

2019 年 10 月第 1 版 开本 787×1092 1/16
2019 年 10 月北京第 1 次印刷 印张 42
定价:118.00 元

序 言

　　汉语作为一种典型的孤立语，汉字作为一种意音文字，与西方的语言文字大相径庭，很早便引起西方宗教界和知识界的兴趣。明末来华的天主教耶稣会士罗明坚和利玛窦 1583—1588 年间在广东肇庆编纂了《葡汉辞典》，这是现存的第一部中西词典，也是最早以罗马字母（又称"拉丁字母"）系统拼写汉语的尝试。利玛窦 1605 年为四篇汉字文章加了罗马字拼音并正式刊行，称为《西字奇迹》。另一位耶稣会士金尼阁 1626 年出版《西儒耳目资》，用罗马字如实描写了当时通行的官话的语音。17 世纪陆续来华的天主教传教士迪亚兹、卫匡国、卜弥格、安文思、何大化、万济国和李明等都用罗马字为当时的官话注音，也留下了弥足珍贵的官话语音文献。与此同时，菲律宾的西班牙天主教传教士也编写了一些汉语文献，其中有一份用罗马字注音的闽南话–西班牙语对照词表。

　　罗常培先生于 1930 年发表《耶稣会士在音韵学上的贡献》，把《西字奇迹》和《西儒耳目资》的拼音方案称为"利–金方案"，并予以高度评价：第一，用罗马字分析汉字的音素，使向来被人认为繁杂的反切，变成简易的东西；第二，用罗马字注明字的字音，使现在对于当时的普遍音，仍可推知大概；第三给中国音韵学研究，开出一条新路，使当时的音韵学者如方以智、杨选杞、刘献廷等，受了很大的影响。

　　现在大家已经知道，第一部正式刊行的汉语语法是万济国 1682 年于福州写定，1703 年于广州首版（其时作者已离世 16 年）的《华语官话语法》（*Arte de la Lengua Mandarina*）。这部语法书近些年才有柯蔚南（W. South Coblin）先生的英译本和姚小平、马又清先生的中译本，在汉语语言学界产生广泛的影响。

　　清康熙后期由于礼仪之争而引发全面禁教，传教士在华的活动几乎销声匿迹。到了 1814 年，英国新教传教士马士曼在赛兰坡出版了《中国言法》（*Elements of Chinese Grammar*），1815—1823 年间，另一位英国传教士马礼逊在澳门出版了第一部汉英–英汉对照字典《华英字典》，西方人编写、出版有关汉语的论著，又开始活跃起来。特别是鸦片战争以后，新教传教士、殖民地官员等蜂拥来到中国沿海及华人众多的东南亚，编印了数以百计的汉语方言文献，其中就有大批罗马字注音的圣经、辞书和课本等，涉及的方言区有粤、闽、客、吴、赣和官话等，涉及的方言点有香港、广州、潮州、梅县、厦门、漳州、福州、兴化（今莆田）、建宁（今建瓯）、邵武、海南、温州、台州、宁波、绍兴、杭州、苏州、上海、汉口、成都、青岛、登州（今蓬莱等地）、献县、北京等几十个，大部分都在南方地区。

海外学者较早利用传教士、汉学家的汉语文献来研究早期的汉语，如 1913 年 Johann Heinrich Vömel 在德国莱比锡大学的博士论文 *Der Hakka-dialekt* 是有关客家方言的第一部博士论文，就利用到巴色会传教士大量的客家方言文献。1915—1926 年间高本汉的《中国音韵学研究》，用到的三十多个汉语方言点的语料，除了他自己亲自调查所得，也有相当部分来自传教士文献。最近几十年来，我们比较熟知的海外学者如罗杰瑞、柯蔚南、桥本万太郎、余霭芹、杨福绵、马西尼、张洪年、柯理思、曹茜蕾、贝罗贝、古屋昭弘、高田时雄、秋谷裕幸等等，也都在上述学术领域做出自己的贡献。

罗常培先生于 20 世纪 30 年代初撰写《厦门音系》时，已经充分注意和利用英国传教士麦都思、杜嘉德、甘为霖的闽南方言文献。1957 年黄典诚先生的《建瓯方言初探》一文便主要是利用闽北韵书《建州八音》和 1922 年上海圣公会出版的建瓯话《新约全书》来勾勒建瓯方言的概貌；1990 年李如龙先生的《建瓯话的声调》一文，除了利用《建州八音》的音读材料之外，还引用了 1901 年 W. C. White 编写的 *A Chinese-English Dictionary of the Kien-Ning Dialect*（《华英建宁方言字典》），以描述建瓯方言声调二百年间的发展演变。最近几十年，比较早而且比较系统地搜集、整理和研究海外早期汉语方言文献的学者是游汝杰先生，他于 2002 年出版《西洋传教士汉语方言学著作书目考述》一书，是有关汉学家、传教士汉语方言文献的版本、目录集成，具有很高的参考价值。

迄今为止，我们两位搜集、整理和研究海外汉语方言文献都已经接近二十年。李炜较早对琉球官话文献进行语言学研究，在《中国语文》等刊物发表了多篇论文，与学生合作的《清代琉球官话课本语法研究》一书于 2015 年由北京大学出版社出版。庄初升对明末以来传教士、汉学家汉语方言文献广泛涉猎，特别是对巴色会传教士的新界客家方言文献尤其熟悉，与学生合作的《19 世纪香港新界的客家方言》于 2014 年由广东人民出版社出版。近十年来，我们主持的重要科研项目几乎都跟上述学术领域直接相关，如李炜主持的 2007 年度国家社科基金一般项目"清代琉球官话系列课本语法研究"和 2012 年度国家社科基金重大项目"海外珍藏汉语文献与南方明清汉语研究"等，庄初升主持的 2007 年度国家社科基金一般项目"从巴色会文献看 19 世纪香港新界的客家方言"、2013 年度国家社科基金一般项目"明末以来西方人创制的汉语罗马字拼音方案研究"和 2014 年度国家社科基金重大项目"海内外客家方言的语料库建设和综合比较研究"等，说明海外汉语方言文献已经引起学界的高度重视，成为汉语语言学的一个重点和热点。

　　《基于域外文献的南方汉语研究论集》一书是 2012 年度国家社科基金重大项目"海外珍藏汉语文献与南方明清汉语研究"的前期成果之一。该书收录了利用海外珍藏汉语文献对早期粤、闽、客、吴及南方官话进行研究的一些代表性成果，其中有我们两位及学生的拙作，更多的是海内外前辈学者、同行学者的大作。全书一共收录论文 36 篇，其中粤语 7 篇、闽语 9 篇、客家话 4 篇、吴语 6 篇、南方官话 10 篇，都已经在海内外各种期刊或集刊公开发表过，涉及语音、词汇、语法等汉语语言学本体研究的方方面面。论文的作者以及首发期刊都积极配合该书的出版工作，在此致以诚挚的谢意。限于篇幅，诸如罗常培《耶稣会士在音韵学上的贡献》等一些长篇大论无法收录，实在非常遗憾。

　　所收论文在海内外不同期刊或集刊发表时，体例各异，但是，这些论文大都是这一领域的重要文献，广被征引，为了保存原貌，便于以后引用，我们与本书的责任编辑王飙编审商定，正文的文字、体例基本不变，但对原文的编校错误作必要的修改；只对参考文献和注释作了一些体例统一的工作。

　　《基于域外文献的南方汉语研究论集》一书得以在商务印书馆出版，我们要特别感谢周洪波总编的大力支持。责任编辑王飙编审做了大量的编校工作，认真严谨，一丝不苟，令人敬佩。中山大学中文系专职副研究员黄燕旋博士，以及在学的研究生张坚、洪妍、吴若凡、汤畅等，协助为这样一本样式各异、图表众多、符号繁杂的图书进行清样校对，也付出不少劳动，在此一并致谢。

　　因为我们的视野和精力所限，该书很有可能挂一漏万，没能把更多具有代表性的优秀成果呈现出来，这是要请学界朋友鉴谅的。

李炜　庄初升

2018 年 10 月 31 日于中山大学

目 录

早期粤语中的变调现象

张洪年

粤语声调系统四声九调，看似复杂，但就变调而言，与吴闽等其他方言相比，反较简单。流行广州、香港、澳门一带的粤语，只有两个变调，一个是高平变调，一个是高升变调。不少学者对这两种变调现象作过种种研究，不过这些研究主要着眼在共时性的描述，对现代粤语中的变调现象进行语音、语法、语义、语用分析。[1] 其实这两种变调现象，由来已久。从现存材料来看，十九世纪的香港粤语中已呈现变调。本文选取在香港编印的 *Cantonese Made Easy* 一书前后两版（1888，1907），按引言及正文举例，对一百年前的高平高升变调，作初步的探讨和分析。

壹 关于 *Cantonese Made Easy*（CME）

1.1 CME 是一本粤语教科书，为学习粤语的英语人士编写，书首开宗明义，有简略数语，说明 CME 的内容和形式：

Cantonese Made Easy: A book of simple sentences in the Cantonese dialect, with free and literal translations, and directions for the rendering of English grammatical forms in Chinese.

全书分十五课，由日常简单用语到有关家庭、宗教、交通、买卖、上学、看病各种对话，短短二三十句话语，不但反映出当时香港社会的现状，同时也记录了一百多年前香港粤语的实况。每课课文分为四栏，一页两栏，左右两页对照。第二栏是汉语，第三栏是拼音，一、四两栏都是翻译，最左一栏是意译，最右一栏是逐字直译，也就是简介中所谓的 free 和 literal 两种翻译。课文之前有四五十页的发音导论，详细描述粤语中声韵调的特点。书后附有比较详细的粤语文法，从词类到句型，分细节讨论。

全书编写以务实为主，课文浅显实用。利用拼音教发音，利用翻译显示中英文遣词造句的异同。文法部分尤其翔实，多列例句，说明粤语中特别的句构词法。对初学粤语的人来说，CME 是一本十分有用的教科书。对研究粤语的人来说，CME 所记所载更是不可多得的历史语料。

1.2 CME 的作者是 J. Dyer Ball（1847—1919），Ball 在中国生长，通晓多种中国方言，任香港高等法院传译。当时的报章 *Academy* 在 1884 年一月十二日载有一段对 Ball 的简介，今移录如下：

> Born in China, of European parentage, favored with exceptional advantages for the acquisition of the dialects of China, having a natural gift for this particular work, and being employed in Her Majesty's Civil Service as Interpreter for the Supreme Court, he [Ball] has had every opportunity to gain an accurate knowledge of Cantonese.

这一段文字也见于 CME1888 书后 Advertisements 部分，页 II—III。Ball 对中国文化及语言热诚爱好，撰有多种著作。除 CME 外，还有东莞方言、香山方言、顺德方言，均有专书著作。以 CME 最受欢迎。详见《粤方言研究书目》。

1.3 CME 前后四版。据第二版所载首版前序，第一版当于 1883 年之前出版，第二版是增订本，1888 年由香港 China Mail Office 出版，序文年份是 1887 年，第三版是 1907 年由 Kelly and Walsch, Ltd. Singapore-Hong Kong-Shanghai-Yokohama 出版，序文年份是 1902 年，第四版是 1924 年出版，同出版公司。我手上资料只有第二和第三版，两书出版前后相差 19 年，但根据书前序文日期，相差则仅 15 年。第二版卷首说明这是修订增补本（Revised and enlarged）。第三版对第二版则作更进一步的增订。修订部分，尤以声调为主。序文说：

> ...attention has been most fully called to those most important tones—the variants which form a part of the very language itself...（页 XII）

换言之，第三版对所谓的变调现象描述更为详尽。

贰　CME 所记录的粤语声调

2.1 粤声九调，平上去各分上下二类，即所谓阴阳二分。而入声分上中下三种，上中即上阴入、下阴入，而下入即阳入。CME 标调形式如下：在音节四角标平上去入。半圆符号标上调式（即阴调）；半圆加杠标下调式（即阳调）。中入则在音节右下角加圈作记。举例如下，例字取自 CME1888 页 XXXIV, XXXVEY, XXXVII。

上平：东 ₌tung　上上：董 ʿtung　上去：冻 tung⊃　上入：急 kap₎　中入：甲 káp。

下平：容 ₌yung　下上：勇 ʿyung　下去：用 yung²　下入：及 k'ɑp₂

2.2 粤语变调，CME 称之为 Variant tones，分两种。但 1888 及 1907 两版对两

种变调的描述和标记都稍有不同，现分述如下：

（一）第一种变调是高平变调，1988 版称为中平调 "medial upper even tone"。平声分上下或阴阳，所谓 upper even tone 就是指上平调，而由上平转化来的变调就是第二个上平调 "the second upper even tone"，合名为中平 "medial even tone"，前加 "medial" 以示区别。但 1907 年的 CME 则直呼为上平变音 "second or higher upper even tone"。这里用的 "higher"，是描述上平变音的音色，和中平调的 "medial" 所指并不一样，上平变调调值较高。Ball 在 1888 页 XXV 中说中平调的特色是：

> ...a slight shriek, differing not only in musical pitch (being nearer to the 上平 ... in that respect than to the 下平 ...) from the other two Even Tones, but also in the manner of its pronunciation, it having a certain quickness or jerkiness of pronunciation.

根据这样的描述，中平调或上平变音的音色高而急。1907 书指出上平下平皆降调（页 XXVII），上平高降，下平低降，上平变音较上平为高，调型似是高平。标调形式，1888 书是在字左下角加小圈，如 "猫" ｡máu，"鎗" ｡ts'öng（页 XXV），而 1907 书则除左下角加圈表示读高调外，还常在字右上角加星号，表示变调，如 "街" ｡kái*，"多" ｡to*（页 92）。不过两书变调标法，偶有不一致的地方，如 1888 书中 "仙" 字（当 "cent" 解），原调阴平，今标 ｡sin*，当读上平变调，有星号而无小圈（页 19）。又如 1907 书中 "听" 字（"听日" 即 "明日"）只加小圈，不注星号：｡t'ing（页 23），用时不得不多加小心。

上举各例都是从上平转读上平变音，但也有的字是从其他声调转读高平变调，而两书标调方式并不一样。例如：伯爷公：1888 pák｡ ｡ye* ｡kung（页 40），1907 pák｡ ｡ye* ｡kung（页 40）。"爷" 字本调是阳平，现加星号当读变调，但究竟读上平 ｡ye 还是读上平变音 ｡ye*？两书似乎有别，而更有意思的是 "公" 字，1888 书维持原调 ｡kung，而 1907 则改读 ｡kung，虽然没有加星号，但显然是上平变音，两书读音不同。

（二）第二种变调是高升变调。CME 称之为 "the Third Rising Tone"，第三种上声，以别于原来的上上和下上。1907 书页 XXXI 对这个变调有较详尽的描述：

> ...this has a distinct fall and a long rise, in fact, being the most prolonged of any of the rising tones, and much emphasis is thrown into the voice on its recovery from the fall, increasing in its volume as it rises to a good crescendo and dying away at the end again.

这个变调是先降而后高升，似乎和今日的高升变调不完全一样。今日的高升变调是全高升，并没有先降的部分。究竟 Ball 的描述是否完全正确？还是他所谓的先降只是强调变调当从低开始？现在很难确定。发生高升变调的字，原调可能是其他任何一种声调。但声调不同，字的用法也不一样。1988 书页 XXVI 中说：

> The Third Rising Tone differs from all the other tones in this that every word that is used in this tone belongs originally to another tone and is generally likewise used in this other tone as well nearly all the tones contribute words which are occasionally, or often, as the case may be, used in the Third Rising Tone.

Ball 指出最常发生高升变调的字是名词，尤其是原属下去（阳去）的常用名词。下平（阳平）转读高升的字也很常见，上去（阴去）的字偶然也有变高升。上上（阴上）和下上（阳上）变化的字则较少见，上平（阴平）的字则绝无仅有。另一方面，Ball 在 1888 和 1907 两书都强调说明：高升变调只发生在口语交谈之中，读书音中并无此现象，同时变调的字往往是独用词；和其他的字连用，则恢复原调。例如"渡"字原调是阳去，单用则读高升变调 ˈtò，连成词"渡船"的"渡"读原调阳去 tò²。由此可见变调不只是一种声调变化的现象，变调其实和字词的用法有关。

高升变调的标调形式，两书不同。1888 书在字右上角标星号表示变调，字左上角加 [符号标明第三上声的读法：ˈ□*，到了 1907 年的修订本时，Ball 不但用星号表示变调，而且按各字原调把标志放在字的四角，属阴调的字，标志是 [；属阳调的字，标志是 ˏ，也就是把原来阳调标记 ˏ 颠倒过来。

2.3 CME 前后两书，注变调的字亦颇有出入。有 1888 书不作变调的字，1907 书读变调，亦有倒过来的例子，十数年间，变化颇大。不过有的前后不同的例子，并不反映读音的变化，而只是 1888 书标调错误，1907 书加以改正而已，现分别举例说明如下：

①粤语中有不少阳上变去的例子，但口语读书音变化不同，如"坐"、"重"各字口语是阳上，读书音是阳去。1888 书有时把口语的阳上误标作高升变调，1907 书则一一改正。由此可见阳上和高升变调调值颇近，因而发生标调错误的现象。例如：

坐：得闲嚟坐 ˈtsʻo* （1888：页96）→ ˏtsʻo （1907：页104）[2]
重：加重严办 ˈchʻung* （1888：页13）→ ˏchʻung （1907：页13）[3]
抱：叫奶妈嚟抱佢 ˈpʻò* （1888：页15）→ ˏpʻò （1907：页15）

②粤语动词可以利用高升变调来表示完成体貌，详见下文。不过 1888 书中有的变调例子，于文意不合，1907 书改为原调。例如：

过：你应承交千八银过我「kwo* （1888：页19）→ kwo² （1907：页19）

这一句是应承句，交钱动作还未发生，不当用完成体变调。所以 1907 书的改动是正确的。

③粤语常利用变调作构词手段，用高升变调标名词（详见下文）。1888 书有时忽略这样变调的例子，误以为原调本如此，1907 书改正。如：对对（作"对对子"解）tui² ‘tui（1888：页 35）→ töü² töü¹* （1907：页 35）。[4] 第一个"对"字是动词，读阴去原调，第二个"对"字是名词，作"对子"解，由阴去变高升。1888 书标作阴上，误。1907 书改为高升变调。不过也有一些例子是 1907 书改错了。例如："渡"（作"渡船"解）「tò* （1888：页 29）→ tò²（1907：页 29）。"渡"当动词或和其他字连用，读阳去，如"渡船"tò² ͺshün（1907：页 29）。不过"渡"字单用作"渡船"解，则读高升变调。1888 和 1907 两书在前言部分都举此字为例，说明变调的现象（见 1888 页 XXVII，1907 页 XXIX）。由此可见 1907 书把「tò* 改作 tò² 是错了。

1907 书的变调改动例子颇多，虽偶有错误，但总体而言是补订 1888 书的不足。作者 Ball 在修订时用功辛勤，用心良苦，也就是说 1907 书中记载的变调现象，更能正确地反映二十世纪初口语中的实况。

叁 关于 CME 记录的高平变调和高升变调

3.1 高平变调

一 1907 的 CME 书中一共记载了 114 个高平变调的例子，而 1888 书中只有 31 例，相比之下，1907 书多了约四倍，十数年间，变化似乎颇大。不过 1888 书列 31 例，其中三分之二都在书首练习发音部分，而且有的例字和后文实例不合。如"猫"字是阴平调，1888 卷首标作ͺmáu（页 XXV），但同书页 77 则作 ͺmáu，前者是高平变调，后者是阴平原调。而 1907 书则前后同调，皆作ͺmáu* （页 XXVII，页 83），其他例子如"鎗"、"香"皆然。[5] 由此可知 1888 书在处理高平变调时，并不一致，错漏的地方，1907 书中加以订正。换言之，同书两版之间的四倍差异，有的可能只是改正错误，并不代表语言真正的变化。

现举一些两书正文中都作高平变调的例子。标音后括号内的数码表示原书页码。

	原调	CME1888	CME1907
一文	阳平	ͺman* （19）	ͺman（19）
一仙	阴平	ͺsin* （19）	ͺsin（19）

		CME1888	CME1907
货<u>仓</u>	阴平	ₒts'ong（23）	ₒts'ong（23）
乌<u>蝇</u>	阳平	ₒying*（58）	ₒying*（61）
多	阴平	ₒto（25）	ₒto（25）
<u>乞</u>儿	阳平	ₒyi*（99）	ₒyi*（106）
伯<u>爷</u>	阳平	ₒye*（41）	ₒye*（41）
雨<u>微</u>	阳平	ₒmei*（9）	ₒmei*（9）

高平变调字的来源以阴平居多，阳平也有一些。上举各例，以阳平来源为主。这些字今日仍读高平，印证 CME 两版，可见变调读法远在一百多年前已经通行。

再举一些例子，由一读而变为二读。1888 书中不变调，而 1907 书中则原调变调并列。由此可见这些词的变调读法是在二十世纪初才开始流行。

	CME1888	CME1907
听<u>日</u>	ꞈt'ing（23）	ꞈt'ing（或 ₒt'ing）（23）
月<u>中</u>	ꞈchung（65）	ꞈchung（或 ₒchung*）（70）
巡理<u>厅</u>	ꞈt'eng（33）	ꞈt'eng（或 ₒt'eng）（33）
出<u>街</u>	ꞈkái（9）	ꞈkái（或 ₒkái）（9）
<u>孙</u>女	ꞈsün（15）	ₒsün（或 ꞈsün）（15）
两仔<u>爷</u>	ꞈye（40）	ꞈye（或 ₒye）（41）
一张<u>刀</u>	ꞈtò（53）	ₒtò*（或 ꞈtò）（55）

两读标音，1907 书中分两种处理方法。一种是先列原调，再举变调，放在括号中，如"巡理厅"的"厅"字。一种是先列变调，再用括号标举原调，如"刀"字。列举次序先后，究竟有什么不同，书中并没有解释，我们也许可以认为放在前边的代表一般读法，放在括号中的比较少用。以"刀"字为例，1907 书中有两读，先列高平变调，高降原调放在括号中。翻检同书其他"刀"字用例，往往只标变调一读，如 CME1907 页 55 有"一把刀"，"刀"字只标变调 ₒtò*。可是由高降转读高平的变化过程，已接近完成，当时读法应以变调为常。另一方面，如"巡理厅"magistry 的"厅"字，旧读原调，新读二调，显然正由高降转向高平，但变调放在括号中，似乎当时读法还是以原调为常。不过同书有"厅"字单用，当"sitting room"解，旧读原调 ꞈt'eng（CME1888：页 52），新读变调 ₒt'eng（CME1907：页 53），而且只有一读，前后两例并举，可见虽同一"厅"字，变调与否，因词而异，变调发生在个别字词身上，在词汇中逐渐扩散。

（二）高平变调的字，绝大部分是名词，而且约有一半是物件名，四分之一和人有关。指人的词尤以亲属词占多数。1907 书中增补亲属词汇，有很多都是读高平变调，如"尊翁"的"翁"。yung*（页141），"表兄"的"兄"。hing*（页143），"舍亲"的"亲"。ts'an（或。ts'an*）（页144），"千金"的"金"。kam*（页141），"二奶"的"奶"。nái*（页141），例子很多。

3.2 高升变调。高升变调的例子，1888的CME一共有101条，而1907书有162条。两书相比，后者多了一半有余，增添量相当可观。

（一）高升变调的来源，以阳平字居多，其他上去入的字也有转读高升。1907书中的162例，来源分配如下：阳平，低降调，73例，占总数45%。阳去52例，阳入4例，它们调值相同，都是中平调，可以合并，共56例，占总数34%。阴去18例，阴入3例，它们的调值也相同，可以合并，共21例，占总数13%。阳上，低升调，12例，占总数8%。

（二）高升变调的字以名词居多，占六成。其间又以物件词占一半，亲属词次多，占16%。现举一些高升变调的例子如下：

	CME1888		CME1907
药<u>丸</u>	⌈yün*（ ͺyün）（25）	→	ͺyün*（25）
绵<u>羊</u>	ͺyöng	→	ͺyöng*（ ͺyöng）（61）
<u>绳</u>	ͺshing	→	ͺshing*（17）

第一例的"丸"字，1888书已有二读，但阳平原调放在括号中，到了1907书，只留下变调的读法。第二例的"羊"字，1888书只有阳平一读，1907书则并列原调变调，而且变调先行，原调反放在括号中。第三例的"绳"字，1888书只有阳平原调，而1907书亦只有一读，但是高升变调。高升变调在当时显然是一个相当普遍的现象，而且有外来词亦转读变调的例子，如CME1888嗻呢"minute"ͺmin ͺni（页64），在CME1907标为。min* ⌐nei（页68）。虽然书中并没有在"呢"字侧加变调标记，但由阴平改读阴上，正是外来词常见的读法。[6]

不过同书也有个别例子呈现由变调改读原调的变化。例如：CME1888菠<u>萝</u>⌈lo*（ ͺlo）（页11）在CME1907标为 ͺlo（页11）。1907书只标阳平一读，并在同页加注说明"萝"字以读原调为宜，也就是说作者显然知道另有变调读法，不过时至1907，变调已不复流行。"菠萝"的"萝"今日仍读阳平，要不是有1888的记载，我们根本不知道一百年前"菠萝"可以说成 ͺpo ⌐lo*。

3.3 变调的演变过程。从音变的过程来说，我们可以有三个时间据点：T₁ T₂ T₃。T₁是在未变之前，T₃在已变之后，T₂是未变体和在变体并存交替的转换期。假如以X代表原调，Y代表变调，我们可以把变调的演变三阶段图解如下。

$$T_1 \qquad\qquad T_2 \qquad\qquad T_3$$
$$X \quad \rightarrow \quad X \sim Y \quad \rightarrow \quad Y$$

CME 前后两版（1888 和 1907）中记载的各种变调例字，正好记录了这三段变化的过程，有的字在 1888 书中还是原调读法，也就是在 T_1 阶段，不过在接着的十数年间，声调开始变化，步伐较快的，到了 1907 书已转化完成，只留下变调一读，也就是到达 T_3 阶段，变化较慢的，在 1907 书中是原调变调并存，是 T_2 阶段。也有一些例子显示出变调早在 1888 之前已经发生，1888 书反映两读交替的 T_2 阶段，到了 1907 才转化完成，属于 T_3。

肆　因变调而产生词性变化等现象

粤语中高平和高升变调，似乎是两个独立的声调变化现象。但细究之下，高平高升变调有一些共同的词性变化规则，现分述如下。

4.1　变调表名词化。变调的字，不论是高平或高升，都以名词居多。CME 书前介绍高平变调部分，列举一些高平高降对比的例子，高平是名词，高降是动词或形容词，前后两版皆如此。见 1888：页 XXXIII，1907：页 XLII。

膏　ₒkò "plaster"（名）　　　　：　高　ˎkò "high"（形）

栏　ₒlán "market"（名）　　　　：　躝　ˎlán "to crawl"（动）

厅　ₒtʻeng "a court"（名）　　　：　听　ˎtʻeng "to hear"（动）

笺　ₒtsin "note paper"（名）　：　煎　ˎtsin "to fry"（动）

猫　ₒmáu "cat"（名）　　　　　：　蹋　ˎmɑu "to squat down"（动）

英　ₒying "a salad"（名）　　　：　英　ˎying "superior"（形）

当然也有一些例外，如"婼"to scorch（动）作高平 ₒnung；又如"乡"village，"丁香"的"香"clove 都是名词，前者读高降 ˎhöng，后者读高平 ₒhöng。高升变调的例子如：

对 "antithetical sentences"（名）ᶜtui　　：　对 "to construct"（动）tui² （1888
（1888 页 35）[7] töü² （1907 页 35）　　　页 35）töü² （1907 页 35）

话 "patois, dialect, language"（名）　　　：　话 "to speak"（动）wɑ² （1907 页
wɑ⁵* （1907 页 XXXII）　　　　　　XXXII）

犯 "prisoner"（名）ᶠfán* （1888 页　　　：　犯 "to commit crime" [8] fán²
31）fán⁵* （1907 页 31）

买办 "comprador"（名）ˈpán*（1888   : 办 "to sentence"（动）pán²（1888

页 23）pán²*（1907 页 23）   页 13）pán²（1907 页 13）

上面列举的例子，高平和高升两类情形稍有不同。高升的例子是一字两用，很清楚看得出是名动相对，以变调区分。但高平一类，因为材料有限，同音对比的例子难找，所以只能多举同音异字的例子，不过高平高降分工，还是十分清楚。动词或形容词保持原调，名词转读变调。以变调表名词的这种用法，除了单词外，在一些复合词中也看得出痕迹，而且以高升变调为主。上文举的"买办"即一例。CME1907 页 100 另举一例：行船 ˌshün "to go a voyage"，行<u>船嘅</u> ˌshün* "a sailor"。"行船"是动宾结构，"船"字不变调，"行船嘅"是"行船嘅人"之省，变调表名化。其他例子如：

		CME1888		CME1907
打<u>杂</u>	"a general assistant"	tsáp₂（93）	→	tsá₂*（100）
打<u>伙记</u>	"inmate of a brothel"	kei²（93）	→	kei²~kei²*（108）
传<u>话</u>	"interpreter"	ˈwá*（33）	→	wá³*（33）
<u>掌</u>柜	"accountant"	ˈkwai*（23）	→	kwai³*（23）
接<u>盘</u>	"contractor"	ˌp'un（94）	→	ˌp'un*（101）

这些复合词都是指从事某种行业的人，动宾结构借变调而名词化。不过利用高平变调表行业的只有一例：大<u>车</u> "chief engineer"、二<u>车</u> "second engineer" 的"车"，CME1888 页 29 都作 ˌch'e，CME1907 页 29 都作 ˌch'e。同书有"车"字作名词或动词用，皆不变调：

车 "carriage"   ˌch'e（CME1888 页 29），ˌch'e（CME1907 页 29）

车 "to go"   ˌch'e（CME1888 页 29），ˌch'e（CME1907 页 29）

从上举各例可以看得出两书标调并不完全一样，有的例子是早期不变调，后期变调，也就是说从 1888 到 1907 期间，正是这些词借变调表名化的过渡期。

CME 书中还有一个高平变调现象和构词有关。我们都知道粤语中常常把形容词后置，表名物化。如"生鱼"倒置成"鱼生"。这种构词形式在 CME 书中颇有一些例子，作者 Ball 以为汉语中形容词有时可以在名词之前，有时可在名词之后，但意思有别。举例如下：

		CME1888：页 59		CME1907：页 63
<u>乾</u>荔枝	"a dry li-chi"	ˌkon	→	ˌkon
荔枝<u>乾</u>	"dried li-chis"	ˌkon	→	ˌkon*
<u>乾</u>龙眼	"dry lung-ngans"	ˌkon	→	ˌkon
龙眼<u>乾</u>	"dried lung-nagans"	ˌkon	→	ˌkon*

从英文翻译可见"乾"字后置，是名物化的用法。而两书相比较，后置的"乾"字正由原调转读高平变调，利用变调表名词化。1888 书中不作变调，是因为当时还未发生调值变化？还是记音的人漏记音变？我们很难决定。不过在 1907 书中另有一例，证明形容词名物化后置而发生变调，在二十世纪初是刚开始不久的现象。

生鱼 "fresh fish" ˌsháng（CME1888 页 59），ˌsháng（CME1907 页 63）

鱼生 "a dish composed of uncooked fish" ˌsháng（CME1888 页 59），ˌsháng

（CME1907 页 63）

上述"乾、生"的例子，在 1907 书中并列同页，"乾"字后置，发生变调，而同类型的"生"字后置，却不变调，显然变调现象因词而异，逐步扩散。"鱼生"的"生"字在 1907 书中还保持高降原调，但今日粤语中只有高平一读，变调先后，变化缓速是不一样的。

类似的例子还有"鸡公、狗公、牛公、马公"的"公"字，在 1888 书中皆保持阴平原调 ˌkung（页 40），而 1907 书则改读变调ᵒkung（页 40），今日仍读高平调。

4.2 名量分化。CME 书中有一些词兼作名词量词，但以变调区分。量词保留原调，名词转读变调，高平高升皆如此，这也是变调表名词化同一模式的现象。例如：

		CME1888	CME1907
1	a. 一枝树枝（量）	ˌchi（49）	ˌchi（50）
	b. 一枝树枝（名）	ˌchi（49）	ᵒchi*（50）
2	a. 一餐饭（量）	ts'an（68）	ˌts'an（72）
	b. 起餐 "meal"（名）	ˌts'án（5）	ᵒts'án（5）
3	a. 一杯茶（量）	ˌpui（68）	ˌpùi（72）
	b. 玻璃杯（名）	ˌpui（10）	ᵒp'ui*（119）
4	a. 一包书（量）	ˌpáu（58）	ˌpáu（62）
	b. 荷包锁（名）	ˌpáu（28）	ᵒpáu（29）
5	a. 一面镜（量）	min²（52）	min²（54）
	b. 船面（名）	「min*（29）	min²*（29）
6	a. 一堂蚊帐（量）	ˌt'ong（56）	ˌt'ong（58）
	b. 祠堂（名）	ˌt'ong（156）	ˌt'ong*（或 ˌt'ong）（58）
7	a. 一台戏（量）	ˌt'oi（55）	ˌt'oi（58）
	b. 台（名）	「t'oi*（17）	ˌt'oi*（17）
8	a. 一行字（量）	ˌhong（58）	ˌhong（61）
	b. 你间行（名）	「hong*（23）	ˌhong*（23）

以上例1—4是名词转高平变调5—8是名词转高升变调。例2a的量词"餐"字前后两版皆作 ts'ɑn。和名词的 ts'ɑn 似有长短元音之别，但较之其他各课"餐"字作量词的例子，短元音 ɑ 疑是手植之误，今日仍读长元音。CME 书中名量兼用而以变调区分互成相比的例子不多。1907 年书有一例，量名同句，而原调变调对举：

　　9. 几多面面？"how many facets？" min²—mɪn²（页 54）

由此可见，名量分工，以变调区分，量词不变，而名词变调，高平高升变化，同出一辙。名量分化在十九世纪末已经发生。而且从"枝、堂"等例来看，前后两书标调不同，名词转读变化，似乎正在这十数年间进行，"堂"字两读 ₌t'ong：₌t'ong，当是转变尚未完成，还在过渡阶段。

4.3　形容词变调。1907 书中颇有一些形容词变调的例子，但不见于 1888 书，先举二例：

　　几<u>大</u> "How old（is he）？" tái²（CME1888 页 98）→ tái²*（CME1907 页 106）

　　几<u>高</u> "How high（is it）？" ₌kò（CME1888 页 98）→ ₒkò（CME1907 页 106）

前一例的"大"字在 1907 书中转读高升变调，后一例的"高"转读高平变调。尤有意思的是，有同一形容词在 1907 书中可兼以两种变调形式出现：

	CME1888（页 60）		CME1907（页 63）
嗰只咁<u>大</u>	tái²	→	tái² "as large as that one" ‖tái²*/ₒtái* "as small as that one"
呢条咁<u>长</u>	₌ch'öng	→	₌ch'öng "as long as this one" ‖₌ch'öng* "like this one so long" / ₒch'öng* "like this one so short"

"大"字本调阳去，"长"字本调阳平，在 1888 书中都只有原调一读，也只有一解，即原义。但根据 1907 记载，这两个字除原读外，皆可变读高升高平。从语义来看，书中英文翻译说明读原调的是字的本义，读变调则衍生别的意思。先看高平变调。"大"字读高平变调，反作"小"的意思，"长"读高平变调，反作"短"的意思。也就是说不管形容词原字声调高低，一转高平，词义也就颠倒过来。这种构词手段，今日粤语中仍有迹可寻，详见袁家骅（1960）。粤语中时有用高调表小称，如"雨微""slight shower"的"微"，由 ₌mei 转 ₒmei（1888 和 1907 同页 9）。"大、长"声调变高，所指转小，正是同一现象。

　　形容词转读高升变调，语义上有什么改动？我们另举一例说明。

　　冇一半咁<u>远</u> "not one half so far" ₌yun（CME1888 页 17）→ ₌yun*（CME1907 页 17）

"冇一半咁远"也就是"没有一半的距离"的意思。"远"字由阳上低升变作高升调，意义已不专指"远"，而是泛指远近距离，既非正面的"远"，也不是相反的"近"，而是一种中性的用法，表路程远近。反过来看"大、长"二字读高升变调，用法相当。"长"字读 ₌ch'öng*，意思是"like this so long"，也就是"像这条的长短"，"大"字读 tái⁵*，英文注解并没有特别标明是大小巨细的意思，但从其他各例类推，"咁大"读高升调，当作"如此大小"解，今日粤语中"大、长"读高升，依然表大小长短。

形容词变调辨义的现象，不多见于 1888 书。是当时还没有这样的变化？还是作者疏忽遗漏？很难断言。不过 1888 书中偶然还有一些例子可供参考。

几耐 "how long" noi⁵*（CME1888 页 23） noi⁵*（CME1907 页 23）
好耐 "for a long time" noi²（CME1888 页 25） noi²（CME1907 页 25）

"耐"字本调阳去，是"长久"的意思。CME 前后两版皆有原调和变调的读法，但用法似乎有别。从英文翻译来看，读本调是"时间长久"原义，读高升变调是问句，问的是时间长短，意不在"长久"。也就是说"好耐"和"几耐"的分别正在形容词义是否中性化，中性化的"耐"表时间长短，变调读高升。这个变调现象，两书都有记载，可见由来已久。

阴平调的形容词也有类似的变化，由高降变高平，表中性泛指的用法。如"多"和"深"：

	CME1888	CME1907
几多 "how many？"	₌to（35）	₀to（35）
好多 "great many"	₌to（35）	₌to（35）
几深 "how deep？"	₌sham（28）	₀sham（28）
好深 "very deep"	₌sham（33）	₌sham（33）

原调表原义，变调表中性，这种区分在 1907 的导论部分已有清楚的说明，这里不待详说。1907 书页 33 有句"又唔係几浅，又唔係几深"，这里"深"字当原义解，"几深"是"很深"的意思，而不是"有多深？"的问句。但标调却作高平。sham 和上述变调表中性的现象不合。书中例子不多，但似乎在"几……"之后出现的阴平调形容词，常读高平变调，这是否是"几"字句的特色，由问句而外延其他非问句的用法，还有待进一步的分析。

4.4 变调表时态。CME 有一些用变调表动作完成的例子。请看：嫁咗（or 嫁）唔曾吖？ "Is she married？" ká⁵ ₌cho（or ⌐ka*）（CME1888 页 15）/ ká⁵ ₌cho（or ká*）（CME1907 页 15）。"咗"字是体貌词尾，附在动词之后，表完成。"嫁咗"即"已嫁了"的意思。但动词本身也可以利用高升变调表完成，相当于"动词 + 咗"，再举一些例子：

	CME1888	CME1907
现时冇，但係<u>过</u>年想请个 "Not at present, but he wishes to engage one after the New year."	kwo*(33)	kwo¹*(33)
我大佬已经<u>中</u>举咯 "My brother has taken his M.A."	⌈chung*(35)	chung¹*(35)
你<u>计</u>数唔曾呀？"Have you made up your accounts?"	⌈kɑi*（23）	kɑi¹*（23）
佢就致<u>行</u>出街呗 "He has only just gone out."	₌háng（93）	₌háng*（100）
佢<u>话</u>我 "He scolded (or told) me."	wá²（38）	wá² ~ wá²*（38）

最后两例，似乎是由 1888 的原调正走向 1907 的变调。其实这两句根据上下文意，可以用完成式，也可以不用。所以变调与否，并非必然。在今日粤语中，依然两可。CME 前后两书的不同，并不一定代表过渡期的声调变化。利用高开变调表完成，其实在早期粤语中，已经是一个相当普遍的现象。

CME 表形容词强化的句型是"形 + 过头"，1888 书中的"过"可读阴去原调，也可读高升变调，但 1907 书一律作变调：

	CME1888	CME1907
<u>热过</u>头 "It's too hot"	yit₂ ⌈kwo*—₌t'ɑu（9）	yit₌ kwo¹*—₌t'ɑu（9）
	yit₂ kwo²—₌t'ɑu（59）	yit₌ kwo¹*—₌t'ɑu（62）

"过"字变调，亦可看作是"动词 + 词尾"（"过咗头"）的变化。

动词变调，有时用法和完成体词尾并不完全相当。如 1907 书页 95 有下面一句：

佢夥计翻<u>嚟</u>咯　　　"His partner has returned."　　　₌fán ₌sai*

这一句可以用完成体，但词尾必出现在动词"翻"之后，如"翻咗嚟"，而不会是"翻嚟咗"。但这一句的变调却发生在补语"嚟"，显然变调的用法和普通词尾稍有不同，有待进一步的研究。

以上讨论是关于高升变调，高平变调是不是也可以表完成？CME 全书并没有提供例句，但 1907 书却在前言中增补一句，很清楚地交待高升变调表完成的功能：

There is ... a Second, or Higher, Upper Even Tone into which words are put and which also at times shows past tense, etc.（页 XXVII）

我们从其他早期材料中也可以找到一些阴平调动词利用高平变调表完成的用例。请看 cheung（1997），这里不赘。

4.5　因句调而造成的变调现象。CME 有一些变调情形和词法句法无关，而是因为句调而发生声调变化的现象，书中例子不多：

係？　　"yes？"　　　　⌐hɑi*？（CME1888 页 85）hɑi⁵*？（CME1907 页 91）

佢係嚟 "Has he come？"　⌐lɑi*（CME1888 页 85）　ₑlɑi*（CME1907 页 91）

1888 和 1907 两书都说明这样的变调是因为问句句调高升，而把高升调套在句末一字的字调上，不过 1907 书对第二例的"嚟"字变调补充说明：...besides the interrogative the 嚟，ₑlɑi*, being in a variant tone also expresses past time.（页 91）也就是说"嚟"字由阳平变高升，一方面是受到疑问句声调的影响，另一方面也是利用变调表完成的结果。一个变调代表两种变化。

因句调而发生高平变调的情形只有一例，而且只见于 1907 书：你知呢啲事幹唔知呀？ "Do you know about these matters？" ₒchi（CME1888 页 100）→ₒchi*（CME1907 页 107）。1907 书改动声调，但并没有说明改动原来标调的原因，句末动词"知"由高降原调变高平，很可能是因为强调语气而发生的变调现象。句末助词"呢"ₒni 和"吖"ₒá，一般都读阴平高降，但 1907 书末补充说，在加强语气时，这两个助词都可变读高平ₒni（页 124）和ₒá*（页 122）。

伍　粤语变调与词汇扩散

5.1　粤语中的高平高升变调，虽然有时和词法句法有关，有规律可循，但总体而言，这些变调是一个词汇层面的现象，先发生在某些词身上，然后外延开去，在词汇中慢慢扩散。CME 前后两书的记音，正可反映这个扩散的痕迹。先举"人"为例。"人"是阳平字，书中一般皆标原调ₑyan。但也有一些例子由原调改读变调，如：

告呢个人 "prosecute this man" ₑyan（CME1888 页 31），ₑyan（CME1907 页 31）

拉嗰个人 "arrest that man"　　ₑyan（CME1888 页 13），ₑyan（或ₑyan*）（CME1907 页 13）

这两个"人"字用法一样，但 1907 书中后一例的"人"可以两读。前一例的"人"是否一定不可以读变调？书中没有交待。但显然"人"字有时可以读原调，有时可以读变调，而且在不同的词条组合中，有的变调，如"男人"ₑyan*，有的不变调，如"唐人"ₑyan，有的在 1907 书中还是两读，如"主人"ₑyan：ₑyan*，详见下文。变调在词汇中扩散外延，变调的词条也因时而陆续添增。

　　"人"字的词条很多，但为什么有的变调，有的不变？其间准则何在？研究粤语变调的学者认为变调可以是一种语用手段，表熟悉，表亲昵，表小称，甚至表轻蔑。变调的词往往是我们常见或很想接触到的事物名称，带变调的词不是一种正式或尊敬用语，使用场合也比较随使（详细讨论请看 Tsou 1994）。我们试以 CME 书中一些例子来说明。

祠堂 "ancestral temple" ˌtʻong（CME1888 页 56），ˌtʻong*（或 ˌtʻong）

（CME1907 页 58）

礼拜堂 "chapel" ˌtʻong（CME1888 页 27），ˌtʻong（CME1907 页 27）

同一"堂"字在两个不同的词条中，一个声调不变，一个在 1907 书中开始转变，两读并用。从社会文化角度来看，祠堂是中国人祭祀祖先的地方，而礼拜堂则是外来洋教聚集的处所。对十九世纪末的粤人来说，礼拜堂自然显得比较陌生，而祠堂是比较常去的庙堂。祠堂的"堂"字变调，而礼拜堂的"堂"字不变，正代表那个时期的人对两种建筑的不同文化认同。今日耶教在香港流行，教堂的"堂"字，在二三十年前还是读阳平原调，现在只有高升变读。变易的发展，正如祠堂的"堂"字一样，在很短的时期内，由阳平变读高升。声调的变化，或多或少可以反映当时人们的社会文化意识。

5.2 再举一些例子说明变调在词汇中扩散的现象：

		CME1888	CME1907
学生	"scholars"	ˌsháng（33）	ˌsháng（33）
医生	"doctor"	ˌsháng（25）	ˌsháng（25）
先生	"teacher"	ˌsháng（35）	ˌsháng（35）

1907 书说明"学生、医生"的"生"都可读 ˌshang，也就是说读短元音 [ɐ]，而不是长元音 [a]；1888 和 1907 两书中，"先生"的"生"又可读 ˌseng。这是高平变调的例子。变调扩散似乎决定于社会等级和受尊重的程度，地位越高，越受尊重，称谓也越正式，以不变调为常；地位低的，用小称对待，可以变调。"学生"的"生"，由高降原调改读高平，可以理解作小称的手段。"生"字变调在 1888 书中并没有记载，在 1907 书中则已发生，而且扩延到"医生"的"生"，但"先生"的"生"并没有受到波及，1907 书还是作原调，同书页 43 并说明"先生"一词是敬语称谓：

先生 ˌsin—ˌsháng, Literally, elder born, but which is applied to teachers, is also used in the same way that <u>Monsieur</u> and <u>Herr</u> are in French and German respectively. It is not confined in its use to preceptors therefore, but is often used for Mr. and also mean Sir or gentleman.

最有意思的是同页加注说：The boys in foreign homes in Hong Kong are styled 先生 ₌sin—₀sháng。也就是说在洋人家中工作的男仆，可以呼为"先生"，但"生"字变读高平。由此可见高平变调表小称带贬义的特殊用法。

5.3 变调带贬义的现象，也见于高升变调，以"婆"字为例：

		CME1888		CME1907
寡母婆	"widow"	₌p'o（15）	→	₌p'o*（15）
媒人婆	"female go-between"	₌p'o（40）	→	₌p'o*（40）
伯爷婆	"old woman"	₌p'o（40）	→	₌p'o*（40）
疍家婆	"boat woman"	₌p'o（40）	→	₌p'o（或₌p'o*（40）
屋主婆	"land lady"	₌p'o（40）	→	₌p'o（40）

前四项"婆"字词条，都语带轻蔑，由原来的阳平（1888）转读高升（1907），正代表变调表蔑称的用法。与此相反的是"屋主婆"。女房东身份理应尊敬，所以不变调。但是请看下面两词：

		CME1888		CME1907
主人婆	"mistress"	₌p'o（40）	→	₌p'o*（40）
事头婆	"mistress"	₌p'o（40）	→	₌p'o（40）

两词同义，指的都是东主人物，应该以礼相待，以礼貌语言称谓，但为什么一个发生变调（1907），一个不变？又如"家婆、老婆"二词：

		CME1888	CME1907
家婆	"mother-in-law"		₌p'o*（142）
老婆	"wife"	₌p'o（27）	₌p'o（27）

"家婆"是丈夫的母亲，待之以礼，为什么称谓变调？表昵称？"老婆"是自己的眷属，本可以昵称或小称相呼，为什么反而不变调？其间变化道理，并不能一言道其所以。

我们回头再举"人"字条，进一步说明变调扩散的例子。有时可以用词义词用来解释，但有的时候，变调似乎是偶发现象。

		CME1888	CME1907
男人	"man ~ husband"	˹yan*（15）	₌yan*（15）
女人	"woman ~ wife"	˹yan*（15）	₌yan*（15）
乜人	"who"	˹yan*（27）	₌yan*（27）
嗰个人	"that man"	˹yan*（13）	₌yan（₌yan*）（13）

呢个人	"this man"	₌yan（31）	₌yan（31）
主人	"master"		₌yan*（少作 ₌yan）（139）
夫人	"（your）wife"		₌yan 或 ₌yan*（140）
尊夫人	"（your）wife"		₌yan 或 ₌yan*（140）
如夫人	"（your）concubine"		₌yan*（41）
内人	"my wife"	₌yan（15）	₌yan（15）
唐人	"Chinese"	₌yan（27）	₌yan（27）
法兰西人	"Frenchmen"	₌yan（27）	₌yan（27）
大人	"His Lordship"	₌yan（31）	₌yan（31）
佛大人	"Mr. Fut"	₌yan（31）	₌yan（31）
司事人	"manages"	₌yan（23）	₌yan（23）
熊人	"bear"	₌yan（49）	₌yan（50）

CME 书中"人"字词很多，有一些例子，前后两书皆读变调，也有一些例子，皆读原调，一律不变。变的如"男人、女人、乜人"，都是日常用语，变调先行，可以明白。"唐人、法兰西人"表国籍，"大人、司事人"表职衔，"佛大人"是面称，都属于正式用语，不能变调是意料中事。"熊人"非人，体大势凶，不是一般人常见或喜爱的动物，所以不能以变调表昵称小称。"夫人、尊夫人、如夫人、内人"都是礼貌语言，自然以不变调为常。但为什么前三者可以变调，而"内人"不变？"主人"是对上而言，为什么转读高升？"呢个人"只一读，而"嗰个人"可以二读，意思有什么分别？还是属于自由变体？总而言之，粤语变调繁复多元，我们可以归纳出的熟称、昵称、小称、蔑称用法只能解释其中一部分的现象而已。

陆 结语

CME（1907）的引言部分页 XXXII 举了下面三个"大"字例，说明粤语变调的情形：

① 一个大人 tái², a big man, a grown up person, also 大人 is a title for high officials such as Your, or His, Excellency, Your, or His, Honour, etc.

② Tái⁵*, i.e., in the Variant Rising Tone of the Lower Retiring as in the phrase 你大个嗰时，when you have grown up. Here the variant tone shows the growing being attained or looked forward to, without its use, when that meaning was to be conveyed, the phrase would fall flat and tame.

③ Tái in the Higher Upper Even Tone as in the phrase 啲咁大个，a tiny mite, 你啲咁大个嗰阵时，when you were a little mite of a child.

"大"字三读，各有所指，可见作者 Ball 对变调现象的重视。他不但能掌握调值变化，而且更能精确地描述变调所带有的语法语义变化。CME 书中记载的变调现象十分丰富，而且 1888 和 1907 两版中标调不同，正反映这十数年间变调发生和扩散的过程。我们上面的描述只是按书中例句分析而得，材料只能作大略的归类，有很多个别例子都未能作进一步讨论，同时我们也没有把 CME 和其他年代的材料放在一起研究，作更详尽的历时性分析。不过仅此数百例，我们还是可以看到粤语声调在十九世纪末的变化痕迹。Dyer Ball 以一人之力，编写 *Cantonese Made Easy*，前后四版，数订其稿。修订之间的更动添补，好供后人用来研究早期粤语的发展过程和规律。本文讨论的变调现象，只是其中一项可以深入探讨的课题。

附 注

[1] 请参看宗福邦（1964），张日昇（1969），张洪年（1972），高华年（1980），Matthews & Yip（1994），Bauer（1997）。

[2] 又如"重"字，1888：页 98 作 ⌐ch'ung*，1907：页 100 作 ˪ch'ung。

[3] 但 1888 书中"抱"亦有标阳上，如页 99"取心抱""to take a daughter-in-law"的"抱"字标 ˪p'ò。

[4] 韵母标音，1888 和 1907 两书用的符号不同，1888 沿用旧音标 ui，而 1907 则改作 öü，见 1907：页 VII。

[5] "鎗"：1888 页 XXV 作 ₒts'öng，页 51、93 皆作 ˪ts'öng。而 1907 书一律作 ₒts'öng。"香"：1888 页 XXXIII 作 ₒhöng，页 50、57、68 皆作 ˪höng，而 1907 书一律作 ₒhöng*。

[6] 参看张洪年（1972）第六章，又"嗰呢"的"嗰"亦由高降 ˪min 改读高平 ₒmin*，拼音前后标记清晰。"呢"字由 ni 改读 nei，元音复化，是二十世纪初粤音变化的一个重要现象。

[7] 1888 书中"对"（名）标阴上调，误，1907 改作高升变调。见上文讨论。

[8] CME 原书两版都没有"犯"字读原调的例子。但"犯"现有变调作名词的用法，依理推据，当有原调原义。今补上以示对比。

参考文献

陈忠敏，论广州话小称变调的来源（文稿）。

高华年（1980）《广州方言研究》，香港：商务印书馆。

袁家骅等（1960）《汉语方言概要》，北京：文字改革出版社。

宗福邦（1964）关于广州话阴平调的分化问题，《中国语文》第 5 期。

张洪年（1972）《香港粤语语法的研究》，香港：香港中文大学出版社。

张日昇（1968）香港粤语中的阴平调及变调问题，《香港中文大学中国文化研究所学报》第 2 卷第 1 期。

张敏、周烈婷（1993）粤方言里的"儿化"现象——从广西玉林的小称变音说起，第四届国际粤方言研讨会论文。

Bauer, Robert & Paul Benedict (1997) *Modern Cantonese Phonology*. New York: Mouton de Gruyter.

Cheung. Hung-nin Samuel (1997) Completing the Completive: (Re) Constructing Early Cantonese Grammar, In C. F. Sun ed. *Studies on the History of Chinese Syntax*, Journal of Chinese Linguistics Monography Series 10. Berkeley.

Tsou, Benjamin K. (1994) A Note on Cantonese Tone Sandhi (CTS) as a Diffusional Phenomenon, In *Interdisciplinary Studies on Language and Language Change*. Taiwan: Pyramid Press.

Matthews, Stephen & Virginia Yip (1994) *Cantonese: A Comprehensive Grammar*. London: Routledge.

（本文发表于《方言》2000 年第 4 期，第 299—312 页）

从《广东省土话字汇》看二百年前粤语古知庄章精组声母的分合类型[*]

万　波　甄沃奇

一、引言

古知庄章精组声母在现代汉语方言中语音形式歧异，分合类型复杂，历史层次丰富，向来为汉语方言学者所瞩目。其今读类型及其所反映的历史层次不但是汉语方言分区的重要标准，也是考察各方言历史演变和相互间历史关系的重要视角。近几十年来，随着方言调查和历史音韵研究的不断深入，相关成果越来越丰富，而电子数据库技术的运用则使我们有可能对汉语方言古知庄章精组声母的读音类型和演变层次作一贯通南北古今的考察研究，本文就是这项研究计划中的子课题之一。

现代汉语东南方言中，客、赣、湘、吴等多数方言古知庄章精组声母均为知二庄精组与知三章组两分格局（张双庆、万波1996；万波1998；庄初升2007；彭建国2009），闽语除闽中方言为知、章、庄精组三分格局外，其余多为知组与精庄章组两分的独特类型，并且知组不论二三等都保留了今读塞音的存古形式（张双庆、万波1996；万波1998；张双庆、万波2002；项梦冰2004），而广州话等多数粤方言则为古知庄章精四组合流型（何丹鹏2007；万波、何丹鹏2008）。但清初粤语韵书《分韵撮要》显示，当时的粤语亦为知庄章精组两分格局（刘镇发、张群显2003；彭小川2004）。据我们对《广东省土话字汇》（1828）一书字音所作穷尽性考察，二百年前的粤语确有 ch[tʃ]、ts[ts] 两套呲音（塞擦音和同部位擦音）。不过当时两套呲音声母各自所涵盖的古声母范围如何？换言之，当时粤语古知庄章精组声母分合类型如何？而这两套呲音声母当时又是否已经开始相混？在这些关系到粤语语音史以及现代粤语与其他汉语方言的历史关系的重要问题上，学界目前仍有很大分歧。如陈万成等《近代广州话里的"私、师、诗"》一文，以擦音"私[精组心母]、师[庄组生母]、诗[章组书母]"为考察对象，认为"南方几个方言本来都是私师合流，诗组自成一类的"，即近代广州话与其他南方方言一

---

* 本文为万波主持之香港特区政府研究资助局优配研究金资助研究计划"汉语方言中古知庄章精组声母的今读类型与历史层次研究"（CUHK451480）阶段性研究成果。

样，为精、庄组与章组两分类型。（陈万成等1990）而彭小川《粤语韵书〈分韵撮要〉及其声母系统》一文认为清初韵书《分韵撮要》是精组与知、章、庄组对立，因为书中除了"师史四"韵外，其余各韵部中声母属精组的字绝大多数都与声母属知、章或庄组的字对立，分列不同的小韵。（彭小川2004：19—20）彭文并且为该书声母系统构拟音值，前者为[ts, ts', s]，后者为[tʃ, tʃ', ʃ]。丁国伟（2006：15—22）在分析《广东省土话字汇》时则提出：

> 比较两组齿音声母字的来源，第一组齿音声母ch/sh由"章组和知组"及"庄组和精组"组成，第二组齿音声母ts/s由"庄组和精组"组成。从这个现象看来，得知较早时候，广州话有两套塞擦音声母，一组是ch/sh，一组是ts/s；及至马礼逊编撰《广东省土话字汇》时，两组塞擦音声母已出现相混，过程是ts/s组声母向ch/sh声母混。

那么在《广东省土话字汇》（*Vocabulary of the Canton Dialect.* 下文简称《字汇》）[1]时代，即约二百年前的粤语中，两套呬音声母是否已经出现相混情况？同时是否只有读ts/s组声母的字才变读ch/sh组声母？而两套呬音声母各自所涵盖的中古声母范围是否为"章组和知组"及"庄组和精组"？本文利用笔者自己建立的《字汇》全文字音电子数据库，[2]通过对《字汇》中所有知庄章精组字音所作穷尽性考察，期望能够解决上述问题。

下文将先简介《字汇》的声韵系统，接着通过对《字汇》一书知庄章精组字音所作穷尽性分析，说明二百年前的粤语古知庄章精组声母字既不同于现代客、赣、湘、吴等多数汉语东南方言知二庄精与知三章组两分格局，也不同于多数闽语知组与精庄章组两分的独特类型，而是与远在北方的官话"济南型"相同，即属于古知庄章组与精组两分类型。据此文章提出了宋元以后曾有过一次大规模的跨越式北民南迁，从而形成了早期粤语的假设。文章最后强调，研究历史音韵必须注意区分个别字音的偶发变读与整个音类的全面相混，否则就容易对某些语言现象的性质产生误判。

二、《字汇》的声韵系统

《广东省土话字汇》成书于1824至1828年间，乃第一本较完整的粤方言词典，也是目前所见最早之罗马字标音粤音资料。作者为罗拔·马礼逊（Robert Morrison），他利用罗马字母记录了当时的广州音。

根据我们的整理归纳，《字汇》声母有17类23个，包括零声母：

p[p, p']	巴怕百 跑朋批	m[m]	麻买猛 墨密每	f[f]	夫锋忿 库欢霍		
t[t, t']	打灯探 铁檀达	n[n]	拿奶泞 匿奴女	l[l]	罗路累 轮浪陆		
ts[ts, ts']	济切情 续速巡			s[s]	散松些 续师事		
ch[tʃ, tʃ']	渣钗摘 炒车至			sh[ʃ]	山柴术 书尝珊	y[j]	任有亦 形狱恩
k[k, k']	家耕楷 咳权极	g[ŋ]	我牛银 硬额逆	h[h]	恐酷晓 血咸匣		
kw[kw, kw']	季刮亏 困狂掘					w[w]	话歪魂 屈荣祸
						[ø]	远热盐 护言莺

从上表可以看出，《字汇》标写声母时，塞音 p、t、k 及塞擦音 ts、ch 不分送气及不送气，[3] 而塞擦音及擦音两套咝音声母也明确标写成 ts、s 及 ch、sh 两组。

《字汇》有 54 个韵母：

	-i	-w/u	-y	-m	-n	-ng	-p	-t	-k
a[a] 差花	ai[ai] 债艾	aou[au] 吵咬		am[am] 耽簪	an[an] 反奸	ang[aŋ] 猛螃	ap[ap] 匣蜡	at[at] 刮七	ak[ak] 择扼
	ei[ɐi] 制矮	âw[ɐu] 舅丑		âm[ɐm] 淋森	ân[ɐn] 珍近	âng[ɐŋ] 杏笙	âp[ɐp] 揖湿	ât[ɐt] 逸吉	âk[ɐk] 德吃
ay[ɛ] 射邪						eng[ɛŋ] 艇睛			ek[ɛk] 剧石
e/ee[i] 矢微		ew[iu] 丢焦		eem[im] 欠严	een[in] 面便	ing[eŋ] 兄京	eep[ip] 劫贴	eet[it] 截别	ik[ek] 值力

euê[œ]	uy[ɵy]	un[ɵn]	eong[œŋ]	ut[ɵt]	eok[œk]
靴	堆水	论闰	丈箱	率律	桌琢

o[ɔ]	oy[ɔi]	oan[ɔn]	ong[ɔŋ]	oat[ɔt]	ok[ɔk]
助我	概腮	干安	江钢	割渴	学错

oo[u]	ooy[ui]	oon[un]	oot[ut]
护夫	梅回	换宽	拨没

u[y]	une[yn]	uet[yt]
诛朱	冤穿	月夺

ow[ou]	ung[oŋ]	op[op]	uk[ok]
澳租	涌东	盒鸽	畜复

ze[ɿ]	im[m̩]	ing[ŋ̍]
师事	唔唔	午五

《字汇》不标声调。

三、古知庄章精组字在《字汇》两套咝音声母中的分布

本节通过对《字汇》中知庄章精组字的声母读音的统计分析，探讨早期广州话两套咝音所涵盖的中古声母范围。[4] 先将统计结果表列如下：

表1 《字汇》中知庄章精四组声母读音统计表 [5]

	ts	百分比	s	百分比	ch	百分比	sh	百分比
共有字数[6]	283		162		266		191	
有效字数[7]	269		150		240		181	
精	110	40.9%	0		0		0	
清	59	21.9%	4	2.7%	2	0.8%	0	
从	56	20.8%	0		0		0	
心	8	3%	125	83.3%	0		3	1.7%
邪	28	10.4%	6	4%	1	0.4%	0	

（续表）

	ts	百分比	s	百分比	ch	百分比	sh	百分比
精组合计	**261**	**97%**	**135**	**87.1**	**3**	**1.3%**	**3**	**1.7%**
庄	3	1.1%	0		24	10%	0	
初	1	0.37%	0		22	9.2%	0	
崇	2	0.74%	3	2%	8	3.3%	5	2.8%
生	0		12	8%	3	1.3%	41	22.7%
庄组合计	**6**	**2.2%**	**15**	**9.7%**	**57**	**23.8%**	**46**	**25.4%**
知	0		0		33	13.8%	0	
彻	0		0		11	4.6%	0	
澄	1	0.37%	0		43	17.9%	0	
知组合计	**1**	**0.37%**	**0**	**0%**	**87**	**36.3%**	**0**	**0%**
章	1	0.37%	0		71	29.6%	0	
昌	0		0		21	8.8%	0	
船	0		0		0		15	8.3%
书	0		0		6	2.5%	64	35.4%
禅	0		0		7	2.9%	53	22.1%
章组合计	**1**	**0.37%**	**0**	**0%**	**93**	**38.8%**	**132**	**72.9%**

先观察表 1 古知庄章精组四组声母在《字汇》中读 ts/s 及 ch/sh 的情况。为清楚起见，可将表 1 简化为表 2：

表 2 《字汇》中知庄章精四组声母在两套塞擦音各占的百分比

	占 ts/s 百分比（共 419 字）	占 ch/sh 百分比（共 421 字）
精组（402 字）	94.5%（396）	1.4%（6）
庄组（124 字）	5.0%（21）	24.5%（103）
知组（88 字）	0.2%（1）	20.7%（87）
章组（226 字）	0.2%（1）	53.4%（225）
知庄章组合计（438 字）	5.4%（23）	94.6%（415）

表 2 显示，古精组字读 ts/s 占 94.5%，读 ch/sh 只占 1.4%。而古庄组字读 ts/s 只占 5%，古知、章组字更各只占 0.2%，三组合共不过占 5.4%；而读 ch/sh 者，古庄、知、章字三组分别占 24.5%、20.7% 及 53.4%，合共占 94.6%。显然，《字汇》中读 ts/s 者主要来自古精组，读 ch/sh 者主要来自古知、庄、章组。不过由于后者各组字在《字汇》中的出现次数不一，如章组字远较知、庄组字为多，所以所占百分比似乎相差较大，但如果比较一下各组分别读 ts/s、ch/sh 的百分比，便会发现它们的比例是非常接近的，而与精组的情形截然相反。请看表 3：

表 3 《字汇》中知庄章精四组声母读 ts/s、ch/sh 的百分比

	读 ts/s 百分比	读 ch/sh 百分比
精组（402 字）	98.6%（396）	1.5%（6）
庄组（124 字）	16.9%（21）	83.1%（103）
知组（88 字）	1.1%（1）	98.9%（87）
章组（226 字）	0.4%（1）	99.6%（225）

根据表 3，《字汇》402 个精组字中，读 ts/s 有 396 个，占精组字总数的 98.6%，读 ch/sh 只占 1.5%。而知组有 88 字，读 ch 者 87 字，占 98.9%，读 ts 者只有 1 字，占 1.1%；章组有 226 字，读 ch/sh 占 99.6%，读 ts/s 占章组字不足 1%；庄组有 124 字，读 ts/s 占 16.9%，较知、章组读 ts/s 的比例为多，这是因为少部分庄组字混入精组，情况与现代普通话相似。但庄组字读 ch/sh 仍占 83%，整体上和知、章组的情况比较接近，而和精组读 ch/sh 只占 1.5% 的情况差距较大，显然，将庄组归入知、章组一类较为恰当。

综上所述，《字汇》声母系统中，读 ts/s 有 94.5% 来自精组，知庄章组相加亦不足 6%；读 ch/sh 有 98.5% 来自知章庄三组，精组只有 1.5%。因此，两套塞擦音和擦音——ts/s、ch/sh 组的中古声母来源可归纳为：ts/s 组主要属精组，ch/sh 组分属知庄章组。由此可推断，古知庄章精组字在当时广州话两套咝音中的分布格局为：知庄章三组合流读舌叶音 ch/sh，与单独读舌尖前音 ts/s 的精组对立。

四、《字汇》中两套咝音变读字的性质

根据上文统计,《字汇》中古精组字主要读 ts/s, 但有少数字例外, 读 ch/sh; 而古庄知章组主要读 ch/sh, 又有少数字例外, 读 ts/s, 我们把这些读 ch/sh 的精组字和读 ts/s 的知庄章组字称作"变读字"。那么, 这些字是否说明当时两套咝音声母已经开始相混? 又是否显示相混的方向只是 ts/s 组单向混入 ch/sh 组?

以下将对所有例外字作一穷尽式的考察, 并比较现代粤语中塞擦音尚未合流的台山、开平及连县(清水)方言读音, [8] 以探讨这种变读的性质。为清楚起见, 下面将精组及知章庄组的例外字分列两表(表 4、表 5)。除列出各字于《字汇》的标音和统计其于《字汇》的出现次数, 并以中古声母及《分韵撮要》[9] 作为参照。

先观察精组混入 ch/sh 声母情况:

表 4　精组混入 ch/sh 声母字表

汉字	中古声母	《分撮》拟音[10]	《字汇》标音	出现次数	台山、开平	连县(清水)
猜	清	ts'ai	chai	14	ts'	ts'
囚	邪	ts'ɐu	chǎw	2	t'	ts'
珊	心	ʃan	shan	8	s	ʂ
擦	清	ts'at	tsat, tsǎt	4	ts'	ts'
梭	心	sɔ	so, sho	2	s	ʂ

表 4 显示,"猜"、"囚"在《分撮》中尚属精组读音, 皆为 [ts'], 但至《字汇》变读 [tʃ]。其中"猜"有 14 个用例, 显示不可能是误记。由此可以推断,"猜"由精组变读知庄章组应发生于《分撮》成书以后至 1828 年之间, 今台山、开平方言均读 [ts'], 连县(清水)读 [tʂ'], 均属知庄章组读法, [11] 与上述现象一脉相承, 可为旁证。而"珊"情况与"猜"相似, 只不过在《分撮》中已变读知庄章组字读音 [ʃ], 至《字汇》亦读 [ʃ], 且有 8 例。因此可以推断最迟于 18 世纪中,"珊"已出现舌叶擦音的变读, 至现代粤语台山等方言仍保留"珊"知庄章组字读音, 如台山及开平读 [s]、连县(清水)读 [ʂ]。[12] 然"囚"在台山、开平读 [t']、连县(清水)读 [ts'], 属精组读法, 与《字汇》的情形并不一致, 而且只有 2 个用例, 到底是当时已出现变读, 还是马氏笔误, 尚待进一步研究。不过, 即使"囚"已出现变读知庄章组的情况, 上述情况也并不能说明《字汇》两套咝音已经开始相混, 其性质只是少数字的例外变读, 这就犹如现代粤语中少数帮

母字读送气音，如"编"、"遍"等，我们并不能因此而认为现代粤语 [p]、[p'] 开始相混一样。此外，今普通话里也有少数庄组字读成舌尖前擦音，如"所"、"搜"、"飕"、"馊"、"搜"、"森"、"涩"、"瑟"、"啬"、"缩"；读成舌尖前塞擦音不送气的，如"阻"、"辎"、"邹"、"滓"、"扎"、"侧"、"责"；读成舌尖前塞擦音送气的，如"厕"、"篡"、"测"、"策"、"册"、"岑"，但是我们同样不能因此认为现代普通话的舌尖前噝音与舌尖后噝音已经开始相混。

"擦"、"梭"的情况与上述三字不同，在《分撮》中分别读 [ts']、[s]，属精组读音，至《字汇》马氏则指"擦"读 ts 或 ch 俱可，即有两读；而"梭"也出现 s、sh 两读，各有 1 例。由此推断，18 世纪中，"擦"、"梭"的读音尚未变化，于 1828 年前出现两读。有趣的是这种两读情况在现代塞擦音尚未合流的方言中也有体现，出现保留精组读音或知庄章组读音两种情况，如今台山、开平读 [ts']、[s]，为知庄章组字读音；连县（清水）"擦"读 [ts']，保留了精组字读音，但"梭"读 [ʂ]，为知庄章组读音。因此，"擦"、"梭"的两读也并不能说明《字汇》两套噝音已经开始相混，其性质只是少数字具有两读，这就犹如现代粤语中"盖"的声母有 [k]、[k']，我们并不能因此而认为现代粤语 [k]、[k'] 开始相混一样。

"梭"在《分撮》中尚属精组读音，读 [s]。至《字汇》出现 s、sh 两读，各有 1 例。由此推断，"梭"应于《分撮》成书至 1828 年期间，出现 [ʃ]、[s] 两读情况，至今台山及开平读 [s] 而不读 [ɬ]；连县（清水）读 [ʂ] 而不读 [s]，都保留了知庄章组的读音。然而，以上各字出现 [s] 及 [ʃ] 的读音，也并不能说明《字汇》两套噝音已经开始相混，理由与上述情况相同。

再看知、庄、章组混入 ts/s 声母情况：

表 5　知、庄、章组混入 ts/s 声母字表

汉字	《字汇》标音	出现次数	中古声母	《分撮》拟音	台山、开平	连县（清水）
滓	tsze	2	庄	tsʅ	t	ts
厕	tsze	2	初	ts'ʅ	ɬ	ts
柿	tsze	2	崇	ts'ʅ	ɬ/s	ts
事	sze	173	崇	sʅ	ɬ	ʂ
史	sze	1	生	sʅ	ɬ	ʂ
师	sze	21	生	sʅ	ɬ	ʂ
狮	sze	1	生	–	ɬ	ʂ
士	sze	9	崇	sʅ	ɬ/s	ts

（续表）

汉字	《字汇》标音	出现次数	中古声母	《分撮》拟音	台山、开平	连县（清水）
搜	sow	1	生	sɐu	ɬ	ʂ
谗	tsam	4	崇	tʃ'am	t'	tʂ'
绉	tsăw	3	庄	tsɐu	ts	tʂ
霜	seong	7	生	sœŋ	s	ʂ
孱	san	1	崇	ʃan	–	–
筝	tsăng	1	庄	tʃeŋ	ts	tʂ
旋	tsew	1	澄	tʃiu	–	–
删	tsun	1	章	tʃnɵŋ	–	–
摔	sut	1	生	–	–	–
率	sut	3	生	ʃɵt	ɬ	s
使	sze	3	生	sʅ	ɬ	ʂ
	shi	3				
	shei	12		ʃɐi	–	
霎	sap	1	生	sap	–	–
	shap	1				
生	săng	1	生	s(ʃ)ɐŋ	s	ʂ
	shăng, shang	42				
少	sew	1	书	ʃiu	s	ʂ
	shew	11				
所	so	1	书	ʃɔ	s	ʂ
	sho	10				

上述知、庄、章组混入 ts/s 声母字可分为只有一读及兼有 ts、s 及 ch、sh 两读两大类。先讨论第一类。这又有四种情况：

首先是"滓"、"厕"、"柿"、"事"、"史"、"师"、"狮"、"士"、"搜"等9字。在《分撮》中均已变入精组读音，读 [ts, ts', s]，[13] 至《字汇》亦读 [ts, ts', s]，可见9字由知庄章组变读为精组读音应发生于《分撮》成书前。现代粤方言中，地处珠江三角洲的台山、开平上述9字亦均变入精组读音，与《分撮》和《字汇》一脉相承，音值为相对应的 [t]、[ɬ]。[14] 而粤北的连县（清水）方言，前3字为精组读法 [ts]，后6字则保留中古晚期知庄章组读音 [ʂ]，说明连县（清水）方言在《分撮》成书前已与珠江三角洲方言有异。

其次是"率"、"谗"2字。《分撮》中尚为知庄章组读音，分别读 [ʃ]、[tʃʻ]，至《字汇》变入精组，读音分别为 [s]、[tsʻ]。二者各有 3 例和 4 例，标音一致，显示不可能是误记，由此可以推断，此 2 字由知庄章组变读为精组读音应发生于《分撮》成书后至 1828 年前。今台山及开平方言此 2 字亦为精组读音，与《字汇》同，音值为相应的 [ɬ]、[tʻ]。连县（清水）"率"亦为精组读音，音值为 [s]；"谗"则为知庄章组读音，音值为 [ʂ]。

再次是"绉"、"霜"2字。《分撮》里均为精组读音，分别为 [ts] 及 [s]，至《字汇》亦读 [ts] 及 [s]。"绉"有 3 例、"霜"有 7 例，均标音一致，显示不可能是误记，由此可以推断，二字由知庄章组变读为精组读音，应发生于《分撮》成书前。不过此 2 字今台山及开平属知庄章组读音，音值为相应的 [tʂ]、[ʂ]，这种情况有两种可能：一是《字汇》后发生的回头演变，二是这两处方言当时就与广州话有差异，到底如何尚需进一步研究。而连县（清水）读 [tʂ]、[ʂ]，均属知庄章组读音。

最后是"筝"字。《分撮》中尚属知庄章组读音，读 [tʃ]，至《字汇》变读精组读音为 [ts]。不过"筝"在《字汇》中仅 1 例，而且今台山、开平及连县（清水）均属知庄章组读音，因此，是马氏笔误还是"筝"在当时确实已出现变读，尚需进一步研究。

再讨论兼有 ts、s 及 ch、sh 两读字例。"使"在《分撮》中有 [sɿ] 及 [ʃei] 两读，分别属精组及知庄章组读音。至《字汇》有三读，其中 shei 应继承自《分撮》[ʃei]，然台山、开平、连县（清水）等方言均未有此读音。而《分撮》读 [sɿ] 者，于《字汇》则变为读 [s] 和 [ʃ]。这种两读情况在现代咝音尚未合流的方言中同样也有体现，如今台山、开平读 [ɬ]，属精组读音；连县（清水）读 [ʂ] 则是保留了知庄章组字读音。

"生"、"少"、"所"3字[15]在《分撮》中均属知庄章组读音，读 [ʃ]。至《字汇》有 s、sh 两读。但从数量上来看，"生"只有 1 例读 [s]，却有 41 例读 [sh]；"少"只有 1 例读 s，却有 11 例读 sh；而"所"也只有 1 例读 s，却有 10 例读 sh，可见读 s 的都是孤例，而读 sh 的数量却颇大。再看今台山及开平读 [s]、连县（清水）读 [ʂ]，均属知庄章组读音。因此《字汇》读 s 者很有可能是误记，否则较难解释这种回头演变现象。当然，是否如此尚需进一步参考其他早期粤语材料才能定说。这样看来，真正能确定有两读的只有"使"一字。

综上所述，《字汇》中少数精组及知、庄、章组字变读、两读的情况，都只是个别字音的偶发变读，并非整个音类的全面相混，尤其是兼有 ts、s 及 ch、sh 两读的字例非常少。因此它们并不能说明《字汇》声母系统中两套咝音声母已开始相混，同时也并不能以此否认《字汇》年代广州话古知、庄、章组读 [tʃ, tʃʻ, ʃ] 与古精组读 [ts, tsʻ, s] 两分的格局。

五、结语

综上所述，根据《字汇》，二百年前粤语的两套噝音分别涵盖中古精组与知庄章组声母，其中古精组字声母主要读成 [ts, tsʻ, s]，而古知庄章组声母主要读成 [tʃ, tʃʻ, ʃ]，呈两分格局。现代粤语仍有部分方言点保留了这种古精组与知庄章组声母两分的格局，如四邑和连县（清水）。《字汇》中虽有少数精组及知、庄、章组字出现变读、两读的情况，但所占比例极少，其性质都属于个别字音的偶发变读，而并非两套噝音在音类上的整体混淆。而且两套噝音偶发变读的方向也并非只是精组由 ts/s 组声母单向变读 ch/sh 组声母，知庄章组也有由 ch/sh 组声母变读 ts/s 组声母的。以前，我们往往根据早期粤语"私师"与"诗"对立，认为早期粤语古知庄章精组声母也与现代客、赣、湘、吴等多数汉语东南方言一样，属于知二庄精组与知三章组两分型方言，因此自然会认为现代粤语古知庄章精组声母即由客、赣、湘、吴等多数汉语两分型合流而来，也就自然认为粤语与客赣等南方方言具有密切的历史关系。但从我们对《字汇》古知庄章组声母分合类型所作考察分析来看，其实不然，早期粤语古知庄章精组声母分合类型完全不同于上述多数现代东南方言，而是与某些平话、土话方言相同（张双庆、万波，1998；庄初升，2004），尤其是与熊正辉（1990）《官话区方言分 ts tʂ 的类型》一文中所言远在北方的济南型官话相同，这就让我们不得不重新思考粤语与其他现代汉语方言的历史关系了。根据韵图等文献资料，济南型官话知庄章组与精组两分类型宋元时期即已形成，而在地理上粤语和官话之间又横亘着客、赣、湘、吴等汉语南方方言，这就让我们有理由假设：或许宋元以后曾有过一次较大规模的跨越式北民南迁岭南事件，从而形成了早期粤语。我们希望以后能找到历史人口统计学的资料来证明这一假设。

以上对《字汇》古知庄章组声母分合类型所作考察分析给我们的启发是，在进行历史音系研究的过程中，必须注意区分个别字音的偶发变读与整个音类的全面相混，否则就会对某些语言现象的性质产生误判，即如前文所讨论过的，把早期粤语中少数精组字由 ts/s 组声母变读 ch/sh 组声母，以及少数知庄章组字由 ch/sh 组声母变读 ts/s 组声母的偶发现象，误为整个音类的全面相混。

附　注

[1] 本文所采用版本为 Ganesha 根据初版《字汇》所翻印。其印刷质量较佳，并且将分成三册的《字汇》合成一本，便于翻阅研究。Robert Morrison. *Vocabulary of the Canton Dialect*（《广东省土话字汇》）. London: Ganesha Publishing Ltd, 2001.

[2] 后又蒙张洪年教授慷慨提供"粤方言历史语料查询系统"，谨致谢忱。

[3] "In the dictionary, Morrison employs a traditional four-tone system of tone marks, but asserts that a knowledge of these is 'useful, not essential', and that: he would recommend the student to defer attention to them, till he has acquired a stock of words and idioms; and then if acquired at all, it must be by the ear from a living teacher. Without a good Chinese assistant, a correct pronunciation is not attainable; nor is at all of importance to reading and understanding Chinese books. The nicer modulations of the living voice cannot be taught by letters. Accents and other Marks may recall to a Native the right tone, but will not enable a Foreigner to acquire it", "The Tons and Aspirates, are quite a secondary nature. Such distinctions do exist, but they are not necessary to write the Language, nor yet to speak it intelligibly." "Introduction", by Kingsley Bolton, Robert Morrison., *Vocabulary of the Canton Dialect*（《广东省土话字汇》）, p 21, 22.

[4] 统计数据过程，笔者先从《字汇》逐字收入汉字及罗马音标，并根据英译推测意义，至于收字的原则，同一字出现多次，相同标音者，只收一次；不同标音者俱收无遗。

[5] 《字汇》字例的中古音韵地位，一般根据《方言调查字表》，如无则据《汉字古音手册》及《广韵》，逐字校勘，以作统计。统计总数方面，由于《字汇》未有记录声调，因此遇上少数两读字，本文将按其中古音、今音推测而统计。

[6] "共有字数"是指《字汇》中所有以该罗马字母标音标示的例字。

[7] "有效字数"是根据"共有字数"，扣除了错误例、方言例、不明例而得出的余数，所占不多。

[8] 据何丹鹏（2007：3—5），四邑话精组读舌尖塞音 [t]、[tʻ]，从、邪、心母读边擦音 [ɬ] 及齿间擦音 [θ]，知庄章组读为 [ts]、[tsʻ]、[s]，而连县（清水）精组读 [ts] 组，知庄章组读 [tʂ] 组。

[9] 本文所据《分韵撮要》版本为《新辑写信必读分韵撮要合璧》（香港陈湘记书局校对重印本，出版年月不详）。

[10] 本文拟音据刘镇发、张群显（2003）。

[11] 四邑话精组读舌尖塞音 [t]、[tʻ] 及边擦音 [ɬ]，知庄章组读 [ts]、[tsʻ]、[s]。连县（清水）精组读 [ts]、[tsʻ]、[s]，知庄章组读 [tʂ]、[tʂʻ]、[ʂ]。参前注 206。见詹伯慧、张日升（1990）《珠江三角洲方言综述》，广东人民出版社，页 117—128；张晓山（1994）连县（清水）四会话与广州话声韵特点比较，《暨南学报（哲学社会科学）》第 3 期，页 136。

[12] 同上注。另，普通话也读 [ʂ] 声母。

[13]《分撮》未收"狮"字，但据中古同一音韵地位的"师"在《分撮》中的读音，以及"狮"在《字汇》中的读音，可推知"狮"在《分撮》时期的广州话里也当读 [s] 声母。

[14] 台山、开平精组读舌尖塞音 [t]、[tʻ] 及边擦音 [ɬ]，知庄章组读 [ts]、[tsʻ]、[s]。另，"柿"、"士"在开平方言中有 [s/ɬ] 两读。

[15] "霎"为生僻字，s、sh 各一读，今台山、开平、连山均无此字的读音纪录，不予讨论。

参考文献

Robert Morrison（2001）*Vocabulary of the Canton Dialect*（《广东省土话字汇》）. London: Ganesha Publishing Ltd.

陈万成、莫慧娴（1990）近代广州话里的"私、师、诗"，《第二届国际粤方言研讨会论文集》，詹伯慧主编，广州：暨南大学出版社。

丁国伟（2006）《1828 年至 1947 年中外粤语标音文献反映的语音现象研究》，香港中文大学博士学位论文。

何丹鹏（2007）《粤语精庄知章组声母今读的历史层次研究》，香港中文大学中国语言及文学系专题研究论文。

李蓝（2007）早期粤语文献中的粤语音系及相关语言学问题，《第十届国际粤方言研讨会论文集》，张洪年、张双庆、陈雄根编，中国社会科学出版社。

李新魁（1987）一百年前的广州音，《广州研究》第 10 期。

刘泽民（1999）客家话的舌齿音声母及其演变——兼论客家话与北方话的分离年代，《兰州大学学报（社会科学版）》第 2 期。

刘镇发、张群显（2003）清初的粤语音系——《分韵撮要》的声韵系统，《第八届国际粤方言研讨会论文集》，詹伯慧主编，北京：中国社会科学出版社。

彭建国（2009）湘语知庄章声母的读音类型与历史演变，《语言科学》第 4 期。

彭小川（1992）粤语韵书《分韵撮要》及其韵母系统，《暨南学报（哲学社会科学版）》第 4 期。

彭小川（2004）粤语韵书《分韵撮要》及其声韵系统，《粤语论稿》，广州：暨南大学出版社。

万波（1998）《赣语声母的历史层次研究》，香港中文大学博士学位论文（北京商务印书馆 2009 年出版）。

万波、何丹鹏（2008）论粤语古精庄知章组声母今读的历史层次及相关音值的来源，第十三届国际粤方言研讨会论文，香港理工大学。

王洪君（2007）《中原音韵》知庄章声母的分合及其在山西方言中的演变，《语文研究》第 1 期。

项梦冰（2004）闽语古精庄知章组字今读的分合（描写篇)，《闽西方言调查研究》第 1 辑，汉城：新星出版社。

熊正辉（1990）官话区方言分 ts tʂ 的类型，《方言》第 1 期。

张双庆、万波（1996a）从邵武方言几个语言特点的性质看其归属，《语言研究》第 1 期。

张双庆、万波（1996b）南雄（乌径）方言音系特点，《方言》第 4 期。

张双庆、万波（1998）乐昌（长来）方言古全浊声母今读的考察，《方言》第 3 期。

张双庆、万波（2002）知庄章组声母在闽语及周边方言里的今读类型考察，《闽语研究及其与周边方言的关系》，香港：香港中文大学出版社。

张晓山（1994）连县（清水）四会话与广州话声韵特点比较，《暨南学报（哲学社会科学版）》第 3 期。

庄初升（2004）《粤北土话音韵研究》，北京：中国社会科学出版社。

庄初升（2007）论赣语中知组三等读如端组的层次，《方言》第 1 期。

（本文发表于《南方语言学》创刊号，第 207—216 页，暨南大学出版社，2009 年）

The Verb Complement Construction in Historical Perspective with Special Reference to Cantonese

Anne O. Yue（余靄芹）

9.1 Introduction

The present analysis concentrates on an aspect of Cantonese grammar different from standard Mandarin but reminiscent of the earlier history of the Chinese language—namely, a type of verb complement structure that is called the causative/resultative or the *shǐchéngshì* 使成式 in Chinese. I trace its history from the earliest documents extant down to the present time. The discussion is divided into two parts: the first part deals with the dating of the emergence of the causative/resultative structure. I argue that this happened during the Han dynasty. The second part deals with the reflexes of this causative/resultative structure in both modern and nineteenth-century Cantonese, which show residues of archaic and ancient features accumulated in several strata, temporally and spatially.

Cantonese, covering the varieties spoken in the city of Guangzhou as well as Hong Kong, is the standard dialect of the Yue group which constitutes one of the major groups of Southern Sinitic dialects or languages.[1] Broadly defined, the Southern dialect groups include most of the dialects spoken south of the Yangzi River—Min, Yue, Hakka, Wu, Xiang, and Gan (but excluding Jiang-Huai and South-western Mandarin). More narrowly defined, this term includes only the 'deep southern' groups of Min, Yue, and Hakka, since Wu, Xiang, and Gan often share more features with the Northern dialect groups (which are essentially the Mandarin dialects) and are sometimes described as Central dialects (Norman 1988: 183, 197–9).

Many phonological, lexical, syntactic, and morphological features distinguish the Southern from the Northern group.[2] In many respects, where the Southern dialects differ from the Northern, the former preserve more archaic features. For example, in terms of phonology, Southern dialects such as Southern Min, Hakka, and particularly Yue preserve a three-way distinction in terms of the point of articulation (labial, dental, and velar) of the nasal or oral plosive ending of the syllable /p, t, k/. This is, in fact, much closer to Middle

Chinese (*c.* seventh century CE) or even to Old Chinese of the Zhou dynasty, whereas Northern dialects bear witness to a high degree of attrition for such a distinction, in the majority of cases with a complete loss of the oral plosives /p, t, k/, and a reduction to a two-way distinction for the nasal ending to /n, ŋ/. In terms of syntactic word order, the verb complement structure to be discussed in this analysis presents a case in which an earlier order sees its residues in several Southern dialects, including Cantonese, as we shall see below.

Complements can be defined as modifying elements that are themselves verb phrases (VP) or sentences occurring after a verb. The nature of the complement depends on the relationship it holds to the verb. The verb complement structure can thus be classified into several major types in Chinese: manner, extent, degree, causative/resultative, aspectual, directional, and potential (see Ch. 4).[3] I next briefly describe these types in terms of their structure, with examples first in Mandarin and then in Cantonese.

(1) The manner complement consists of a stative VP most commonly introduced with a marker such as *.de* 得 in Mandarin or *dak*^{1} 得 in Cantonese; for example: *tā pǎo de hěn kuài* 他跑得很快 3SG-run-DE-very-fast or *kui*^{5} *jau*^{2} *dak*^{1} *ho*^{2} *faai*^{3} 佢走得好快 3SG-run-DAK-very-fast 'he runs very fast'.[4]

(2) The extent complement consists of a sentence or a VP introduced with a marker such as *.de* 得 in Mandarin or *do*^{3} 到 in Cantonese; for example: *tā pǎo de lèi-sǐ le* 他跑得累死了 3SG-run-DE-tired-very-PRT or *kui*^{5} *jau*^{2} *do*^{3} *gui*^{6}-*saai*^{3} 佢走到瘤嗮 3SG-run-DOU-tired-completely-PRT 'she ran to such an extent that she became exhausted'.

(3) The degree complement consists of an 'intensive' VP or its reduced form usually introduced with a marker such as *.de* 得 in Mandarin or *do*^{3} 到 in Cantonese; for example: *zhè jǐ tiān rè de yàomìng* 这几天热得要命 (this-several-day-hot-DE-terribly) or *ni*^{1} *gei*^{2} *yat*^{6} *yit*^{6} *do*^{3} *a*^{1} 呢几日热到吖 this-several-day-hot-DOU-PRT 'it is terribly hot these few days'.

(4) The causative/resultative complement appears as the second verb of a $V_1 + V_2$ structure, where V_2 is the result of V_1 and where the potential marker, such as de 得 (affirmative potential 'able') and bù (negative 'unable') in Mandarin, or *dak*^{1} 得 (affirmative) and *m*^{4} 唔 (negative) in Cantonese, may occur between V_1 and V_2; for example: *xǐ de gānjìng xǐ bù gānjìng* 洗得干净洗不干净 wash-DE-clean-wash-NEG-clean or *sai*^{2} *m*^{4} *sai*^{2} *dak*^{1} *gon*^{1} *jeng*^{6} 洗唔洗得干净 wash-NEG-wash-DAK-clean 'can it be washed clean?'

(5) Both the aspectual and the directional complement, strictly speaking, are subtypes of the causative/resultative complement. The aspectual complement has a grammaticalized verb or function word that carries aspectual meaning rather than its original lexical meaning as V_2; for

example: *zuò-xiaqu ba* 做下去吧 do-down-go-PRT or *jo⁶ lok⁶ heui³ la¹* 做落去啦 do-down-go-PRT 'do continue to work'.[5] The directional complement has a V_2 which indicates the direction of the movement of V_1; for example: *pá-bù-shanglai* 爬不上来 climb-NEG-up-come or *m⁴ kam² dak¹ seung⁵ lai⁴* 唔擒得上来 NEG-climb-DAK-up-come 'cannot climb up'.

(6) The potential complement occurs only along with the causative/resultative or the aspectual and the directional complement. If the latter types of complements are represented as V-C, the potential complement has the form V-AFF-C or V-NEG-C, for both of which examples have already been given.

Henceforth, my discussion is limited to the so-called causative/resultative and the aspectual type having the structure of $V_1 + V_2$ (where semantically V_1 is a transitive verb denoting the cause and V_2 an intransitive or a stative verb denoting the result of an action or state). As seen above, this construction creates the potential form by inserting the potential marker *de* 得 (*dak¹* in Cantonese) between the verb and its complement, otherwise not tolerating the insertion of any other element between V and C except the object NP.[6] A sentence with V-C structure has the following basic form: NP_1 + V-C + NP_2, where NP_1 is the agent and NP_2 the patient. Occasionally, the verb complement structure in question may have the form V-C_1-C_2, where at least one of the complements is an aspectual complement.

This verb complement structure is of particular interest when it occurs with an object noun phrase. Nineteenth-century Cantonese documents reveal a word order of V-O-C, which differs from the modern popular word order of V-C-O, but which concurs with the word order found in many other Southern dialects (such as Hakka, Wu, Xiang) or in the Chinese language, in general, earlier in its history.

9.2 Historical background of the verb complement structure

To claim that the Cantonese causative/resultative form can be traced back to Archaic and Medieval constructions, it is necessary to establish an approximate time-frame for the emergence and the development of this construction in Chinese. This is a controversial subject, with different scholars holding different views. The appearance of this construction has been considered to be as early as the pre-Qin period (before the third century BCE) or as late as the Tang dynasty (seventh to tenth centuries CE).[7] I re-examine the major arguments in the following sections and focus on aspects relevant to Cantonese.

9.2.1 The pre-Qin period

Although in many pre-Qin texts (prior to the end of the third century BCE), a combination of V₁ + V₂ is very common, the syntactic relationship is generally coordinating with its preceding subject functioning as experiencer or agent, and the NP following, if any, the patient, as for example in the opening lines of the *Book of Yao* or *Yáo Diǎn* 尧典 in the 'Book of Documents' or *Shàng Shū* 尚书 :[8]

(1)	平	章	百姓...	协	和	万	邦
	píng	*zhāng*	*bǎixìng...*	*xié*	*hé*	*wàn*	*bāng*
	examine	commend	100:names	co-ordinate	harmonize	10,000	state

'Examine and commend the various officials ... co-ordinate and harmonize the various states.'

The combination of Verb plus Resultative Complement (henceforth V-C) structure is a later development. As mentioned above, there is much controversy concerning the first appearance of such a V-C structure, which is generally defined as C being the result of V or V being the cause of C. Some scholars regard expressions such as *jiǎo jué* 剿绝 'extinguish and terminate' in (2) or *pū miè* 扑灭 'beat and extinguish' in (3) or *luàn zhèng* 乱正 'rule and straighten out disorder' in (4) in the *Shàng Shū* 尚书 as V-C structures (Yu 1957; Zhou 1958):

(2)	天	用	剿	绝	其	命
	tiān	yòng	*jiǎo*	*jué*	qí	mìng
	Heave	thus	extinguish	end	3SG	mandate

'Heaven thus extinguishes and terminates its mandate.' (甘誓 Gān Shì.)

(3)	若	火	之	燎	于	原	不	可	向	迩	其	犹	可	扑	灭
	ruò	huǒ	zhī	liáo	yú	yuán	bù	kě	xiàng	ěr	qí	yóu	kě	*pū*	*miè*
	like	fire	GEN	burn	at	plain	NEG	able	towards	near	3SG	still	able	beat	destroy

'Like fire burning in the prairie, which cannot be approached, let alone extinguished.' (盘庚 Pángēng.)

(4)	殷	其	弗	或	乱	正	四	方
	yīn	qí	fú	huò	*luàn*	*zhèng*	sì	fāng
	(name)	3SG	NEG	perhaps	rule	straighten	four	area

'Is Yin not able to rule and straighten out the four corners of the earth?' (微子 Wēizǐ.)

Such a claim is usually made on a semantic basis. In other words, semantically such structures may have a second reading: the subject NP may also be interpreted as the agent of

V_1, and the object NP, the patient of V_1, but at the same time the experiencer of V_2. Therefore, to prove conclusively that a $V_1 + V_2$ combination is a V-C structure on syntactic grounds, it must be shown that V_2 is an intransitive verb. The distinction between a V-C structure and a $V_1 + V_2$ structure can best be captured in the possibility of paraphrasing the latter coordinative one with $V_1 + ér$ 而 (conjunction 'and') $+ V_2 + O$ and the former causative/resultative one with $V_1 + O + V_2$. Unfortunately, such a paraphrase type of structure as $V_1 + O + V_2$ is found neither in the *Shàng Shū* 尚书 [9] nor in the majority of pre-Qin texts, so it is difficult to claim that V-C structures already existed during that time.

9.2.2 Pivotal constructions as a transitional type

We may say that structures such as $V_1 + O + V_2$, where V_2 is an intransitive verb, are the forerunners of the V-C structure of later times.[10] The following examples from the *Zuǒ Commentary* 左传 are interpreted by Shimura (1974: 5) as $V_1 + O + V_2$, where an object pronoun *zhī* 之 occurs between two verbs, the one preceding indicating the cause, the one following indicating the result: [11]

(5)　城　　射　　之　　殪… 又　　射　　之　　死
　　　chéng *shè*　zhī　*yì*… yòu　*shè*　zhī　*sǐ*
　　　(name) shoot 3SG die　again　shoot 3SG die
　　　'Cheng shot him dead…and shot him dead.'(左昭 Zuǒ Zhāo 21/6.)

Each of these examples, however, may also be interpreted as consisting of two split predicates: $V_1 + O$, V_2 (such as *Chéng shè zhī, yì* 城射之 , 殪 'Cheng shot him, and he died'; *yòu shè zhī, sǐ* 又射之 , 死 'and shot him again, so he was dead').[12] It was not until the Han period (third century BCE to third century CE), the time of the *Historical Records* or *Shǐ Jì* 史记 (108-93 BCE), that not all such cases could be interpreted as having split predicates. Although the first of the following examples from the *Shǐ Jì* 史记 , (6), can still be so interpreted (namely, *jī* O-NP, *sǐ* 击 O-NP, 死 'attack X, who died'), the second, (7), cannot:

(6)　章邯　　已　　破　　伍徐　击　　陈　　柱国　　房君　　死
　　　zhānghán　yǐ　　pò　　wǔxú　jī　　chén　zhùguó　fángjūn　sǐ
　　　(name)　already destroy (name) strike (name) state:pillar (name) die
　　　'Zhang Han has already destroyed Wu Xu, and fought with the State Pillar official Fang Jun of the state of Chen (until he was) dead.' (陈涉世家 Chén Shè Shìjiā 18.)

(7)

中尉	条	侯	周亚夫	与	梁	相	山都	侯
zhōngwèi	tiáo	hóu	zhōuyàfū	yǔ	liáng	xiàng	shāndū	hóu
commandant	(name)	marquis	(name)	and	(name)	minister	(name)	marquis

王恬开	见	释之	持	议	平
wángtiánkāi	jiàn	shìzhī	*chí*	yì	*píng*
(name)	see	(name)	uphold	argument	fair

'Commandant Zhou Yafu, Marquis of Tiao, and Wang Tiankai, Marquis of Shandu and Minister of Liang, saw that Shizhi kept his argument fair.' (张释之冯唐列傳 Zhāng Shìzhī Féng Táng Lièzhuàn 42.)

In (7), the analysis of the embedded clause as *chí yì, píng* 持议 , 平 '??keep the argument, which is fair' does not make sense at all. [13] On the other hand, these two examples may be interpreted as having the structure of a pivotal construction $V_1 + NP + V_2$ where the NP is at once the object of V_1 and the subject of V_2. [14]

Such transitional types are not popular until the post-Han Six Dynasties period (420–589 CE). [15] However, sometimes it is still difficult to argue that all instances of $V_1 + NP + V_2$ are necessarily of the pivotal type. In the *New Account of Tales of the World* or *Shì Shuō Xīn Yǔ* 世说新语 , presumably written during the early part of the fifth century CE, similar examples are observed in the combination *zuò* 作 'make' + O + *chéng* 成 'achieve', which number at least five tokens in the fourth chapter of *Wénxué Dìsì* 文学第四 :[16]

(8a)

夏侯湛	作	周诗	成
xiàhóuzhàn	*zuò*	zhōushī	*chéng*
(name)	make	Zhou:poetry	completed

'Xiahou Zhan wrote the *Zhou Poetry* which was completed.' (Wénxué Dìsì 文学第四 4/71.)

Another example in the same chapter has V2 actually occurring as a verb phrase:

(8b)

左太冲	作	三	都	赋	初	成
zuǒtàichōng	*zuò*	sān	dū	fù	chū	*chéng*
(name)	make	three	capitals	rhapsody	just	completed

'Zuo Taichong composed the *Rhapsody on the Three Capitals* which was just finished.' (Wénxué Dìsì 文学第四 4/68.)

On the other hand, such examples can still be analysed into split predicates of $V_1 + NP$, VP_2.[17]

However, in the *Shì Shuō Xīn Yǔ* 世说新语, there are examples that cannot be interpreted as consisting of split predicates but must be interpreted as being of the pivotal type, for example:

(9) 道真   食   豚   尽   了   不   谢   姁

    dàozhēn   *shí* tún   *jìn*   liǎo   bù   xiè   yù

    (name)   eat   pig   exhaust complete NEG thank old:woman

    'Daozhen ate the whole pig; after finishing (he) did not thank the old woman.' (任诞 Rèn Dàn 17.)

Here the verb *liǎo* 了 'complete, exhaust, following *jìn* 尽 'exhaust wholly' renders it impossible to interpret the sentence as *shí tún, jìn* 食豚, 尽 'eat the pig, it is completed' or *shí tún, jìn liǎo* 食豚, 尽了 'eat the pig, finished and completed'. Similar examples from the *Yōumíng Lù* 幽明录 (written during the Southern dynasty of Song, 420–49), such as in (10) and (11), and the *Xiányú Jīng* 贤愚经 (compiled during the Northern dynasty of Wei, 439–534), such as in (12), are first quoted in Ohta (1958: 207):

(10) 我   憎   汝   状   故   破   船   坏   耳

    wǒ   zèng rǔ   zhuàng   gù   *pò*   chuán *huài* ěr

    lSG hate 2SG behaviour therefore break boat ruined PRT

    'We hate your crime, and so destroyed the boat.' (*Yōumíng Lù* 幽明录 .)

(11) 当   打   汝   口   破

    dāng   *dā*   rǔ   kǒu   *pò*

    should strike 2SG mouth broken

    'should wreck your mouth.' (*Yōumíng Lù* 幽明录 .)

(12) 今   当   打   汝   前   两   齿   折

    Jīn   dāng   *dǎ*   rǔ   qián liǎng chǐ   *zhé/shé*

    now   should strike 2SG front two   teeth broken

    'now your two front teeth should be broken.' (*Xiányú Jīng* 贤愚经 .)

These examples illustrate a further step toward the development of the V-C structure through the pivotal construction. The use of *ěr* 耳 (a complex final particle of restriction: 'and that's all') in the first example of *Yōumíng Lù* 幽明录 in (10) and the use of the optative verb *dāng* 当 'should' in (11) and (12) in the other two preclude them from any possibility of being analysed as having split predicates of $V_1 + O, V_2$, since they take the whole predicate in their scope.

9.2.3 Emergence of the V-C structure

In the last section, it was shown that the transition to the V-C structure through the pivotal construction $V_{tr} + O + V_{intr}$ is evidenced as early as Han times, with some rare examples in the *Historical Records* 史记 . More and more examples surfaced after the Han. As to exactly when we have solid evidence for the emergence of the V-C structure in the form of $V_{tr} + V_{intr} + O$ is extremely difficult to determine, since it is often difficult to show that the V_2 in a $V_1 + V_2 + O$ structure is necessarily an intransitive verb. Ohta (1958: 206) presents an argument to solve this problem by citing the pair of verbs *shā* 杀 and *sǐ* 死 ; the former he claims is used exclusively as a transitive verb 'kill' and the latter as an intransitive verb 'die' irrespective of historical period. Therefore, examples with *sǐ* 死 as V_2 should provide evidence of the emergence of the V-C structure. However, it has since been pointed out that examples of *sǐ* 死 used as a transitive or a causative verb did exist in pre-Qin texts, such as in the *Zuǒ Commentary* 左传 (fifth-fourth century BCE) or in the *Hán Fēizǐ* 韩非子 (third century BCE), as pointed out by Li Ping (1987), although they are in the minority. This is exemplified in (13a):

(13a) 以　范氏　为　死　桓主　而　专　政　矣...
　　　 yǐ　fànshì　wéi　*sǐ*　huánzhǔ　ér　zhuān　zhèng　yǐ...
　　　 take　(name)　as　kill　(name)　and　dictate　rule　PRT

死　吾　父　而　专　于　国
sǐ　wǔ　fù　ér　zhuān　yú　guó
kill　1SG　father　and　dictate　at　state

'presumed that Fan killed Huanzhu and usurped the rule... killed my father and ruled the state'.
(左襄 Zuǒ Xiāng 21/5.)

In this case, *sǐ* 死 may be interpreted as causative 'kill' in usage.

Unlike the case of *sǐ* 死 , there seem to be hardly any examples of *shā* 杀 used as an intransitive verb, at least during pre-Qin times; example (13b) seems to be exceptional.

(13b) 不　食　而　饿　杀
　　　 bù　shí　ér　è　*shā*
　　　 NEG　eat　and　starve　die

'did not eat, starved and died'. (韩非子·内储说上七术第三十 *Hán Fēizǐ*, Nèi Chǔ Shuō Shàng Qī Shù 30/13.)

Instead of viewing this example as proof for *shā* 杀 functioning also as an intransitive verb, it should be taken as the beginning of a transition whereby a transitive verb may function as the complement verb in a V₁ + O + V₂ sequence, thereby losing its transitivity, as found in an example from the *Bǎi Yù Jīng* 百喻经, compiled some time during the Southern dynasties (420-580 CE):

(14)　（雄鸽）　　即　　　便　以　　隽　啄　　雌鸽　　　杀

　　　(xiónggē)　 jí　 biàn yǐ　 jùn *zhuó* cígē　 *shā*

　　　(male:pigeon) immediately then with beak peck fem.:pigeon die

　　　'The (male pigeon) then with his beak pecked the female pigeon which died'. (二鸽喻 Èr Gē Yù.)

Syntactically speaking, it is not possible to interpret *shā* 杀 as a transitive verb here in a construction which must be taken as pivotal. For *shā* 杀 to be interpreted as transitive, either the object pronoun *zhī* 之 3SG must follow (as in *zhuó cígē shā zhī* 啄雌鸽杀之 'peck the female pigeon and kill it') or the sentence has to be broken up into the two clauses of *(xiónggē) jí biàn yǐ jùn zhuó cígē, cígē shā* (雄鸽) 即便以隽啄雌鸽 , 雌鸽杀 '(the male pigeon) then with his beak pecked the female pigeon, and the female pigeon was killed'.

In fact, by the time of the *Bǎi Yù Jīng* 百喻经, there is variation in usage between V₁ + O + V₂ and V₁ + V₂ + O. For example, the title of a fable *Yǐ lí dǎ pò tóu yù* 以梨<u>打破</u>头喻 'The fable of using a pear to hit and crack open the head' has *dǎ-pò tóu* 打破头 (hit-broken-head) occurring in the V₁ + V₂ + O frame but the narration has the V₁ + O + V₂ frame in *yǐ lí dǎ wǒ tóu pò nǎi ěr* 以梨<u>打</u>我头<u>破</u>乃尔 (hit-1SG-head-broken) 'use a pear to crack open my head like this'. Could we interpret instances of V₁ + V₂ + O as V-C + O as early as this period? Syntactically speaking, it is quite difficult to answer this question, since the variation in usage could equally be an indication of a transition from the earlier coordinating structure toward a pivotal structure.

In connection with the discussion of the transitivity of the verb *shā* 杀 compared with the intransitivity of the verb *sǐ* 死 as evidence for determining the emergence of the V-C structure, Mei (1991) makes an important observation, noting the complementary distribution of the combination 'V *shā* 杀' with that of 'V *sǐ* 死' during Qin-Han times, the former appearing in the pattern Agent + V *shā* 杀 + Patient and the latter in the pattern Patient + V *sǐ* 死. He points out that it was not until the fifth century that the latter appeared in the pattern

Agent + V 死 + Patient. While these facts certainly throw new light on the issue of the nature of this pair of verbs and help to determine the dating of the emergence and formation of the V-C structure, other factors will have to be taken into consideration too, since the V-C structure encompasses a great variety of verbs and its emergence with V *sǐ* 死 or V *shā* 杀 may not necessarily be the first instance. In other words, it is not clear whether V *sǐ* 死 or V *shā* 杀 is the leader in the development of the V-C structure or not.

Liu (1984) points out the interrelationship between the decline of causative usage and the rise of the V-C structure, the latter appearing as compensation for the gradual falling into disuse of the former. Mei (1991) adds the decline of the contrast in voicing of initial consonants for distinguishing transitivity from intransitivity as another contributing factor which began around the time of the Eastern Han and was completed around the sixth century. While these are important observations, the actual, unambiguous establishment of the V-C structure is none the less not easy to pinpoint.

Shimura (1974) has suggested that V_2 became grammaticalized and V_1 + V_2 acquired a new meaning which is not equivalent to the combination of the meaning of V_1 plus that of V_2. While this seems reasonable as a test for whether the combination has acquired a non-co-ordinating status, it would mean a different definition of a V-C structure from the one we started with—C being the result of V—and would not distinguish it from a compound. Even then, examples of this type are not easy to come by, since most V-C structures, even in Modern Standard Chinese, not to mention at the time when the earliest types appeared, have a concrete meaning for both components. Whereas Shimura treats the combination *chóushā* 愁 杀 'die of grief', found in, for example, 古诗十九首 *Gǔ Shī Shíjiǔ Shǒu* (Nineteen Ancient Poems) (the majority of which date from the Eastern Han period of 25–220 CE) as one of the earliest examples of such a type in which *shā* 杀 'kill' has but an intensive meaning, one could also argue that 'kill' is used here in a metaphorical sense, without losing its original meaning:

(15) 白　　杨　　多　　悲　　风　　萧　　萧　　愁　　杀　　人
　　　bái　yáng　duō　bēi　fēng　xiāo　xiāo　*chóu*　*shā*　rén
　　　white　poplar　many　lament　wind　sough　sough　grief　kill　person
　　　'the white poplar with wailing winds, bringing grief/killing with grief in its sigh'. (古诗十九首 *Gǔ Shī Shíjiǔ Shǒu* 14.)

The only example we came across that would qualify as a V-C structure, as originally defined, is from the *Shǐ Jì* 史记 of the Han period, showing V_2 becoming an intransitive verb. In the following example quoted in Yang and He (1992), the meaning of *xià* 下 in *shuōxià* 说下 'persuade (talk down)' cannot be taken in its usual verbal transitive sense of 'lower (something), make low, subjugate to,[18] give in to,[19] capture (a place)'[20] as found in various pre-Qin texts:

(16a) 汉　　　王　　使　　郦生　　往　　说下　　　齐　　　王　　广

hàn　　　wáng　shǐ　　líshēng　wǎng　*shuō-xià*　qí　　　wáng　guǎng

(name)　king　send　(name)　go　　talk-down　(name)　king　(name)

及　其　相国　　　横

jí　qí　xiàngguó　héng

and　3SG　state:minister　(name)

'King Han sent Lisheng to go and persuade King Guang of Qi and his State Minister Heng to abdicate (= get down).' (田儋列传 Tián Dān Lièzhuàn 34.)

The V_2 *xià* 下 in this combination can only be interpreted as having the intransitive meaning of 'descend'. That it cannot carry the depreciative meaning of 'lower' or 'make low' is also evident in the following context to (16a) in which the reaction of Tian Heng is described:

(16b) 横　　　以　为　然　解　　其　历下　　军

héng　　　yǐ　wéi　rán　jiě　　qí　lìxià　　jūn

(name)　take　as　so　disband　3SG　(name)　army

'Heng agreed and disbanded his army in Lixia.' (Ibid.)

It is thus more appropriate to interpret the V_2 *xià* 下 as 'descend' in (16a).

In conclusion, since a genuine V-C structure is found in the *Shǐ Jì* 史记, albeit rarely, it is safe to claim that the V-C structure had appeared by the Han dynasty.[21] In addition, since the *Shǐ Jì* 史记 is a literary work, the V-C structure may have come into use in the colloquial language even earlier, although we do not have *bona fide* examples from colloquial sources that predate the *Shǐ Jì* 史记. It is important to keep in mind that the appearance of this new structure by no means suggests that it immediately replaced older co-ordinating structures or indicates that it was preferred. $V_1 + V_2$ combinations were very popular indeed during Han times but mostly as co-ordinating structures. We can support the thesis that such combinations of $V_1 + V_2$, co-ordinating in character, were still very much alive and productive by citing the following example, from the same chapter of the *Shǐ Jì* 史记, in which there is a combination of three transitive verbs—$V_1 + V_2 + V_3$:[22]

(17) 田荣   怒   追   击   杀   齐   王   市   于   即墨

tiánróng   nù   *zhuī*   *jī*   *shā*   qí   wáng   shì   yú   jímó

(name)   angry   pursue   strike   kill   (name)   king   (name)   at   (name)

'Tian Rong was angry, he pursued, attacked and killed King Shi of Qi in Jimo.' (田儋列传 Tián Dān Lièzhuàn 34.)

Apart from the form of $V_{tr} + V_{intr} + O$, the V-C structure could also take the form of $V_{tr} + O + V_{intr}$. In section 9.2.2, we discussed $V_1 + O + V_2$ as a pivotal construction, transitional to the V-C structure. It must not be forgotten that while a pivotal construction has the form $V_1 + O + V_2$ (or $V_1 + O + VP_2$), the converse is not true. In other words, not all $V_1 + O + V(P)_2$ structures are pivotal. We shall presently show that some of them are, in fact, V-C structures. The following examples from the *Shì Shuō Xīn Yǔ* 世说新语 are quoted in Li Ping (1987):

(18) 看   书   竟

kàn   shū   *jìng*

read   book   finish

'finished reading (books)'. (雅量 Yǎ Liàng 35.)

(19) 王   饮   酒   毕

wáng   *yǐn*   jiǔ   *bì*

(name)   drink   liquor   finish

'Wang finished drinking (liquor).' (方正 Fāng Zhèng 63.)

(20) 客   饮   酒   不   尽   者

kè   *yǐn*   jiǔ   bù   *jìn*   zhě

guest   drink   liquor   NEG   exhaust   PRT$_{NOM}$

'those guests who did not finish drinking (liquor)'. (汰侈 Tài Chǐ 1.)

These examples cannot be interpreted either as containing split predicates of $V_1 + O$, (NEG) V_2 or as pivotal constructions: although the NP is the object of V_1, it is not the subject of V_2. The only reasonable analysis is to regard it as a V-C structure with the object flanked by the verb and its complement. Note that the complement in each case is a verb with the meaning of 'finish' referring to the action of the verb rather than to the object NP, so for this reason the examples cannot be taken as pivotal constructions. This kind of example also occurs in the *Bǎi Yù Jīng* 百喻经 from the same period of Early Medieval Chinese.

9.2.4 The negative form of the V-C structure and variations

It is not the intention of this analysis to trace the entire history of the development of the V-C structure, but simply to point out that the Han dynasty was the time of emergence of both the pivotal construction of the type $V_{tr} + O + V_{intr}$, transitional to the V-C structure, and the V-C structure itself. Post-Han literary works indicate that, while the V-C structure is abundantly recorded up to modem times, the pivotal structure is sparingly recorded in colloquial documents up to the time of the *Water Margin* or *Shuǐ Hǔ Zhuàn* 水浒传 (compiled in the fourteenth century).

I next consider the negative form and the possibility of dialectal variation. I limit the discussion to simple negation marked with *bù* 不 in VPs which may suggest a possible connection with the V-C structure of later times. This concerns VPs that contain more than one verb in close combination of the type *bù* V_1 *bù* V_2, or *bù* V_1 V_2, as seen in nine pre-Qin texts. Although this simple negative marker is among the highest in frequency in these texts, its occurrence in the two combinations in question is relatively rare. Apart from one text, *the Dào Dé Jīng* or *Classic of the Way and Virtue* 道德经, in which no example is found,[23] in terms of frequency of one type compared with the other, the texts fall roughly into two groups: Group 1 has more examples of the *bù* V_1 *bù* V_2 pattern than Group 2 with the *bù* V_1 V_2 pattern. Group 1 includes *Mèngzǐ* or *The Works of Mencius* 孟子 compiled during the Warring States period of the fifth to the third centuries BCE (4: 1), *Lún Yǔ* or *The Analects* 论语 compiled during the fifth century BCE (6: 2) and *Zhuāngzǐ* 庄子 of the third century BCE (9: 5), while Group 2 includes *Shàng Shū* or *the Book of Documents* 尚书 (2: 7), the *Zuǒ Commentary* 左传 (5: 6), *Zhàn Guó Cè* or *Intrigues of the Warring States* 战国策 (compiled during Western Han of 206 BCE-24 CE) (3: 8), *Xúnzǐ* 荀子 of the third century BCE (16: 23), *Mòzǐ* 墨子 of the fifth century BCE (9: 24), and *Hán Fēizǐ* 韩非子 of the third century BCE (3: 24). It is quite apparent that the first type is strictly co-ordinate in structure and probably antedates the latter, which is also co-ordinate in structure but from which the negative V-C structure eventually evolves. I found only two such examples with an object, both of the *bù* 不 V_1 V_2 type:

(21) 不　　宽　　绰　　厥　　心
　　　bù　　kuān　　chuò　　jué　　xīn
　　　NEG　broaden　spacious　2SG　heart
　　　'(You) do not broaden your heart.' (书 • 无逸 Shū, Wú Yì.)

(22)

夫	犯	法	废	令	不	尊	敬	社
fū	fàn	fǎ	fèi	lìng	bù	*zūn*	*jìng*	shè
PRT	break	law	dispense	order	NEG	honour	respect	God:of:land

稷	者
jì	zhě

God:of:grain PRT$_{\text{NOM}}$

'Those who break the law and order and do not respect the state.' (韩非子·外储说右上 *Hán Fēizǐ*, Wài Chǔ Shuō Yòu Shàng 34.)

While the *bù* V$_1$ V$_2$ type is also the mould for the negated V-C structure, it is a different negative form that in later history distinguishes the V-C structure from co-ordinate verbal structures. The negation strategy that merits attention is the type that places the negative marker before V$_2$: V$_1$ NEG V$_2$, which later develops into the negative potential form particular to the V-C structure, discussed in section 9.3.1. There are no solid examples of such a type in the pre-Qin period, although the *Gōngyáng* 公羊 and the *Gǔliáng* 穀梁 Commentaries to the *Chūn Qiū or Spring and Autumn Annals* 春秋 list the following examples respectively:

(23)

诛	不	得	辟	兄
zhū	bù	*dē*	bì	xiōng
execute	NEG	able	ruler	elder:brother

'cannot kill your elder brother (addressing a ruler)', (庄子 *Zhuāngzǐ* 32/3.)

(24)

田	不	得	禽...	而	射	不	中
tián	bù	*dé*	qín...	ér	shè	bù	zhòng
hunt	NEG	obtain	game	and	shoot	NEG	hit:target

'hunt and does not get any game... and shoot and does not hit the target'. (昭 Zhāo 8/6.)

There is also one example of *zhàn-bù-shèng* 战不胜 'fight-NEG-win' in the *Zhàn Guó Cè* occurring in five places in the text, one of which even has an object NP following:

(25)

秦	王	怒	于	战	不	胜...	战	不	胜	秦
qín	wáng	nù	yú	*zhàn*	bù	*shèng...*	*zhàn*	bù	*shèng*	qín
(name)	king	angry	at	fight	NEG	win...	fight	NEG	win	(name)

'The king of Qin will be angry at going into battle and not winning... if going into battle and not winning over the Qin.' (战国策 *Zhàn Guó Cè* 173B.)

Except for (23), these examples may be interpreted as V$_1$ (*ér*) *bù* V$_2$, namely, a co-ordinating structure. By the time of the Han, V_1 + NEG + V_2 generally occurs in the form of V_1 + *bù* + *dé* with the meaning of 'V_1 and does not obtain (it)', as evidenced in the following examples:

(26) 吏　　　追　　　不　　　得
　　　lì　　zhuī　　bù　　dé
　　　official　pursue　NEG　obtain

'The officials chased but did not get (him).' (韩非子 • 外储说左下 *Hán Fēizǐ*, Wài Chǔ Shuō Zuǒ Xià 33/7.)

(27) 靖郭君　　　辞　　　不　　　得
　　　jìngguōjūn　cí　　　bù　　dé
　　　(name)　　decline　NEG　obtain

'Jingguo-jun declined but did not succeed.' (战国策 *Zhàn Guó Cè* 101.)

The verb *dé* 得 'obtain' merits special attention in the history of the formation of the V-C structure, since the change of its role from a verb to a potential marker brought into play an important type of V-C structure in which the complement is highly productive in its combinatory power (see also Ch. 4; Sun 1996). Of particular interest is the fact that, during pre-Qin times, this verb, which had actually already acquired two functions—one as the main verb of a predicate and the other as an optative verb 'be able' preceding another verb (see Ch. 7)—seldom follows a main verb, although it may follow another optative verb, as shown in the following example:

(28) 可　　得　　食　　乎
　　　kě　　dé　　shí　　hū
　　　can　obtain　eat　Q

'Can it be obtained and eaten?' (左宣 Zuǒ Xuān 12/3.)

Furthermore, the negative marker always precedes it:

(29) 不　　得　　与　　之　　言
　　　bù　　dé　　yǔ　　zhī　　yān
　　　NEG　obtain　with　3SG　speak

'did not get to speak with him'. (论 • 微子 *Lún*, Wēizǐ 18/5.)

There is not a single instance of *dé* 得 occurring as V_2, either in the pattern V_1 *bù* V_2

already examined, or in the pattern V₁ V₂ in the five pre-Qin texts *Shàng Shū* 尚书, *Zuǒ Commentary* 左传, *The Analects* 论语, *Mencius* 孟子, and *Xúnzǐ* 荀子. Apart from the examples already cited for V₁ *bù dé* 不得 earlier, there are only two examples of V₁ *dé* 得 (one in *Mòzǐ* 墨子 and one in *Zhuāngzǐ* 庄子) in the remaining texts examined:[24]

(30)

能	捕得	谋	反	卖	城	踰	城
néng	*bǔ-dé*	móu	fǎn	mài	chéng	yú	chéng
can	capture-obtain	scheme	rebel	betray	city	cross	city:wall

敌	者	一	人
dí	zhě	yī	rén
enemy	PRT_NOM	one	person

'was able to capture and get one of the enemy who schemed to rebel, to betray the city and who climbed over the city wall'. (墨 • 号令 *Mò*, Hào Lìng 70.)

(31)

而	无	见得
ér	wú	*jiàn-dé*
and	NEG	see-obtain

'and did not get to be seen'. (庄 • 应帝王 *Zhuāng*, Yìng Dìwáng 7.)

This permutation in position strongly suggests that some major syntactic change had begun and that the verb *dé* 得, while retaining its meaning of 'obtain', was moving towards assuming the role of a complement. This assumption is supported by the fact that, around the time of the Han dynasty, the verb *dé* 得 serving as V₂ in such structures became grammaticalized into a potential marker, as observed in examples such as (32) where its verbal meaning 'obtain' would no longer make sense:

(32)

今	壹	受	诏	如	此,	且	使	妾
jīn	yī	shòu	zhào	rú	cǐ,	qiě	shǐ	qiè
now	once	receive	summons	like	this	moreover	make	1SG

摇	手	不	得
yáo	shǒu	bù	*dé*
wave	hand	NEG	able

'Now I unexpectedly received such a summons, which made me unable to raise my hand (in opposition).' (汉书 • 外戚列传 67, 考成许皇后 *Hàn Shū*, Wài Qī Lièzhuàn 67, Kǎochéng Xǔ Huánghòu.)

After the Han, both the negative and the V_2 in the V_1 + NEG + V_2 construction were no longer limited to *bù* 不 and *dé* 得 respectively.

Comparing examples (23), (24), and (30), with (32), there is a difference in word order of the object NP which occurs after V_1 (*bù* 不) *dé* 得 in the first three, that is, V *bù dé* O, but is flanked by V_1 and *dé* 得 in the last example, that is, V O *bù dé*. Although the latter type of word order was not found in the pre-Qin texts we examined, one is reminded of its occurrence in the opening poem of the *Shī Jīng* 诗经 (*Book of Odes*):

(33) 求　　　之　　不　　　得
　　　qiú　　*zhī*　*bù*　　*dé*
　　　seek　　3SG　NEG　　obtain
　　　'seeking her and not obtaining'. (关雎 Guān Jū.)

None the less, this line could be interpreted as containing two VPs: V_1O, (*ér* 而) *bù dé* 不得. Furthermore, since word order in verse is treated with more flexibility and freedom, and since *dé* 得 occurs in a rhyming position in the first line of a stanza, this line cannot be taken as evidence for the word order in question. Thus, there is, in fact, no solid evidence that this type of word order occurred before the Han dynasty.

An alternative interpretation of the permutation of *dé* 得, as well as the variation in the word order of the object NP, is the possibility of dialectal difference. A third possibility is that it could be due to a stylistic difference—as a requirement of the literary as opposed to the colloquial genre. This is, however, purely speculation, albeit reasonably based, since there is as yet no other independent evidence found in the pre-Qin period to support it.

9.2.5 Summary

To recapitulate the discussion in this section: I have examined evidence for the emergence of the V-C structure and concluded that it must have occurred by Han times, through examples of V_2 occurring as an intransitive verb in the V_{tr} + O + V_{intr} type of pivotal construction (see examples (7), (9), (10), (11), (12), (14)), as well as in a V_1 + V_2 or genuine V-C structure of the form V-C-O (see example (18)–(20)); and of the grammaticalization of V_2 into the complement *dé* 'able' in a V_1 + V_2 combination in its negative form (V-O *bù dé*) (see example (32)). Furthermore, the permutation in position of the verb *dé* 得 into a potential mode marker correlates with this observation. Table 9.1 recapitulates the summary.

Table 9.1 Emergence of the V-C structure

Type	*Pattern*	*Sources*	*Date (century)*
Pivotal	V_{tr} + O + V_{intr}	*Shǐ Jì,* *Shì Shuō Xīn Yǔ,* *Yōuming Lù,* *Xiányú Jīng,* *Bǎi Yù Jīng*	2nd-1st BCE; 5th-6th CE
VCO	V_{tr} + V_{intr} + O	*Shǐ Jì*	2nd-1st BCE
Potential	V + O + *bù dé* 不得	*Hàn Shū*	1st CE
VO (NEG) C	V_{tr} + O + NEG + V_{intr}	*Shì Shuō Xīn Yǔ,* *Bǎi Yù Jīng*	5th-6th CE

9.3 Ancient residues in the Yue dialect of Hong Kong Cantonese

Because of the controversy over the dating of the emergence of the V-C structure, I have gone to great lengths to establish an approximate time-frame for it, and also for that of the V-O-C word order, on syntactic grounds. I did so in order to provide background information on certain Archaic and Medieval residues found in the syntactic patterns of the Yue dialect of Hong Kong Cantonese. The use of *dé* 得 as a preverbal optative verb 'be able', so popular during pre-Qin times, declined after the Han, assuming thereafter a postverbal position as a complement in Early Medieval Chinese. Hence, it is interesting to find that its earlier optative verb usage, especially in the negative form, can still be found in Cantonese documents of the nineteenth century and even early in the twentieth century.[25] For example:

(34) 百姓　　　　　唔　　得　　见
　　　baaksing　　　m　　dak　　gin
　　　common:people　NEG　able　see
　　　'Common people cannot see.' (Anon. 1841: 11.1.)

(35) 唔　得　　圆　　　　句　　　　说　　话
　　　m　tük　ün　　　　ku　　　shüt　wa
　　　NEG　able　complete　sentence　speak　word
　　　'The language will not be complete.' (Bonney 1854: 32.)

(36)

唔	论	佢	有	乜野	病	就	得	好
m	leun	keui	yau	matye	beng	jau	dak	hou
NEG	say	3SG	have	what	illness	then	can	be:well

'No matter what illness he has, he can get well.' (Anon. 1863: 23.)

(37)

唔	得	近	前
m	dak	gan	chin
NEG	able	near	front

'cannot get near'. (Anon. 1863: 22.)

(38)

你	点	得	知	神	係	爱	人	呢
nei	dim	dak	ji	san	hai	oi	yan	ne
2SG	how	can	know	God	be	love	people	PRT

'How do you know God loves men?' (Condit 1880: 38.)

(39)

总	係	第	四	第	五	两	音	係	唔	得	正
tsuŋ	hai	tai	si	tai	ŋ	løn	jam	hai	m	tak	tsɛŋ
always	be	ORD	four	ORD	five	two	sound	be	NEG	able	correct

'It's always the 4th and the 5th tone which are not accurate.' (Jones and Woo 1912: 18.)

In fact, a fossilized expression of this form, 唔得闲 *m dak haan* 'does not get leisure' (that is, 'have no time', 'be busy'), is still in popular use today.

The same kind of antiquity of origin cannot be claimed, however, for certain types of V-C structure observed in Cantonese, since it was not until the post-Han Nanbeichao period that the V-C structure began to spread, becoming popular during Tang and Song times.[26] For the resultative type of V-C form with an overt object NP, Ly (1944) lists the following types with examples mostly from the Tang and Song periods (unless otherwise specified): V-O-C, V-C-O, V-O-*dé*, V-*dé*-O, V-O-*bùdé*, V-*bùdé*-O, *bù*-V-*dé*-O, V-O-*dé*-C (Song, rare), V-*dé*-O-C, V-*dé*-C-O (pre-modern), V-O-*bù*-C, V-*bùdé*-O-C (pre-modern, rare), V-*bù*-C-O (pre-modern), and V-C-O-*bùdé* (Song, rare). In the modern dialects, while V-O-C has almost disappeared (except in structures with the directional complement), V-C-O is universal for the non-potential type. For the potential form the patterns V-O-*dé*, Y-O-*bùdé*,[27] V-O-*dé*-C, V-*bùdé*-O-C, and V-C-O-*bude* do not seem to exist any more; and for those patterns that still exist, apart from V-*de*-O, V-*de*-C-O, and V-*bù*-C-O which seem to be universal among the dialects (see also Ch. 4), there are different preferences between the northern and the southern Sinitic languages: while the northern dialects use V-*bùdé*-O (for example, *chī-bù-*

de-fàn 吃不得饭 'unable to eat any food', in Mandarin), the southern use *bù*-V-*dé*-O (for example, *m⁴ sik⁶ dak¹ faan⁶* 唔食得饭 'unable to eat any food' in Cantonese).

Of special interest are the patterns V-*dé*-O-C, V-O + NEG + C (see example (20) in the last section) and NEG + V + *dé* + O + C, all with the object NP occurring between the verb and its complement. These had all appeared by Tang and Song times:[28]

(40)　十三　　　学得　　　琵琶　　成
　　　shí-sān　*xué*-dé　pípa　　*chéng*
　　　thirteen　study:able　pipa　　completed
　　　'mastered the *pipa* at thirteen'. (白居易：琵琶行 Bái Jūyì, Pípa Xíng.)

(41)　后妻　　　设得　　　计　　成
　　　hòuqī　　*shè*-dé　jì　　*chéng*
　　　step-wife　devise:able　plan　completed
　　　'The step-wife devised a plan.' (舜子变 Shùnzǐ Biàn.)

(42)　如今　　未　曾　看得　　正当　　　底　　道理　　出
　　　rú-jīn　wèi　céng　*kàn*-dé　zhèngdàng　dǐ　　dàolǐ　　*chū*
　　　now　not yet　see-able　proper　　GEN　principle　come:out
　　　'Now (one) has not yet found out the proper principle.' (朱子语类卷七 Zhūzǐ Yǔlèi, ch. 7.)

These patterns still linger on in the Yue dialect of Cantonese, as well as some other southern Sinitic languages such as the Hakka dialect of Dabu 大埔 , the Xiang dialects of Dongkou 洞口 and Changsha 长沙 , and the Wu dialect of Jinhua 金华 .[29] In the following section, I use Cantonese as an example of this earlier pattern.

9.3.1 Modern Cantonese

The V-C structure in modern Cantonese has the following affirmative form when an object NP is present and not topicalized.

Pattern Ia. V-C-O:

(43)　打死　　　只　　乌蝇
　　　da²-sei²　jek³　woo¹ying¹
　　　hit-die　　CL　　fly
　　　'(hit and) kill the fly'.

(44)
学	识	粤语	唔	容易
hok^6	sik^1	$yuet^6yue^5$	m^4	$yung^4yi^6$
study-know		Cantonese	NEG	easy

'It is not easy to learn and master Cantonese.' (Zheng et al. 1993: 133.)

(45)
搵倒	佢
wan^2-do^2	kui^5
look:for-succeed	3SG

'(Look and) find him.'

Since there is variation in the pattern depending on whether the object NP is a pronoun, all the following examples will include one with a pronoun as object. The negative counterpart has the negative marker preceding the entire structure, while the negative marker may be one of four forms—the simplex (simple negative) m^4 唔 'does not, will not'; the complex (negative + past) mo^5 冇 'did not'; the complex (negative + imperfective) mei^6 未 'not yet'; and the contracted negative imperative mai^5 咪 'don't' (the gloss for all four will not be repeated but merely represented by NEG in the following examples).

Pattern Ib. NEG-V-C-O:

(46)
唔 / 冇 / 未 / 咪	打死	只	乌蝇
m^4/mo^5/mei^6/mai^5	da^2-sei^2	jek^3	woo^1ying^1
NEG	hit-die	CL	fly

'NEG kill the fly.'

(47)
唔 / 冇 / 未 / 咪	搵倒	佢
m^4/mo^5/mei^6/mai^5	wan^2-do^2	kui^5
NEG	look:for-succeed	3SG

'NEG (look and) find him.'

When a V-C occurs in the potential form, the negative cannot be the imperative mai^5 or the past form mo^5; however, it has the following varieties (where * = 'unacceptable' and ? = 'acceptable with older speakers').

Pattern IIa. V-dak^1-C-O:

(48)
打得死	只	乌蝇
da^2-dak^1-sei^2	jek^3	woo^1ying^1
hit-DAK-die	CL	fly

'can kill the fly'.

(49) 揾得倒 佢

wan^2-dak^1-do^2 kui^5

look:for-DAK-succeed   3SG

'can (look and) find him.'

There are two negative patterns, IIb(1) and IIb(2), the former more restricted in usage than the latter. With the IIb pattern, the negative imperfective mei^6 'not yet' cannot be used.

Pattern IIb(l). V-NEG-C-O:

(50) 打唔 /* 未死   只 乌蝇

da^2-m^4/*mei^6-sei^2 jek^3 woo^{1}ying^1

hit-NEG-die   CL fly

'cannot kill the fly'.

(51) 揾唔 /* 未倒   佢

wan^2-m^4/*mei^6-do^2 kui^5

look:for-NEG-succeed   3SG

'cannot/cannot yet (look and) find him'.

Pattern IIb(2). NEG-V-dak^1-C-O:

(52) 唔 / 未 打得 死 只 乌蝇

m^4/mei^6 da^2-dak^1 sei^2 jek^3 woo^{1}ding^1

NEG   hit-DAK   die CL   fly

'cannot/cannot yet kill the fly'.

(53) 唔 / 未 揾得倒   佢

m^4/mei^6 wan^2-dak^1-do^2 kui^5

NEG   look:for-DAK-succeed   3SG

'cannot/cannot yet (look and) find him'.

There is reason to believe that IIb(2) is the older, native form on two counts: it is the only pattern that is possible for structures with the directional complement m^4 seung^5 dak^1 hui^3 uk^{1}deng^2 唔上得去屋顶 (NEG-ascend-DAK-go-roof) 'cannot get up to the roof' but not *seung^5 m^4 hui^3 uk^{1}deng^2 * 上 唔 去屋顶 (*ascend-NEG-go-roof), and it occurs with more options for the negative (m^4 唔 or mei^6 未).

The next three patterns are possible only if the object NP is a pronoun. Moreover, if it is in the negative, only the simple negative is used.

Pattern IIIa. V-*dak*¹-O-C:

(54) *打得　　只　　乌蝇　　死

　　　**da*²-dak¹　jek³　woo¹ying¹　*sei*²

　　　hit-DAK　　CL　　fly　　　die

　　　(Attempted meaning: 'can kill the fly'.)

(55) 搞得　　　　佢　　掂

　　　*gaau*²-dak¹　kui⁵　*dim*⁶

　　　do-DAK　　3SG　straight

　　　'can make it straight'.

Pattern IIIb(1). NEG-V-*dak*¹-O-C:

(56) *唔 /* 未　　打得　　只　　乌蝇　　死

　　　*m⁴/*mei⁶　*da*²-dak¹　jek³　woo¹ying¹　*sei*²

　　　NEG　　　hit-DAK　CL　　fly　　　die

　　　('cannot kill the fly'.)

(57) 唔 /? 未　　搞得　　　佢　　掂

　　　m⁴/?mei⁶　*gaau*²-dak¹　kui⁵　*dim*⁶

　　　NEG　　　do-DAK　　3SG　straight

　　　'cannot/cannot yet make it straight'.

Pattern IIIb(2). V-O-NEG-C:

(58) *打　只　　乌蝇　　　唔 / 未　　死

　　　**da*²　jek³　woo¹ying¹　m⁴/mei⁶　*sei*²

　　　hit　CL　　fly　　　　NEG　　die

　　　('cannot kill the fly'.)

(59) 揾　　　佢　　唔 /* 未　　倒

　　　*wan*²　kui⁵　m⁴/*mei⁶　*do*²

　　　look:for　3SG　NEG　　　succeed

　　　'cannot (look and) find him'.

To sum up, in modern Cantonese, the V-C structure with an object NP has the same basic word order for both the affirmative and the negative of (NEG) V-C-O, only if it is not in the potential form. If it is in the potential mode, there is greater variety in word order and the word order patterns are not symmetrical for the affirmative as compared with the negative. There are only two structures for the affirmative of V-*dak*¹-C-O and V-*dak*¹-O-C while more patterns are possible in the negative, namely six, as when the object is a pronoun, it can occur in as many as four negative patterns (IIb(1), IIb(2), IIIb(1), IIIb(2)).

9.3.2 Earlier Cantonese documents

Why is there such an asymmetry of patterning in the potential form? Before answering this question, let us first observe the occurrence of various patterns from the earliest extant documents on Cantonese from the nineteenth century down to the present day. (The written documents are listed in Appendix 9.1—and included in the Bibliography—and examples from these documents are given in Appendix 9.2.) Table 9.2 summarizes this information.

Table 9.2 Occurrence of V-C patterns in written Cantonese

Document	Ia VCO	Ib mVCO	IIa VdakCO	IIb(1) VmCO	IIb(2) mVdakCO	IIb(3) mV$_1$dakCO VP$_2$	IIIa(1) VdakOC	IIIb(1) mVdakOC	IIIb(2) VOmC	IVa VOC
1 (1841)	18		1							
2 (1841)						1	1			
3 (1842)	31									1
4 (1854)					1			1	2	
5 (1863)	x						2			
6 (1877)								1		
7 (1877)				1	3		1	1		
8 (1880)	3	2	1							
9 (1888)				1	2				1	
10 (1888)	1		1						1	
11 (1894)					1					
12 (1900)	1	1			4					
13 (1904)	2	1	1		1		1			
14 (1904)	1									
15 (1906)	1						1	4		
16 (1912)		2								
17 (1924)	1									

18 (19**)			1	3	5			1		
19 (1931a)	1								1	
20 (1931b)			1							
21 (1936)	1	1						1		
22 (1938)	2	1	1	2	2		1	1	2	
23 (1940)										
24 (1943)	x			x						
25 (1946)										
26 (1947)	x	x	x	x						
27 (1949)	x		x							
28 (1953)	x	x		x						
29 (1954)	x									
30 (1955)	x			x						
31 (1959)	x	x								
32 (1963)	52	4	2	2	7					
33 (1963)	43	2	1		1		2	1	1	
34 (1967)	24		2	3	3					
35 (1970)	x	x		x						
36 (1977)	20			2	2					
Subtotal₁							9	11	8	1
						Subtotal₂	28			

Notes: 1. m = NEG, x = unspecified number of occurrences.

2. Dates in parentheses in column 1 are dates of publication. For details of sources see Appendix 9.1.

3. There are no occurrences of the V-C structure in sources 23 (1940) and 25 (1946), while Zheng et al. (1993) is not included in this survey.

Apart from two documents where no examples of the V-C structure are found, several salient points can be gathered from Table 9.2. First of all, pattern III is not recorded in any documents after 1938 except for one from 1963. It was found in fourteen texts, including the 1963 one, with a total of twenty-eight examples. Moreover, the majority of the pre-1938 texts, nine of them, also had examples of pattern II, the difference between pattern II and pattern III being the word order of C-O rather than O-C. The five texts that did not show pattern II are Anon. (1863), Anon. (1877), Wisner (1906), Wells (1931a), and Belt and Hoh (1936), but the paucity of total examples for pattern III, only twenty-eight, renders it difficult to conclude whether the absence of pattern II is accidental or a matter of preference. (Note that three pre-1938 texts contained neither pattern. These are Williams (1842), Brouner and Fung (1904), and Ball (1924).)

On the other hand, there is no doubt that pattern III is an older form which gradually fades away to a very limited usage. This can be shown by the following two facts: first, recall that in contemporary Cantonese, the pattern with the object preceding the complement may only occur if the object is a pronoun. Referring to the examples listed in Appendix 9.2, this new constraint does not generally apply in the nineteenth- and twentieth-century texts observed, although there are more examples where the object is a pronoun. For pattern IIIa, there are six examples with pronoun objects and three without; for IIIb(1), there are seven examples of the former type and four of the latter type; and for IIIb(2), there are four for each type. Below I give examples with object NPs that are not pronouns:

(60) 唔　　慌　　有人　　　聽得　　你　　銀　　倒　　咯

'm　　fong　yauyan　　*chan*-tak　ni　　ngan　　*to*　　lok

NEG　afraid　exist:person　earn-DAK　2SG　money　succeed　PRT

'There is no occasion to fear that anybody will get away [with] the profits of your money.' (Bridgman 1841: 6.43.)

(61) 唔　　做　　得　　咁　　嘅　　事　　　　好

'm　　*tsoo*　tuk　kom　kay　sz　　　　*ho*

NEG　do　　able　so　　GEN　business　good

'cannot do that business well'. (Bonney 1854: 176.)

(62) 呢　　个　　人　　旧年　　　种痘　　　　唔　　出

ni　　ko　　yan　　kau-nin　　*chung-tau*　m　　*ch'uut*

this　CL　　person　last:year　vaccinate　NEG　come:out

'This man was vaccinated last year but it did not take.' (Fulton 1888: 10.)

Furthermore, the data show a fuller range of patterns where C precedes O. Pattern IV in the non-potential form, namely, V-O-C, is no longer found in contemporary Cantonese, although it did occur during the Tang and Song period and in nineteenth-century Cantonese.

Just one example turns up from 1842 among all thirty-six texts examined, with a directional complement:

(63) 扫　　个　　一　　块　　泥　　去
　　　so　　ko　　yat　　fai　　nai　　hu
　　　sweep　that　one　CL　mud　away
　　　'sweep away that clod of dirt'. (Williams 1842: 140.)

Second, Table 9.2 shows that the negative form IIb(2), where the negative occurs before V, antedates IIb(1), where the negative occurs after V. This is easily seen in the fact that before the 1930s, there are more examples with pattern IIb(2) than with IIb(i) (seventeen versus five), but after that date the reverse is true, with the exception of the texts from 1960 and 1963. There are four texts (Bonney 1854; Ball 1894; Anon. 1900; Ball 1904) where only pattern IIb(2) occurs (NEG-V-DAK-C-O) and there are three texts where there are more examples of pattern IIb(2) than IIb(1) (V-NEG-C-O) (Bruce 1877; Fulton 1888; Anon. 19?). The pattern listed as IIb(3), found only in one text (Bridgman 1841), can be subsumed under IIb(2), thus yielding one more text with only pattern IIb(2).

O'Melia (1938: 301) gives variations of V-NEG-C, NEG-V-dak^1-C and V-NEG- dak^1-C but does not explain if there is any difference in terms of frequency of usage. Chao (1947: 102-3), on the other hand, does explain that NEG-V-dak^1-C is a second negative potential form when the verb has a complement, but in the text, only the V-NEG-C form is given. Again, caution is necessary in interpreting the figures, given that the limited number of total examples does not rule out the accidental factor. This is, however, an unavoidable dilemma when dealing with historical materials. The available figures, in any case, do lend support to our earlier argument on different grounds in section 9.3.1 for assuming IIb(2) to be the older, native form.

A parallel should be found with respect to pattern III. However, the data do not show anything revealing. Patterns IIIb(1) and IIIb(2) do not seem to show significant differences in terms of chronology. We can only speculate that by analogy with pattern II, the variants of pattern III probably follow the same hierarchy in terms of time depth, IIIb(1) being older than IIIb(2). On the other hand, pattern IIIb(2) has precedence in the *Shì Shuō Xīn Yǔ* 世说新语 as exemplified in example (20) in section 9.2.3.

9.4 Conclusion—syntactic stratification in Cantonese

Now we can attempt to answer the question posed at the beginning of the last section. The asymmetry and complexity in the potential form of the V-C structure in modern Cantonese is the result of the accumulation of several syntactic strata temporally and spatially. A number of factors are involved. First, there is difference in time depth among the different patterns, the oldest being pattern IV with the word order V O C. This is reminiscent of the pivotal V_{tr} + O + V_{intr} pattern, already present during Han times, which is transitional to the genuine V-C structure including the form of VO (NEG) C, already present in the fifth and sixth centuries. Pattern III in the potential form, (NEG)V-dé-OC, is the next oldest, and can be traced at least as far back as the Tang and Song period or even earlier (the fifth century and time of the *Shì Shuō Xīn Yǔ* 世说新语), with its positive form probably popular by the Tang dynasty. Further investigation of the two negative forms of Pattern III is needed before we can decide when each of them emerged. Although Ly (1944) lists IIIb(2) (VO-NEG-C) with examples from both Tang and Song documents, he does not mention IIIb(1) (NEG-V-dé-O-C) at all. We, however, found examples of this in the *Zhūzǐ Yǔlèi* 朱子语类.[30] Pattern II, also in the potential form, is of more recent origin: both its positive form V-*de*-C-O and one of its negative forms, IIb(1): V-NEG-C-O, can be traced to pre-modern times or the beginning of the Ming dynasty (mid- to late fourteenth century).

Since, on internal grounds, we have established that Pattern IIb(2) is older than IIb(1), it would imply that it should have appeared by pre-modern times. However, Ly (1944) lists no such examples. There is a possibility that it is a dialectal form, but this thesis is yet to be proved. Hopefully in the immediate future, there will be more studies on dialectal grammar based on historical documents, enabling us to provide evidence of dating on more solid ground than mere speculation, and deduction from hypotheses.

Appendix 9.1: Sources for Cantonese

The sources for Cantonese listed below are arranged chronologically.

1. Anon. (1841) (Untitled)

2. Bridgman, E. C. (1841) *Chinese Chrestomathy in the Canton Dialect*. Macau: S. Wells Williams.

3. Williams, S. W. (1842) *Easy Lessons in Chinese*. Macau: Office of the Chinese Repository.

4. Bonney, Samuel W. (1854) *A Vocabulary with Colloquial Phrases of the Canton Dialect*. Canton:

Office of the Chinese Repository.

5. Anon. (1863) 耶稣言行撮要俗话. Canton: 双门底福音堂梓行.

6. Anon. (1877) 散语四十章 (由自迩集翻译羊城俗话) Hong Kong: St. Paul's College.

7. Bruce, Donald (1877) *Easy Phrases in the Canton Dialect of the Chinese Language* (2nd edn.), 英华常语合璧 . San Francisco: Bruce's Printing House.

8. Condit, I. M. (1880) *English and Chinese Reader* 英语入门. Shanghai: Meihua Shuguan.

9. Fulton, A. A. (1888) *Progressive and Idiomatic Sentences in Cantonese Colloquial*. Shanghai: American Presbyterian Mission Press.

10. Stedman, T. L., and Lee, K. P. (1888) *A Chinese and English Phrase Book in the Canton Dialect.* New York: William R. Jenkins.

11. Ball, J. Dyer (1894) *Readings in Cantonese Colloquial.* Hong Kong: Kelly & Walsh, Ltd.

12. Anon. (1900) 约翰福音中西字. Shanghai: American Presbyterian Mission Press.

13. Ball, J. Dyer (1904) *How to Speak Cantonese* (3rd edn.) Hong Kong: Kelly & Walsh, Ltd.

14. Brouner, W. B., and Fung, Y. M. (1904) *Chinese Made Easy.* New York and London: MacMillan.

15. Wisner, O. E (1906) *Beginning Cantonese* 教话指南. Canton.

16. Jones, Daniel, and Woo, Kwing-Tong (1912) *A Cantonese Phonetic Reader.* London: University of London Press.

17. Ball, J. Dyer (1924) *Cantonese Made Easy* (4th rev. and enl. edn.) Hong Kong: Kelly & Walsh, Ltd.

18. Anon. (19?) *Cantonese New Testament* 新约全书 (rev. version) The American Bible Society and the British and Foreign Bible Society.

19. Wells, H. R. (1931a) *Cantonese for Everyone* 英粤通语 (rev. and enl. edn.). Hong Kong: Kelly & Walsh, Ltd.

20. Wells, H. R. (1931b) *Commercial Conversations in Cantonese and English* 英粤商业杂话. Hong Kong: Kae Shean Publishing Co.

21. Belt, Walter, and Hoh, Fuk Tsz (1936) *The Revised and Enlarged Edition of A Pocket Guide to Cantonese* 增订粤语撮要. Canton: Lingnan University.

22. O'Melia, T. A. (1938) *First Year Cantonese* 综合粤语学习法 (一年级) (4 parts). Hong Kong: Catholic Truth Society.

23. Kageyama, Takashi 影山巍 (1940) 实用速成广东话. Tokyo: 文求堂书店.

24. Koosaka, Jun'ichi 香坂顺一, and Lin, Yaobo 林耀波 (1943) 广东语会话典. Taipei: 东都书籍株式会社.

25. Chiang, Ker Chiu 蒋克秋 (1946) *Cantonese for Beginners with a Vocabulary, Book 1* (4th edn.) 粤语易解. Singapore: Chin Fen Book Store.

26. Chao Yuen Ren (1947) *A Cantonese Primer* 粤语入门. Cambridge, Mass.: Harvard University Press.

27. Chiang, Ker Chiu 蒋克秋 (1949) *Cantonese for Beginners with a Vocabulary*, *Book 2* (5th edn.) 粤语易解. Singapore: Chung Hwa Institution.

28. Oakley, R. H. (1953) *Rules for Speaking Cantonese*. Kuala Lumpur: Charles Grenier & Son Ltd.

29. Bruce, Robert (1954) *Cantonese Lessons for Malayan Students* 粤语入门. Kuala Lumpur: Government of the Federation of Malaya.

30. Chan, Yeung Kwong (1955) *Everybody's Cantonese* (4th edn.) 大众粤语. Hong Kong: Man Sang Printers.

31. Whitaker, K. P. K. (1959) *Structure Drill in Cantonese*. London: Percy Lund, Humphries & Co. Ltd.

32. Huang, Parker, and Kok, Gerard P. (1963) *Speak Cantonese*. New Haven, Conn.: Yale University Press.

33. Wong, S. L. (1963) *Cantonese Conversation—Grammar, Book I* (2 parts). Hong Kong: Hong Kong University Press.

34. Wong, S. L. (1967) *Intermediate Cantonese Conversation, Book II*. Hong Kong: Hong Kong University Press.

35. Boyle, Elizabeth L. (1970) *Cantonese Basic Course* (2 vols.). Washington, DC: Department of State.

36. Nakajima, Motoki 中岛干起 (1977) 粤语课本 I, II, III. 东京外国语大学.

37. Zheng, Ding'ou 郑定欧 et al. (1993) 今日粤语. Guangzhou: Jinan University Press.

Appendix 9.2: Examples of tokens from written sources

Except for pattern III, the following list of examples from written sources does not exhaust all tokens from the texts but is meant merely as a sample. The English translation follows what is given in the texts, where it is given. The reader is referred to Table 9.2 in section 9.3.2 for comparison.

Pattern Ia. V-C-O

duk yun yau hok si 读完幼学诗 'finish reading *Beginners' Verse*'. (Anon. 1841: 9.13.)

ní t'ing kîn ngó ngò chung 你听见我挈钟 'You hear my bell ring'. (Williams 1842: 88.)

ya chang mong gin keui ge sing 也曾望见佢嘅星 'had also seen his star'. (Anon. 1863: 5.)

matseui jing laan hiu ngo bou syu ne 乜谁整烂晓我部书呢 'who tore my book?' (Condit 1880: 35.)

ni hang pi fan ngo m ni 你肯俾翻我唔 'will you let me have them?' (Stedman and Lee 1888: 81.)

mák lán tsz-kéi shám 擘烂自己衫 'tore his clothes'. (Ball 1894: 32.)

mou yan juk jyu keui 冇人捉住佢 'no man laid hands on him'. (Anon. 1900: 42.)

Pattern Ib. NEG-V-C-O

mok jing wujou keui 莫整污糟佢 'don't soil it'. (Condit 1880: 39.)

jau m da jit keui geuk gwat 就唔打折佢脚骨 'they brake not his legs'. (Anon. 1900: 98.)

yau si haam dou m gin dou yu tim 有时喊都唔见到鱼添 'there are times when you never see any fish at all'. (Ball 1904: 108.)

ŋɔ m sik kwɑ:n jin t'uŋ 我唔食惯烟筒 'I am not used to smoking a pipe'. (Jones and Woo 1912: 52.)

m juŋ tou k'øy 唔用到佢 'have no use of them'. (Jones and Woo 1912: 44.)

mat neǐ m sóh maai kòh lǔng à 乜你唔镇埋个杠呀 'why didn't you lock the trunk?' (Belt and Hoh 1936: 58.)

ngǒh m t'ái kìn nĕi ni 我唔睇见你呢 'I did not see you'. (O'Melia 1938: 1.288.)

Pattern IIa. V-dak^1-C-O

nei nim dak guo go bou syu m nim dak ne 你念得过个簿书唔念得呢 'are you able to study that book or not?' (Bridgman 1841: 8.5.)

mou yat go hoyi teng dak dou keui ge a 冇一个可以听得倒佢嘅呀 'no one could hear him'. (Condit 1880: 71.)

ming yat sai tak hi ni tik sau kan ma 明日洗得起呢的手巾吗 'can you have these handkerchiefs washed for me by tomorrow?' (Stedman and Lee 1888: 79.)

Pattern IIb(1) V-NEG-C-O

ts'am 'm chéuk kó yat t'iú tái 'I cannot find that girdle'. (Williams 1842: 132.)

ngo tai m cheut nei gam lou 我睇唔出你咁老 (I did not think you were so old'. (Bruce 1877: 13.)

ni chek lo tsoi m sɑɑi tik ye 呢只箩载唔嗮啲嘢 'this basket will not hold all the things'. (Fulton 1888: 39.)

wan m cheut dimyeung faatji 搵唔出点样法子 'could not find out how'. (Anon.: 1841.)

tá m sź k'ǔi 打唔死佢 'did not kill it'. (O'Melia 1938: 1.299.)

Pattern IIb(2) NEG-V-dak^1-C-O

'm kow tuk hee now 唔绞得起挠 'cannot raise the anchor'. (Bonney 1854: 140.)

ngo m chou dak cheut go gin si 我唔做得出个件事 'I can't think of doing that'. (Bruce 1877: 47.)

m t'eng tɑk kin k'ü kong mɑt ye 唔听得见佢讲乜野 'I did not hear what he said'. (Fulton 1888: 14.)

m wan tak to hing-tai 唔搵得倒兄弟 'could not find his brothers'. (Ball 1894: 30.)

ling ngo m wan dak jeuk keui ne 令我唔搵得着佢呢 'that we shall not find him' (Anon. 1900: 37.)

bat neng sik dak saai gwai gwok lai faat 不能识得嗮贵国礼法 'I am not able to know the whole of your code of politeness'. (Ball 1904: 170.)

hoksaang m sing dak gwo sinsaang 学生唔胜得过先生 'Students cannot surpass teachers'. (Anon. 1841: 141.)

k'ǔi yat têng m shîk tak saài kóh ti fâan 佢一定唔食得嘅個的饭 'he certainly cannot eat all that rice'. (O'Melia 1938: 1.228.)

keuih mgaaidakhoi tiuh taai 'he couldn't untie his tie'. (Huang and Kok 1963: 230.)

mrh fan-dhak-zreok gaau gea 唔瞓得着觉嘅 'cannot fall asleep' (Wong 1963: 1.102.)

ngror mrh mrenqbraak-dhak-saai gam dhoh mrenqcrih 我唔明白得晒咁多名词 'I can't possibly learn so many terms'. (Wong 1967: 68.)

ngóh juhng meih tái dak dihm di jung mán bou jí 我重未睇得掂啲中文报纸 'I still cannot read Chinese newspapers'. (Nakajima 1977: 2.81.)

Pattern IIb(3) NEG-V₁-dak¹-C-O-VP₂

'm wá tak shat ní chí 唔话得实你知 'cannot inform you with certainty'. (Bridgman 1841: 5.45.)

Pattern IIIa. V-dak¹-O-C

'm fóng yau yan chán tak ní ngan tò lók 唔慌有人聽得你银倒咯 'there is no occasion to fear that anybody will get away [with] the profits of your money'. (Bridgman 1841: 6.43.)

hou noi chi chou dak keui hei 好耐至做得佢起 'it takes up too much time'. (Bruce 1877: 49.)

gu seun dak keui gwo lok 估信得佢过咯 'thought you could trust him' (Ball 1904: 208.)

něi sùn tak ni kòh yān kwòh m̄ ni 你信得呢个人过唔呢 'can you trust this person'. (Wisner 1906: 12.)

lěung kòh sin tím maǎi tak yat kan tó àh 两个先, 点买得一斤倒呀 'two cents, how could that buy a pound?' (O'Melia 1938: 3.97.)

ang jrae ngror dhou gaau dhak fhaann kreoe gwhaay 更曳我都教得翻佢乖 'no matter how naughty he is, I will teach him to be good' (Wong 1963: 2.52.)

Pattern IIIb(1) NEG-V-dak¹-O-C

'm tsoo tuk kom kay sz ho 唔做得咁嘅事好 'cannot do that business well'. (Bonney 1854: 176.)

m wan dak deifong dou 唔揾得地方倒 'cannot find the place'. (Anon. 1877: 37.)

ngo m fan dak keui hoi 我唔分得佢开 'I can't tell them apart'. (Bruce 1877: 49.)

keui hou m deui dak ngo jyu ge 佢好唔对得我住嘅 'he let me down'. (Wisner 1906: 8.)

m sùn tak k'uǐ kwòh 唔信得佢过 'I am unable to believe him'. (Belt and Hoh 1936: 77; O'Melia 1938: 4.162.)

m gon dak keui cheut 唔赶得佢出 'could not drive him out'. (Anon. ?: 98.)

sritrawv mrh sae dhak forgei jhuk 事头唔使得伙计郁 'the boss can't make his shop-assistants work'. (Wong 1963: 2.30.)

Pattern IIIb(2). V-O-NEG-C

tsum kü'm chɑy-uk 寻佢唔着 'cannot find him'. (Bonney 1854: 68.)

ni ko yan kau nin chung tɑu m ch'uut 呢个人旧年种痘唔出 'this man was vaccinated last year but it did not take'. (Fulton 1888: 10.)

kon ch'e m to 赶车唔到 'miss our connection'. (Stedman and Lee 1888: 143.)

wan kung m to 揾工唔倒 'could not find work'. (Wells 1931a: 120.)

něi ue kwoh tá k'ǔi m sź 你如果打佢唔死 'if you do not kill it when you hit it'. (O'Melia 1938: 1.300.)

warn kreoe mrh doo 揾佢唔倒 'I couldn't find him'. (Wong 1963: 2.108.)

Pattern IV. V-O-C

sò kó yat fɑi nai hü 扫个一块泥去 'sweep away that clod of dirt'. (Williams 1842: 140.)

NOTES

[1] Since these major dialect groups are mutually unintelligible, they are more appropriately termed languages, although traditionally they have been called dialects.

[2] For a discussion of these features, see Norman (1988) and Yue-Hashimoto (1993a).

[3] Measure expressions indicating frequency and duration may be considered complements, too, since they may be marked with the existential verb *yǒu* 有 which can be negated (note that in modern Chinese, verbs are the only grammatical category that can be negated); for example in Mandarin: *Tā lái-le yǒu sān tiān le ma?—Bù, tā lái-le méi sān tiān, cái liǎng tiān bàle* 他来了有三天了吗？ — 不，他来了没三天，才两天罢了 'Has he been here for three days already?— No, he hasn't been here for three days, just two days.' (The underlined phrases indicate duration expressions.)

   For a succinct description of the various types of complements mentioned here as well as the rationale for the classification, see Cheung (1972: ch. 3), and especially Yue-Hashimoto (1993a: ch. 11).

[4] The Mandarin romanization follows the *pīnyīn* system. The romanization for the Cantonese examples follows the original texts. Where none is provided, the Sidney Lau system is used. Note that morpheme-by-morpheme glossing has been added to the original examples from the Cantonese historical materials.

[5] Further examples of the Cantonese aspectual complement include complements such as [fan^{55}] 番 / 翻 with resumptive meaning (< 'return'), [saai^{44}] 徙 / 晒 with inclusive meaning ('all'), [maai^{11}] 埋 with conclusive meaning ('finish all'), and [dou^{35}] 倒 with achievement meaning (< 到 'reach').

[6] Cheung (1972) lists another condition under which the V and die C can be separated—by the degree adverb *gam*^{3} 咁 'so' such as *jing*^{6} *gam*^{3} *lyun*^{1} 整咁孿 (p.108) 'make it so crooked'. I consider this, however, a variant of the manner or the extent complement with *dak*^{1} 得 or *dou*^{3} 到 understood; namely, a variant of *jing*^{6} *dak*^{1} *gam*^{3} *lyun*^{1} 整得咁孿 or *jing*^{6} *dou*^{3} *gam*^{3} *lyun*^{1} 整到咁孿.

[7] For example, Yu (1957), Zhou Chiming (1958), and Pan (1980) argue for its appearance during the Yin period (14th-13th centuries BCE), Zhu Minche (1958) and Guan (1981) for the Zhou period (11th century-771 BCE), He (1984) for the Spring and Autumn period (770-476 BCE), Yang Jianguo (1959) for the Warring States period (475-221 BCE), Wang Li (1989) for the Han period (206 BCE-220 CE), while Liu Lichuan (1984) and Mei (1991) argue for its established usage during the Six Dynasties period (420-589), and Ohta (1958) and Shimura (1974) for the Tang period (618-907). Although the divergence in opinion may lie in tracing its emergence rather than in establishing its usage, the time-span difference is too great to be easily reconciled.

[8] The dating of the various chapters of the *Book of Documents* is controversial, ranging from the twelfth century BCE for some to the second century CE for others.

[9] Although the V$_1$+ *ér* V$_2$ type is found in, for example, *kuān ér lì, róu ér lì* 宽而栗 , 柔而立 (Gāo Yáo Mó 皋陶谟) 'tolerant and cautious, soft and independent'.

[10] Li Ping (1987:133) claims that V$_1$ O V$_2$ is preceded by structures such as V$_1$ O V$_2$ *zhī*, found in the *Historical Records* 史记 *Shǐ Jì*—for example *gōng qín xìnliáng jūn pò zhī* 攻秦信梁军破之 'attacked the Qin army led by Xinliang (and) destroyed it' (Zhào Shìjiā 赵世家 13). However, all such structures could be interpreted as V$_1$ O, V$_2$ *zhī* 之 and so cannot be absolutely determined as a predecessor form of V$_1$ O V$_2$.

[11] The dating of the *Zuǒ Zhuàn* or *Zuǒ Commentary* is uncertain, possibly around the end of the fifth and the beginning of the fourth centuries BCE.

[12] These examples may not be interpreted as pivotal constructions (see below), since the object NP is the pronoun *zhī* 之 , which mainly only occurs as die object during this period of time.

[13] If such an analysis is effected, it would make the verb *píng* 平 take the proper nouns *Zhou Yafu* and *Wang Tiankai* as its subject instead of 'argument', which does not make sense here.

[14] Our definition of a pivotal construction differs from the traditional one which includes imperative verbs or verbs of command or causative verbs as V$_1$, so that examples like *mìng zhī yòu* 命之宥 'make (allow) them (to) toast his majesty' (Zuǒ Zhuāng 左庄 18/1) qualify. In our opinion, such examples allow the object pronoun *zhī* 之 to occur between V$_1$ and V$_2$ and since *zhī* 之 cannot

function as the subject pronoun at the same time, it cannot qualify as a pivot. It is important to note that it is exactly these types of examples that take imperative complements: in other words, if V_2 is negated, the negative cannot be a simple negative but a negative that occurs in the imperative—for example, *huáigōng mìng wú cóng wáng rén* 怀公命无从亡人 'duke Huai gave the order not to follow those in exile' (Zuǒ Xī 左僖 23/4), or *zǐzhǎn mìng shī wú rù gōng gōng* 子展命师无入公宫 'Zizhan ordered the army not to enter the residence of the duke' (Zuǒ Xiāng 左襄 25/5), where the negative *wú* 无 is used in the imperative and where the occurrence of a simple negative like *bù* 不 would be ungrammatical. Notice also that a sentence like *shī wú rù gōng gōng* 师无入公宫 cannot be a statement but only a command to be interpreted as *shī, wú rù gōng gōng* 师，无入公宫 'You soldiers, do not enter'. The same distinction remains in modern Chinese. For details of the distinction between a pivotal construction and a construction with an imperative complement, see Yue-Hashimoto (1993a, ch. 14; 1998).

Sun Jingtao suggested (at my UBC lecture) an alternative interpretation of example (7) as having an S-P predicate for the structure described here as $V_1 + NP + V_2$, which seems equally feasible. In that case, one may claim that this type of S-P predicate is a forerunner of the V-C structure.

[15] Li Ping (1987:133–4) mentions a type of structure $V_1 + O + V_2 + zhī$ found in the *Shǐ Jì* 史记, which he considers to be replaced by the $V_1 + O + V_2$ structure: *gōng qín xìnliáng jūn pò zhī* 攻秦信梁军破之 'attacking the Xinliang army of the Qin and destroying it' (Zhào Shìjiā 赵世家 13). In other words, he regards the latter as being derived from the former through the disappearance of the object pronoun *zhī* 之 which at the same time renders the transitive verb V_2 intransitive. This argument would have been persuasive if there were examples in the *Shǐ Jì* 史记 in which the same verb occurs as V_2 in both types of structure. However, such examples are not found in the *Shǐ Jì* 史记, although examples of the former type abound.

[16] The author is generally assumed to be Liu Yiqing 刘义庆（403–44) of the Southern dynasty of Song, during the Nanbeichao period.

[17] For example, *zhōu zhòngzhì yǐn jiǔ zuì* 周仲智饮酒醉（Yǎ Liàng 雅量 21) 'Zhou Zhongzhi drank (liquor) and got drunk' may also be analysed as having split predicates of *yǐn jiǔ, zuì* 饮酒，醉.

[18] As found in the *Zuǒ Commentary*. See Yang and Xu (1985:19).

[19] As found in the *Analects* 论语. See Li et al. (1993: 9).

[20] As found in the *Zhàn Guó Cè* 战国策. See *Hànyǔ Dàzìdiǎn* vol. 1 汉语大字典一 (1986: 7).

[21] While our conclusion concurs with Wang Li (1989: 262), it is reached by syntactic evidence and not by the semantic argument preferred by Wang.

[22] He Leshi (1984: 233–4) seems to have been the first to point out such combinations in the *Shǐ Jì*

史记 ; however, her analysis is different from ours in that she considers them either $V_1 + V_2 + C$ or $V + C_1 + C_2$. Our example (17) would fell into her first type and *zhāng hán suì jī pò shā zhōu shì děng jūn* 章邯遂击破杀周市等军 (Wèi Bào Péng Yuè Lièzhuàn 魏豹彭越列傅 30), 'Zhang Han then attacked, destroyed, and killed the troops of Zhou Shi and others', into her second type. We consider all of them potentially co-ordinating in structure, as shown in our translation.

[23] If we consider examples in complements of optative verbs, there is one sole example in both the version transmitted by Wang Bi 王弼 and the two Ma Wang Dui 马王堆 manuscript copies: *sān zhě bù kě zhì (zhì) jì (jié)* 三者不可至 (致) 计 (诘) (14) 'the three cannot be fathomed' (the characters given in parentheses are those which appear in the Wang Bi text).

[24] This example, *sǐ dé yú zhuàn dùn zhī shàng* 死得于腞楯之上 (*Zhuāng*, Dá Shēng 庄·达生 19), looks like the type in question but actually should be analysed as V_1, *dé* 得 with the reading 'in death, has to be on a carved hearse'.

[25] For the use of preverbal *dé* 得 in modem Pekinese or in the obligatory sense, see Ohta (1958: 197), and Sun (1996).

[26] Since I have not examined the documents of post-Han periods in any detail, the assertion here follows Ly (1944) and Zhou (1958).

[27] However, the pattern V O NEG C occurs in some Southern Sinitic languages, as described below.

[28] Example (40) is first cited in Ohta (1958).

[29] See He Wei (1993), Tang (1960), Zhang Daqi (1985), and Cao (1988) for details.

[30] However, we have not yet checked Tang documents for Pattern IIIb(1).

（本文发表于 Hilary Chappell 主编 *Sinitic Grammar: Synchronic and Diachronic Perspectives*，第 232—265 页，牛津大学出版社，2001 年）

早期广州话完成体标记"晓"的来源和演变 [*]

郭必之　片冈新

1．问题的提出

　　一般讨论广州话的专著在谈及完成体标记[1]时，都会包括以下两个项目：（一）"咗"，读 [tʃɔ³⁵]，[2] 常黏附在动词、动结式、动趋式短语或形容词之后，[3] 大致相当于普通话的"了₁"，例如"食咗饭喇"（吃了饭了）；（二）依附在动词后头的高升变调 35，例如"落咗堂未"（下了课没有）[lɔk²² tʃɔ³⁵ tɔŋ¹¹ mei²²] 也可以说成 [lɔk²²⁻³⁵ tɔŋ¹¹ mei²²]。"咗"和高升变调在表达动作完成方面基本没有分别，但后者出现的范围比较局限，尤其在香港粤语里。张洪年指出："（变调）这个现象可能是广州粤语的残留，现在的香港人已经不大用了，特别是阴平阴入的字，大多数都把'咗'字说出来。"[4]

　　作为完成体标记，"咗"和高升变调的使用范围几乎遍及整个广府片粤语区。[5]据近人调查，以"咗"表完成的方言点有广州市区、香港市区、新界蕃田、新界泰亨、新界三门仔、澳门市区、番禺市桥、花县花山、从化城内、佛山市区、三水西南、高明明城、清远、佛冈、英德、韶关、曲江马坝、仁化、乐昌和肇庆高要；[6] 而高升变调则活跃于西江流域肇庆一带。[7] 如果只根据这些材料，再配合历史语言学中的比较法（comparative method），我们会毫不犹豫地把原始（proto-）广府片粤语的完成体标记拟构为 *tʃɔ阴上。

　　众所周知，研究一种语言的历史，除了拿它跟具发生学关系（genetically related）的语言进行比较外，还需要参考文献信息。近十几年来，学界开始注意到利用由西洋传教士记录的文献去研究早期汉语方言的重要性。游汝杰曾经这样评论这些材料的价值：

---

[*]　本文为"近代粤语的演变——早期广东话话语材料研究"计划（由香港特区政府研究局资助，编号：CUHK 6055/02H，主持人：张洪年教授）的阶段性成果。初稿曾经在香港语言学学会"第四届粤语讨论会"（WOC-4，香港城市大学，2005 年 4 月）和"中国东南部方言比较研究计划第十一届年会"（上海复旦大学，2005 年 9 月）上宣读过。李行德、施其生、张洪年、张双庆、陈以信、汤志祥、叶凤霞、邓思颖、钱志安、钟东、关瑾华（笔画序，按：发表时为繁体字）诸位师友，或反复论难，或惠示语料，笔者受益匪浅。两位评审员提出了很多值得参考的建言，我们也得到很大的启发。在此一并表示衷心的感谢。文中如有任何错误，均由作者负责。

19世纪下半期至20世纪上半期来华的西洋传教士，翻译、编写、出版了种类繁多的汉语方言圣经译本（其中有一部分为罗马字本）和方言学著作（有罗马字对音），这些文献记录、描写并研究了当时各地汉语方言口语，在广度、深度和科学性方面远远超过清儒的方言学著作，也是同时代的其他文献，如地方志和方言文学作品所望尘莫及的。[8]

西洋传教士没有传统中国"雅言中心观"[9]的桎梏，能够以平等的心态对待各种方言。另一方面，为了达到实用的目的，他们的作品比较讲求反映当时语言的真貌。以上种种，解释了为什么传教士在方言学著述方面，拥有比清儒更高的水平。在广东省，粤语一直是强势方言，使用人口众多，而且有香港这一块英国殖民地，传教士留下的方言文献数量也因此特别可观。据游汝杰的统计，单单是广州话《圣经》就有146种之多，其中129种为汉字本，17种为罗马字本；此外还有词典、课本、语法等90种。[10]可以说，这些材料都是窥探粤语史的重要窗口。那么到底一百多年前的广州话，是否如比较法预期中那样、用 *tʃɔ阴上作为完成体标记呢？

结果教人相当意外，最早编成的几部广州话文献几乎统统都不用"咗"。[11]它们有的不用标记，[12]有的用"了"，[13]而最主要的标记——即本文的主题——是"哓"。对大部分以广州话为母语的人来说，"哓"恐怕是相当陌生的。就文献的记录而言，"哓"似乎在1840年左右才进入广州话，1940年左右逐渐消失，活跃的时间只有一百年。这个完成体标记的来源是什么？它有什么语法特点？为什么会在1940年左右消失？现在还有没有粤语方言以"哓"或它的同源词作为完成体标记？厘清这些问题，对研究粤语史、甚至汉语语法史都会有深远的意义。

我们会首先罗列古文献中"哓"的各种用法，并拿它和今天广州话的"咗"加以比较。接着尝试到其他粤语方言里寻找线索，进而从音韵和语法两个层面出发，给出"哓"的语源和它演变的路线。

2. 基本材料介绍

在正式进入正题之前，先介绍一下各种早期广州话语料的资料，按出版时间的先后排列：

1. Devan, T. T. 1847. *The Beginner's First Book in the Chinese Language (Canton Vernacular)*. Hong Kong: n.p. (简称 Devan 1847).

2. Bonney, S. W. 1854. *A Vocabulary with Colloquial Phrases, of the Canton Dialect*. Canton: The Chinese Repository (简称 Bonney 1854).

3. Williams, S. Wells (卫三畏). 1856. *Tonic Dictionary of the Chinese Language in the Canton Dialect*. Canton: The Office of the Chinese Repository (简称 Williams 1856).

4. Preston, C. F. 1863.《耶稣言行撮要俗话》。广州：福音底双门堂 (简称 Preston 1863)。[14]

5. French. 1866.《述史浅译》。Cantonese translation of *Bible History for the Least and Lowest*. Canton: American Presbyterian Mission Press (简称 French 1866).[15]

6. Louis, W. 1867. *Das Evangelium des Lucas im Volksdialekte der Punti Chinesen* (《路加传福音书本地俗话》). Hong Kong: Rheinischen Missions Gesellschaft. Printed on behalf of the British and Foreign Bible Society in England (简称 Louis 1867).[16]

7. Piercy, G. 1871.《天路历程》。Cantonese translation of *The Pilgrim's Progress* by Bunyan. Canton: English Wesleyan Methodist Mission Society (简称 Piercy 1871).

8. Dennys, Nicholas B. 1874. *A Handbook of the Canton Vernacular of the Chinese Language: Being a Series of Introduction Lessons, for Domestic and Business Purposes*. London: Trubner & Company (简称 Dennys 1874).

9. Burdon, J. S. 1877.《散语四十章》。Hong Kong: St. Paul's College. Partial Cantonese translation from《语言自迩集》: *A Progressive Course Designed to Assist the Student of Colloquial Chinese as Spoken in the Capital and the Metropolitan Department Prepared by Thomas Francis Wade and Walter Caine Hillier* (简称 Burdon 1877).[17]

10. Ball, James D. 1888. *Cantonese Made Easy: A Book of Simple Sentences in the Cantonese Dialect, with Free and Literal Translations, and Directions for the Rendering of English Grammatical Forms in Chinese* (2d ed.). Reprinted by Taipei: Ch'eng Wen Publishing Company, 1971 (简称 Ball 1888).

11. Stedman, Thomas L., and K. P. Lee (李桂攀). 1888. *A Chinese and English Phrase book in the Canton Dialect: Dialogues on Ordinary and Familiar Subjects for the Use of the Chinese Resident in America, and of Americans Desirous of Learning the Chinese Language; with the Pronunciation of Each Word Indicated*

in Chinese and Roman Characters. New York: W. R. Jenkins (简称Stedman and Lee 1888).

12. 麦仕治。1893。《广州俗话书经解义》。广州：羊城十八甫文宝阁（简称《麦书》〔1893〕）。

13. 麦仕治。*c.*1893。《广州俗话诗经解义》。广州：羊城十八甫文宝阁（简称《麦诗》〔*c.*1893〕）。

14. Ball, James D. 1912. *How to Speak Cantonese: Fifty Conversations in Cantonese Colloquial; with the Chinese Character, Free and Literal English Translations, and Romanised Spelling with Tonic and Diacritical Marks, etc.* 4th edition. Hong Kong: Kelly and Welsh（简称 Ball 1912）。

15. Wisner, O. F. 1927. *Beginning Cantonese (Rewritten): Part One (Chinese)* (2d ed.). Canton: China Baptist Publication Society（简称 Wisner 1927）。

16. 谭季强。1930s。《分类通行广州话》。国立北京大学中国民俗学会民俗丛书122。台北：东方文化书局影印，1975 年（简称谭季强 1930s）。

余霭芹最近建议把粤语的历史语料分为五类：（一）关于广州方言；（二）关于中国；（三）粤人写的资料；（四）教科书；（五）圣经及宗教性的资料。[18]上述十六种材料以第四和第五类为主，麦仕治和谭季强的作品则属于第三类。值得一提的是：麦仕治的两部著作，由于针对的读者是"教育得稍识个字者"，希望他们"明白此书中之趣味"，所以"逐句书句，音注以俗话"（《麦书·序》）。这种体制，和西洋传教士编订的教科书其实没有太大差别。更重要的是这两部书篇幅长、语料足，对研究粤语语法史有不可或缺的价值。

3. "哓"在早期广州话里的用法

和"咗"一样，"哓"在早期的文献中并没有固定的写法。大部分材料把它写作"哓"，Stedman and Lee（1888）写作"咻"，《麦书》和《麦诗》则作"侥"。为了行文方便，除援引实例外，其他情况下本文一律把它写作"哓"。读音方面，Stedman and Lee（1888）把它标成 *heu*，念阴平调；其他材料一律标作 *hiu*，阴平调。按照后一种读法，"哓"应该和"侥"、"浇"、"嚣"同音。

"哓"最早的用例见于 Devan（1847）。较后出版的 Williams（1856）也收录了这个词，并稍作解释："a word denoting past time."（Williams 1856：86）下面举一些实

际的例子。我们根据宾语的有无、补语的有无以及它们出现的位置，把例句分为四类。句末列出原书的英文翻译。没有英文对照的，我们就把它翻译为现代书面汉语：

【一】V / Adj + 晓（A 类）

（1）你错晓咯。*You were mistaken.*（Devan 1847:100）

（2）嗰间房嘅台椅都烂晓。那屋里那些桌子都烂了。（Burdon 1877, Ch.7）[19]

（3）唔见晓咯。*It is lost.*（Ball 1888:81）

（4）共又唔好来个忘记侥。而且不要忘记了。（《麦书》〔1893〕1.13a）[20]

（5）只艇嚟晓咯。那条小船来了。（Wisner 1927:95）

"A 类"包括所有以"晓"作完成体标记，但既没有宾语、又没有补语的谓词性成分。在我们看过的例子中，"晓"总是出现在谓词的后头，这点和现代广州话的"咗"是没有分别的。不过，下例中的"晓"，却似乎不能用现代广州话的"咗"去代替：

（6）我有行晓。*I have walked.*（Dennys 1874:30）

现代广州话"有 +VP"结构的"有"是一个助动词，它的作用是强调"'肯定一种情况存在'，即肯定有这么一回事"，[21] 后头的动词短语一般不带体标记。[22] 例（6）的"有行晓"，到底是 Dennys 根据的材料有误，还是反映了"晓"的性质和"咗"不完全一样，目前不能确定。

【二】V + 晓 + O（B 类）

（7）佢去晓边处呀？*Where has he gone?*（Devan 1847:95）

（8）佢已经开晓你眼。他打开了你的眼睛了。（Preston 1863:65）

（9）佢脱晓衣服嚟瞓。他脱了衣裳躺。（Burdon 1877, Chap. 11）

（10）呢啲白衫，洗咻几多银呢？*How much is it for washing those shirts?*（Stedman and Lee 1888:83）

（11）将侥只杯传交俾过个位礼赞大臣之后…… 把杯子交了给那位礼赞大臣之后……（《麦书》〔1893〕5.31b）[23]

我们把带完成体标记"晓"的动宾结构归入"B 类"。"晓"无一例外地出现在动词和宾语之间，组成"V + 晓 + O"结构，这和现代广州话的"咗"是一样的。事实上，文献中不难找到"晓"、"咗"在动宾结构中互换的例子：

（12）抌晓嗰的字纸落火炉喇……嗰的有用嘅物件就抌咗佢喇。把那些草稿扔进火炉里去吧……把那些没用的东西扔掉吧。（Wisner 1927:140）

（13）镇邦街烧咗一橛，连阜安棉安街都烧晓好多。镇邦街被烧了一部分，而阜安棉安街也被烧了很多。（谭季强 1930s:11）[24]

这两个例子可以说明："晓"、"咗"在某些情况下，肩负着完全一样的功能。

【三】V + C + 晓（C 类）

（14）我食厌晓波罗咯。*I am tired of eating pineapple.*（Devan 1847:91）

（15）故此唔害得成二徒就出去晓。加害不成二徒就出去了。（Piercy 1871:104）

（16）係佢吹熄晓。他给吹灭了。（Burdon 1877, Ch.8）

（17）避去佬上天所降责的时灾时祸。避开了由上天降责下来的灾祸。（《麦书》〔1893〕2.33a）

（18）就先先同我来约定佬日子。就先跟我约好日子。（《麦诗》〔*c.*1893〕1.21b–22a）

（19）我打烂晓个花罉呀。我把花瓶给打破了。（Wisner 1927:180）

"晓"出现在整个动补结构之后，我们把它称为"C 类"。"C 类"有的时候还可以带宾语，组成"V + C + 晓 + O"，如例（14）、（17）、（18）和（19）。粤语补语的类型十分丰富，张洪年曾建议把它们分为九类。[25] 在现代广州话里，体标记一般出现在整个动补结构的后面，[26] 例如：

（20）我打烂咗个花罉呀。我把花瓶给打破了。【结果补语】

（21）瞓着咗觉。睡着了。【状态补语】

但当方向补语带体标记时，表现却不一样。如果动补结构不带宾语，而补语是"嚟"或"去"，体标记一般会出现在动补之间，如"返咗嚟"（回来了）、"行紧去"（正在去）。[27] 这条规则似乎并不完全适用于早期的广州话。例（15）有"出去晓"、例（17）有"避去晓"，同属"V + 去 + 晓"结构。这种现象，在《麦书》和《麦诗》中特别常见。这里多举四个例子：

（22）兼又离远去佬、唔肯亲近个的年高有德的老人。而且又疏离、不肯亲近那些年高有德的老人。（《麦书》〔1893〕2.21b）

（23）咁逃走去佬。这样跑掉了。（《麦书》〔1893〕5.50b）

（24）就唔能来捆绑得起，咁拈去佬。不能把它绑起来拿走。（《麦诗》〔*c.*1893〕1.20b）

（25）共又唔在我死去俵之后呢？又（为什么）不在我死了以后呢？（《麦诗》〔c.1893〕
3.26b）

我们认为：这种结构之所以和现代广州话相异，关键在于"去"，而不在于"哓"。因
为当时的"去"和其他体标记如"了"、"晒"[28]结合时，同样出现在它的前面，构成
"V＋去＋了／晒"：

（26）飞去了。*Flown away.*（Bonney 1854:70）
（27）俱被个的凶恶的贼人来抢夺去晒。都被那些凶恶的贼人抢走了。（《麦书》
〔1893〕3.2b）

还有一些拿"去"和"哓"／"晒"对举的例子，也很值得注意：

（28）咁来旱干晒，枯槁去。这样把它干湿。（《麦诗》〔c.1893〕1.35a）
（29）尔就丢弃俵我，犹之乎好似尔丢弃去一件唔要的物一样。你丢弃我，就好像丢
弃一件没用的物件一样。（《麦诗》〔c.1893〕3.40b）

看来早期广州话的"去"不单可以表方向，还有"完成"的意味。[29] 无论如何，"C 类"
的例子似乎不能说明"哓"和"咗"在语法功能上有什么差别。

【四】V＋哓＋C（D类）

（30）睇见佢就过哓去。*When he saw him, he passed by on the other side.*（Louis 1867:50）
（31）嗰时自是跌哓落去。那时自是掉了下去。（Piercy 1871:101）
（32）来挤俵入去在嗰一个金縢匣内处。放到了那一个金縢匣里去。（《麦书》〔1893〕
3.23a）
（33）就享坐俵有七十五年皇帝咁耐呢的福泽。享受了当七十五年皇帝这么久的一种福泽。
（《麦书》〔1893〕5.2a）
（34）咁垂俵落来，就泵泵下。就这样垂了下来，摇摇摆摆的样子。（《麦诗》〔c.1893〕
1.30b）

"D 类"是指"哓"出现在动补结构的中间。这类例子所牵涉的补语成分，大部分都
属方向补语。刚才看过 C 类有很多"V＋去＋哓"结构，但原来"V＋哓＋去"也一
早出现了（例 30）。有一点需要注明：麦仕治的作品中并不是没有"V＋哓＋去"结构，
只是数量不多而已。下面是其中两个例子：

（35）出嘵去郊外。到了郊外去了。（《麦诗》〔*c*.1893〕2.3a）[30]

（36）就流嘵去。就流走了。（《麦诗》〔*c*.1893〕3.33b）[31]

文献中并存着两种结构，反映出"V＋嘵＋去"和"V＋去＋嘵"当时正处于"竞争"的状态。不用说，最后是"D类"胜出了这场比赛。

要是遇到复合方向补语（例31、32、34），"嘵"一律置于动词和补语之间，和现代广州话并无二致。[32]例（33）的"有"，据余霭芹的理解，是"一种用在动词或动补结构后作肯定性的补语"。[33]我们暂时把它归入"D类"。

看过上述三十多个在早期广州话语料中带"嘵"的例子后，我们马上得到一个印象："嘵"和"咗"出现的场合似乎没有明显的分别。[34]换言之，"嘵"、"咗"可能只是词汇层面上的差异。

刘丹青认为，一个成熟的体标记可以从以下四方面体现出来：（一）谓词提供了新信息，甚至是焦点所在；（二）没有可能式；（三）可以接在动补结构后面；（四）不能接同类意义的纯体标记。[35]文献中的"嘵"大多数都符合这些条件。因此把它们都视为"纯体助词"，并无不妥。[36]问题是也有少数例子，显示出"嘵"还没有完全虚化的痕迹：

（37）倘若尔地果能去得嘵自己顾自己有益呢一段私心。假如你们可以去除得到自己顾自己这一种自私的想法。（《麦书》〔1893〕2.30b）

句中"去得嘵自己顾自己有益呢一段私心"应该被分析为"V＋得＋嘵＋O"。这个"得"分明是个能性补语标记。[37]句子前面的助动词"能"是一个相当有力的旁证。如果我们的看法没错，"嘵"只能视为补语。用现代的广州话来说，"去得嘵"就是"去除得晒"或"去除得倒"。例（37）在"嘵"的发展史上扮演着非常重要的角色。本文后半部讨论"嘵"的演变途径时，还要提到这个例子。

"V＋得＋嘵＋O"结构在文献中毕竟只有一个。我们能否通过其他途径，找到别的以"嘵"作补语的例子呢？请看以下三例：

（38）都总唔能来除得佢去嘵。不能把它扫光。（《麦诗》〔*c*.1893〕1.20b）

（39）我就同尔劏嘵、煮熟、烩到焓到合尔口味来食。我就替你切好、煮熟、烧得合你的口味来吃。（《麦诗》〔*c*.1893〕2.6b）

（40）嗰的日子，就过晒去嘵。那些日子，都已经过去了。（《麦诗》〔*c*.1893〕2.22a）

例（38）和例（40）反映着同一个现象，我们先一并讨论。（38）牵涉可能式"除得佢去"，（40）则有体标记"晒"。引用刘丹青对体标记所订下的条件，上面例子的"哓"便肯定不会是纯体助词。我们怀疑这里的"去哓"是一个复合补语，"哓"是补语的一部分。因为按照这样的理解，"除得佢去哓"才符合语法：它跟"除得佢去"有着同样的结构，即"V＋得＋O＋C"。[38] 前文我们也讨论过一些"V＋去＋哓"的例子，但由于出现的环境不一样，所以这里的"去哓"和前述的"去哓"可能属于不同的结构。例（39）"劙哓"和"煮熟"对举，两者的语法结构应该十分相似。"煮熟"毫无疑问是动补结构，那么"劙哓"的"哓"就应该是个补语。

刘丹青把由补语虚化至体标记的过程划分为四个阶段，其中第二个阶段是"唯补词"："不能作谓语，紧接在动词后，有或专门或宽泛的结果义，可以作为句子焦点，多数可以重读，都有可能式，兼有某种体意义，但后面可以有（但不是必须有）纯体助词（没有纯体助词的方言除外）。"[39] 我们建议把像例（37）、（39）这种"哓"归入唯补词一类。它们代表了"哓"发展为纯体助词之前的面貌。

纵使我们掌握了"哓"虚化途径的一些线索，但对它的"本字"依然没有什么头绪。解决这个问题，必须通过方言之间的比较。

4．和其他粤语方言的比较

"哓"在广州话中已经消失了，但其他粤语方言中可能仍然使用它。首先引起我们注意的，是东莞莞城话（下文简称"东莞话"）。东莞话的完成体标记是 [hau^{324}]，一般写作"敲"。詹伯慧、陈晓锦编纂的《东莞方言词典》为这个词收录了两个义项：

（一）"用在动词或形容词后面，表示动作或变化已经完成：食~饭 / 放~学就去嬲玩 / 荔枝黄熟~"
（二）"用在形容词后面，表示得很，非常之意：甜啲~非常甜 / 皓苏~非常亮"[40]

第一个义项是完成体标记，第二个义项是形容词重叠式的第二个成分。这两个义项看来没有什么直接的联系，应该分开处理。下文只集中讨论"敲"作完成体标记的用法。

"敲"在东莞话里至少已经存活了三百多年。屈大均（1630—1696）《广东新语》卷十一《土言》有这样的记载："东莞谓事讫曰効。"[41] 屈氏是广东番禺人。"効"现代番禺市桥话念 [hau^{22}]，[42] 和东莞的"敲" [hau^{324}] 十分接近。[43] 加上词义（事讫）上的高度配合，我们相信《广东新语》的"効"和今天东莞话的"敲"是同一个词。有趣的是，屈大均特别标明东莞用"効"，同时又没有提及广州话的情况。这可能是当时广州话有另一个完成体标记。十九世纪末 Saunders 在 *The China Review* 上简单介绍过东莞石龙的音系和词汇。他把完成体标记写成"休"*hau*，[44] 可惜没有提供任何实际的例子。

《东莞方言词典》里有不少带"敲"的例句。我们发现：东莞话的"敲"和广州话的"哓"在语法层面上没有任何差别。只要把下列例句中的"敲"换成"哓"，就是广州话的说法：

（41）银包唔见敲。钱包不见了。【A 类：V + 敲】

（42）辛苦敲你成日真系多谢啦。辛苦了你一整天，真的很感谢。【B 类：V + 敲 + O】

（43）打烂敲就搞唔掂。把它打破了就不得了。【C 类：V + C + 敲】

（44）改革开放令千家万户富敲起嚟。改革开放使千家万户富了起来了。【D 类：V + 敲 + C】

新界围头话和东莞话有密切的联系。Barnett 曾经注意到围头话"陈"、"文"、"岈"等字由 -n 尾并入 -ŋ 尾，可能源自东莞话。[45] 稍后沙加尔对新界吉庆围话进行了一次系统的调查，指出这种围头话和东莞石龙话"拥有很多共同的特征"。他同意 Barnett 的观察。[46] 张双庆、庄初升的《香港新界方言》记录了蕃田、泰亨和蚝涌三种围头话的资料。它们是否都像东莞话一样，以"敲"作为完成体标记呢？请看表 1。

表 1　三种新界围头话的完成体标记 [47]

	去了	饿死了	花开了两朵了
广州话	去哓	饿死哓	啲花开哓两朵
蕃田话	去来啰	饿死哓	花开哓两□ [tyœn³⁵] 了
泰亨话	去哓	饿死哓	花开哓两□ [tyœn³⁵]
蚝涌话	去后	饿死后	花开后两朵

蕃田话和泰亨话都用"哓"[tʃɔ³⁵]，可能是广州话的借词。蚝涌话的"后"[hɐu³³] 看来和东莞话的"敲"有关，这点我们在下文比较它们的音韵地位时会作深入的论证。[48]

据《珠江三角洲方言词汇对照》，中山（旧称香山）石岐话的完成体标记是"哺"[pʰu⁵⁵]，[49] 本字不明。赵元任在上世纪四十年代所做的调查则记录了三个标记：[pʰou⁵⁵]、[hou⁵⁵] 和 [ou⁵⁵]。他没有说清楚这三个标记的关系，只写道它们都是"动词的词尾，相当于广州的'嗰'、苏州的'仔'、常州的'则'、北平的'了'。"[50] 把时间推得更前一点，Ball 在 1897 年一篇报道香山小榄方言的文章中指出：香山话从不用"咕"表完成，用的是"噭"，并注明这可能和广州话的"晓"是同一个词。[51] 他把"噭"拼写为 *háu*，转换成国际音标就是 [hau⁵⁵]。如果不作一番考证，我们很难想象中山话的完成体标记在不到一百年的时间内，竟然至少发生了两次重大的变化，即：[hau⁵⁵] > [pʰou⁵⁵] / [hou⁵⁵] / [ou⁵⁵] > [pʰu⁵⁵]。[52]

澳门本来是香山县的一个渔港，因此老派的澳门粤语基本上就是中山粤语的一个分支。林柏松比较过老派澳门话和新派澳门话的异同，他提到："动词＋'敲'（hau⁵⁵）表动作完成，是新澳门话的一个特色，它可能是受邻近水上话'敲'（hɐu⁵³）的影响而变成的。"[53] 澳门话的完成体标记 [hau⁵⁵] 居然和 Ball 百多年前记录的香山话一模一样。但耐人寻味的是，林先生强调"敲"是新派澳门话的用法，而且认为这个新式的完成体标记可能借自邻近水上话的 [hɐu⁵³]。究竟澳门话的"敲"是存古（承继香山话百多前的说法）还是创新（借自邻近的水上话），需要仔细推敲。

南海地区的粤语方言一共有八个完成体标记，[54] 其中四个在读音上和"晓"相仿佛，或者可以视之为关系词。[55] 这四个完成体标分别是：（一）[jɐu⁵³]，流行于小塘狮北；（二）[hɐu⁵³] 或 [hɐu⁵⁵]，流行于凤鸣三山、罗村务庄、小塘鹤巢里等地；（三）[ɐu⁵³]，流行于官窑的刘边、唐边、黄洞等地；（四）[ɛ⁵³]，流行于西樵、丹灶、沙头等地。完成体标记如此丰富，一方面代表了语言接触相当厉害，语言部件的借用非常频繁；另一方面则反映了虚词语音的弱化在不同地区有不同表现。

以上我们先后介绍了东莞、蚝涌、中山、澳门、南海五种粤语方言的完成体标记，发现它们拥有几个共同的特征：（一）声母主要是 /h/；（二）韵尾都是 /u/；（三）以阴平调为主。唯一的分别是主元音。要寻求它的本字，首先便要确立它的音韵地位。表 2 列出东莞、蚝涌、中山（包括早期的香山和二十世纪以后的中山）、澳门四种方言完成体标记 [56] 以及早期广州话"晓"的读音，并分别与"休"（中古流摄开口三等）、"敲"（中古效摄开口二等）、"掉"（中古效摄开口四等）、"好"（中古效摄开口一等）四字进行比较。

表 2　东莞等六种粤语方言完成体标记的音韵地位 [57]

	完成体标记	休	敲	掉	好
广州话	hiu⁵⁵	jɐu⁵⁵	hau⁵⁵	tiu²² ~ tɐu²² [58]	hou³⁵
东莞话	hau²¹³	hau²¹³	hau²¹³	tiu³²	hɔu³⁵
蚝涌话	hɐu³³	jɐu²³	hau³⁵ "巧"	——	hɐu³⁵

	完成体标记	休	敲	掉	好
香山话	hau^{55}	iɐu^{55}	hau^{55}	tiu^{33}	hou^{213}
中山话	hou^{55}	iɐu^{55}	hau^{55}	tiu^{33}	hou^{213}
澳门话	hau^{55}	iɐu^{55}	hau^{55}	tiu^{22}	hou^{13}

比较的重点在韵母方面。在每一列中（每列代表不同的方言），凡是和完成体标记拥有相同韵母的字，我们都用灰色底色加以强调。例如广州话"唨"、"掉"同韵，于是这两个字都被打上灰色。

这五种方言的完成体标记虽然读音相近，但音韵上却并没有显示出规则的对应。我们根据韵母的归并模式，把它们归纳为四个类型：

一、广州型：完成体标记和"掉"同韵。同类型的还有早期的香港话。[59]

二、东莞型：完成体标记和"休"同韵。同类型的还有蚝涌话。

三、中山型：完成体标记 [hou^{55}] 和"好"同韵。

四、澳门型：完成体标记和"敲"同韵。同类型的还有十九世纪的香山话。

先谈广州型。广州话"唨"以 / i / 作为主元音，读同效摄开口四等字，和其他类型以 / a /、/ ɐ / 等低元音为主元音的情况不太一样。"唨"和其他类型的完成体标记不单在音韵上没有平行的例证，我们甚至很难解释这个 -iu 韵母到底和其他类型的韵母（-au、-ɐu 等）有什么承传关系。从类型学看，无论是 *-iu ＞ -au，还是 *-au ＞ -iu，[60] 都是极其罕见的。幸亏在广州话中有几个和"唨"同韵的字带有异读，使我们知道 -iu 有来源于 -ɐu 的可能。

广州话"掉"、"寮"、"撩"、"嚼"等字都有两个读音，韵母既可念 -iu，也可念 -ɐu。[61] 很多时候我们根本看不出这些异读之间的分别，或者只觉得 -ɐu 韵一读比较少用而已。[62] 表 3 把这些字的异读都罗列出来。

表 3　广州话 -ɐu 韵母和 -iu 韵母的异读

	异读 1	异读 2
掉	tiu^{22}	tɐu^{22}
寮（空～～，空洞洞）	liu^{55}	lɐu^{55}
撩（拨取）	liu^{35}	lɐu^{35}

（续表）

	异读 1	异读 2
噍（咀嚼）	tʃiu²²	tʃɛu²²
撬	kiu²²	kɛu²²
绕（缠着）	kʰiu¹³	kʰɛu¹³
夹	kip³³	kɛp³³
哓	hiu⁵⁵	（hɛu⁵⁵）

异读 1 和异读 2 应该代表着两个"同源层次"。王福堂说："同源层次中的新音类是旧音类演变的结果，而演变应该是可以用音理来说明的。这里把语音变化的过程看成是一个环环相接的链，那么旧的语音形式总是这个音链的上环，新的语音形式总是这个音链的下环，两者的位置不会倒置。"[63] 套用王先生的话，-ɛu 属于旧音类，是音链的上环；-iu 则为新音类，是由 -ɛu 演变而来的。-ɛu > -iu 是一种非常普通的音变，曾经在不少汉语方言中发生过，包括新界的客语方言。[64] 放在这样的框架下，我们可以认为："哓"本应也有 [hɛu⁵⁵] 一读。[hɛu⁵⁵] 其后发展为 [hiu⁵⁵]，而这个新兴的 [hiu⁵⁵] 不久就取代了 [hɛu⁵⁵] 的地位。前文说过，Stedman and Lee（1888）把广州话的完成体标记标写为 ˌheu。换成国际音标，正好就是我们所拟构的 [hɛu⁵⁵]。然而，[hɛu⁵⁵] 还不是我们的最终目标。

中古麻韵三等字广州话普遍念 -ɛ 韵母，这个 -ɛ 其实是由 -ia 演变而来的，只要和开平、恩平、东莞等方言比较一下就可以一目了然。庚韵三等字和麻三是一个平行的韵，经历了 -iaŋ > -iɛŋ 的音变，主元音在介音 -i- 的带动下由 /a/ 提升至 /ɛ/。介音丢失以后，就成了今天的 -ɛŋ。[65] 广州话的 /ɛ/ 既然有如此来历，那么我们也不妨把 [hɛu⁵⁵] 更早的形式拟构为 *hiau^阴平。如果属实，广州话"哓"的音变应该包含了两个步骤，即：*hiau^阴平 > hɛu⁵⁵ > hiu⁵⁵。这个拟构一方面能照顾到东莞话和早期中山话完成体标记的读音（分别只在于介音的有无），另一方面又解释了广州话的特殊发展方向。*hiau^阴平可能是各种类型的"哓"/"敲"的来源。[66]

中山话的完成体标记，Ball 1897 年的记音是 [hau⁵⁵]，赵元任 1948 年的调查写作 [hou⁵⁵]。两者有三种可能的关系：（一）最直接的方案，是认为 [hau⁵⁵] 演变为 [hou⁵⁵]，但我们找不到任何平行的例子。（二）Ball 记录的是香山小榄话，而赵先生记录的则是中山石岐话，可能这两种次方言用了不同的完成体标记。不过，我们细心比较过小榄和石岐 -au、-ou 两韵的分布，看不出有什么明显的分别。（三）[hau⁵⁵] 和 [hou⁵⁵] 不是同一个词。[hou⁵⁵] 可能是由 "好" [67] 经感染作用（contamination）而产生的。[68] 第三个方案在音、义两方面都讲得通，比较可行。既然语源不同，那么我们可以把中山型剔除掉。"晓" 在粤语方言的表现现在只剩下三个类型。

澳门话的 "敲"，我们认为就是 Ball 所说的 "嚓"。林柏松认为："'敲'……是新澳门话的一个特色"，似乎没有留意到 Ball 的记录。而且林先生也没有说明为什么水上话的 [hɛu⁵³] 借入澳门话之后会变成 [hau⁵⁵]。澳门型的 "敲" 和东莞型的 "敲"，声母、韵母、甚至调类都完全一样，应该怎样理解它们的关系呢？这是因为澳门话和东莞话同样都保留了 "敲" 较早期的面貌。用发生学的术语说，就是共同存古（shared retention）的表现。

南海话的 [hɛu⁵³]、[ɛu⁵³] 和 [ɛ⁵³] 代表一个词演变的三个阶段：[hɛu⁵³] 是原来的面貌，它毫无疑问和早期广州话的 [hɛu⁵⁵] 有关；h- 声母脱落了以后就是 [ɛu⁵³]；[ɛu⁵³] 如果进一步弱化为单元音，那就是 [ɛ⁵³]。和上述三个完成体标记不同，[jɛu⁵³] 只见于一个方言点（小塘狮北）中。分布如此狭窄，我们怀疑它是通过语言接触，从邻近方言中借来的。换句话说，[jɛu⁵³] 和 [hɛu⁵³]、[ɛu⁵³]、[ɛ⁵³] 纵使读音相近，但也许有不同的源头。根据目前仅有的数据，我们暂时可以把凤鸣三山、罗村务庄等地所用的 [hɛu⁵⁵] 归入 "广州型"。

东莞话的 "敲" 早见于三百多年前的《广东新语》，在诸种以 "敲" / "晓" 作为完成体标记的方言中，历史最为悠久。在表 2 中我们可以看到，东莞的完成体标记除了和 "敲" 同音外，也跟 "休" 同音。事实上，张洪年在考证广州话 "晓" 的语源时，就提出过 "晓" 来自 "休" 的想法。他立论的主要根据，是 Stedman and Lee（1888）一书把完成体标记写作 "咻"，[69] 而不是东莞话。"休" 的确可能就是我们要找的本字，但在得出最终结论之前，必须找到更具体的证据，以及解决方言间韵母不对应等问题。

"休" 具有以下几项特质，足以使人相信它就是广州话 "晓"、澳门话 "敲" 和东莞话 "敲" 的本字。首先要谈的是古文献的写法。除了 Stedman and Lee（1888）和前面提过的 Saunders（1896—1897）外，粤语讲唱文学木鱼书也有把完成体标记写作 "休" 的例子：

（45）过了小春廿月到。过休十二月，又是一年辰。(《日边红杏》)[70]

"过休十二月" 相当于现在广州话的 "过咗十二月"。文中 "休" 和 "了" 对举，意思明显不过。《日边红杏》的撰作年代已不可考，[71] 但作者把完成体标记写作 "休"，表示广州话的"晓"也曾经有过类似"休"的读音。

其次我们注意到词义上的配合。"休"的本义是休息、停止。《说文·木部》:"休,息止也。"[72] 后来引申为完结。下面三个例子中的"休",都有完结的意思:

（46）陶渊明《归去来兮辞》:"善万物之得时,感吾生之行休。"今人龚斌《陶渊明集校笺》对"行休"的注释:"指年命将尽,与《游斜川》诗'吾生行归休'句同意。逯《注》:'行休,即将退休。'非是。"[73]"行休"可分析为"V＋完成动词",[74] 和《世说新语》的"言毕"、"食竟"、"听讫"具有相同的结构。

（47）敦煌曲子词《定风波》（伯3093）:"更遇盲依（医）与宣谢（泻）,休也,头面大汗永分离。"[75]

（48）《水浒全传》第五十一回:"若孩儿有些好歹,老身性名也便休矣。"[76]

不单古文献如是,某些现代汉语方言的"休"也可以作完成动词用。像江西赣州蟠龙客语的"休命"[ɕiu²⁴ miã⁵³],就有"完蛋"之义。[77] 我们知道,完成动词普遍都具备发展为完成体标记的性质。世界上很多语言都体现了这一点。详细情形我们会在下一节检讨"休"的语法化途径时再作交代。

读音方面,我们先前已经根据广州话的情况,把"晓"的原始形式拟构为 *hiau阴平。这个标记在广州话和南海话里都经历过元音高化（ *iau ＞ ɛu）,广州话更进一步发展为 [hiu⁵⁵]。东莞话和澳门话的特征是丢掉介音,但主元音没有变化。蚝涌话虽然把韵母读为 -ɛu,但却合乎方言自身的对应规律。[78] 此外,"休"是中古晓母字,各方言读 /h/ 其实是正常不过的。各方言"晓"的演变途径可以概括如下:

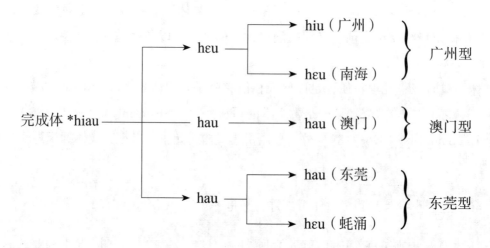

现在还有一个问题需要解决:为什么广州话会把"休"读作 [jɛu⁵⁵] 呢? 我们认为

[jɐu⁵⁵] 和 [hiu⁵⁵] 属于同源层次的变体。先谈声母的情况。文读音 [jɐu⁵⁵] 以半元音 j- 作为声母,这个 j- 并非由 h- 演变而来,而是 *hiau 的 h- 声母在文读演变的过程中脱落所造成的。广州话把中古晓母字念成 j- 声母的,还有"旭"、"衅"、"欣"三个字,[79] 均属开口三等。同样地,南海沙头话和顺德大良话有大量中古喻三、喻四字读 h- 声母的例子,如南海的"雨"[hy¹³]、"圆"[hyn⁴⁴]、"异"[hi²²],[80] 顺德的"远"[hyn¹³]、"姨"[hi⁴²]、"盐"[him⁴²]、"叶"[hip²¹] 等。[81] 这些字在广州话以及大部分粤语方言中都念 j- 声母。套用比较法,可以把它们的原始形式拟构为 *hi-("异"、"盐"等字)或 *hy-("雨"、"远"等字)。如果属实,那么就代表广州话某些字曾经经历过一个 *hi-, *hy- > j- 的音变。[82] 这个音变和"休"的弱化是完全平行的。韵母方面,-iu 韵和 -ɐu 韵都是由 *-iau 韵发展而来的。它们之所以有不同的演变路向,可能和体标记的性质有关。体标记是个非常常用的虚词。虚词的演变速度较慢、演变方向也往往跟实词不一样。[83] 我们推测:当一般尤韵字已经参加了 -iau > -iou 这条音变规律时,[84] 完成体的"休"还依然念 -iau。澳门话把完成体标记念作 [hau⁵⁵],主元音依然维持 /a/,没有跟随一般尤韵字变作 -ɐu,便是滞古的最佳明证。稍后 -iau > -iou 这条规律失效了,"休"就接受了另一种音变,即:-iau > -ɛu > -iu。这样"休"和其他尤韵字就分隶两韵了。

完成体"休":　　　*-iau ＞ -iau ＞ -ɛu ＞ -iu
"休"及其他尤韵字: *-iau ＞ -iou ＞ -ɐu

"休"虽然有 [jɐu⁵⁵]、[hiu⁵⁵] 两读,和文白异读的现象颇相类似,但由于一般人根本不知道 [hiu⁵⁵] 的本字就是"休",所以不会产生徐通锵所谓的"叠置式音变"。[85] 作为完成体标记,"休"的衰落并不是来自文读音的挑战,而是另一个词完全取代了它。

可以看到,"休"无论是书写方式,还是词义、读音等几方面,都和"哓"相对应,我们相信它就是"哓"的本字。

5."休"的语法化路径及其消亡的过程

前面提过,"休"的本义是"休息、停止",引申为"完结、完成"。事实上,世界上不少语言的完成体标记都来源于表完成的词语,好像 Cocama 语、Kongo 语、Tucano 语、Tem 语、寮语(Lao)、拉祜语(Lahu)、拉萨藏语等等。[86] 汉语方面,"已"、"讫"、"竟"、"毕"、"罢"这些在古代流行一时的完成体标记,本身统统都是完成动词。[87] 现代汉语所使用的"了"也是一样。因此，"休"带"完成"义，就表示它具备了发展为完成体标记的潜质。

"休"在语法化前还应该经历了一个充当结果补语（或者"唯补词"）的阶段。例（37）是一个很好的例子，它保存了"休"较原始的用法。刘丹青曾经以苏州话的"好"为例，说明"好"怎样由谓词、结果补语，最终发展成一个成熟的体标记。[88]"休"的演变过程大概和"好"是平行的。

在十九世纪中后叶的广州话语料中，"休"大部分情形下都以一个成熟体标记的姿态出现：可以出现在动补结构后头、没有可能式、跟其他纯体标记发生排斥。实词的意义既不存在，那就是说"休"当时已经经历了语法化的洗礼。"休"的演变历程可以概括为以下几个阶段：

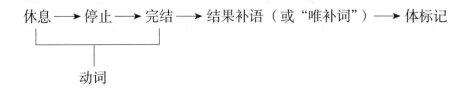

和其他体标记比较起来，"休"的语法化途径没有什么特别的地方。可以说，"休"的语法化在某程度上体现了人类语言演变的共性。[89]

接着要谈的是早期广州话的"晓"和其他完成体标记的关系。

Bridgman（1841）和 Devan（1847）出版的年份只差几年，但前者只用"了"，后者只用"晓"，是否表示"了"在几年间被"晓"取替了呢？我们认为不是。Bridgman 书中有不少内容是外国人向中国老师请教古文的对话。Devan 本身是个医生，该书的编写方针是以医生和病人的对话为中心的。可能由于读者的对象不同，所以影响了那两部书的用辞。社会语言学中有所谓"高层语言"（high language）和"低层语言"（low language）的区分。[90]"高层语言"是指统治阶级或强势社团所用的语言。相反，"低层语言"就是低下阶层所用的语言。或者我们可以这样猜测："了"属于高层语言，在较正式的场合中使用；而"晓"则是低层语言，用于日常生活的口语中。[91]换言之，"了"、"晓"的分野并不是历史先后的问题。张洪年认为"晓"很早就存活在广州话的口语中，甚至超越文献所记载的上限。[92]我们同意他的见解。

踏入二十世纪二十年代以后，"晓"在文献中以完成体标记出现的比例越来越少，到了四十年代就完全消失了。"晓"走向衰亡，有两个主要原因。首先是"咗"的出现。[93]"咗"最早见于 Williams（1856），写作"阻"。作者对这个词的解释是："A sign of the past tense, placed after the verb like *hiu*."（页 26）这句话为"咗"（阻）/"晓"功能的相似性下了一个很实在的注脚。"咗"、"嗋"在十九世纪末、二十世纪初一直处于竞争的状态。到了二十世纪四十年代,"咗"终于胜出了这场比赛,完全取代了"嗋"作为广州话完成体标记的位置。这种虚词更替、但并不影响句法结构的现象,在汉语发展的历史长河中不时出现。梅祖麟作过一个很生动的譬喻:"句法结构不变,词汇中的新陈代谢就像接力赛跑,一个运动员跑累了,另一个接棒跑下去。汉语语法史常有这种现象,所以有些现代汉语句型的渊源,一直可以追溯到五世纪,完成貌就是明显的例子。"[94]语法化过程中有所谓"择一原则"(specialization),即"能表达同一语法功能的多种并存形式经过筛选和淘汰,最后缩减到一二种。"[95]"咗"之取代"嗋",也可以视为广州话"择一"的表现。

"嗋"总是黏附在谓词的后头。由于这种虚词经常出现在口语中,久而久之,它的语音会受到磨损,最后弱化至以变调的形式依附在谓词中。张洪年曾经深入观察过"嗋"弱化的过程。他认为弱化分三个阶段进行:

第一阶段:V + 体标记[96]
第二阶段:V* + 体标记("*"代表变调)
第三阶段:V*

每一个阶段都可以在早期的语料中找到证据。至于变调的规则,则要视乎前头谓词调值的高低:

$$V [+ 高] + 嗋 [+ 高] \rightarrow V^{55}$$
$$V [- 高] + 嗋 [+ 高] \rightarrow V^{35}$$

据张文的统计,Ball(1912)用"嗋"的例子有八个,占全部完成体标记16%;变调的例子则有二十二个,占全部完成体标记44%。[97]后者差不多是前者的三倍。这说明,以变调表完成,在二十世纪初的广州话中曾经一度是主流。[98]语音弱化,是"嗋"走向衰亡的另一个原因。[99]

6. 结论

或者有人会觉得考察个别词语演变的意义并不很大。但本文把早期的广州话"嗋"放在一个较宽阔的层面上观察,有别于一般"考本字"的文章:[100]一方面我们努力地从十九世纪末、二十世纪初的广州话文献中发掘相关例子，另一方面又着重和当代方言进行比较。视野给开拓了，我们自然可以看到更深邃的景观。

总的来说，本文厘清了三个问题：（一）"哓"的语源；（二）"哓"在各种粤语方言里的发展（音韵上和语法上的）；（三）"哓"在早期广州话语料中所显示的语法特色。"哓"的故事告诉我们：词汇、语音和语法是三位一体的，研究历史词汇时不能不兼顾音韵和语法的因素。其实李方桂早在 1974 年的一次演讲中就已经指出：

> 一个方言往往有一个方言的词汇，是跟别种方言的词汇不同。在一个方言里有多少个词汇，而且属于这个方言区的，别的方言不用的，这类材料应大量地搜集，因为如果有些词汇是属于这个方言所特有的，那么，一定在它的音韵上具有相当的重要性。……研究汉语音韵学，不仅是研究它的语音情形，我想与语法这门学问也有相当的关系。[101]

李先生主张把音韵学、语法学、词汇学联合起来解决语言学上的种种问题，并以它作为音韵学发展其中一个主要的方向。这番话在三十年后的今天读起来仍然有其深远意义。

附 注

[1] 英语的 "aspect" 有多种译法，例如"动相"、"情貌"、"动态"、"情态"等，这里我们采用刘丹青的方案，译作"体"。参阅刘著：《东南方言的体貌标记》，载张双庆（主编）：《动词的体》（香港：香港中文大学中国文化研究所吴多泰中国语文研究中心，1995 年），页 9—33。

[2] 本文广州话的标音，除特别标明者外，均依李新魁等：《广州方言研究》（广州：广东人民出版社，1995 年）的系统。引用时作了两个改动：（一）送气符号由 ['] 改为 [ʰ]；（二）阴平调一律标为 55。换言之，没有 55 和 53 的区别。

[3] 关于"咗"出现的场合，可参考以下几种具代表性的著作：张洪年：《香港粤语语法的研究》（香港：香港中文大学出版社，1972 年），页 144—7；Stephen Matthews（马诗帆）and Virginia Yip（叶彩燕）: *Cantonese: A Comprehensive Grammar*（London: Routledge, 1994）, pp. 204–5；李新魁等：《广州方言研究》，页 554；彭小川：《广州话的动态助词"咗"》，载胡明扬（主编）：《汉语方言体貌论文集》（南京：江苏教育出版社，1996 年），页 226—39；Hilary Chappell（曹茜蕾）: "The perfective aspect marker jó in Cantonese Yue spoken narratives", in *Studia Linguistica Serica*, ed. Benjamin K. T'sou（Hong Kong: Language Information Sciences Research Centre, City University of Hong Kong, 1998）, pp.145–73。

[4] 张洪年:《香港粤语语法的研究》,页 145。

[5] 广府片粤语分布在广州、番禺、顺德、南海、佛山、三水等二十多个县市境内,参阅熊正辉:《广东方言的分区》,《方言》1987 年第 3 期,页 161。

[6] 参考詹伯慧、张日昇(主编):《珠江三角洲方言词汇对照》,珠江三角洲方言调查报告之二(香港:新世纪出版社,1988 年),页 277,"睡了"条;同编者:《粤北十县市粤方言调查报告》(广州:暨南大学出版社,1994 年),页 609,"睡了"条;同编者:《粤西十县市粤方言调查报告》(广州:暨南大学出版社,1998 年),页 613,"睡了"条;张双庆、庄初升:《香港新界方言》(香港:商务印书馆,2003 年),页 724,"饿死了"条。

[7] 黎纬杰:《粤方言的变调表完成体》,载詹伯慧(主编):《第二届国际粤方言研讨会论文集》(广州:暨南大学出版社,1990 年),页 182。

[8] 游汝杰:《西洋传教士汉语方言学著作书目考述》(哈尔滨:黑龙江教育出版社,2002 年),页 5。

[9] "雅言中心观"是指古代中国人从雅言(标准语)角度去观察"方言"(非标准语,包括汉语和少数民族语言)的一种观念。这种观念支配了中国语言学近二千年。何大安《从中国学术传统论汉语方言研究的过去、现在与未来》(《"中研院"历史语言研究所集刊》第 63 卷第 4 期〔1993 年〕,页 714—7)对此有详细的分析。

[10] 游汝杰:《西洋传教士汉语方言学著作书目考述》,页 17、21。

[11] 就我们手头上的数据看,"咗"最早见于 S. W. Williams(卫三畏)的 *Tonic Dictionary of the Chinese Language in the Canton Dialect*(1856),到了二十世纪三十年代以后才开始成为主流。参考 Hung-nin Samuel Cheung(张洪年), "Completing the completive:(Re)constructing early Cantonese grammar", in *Studies on the History of Chinese Syntax*, ed. Chaofen Sun, Journal of Chinese Linguistics Monograph Series No.10(Berkeley: Project on Linguistic Analysis, 1997),p.152 表 2 的统计。

[12] 如 E. C. Bridgman(禆治文)*Chinese Chrestomathy in the Canton Dialect*(Macao: S. W. Williams, 1841)。此书一般用"了"作为完成体标记,但也有些情况不用标记。见 Cheung, "Completing the completive", pp.153–4.

[13] 如 S. W. Bonney, *A Vocabulary with Colloquial Phrases, of the Canton Dialect*(Canton: The Chinese Repository, 1854)。

[14] 原书没有注明作者,此系据 James D. Ball, *Reading in Cantonese Colloquial: Being Selections from Books in the Cantonese Vernacular with Free and Literal Translations of the Chinese Character and Romanised Spelling*(Hong Kong: Kelly and Walsh, 1894),p. XXVI 补。

[15] 原书并无注明作者,但 Ball 曾经提及此书,并指出作者是 Mrs. French,见 *Reading in Cantonese Colloquial*, p. XXVI。

[16] 原书没有注明作者,此系据 H. W. Spillett, *A Catalogue of Scriptures in the Languages of*

China and the Republic of China（London: British and Foreign Bible Society, 1975），p.130 补。

[17] 原书没有注明作者，此系据 Ball, *Reading in Cantonese Colloquial*, p. XXVIII 补。

[18] Anne O. Yue（余霭芹），"Materials for the diachronic study of the Yue dialects", in *The Joy of Research: A Festschrift in Honor of Professor William S-Y. Wang on His Seventieth Birthday*, ed. Feng Shi and Zhongwei Shen (Tianjin: Nankai University Press, 2004), p.271.

[19] 所有采自 Burdon（1877）的例子，都用原书的官话翻译。

[20] 1.13a 代表卷一页十三上。下仿此。

[21] 施其生：《论"有"字句》，载施其生：《方言论稿》（广州：广东人民出版社，1996 年），页 52。

[22] 张洪年《香港粤语语法的研究》已经指出："'咗'字一般不能和'有、冇、未'诸字并用。"（页 147）但他没有详细解释原因。

[23] 余霭芹这样评论《麦书》中的"将字句"："'将'字句的处置式用得异常普遍，而且'将'字尚有动词性，可带体貌标志。"见所著：《粤语方言的历史研究——读〈麦仕治广州俗话《书经》解义〉》，《中国语文》2000 年第 6 期，页 502。

[24] 这两个例子 Cheung, "Completing the completive", p.142 曾经引述过。

[25] 张洪年：《香港粤语语法的研究》，第三章。这九类分别是"结果补语"、"状态补语"、"强化补语"、"方向补语"、"能性补语"、"回复补语"、"描写补语"、"程度补语"和"黏附性词组补语"。

[26] 基本上只有结果补语、状态补语和方向补语可以带体标记。

[27] 参阅张洪年：《香港粤语语法的研究》，页 117—8 的分析。

[28] "晒"有的时候像补语，有的情况又像体标记。这里采用了张洪年《香港粤语语法的研究》页 159—61 的处理方法。

[29] 闽语即以"去"表"完成"，参阅李如龙《泉州方言的"体"》和陈泽平《福州方言动词的体和貌》两文，载张双庆（主编）：《动词的体》，页 195—224,225—53。不过闽语的"去"可以出现在动补结构之后，显然是一个成熟的体标记。至于为什么早期广州话的"去"有"完成"的意思，由于已超出本文考察的范围，所以不拟详探。

[30] 张洪年《香港粤语语法的研究》在讨论现代广州话体标记跟动补结构的结合时说："假如是简单的方向补语，而又带有表示处所的宾语时候，那么'词尾'（即本文的'体标记'）就加在动词之后、补语之前"（页 117），如"行咗落三楼"（下到三楼去）。麦仕治作品的"V＋去＋哓"结构，数量纵使很多，却从来不带处所宾语。例（35）带处所宾语，则采用较少见的"V+哓＋去"结构。这间接说明了张洪年提出的规律应该可以套用到麦氏的语言里去。

[31] 有一个和例（36）构成最小对立（minimal contrast）的例子："咁流去傆略。"（《麦诗》〔*c.*1893〕3.60b）我们有理由相信："流哓去"和"流去哓"在没有处所宾语的条件下是自

由变体（free variants）。

[32] 参考张洪年:《香港粤语语法的研究》，页 117—78。

[33] 余霭芹:《粤语方言的历史研究》，页 502。

[34] 例（6）的"我有行哓"是个孤例，或可当例外处理。

[35] 刘丹青:《东南方言的体貌标记》，页 15—7。Anne Yue-Hashimoto（余霭芹）在 *Comparative Chinese Dialectal Grammar: Handbook for Investigators*（Paris: CRLAO, EHESS, 1993），p.69 中则提到了体补语（aspectual complement）和体词缀（aspectual suffix）的分别。她认为体词缀和词干是不能分割的（inseparable），但体补语却可以和词干分开处理。

[36] 刘丹青《东南方言的体貌标记》给"纯体助词"下的定义是:"意义广泛虚化，只表示前面动词的体，有广泛的配搭面，可用在半实或半虚的体标记后，在有轻声的方言中一般念轻声。"（页 21）

[37] 针对现代广州话能性补语的情况，张洪年《香港粤语语法的研究》说:"所谓能性补语，就是在本来一个谓补结构中，插进一个词嵌（infix）而成。这个词嵌，若是表示正面意思的，就是'得'，表示反面的，就是'唔'。"（页 119）

[38] 可能有人会想到"去哓"的"哓"是个句末助词:"去哓"相当于现在的"去啦"。这个解释的确相当吸引人。问题是如果成立的话，我们将无法说明这个句末助词的来源，以及它和完成体标记"哓"的关系，现代各种粤语方言也不支持这种想法。

[39] 刘丹青:《东南方言的体貌标记》，页 20。

[40] 詹伯慧、陈晓锦:《东莞方言词典》（南京: 江苏教育出版社，1997 年），页 120。

[41] 屈大均:《广东新语》（北京: 中华书局，1985 年），页 338。

[42] 詹伯慧、张日昇（主编）:《珠江三角洲方言字音对照》，页 137。按:"効"即"效"之俗字，见《广韵·效韵》"効"字下的解说。

[43] 番禺话没有曲折调，所以只能以相近的中平调去模仿东莞话的读音。

[44] C. J. Saunders, "The Tungkwun dialect of Cantonese", *The China Review* 22.1（1896–1897），p.471.

[45] K. M. A. Barnett, "Do words from extinct Pre-Chinese languages survive in Hong Kong place names", *Journal of the Hong Kong Branch of the Royal Asiatic Society* 14（1974），pp. 137, 156.

[46] Sagart，Laurent（沙加尔），"Phonology of a Cantonese dialect of the New Territories: Kat Hing Wai", *Journal of the Hong Kong Branch of the Royal Asiatic Society* 22（1982），p.158. 按: 原文用英文发表，引文系由笔者翻译。

[47] 据张双庆、庄初升:《香港新界方言》，页 746、724、751 重绘。

[48] 蒙汤志祥教授告知，完成体标记"后"也出现在南头话和宝安话中。一般认为南头话、宝安话和东莞话具有较密切的发生学关系。但由于汤教授的资料还没有公开发表，这里不便引用。

[49] 詹伯慧、张日昇（主编）：《珠江三角洲方言词汇对照》，页 277 "睡了"条。

[50] 赵元任：《中山方言》，《中央研究院历史语言研究所集刊》第 20 本上册（1948 年），页 71，注 13。

[51] James D. Ball, "The Höng Shan or Macao dialect", *The China Review* 22（1897），p.515.

[52] 本文其中一位评审员引用赵元任 1929 年未发表的田野报告。赵先生把当时中山话的 "休" 记作 [hɐu]。我们不清楚这个形式到底是来源于 [hau]，还是 [hou] 的前身。

[53] 林柏松：《近百年来澳门话语音的发展变化》，《中国语文》1988 年第 4 期，页 276。

[54] 彭小川：《南海方言的语法特点》，载彭小川：《粤语论稿》（广州：暨南大学出版社，2004 年），页 99—101。

[55] 关系词是指不同语言之间语音、语义都有对应关系的词（或语素），但不能确定它们属于同源还是借用的关系。

[56] 南海地区的方言除沙头话外均没有详细的记录，暂时无法作出可靠的音韵比较。

[57] 表中 "完成体标记" 一栏，广州话、香山话、中山话的读音系根据早期文献的转写，其余三个方言点则依照现代的记音（资料的详细出处见前）。至于 "休"、"嗽"、"掉"、"好" 四字，一律是现代的念法。这四个字在上述粤语方言中的读音，过去一百年都没有什么变动。

[58] 李新魁等：《广州方言研究》，页 164；Robert S. Bauer（包睿舜）and Paul K. Benedict（白保罗）: *Modern Cantonese Phonology*, Trends in Linguistics: Studies and Monograph 102（Berlin: Mouton de Gruyter, 1997），p.60。

[59] 指在香港出版的文献所反映的读音。

[60] James A. Matisoff（马蒂索夫）曾报告过一种由原始藏缅语 *-a 发展为西夏语 -i 的音变，他称之为 "brightening"。见所著：" 'Brightening' and the place of Xixia（Tangut）in the Qiangic branch of Tibeto-Burman"，载林英津等（编）：《汉藏语研究：龚煌城先生七秩寿庆论文集》（台北："中研院"语言学研究所，2004 年），页 327—52。西夏语拥有大量 brightening 的例证。相对地，广州话只有一个 "哓" 可能经历过类似的音变，而且没有平行的例子，所以不好引用马氏的理论。

[61] 在我们接触到的文献中，似乎只有吉川雅之谈过广州话中 -iu 韵和 -ɛu 韵的关系，见所著：《音韵变化と粤语研究・广东语教育：周边韵母の承认を例に》，载上田博一编：《日本语学と言语教育》（东京：东京大学出版会，2002 年），页 193—221。和我们的意见不同，吉川先生认为 -ɛu 是由 -iu 演变而来的（页 204）。

[62] 李新魁等：《广州方言研究》，页 164 把 "掉"、"寥" 读 -ɛu 韵母的例子处理为白读音。

[63] 王福堂：《汉语方言语音中的层次》，《语言学论丛》第二十七辑（2003 年），页 8。

[64] 张双庆、庄初升：《一百多年来新界客家方言音系的演变》，《中国文化研究所学报》新 12 期（2003 年），页 449。

[65] 李新魁等:《广州方言研究》,页 132。

[66] 中古尤韵三等字,现代广州话主要念 -ɐu 韵母,而在 McCoy 的原始粤语(Proto-Cantonese)中则有两种反映:*-əu 和 *-iau,其中后者和我们的拟构完全呼应。见 William J. McCoy Jr., "Szeyap Data for a First Approximation of Proto-Cantonese"(Ph.D. diss., Cornell University, 1966),p.157.

[67] 在中山话里,"好"和完成体标记 [hou⁵⁵] 声、韵俱同,只是声调有别而已。参考表 2。

[68] 这里所指的是声调上的感染。中山话一早已经有念阴平调的 [hau⁵⁵]。当新的完成体标记产生时,就模仿它的声调,形成"同一个词类同一个声调"的现象。同样的例子还有广州话的人称代词系统,参阅李荣:《语音演变规律的例外》,载所著:《音韵存稿》(北京:商务印书馆,1982 年),页 109—11。

[69] Cheung, "Completing the completive", p.143.

[70] 佚名:《日边红杏》(广州:五桂堂,出版年份不详),卷四,页二下。

[71]《日边红杏》由广州五桂堂出版。五桂堂创立于光绪中叶,至 1972 年才正式结业(参阅梁培炽:《香港大学所藏木鱼书叙录与研究》〔香港:香港大学亚洲研究中心,1978 年〕,页 253—6),因而无法确定《日边红杏》的撰作年代。

[72] 汉许慎(撰)、宋徐铉(校定):《说文解字》,陈昌治刻本(香港:中华书局影印,1989 年),卷六上,页二三下(总页 125)。

[73] 晋陶渊明(撰)、龚斌(笺):《陶渊明集校笺》(上海:上海古籍出版社,1996 年),卷五,页 399,注 37。

[74] "完成动词"是梅祖麟的术语,指表完成的动词,如"了"、"讫"、"毕"等。见梅著:《现代汉语完成貌句式和词尾的来源》,载《梅祖麟语言学论文集》(北京:商务印书馆,2000 年),页 67。

[75] 王重民(辑):《敦煌曲子词集》(上海:商务印书馆,1950 年),卷一,页 19。

[76] 元施耐庵(集撰)、明罗贯中(纂修):《水浒全传》(香港:中华书局,1976 年),页 843。

[77] 许宝华、宫田一郎(主编):《汉语方言大词典》(北京:中华书局,1999 年),第二卷,页 2026。

[78] 参看表 2。"后"和"休"都读 -ɐu 韵母。

[79] 李新魁等:《广州方言研究》,页 209。

[80] 参阅彭小川:《沙头话古云、以母字今读初析》,载《粤语论稿》,页 208—13。

[81] James D. Ball, "The Shuntak Dialect", *China Review* 25(1900—1901),p.66 为当时顺德话的"有"字记录了两种读音:零声母的 *yau* 是字音,而带 h- 声母的 *hau* 则是日常会话(commonest speech)的读音。前者很可能是由后者弱化而来的。

[82] 但我们不清楚这种音变背后的动因。也许是方言混杂的缘故。

[83] 梅祖麟说过:"虚词在各种语言里都特别保守,往往属于更深一层的音韵层次。"见《方

言本字研究的两种方法》，载《梅祖麟语言学论文集》，页 416。魏培泉讨论古汉语指示词"之"、"这"的关系时也曾经指出："王力以为'这'是从'之'来的。虽然韵母上不大相合，但是这种指示词在元音的高低上有变化却并非不可能的，不能像一般实词的音变那样严格的要求。"见所著：《汉魏六朝称代词研究》（台北：台湾大学中国文学研究所博士学位论文，1990 年），页 90。其实像体标记这类虚词，很多汉语方言都体现了存古（如苏州话的完成体标记"仔"）、弱化（如北京话的完成体标记"了"）等不依常规的演变方式。广州话的"休"并不是个孤例。

[84] 关于 -iou 韵的拟构，见李新魁等：《广州方言研究》，页 144。他们认为广州市郊的蚌湖、龙归把部分尤韵三等字读为 -ou 韵是存古的表现。

[85] "叠置式音变"的定义是："在存在文白异读的叠置系统中……'不同系统的同源音类的叠置'则是不同系统的因素共处于一个系统之中，因而相互展开了竞争，如果其中某一个系统的因素在竞争中失败，退出交际的领域，那么在语言系统中就消除了叠置的痕迹，实现了两种系统的结构要素的统一。我们把这种竞争的过程称为叠置式音变。"见徐通锵：《历史语言学》（北京：商务印书馆，1991 年），页 353。

[86] 详情见 Joan Bybee, Revere Perkins, and William Pagliuca: *The Evolution of Grammar: Tense, Aspect, and Modality in the Languages of the World*（Chicago / London: The University of Chicago Press, 1994），p.58; Bernd Heine and Tania Kuteva, *World Lexicon of Grammaticalization*（Cambridge: Cambridge University Press, 2002），p.138。

[87] 梅祖麟：《现代汉语完成貌句式和词尾的来源》，载《梅祖麟语言学论文集》，页 67；李宗江：《"完成"类动词的语义差别及其演变方向》，《语言学论丛》第三十辑（2004 年），第 2.3.2 节"后加时态标记"（页 157—60）。

[88] 刘丹青：《东南方言的体貌标记》，页 13—7。

[89] 最近吴福祥提出用"人类语言演变的范围"去检视汉语历史语法的演变，分辨"哪些体现了语法演变的统计共性，哪些是汉语语法演变的真正特性"。见所著：《汉语历史语法研究的检讨与反思》，《汉语史学报》第 5 辑（2005 年），第六节"演变的特性与共性"（页 23—6）。

[90] 请参看 Charles A. Ferguson: "Diglossia", in *Language in Culture and Society: A Reader in Linguistics and Anthropology*, ed. Dell Hymes（New York: Harper and Row, 1964），pp.429–39 对这个课题富开创性的论述。

[91] 赵元任在《现代吴语的研究》（北京：清华学校研究院，1928 年）中，就把常州话分为"街谈"和"绅谈"。"街谈"是一般市民的用语，而"绅谈"是来自东南乡少数官绅的用语。"绅谈"、"街谈"可以分别被视为常州话的"高层语言"和"低层语言"。中国境内还有很多类似的例子，可参考游汝杰、邹嘉彦：《社会语言学教程》（上海：复旦大学出版社，2004 年）。

[92] Cheung, "Completing the completive", pp. 159–60.

[93] 张洪年尝试为粤语的"咗"和吴语的"仔"挂钩,认为它们都来自六朝江东方言的"著",见"Completing the completive", pp. 158-9。但我们认为张先生引用的证据略嫌不足。"咗"的语源始终是个谜。

[94] 梅祖麟:《现代汉语完成貌句式和词尾的来源》,页 72。

[95] 沈家煊:《"语法化"研究综观》,载吴福祥(主编):《汉语语法化研究》(北京:商务印书馆,2005 年),页 7。

[96] 原文是"V + suffix(后缀)"。为了全文的连贯性,我们把"后缀"改为"体标记"。

[97] Cheung, "Completing the completive", pp. 148–52.

[98] 从历史材料看,以变调表小调,有的来自"V + 晓",也有的源于"V + 咗"。我们打算在另一篇文章中深入讨论这个问题。

[99] 体标记弱化为变调,变调最后趋向消失,而新标记就在这时候进入语言的体系中,如是者循环不息。其实不单体标记如是,许多汉语方言的小称形式也曾经有过类似的经历,参阅郭必之《南部吴语几种小称形式的内在关系及其来源》(载林英津等〔编〕:《汉藏语研究》,页 769—86)一文对南部吴语的报道。我们认为体标记和小称的发展是平行的。这种仿佛"轮回"的语言演变方式,日后应该多加关注。

[100] 梅祖麟认为,汉语方言学中的"考本字"包含了两种方法:"寻音法"和"觅字法"。本文所采用的是前者。"寻音法"有两个功能是"觅字法"没有的,即:(一)分辨音韵层次;(二)探索方言的语法史。见梅著:《方言本字研究的两种方法》,页 414—5。

[101] 李方桂:《汉语研究的方向——音韵学的发展》,载痖弦(主编):《中国语言学论集》(台北:幼狮文化事业公司,1977 年),页 230。

(本文发表于《中国文化研究所学报》第 46 期,第 91—115 页)

Cantonese Made Easy：早期粤语中的语气助词 *

张洪年

1. 引言

　　句末使用语气助词是汉语语法的一大特点，也是研究汉语语法一个比较困难的课题。语气助词，顾名思义，主要是表达说话语气的轻重虚实。不同的助词，可以表强调，表婉转，表陈述，表疑问等。它的具体实义，有时不容易掌握。语音表现形式，也比较多变化。尤其是在声调方面，往往会根据上下文意而高低有所改动。所以历来研究汉语方言语法，对处理语气助词的文章相对地比较少。从历史语法角度探讨方言语气助词的使用，更是罕见。其间原因很简单。用口语写成的历史方言材料本不多见，而在少有的历史方言材料中，当日语气助词的确实用法，今日应如何理解，如何分析，还有待斟酌。本文试选取一本十九世纪写成的粤语教学课本作材料，对早期粤语中的语气助词，作一初步探讨。

　　粤语中的语气助词数量特别多，用法灵活多变化。声调升降稍一改动，往往会影响说话的语气和句子的讯息。对初学粤语的人来说，如何掌握语气助词是一种考验；对研究粤语的学者来说，如何分析语气助词更属一种挑战。一九六零年代初，詹伯慧在《汉语方言概要》的《粤语》一章中对广州话语气助词的使用，作了详细的描述。张洪年（1972）对六零年代香港粤语中的助词现象，也作过比较深入的分析。1991年梁仲森出版《香港粤语助词的研究》，2003年方小燕出版《广州方言句末语气助词》，更是有系统地对两地粤语中的语气助词作了全面性的论述。

---

* 本文初稿曾在 2006 年庆祝李方桂全集出版及中国语言学集刊出版国际学术会议上宣读。其后多次修改，蒙姚玉敏、片冈新等提供意见，至为感激。又文稿外审，得到学者提供宝贵修改意见并有关参考书目，在此一并致谢。本文是香港研究资助局（Research Grants Council）资助研究项目的成果之一（项目编号 CUHK6055/02H），是我对早期粤语发展研究计划的一部分。

2．CME 简介

嚟呢處咩 做也你唔嚟呢
也人嚟吖 也誰吖, or 邊個吖
有人嚟咩 (or 行人呀 or 冇邊
嗰個係也人呢 [個吖
唔為呀 我點知呀
佢係唔好人呀 佢係好惡人嚛
叫佢扯咯
佢去咗咯 去好耐咯
掩埋門 咪閂吖
開門呀 做也你鎖呢
叫亞媽嚟見我喇
快啲嚟 越快越好咯
睇店呢 嚟未曾呀
聽日嚟喇 後日嚟都好吖 (or
　　都做得吖
有少少睹
好頸咩 佢係噉話
佢話也野 講過我聽喇
佢話唔想嚟咯
解明過佢聽 至必要同我去
唔論大細 有幾多人呢
有十幾個 or 有十零個咯 or
　　十個有多.
喊嚇哈 有六十人咯
有細佬仔冇呢
有個(or 壹個)仔咯
嗰個係仔嚤女呢
佢喺我處打工嚰
邊個係你事頭呢
佢係本地人, 即係城人咯
佢唔係同你同鄉嚰
佢喺邊處住呢
離呢處有好遠咯

1. ₅Lai ₅ni-shü² á². Tsó²-mat₅ ⁵néi m ₅lai ₅ni?
2. Mí-'yan⁺ ₅lai á? Mí-'shui⁺ á? ⁵Pín ko⁷ á?
3. ⁵Mó yan ₅lai á, or simply ⁵Mó ₅yán á, or ⁵Mó
4. ⁵Ko-ko⁷ hai² mí-'yan⁺ ₅ni? [₅pín ko⁷] á.
5. M ⁵chí á². ⁵Ngo ₅tím ₅chí á²?
6. ⁵K'ui hai² m-'hò yan á². ⁵K'ui hai² ₅hò ok₅
7. Kíu², ⁵k'ui ₅ch'e lok₅. [₅yan ká².
8. ⁵K'ui hui²-₅cho lok₅. Hui² ₅hò noi² lok₅.
9. ⁵Yím ₅mái ₅min, ¹mai ₅shán á.
10. Hoi ₅mún á⁷. Tsó²-mat₅ ₅néi ₅so ₅ni?
11. Kíu⁷ A⁷-₅Má ₅lai kín⁵ ₅ngo lá.
12. Fái⁷-₅ti ₅lai : yüt₅ fái yit⁵, ₅hò lok₅.
13. ⁵Kíu-tím⁷ ₅ni ; ₅lai méi²-₅ts'ang á⁷?
14. ₅T'ing-yat₅ ₅lai lá, hau² yat₅ ₅lai ₅tò ₅hò á, (or ₅tò tsó² tak₅ á).
15. ⁵Yau ⁵shíu ⁵shíu cho.
16. ⁵Hò lá² ma²? ⁵K'ui hai² ⁵kòm wá². [₅lá.
17. ⁵K'ui wá² mí-⁵ye? ⁵Kong kwo⁷ ₅ngo ₅t'eng†
18. ⁵K'ui wá² ₅m ⁵sòng ₅lai lok₅.
19. ⁵Kái ₅ming kwo⁷ ⁵k'ui ₅t'eng† shí²-pít, yíú ₅t'ung ⁵ngo lui².
20. M lun² tái² sai² ⁵yau ⁵kéi ₅to ₅yan ₅ni?
21. ⁵Yau shap₅ ⁵kéi ko⁷, or ⁵yau shap₅ ₅leng† ko⁷ lok₅, or shap₅ ko⁷ ⁵yau ₅to.
22. Hám²-páng²¹-lúng² ⁵yau luk₅-shap₅ yan lok₅.
23. ⁵Yau sai⁷ (or more often ₅sam) man-tsai ⁵mò
24. ⁵Yau ko⁷ (or yat₅ ko⁷) ₅tsai lok₅. [₅ni?
25. ⁵Ko-ko⁷ hai² ₅tsai, péi² ⁵nui ₅ni?-
26. ⁵K'ui ⁵hai ₅ngo shü² ⁵tá-₅kung ke⁷.
27. Pín-ko⁷ hai² ⁵néi sz²-₅t'nu⁺ ₅ni? [₅yan lok₅.
28. ⁵K'ui hai² ⁵pún téi² yan, tsik₅ hai² ⁵sheng⁺†
29. ⁵K'ui ₅m hai² ₅t'ung ⁵néi t'ung ₅hòng-ke⁷.
30. ⁵K'ui ⁵hai ₅pín shü² chü² ₅ní?
31. ⁵Léi ₅ni shü² ⁵yau ⁵hò ⁵yün lok₅.

2.1 前人对粤语语气助词的研究，以共时描述为主，时间上限是一九五零或六零年代。五十年代以前的粤语，我们所知有限。但是粤语中语气助词丰富的现象，当不始自五十年代。近年大批早期材料陆续面世，当可为证。现摘取一段十九世纪的教学材料为例，句中的语气助词加圈为标记。引文共三十二句，几乎每句都有语气助词，由此可见使用之频繁。

这一段课文录自 *Cantonese Made Easy*（下文简称 CME），作者是 James Dyer Ball（1847—1919）。Ball 是英国人，在香港生长，能操多种方言，并曾编写各种不同方言的教学材料。[1] 有关粤语教学就出版多种教材，其中尤以 *Cantonese Made Easy* 最为重要，前后四版，而第四版更是在 Ball 逝世后出版，更可见其受欢迎之广。

　　第一版：1883 Hong Kong: China Mail Office
　　第二版：1888 Hong Kong: China Mail Office

第三版：1907 Singapore-Hong Kong-Shanghai-Yokohama: Kelly & Walsh, Ltd.

第四版：1924 Hong Kong: Kelly & Walsh, Ltd.

CME 二十九年间四版，前后颇有修订。但在语气助词使用方面，却改动不大。本文研究以 1888 年版为准。[2] 本来在 Ball 以前已经颇有一些为西洋人学习粤语而编写的字典或教科书，[3] 二十世纪以后，粤语教材更见普遍。我们这里只选用 Ball 的 CME，主要原因是语气词用法可能因人而异，杂采众家说法，或许不容易整理头绪。Ball 对粤语语感敏锐，观察精微，而 CME 一书对语气助词的分析，远较其他教材详细。所以我们以 CME 作探讨的首要对象，以此为切入点，先作分析，以便将来再和其他材料比较，进行更深入的研究。

2.2 CME 一书共十五课，每课三十二条。采用对话形式，以浅白口语，把中国社会中各种情形，包括家庭、教育、医药、司法、宗教等等，都大略交代，作为进阶的认识。每课课文，分四栏排列。汉字一栏，拼音一栏，左右再分列两栏翻译。一栏是逐字直译，一栏是每一个句子的意译。因为每句都附有罗马注音，声韵调并连同变调，都一一注明。[4] 所以我们根据全书记录，可以对当时整个语音系统有一个全面而确实的了解。语气助词在书中归为 finals，也就是附于句末的助词。课文中每一个语气助词的发音及音调高低，都标注得十分清楚。从翻译部分我们可以知道助词使用的上下文意和语境。书后更附有语法讲义，前后几十页，关于语气助词的用法，也颇有说明。整体而言，CME 对我们研究早期粤语的语气助词，是一项十分重要的语料。

3. CME 书中出现的语气助词

3.1 我们先看 CME 使用语气助词的大概。表 1 的统计是把十五课课文中使用语气助词的数字开列。

表 1

课文	句子	带助词	%
1	48	37	77%
2	53	43	81%
3	43	34	79%
4	44	35	80%

（续表）

课文	句子	带助词	%
5	45	36	80%
6	40	24	68%
7	35	12	34%
8	42	19	45%
9	44	41	93%
10	38	36	95%
11	40	33	83%
12	44	39	87%
13	49	28	61%
14	48	32	67%
15	56	41	73%
	669	**490**	**73%**

综观全书单句六百六十九句，句末有语气助词的共四百九十句，占总数的 73%。有的课文如第十课，共三十八句，用助词的有三十六句，占 95%；最低的也有 34%，如第七课。邓思颖（2002）曾对当今粤语口语中使用语气助词的现象进行研究。他把电视和广播电台的节目录音誊写，一共得到八百九十三句，而使用语气助词的句子有六百零一句，占 67%。单从百分比来看，这两种语料前后相差一百多年，但都呈现同样的语言现象，也就是语气助词极其常见。从十九世纪的 CME 到今日二十一世纪，粤语多用语气助词的习惯，一直未变。

粤语语气助词使用既频，而助词本身数目亦多。根据梁仲森（2005）的研究，现代粤语共有九十五项语气助词，变化繁复，这里不容细举。然而一百年前的粤语究竟有多少语气助词？CME 书后附有一列，共七十六项，数目虽比梁书开列的少，但仍然颇为可观。

本文研究即以 CME 开列的语气助词、和全书近七百句的实例为基本材料，进行研究。根据例句使用的上下文语境，和书中所附的英文翻译，我们可以比较确切地理解各语气助词的具体语用和语义。而 Ball 的语法讲义，对我们整理十九世纪粤语语气助词的系统，也极备参考之用。

35. Má², 嗎, interrogative : asking certainly as to any matter.

36. ₅Má, 嘛, same as last, or the meaning might be expressed by " (*I told you so before*), *now isn't it so ?*"

37. ⁵Má, 嗎, interrogative, and expecting an affirmative reply.

38. Má², 嗎, affirmatively-interrogative.

39. ₅Me, 咩, interrogative, or expressing some surprise as well, as—" Is it so ?"

40. ₅Mo, 麼,
41. ⁵Mo, 麼, } interrogative, implying doubt.
42. Mo², 麼,

43. ₅Mo, 麼,
44. ⁵Mo, ⁵麼, } simply interrogative, used after hearing anything said, having the sense of,
45. Mo², 麼, "Oh ! that's what it is, is it ?"

46. ₅Ná, 那,
47. Ná², 那, } emphatically demonstrative.

48. ₅Ne, 嘅,
49. ⁵Ne, 嘅,
50. Ne², 嘅, } emphatically demonstrative, used when one might say in English, " There
51. ⁵Ne, 嘅, now, what I said was true you see."
52. Ne², 嘅,

53. ₅Ne, *or more commonly* ₅ni, 呢, } interrogative, or emphatically demonstrative.
54. ₀Ne, *or* ₀ni, 呢,

55. ₅O, 啊,
56. O², 啊, } strongly emphatically affirmative. The first is rarely used.
57. O², 啊,

58. Pe², 嘎, interrogative.

59. Péi², 嘎², affirmative.

60. Po², 嚕, very emphatic, used often after the final 囉 lo².

61. Wá², 嘩,
62. ⁵Wá, 嘩, } denoting that the statement preceding it has been made by some one
63. Wá², 嘩, before.

64. Wo², 喎,
65. ₅Wo, 喎, } same as above.
66. Wo², 喎,

67. ₅Yá, 吔,
68. Yá², 吔, } affirmative.

69. ₅Yá, 吔,
70. ⁵Yá, 吔, } expressing slight surprise.
71. Yá², 吔,

72. Yák, 喫,
73. Yák₀, 喫, } affirmative.
74. Yák₂, 喫,

75. Yo²,
76. Yo², } expressive of surprise.

1.	係 Hai²	*Yes, (affirmative).*
2.	喺 'Hai?	*Yes? (indicative of great surprise.)*
3.	係哩 Hai² ‚le	*Yes, (you are right it is so.)*
4.	係啊 Hai² o'	*Yes, (indeed it is so.)*
5.	係嗯 Hai² ‚ne	*Yes, (didn't I say it was so, or I told you so.)*
6.	係咩 Hai² ‚me?	*Yes? (yes? Oh! is it so?)*
7.	係嗎 Hai² ‚má?	*Yes? ('tis so, isn't it?)*
8.	係嗎 ' Hai² má' ?	*Yes? (it is indeed so, is it not?)*
9.	係麼 Hai² mò' ?	*Yes? (the same.)*
10.	係吖 Hai² ‚á	*Yes, ('tis so)*
11.	係呀 Hai² á'	*Yes, (it is so indeed.)*
12.	係啩 Hai² ‚kwá	*It's so I think.*
13.	係啩 Hai² kwá'	*I think, yes—I think it so, is it not?*
14.	係囉 Hai² ‚lo	*Yes, all right.*
15.	係咯 Hai² lok₀	*Yes, that's it.*
16.	係囉 嗎 ' Hai² lo' má' ?	*It's so, is it not, eh?*
17.	係囉 咩 Hai² lo' ‚me?	*Oh! it's so, is it indeed?*
18.	係囉 ' Hai² lo'	*Yes, 'tis so.*
19.	係囉 啩 Hai² lo' kwá'	*'Tis so I think.*
20.	係囉 啩 Hai² lo' ‚kwá	*It's so, isn't it?*
21.	係嗜 Hai² ‚e	*Indeed it's so?*
22.	係唔係 呢 Hai² ‚m hai² ‚ni?	*There, isn't it so now?*
23.	係唔係 嗯 Hai² ‚m hai² ‚ne?	*Is it so, or not? or simply Is it so?*
24.	係唔係 呀 Hai² ‚m hai² á'?	*Is it so, or not? or simply Is it so?*
25.	係唔係 吖 Hai² ‚m hai² ‚á?	*There, didn't I tell you it was so.*
26.	係唔係 啊 Hai² ‚m hai² o'?	*Do tell me is it so, or not?*

3.2 说话的语气本来就不容易用文字记录，粤语语气助词所反映的语气，更不容易通过英语来说明。Ball 深明这个中难处。他在 CME 中指出：

> Though the Final Particles so freely used in Chinese have in most cases no exact meaning as separate words, yet they often throw a strong emphasis upon the sentence, and express in the clearest manner whether it is Interrogative or Affirmative; whether the speaker is simply assenting to some propositions that is stated, or expressing surprise at it; whether a simple statement is being made, or whether it is being stated in the most positive manner, and with all the possible emphasis; or whether the speaker is not very sure of what he says, and with this uncertainty asks in an indirect manner whether it is so, or not. It will thus be seen that such words as these express different feelings, and modulations of intensity of such feelings, and bring out different shades of meaning as they are used singly, or in combinations (very much as stops are used in an organ to modulate, and intensify the sound of music). It will be seen that such words as these are very difficult, or impossible even of translation into English where accent and emphasis alone do their work to a great extent. [5]

Ball 在书后语法部分列举二十六个短句，都是以"係"为例。[6] 一个简单的"係"相当于英语的 "yes"，但一经配搭不同的助词，表达的语气就大有分别。Ball 尝试用不同的英语句子，或是另加说明，来解释语气和意义上的差异。

外语对译，本不易拿捏。Ball 在列举例句之时，更慎重指出翻译或说明的不足：

> Of course the learner will understand that the English words that appear …, opposite the Chinese, do not appear in the Chinese, but where a certain state of feeling is given expression in English in certain words, the same feeling would probably cause the Chinese words that are opposite the English to be uttered. It is thus rather a free translation without which it would be impossible to convey anything of the sense of these enclitic particles. [7]

不过，倘若没有 Ball 的尝试和努力，我们就没有认识旧日粤语实况的可能。本文的讨论还是根据 Ball 的语感和翻译，重新整理十九世纪的语气助词使用概况。

1. ₍A, 吖, interrogative, emphatic, or merely euphonic.

2. A', 呀, emphatic, or merely euphonic.

3. A², 呀, emphatic, more so than the last.

4. ₍Chá, 喳, cautionary, or restraining.

5. 'Chá, 喳, stronger, or more urgent than the last.

6. Chá', 咋, cautionary, or restraining, or delaying, but rarely implying doubt.

7. ₍Che, 呮, or 嗻, implying limitation.

8. Che', 啫, implying limitation, &c.

9. 'Chá, 啫, implying limitation, but stronger than the last.

10. ₍Chí, 吱, emphatic.

11. 'Cho, or 'chö, 咀 emphatic.

12. ₍E, 嗱, interrogative.

13. ₍Ká, 唎 ⎫
14. Ká', 嚤 ⎬ emphatic-affirmative.

15. Ke', 嘅, somewhat similar to the last, or simply euphonic.

16. Ko', 个, same as last.

17. ₍Kwa, 啩, implying doubt, or some degree of probability; there is also an expectancy of a reply sometimes expressed in it,—a reply which will solve the doubt, or intensify the probability.

18. Kwá', 啩, the same as last.

19. ₍Kwo, 過 ⎫
20. Kwo', 嗰 ⎬ the same as last.

21. ₍Lá, 喇, emphatic, or simply euphonic.

3.3 Ball 在 CME 中列举七十六项语气助词（页 111—115），但是他同时指出这些助词有一半以上不见于任何词典。[8] 我们翻检全书，把各课文中所有出现过的语气助词一一排列出来，也只有二十七项。我们下面先把原来的七十六项助词按拼音排列。拼音中的声调以数目字标写，容后再作讨论。但是书中不曾出现的助词，则以暗格表示。见表 2。

表 2

a1	吖	la1	喇	mo2	么	wa3	嗱
a3	呀	la3	嗱	mo3	么	wa5	嗱
a6	呀	lak9	㪐	mo4	么	wa6	嗱
cha1	嗏	le1	哩	mo5	么	wo3	喎
cha2	嗏	le2	哩	mo6	么	wo4	喎
cha3	咋	le3	唎	na4	那	wo6	喎
che1	呮，瓥	le4	哩	na6	那	ya1	吔
che3	嗻	le5	哩	ne1	嘅	ya3	吔
cha2	嗻	le6	唎	ne2	嘅	ya4	吔
chi1	吱	lo1	啰	ne3	嘅	ya5	吔
cho2	咽	lo3	啰	ne5	嘅	ya6	吔
e1	唉	lok8	咯	ne6	嘅	yak7	吃
ka1	咖	ma1	吗	ni1	呢	yak8	吃
ka3	嘞	ma2	吗	ni10	呢	yak9	吃
ke3	嘅	ma3	吗	o1	啊	yo3	X
ko3	個	ma4	嘛	o3	啊	yo6	X
kwa1	啩	ma5	吗	o6	啊		
kwa3	啩	ma6	吗	pe3	噽		
kwo1	喎	me1	咩	pei6	噽		
kwo3	喎	mo1	么	po3	嶓		

查表中所列而真正在课文出现的语气助词只有二十六项，而非二十七项。原因是课文中有助词“啫”chek7，但是并没有收入书后的语气助词总表中。所以，要是把这一条也算进去，总数当是七十七项。我们且把这二十七项语气助词重新开列如下：

1. 吖	a1	10. 嘅	ke3	19. 吗	ma5
2. 呀	a3	11. 個	ko3	20. 咩	me1
3. 呀	a6	12. 啩	kwa3	21. 咯	lok8

4.	嗏	cha2	13.	喇	la1
5.	咋	cha3	14.	嚹	la3
6.	呎、嚧	che1	15.	囉	lo1
7.	啫	che3	16.	囉	lo3
8.	啫	chek7	17.	吗	ma1
9.	嘿	ka3	18.	吗	ma3

22.	呢	ni1
23.	啊	o3
24.	啊	o6
25.	嘫	po3
26.	唦	wo3
27.	唦	wo6

4. 语气助词和声调的关系

4.1 Ball 书中开列这许多语气助词，有许多是同一个音节的不同声调变化。Ball 说：同一个语气助词可以用不同的声调来说，表达的意思轻重有别。[9] 也就是说一个助词可以有不同的变体（variant），由声母韵母组成的基本音节不变，但是声调可以配合语气而发生变化。我们按此道理可以把原来七十六助词重新分析，只看声韵部分，不管声调，归纳为三十二个音节。[10]

a	e		o	
cha	che	chi	cho	chek
ka	ke		ko	
kwa			kwo	
la	le		lo	lak	lok
ma	me		mo	
na	ne	ni		
	pe	pei	po	
ya			yo	yak
wa			wo	

4.2 从声调角度来讨论，我们先要了解一下当日的声调系统。根据 CME 书中描述，十九世纪的声调大抵和今日相似，分四声九调。四声也就是平上去入，各分阴阳，阴入再分上下。[11] 至于各调调型和调高，Ball 在其他文章中曾作描述。我们这里且把 CME 的声调系统图表如下。表中先分四声。四声各分上下，"上下"是 Ball 的叫法 —— the upper and lower series，[12] 相当于传统的阴阳之分。Ball 的标调法，是在字的四角加半圆圈，左下角表平声，左上角表上声，右上角表去声，右下角表入声。半圈底下打杠表阳声调，不打杠表阴声调。我们在文章中简为 1 至 9 调。[13]

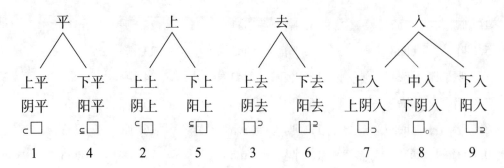

我们从七十七项助词表中抽取若干相同音节的助词，按平上去（1-2-3, 4-5-6）排列，看看是否声调变化并不真正影响助词的基本意义。

（1）吖 a1
interrogative, emphatic,
or merely euphonic

吖 a3
emphatic, or merely
euphonic

呀 a6
emphatic, more so than the last

（2）嗏 cha1
cautionary, restraining

嗏 cha2
stronger, more urgent
than the last

咋 cha3
cautionary, restraining,
delaying, but rarely
implying doubt

（3）吖、嗏 che1
implying limitation

啫 che3
implying limitation, & c.

（4）啩 kwa1
implying doubt, or some degree
of probability

啩 kwa3
the same as last

（5）哩 le1
emphatic

哩 le2
affirmative

哩 le3
same as last

（6）么 mo1
interrogative, doubt

么 mo2
interrogative, doubt

么 mo3
interrogative, doubt

（7）嘅 ne1
emphatically
demonstrative

嘅 ne2
emphatically
demonstrative

嘅 ne3
emphatically
demonstrative

根据 Ball 的英文注释，同一个音节的语气助词，可以有几个声调变体，语气可能有强弱之分，但是所表达的意思大致相同。按此道理，七十七项语气助词，实际上只有三十二个音节。也就是说 CME 语气助词，不管声调变化，共有三十二项，而真正在课文中出现的只有十五项，现开列如下，见表 3：

表 3

吖 a1		呀 a3
		呀 a6
	啫 cha2	咋 cha3
呮 / 嚧 che1		啫 che3 chek7
		嘎 ka3
		嘅 ke3
		個 ko3
		啩 kwa3
喇 la1		嘞 la3
囉 lo1		囉 lo3
		咯 lok8
吗 ma1		吗 ma3
	吗 ma5	
咩 me1		
呢 ni1		
		啊 o3
		啊 o6
		嘑 po3
		喎 wo3
		喎 wo6

4.3　阴声调和阳声调的对比

4.3.1 粤语声调分阴阳两大类。CME 的语气助词，有的是阴阳两类兼有，如上面所举各例。一般而言，阴声调调值较高，阳声调调值较低。根据 Ball 的描述，阴阳四

调的调型和调值大略如下：[14]

我们也可以因而把粤语声调重新排列如下：

平		上		去		入		
上平	下平	上上	下上	上去	下去	上入	中入	下入
阴平	阳平	阴上	阳上	阴去	阳去	上阴入	下阴入	阳入
₍□	₌□	꜀□	꜁□	□꜄	□꜅	□꜄	□。	□꜆
1	4	2	5	3	6	7	8	9
53:	31:	35:	13:	33:	22:	5:	3:	2:

我们查看七十六项助词总表，同一音节而兼有阴阳声调并存的助词，颇有一些例子。阴阳相对的关系，Ball 已经注意到这一点。他在书里特别举 le 为例子，说明声调变化的现象。le 共有阴阳六调，都表示"肯定"。

（8）le1 哩：affirmative

le2 哩：same as last

le3 唎：imperative, or emphatically affirmative

le4 哩

le5 哩

le6 唎

1-2-3 调属阴调，即阴平，阴上，阴去；4-5-6 属阳调，即阳平，阳上，阳去。阴阳二分的用法，Ball 特别加以说明：

The best way to indicate the difference between these two series of Les may be best illustrated by supposing a traveler was telling a tale the truth of which he could see was doubted by his auditors. He might use any of the second series of Finals in replying to any question put to him in which he could plainly see there was doubt felt by the questioner; but supposing his tale concluded and corroborative evidence proving that his marvels were truths, then the former series would be employed by him, their use giving a slight trace of jubilant triumph, which, if expressed in English colloquial, might be, "There you see that's just what it is." [15]

这也就是说：当说话人发现对方不尽相信自己的说话时，他会用阳调的 le 回答对方的质疑。不过，要是他能列出证据证明自己所说并非胡言乱语，他就会用阴调 le，语气比较轻松，胜券在握。换言之，阳调的助词，比较谨慎，语气较重，志在说服对方。阴调的助词，比较轻快，意气高扬。

这种阴阳区别，阳重阴轻，是否确实如此，我们且到 CME 书中寻找实例。

4.3.2 翻阅 CME 全书十五课，助词阴阳声调的最小对比，我们只找到三例。各有两句，一句句末是阴调语气助词，一句是阳调助词。[16]

（9）（我慌佢食鸦片烟嘅.）　　　　　　　　　　　　　　（CME, 11.27）[17]

　　　I am afraid that he smokes opium.

　　　a. 怕係 呀 a3. [18]

　　　Perhaps he does.

　　　b. 或者係都唔定 呀 a6.

　　　I am afraid he does.

（10）a. 今日好热 啊 o3.　　　　　　　　　　　　　　　（CME, 3.8）

　　　It's very hot today.

　　　b. 事头呢？出街啰 . 佢出街有几耐呢？几时翻嚟呢？

　　　佢又冇话几时翻嚟 啊 o6.　　　　　　　　　　　（CME, 4.24–27）

　　　Where is your master? He is out. How long has he been gone?

　　　When will he be back?

（11）a. 佢哋呢，和尚呢，做乜野呢？成日念经 唎 wo3.　　（CME, 12.6–7）

　　　What do they, the priests, do? Read the sutras the whole day long, so they say.

　　　b. 佢话乜野呢？冇银 唎，银两紧 唎 wo6.　　　　　（CME, 5.1–2）

　　　What does he say? He says he has no money. He says he is hard up for money.

我们先看例（9）的两句。（a）句以"怕"开头，表"恐怕"意，英文翻译作"perhaps"，语气是表"不敢肯定"。（b）句虽然也用"或者"开头，以"唔定"结尾，但是从上下文看，说话人在揣测之余，不乏肯定的意味。相比之下，（b）句语气比较强，助词"呀"的声调比（a）句的较低，这也就是说读阳去的 a6 要比读阴去的 a3 显得有力。

例（10）的两句，上下文境各不相同。助词"啊"的功能是"strongly emphatically affirmative"。[19]（a）和（b）两句用"啊"都有加强语气的功能。（a）句是形容句，后加助词"啊"o3，强调天气的炎热，是一个描写句。（b）句是说话人无法答复别人的提问，只有强调自己的不知情，作为解释。"老板没说，我怎么会知道呢？"句子近似反诘，语气理应较重。句末用阳调的o6。[20]（a）（b）两句相比，阳调的o6是比阴调的o3更能突出说话人的语气心态。

例（11）的"啵"，Ball 认为是 "denoting that the statement preceding it has been made by someone before"。[21]"啵"是粤语中一个独特的语气助词，表示说话人在转述别人的话语，有"别人所云，如是我闻"的意思。（a）句的意思是"成日念经"是和尚自己的说法，说话人不一定赞同，也不必为这话负责。英文翻译作 "so they say" 正是这个意思。（b）句也是因引用别人的说话，一来没钱，二来周转不灵，手头很紧。两句相比，（b）句的情况特别严重。（a）句用的是阴调的 wo3，（b）句用的是阳调的 wo6。

4.3.3 上举三例，都是阴去和阳去的对比。阴去是中平调，阳平是低平调，高低分别十分清楚。从句子文义来看，句末助词的声调高低和语气轻重似乎有着必然的关系。Ball 对声调阴阳系列分工的描述，颇有道理。可惜，这样的对比例子很少，也没有阴平和阳平的对比，阴上和阳上的对比，或阴入阳入的对比，希望以后可以再从其他的语料中找到实例研究。

4.4 阴平和阴去的对比

4.4.1 CME 材料中的二十七项语气助词，按声调排列，分布如下：

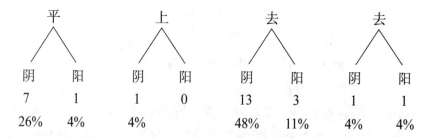

从数字显示，阴去的语气助词最多，共十三项，占 48%，差不多是课文中出现助词的一半。与阴去相对的阳去只有三项，占 11%。反而阴平的助词倒有七项，占 26%。其他声调的助词，出现极少。从调高的角度来看，阴平是高降调 53:，阴去是中平调 33:，阳去是低平 22:，正是高中低三种音高的对比。

阴平	阴去	阳去
53:	33:	22:
高 ——	中 ——	低

我们翻看 Ball 列举的七十六项语气助词，阴平助词占 25%，阴去占 28%，阳去占 16%，其他声调的词共占 31%。也显示同样的高中低的对比。三调高之中，尤以高调的阴平和中调的阴去助词最多。

4.4.2 Ball 在语法部分讨论语气助词的时候，特别提到这调高的区分。他指出有的语气助词有上平和上去两种说法。所谓上平也就是高调的阴平，所谓上去就是中调的阴去。而上平的变体要比中平的变体显得语气更强。

> If the same final is put into a 上平 and 上去 , the former has generally more emphasis of meaning than the latter. [22]

我们查看他的七十六项总表，每个语气助词后面都附有英文批注，而 "emphatic" 一词随处可见，并不只限于上平助词。如 "吖 / 呀" 阴调平上去三声都注有 "emphatic"，[23] "喊" 阴调平上去和阳调上去都作 "emphatically demonstrative"。[24] 所以总表中的注释，并不能说明阴平和阴去分工的情形。我们只有从课文中找寻例句，从上下文来看阴平和阴去的区分是否果如 Ball 的描述，可以分辨语气轻重。

4.4.3 che1 呎 / 囖 : che3 啫

"呎 / 囖 / 啫" 的写法虽然不同，声调有别，但是 Ball 都注释为 "implying limitation"，也就是 "只不过……而已" 的意思，所以应该算是一个语气助词 che 的声调变体。阴平和阴去的变体究竟有没有区别语气的功能？我们从书里找到下面一些例子。

（12）闲事囖 che1, 冇相干咯 . (CME, 3.29)
    It's only a trifling matter. It's no matter.

（13）我讲笑话啫 che3，你见怪咩？ (CME, 4.17)
    I am only jesting. Do you think it strange?

（14）我唔係做学生吖 . 我不过嚟坐吓个呎 che1, 嚟见吓个教馆先生啫 che3.
    I do not belong to this school. I have only come to visit—to see the teacher.

    (CME, 15.17)

（12）和（13）两句的 che，一个阴平，一个阴去，都表示 "only"，虽然声调有别，但是语气上是否轻重有别，从上下文并看不出来。句（14）的 che1 和 che3，却显得出前后两句说话的语气重点。前一半是否认别人的看法 —— 我不是学生，我只不过是来看看而已。因为是要纠正别人的错误印象，所以语气较重。后一句是补充前半的说话，说明自己来学堂的目的 —— 只是来看看教书先生罢了，语气放软。倘若两句都用高调的 che1，说话似乎有点不客气。[25] 所以从话语角度来看，语气轻重是会影响语气助词的声调高低。Ball 的看法颇有道理。

4.4.4 lo1 啰 : lo3 啰

阴平调的 lo1 和阴去调的 lo3，Ball 都解作是 "affirmative" 或 "euphonic" 的标志，表示肯定的语气，或者是使语气放缓，听起来比较悦耳。CME 课文中用 lo3 的很多，用 lo1 的只有一句。

（15）佢肚饿 啰 lo3… 俾野佢饮 啰 lo1.　　　　　　　　　　　（CME, 6.21–22）

　　　　He is hungry… Give him something to drink.

（15）其实是同一课文的两句对话，前后相承。前一句是描述句，后一句是祈使句或命令句，语气自然很不一样。用高调的 lo1，可以强化命令的语气，带出事情的迫切。描述句并没有迫切性，用较低的 lo3，也许比较合适。请比较下面这一句：

（16）你发热 啰 lo3. 我俾药水你食.　　　　　　　　　　　（CME, 11.16）

　　　　You have fever. I will give you a draught.

（16）同样是前后相承的两句，前句描述事件，后句叙说行动。描述部分用的助词是阴去的 lo3。行动句没有助词，不过我们可以猜想假如说话人在句末加上一个 lo，以表示强调，这个助词应当是一个高调的 lo1。CME 各课文中出现 lo3 的二十七处，很多都是和描述句有关。但是 lo1 仅（15）一句。但是关于祈使句用阴平高调的情形，还可以参看下一节的讨论。[26]

4.4.5 a1 吖 : a3 呀

"吖" a1 和 "呀" a3 是 CME 书中十分常见语气助词，阴平的 a1 出现共四十七次，而 a3 出现七十六次。CME 对 a1 的解释是 "interrogative, emphatic, or merely euphonic"，对 a3 的解释是 "emphatic, or merely euphonic"。也就是说两者的功能都在表强调，或是让说话听起来比较和谐悦耳。查阅 CME 全书，a1 和 a3 都可能出现在问句之末。即使是在今日粤语中，问句句末不带助词，语气会显得突兀或不礼貌，这也就是 Ball 所谓 euphonic 的功能。不过 a1 和 a3 的分别，在 CME 课文中并不特别显著。但是也有一些例子可以说明声调区别语气轻重的功能。例如：

（17）佢饮酒唔饮 呀 a3？　　　　　　　　　　　　　　（CME, 11.25）

　　　　Does he drink?

（18）你信唔信 吖 a1？冇人信嘅.　　　　　　　　　　（CME, 12.8）

　　　　Do you believe it? No one does.

（17）和（18）都是正反问句，句末带有助词 a。两者相比，句（17）是一个简单的正反问句，句末的"啊" a3 应该是缓和语气 "euphonic"，而非加强问话 "emphatic"。反观句（18），前后两句，后句批驳前句，所以前句比并非为提问而提问，实质上是等同质询，所以语气自然很重。高声调的 a1 正可发挥这样的语气功能。

我们再看一些不是问句的句子，看看是否也呈现以声调高低辨义的现象。

（19）头瘌呀 a3. （CME, 11.6）
My head aches.

（20）我肚都痛吖 a1. （CME, 11.10）
I have also the stomach-ache.

（21）好重利呀 a3. 唔係吖 a1. 几平利呀 a3. （CME, 9.31）
That's very heavy interest. No! It's rather little interest.

（19）和（20）两句出自同一课文，内容是有关看病的对话。（19）是病人向医生报告自己的病状 —— 头疼，（20）是在医生追问之下再补充的病情 —— 还有肚子疼。后一句自然比前一句语气要重，语气词似乎也反映这语气的分别。（21）同一句有三个短句。第一个和第三个短句都是描述句；而中间一句是否定句，反驳第一句的意见，用高声调的 a1 理所当然。

4.4.5 节提到祈使句多用阴平高调助词。这情形在 a1:a3 的比对中，更是明显。下面是 CME 课文中的表禁止的祈使句，三句带 a1，只有一句带 a3。可见高声调的 a1 更能表现命令的语气。

（22）咪饮咁多水吖 a1. （CME, 11.20）
Don't drink so much water.

（23）唔好咁悭吖 a1. （CME, 9.24）
Don't be so stingy.

（24）掩埋门，咪闩吖 a1. （CME, 2.9）
Don't fasten it.

（25）咪行埋烟通个处呀 a3. （CME, 13.19）
Don't go near the funnel.

4.5 从上述的讨论来看，语气助词所表达的语气轻重和助词的声调有关。这一点并不难理解。说话的时候，说话人的心态，对事情的感觉，对听话人的预期，往往是通过语调来表达说话轻重。这本是语言中常见的现象，而这种现象在汉语里表现更为突出。汉语是一个有声调的语言,说话的时候,字调一加上语调,变化会显得复杂,而句末语气词最能体现这种语调变化。语气助词多没有实义,所以最容易通过声调高低升降来表现话语的轻重强弱,于是造成一个语气助词可能有不同的声调归类。赵元任(1968)讨论汉语语法,已经把有的语调类型独立成类,视为助词一类,是介乎语音和语法之间的一种手段,可以和其他自成音节的词语结合,表示不同的语气功能。[27] 麦耘对粤语中的语气助词的语调性质,曾撰专文讨论。[28]

CME 书中的语气助词,按声调分,最常见的有高调(阴平调),中调(阴去调),和低调(阳去调)三类。从语气轻重角度来看,高调比中调强,低调也比中调强。中调似乎是一个标准调高,CME 课文所用的二十七项助词,差不多一半都是中调,占 48%。(见 4.4.1 节)比中调高的声调,表达的语气较强;比中调低的声调,也表达较强的语气。换言之,偏离标准,都是别有意义。我们可以用下面图表说明这现象:

高 >　　中　　< 低

至于高低二调,谁轻谁重,CME 并没有足够的对比例句可以让我们分析归纳,这里只能存疑。

5. 语气助词和元音的关系

5.1 粤语的语音系统相当复杂。根据 CME 书中的注音,当时的粤语有二十二声母,五十六韵母,八个元音,和九个声调。[29] 韵母分阴阳入三大类,阴声韵以元音收尾,阳声韵以鼻音收尾,入声韵以塞音收尾。CME 所列七十六语气助词,在音韵结构上有一个特点,也就是除了少数的几个入声韵尾助词以外,一律都是阴声韵,完全没有阳声韵。而且阴声韵母都是单原音。书里列有"噂",读音是 pei6,表肯定 "affir-mative",[30] 是唯一的复元音助词,但是课文中并没有实例,无法作进一步的分析。除此以外,其余的七十个语气助词都是单元音韵母。当日粤语韵母有八个元音,但是语气助词却只见四个元音:i e a o。我们把这七十个助词按元音重新排列如下,见表 4:

表 4

i	e	a	o
chi(1)	che(3)	cha(3)	cho(1)
	ke(1)	ka(2)	ko(1)

（续表）

i	e	a	o
		kwa（2）	kwo（2）
	le（6）	la（2）	lo（2）
	me（1）	ma（6）	mo（6）
ni（2）	ne（5）	na（2）	
	pe（1） pei（1）		po（1）
		wa（3）	wo（3）
		ya（5）	yo（2）
	e（1）	a（3）	o（3）

表中所列共二十七个音节，每个音节后的数字，代表书中列出的助词数目，总数是七十。例如 a（3）代表三个助词：a1, a2, a5，其实都是声调的变体。

表中所列，元音排序，显得很有秩序。而且有些助词的音节组合，声母相同，而韵母的元音呈开合之分，而具体用法又非常类似，或是完全相同。例如："噧"wa 和 "啝"wo，CME 的定义都是 "denoting that the statement preceding it has been made by some one before"。[31] 这样看来，wa 和 wo 可以归位一个语素中的两个变体，分别只在元音的前后不一样。我们是否可以用这样方法把二十七音节助词重新归并？而元音的音质不同又和语气因有什么关系？我们从 CME 课文抽取一些实例来分析。

5.2 ke – ka – ko

我们先选取 k- 声母的语气助词实例来看。

（26）字大多浅嘅 ke3, 但意思有时好深嘅 ke3.　　　　　　　　　（CME, 15.11）
    The words are most of them simple, but the meaning is sometimes abstruse.

（27）佢系好恶人嘿 ka3.　　　　　　　　　　　　　　　　　（CME, 2.6）
    He is a very bad man.

（28）呢间屋好大间個 ko3.　　　　　　　　　　　　　　　　（CME, 7.7）
    This is a very large house.

三个语气助词的汉字写法都不一样，元音是 e – a – o 的对比。Ball 给这三个助词的定义是：

（29）嘛 ka3 – emphatic, affirmative

　　　嘅 ke3 – somewhat similar to the last, or simply euphonic

　　　個 ko3 – same as last

也就是说三个助词都是表强调，表肯定，实质上并无区别。但是从实例来看，用法似乎不尽相同。句（26）用 ke，是描述句，语气一般。相比之下，句（27）用 ka，虽然也是描述句，但是重点在强调"他是坏人一个"，所以下一句是"叫佢扯咯"'Tell him to go away.'（叫他滚吧），语气理应较重。句（28）用"個"ko3，是否语气更强，上下文并没有交代。而且全书十五课，只有这一个 ko3 的用例，不能进一步深究。[32] 不过，从英文翻译来看，（27）和（28）两句都在形容词前加上"very"："a very bad man"，"a very large house"，而（26）ke 字句，只是简单的"simple"和"abstruse"，并没有前加"very"，以示强调。由此可见语气轻重确然有别。

5.3　chi – che – cha – cho

这是助词表上唯一的四个元音俱全的系列。Ball 对这些助词的解释是：

（30）chi1 吱：emphatic

　　　che1/3 只 / 嚧 / 啫：implying limitation[33]

　　　cha1/2/3 嗻 / 咋：cautionary, restraining, delaying, but rarely implying doubt[34]

　　　cho2 喌：emphatic

从课文去找，没有 chi1 或 cho2 的例句。但是 che3 和 cha3 却有下面这两句，都是阴去调值。

（31）我讲笑话啫 che3. 你见怪咩？　　　　　　　　　　　（CME, 4.17）

　　　I am only jesting. Do you think it strange?

（32）等吓咋 cha3. 呢条错咯.　　　　　　　　　　　　　　（CME, 10.10）

　　　Wait a bit, this item is wrong.

che3 表示"limitation"，cha3 表示"restraining"，都带有减少或轻化的意味。句（32）的意思是"等一下！这条错了""等一下"或"稍等"本来是客气的说法，但是因为发现错误，所以紧接一句是"要计过咯"（要再算一次）"It must be gone over again."事态显得严重，语气自然加强。低元音的 cha 听起来似乎比高元音的 che 更有力。这两个例子可以说明 e – a 的分别。[35]

5.4 e－a－o

元音韵母的语气助词有以下几项：

（33）嗳 e1 – interrogative

呀 a1 – interrogative, emphasis, or merely euphonic

呀 a3 – emphatic, or merely euphonic

啊 o1 – strongly emphatically affirmative

啊 o3 – strongly emphatically affirmative

五项之中，只有 a3 "呀" 和 o3 "啊" 既同声调，用法也都是表示加强语气。我们试从以下实例来看 a3 和 o3 在语气上是否还有分别。

（34）我见好冷呀 a3.　　　　　　　　　　　　　　　（CME, 3.30）

I feel very cold.

（35）今日好热啊 o3.　　　　　　　　　　　　　　　（CME, 3.8）

It's very hot today.

（36）有平啲嘅冇呀 a3？ 呢个平啲啊 o3.　　　　　　　（CME, 9.5–6）

Have you any cheaper ones? This is cheaper.

（34）和（35）两句分别似乎不大，都是描述句加助词，语气生动活泼。句（36）是市场上讨价还价的话语。前一句嫌贵，想讨一个便宜的价钱。后一句不肯降价，说"这个已经是够便宜的啰"。所以语气上，后一句要比前一句重。使用助词，前句用 a3，后句用 o3。也就是说后元音 o 比前元音 a 更强有力。

5.5 le－la－lo

这一列 e-a-o 的对比在书里是这样的解说：

（37）哩 le – affirmative

嘛 la – emphatic, euphonic

啰 lo – affirmative, euphonic

在课文中找到两句实例可以对比元音前后和语气的关系。

（38）听日月尾嘛 la3.　　　　　　　　　　　　　　　(CME, 3.13)

Tomorrow is the end of the month.

（39）第二个月（係）冷啰 lo3.　　　　　　　　　　　(CME, 3.12)

Next month will be cold.

句（38）是陈述句，说明"明天是月尾"这事实。句（39）也是陈述句，但是语带夸张，强调"下个月会很冷"这个可能。句子中加插"係"就是表示这种加强语气的说法。句末用后元音 o，也是同样的道理。这两个例子和上一节的句（36）都说明 o- 语气助词比 a- 语气助词更能增强说话的语气。

5.6 其他

CME 书里还有别的一些元音排序的对比。例如：

me – ma – mo
（40）咩 me1 – interrogative, or expressing some surprise as well as, "Is it so?"

嗎 ma1 – simply interrogative, or interrogative combined with surprise. [36]

么 mo1 – interrogative, implying doubt. [37]

ni – ne – na
（41）呢 ni1 – interrogative, emphatically demonstrative. [38]

嘅 ne1 – emphatically demonstrative, used when one might say in English,

"There now, what I said was true, you see."

那 na4 – emphatically demonstrative. [39]

ya – yo [40]
（42）吔 ya6 – slight surprise

X yo6 – expressive of surprise

可惜这些对比在书里都没有实例可以显示助词的确实用法和语气。不过，就从英文翻译来看，还是可以见到元音和语气的关系。比如（42）的 ya6 是 "slightly surprise"，而 yo6 却是 "expressive of surprise"，元音从 a 到 o，语气逐渐加重。

5.7 从 CME 的用例和解释来看，语气助词的元音不出 i – e – a – o，而且自成系统。从高到低，从前到后，语气越来越强。我们可以用下面图标来说明：

$$i < e < a < o$$
$$轻 \quad \rightarrow \quad 重$$

元音的变化，是因舌位上下移动而有所不同。舌位向下，口腔张大，发音也就比较用力。i – e – a – o 的不同，正显示口腔用力的多少。说话的时候，语气重自然会多用力。

句末的语气助词往往会因此而发生元音音质上的变化。同一声母的几个助词音节可能只是一个助词的声调变体，表示不同程度的语气轻重。元音分 i – e – a – o 四阶段，是否意味语气也因而可以分成轻重四度？从 CME 的例句来看，似乎有这种可能。

6．语气助词和韵尾的关系

CME 助词总表中还有几项是属于入声韵：chek7、[41]lak9、lok8、yak7、yak8、yak9。真正见于课文的只有 chek7[42] 和 lok8。以 chek7 为例，用法和没有 -k 为的 che1 似乎相同，都是表"只不过……"的意思。chek7 的声调是阴入，调值和阴平相近，都属于高调。请比较下列两句：

che1 – chek7

（43）有少少 喳 che1. （CME, 2.16）

There is only a very little.

（44）唔係几好，中中哋 嚖 chek7. （CME, 1.18）

It is not very good, only middling.

从句子内容和翻译来看，都看不出语气上有强与弱的分别。che1 和 chek7 可以看成同一个助词的两个变体。但是 CME 全书十五课，用"嚖"chek7 的例句只有一句，无法进一步分析。但是请看下面的例子：

lo3 – lok8

（45）见干 啰 lo3，又见好痛添 咯 lok8. （CME, 11.19）

I feel my throat dry, and it is very painful.

（46）佢好耐见软弱 啰 lo3. 食咗药丸……越发敝 咯 lok8. （CME, 11.29, 31–32）

He has been feeling weak for a long time. After taking the pills ... he was much worse.

（45）和（46）都各有两句，一句收"啰"lo3，一句收"咯"lok8。从声调上来说，阴去的 3 调和中入的 8 调，调值都是中平调，所以"啰"lo3 和"咯"lok8 的分别只在塞音韵尾的有无。从文意来看，句（46）是病人诉说自己的病情。前句说喉咙干，后一句补说喉咙疼痛。所以后一句语气当比前一句为重。句（46）也是和看病有关。前一句说身体感到虚弱，后一句说吃药以后，病情反而加重。语气当然也是后句转强。（45）和（46）都是前句用 lo3，后句用 lok8，似乎加上塞音韵尾，显得更有力。CME 助词总表中指出"啰"lo3 表 affirmative"肯定"，表 emphatic"强调"，而"咯"lok8 的用法相同，"but intensified in its sense"。[43] 也就是说 lok8 更能进一步强化说话的语气。

根据 Ball 的说明，并参考实际用例，我们可以说 lo3 和 lok8 当属于一个助词的两个语音变体，有塞音韵尾的语气特别重。我们也许可以进一步说 -k 尾的功能在于强化，就像声调的升高降低变化一样，利用语音变化来调整语气助词所表达的语气轻重。我们试举三例来说明这变化现象：

（47）叫佢翻去 嚹 la3.　　　　　　　　　　　　　　　　　　（CME, 5.19）
　　　Tell him to go back.

（48）要问佢就知 啰 lo3.　　　　　　　　　　　　　　　　　　（CME, 12.31）
　　　You must ask him to know.

（49）若係再制就加重严办 咯 lok8.　　　　　　　　　　　　　（CME, 5.32）
　　　If he does, he will be more severely punished.

三句都在说明事情的下一步应该做些什么。只从英文翻译来看，三句话的轻重分别很清楚。句（47）只表示一个请求。句（48）有 "must"，语气较强，句（49）提到 "加重严办"，可见事非寻常。所以三句的语气强度排序应当是（47）—（48）—（49），语气越来越强。而三句的语气助词正是 la3 – lo3 – lok8 这样的排序。两者相对，说明语气的强度会影响元音和韵尾的表现。不过，关于韵尾部分，因为实例不多，无法知道是否确实如此。而且粤语塞音韵尾有 -p, -t, -k 三类，CME 材料中不见收 -p, -t 韵尾的语气助词。这三缺二的现象是因为我们材料不足而未能尽窥全貌，还是因为某些语音性质而自动造成 -p, -t 的缺位，我们还得搜集更多的资料，再作深入的探讨。不过，就今日粤语来看，收塞音的语气助词，也只有收 -k，没有收 -p 或 -t 的例子，情形和当年一样。也许粤语本来就没有入声语气助词，所谓收 -k 尾的其实来自收喉塞音 -ʔ。说话人为了加强语气，句末喉头紧锁，于是开音节的助词，就成了 -ʔ 音节。而 -ʔ 和 -k 相类似，渐渐转化成收 -k 的音节形式。这种可能性，也还待进一步研究。

7. 语气助词的组合

以上几节都在讨论语气助词和声调与韵母的关系。然而声母是否也在助词体系中扮演某一种角色？冯淑仪（2000）和饭田真纪（2005）曾对这问题进行讨论。她们认为现代粤语句末助词可以分成几大类，各有语法或语气功能。这些类别往往可以按声母区分，而各类之间的聚合与组合有一定的规律。我们这里借用她们的说法，取其重点来看 CME 材料中语气助词组合的大体情形。

　　根据饭田的分析，从话语层面来看，语气助词可以突出说话人对事体的看法，也可以表示他对听话人的期望。前一类又可以再分两类，一类是说话人陈述事实，强调事体的一般性，表达的助词主要是"嘅"ke3；另一类是说话人对事体更主观的看法，或强调事体的新情况，如"嗽"la3，或把事体放在一个比较低的层次来看待，如"啫"che1。后一大类包括表陈述、表疑问、表祈使等，都在说明说话人和听话人之间的关系和互动，许多表语气的如"呀"a3、"咩"me1、"啝"wo3 等等，都属于这一类。饭田有一个图表说明这三类的关系：[44]

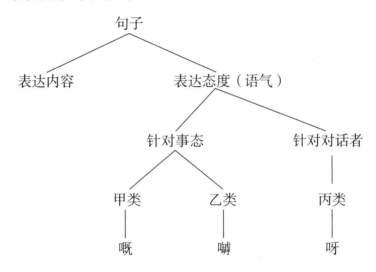

前人研究粤语都注意到语气助词连用的现象。[45] 饭田根据许多语料，分析语气助词之间的组合，认为连用的次序是按甲、乙、丙三类的排序。三类各有自己的范畴意义，组合的原则是从客观到主观，从说话人对事态的看法到他和听话人之间的互动。甲类以 k- 声母为主，乙类以 l-、che- 声母为主。组合排列，是 k- 在前，后接着是 l-、ch- 等。饭田的说法为研究粤语语气助词开出一个新的探讨途径，但是能否有效地解释所有连用的现象，还有待进一步的研究和印证。[46]

CME 书中也有一些语气助词连用的例，但例句不多。现列举如下：

ke3-la1

（50）定嘅喇.   （CME, 15.7）

　　　Certainly.

ke3lok8

（51）我地唐人过年算至紧要嘅咯.   （CME, 15.7）

　　　We Chinese think it of the utmost importance to keep the New Year.

（52）你都唔识好丑嘅咯.   （CME, 9.19）

　　　You don't know good from bad.

ke3me1

（53）做乜你唔曾入教 呢咩 ？   （CME, 12.17）

      Why have you not become a convert?

la3kwa3

（54）系旧嘅 嚹啩 ？   （CME, 9.21）

      I am afraid it is old. Is it not?

la3ma6

（55）好 嚹吗 ？   （CME, 2.16）

      It's good, is it?

lo3kwa3

（56）年尾放假 啰啩 .   （CME, 15.6）

      There will be holidays at the end of the year, I suppose.

lo3po3

（57）你对手污糟 啰嚩 .   （CME, 7.17）

      Your hands are dirty.

上举八例，都只是两个助词连用，而其间排列次序，和饭田提出的语序正相吻合。但是因为例句不多，又不见多词组合的例子，所以早期粤语中语气助词连用的规律，以致语气助词的分类，还待搜集更多语料，研究个中实况，才能进一步讨论。

8. 余论

粤语大量使用语气助词，从历史语料到今日语料，都可以得到确实的明证。根据 1888 年 CME 的记录，当时的语气助词数目高达七十多项，用法灵活。Ball 认为：

    It is curious, and most interesting to notice how small and insignificant a word at the end of a sentence will change the meaning of the whole sentence, like the rudder at the stern of the ship governing the motions of the whole vessel. [47]

相对整个句子的具体内容来说，语气助词似乎是细琐的赘语，随意加添。但是句子临末加上一个助词，马上勾勒出说话人的语气和整个说话的用意。Ball 把语气助词比作船后的舵，不无道理。船就是说话的具体内容，但是船没有舵，航驶就没有方向。说话不用语气助词，也许会语焉不详，话语的实际用意，听话的人不一定能听得明白。不过，所谓语气又当如何理解？我们从 CME 书中看到语气助词在语音结构上稍一变动，句子所表示的态度或意图也就有所不同。语音和语气之间有着一定的关联或对应。我们从书中实例的注音可以看到语音变动的痕迹，但是语音变动如何影响语气轻重变化，Ball 并没有交代。我们试用 CME 全书十五课课文，对这问题作初步的探讨。七八十项的助词，经过整理分析之后，我们可以看到语气助词的运作似是按着两条语音规律来进行。一条是声调的变化：从中调往上或往下调动都表示语气的加重。

I.　高　>　中　<　低

另一条是元音的排序：i-、e-、a-、o-，从前元音到后元音，从高元音到低元音，递进式的加强语气，同一个元音可以再加上塞音 k- 尾，语气更重。

II.　i　<　e　<　a　<　o
$$\underset{ek}{\smile} \qquad \underset{ok}{\smile}$$

根据这两条规律，我们可以大大简化整个语气助词体系。从声调层面整理，七十七个语气助词可以归纳为二十七个基本音节。再从元音层面入手，我们可以把下面的音节中同声母而韵母呈现 i－e－a－o 的组合，归位同一个助词的元音变体，于是体系中只有十个助词：

i	e	a	o
chi (1)	che (3)	cha (3)	cho (1)
	ke (1)	ka (2)	ko (1)
		kwa (2)	kwo (2)
	le (6)	la (2)	lo (2)
	me (1)	ma (6)	mo (6)
ni (2)	ne (5)	na (2)	
	pe (1)		po (1)
		wa (3)	wo (3)
		ya (5)	yo (2)
	e (1)	a (3)	o (3)

按声母排序，这十个助词是：

ch-, k-, kw-, l-, m-, n-, p-, w-, y-, ø-

最后一个是零声母，也就是元音助词。辅音声母中塞音和塞擦音一律都是不送气。这样的简化或系统化，事实上是在说：语气助词是以声母为核心，因声母而区分句子的语气。而元音（或塞音尾）和声调的变化只是在语气轻重程度上的调整。冯淑仪（2000）研究现代粤语的语气词有类似的观察。不过，这样的分析，也许会有失于过度简化，反而会掩盖其间有趣或复杂的现象。譬如 ma 和 me 同属 m- 系列，是否同一表态？我们知道 ma 一般是表疑问，而 me 是表反问，用法迥然有别。l- 系列有 le、la、lak 等，既可表肯定，也可表新情况，分析时，当归为一个助词，还是分为两个助词？其间分合，还要作更详尽的语料搜集和分析。

Ball 在书中提到，当日西方学者研究汉语，往往只着重书面语，对口语里的种种现象，往往一无所知。他认为句末助词是粤语的优美特质，西方学者视若无睹，入宝山而空手回，深为可惜。[48] 其实在十九世纪或二十世纪初之际，又有多少中国学者留意到粤语中如此丰富的语气助词现象？倘若没有 Ball 或其他一些有心人，细心观察当日粤语的实况，进行记录，留下详细的语料和分析，我们今日又如何能够重窥十九世纪的语言世界？历史方言研究一定要有可靠的实际语料，CME 虽然只是一部学习粤语的初阶教材，但是十五课课文，却是一个宝藏，从口语对话到语法解释，从注音到翻译，如实记载一个活的语言。语气助词只是多少语言现象中的一个。我们的研究只是一个开始，还要再参考其他同时代的口语材料，作更深入的分析，才能对十九世纪的语气助词有更全面的认识。这种认识对我们研究今日粤语的助词性能，重构粤语语法演变的规律，或者是从理论角度来讨论语气助词的范畴意义和标志，都有一定的意义和启发。

附录：*Cantonese Made Easy* 第二课

LESSON II.—General.

1. Come here. Why don't you come?	嚟呢處呀, 做乜你唔嚟呢.
2. Who has come? Who is it?	乜人嚟吖, 乜誰吖, or 邊個吖.
3. No one has come.	冇人嚟吖 (or 冇人呀 or 冇邊
4. Who is that?	嗰個係乜人呢[1] [個吖.
5. I don't know. How should I know?	唔知呀, 我點知呀.
6. He is not a good man. He is a very bad man.	佢係唔好人呀, 佢係好惡人嚹.
7. Tell him to go away.	叫佢扯咯.
8. He has gone. He went long ago.	佢去咗咯, 去好耐咯.
9. Close the door, don't fasten it.	掩埋門, 咪閂吖.
10. Open the door. Why did you lock it?	開門呀, 做乜你鎖呢.
11. Tell the Amah to come to me.	叫亞媽嚟見我喇.
12. Come quickly: the quicker the better.	快啲嚟, 越快越好咯.
13. Where's the coolie; has he come?	管店呢, 嚟未曾呀.
14. Come to-morrow, or it will do to come the day after to-morrow.	聽日[2] 嚟喇後日嚟都好吖 (or 都做得吖).
15. There is only a very little.	有少少啫.
16. It's good is it? He says so.	好嘞嗎, 佢係噉話.
17. What does he say? Tell me.	佢話乜野, 講過我聽喇.
18. He says he doesn't wish to come. [with me.	佢話唔想嚟咯.
19. Explain to him that he must certainly go	解明過佢聽, 是必要同我去.
20. How many persons are there old and young?	唔論大細, 有幾多人呢.
21. More than ten.	有十幾個 or 有十零個咯 or 十個有多.
22. Altogether there are sixty men.	喊嚹哈有六十人咯.
23. Are there any children?	有細佬仔冇呢.
24. There is a boy.	有個 (or 壹個) 仔咯.
25. Is that a boy, or a girl?	嗰個係仔嘛女呢.
26. He is in my employ.	佢喺我處打工嘅.
27. Who is your master?	邊個係你事頭呢.
28. He is a native of the place, that is a Cantonese.	佢係本地人, 即係城人咯.
29. He is not a fellow-villager of yours.	佢唔係同你同鄉嘅.
30. Where does he live?	佢喺邊處住呢.
31. A long way from here.	離呢處有好遠咯.
32. Do you go by land, or by water?	打路去嘛搭船去呢.

1. Or as in No. 2.
2. 聽日 ₍t'ing yat₎ very often also means any indefinite time in the future.

LESSON II.—General.

1. ˌLai ˌni-shü² á². Tsò²-mat, ˢnéi ˌm ˌlai ˌni?
   Come this place.² Why you not come eh?[53]

2. Mi-ˈyan* ˌlai á? Mi-ˈshui* ˌá? Pín ko² á?
   What man come eh?[1] Who eh?[1] Which one eh?[1]

3. ˢMò ˌyan ˌlai ˌá, or simply ˢMò ˌyán ˌá, or ˢMò
   No man come,[1] or no man,[2] or no which one.[2]

4. ˈKo-ko² hai² mi-ˈyan* ˌni? [ˌpín ko² ˌá.
   That is what man eh?[53]

5. ˌM ˌchí á². ˢNgo ˈtím ˌchí á²?
   Not know.² I how know eh?[2]

6. ˢK'ui hai² ˌm-ˈhò ˌyan á². ˢK'ui hai² ˈhò ok。
   He is not good man.² He is very wicked man.[14]

7. Kíti², ˢk'ui ˈch'e lok。 [ˌyan ká²
   Tell him to-be-off.[39]

8. ˢK'ui hui²-ˈcho lok。 Hui² ˈhò noi² lok。
   He gone [s. of p. t.].[32] Gone very long.[32]

9. ˈYím ˌmái ˌmún, ˢmai ˌshán á.
   Close to door, don't fasten it.[1]

10. ˌHoi ˌmún á². Tsò²-mat, ˢnéi ˌso ˌni?
    Open door.² Why you lock eh?[53]

11. Kíu² á²-ˢMá ˌlai kín ˢngo ˌlá.
    Call Amah come see me.[21]

12. Fái²-ˌti ˌlai: yüt, fái ˈyüt, ˈhò lok。
    Quickly come: still quicker still better.[32]

13. ˈKün-tím² ˌni; ˌlai méi²-ˌts'ang á²?
    House (or shop) coolie eh;[53] come not yet eh?[3]

14. ˌT'ing-yat, ˌlai ˌlá, hau² yat, ˌlai ˌtò ˈhò ˌá,
    (or ˌtò tsò² tak, ˌá).
    To-morrow come.[21] Day after to-morrow also good,[1] (or also do can).[1]

15. ˢYau ˢshíú ˢshíú ˌche.
    Have little little only.[7]

16. ˈHò lá² má²? ˢK'ui hai² ˈkòm wá². [ˌlá.
    Good?[23] [37] He does so say.

17. ˢK'ui wá² mi-ˢye? ˢKong kwo² ˢngo ˌt'eng†
    He says what thing? Tell over to-me to-hear.[21]

18. ˢK'ui wá² ˌm ˢsöng ˌlai lok。
    He says not wish come.[32]

19. ˈKái ˌming kwo² ˢk'ui ˌt'eng† shí²-pít, yíú²
    ˌt'ung ˢngo hui².
    Explain clearly to him to-hear certainly must with me go. [eh?[53]

20. ˌM lun² tái² sai² ˢyau ˈkéi ˌto yan ˌni?
    No matter (whether) big small have how many men

21. ˢYau shap, ˈkéi ko², or ˢyau shap, ˌleng†
    kò² lok。, or shap, ko² ˢyau ˌto.
    Have ten odd ones, or have ten plus others,[33] or ten ones have more.

22. Hám²-páng²¹-láng² ˢyau luk, shap, yan lok。
    In-all have sixty men.[32]

23. ˢYau sai (or more often ˌsam) ˌman-ˈtsai ˢmò
    Have children not eh?[53]

24. ˢYau ko² (or yat, ko²) ˈtsai lok。 [ˌni?
    Have one boy.[32]

25. ˈKo-ko² hai² tsai, péi² ˈnui ˌni?
    That is boy, or girl eh?[53]

26. ˢK'ui ˈhai ˢngo shü² ˈtá-ˌkung ke².
    He at my place works.[15]

27. ˌPín-ko² hai² ˢnéi sz²-ˈt'au* ˌni? [ˌyan lok。
    Which one is your master eh?[33]

28. ˢK'ui hai² ˈpún téi² ˌyan, tsik, hai² ˈsheng*†
    He is native soil man, that is city man.[32]

29. ˢK'ui ˌm hai² ˌt'ung ˢnéi ˌt'ung ˌhöng-ke².
    He not is with you same villager.[15]

30. ˢK'ui ˈhai ˌpín shü² chü² ˌni?
    He at what place lives eh?[53]

31. ˌLéi ˌni shü² ˢyau ˈhò ˢyün lok。
    Separated-from this place have very far.[32]

32. ˈTá lò² hui², péi² táp。 ˌshün hui² ˌni?
    By road go, or on ship go eh?[53]

---

1. This word is pronounced pá² when spoken rapidly.

附 注

[1] 关于 Ball 的生平，请参看 H. J. Lethbridge 在 1982 重版 *Things Chinese* 的 Introduction。

[2] 关于语气助词的使用，各版本之间还是略有差别。例如 1888 版第六课第 19 句作"你出年娶咩"，而 1907 版则作"你出年娶老婆喇咩"，句末助词稍有不同。

[3] 现存最早的粤语教材是 Robert Morrison 在 1828 年出版的粤语词典 *A Vocabulary of the Canton Dialect*。1841 年有 Elijah C. Bridgman 的 *Chinese Chrestomathy*，全书七百多页。

[4] 请参看附录。

[5] CME，页 112。

[6] CME，页 115—116。

[7] CME，页 125。

[8] "Considerably more than half of the above Finals and their Variants do not appear in any dictionary." CME，页 125。

[9] CME，页 115。

[10] 表中音节排列，根据声母横排。CME 全书所列语气助词只有两类音节：以元音为韵母的开音节，和以塞音 -k 收尾的音节。翻阅全书，没有收 -p 或收 -t 的韵尾，也没有收鼻音韵尾的音节。也就是说语气助词以阴声韵为主，入声韵只有收 -k 一类。传统音韵排列，阴阳入相配，自成组合。但粤语助词的语音组合，阴阳并不配搭。chek 排入 ch- 一栏，lak 和 lok 排入 l- 一栏，yak 排入 ya 一栏。请参看下文 5.1 节。

[11] CME 对声调的处理，十分详尽。书前总论部分以二十页篇幅（页 XVIII 至 XXXVIII）描述各声调的音高变化。请参看张洪年（2006）对 CME 声调系统的讨论。

[12] CME，页 XXIV。

[13] 助词总表中，"呢"有两条，一条注音是 ni1，另外一条作 ni10。调号 10 代表变调，属高平调。

[14] 请参看 Ch'an Chan Sene & J. D. Ball（1900）。

[15] CME，页 113。

[16] 查 CME 书中描述各种语气助词用法，验诸今日粤语，大体依然。下文所引十九世纪用例的发音和意义，多仍见于二十世纪以后的口语。但本文只是断代研究 CME 当年的语言，以一人一时的记录为依归，所以不列举今日用法，以资比较佐证。倘有必要，则在注中说明。

[17] CME，11.27 表示 CME 第十一课第二十七句。下文说明举例出处，皆同此例。

[18] 例句皆用汉字，语气助词后标注音，数目字表调，1-2-3 属阴调，4-5-6 属阳调。句后再附英文翻译。

[19] CME，页 124。

[20] 今日粤语，句末可以用 wo3，表示引述句。请参看例句（11b）。

[21] CME，页 124。

[22] CME，页 115。

[23] CME，页 112。

[24] CME，页 114。

[25] 今日粤语没有中平调的 che3，所以（13）和（14）两句的 che3 都会说成高平调的 che1。

[26] 今日粤语用 lo1 的情形很多，但用法有别。例如 "佢唔肯去 lo1。"（他不肯去呗。）"我都觉得佢有啲唔妥当 lo1。"（我也觉得他有点不太对劲吧。）说话者虽然是表示意见，但是却不太愿意为说话负上责任，用 lo1 表示有所保留。这种用法，似乎是八十年代以后新兴的用法，并不见于早期粤语。

[27] Chao Yuen Ren（1968），页 812—814。

[28] 麦耘（1998）对字调和语调之间的相互关系，有详细的讨论。

[29] CME 的声韵系统，请参看张洪年（2006）的研究。

[30] CME，页 114。

[31] CME，页 114。

[32] 今日粤语中有 ke3 和 ka3，用法相当，但并没有 ko3 这种说法。

[33] 根据 CME 页 113 的描述，che 有三种写法，两种说法：che1 写作 "㗎" 或 "嚧"，che3 写作 "啫"。

[34] 根据 CME 页 112—113 的描述，cha 有两种写法，三种说法：cha1 和 cha2 写作 "嗻"，cha3 写作 "咋"。

[35] 今日粤语中相当的助词只有 che1 和 cha3 两种形式。

[36] 今日粤语只有 ma3 的说法。

[37] 今日粤语没有 mo1 的说法。

[38] 查今日粤语中相当于早期 ni1 的只有 ne1，但不带强调语气。

[39] 今日粤语没有 na4 的说法。

[40] ya 和 yo 都不见于今日粤语。

[41] 如上文所述，chek7 并不见于助词总表，但是却出现在课文中。

[42] CME1888 版本 "嗾" 作 chek7，但是 1907 版本作 chek8。

[43] CME，页 113。

[44] 饭田真纪（2008）。饭田原分四大类，除表中三类外，还有一类，是 "表达内容"，和 "表达态度" 相对，包括 "住"、"嚫"、"先"、"添"。饭田认为这些助词的重点在句子的实质内容，而不在表示说话者对这命题内容的看法，或表达方式。严格来说，这些都属于语气助词。CME 的助词总表中并不收这四助词，所以，我们的讨论也不包括这一类。饭田的第一类是 A 类，第二类包括 B、C、D 三小类；我们既不处理 A 类，所以把她的 B、C、D 三类改为甲、乙、丙三类。

[45] 请看梁仲森（2005）的研究。

[46] 例如同属丙类的"呀"a3"吗"ma3 可以连用，如："你嚟呀吗？"如何解释"呀"在"吗"前？又梁仲森以为粤语中可以八九个助词一起连用，我们应当如何处理？

[47] CME，页 112。

[48] CME，页 112。

参考文献

Cheung, Hung-nin Samuel（2006）One Language, Two Systems: A Phonological Study of Two Cantonese Language Manuals of 1888. *Bulletin of Chinese Linguistics* 1.1:171–200.

Ball, J. Dyer（1888）*Cantonese Made Easy: A Book of Simple Sentences in the Canton Dialect*. 2nd Edition. Hong Kong: China Mail Office.

Ball, J. Dyer（1982）*Things Chinese*, with an introduction by H. J. Lethbridge. Hong Kong: Oxford University Press.

Ch'an, Chan Sene & J. D. Ball（1900）Rules for the Use of the Variant Tones in Cantonese. *The China Review* 24:209–226.

Chao, Yuen Ren（1968）*A Grammar of Spoken Chinese*. Berkeley & Los Angeles: University of California Press.

Fung, Roxana Suk Yee（2000）Final Particles in Standard Cantonese: Semantic Extension and Pragmatic Inference. Ph.D. Dissertation. Ohio State University.

邓思颖（2002）粤语句末助词的不对称分布，《中国语文研究》第 2 期。

饭田真纪（2007）粤语句末助词的体系，《第十届国际粤方言研讨会论文集》，北京：中国社会科学出版社。

方小燕（2003）《广州方言句末语气助词》，广州：暨南大学出版社。

梁仲森（2005）《当代香港粤语语助词的研究》，香港：香港城市大学语言资讯科学研究中心。

麦耘（1998）广州话语调说略，《广州话研究与教学》第三辑，广州：中山大学出版社。

袁家骅等（1960）《汉语方言概要》，北京：文字改革出版社。

张洪年（1972/2006）《香港粤语语法的研究（修订版）》，香港：香港中文大学出版社。

（本文发表于《中国语言学集刊》第三卷第二期，第 131—169 页，2009 年）

粤语间接宾语标记的发展和相关语法现象

钱志安

1. 引言

本文探讨粤语历时语法的发展，以及当中涉及的机制和因素。传统的方言研究主要集中在词汇和语音，语法不太受重视，甚至有学者认为汉语方言之间的语法差异不大。自上世纪 80 年代，汉语方言语法开始引起语言学家的注意。[1] 当中较为全面描述汉语方言语法的著作包括黄伯荣（1996）的《汉语方言语法类编》、余霭芹（Yue-Hashimoto 1993）的 *Comparative Chinese Dialectal Grammar: Handbook for Investigators* 以及近期刘丹青（2008）在 Comrie & Smith（1977）的框架下专为汉语方言语法研究增写的《语法调查研究手册》。这些著作除了提供方言资料之外，也可以让我们进一步了解方言语法在类型学上（汉语南北方言之间或跟其他语言之间）的特点。

从时间层面上，方言语法调查可分为两大类别：历时（diachronic）和共时（synchronic）。根据拉波夫（Labov 1999），研究历时语法有"非实时"（apparent time）和"实时"（real time）两种方式。

非实时方式透过对不同年龄说话人进行调查，从而推断不同时期的语言特征。例如，一位 80 岁的说话人所用的语言代表了上世纪 30 年代的语言。明显地，非实时方式有它的局限和缺点。首先，这种调查不可能收集到时间很久远（如 150 年前）的语言数据；此外，更重要的是，说话人的语言一直在变化，换句话说，80 岁说话人在2010 年所用的语言并不完全等同他出生时期（即 1930 年）的语言，这在一些几代同堂的家庭里尤为明显，年轻一辈跟年长家庭成员的语言互相影响。因此，使用非实时调查方式要注意语言变化这个因素。

实时方式采用不同时代的语言数据来分析和比较。例如，研究上古汉语会用先秦文献。透过早期材料，我们可以了解语言的变化，甚至可以发现一些已消失的语言现象。同时，我们也可以归纳出有关语言现象演变的机制和原因。实时方式也适用于汉语方言历时语法研究。余霭芹（Yue 2004）指出，如果没有早期方言材料，我们就不知道早期粤语最常用的反复问句句式是 VP-Neg（如"你食饭唔呢? 你吃饭不吃饭呢?"）。

跟其他方言如吴语、官话和闽语相比，粤语的早期方言材料最远只可以追溯至 19

世纪初。[2] 这些方言材料有各式各样的内容[3]：介绍中国文化、教学指南、对话练习、圣经翻译等。值得注意的是，很多材料都不是由语言学家或语文工作者编撰，而是由外国传教士编写的[4]。因此，有人会质疑这些材料记录的语言是否准确。余霭芹（Yue 2001a）比较过早期传教士和赵元任记录的潮安方言，发现传教士记录的资料颇为可靠，对了解早期方言的面貌有一定的参考价值。

透过早期材料来探索粤语历时发展的研究已有不少，如反复问句（Yue 1993；陈万成 1994；Cheung 2001）、方向补语（Yiu 2005）、体貌词（Cheung 1997；郭必之、片冈新 2006）、指示代词（张洪年 2006）、音系分析（Cheung 2006），动补结构（Yue 2001b）、外来词（张洪年 2000）、比较句的发展（Yue 1997），词汇反映的社会文化（Tsou 2006）和双宾动词"畀"的语法化（Chin 2009）等。透过早期材料，本文分析粤语间接宾语标记的发展。

2．双宾句和间接宾语标记

间接宾语标记涉及的句型为"双宾句"。"双宾句"在不同的语法理论框架中有不同的理解。比如说，朱德熙（1982）在《语法讲义》里指出"我送他一本书"是双宾句，"我送一本书给他"是连谓句。因为"我送一本书给他"中，"他"前面有介词"给"。本文讨论的"双宾句"是那些用来表达含有"给予"行为的句式。根据朱德熙（1979），在深层的语义里，"给予"行为包括以下三种状况：

（a）存在着"与者"（A）和"受者"（B）双方；

（b）存在着与者所与亦即受者所受的事物（C）；

（c）A 主动地使 C 由 A 转移至 B。

"给予"类的行为包含三个个体（A、B、C），从语法角度来看，A 是主语，B 是间接宾语，C 是直接宾语。从语义角色来看，主语是施事者，直接宾语指的是事物，间接宾语指的是接受者，有关例子见句（1）。

（1）	张三	送	小王	五百元
句法功能	主语	动词	间接宾语	直接宾语
语义角色	施事者	"给予"动词	接受者	事物

句（1）是"给予"类双宾句，所谓"给予"，即事物由施事者转移到接受者。在本文里，双宾句是一个以语义为主的概念。因此，"我送他一本书"和"我送一本书给他"都是双宾句，这是由于"送"这个双宾动词必须带两个宾语，但是在句式的表达上，间

接宾语前面可有介词"给"。

除了"给予"类双宾句，还有一种"取得"类双宾句。"取得"类双宾句所描述的动作方向刚好和"给予"类相反，如句（2）。

（2）张三偷小王五百元。

"张三"仍然是施事者，"五百元"仍然是"事物"，"小王"这个间接宾语可以理解为"来源"。

这两类双宾句的主要区别在于动词的语义，一类为"给予"类，另一类为"取得"类。本文讨论的间接宾语标记，涉及的是"给予"类双宾句。本文用的"双宾句"指的是"给予"类双宾句，"双宾动词"指的是"给予"类动词。

一直以来，粤语双宾句的研究主要集中在间接宾语和直接宾语相对位置跟普通话的差异，在粤语"给予"类双宾句中，直接宾语在前，间接宾语在后，如句（3），两个宾语的语序刚好跟普通话（句（1））相反 [5]。

（3）张三送五百文畀老王 [6]。 张三送老王五百块

这种语序差异在很多粤语语法研究有所提及（如黄伯荣 1959；张洪年 1972/2007；清水茂 1972；高华年 1980；袁家骅 1980/2001；黄家教、詹伯慧 1983；Tang 1998；刘丹青 2001；邓思颖 2003；Yue 2003等）。有学者进一步讨论这种语序差异在汉语方言地理类型学中的分布和意义（Hashimoto 1976；Yue-Hashimoto 1993）。

除了两个宾语的语序，另一个值得探讨的课题是"间接宾语标记"。在句（3）中，间接宾语"老王"前有"畀"这一个词。在普通话中，"给予"类双宾句都有一个共同点，就是间接宾语前出现"给"这一个词 [7]，如句（4）和（5）。

（4）张三 给 小王送了五百块。
（5）张三送 给 小王五百块。

我们把这个出现在间接宾语前面的词语称为"间接宾语标记"，是由于它总是出现在间接宾语之前，并由同一个词语来表示。在大部分的现代汉语方言里，出现在间接宾语前面的词语都是该方言中表示"给"的双宾动词，有关例子如下：

（6）梅县客语（李如龙、张双庆 1992）：分一本书 分 佢 给我一本书
（7）雷州闽语（林伦伦 2006）：我乞本书 乞 伊 我给你一本书
（8）长沙湘语（李永明 1991）：你不把半个工钱 把 我 你不给我半个工钱
（9）上海吴语（许宝华、汤珍珠 1988）：拨张纸头 拨 我 给我一张纸

基于以上的观察，我们认为这个出现在间接宾语前面的词语是一个语法标记，是由表示"给予"的双宾动词语法化而成的。由双宾动词语法化为间接宾语标记在其他语言颇为常见（Newman 1996；Heine & Kuteva 2002）。在亚洲，这现象不独见于汉语，周边的东南亚语言，如越南语、泰语（Matisoff 1991）、马来语（Yap 1999）也可找到相关的现象。

3. 粤语的间接宾语标记

3.1 现代粤语

现代粤语的间接宾语标记也是由双宾动词"畀"[pei^{35}] 或者 [pɐi^{35}] 语法化而成，主要见于：（1）广府片[8]，如香港、广州、佛山、增城、信宜、高州、北海和南宁；（2）北三角洲片，如南海、顺德、高要和藤县；（3）南三角洲片，如东莞和化州；（4）两阳片，如阳春。[9]

（10）香港：k'ɵy^{13} pei^{35} tsɔ^{35} pun^{35} sy^{55} $\boxed{\text{pei}^{35}}$ ŋɔ^{13}

　　　佀　畀　咗　本　书　畀　我

　　　（意思为：他给了我一本书）

（11）东莞：t'uŋ^{31} ŋɔ^{13} tɔi^{42} tsi^{324} pɐt^{4} $\boxed{\text{pɐi}^{35}}$ kɔ^{35} vɔi^{42} tai^{42} tsɵ^{35} tsɔi^{35}

　　　同　我　递　枝　笔　畀　嗰　位　大　姐　仔

　　　（例子取自陈晓锦（1993），意思为：替我递一枝笔给那位小姐）

（12）信宜：nei^{23} kɔŋ^{35} $\boxed{\text{pei}^{35}}$ k'ɵi^{23} tei^{53} tsi^{53}

　　　你　讲　畀　佀　哋　知

　　　（例子取自罗康宁（1987），意思为：你说给他们）

3.2 早期粤语

100 多年前的粤语，间接宾语标记不是"畀"，而是趋向动词"过"，如句（13）至（15）。

（13）我交现钱过你。我交现金给你（Bridgman 1841）

（14）借一个镬过我。借我一个锅子（Dennys 1874）

（15）个大佬番去送好多银过的父老。大哥回去送很多钱给父老（Wells 1941）

表 1 列出间接宾语标记"过"和"畀"在 44 份由 1828 年至 1970 年出版的粤语文字材料里的分布。附录列出这 44 份材料的书目。

表 1　间接宾语标记"过"和"畀"在过去 150 年粤语中的分布

	过	畀
频率	576	479

　　从整体分布来看，这两个标记数量相差不大，"过"比"畀"多约 100 次。语料当中有三部在不同时期（1873 年、1931 年和 1997 年）用粤语翻译的《路加福音》，由于它们的内容相同，同时三部译本依次相隔大约 60 年，这正好让我们比较这三个时期粤语间接宾语标记的使用情况，表 2 列出其中 5 个例句。

表 2　1873、1931 和 1997 年《路加福音》粤语译本中的间接宾语标记

章节	1873	1931	1997
第十章， 第三十五节 [10]	拧出二钱嚟，交过店主	拧两个银钱出来，交过店主话	第二日拎两个银币，交畀客栈嘅主人
第十一章，第五节	请你借三个饼过我	请你畀三个饼过我	请畀三个饼我
第十一章，第十一节	倒转畀蝎过佢呢	反畀蝎过佢	就畀蝎佢呢
第十三章， 第三十二节	你去话过个只狐狸知	你哋去话过个只狐狸知	你哋去话畀嗰只狐狸知
第十四章，第九节	让位过呢个人喇	让位过呢个人喇	请让座畀呢位啦

　　从表 2 的例句，我们看到在 1873 年和 1931 年两个版本中，间接宾语标记都是"过"，在 1997 年的版本，"畀"取代了"过"。同时我们也留意到在旧版的福音书（1873 年和 1931 年的版本）中，当双宾动词是"畀"时，间接宾语标记"过"也会出现。但是在 1997 年版本中，当"畀"作为间接宾语标记时，以"畀"作为双宾动词的双宾句中的间接宾语标记就不出现了。有关间接宾语标记省略的现象，我们会在第五节再讨论。由以上三部福音书的粤语译本，我们可以看到"畀"取代"过"成为间接宾语标记的概况。高岛谦一和余霭芹（Takashima & Yue 2000）指出"畀"完全取代"过"作为间接宾语标记的角色大概是 1940 年代之后。表 3 比较间接宾语标记"畀"和"过"1940 年之前和之后的分布。

表 3　间接宾语标记"畀"和"过"在 1940 年之前和之后的分布

	过	畀
1940 年之前	504	181
1940 年之后	72	298

1940 年之前已经使用间接宾语标记"畀",但不及"过"多,两者的比例大约 1:3。1940 年之后,"过"渐渐式微,现今年轻一代已经不用间接宾语标记"过"。[11] 此外,部分语料(如麦仕治 1893a,1893b)更出现"畀"、"过"同用的情况 [12],如句(16)和(17)。

(16)佢赠送呢一个木瓜 畀过 我 他送给我这一个木瓜
(17)就赐个一条大天命来 畀过 我地文王 就赐给我们的文王那一条大天命

4. 粤语间接宾语标记"过"发展为"畀"的原因和机制

根据 Heine & Kuteva(2002)对多种不同语言的调查,间接宾语标记的来源有三种:(1)动词"给"(GIVE);(2)向格(allative);(3)受益格(benefactive)。虽然汉语是孤立语,各种语法功能并没有格的变化,但是我们可以把"向格"理解为由趋向动词透过语法化演变出来的语法标记。Rice & Kabata(2007)调查过 40 多种语言,当中有 10 多种使用向格标记来做间接宾语标记,典型的例子有英语的 to 和日语的に。由此可见,早期粤语使用趋向动词"过"作为间接宾语标记属于普遍的语法化现象 [13]。既然趋向动词和"给予"动词都可以语法化为间接宾语标记,为什么粤语的间接宾语标记"过"会由"畀"取代呢?以下我们从语法和语义两个层面来探讨有关的发展。

4.1 语法因素

我们先介绍一种跟双宾句有关的句型:受益句。比较句(18)和(19)。

(18)佢织咗条颈巾畀老公 她给她丈夫织了一条围巾
(19)佢送咗条颈巾畀老公 她给她丈夫送了一条围巾

句(18)和(19)的句型可以归纳为 $NP_1 + V + NP_2 + 畀 + NP_3$,但是在深层语义结构中,它们属于两种不同的句式,当中主要的差异是动词的语义特征。"送"在句(19)中是双宾动词,带有"给予"义。在语法结构上,它必须带两个宾语,即"间接宾语"和"直接宾语"。除非在特定语境之下,否则这两个宾语是不能缺少的。相反,句(18)中的动词"织"并不是双宾动词,换句话说,句(18)的"畀老公"可以省略,如"佢织咗条颈巾"。所以"老公"在两个句子中的语义角色并不一样,在句(18)中,它是"受益者"(beneficiary),在句(19)中,它是"接受者"(recipient)。这两种句式可以用以下的公式表示,圆括号表示有关句子成分可以省略:

（20）双宾句：NP$_1$ + V$_{[+给予义]}$ + NP$_2$ + 畀 $_{[间接宾语标记]}$ + NP$_3$

（21）受益句：NP$_1$ + V$_{[-给予义]}$ + NP$_2$（+ 畀 $_{[受益者标记]}$ + NP$_3$）

我们在第二节已经指出，在早期粤语里，双宾句的间接宾语标记主要由"过"来担当，当时的受益句的受益者标记，绝大部分都是"畀"。例子如下：句（22）和（23）是受益句，句（24）和（25）是双宾句。

（22）拧白糖羹 俾 我。给我拿白糖勺子（Dennys 1874）

（23）攞一块面包 俾 我。给我拿一片面包（Caysac 1926）

（24）你去交银 过 佢。你去给他交钱（Bridgman 1841）

（25）卖啯啲米 过 我。卖那些米给我（Dennys 1874）

因此，这两种句式在早期粤语可以归纳为：

（26）双宾句：NP$_1$ + V$_{[+给予义]}$ + NP$_2$ + 过 + NP$_3$

（27）受益句：NP$_1$ + V$_{[-给予义]}$ + NP$_2$ + 畀 + NP$_3$

语法标记"过"和"畀"在 19 世纪粤语里有明显的分工。这在部分语料中特别明显，有关资料见表 4。

表 4　早期粤语中的间接宾语标记和受益者标记的分布

作者	年份	间接宾语标记		受益者标记	
		过	畀	过	畀
Morrison	1828	8	4	0	2
Bonney	1853	9	0	0	5
散语四十章	1877	3	0	1	2
Ball	1888	8	0	0	5
Ball	1894	14	1	2	1
Wisner	1906	21	3	7	11
LeBlanc	1910	7	1	0	2
Ball	1912	13	9	0	7
Cowles	1920	6	0	1	8
Ball	1924	12	0	0	5

以上十部语料中，四部由 Dyer Ball 在不同时期编写。两种语法标记在这四部语料

中有不同的分布，我们因此可以追踪间接宾语标记的发展过程。表 5 列出这两种标记在这四部语料中的分布。

表 5　Dyer Ball 四部语料中的间接宾语标记和受益者标记

作者	年份	间接宾语标记		受益者标记	
		过	畀	过	畀
Ball	1888	8	0	0	5
Ball	1894	14	1	2	1
Ball	1912	13	9	0	7
Ball	1924	12	0	0	5

在 1888 年的语料中，间接宾语标记全都是"过"，受益者标记则为"畀"，分工十分明显。6 年后，14 句双宾句中，有 1 句（约 6%）用间接宾语标记"畀"。18 年后，22 句双宾句中，9 句（约 41%）用"畀"作为间接宾语标记。由此可见，间接宾语标记"畀"的用法有上升的趋势。按照前面几部材料的发展趋势，1924 年材料中，以"畀"作为间接宾语标记的双宾句应该有 10 句以上。不过，1924 年的语料的间接宾语标记全用"过"，并没有"畀"。这是一个很值得探讨的现象。1924 年和 1888 年的语料都是 *Cantonese Made Easy*，1888 年的是第二版（第一版是 1883 年），1924 年的是第四版（第三版是 1907 年）。第四版的书名下面写着 *Fourth Edition, Revised and Enlarged*。第四版里有前三个版本的前言，从这些前言，我们知道每一个新版本大致沿用前一版本的内容，并作出一些修改。根据第四版的前言，由于 1922 年的火灾，所有的资料都付诸一炬，因此第四版大部分内容都是直接套用第三版的内容。在第四版开始的部分，Ball 附上 22 页的校勘表，注明他修改过的内容。校勘表第 21 页列出间接标语标记的语法要点。Ball 指出："过，sometimes translates the word *to*. The real meaning of 过，is *over, to pass*，so that after verbs of giving, sending, throwing, etc., it may be inserted between the verb and the indirect object"。这里作者特别说明粤语里间接宾语标记"过"的用法，但是并没有提到"畀"。由此可见，1924 年这份语料记载的间接宾语标记用法主要是承袭了前几个版本的用法[14]，因此我们看不到预期的变化。无论如何，从 Ball 的其他语料，我们仍然可以看到间接宾语标记在 24 年的时间里（1888—1912 年）由"过"发展到"畀"的情况。这种交替是一种类推的语法演变，受益者标记"畀"渗透到双宾句的间接宾语标记，使它由"过"过渡到"畀"。至于为什么是受益者标记影响间接宾语标记，而不是受益者标记向间接宾语标记靠拢呢？我们可以从两个标记的语义成分来解释。

4.2 语义因素

由于"过"和"畀"这两种间接宾语标记来源不一样，因此它们的语义成分也不尽相同："过"源于趋向动词，表示物体由一个地点转移到另一个地点，主要是物体在空间上的转移。"畀"由双宾动词语法化而来，当中除了涉及物体的空间转移之外，最重要的是物体"拥有权"的转移。因此，在语义层面上，"畀"比"过"更适合来担当间接宾语标记。这种语义分别仍见于广东省从化市街口话中[15]。作者 2008 年曾经到从化市调查街口话的间接宾语标记。在街口话里，间接宾语标记"过"逐渐由"畀"所取代，这主要是受广州话和香港粤语影响。值得注意的是，部分双宾动词如"租"、"借"仍然使用间接宾语标记"过"，很少用"畀"，其他的双宾动词，如"递"、"送"等则可用"畀"。这种差异主要是由于"借"和"租"并没有转移物体的拥有权，物体的拥有者仍然属于施事者，因此，"过"比"畀"更适合担当间接宾语标记的功能。有关资料请看表 6。

表 6　从化街口话间接宾语标记"畀"和"过"的比较

	1			2			3			4		
	过	过/畀	畀	过	过/畀	畀	过	过/畀	畀	过	过/畀	畀
借	8	0	1	3	7	0	3	1	6	0	0	10
租	5	0	0	4	1	1	1	1	4	0	0	6
送	0	1	4	3	0	2	1	2	2	0	0	5
递	0	2	4	4	0	4	0	0	8	0	0	8

调查一共有四个人，都是从化本地人。第四位最年轻，20 来岁，以前在广州上大学，由于受广州话影响，他的街口话已经不再用"过"，全用"畀"。[16] 另外三位的年龄在 60 岁以上，长期在从化生活工作。我们看到第一位和第二位主要用"过"作为双宾动词"借"和"租"的间接宾语标记，"送"和"递"则以"畀"为主要间接宾语标记。第三位曾经在广州工作过三年，受了广州话影响，所以"借"和"租"两个动词使用"畀"的频率都比"过"高，也比另外两位的高。[17] 以上的调查反映间接宾语标记"过"发展为"畀"的情况，并支持我们对两个间接宾语标记语义差异的解释。

综合以上的分析，我们可以这样理解：受益句中的动词缺乏"给予"义，当带出受益者时，需要用上一个"给予"义较为明确的标记，因此，受益者标记在早期粤语就已经由"畀"担当；反之，双宾动词有内在的"给予"义，包含了拥有权转移的深层意义，因此用表示空间转移的趋向动词来标示接受者已经足够。后来，由于类推关系，双宾句的间接宾语标记渐渐由"畀"取代"过"。

5．间接宾语标记省略现象

另一个跟粤语间接宾语标记有关的句法特征是双宾句中间接宾语标记的省略。在香港粤语中，如果双宾句的双宾动词是"畀"，间接宾语标记"畀"可以省略，如"佢畀本书我（他给我一本书）"。一般的讨论都把这种现象视为"同音省略"（haplology）（Xu & Peyraube 1997；Tang 1998；钱志安、邹嘉彦 2005），因为双宾动词和间接宾语标记都是同一个词语——"畀"，而且距离十分接近。作者（Chin 2009）曾经调查过 40 位香港人，具体了解间接宾语标记省略的现象。表 7 列出这 40 人使用间接宾语标记"畀"的语感调查。

表 7　间接宾语标记省略的语感调查

	可接受		尚可接受		不能接受	
	零标记	畀	零标记	畀	零标记	畀
句子 1	33	6	5	17	2	17
句子 2	30	10	10	16	0	14
句子 3	15	14	22	20	3	6
句子 4	8	12	25	19	6	8

四个句子的双宾动词都是"畀"，语法形式为：NP$_1$ 畀 NP$_2$（畀）NP$_3$。句子 1 和句子 2 中的直接宾语（即 NP$_2$）较短，如"一本书"，"礼物"；句子 3 和句子 4 的较长，如"两万一千五百块"。从表七，我们看到，对于句子 1 和句子 2，调查对象普遍接受"零标记"（分别有 33 人和 30 人），使用间接宾语标记"畀"的接受度则很低，只有6 人和 10 人，不接受的分别有 17 人和 14 人（即倾向不用"畀"）。但是，当句子的直接宾语较长（即双宾动词"畀"和间接宾语标记"畀"的距离较大时），使用间接宾语标记"畀"的接受度增加不少，有 14 人（句子 3）和 12 人（句子 4）；不能接受的只有 6 人和 8 人。相反，零标记的接受度比句子 1 和句子 2 的低，只有 15 人和 8 人，不接受零标记的人比句子 1 和句子 2 的多。这个调查结果基本上支持同音省略的解释。[18]

如果同音省略这个假说成立的话，我们可以推论 19 世纪粤语里，双宾动词"畀"的双宾句中应该不会有间接宾语省略的现象。因为当时的间接宾语标记以"过"为主。

换句话说，双宾动词跟间接宾语标记不是同一个词语。不过，潘秋平（2007）指出1841 年 Bridgman 编撰的 *Chinese Chrestomathy in the Canton Dialect* 有以下的句子：

（28）畀棉布汗衫我　给我一件棉衬衣
（29）畀个价钱我　给我一个价钱

由于当时的间接宾语标记和动词"畀"并不一样，因此间接宾语标记的省略似乎不能单用同音省略来解释。潘秋平这个观察很有意思，但他没有解释当时间接宾语标记省略的原因。我们之前引用高岛谦一和余霭芹（Takashima & Yue 2000）的调查结果，指出"畀"取代"过"作为间接宾语标记的过程，大概在 1940 年代左右完成。因此我们再整理和统计 1940 年代之前的语料，发现零标记出现 305 次（占 28.4%），"过"出现 533 次（占 50%），"畀"出现 228 次（占 21.6%）。在这 305 个零标记双宾句里，247 个以"畀"作为双宾动词，占了零标记双宾句的 81%，比例相当高。这 247 个零标记占使用双宾动词"畀"为双宾句的 56.7%。这些数据都指出早期粤语间接宾语标记省略主要出现在双宾动词为"畀"的双宾句，省略的原因可以解释为："畀"是双宾动词类中的核心成员，由它组成的双宾句，"给予"义比其他双宾动词更明显和丰富，句中的间接宾语标记因此可以省略。这种解释说明有关现象并不只是"语音—句法"问题。

6. 结语

本文讨论的两种间接宾语标记在语言类型学上都很常见，因此，我们需要了解两者交替的原因和机制。有关的演变可以从共时和历时两个层面去探讨：早期的粤语材料揭示演变的时间和轨迹和涉及的语法和语义因素；现代方言资料（如从化市街口话）进一步支持我们从历时层面归纳出来的语义条件。我们看到有关语法演变跟动词的语义有关，虽然"畀"、"租／借"和"递／送"都是双宾动词，含有"给予"义，但是它们的"给予"义有所不同："畀"是核心成员，"给予"义最明显；"借／租"并没有涉及物体拥有权的转移，这些给予类动词的语义差异跟间接宾语标记语法演变有关，同时也可以解释相关的间接宾语标记省略现象。

附录　早期粤语文献

蒋克秋（1949）《粤语易解卷二》，新加坡。
蒋克秋（1951）《粤语易解卷三》，新加坡。

路加福音（1931）《（广东话）新旧约全书》，香港圣经公会，香港。

路加福音（1997）《新广东话圣经》，香港圣经公会，香港。

《路加传福音书》（1873），美华书院，上海。

麦仕治（1893a）《广州俗话诗经解义》。

麦仕治（1893b）《广州俗话书经解义》。

《散语四十章》（1877），圣保罗书院，香港。

Ball, Dyer (1888) *Cantonese Made Easy*. 2nd ed. Hong Kong: China Mail Office.

Ball, Dyer (1894) *Readings in Cantonese Colloquial*. Hong Kong: Kelly & Walsh Limited.

Ball, Dyer (1912) *How to Speak Cantonese*. 4th ed. Hong Kong: Kelly & Walsh Limited.

Ball, Dyer (1924) *Cantonese Made Easy*. 4th ed. Hong Kong: Kelly & Walsh Limited.

Belt, Walter and Hoh, Fuk Tsz (1936) *The Revised and Enlarged Edition of a Pocket Guide to Cantonese*. Guangzhou: Lingnan University.

Bonney, S. W. (1853) *Phrases in the Canton Colloquial Dialect*. Canton: Canton.

Bridgman, E. C. (1841) *Chinese Chrestomathy in the Canton Dialect*. Macao: S. Wells Williams.

Brouner, Walter Brooks & Fung Yuet-Mow (1935) *Chinese made easy*. E. J. Brill ed. Leiden.

Bruce, R. (1954) *Cantonese Lessons for Malayan Students*. Kuala Lumpur: Charles & Son Ltd.

Bunyan, John (1871) *The Pilgrim's Progress: From this World to that which is to Come* (《天路历程》), translated by George Piercy. Canton: South China Religious Tract Society.

Caysac, Georges (1926) *Introduction a l'etude du Dialecte Cantonais*. Hong Kong: Imprimerie de Nazareth.

Chan Yeung Kwong (1955) *Everybody's Cantonese*. Hong Kong: The Man Sang Printers.

Chao, Yuen-Ren (1947) *Cantonese Primer*. New York: Greenwood Press.

Chapman，Tim (1973) *A Practical Guide to Cantonese Conversation*. Hong Kong: Hong Kong.

Cowles, Roy T. (1920) *Inductive Course in Cantonese*. 2nd ed. Hong Kong: Kelly & Walsh Limited.

Dennys, N. B. (1874) *A Handbook of the Canton Vernacular Chinese Language*. London: Trubner & Co.

Devan, T. T. (1847) *The Beginner's First Book in the Chinese Language (Canton Vernacular)* Hong Kong: China Mail Office.

Fulton, A. A (1888) *Progressive and Idiomatic Sentences in Cantonese Colloquial*. Hong Kong: Kelly & Walsh Limited.

Happer, Little (1874) *That Sweet Story of Old* (《悦耳真言》). Canton: Xiguan Tongde Dajie Fuyintang.

Hobson, Benjamin (1850) *Canton Dialogues*.

Lau, Sidney (1972a) *Elementary Cantonese: Volumes I and II*. Hong Kong: Government Training Division.

Lau, Sidney (1972b) *Intermediate Cantonese: Volumes I and II*. Hong Kong: Government Training Division.

Leblanc, Charles (1910) *Cours de Langue Chinoise Parlee Dialecte Cantonnais*. Honoi-Haiphong: Imprimerie d'Extreme-Orient.

Morrison, Robert (2001) *Vocabulary of the Canton Dialect*. London: Ganesha (reprint of the 1828 edition).

O'Melia, Thomas A. (1941) *First Year Cantonese*. Hong Kong: Maryknoll House.

Oakley, R. H. (1953) *Rules for Speaking Cantonese*. Kuala Lumpur: Charles Grenier & Son Ltd.

Stedman, T. L. & Lee, K. P. (1888) *A Chinese and English Phrase Book in the Canton Dialect*. New York: William R. Jenkins.

Wells, H. R. (1931) *Commercial Conversations in Cantonese and English* (《英粤商业杂话》). Hong Kong: Kae Shean Printing Co.

Wells, H. R. (1941) *Cantonese for Everyone*. Hong Kong: International Commercial Printing Press.

Whitaker, K. P. K. (1954) *Cantonese Sentence Series*. London: Arthur Probsthain.

Whitaker, K. P. K. (1959) *Structure Drill in Cantonese*. London: Percy Lund, Humphries.

Wisner, O. F. (1906a) *Cantonese Romanized 1*.

Wisner, O. F. (1906b) *Cantonese Romanized 2*.

Wisner, O. F. (1927) *Beginning Cantonese* (《教话指南》). Canton.

Wu T. C. (1960) *Daily Cantonese* (《日用粤语》). Hong Kong: Too Hung Engraving & Printing Co.

Yuen Y. C. 袁英才 (1960) *A Guide to Cantonese*. Hong Kong: Caslon Printers Limited.

附　注

[1] 当中的佼佼者为朱德熙（1985,1991）和 Zhu（1990）的反复问句句式在汉语方语中的分布。

[2] 这里所谓的"早期"是一个简单的概念，主要是相对 20 世纪末和 21 世纪初的粤语来说。

[3] 有关早期粤语方言材料的性质和详细描述，参看 Yue（2004）。

[4] 有关传教士编写的方言材料，见游汝杰（2002）。另有关传教士撰写的资料对汉语史研究的贡献，见罗常培（1930），许光华（2000），李燕萍、片冈新（2006）。

[5] 在"取得"类双宾句中，两个宾语的语序在粤语和普通话中则相同。

[6] 除非特别注明，否则本文所用的粤语例子均来自作者本人。

[7] 句（1）中的间接宾语前并没有"给"，根据朱德熙（1979）的分析，句（1）是句（5）的简缩句，这种省略间接宾语前"给"的原因是主动词是核心给予类动词，所以，句子可以不用间接宾语标记"给"。

[8] 关于粤方言的分类，参见余霭芹（2006）。

[9] 四邑的台山方言（Yue-Hashimoto，2005）和开平方言（邓钧，2000）的间接宾语标记分别

为 [ʔi] 和 [ei]。此外，广西壮族自治区的一些粤方言（包括平话）的间接宾语标记为 [hai]，这是壮傣语跟广西粤语长期语言接触的结果（参见 Chin 2009；覃远雄 2007）。

[10] 这五个例句的大意为：（1）拿出两个银币来，交给店主；（2）请你借我三个饼；（3）反而给他一只蝎子；（4）你去告诉那只狐狸；（5）给这个人让座吧。

[11] Chin（2009）调查过 40 位以香港粤语为母语的人士（最年长为 60 岁），他们都不用"过"作为间接宾语标记，年轻一辈（约三四十岁）更认为用"过"作为间接宾语标记不合语法。

[12] 根据钱乃荣（2003），20 世纪 30 年代的上海方言也同时使用"拨"和"拉"，如"我无得铜钱借拨拉伊"（p.309）。"拨"是双宾动词，"拉"是趋向动词，源自"来"（参见石汝杰（2006a，2006b，2006c））。

[13] 在汉语中以趋向动词作为间接宾语标记有甲骨文的"于"（Chin 2009，2010），明清时代吴语的"来"（石汝杰 2006a，2006b，2006c），现代晋江话（董同龢 1959）、泉州话（李如龙 1996）和邵武话（郭必之 2008）的"度"。

[14] 1924 年的语料里有一个句子："我使费大，唔界得咁多过你"，1888 年的版本没有这个句子，只有"你使费少，唔使要咁多"。可见在 1924 年的语料里，作者仍然使用间接宾语标记"过"。

[15] 从化市在广州的东北方，距离大概 56 公里，面积大约 20 平方公里，人口 11 万左右。有关从化方言的资料，参看《从化县志》（1994）。

[16] "过 / 界"表示有关句子既可以用"过"，也可以用"界"作为间接宾语标记。这种用法反映"过"过渡到"界"的情况。

[17] 关于从化街口话间接宾语标记"界"和"过"的交替状况，见 Chin（2010b）。

[18] 当双宾动词不是"界"的时候，无论直接宾语有多短，间接宾语标记总是出现的。有关讨论，请参考 Chin（2009）。

参考文献

陈万成（1994）近代粤语反复问句的演变及相关问题，《第一届国际粤方言研讨会论文集》，单周尧编，香港：现代教育出版社。

陈晓锦（1993）《东莞方言说略》，广州：广东人民出版社。

从化县地方志编纂委员会（1994）《从化县志》，广州：广东人民出版社。

邓钧（2000）《开平方言》，长沙：湖南电子音像出版社。

邓思颖（2003）《汉语方言语法的参数理论》，北京：北京大学出版社。

董同龢（1959）四个闽南方言，《"中研院"历史语言研究所集刊》，第 30 期。

高华年（1980）《广州方言研究》，香港：商务印书馆。

郭必之（2008）邵武话动态助词"度"的来源——兼论邵武话和闽语的关系，《中国语文》第 2 期。

郭必之、片冈新（2006）早期广州话完成体标记"晓"的来源和演变，《中国文化研究所学报》第 46 期。

黄伯荣（1959）广州话补语宾语的词序，《中国语文》第 3 期。

黄伯荣（1996）《汉语方言语法类编》，青岛：青岛出版社。

黄家教、詹伯慧（1983）广州方言中的特殊语序现象，《语言研究》第 2 期。

李如龙（1996）泉州方言"给予"义的动词，《方言与音韵论集》，香港：香港中文大学吴多泰中国语文研究中心。

李如龙、张双庆（1992）《客赣方言调查报告》，厦门：厦门大学出版社。

李燕萍、片冈新（2006）马礼逊对中文的认识，《中国语文研究》第 22 期第 2 本。

李永明（1991）《长沙方言》，长沙：湖南出版社。

林伦伦（2006）《粤西闽语雷州话研究》，北京：中华书局。

刘丹青（2001）汉语给予类双及物结构的类型学考察，《中国语文》第 5 期。

刘丹青（2008）《语法调查研究手册》，上海：上海教育出版社。

罗常培（1930）耶稣会士在音韵学上的贡献，《中央研究院历史语言研究所集刊》第 3 期。

罗康宁（1987）《信宜方言志》，广州：中山大学出版社。

麦仕治（1893a）《广州俗话诗经解义》。

麦仕治（1893b）《广州俗话书经解义》。

潘秋平（2007）粤方言给予义双宾语结构的来源，《第十届国际粤方言研讨会论文集》，张洪年、张双庆、陈雄根编，北京：中国社会科学出版社。

钱乃荣（2003）《上海语言发展史》，上海：上海人民出版社。

钱志安、邹嘉彦（2005）粤语"畀"字句语法化演变过程初探，《第九届国际粤方言研讨会论文集》，邓景滨、汤翠兰编，澳门：中国语文学会。

覃远雄（2007）平话、粤语与壮语"给"义的词，《民族语文》第 5 期。

清水茂（1972）粤方言双宾语の词序，《鸟居久靖先生华甲纪念论集 —— 中国の言语と文字》，天理：天理大学。

石汝杰（2006a）《缀白裘》的语言，《明清吴语和现代方言研究》，上海：上海辞书出版社。

石汝杰（2006b）《缀白裘》里的"拉"，"来"以及相关结构，《明清吴语和现代方言研究》，上海：上海辞书出版社。

石汝杰（2006c）《山歌》的语音和语法问题，《明清吴语和现代方言研究》，上海：上海辞书出版社。

许宝华，汤珍珠（1988）《上海市区方言志》，上海：上海教育出版社。

许光华（2000）16 至 18 世纪传教士与汉语研究，《国际汉学》第 6 期，任继愈编，北京：商务印书馆。

游汝杰（2002）《西洋传教士汉语方言学著作书目考述》，哈尔滨：黑龙江教育出版社。

余霭芹（2006）粤音构拟之二：声母，《山高水长：丁邦新先生七秩寿庆论文集》（下册），何大安、张洪年、潘悟云、吴福祥编，台北："中研院"语言研究所。

袁家骅（1980/2001）《汉语方言概要》，北京：语文出版社。

张洪年（1972/2007）《香港粤语语法研究》，香港：香港中文大学。

张洪年（2000）早期粤语里的借词现象，《语言变化与汉语方言：李方桂先生纪念论文集》，丁邦新、余霭芹编，台北／西雅图："中研院"语言研究所／华盛顿大学。

张洪年（2006）早期粤语"个"的研究，《山高水长：丁邦新先生七秩寿庆论文集》（下册），何大安、张洪年、潘悟云、吴福祥编，台北："中研院"语言研究所。

朱德熙（1979）与动词"给"相关的句法问题，《方言》第 2 期。

朱德熙（1982）《语法讲义》，北京：商务印书馆。

朱德熙（1985）汉语方言里的两种反复问句，《中国语文》第 1 期。

朱德熙（1991）V-neg-VO 与 VO-neg-V 两种反复问句在汉语方言里的分布，《中国语文》第 5 期。

邹嘉彦（2006）从合逊《广东对话》看十九世纪中叶广东的语言、文化和社会，游如杰译，《语言研究集刊》第三辑，上海：上海辞书出版社。

Bridgman, E. C. (1841) *Chinese Chrestomathy in the Canton Dialect*. Macao: S. Wells Williams.

Caysac, Georges (1926) *Introduction a l'etude du Dialecte Cantonais*. Hong Kong: Imprimerie de Nazareth.

Cheung, Samuel Hung-nin (1997) Completing the Completive—(Re)constructing Early Cantonese Grammar. In Chaofen Sun (ed.) *Studies on the History of Chinese Syntax*, *Journal of Chinese Linguistics monograph*, No. 10, pp. 133–165.

Cheung, Samuel Hung-nin (2001) The Interrogative Construction: (Re)constructing Early Cantonese Grammar. In Hilary Chappell (ed.) *Sinitic Grammar: Synchronic and Diachronic Perspectives*, pp.191–231. Oxford: Oxford University Press.

Cheung, Samuel Hung-nin (2006) One Language, Two Systems: A Phonological Study of Two Cantonese Language Manuals of 1888（一语两制：1888 年两本粤语教科书的语音研究）. *Bulletin of Chinese Linguistics*（《中国语言学集刊》）, 1(1), 171–200.

Chin, Andy (2009) *The Verb GIVE and the Double-object Construction in Cantonese in Synchronic, Diachronic and Typological Perspectives*. PhD dissertation, University of Washington.

Chin, Andy (2010) Two Types of Indirect Object Markers in Chinese: Their Typological Significance and Difference. *Journal of Chinese Linguistics*, 38(1), 1–25.

Chin, Andy (to appear) The *Go*-type and the *Give*-type Indirect Object Markers in the Conghua Dialect. In A. Yue & S. Coblin (eds.) *Studies in Honor of Jerry Norman*, pp.241–271. Hong Kong: Ng Tor-tai Chinese Language Center, Institute of Chinese Studies, the Chinese University of Hong Kong.

Comrie, Bernard & Smith, Norval (1977) Linguistic Descriptive Studies: Questionnaire. *Lingua*, 42, 1–72.

Dennys, N. B. (1874) *A Handbook of the Canton Vernacular Chinese Language*. London: Trubner & Co.

Hashimoto, Mantaro (1976) The Double Object Construction in Chinese. *Computational Analyses of Asian & African Languages*, 6, 33–42.

Heine, Bernd & Kuteva, Tania (2002) *World Lexicon of Grammaticalization*. Cambridge: Cambridge University Press.

Labov, Willliam (1999) *Principles of Linguistic Change: Internal Factors*. Oxford: Blackwell.

Matisoff, James (1991) Areal and Universal Dimensions of Grammatization in Lahu. In Elizabeth Closs Traugott & Bernd Heine (eds.) *Approaches to grammaticalization*, Volume 2, pp.383–453. Amsterdam: John Benjamins.

Newman, John (1996) *Give: A Cognitive Linguistic Study*. Berlin: Mouton de Gruyter.

Rice, Sally & Kabata, Kaori (2007) Crosslinguistic Grammaticalization Patterns of the ALLATIVE. *Linguistic Typology*, 11(3), 451–514.

Takashima, Ken-ichi & Yue, Anne. (2000) Evidence of Possible Dialect Mixture in Oracle-bone Inscriptions. In Ting Pang-hsin & Anne Yue (eds.) *In Memory of Professor Li Fang-Kuei: Essays on Linguistic Change and the Chinese Dialects* (《语言变化与汉语方言: 李方桂先生纪念论文集》), 1–52. Taipei/Seattle: Institute of Linguistics, Academia Sinica and University of Washington.

Tang, Sze-wing. (1998) On the 'Inverted' Double Object Construction. In S. Matthews (ed.) *Studies in Cantonese Linguistics*, pp.35–52. Hong Kong: Linguistic Society of Hong Kong.

Wells, H. R. (1941) *Cantonese for Everyone*. Hong Kong: International Commercial Printing Press.

Xu, Liejiong & Peyraube, Alain (1997) On the Double-object Construction and the Oblique Construction in Cantonese. *Studies in Language*, 21(1), 105–127.

Yap, Foong-Ha (1999) *The Polysemy of 'GIVE' Constructions in Malay and Other Languages: A Grammaticalization Perspective*. Ph.D. dissertation, University of California, Los Angeles.

Yiu, Yuk Man Carine (2005) *Spatial Extension: Directional Verbs in Cantonese*. Ph.D. dissertation. Hong Kong University of Science and Technology.

Yue, Anne (1993) The Lexicon in Syntactic Change—Lexical Diffusion in Chinese Syntax. *Journal of Chinese Linguistics*, 21(2), 213–253.

Yue, Anne (1997) Syntactic Change in Progress—Part I: The Comparative Construction in Hong Kong Cantonese. In Anne Yue & Mitsuaki Endo (eds.) *In Memory of Mantaro J. Hashimoto* (《桥本万

太郎纪念中国语学论集》), 329–375. Tokyo: Uchiyama shoten.

Yue, Anne (2001a) The Historic Role of the Late Professor Y. R. Chao's 1929 Field Materials. *Language and Linguistics*, 2(1), 197–228.

Yue, Anne (2001b) The Verb-Complement Construction in Historical Perspective with Special Reference to Cantonese. In H. Chappell (ed.) *Synchronic and Diachronic Perspectives on the Grammar of Sinitic Languages*, pp.232–265. Oxford: Oxford University Press.

Yue, Anne (2003) Grammar of Chinese Dialects. In G. Thurgood & R. LaPolla (eds.) *The Sino-Tibetan Languages*, pp.84–125. London: Routledge.

Yue, Anne (2005) *The Dancun Dialect of Taishan* (《台山淡村方言研究》). Hong Kong: Language Information Sciences Research Center, City University of Hong Kong.

Yue, Anne (2004) Materials for the Diachronic Study of the Yue Dialects. In Shi Feng & Shen Zhongwei (eds.) *The Joy of Research: A Festschrift in Honor of Professor William S-Y. Wang on his Seventieth Birthday* (《乐在其中——王士元教授七十华诞庆祝文集》), 246–271. Tianjin: Nankai University Press.

Yue-Hashiomoto, Anne (1993) *Comparative Chinese Dialectal Grammar: Handbook for Investigators*. Paris: EHESS-CRLAO.

Zhu, Dexi (1990) Dialectal Distribution of V-neg-VO and VO-neg-V Interrogative Sentence Patterns. *Journal of Chinese Linguistics*, 18(2), 209–230.

（本文发表于《语言学论丛》第四十二辑，第 189—210 页，商务印书馆，2010 年）

Directional Verbs in Cantonese: A Typological and Historical Study[*]

Carine Yuk-man Yiu（姚玉敏）

1. Talmy's typology of motion events

Talmy (1985, 2000b) suggests that languages are classified into verb-framed languages and satellite-framed languages according to how path is encoded. While path is expressed in the verb in verb-framed languages (e.g. Romance, Semitic, Japanese, Tamil, Polynesian, Bantu, some branches of Mayan, Nez Perce and Caddo), it is specified in the satellite[1] in satellite-framed languages (e.g. most Indo-European minus Romance, Finno-Ugric, Chinese, Ojibwa and Warlpiri).

(1)   La   botella salió flotando.

the   bottle   exit   floating

'The bottle exited floating.'

(2)   The bottle floated out.

Examples (1) and (2) show that path is expressed in the main verb *salir* 'to exit' in Spanish and in the verb particle *out* in English.

Scholars have held different views with regard to the typological status of Chinese. According to Talmy (2000b:109), Chinese is a satellite-framed language as path is expressed in a satellite.[2] For example,

---

*   An earlier version of this paper was presented at the 16th International Conference on Yue Dialects (The Hong Kong Polytechnic University, December 15–16, 2011). I am grateful to Samuel H.-N. Cheung, Dingxu Shi, the two anonymous reviewers of *Language and Linguistics* for their valuable suggestions and comments. All errors are of course my own. This work was supported by funding from the General Research Fund of the Research Grants Council of Hong Kong for the project entitled "Directional verbs in early Cantonese colloquial texts: A study of metaphorical extension and word order change" (Project No. 644608).

(3)   瓶子漂出了洞穴。

Píngzi   piāo   chū   le   dòngxué.[3]

bottle   float   exit   ASP   cave

'The bottle floated out of the cave.'

In example (3), manner is expressed in the main verb *piāo* 漂 'to float' while path is incorporated in the satellite *chū* 出 'to exit'.

The following path satellites are listed in Talmy (2000b: 109) for Chinese.[4]

qù 去	'thither'	*guò* 过	'across/past'
lái 来	'hither'	*qǐ* 起	'up off'
shàng 上	'up'	*diào* 掉	'off (he ran off)'
xià 下	'down'	*zǒu* 走	'away'
jìn 进	'in'	*huí* 回	'back'
chū 出	'out'	*lǒng* 拢	'together'
dào 到	'all the way (to)'	*kāi* 开	'apart/free'
dào 倒	'atopple (i.e., pivotally over)'	*sàn* 散	'ascatter'

Tai (2003) suggests, on the contrary, that directional complements *quxiang buyu* 趋向补语 should not be considered as satellites because they can serve as a main verb in the sentence. For example,

(4)   John 飞过英吉利海峡。

John   fēi   guò   Yīngjílì   Hǎixiá.

John   fly   pass   English   Channel

'John flew across the English Channel.' (Tai 2003: 309)

(5)   John 过了英吉利海峡。

John   guò   le   Yīngjílì   Hǎixiá.

John   pass   ASP   English   Channel

'John crossed the English Channel.' (Tai 2003: 310)

(6)   *John 飞了英吉利海峡。

John   fēi   le   Yīngjílì   Hǎixiá.

John   fly   ASP   English   Channel

'John flew across the English Channel.' (Tai 2003: 310)

In examples (4) and (5), path is expressed in *guò* 过 'to pass', which functions as a complement in (4) but as a main verb in (5). The grammaticality contrast in (5) and (6) illustrates that *guò* 过 'to pass' in the former can stand alone as a main verb without the manner verb *fēi* 飞 'to fly' while the use of *fēi* 飞 'to fly' without *guò* 过 'to pass' in (6) gives rise to ungrammaticality. Based on the facts presented in (4)–(6), Tai concludes that Chinese is primarily a verb-framed language as it encodes path in a verb.[5]

Another proposal is put forward in Lamarre (2003), in which it is shown that Chinese is neither a verb-framed nor a satellite-framed language. Instead, it exhibits a split system of conflation in that whether path is encoded in the main verb or in the satellite depends on the type of events denoted. Precisely, when encoding an agentive motion event, path is expressed in the satellite; when expressing a self-agentive motion event, path can be specified in the main verb or in the satellite;[6] and when denoting a non-agentive motion event, there is a tendency to express path in the satellite.[7]

(7)　　我把它扔进了废纸篓。

Wǒ　bǎ　tā　rēng　jìn　le　　fèizhǐlǒu.

I　　DM　it　throw　enter　ASP　wastepaper basket

'I threw it into the wastepaper basket.' (Lamarre 2003: 6)

(8)　　你回来。

Nǐ　　huí　lái.

you　return　come

'You come back.' (Lamarre 2003: 7)

(9)　　他走回来了。

Tā　zǒu　huí　lái　le.

he　walk　return　come　SFP

'He walked back.'

(10)　　河水流出来了。

Hé　　shuǐ　liú　chū　lái　le.

river　water　flow　exit　come　SFP

'The river water flew out.'

Example (7) represents an agentive motion event, a motion event in which the figure, i.e. *tā* 它 'it', is caused by the external force, i.e. *wǒ* 我 'I', to move into the wastepaper basket.

The cause of the movement is denoted by the verb *rēng* 扔 'to throw' whereas the path is expressed in the satellite or the directional complement *jìn* 进 'to enter'. Examples (8) and (9) involve self-agentive motion events, motion events in which the figure, i.e. *nǐ* 你 'you' or *tā* 他 'he', carries out the movement intentionally. In both examples, *huí* 回 'to return' denotes the semantic component of path. Syntactically, it serves as a main verb in the former but as a complement in the latter. Example (10) illustrates the use of a satellite to encode path in non-agentive motion events, in which the subject might or might not be caused by some unspecified entity to move in a certain direction.

Much effort has been put into investigating the typological status of Mandarin. However, important questions such as how other Chinese dialects express path and whether they behave in the same way as Mandarin are not addressed by scholars. This paper will provide a detailed description of the expression of path in another Chinese dialect – Cantonese, a regional variety of Chinese spoken mainly in the provinces of Guangdong and Guangxi. On the one hand, Cantonese resembles Mandarin in exhibiting both characteristics of verb-framed and satellite-framed languages in expressing path in the main verb or in the satellite. On the other hand, Cantonese shows a number of properties which are not observed in Mandarin such as the use of directional verbs to encode path in agentive motion events.[8]

2. Previous works on directional verbs and directional complements in Cantonese

Iida (2001) divides directional verbs into two types, namely, the *heoi³* 去 type and the *soeng⁵* 上 type. The former includes *lai⁴* 嚟 'to come' and *heoi³* 去 'to go' while the latter consists of *lok⁶* 落 'to descend', *jap⁶* 入 'to enter', *ceot¹* 出 'to exit', *gwo³* 过 'to pass', *faan¹* 翻 [9] 'to return' and *maai⁴* 埋 'to approach'. According to Iida, it is possible for *di¹* 啲 to be combined with members of the *soeng⁵* 上 type to express comparison (e.g. *jap⁶ di¹* 入啲 'to move toward the inside a little bit') but such a usage is not found in members of the *heoi³* 去 type (e.g. *lai⁴ di¹ 嚟啲 'to move toward the speaker a little bit'). However, it is observed that some members of the *soeng⁵* 上 type cannot be used with *di¹* 啲 (e.g. *faan¹ di¹ 翻啲 'to move back a little bit').[10] As a result, the proposed distinction, i.e. the possibility to be used with *di¹* 啲, fails to differentiate the two types of directional verbs.

He (2000) discusses the various word orders exhibited in a sequence that involves a main verb (V), an aspectual suffix (ASP), one or more than one directional complement (DC) and an object (O) such as V-ASP-DC (e.g. *soeng⁵ zo² heoi³* 上咗去 ascend-ASP-go 'ascended and away from the speaker'), V-ASP-DC-DC (e.g. *haang⁴ zo² ceot¹ heoi³* 行咗出去 walk-ASP-exit-go 'walked out and away from the speaker'), V-DC-O (e.g. *geoi² hei² biu¹jyu⁵* 举起标语 lift-rise-sign 'to lift up the sign') and V-ASP-DC-O (e.g. *haang⁴ zo² soeng⁵ lau²* 行咗上楼 walk-ASP-ascend-floor 'walked upstairs'). He further proposes a syntactic structure from which the various word orders are derived. In the proposed structure, the main verb and the first directional complement are under the same branch, a combination which is a sister to the second directional complement. For example, *tiu³ lok⁶ heoi³* 跳落去 jump-descend-go 'to jump down and away from the speaker' is schematically represented as: [ᵥ [ᵥ tiu³ lok⁶] heoi³]. The question that immediately arises is why *lok⁶* 落 'to descend' and the main verb *tiu³* 跳 'to jump' form a unit instead of *lok⁶* 落 'to descend' and *heoi³* 去 'to go' as it is impossible to say **tiu³ lok⁶* 跳落 jump-descend 'to jump down'. *Lok⁶ heoi³* 落去 descend-go 'to descend and away from the speaker' in *tiu³ lok⁶ heoi³* 跳落去 jump-descend-go 'to jump down and away from the speaker' is referred to as a compound directional complement in Cheung (2007). If an aspectual suffix is to appear, it will appear between the main verb *tiu³* 跳 'to jump' and the compound directional complement *lok⁶ heoi³* 落 去 descend-go 'to descend and away from the speaker', as in *tiu³ zo² lok⁶ heoi³* 跳 咗 落 去 jump-ASP-descend-go 'jumped down and away from the speaker'. The position in which *zo²* 咗 appears further suggests that *lok⁶* 落 'to descend' and the main verb *tiu³* 跳 'to jump' do not form a unit but *lok⁶* 落 'to descend' and *heoi³* 去 'to go' do. The presence of an object further complicates the picture. While *zo²* 咗 appears after the verb *haang⁴* 行 'to walk' in *haang⁴ zo² soeng⁵ lau²* 行咗上楼 walk-ASP-ascend-floor 'walked upstairs', it occurs after the directional complement *hei²* 起 'to rise' in *geoi² hei² zo² biu¹jyu⁵* 举起咗标语 lift-rise-ASP-sign 'lifted up the sign'. The different positions in which *zo²* 咗 appears seem to suggest that the relationship between the verb and the directional complement differs depending on the type of motion events that is involved, i.e. self-agentive vs. agentive motion events. Therefore, the different word orders exhibited might not be derived from a single underlying structure as proposed by He.

Cheung (2007) is one of the few comprehensive studies on directional complements in Cantonese, in which twelve directional complements are divided into three types of simple directional complements *jiandan de fangxiang buyu* 简单的方向补语. The three types of simple directional complements are as follows:[11]

Table 1: Cheung's (2007) three types of simple directional complements

Type 1	Type 2	Type 3
*lai*⁴ 嚟 'to come'	*soeng*⁵ 上 'to ascend'	*faan*¹ 翻 'to return'
*heoi*³ 去 'to go'	*lok*⁶ 落 'to descend'	
	*ceot*¹ 出 'to exit'	
	*jap*⁶ 入 'to enter'	
	*hoi*¹ 开 'to depart'	
	*maai*⁴ 埋 'to approach'	
	*gwo*³ 过 'to pass'	
	*hei*² 起 'to rise'	
	*dou*³ 到 'to arrive'	

Two or three simple directional complements can be further combined to form a compound directional complement *fuhe de fangxiang buyu* 复合的方向补语. In a compound directional complement that is made up of two simple directional complements (hereafter referred to as double directional complements), a Type 2 complement or a Type 3 complement is followed by a Type 1 complement. The nineteen possible combinations of double directional complements are listed in Table 2 below:[12]

Table 2: Double directional complements in Cantonese [13]

Type 1	Type 2									Type 3
	*soeng*⁵ 上 'to ascend'	*lok*⁶ 落 'to descend'	*ceot*¹ 出 'to exit'	*jap*⁶ 入 'to enter'	*hoi*¹ 开 'to depart'	*maai*⁴ 埋 'to approach'	*gwo*³ 过 'to pass'	*hei*² 起 'to rise'	*dou*³ 到 'to arrive'	*faan*¹ 翻 'to return'
*lai*⁴ 嚟 'to come'	+	+	+	+	+	+	+	+[14]	+	+
*heoi*³ 去 'to go'	+	+	+	+	+	+	+	−[15]	+	+

For compound directional complements that contain three simple directional complements (hereafter referred to as triple directional complements), a Type 3 complement is followed by a Type 2 and a Type 1 complement.[16] The fourteen possible combinations of triple directional complements are shown in Table 3 below:

Table 3: Triple directional complements in Cantonese

faan¹ soeng⁵ lai⁴ 翻上嚟 return-ascend-come	*faan¹ soeng⁵ heoi³* 翻上去 return-ascend-go
faan¹ lok⁶ lai⁴ 翻落嚟 return-descend-come	*faan¹ lok⁶ heoi³* 翻落去 return-descend-go
faan¹ ceot¹ lai⁴ 翻出嚟 return-exit-come	*faan¹ ceot¹ heoi³* 翻出去 return-exit-go
faan¹ jap⁶ lai⁴ 翻入嚟 return-enter-come	*faan¹ jap⁶ heoi³* 翻入去 return-enter-go
faan¹ hoi¹ lai⁴ 翻开嚟 return-depart-come	*faan¹ hoi¹ heoi³* 翻开去 return-depart-go
faan¹ maai⁴ lai⁴ 翻埋嚟 return-approach-come	*faan¹ maai⁴ heoi³* 翻埋去 return-approach-go
faan¹ gwo³ lai⁴ 翻过嚟 return-pass-come	*faan¹ gwo³ heoi³* 翻过去 return-pass-go

As noted above, Cheung's (2007) discussion is one of the few comprehensive studies on directional complements found in the literature. It has drawn our attention to a number of interesting phenomena associated with directional complements such as the position of the aspect marker and the position of the directional complement in relation to a common noun object and a locative object and the order of simple directional complements in a compound directional complement. However, no discussion is provided to explain the above observations.

Yiu (2005) is to this day the most comprehensive study on the syntactic and semantic characteristics of directional verbs and directional complements in Cantonese. She addresses a number of issues raised but unexplained in Cheung (2007). For example, she divides the twelve directional verbs into three types, according to the component of a movement they project for, namely, source, path and goal. She further shows that the order in which the simple directional complements appear reflects the temporal sequence in which a movement takes place. In addition, Yiu probably is the first one who has brought attention to the causative or agentive use of directional verbs in Cantonese (e.g. *lok⁶ dai¹ go³ coeng¹ lim²* 落低 个窗帘 descend-low-CL-curtain 'to lower the curtain'), a use which indicates that the theme object is caused to move in the direction denoted by the directional verb. However, since the focus of her study is primarily on Cantonese, some of the proposals made therein need to find further support from other Chinese dialects and languages.[17]

From the above discussion, it can be observed that previous works often focus on the syntactic and semantic characteristics associated with directional complements. Not much attention has been given to the core usage and meaning of directional verbs, i.e. their use as a main verb and their expression of the directional meaning, a task that will be undertaken in the next section.

3. Characteristics of directional verbs in Cantonese[18]

As noted in the last section, the study of Cheung (2007) includes the following twelve directional verbs: *soeng*[5] 上 'to ascend', *lok*[6] 落 'to descend', *ceot*[1] 出 'to exit', *jap*[6] 入 'to enter', *hoi*[1] 开 'to depart', *maai*[4] 埋 'to approach', *gwo*[3] 过 'to pass', *hei*[2] 起 'to rise', *dou*[3] 到 'to arrive', *faan*[1] 翻 'to return', *lai*[4] 嚟 'to come' and *heoi*[3] 去 'to go'. He further divides them into three types. However, no justification has been provided regarding the criteria adopted for the classification. This study will focus on the same group of directional verbs[19] and classify them into two groups based on whether the location of the speaker is involved in defining the direction. While the direction of *lai*[4] 嚟 'to come' and *heoi*[3] 去 'to go' is defined in relation to the location of the speaker,[20] the orientation point of the other directional verbs does not involve the location of the speaker. The former are referred to as deictic directional verbs whereas the latter are non-deictic directional verbs (cf. Lamarre 2008 and 2009a, Liu 2008). For example,

(11) 佢嚟 / 去办公室。

  Keoi[5]   lai[4]/heoi[3]   baan[6]gung[1]sat[1].

  s/he   come/go   office

  'S/he comes/goes to the office.'

(12) 佢上三楼。

  Keoi[5]   soeng[5]   saam[1]   lau[2].

  s/he   ascend   third   floor

  'S/he ascends to the third floor.'

The directional verbs *lai*[4] 嚟 'to come' and *heoi*[3] 去 'to go' in (11) indicate that the movement is toward and away from the location of the speaker, i.e. *baan*[6]*gung*[1]*sat*[1] 办公室 'the office', while the directional verb *soeng*[5] 上 'to ascend' in (12) specifies an upward movement toward the location denoted by the locative object *saam*[1] *lau*[2] 三楼 'the third floor' and does not involve the location of the speaker.

There are three characteristics that distinguish the above directional verbs from verbs such as *hai*[2] 喺 'to be at', *hoeng*[3] 向 'to face', *sing*[1] 升 'to rise', *dit*[3] 跌 'to drop', *haang*[4] 行 'to walk' and *tiu*[3] 跳 'to jump', which denote state, direction and movement. The three characteristics are: (i) the expression of motion, (ii) the ability to take a locative object and (iii) the potential to form compound directional complements.

3.1 Expression of motion

The characteristic of expressing motion differentiates the twelve directional verbs in this study from verbs which indicate location or state such as hai^2 喺 'to be at' and $hoeng^3$ 向 'to face'.

(13)　佢上咗 / 过 / 紧三楼。

　　　Keoi^5　soeng^5　zo^2/gwo^3/gan^2　saam^1　lau^2.

　　　s/he　ascend　ASP ASP ASP　third　floor

　　　'S/he ascended/has ascended/is ascending to the third floor.'

(14)　* 本书喺咗 / 过 / 紧书架。

　　　Bun^2　syu^1　hai^2　zo^2/gwo^3/gan^2　syu^{1}gaa^2.

　　　CL　book　be at　ASP ASP ASP　bookshelf

　　　'The book was/has been/is being on the bookshelf.'

(15)　* 个窗向咗 / 过 / 紧后院。

　　　Go^3　coeng^1　hoeng^3　zo2/gwo3/gan2　hau^{6}jyun^2.

　　　CL　window　face　ASP ASP ASP　backyard

　　　'The window faced/has faced/is facing the backyard.'

One characteristic of movement verbs is that they can always be used with an aspectual suffix, such as the perfective aspectual suffix zo^2 咗, which denotes the completion of an event, the experiential suffix gwo^3 过, which emphasizes the notion of having undergone a certain experience in the past, and the progressive aspectual suffix gan^2 紧, which specifies the continuation of an event. In example (13), $soeng^5$ 上 'to ascend' specifies an upward movement, while in examples (14) and (15), neither hai^2 喺 'to be at' nor $hoeng^3$ 向 'to face' implies any movement. Instead, hai^2 喺 'to be at' indicates the location of the book, i.e. on the bookshelf, while $hoeng^3$ 向 'to face' denotes the state of the window, i.e. it is facing the backyard. As a result, only the directional verb $soeng^5$ 上 'to ascend' in (13) can be used with zo^2 咗, gwo^3 过 and gan^2 紧 whereas hai^2 喺 'to be at' and $hoeng^3$ 向 'to face' in (14) and (15) cannot.[21]

3.2 Ability to take a locative object

The second characteristic that differentiates the directional verbs studied from verbs such as dit^3 跌 'to fall' and $saang^1$ 生 'to grow', which also denote direction, is that the former, in general, can take a locative object whereas the latter cannot.

(16) 佢上三楼。

Keoi⁵ soeng⁵ saam¹ lau².

s/he ascend third floor

'S/he ascends to the third floor.'

(17) 佢跌 *(落) 水。

Keoi⁵ dit³ *(lok⁶) seoi².

s/he fall descend water

'S/he falls into the water.'

(18) 啲树枝生 *(上) 屋顶。

Di¹ syu⁶zi¹ saang¹ *(soeng⁵) uk¹ deng².

CL branch grow ascend house top

'The branches grow up to the top of the house.'

Although the verbs *soeng⁵* 上 'to ascend', *dit³* 跌 'to fall' and *saang¹* 生 'to grow' all denote direction, i.e. an upward movement in the cases of *soeng⁵* 上 'to ascend' and *saang¹* 生 'to grow' and a downward movement in the case of *dit³* 跌 'to fall', only *soeng⁵* 上 'to ascend' can be immediately followed by the locative object *saam¹ lau²* 三楼 'the third floor', whereas *dit³* 跌 'to fall' and *saang¹* 生 'to grow' cannot be followed by the locative objects *seoi²* 水 'the water' and *uk¹ deng²* 屋顶 'the roof top'. Instead, a directional complement, i.e. *lok⁶* 落 'to descend' and *soeng⁵* 上 'to ascend', is used to introduce the locative object.[22]

The characteristic of taking a locative object also differentiates most of the directional verbs of this study from movement verbs such as *haang⁴* 行 'to walk', *tiu³* 跳 'to jump' *paa⁴* 爬 'to climb', etc.

(19) 佢行 *(入) 房。

Keoi⁵ haang⁴ *(jap⁶) fong².

s/he walk enter room

'S/he walks into the room.'

(20) 佢跳 *(过) 张台。

Keoi⁵ tiu³ *(gwo³) zoeng¹ toi².

s/he jump pass CL table

'S/he jumps over the table.'

(21) 佢爬 *(上) 阁楼。

Keoi⁵ paa⁴ *(soeng⁵) gok³lau².

s/he climb ascend attic

'S/he climbs up to the attic.'

In examples (19)–(21), the verbs *haang*⁴ 行 'to walk', *tiu*³ 跳 'to jump' and *paa*⁴ 爬 'to climb' are referred to as verbs of manner of motion in Levin & Rappaport Hovav (1992), and they denote the manner in which the movements are carried out. For example, *haang*⁴ 行 'to walk', *tiu*³ 跳 'to jump' and *paa*⁴ 爬 'to climb' all involve the use of feet. While *haang*⁴ 行 'to walk' and *paa*⁴ 爬 'to climb' specify that the feet are constantly in contact with some kind of surface, *tiu*³ 跳 'to jump' implies that the feet are in contact with the surface at the starting point and at the endpoint of the movement but are lifted up in the air, having no contact with the surface along the path. These movement verbs differ from directional verbs in that no direction is encoded in them and they cannot themselves take a locative object.[23] As a result, they have to rely on the use of a following directional complement, i.e. *jap*⁶ 入 'to enter', *gwo*³ 过 'to pass' and *soeng*⁵ 上 'to ascend', to specify the direction of the movement and to serve as a link between them and the locative object.

3.3 Potential to form compound directional complements

The third characteristic that distinguishes the directional verbs studied from verbs that denote location, state, or direction is that a non-deictic directional verb can be followed by a deictic directional complement.[24] Furthermore, a non-deictic directional complement and a deictic directional complement can be combined to form a compound directional complement. In contrast, verbs which denote location, state, or direction in general cannot be followed by a deictic directional complement. Neither can they be combined with a deictic directional complement to form a compound directional complement.[25] For example,

(22) 佢就快上嚟 / 去 (三楼)。

Keoi⁵ zau⁶ faai³ soeng⁵ lai⁴/heoi³ (saam¹ lau²).

s/he then quick ascend come/go third floor

'S/he will soon ascend and toward/away from the speaker (to the third floor).'

(23) 佢就快行上嚟 / 去 (三楼)。

Keoi⁵ zau⁶ faai³ haang⁴ soeng⁵ lai⁴/heoi³ (saam¹ lau²).

s/he then quick walk ascend come/go third floor

'S/he will soon walk up and toward/away from the speaker (to the third floor).'

(24) * 本书喺嚟 / 去书架。

Bun² syu¹ hai² lai⁴/heoi³ syu¹gaa².

CL book be at come/go bookshelf

'The book is on the bookshelf.'

(25) * 个窗向嚟 / 去后院。

Go³ coeng¹ hoeng³ lai⁴/heoi³ hau⁶jyun².

CL window face come/go backyard

'The window faces the backyard and toward/away from the speaker.'

(26) * 佢跌嚟 / 去水。

Keoi⁵ dit³ lai⁴/heoi³ seoi².

s/he fall come/go water

'S/he falls into the water and toward/away from the speaker.'

(27) * 啲树枝生嚟 / 去屋顶。

Di¹ syu⁶zi¹ saang¹ lai⁴/heoi³ uk¹ deng².

CL branch grow come/go house top

'The branches grow toward the top of the house and toward/away from the speaker.'

(28) * 架火箭就快升嚟 / 去空。

Gaa³ fo²zin³ zau⁶ faai³ sing¹ lai⁴/heoi³ tin¹hung¹.

CL rocket then quick rise come/go sky

'The rocket will soon be launched toward the sky and toward/away from the speaker.'

In example (22), the main verb *soeng⁵* 上 'to ascend' can be followed by the complements *lai⁴* 嚟 'to come' and *heoi³* 去 'to go', which specify whether the speaker is or is not at the destination of the movement. Example (23) shows that the combinations of *soeng⁵lai⁴* 上 嚟 ascend-come 'to ascend and toward the speaker' and *soeng⁵heoi³* 上 去 ascend-go 'to ascend and away from the speaker' can function as a complement of the main verb *haang⁴* 行 'to walk'. It should be noted that when *lai⁴* 嚟 'to come' and *heoi³* 去 'to go' are combined with the non-deictic directional verbs or non-deictic directional complements, the locative objects can be omitted without giving rise to ungrammaticality. The presence of the locative object serves to pinpoint the location of the speaker, without which the deictic directional complement indicates only that the movement is toward the speaker (in the case of *lai*[4] 嚟 'to come') or away from the speaker (in the case of *heoi*[3] 去 'to go'). In examples (24)–(28), none of the verbs, i.e. *hai*[2] 喺 'to be at', *hoeng*[3] 向 'to face', *dit*[3] 跌 'to fall', *saang*[1] 生 'to grow' and *sing*[1] 升 'to rise', can be followed by either of the two deictic directional complements. Neither can they be combined with a deictic directional complement to form a compound directional complement.[26]

4. The use of directional verbs in Cantonese

This section will examine the use of Cantonese directional verbs in self-agentive and agentive motion events. In a self-agentive motion event, the subject refers to a volitional entity which carries out the movement at his/her own will, while the object (if there is any) denotes a location. In an agentive motion event, the subject is an agent who causes another entity to move in a certain direction and the orientation point might or might not manifest itself as a locative object in the sentence.

4.1 Self-agentive motion events

In a self-agentive motion event, the directional verb denotes the direction of the movement undergone by the subject or theme. A movement is made up of three components, namely, the source, the path, and the goal, as illustrated in Figure 1.

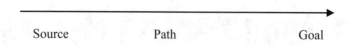

Source   Path   Goal

Figure 1: Three components of a movement

The source is the location in which a movement starts; the path is the course of the movement; and the goal is the location at which the movement ends. The meaning of a directional verb thus includes an inherently specified source (such as *hei*[2] 起 'to rise'), goal (such as *dou*[3] 到 'to arrive', *faan*[1] 翻 'to return', *lai*[4] 嚟 'to come' and *heoi*[3] 去 'to go') or path (such as *soeng*[5] 上 'to ascend', *lok*[6] 落 'to descend', *ceot*[1] 出 'to exit', *jap*[6] 入 'to enter', *hoi*[1] 开 'to depart', *maai*[4] 埋 'to approach', *gwo*³ 过 'to pass').[27] In Cantonese, one of the ways to express comparison is by using the classifier *di*¹ 啲 after adjectives such as *gou*¹ *di*¹ 高啲 'higher'. Table 4 below shows that directional verbs in the left-hand column, i.e. those whose meaning includes an inherently specified path, can be used with *di*¹ 啲 but those in the right-hand column, i.e. those whose meaning involves an inherently specified source and goal, cannot.[28]

Table 4: Directional verbs and *di*¹ 啲

Directional verbs compatible with *di*¹ 啲	Directional verbs incompatible with *di*¹ 啲
*soeng*⁵ 上 'to ascend'	*hei*² 起 'to rise'
*lok*⁶ 落 'to descend'	*dou*³ 到 'to arrive'
*ceot*¹ 出 'to exit'	*faan*¹ 翻 'to return'
*jap*⁶ 入 'to enter'	*lai*⁴ 嚟 'to come'
*hoi*¹ 开 'to depart'	*heoi*³ 去 'to go'
*maai*⁴ 埋 'to approach'	
*gwo*³ 过 'to pass'	

A comparison can be made only when two or more than two entities are involved. A path involves a number of points or locations traversed by the theme. As a result, the height (e.g. *soeng*⁵ *di*¹ 上啲 'higher'), the closeness (e.g. *maai*⁴ *di*¹ 埋啲 'closer'), etc., of those points can be compared. In contrast, directional verbs in the right-hand column involve only one single point, i.e. the source or the goal, therefore, a comparison between the points is impossible. Moreover, the difference in the inherently specified component of a movement projected by directional verbs is also exemplified in their locative object. Except for *hoi*¹ 开 'to depart' and *maai*⁴ 埋 'to approach', the rest in the left-hand column can have a locative object which denotes the path of a movement (cf. (29)–(33)) while those in the right-hand column, except for *hei*² 起 'to rise', can only have a goal object (cf. (34)–(37)).

(29) 佢上紧楼梯。

Keoi⁵   soeng⁵   gan²   lau⁴tai¹.

s/he   ascend   ASP   staircase

'S/he is ascending along the staircase.'

(30) 佢落紧楼梯。

Keoi⁵   lok⁶   gan²   lau⁴tai¹.

s/he   descend   ASP   staircase

'S/he is descending along the staircase.'

(31) 佢出咗闸。

Keoi⁵   ceot¹   zo²   zaap⁶.

s/he   exit   ASP   gate

'S/he exited through the gate.'

(32) 佢入咗闸。

Keoi⁵   jap⁶   zo²   zaap⁶.

s/he   enter   ASP   gate

'S/he entered through the gate.'

(33) 佢过咗海。

Keoi⁵   gwo³   zo²   hoi².

s/he   pass   ASP   sea

'S/he crossed the sea.'

(34) 佢到咗办公室。

Keoi⁵   dou³   zo²   baan⁶gung¹sat¹.

s/he   arrive   ASP   office

'S/he arrived at the office.'

(35) 佢翻咗办公室。

Keoi⁵   faan¹   zo²   baan⁶gung¹sat¹.

s/he   return   ASP   office

'S/he returned to the office.'

(36) 佢嚟咗我屋企。

Keoi⁵   lai⁴   zo²   ngo⁵   uk¹kei⁵.

S/he   come   ASP   my   house

'S/he came to my house.'

(37) 佢去咗我屋企。

Keoi⁵   heoi³   zo²   ngo⁵   uk¹kei⁵.

s/he   go   ASP   my   house

'S/he went to my house.'

The locative object of *soeng*[5] 上 'to ascend', *lok*[6] 落 'to descend' and *ceot*[1] 出 'to exit' can also refer to the source of a movement.[29]

(38) 佢上咗水。

Keoi[5]   soeng[5]   zo[2]   seoi[2].

s/he   ascend   ASP   water

'S/he ascended from the water (to the shore).'

(39) 佢落咗车。

Keoi[5]   lok[6]   zo[2]   ce[1].

s/he   descend   ASP   car

'S/he moved out from the car.'

(40) 佢出咗课室。

Keoi[5]   ceot[1]   zo[2]   fo[3]sat[1].

s/he   exit   ASP   classroom

'S/he exited from the classroom.'

In the above self-agentive examples, path is denoted by the directional verbs, a characteristic which is associated with verb-framed languages. The next section discusses the use of directional verbs to encode path in agentive motion events, a use of directional verbs which is in general not exhibited in Mandarin and which has not been systematically studied by scholars.

4.2 Agentive motion events

In an agentive motion event, the directional verb refers to the action which is carried out intentionally by the agent subject and which causes the theme object to move in a certain direction, as illustrated in (41)–(46) below:[30]

(41) 佢上咗三箱货喺个架 (度)。

Keoi[5]   soeng[5]   zo[2]   saam[1]   soeng[1]   fo[3]   hai[2]   go[3]   gaa[2]   (dou[6])

s/he   ascend   ASP   three   CL   goods   at   CL   shelf   LOC

'S/he moved three boxes of goods up onto the shelf.'

(42) 佢落咗糖喺杯咖啡 (度)。

Keoi[5]   lok[6]   zo[2]   tong[4]   hai[2]   bui[1]   gaa[3]fe[1]   (dou[6]).

s/he   descend   ASP   sugar   at   CL   coffee   LOC

'S/he put sugar into the cup of coffee.'

(43) 佢出咗三张牌喺台 (度)。

Keoi⁵ ceot¹ zo² saam¹ zoeng¹ paai² hai² toi² (dou⁶).

s/he exit ASP three CL card at table LOC

'S/he put three cards onto the table.'

(44) 佢入咗啲钱喺个信封 (度)。

Keoi⁵ jap⁶ zo² di¹ cin² hai² go³ seon³fung¹ (dou⁶).

s/he enter ASP CL money at CL envelope LOC

'S/he put the money into the envelope.'

(45) 佢开咗架船去码头 (度)。

Keoi⁵ hoi¹ zo² gaa³ syun⁴ heoi³ maa⁵tau⁴ (dou⁶).

s/he depart ASP CL ship go pier LOC

'S/he sailed the ship to the pier.'

(46) 啲洗粉去咗啲渍出嚟。

Di¹ sai²fan² heoi³ zo² di¹ zik¹ ceot¹ lai⁴.

CL detergent go ASP CL stain exit come

'The detergent removed the stain.'

In (41)–(46), except for the orientation point of *heoi³* 去 'to go' in (46) which is manifested as the compound directional complement *ceot¹ lai⁴* 出 嚟 exit-come 'to exit and toward the speaker', those of the others are spelt out as the objects of the preposition *hai²* 喺 'at' or are introduced by a directional complement such as *heoi³* 去 'to go' in (45).[31] That the directional verbs in (41)–(46) function as a main verb can be seen by their use with the perfective aspectual suffix *zo²* 咗 . Furthermore, they can also have a complement, as in (47)–(51), or a verbal particle,[32] as in (52).

(47) 佢上漏咗三箱货喺个货架 (度)。

Keoi⁵ soeng⁵ lau⁶ zo² saam¹ soeng¹ fo³ hai² go³ fo³ gaa² (dou⁶).

s/he ascend leave out ASP three CL goods at CL goods shelf LOC

'S/he moved three boxes of goods less up onto the shelf.'

(48) 佢落错咗包盐喺杯咖啡 (度)。

Keoi⁵ lok⁶ co³ zo² baau¹ jim⁴ hai² bui¹ gaa³fe¹ (dou⁶).

s/he descend wrong ASP CL salt at CL coffee LOC

'S/he wrongly put the packet of salt in the cup of coffee.'

(49) 佢出多咗三张牌喺台 (度)。

Keoi⁵ ceot¹ do¹ zo² saam¹ zoeng¹ paai² hai² toi² (dou⁶).

s/he exit more ASP three CL card at table LOC

'S/he put three more cards onto the table.'

(50) 佢入翻十蚊喺个信封 (度)。

Keoi⁵ jap⁶ faan¹ sap⁶ man¹ hai² go³ seon³fung¹ (dou⁶).

s/he enter return ten dollar at CL envelope LOC

'S/he put ten dollars back into the envelope.'

(51) 佢开迟咗架船去码头 (度)。

Keoi⁵ hoi¹ ci⁴ zo² gaa³ syun⁴ heoi³ maa⁵tau⁴ (dou⁶).

s/he depart late ASP CL ship go pier LOC

'S/he sailed the ship to the pier late.'

(52) 啲洗粉去哂啲渍出嚟。

Di¹ sai²fan² heoi³ saai³ di¹ zik¹ ceot¹ lai⁴.

CL detergent go all CL stain exit come

'The detergent removed completely the stain.'

The basic word order in Cantonese is SVO. When the resultant state of the object is to be highlighted, the disposal construction is used. In the Cantonese disposal construction, the patient object is moved to the preverbal position and is marked by the disposal marker *zoeng*¹ 将 . The preposed object has to be specific while the verb cannot be bare. One major difference between Cantonese and Mandarin in the use of the disposal construction is that the verb has to be transitive in the former but can be transitive or intransitive in the latter. For example, when a transitive verb such as *daa*² 打 'to hit' in Cantonese and *dǎ* 打 'to hit' in Mandarin is involved in the disposal construction, the Cantonese sentence *keoi*⁵ *zoeng*¹ *zek*³ *man*¹ *daa*² *sei*² *zo*² 佢将只蚊打死咗 s/he-DM-CL-mosquito-hit-die-ASP 'S/he killed the mosquito by hitting it' and the Mandarin equivalent *tā bǎ wénzi dǎ sǐ le* 他把蚊子打死了 he-DM-mosquito-hit-die-SFP 'He killed the mosquito by hitting it' are both acceptable. In contrast, Mandarin allows an intransitive verb to be used as the main verb in the disposal construction *tā bǎ ge zéi pǎo diào le* 他把个贼跑掉了 he-DM-CL-thief-run-away-SFP 'He let the thief run away', whereas Cantonese does not, *keoi*⁵ *zoeng*¹ *go*³ *caak*² *paau*² *lat*¹ *zo*¹ 佢将个贼跑甩咗 s/he-DM-CL-thief-run-away-ASP 'S/he let the thief run away'. The use of the directional verbs in the disposal constructions in (53)–(58) suggests that the directional verbs resemble transitive verbs when they are used causatively. For example,

(53)　佢将三箱货上漏咗喺个架 (度)。

Keoi⁵	zoeng¹	saam¹	soeng¹	fo³	soeng⁵	lau⁶	zo²	hai²	go³	fo³
s/he	DM	three	CL	goods	ascend	leave out	ASP	at	CL	goods

gaa² (dou⁶).

shelf LOC

'S/he moved three boxes of goods less up onto the shelf.'

(54)　佢将包盐落错咗喺杯咖啡 (度)。

Keoi⁵	zoeng¹	baau¹	jim⁴	lok⁶	co³	zo²	hai²	bui¹	gaa³fe¹	(dou⁶).
s/he	DM	CL	salt	descend	wrong	ASP	at	CL	coffee	LOC

'S/he wrongly put the packet of salt into the cup of coffee.'

(55)　佢将三张牌出错咗喺台 (度)。

Keoi⁵	zoeng¹	saam¹	zoeng¹	paai²	ceot¹	co³	zo²	hai²	toi²	(dou⁶).
s/he	DM	three	CL	card	exit	wrong	ASP	at	table	LOC

'S/he wrongly put three cards onto the table.'

(56)　佢将十蚊入翻喺个信封 (度)。

Keoi⁵	zoeng¹	sap⁶	man¹	jap⁶	faan¹	hai²	go³	seon³fung¹	(dou⁶).
s/he	DM	ten	dollar	enter	return	at	CL	envelope	LOC

'S/he put ten dollars back into the envelope.'

(57)　佢将架船开迟咗去码头 (度)。

Keoi⁵	zoeng¹	gaa³	syun⁴	hoi¹	ci⁴	zo²	heoi³	maa⁵tau⁴	(dou⁶).
s/he	DM	CL	ship	depart	late	ASP	go	pier	LOC

'S/he sailed the ship to the pier late.'

(58)　啲洗粉将啲渍去哂出嚟。

Di¹	sai²fan²	zoeng¹	di¹	zik¹	heoi³	saai³	ceot¹	lai⁴.
CL	detergent	DM	CL	stain	go	all	exit	come

'The detergent removed completely the stain.'

The semantic roles borne by the subject and the object of a directional verb in self-agentive and agentive motion events are summarized in Table 5 below:

Table 5: The semantic roles borne by the subject and the object of a directional verb

Types of motion events	Arguments of directional verb	
	Subject	Object
Self-agentive	Theme	Locative
Agentive	Agent	Theme

This section has shown that directional verbs can be used to encode path in both self-agentive and agentive motion events, a characteristic which is exemplified in verb-framed languages. It will be illustrated in §5 that Cantonese also exhibits the characteristic of satellite-framed languages in expressing path in a satellite or a directional complement.

5. The use of simple directional complements in Cantonese

In addition to functioning as a main verb, a directional verb can also appear after another verb as a complement in self-agentive and agentive motion events.

5.1 Self-agentive motion events

In self-agentive motion events, the main verb denotes the manner in which the movement is carried out. The simple directional complement denotes the direction of the movement and provides the movement with an endpoint either by introducing a locative object for the main verb (in cases of non-deictic directional complements)[33] or by defining the direction of the movement in relation to the speaker's location (in cases of deictic directional complements). While the theme subject is the entity that undergoes a change of location, the locative object often represents the goal of the movement.

(59) 佢跑咗 *(上) 三楼。
Keoi⁵ paau² zo² *(soeng⁵) saam¹ lau².
s/he run ASP ascend third floor
'S/he ran up to the third floor.'

(60) 佢跑咗 *(落) 三楼。
Keoi⁵ paau² zo² *(lok⁶) saam¹ lau².
s/he run ASP descend third floor
'S/he ran down to the third floor.'

(61)　佢行咗 *(出) 客厅。

Keoi⁵　haang⁴　zo²　*(ceot¹)　haak³teng¹.

s/he　walk　ASP　exit　living room

'S/he walked out into the living room.'

(62)　佢行咗 *(入) 房。

Keoi⁵　haang⁴　zo²　*(jap⁶)　fong².

s/he　walk　ASP　enter　room

'S/he walked into the room.'

(63)　佢跳咗 *(埋) 呢边。

Keoi⁵　tiu³　zo²　*(maai⁴)　nei¹　bin¹.

s/he　jump　ASP　approach　this　side

'S/he jumped to this side.'

(64)　佢行咗 *(过) 办公室。[34]

Keoi⁵　haang⁴　zo²　*(gwo³)　baan⁶gung¹sat¹.

s/he　walk　ASP　pass　office

'S/he walked over to the office.'

(65)　佢爬 *(到) 咗山顶。[35]

Keoi⁵　paa⁴　*(dou³)　zo²　saan¹　deng².

s/he　climb　arrive　ASP　hill　top

'S/he climbed to the top of the hill.'

(66)　佢游咗 *(翻) 岸边。

Keoi⁵　jau⁴　zo²　*(faan¹)　ngon⁶　bin¹.

s/he　swim　ASP　return　shore　side

'S/he swam back to the shore.'

(67)　佢跑咗 *(嚟) 终点。

Keoi⁵　paau²　zo²　*(lai⁴)　zung¹dim².

s/he　run　ASP　come　finishing line

'S/he ran to the finishing line and toward the speaker.'

(68)　佢跑咗 *(去) 终点。

Keoi⁵　paau²　zo²　*(heoi³)　zung¹dim².

s/he　run　ASP　go　finishing line

'S/he ran to the finishing line and away from the speaker.'

In examples (59)–(68), the action verbs *paau²* 跑 'to run', *haang⁴* 行 'to walk', *tiu³* 跳 'to jump', *paa⁴* 爬 'to climb' and *jau⁴* 游 'to swim' are the main verbs in the sentences, specifying the manner in which the movements are carried out. They cannot introduce a locative object. Instead, a directional complement is used as a link between the main verb and the locative object. It should be noted that in these self-agentive sentences, the action verb can be omitted without giving rise to ungrammaticality, while the presence of the directional complement is necessary. On the other hand, the locative object after a non-deictic directional complement, in general, cannot be omitted while that after a deictic one can be.[36]

The directional complements *soeng⁵* 上 'to ascend', *lok⁶* 落 'to descend', *ceot¹* 出 'to exit', *jap⁶* 入 'to enter' and *gwo³* 过 'to pass' can introduce a path object.[37] For example,

(69) 佢跑紧上楼梯。

Keoi⁵   paau²   gan²   soeng⁵   lau⁴tai¹.

s/he   run   ASP   ascend   staircase

'S/he is running up along the staircase.'

(70) 佢跑紧落楼梯。

Keoi⁵   paau²   gan²   lok⁶   lau⁴tai¹.

s/he   run   ASP   descend   staircase

'S/he is running down along the staircase.'

(71) 佢跑咗出闸。

Keoi⁵   paau²   zo²   ceot¹   zaap⁶.

s/he   run   ASP   exit   gate

'S/he ran out through the gate.'

(72) 佢跑咗入后闸。

Keoi⁵   paau²   zo²   jap⁶   zaap⁶.

s/he   run   ASP   enter   gate

'S/he ran in through the gate.'

(73) 佢游咗过河。

Keoi⁵   jau⁴   zo²   gwo³   ho⁴.

s/he   swim   ASP   pass   river

'S/he swam across the river.'

The directional complements *soeng⁵* 上 'to ascend', *lok⁶* 落 'to descend' and *ceot¹* 出 'to exit' can also introduce a locative object which indicates the source of the movement.[38] For example,

(74) 佢跳咗上水。

Keoi[5] tiu[3] zo[2] soeng[5] seoi[2].

s/he jump ASP ascend water

'S/he jumped up from the water (to the shore).'

(75) 佢跳咗落车。

Keoi[5] tiu[3] zo[2] lok[6] ce[1].

s/he jump ASP descend car

'S/he jumped out from the car.'

(76) 佢走咗出课室。

Keoi[5] zau[2] zo[2] ceot[1] fo[3]sat[1].

s/he run ASP exit classroom

'S/he ran out from the classroom.'

5.2 Agentive motion events

In agentive motion events, the co-event verb indicates the cause of the movement which is instigated by the agent subject and which brings about the change of location of the theme object. The simple directional complement specifies the direction of the movement undergone by the theme object that follows. Locative objects are often not involved. [39]

(77) 佢打落咗三架战机。

Keoi[5] daa[2] lok[6] zo[2] saam[1] gaa[3] zin[3]gei[1].

s/he hit descend ASP three CL rival plane

'S/he shot down three rival planes.'

(78) 佢踢出咗一个波。

Keoi[5] tek[3] ceot[1] zo[2] jat[1] go[3] bo[1].

s/he kick exit ASP one CL ball

'S/he kicked out one ball.'

(79) 佢射入咗三球。

Keoi[5] se[6] jap[6] zo[2] saam[1] kau[4].

s/he shoot enter ASP three ball

'S/he shot in three balls.'

(80) 佢推开咗张台。

Keoi⁵ teoi¹ hoi¹ zo² zoeng¹ toi².

s/he push depart ASP CL table

'S/he pushed away the table.'

(81) 佢拉埋咗张台。

Keoi⁵ laa¹ maai⁴ zo² zoeng¹ toi².

s/he pull approach ASP CL table

'S/he pulled the table close to a certain location.'

(82) 佢拉过啲张台。

Keoi⁵ laa¹ gwo³ di¹ zoeng¹ toi².

s/he pull pass CL CL table

'S/he pulled the table past a certain location a little bit.'

(83) 佢执起咗张纸。

Keoi⁵ zap¹ hei² zo² zoeng¹ zi².

s/he pick rise ASP CL paper

'S/he picked up the piece of paper.'

(84) 佢拧翻咗张台。

Keoi⁵ ning¹ faan¹ zo² zoeng¹ toi².

s/he bring return ASP CL table

'S/he brought back the table.'

(85) 佢带嚟咗好多麻烦。[40]

Keoi⁵ daai³ lai⁴ zo² hou²do¹ maa⁴faan⁴.

s/he bring come ASP much trouble

'S/he brought much trouble.'

(86) 间公厂排去咗好多污水。

Gaan¹ gung¹cong² paai⁴ heoi³ zo² hou²do¹ wu¹seoi².

CL factory discharge go ASP much polluted water

'The factory discharged much polluted water.'

There are three major differences exhibited in the use of the simple directional complement in self-agentive and agentive motion events. First, the verb and the simple directional complement do not form a compound in the former but they do in the latter. Such a contrast can be shown by the different positions in which the aspectual suffix *zo²* 咗 appears. In self-agentive motion events, the verb and the simple directional complement, except for dou^3 到 'to arrive', do not form a compound and zo^2 咗 appears between them. In agentive motion events, the verb and the simple directional complement form a compound and zo^2 咗 occurs after the compound. Second, the former involves a theme subject and a locative object while the latter has an agent subject and a theme object, a pattern of semantic roles that is also exhibited in directional verbs, as shown in Table 5. Third, the omission of the main verb is possible in the former, but is, in general, not allowed in the latter.[41] The above differences suggest that different structures are involved in the two kinds of motion events, as illustrated schematically in Figure 2 below:

Self-agentive $\left\{\begin{array}{l} \text{[Theme subject + [VP [Main verb + } zo^2 \text{ 咗] + [Directional complement} \\ \text{+ Locative object]]]} \end{array}\right.$

Agentive $\left\{\begin{array}{l} \text{[Agent subject + [VP [Main verb + Directional complement + } zo^2 \text{ 咗]} \\ \text{+ [Theme object]]]} \end{array}\right.$

Figure 2: Two structures exhibited in self-agentive and agentive motion sentences

In the above examples of agentive motion events, the goal of the movement is implied but not explicitly specified. If the destination of the theme object is to be stressed, the verb-directional compound can be restructured as the verb complement construction in which the co-event verb is followed by the theme object, which is in turn followed by the directional complement and the locative object.

(87) 佢打咗三架战机落海。

Keoi^5 daa^2 zo^2 saam^1 gaa^3 zin^{3}gei^1 lok^6 hoi^2.

s/he hit ASP three CL plane descend sea

'S/he shot three planes down into the sea.'

(88) 佢踢咗一个波出界。

Keoi^5 tek^3 zo^2 jat^1 go^3 bo^1 ceot^1 gaai^3.

s/he kick ASP one CL ball exit boundary

'S/he kicked a ball out of the sideline.'

(89) 佢射咗三球入门。

Keoi^5 se^6 zo^2 saam^1 kau^4 jap^6 mun^4.

s/he shoot ASP three ball enter goal

'S/he shot three balls into the goal.'

(90)　佢拉咗张台开去。

　　　Keoi⁵　laa¹　zo²　zoeng¹　toi²　hoi¹　heoi³.

　　　s/he　pull　ASP　CL　table　depart　go

　　　'S/he pushed the table away from here.'

(91)　佢拉咗张台埋墙。

　　　Keoi⁵　laai¹　zo²　zoeng¹　toi²　maai⁴　coeng⁴.

　　　s/he　pull　ASP　CL　table　approach　wall

　　　'S/he pulled the table close to the wall.'

(92)　佢拉咗张台过呢边。

　　　Keoi⁵　laa¹　zo²　zoeng¹　toi²　gwo³　nei¹　bin¹.

　　　s/he　pull　ASP　CL　table　pass　this　side

　　　'S/he moved the table over to this side.'

(93)　佢拧咗张台翻屋企。

　　　Keoi⁵　ning¹　zo²　zoeng¹　toi²　faan¹　uk¹kei⁵.

　　　s/he　bring　ASP　CL　table　return　home

　　　'S/he brought the table back home.'

(94)　佢带咗好多麻烦嚟 (呢度)。

　　　Keoi⁵　daai³　zo²　hou²do¹　maa⁴faan⁴　lai⁴　(nei¹dou⁶).

　　　s/he　bring　ASP　much　trouble　come　here

　　　'S/he brought much trouble to here.'

(95)　间公厂排咗好多污水去河度。

　　　Gaan¹　gung¹cong²　paai⁴　zo²　hou²do¹　wu¹seoi²　heoi³　ho⁴　dou⁶.

　　　CL　factory　discharge　ASP　much　polluted water　go　river　LOC

　　　'The factory discharged much polluted water into the river.'

Although *lai*⁴ 嚟 'to come' and *heoi*³ 去 'to go' can be combined with the main verb to form a compound word (cf. (85) and (86)), it is more natural for them to appear after the theme object, as shown in (98) and (99). Furthermore, the simple directional complements *lai*⁴ 嚟 'to come' and *heoi*³ 去 'to go' can only be combined with a small number of verbs to form a compound.[42] For example,

(96)　*佢拧嚟咗本书。

Keoi⁵　ning¹　lai⁴　zo²　bun²　syu¹.

s/he　bring　come　ASP　CL　book

'S/he brought the book here.'

(97)　*佢送去咗一份礼物。

Keoi⁵　sung³　heoi³　zo²　jat¹　fan⁶　lai⁵mat⁶.

s/he　send　go　ASP　one　CL　gift

'S/he sent away the gift.'

(98)　佢拧咗本书嚟。

Keoi⁵　ning¹　zo²　bun²　syu¹　lai⁴.

s/he　bring　ASP　CL　book　come

'S/he brought the book here.'

(99)　佢送咗一份礼物去。

Keoi⁵　sung³　zo²　jat¹　fan⁶　lai⁵mat⁶　heoi³.

s/he　send　ASP　one　CL　gift　go

'S/he sent away the gift.'

In examples (96) and (97), the sentences are ungrammatical. The simple directional complements *lai⁴* 嚟 'to come' and *heoi³* 去 'to go' cannot follow the verbs *ning¹* 拧 'to bring' and *sung³* 送 'to send'. In examples (98) and (99), when the two deictic directional complements appear in the sentence-final position, the sentences become grammatical. The above contrast in grammaticality shows that the simple directional complements *lai⁴* 嚟 'to come' and *heoi³* 去 'to go' cannot be randomly combined with any verb to form a compound, and always tend to appear in the sentence-final position.

The two word-order patterns illustrated in agentive motion are schematically represented in Figure 3 below:

Agentive {

(i):　[Agent subject + [VP [Main verb + Directional complement + *zo²* 咗] + [Theme object]]] OR

(ii):　[Agent subject + [[VP [Main verb + *zo²* 咗] + [Theme object]] + [Directional complement + Locative object]]]

Figure 3: Two word-order patterns exhibited in agentive motion sentences

Section 5 has illustrated the use of simple directional complements to encode path in both self-agentive and agentive motion events, a characteristic which is exemplified in satellite-framed languages. The next section will show the expression of path in compound directional complements. While both Cantonese and Mandarin allow the use of compound directional complements which consist of two simple directional complements, only the former exhibits the use of compound directional complements that are made up of three simple directional complements.

6. The use of compound directional complements in Cantonese

A compound directional complement is a complement which consists of two or three simple directional complements.[43] The order in which the simple directional complements are combined is fixed with the non-deictic directional complement(s) preceding the deictic one. Similar to simple directional complements, compound directional complements are used in self-agentive and agentive motion events to denote path. On the other hand, compound directional complements differ from the simple directional complements in that the former and the verb do not form a compound while the latter and the verb might.

6.1 Self-agentive motion events

In a self-agentive motion event, the main verb denotes the manner in which the movement is carried out by the theme subject while the compound directional complements denote the spatial configuration of the trajectory traversed by the theme subject.

(100) 佢跑咗上嚟 / 去 (三楼)。

　　　Keoi^5　paau^2　zo^2　soeng^5　lai^4/heoi^3　(saam^1 lau^2).

　　　s/he　　run　　ASP　　ascend　　come/go　　third floor

　　　'S/he ran up here/there (to the third floor).'

(101) 佢跑咗落嚟 / 去 (三楼)。

　　　Keoi^5　paau^2　zo^2　lok^6　lai^4/heoi^3　(saam^1 lau^2).

　　　s/he　　run　　ASP　　descend　　come/go　　third floor

　　　'S/he ran down here/there (to the third floor).'

(102) 佢行咗出嚟 / 去 (客厅)。

Keoi⁵　haang⁴　zo²　ceot¹　lai⁴/heoi³　(haak³teng¹).

s/he　walk　ASP　exit　come/go　living room

'S/he walked out here/there (to the living room).'

(103) 佢行咗入嚟 / 去 (睡房)。

Keoi⁵　haang⁴　zo²　jap⁶　lai⁴/heoi³　(seoi⁶fong²).

s/he　walk　ASP　enter　come/go　bedroom

'S/he walked into here/there (into the bedroom).'

(104) 佢跑咗开嚟 / 去 (张台度)。

Keoi⁵　paau²　zo²　hoi¹　lai⁴/heoi³　(zoeng¹　toi²　dou⁶).

s/he　run　ASP　depart　come/go　CL　table　LOC

'S/he ran away to here/there (to the table).'

(105) 佢企咗埋嚟 / 去 (张台度)。

Keoi⁵　kei⁵　zo²　maai⁴　lai⁴/heoi³　(zoeng¹　toi²　dou⁶).

s/he　stand　ASP　approach　come/go　CL　table　LOC

'S/he stood close to here/there (to the table).'

(106) 佢行咗过嚟 / 去 (办公室)。

Keoi⁵　haang⁴　zo²　gwo³　lai⁴/heoi³　(baan⁶gung¹sat¹).

s/he　walk　ASP　pass　come/go　office

'S/he walked over here/there (to the office).'

(107) 佢行到嚟 / 去学校。[44]

Keoi⁵　haang⁴　dou³　l ai⁴/heoi³　(hok⁶haau⁶).

s/he　walk　arrive　come/go　school

'S/he arrived here/there (at the school).'

(108) 佢游咗翻嚟 / 去 (岸边)。

Keoi⁵　jau⁴　zo²　faan¹　lai⁴/heoi³　(ngon⁶ bin¹).

s/he　swim　ASP　return　come/go　shore side

'S/he swam back here/there (to the shore).'

In the above examples, the subjects bear the role of theme, whose movements are of concern, whereas the optional objects indicate the destinations of the movements. While the non-deictic complements provide information regarding the spatial configurations of the movements, *lai*⁴ 嚟 'to come' and *heoi*³ 去 'to go' indicate whether the movement is toward or away from the speaker. Co-event verbs are used to specify the manner in which the movements are carried out and can be omitted.

As mentioned above, lai^4 嚟 'to come' and $heoi^3$ 去 'to go' have an implied speaker orientation point while the non-deictic directional verbs lack it. In the former, unless the location of the speaker is stressed, a locative object, and more specifically one that denotes the goal of the movement, need not appear after the deictic directional complement. In the latter, the orientation point is defined in relation to a physical location which is indicated by a locative object. As a result, the locative object of a non-deictic directional complement, in general, cannot be omitted. With the presence of lai^4 嚟 'to come' or $heoi^3$ 去 'to go' as the last member in a compound directional complement, a locative object becomes optional after the compound directional complement.

The following examples illustrate the use of triple directional complements in self-agentive motion events.

(109) 佢跑咗翻上嚟 / 去 (三楼)。

     $Keoi^5$ $paau^2$ zo^2 $faan^1$ $soeng^5$ $lai^4/heoi^3$ ($saam^1$ lau^2).

     s/he   run   ASP   return   ascend   come/go   third floor

     'S/he ran back up here/there (to the third floor).'

(110) 佢跑咗翻落嚟 / 去 (三楼)。

     $Keoi^5$ $paau^2$ zo^2 $faan^1$ lok^6 $lai^4/heoi^3$ ($saam^1$ lau^2).

     s/he   run   ASP   return   descend   come/go   third floor

     'S/he ran back down here/there (to the third floor).'

(111) 佢行咗翻出嚟 / 去 (客厅)。

     $Keoi^5$ $haang^4$ zo^2 $faan^1$ $ceot^1$ $lai^4/heoi^3$ ($haak^3teng^1$).

     s/he   walk   ASP   return   exit   come/go   living room

     'S/he walked back out here/there (to the living room).'

(112) 佢行咗翻入嚟 / 去 (睡房)。

     $Keoi^5$ $haang^4$ zo^2 $faan^1$ jap^6 $lai^4/heoi^3$ ($seoi^6fong^2$).

     s/he   walk   ASP   return   enter   come/go   bedroom

     'S/he walked back in here/there (to the bedroom).'

(113) 佢行咗翻开嚟 / 去 (张台度)。

     $Keoi^5$ $haang^4$ zo^2 $faan^1$ hoi^1 $lai^4/heoi^3$ ($zoeng^1$ toi^2 dou^6).

     s/he   walk   ASP   return   depart   come/go   CL   table   LOC

     'S/he walked away back here/there (to the table).'

(114) 佢企咗翻埋嚟 / 去 (张台度)。

Keoi⁵ kei⁵ zo² faan¹ maai⁴ lai⁴/heoi³ (zoeng¹ toi² dou⁶).

s/he stand ASP return approach come/go CL table LOC

'S/he stood back close to here/there (to the table).'

(115) 佢行咗翻过嚟 / 去 (办公室)。

Keoi⁵ haang⁴ zo² faan¹ gwo³ lai⁴/heoi³ (baan⁶gung¹sat¹).

s/he walk ASP return pass come/go office

'S/he walked back over here/there (to the office).'

The Type 3 directional complement *faan*¹ 翻 'to return' is added to the double directional complements to derive the triple directional complements, indicating that the movement is oriented back to the location from which the theme subjects have moved away at an earlier time; the Type 2 directional complements provide information regarding the spatial configurations of the movements; and the Type 1 complements *lai*⁴ 嚟 'to come' and *heoi*³ 去 'to go' define the direction of the movement in relation to the location of the speaker, appearing in the outermost position. The co-event verbs in the above self-agentive motion sentences describe the manner in which the movements are carried out.

6.2 Agentive motion events

In an agentive motion event, the co-event verb refers to the cause instigated by the agent subject, which leads to the change of location of the theme object, while the compound directional complement specifies the direction of the movement. The following examples illustrate the use of double directional complements in agentive motion events.[45]

(116) 佢搬咗啲货上嚟 / 去 (货架)。

Keoi⁵ bun¹ zo² di¹ fo³ soeng⁵ lai⁴/heoi³ (fo³ gaa²).

s/he move ASP CL goods ascend come/go (goods shelf)

'S/he moved the goods up here/there (onto the shelf).'

(117) 佢搬咗啲货落嚟 / 去 (楼下)。

Keoi⁵ bun¹ zo² di¹ fo³ lok⁶ lai⁴/heoi³ (lau⁴ haa⁶).

s/he move ASP CL goods descend come/go (downstairs)

'S/he moved the goods down here/there (to downstairs).'

(118) 佢揸咗架船出嚟 / 去 (海中心)。

Keoi⁵ zaa¹ zo² gaa³ syun⁴ ceot¹ lai⁴/heoi³ (hoi² zung¹sam¹).

s/he drive ASP CL ship exit come/go (sea center)

'S/he sailed the ship out here/there (to the deep water).'

(119) 佢搬咗啲货入嚟 / 去 (货仓)。

Keoi⁵ bun¹ zo² di¹ fo³ jap⁶ lai⁴/heoi³ (fo³coeng¹).

s/he move ASP CL goods enter come/go (warehouse)

'S/he moved the goods into here/there (to the warehouse).'

(120) 佢泊咗架船开嚟 / 去 (码头)。

Keoi⁵ paak³ zo² gaa³ syun⁴ hoi¹ lai⁴/heoi³ (maa⁵tau⁴).

s/he anchor ASP CL ship depart come/go (pier)

'S/he anchored the ship over here/there (at the pier).'

(121) 佢泊咗架船埋嚟 / 去 (码头)。

Keoi⁵ paak³ zo² gaa³ syun³ maai⁴ lai⁴/heoi³ (maa⁵tau⁴).

s/he anchor ASP CL ship approach come/go (pier)

'S/he anchored the ship close to here/there (to the pier).'

(122) 佢揸咗架巴士过嚟 / 去 (车房)。

Keoi⁵ zaa¹ zo² gaa³ baa¹si² gwo³ lai⁴/heoi³ (ce¹fong⁴).

s/he drive ASP CL bus pass come/go (garage)

'S/he drove the bus over here/there (to the garage).'

(123) 佢还咗本书翻嚟 / 去 (图书馆)。

Keoi⁵ waan⁴ zo² bun² syu¹ faan¹ lai⁴/heoi³ (tou⁴syu¹gun²)

s/he return ASP CL book return come/go (library)

'S/he returned the book back here/there (to the library).'

In the above examples, the co-event verb is followed by the theme object which is, in turn followed by a double directional complement and an optional locative object.

The following examples show the use of triple directional complements in agentive motion events.

(124) 佢搬咗啲货翻上嚟 / 去 (货架)。

Keoi⁵ bun¹ zo² di¹ fo³ faan¹ soeng⁵ lai⁴/heoi³ (fo³ gaa²).

s/he move ASP CL goods return ascend come/go (goods shelf)

'S/he moved the goods back up here/there (onto the shelf).'

(125) 佢搬咗啲货翻落嚟 / 去 (楼下)。

Keoi⁵	bun¹	zo²	di¹	fo³	faan¹	lok⁶	lai⁴/heoi³	(lau⁴ haa⁶).
s/he	move	ASP	CL	goods	return	descend	come/go	(downstairs)

'S/he moved the goods back down here/there (to downstairs).'

(126) 佢揸咗架船翻出嚟 / 去 (海中心)。

Keoi⁵	zaa¹	zo²	gaa³	syun⁴	faan¹	ceot¹	lai⁴/heoi³	(hoi² zung¹sam¹).
s/he	drive	ASP	CL	ship	return	exit	come/go	(sea center)

'S/he sailed the ship back out here/there (to the deep water).'

(127) 佢搬咗啲货翻入嚟 / 去 (货仓)。

Keoi⁵	bun¹	zo²	di¹	fo³	faan¹	jap⁶	lai⁴/heoi³	(fo³coeng¹).
s/he	move	ASP	CL	goods	return	enter	come/go	(warehouse)

'S/he moved the goods back into here/there (to the warehouse).'

(128) 佢泊咗架船翻开嚟 / 去 (码头)。

Keoi⁵	paak³	zo²	gaa³	syun⁴	faan¹	hoi¹	lai⁴/heoi³	(maa⁵tau⁴).
s/he	anchor	ASP	CL	ship	return	depart	come/go	(pier)

'S/he anchored the ship back over here/there (at the pier).'

(129) 佢泊咗架船翻埋嚟 / 去 (码头)。

Keoi⁵	paak³	zo²	gaa³	syun⁴	faan¹	maai⁴	lai⁴/heoi³	(maa⁵tau⁴).
s/he	anchor	ASP	CL	ship	return	approach	come/go	(pier)

'S/he anchored the ship back close to here/there (at the pier).'

(130) 佢揸咗架车翻过嚟 / 去 (车房)。

Keoi⁵	zaa¹	zo²	gaa³	baa¹si²	faan¹	gwo³	lai⁴/heoi³	(ce¹fong⁴).
s/he	drive	ASP	CL	bus	return	pass	come/go	(garage)

'S/he drove the car back over here/there (to the garage).'

The structures exhibited by compound directional complements in sentences that encode self-agentive and agentive motion events are schematically represented in Figure 4 below:

Self-agentive { [Theme subject + [VP [Main verb + ASP] + [Compound directional complement + (Locative object)]]]

Agentive { [Agent subject + [VP [[Main verb + ASP] + [Theme object]] + [Compound directional complement + (Locative object)]]]

Figure 4: Structures exhibited by compound directional complements in self-agentive and agentive motion sentences

Figure 4 shows that in both types of motion events, the compound directional complement and the main verb do not form a compound, a possibility that exists when simple directional complements are used to express path in agentive motion events (cf. Figure 3). As a result, an aspectual suffix follows immediately after the main verb and before the compound directional complement.

Sections 3-6 have provided a detailed description of the characteristics of directional verbs and the use of directional verbs and directional complements (including both simple and compound ones) in Cantonese. It is demonstrated that Cantonese exhibits both characteristics of verb-framed and satellite-framed languages in encoding path in the verb or in the satellite. In the next section, two issues will be addressed. First, how does Cantonese fit into Talmy's typology of motion events? Second, how are the differences exhibited by Cantonese and Mandarin accounted for?

7. Discussion

Lamarre (2003) notes that one major difference between Chinese and verb-framed languages such as Japanese and French is that an agentive motion event is expressed by a combination of a co-event verb and a path satellite in Chinese but by a single path verb in Japanese and French.

(131) …doraibuwei ni   kuruma-o   ireta

  garage   at   car-ACC   enter

  '…drove the car into a garage…'

(132) Je vais sortir la voiture du   garage.

  I will exit the car   from-the garage

  'I will drive the car out from the garage.'

The Japanese path verb *ireru* 'to enter' in (131) and the French path verb *sortir* 'to exit' in (132) express the meaning of causing X, i.e. the car, to move in a certain direction, i.e. into the garage and out from the garage. However, path verbs such as *jìn* 进 'to enter' in Chinese lack such an agentive use (cf. (133)). Instead, a combination of a co-event verb and a directional complement such as *fàng* 放 'to put' and *jìn* 进 'to enter' is used (cf. (134)).

(133) * 他进了信在信封里。

    Tā   jìn   le   xìn   zài   xìnfēng   lǐ.

    he   enter   ASP   letter   at   envelope   inside

    'He put the letter into the envelope.'

(134) 他把信放进了信封里。

    Tā   bǎ   xìn   fàng   jìn   le   xìnfēng   lǐ.

    he   DM   letter   put   enter   ASP   envelope   inside

    'He put the letter into the envelope.'

In contrast, Cantonese stands out from Mandarin in having a group of path verbs which exhibits the agentive use.

(135) 佢入咗封信喺信封。

    Keoi^5 jap^6 zo^2 fung^1 seon^3 hai^2 seon^{3}fung^1.

    s/he   enter   ASP   CL   letter   at   envelope

    'S/he put the letter into the envelope.'

(136) 佢放咗封信入信封。

    Keoi^5 fong^3 zo^2 fung^1 seon^3 jap^6 seon^{3}fung^1.

    s/he   put   ASP   CL   letter   enter   envelope

    'S/he put the letter into the envelope.'

Examples (135) and (136) illustrate that Cantonese has an option of encoding path in a main verb or in a directional complement in agentive motion events.

Table 6 below summarizes the ways in which path is expressed in self-agentive and agentive motion events in Cantonese and Mandarin.

Table 6: Expression of path in self agentive and agentive motion events in Cantonese and Mandarin

	Cantonese		Mandarin	
	Verb-framed	Satellite-framed	Verb-framed	Satellite-framed
Self-agentive motion events	✓ （佢入咗闸）	✓ （佢行咗入房）	✓ （你回来）	✓ （他走回来了）
Agentive motion events	✓ （佢入咗封信喺信封）	✓ （佢放咗封信入信封）		✓ （他把信放进了信封里）

In Table 6, it is shown that both Cantonese and Mandarin can express path in a verb or in a directional complement in self-agentive motion events. The two dialects, however, differ significantly in encoding path in agentive motion events. While Cantonese can use a single directional verb or a combination of a co-event verb and a directional complement to denote an agentive motion event, only the latter is allowed in Mandarin. The question that immediately arises is why directional verbs in Cantonese exhibit an agentive use but those in Mandarin do not.

Scholars (cf. Li 1993, Xu 2006, Ma 2008, Peyraube 2009) have shown that Classical Chinese underwent a typological change from a verb-framed language to a satellite-framed language. For example, *chū* 出 'to exit' in Classical Chinese could be used to denote path in self-agentive and agentive motion events, uses which are identical to those observed in directional verbs in Cantonese.

(137) 既醉而出… (*Shījīng* 诗经 220)[46]

Jì   zuì   ér   chū…

already drunk   and   go-out

'If they, when drunk, go out (retire)...'

(138) 我出我车… (*Shījīng* 诗经 168)

Wǒ   chuì   wǒ   jū…

we   bring-out our   carriage

'We bring out our carriages…'

Example (137) denotes a self-agentive motion event and *chū* 出 'to exit' indicates the movement undergone by the subject. Example (138) refers to an agentive motion event and *chuì* 出 'to exit' expresses the meaning of causing the object *wǒ jū* 我车 'our carriages' to move from the inside to the outside. The striking similarity between Cantonese and Classical Chinese in terms of the use of directional verbs in agentive motion events suggests that although both are descendants of the same ancestral language, Cantonese has retained more characteristics of Classical Chinese than Mandarin. In particular, while the use of directional verbs in self-agentive motion events has been preserved in both dialects, the corresponding agentive use has been kept in Cantonese but has become obsolete in Mandarin. As a result, the verb complement construction (such as *gǎn chū* 赶 出 'to expel') is the only way used in Mandarin to express the agentive meaning originally conveyed by directional verbs in Classical Chinese, an option which is still available in Cantonese. The picture which emerges from the above discussion is that Classical Chinese, as claimed by scholars, was a verb-framed language and it underwent a typological shift to a satellite-framed language. Being descendants of Classical Chinese, Cantonese has progressed slower than Mandarin in becoming a satellite-framed language. It is further noticed that both Cantonese and Classical Chinese are largely monosyllabic while Mandarin is increasingly disyllabic,[47] a contrast which seems to be correlated with the availability of the agentive use. For example, some monosyllabic adjectives in Cantonese can also be used as a main verb denoting change of state in agentive events such as *gon¹ zo² di¹ saam¹* 干咗啲衫 dry-ASP-CL-shirt 'dried the clothes'. However, such an agentive use is not observed in disyllabic adjectives such as **gon¹zeng⁶ go³ dei⁶* 干净个地 clean-CL-floor 'to clean the floor'. Furthermore, one of the factors that contributed to the rise of the verb complement construction in Classical Chinese was the disappearance of the causative use of verbs (cf. Mei 1991, Jiang 2000), a process during which causation, which was originally expressed by a monosyllabic element, has gradually been conveyed by a disyllabic complex predicate. If our speculation that syllabicity correlates with the causative use turns out to be true, it would help explain why Mandarin—which is becoming disyllabic—lacks it, while Cantonese—which is basically monosyllabic—exhibits it.

Croft et al. (2010) illustrate that the languages they have examined (including Bulgarian, Japanese, Icelandic, Dutch and English) use more than one of Talmy's types to encode complex events. For example, Japanese, a verb-framed language according to Talmy (2000b), uses a number of strategies to express directed motion events, including the satellite framing construction, compounding and coordination.

(139) Watashi wa ie ni kake-konda.[48]

I TOP house to run-go.into:PST

'I ran into the house.' (Croft et al. 2010 ex. (79a))

(140) Bin ga doukutsu no naka ni ukande-itta.

bottle NOM cave GEN inside to float-go:PST

'The bottle floated to the inside of the cave.' (Croft et al. 2010 ex. (80a))

(141) Watashi wa taru o korogashi te chikashitsu ni ireta.

I TOP barrel ACC roll and basement to put.into:PST

'I rolled the barrel into the basement.' (Croft et al. 2010 ex. (87))

Moreover, Croft et al. propose adding two new types, ie. symmetrical framing[49] and double framing languages, to Talmy's two-way classification. Symmetrical framing is proposed to encompass serial verb languages in which both event and frame are expressed in forms that may occur as predicates on their own. It further consists of three sub-types: serial strategy, compounding and coordination. Mandarin is used by the authors to illustrate the use of the serial strategy to express the core schema and the co-event. For example,

(142) 他们跑出来了。

    Tāmen pǎo chū lái le.

    they   run   exit come SFP

    'They came running out.'

In the above example, the verb *pǎo* 跑 'to run' expresses manner while the directional complements *chū* 出 'to exit' and *lái* 来 'to come' denote the non-deictic and the deictic path. All of them can occur as predicates on their own, as illustrated in the following examples:

(143) 他们还在跑。

    Tāmen háizài pǎo.

    they   still   run

    'They are still running.'

(144) 他出了教室。

    Tā chū le   jiàoshì.

    he exit ASP classroom

    'He exited from the classroom.'

(145) 他来了。

    Tā lái le.

    he come SFP

    'He came.'

According to Croft et al. (2010), compounding is more grammaticalized than the serial strategy. The forms that express the core schema and the co-event in the former are morphologically bound or more tightly integrated than those in the latter. The compounding strategy is used in Kiowa. For example,

(146) Ɔ̀: pàl sép cándé-à: nɔ̀ pàhị́: bà-tʰídạ́y.

　　　nearer rain reach-come and.DS clearly get.wet.PF

　　　'The rain is coming closer and it is clear we will get wet.' (Croft et al. 2010 ex. (27))

In the above example, the path component is expressed by *cándé* 'to reach' and the deictic component by-*à*: 'to come', and together the two form a compound.

　　　The third sub-type of symmetrical framing is coordination. Amele uses a combination which involves the path component and the deictic component to express a complex event. For example,

(147) Cois hina gad cesel -i nu-ug-a.

　　　OK 2SG may return-PRED(SS) go-2SG-IMP

　　　'Alright you can go home [back] now.' (Roberts 1987 quoted in Croft et al. 2010 ex. (28))

　　　The other new type proposed is the double framing construction, as illustrated by the following Russian example, in which the path and the framing expressions are expressed by the satellite, i.e. *iz* 'from', and by part of the path verb, i.e. *vy* 'out'.

(148) Ja vy-bežal iz doma.

　　　I out-ran from house: GEN

　　　'I ran out of the house.' (Talmy 1985:105 quoted in Croft et al. 2010 ex. (30))

　　　Croft et al. further point out that the different strategies adopted by languages for the expression of motion events appear to represent a grammaticalization path of morphosyntactic integration which reflects event integration. The following two grammaticalization paths which end in univerbation of the event and the frame morphemes emerge from their study.

(149) Coordination > Serialization > Satellite framing > Verb Satellite fusion

(150) Coordination > Verb framing > Verb Adverb fusion

The strategy/strategies on the right represent(s) a higher degree of morphosyntactic integration of elements than that/those on the left. Dutch and Japanese are used to illustrate the two paths.

　　　As noted by the authors, it is not clear whether the directional satellites of Indo-European were originally serial verbs. However, there is evidence which shows that the satellites are attracted to the verb, leading to the fusion of both event and frame in a single predicate, as illustrated by the following examples from Dutch.

(151) De   fles   dreef   de   grot   in.

the   bottle   floated   the   cave   in

'The bottled floated into the cave.' (Croft et al. 2010 ex. (97))

(152) De   fles   is   de   grot   in-gedreven.

the   bottle   is   the   cave   in-floated

'The bottle has floated into the cave.' (Croft et al. 2010 ex. (98))

In 'in' in (151) is a path satellite in the simple past or present of a main clause without an auxiliary. In (152), when the auxiliary *is* 'is' is present, the path expression is prefixed to the manner verb *gedreven* 'to float', i.e. *in-gedreven* 'to float in'.

The following examples from Japanese demonstrate the grammaticalization path in (150). Unlike Spanish, Japanese does not express manner or process in an adverbial verb. As a result, the process directly leads via verb framing constructions to verbal compound constructions.

Example (153) below illustrates the strategy of coordination:

(153) Kanojo   wa   arui   te   douro   o   yokogitta.

she   TOP   walk   and   street   ACC   cross:PST

'She walked and crossed the street.' (Croft et al. 2010 ex. (109a))

Example (153) represents a self-agentive motion event, in which the verbs *aruku* 'to walk' and *yokogiru* 'to cross' are linked by the conjunction *te* 'and'.

Example (154) shows the strategy of compounding:

(154) Kanojo   wa   douro   o   aruite-yokogitta.

she   TOP   street   ACC   walk-cross:PST

'She walked across the street.' (Croft et al. 2010 ex. (109b))

The verbs *aruku* 'to walk' and *yokogiru* 'to cross' in (154) are fused together, becoming a compound.[50]

The grammaticalization path depicted in (149) is supported by the development of Chinese. Scholars (cf. Wang 1980[2001], Mei 1991, Jiang 2000, Peyraube 2009, Zhang & Li 2009) have suggested that the verb complement construction was derived from the serial verb construction, which in turn originated from the coordinate construction. For example, the phrase *qū ér chū* 趨而出 'to move forward and to exit' is a coordinate structure in which the verbs *qū* 趋 'to move forward' and *chū* 出 'to exit' are linked by the conjunction *ér* 而 'and'. Later on, the coordinate verbs were reanalyzed as a serial verb structure and then a verb complement structure. In the latter two stages, *ér* 而 'and' could no longer be inserted between the verbs. Much discussion has been devoted to the timeframe during which Classical Chinese shifted from a verb-framed language to a satellite-framed language. In contrast, little attention has been given to the last stage in which the verb and the satellite are fused together, an issue which we now turn to.

As noted by Croft et al. (2010), the difference between the serial strategy and compounding is that the former is not as morphologically bound or at least less tightly integrated than the latter. It is pointed out in §5.2 that the aspectual suffix zo^2 咗 in Cantonese appears after the verb and the complement when the complement denotes path in agentive motion events (cf. (155)).

(155) 佢射入咗一个波。

　　　 Keoi⁵　　se⁶　　jap⁶　　zo²　　jat¹　　go³　　bo¹.

　　　 s/he　　shoot　enter　ASP　one　CL　ball

　　　 'S/he shot in one ball.'

In contrast, zo^2 咗 occurs after the verb and before the directional complement in sentences that express self-agentive motion events (cf. (156)–(158)).

(156) 佢行咗入课室。

　　　 Keoi⁵　haang⁴　zo²　　jap⁶　　fo³sat¹.

　　　 s/he　　walk　ASP　enter　classroom

　　　 'S/he walked into the classroom.'

(157) 佢行咗入嚟课室。

　　　 Keoi⁵　haang⁴　zo²　　jap⁶　　lai⁴　　fo³sat¹.

　　　 s/he　　walk　ASP　enter　come　classroom

　　　 'S/he walked into the classroom here.'

(158) 佢行咗翻入嚟课室。

　　　 Keoi⁵　haang⁴　zo²　　faan¹　　jap⁶　　lai⁴　　fo³sat¹.

　　　 s/he　　walk　ASP　return　enter　come　classroom

　　　 'S/he walked back into the classroom here.'

The following Mandarin example shows that the aspectual suffix *le* 了 appears after the verb and the complement in agentive motion sentences.

(159) 他踢进了一个球。

Tā   tī   jìn   le   yí   ge   qiú.

he   kick   enter   ASP   one   CL   ball

'He kicked in a ball.'

Similarly, *le* 了 occurs after the verb and the complement in the following self-agentive motion sentence.

(160) 他走进了教室。 [51]

Tā   zǒu   jìn   le   jiàoshì.

he   walk   enter   ASP   classroom

'He walked into the classroom.'

Additional evidence which shows that the relationship between the co-event verb and the directional complement in Cantonese is rather loose is shown by the possibility of separating the verb and the directional complement. [52]

(161) 佢踢入咗一个波。

Keoi^5 tek^3 jap^6 zo^2 jat^1 go^3 bo^1.

s/he   kick   enter   ASP   one   CL   ball

'S/he kicked in a ball.'

(162) 佢踢咗一个波入龙门。

Keoi^5 tek^3 zo^2 jat^1 go^3 bo^1 jap^6 lung^{4}mun^4.

s/he   kick   ASP   one   CL   ball   enter   goal

'S/he kicked a ball into the goal.'

While *jap^6* 入 'to enter' in (161) indicates the resultant state of the object *jat^1 go^3 bo^1* 一个波 'a ball', i.e. its location in the inside of an unspecified location, it indicates the inward movement undergone by the object and introduces the goal object *lung^{4}mun^4* 龙门 'the goal' in (162).

It is further observed that it is possible for a compound directional complement to appear after the main verb and before the theme object in Mandarin.

(163) 他踢进来一个球。

    Tā   tī   jìn   lái   yí   ge   qiú.

    he   kick   enter   come   one   CL   ball

    'He kicked a ball into here.'

(164) 他踢进一个球来。

    Tā   tī   jìn   yí   ge   qiú   lái.

    he   kick   enter   one   CL   ball   come

    'He kicked a ball into here.'

(165) 踢一个球进来！

    tī   yì   ge   qiú   jìn   lái!

    kick   one   CL   ball   enter   come

    'Kick a ball into here!'

The compound directional complement *jìn lái* 进 来 'to enter and to come' occurs after the verb and before the object in (163), but after both the verb and the object in (165). In (164), the object *yí ge qiú* 一个球 'a ball' is inserted between *jìn* 进 'to enter' and *lái* 来 'to come'.[53] Among the three word order patterns, only the one displayed in (165) is allowed in Cantonese.

(166) * 佢踢入嚟一个波。

    Keoi^5 tek^3 jap^6 lai^4 jat^1 go^3 bo^1.

    s/he   kick   enter   come   one   CL   ball

    'S/he kicked a ball into here.'

(167) * 佢踢入一个波嚟。

    Keoi^5 tek^3 jap^6 jat^1 go^3 bo^1 lai^4.

    s/he   kick   enter   one   CL   ball   come

    'S/he kicked a ball in here.'

(168) 佢踢一个波入嚟。

    Keoi^5 tek^3 jat^1 go^3 bo^1 jap^6 lai^4.

    s/he   kick   one   CL   ball   enter   come

    'S/he kicked a ball in here.'

Zhang (1991) points out that compound directional complements have emerged in the history of the standard language in the following chronological order: Stage I: V + O + DC + DC > Stage II: V + DC + O + DC > Stage III: V + DC + DC + O. While Mandarin has gone through all three stages, Cantonese is still lagging behind at Stage I. The contrasts between Cantonese and Mandarin in simple as well as compound directional complements suggest that the verb complement construction in Mandarin is more grammaticalized than that in Cantonese. Both simple and compound directional complements and the main verb in Mandarin form a compound. In contrast, only simple directional complements and the main verb have undergone the univerbation process when expressing agentive motion events in Cantonese. In all other cases, the simple and the compound directional complements have yet to be fused together in Cantonese.

Table 7 below summarizes the integration of the verb and the directional complement (including simple and compound directional complements) in self-agentive and agentive motion events in Cantonese and Mandarin.

Table 7: Integration of the verb and the directional complement in self-agentive and agentive motion events in Cantonese and Mandarin[54]

	Cantonese	Mandarin
Simple directional complement		
● Self-agentive	✗	✓
● Agentive	✓	✓
Compound directional complement		
● Self-agentive	✗	—
● Agentive	✗	✓

In Table 7, it is demonstrated that Mandarin can use compounding to express path in both self-agentive and agentive motion events whether a simple or a compound directional complement is involved; and Cantonese might use compounding to encode path only in agentive motion events that involve simple directional complements. All in all, Mandarin has progressed much further on the grammaticalization path than Cantonese in combining the verb and the satellite together.

In section 5.2, it is illustrated that two word-order patterns are exhibited in sentences that denote agentive motion events in Cantonese. Figure 3 is repeated below as Figure 5:

Agentive
(i): [Agent subject + [VP [Main verb + Directional complement + zo^2 咗] + [Theme object]]] OR

(ii): [Agent subject + [[VP [Main verb + zo^2 咗] + [Theme object]] + [Directional complement + Locative object]]]

Figure 5: Two word-order patterns exhibited in agentive motion sentences

While (i) illustrates that the main verb and the directional complement have been fused together as a compound, taking one theme object, (ii) shows the serial structure in which the main verb and the directional complement have their own object. The serial strategy is not as morphologically bound or at least less tightly integrated than compounding according to Croft et al. (2010). The question is how (i) is derived from (ii), an issue which is to be addressed below with data from early Cantonese, the Cantonese language spoken in the 19th and the early 20th centuries.

(169) 放个吊桶落井

fong^3　go^3　diu^3 tung^2　lok^6　zeng^2

put　CL　bucket　descend　well

'Let the bucket down into the well.' (Bridgman 1841)

(170) 放落啲嘢

fong^3　lok^6　di^1　je^5

put　descend　CL　thing

'to put the things down' (O'Melia 1941)

(171) 嗰啲嘢放落台上

go^2　di^1　je^5　fong^3　lok^6　toi^2　soeng^6

that　CL　thing　put　descend　table　LOC

'to drop those things down on the table' (O'Melia 1941)

(172) 放嗰啲鸡蛋落嗰只笋处喇。

fong^4　go^2　di^1　gai^{1}daan^2　lok^6　go^2　zek^3　lo^1　cyu^3　laa^3

put　that　CL　eggs　descend　that　CL　basket　LOC　SFP

'to put the eggs into the basket' (Wisner 1927)

(173) 我放落啲嘢喺你处

ngo⁵   fong³   lok⁶   di¹   je⁵   hai²   nei⁵   cyu³.

I   put   descend   CL   thing   at   your   place

'I put some things in your place.' (O'Melia 1941)

Examples (169)–(173) represent the three stages the verb and the directional complement have to go through before they are fused together. Example (169) illustrates the first stage in which the verb *fong³* 放 'to put' and the directional complement *lok⁶* 落 'to descend' appear in a serial verb sentence, each taking its own object. The second stage is shown in (170)–(172), during which the verb and the directional complement are juxtaposed, taking only a theme object or a locative object (cf. (170)–(171)). However, the relationship between the verb and the directional complement is still rather loose and they can still be restructured as a serial verb construction, as illustrated in (172). Example (173) represents the final stage in which the verb and the directional complement are fused together as one unit, subcategorizing for a theme object, and the locative object is introduced by *hai²* 喺 'at'. During the univerbation process, the meaning of the directional complement has changed. *Lok⁶* 落 in (170)–(172), for instance, does not denote a downward movement but emphasizes the resultant state after the downward movement, i.e. the location of the theme object after the movement. The three stages of the univerbation process can be summarized below:

Stage I: the co-event verb and the directional complement take their own object, i.e. a theme object and a locative object; the directional complement expresses a path meaning (cf. (169))

Stage II: the co-event verb and the directional complement are juxtaposed, taking either a theme object or a locative object; the directional complement denotes a resultative meaning (cf. (170)–(171), (173))

Stage III: the co-event verb and the directional complement are fused together, subcategorizing for a theme object and the locative object is introduced by a preposition or another directional complement[55]

During the fusion process, it is observed that the removal of the theme object from the position after the co-event verb and before the directional complement is necessary for the process to take place.

(174) ⋯人拧灯嚟，岂系挤落斗下

Jan⁴ ning¹ dang¹ lai⁴, hei² hai⁶ zai¹ lok⁶ dau² haa⁶

man bring candle come why be put descend bushel below

'Is a candle brought to be put under a bushel...' (1872 *Make Chuan Fuyinshu*)

(175) 呢三条手巾收埋柜处⋯

Nei¹ saam¹ tiu⁴ sau²gan¹ sau¹ maai⁴ gwai⁶ cyu³...

these three CL handkerchief put approach wardrobe LOC

'These three handkerchiefs, put in the wardrobe...' (Fulton 1931)

In example (174), the noun *dang¹* 灯 'a candle' is the object of both *ning¹* 拧 'to bring' and *zai¹* 挤 'to put'. It appears in the first clause and is omitted in the second clause. In example (175), the object *nei¹ saam¹ tiu⁴ sau²gan¹* 呢三条手巾 'these three handkerchiefs' is preposed to the sentence-initial position. The omission of the object in both examples makes possible the juxtaposition and the fusion of the verb and the directional complement. The omission of the object is also frequently observed in early Cantonese.

Table 8: Number of tokens of presence and absence of theme object between the co-event verb and the directional complement

	上	落	出	入	埋	去
with a theme object	3	12	0	6	0	29
without a theme object	3	36	1	9	9	27

Table 8 shows the presence and the absence of the theme object after the co-event verb and before the directional complement in the Early Cantonese Tagged Database.[56] It is shown that for *soeng⁵* 上 'to ascend' and *heoi³* 去 'to go', the number of tokens of the presence and the absence of the theme object for the former is identical (3), whereas the number of tokens of the presence of a theme object for the latter is slightly higher than that of the absence of the theme object (29 vs. 27). In the remaining cases, the number of tokens of the absence of the theme object is higher than that of the presence of the theme object, especially in the cases of *lok⁶* 落 'to descend' and *maai⁴* 埋 'to approach'. Table 8 illustrates that except for the cases of *soeng⁵* 上 'to ascend' and *heoi³* 去 'to go', the theme object is often omitted after the co-event verb and before the directional complement. As a result, the co-event verb and the directional complement can be juxtaposed, a pre-requisite which allows them to be further fused together.[57]

8. Conclusion

This study has shown that the Cantonese directional verbs examined constitute a unique group, denoting movements with an inherently specified direction. They differentiate themselves from other verbs in the following aspects: (i) the expression of motion, (ii) the ability to take a locative object and (iii) the potential to form compound directional complements. More importantly, some members of the group can be used to express path in agentive motion events, a use which is exemplified in verb-framed languages such as Japanese, French and Classical Chinese, but which has rarely, if ever, been reported in other Chinese dialects. In expressing self-agentive motion events, both Cantonese and Mandarin exhibit the characteristics of verb-framed and satellite-framed languages in using a single directional verb or a combination of a co-event verb and a directional complement to encode path. The two dialects differ significantly in the representation of agentive motion events. In particular, Cantonese can use a single directional verb to express path in agentive motion events but Mandarin cannot. Scholars have argued that Classical Chinese was a verb-framed language and underwent a typological shift to a satellite-framed language. Such a change, however, did not happen overnight and modern Chinese dialects seem to have participated in the change at their own pace with some closer to the finishing line than others. That Cantonese has progressed slower than Mandarin in becoming a satellite-framed language coincides with the different stages of grammaticalization that the two dialects have undergone in developing the verb-complement construction. Specifically, the degree of integration of the verb and the complement is higher in Mandarin than in Cantonese.

Notes

[1] Talmy (2000b: 222) notes that "the satellite to the verb…is the grammatical category of any constituent other than a nominal or prepositional-phrase complement that is in a sister relation to the verb root. The satellite, which can be either a bound affix or a free word, is thus intended to encompass all of the following grammatical forms: English verb particles, German separable and inseparable verb prefixes, Latin or Russian verb prefixes, Chinese verb complements, Lahu

nonhead 'versatile verbs', Caddo incorporated nouns, and Atsugewi polysynthetic affixes around the verb root." In Chinese, a complement is a lexical word which is often a verb or an adjective, and which appears after the main verb, providing information regarding the result or state of an entity. When a directional verb follows a main verb, denoting the direction in which the movement specified by the main verb is carried out, it is traditionally referred to as a directional complement or a satellite in Talmy's term.

[2] Talmy (2000b: 103–109) states that satellites do not require a ground NP whereas prepositions do. Lamarre (2009a) points out that in Chinese prepositional phrases are neatly distributed before or after the verb according to the relationship they bear to the motion (if the prepositional phrase indicates the source or direction, it appears before the verb; if it denotes the goal, it occurs after the verb). In contrast, path satellites or directional complements appear only after the verb. Therefore, the categorical status of prepositions and that of path satellites do not overlap. To put it simply, directional complements are satellites rather than prepositions.

[3] *Pinyin*, and *Jyutping*, developed by the Linguistic Society of Hong Kong, will be adopted for the romanizations of Mandarin and Cantonese examples. Also, the following list of abbreviations will be used in the discussion: ACC=accusative case, ASP=aspect marker, CL=classifier, DC=directional complement, DM=disposal marker, DS=different subject marker, GEN=genitive case, IMP=imperative, LOC=localizer, NOM=nominative case, NP=noun phrase, O=object, PF=perfective, PRED=predicate marker, PST=past tense, SFP=sentence-final particle, S=subject, SG=singular, SS=same subject marker, TOP=topic, V=verb and VP=verb phrase.

[4] Thanks to the reviewer who has drawn my attention to the fact that the list is taken from Chao (1968).

[5] A reviewer has pointed out that *fēi* 飞 'to fly' is mostly used intransitively but in some situations it can take a direct object, as in *wǒ fēi Yīngguó* 我飞英国 'I fly to England', especially if the speaker is a pilot. The occurrence of a nominal after an intransitive verb and the semantic relationship held between the intransitive verb and the nominal seems to be determined by pragmatics or context rather than by syntax. For example, the noun *Yīngguó* 英国 'England' in *fēi Yīngguó* 飞英国 'to fly to England' denotes the destination while *Guótài* 国泰 'Cathy Pacific' in *fēi Guótài* 飞国泰 'to fly Cathy Pacific' represents the instrument. Since the issue is not directly related to the present study, I will leave it for future exploration.

[6] Agentive and self-agentive motion events are also referred to as caused and spontaneous motion events (cf. Choi & Bowerman 1991, Matsumoto 2003, Lamarre 2009a).

[7] However, statistics are not provided for the observations in Lamarre (2003).

[8] Scholars have proposed that Talmy's binary classification should be expanded to include a third type of languages, namely, equipollently-framed languages (cf. Slobin & Hoiting 1994, Zlatev & Yangklang 2004). In equipollently-framed languages, path and manner are both expressed by equivalent grammatical forms. In the following Thai example from Zlatev & Yangklang (2004:160): *chán dɔɔn khâam thanŏn khâw paj naj sŭan* I-walk-cross-road-enter-go-in-park 'I walked across the road and into the park', while the main verb *dɔɔn* 'to walk' denotes manner, the verbs *khâam* 'to cross', *khâw* 'to enter' and *paj* 'to go' denote non-deictic and deictic path. Similarly, Cantonese also exhibits the use of the serial verb construction. However, it is often difficult to determine whether the verbs in the serial verb construction in Cantonese have the same status. For example, the aspectual marker zo^2 咗 is attached to the first verb $ning^1$ 拎 'to bring' but not to the second verb lai^4 嚟 'to come' in $keoi^5$ $ning^1$ zo^2 bun^2 syu^1 lai^4 佢拎咗本书嚟 s/he-take-ASP-CL-book-come 'S/he brought a book', while the progressive marker gan^2 紧 is likely to be attached to the second verb se^2 写 'to write' than to the first verb or the coverb $jung^6$ 用 'to use' in $keoi^5$ $jung^6$ zo^2 sau^2 ze^2 gan^2 zi^6 佢用左手写紧字 s/he-use-left-hand-write-ASP-character 'S/he is writing characters with her left hand.' Because of the difficulty stated above, the present study will follow the bipartite classification of verb-framed and satellite-framed languages proposed by Talmy rather than adopting the tripartite scheme.

[9] The character for *faan¹* 'to return' should be 返 . However, the use of 翻 has become increasingly popular. In this study, the character 翻 rather than 返 will be used to refer to *faan¹* with the meaning of 'to return'.

[10] In addition to members of the $heoi^3$ 去 type, i.e. lai^4 嚟 'to come' and $heoi^3$ 去 'to go', $faan^1$ 翻 'to return', dou^3 到 'to arrive' and hei^2 起 'to rise' also cannot be combined with di^1 啲 to express comparison.

[11] Scholars have different opinions with regard to the number of core directional verbs. Li Xinkui et al. (1995) include dai^1 低 'low' in addition to the ones in Table 1 while Yuan (1995) excludes dou^3 到 'to arrive'.

[12] Cheung (2007: 119–122) does not mention gwo^3 lai^4 过嚟 pass-come 'to pass over and toward the speaker' and gwo^3 $heoi^3$ 过去 pass-go 'to pass over and away from the speaker'. But since they are possible combinations, we will include them in our discussion. On the other hand, Cheung (2007) includes dou^3 lai^4 到嚟 arrive-come 'to arrive and toward the speaker' and dou^3 $heoi^3$ 到去 arrive-go 'to arrive and away from the speaker' as possible combinations of double

directional complements. However, it is observed that dou^3 到 'to arrive' behaves differently from the others. In particular, simple directional complements which can appear in double directional complements can also occur in triple directional complements except for dou^3 到 'to arrive' and hei^2 起 'to rise', of which the latter is seldom used even as a double directional complement as noted in Cheung. Therefore, it is not clear whether dou^3 到 'to arrive' in $haang^4$ dou^3 lai^4 行到 嚟 walk-arrive-come 'to walk toward the speaker' and $haang^4$ dou^3 $heoi^3$ 行到去 walk-arrive-go 'to walk away from the speaker' is a genuine directional complement or a complement marker. However, without further evidence, we will include them in this study.

[13] '+' indicates that the combination is possible whereas '−' means the combination is not possible.

[14] According to Cheung (2007: 121), hei^2 lai^4 起嚟 rise-come 'to rise and toward the speaker', as in tiu^3 hei^2 lai^4 跳起嚟 jump-rise-come 'to jump up and toward the speaker', is seldom used as a double directional complement. Because of its low frequency of use, hei^2 lai^4 起嚟 rise-come 'to rise and toward the speaker' will be excluded from the following discussion on compound directional complements.

[15] As noted in Cheung (2007: 121), the use of hei^2 $heoi^3$ 起去 rise-go 'to rise and away from the speaker' as a double directional complement does not seem to exist in Cantonese. But such a use is found in other dialects. Cf. note 24.

[16] Although $ning^1$ $faan^1$ hei^2 lai^4 拎 翻 起 嚟 bring-return-rise-come 'to bring back up and toward the speaker' seems to be as good as the other triple directional complements such as $ning^1$ $faan^1$ gwo^3 lai^4 拎翻过嚟 bring-return-pass-come 'to bring back over and toward the speaker', $faan^1$ hei^2 lai^4 翻起嚟 differs from triple directional complements in a number of ways. For example, the former does not allow a theme object to appear after the verb and before it such as *$ning^1$ bun^2 syu^1 $faan^1$ hei^2 lai^4 拎本书翻起嚟 bring-CL-book-return-rise-come 'to bring the book back up and toward the speaker', whereas the latter does, as in $ning^1$ bun^2 syu^1 $faan^1$ gwo^3 lai^4 拎本书翻过嚟 bring-CL-book-return-pass-come 'to bring the book back over and toward the speaker'. Moreover, $faan^1$ hei^2 lai^4 翻起嚟 can not be used in the potential construction, e.g. *$ning^1$ dak^1 /m^4 $faan^1$ hei^2 lai^4 拎得 / 唔 翻 起 嚟 bring-can/not-return-rise-come 'can/cannot bring back up and toward the speaker', an option that is available to triple directional complements such as $ning^1$ dak^1/m^4 $faan^1$ gwo^3 lai^4 拎得 / 唔翻过嚟 bring-can/not-return-pass-come 'can/cannot bring back over and toward the speaker'. Therefore, $faan^1$ hei^2 lai^4 翻起嚟 is not considered a triple directional complement. Also, dou^3 到 'to arrive' cannot appear in triple directional complements and is excluded here.

[17] Yuan (1995) is a detailed study on directional verbs and directional complements in Cantonese. However, the discussion focuses primarily on self-agentive motion events, details of which have been already outlined in this section. Therefore, a further elaboration of the article is not provided.

[18] The Cantonese examples in this study were constructed by the author and their acceptability was checked against by speakers of Cantonese whose age ranges from twenty to seventy. The variety of Cantonese reflected in the examples represents the variety spoken in Hong Kong.

[19] The directional verbs examined in this study belong to the group of verbs of inherently directed motion in Levin & Rappaport Hovav (1992).

[20] Thanks to the reviewer who has drawn my attention to the fact that if the subject is ngo^5 我 'I', the deictic reference would become the location of the addressee.

[21] The ability to be used with zo^2 咗 , gwo^3 过 and gan^2 紧 is also observed in the other eleven directional verbs.

[22] Except for hei^2 起 'to rise' and hoi^1 开 'to depart', the other ten directional verbs can be followed by a locative object. Moreover, Yiu (2005) notes that without a given context it is unnatural to omit the locative object of non-deictic directional verbs, e.g.??$keoi^5$ $soeng^5$ zo^2 佢 上 咗 s/he-ascend-ASP 'S/he ascended'. Such omission, nevertheless, is fine with deictic directional verbs, e.g. $keoi^5$ lai^4 zo^2 佢嚟咗 s/he-come-ASP 'S/he came'. A similar observation is made in Lamarre (2009a) for Mandarin.

[23] It might be argued that $haang^4$ 行 'to walk, tiu^3 跳 'to jump' and paa^4 爬 'to climb' can be immediately followed by a locative object without the use of a directional complement, e.g. $haang^4$ $saan^1$ 行山 walk-mountain 'hiking', tiu^3 $seoi^2$ 跳水 jump-water 'water-diving' and paa^4 $saan^1$ 爬 山 climb-mountain 'mountain-climbing'. However, examples such as these refer only to the types of activities rather than a specific instance of the activities. In other words, $haang^4$ $saan^1$ 行山 'hiking', tiu^3 $seoi^2$ 跳水 'water-diving' and paa^4 $saan^1$ 爬山 'mountain-climbing' are compounds rather than verb-object phrases. Therefore, the use of a directional complement to link up the verb with the locative object is not necessary. In contrast, if the direction of $haang^4$ 行 'to walk', tiu^3 跳 'to jump' and paa^4 爬 'to climb' is to be specified, the use of a directional complement is required as in $haang^4$ $soeng^5$/lok^6 $saan^1$ 行 上 / 落 山 walk-ascend/descend-the mountain 'to walk up/down the mountain', tiu^3 lok^6 $seoi^2$ 跳落水 jump-descend-water 'to jump down into the water' and paa^4 $soeng^5$ $saan^1$ 爬 上 山 climb-ascend-mountain 'to climb up the mountain'.

[24] All non-deictic directional verbs, except for hei^2 起 'to rise' and dou^3 到 'to arrive', can be

followed by either of the two deictic directional complements, i.e. *lai*⁴ 嚟 'to come' and *heoi*³ 去 'to go'. However, the combinations of *qǐlái* 起来 and *qǐqù* 起去 are found in other Chinese dialects such as Minnan and Guizhou Dafanghua (cf. Li 1998).

[25] Although some verbs which denote manner and movement such as *paa*⁴ 爬 'to climb' might be combined with *lai*⁴ 嚟 'to come' and *heoi*³ 去 'to go', as in *paa*⁴ *lai*⁴/*heoi*³ 爬嚟 / 去 crawl-come/go 'to crawl toward the speaker and away from the speaker', the resulting combination cannot function as a compound complement of a main verb, e.g. **haang*⁴ *paa*⁴ *lai*⁴/*heoi*³ 行爬嚟 / 去 walk-crawl-come/go.

[26] The verbs and the deictic directional complements in (24)–(28) cannot be combined to form compound directional complements. Therefore, examples such as **bun*² *syu*¹ *fong*³ *hai*² *lai*⁴ *syu*¹*gaa*² 本书放喺嚟书架 CL-book-put-at-come-bookshelf 'The book is placed on the bookshelf and toward the speaker', **go*³ *coeng*¹ *ceoi*¹ *hoeng*³ *lai*⁴ *hau*⁶*jyun*² 个窗吹向嚟后院 CL-window-blow-face-come-backyard 'The window faces the backyard and toward the speaker as a result of X's blowing on it', **keoi*⁵ *tiu*³ *dit*³ *heoi*³ *seoi*² 佢跳跌去水 s/he-jump-fall-go-water 'S/he jumps into the water and away from the speaker', **di*¹ *syu*⁶*zi*¹ *faat*³ *saang*¹ *heoi*³ *uk*¹ *deng*² 啲树枝发生去屋顶 CL-branches-grow-grow-go-roof top 'The branches grow toward the roof top and away from the speaker', **gaa*³ *fo*²*zin*³ *zau*⁶ *faai*³ *se*⁶ *sing*¹ *heoi*³ *tin*¹*hung*¹ 架火箭就快射升去天空 CL-rocket-then-soon-shoot-rise-go-sky 'The rocket will soon be launched toward the sky and away from the speaker' are ungrammatical.

[27] Lamarre (2008) notes that in Mandarin *qǐ* 起 'to rise' is source-oriented while *shàng* 上 'to ascend' is goal-oriented.

[28] As noted in §2 above, a similar observation is made in Iida (2001).

[29] When *hoi*¹ 开 'to depart' appears in the compound form *lei*⁴*hoi*¹ 离开 'to leave', it can be followed by a locative object which denotes the source of the movement *lei*⁴*hoi*¹ *baan*⁶*gung*¹*sat*¹ 离开办公室 leave-office 'to leave the office'.

[30] *Maai*⁴ 埋 'to approach', *gwo*³ 过 'to pass', *dou*³ 到 'to arrive', *faan*¹ 翻 'to return' and *lai*⁴ 嚟 'to come', in general, do not take a theme object. Therefore, they are excluded from the discussion here. Also, in some cases, when a directional verb is followed by a theme object, a metaphorical meaning rather than a directional meaning is conveyed. For example, *hei*² 起 'to rise' in *hei*² *san*¹ 起身 rise-body 'to get up' expresses the meaning of causing the body to be in an upright position. However, in *hei*² *gaan*¹ *uk*¹ 起 间 屋 rise-CL-house 'to build a house', *hei*² 起 expresses the metaphorical meaning of 'to build' rather than the directional meaning of 'to rise'. Metaphorical

meanings of directional verbs are excluded from the discussion here.

[31] It is noted above that the meaning of *hei²* 起 'to rise' is source-oriented. As a result, it cannot have a goal object. On the other hand, *hei²* 起 'to rise' can have a prepositional phrase which appears in front of it, indicating the location at which the change of state takes place, e.g. *keoi⁵ hai² dei⁶haa⁵ dou⁶ hei² zo² san²* 佢喺地下度起咗身 s/he-at-floor-LOC-rise-ASP-body 'S/he got up from the floor.' The prepositional phrase *hai² dei⁶haa⁵ dou⁶* 喺地下度 at-floor-LOC 'on the floor', however, cannot occur after *hei² san¹* 起身 rise-body 'to get up', referring to the destination after the change of state takes place. Another point to note is that it also seems possible to say that *hoi¹* 开 'to depart' and *heoi³* 去 'to go' in the above examples express the metaphorical meanings of 'to sail' and 'to remove'. However, since a simple/compound directional complement can be used in the sentences to denote the destination (cf. (45)–(46) and (51)–(52)), I will assume that *hoi¹* 开 'to depart' in (45) and (51) and *heoi³* 去 'to go' in (46) and (52) specify physical movements.

[32] According to Matthews & Yip (1994), verbal particles are grammatical words whose functions resemble those of phrasal verbs in English.

[33] It is mentioned in note 22 that the directional verbs *hei²* 起 'to rise' and *hoi¹* 开 'to depart' cannot take a locative object. Such a property is also exhibited when they function as a simple directional complement. Therefore, they are excluded from the discussion on self-agentive motion events.

[34] It is not clear why when *gwo³* 过 expresses the meaning of 'to pass', *zo²* 咗 appears after the V-*gwo³* 过 combination such as *keoi⁵ haang⁴ gwo³ zo² baan⁶gung¹sat¹* 佢行过咗办公室 s/he-walk-pass-ASP-office 'S/he walked past the office'; and when *gwo³* 过 means 'to pass over' such as *keoi⁵ haang⁴ zo² gwo³ baan⁶gung¹sat¹* 佢行咗过办公室 s/he-walk-ASP-pass over-office 'S/he walked over to the office', *zo²* 咗 occurs between the verb and *gwo³* 过 'to pass over'.

[35] Instead of appearing after the main verb, *zo²* 咗 follows the verb and the directional complement *dou³* 到 'to arrive'.

[36] It is mentioned in note 22 that the same contrast is observed in non-deictic and deictic directional verbs.

[37] Please refer to (29)–(33) for the introduction of a path object by these five directional verbs.

[38] Please refer to (38)–(40) for the introduction of a source object by these three directional verbs.

[39] The directional complement *soeng⁵* 上 'to ascend' often expresses a metaphorical meaning when it is followed by a theme object, e.g. *oi³ soeng⁵ Hon⁴kek⁶* 爱上韩剧 'to fall in love with Korean movies' while *dou³* 到 'to arrive' can hardly be followed by a theme object. Therefore, they are

excluded here.

[40] It might be argued that *lai*^{4} 嚟 'to come' in *daai*^{3} *lai*^{4} 带嚟 bring-come 'to bring and toward the speaker' might express a metaphorical meaning rather than a directional meaning. However, since a locative object can be added to indicate the location to which the trouble was brought, it is assumed that *lai*^{4} 嚟 'to come' expresses a directional meaning in (85) (cf. 94).

[41] There are exceptions in which the omission of the co-event verb is possible in sentences that express agentive motion events. For example, in *se*^{6} *jap*^{6} *zo*^{2} *jat*^{1} *go*^{3} *bo*^{1} 射入咗一个波 shoot-enter-ASP-one-CL-ball 'shot in a ball', the verb or the complement can be omitted without giving rise to ungrammaticality (e.g. *se*^{6} *zo*^{2} *jat*^{1} *go*^{3} *bo*^{1} 射咗一个波 shoot-ASP-one-CL-ball 'shot a ball' and *jap*^{6} *zo*^{2} *jat*^{1} *go*^{3} *bo*^{1} 入咗一个波 enter-ASP-one-CL-ball 'shot in a ball').

[42] Besides *daai*^{3} 带 'to bring', it is hard to come up with another verb which can be combined with *lai*^{4} 嚟 'to come' to form a compound. On the other hand, the V-*heoi*^{3} 去 compounds might also include *sat*^{1}*heoi*^{3} 失去 'to lose', *ceoi*^{4}*heoi*^{3} 除去 'to remove', *gaam*^{2}*heoi*^{3} 减去 'to subtract', compounds which are lexicalized and cannot be restructured as a verb-object-complement-(locative object) construction. It seems that V-*lai*^{4} 嚟 /*heoi*^{3} 去 compounds are more often used in a formal context such as news reports than in daily conversations. Therefore, they might have entered Cantonese as a result of influences from Mandarin. On the other hand, J. Wang (2006) observes that there is a strong tendency for *lái* 来 'to come' and *qù* 去 'to go' in *Zhuzi Yulei* 《朱子语类》, which is a collection of discussions between the Southern Song neo-Confucian philosopher Zhuxi 朱熹 and his disciples, to occur in the sentence-final position, a phenomenon which is identical to that found in Cantonese. Therefore, it is possible that such a characteristic observed in *Zhuzi Yulei*, i.e. the tendency for *lái* 来 'to come' and *qù* 去 'to go' to occupy the sentence-final position, has been preserved in Cantonese.

[43] The discussion of compound directional complements in this study follows the classification of simple directional complements in Cheung (2007). Please refer to §2 for further details on Cheung's classification.

[44] It is unnatural to insert *zo*^{2} 咗 between the verb *haang*^{4} 行 'to walk' and the double directional complement. However, based on the situations observed in other double directional complements, it will be assumed that *dou*^{3} *lai*^{4}/*heoi*^{3} 到嚟 / 去 arrive-come/go 'to arrive here/there' and the verb do not form a compound.

[45] When a theme object is present, it appears between *hei*^{2} 起 'to rise' and *lai*^{4} 嚟 'to come', e.g. *ning*^{1} *hei*^{2} *bun*^{2} *syu*^{1} *lai*^{4} 拧起本书嚟 pick-rise-CL-book-come 'to pick up the book', rather than

after the main verb as in the cases of other double directional complements, e.g. *ning*^{1} *bun*^{2} *syu*^{1} *soeng*^{5} *lai*^{4} 拧本书上嚟 pick-CL-book-ascend-come 'to pick up the book'. On the other hand, the reviewer has pointed out that sentences in which *hei*^{2} *lai*^{4} 起嚟 'to rise and to come' occurs after an object such as *pou*^{2} *zek*^{3} *gung*^{1}*zai*^{2} *hei*^{2} *lai*^{4} 抱只公仔起嚟 carry-CL-stuffed animal-rise-come 'to lift up the stuffed animal' should not be ruled out. However, the occurrence of a locative object after *hei*^{2} *lai*^{4} 起嚟 'to rise and to come', i.e. ??*pou*^{2}*zek*^{3}*gung*^{1}*zai*^{2} *hei*^{2} *lai*^{4} *toi*^{2} *dou*^{6} 抱只公仔起嚟枱度 carry-CL-stuffed animal-rise-come-table-LOC 'to lift the stuffed animal up to the table', sounds awkward. In contrast, the occurrence of a locative object after a double directional complement is allowed, e.g. *ning*^{1} *bun*^{2} *syu*^{1} *soeng*^{5} *lai*^{4} *toi*^{2} *dou*^{6} 拧本书上嚟台度 pick-CL-book-ascend-come-table-LOC 'to pick the book up here to the table'. Since *hei*^{2} *lai*^{4} 起 嚟 'to rise and to come' exhibits properties that are different from double directional complements, it is highly likely that *hei*^{2} *lai*^{4} 起嚟 'to rise and to come' is not a double directional complement and is excluded here. Please refer to Yiu (2008) for a discussion on the comparison between *hei*^{2} *lai*^{4} 起嚟 'to rise and to come' and double directional complements.

[46] Examples (137) and (138) are taken from Xu (2006: 65), according to whom the pronunciations of 出 are different when expressing a self-agentive event and an agentive event, i.e. *chū* vs. *chuì*.

[47] Masini (1993: 121) notes that in (1649) *Shuihuzhuan*《水浒传》, (1765) *Hongloumeng*《红楼梦》and (1840) *Ernu Yingxiong Zhuan*《儿女英雄传》, the ratio between monosyllables and polysyllables is approximately 1:1. The ratio stays more or less the same in (1935) *Luotuo Xiangzi* 《骆驼祥子》, but has increased drastically in the literary works written after 1949, in which the ratio between monosyllables and polysyllables is 14.2% and 85.8% (of which 73.7% is disyllables).

[48] Croft et al. (2010) note that a *te*-compound *hashitte-haitta* 'run-went into' can also be used in this example. However, the one with an *i*-compound is more pervasive and more natural.

[49] Symmetrical framing includes the use of two single verbs in serial verb languages, the use of a compound verb in bipartite verb languages and the use of two preverbs in Jaminjungan languages. It is equivalent to the equipollently framing proposed by some scholars (cf. Slobin & Hoiting 1994, Slobin 2004, Zlatev & Yangklang 2004).

[50] It seems that the contrast between the coordinate structure in (153) and the compound structure in (154) can be differentiated by the insertion of an object between the two verbs. In (153), *douro* 'the street' appears between the two verbs but it occurs before the two verbs in (154).

[51] Mandarin does not allow the occurrence of a locative object after a compound directional complement, e.g.**tā zǒu shàng lái sān lóu* 他 走 上 来 三 楼 he-walk-ascend-come-three-floor

'He walked up here to the third floor.' It seems that the ability of a directional verb, including both deictic and non-deictic directional verbs, to take a locative object in some dialects such as Pekingese and Wu has disappeared. Instead, *dào* 到 'to arrive' is much more frequently used in these dialects to introduce a postverbal locative object. In contrast, both deictic and non-deictic directional verbs in dialects such as Cantonese and Min can still have a locative object. The above contrast exemplified in the dialects might be a result of the change of argument structure. In particular, in some dialects, the argument structure of directional verbs has undergone structural change, and as a result, the directional verbs in these dialects can no longer take a locative object; while in other dialects, the argument structure of directional verbs has not undergone any change and the directional verbs can still have a locative object. Please refer to Lamarre (2009b) and Liu (2003) for a relevant discussion on the use of *dào* 到 'to arrive' to introduce a locative object in some Chinese dialects.

[52] Please refer to §5.2 for more examples on the alternation between verb-directional complement-object and verb-object-directional complement-locative object.

[53] Please refer to Zhang & Fang (1996) for a detailed discussion on the use of the three word orders exhibited by compound directional complements in Mandarin. Thanks to the reviewer for drawing my attention to the fact that in Northern Mandarin, the use of V + O + DC + DC is restricted to the irrealis mood. A similar point is also made in Zhang & Fang (1996). Moreover, according to them, V + DC + DC + O in general is interpreted as a declarative sentence while V + DC + O + CD can be interpreted as a declarative sentence or an imperative sentence.

[54] In Table 7, ' ✓ ' indicates that the integration of the verb and the complement is possible; ' × ' means that the integration is not possible; and '—' means the integration is not relevant as a locative object cannot follow a compound directional complement in Mandarin.

[55] This example from Dennys (1874): *nei⁵ jau⁵ fong³ jap⁶ go² di¹ lok⁶ go² bun² syu¹ lai⁴ mou⁵ ne¹* you-have-put-enter-that-CL-descend-that-CL-book-SFP-have not-SFP 你有放入嗰啲落嗰本书嚟冇呢 'Did you insert that in the book?', shows that after the co-event verb *fong³* 放 'to put' and the directional complement *jap⁶* 入 'to enter' are fused together, taking the theme object *go² di¹* 嗰啲 'that', the directional complement *lok⁶* 落 'to descend' is used to introduce the locative object *go² bun² syu¹* 嗰本书 'that book'.

[56] Please refer to the following website for further details of the Early Cantonese Tagged Database: http://pvs0001.ust.hk/WTagging/

[57] Verbal attraction is a process during which units being part of or forming arguments of the

predicate are attracted to the verb and the endpoint is reached when the relevant unit either becomes a verbal affix or merges entirely with the verb (cf. Heine & Reh 1984: 50). For self-agentive motion events in which a theme object is not involved, the directional complement might simply be attracted to the verb, giving rise to the fusion of the co-event verb and the directional complement, as illustrated in the case in Mandarin.

References

Anonymous (1872) *Make Chuan Fuyinshu: Guangdong Tu Bai* [*Gospel of Mark*]. Shanghai: Meihua Bookstore.

Beavers, John, Beth Levin & Shiao Wei Tham (2010) The typology of motion expressions revisited. *Journal of Linguistics* 46.2: 331−377.

Bridgman, Elijah Coleman (1841) *Chinese Chrestomathy in the Canton Dialect*. Macao: S. W. Williams.

Brown, Penelope (2004) Position and motion in Tzeltal frog stories: the acquisition of narrative style. *Relating Events in Narrative*, Vol. 2: *Typological and Contextual Perspectives*, ed. by Sven Strömqvist & Ludo Verhoeven, 37−57. Mahwah: Lawrence Erlbaum Associates.

Chao, Yuen Ren (1968) *A Grammar of Spoken Chinese*. Berkeley: University of California Press.

Chen, Liang & Jiansheng Guo (2009) Motion events in Chinese novels: evidence for an equipollently-framed language. *Journal of Pragmatics* 41.9: 1749−1766.

Cheung, Hung-nin Samuel (2007) *Xianggang Yueyu Yufa de Yanjiu* [*A Grammar of Cantonese as Spoken in Hong Kong*] (Revised edition) Hong Kong: The Chinese University Press.

Choi, Soonja & Melissa Bowerman (1991) Learning to express motion events in English and Korean: the influence of language-specific lexicalization patterns. *Cognition* 41.1-3: 83−121.

Croft, William A., Jóhanna Barðdal, Willem Hollmann, Violeta Sotirova & Chiaki Taoka (2010) Revising Talmy's typological classification of complex event constructions. *Contrastive Studies in Construction Grammar*, ed. by Hans C. Boas, 201−236. Amsterdam & Philadelphia: John Benjamins.

Dennys, Nicholas Belfield (1874) *A Handbook of the Canton Vernacular of the Chinese Language*. Hong Kong: China Mail Office.

Fan, Kwok, Thomas Hun-tak Lee, Caesar Lun, K. K. Luke, Peter Tung & K. H. Cheung (1997) *Guide to LSHK Cantonese Romanization of Chinese Characters*. Hong Kong: Linguistic Society of Hong Kong.

Filipović, Luna (2007) *Talking about Motion: A Crosslinguistic Investigation of Lexicalization Patterns*. Amsterdam & Philadelphia: John Benjamins.

Fulton, Albert Andrew (1931) *Progressive and Idiomatic Sentences in Cantonese Colloquial*. Hong Kong: Kelly & Walsh Limited.

Gao, Huanian (1980) *Guangzhou Fangyan Yanjiu* [*Study of the Cantonese Dialect*]. Hong Kong: The Commercial Press.

Harris, Alice C. & Lyle Campbell (1995) *Historical Syntax in Cross-linguistic Perspective*. Cambridge & New York: Cambridge University Press.

He, Yuanjian (2000) A comparative study of verb, aspect and directional systems between Mandarin and Cantonese. Paper presented at the Annual Research Forum of the Linguistic Society of Hong Kong, December 10, 2000. Hong Kong: The City University of Hong Kong.

Heine, Bernd & Mechthild Reh (1984) *Grammaticalization and Reanalysis in African Languages*. Hamburg: H. Buske.

Iida, Maki (2001) Yueyu quxiang dongci de jufa biaoxian [The syntax of directional verbs in Cantonese]. Paper presented at the Workshop on Cantonese Linguistics, April 28, 2001. Hong Kong: The Hong Kong Polytechnic University.

Jiang, Shaoyu (2000) Hanyu dongjieshi chansheng de shidai [The emergence of the verb-resultative construction in Chinese]. *Hanyu Cihui Yufashi Lunwenji* [*A Collection of Articles on History of Chinese Vocabulary and Grammar*], 240−262. Beijing: The Commercial Press.

Kopecka, Anetta (2006) The semantic structure of motion verbs in French: typological perspectives. *Space in Languages: Linguistic Systems and Cognitive Categories*, ed. by Maya Hickmann & Stéphane Robert, 83−101. Amsterdam & Philadelphia: John Benjamins.

Lamarre, Christine (2003) Hanyu kongjian weiyi shijian de yuyan biaoda: jian lun shuqushi de jige wenti [How does Chinese encode motion events? And a few issues connected with the so-called "directional complements"]. *Xiandai Zhongguoyu Yanjiu* [*Contemporary Research in Modern Chinese*] 5: 1−18.

Lamarre, Christine (2004) Hanyu quxiang dongci de yufahua he quxiangci fanchou [The grammaticalization of directional verbs in Chinese and the category of directional verbs]. Paper presented at the 5th International Symposium on Taiwanese Languages and Teaching, May 22-23, 2004. Taichung: Providence University.

Lamarre, Christine (2008) The linguistic categorization of deictic direction in Chinese: with reference to Japanese. *Space in Languages of Chinese*: *Cross-linguistic, Synchronic and Diachronic*

Perspectives, ed. by Dan Xu, 69–97. New York: Springer.

Lamarre, Christine (2009a) The typological status of Sinitic directionals. Paper presented at the Workshop on Chinese Directionals: History and Dialectal Variations, in conjunction with the 6th Cross-Strait Conference on Chinese Historical Grammar, August 26–27, 2009. Taipei: Academia Sinica.

Lamarre, Christine (2009b) Lun beifang fangyan zhong weiyi zhongdian biaoji de yufahua he juweiyi de zuoyong [The grammaticalization of goal markers and the constructional meaning of goal in the northern dialects]. *Yufahua yu Yufa Yanjiu* [*Studies of Grammaticalization and Syntax*] 4: 145–187. Beijing: The Commercial Press.

Langacker, Ronald W. (1987) *Foundations of Cognitive Grammar*, Vol. 1: *Theoretical Prerequisites*. Stanford: Stanford University Press.

Levin, Beth & Malka Rappaport Hovav (1992) The lexical semantics of verbs of motion. *Thematic Structure: Its Role in Grammar*, ed. by Iggy M. Roca, 247–269. Berlin & New York: Foris.

Li, Fengxiang (1993) *A Diachronic Study of V-V Compounds in Chinese*. Buffalo: State University of New York dissertation.

Li, Lan (1998) Guizhou Dafanghua zhong de *dao* he *qi* [*Dao* and *qi* in Dafanghua of Guizhou]. *Zhongguo Yuwen* [*Studies of the Chinese Language*] 1998.2: 113–122.

Li, Xinkui, Jiajiao Huang, Qisheng Shi, Yun Mai & Dingfang Chen (1995) *Guangzhou Fangyan Yanjiu* [*A Study of the Guangzhou Dialect*]. Guangzhou: Guangdong People's Publishing House.

Liu, Danqing (2003) *Yuxu Leixingxue yu Jieci Lilun* [*Word Order Typology and a Theory of Adposition*]. Beijing: The Commercial Press.

Liu, Danqing (2008) Syntax of space across Chinese dialects: conspiring and competing principles and factors. *Space in Languages of Chinese*: *Cross-linguistic, Synchronic and Diachronic Perspectives*, ed. by Dan Xu, 39–67. New York: Springer.

Lü, Shuxiang (ed.) (1980[1996]) *Xiandai Hanyu Babai Ci* [*Eight Hundred Words in Modern Chinese*]. Beijing: The Commercial Press.

Ma, Yunxia (2008) *Hanyu Lujing Dongci de Yanbian yu Weiyi Shijian de Biaoda* [*The Development of the Path Verbs and the Expression of the Motion Event*]. Beijing: Minzu University of China Press.

Masini, Federico (1993) *The Formation of Modern Chinese Lexicon and its Evolution toward a National Language*: *The Period from 1840 to 1898*. Berkeley: Project on Linguistic Analysis, University of California.

Matsumoto, Yo (2003) Typologies of lexicalization patterns and event integration: clarifications and reformulations. *Empirical and Theoretical Investigations into Language: A Festschrift for Masaru Kajita*, ed. by Shuji Chiba et al., 403–418. Tokyo: Kaitakusha.

Matthews, Stephen (2006) On serial verb constructions in Cantonese. *Serial Verb Constructions: A Cross-linguistic Typology*, ed. by Alexandra Y. Aikhenvald & R. M. W. Dixon, 69–87. Oxford & New York: Oxford University Press.

Matthews, Stephen & Virginia Yip (1994) *Cantonese: A Comprehensive Grammar*. London & New York: Routledge.

Mei, Tsu-Lin (1991) Cong Handai de "dongsha", "dongsi" lai kan dongbu jiegou de fazhan: jian lun zhonggu shiqi qici de shishou guanxi de zhonglihua [The historical development of the "verb-resultative complement" construction, with a note on the neutralization of the pre-verbal agent/patient distinction in Middle Chinese]. *Yuyanxue Luncong* [*Essays on Linguistics*] 16: 112–136. Beijing: The Commercial Press.

O'Melia, Thomas A. (1941) *First Year Cantonese*. Hong Kong: Maryknoll House.

Peyraube, Alain (2009) On the history of Chinese directionals. Paper presented at the Workshop on Chinese Directionals: History and Dialectal Variations, in conjunction with the 6th Cross-Strait Conference on Chinese Historical Grammar, August 26–27, 2009. Taipei: Academia Sinica.

Ragnarsdóttir, Hrafnhildur & Sven Strömqvist (2004) Time, space & manner in Swedish and Icelandic narrative construction in two closely related languages. *Relating Events in Narrative*, Vol. 2: *Typological and Contextual Perspectives*, ed. by Sven Strömqvist & Ludo Verhoeven, 113–141. Mahwah: Lawrence Erlbaum Associates.

Roberts, John R. (1987) *Amele*. London & New York: Croom Helm.

Shen, Jiaxuan (2003) Xiandai Hanyu dongbu jiegou de leixingxue kaocha [The resultative construction in Chinese: a typological perspective]. *Shijie Hanyu Jiaoxue* [*Chinese Teaching in the World*] 2003.3: 17–23.

Slobin, Dan I. (2004) The many ways to search for a frog: linguistic typology and the expression of motion events. *Relating Events in Narrative*, Vol. 2: *Typological and Contextual Perspectives*, ed. by Sven Strömqvist & Ludo Verhoeven, 219–257. Mahwah: Lawrence Erlbaum Associates.

Slobin, Dan I. & Nini Hoiting (1994) Reference to movement in spoken and signed languages: typological considerations. *Berkeley Linguistics Society* (*BLS*) 20: 487–505. Berkeley: Berkeley Linguistics Society.

Tai, James H-Y. (1985) Temporal sequence and Chinese word order. *Iconicity in Syntax*, ed. by John

Haiman, 49–72. Amsterdam & Philadelphia: John Benjamins.

Tai, James H-Y. (2003) Cognitive relativism: resultative construction in Chinese. *Language and Linguistics* 4.2: 301–316.

Talmy, Leonard (1985) Lexicalization patterns: semantic structure in lexical forms. *Language Typology and Syntactic Description*, Vol. 3: *Grammatical Categories and the Lexicon*, ed. by Timothy Shopen, 57–149. Cambridge & New York: Cambridge University Press.

Talmy, Leonard (2000a) *Toward a Cognitive Semantics*, Vol. 1: *Concept Structuring Systems*. Cambridge: MIT Press.

Talmy, Leonard (2000b) *Toward a Cognitive Semantics*, Vol. 2: *Typology and Process in Concept Structuring*. Cambridge: MIT Press.

Talmy, Leonard (2009) Main verb properties and equipollent framing. *Crosslinguistic Approaches to the Psychology of Language: Research in the Tradition of Dan Isaac Slobin*, ed. by Jiansheng Guo, Elena Lieven, Nancy Budwig, Susan Ervin-Tripp, Keiko Nakamura & Şeyda Özçalişkan, 389–401. New York: Psychology Press.

Thepkanjana, Kingkarn (1986) *Serial Verb Constructions in Thai*. Ann Arbor: University of Michigan dissertation.

Wang, Jin-Hui (2006) Fuhe quxiang buyu zai Songdai de fazhan: yi *Zhuzi Yulei* zuowei kaocha [Development of complex deictic complement in the Sung dynasty: a study of *Zhuzi Yulei*]. *Bulletin of Chinese* 37: 49–90.

Wang, Li (1980[2001]) *Hanyu Shi Gao* [*An Outline of Chinese Language History*]. Beijing: Zhonghua Book Company.

Wilkins, David P. (2004) The verbalization of motion events in Arrernte. *Relating Events in Narrative*, Vol. 2: *Typological and Contextual Perspectives*, ed. by Sven Strömqvist & Ludo Verhoeven, 143–157. Mahwah: Lawrence Erlbaum Associates.

Wisner, O. F. (1927) *Beginning Cantonese*. (no publication detail)

Xu, Dan (2006) *Typological Change in Chinese Syntax*. Oxford & New York: Oxford University Press.

Yiu, Carine Yuk-man (2005) *Spatial Extension: Directional Verbs in Cantonese*. Hong Kong: The Hong Kong University of Science and Technology dissertation.

Yiu, Carine Yuk-man (2008) Yueyu kaishiti *qishanglai* de chansheng [The formation of the inchoative aspect marker *heisoenglai* in Cantonese]. *Bulletin of Chinese Linguistics* 2.2: 127–147.

Yuan, Guowei (1995) Guangzhouhua de quxiang dongci [Directional verbs in Cantonese].

Guangzhouhua Yanjiu yu Jiaoxue [*Study and Teaching of Cantonese*] 2: 41–51. Guangzhou: Sun Yat-sen University Press.

Zhang, Bojiang (1991) Guanyu dongqushi dai binyu de jizhong yuxu [Word orders of object in the verb-directional complement construction]. *Zhongguo Yuwen* [*Studies of the Chinese Language*] 1991.3: 183–191.

Zhang, Bojiang & Mei Fang (1996) *Hanyu Gongneng Yufa Yanjiu* [*Functional Studies of Chinese Grammar*]. Nanchang: Jiangxi Education Press.

Zhang, Min & Yuxiang Li (2009) Xianqin Lianghan Hanyu quxiang dongci jiegou de leixingxue diwei ji qi bianqian [The typological status and change of the directional verb construction in Pre-Qin and Han]. Paper presented at the Workshop on Chinese Directionals: History and Dialectal Variation, in conjunction with the 6th Cross-Strait Conference on Chinese Historical Grammar, August 26–27, 2009. Taipei: Academia Sinica.

Zlatev, Jordan & Peerapat Yangklang (2004) A third way to travel: the place of Thai in motion-event typology. *Relating Events in Narrative*, Vol. 2: *Typological and Contextual Perspectives*, ed. by Sven Strömqvist & Ludo Verhoeven, 159–190. Mahwah: Lawrence Erlbaum Associates.

（本文发表于《语言暨语言学》第十四卷第三期，第 511—569 页，2013 年）

The Min Translation of the *Doctrina Christiana*[1]

Anne O. Yue（余靄芹）

0. INTRODUCTION

The *Doctrina Christiana* rendered in Spanish and Tagalog was the first book printed in the Philippines in 1593 by the Dominican priests. It has been lost for centuries until a copy came into the possession of Lessing J. Rosenwald in 1948, who presented it to the Library of Congress. A Chinese edition of this same book, *Doctrina Christiana en letra y lengua China* (henceforth *Doctrina*), was supposed to be published around the same time. It was not until 1950 that an account of the discovery of a copy of this edition in the Vatican Library surfaced in the Manila *Sunday Times Magazine*. Like the Spanish-Tagalog version, this Chinese edition is xylographic, namely, printed from hand-carved wood blocks. "Whereas in the Spanish-Tagalog edition there is no indication of who made the book, the Chinese version states that it was executed by Keng Yong, a Chinese, in the Chinese quarter of the Parian, northeast of the walled city of Intramuros."[2] And this Chinese version turns out to be written in the Min dialect. The entire book consists of only thirty-one double pages, and the script is legible. Each double page (except the first) has two leaves, with nine columns to each leaf. Only Chinese characters are used and the only punctuation mark appears as a small circle to the lower right of a certain character ending a clause or a sentence. Despite its small size, it contains enough materials to show some typical usage of vocabulary and syntax that can be identified with the Min dialect. Furthermore, the antiquity of its date makes it an important piece of historical document for the study of the Min dialect. It was also written in the same century as, though several decades later than, the Jiajing 嘉靖 (1566) and the Wanli 万历 (1581) edition of the *Litchi Mirror Tale* 荔镜记 (*Li Jing Ji*) / 荔枝记 (*Lizhi Ji*), and would provide a good comparison with them.

Van der Loon 1966 (Part 1) and 1967 (Part 2) constitute the first major work devoted to research of this document. This work is important in two respects: it establishes the date and the authors of the text and reconstructs the phonological system of the Min dialect on which the text is based. Van der Loon 1966 painstakingly analyzed external events as well as internal linguistic styles in establishing the dating and authorship of the text. Van der Loon's conclusion is that it is "a heterogeneous text, the first part of which was probably translated soon after 1587 by the Chinese interpreters working with [Miguel de] Benavides and [Juan] Cobo [of the Dominican mission]; … the tract on the rosary, occupying most of the rest of the book, is an independent composition not older than the beginning of the seventeenth century" (p.25). Furthermore, he thinks that Keng Yong was responsible for the printing of the book, which took place presumably before 1607. Van der Loon's arguments are rather convincing and we have no other evidence to prove otherwise. Van der Loon 1967 made use of a Spanish manuscript in the British Museum, which contains a romanized text and Spanish translation of the *Docrina* (with no Chinese characters) that is "an almost verbatim transcription of the edition as printed by Keng Yong"(p.99), modern Southern Min or as he puts it the Hokkien dialects such as standard Amoy, Zhangzhou, Quanzhou and Chao'an, as well as the series of Southern Min rime dictionaries called the *Shiwu Yin* 十五音 , to reconstruct the phonetic value of the initials and the finals of the dialect underlying the *Doctrina*, which van der Loon showed to be the Haicheng 海澄 dialect, and which will not be of our concern here. Except for a list of grammatical particles given in Appendix I, van der Loon 1967 did not touch upon syntax, which will be the major concern of the paper.

As far as the analysis of the different parts of the text is concerned, we differ somewhat from van der Loon 1966. While we agree with him that there is a difference in the choice of vocabulary through the use of colloquial (more precisely, "Hokkien colloquial in the Ming period", as he put it) versus classical or Mandarin characters, his claim that the former is used in the first part (up to p.12A ending with the catechism) while the latter two are used in the second part is exaggerated. The line cannot be drawn so definitely, as can be shown in the examples cited in the following sections of this paper. Instead, we shall describe the entire document in terms of contents in five major sections. Van der Loon 1966 has already identified all segments of the book, and we shall largely follow him. The first section (two-and-a-half pages) consists of five prayers and invocation, all ending with the phrase 哑民西士 'amen Jesus'. The first leaf of the first page was blank, while the second leaf consists of only two lines of the sign of the cross. Next comes the Lord's Prayer. The third one is the Hail Mary or Sancta Maria 山礁妈厘哑, the fourth is the Apostles' Creed, while the fifth one is salve Regina.[3] The second section (almost seven pages) consists of explanation of six sets of basic tenets of faith, each set ending with the phrase 哑民西士. The first set relates to fourteen articles of faith in God or Deus (Spanish 'dios') 僚氏, the first seven pertain to Deus in general and the last seven to Jesus Christ 西士奇尼实道. The second set includes the Ten Commandments, the third set includes the five commandments of the Holy Church (Spanish 'sancta yglesia') 山礁益礼社, the fourth set includes the seven sacraments 沙胶览民厨, the fifth set includes fourteen rules of conduct toward other people (works of mercy), and the last set refers to the Seven Deadly Sins. This section ends with the Confiteor.

The third section (about three pages) is Catechism.

The fourth is a long section (about fifteen plus pages) explaining the working of the Rosary, which may be divided into three series, each narrating certain events in the life of Jesus and Saint Mary, followed by a prayer referring to the same event. The first series is concerned with the Holy Conception, the visit of St. Isabelle 山礁依沙迷 , the birth of Jesus, the visit to the temple when the temple. The second series is concerned with events of the thirty-three-year-old Jesus leading to his death on the cross—the prayer in the garden, the arrest, the torture, the carrying of the cross and the crucifixion. The third series is concerned with the resurrection of Jesus—his apparition to St. Mary on the third day after his death, his ascent to heaven on the fortieth day, the visit of the Holy Ghost to the apostles ten days later, the death of Sancta Maria and her enjoyment of glory in heaven.

The fifth and the last section (three-and-a-half pages) describes various rules for followers of the church. It consists of six parts: the first is concerned with what is termed a complete attendance of the mass or missa 绵卅 , the second lists all the days that require attendance of the missa, the third deals with fasting, the fourth with what to do upon death, the fifth talks about the terror of hell followed by a prayer, and the last gives admonition about saying prayers.

The style of the entire document may be described as consisting of three levels: the colloquial, the literary vernacular, and the classical. The greater part of the document, for example, sections one, two and five, are largely rendered in a mixture of the colloquial and the literary vernacular style. The fourth section, which contains a great amount of narration, has the highest percentage of classical usage. The third section, which comprises the Catechism, is more colloquial in style than the rest and is by far the most interesting and important for our study, although it consists of only three double-pages.

The three levels of style may be defined linguistically in terms of vocabulary and syntax. By 'colloquial', we mean vocabulary items and syntactic structures unique to what we identify as the Min dialects (see section 1 below) or the Southern dialects[4] as we know them today. By 'literary vernacular', we refer to a written style that probably approximates the standard spoken language of the time. By 'classical', we refer to pre-Qin lexical and syntactic usage.

We shall describe the colloquial and the literary vernacular style (henceforth 'the literary style') in usage with respect to function words, vocabulary and syntax in sections 1 and 2 below, and the classical style in the last section. Furthermore, descriptions in sections 1 and 2 will be given in comparison with usage found in the Jiajing edition of the *Lichi Mirror Tale* (henceforth *LJJ*)[5] as well as the colloquial Min *Grammar* of the seventeenth century (henceforth the *Grammar*). This last text, which is rendered in Chinese characters and romanization with tone marks as well as glossed in Spanish but with no indication of authorship, has not been exactly identified. Although there was a date, the 48th year of Wanli 万历四十八年, written on p.31B, its designation is puzzling, since Wanli lasted only forty-seven years and its last year (47th) was 1619. However, the Emperor Guangzong 光宗 who succeeded Shenzong 神宗 was on the throne for only one year when he was succeeded by Xizong 熹宗 in 1621. Perhaps this one year was considered an interim and included as an extension of Shenzong's reign by the Chinese immigrants. If this is the case, the *Grammar* may be dated as of 1620. According to Prof. Alain Peyraube, some experts claimed that it was probably written by Fra Melcior de Mancano, para el uso de Fra Raymundo Feijoo de l'order de Predicadoses (Dominicans), but there is no such indication in the document. This text from the Library of Barcelona in Spain, which was unavailable to van der Loon at the time of his study, is valuable in providing a comparison to the two versions of romanized text of the *Doctrina* from the British Museum that van der Loon 1967 made use of in "deciphering" colloquial Min words given in Chinese characters in the *Doctrina* and to the *LJJ*, although it consists of only thirty-three double pages and does not appear in very good condition.

1. FUNCTION WORDS AND VOCABULARY

Since the *Doctrina* is written in Chinese characters, it is at the moment difficult to identify the exact dialect in which it was rendered. However, since it was an important religious document to be used among the Chinese immigrants, who were mainly from the Southern Min area identified by van der Loon 1966 as Southern Fujian with Haicheng 海澄 as the main port of embarkation, it reflects mostly the Southern Min dialect of the time, but it probably does not reflect any single dialect but a semi-colloquial, semi-literary idiom understood by all Min speakers, including perhaps even some from Northern Min (see section 1.9 below for lexical items like 大手, which is similar to the modern Fuzhou 大边手).

1.1 Personal Pronouns

The personal pronouns are indicated with 俺, 阮, 我 and 咱 for the first person, 你 and 汝 for the second person, and 伊 and 他 for the third person. While 汝 and 伊 are known to be typically used for colloquial Min, Northern or Southern, the form 阮 seems to be particular to the Southern Min dialects. Except for 俺, 咱 and 汝, all of them are found in the *LJJ*, where 恁 instead of 汝 is used. The use of 俺 and 咱 reflects the influence of the standard language of the time—presumably some variety of Mandarin. On the other hand, the character 俺 has also been used in Southern Min to represent the first person inclusive plural.

The *Grammar* identifies these forms as follows: 我 /gùa/=1st person singular, 阮 /gùan/=1st person plural; 汝 /lù/=2nd person singular, (恁 /lǔn/=2nd person plural,) 伊 /ý/=3rd person singular (因 /ýn/= 3rd person plural).

The plural marker of the standard language of the time appears as 等 in the combination 我等 for the first plural. The same is true in the *LJJ*.

In terms of distribution, all except 俺, 咱 and 我等 occur in almost all possible syntactic positions such as the subject, the object and the attributive, as indicated by the following examples[6]—in the subject position:

阮惜你甚甜 (3)   我可怜施水乞伊 (7)

汝不须惊疑 (13)   你在天上 (1)

伊是俺本头 (2)[7]   他无艰难 (1S)

in the object position after a verb:

本头僚氏救阮 (1)   人有得罪我 (8)

我今求汝 (14)   僚氏赐福乞你 (2)

我可怜去赈济伊 (7)　　　　　　　　就往探他 (14)

or after a preposition:

你共我解罪 (10)　　　　　　　　降下与汝报喜 (14)

巴礼共伊抹山厨油 (7)　　　　　　我可怜为伊赎身 (7)

亦有多妇人为他涕泣哀伤 (21)　　替他负去 (21)

[巴礼 =padre/father, 山厨 =sancto/saint]

in the attributive position:

阮罪 (1)，阮娘奶 (3)　　　　　　我罪 (9)，我厝 (8)

汝子 (14)，汝言语 (31)　　　　　你子 (2)，你名 (I)

伊子 (16)，伊母 (17)，伊娘奶 (11)，伊面 (24)　　　他孕子 (14)，他母 (15)，他面 (18)

Although one expects the colloquial set of pronouns to occur with other colloquial lexical items, and the Literary set to occur with other literary lexical items, as we can see, in general, the distribution is very similar for the colloquial as well as for the literary forms, and both sets appear to intermix in occurrence. However, the third person pronoun 他 does not seem to occur with as many colloquial lexical items as does 伊 and it occurs only in the last two sections of the text. In addition, there is no example of 阮 or 你 occurring as object of a preposition.

The form 俺 occurs only in the subject or the attributive position, such as 俺有冤家(1) or 俺爹(1), 俺本头(2); 我等 occurs only as a modifier: 乃我等真正本头哑(17) or 汝乃我等慈母(20); while 咱 occurs only twice in the document as a modifier in 咱第一本头僚氏(30) and 咱爹(31). It is interesting that the romanized text of the British Museum which is given as Appendix II in van der Loon 1967 (henceforth 'the romanization') gives /lan/ but with a few instances of /guan/ for 俺, the form /guan/ identifies it with 阮 which is also rendered /guan/, while it gives /lan/ for 咱.

It is thus evident that whoever made the romanization did not follow the reading of characters, provided that the same characters appeared in the version of *Doctrina* that was used, but rendered the meaning of the characters into his own colloquial, dialectal version. Further evidence can be cited from the romanization of both 你 and 汝 as /lu/, of 与 as /tong/ or /cang/, of 子 as /kia/ or /qia/, of 人 as /lang/ (as /yin/ only in literary compounds such as 天人, 牧羊人, 贫人, 妇人 and as /xin/ only in 人情),[8] of 一 as /cheg/ (as /it/ only when it is ordinal), of 识 as /bar/, 不可 as /m~um tang~tan~t'ang~t'an (cf. 可以 as /co y/ and there is one instance of 不可 rendered /purco/), of 二 as /no/ (but as /xi/ or /yi/ if ordinal), of 肉 as /ba/, of 打 as /pa/, of 独 in 独自 as /ca/ or /ka/, of 要 as /ay/, 香 as /pang/. Sometimes the romanization fluctuates between a phonetic rendering and a semantic rendering, as for example in giving /hou/ or /bo/ for 否, /bu/ or /bo/ for 无, /u/ or /tou/ for 与, /chi/ or /ge/ for 之 (whereas 箇 is also rendered /ge/), /chu/ or /ki/ for 自, /yu/ or /u/ for 有, /boc/ or /bo/ for 莫, /pur/ or /m/ for 不, /chay/ or /tu/ for 在, /leng/ or /e/~/ei/ for 能. On the other hand, while 伊 is rendered /y/, 他 is also always rendered phonetically as /ta/ or /t'a/. In this connection, there is a definite distinction in rendering colloquial versus literary words, sometimes manifested in phonetic doublets such as /mia/ for 名 in colloquial context (for example 名叫) and /beng/ for the same in literary context (for example 名曰), /se/ for 生 as in 生子 and /seng/ for the same in 平生, 复生, 学生 or 生事, /chiu/ for 手 in 大手边 and /siu/ for the same in 他手 or 手足, /ti/ or /t'i/ for 天 in 天上, 上天, 天地 and /tian/ for 天人, 天下, 天堂 or 升天. We have also seen (in note 8) that sometimes literary expressions are rephrased as colloquial. Although there is always the possibility that different written Min versions of the *Doctrina* existed,[9] the romanization clearly demonstrates an inclination toward favoring colloquial expressions, despite whatever is given as the written form.

1.2 Interrogative Forms

All interrogative forms occur in the Catechism section. The [+human] interrogative pronoun is represented by the graphs 是谁, which appears in the subject position of a copular sentence: 濂水人尊敬是谁 (10) [濂水人=/liān chùi lāng/ 'Christian' in the *Grammar*]. From this text alone, it is difficult to judge if the interrogative pronoun 'who' is represented with just the graph 谁 or the two graphs 是谁 and whether 谁 or 是谁 is/are used to represent a colloquial Min form or a literary form in the standard dialect of Mandarin. For the latter question, one can argue either way: it may represent a Min form, since all other interrogative pronouns found in the same section are colloquial Min forms; on the other hand, it may be taken at its face value to represent a Mandarin form, since all other interrogative forms are represented by graphs with colloquial designation, as we shall see below, and since this interrogative pronoun, [+human], may be intended as on a more elevated stylistic level than all the others, which are [-human]. Lacking supporting evidence from phonetic representation, either interpretation seems to be reasonable. Only the form 谁 occurs in the *LJJ*, for example, 占: 交付乞谁 (3B唱)；末: 谁厝娘仔 (5B唱). The answer to the first question may be found in the *Grammar* which gives the transcription /sǐchuî/ for 是谁. Although 是, spelt /sǔ/, alone is also used as the copula, phrases such as 乞是谁 /kît sǐ chuî/, 甲是谁 /cɑbsǐchuî/ (4) indicate that /sǐ chuî/ is to be taken as a unit. The romanization for the *Doctrina* gives /chichui/ and /sichui/ for 是谁.

The [-human] interrogative pronoun for 'what' represented with 是乜 (/simi/ in the romanization) or 乜物 (/mimi/ in the romanization), the latter is probably more native Min than the former, which may come from the literary language of the time. This can be supported by the fact that only 乜 is used in the *LJJ* for the same. However, the *Grammar* lists 是乜 /sǐmǐ/; for example: 是乜人来 /sǐmǐlānglāy/, 是乜月 /sǐmǐguè/(4). Either form contains the graph 乜, which evidently carries the meaning of 'what'. This interrogative occurs in the predicative nominal or the attributive position:

僚氏是乜物 (10)　　　　　　　名叫是也 (11)

叫是乜名 (10)　　　　　　　是乜罪靠 (11)

In the *LJJ* but not in this document, 乜 occurs alone too as 净: 名叫乜 (5B 白) or 丑: 媒姨因也来障晏 (17A 白); besides serving as attributive, as in 末 : 乜人在只外 (2A 白), or 丑 : 只一盏正是乜灯 (8A 白).

Another interrogative compound that contains the graph 乜 is the interrogative adverb 乜事 (/mitay/ in the romanization) 'what matter' or 'why':

伊做人乜事 (11)　　　　　　　　落去临暮内乜事 (12)

which also occurs in the *LJJ*— 旦 : 许处正是人乜事 (7B 白).

The interrogative adjective 'which' is represented with 值 (/ti/ in the romanization), as in 值一箇别孙仔做人 (11) [别孙仔 =Persona/Person]; while the interrogative adverbs for place and for time are compounds formed with 值 — 值时 for 'when' and 值处 for 'where':

值时活起来 (12)　　　　　　　僚氏值时赦人罪靠 (12)

身值处去 (12)　　　　　　　值处落 (12)

Similar usage is found in the *LJJ*, and even with 值 occurring alone:

丑: 阮只处值人不作伊田值人不住伊厝值人不食伊饭值人不牵伊牛值人不看伊羊 (71B 白)

介：你值时讨一个媳妇 (5A 白)　　　且：陈三今在值 (58A 白)

while the *Grammar* gives 值 /tǐ/ and 值时 /tǐsī, tǐsȳ/, for example, 是值一人 /sȳtǐchèglāng/ (4), 你值时来 /lùtǐsīlāy/(9)

Other interrogative forms found both in this book and the *LJJ* but seem to lack modern correspondents are the interrogative pronoun of manner represented with 俪年 (/chayni/ in the romanization) or 做年 (/choni/ in the romanization) 'how' in this text:

只山礁益礼杜俪年说 (10)

做年会生子 (11)

众山厨做年相福荫 (12)

and with 做俪 in the *LJJ*— 末：俗人可做俪说 (5A 白).

1.3 Other Pro-forms

Other forms that function like pro-forms seem to be from the literary stratum, as far as graphic representation is concerned at least. For example, 别 is used for 'other', as in:

不可思想别人妻 (6)　　　　　　　不要别物 (24)

人 is used to indicate 'others': 人做不着 (8); while 独自 seems to be used in the sense of oneself rather than 'alone', the latter being the common meaning in the literary language: 惜别人亲像惜你独自 (6).

The classical relative pronoun for object Noun Phrase (NP), 所, appears, as is the case in many semi-colloquial, semi-literary documents; therefore, it is considered a usage in the literary style rather than the classical style. For example:

地上所有箇物 (6)　　　　　　　所累子孙 (11)

所 as relative pronoun is not used in the *LJJ*.

1.4 Demonstratives

There are three sets of demonstratives in terms of style. The colloquial set is represented by 只 (/chi/ in the romanization) for the proximal form and by 许 (/hu/ in the romanzation) for the distal form, for example:

只地上 (1)   只名濂水人 (10)

在许阿实爹内落 (7)   许时杰氏救人罪靠 (12)

which accords with the use in the *LJJ* as well as the modern Min dialects. The following examples are from the *LJJ*, in which these demonstratives occur either alone or as attributive:

净：只是乜灯 … 许是乜灯 (10A 白)   占：茶在只 … 饭在只 (89A 白)

末：只街头巷尾 (5B 唱)   旦：见许赏灯人尽都欢书 (10A 唱)

The literary set is represented by 是 for the proximal form. However, it is used only for the stylized expression of time 是时 , which may actually be better interpreted as a definite article plus the word for time, namely, '(at) the time' 是时豪光璀璨 (15). While the *LJJ* agrees with this text in the usage of the colloquial demonstratives, it uses 这 for the literary proximal demonstrative, for example, 旦 : 前日楼前见许马上一位官人好亲像这人 (31B 白) or 丑 : 到这里有二十里路 (14A 白).

The *Grammar* has /chǐ/ for 只 and /hù/ for 许 , with examples such as 只一人 /chǐchèglāng/, 许一人 /hùchèglāng/(4), 许一时我困 /hùchègsīguàcǔn/, 巴礼在只处 /pálètùchǔtě/(9), 巴礼在许处 / pálètùhùtě/(10)

The classical pair will be discussed in section 3.

1.5 Negatives

Like in the modern Min dialects, there are simple and compound negative markers. They include 不 (/m/ in the romanization) as in 不可害死人 (5), 天地是僚氏否. 答曰. 不是 (10); 袂(/bei/ in the romanization) as in 天地会保庇人否. 答曰. 袂 (10); 无(/bo/ in the romanization for the colloquial) as 有箇可大否. 答曰. 无箇可大 (11); 未(/bue/ in the romanization) as in 识道理未明 (8), 莫 (/bo/ in the romanization for the colloquial as in 你莫放乞阮做 (1), and the negative pro-form 否 (/bo/ in the romanization for the colloquial) used in questions. Evidently, these negatives correspond well to their modern counterparts, namely, 不 corresponds to the modern simple negative, 袂 to the negative for the affirmative counterpart 会, 无 to the negative for the affirmative counterpart 有 and 未 to the negative for the perfective. The prohibitive form 莫 may designate a classical usage or may simply be a graphic representation of the prohibitive in the colloquial language. All of these negative forms with the exception of 否, occur in the *LJJ* and the *Grammar*, the latter of which gives the following transcription for these negatives: 不 /m̀/, 袂 /běi/, 无 /bō/, 未/buê/, 莫 /bò/; while the former gives such examples as:

旦：我不愿嫁乞伊 (18B 唱)　　　　净：不通啼 (17A 白)

旦：恁行开去莫得来相缠 (11A 唱)　　丑：我句袂做媒人 (3A 白)

生：未得知值日相见 (16A 唱)

The distribution of the simple negative 不 is similar to that in the modern Min dialects, occurring before the copula, verbs of cognition and optative verbs, such as:

不着 (9)　　　　　　　　　　不识男人气味 (11)

汝不须惊疑 (13)　　　　　　　不得身离 (29)

不合该看绵卅 (29)　　　　　　不敢再得罪汝 (31)

but it also occurs before other simple verbs:

不食肉, 不减飡 (30), 不要只世上假欢喜 (23), 不看 (29), 不孝, 不听, 不解 (31)

although in such cases the style is often idiomatic, literary or classical:

欢喜不胜 (18), 血流不止 (19)—idiomatic

他不开口 (19)—literary

其身尸不见 (26), 不欲再路前恁 (31)—classical

This simple negative is also used in the negative potential form for resultative structures with the word order of **V-neg-C(omplement)**, such as 做不着 (11), 寻不见 (17), 看不见 (24). The same can be found in the *LJJ*, as for example in 占：事志做未成 (25B 白). The *Grammar* gives the following examples of 不 in both functions: 汝都不识来 /lùtóum̀bârlāi/ (10), 看不见 /cǔɑm̀kǐ/(12).

The modal negative 袂 occurs only twice in the Catechism section, in answer to a question with its affirmative counterpart 会. Another example besides the one given above is: 人神魂会死否. 答曰. 袂死 (12). It is quite interesting that in the romanization for the *Doctrina*, the 否 in this question is rendered /bei/, which is the form given for 袂, whereas elsewhere 否 is given as /hou/ (seven instances) or /bo/ (three instances). On the other hand, in the *Doctrina*, the modal negative 未 never occurs in a context where its affirmative counterpart also occurs, although it is clear that it carries the meaning of 'not yet': 人来看绵

卅. 巴礼未高冒牙. 未与众人打十字号若先出去. 有罪(28) The *Grammar* gives examples such as 我袂去 /guàběicŭ/(11), 我袂写字 /guàběisiàxī/ (8) and 未食饭 /buêchiàpuî/(13).

The negative 无 occurs frequently but seems to occur only in the function of negative for the existential/possessive with a NP and not a VP following:

有娘父否. 答曰. 无 (11)   无人留宿他 (15)   不可无关心 (28)

however, it occurs before the verb 有 once: 无 有 可 比 (23). In the *Grammar*, 无 is the negative for both types: 无人来 /bōlānglāy/(11), 汝有钱亚无 /lùùchīābō/(14), 你有打伊亚无 /lùùpàýābō/ (7).

At the beginning of this section, we mentioned that 莫 may represent either a classical or a colloquial usage. Although the graph itself conjures up the image of classical association, as may be so interpreted in such examples as:

莫怨恨, 莫报怨 (8)   莫使恶鬼来迷我 (19)

it also occurs in colloquial Min expressions:

你莫放乞阮做 (1)   莫乞伊再做 (8)

where 乞, 阮 and 伊 are typical colloquial Min forms. In the *LJJ*, 莫 is always used together with 得 to form the prohibitive:

占: 恁莫得去充着伊 (7B 白)

which is also expressed with 不通: 净: 不通啼 (17A 白). In the *Grammar*, both 莫 and 不可 (equivalent to 不) are used for the prohibitive 莫打简仔 /bòpàkĭnnià/(8), 不可偷提 /m̆tángtáutè/ (13) The romanization for the *Doctrina*, as we have seen, agrees with the transcription for 莫 in its colloquial use. In addition, it transcribes 不可 as equivalent to 不通, namely, /m t'ang~tang~t'an~lan/, just as in the *Grammar*.

1.6 Function Words

1.6.1 Markers for comparison

Certain function words particular to the Southern Min dialects occur in this text. For example, for a comparative clause expressing similarity, 亲像 is used as a marker with the meaning of 'like, just as':

顺守你命亲像在天上 … 你亦赦阮罪 . 亲像阮赦得罪阮人 (1)

for expressing the Equal Degree of comparison, the marker 平 is used before the stative verb or adjective:

都平大 . 都平好 . 都平贤 (11)

and for expressing a comparison with the meaning of 'comparatively', 可 is used:

有箇可大否 . 答曰 . 无箇可大 (11).

This 可 is comparable to the graph 较 used for the same purpose in the modern Min dialects. The same is found in the *Grammar*, where 可 is glossed 'more' in Spanish, with such examples as 可多 /cǎcheî/ 'more'(5), 汝可好 /lùcǎhò/ 'you are better'(6). The romanization of the *Doctrina* also renders 可 as /ca/.

In the *LJJ*, 亲像 is used in a similar way, as for example in 净 : 丈夫人无厶亲像衣裳讨无带 (4B 唱) or 占 : 我见你亲像一人 (31A 白); however, a reduplicated form 平平 is used instead of 平 for expressing the Equal Degree— 净 : 恁今平平乞人饲 (43B 白), while 可 is not used in the lexical sense of 'comparatively' at all. Whereas in the *Grammar*, both 并 /pēⁿ/ and its reduplicated form 并并 /pēⁿpēⁿ/ are used: 汝共我并大 /lùcângguàpēⁿtôi/, 恁二人都并怯 /lǔnnòlāngtóupēⁿkiâp/, 僚氏父共僚氏子都并并大 /diósǐ pècângdiōsǐkiǎ tóupēⁿpēⁿtói/(11), 恁 人 并 并 贤 /lǔnlāngpēⁿpēⁿgāu/(6). The romanization of the *Doctrina* gives /chinchio/ for 亲像 and /pe/ for 平 .

1.6.2 乞

The marker 乞 is typically used in a three-fold related function found it the Southern dialects,[10] although the marker itself bears the earmark of Min. First, it is used as a benefactive marker after the verb or a Verb Phrase (VP):

今旦日你赐乞院 (1)　　　　　　　　　做一件好事乞伊 (12)

Although it is not used in this document as the verb 'to give', it does occur once before a verb and seem to function like the verb 'to give':

恳求僚氏天父乞赦世人罪恶 (18)

Second, it is used as a passive marker:

乞人钉死在居律上 (11) [居律 = 'cross']

although the literary marker 被 also occurs frequently in this function—more so than 乞 :

被人钉在居律上 (22)　　　　　　　　被恶人讨莿篱篱箱箱他头 (20)

even in its pre-modern usage of allowing a complicated VP to follow:

第四件 . 是俺本头西士 . 奇尼实道 . 被恶人做一居律士 .

极大极重 . 令西士奇尼实道 . 自负往彼山 (21)

Third, it is used as the causative verb 'to let, to allow':

乞人专心信僚氏道理 (7)　　　　　　莫乞伊再做 (8)

In the *Grammar*, 乞 is given as /kît/ and the examples illustrate both its passive and benefactive usage: 简仔乞我打 /kĭnnĭɑkîtguàpà'/(8), 乞人 /kîtlāng/ glossed as 'for people'(3). The romanization for the *Doctrina* gives /kir/ for 乞 .

In the *LJJ*, 乞 is used as the verb 'to give' as well as the marker for the benefactive, the causative verb, and the passive; for example:

净 : 乞我缘分对着伊 (8B 唱)

旦 : 打一顿乞伊 (20A 白)

旦 : 不通乞哑公哑妈知 (25B 白)

丑 : 婆仔乞人打了 (21A 白)

1.6.3 共

共 is used for the benefactive/comitative. It is also used to represent a word for the same functions in the nineteenth century documents of the Yue dialects. The Min and the Yue form represented with this graph are probably cognates. Some examples of it use for the Min form in the document in question are:

巴礼共人解罪愆 (12)　　　　　　　　巴礼王共人打十字号 (7)

in its benefactive function and:

我共僚氏合山礁妈厘哑 . 微里矧 . 山绵牙亚勝江奚 . 山羡茅知实踏... 并山哆罗明敖 . 共众山厨氏 . 亦共巴礼你认我罪(9)

[微里矧 =virgen/virgin, 山绵牙亚胜江奚 =St. Miguel archāgel, 山羡茅知实踏 =St. Juan baptista, 山哆罗明敖 =St. Domingo]

in its comitative function. Both of these functions of 共 are found in the *LJJ* and the *Grammar*. Its benefactive function is displayed in the *Grammar* 汝共我煮饭 /lùcângguàchùpûiⁿ/(11) and in the *LJJ* in the following examples:

丑: 我去共阮哑娘说 (10A 白)

旦: 益春书写了共我叫小七出来 (95B 白)

外: 正是仔在潮州王长老厝共伯卿娶来个 (105A 白)

and its comitative function is seen in such example as 僚氏父共僚氏子都并并大 /diōsǐpècângdiōsǐkiǎtóupēⁿpēⁿtói/(11) in the *Grammar* and 净 : 益春你是病仔卜食苦桃共涩李 (17A 白) in the *LJJ*. The romanization agrees with the *Grammar* in the transcription for 共 .

1.6.4 将

The market for the disposal from is 将 , which is common among the Southern dialects, although the disposal construction itself is not as widely used as it is in Northern Chinese. In the present document, it appears in the last section of the text, for example:

后将居律氏竖起 (22)　　　　　　被人 … 将他手足钉在居律上 (22)

It is used in the same way in the *LJJ*, for example:

旦，占: 不免将荔枝挨落乞伊 (28 白)

生: 不免将这镜来打破 (33A 白)

However, there is no example in the *Grammar*. The romanization gives /chiang/ for 将 .

l.7 Modals

The Min dialects have a distinctive set of modal markers that occur before the verb. They differ from Optative Verbs by not allowing the following verb to be negated.[11] In addition, they constitute affirmative versus negative pairs for each marker. Since the negative forms of the pairs have already been discussed in section 1.5, we shall only give the modals in the affirmative, including:

The affirmative marker 卜: 魔鬼卜迷阮心悴 (1);

The potential marker 会: 天地会保庇人否．答曰袂 (10);

The imperative marker 着: 众人着信先七件 (3);

The affirmative/existential marker 有 appearing before stative verbs: 极有欢喜(16)，有灵通(25).

The romanization gives /po/ and /bue/ for 卜, /ei/ or /ey/ for 会, /tio/ for 着 and /u/ for 有 in their colloquial usage. While the affirmative marker, the potential marker and the imperative marker are also found in the *LJJ*, 有 is not used as a modal marker there. For example:

净: 雄人厶卜租人 (5A 白)　　　　　占: 看值日会甜 (17A 白)
丑: 也着请哑娘出来食一口槟榔 (18A 白)

1.8 Nominal Suffix

The nominal suffix 仔 is probably a diminutive suffix, for example: 鸽仔 (16). It is found in the *LJJ* and the *Grammar* as well as the modern Southern Min dialects. In the *LJJ*, many examples, such as 傀儡仔 (净, 6A 白), 婆仔 (丑, 14B 白), 病仔 (净, 17A 白), 官荫人仔，白贼仔 (旦, 38A 唱), 姅仔 (生, 28A 白), occur; while 帽仔 /bôguǐa/, 刀仔 /tóguǐa/, 圭仔 /kéiguǐa/(6) are given in the *Grammar*.

1.9 Colloquial Lexical Items

The following is a list of lexical items not discussed earlier but special to the Min dialects or to the Southern dialects:

呾话 for 'to speak'(/ta ua/ or /ta oe/ in the romanization), as in 我 … 呾话悴 … 多多过 (9) which is typical of Southern Min and also used in the *LJJ*, which uses 喏 or 喏话 as in 生: 恁哑娘都不喏 (41B 白) or 丑: 你颠狂喏话 (13A 白); it is written as 诅 /tân/(11) in the *Grammar*.

惜 for 'to love' (/sio/ in the romanization) as in 惜僚氏胜过各众物 (5) and 欢喜 for 'to be glad' (/huahi/ in the romanization), as in 欢喜感谢僚氏恩德 (14) which are also used in the *LJJ* and the Yue dialects; the former, romanized as /sîo/, is used in the *Grammar* too;

厝 for 'house' (/chu/ in the romanization), as in 我可怜留宿我厝 (8); also used in the *LJJ*;

目睭 for 'eyes' (/bacchiu/ in the romanization) as in 慈悲目睭看顾阮 (3), also used in the *LJJ*; 大手 for the 'right hand' (/toachiu/ in the romanization), as in 在僚氏娘父大手边坐

(12), which is similar to the modern Fuzhou 大边手 ;

今旦日 for 'today' (/kintoayit/ or /quintoaxit/ in the romanization, as in 今旦日你赐乞阮 (1), also used in the *LJJ* and the *Grammar*, the latter giving /gúinŭaxĭt/(7);

娘奶 is used for 'mother' (/nioley/ in the romanization), as in 你是阮娘奶 (3), which is akin to modern Fuzhou; while 娘父 is used for 'father' (/niope/ in the romanization), as in 真正娘父赦我罪过 (31), which is not found in the modern dialects; both are not used in the *LJJ*, which uses 哑妈 , 哑公 or 爹妈 , the former two seem to be employed in informal context, used more frequently by female (as for example used by the heroine, her maid, and the hero disguised as a mirror polisher) and the last in more formal context and more frequently by male (as for example, used by the hero and his elder brother, who is a high official, to address or to refer to their parents).

悷 , a time word 'at the time when' /chun/ in the romanization), as in 巴礼共人解罪悷 (12); it is also used in the *LJJ*, and in the *Grammar* there are several examples: 你食饭悷许当时我来 /lùchiȧpûichûnhùtá^{n}sīguȧlāi/, 你念经悷许时我来 /lùliâmkéngchûnhùsīguȧlāi/, 你来悷许一时我困 /lùlāychûnhùchègsīguȧcᶜŭn/(9).

那 , for 'only' (/na/ in the romanization), as in 那有只一子 (2); in the *LJJ*, it also has the same meaning, in for example, 占 : 阮厝是有一镜卜磨 , 那是阮镜有主客 (31A 白); however, it is also used for the meaning of 'which' as shown in the interrogative for place 那里 : 丑 : 敢问贤友贵处那里 (1B 白).

2. SYNTAX

2. 1 Affirmation and Negation

In the modern Min dialects, modal affirmatives and negatives are used with verbs to make assertion, assume possibility, give command, express perfectivity, ascertain existence, or to negative them. These models, as observed in their modern function, most probably derive from full verbs,[12] and at least one of them, the existential modal, still retains its verbal status in its simultaneous function as existential/possessive verb. On the other hand, it is difficult to prove, given the limited amount of data, whether at the time of this book, they function as full verbs.

They function in pair, as already mentioned in sections 1.5 and 1.7. For example, the modal 会 indicates possibility,[13] and we have already seen that its negative counterpart is 袂 . The *Grammar* gives a pair of examples: 我袂写字 /guàběisǐaxī/, 我会写字 /guàǎysiàxī/ (8). However, not all members of these pairs appear in the text in question; in fact, more often they do not. For example, the modal 卜 is used for assertion, but its negative counterpart marker does not appear in the text. Since the modern Min dialects do have a corresponding negative marker, it is more reasonable to believe that it also existed at that time on the basis of cross dialectal reconstruction rather than to assume that it had not yet come into existence at the time.

The existential modal 有 is of particular interest in terms of its functions in the modern Min dialects. It occurs with stative verbs to express existence, it occurs with action verbs to express past action, and it occurs with certain action verbs such as 'to plant', 'to learn', 'to raise', etc. to express affirmation. All three cases pertain to existence, past or non-past. Only the first two cases occur in the text in question. Examples have already been cited for the first case in section 1.7, and only one instance for the second case is found: 后有受艰难否 . 答曰 . 有 受 艰 难 (11). The negative counterpart for this modal is not found in the text. Although there are many instances of 无 in this text, they all pertain to the verb negating existence/possession, occurring with a following NP, as mentioned in section 1.5.

We have seen that the modal for command is 着 . As can be expected, it occurs most frequently in the second section of the book concerned with the Ten Commandments, etc. The negative counterpart is expressed with 不可: 不可生事害人, 亦不可说白贼(5).

While all of the above occur in the *LJJ*, the negative modal for command there is 莫得 or 不通 , although 通 does not occur as the affirmative counterpart, as is the case in the modern Min dialects.

As is well known, while imperceptivity is expressed with the negative modal 未, in the modern Min dialects as well as in the present document. the *LJJ* and the *Grammar*, as described in section 1.5, for the document in question, perfectivity is not expressed in a similar way, neither by a modal as seen in other functions describe above, nor by a post-verbal marker/suffix as observed in the Northern dialects or other Southern dialects. The Min dialects are unique in this respect in that they still reflect an earlier historical stage before the modern perfective aspect has evolved from a complement verb to a marker/suffix. To be more precise, it really represents a transitional stage at which the form for the perfective—in this case for the Min dialects, 了—evolved from a full fledged verb to a suffixal marker.[14]

In this document, 了 is seen used as a noun to mean 'end', as in 永世无了(2); as a complement verb to mean 'to finish, to end', occurring after the object NP, such as: 腰加厘实爹 (=Eucharist). 是巴礼做绵卅. 念经了. 俺本头西士奇尼实道在许阿实爹内落 (7), and as a perfective aspect marker, as in:

伊死了 (12)　　　　　　　　上天去了 (12)　　　　　　　　我当今反悔了 (9)

In the *LJJ*, 了 does not appear as a verb but as an aspect marker:

占: 人客镜磨光未　　　　　生: 只镜磨光了 (33A 白)
占: 亚娘月上了 (46A 白)
占: 更深了返来去 (49A 白)
丑: 益春筵席安排便未　　　占: 安排便了 (103B 白)

The clearest distinction between the verb 'to finish' and the perfective is given in the *Grammar*, where the former is given as 了 /liǎo/ and the latter as 膀/là/, though neither is glossed. 了膀 /liǎolà/ is also given as combination, though not glossed either. The following examples illustrate their different function:你来膀/lùlāylà/, 我念经了膀/guǎliǎ mguéngliǎolà/(7); although 了 is not used alone in the examples of the *Grammar*.

2.2 The Potential Form

We have already observed in section 1.5 that the negative potential form for resultative structures has the word order of **V + neg + C**, which is similar to the same structure in Northern Chinese. The affirmative potential form with the word order **V + 得**, however, seems to indicate an older origin, as observed in the following examples: 那是僚氏会保庇得人. 会责罚得人(10). Both examples contain the modal 会. It is uncertain, due to the scarcity of data, whether this modal always occurs with this potential form.

No example is found for the negative potential for non-resultative structures.

In the *LJJ*, structures of **V + 得** as the potential do not occur, and 得 as the potential marker is found only with the negative prohibitive mentioned above.

2.3 Resultative Complement

The word order of the complement of resultative structures with object NP present reflects an earlier historical stage, which placed the complement after the object NP for both the affirmative and the negative. In other words, the word order is **V + O (+ neg) + C**. This word order can still be observed in some modern Min dialects as well as some other Southern dialects (for example, Yue, Xiang, Wu) under specific conditions. In the present text, we find five examples in the affirmative—three with 了 as the complement:

念经了 (7)，求人情了，要看绵卅时巴礼若抱册过左手边了 (28)

one each with 真 and even a disyllabic stative verb 完全：

着看绵卅完全 (6)   我可怜教示伊真 (8)；

and two in the negative:

寻他不见 (18)   人识道理未明 (8)

This structure is also found in the *LJJ*; for example, 生：不得伊着俩甘心 (11B 白).

2.4 Measure Expressions

Measure expressions for verbs—Duration, Frequency, etc.—follow a different word order in the Northern versus the Southern dialects today. In the Northern dialects, they follow the main verb (and its object NP if there is one) in an affirmative sentence but precede it in a negative or emphatic sentence (for example in standard Mandarin, 病了三天 but 三天都病了 or 三天 [都] 没病 and not * 没病三天); whereas in the Southern dialects, they follow the main verb despite the affirmative versus negative distinction unless the sentence is emphatic, in which case the word order is the same as in the Northern dialects. Emphasis is usually rendered with a special marker. In this text, however, such measure expressions are found to precede the main verb in an affirmative sentence without any emphatic marker:

与山须习 (=Saint Joseph)   三昼夜烦恼 (17)
三昼夜极烦恼 (18)   三次念经 (19)

No example in the negative occurs. This construction in this word order is not found in the *LJJ*.

2.5 The Comparative

In section 1.6, we already discussed the function words used for expressing various kinds of comparison. However, they are used in a lexical context and do not mark any particular kind of comparative construction in the syntactic sense.

Only the comparative degree and the superlative degree of the comparative construction are found in this document. For the latter, it is just like the same construction across all Chinese dialects, using the marker 最 with the stative verb:

因为汝最谦细 (14)   汝最好命 (14)

The most interesting for inter-dialectal comparison is the comparative construction in the comparative degree. In this document, it is marked with a post-verbal 过. Although this marker is not found in the modern Southern Min dialects but in other Southern dialects such as Yue, the word order of **NP1+ Vst (=Stative Verb) + 过 + NP2** is typical of the Southern dialects—namely, the two terms of comparison flank the stative verb. In the *Doctrina*, we found examples used only with the verb 胜 occurring four times:

僚氏赐福乞你胜过众妇人 (2)
惜僚氏胜过各众物 (6)
僚氏赐福与汝胜过众妇人 (14)
受大敖罗里耶．胜过众天人 (27) [敖罗里耶 =gloria/glory]

In this text, there is no comparative construction with the comparative marker occurring before the stative verb or without a comparative marker, as can be found in more conservative modern Min dialects. Namely, there is no comparative sentence in the form **NP1 (+ 较) + Vst + NP2** where 较 signifies the comparative marker. On the other hand, there is no comparative construction marked with 比 cast in the word order of the Northern Chinese type of **NP1 + 比 + NP2 + Vst** as can be found in some modern Min dialects such as Taiwanese. This raises the question of the nature of the comparative construction found in this text. Is the construction with 胜过 simply a stylized expression reminiscent of the literary language? Again for lack of sufficient data, it is a question that cannot be answered with certainty without relying on other evidence. On the other hand, as we have seen in section 1.6.1, markers for other types of comparison, such as the Equal Degree of comparison, are typically colloquial Min; therefore, it would be curious that only for the comparative degree of the comparative construction, a non-colloquial marker would be favored.

In the *Grammar*, the comparative marker 过 is also found with the verb 胜 in its example:

僚氏胜过宝贝 /dīosỷsĕngguepòpûe/(6).

In the *LJJ*, on the other hand, the comparative construction in the comparative degree shows a greater variety of verbs used with the marker 过:

末: 好元宵强过别冥 (SB 唱)
生: 你只计赛过孙吴 (45A 白)
生: 饭今袂食涩过吞沙 (51B 唱)

and thus can be considered actively used in the colloquial language of the time. The limited usage in the *Doctrina* may therefore be accidental.

2.6 Neutral Question Forms[15]

Neutral Question forms without interrogative words belong to the **VP-neg** type, with 否 occurring at the end of the question. They are found mainly in the section of Catechism. For example:

你是濂水人否，天地是僚氏否，天地有起头否，天地会保庇人否 (10)
有箇可大否，有娘父否，有娘奶否 (11)
死后有日再活起来否，后有日再落来否，人神魂会死否 (12)

These examples include a variety of classes of verbs: the verb 'to be' 是 , the possessive verb 有 , the modal 会 , the stative verb 大 , the transitive verbs 活起来 and 落来 . They are particularly important in that they show that in pre-modern times, the **VP-neg** form is the predominant form for Neutral Questions in the Min dialect. There was not a single example of the **V-not-V** form or the **ADV-VP** form. The romanization for 否 gives eight instances of /hou/, which is clearly a literary pronunciation, three instances of /bo/ and one instance of /bei/, the latter two of which indicate a colloquial pronunciation. The one instance of /bei/ occurs in a question whose answer contains 袂 , also rendered /bei/: 人神魂会死否 . 答曰 . 袂死 (12).

In the *LJJ*, the majority (29 out of about 50) of the Neural Question form agree with what is found in the *Doctrina*, although 否 never occurs as **neg**, which appears 不 , 无 , 未 , 袜 or 袂 — 生: 只荔枝是娘仔你个不 (59B 白), 旦: 陈三有乜话说无 (56B 白), 丑: 筵席安排便来 (103B 白), 占: 会唱歌袜年 (32A 白). Out of these twenty-nine examples, five carry a particle (也 , 哑 or 亚) before the **neg**, such as— 旦: 情见官人哑不 (99A 白),

占：恁有好酒哑无 (80A 白). In addition, there are three rare examples of the **V-not-V** form in its variant of **VO-neg-V**, such as, 外：有文书没有 (1B 白) and sixteen examples of the **ADV-VP-neg** form, such as, 净：伊可见我不 (13A 白); both types of which may have a particle occurring before the neg, such as— 外：有哑没有 (102B 白), 占：可曾意着许马上官人亚不 (47A 白).[16]

The *Grammar* differs from the *Doctrina* in two respects. While the majority of the Neutral Questions are of the **VP-neg** type, there is always the particle 亚/ā/ occurring between **VP** and **neg**. In other words, the structural formula is **VP-ā-neg**. For example:

汝爱食饭亚不 lùaўchîapûiāм̌ (13)

你有打伊亚无 lùùpàỳābō (7)　　　　　汝有钱亚无 lùùchîⁿ ābō (14)

食饭亚未 chìapûiābûe (13)

汝念经了亚未 lùliâmkéngliàoābûe (13)

汝会去亚袂 lùěicuāběi (13)

只事会做得亚袂 chǐsûěichâttêtāběi (14)

Secondly, there is an example of the **V-not-V** form which also contains 亚 before the negative: 汝信亚不信 /lùsǐnām̌sǐn/(13). In these two respects, the *Grammar* is more similar to the *LJJ*, although the usage of the particle is obligatory in the former but optional in the latter.

2.7 The Attributive and the Nominalizing Construction

Although both the possessive/attributive and the nominalizing marker is expressed with 箇 , which is also a classifier, characteristic of the modern Southern dialects and in line with the syntactic feature of modern Chinese in the merger of the two markers, there is a trace of some distinction between the usage of markers with respect to the two types of constructions in this text.

Let us first examine the use of 箇 as the marker in an attribute construction. The head in such a construction is almost always a noun:

亦受僚氏箇福 (2)　　　　　　　　西士奇尼实道箇身 (13)

日日所用箇物 (1)　　　　　　　　地上所生箇物 (6)

although it may be a VP with the proposed relative pronoun 所 for the object NP: 做人箇所行 (4). The modifiers may be a noun or a VP, as can be observed from the above examples.

When a pronoun modifies a noun, no attributive marker is used, just as in the modern dialects 我厝 (8), 我罪 (9), 俺爹, 你国, 阮心 (1), 阮娘奶, 你子 (3), 阮妈 (10), 伊娘奶 (11), 汝腹内 (13), 他圣母 (14). This the case also when impersonal pro-forms are used 别人妻, 别人财物 (6) or when the noun 'Deus' is used as modifier: 僚氏子 (14), 僚氏恩德 (15). Furthermore, when the head noun is the literary time word 时 or the colloquial time word 恂, no attributive marker is used, which seems to indicate a literary style: 他死时 (22), 要升天时 (24). However, there is also one instance where no attributive marker occurs between the VP serving as modifying clause and its head noun 亲像阮赦得罪阮人 (1). Since this example contains colloquial Min words such as 亲像 and 阮, the pattern it displays may very well be remnant of a colloquial style in which the attributive construction needs no attributive marker. Such is the case in the modern Southern Min dialects when a VP is the modifier and the head noun contains a demonstrative.[17] In the *Grammar*, the rule of head noun with a demonstrative applies: 查暮日汝来许今时 /cȟabôuzïtlùlāyhùcáⁿsī/(7), 冥昏你来许当时 /mēhúilùlāyhùtáⁿsī/(8), so does the rule of time word: 你食饭恂许当时我来 /lùchiàpûichûnhùtáⁿsīguàlāi/(8), 你念经恂许时我来 /lùliâmkéngchûnhùsīguàlāi/, 你来恂许一时我困 /lùlāychûnhùchègsīguàcᶜŭn/(9).

The nominalizing construction is always marked with 箇:

是卑尼厨山化箇，是山礁妈厘哑美里矧生箇 (2)

亲像伊独自做箇 (12)

[卑尼厨山厨 = holy spirit/spirit sante]

and sometimes with 的:

乃卑尼厨山厨化的 (13)　　　　　　　　俱是他化的 (22)

When 的 is used, it is apparent that style is literary, or more precisely, half classical and half literary.

In comparison, the usage in the *LJJ* is quite simple—it employs 个 for both the attributive and the nominalizing marker:

净：只一位娘仔正是后沟王九郎个诸娘仔 (12 白)

旦：尔将许谢个花却一枝来我看 (48A 白)

生：只是阮师父亲传乞阮个 (32A 白)

外：正是仔在湖州王长老厝共伯卿娶来不 (105A 白)

although the literary 的 is sometimes, but very rarely, used— 生 : 告老爹容小的分诉 (84A 白).

The *Grammar* gives three variant graphs for this attributive cum nominalizing marker, 個, 箇 or 个; for example, 卖鱼個人 /bêihūguàlāng/, 作石個人 /chôcsiòguàlāng/(5), 念经箇 人 /liâmkéngguàlāng/(8), 后念经个人 /ăuliâmkéngguàlāng/(8), 打铁个人 /pà°tǐguèlāng/ (13); 阮个 /guǎnguè/(3), 天地是僚氏化个 /týtêisǐdīosǐhuǎguè/(9), 只话是我诅个 /chǐŏasy̌guàtǎ^n guè/(9). What is of interest here is that the attributive marker is given the transcription /guà/ while the nominalizing marker is rendered /guè/. Since the tone agrees in both forms, it is obvious that the latter, occurring often in the final position of a phrase or sentence, is a weakened form of the former. The phonetic laxing of the vowel, from low toward mid, is the result of probably weakened stress, which is not shown in the transcription (neither is tone sandhi indicated).

3. THE CLASSICAL STYLE

The classical style is heavily concentrated in the last two sections of the text and blends with the literary and the colloquial style. Even in the Catechism section, such classical expression as 答曰 appears, though probably as a stylized and crystallized phrase.

Usage of classical vocabulary abounds. The demonstratives 彼 and 此 appear:

在彼礼拜中 (16)   思彼一件事实 (28)

听见此话 (15)   此五件 (18)

已上此等好日 (29)

As well as 斯: 斯时僚氏子便投胎于腹中 (14).

The pronouns 之 and 其 are used, and as expected, the former in the object and the latter in the attributive position:

便往探之 (15)   封之为太后 (27)

降下其家时 (25), 其身尸不见 (26), 其罪同 (28)

The interrogative 何 is used both pronominally and attributively:

因何赐此最大人之母来探我 (14-5)

汝何故使我与汝父受此等烦恼 (17)

如此者虽念有何益哉 (28)

Another interrogative is 安：则其受益安有量哉 (31).

Typical of classical Chinese, 之 is used as an attributive marker:

论地狱之艰难 (30)　　　　　　人遇减飡之日早饭不可食 (30)

while 者 is used as a nominalizing marker:

有一得道老者，年高者 (17)、入教者 (31)

When the head noun is 时, however, the attributive marker may be optional:

或临难俭死之时 (30)[18]　　　　要看绵卅时 (28)

Copular/classificatory verbs include 乃, 如 and 为. The latter two occur before stative verbs or stative verb phrases while the former occurs in the copular function as well:

我乃僚氏卑仆 (13)　　　　他乃年老 (14)

中夜如昼 (15)　　　　汝赐我能如汝烦恼 (18)

山礁妈厘亚. 微里矧为最清洁为最标致 (14)

Other verbs of classical usage are 曰, 称, 谓, 与, 往, 至, 讫, the last one occurring as a complement:

乃称之曰 (13)　　　　天人复谓妈厘亚曰 (13)

汝与之表名曰 (13)　　　　同往西吕沙陵礼拜内 (17)

至半夜时 (15)　　　　与之慰闷讫 (26)

[西吕沙陵 =Jerusalem]

Adverbs (既, 复, 均, 俱, 皆), conjunctions (故, 则, 而) and the classical preposition 于 occur, the last in both temporal and locative contexts:

他既出世 (13)　　　　均为之痛伤 (22)

因为俱是他化的 (22)　　　　众人皆起立 (28)

故当真心诚意 …(31)　　　　至则参拜西士氏 (15)

无益而有罪矣 (28)

于将死时 (26)   斯时僚氏子便投胎于腹中 (14)

The exclamatory particle 哉 and the aspectual particle 矣 are also found:

乃离身死矣 (22)   如此者虽念有何益哉 (28)

In the above examples, classical vocabulary items occur not only in sentences submerged in the classical style, but also in sentence mixed in style, such as 他乃年老 (15), 因为俱是他化的 (22).

In contrast, the *LJJ* does not use classical vocabulary or the classical style except in crystallized phrases in the verse.

4. EPILOGUE

From the examples discussed in sections 1 through 3, the difference in style—colloquial versus literary—in the *Doctrina* is ascribable to different factors and not limited simply to the earlier versus the latter part of the text presumably written by different authors. A second factor is the different character of the contents of the text—catechism versus prayers versus explanations and narratives—demanding different treatment and attention, For example, a classical style would not be appropriate for the catechism, which is best garbed in the colloquial language. Prayers could be intimate or formal and could be invoked in a mixture of styles. The same can be said of narration, where a change of style might arrest attention.

Although we are not sure if the *Doctrina* is the predecessor of using this mixture of style of the colloquial, the literary and the classical, it has become indeed characteristic of the translation of the Bible and other religious texts in various Chinese dialects in the ensuing centuries to adopt this style.

In comparing the syntax of this text with texts around the same period such as the *Grammar* or the Jiajing edition of the *LJJ*, one can draw the conclusion that in general these texts are sufficiently similar in their "vernacular" (as opposed to classical or standard literary) syntactic structure as to be representative of the semi-spoken colloquial and semi-written vernacular style of Southern Min of the latter part of the sixteenth through the beginning of the seventeenth century. Some differences are observed in the choice of a reduplicative versus a non-reduplicative form for the marker of comparison of the Equal Degree, or the appearance versus non-appearance of the **V-not-V** and the **ADV-VP** neutral question form. This latter distinction suggests that the *Doctrina*, in which neither the **V-not-V** nor the **ADV-VP** form appears, does not include the neutral question form (the **V-not-V**) from the standard language of the time,[19] or that (**ADV-VP**) from the Zhangzhou 漳州 area.[20] This is significant in two respects. First, the exclusion of the **V-not-V** question form implies that, except for passages of classical usage, the *Doctrina* is basically native in style in its syntax, with little contamination from the standard language of the time (except for contain lexical items as we have seen). Second, the non-inclusion of the **ADV-VP** question form suggests either that the text is meant for the majority of Southern Min speakers who were not from the Zhangzhou area, or that the **ADV-VP** question form at that time had not been firmly established, in other words, had not yet transformed from its earlier transitional structure of **ADV-VP-neg**, which appeared in the *LJJ*, as we have seen. The former suggestion would support the argument of van der Loon 1967 for a dialect different from Zhangzhou to be the base dialect which was studied by the earliest Spanish missionaries, including the one presented in the *Doctrina*. However, pending syntactic materials from the Haicheng dialect, which van der Loon 1967 concluded to be this base dialect, there is yet no direct evidence for any representative dialect as far as grammar is concerned.

The remaining major tasks that lie outside the scope of this paper are the comparison of the syntax of the time of the *Doctrina* with that of the modern Min dialects and the reconstruction of the syntactic history of Min from the sixteenth century onward. Here we shall merely give an example indicating the significance of research in such directions. In comparing modern Southern Min with the *Doctrina*, there appears a fascinating yet intricate aspect relating to the **VP-neg** neutral question form. As we have observed in section 2.6, the **VP-neg** is not only the sole neutral question form in the *Doctrina*, but it also does not include any occurrence of a particle in the structural formula. In the romanization, however, there are two instances where the particle /a/ is added before the neg:

天	地	有	起	头	否		僚氏	有	起	头	否 (10)
ti	tei	u	ki	tau	a bo		Diosi	u	ki	tau	a bo

Since the neutral questions occur only in the Catechism or the most colloquial section of the *Doctrina*, this strongly suggests that the Witten text is not in perfect accord with the spoken language of the time used in the romanization, which fact of course agrees with the general character of the text of embracing a mixture of styles as we described earlier. On the other hand, it may imply the presence of dialectal difference among the speakers toward whom the text was targeted, and such difference manifests itself in the romanization or the person(s) reading out the text. This last observation rests on the assumption that the presence versus absence of a particle in the **VP-neg** question indicates dialectal difference. We have seen that this question form appears only as **VP-ā-neg** in the *Grammar* but mostly as simply **VP-neg** (twenty-two instances) in the *LJJ*, although the **VP-prt-neg** form (five instances) also occurs in the latter. In the Wanli edition of the *Lizhi Ji* (1581) however, there are fourteen examples of the **VP-prt-neg** type versus twelve instances of the simple **VP-neg** type. In the *Golden Flower Girl* 金花女 of the Wanli period, the occurrence of the **VP-prt-neg** form (eight instances) is even higher in frequency than that of the simple **VP-neg** form (only one instance). Yet, in the *Su Liuniang* 苏六娘 text of about the same time, only the simple **VP-neg** type (six instances) appears, and in the Shunzhi 顺治 edition (1651) of the *Lizhi Ji*, the simple **VP-neg** type is in the overwhelming majority (thirty-three versus two). The modern Southern Min dialects in the Quanzhou 泉州 -Chaozhou 潮州 region show variation in usage between the two forms. Some dialects use both as free variations: Xiamen has **VP-(a$?^{32}$)-neg**, Zhangping 漳平 has **VP-(a^{55})-neg** and Chaozhou has **VP-(a^{33})-neg**. Some use the simple **VP-neg** as the predominant form but sometimes use a form with partiele too: Shantou 汕头 , Jieyang 揭阳 , and Quanzhou are representatives. So far we have the record of only one dialect—Raoping 饶平 which uses the **VP-prt-neg** as the predominant form. However, the picture as shown in these modern dialects is but a hint to more complicated historical facts, which may not be transparent merely through the modern eye. For example, although modem Shantou prefers the simple **VP-neg** form over the **VP-pr-neg** form, Fielde 1878 gives fifty-three instances of the latter type of questions versus twenty-three of the former type. In other words, the situation reverses in about a century's time.[21] In conclusion, the choice of these two forms seems to correlate, or seems to suggest a correlation, with dialectal difference, although such difference is blurred, either for the lack of more dialectal materials or due to mixture of usage as a result of language contact.

One more question remains to be solved. The comparative construction in the comparative degree as presented in the *Doctrina* and its contemporaneous texts such as the *LJJ* and the *Grammar*, gives a structure with the marker 过 , namely, **NP1 + Vst + 过 + NP2**, which is typical of the Yue dialects but which does not appear in any modern Min dialects, although some allow for a structure **NP1 (+ 较) + Vst + NP2**. Is this **NP1 (+ 较) + Vst +**

NP2 structure a direct descendant of the **NP1 + Vst + 过 + NP2** structure? Or, is the former an innovation that had forced out the latter? The history of the comparative in Min need to be studied in depth before we can answer these questions in a meaningful way.

NOTES

[1] I am indebted to Dr. Min Zhang, who provided me with a copy of this version of the *Doctrina Christiana* and to Prof. Alain Peyraube, who provided me with a copy of the Min *Grammar* published in the early seventeenth century. An outline of this paper was presented at the Second Chao Yuen Ren Center for Chinese Linguistics Symposium held at the University of California, Berkeley, March 18-19, 1995. Thanks are due to Professors Tsulin Mei and Benjamin T'sou for their comments. My gratitude must also extend to Prof. Chinfa Lien for drawing my attention to van der Loon's study and to Prof. Jerry Norman for his assistance in deciphering the Spanish explanation in the Min *Grammar*.

[2] Quotation from the Library of congress information bulletin; vol. 9，no. 13, March 27, 1950, p. 24.

[3] The transliteration is not always consistent. Here Sancta Maria is rendered 仙礁妈厘哑 .

[4] The Southern dialects in its narrow sense refer to the Min, the Yue, and the Hakka dialects, and in its broad sense, include the Wu dialects in addition to these three groups.

[5] We select the Jiajing rather than the Wanli edition for comparison for two reasons: the former edition available to us is in better shape than the latter, and there seems to be no great difference in usage in terms of vocabulary and syntax between the two editions. Although at times the Wanli edition seems to employ the literary language more—for example, there is a line with a simile given by the character Lin Da 林大 found in both editions but using different markers as follows:

净：丈夫人无厶亲像衣裳讨无带 (4B 唱 , Jiajing ed.)
林：丈夫人无么恰似衣裳讨无带 (4B 白 , Wanli ed.)

[all examples are given first with the role or character followed by a colon, the example sentence, and in parentheses the page number and the type of speech, sung 唱 or spoken 白 .]

it is quite evident that 亲像 is characteristic of colloquial Min while 恰似 comes from the literary language—there is no lack of examples in colloquial Min, and the marker 亲像 is used freely in this edition too: 旦 : 值时亲像灯月（6A 白). There is difference in the choice of lexical items too: for example, 'to look at' is represented mostly with 看 (as in 看灯) and seldom with 体 in the Jiajing edition but almost always with 体 (as in 体灯) in the Wanli edition, not to mention that many verses and dialogues are arranged and rendered quite differently. A comparison between the two editions goes beyond the scope of the present paper and henceforth we shall limit ourselves to the discussion of the Jiajing edition only.

[6] The Arabic numerals enclosed within parentheses indicate the page number of individual examples occurring in the document.

[7] According to Douglas 1899, /pùnthâu/, which is the equivalent for 本头 here, means 'master of female slave, especially said by herself'(p. 387).

[8] There is an instance where the literary compound 贫人 is romanized as /kenglang/, which is a colloquial equivalent.

[9] We are quite certain that different versions in characters existed. The version that van der Loon 1967 quoted in his Appendix II differs slightly from the one we used. For example, on p.15B of his quoted text, 度 was used in the sentence 我送度汝, whereas in the text we have, the character 与 was used in exactly the same sentence.

[10] For example, this three-fold function is found in the Yue and the Hakka dialects. See Yue 1993a, p.131 for details.

[11] By Optative Verbs is meant verbs that take verbal complements. An example is 敢. In this document, there is no example of a negated Optative Verb followed by a negative VP.

[12] Or perhaps may be better analyzed as such. However, we shall not be concerned with this problem here.

[13] The graph 会 also represents the word for capability, 'can, know how to', as observed in this example: 做年会生子 (11).

[14] See Mei 1981 for an exposition of the historical development of the perfective aspect marker.

[15] For a definition of the Neutral Question Form and for classification of its types, see Yue 1988 and 1992.

[16] For a discussion of the Neutral Question forms in the various editions of the *Litchi (Mirror) Tale*, see Yue 1991 and 1993b.

[17] See Yue 1993a for details. This zero marking for the attributive construction under the said condition is also found in the Yue dialects. See Yue 1995.

[18] The character 俭 is probably meant for 险.

[19] See Zhang 1990 for evidence that the **V-not-V** neutral question form was introduced into the standard language during the Tang-Song times.

[20] See Yue 1991 and 1993b for the introduction of the **ADV-VP** form into Southern Min.

[21] See Yue 1993b for details.

REFERENCES

Douglas, Carstairs (1899) *Chinese-English Dictionary of the Vernacular or Spoken Language of Amoy, with the principal variations of the Chang-chew and Chin-chew dialects.* London: Publishing Office of the Presbyterian Church of England.

Fielde, A. M. (1878) *First Lessons in the Swatow Dialect.* Swatow: Swatow Printing Office Company.

Hou, Jingyi 侯精一 ed. (1993)《中国语文》四十周年纪念刊文集, 北京：商务印书馆.

Mei, Tsu-lin 梅祖麟 (1981) 现代汉语完成貌句式和词尾的来源. 语言研究 1: 65–77.

Van der Loon, P. (1966) The Manila incunabula and early Hokkien studies, Pt. 1. *Asia Major New Series*, XII-1: 1–43.

Van der Loon, P. (1967) The Manila incunabula and early Hokkien studies, Pt. 2. *Asia Major New Series*, XIII-1: 95–186.

Wu, Shouli 吴守礼 & Lin Zongyi 林宗毅 eds. (1976) 明清闽南戏曲四种. 台北：定静堂.

Yue-Hashimoto, Anne 余蔼芹 (1988) 汉语方言的比较研究. 台北："中研院"历史语言研究所集刊 59-1: 23–41.

Yue-Hashimoto, Anne 余蔼芹 (1991) Stratification in comparative dialectal grammar: a case in Southern Min. *Journal of Chinese Linguistics* 19-2: 172–201.

Yue-Hashimoto, Anne 余蔼芹 (1992) 广东开平方言的中性问句. 中国语文 229: 279–86. Also in Hou 1993: 84–91.

Yue-Hashimoto, Anne 余蔼芹 (1993a) *Comparative Chinese Dialectal Grammar— Handbook for Investigators (Collection des Cahiers de Linguistique d'Asie Orientate 1).* Paris: Ecole des Hautes Etudes en Sciences Sociales, Centre de Recherches Linguistiques sur l'Asie Orientale. vii+313pp.

Yue-Hashimoto, Anne 余蔼芹 (1993b) Language contact and linguistic change—recent development of the Southern Min neutral question forms. Paper for the 2nd International Conference on Chinese Linguistics, Paris, June 23–5.

Yue-Hashimoto, Anne 余蔼芹 (1995) 广东开平方言的"的"字结构——从"者""之"分工谈到语法类型分布. 中国语文 247: 289–97.

Zhang Min 张敏 (1990) 汉语方言反复问句的类型学研究：共时分布及其历时蕴含. 北京大学博士学位论文.

（本文发表于 *Contemporary Studies on the Min Dialects*，第 42—76 页，香港中文大学出版社，1999 年）

罗马所藏 1602 年手稿本闽南话－西班牙语词典

——中国与西方早期语言接触一例[*]

马西尼

游汝杰译　邹嘉彦校

自 16 世纪末期开始，在亚洲东部地区因传教与中国人接触的西方人，几乎无不声称或打算编写中文词典。此后编写一本优秀的中文词典成为人们长期追求的目标，一直到 20 世纪初期马礼逊出版著名的 6 卷本大词典。

因传教活动关系，西方人需要实用的研究当地语言的基本工具书。最初碰到的问题是如何记录这些外国的语音，列出供记忆的词表。利玛窦（Matteo Ricci）在郭居静（Lazzaro Cattaneo）等传教士的协助下，为官话制订了一个可靠的拼音方案，方案中有送气符号和声调符号。这一方案稍加修改，最后为金尼阁（Nicolas Trigault）的《西儒耳目资》所采用，此书于 1626 年在杭州出版。此后几百年此书所用官话拼音方案一直被当作标准拼法。[1]

不过在利玛窦经澳门到中国之前，在菲律宾的传教士们为学会汉语和汉字，已经开始努力工作了。大多数传教会，即奥古斯汀会、多明我会和耶稣会，都声称已经编写好词典，这些教会是 1565 年至 17 世纪初期抵达菲律宾传教的。

第一本词典是《中国语言词汇集》（*Arte y Vocabulario de la lengua China*），据称编者是西班牙奥古斯汀会的 Martin de Rada（1533—1578）。他说他曾于 1575 年和 1576 年两度到福建旅行。可惜他编写的词典已逸失，与别的一些词典一样只有书名残留至今。[2]

这一时期编写的词典，只有少数几种至今犹存。其中一种今存罗马 Angelica 图书馆，作者是西班牙耶稣会的 Pedro Chirino（1557—1635）。这本手稿于 1602 年由作者从菲律宾带到罗马。这是一本记在笔记本上的手稿，共 88 页（其中只有 83 页有文字），包括几百条中文词语，并有某种闽南话及相应的 Castillian 西班牙语注音。这些词语对于研究中国和西方早期的语言接触是非常有用的。它也可以用于研究当时闽南话的语

---

* 本文初稿是用意大利语发表，题目为 "Materiali Lessicografici sulla lingua cinese redatti dagli occidentali fra '500 e '600: I dialetti del Fujian", in *Cina* 28, *Roma*, 2000, pp. 53-79.

音和词汇特点。手稿上的汉字是文化程度不高的人写的，所以它对于验证最初出现的一些简体字也是有用的。

西班牙的多明我会继奥古斯汀会之后来到菲律宾传教。他们在 1578 年到达菲律宾群岛，一直到 1626 年离开，当年他们设法登陆中国的台湾，在 1642 年荷兰人占领台湾后，他们最终转移到中国大陆。[3] 他们在那儿所遇见的是福建人，多明我会便创制了闽南话罗马字拼音方案。

西班牙多明我会在 16 世纪末和 17 世纪初，曾将这些罗马字拼音方案用于各种宗教文献。开头在菲律宾，后来到中国内地的多明我会编写了至少 16 本有关汉语词汇的著作，我们只知道这 16 本书的书名。其中非闽南话著作暂不讨论，我现在只是把其中的闽南话著作的情况略为说一说。正如上文所说，有关闽南话的著作是最早的，因为最早与传教士接触的中国人是福建人。

这些书的书名如下：

a）*Vocabulario Sinico*, 又名 *Diccionario español-chino vulgar*[4], Miguel de Benavides（1550—1605）著；

b）*Dictionarium Sinicum*, 又名 *Diccionario chino*[5], Domingo de Nieva（1563—1606）著；

c）*Vocabulario chino*[6], Juan Cobo（?—1592）[7] 著。

还有下列闽南话词典，我们也仅仅知道其书名，大部分不知其作者是谁。

其中有五种曾收于马尼拉的 San Tomás 大学的档案馆目录。这五种中有两种毁于 1941 年第二次世界大战时。今存以下几种应无问题：

1. *Diccionario chino-español*。

2. *Diccionario español-chino*。

3. *Vocabulario de la lengua española-china*。[8]

4. 又一种见于巴黎国家图书馆。书名为 *Dicionario de la lengua Chin-cheo*，写于 1609 年。最初为 Abel Remusat 藏书，后为 Stanislas Julien 所收藏，最后归 L. d'Hervey de Saint Denis 所有。[9]

5. 又一种见于大英博物馆图书馆（Add 25.317, ff. 2a-224b），书名为 *Bocabulario de lengua sangleya por las letraz de el A.B.C.*，最初为 Heinrich Julius Klaproth 藏书，1863 年 7 月 11 日由大英博物馆购得。[10]

6. 又一种见于罗马的 Angelica 书目，书名为 *Dictionarium Sino-Hispanicum*, Pedro Chirino 著，作者是在菲律宾的西班牙耶稣会会士。[11]

前三种我未曾寓目，其编写的年代可能比后三种要古老得多。

第五种今藏于大英博物馆图书馆。P. van der Loon 研究过这本词典，并有所概述：这是一本汉语闽南话－西班牙语 Castillian 话词典，几无汉字，记录约三百个音节，标出送气音和鼻音，但大多不标声调。P. van der Loon 详细研究了用于 1605 年在马尼拉印刷的 *Doctrina christiana en letra y lengua china* 的罗马字拼音方案，他在梵蒂冈图书馆找到原本（Riserva，V，73，ff. 33，只有中文部分），又在大英博物馆找到该馆所藏两种稿本。在同一档案中另藏上文述及的 *Bocabulario*，还有 *Doctrina* 的两个抄本，一本有罗马字拼音和西班牙语译文（Add 25.317，ff. 239a–279a），另一本只有罗马字拼音（Add 25，317，ff. 281a–313a）。[12]

van der Loon 已认定 *Doctrina* 所见语言是闽南地区的潮州话，他相信 *Doctrina* 和 *Bocabulario* 的作者是 Domingo de Nieva，他也是 *Dictionarium Sinicum* 的作者（参见上文的 b）。

据 van der Loon 说，多明我会会士虽然负责编写词典，但是不会读汉字。然而他们创制的罗马字拼音方案系统性很强。他们用了 13 个附加的发音符号，包括用 7 个符号表示不同的调值（见表 2），用一个符号，即提升半格的 h，表示送气，另用一个符号，即斜线，表示鼻音。

上述最后一本词典（第六种）是耶稣会而不是多明我会传教士编写的。这就是本文所要讨论的词典。就我所知，这是 16 世纪晚期以来，耶稣会传教士所编的唯一的非官话词典。要不是利玛窦和罗明坚（Michele Ruggieri）所编的著名的汉葡词典早十年问世，这将是第一本汉外词典。[13]

1. Pedro Chirino 和他的词典

罗马 the Biblioteca Angelica 所藏 *Dictionarium Sinico-Hispanicum*（Ms. Ltal. -lat. n. 60）[14] 是西班牙耶稣会会士 Pedro Chirino（1557—1635）编写的。他于 1557 年生于 Ossuna，1580 年他在安达卢西亚省开始耶稣会修道士的见习期。他曾要求委派到美洲传教，但是没有获得批准，后来他就开始在 Jerez della Frontera 当使徒。1589 年他受命向菲律宾传达耶稣会会长 Claudio Acquaviva 的指示，将马尼拉耶稣会住所（the Jesuit Residence）改为学院，以利解决在菲律宾居住的西班牙人的教育问题。他于 1590 年到达马尼拉，在马尼拉地区他曾参加一些传教活动，后来他被任命为宿务耶稣会学院（Jesuit College）院长。他从 1595 年开始学习中文，意图在改变宿务的中国人的观念，使其皈依耶稣教。[15] 从当时 Chirino 写的一份报告，我们知道，在一位由马尼拉总督派往宿务的中国信徒 Don Luis de los Mariñas 的帮助下，他很快就能用中文授课，并在 1596 年为第一批中国人施洗浸礼。[16] 在 1602 年，作为菲律宾副省长的代理人，

Chirino 被派往罗马,向会长报告在菲律宾的传教事业。Chirino 利用这个机会写了一份详细的报告,耶稣会会长很快就出版了这份报告,报告的题目是 *Relación de Islas Filipinas i de lo que en ellas trabaiado los Padres de la Compañia de Jésus*。[17]Chirino 又利用这个机会把他所编词典的手稿带到罗马,交给奥古斯汀会红衣主教 Angelo Rocca。Rocca 是圣彼得大教堂司事和著名的藏书家,他的个人藏书,后来成为 Angelica 图书馆的基本藏书,这个图书馆最终成为世界上最早的公共图书馆之一。[18]

Chirino 于 1606 年回到马尼拉,1635 年 9 月 16 日在马尼拉去世。[19]

2. 书稿

书稿(21.8×16.6 厘米)由 88 张纸合订而成,其中只有 83 张纸和封面上写有文字,根据洋装书自左至右阅读的习惯,页码用铅笔自左至右记在右上角。所以有文字的每一页按中文书的习惯只出现在书的正面,但页码标在背面的右上角。这种现象很容易解释,页码是一个西方人添加上去的,他并不知道中文的书写习惯是从右到左。

每一张纸都只是一面有文字,只有第 71 页是例外,两面都写字。第 71(a-b)、72、73 和 74 页笔迹有所不同,并且在正字法方面与其余部分不同,例如"水"("agua")标为 *Chuy*,但在第 3 页上却标为 *Chui*。

每一个字都有 Castillian 的翻译,译文写在左边,中文注音写在右边。多音节的词语按语素逐一用 Castillian 译出,它们与组成中文多音节词语的语素显然没有任何关系。有些词语的注音与所注的中文字并不相符,实际上所注是口语中的词语的语音,例如第 29 页上的第一个词是 *sai fu*"师傅",可是在同一页和下一页有许多以"匠"结尾的词,对"匠"的注音也是 *sai fu*。另有些例子,用不同的语音来注同一个汉字,例如 26 页上的"一",有两种读法:*chit* 和 *cheg*。

这本词典上的词和词语是按不同的标准编排起来的(见表 1)。表上第 Ⅰ 栏是页码,第 Ⅱ 栏是内容,第 Ⅲ 栏是该页所见字数,第 Ⅳ 栏是单音节词的数量,第 Ⅴ 栏是双音节词的数量,第 Ⅵ 栏是三音节词的数量,第 Ⅶ 栏是短语和句子的数量,第 Ⅷ 栏是词语的总数,第 Ⅸ 栏是句子的数量(请与第 Ⅲ 栏所示字数比较)。表 1 底端列出每一栏的总数。如果没有特别说明,每一个词、词语或句子都是先用中文写出,再写出罗马字拼音,最后是写出 Castillian 西班牙语。所有词、词语或句子都用中文的书写习惯,即从上到下,从右到左。

从表 1 可知,这本词典(或可称为"笔记")包含 1920 个字,966 个词,其中单音节词有 639 个,双音节词有 304 个,三音节词有 17 个,另有 6 个短语,116 个句子(未按组成这些句子的词的多寡来分类)。单音节词、双音节词和三音节词之间的比例关系，与十七、八世纪其他汉语方言文献的统计结果是一致的。[20] 以上的数字只能看作大略的说明，因为确定某一个说法是词（单音节、双音节和三音节词等）、短语或句子，常常是非常困难的。

从表1可知，编者的意图是让读者循序渐进，熟悉这种语言。开头是一些常用字，然后是热带地区常见的物件、动物、植物、鱼类和昆虫。只是开头的几页是按字形编排的，部首相同的词排在一起。开头五页按五个不同的部首分页，每一部首占一页：第一页为"金"，第二页为"木"，第三页为"水"，第四页为"火"，第五页为"土"。从第六页开始，即按义类编排，可见编者的用意是将这本词典作为学习口语，而不是书面语的入门书。还应该指出，从这本词典所收的词汇和句子来看，没有任何表示外国的概念或观念的词或词语，也没有提到 Chirino 的祖国和他的宗教信仰。

这本词典上的字显然是没有受过教育的中国人写的。有些部首的写法前后不一致，如部首"彳"常常和"双人旁儿"相混。常用简体字，而不用正体字：例如用"旧"代替"舅"（f. 21），用"铁"代替"鐵"（f. 1）。后一种现象是非常有意思的，特别值得注意。这本词典中的有些简体字，在中国文字学史的正规文献上，出现的时代要晚得多。

例如"旧"，据现代的词典学参考书[21]，是下列三个字的简化形式：舊臼舅。在 Chirino 的词典里，只用于第三个字"舅"[22]。又如"铁"是"鐵"的简化形式，最早见于《正字通》，以及《雍熙乐府》中的一首诗，后者出版于1566年，年代仅比 Chirino 的词典略早几年。[23]

表1　Chirino 词典内容说明

栏目内容：

I. 页码；II. 内容；III. 见于该页的字数；IV. 单音节词的数量；V. 双音节词的数量；VI. 三音节词的数量；VII. 短语的数量；VIII. 词语的总数；IX. 句子的数量

I	II	III	IV	V	VI	VII	VIII	IX
1	"金"字旁的字	20	20				20	
2	"木"字旁的字	20	20				20	
3	"水"字旁的字	20	20				20	
4	"火"字旁的字	20	20				20	
5	"土"字旁的字	20	20				20	
6	动物	21	17	2			19	

（续表）

I	II	III	IV	V	VI	VII	VIII	IX
7	鱼	27	9	9			18	
8	虫	23	17	3			20	
9	虫	26	10	8			18	
10	天气	20	20				20	
11	物件	22	18	2			20	
12	物件	20	20				20	
13	物件	23	11	7			18	
14	植物和水果	12	12				12	
15	植物和水果	22	10	6			16	
16	植物和水果	18	14	2			16	
17	植物和水果	27	4	10	1		15	
18	人体各部分	16	16				16	
19	人体各部分	22	18	2			20	
20	人体各部分	24	16	4			20	
21	亲属关系	24	16	4			20	
22	亲属关系	24	16	2			18	
23	代词、色彩	18	12	3			15	
24	布料	19	13	3			16	
25	布料	31	5	8	2	1	16	
26	数词 1—10，以及从 20—100 的十位数	28	10	9			19	
27	别的数词、度量衡	28	12	8			20	
28	各类名称	25	9	8			17	
29	职业（以"匠"结尾的 14 个）	32		16			16	
30	职业（以"匠"结尾的 5 个）	15		6	1		7	
31	性质形容词	16	16				16	
32	形容词和动词	16	16				16	
33	形容词和动词	16	16				16	
34	形容词和动词	17	15	1			16	

（续表）

I	II	III	IV	V	VI	VII	VIII	IX
35	动词	16	16				16	
36	动词	16	16				16	
37	动词	17	15	1			16	
38	动词短语（如"完了"）	32		16			16	
39	动词或形容词短语	26		13			13	
40	11个动词短语和1个动词	22	2	10			12	
41	动词短语	24		12			12	
42	动词短语	24		12			12	
43	11个动词短语和一个名称	24	1	10	1		12	
44	句子	41						12
45	句子	27						6
46	句子（只有一个有翻译）	29						6
47	句子（只有一个有翻译）	33						8
48	句子（没有翻译）	28						5
49	句子	36						5
50	句子（没有翻译）	28						7
51	词和动词短语	23		5			5	4
52	句子	28						6
53	句子	27						5
54	8个词和1个短语	20		8		1	9	
55	各种名称	18	4	7			11	
56	各种名称（7个以"食"为偏旁的字）	21	7	4		2	13	
57	7个不同的名称和2个句子	22		7			7	2
58	各种名称	18	8	5			13	
59	各种名称（4个以"手"为偏旁的字）	20	4	8			12	
60	7个含"打"字的句子和另一个句子	20		7			7	1
61	各种名称和短语	20		7			7	2
62	各种名称和短语	24	7			1	8	1

（续表）

I	II	III	IV	V	VI	VII	VIII	IX
63	各种名称（其中 8 个以"相"开头）	23	1	11			12	
64	各种名称（其中 5 个以"相"开头）	22		11			11	
65	基本方位词和季节名称	13	11	1			12	
66	形容词和名称	20	20				20	
67	各种名称（其中 3 个以"相"开头）	20	5	6			11	1
68	句子	27						3
69	各种名称	20	1	5	3		9	
70	各种名称	19	1	6	2		9	
71	正面：句子	30			1		1	5
72	背面：不加注音和释义的单音节词	10	10				10	
73	背面：不加注音和释义的单音节词	20	20				20	
74	背面：单音节词，部分有注音和释义	20	20				20	
75	动词短语	22				1	1	6
76	短语和句子	20	2	4	2		8	1
77	句子	27			2		2	4
78	句子	32						6
79	句子，只有第一个有部分翻译	35						5
80	句子，有的有翻译	36						4
81	句子和两个词，有的有翻译	27		2			2	4
82	句子，有的有翻译	34						5
83	句子和词，有的有翻译	27		3	2		5	2
84	总计	1920	639	304	17	6	966	116

3. 罗马字拼音系统

Chirino 的罗马字拼音系统，在符号使用上有以下特点：

送气音十分系统地用"h"写在塞音 /p/，/t/，/c/，/ç/，/q/ 的后面，即 /ph/，/th/，/ch/，/çh/，/qh/。van der Loon 曾研究过的 *Doctrina* 和 1607 年出版的 *Bocabulario* 也是用"h"表示送气的。在中国的耶稣会会士后来编写的别的词典或词汇学文献则是用一个希腊文字母写在符号的上面，或者用一个撇号写在声母的前面，后来把撇号挪到声母的后面，表示送气，所使用的方法跟威妥玛式或远东法兰西学院（the École Française d'Extrême-Orient）拼法完全一样。

声调似乎没有系统的标示法，不过在某些场合还是用了一些附加符号。可能这是最初为标示声调所做的努力，例如：sia 加声调后有三个音节 sià 城，siā 锡，siá 社。通过与闽语三个主要次方言（厦门话、潮州话、福州话）的比较，可以假设：短横在上表示阴入，长横在下表示阳入，一捺在上表示阳平；有时也用曲折号，可能是用来表示阴去，如 sǔa 线。[24] 因为只有十来个音节用了声调符号，所以以上所说还只是一种假设。

表 2 声调符号

声调	年份	平声		上声	去声		入声	
		阴	阳		阴	阳	阴	阳
Chirino	1602	´			˘		`	‾
Doctrina 和 *Bocabulario*	1605/1607	´	‾	˘	`	^	˘	‾
西字奇迹 [25]	1605	‾	^	`		´		
西儒耳目资	1626		^	`		´		

这本词典所采用的罗马字拼音系统请见表 3 和表 4。表 3 为声母表，先写出大致的音值，后面括号中是 Chirino 所用的声母符号。表 4 为韵母表，表中的韵母只是对 Chirino 所用的韵母有所修正，我不想构拟当时可能的音值。因为我目前还没有将它的音韵与当时其他闽语进行比较，所以我不打算确定每一个语音的实际音值。Chirino 在宿务的时候可能已经与使用不同闽语的人群有所接触。然而有必要指出，Chirino 的罗马字拼音系统与 van der Loon 曾研究过的罗马字拼音系统有所不同。[26]

表 3 Chirino 词典的声母

Voiceless unaspirated	p (p)	t (t)	ts (çh)	k (c, ç, qu)
Voiceless aspirated	p' (ph)	t' (th)	ts' (ch)	k' (qh)
Voiced	b (b)		dz (tz)	
Nasals	m (m)	n (n)		g (ng)
Fricatives			s (s)	
Approximant				h (h)
Sonorants		l (l, d)		

表 4　Chirino 词典的韵母

	-b	-c	-g	-m	-n	-ng	-p	-r	-t
a		ac		am	an	ang	ap	ar	at
ai									
ao									
au									
e		ec	eg			eng			et
ee									
ei									
i				im	in	ing	ip		it
ia	iab			iam	ian	iang	iap		
iao									
iau									
ie					ien	ieng			iet
io						iong			
iu									
o		oc	og			ong			
oa				oam	oan				
oai									
oe									
ou									
u					un			ur	
ua				uam					
ue									
uei									
ui				uim	uin				uit
uia				uiam					
uio									

4. 结语

没有证据可以指出当时中国知识界已经注意到这一种或别的闽语罗马字拼音系统。

它们只是为实用的目的而制订，即用于宗教图书的拼写，如 1605 年的 *Doctrina*，或者为了向当地人民传福音而研究语言，制订拼写法，如 Chirino 的罗马字拼音系统和用于 1607 年的 *Bocabulario* 的拼写法。这些系统很快就被制订者耶稣会会士和多明我会会士放弃，他们不久更去了内地，将精力转向官话。他们致力制订官话拼音系统、编写官话词典和语法书，因为官话是他们传教对象，即知识分子所用的语言。这种情形一直维持到 19 世纪初年，那时候新教传教士投身于研究南方语言，创制各种不同的罗马字拼音系统。这些拼音系统中只有闽南白话字得以广泛传播，一直到今天福建省一些当地人还懂这种白话字。[27]

附 注

[1] 关于 Ricci, Ruggieri, Cattaneo 的官话罗马字拼音系统，参见 Yang, Paul Fumien S. J., "The Portuguese-Chinese Dictionary by Matteo Ricci: A Historical and linguistic Introduction", *Proceedings of the Second International Conference on Sinology. Section on Linguistics and Palaeography*. Taipei: Academia Sinica, 1989。F. Masini, "Some preliminary remarks on the study of Chinese lexicographic materials prepared by Jesuit missionaries in the XVIIth century", in F. Masini ed., *Western Humanistic Culture Presented to China by Jesuit Miwiofwiia*, Rome. 1996, pp.235–245。Joseph A. Levi, *Dicionario Portuguese-Chinese de Mateo Ricci*. University Press of the South, 1998。有关《西儒耳目资》的中文、日文和西文的书目参见 F. Masini, "Some preliminary remarks on the study of Chinese lexicographic materials prepared by Jesuit missionaries in the XVIIth century"，见注 [7]。

[2] 关于 Miguel López de Legazpi 的探险事迹参见 N. P. Cushner, *Spain in the Philippines*. Institute of Philippine Culture, Ateneo de Manila, Quezon City, 1971。P. Femandez, *History of the Church in the Philippines (1521–1898)*. Navotsa Press, Metro Manila, 1979。H. de la Costa, *The Jesuit in the Philippines 1581–1768*. Harvard University Press, 1967。感谢 Giuliano Bertuccioli 教授允许我引用他的有关菲律宾的材料，特别是有关 Pedro Chirino 的笔记。

[3] 参见 J. Dehergne, "L'ile Formose au XVIIᵉ sièle", in *Monumenta Nipponica* 4, 1941, pp.270–277。

[4] 参见 Streit, *Bibliotheco Missionum*, vol. IV, p.358, J. M. Gonzáles, *Historia de las Missiones Dominicanas de China*. Madrid, 1967, vol. V, p.386。

[5] 参见 Streit, *op. cit.*, vol. IV, p.364, J. M. Gonzáles, *op. cit.*, vol. V, p.391。

[6] 参见 Streit, *op. cit.*, vol. IV, p.472, J. M. Gonzáles, *op. cit.*, vol. V, p.386。

[7] 有关这些传教士的事迹，也见于 Diego Aduarte, *Historia de la Provincia del Santo Rosario de la Orden de Predicatores en Filipinas, Japón y China, Zaragoça* 1693, now edited by M, Ferrero, C. S. I. C., Madrid 1963。其中有些人的事迹也见于 F. Mateos, "Apuntes para la Historia de la Lexicografía Chino-Española", in M. Ariza, A. Salvador, A. Viudas ed., *Actas del I Congreso International de Hisioria de la lengua Espanola*, Cáceres, 30 de marzo-4 de abril de 1987, Arco-Libros. S. A, pp. 927–941。

[8] J. M. Gonzáles, Historia de las Missiones Dominicanas de China, Madrid 1967, vol. V, pp.412–414. González 指出，马尼拉的 San Tomás 大学档案馆所藏这三本词典的书号分别为 t.215, t.216 和 t.214。

[9] 参见 A. Remusat, *Mélanges Asiatiques*, vol. II, Paris 1826, pp.90-93; Cardier, *Bibliotheca Sinica.*, col. 1629. Courant Chinois。

[10] Cordier, op.cit., col. 1632.

[11] 参见 "The Manils Incunsbola and Early Hokkien Studies", in *Asia Mayor* XII, pp.95–186, cf. Part II, p.99。

[12] Ivi, pp.143–186.

[13] 手稿藏于罗马耶稣会历史档案馆，1934 年被 Pasquale D'Elia 发现，Dizionario Portoghese-cinese, D'Elia 和杨福绵认为，这本手稿是 Ricci 和 Ruggieri 1583—1588 年在广东肇庆写的，1588 年由 Ruggieri 带到罗马。参见 *ARSI, Jap. Sin.* I, 198, ff.32–156。又，参见 F. Masini, "*Some preliminary remarks on the study of Chinese lexicographic materials prepared by Jesuit missionaries in the XVlIth century*", p.239, n.9。

[14] 手稿的完整题目是: *Dictionarium Sinico-Hispanicum quo P. Pedro Chirino Societatis Jesu Linguam Sinensium in Filipinis addiscebat ad convertendos eos Sinenses qui Filipinas ipsas inodunt, et quadraginta millium numerum excedunt. Quem R. mo D. Mons. Sacrista obesequia ergo ipsemet Petrus suppliciter obtulit prid.* Cal. Aprilis 1604。又可参见 E. Narducci, *Catalogus codicum manoscriptorum Praeter Graecos et Orientales in Bibliotheca Angelica*, vol. l, Roma 1893, p.21，也参见 van der Loon, *art. cit.*, p.98。

[15] 在 1604 年的报告中 Chirino 说，当地约有两百个中国人，但在词典的序言里他说有四十万人。

[16] 参见 de la Costa, *op. cit.*, pp.166–167, 200, 222。

[17] Roma, Estevan Paulino, 1604, pp.196；再版 Manila, 1969。

[18] 据《序言》, Chirino 在 1604 年 3 月 5 日完成他的 *Relación de Islas Filipinas*，过了没多久，即在 3 月 31 日，把手稿奉献给红衣主教 Rocca。为什么一个耶稣会传教士会把一本

词典手稿交给一位奥古斯汀会红衣主教？可能的解释是：这位红衣主教是一位饱学之士，语言学专家，第一本官方出版的《圣经》（1590 年）的编辑，多少对 Chirino 的 *Relación* 的出版有些助益。事实上，一直到 1595 年，Rocca 多年来掌管梵蒂冈印刷厂，并与包括 Estevan Paulino 或 Stephanum Paulinum 在内的罗马所有的主要印刷厂都有联系，Chirino 的 *Relación* 和 Rocca 的至少一本书就是在上述印刷厂出版的。我们可以推想，Chirino 将词典交给 Rocca，是希望词典能在罗马出版。Rocca 在一本匿名小册子里曾提到这本手稿：*Bibliotheca Angelica litteratorum litterarumque amatorum commoditati dicata Romae in aedibus augustinianis*, Romae, apud Stephanum Paulinum, 1608，在第 86 页他就写：Codices excortice arundines Sinis conscripti, & Siniacè item Sinis impressi cum dictionarium Sinohispanico manuscripto. 这本手稿不见于 Angelica 图书馆的首批目录：*Index Manascriptorum Bibliotheca Angelica autorum et materiarum ordine alphabetico dispositus*. A Padri Basilio Rassegnier, 1734 (ms. 2393)，但见于 Guilelmus Bartolomei 在 1847 (ms. 1078, f.48V) 编辑的目录。有关图书馆一般历史和有关 Rocca 的文献参见 P. Munafò, e N. Muratore, *La Biblioteca Angelica*, Istituto Poligrafico e Zecca dello Stato, Roma, 1989。

[19] 关于 Chirino 的生平事迹见于上文述及的有关基督教在菲律宾传教活动的参考书，也见于下述著作（引自 Archivo Biográfico de España, Portugal e Iberosmérica, II /229, 353, 354): *M. Méndez Bejarano, Diccionario de Escritores, Maestros y Oradores naturales de Sevilla*, Girones, vol. I, Sevilla 1922, n.672; F. Rodriguez Marin, *Nuevos datos para las Biografias de cien escritores de los siglos XVI y XVII*, Tip.de la Revista de Archivos, Bibliotecas y Museos, Madrid, 1923, ad indicem。

[20] 参见 F. Masini, *The Formation of Modern Chinese Lexicon and its Evolution toward a National Language: The Period from 1840 to 1898*, Monograph No.6 of the *Journal of Chinese Linguistics*, Berkeley, 1993, p.121, n.2。中文译本：马西尼著、黄河清译《现代汉语词汇的形成——十九世纪汉语外来词研究》，汉语大词典出版社，1997 年。

[21]《汉语大字典》，湖北辞书出版社，四川辞书出版社，1986—1990，8 卷；《汉语大词典》，汉语大词典出版社，1986—1994，13 卷。这些书上没有简化字在历史上首出的资料。《中文大辞典》，台北中华学术院印行，1973 年，1980 年重印，10 卷，包括《宋元以来俗字谱》载录的所有简化字。《宋元以来俗字谱》为刘复和李家瑞 1930 年初版，1957 年重印，全书包括 6240 个简化字。

[22] 参考《中文大词典》，14 052 条。

[23] 参考《中文大词典》，41 220 条；《汉语大词典》第 11 卷，1232 页；《汉语大字典》第 6 卷，4187 页。

[24] 各声调的调值据它们在现代闽语厦门话和（/ 或）潮州话的调值作了修正。见《汉语方音字汇》（第二版），北京大学中国语言文学系语言学教研室编，文字改革出版社，1989 年。

[25]《西字奇迹》是一本简短的教科书（正背面共6页），利玛窦著，1605年初版于北京，全书包括三个圣经故事，皆译成中文，并配以罗马字拼音。《西儒耳目资》一书是金尼阁（1577—1628）在韩云和王征的协助下写成的，1626年出版于杭州。参见马西尼《一些初步想法……》、《欧洲出版的第一本中文词典》，以及这两种著作所列的详细书目。

[26] 相关的闽语音韵特征大多可以在下述两种著作中找到：《汉语方音字汇》（第二版），北京大学中国语言文学系语言学教研室编，文字改革出版社，1989年；袁家骅等著《汉语方言概要》（第二版），文字改革出版社，1983年。

[27] 关于闽南白话字请参见《介绍流行悠久的闽南白话字》，载《语文建设通讯》，香港，1994，45，pp.72—79。

（本文发表于邹嘉彦、游汝杰主编《语言接触论集》，第211—234页，
上海教育出版社，2004年）

福安话韵母的历史音变及其共时分析方法 *

陈泽平

一　福安话的变韵

近年来对闽东区福宁片（北片）方言的调查工作取得了很大进展，到目前为止，所见到的调查成果都显示包括福安话在内的闽东北片（福宁片）方言有复杂的韵母系统。本文拟从闽东区南北两片方言的比较入手，梳理福安话韵母系统特别是元音系统的演变脉络和层次，然后讨论共时音系的处理原则。

先列出《福安市志·方言》的韵母表作为讨论基础，见表1：

表1　《福安市志·方言》福安韵母表

<table>
<tr><td rowspan="3">阴声韵</td><td>a</td><td>加爬马架咬</td><td>ε</td><td>低题底帝丽</td><td>e</td><td>车斜且社夜</td><td>œ</td><td>初驴楚错助</td></tr>
<tr><td>ø</td><td>於去芋</td><td>ɔ</td><td>坡婆宝套抱</td><td>o</td><td>瓜华寡挂画</td><td>i</td><td>批离吕剃滤</td></tr>
<tr><td>u</td><td>锅蒲鼓过暮</td><td></td><td></td><td></td><td></td><td></td><td></td></tr>
<tr><td rowspan="3"></td><td>ai</td><td>梯才彩菜在</td><td>ei</td><td>悲棋○记技</td><td>øi</td><td>猪锤腿醉跪</td><td>ɔi</td><td>堆雷○碎代</td></tr>
<tr><td>au</td><td>遭茅找灶闹</td><td>ɛu</td><td>雕条○凑豆</td><td>eu</td><td>抽求狗救柱</td><td>ou</td><td>都塗敨兔土</td></tr>
<tr><td>uai</td><td>乖怀拐怪坏</td><td>uoi</td><td>杯梅每妹卫</td><td>ieu</td><td>飘嫖表票庙</td><td>iau</td><td>了</td></tr>
<tr><td rowspan="3">阳声韵</td><td>aŋ</td><td>摊残斩赞病</td><td>ɛiŋ</td><td>针填○店县</td><td>eiŋ</td><td>冰陈点镇阵</td><td>œŋ</td><td>东朋○冻洞</td></tr>
<tr><td>øŋ</td><td>宫穷梗供近</td><td>ɔuŋ</td><td>帮堂○顿丈</td><td>ouŋ</td><td>锋蒙选宋顺</td><td>iŋ</td><td>边棉紧见键</td></tr>
<tr><td>uŋ</td><td>冤完挽怨旺</td><td>iaŋ</td><td>厅名饼镜命</td><td>ioŋ</td><td>张墙厂唱尚</td><td>uaŋ</td><td>官瞒管惯万</td></tr>
<tr><td rowspan="4">入声韵</td><td>ak</td><td>答达</td><td>ɛik</td><td>涩十</td><td>eik</td><td>滴直</td><td>œk</td><td>北白</td></tr>
<tr><td>øk</td><td>竹逐</td><td>ɔuk</td><td>啄夺</td><td>ouk</td><td>足族</td><td>ik</td><td>揭杰</td></tr>
<tr><td>uk</td><td>国局</td><td>iak</td><td>峡页</td><td>iok</td><td>脚剧</td><td>uak</td><td>法乏</td></tr>
<tr><td>ɔk</td><td>托镯</td><td>ok</td><td>复佛</td><td></td><td></td><td></td><td></td></tr>
</table>

本文对这个表中的韵母例字做了调整，舒声韵一般选五个例字，按阴平、阳平、上声、阴去、阳去顺序每调选一字；入声韵选二字，阴入、阳入各一字。"ø"韵字数

---

*　本项研究得到国家社科基金项目"闽东方言语音变异的现代音系学研究"（项目批准号：09BYY055）资助。作者感谢匿名审稿者的修改建议。

太少，只能选出"去、芋、於"三个字，"iau"韵只有一个"了"字。"ei、ɔi、ɛu、ɛiŋ、œŋ、ɔuɔ"的上声调无字，特用"〇"表示空缺。

福安话与福州话在调类和声母上大体上一致，二者的韵母系统尽管整体格局不同，但其实也对应得相当有规律，这无疑表现出了闽东区方言的内部一致性。一部分韵母出现规律性的缺调，提示福安方言发生过类似南片（侯官片）福州话那样以调类为条件的韵母音值变化，即所谓的"变韵"。

最早报告闽东北片存在变韵现象的是 Norman（1977—1978）。其实只要参考明末清初的方言韵书《戚林八音》，对比福安、福州的同音字汇，循着两地常用字在韵母类别上的错位关系，不难从中整理出福安话变韵的线索。福州话和福安话都是七个声调：阴平、阳平、上声、阴去、阳去、阴入、阳入。福州话的变韵发生在阴去、阳去、阴入三调，而福安话除了上声，其余六调都变韵。例见表2、表3：

表2 《戚林八音》的"宾"韵类

调类	阴平	阳平	上声	阴去	阳去	阴入	阳入
例字	冰心金经	明神林灵	丙品审警	鬓镇证敬	咏定另孕	必匹踢式	蜜直辑入
福安	eiŋ	eiŋ	iŋ	eiŋ	eiŋ	eik	eik
福州	iŋ	iŋ	iŋ	eiŋ	eiŋ	eiʔ	iʔ
《八音》[1]	*iŋ	*iŋ	*iŋ	*iŋ	*iŋ	*ik	*ik

表3 《戚林八音》的"灯"韵类

调类	阴平	阳平	上声	阴去	阳去	阴入	阳入
例字	斑森针牵	爿填沉闲	版点剪省	店惯荐	办慢殿县	八贴节血	拔密截贼
福安	ɛiŋ	ɛiŋ	eiŋ	ɛiŋ	ɛiŋ	ɛik	ɛik
福州	eiŋ	eiŋ	eiŋ	aiŋ	aiŋ	aiʔ	eiʔ
《八音》	*eŋ	*eŋ	*eŋ	*eŋ	*eŋ	*ek	*ek

经过与《戚林八音》及今福州话的全面比对，我们认为福安话的变韵现象涉及下列韵母，见表4：

表4 福安话变韵现象所涉韵母

	阳声韵			入声韵			阴声韵				
A上	iŋ	uŋ	*yŋ	*ik	*uk	*yk	i	u	*y	*ui	*iu
B全	eiŋ	ouŋ	øŋ	eik	ouk	øk	ei	ou	(*øy)	oi (*oi)	eu
C缺上	ɛiŋ	ɔuŋ	œŋ	ɛik	ɔuk	œk	(au)[2]		ɔi		ɛu

表 4 中加 "*" 号的，是构拟的变韵初始音值，与今福州话的对应韵母一致。

参与变韵的韵母分为 ABC 三组。"A → B" 是第一级变韵，"B → C" 是第二级变韵。两级变韵之间存在推链关系。A 组都是高元音韵母，都只剩下上声字。B 组韵母以半高元音为主元音，虽然各调俱全，但都有两个来源，其平声（包括阴平、阳平）、去声字（包括阴去、阳去）实际上都是来自同列的 A 组韵母的变韵。C 组韵母以半低元音或低元音为主要元音，都是与同列 B 组上声调配对的变韵，上声调空缺。示意如下：

A	B	C	
上	平＿＿去		（第一级变韵）
	上	平＿＿去	（第二级变韵）
iŋ	→ eiŋ		（第一级变韵）
	eiŋ	→ εiŋ	（第二级变韵）

"变韵" 是变韵调音节的韵母在特定调值作用下对本韵音值的逐渐偏离，这有一个历时过程。陈泽平（1984）用比较法构拟出福州话的变韵过程。例如高元音先逐步低化，低化一度之后开始复化，派生出次要的高元音韵尾。例如：i → e → ei。这个构拟放在北片（福宁片）方言资料中检验，也是合适的。

基于原来的韵母结构格局，变韵形成了一个 "推链"。例如 "iŋ" 在变韵调逐步变成 "eiŋ"，迫使韵母系统中原有的 "eiŋ" 韵母在变韵调低化为 "εiŋ"，以保持两类韵母的区别，福安话中这种推链式的变韵格局也与福州话等南片（侯官片）方言相同。

入声韵的变韵与阳声韵平行，但入声韵只分布在两个入声调，所以列在 A 组的都只是构拟形式。

变韵的始作俑者是一组高元音。按照语音自然类在音系中平行活动的原理，"*y" 的变韵形式应该是 "*øy"，"*ui" 的变韵应该是 "*oi"，二者合并为 "øi"。

福州话变韵机制触及的韵母中不包括低元音韵母和有介音的韵母，福安话也是如此。所以，"*ui" 和 "*iu" 的结构都应该分析为 "韵腹 + 韵尾"。

福安话与福州话的变韵在机制、范围、过程上高度一致，二者应该是密切相关的。

变韵发生于过去，由于无法获知变韵启动时期的调值面貌，陈泽平（1984）干脆放弃了这种努力。曾有学者推测是低调或长调引起变韵，但仅是较早得到报告的福州、福清等地的变韵调调值就很难概括周全。平山久雄（1998）曾经用调值调型轮转变化的构想来解决矛盾，由于绕的圈子比较大，不太有说服力。随着调查工作的进展，闽东各处发现有变韵的方言越来越多，变韵调调值五花八门，有高有低、有升有降、有曲调、有平调、有长调、有短调。想简单地从五度调值表中去概括变韵调值的共同区别性特征，拿出一个适用于各点方言的统一答案，这种设想肯定是要失望的。由于实在无法从五度调值中找到简单的答案，有的学者甚至宣布变韵跟调值没有关系，而是分调类进行的词汇扩散式音变。

变韵以调类为条件，声调分类的依据就是调值差异，变韵发生的机制必然是与构成特定调值的某个成素有关，这是逻辑推论，不论我们是否已经发现了或不远的将来是否能发现这个相关的调值成素究竟是什么。我们在这里故意使用一个不太通用的名词"成素"，是想强调它是构成这种声调特质的成分之一，未必只是相对音高或长短，5度标调法也许不足以表达这种调值成素。至于这个调值成素究竟是什么，在声学或发音生理机制上应该怎么描述，仍是一个有挑战性的课题。我们这里也还拿不出答案，但有些想法也许有助于研究的进展：

1）我们观察到，不论在侯官片还是在福宁片，这个变韵的音变过程没有无限制地进行下去，不断地促使元音变化，到达某个系统的平衡点后，这个过程就停止了。推动变韵的调值成素与这样一个变韵的度之间，应该存在生理语音学的解释。

2）由于观察到变韵中的"推链"，似乎能说明同一方言中发生变韵的韵母不是同步起变的，最初启动变韵的可能仅是高元音。

3）由于我们观察到有的方言中不同调的变韵音值有差别，说明同一方言中有几个变韵调的，变韵的发生可能有先有后，这意味着变韵可能最先在某一个调启动，其他调是受其影响后跟进。如果确实存在这样的初始变韵调类，似乎最可能是阳去调。因为阳去总是变韵音值发展最充分的调类之一。

4）闽东各点方言的变韵有可能是平行发生的，但更可能是先发生于某一两个区域性权威方言，附近的方言受其影响而陆续跟进。例如永泰城关话的变韵与福州相似，但坂东话却没有变韵。这显然是因为城关话受到了福州话的影响（参看陈泽平1984）。寿宁城关话没有变韵，但靠近福安的斜滩话却有变韵，这是受了福安话影响的结果（参看秋谷裕幸2010）。

因此，研究启动变韵的调值成素，也许应该避免使用全面归纳各种变韵调调值的简单方法；而要通过分析，对准权威方言点，在最先启动变韵的调类和元音类上下功夫，然后再逐步梳理出变韵在韵类、调类上的扩散途径和顺序，以及变韵式音变在地理上的扩散波。

二 音系自调节音变

上一节的分析指出，福安话与福州话的变韵在机制、范围、过程上高度一致。接触过福安话的读者也许对这个结论存在疑问，认为福安话的韵母变化内容远不止本文用示意图概括说明的那些，要更为复杂多样，本节将做出解答。

原本相同的韵母按调类分化出两种（或多种）不同的音值，汉语方言中的这种现象其实也并非绝无仅有，可以参看远藤光晓（1994）和曹志耘（2009）。闽东方言中这种现象表现得尤为突出，在讨论闽东方言音韵的语境中，大家现在都已经习惯叫做"变韵"现象。"变韵"又与"本韵"相对而言，"变韵"特指在特定调值作用下发生了变异的韵母音值，维持该韵母原来音值的是"本韵"。福州话的"本韵"与"变韵"互补分布在不同的调类，构成一个韵位。福州话变韵调的字在连读变调条件下，韵母音值回归本韵，这是"连读变韵"，有时亦简称"变韵"。

无论在何种意义上使用"变韵"这个术语，都与声调条件有关。如果观察到方言中某个音类呈现出按调类互补分布的不同音值，我们说这是一种变韵现象。而与调类无关，即全调性的、一般性的韵母音变，不能也叫做"变韵"。必须区分变韵与一般性的历史音变，才能对变韵的性质和特征做出正确的判断。

闽东福宁片方言的韵母系统在数百年间发生了很多变化，近百年来的变化尤为剧烈。以声调为条件的变韵只是其中比较特殊的一组变化，除此之外，还有其他一些也会影响韵母系统整体面貌的历史音变。例如福安话在近百年内三种鼻音韵尾合并为一种，四种塞音韵尾也合并为一类，材料确凿，脉络清晰，却与声调的作用毫无关系。[3]

还有一些韵母变化可能与变韵有关，而其实只是系统自我调整性质的自然音变，却容易与变韵混为一谈，这是本节要着重分析讨论的。

福安话大面积的变韵音变确实使得这个语音系统呈现出一种很不合理的结构。例如：高元音韵母"i"除了上声调，其余各调的字都复元音化了，变成"ei"韵母，在声韵调配合的音节层面上，就造成大量空格。复元音韵母"ei"的上声空格只占所有可能的音节数的五分之一，这是系统还能够容忍的；但高元音韵母"i"的音节表上空格占了五分之四，造成音节资源的极大浪费。人类语言共性研究结果证明，高元音 [i]、[u] 都属于最无标记的元音，在任何语言中都扮演重要角色。汉语各方言的语音系统中，由 [i]、[u] 构成的单韵母都是管字较多的韵母。而福安话变韵凝固之后，"i"、"u"（以及配上辅音韵尾的"iŋ"、"ik"、"uŋ"、"uk"）呈现出大量空格，这是难以长期维持的畸形面貌。于是，系统的自调整功能启动了，音值相似的韵母"*ie"流入"i"空格，

"*uo"流入"u"空格。平行的变化也发生在带有辅音韵尾的阳声韵和入声韵:

*ie	>	i	*uo	>	u
*ieŋ	>	iŋ	*uoŋ	>	uŋ
*iek	>	ik	*uok	>	uk[4]

只要将福安话与邻近的霞浦话等以及闽东南片(侯官片)的福州话、福清话等进行对比,上述带星号的原始形式不难判定,戴黎刚(2008)做了细致的比较工作,可以参考。

我们在这里要强调指出的是,这一组音变是由变韵造成的畸形局面而引发的韵母系统自我调节,它与变韵有关,但不是在特殊调值作用下的变韵音变的一部分。这是一种"后变韵"的第二波历史音变。与变韵相比,它有如下三个特点:第一,韵母音值从有标记形式向无标记形式转移("i"比"ie"更自然,更容易发音);第二,音变是全调的,由大面积空格引发的调整型自然音变势力强大,既全面填补了原来分布在阴平、阳平、阴去、阳去、(阴入、阳入)上的空格,这股潮流也夹带着上声字挤入不是空格的上声音节,成为原有"i"韵母上声字的来历不同的同音字。第三,这种系统自我调谐性质的自然音变是"范性"音变,不具有变韵的"弹性"。

物理学上,把外力撤销后即恢复原状的形变称为"弹性形变",不能恢复原状的形变是"范性形变"。福州话的变韵调字在连读变调的条件下,韵母音值自动回归本韵(参看陈泽平1984),这是变韵音变的"弹性"。福安话的变韵则分两种情况:属于第一级变韵的字大多数仍表现出这种"弹性",例如:

汽 kʰei	汽油 kʰi jeu	字 tsei	字典 tsi tiŋ
渡 tou	渡头 tu lau	姑 kou	姑奶 ku nɛ
清 tsʰeiŋ	清水 tsʰiŋ tsi	清 tsʰeiŋ	清气 tsʰiŋ ŋei
同 touŋ	同学 tuŋ ɔuk	公 kouŋ	公道 kuŋ nɔ
日 neik	日头 nik lau	七 tsʰeik	七寸 tsʰik ɔuŋ
木 mouk	木虱 muk sɛik	腹 pouk	腹肚 puk lu

而第二级变韵的字则大多数已失去"弹性",不再回归本韵音值。例如:

| 前日 sɛiŋ neik | 缸斗 kɔuŋ nou | 杏花 kœŋ ho |

福安话中系统自调整性质的音变一律是"范性"音变,例如:

刺 tsʰi(<-ie)	刺瓜 tsʰi o	布 pu(<-uo)	布鞋 pu ɛ
本 puŋ(<-uoŋ)	本事 puŋ sou	关 kuŋ(<-uoŋ)	关门 kuŋ muŋ
天 tʰiŋ(<-ieŋ)	天气 tʰiŋ ŋei	年 niŋ(<-ieŋ)	年节 niŋ tsɛik

绿 luk(<-uok)　　绿豆 luk lau　　　　烛 tsuk(<-uok) 烛台 tsuk lɔi

与 "i" 和 "u" 相比，"y" 是一个有标记的高元音，世界上很多语言没有这个元音，一些汉语方言中没有 "y" 韵母。根据邻近方言的比较以及变韵机制的平行性，我们仍然假定福安话原来有一套以 "y" 为主要元音的韵母：

*y → øy > øi / 非上声

*yŋ → øŋ/ 非上声

*yk → øk

变韵凝固之后，"*y" 只剩下上声音节，没有其他韵母流入空格，形单影只的上声调的 "y" 难以长期独立生存，大部分并入 "i"，其过程很可能是 *y>*yi> >i，如："女汝吕旅缕侣滤主煮水取鼠杼黍暑署举语御许栩与予愈雨宇羽禹" 等字。[5] 在 "øy" 中作为次要元音的 "y" 也随之转化为 "i"，即从 "øy" 变成 "øi"。

"*yŋ" 韵的上声字本来就少，主要并入 "uŋ" 韵，可能包括："种肿恐拱勇涌俑" 等。

"*y" 转化为 "i" 或 "u"，也属于从有标记形式向无标记形式流动的自然音变。现在的福安话韵母系统中已经没有 "y" 这个音位了。

顺便在这儿交代，"*iu" 韵（中古流摄）的上声并入 "iou" 韵（中古效摄），如："酒肘丑纽柳手首守久九朽有友" 等。"*ui" 韵的上声字也就近并入 "uoi"，如："垒蕊累(~计)傀磊鬼诡几轨毁委苇萎" 等。以上是福安话韵母系统由变韵导致的第二波音变。经过这样的系统调整，福安话音节表上由变韵造成的大面积空格已经大体上填满。

第三波音变也是系统自调整性质的自然音变，只涉及两个阴声韵：*ia> e 和 *ua> o。演变过程很可能有一个中间阶段，即：

*ia > *ie > e

*ua > *uo > o[6]

如果存在这样一个中间阶段，这一波的变化必然是在前一波演变 ie > i 、uo > u 之后才发生的。所以单独列为第三波变化。重要的是，因而也属于自然音变，不是变韵。并且这也是全调性的演变；演变方向也是发音从复杂到简单，从有标记到无标记；在连读音变中保持韵母音值不变，例如：

车 tshe (<*-ia)　　　车票 tshe βiu

大 to (<*-ua)　　　　大学 to ɔuk

这两项变化不涉及对应阳声韵和入声韵。

至此，我们已经分析了福安话韵母的元音结构的演变大略。我们再次强调，应该区分哪些变化是有声调条件的变韵，哪些变化是与声调条件无关的一般性自然音变。只有明确了变韵的范围，才不至于对变韵的性质、规律和特征做出错误的概括。

三　如何处理福安话韵母表

让我们先从福州话说起。试拿一组福州话的单字音来举例分析[7]：

丁 $tiŋ^1$　　陈 $tiŋ^2$　　顶 $tiŋ^3$　　镇 $teiŋ^5$　　阵 $teiŋ^6$

灯 $teiŋ^1$　　澄 $teiŋ^2$　　等 $teiŋ^3$　　店 $taiŋ^5$　　殿 $taiŋ^6$

在这一组字音中归纳韵母，有两种可能的方案：A 方案按"韵位"归纳成两个韵母：iŋ/eiŋ，eiŋ/ aiŋ，如例字分行所示。这样的韵母是"韵位"的概念，即允许一个韵母内部包含不同的音值，不同的音值互补分布在不同的调类上。这种韵母系统的处理方法虽然特别，但适合福州话的音系特点，向来没有争议。研究福州话的文献都采用这样的分析方法。

B 方案按音值同一性归纳韵母，划分成三个韵母：iŋ，eiŋ，aiŋ。这样处理的韵母表比较直观、简单，但却不经济，不仅韵母数量多了一个，而且在声韵调配合的音节表上形成大量空格：

丁 $tiŋ^1$　　陈 $tiŋ^2$　　顶 $tiŋ^3$　　——　　——

灯 $teiŋ^1$　　澄 $teiŋ^2$　　等 $teiŋ^3$　　镇 $teiŋ^5$　　阵 $teiŋ$

　　　　　　　　　　　　　　　　店 $taiŋ^5$　　殿 $taiŋ^6$

福州话适合采用 A 方案归纳韵母有其历时方面的理据，因为同一韵位中包含不同音值本来就是元音结构以调类为条件的音变结果。按韵位归纳韵母系统不仅能减少韵母总数，整合音节表，而且与传统方言韵书《戚林八音》的分韵大致吻合，这一点对于展开闽东区各方言点的韵母比较研究有极大的便利之处。

同样存在变韵的福安方言，《福安市志·方言》（1999）却用按音值同一性的 B 方案来归纳韵母，韵母表中包含 47 个韵母（不计独立成音节的鼻音），如本文开头处所示。叶太青（2007）则尝试引入"韵位"的概念处理福安话韵母，列出一份 49 个韵母的福安话韵母表，即表 5：

表 5　叶太青（2007）福安韵母表

	甲							乙		丙		
阴声韵	a	e	ɛ	o	ɔ	ø	œ	i	ui	i / ei	ui / oi	øi / ɔi
		ie						u	iu	u / ou	iu / eiu	eu / ɛu
								ai	au	i / øi		
								iau	uai			

（续表）

	甲	乙	丙
阳声韵	aŋ iaŋ　ioŋ uaŋ	iŋ uŋ	iŋ/eiŋ　　eiŋ/aiŋ　　iŋ/øŋ uŋ/ouŋ　　ouŋ/ouŋ　　øŋ/œŋ
入声韵	ak　　ok　ɔk iak　　iok uak	ik[8] uk	(ik) / eik　　(eik) / ɛik (uk) / ouk　　(ouk) / ɔuk (ik) / øk　　(øk) / œk

原作者说明："福安话的韵母系统可以分为韵母表中的甲乙丙三类，其中的丙类韵母就是韵位。每一个韵位都由一个本韵和一个变韵组成，斜线符号'/'前为本韵，后为变韵。本韵分布在上声调上，变韵分布在其他六个调类上。"放在括号内的六个入声韵音值只是为了说明变韵机制而加上的，实际上不存在。比《福安方言志》多出的"ie"韵母只有"艾、外"两个字，可能是外方言混入的。

戴黎刚（2008）也是根据本韵、变韵的对应关系，重新整合《福安市志·方言》的同音字汇，提出一个40韵母的韵母表，即表6：

表 6　戴黎刚（2008）福安韵母表

	a	e	ε	o	ɔ	ø	œ	
阴声韵	a ai uai iau	e eu/εu ieu、ieu/eu	ε	o ou/au uoi、uoi/øi	ɔ ɔi	ø	œ	i、i/ei、i/øi u、u/ou
阳声韵	aŋ iaŋ uaŋ	eiŋ/εiŋ		ioŋ ouŋ/ ɔuŋ		øŋ/œŋ (øŋ/εiŋ)		iŋ、iŋ/eiŋ、iŋ/øŋ uŋ、uŋ/ouŋ
入声韵	ak iak uak	eik	εik	ok iok ouk	ɔk ɔuk	øk	œk	ik uk

原作者说明："福安话韵母的音类总数是47个，但是韵母只有40个"。可见表6中用"、"号隔开的一组"音类"都被看作同一韵母。

叶（2007）与戴（2008）对福安话韵母系统的处理方式都属于按韵位归纳的A方案，即允许同一个韵母在不同的声调上有不同的音值。

同一个福安方言，大家对语言事实（单字音）的认定基本上一致，却处理出三个不同的韵母表。这是一个令人感兴趣的音系学问题，值得进一步深入讨论。

这里只以"i、ei、øi、ɔi"的音节表为例，具体说明三种韵母表的不同处理方式。

《福安市志·方言》按音值的同一性归纳韵母，四个韵母的音节构成如下：

表7　i

	p	pʰ	m	w	t	tʰ	n	l	ts	tsʰ	s	k	kʰ	ŋ	h	j	0
1	禈	批					A		支		施	鸡	稽		嘻		
2	琵		弥		池	啼		离			匙	茄					兮
3a	比	痞	米		抵	耻			址		死	几	起	耳	喜	予	以
3b							女	旅	水		暑	举		语	许		雨
3c								里	紫	扯			启				椅
5	臂				淛	剃	呢	滤	际	取	世	计	契		费		B
6	避				弟			例		刺	誓			义	系		缢

A：歪。B：花残。

表8　ei

	p	pʰ	m	w	t	tʰ	n	l	ts	tsʰ	s	k	kʰ	ŋ	h	j	0
1	悲	菲			知	A				痴	诗	基	欺		稀		伊
2	脾	疲	微		迟	持	呢	梨			时	棋	骑	疑			姨
3																	
5	泌	屁	未		智		饵	利	志	饲	四	记	器		B		亿
6	篦			味	治		二	痢	字	市	是	妓	柿	耳			易

A：粘液。B：那里。

表9　øi

	p	pʰ	m	w	t	tʰ	n	l	ts	tsʰ	s	k	kʰ	ŋ	h	j	0
1					猪				书	趋	舒	居	区		虚		威
2	肥			围	除	锤	A	骡			徐	渠	C	鱼			余
3					短	腿		儒		髓							
5	沸	屁			著	赘	B		醉	处	穗	贵	愧		纬		慰
6	吠			胃	箸			类	住		遂	跪	溃	魏			喻

A：踩。B：伸手。C：等一下。

表 10　ɔi

	p	p^h	m	w	t	t^h	n	l	ts	ts^h	s	k	k^h	ŋ	h	j	0
1					堆	推				催	衰		魁				
2					颓			雷									
3																	
5					对	退			最	碎	帅						
6					袋		内	擂	罪		坐						

《福安市志·方言》按 B 方案归纳韵母，有些韵母缺调，如“ei”、“ɔi”两表所示。叶（2007）把“i”韵母的上声字按历史来源分拆为三组，表中的“3a”划给上声空缺的“ei”，把“3b”划给“øi”。“øi”表中原有的上声字“短、腿、儽、髓”等则也按照历史来源另行配给上声空缺的“ɔi”韵，从而重组出“i、i/ei、i/øi、øi/ɔi”四个韵母。其中包含两种音值的韵母斜线左边是上声调的“本韵”，右边是其他调的“变韵”。叶（2007）的“本韵 / 变韵”搭配是有历时分析依据的，通过与周边方言的比较以及联系中古音系进行比较都可以得到证明。但蹊跷的是，经过了这样的大调整，他的韵位归纳没有表现出经济性。四个韵母音值拆分搭配之后，还是四个韵母。

戴（2008）在“本韵 / 变韵”搭配关系的分析证明上更加细密、成系统。分析出“i”的不同层次后，也做了类似的韵位归纳，而且更进一步，把“本韵”相同的“i、i/ei、i/øi”都合起来算是一个韵母，“øi/ɔi”配成另一个韵母。以同样的原则处理其他韵母，从而把韵母总数降为 40 个。但下文将说明这一处理是错误的。

汉语的音节由声韵调三个音系单位构成。韵母本质上都是韵位，只不过多数情况下韵位内部的音值基本上统一，没有必要使用这个术语来强调韵母的音系学属性。韵位概念是音位概念的扩大和变通，但结构主义的共时分析原则没有变。辨义对立的不同语音形式应该分析为不同的韵位，互补分布的音值可以归纳为同一韵位。原则上，属于同一韵位的不同音值可以用同一个抽象的语音符号来标记。

戴（2008）的韵母表显然不符合分布分析的对立原则。他将“i、i/ei、i/øi”合并为一个韵母，这样的“韵母”虽然在上声调出现的都是 i，但在其他调类，所管字的韵母音值既有 i，也有 ei 或 øi，这三种音值各有一批专属的语素，例如：

施	诗	舒	池	迟	除	计	记	贵
si^1	sei^1	$søi^1$	ti^2	tei^2	$tøi^2$	ki^5	kei^5	$køi^5$

三种音值既不能互相自由替换，也不能根据环境条件预测该出现的是哪一种，它们显然不能放在同一个音系单位内，用同样的符号来标记。所以说，戴氏的福安话 40 韵

母表不能成立。

那么，将"i"、"i/ei"、"i/øi"分析成各自独立的韵母，即叶（2007）的福安韵母表可行吗？这个问题可以归结为，同一个上声调的"i"，能否根据其不同的历时背景分裂成三个音系单位？答案也是否定的。[9]

在汉语方言的音系分析中，某些特殊情况下需要将同一个音素分别配入不同音位。例如北京话的[ɛ]，在[iɛ]、[yɛ]中属于/e/音位，在[iɛn]中属于/a/音位。这样的分析是基于共时组合条件的差别，也符合其历时背景。根据音位分析的"双向单一性原则"，相同组合条件下出现的相同的韵母音值只能属于同一个韵位。福州话的每个韵位的本韵与变韵互补分布在不同的调类，即与不同的声调组合，不会发生混淆。但福安话同一个上声调的"i"，在共时平面上没有音值上的差异，没有语音环境的差异（例如"紫、水、址"都读 tsi3 ），就不能人为地切割为 3 份，分别配入不同的韵母。

浙江温岭话同一个单字调值分析为阳平和阳去两种调位，符合其历时背景，也与周边其他吴语方言协调，但最关键的依据还是这两类字的连读变调规律不同，共时平面上的连读变调规则支持这种分析。[10] 系统分析只能放在共时平面上进行，照顾历时背景不能喧宾夺主，不能取代共时分析。那么，福安话中是否也有这样的连读音变规则支持叶（2007）的分析呢？

上一节我们着重区分了形成福安话韵母目前这个面貌的两类音变：特殊调值推动的变韵音变和系统自调谐的自然音变。前者在共时的连读音变规则中得到反映，后者虽在音变顺序上后发，但在共时的连读音变中了无痕迹。"i"韵母的三种来源叠合就是由这样的自然音变造成的结果，这种变化是"范性"的，不可逆的，现在的共时平面上找不到任何区分的痕迹，就像北京话的"之、脂、支"三源合一一样，没有理由把它拆分到三个不同的韵母中去。

福安话韵母系统与福州话的不同之处就在于，福州话的变韵既是历时音变的结果，又是现在共时音系的规则；而福安话的变韵导致系统启动自调谐机制来恢复平衡，这一连串后续的自然音变已经阻断了变韵与现在的共时平面之间的联系。所以按韵位归纳韵母系统的 A 方案已经无法施用于福安话，只能采用 B 方案。更何况，既然后续的自然音变已经大体上填平了福安话音节表上的空格，恢复了系统平衡，B 方案已经具备合理性。叶（2007）的韵母表无法减少韵母总数的原因正在于此。

上述分析说明了：用归纳"韵位"的办法来分析韵母系统的 A 方案适用于福州话以及福州周边的侯官片方言，但没必要也不可能施用于福安话，以及情况与福安话相似的其他福宁片方言。合理的音系分析总是能在两个方面得到验证：在符合对立原则的基础上，它能最经济、简洁地描写说明音系活动，并且它总是能与母语者的语感一致。流传了一百多年的福安方言传统韵书《安腔戚林八音》以及上世纪30年代编成的《七音字汇》，还有十多年前由地方政府组织编写的《福安方言志》、《周宁方言志》等都一贯地用B方案分析韵母系统，颇能说明这一点。

　　本文针对闽东方言南北两片韵母系统处理方案的讨论，重申了音系分析的共时原则。

附　注

[1]《戚林八音》的音值构拟根据陈泽平（1984）。

[2] "au" 韵有 "找、吵、咬、挠" 4个上声字，前3个都另有白读音，文读大概是后来从外方言借入的。

[3] 关于福安话辅音韵尾的历史情况可以参阅马重奇（2001），本文讨论福安话韵母系统的变化时，参照目前的韵母系统，把元音结构相同的阳声韵和入声韵都合并起来，集中讨论元音结构的变化。

[4] 本文用 "→" 表示变韵音变，用 ">" 表示自然音变。

[5] 秋谷裕幸先生告诉我，西班牙传教士编纂的福安方言词典《班华字典》中还有独立的 yi 韵母，该韵基本上只有上声字。

[6]《简易识字七音字汇》反映二十世纪早期福安方言字音面貌，这两个韵的罗马字标音就是 "ie" 和 "uo"。

[7] 自然数表示调类：阴平1、阳平2、上声3、阴去5、阳去6。

[8] 原文 "ik、uk" 排在甲栏，本文移到乙栏，这个移动应该符合原作者的本意。

[9] 本文作者对叶（2007）负有指导责任，以下的讨论也是自我批评。

[10] 李荣《温岭方言的连读变调》，《方言》1979年01期。

参考文献

包智明、侍建国、许德宝（1997）《生成音系学理论及其应用（第二版）》，北京：中国社会科学出版社。

曹志耘（2009）汉语方言中的调值分韵现象，《中国语文》第2期。

陈泽平（1984）福州话的韵母结构及其演变模式，《语言学论丛》第十三辑，北京：商务印书馆。

陈泽平（1998）《福州方言研究》，福州：福建人民出版社。

戴黎刚（2007）闽东周宁话的变韵及其性质，《"中研院"历史语言研究所集刊》78-3。

戴黎刚（2008）闽东福安话的变韵，《中国语文》第3期。

李荣（1979）温岭方言的连读变调，《方言》第 1 期。

马重奇（2001）福建福安方言韵书《安腔八音》，《方言》第 1 期。

平山久雄（1998）汉语福州方言の声调と"变韵"，《アジア・アフリヵ文法研究》27。

秋谷裕幸（2010）《闽东区福宁片四县市方言音韵研究》，福州：福建人民出版社。

秋谷裕幸（2008）《闽东语福宁方言群の调查研究》，爱媛大学（平成 20 年）研究成果报告书。

沙平（1999）福建省宁德方言同音字汇，《方言》第 4 期。

王福堂（2005）《汉语方言语音的音变和层次（修订版）》，北京：语文出版社。

王理嘉（1991）《音系学基础》，北京：语文出版社。

叶太青（2007）《闽东北片方言语音研究》，福建师范大学博士学位论文。

远藤光晓（1994）元音与声调，《中国境内语言暨语言学》2。

福建省福安市地方志编撰委员会（1999）《福安市志》，北京：方志出版社。

Norman, Jerry (1977-78) A Preliminary Report on the Dialects of Mindong, *Monumenta Serica*, 33.

（本文发表于《中国语文》2012 年第 1 期，第 58—67 页）

潮州方言百余年来韵母演变的研究 *

徐宇航

提要 潮州方言韵母在百余年间经历了"鼻音、塞音韵尾种类减少""uan/uat 韵母主要元音高化"和"ŋ韵母搭配规则变更"三类主要变化。以往学者只留意到"鼻音、塞音韵尾种类减少"特征。本文则借 19 世纪中到 20 世纪初罗马字语料与方言韵书，全面讨论潮州方言韵母的演变。研究发现，潮州方言百余年间除了 -n > -ŋ/-t > -k 演变，还有 a > ɛ 规则的存在。ŋ韵母在百余年间也发生了 ŋ > uŋ/ŋ > ɯŋ 音变，这种音变与ŋ韵母和声母的"搭配规则变更"相关。

关键词 潮州方言　韵母　历时演变　罗马字语料　方言韵书

1. 引言

本文通过 19 世纪欧美传教士、汉学家编写的罗马字潮州方言语料[1]，以及 20 世纪初潮籍文人所编写的方言韵书，考察潮州方言韵母的历时演变。19 世纪的罗马字语料侧重方言实际音值的记录，20 世纪的方言韵书有强烈的字书分类观念，两者相互补充，为考察方言的历时演变提供宝贵线索。据研究，19 世纪罗马字语料的基本音系为潮州府城音系（徐宇航 2013：223—244），故本文讨论之潮州方言指潮州府城（今潮州市区）方言。比较 19 世纪与今天的潮州方言，声母与单字调系统变化甚微，韵母则在百余年间有较大演变。潮州方言百余年来韵母的演变包括"鼻音、塞音韵尾种类减少""uan/uat 韵母主要元音高化"和"ŋ韵母搭配规则变更"。以往学者只留意到潮州方言"鼻音、塞音韵尾种类减少"特征。本文则借 19 世纪中期到 20 世纪初罗马字语料与方言韵书的记录，全面讨论潮州方言韵母的演变。

---

* 本文为社科基金重大项目"海外珍藏汉语文献与南方明清汉语研究"（12&ZD178）与社科基金重点项目"粤、闽、客诸方言地理信息系统建设与研究"（13AYY001）子项目"潮州地区方言的地理语言学研究"（14FZ13）阶段性成果。初稿曾于 2014 年"海外珍藏汉语文献与南方明清汉语研究"讨论会发表，庄初升教授、李炜教授提出宝贵意见，特此致谢。《语言学论丛》匿名评审专家审稿细致、意见精湛，一并致谢，亦感谢厦门大学硕士研究生张坚对本文提出修改意见。文章任何疏漏，概由笔者负责。

2．鼻音、塞音韵尾种类减少

根据罗马字语料的记录，19 世纪潮州方言存在 -m/-p、-n/-t、-ŋ/-k 三套鼻音、塞音韵尾，今天的潮州方言只见 -m/-p、-ŋ/-k，不见 -n/-t，-n/-t 归入 -ŋ/-k，鼻音、塞音韵尾系统从"三分"走向"二分"。此音系变化早为前贤所发现，如李竹青、李如龙（1994：181—194）、张屏生（1994：195—222）、林伦伦（2005：74—80）等已有精彩描写。-n/-t 归入 -ŋ/-k，实现韵尾系统的合并，实则为音变规则"-n > -ŋ/-t > -k"的实现。吴芳（2009/2013：106—123）、徐宇航（2012：136）在上述论文的基础上，通过对罗马字语料，特别是对传教士 Fielde 出版于 1878 和 1883 的两本语料的考察后得出，"-n > -ŋ/-t > -k"演变以 an/at 类为先。

本文更细致考察 Fielde 所编 *First Lessons in the Swatow Dialect* 和 *A Pronouncing and Defining Dictionary of the Swatow Dialect Arranged according to Syllables and Tones* 两本语料后，对上述结论有以下的补充："-n > -ŋ/-t > -k"演变以 an/at 类为先，只是对部分现象的描述。我们发现，潮州方言以 a 为主元音带 -n/-t 韵尾的韵母，包括 an/at，以及在潮州府城相当罕见、在汕头港沿岸极为常见的 uan/uat，皆已开始"-n > -ŋ/-t > -k"演变。除了 an/at，主元音同样是 a 的合口三等字"宣""圈""萱""喧"在 Fielde（1883）、Duffus（1883）中也存在 uang 的记录[2]。因此，率先实现"-n > -ŋ/-t > -k"音变的音类包括 an/at，但不限于 an/at，主元音为 a 的音节皆可能参与这个演变，即规则"-n > -ŋ/-t > -k"可拓展为"-n > -ŋ/a_""-t > -k/a_[3]"。细化这个规则的重要性在于突出主元音 a 对"-n > -ŋ/-t > -k"演变的制约作用，这种制约作用对下文讨论"uan/uat 韵母主要元音高化"有重要意义。

3．uan/uat 韵母主要元音高化

如上文所言，揭示"-n > -ŋ/-t > -k"演变开端的语料主要是 Fielde（1878）和 Fielde（1883）。然而在这两本语料中也出现了 wn/wt 韵母（主要为山摄合口字读音），这两种韵母在同时代的其他语料记为 uan(wan) 和 uat(wat)。上文认为 Fielde（1878）和 Fielde（1883）记音细致，捕捉到"-n > -ŋ/-t > -k"演变的先驱，是同类语料中的翘楚。如此，对于 Fielde（1878）和 Fielde（1883）所记的 wn/wt 韵母，也须特别对待。根据研究（徐宇航 2012），本文所参考的 10 本 19 世纪潮州方言罗马字语料，虽基础音系皆为潮州府城方言音系，但在具体音类的记录、描写上，基本可分为两个系

列，一为具有强烈府城意识，音类记录、描写尽力贴近府城方言的语料，包括 Fielde（1878）和 Fielde（1883）；一为因方言协助人等因素，而侧重描写汕头港沿岸方言的语料，包括 Goddard（1883）、Duffus（1883）、Ashmore（1884）、Lim（1886）、Gibson（1886）、Matthew（1889）、Genesis（1896）、Steele（1924）。我们认为，Fielde（1878）和 Fielde（1883）所记录的 wn/wt 韵母，正是府城方言异于汕头港沿岸方言的主要特征，wn/wt 不应简单等同 uan/uat。理由有二：第一，在 Fielde（1878）和 Fielde（1883）中除了 wn/wt 类语音，也存在以 uan/uat 中 ua 字母记录语音的情况。如山摄合口末韵字"末""活"记为 uah，咸摄合口凡韵字"犯"记为 uam，宕摄开口阳韵字"装"的文读音、合口唐韵字"光"的文读音，均记为 uang。既然 Fielde（1878）和 Fielde（1883）仍有 ua 类的记音，如果 wn/wt 完全等同 uan/uat，语料没有理由舍近求远，选择两套符号记录完全一致的读音。第二，在 Fielde（1878）的音系说明中，我们找到对符号 w 的论述。Fielde（1878）以英文单词 one 中的 o 描写 w 的读音[4]，one 读 wʌn，此间的 o，大致相当于 wʌ 读音。换言之，语料以 wʌ 描写符号 w，其中的元音 ʌ，舌位比 a 高，较接近 ε（徐宇航 2013：223—244）。基于此，我们认为 wn/wt 类读音，不完全等同 uan/uat。

如此，记音细致的 Fielde（1878）和 Fielde（1883）又为我们展现了潮州方言的另一项音变：uan/uat 主元音高化，演变规则为：a > ε/u_n；a > ε/u_t。此演变形成今天潮州府城方言山摄合口字读 uεŋ/uεk，异于汕头、澄海、揭阳等地的 uaŋ/uak 韵母。不过，Fielde 的记音反映当时这一对韵母只演变为近似 uʌn/uʌt，尚未完全演变为 uεn/uεt。

同时，由于贴近潮州府城方言的 Fielde（1878）和 Fielde（1883）收录 wn/wt，侧重描写汕头港沿岸方言的其他语料则有 uan/uat、uang/uak 的描写区别，如"圈"字在 Fielde（1883）中有 khwn（第 329 页）和 khuang（第 320 页）两种记录，而在其他语料中则有 uan（Gibson 1886：22；Steele 1924：123）、uang（Lim 1886：25）两种记录，可知，wn 已然存在之时，uan 和 uaŋ 还处于动摇状态。由此可见，uan/uat 韵母主要元音高化与鼻音、塞音韵尾演变是两项起始时间有异，独立进行，但相互影响的音变。百余年间潮州方言产生"a > ε/u_n；a > ε/u_t"与"-n > -ŋ/a_；-t > -k/a_"演变，且"a > ε/u_n；a > ε/u_t"早于[5]"-n > -ŋ/a_；-t > -k/a_"。由于"-n > -ŋ/-t > -k"从主元音为 a 的音节开始，参与"a > ε/u_n；a > ε/u_t"音变的山摄合口字因主元音的高化，延缓了其"-n > -ŋ/-t > -k"演变的时间。也因此，在 Fielde（1878）和 Fielde（1883）中，我们没有找到任何 wng/wk 记录。

4. 搭配规则变更

潮州方言百余年来韵母系统经历"uan/uat 主要元音高化""鼻音、塞音韵尾种类减少"之外，还有另外一项重要的演变：ŋ 韵母音节在声母与韵母搭配规则上的变更。吴瑞文、林英津（2007：1—20）、林晴（2012：16—20）曾提及这项音变，但尚未详述该音变原理及过程。ŋ 韵母存在及其搭配规则在潮汕地区具有内部差异，也是潮汕方言与福建等地闽南方言的重要音值差别，具有区域特征，存在讨论价值。本文借罗马字语料与方言韵书，梳理这项音变。

19 世纪罗马字语料记录了诸多 ŋ 韵母音节，这些音节主要分布在山、臻、宕、江摄等阳声韵摄。在有层次叠加的音类中，ŋ 为白读层韵母。由传教士 John Campbell Gibson（1849—1919）编写的语料 *A Swatow Index of the Syllabic Dictionary of Chinese by S. Wells Williams, of Amoy by Carstairs Douglas*（《卫三畏《汉英拼音字典》及杜嘉德《厦门方言字典》之汕头方言索引》）前言部分还特别指出，ŋ 韵母与带主元音的 ɯŋ 不同："潮州方言的 m，n 和 ng 可不带元音单独组成音节，也可与声母 h 相连，发成一个类似呼气（murmur）的音节，如 hm，hngh。在这种音节中，没有出现有响度的元音，要与英语中 hung 和 sung 区别开"[6]。比较语料记录与今天潮州方言可知，ŋ 韵母音节与声母搭配的类型和规则在百余年间发生变化。我们统计语料记录，比较 19 世纪与今天的 ŋ 韵母，结果如表 1 所示。

表 1　潮州方言 ŋ 韵母在 19 世纪与 21 世纪的分布 [7]

韵目	19 世纪		21 世纪		
	ŋ	uŋ	ŋ	ɯŋ(ɤŋ/əŋ)[8]	uŋ
桓 (山合一)	断缎段卵钻酸算蒜管			断缎段卵钻酸算蒜管	
仙 (山开三)	全转传砖穿软卷			全转传砖穿软卷	
元 (山合三)	饭晚劝园远		园远	劝	饭晚
魂 (臻合一)	门村本(白)顿(白)孙(白)损(白)昏(白)	本(文)顿(文)孙(文)损(文)昏(文)	昏(白)	村顿(白)孙(白)损(白)	门本顿(文)孙(文)损(文)昏(文)
文 (臻合三)	问(白)	问(文)			问
唐 (宕开一)	汤烫当堂唐塘糖郎葬仓桑钢缸糠			汤烫当堂唐塘糖郎葬仓桑钢缸糠	

（续表）

韵目	19 世纪		21 世纪		
	ŋ̍	un	ŋ̍	ɯŋ(ɤŋ/əŋ)[8]	uŋ
唐(宕合一)	光荒广黄		荒黄	光广	
阳(宕合三)	方(地～)		方(地～)		
江(江开二)	扛肛		扛肛		
麻(假开二)	要		要		
鱼(遇合三)	女		女		
脂(止开三)	指		指		

4.1 ŋ̍韵母的分布与演变规则

观察表 1 可知，19 世纪 ŋ̍韵母分布范围广，辖字多，声母种类丰富，声调分布齐全。同时，ŋ̍韵母在百余年间发生了音值变迁，主要表现在 ŋ̍减少，ɯŋ、uŋ 增多。ɯŋ 为非唇音声母字演变的结果，uŋ 为唇音声母字演变的结果。由于 19 世纪 ŋ̍韵母字还涉及文白异读，文读层与白读层皆因语音演变而形成音值差异。因而讨论 ŋ̍音变时，还须梳理层次叠置夹杂语音演变所形成的音类异同。

先看 19 世纪读 ŋ̍、un，今天读 uŋ 的唇音声母字的读音演变。此类字主要分布在山摄（元韵）、臻摄（魂韵、文韵），具体涉及"饭""晚""本""门""问"等字。这些字的声母为 p（"饭""本"）和 m（"晚""门""问"），皆为唇音，其演变涉及声、韵母搭配规则变更：唇音声母字 ŋ̍韵母增生主元音 u，形成 uŋ 韵母，即：

规则：ŋ̍ > uŋ / # p、m_

须说明，如表 1 所示，19 世纪"本""问"二字有文白异读，白读韵母为 ŋ̍，文读韵母为 un，今天则只有 uŋ 韵母，没有异读现象。这是因为今天潮州方言"本""问"由 ŋ̍演变而来的 uŋ，恰好与历经韵尾演变 -n > -ŋ 的文读音 uŋ 形式一致，形成"异层同读"，也称"文白合流"[9]。由于 19 世纪不具异读的唇音声母字亦参与 ŋ̍ > uŋ 演变，而臻摄其他声母字今天仍保持 ɯŋ、uŋ 异读，因此唇音声母字读 uŋ，可能源于 ŋ̍，也可能源于 un，层次差异因语音演变而消失。

与唇音声母字并行的另一种音变则是 19 世纪的 ŋ̍韵母到今天 ɯŋ 韵母的演变。这种演变也涉及声、韵母搭配规则的演变。19 世纪能与 ŋ̍韵母搭配的声母类型众多，潮州方言除去唇音的 14 个声母，除了 l、dz、ŋ、g 我们尚未在语料中找到例字外，其他

10 个声母，包括 t、th、n、ts、tsh、s、k、kh、h、Ø[10]，皆能与 ŋ 搭配组成音节。这种 ŋ 韵母能与多种声母组合成音节的规则，在百余年间发生了演变。今天的潮州方言 ŋ 韵母与声母的组合限制增强，除了 h、Ø 声母能与 ŋ 组合外，其他声母皆无法与 ŋ 直接组合成音节。当其他声母需要与 ŋ 组合时，音节结构就会发生演变，形成 ɯŋ 韵母。该演变规则可表述为：

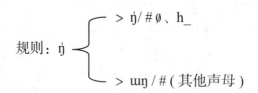

规则：ŋ
> ŋ/ # Ø、h_

> ɯŋ / #（其他声母）

上述演变规则在潮州方言表现得非常彻底，除 h、Ø 声母音节，其他 19 世纪读 ŋ 韵母音节皆发生 ŋ > ɯŋ 音变，转读 ɯŋ。形成今天潮州方言部分山、臻摄字与宕、江摄字韵母合流的现象。

同时，规则"ŋ > ŋ/ # Ø、h_；ŋ > ɯŋ/ #（其他声母）"的实现也影响了潮州方言其他音节的分布。观察 19 世纪罗马字语料我们发现，19 世纪潮州方言臻摄痕韵、真韵、殷韵的晓影系主要读音为 ɯn。由于潮州方言发生"-n > -ŋ"韵尾系统改变，上述 19 世纪读 ɯn 韵母的臻摄字，今天应读 ɯŋ。不过，由于规则"ŋ > ŋ/ # Ø、h_；ŋ > ɯŋ/ #（其他声母）"的存在，19 世纪读 ɯn 的臻摄字，并不完全演变为 ɯŋ，而是依声韵母搭配规则，进行音类重新组合。ɯn 韵母字的历史演变如表 2 所示。

表 2　潮州方言痕、真、殷韵晓影系字在 19 世纪与 21 世纪的分布

韵目	19 世纪	21 世纪	
	ɯn	ɯŋ	ŋ
痕（臻开一）	跟根恳垦龈很恨恩	跟根恳垦龈很恨	恩
真（臻开三）	巾仅银	巾仅银	
殷（臻开三）	斤筋瑾勤芹近欣隐	斤筋瑾勤芹近	欣隐

如表 2 所示，潮州方言百余年来"增生"了新的 ŋ 韵母，"欣""恩""隐"并不遵循"-n > -ŋ"规则，由 ɯn 演变为 ɯŋ。而是受"ŋ > ŋ/ # Ø、h_；ŋ > ɯŋ/ #（其他声母）"制约，先实现 ɯn > ɯŋ，再根据声、韵母搭配规则，h、Ø 声母字回归 ŋ 读音，即"ɯŋ > ŋ/ # Ø、h_"。

这种 ŋ̍ 韵母增生现象在潮汕地区内部存在差异。潮州府城受 "ɯŋ > ŋ̍/ # Ø、h_" 规则影响最深，h、Ø 声母后的 ɯŋ 韵母多转读 ŋ̍ [11]。其他地区受此规则影响的程度则有区别。我们将 "欣""恩""隐" 在其他潮汕方言点的读音情况做了统计，结果如下。

表 3　"欣""恩""隐" 在潮汕方言的韵母读音 [12]

	潮州	登塘	凤塘	金石	庵埠	澄海	汕头	泰国潮州话
ŋ̍	欣恩隐	欣恩	欣					
ɯŋ			隐	恩隐	欣恩隐	欣恩隐	欣恩隐	欣恩隐

表 3 登塘、凤塘位于潮州府城西面，受潮州方言影响，部分实现了"ɯŋ > ŋ̍/ # Ø、h_"规则。金石、庵埠位于潮州南面，与汕头距离较近，澄海更是归汕头管辖，其方言特点受汕头影响甚于潮州，没有实现"ɯŋ > ŋ̍/ # Ø、h_"规则。海外潮州方言亦未受该规则影响。可见，"ɯŋ > ŋ̍/ # Ø、h_"是 ŋ̍ 韵母历时演变后依演变条件重新匹配的晚近规则，始于潮州府城，波及周边地区，是府城方言与周边方言语音差异的体现。

4.2　ŋ̍ 韵母历时音变的动因探究

4.2.1　潮州方言与福建等地闽方言 ŋ̍ 韵母演变差异解释

4.2.1.1　差异解释

在语音的历时演变中，音变规则因现实语言的验证而为必然，音变动因则只是一种解释。然而，有了语音规则，人们总会关心音变动因何在。事实上，语言演变的制约因素极为复杂，包括语言自身因素，亦包括非语言因素。我们考察音变动因，主要着力与语言自身相关的原因。因此，要让音变动因具有必然性，同样须在现实语言、语料中找证据。具体到 ŋ̍ 韵母历时音变，潮州方言 ŋ̍ 韵母在百余年间主要有从 ŋ̍ 向 uŋ 和从 ŋ̍ 向 ɯŋ 两种演变。与潮州方言临近的潮汕其他方言，如汕头、揭阳方言，也实现 ŋ̍ > uŋ/ŋ̍ > ɯŋ 演变。然而，同样具有 ŋ̍ 韵母的福建、浙南、台湾等地闽语，却没有实现 ŋ̍ > uŋ/ŋ̍ > ɯŋ 的演变，今天仍保持诸多 ŋ̍ 韵母。因此，解释潮州方言 ŋ̍ 韵母的演变，首先要解释为何在类似的环境里，潮州方言发生 ŋ̍ > uŋ/ŋ̍ > ɯŋ 演变，福建、浙南、台湾等地闽语却没有发生平行的变化。

我们认为，潮州方言发生 ŋ̍ > uŋ/ŋ̍ > ɯŋ 演变，与百余年间发生的韵尾系统演变 -n > -ŋ 关系密切，是韵尾系统演变之后，音系中存在元音空间位置相近的 ŋ̍、uŋ、ɯŋ 韵母，彼此相互感染、合并的结果。至于为何主流音变是从 ŋ̍ 到 uŋ/ɯŋ，而非从 uŋ/ɯŋ

到 ŋ，则与汉语主流音系结构是 (C)V(C)[13] 相关，即"结构模式会制约音位的变化，使之尽可能地维持结构模式的要求"[14] 之体现。如此，ŋ > uŋ/ŋ > ɯŋ 演变的演变动因可归结为两点。第一，韵尾系统 -n > -ŋ 的演变；第二，音系中存在与 ŋ 元音空间位置较为接近的 uŋ、ɯŋ（包括由 -n > -ŋ 演变所形成与音系中原有的韵母）。我们以这两条演变动因检测与潮州方言存在同一批 ŋ 韵母的福建、浙南、台湾等地闽语，以此验证我们对潮州方言 ŋ > uŋ/ŋ > ɯŋ 演变动因的预测。

4.2.1.2 同类方言论证

要证明上述预测，我们必须证明，没有发生 ŋ > uŋ/ŋ > ɯŋ 演变的福建等地闽语，韵尾系统没有发生 -n > -ŋ 演变，且这些方言中亦无与 ŋ 韵母元音空间位置接近的 uŋ、ɯŋ 存在。据此思路，我们检索"中国五省及东南亚闽方言调查"项目成果。在乐东、厦门、大田、宁德、寿宁、尤溪、平南、建瓯、建阳、惠东、揭阳、文昌、永安、汕头、沙县、泉州、泰国、泰顺、海丰、海口、海康、漳州、潮阳、电白、石陂、福安、福州、福鼎、紫湖、苍南、莆田、菲律宾、隆都、马来西亚、鹿港、龙岩这 36 个闽语点中，剔除潮汕方言[15] 和没有与潮州方言共存 ŋ 韵母的方言，选取与潮州方言基本共存同一批 ŋ 韵母的厦门、泉州、苍南、菲律宾（泉州）、鹿港方言，及仅在宕、江等摄与潮州方言部分共存 ŋ 韵母的大田、漳州方言，另加入同样具有 ŋ 韵母的漳平永福方言[16]，对这些方言的韵尾变化情况与有无 uŋ、ɯŋ 做穷尽式统计，结果如下。

表 4　福建、浙南、台湾等地闽语韵尾变化与 uŋ、ɯŋ 韵母分布

	厦门	泉州	苍南	菲律宾（泉州）	鹿港	漳平	大田	漳州
-n > -ŋ	无	无	无	无	无	无	有	无
uŋ	无	无	无	无	无	无	无	无
ɯŋ	无	无	无	无	无	无	无	无

表 4 韵尾变化 -n > -ŋ 与 uŋ 形成一套条件，制约唇音声母 ŋ 的演变，-n > -ŋ 与 ɯŋ 形成另一套条件，制约非唇音声母 ŋ 的演变，uŋ 与 ɯŋ 平行存在，彼此无蕴涵关系。从表 4 的统计数据可知，与潮州方言共存 / 部分共存 ŋ 韵母，并没有发生 ŋ > uŋ/ŋ > ɯŋ 演变的福建等地闽语，皆不存在 uŋ（唇音声母字）、ɯŋ（非唇音声母字）韵母。同时，绝大多数方言也没有发生 -n > -ŋ 演变。可见，潮汕方言的 ŋ > uŋ/ŋ > ɯŋ 音变，与韵尾系统变迁、因元音空间位置接近而合并的现象，关系密切。

4.2.2 潮州方言 ŋ 韵母演变音理解释

4.2.2.1 音理解释

上述对潮州方言与福建等地闽方言 ŋ 韵母演变差异的解释，实为类比法论证 ŋ 韵母演变与韵尾系统及语音相似的关系。然而，ŋ 韵母因搭配规则演变而向 uŋ、ɯŋ 演变，在音变原理存在可能，则能为该演变现象的发生提供更实质的解释。我们认为，ŋ > uŋ/ŋ > ɯŋ 演变的动力，来自发音部位靠前的声母与发音部位靠后韵母拼合时发音器官运动的要求。在 ŋ 音节中，由于 ŋ 独立充当音节韵母，具有元音性质。这个相当于元音的软腭鼻音 ŋ，类似一个舌位极高的后元音。此时，如须与发音部位靠前的声母拼合，从声母到韵母间，易产生一个舌位动程，正是这种舌位动程，拉动了 ŋ 韵母音节的演变。这种演变将鼻音 ŋ 从音节韵母调整为韵尾，在声母与 ŋ 之间增生一个承载舌位动程的元音，并将音节调整为主流音系结构 CVC。在增生元音的选择上，与 ŋ 发音部位（即上述元音空间）接近的元音具有优先权。潮州方言音系中存在舌位偏后的高元音 u、ɯ，它们与鼻音韵尾 -ŋ 在发音部位上具有协同性，加之因韵尾演化，音系中已有 uŋ、ɯŋ 韵母，故 u、ɯ 成为 ŋ 演变的选择，形成 ŋ > uŋ/ŋ > ɯŋ。

4.2.2.2 语料证据

如果上述音变原理是 ŋ 韵母历时演变的动因，则须证明以下两个推断。第一，在声母与韵母搭配中，具有与 ŋ 韵母发音部位接近的舌面后、喉音声母音节，最稳固，最不容易演变。第二，与 ŋ 韵母发音部位距离最远的唇音、舌尖前声母音节，最容易演变，应为演变的先驱。与 ŋ 韵母发音部位接近的声母音节最稳固的推断，实为上述"ŋ > ŋ/ # Ø、h_"的表现，即：今天的潮州方言，只有喉音声母 h，带喉塞 ʔ 的零声母字保持 ŋ 韵母。而与 ŋ 韵母发音部位距离最远的唇音、舌尖前声母音节，最容易演变，则须在历史语料中找证据。

19 世纪罗马字语料展现了潮州方言丰富的 ŋ 韵母，今天潮州方言共时表现则告知 ŋ 韵母演变的终点：uŋ、ɯŋ。在起点与终点之间，我们需要更多的材料，才能获悉何种音节最先变化。此时，20 世纪初的方言韵书给我们新的启示。《潮声十五音》和《潮语十五音》是 20 世纪初潮籍文人编写的两部反映潮汕地区方言音系的韵书，《潮声十五音》编写年代早于《潮语十五音》，两部韵书关系密切。《潮语十五音》"依《潮声十五音》删繁补简……字数较《潮声十五音》增十之二三"[17]，据相关研究[18]，由于《潮语十五音》与《潮声十五音》的承袭关系，它们在音系上表现出了高度一致，两部韵书具有相同的声母、声调描写。不过，两部韵书在韵母描写和字音归类上，却存在差异。这种差异恰好为我们论证 ŋ 韵母的历时演变提供了重要线索。

首先看唇音声母字 ŋ > uŋ 的演变。从发音部位考量，唇音声母发音部位为双唇，

与 ŋ 韵母发音部位距离最远。要证明上文基于音变原理的推断，唇音声母字应为最先演变的音类。这种演变在《潮声十五音》和《潮语十五音》可找到证据。由于《潮声十五音》的"扛""钩"韵，《潮语十五音》的"扛"韵皆既收山摄字，也收宕摄字（详见下文表6），可推断两本韵书编写时，潮州方言已发生 -n > -ŋ/-t > -k 音变，音系中仅有 -ŋ/-k 韵尾，没有 -n/-t 韵尾。两部韵书"扛"韵读 ŋ/uɯ[19]，"君"韵读 uŋ。因此，唇音声母 ŋ 发生 ŋ > uŋ 演变，未变时归"扛"韵，演变后归"君"韵。以下观察唇音声母字"饭""本""晚""门""问"在两部韵书中的归类。

表5　唇音声母字在《潮声十五音》与《潮语十五音》的归类

		饭	本	晚	门	问
《潮声十五音》	扛 (ŋ)	有	有	有	有	有
	君 (uŋ)	有	有	无	无	无
《潮语十五音》	扛 (uɯ)	无	无	无	无	无
	君 (uŋ)	有	有	有	有	有

表5中"有"表示此韵收该字，"无"表示该韵未收此字。这种字音归类清晰展示了唇音声母 ŋ 音节的历时演变情况。从表5可见，在《潮声十五音》时代，读 p 声母的"饭""本"二字已有 ŋ、uŋ 两读，既出现在"扛"韵，也出现在"君"韵，这种现象展现了 ŋ > uŋ 演变的两可阶段[20]。此时，读 m 声母的"晚""门""问"尚未发生 ŋ > uŋ 演变，只出现在"扛"韵。到了《潮语十五音》时代，"饭""本""晚""门""问"各字皆已发生 ŋ > uŋ 演变，全部归"君"韵，不再出现在"扛"韵，与今天的潮州话完全一致。这种字音归类的区别，刚好显示了唇音声母 ŋ 音节从 ŋ 到 ŋ、uŋ 两可，再到只读 uŋ，不读 ŋ 的过程，也论证了 ŋ 韵母演变以唇音声母 p 为先驱的语音事实，符合上文"与 ŋ 韵母发音部位距离最远的唇音、舌尖前声母音节，最容易演变"的推断。

再看非唇音声母字 ŋ > uɯ 的演变。如上文所言，《潮声十五音》和《潮语十五音》声母、声调描写一致的同时，在韵母描写上存在差异。其中，《潮声十五音》比《潮语十五音》多了"钩"韵。《潮声十五音》有"扛""钩"两韵，《潮语十五音》则仅有"扛"韵，没有"钩"韵。《潮声十五音》中的"钩"韵字，在《潮语十五音》中归"扛"韵，"扛""钩"两韵无别。《潮声十五音》与《潮语十五音》"扛""钩"韵收字情况如表6所示。

表 6 《潮声十五音》与《潮语十五音》"扛""钩"韵收字 [21]

	扛韵 (ŋ)	钩韵 (ɯŋ)
《潮声十五音》	饭段缎状问郎唐**塘长堂**肠胀糖餹黄门们床牀园卵丈断远贯鑶劝当脱葬钻算蒜剌伙	钩均觔斤根筋巾神跟肋恩侃欣侏掀忻炘勲燻薰纁熏勋殷愍轩靬仚近壎袄谨瑾仅槿恳垦龈隐尹很乞吃仡纥讫迄勤憨芹**塘长堂**银垠狺断近恨艮觐
《潮语十五音》	扛韵 (ɯŋ)	
《潮语十五音》	女软郎卵斤觔均光缸釭扛跟巾筋根卷捲婘睠槿仅谨瑾觐贯鑶艮近康穄粇糠恳垦劝乞芹勤憨当**塘长堂**溏唐胀肠断丈镭汤烫脱档餹糖砖庄莊樟脏臟装妆粧攒钻葬状酸媛骦霜桑礵孙丧耍算蒜甗恩侃隐尹仡纥讫迄吃银狺断龈仓舱村疮剌伙床牀欣侏掀忻炘勲燻薰纁熏勋殷轩靬昕愍壎袄呍很甀恨	

我们认为，从《潮声十五音》的"扛""钩"有别，到《潮语十五音》的"扛""钩"无别，正是 ŋ > ɯŋ 历时音变的展现。如表 6 所示，《潮声十五音》中"扛"韵辖字，多为古山、宕摄字；"钩"韵辖字，多为古臻摄字。[22] 根据音类分布规律，"扛"韵读 ŋ，"钩"韵读 ɯŋ。《潮语十五音》"扛"韵则山、臻、宕摄字兼收，应读 ɯŋ[23]。考察《潮声十五音》收字情况可知，诸多 19 世纪罗马字语料记录的 ŋ 音节收于《潮声十五音》"扛"韵的同时，"堂""塘""长"这三个在今天潮州方言中同读 tɯŋ 之字，既收于"扛"韵，也收于"钩"韵。同时出现在"扛"韵和"钩"韵的"堂""塘""长"各字，正是 ŋ 向 ɯŋ 发展的重要标志，显示了《潮声十五音》编写时代中，"扛""钩"虽有别，但已出现混同，且这种混同首先出现在读舌尖前 t 声母的"堂""塘""长"等字。这种"扛""钩"混同的趋势继续发展，体现于稍后的《潮语十五音》。因而《潮语十五音》展现"扛""钩"无别，所有"钩"韵字读归"扛"韵的语音格局。可见此时"扛"韵的 ŋ 已发展为 ɯŋ，"扛""钩"合二为一，实现 ŋ > ɯŋ 音变。

如此，罗马字语料的 ŋ、ɯŋ 之别，《潮声十五音》与《潮语十五音》"扛""钩"二韵从有别到无别，实为潮州方言 ŋ 韵母音节演变过程的写照。《潮声十五音》中读 t 声母的"堂""塘""长"各字既可归"扛"韵，又可归"钩"，显示了非唇音 ŋ 音节的历时音变，以舌尖前 t 声母字为先驱的事实。这种事实又印证了上述"与 ŋ 韵母发音部位距离最远的唇音、舌尖前声母音节，最容易演变，应为演变先驱"的推断，即：论证了音变原理对 ŋ 韵母演变的制约作用。

因此，在 ŋ 韵母的 ŋ > uŋ/ŋ > ɯŋ 演变中，发音部位靠前的声母与发音部位靠后韵母拼合时，发音器官运动的要求是其最重要的动因。在 ŋ > uŋ/ŋ > ɯŋ 演变中，与 ŋ 韵

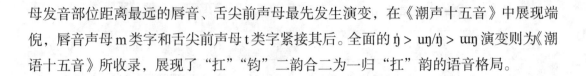

母发音部位距离最远的唇音、舌尖前声母最先发生演变，在《潮声十五音》中展现端倪，唇音声母 m 类字和舌尖前声母 t 类字紧接其后。全面的 ŋ > uŋ/ɯ > ɯŋ 演变则为《潮语十五音》所收录，展现了"扛""钩"二韵合二为一归"扛"韵的语音格局。

5. 潮州方言百余年来韵母演变规则及其次序

基于上文论述，潮州方言韵母在百余年间经历"鼻音、塞音韵尾种类减少""uan/uat 韵母主要元音高化"和"ŋ 韵母搭配规则变更"三种变化，受制于演变规则："-n > -ŋ/a_；-t > -k/a_""a > ɛ/u_n；a > ɛ/u_t""ŋ > uŋ/#p、m_；ŋ > ŋ/# Ø、h_；ŋ > ɯŋ/#（其他声母）"和"ɯŋ > ŋ/#Ø、h_"。同时，潮州方言韵母多项演变的起始时间有别：以"uan/uat 韵母主要元音高化"为先，"鼻音、塞音韵尾种类减少"其次，"ŋ 韵母搭配规则变更"最迟，即：

（1）a > ɛ/u_n；a > ɛ/u_t

（2）-n > -ŋ/a_；-t > -k/a_

（3）ŋ > uŋ/#p、m_；ŋ > ŋ/# Ø、h_；ŋ > ɯŋ/#（其他声母）

（4）ɯŋ > ŋ/# Ø、h_

规则（1）必先于（2），（2）必先于（3），（3）必先于（4）。（1）必先于（2），（2）必先于（3）可从历时语料的记录得以证实。如 19 世纪罗马字语料所示，当 wn/wt 已存在时，（2）才刚刚发生，以主元音为 a 的音节率先实现规则。而当（2）经已开始之时，ŋ 韵母仍可与多数声母搭配，规则（3）尚未产生。（3）必先于（4）可从共时语言分布和规则制约条件得以证实。从共时语言分布上讲，目前潮州府城、潮安、汕头、澄海等地方言，其韵母皆受到（3）影响，由 ŋ 走向 uŋ、ɯŋ，仅当声母为 h 或零声母时才存留 ŋ。然而，仅有潮州府城较全面实现（4），潮安部分地区，汕头、澄海则并未受影响。从规则制约条件上讲，（4）的演变条件来自（3），（3）的声、韵母搭配规则，是产生（4）的基础。故（3）必先于（4）。

6. 总结

本文借罗马字语料与方言韵书的记录，考察潮州方言韵母在百余年间的演变。研究发现，潮州方言韵母在百余年间经历了"鼻音、塞音韵尾种类减少""uan/uat 韵母主要元音高化"和"ŋ 韵母搭配规则变更"三类主要演变。"鼻音、塞音韵尾种类减少"以主元音为 a 的音节为先，部分山摄字因"uan/uat 韵母主要元音高化"延缓了其参与韵尾演变的时间。同时，ŋ韵母在百余年间发生 ŋ > uŋ/ŋ > ɯŋ 音变。这种音变受到声、韵母搭配规则制约，能为音变原理所解释，并以唇音 p 和舌尖前 t 声母字为演变先驱。ŋ韵母演变是潮州方言的自我创新，这种创新形成了潮州方言有别于漳、泉系闽南方言的读音特色，且在潮汕方言内部存在差异。

附 注

[1] 本文参考的罗马字语料有 10 本，由 19 世纪传教士、汉学家和海峡殖民地潮籍职员编写，分别是：

Fielde, Adele Marion (1878) *First Lessons in the Swatow Dialect*. Swatow: Swatow Printing Office Company.

Fielde, Adele Marion (1883) *A Pronouncing and Defining Dictionary of the Swatow Dialect Arranged according to Syllables and Tones*. Swatow: American Presbyterian Mission Press.

Duffus, William (1883) *English-Chinese Vocabulary of the Vernacular or Spoken Language of Swatow*. Swatow: English Presbyterian Mission Press.

Ashmore, William (1884) *Primary Lessons in Swatow Grammar*. Swatow: English Presbyterian Mission Press.

Lim, Hiong Seng (1886) *A Handbook of the Swatow Vernacular*. Sincapore-Printed at the Koh Yew Heanm Press.

Gibson, John Campbell (1886) *A Swatow Index of the Syllabic Dictionary of Chinese*. Swatow: English Presbyterian Mission Press.

Goddard, Josiah (1883) *A Chinese and English Vocabulary in the Tie-Chiu Dialect*. Shanghai：American Presbyterian Mission Press. 此书为第二版印刷语料，第一版于 1847 年出版。

Duffus, William and Gibson, John Campbell (1889) *Sin-Ieh Ma-Thai Hok-Im Tsu̧ Tshuan-Tsu̧(Ek-So Tie-Chiu Peh-Ue)*.Swatow: English Presbyterian Mission Press.

The author is unfound (1896)*Ku-Ieh Tshang-Si Ki Tshuan-Tsu̧*(Ek-Tso Tie-Chiu Peh-Ue). Swatow: English Presbyterian Mission Press.

Steele, John (1924) *The Swatow Syllabary with Mandarin Pronunciations*. Swatow: English Presbyterian Mission Press. 此书另版出版于 1909 年，编写年代为 19 世纪末。

语料书名虽有"汕头（Swatow）"、"潮州（Tie-Chiu）"之别，实以潮州府城方言为基础音系，参考《十九世纪的潮州方言音系》（徐宇航 2013：223—244）。语料标调类不标实际调值，故本文以调类符号标声调。

[2] "灌""宣""圈""喧"记为 uang 分别出现于 Fielde（1883：508、320、508），同时语料 Duffus（1883）也出现"宣"记为 uang 的例子，如 suang-iaⁿ（义为"宣扬"，第 73 页）。这几个字也有主元音高化音变的可能，因此 Fielde(1883)也收录它们 wn 的读法，如"圈"，

khwn（第 329 页）和 khuang（第 320 页）。但只要存在主元音未高化，保持 a 作为主元音的韵母，就有实现韵尾演变的可能。19 世纪潮州方言以 a 为主元音的带 n/t 韵尾韵母包括 an/at、uan/uat，潮州方言并无 ian/iat 韵母。同时，部分 uan/uat 在潮州府城方言已有元音高化现象（见下文分析），尚未发生元音高化的音节才保持 uan/uat。

[3] 从 19 世纪语料与今天潮州方言现状看，鼻音韵尾与塞音韵尾的具有平行演变特点，即既发生 -n > -ŋ，也发生 -t > -k 。不过，在罗马字语料中，塞音韵尾 -t > -k/a_ 规则的例子仅有"达""扎""辖"等 ak 韵母音节，并无 uat 变为 uak 的例子。这一方面因为入声韵音节较阳声韵少，另一方面因为部分 uat 韵母音节实际上在早于 19 世纪已演变为 uaʔ，这种音节不再参与 -t > -k，另有部分 uat 主元音已高化为 ɛ，不再读 uat。这里由鼻音塞音韵尾平行演变特点将 -t > -k/a_ 与 -n > -ŋ/a_ 对举，特此说明。

[4] 参考 Fielde（1878：5—6）"Sounds of the Letters"。

[5] 本文的"早于"指的是 a > ɛ/u_n；a > ɛ/u_t 规则开始的时间比 -n > -ŋ/-t > -k 早，并非指前者结束的时间比后者早，下同。

[6] 参考 Gibson（1886：13）"Introduction"。

[7] 19 世纪语料来自上述 10 本罗马字语料，21 世纪语料来自国家社会科学基金重点项目"粤、闽、客诸方言地理信息系统建设与研究"（13AYY001）子项目"潮州地区方言的地理语言学研究"（14FZ13）。潮州方言少数阴声韵读 ŋ，是 ɯ 元音演变的结果，但这种 ɯ>ŋ 早于 19 世纪经已发生。故这些由阴声韵 ɯ 演变而来的 ŋ 在 19 世纪与阳声韵音节表现一致，本文一并讨论其演变规则，特此说明。

[8] ɤŋ、əŋ 韵母与 ɯŋ 不具音位差别，下文统一以 ɯŋ 表示。

[9] 这两个术语分别来自杜佳伦（2013:409—456）和曾南逸（2013:228—236），两者异曲同工，指的都是文读音与白读音因语音变化等因素而形式一致，无法分辨。

[10] 潮州方言零声母字，实际上具有 [ʔ] 声母，作为发音的起点。

[11] 表 2 中同样读 h 声母的"很""恨"二字并没转读 ŋ 韵母，前者由于方言少用"很"，而直接模仿通语读音所致；后者如读 hŋ35 则与"远"字的白读音完全相同，因别义而没转读。不过，在调查中，发音人表示词汇"仇恨"中，"恨"可读 hŋ35，亦可读 hɯŋ35，可见规则对"恨"字也起作用。

[12] 本表潮州、登塘、凤塘、金石、庵埠方言语料来自国家社会科学基金重点项目"粤、闽、客诸方言地理信息系统建设与研究"（13AYY001）子项目"潮州地区方言的地理语言学研究"（14FZ13），其中登塘、凤塘、金石、庵埠皆属潮安地区；澄海方言语料来自林伦伦（1996：35）；汕头方言语料来自林伦伦、陈小枫（1996：60）；泰国潮州话语料来自香港政府研究资助局资助研究计划"中国五省及东南亚闽方言调查"（2002 年 3 月）。

[13] C 表示辅音声母及以辅音为韵尾的情况，V 表示元音，（）表示辅音声母、韵尾非必须。

[14] 徐通锵（1991/2008），《历史语言学》，北京：商务印书馆，183 页。

[15] 由于潮汕方言受到潮州、汕头两大首府的影响，皆实现了 ŋ > ɯŋ 演变，与其他地区闽语形成区别，故率先将其剔除。

[16] 语料来源于张振兴（1992）《漳平方言研究》，中国社会科学出版社，北京。

[17] 参考蒋儒林（1921）凡例。

[18] 陈伟达（2006）；马重奇（2008a，b）；徐宇航（2012）等。

[19] "扛"韵在《潮声十五音》读 ŋ，读 ɯŋ 是《潮语十五音》的情况，详见表6。

[20] 逻辑上，"饭""本"的 uŋ 读音亦有可能来自文读音 un 的演变。不过，19 世纪同样具有文白异读的"问"却没有在君韵出现 uŋ，可见方言韵书未必将文白读音全部记录。换言之，"饭""本"的 uŋ，可能来自 ŋ，也可能来自 un。但比较"问"的记录，uŋ 由 ŋ 演变而来的概率更大。

[21] 我们统计两本韵书的收字时，剔除罕见方言字，集中表述与本文论述相关的例字。

[22] 由于 19 世纪山、臻摄字读 -n/-t 韵尾，宕、江、曾、梗、通摄字多读 -ŋ/-k 韵尾。同时，这些韵摄中都有 ŋ 类音节的存在。因此，要将"扛""钩"有别作为 ŋ 与非 ŋ 音节区别的证据，逻辑上我们还须排除"扛""钩"有别是韵尾之别。理由非常简单。先为"扛"韵同时辖山、宕摄字，19 世纪山摄读 -n/-t 韵尾，宕摄读 -ŋ/-k 韵尾。同一韵辖两种不同韵尾字尤为不合理，只能推断当时的韵尾合并已经完成。再则在"钩"韵辖字中存在"堂""塘""长"等字，这些字无论在 19 世纪语料中，还是在今天的潮州方言中，皆读 ŋ 或 -ŋ，无 -n 韵尾读音。"钩"韵既然能收完全读 -ŋ/ŋ 类的读音，我们只能推论，当时的潮州方言已完成"-n > -ŋ"音变，音系中仅有 -ŋ，没有 -n，"钩"韵所收音节，非 -n 韵尾音节。因而"扛""钩"之别，不可能是韵尾之别，只能是 ŋ 与非 ŋ 音节的区别。

[23] 从逻辑上讲，由于《潮语十五音》已发生 ŋ > uŋ/ŋ > ɯŋ 演变，零声母、h 声母后的非唇音声母字仍读 ŋ，应再归一类。然而该韵书取巧，并未收"黄""园"等零声母、h 声母字，故没有再设一类韵母。

参考文献

陈伟达（2006）《〈潮语十五音〉音系研究》，福建师范大学硕士学位论文。

杜佳伦（2013）闽语古全浊声类的层次分析，《语言暨语言学》第 14（2）期。

蒋儒林（1921）《潮语十五音》，香港：香港陈湘记书局。

李竹青、李如龙(1994)潮州方言语音的演变，《潮州学国际研讨会论文集》（上册），郑良树主编，广州：暨南大学出版社。

林伦伦（1996）《澄海方言研究》，汕头：汕头大学出版社。

林伦伦（2005）从《汕头话口语语法基础教程》看 120 年前的潮州话音系，《语言科学》第 15 期。

林伦伦、陈小枫（1996）《广东闽方言语音研究》，汕头：汕头大学出版社。

林晴（2012）《潮州方言的鼻化韵》，北京大学硕士学位论文。

马重奇（2008）《潮声十五音》与《潮语十五音》音系比较研究，《古汉语研究》第 1 期。

马重奇(2008)粤东潮汕五种闽南方言韵书音系比较研究，《福建师范大学学报》(社科版)第 4 期。

吴芳（2009）《粤东闽语 -n、-ŋ 韵尾的方言地理类型研究》，暨南大学博士学位论文。

吴芳（2013）从历史文献看粤东闽语 -n、-ŋ 韵尾在 19 世纪以后的演变，《韩山师范学院学报》第 4 期。

吴瑞文、林英津（2007）闽南方言辅音韵尾今读的历史分析，《中国语文研究》第 23 期。

徐通锵（1991/2008）《历史语言学》，北京：商务印书馆。

徐宇航（2012）《潮州方言一百多年来语音演变的研究》，香港中文大学博士学位论文。

徐宇航（2013）十九世纪的潮州方言音系，《香港中文大学中国文化研究所学报》第 57 期。

曾南逸（2013）文白异读消亡的三种可能模式——以晋江安海苏厝方言正在发生的演变为例，《语言研究集刊》第 13 辑，上海：上海辞书出版社。

张屏生（1994）《潮正两音字集》音系初探，《潮州学国际研讨会论文集》（上册），郑良树主编，广州：暨南大学出版社。

张世珍（1913）《潮声十五音》，汕头图书报石印社，汕头。

张振兴（1992）《漳平方言研究》，北京：中国社会科学出版社。

Dialect Grammar in Two Early Modern Southern Min Texts: A comparative study of dative *kît* 乞, comitative *câng* 共 and diminutive-*guìa* 仔*

Hilary Chappell (曹茜蕾)

1. INTRODUCTION

Early 17th century missionary texts on Southern Min (or Hokkien) dialects provide an invaluable source for the diachronic study of the grammar of their modem counterparts as they are largely written in the special dialect characters for vernacular Hokkien and have romanized versions. The significance of these early documents cannot be underestimated, given the small number of works written in the colloquial form of Southern Min dialects that are available to us from earlier periods.

According to van der Loon (1967), the translation of the Catholic religious text, the *Doctrina Christiana*, into a Southern Min dialect was published by 1607 in Manila. A lexicon (*Bocabulario*) and a grammar (*Arte*) were also compiled during the second decade of the 17th century, in 1617 and 1620 respectively. Van der Loon describes each of these three works as a collaborative effort of Spanish Dominican missionaries and Chinese interpreters living in a Chinese Sangley community near Manila in the late 16th and early 17th centuries.[2]

There are also several Southern Min colloquial plays and manuals in existence which date back to the Ming and Qing dynasties, such as the *Lìjìngjì* 荔镜记 'The Romance of the Lychee Mirror'. These are written in a mixture of the Chaozhou and Quanzhou vernaculars and have been examined in studies such as Yue-Hashimoto (1991) and Yue (1999) on interrogative structures and grammar; Lien (1994a, 1995) on resultative verb compounds; and Mei (1998) on pronoun fusion in Southern Min. Lien (1995) also considers hybrid

---

* This research was funded by an Australian Research Council Large Grant, A59701190.

literary genres such as Taoist liturgical texts. However, such texts provide few clues as to the pronunciation of the characters and words in these epochs, let alone facilitate easy reconstruction of the phonological systems. Nor do they allow us to discern when Mandarin characters (as opposed to the special dialect characters) should be given the literary or the colloquial reading in Southern Min. The romanized versions of the Southern Min *Doctrina Christiana* clarify this problem in most cases. Consequently, the rediscovery of the missionary texts in romanized and character form is a great boon to researchers in Chinese dialectology.[3] Problems in interpretation for 19th and early 20th century documents on Australian languages have been described in McGregor (in press) with respect to missionary archives on Dampier Land languages and the degree of authenticity in representing the grammar and phonological systems.

2. BACKGROUND TO THE DOCUMENTS USED IN THE ANALYSIS

The following three early modern Southern Min documents have been consulted for this analysis. Next, I briefly describe their contents:

(i) The translation of the Spanish version of the *Doctrina Christiana* into a Min dialect in character form is attributed to Dominican missionaries by van der Loon (1967). It was blockprinted not earlier than 1607 by Keng Yong of the Parian, near Manila, although the translation of some parts of it were possibly made as early as 1587.

In addition, two somewhat different romanized versions of the *Doctrina Christiana* also exist and form part of an untitled 337 page Spanish manuscript, which is held in the British Museum (Add. 25,317). Both the Spanish romanizations and Chinese characters for the *Doctrina Christiana* have been collated and reproduced in Appendix II to van der Loon (1967). I refer to this appendix in my analysis. The *Doctrina Christiana* has the following contents: the Sign of the Cross, the Lord's Prayer, the Hail Mary, the Apostles' Creed, Salve Regina, the Fourteen Articles of Faith, the Ten Commandments, the Commandments of the Holy Church, the Sacraments of the Holy Church, the Fourteen Works of Charity, the Seven Mortal Sins, the Confiteor, the Catechism, the Mysteries of the Rosary, followed by the rules for hearing mass, days of fasting and abstinence, and the Act of Contrition.[4]

In a classic piece of investigative work, van der Loon pinpoints the dialect used and described in this manuscript by Spanish Dominican missionaries in the Philippines as the vernacular of Haicheng (海澄), in the prefecture or Zhangzhou (漳州) as used around the turn of the 17th century (1967: 132). He shows that it differed in certain phonological features from the dialect of Zhangzhou city, although it belongs to this subgroup of Southern Min (see Ting 1980: 5). Van der Loon concludes that the Sangleys, or Chinese traders, must have migrated from this port town in southern Fujian province, with many eventually settling in and around Manila.

Van der Loon also documents the lack of linguistic uniformity of this text revealed by its use of two orthographies: the special characters used for vernacular Hokkien during the Ming dynasty are strongly in evidence in the first part of this text up to the end of the catechism. This half is characterized as the basic *Doctrina* by van der Loon (1966: 22) and was probably translated in the 1590s during the early years of the Dominicans' mission, even though it may only have been blockprinted at a much later date, sometime before 1607. Van der Loon points out that while the use of the vernacular in written works was widespread by the time of the late Ming period (1966: 13), subsequently this practice was more thoroughly suppressed in southern Fujian province than anywhere else in China.

In the second part, the use of Hokkien characters is more limited, apart from the Act of Contrition, leading to the conclusion that there were at least two different sets of authors: most likely the missionaries, Miguel de Benavides and Juan Cobo, helped by Chinese interpreters, were responsible for the basic *Doctrina* while other Dominican missionaries translated the second section on the rosary, also with the help of Chinese collaborators, in the early17h century.[5]

Van der Loon mainly investigates the phonology of the Min dialect represented by the *Doctrina Christiana*. Yue (1999) takes issue with his bipartite division, showing that, in terms of both syntax and the lexicon, finer distinctions can be made, the colloquial-literary division between these two parts of the *Doctrina* not being in fact so rigid. She describes the *Doctrina* in terms of five main sections and claims that the section, Mysteries of the Rosary, being narrative in form, contains the highest proportion of classical (pre-Qin) elements, while the Catechism is the most colloquial in its rhetorical question-answer format, with the remaining sections showing a mixture of both colloquial Min and literary vernacular styles. Note that Yue (1999: 4) defines 'literary vernacular style' as 'a written style that probably approximates the standard language of the time'. In view of this, I place the whole text under scrutiny for the purpose of seeking historical evidence on different stages of grammaticalization.

(ii) *Arte de la lengua Chiõ Chiu*. The British Museum copy of this manuscript is catalogued as: "*Arte de la lengua Chiõ Chiu, otherwise called Chin-Chen from a town of that name in the province of Fokien, in China*". This is the copy referred to by van der Loon (1966, 1967). The place name *Chiõ Chiu* clearly refers to Zhangzhou (1967: 97, 100) but van der Loon (1967: 105) is unable to precisely date the British Museum copy. From various clues, he deduces that it was probably made after the *Bocabulario* (Lexicon) was compiled in 1617.

A new copy of this manuscript has recently come to light from the Biblioteca Universitaria Provincial Barcelona.[6] It is likely that the Barcelona copy is longer, if not more complete, than the British Museum copy since it has allowed scholars to precisely date the manuscript as written in the year 1620 (Yue 1999; Mei Tsu-Lin, pers. comm.). This analysis makes use of the Barcelona copy of the *Arte*.

(iii) There is a third additional text which is worth mentioning here: *Grammatica Linguae Sinicae Popularis in provincia Chin Cheu* is a translation and redaction of *Arte de la lengua Chiõ Chiu* described above. Specifically, it is a Latin translation from the original Spanish made by a Dominican chaplain, Bernardo Ribera, on behalf of Gottlieb Bayer who revised and published it in 1730 as part of his larger two volume work on the Chinese language *Museum Sinicum* (see also van der Loon 1967: 107).[7] Note that Bayer omits all tone diacritics and Chinese characters, rendering it far less useful than the original. I have referred to it wherever the relevant part of the Barcelona manuscript is barely legible.

3. THE MIN DIALECT GROUP

The Min group forms a very diverse group of dialects whose subdivisions are in the main not mutually intelligible. This dialect group makes up 4.1% of China's population. Its speakers principally live in the southeastern coastal province of Fujian with some incursions into the Guangdong region.

Regarding the history of the Min dialects, Bielenstein (1959) uses prefectural records to show that Fujian province was colonized at a much later period than other parts of South China due to its remoteness and inaccessibility The first major migration occurred during the 3rd century AD, following two different paths from (modern day) Jiangxi in the west and

Zhejiang in the north, while the second major migration occurred in the 7th century moving down the coast from these same two areas. However, the main formation period for Min took place earlier during the Han dynasty, most likely in Wu territory, with it emerging as an identifiable dialect group by the time of the Tang dynasty (7th–9th centuries).[8]

Norman (1988, 1999) proposes the following classification for the heterogeneous Min group: the primary division is into Inland and Coastal (or Western and Eastern) Min, reflecting the two major historical routes of migration and settlement in the Fujian area, described above. Inland (Western) Min is specifically subdivided into Northwestern, Far Western and Central Min, while Coastal (Eastern) Min is subdivided into Northern and Southern Min.[9] The Fuzhou, Gutian, Ningde, Zhouning, Fuding and Fuqing dialects are examples of Northern Coastal Min used in this analysis (which I abbreviate to 'Northeastern Min'), while Taiwanese, Quanzhou, Zhangzhou, Amoy (Xiamen), Datian, Yongchun, Dongshan, Shantou (Swatow), Chaozhou [Teochiu], Chaoyang, Suixi and Hainanese dialects are examples of Southern Coastal Min (which I abbreviate to 'Southern Min'). Putian is considered an isolate by some (cf. Chen and Li 1991), as belonging to Southern Min by others (Ting 1980), or as a dialect intermediate between Northeastern and Southern Min (Norman 1999).[10]

Xiamen or Amoy developed into one of China's major seaports during the Ming dynasty, and gradually became the economic centre of Fujian province, being opened up to foreign trade as a treaty port in 1841 by the British. Its dialect also developed into the unofficial standard for Southern Min, blending many features from the surrounding dialect areas of Zhāngzhōu and Quánzhōu (Ting 1980: 5–7). Migration to Taiwan from these districts in southern Fujian took place from the early Qing dynasty onwards, that is, from the mid-17th century, with the result that Southern Min speakers form the major linguistic group today, constituting 73.3% of the population in Taiwan (Huang 1995: 21).

It is thus reasonable to use these modern Southern Min dialects to make a typological comparison with the 17th century Hǎichéng dialect represented in the *Arte* and the *Doctrina Christiana*, particularly given that Taiwanese and Amoy are the best described in this dialect group, while there is no contemporary description of the Hǎichéng dialect to my knowledge (see also Yue 1999). Reference is made to other Min dialects, as listed above, according to the data available.[11]

4. GRAMMATICAL ANALYSIS

4.1 The Grammatical Function Word *kir* [khit] 乞 < 'to give'

In the *Doctrina Christiana*, passive, causative and certain kinds of dative constructions are all formed with the exponent *kir* 乞 (*khit*), a verb which means 'to give, to cause, to entreat'. In the *Arte*, which provides the romanization *kît*, only its passive and dative uses are discussed, although van der Loon lists or exemplifies both the verbal meanings 'to give, to ask' and the causative meanings 'to enable, to let (somebody do something)' in Appendix I (1967: 140). The use of *kir* 乞 (*khit*) as a verb can be traced back to the Han and Wei dynasties (Zhang 1989).

It is typical of Southern Sinitic languages for passives, causatives and datives to share the same grammatical exponent, generally evolving from one of the verbs of giving (see Yue-Hashimoto 1993: 131). This is true of the Shanghai and Suzhou dialects of Wu, standard Hong Kong Cantonese, Meixian Hakka and Min dialects, while Standard Northern Chinese, that is, Mandarin, generally uses a different set of sources from Southern Sinitic languages.[12] Nonetheless, it too has identical exponents for causative and passive structures in the colloquial register but a separate morpheme for dative constructions (*gěi* < 'give'). Norman (1982) and Hashimoto (1986) attribute this North-South contrast to an Altaic superstratum which triggered the development of the causative verbs *ràng* 'let' and *jiào* 'tell' into passive exponents in standard Mandarin. All these lexical sources for passive markers in Chinese languages are quite common crosslinguistically: *be ~ become*, verbs of giving, perception verbs and contact verbs (see Heine et al. 1993).

In fact, there are three possibly verbal usages of *kir* 乞 (*khit*) in the *Doctrina Christiana* where it precedes the verb *sia* 'forgive' (see also Yue 1999). Note also that the romanization differs in one case from that used for its grammaticalized functions—*kiet* versus *kir ~ kît*. In this context, it shows the other main meaning of 'beg, ask':

Doctrina Christiana of the 17th century: Verb$_1$ + Verb$_2$

(1) 乞   赦   人   罪

    kiet   *sia*   -   -

    beg   forgive   people   sin

    '(Jesus then prayed to God, the Father) and begged forgiveness for people's sins.'

[DC 19a, p.170] [13]

292

In the contemporaneous *Lìjìngjì* [The Romance of the Lychee Mirror] (1581), written in a mixture of the Quánzhōu and Zhāngzhōu vernaculars, the same grammaticalized uses of *kir* 乞 (*khit*) can be found, according to Jiang (1989) and Yue (1999). Contrasting to this, in contemporary Taiwanese Southern Min, the three construction types are all formed using the exponent *hō* which, in its turn, is related to a verb 'to give' (Tsao 1988). I next discuss dative, causative and passive uses of *kir* 乞 (*khit*), in that order. There are 24 tokens of *kir* 乞 (*khit*) in the *Doctrina*, which can be classified into three uses as a verb of giving, three passives, five causatives, and thirteen uses where it introduces a dative or indirect object. Clearly its last use is the main one in this text, while it can be conjectured that there are incipient developments in the direction of a causative and passive use, with the verbal use possibly on the wane.

4.2 Dative Constructions

The *Arte* explains (1620: 3a) that only the genitive, dative and ablative cases use particles to mark these functions while other cases such as the nominative, accusative and vocative are not declined but rely purely on position. Specifically, the genitive uses the postpositioned particle *gùe* (个), while the dative uses preposed *kît* 乞, and the ablative one of the three particles *câng, câb*, or *tāng* (共, 甲, 同).[14] Only examples with pronouns and *lâng* 'person' are presented in the chapter on case in the *Arte*.

In this section, I examine dative or ditransitive constructions in Southern Min dialects which employ a special marker for the recipient (Goal or indirect object). Let us begin with an historical overview.

From Late Medieval Chinese (7th-11th centuries) up until the end of the Modern Chinese period (18th century), the following word orders were available for datives according to Peyraube (1988, 1996):

(2)   Dative structures in Late Medieval Chinese (7th–11th centuries)

    (i) Verb   +   Indirect Object   +   Direct Object

    (ii) *Verb*   +   [**Prep *yǔ* 与 + Indirect Object**]   +   Direct Object

    (iii) Verb   +   Direct Object   +   [**Prep *yǔ* 与 + Indirect Object**]

    (iv) [**Prep *yǔ* 与 + Indirect Object**]   +   Verb   +   Direct Object

Peyraube argues that the use of *yǔ* 与 is not a case of a lexical replacement of *yú* 于 found in Archaic Chinese. Rather, the source of the structures in (ii) and (iii) where the indirect object (or recipient) is marked by *yǔ* 与 is a serial verb construction $V_1 + V_2 + IO +$ DO which emerged during the Six Dynasties period circa 4th-5th centuries AD. Its special semantic features were: V_1=verb of giving specifying manner and V_2=one of three general verbs of giving including *yǔ* 与, *yǔ* 予, *wèi* 遗. The $V_2 + IO$ in this construction became postposed after the DO to create the structure in (iii) by analogy with other existing serial verb constructions during this same period, while the V_2, lexically restricted to *yǔ* 与 by the early Tang dynasty, had grammaticalized into a preposition introducing the IO by the 9th century. In contemporary Mandarin, *yǔ* 与 has been replaced by *gěi* 给 'to give'. It appears that the Late Medieval period bears most relevance for the study of datives in Southern Min dialects which possess all the structures shown in (2), although using different forms as will be shown.

In the *Doctrina Christiana*, there were thirteen examples of ditransitive constructions formed with *kît* 乞 (*khit*) but only three had the patient noun preceding a recipient noun:

$$NOUN_{AGENT} + VERB + NOUN_{PATIENT} + KHIT + NOUN_{RECIPIENT}$$

Doctrina Christiana:

(3)

做	一	件	好	事	乞	伊
cho	*cheg*	*kia*	*ho*	*su*	*kir*	*y*
do	one	CLF	good	deed	give	3SG

'do a good deed for them' [DC12a, p.162]

There were ten examples in the *Doctrina Christiana* where the dative-marked noun directly followed the verb, having the form: $NOUN_{AGENT} - VERB - KHIT - NOUN_{RECIPIENT}$ (– $NOUN_{PATIENT}$). In this construction, *kît* 乞 acts like a complement verb or verbal enclitic and the patient noun, if present, can either follow the recipient noun as in (4), or come before the verb in the immediately preceding context as in (5):

Doctrina Christiana:

(4)

求	僚氏	保庇	生人。	赐	乞	伊	呀劳舍
kiu	*Diosi*	*po pi*	*se lang*	*su*	*kir*	*y*	*Galaçia*
entreat	God	protect	live:person	bestow	give	3SG	grace

'(I) entreat God to protect the living and bestow upon them Grace.' [DC 8a-b, p.156]

(5)

人	欠	衣裳。	我	可怜	舍施	乞	伊。
lang	*kiam*	*y chio*	*gua*	*co leng*	*sia si*	*kir*	*y*
person	lack	clothes	ISG	take: pity	bestow	DAT	3SG

'If people lack clothes, I take pity on them and give freely to them.' [DC 7b, p.155]

The main use of *kît* 乞 in this category appears however to be its development as a marker of the cause rather than the recipient particularly in a kind of verb compound where V₁= verb of giving and V₂= *kît* 乞 and no patient noun occurs. In this compound, V₁ is typically *su* 赐 'bestow' (6 examples) or *pang* 放 'let go, set free' (1 example) and it takes on the causative meaning 'to enable, make' in most of these examples (a total of seven examples out of ten in the dative category where no patient noun occurred). This use—dative or causative—recalls the serial verb constructions of the Six Dynasties period of Early Medieval Chinese which eventually produced the prepositional dative marker *yǔ* 与 (see Peyraube 1996 and preceding description). It is exemplified by (6):

Doctrina Christiana

(6)

亦	保庇	濂	水	死	人	赐乞	伊	受	嗷啰哩仔
ya	*po pi*	*liam*	*chui*	*si*	*lang*	*su kir*	*y*	*siu*	*Goloria*
also	protect	baptise	water	dead	person	bestow-give	3SG	receive	glory

'and also to protect the Christian dead, enabling them to receive glory' [DC 8b, p.156]

In modern Taiwanese, *khit* cannot be used in these two kinds I of dative constructions. Instead, *hō·* is used to mark the recipient in a postverbal slot either directly following the verb or the patient noun (see Tsao 1988). Specifically the possible word orders corresponding to Medieval Chinese outlined above are:

(7) Constructions with *hō·* in Taiwanese Southern Min corresponding to Medieval Chinese

(i) VERB + **NOUN**Recipient + **NOUN**Patient

(ii) VERB + [*hō·* + **NOUN**Recipient] + **NOUN**Patient

(iii) VERB + **NOUN**Patient + [*hō·* + **NOUN**Recipient]

but:

{(iv) [*kā* + **NOUN**Benfactive/Goal] + VERB **NOUN**Patient}

The recipient noun is obligatorily marked by *hō·* when it follows the patient noun as in structure (iii). When the recipient follows the verb directly, *hō·* may be used to introduce it as in structure (ii), or may be omitted as in double object structure given under (i) (Tsao

1988, Cheng 1997). The use of *hō·* is exemplified by (8) and (9) for the structure VERB + [*hō·* + **NOUN**~Recipient~] + **NOUN**~Patient~. The preverbal position for the prepositional phrase is not available however for *hō·* in the function of a benefactive but only as a passive marker (see section 4.4 below). Instead we find several other prepositions introducing benefactive and goal nouns such as *kā* (discussed below in section 3).

Taiwanese Southern Min:

(8)   *i*   *chhôan*   *hōu*   *guā*   *chit-poe*   *tê*

       he   pass   to   me   one-CLF   tea

       'He passed me a cup of tea.' [Tsao 1988: 179]

The same applies to the Xiamen dialect, shown in an example form Zhou (1991: 234, his characters and romanization):

Xiamen Southern Min:

(9)   交   互   我   一   张   批

       kau~1~   *hɔ~5~*   *gua~3~*   *tsit~7~*   *tĩũ~1~*   *phue~1~*

       hand   to   1SG   one   CLF   letter

       'Hand a letter over to me.'

Next, an example of the second type of dative construction in Taiwanese Southern Min is presented, which has the form VERB + **NOUN**~Patient~ + [*hō·* + **NOUN**~Recipient~] where the prepositional phrase with *hō·* is postposed after the patient noun:

(10)   我   教   一   个   撇步   与   你

       goá   *kà*   *chit*   *ê*   *phiët- pō·*   *hō·*   *lí*

       1SG   teach   one   CLF   trick   to   2SG

       'I'll teach you a trick.'

In the Suixi Southern Min dialect of Leizhou, the verb 'to give' which is *k'i* ꜒ can also be used as a dative marker in both construction types (ii) and (iii) (Yue-Hashimoto 1985: 353, 358-360). Similarly, Nakajima (1977: 221, 1979: 297) and Chen and Li (1991: 42, 95, 299-302) give examples showing that Fuzhou 乞 *k'øyk²³*, Gutian *k'ei? ~ k'i?*, Zhouning *k'e?*, Fuqing *k'ø?* (all Northeastern Min); and the Putian isolate *k'œ?*, Datian *k'i ~ k'e*, Dongshan *k'ə?⁸* and Chaoyang *k'i?²* (all Southern Min) are all used both as verbs of giving and dative markers in the V-*khit* 乞 + Recipient Noun form (and some, but not all, as passive markers too). In contrast to this, the Southern Min dialects of Taiwanese, Xiamen, Zhangzhou and Yongchun primarily use the marker *hō·* in these functions. Note that Songxi (Western Min) is the only dialect from the other two groups of Central and Northern Min represented in Chen and Li's corpus of Min dialects which makes use of a cognate form with *khit* 乞 for at least the dative and passive uses. Therefore, we can conclude that the dative use of the cognates of *khit* 乞 is a consistent and widespread feature of Northeastern Min, but less so in Southern Min where *khit* 乞 and *hō·* are competing forms, while it is not at all well-attested for Inland or Western Min. *Khit* 乞 is also employed across the board for the passive in the Northeastern Min. Further discussion of the grammaticalization of *khit* 乞 is provided at the end of the section.

There is also another marker of the dative or recipient in the two early modern Southern Min texts: in the *Doctrina Christiana*, the beginning of each section in the Mysteries of the Rosary contains a ditransitive sentence with the romanization *tou* underneath either the character 与 [*yǔ* 'give' in Mandarin] or 度 in Southern Min, which is phonetically [*t'ɔ⁷*], also meaning 'to give (to)'.[15] The prayer for the relevant beads of the rosary is being offered to Mary in each case, pronominally coded as *lu* 'thou, thee' in the example below:

Doctrina Christiana:

(11) 我　　送　　与　　汝

　　　gua　sang　tou　lu

　　　'I offer it up to thee.' [DC 24a, p.177]

There are 15 examples in the *Doctrina Christiana* of this postverbal complement use of *tou*, always in this same sentence. In contemporary Taiwanese, *hō·* has to mark the recipient noun as explained above:

Taiwanese Southern Min:

(12) 我　　送　　与　　汝

　　　goá　sang　hō·　lí

　　　'I offer it to you.'

In addition to this, the morpheme *tôu* 度 [*t'ɔ⁷*] is exemplified as a verb of giving in the *Arte* and glossed as such in van der Loon (1967: 14l):

Arte:

(13)　汝　　有　　钱　　　一　　个　　度　　我

　　　lù　　*ù*　　*chī*ⁿ　　*chèg*　*guè*　*tôu*　*guà*

　　　2SG　have　money　one　CLF　give　me

　　　'If you have money, give me a dollar (coin).'

　　　(*Si tienes dinero un toston me da.*) [*Arte* 1620: 12]

This points to two conclusions: (i) in the early 17th century, the grammaticalization of *tôu* 度 had not progressed as far as that for *khit* 乞 since it still had a clearly verbal usage in addition to the dative marking function where it directly follows the verb. There is no evidence of the dative structure (iii) for *tôu* 度 as found in Medieval Chinese with a recipient NP postposed after the patient noun which would suggest the second stage of development (Peyraube 1988); and (ii) there are elements of more than one Southern Min dialect in these 17th century texts, a point borne out in the exegesis of the grammar of the *Doctrina Christiana* given in Yue (1999). Yue (p.5, p.29) supposes that the *Doctrina Christiana* was intended for widest religious audience, and thus its language possibly represents a mixed Southern Min dialect in currency during the late 16th and early 17th centuries in Southern Fujian, one that was comprehensible to the largest variety of dialect speakers. The verb [*t'ɔ⁷*] is found in the Quanzhou dialect of Southern Min.

In the Quanzhou dialect, the morpheme [*t'ɔ↓*] can be used as a passive marker alongside *k'it⁷* (Lin 1993: 243; Zhou 1993; and see section 4.4 below on the passive). Lin (1993: 259, 262) uses the character 与 (*yǔ* in Mandarin) to represent this and later provides an example of the double object construction with the same morpheme used as the verb 'to give'. This is supported by Douglas (1873: 562) who defines *thò·* as a verb meaning 'bestow, give' in the Quanzhou dialect equivalent to Amoy *hō·*, 'to give, cause, sign of the passive in many phrases'.

For dative constructions in the language of the *Doctrina Christiana* and the contemporary Southern Min dialects of Taiwanese and Quanzhou, it can be concluded that although the forms may be different, in each case the source is the same: verbs of giving have grammaticalized in to prepositional markers of the recipient (or Goal) in the postverbal position. Next, the development of causative and passive constructions from the dative use of these verbs of giving is discussed.[16] Tsao (1988: 190), in particular, argues that the passive use of *hō·* in contemporary Taiwanese developed out of this dative use, whereby the goal marking function of *hō·* was reanalysed as an agent marking one. The input to this reinterpretation from dative > agent may well have been its causative use, however, in pivot constructions. Consider the following example of the *hō·* causative:

Taiwanese Southern Min:

(14) 我　　有　　企　　起来　　与　　彼　　的　　人　　过

goá　　ū　　khiā　-khí-lâi　hō·　　hia　　ē　　lâng　　koè

1SG　have　stand　DIR　CAUS　those　CLF　person　pass

'I stood up in order to let those people pass.' [Cheng 1997: 222]

The causee in (13) is an agent of the motion verb *koè* 'pass' and the patient of the causative verb *hō·* which can be understood in the enabling sense of 'allow for, let, so that'. The semantic development from give > dative > causative > passive is typical for verbs of giving as attested crosslinguistically (Heine et al. 1993). First the causative use of *khit* is discussed and compared with *hō·*.

4.3 Causatives

There are five causative uses of *khit* in the *Doctrina Christiana*. Causative constructions formed with *khit*, or *hō·* in contemporary Taiwanese, belong to the permissive type (see Shibatani 1973; Talmy 1976), expressing that the causative agent let, allowed or enabled the situation to happen. In this sense, four uses of *khit* occur with verbs that are semantically stative, such as *bat* 识 'to know', *sin* 信 'to believe' and *siu* 受 'to receive', thus allowing disambiguation from the passive use. Only one use occurs with an active verb *cho* 做 'do' but in an imperative: 'Do not let them do it again.' [DC 8a, p.155]

$$(NOUN_{CAUSER}) + KHIT_{CAUS} + NOUN_{CAUSEE} + VERB$$

Doctrina Christiana:

(15) 先　　七　　件　　乞　　人　　议　　僚氏　　根因。

seng　chit　kia　kir　lang　bar　Diosi　kinyn

first　seven　item　CAUS　person　know　God　origin

'The first seven itemns enable people to know that God is the origin.'

[DC 3a, p.148, Fourteen Articles of Faith]

This is rendered in contemporary Taiwanese by the following translation:

Taiwanese Southern Min:

(16) 头　七　件　与　人　识　上帝　是　咱　的　起头

thâu　chhit　kiaⁿ　hō·　lâng　bat　Siōng-te　sī　lan　ê　khí-thâu

first　seven　item　CAUS　person　know　God　be　1PL$_{inc}$　POSS　origin

'The first seven items enable people to know that God is the origin.'

The verb su 賜 'bestow' is however by far the most common in its causative usage in the *Doctrina Christiana*. Of thirty examples, only nine retain the verbal meaning of 'bestow, grant' while twenty-one show the development of a similar permissive causative meaning 'enable', doubtlessly via semantic shift from '(a person in a superior position) granting someone the conditions or capacity to do something'. A seemingly curious phenomenon is the appearance of ten compound causative verbs with V_1= su 賜 'bestow' and V_2= either khit 乞 'give' (eight) or u 与 'give' (two) recalling the grammaticalization of yǔ 与 'give' into a preposition from V_2 position in similar serial verb constructions by Late Medieval Chinese (Peyraube 1988, 1995). The examples with khit as a kind of verb complement with a dative function are treated in the previous section (see example (6) and Chappell (to appear (c)). There are also ten examples of su 使 'cause, send' used mainly in the directive sense of 'make someone do something'.

It is interesting to note that the permissive causative use of khit occurs in the *Lìjìngjì*, The Romance of the Lychee Mirror (1581), with a verb meaning 'to know' as given in Yue (1999, p.15):

Lìjìngjì (Romance of the Lychee Mirror 1581)

(17)　旦：不通　乞　哑公　哑妈　知　(白25B)

　　　NEG-IMP　CAUS　grandfather　grandmother　know

　　　Heroine: 'You mustn't let grandad and grandma know.'

The semantic transition to a passive interpretation can be clearly seen in an alternative English translation of "You mustn't let it be known by grandad and grandma". The passive use of khit is the subject of the next section.

4.4 Passives

A brief historical overview of the development of the passive structures in Chinese precedes the discussion of the use of khit and hō· in Southern Min dialects.

Beginning with the Early Medieval period (2nd-6th centuries AD), the form with *wéi* + Agent Noun+ *suō* + Verb (为...所) was the main passive structure until it was gradually overtaken by the *bèi* 被 passive, the dominant form during the Tang dynasty (618–907 AD) as reflected in vernacular texts (Peyraube 1989).

Earlier, during the period from the Late Archaic to the Early Medieval, *bèi* is found used as a full verb in simple S-V-O structures with the meanings of 'receive', 'suffer' (L. Wang 1935, 1: 35; Peyraube 1989). In Peyraube's view, its passive use developed out of a serial verb construction by analogy with the *wéi...suǒ* form. Moreover, by the middle of the Tang dynasty, it had become fully grammaticalized as a prepositional marker of the passive with the form introducing an agent in the majority: *bèi* + Agent Noun + Verb (Peyraube 1996: 178).

During the modern period from the 13th century onwards, *bèi* became relegated more and more to the written language so that it can be aptly described as a passive of more formal genres in its contemporary usage (see Chappell 1986, to appear (b)). In the modern period, the causative verbs *ràng* 'let' and *jiào* 'tell' also developed passive uses in Mandarin. Other markers of the passive such as 乞 *qǐ* 'to request, give', attested from the Yuan dynasty (13th century), did not last in the colloquial Northern Chinese koiné of the capital, disappearing from vernacular literature in approximately the 18th century (see Hashimoto 1986; Jiang 1989; Zhang 1989). However, it appears that the use of 乞 *qǐ* 'to request, give' has clearly been maintained in many contemporary Southern Min dialects, including the language of the *Doctrina Christiana* which has three such uses of *khit* 乞.

Let us next examine some examples of the passive use of *khit* 乞 in the *Arte* and the *Doctrina Christiana*. The *Arte* (1620: 8) explains that the passive can be formed by the particle *kît*: the thing which is the patient is placed in the first position, followed by *kît*, then the person who does the action and the verb. The following example of the active-passive contrast is provided:

Arte:

(18) 我　　打　　简仔

　　 guà　 *pà*　 *kǐn nìa*

　　 1SG　 hit　 child

　　 'I beat the child.'

　　 [*yo açore el muhacho*]

(19) 简仔　　乞　　我　　打

    kĭn nìa　*kît*　*guà*　*pà*

    child　PASS　1SG　hit

    'The child was beaten by me.'

    [*el muhacho fue por me açotado*] [*Arte* 1620: 8]

This is the only example of a passive sentence in the *Arte*. The three examples in the *Doctrina* all have the structure: (NOUN$_{PATIENT}$) + *KHIT*$_{PASS}$ + NOUN$_{AGENT}$ + VERB:

Doctrina Christiana:

(20) 乞　　本事　　卑劳厨。柱　　法　　钉死　　在　　居律　　上

    kir　*Punsu*　*Pilato*　*ong*　*huar*　*teng-si*　*tu*　*Culut*　*chĩõ*

    PASS　Pontius　Pilate　unjust　law　nail-die　at　cross　on

    'crucified by the unjust law of Pontius Pilate' (from the Aposties' Creed) [DC 2a, p.146]

This can be translated into contemporary Taiwanese Southern Min by example (21):

Taiwanese Southern Min:

(21) 与　　彼拉多　　柱　　法　　钉死 仁　　十字架　　上

    hō·　*Pi-liáp-to*　*ong-*　*hoat*　*tèng-sí ti*　*sip-jī-kè*　*(siōng)*

    PASS　Pilate　unjust　law　nail-die at　cross　(on)

    'crucified by the unjust law of Pontius Pilate'

As can be seen by comparing (20) and (21), the main difference between the *Doctrina Christiana* and modem Taiwanese is lexical, with the use of *khit* as opposed to *hō·*. Note that there are also eleven examples of passives formed with the literary *pi* 被 and that these all occur in the second half of the *Doctrina Christiana* in the more classical section on the Mysteries of the Rosary.

    In Southern Min dialect texts such as the *Lìjìngjì*, The Romance of the Lychee Mirror, from the Ming period, which is a mixture of Quanzhou and Zhangzhou dialects, the passive is also expressed with 乞 *khit* (Jiang 1989: 376; Yue 1999: 15—her example).

Lìjìngjì [Romance of the Lychee Mirror 1581]:

(22) 丑：婆仔　　乞　　人　　打　　了 (白21A)

    female: attendant　PASS　person　hit　finish

    Clown: 'The maid has been beaten up by someone.'

Regarding the synchronic situation Zhou (1993), in particular, describes dialectal differences in the use of passive markers in Southern Min and claims that the Xiamen and Zhangzhou areas are quite close in their use of three main passive patterns, with: (i) *hō·* + NP 与; (ii) *hō·* + *lâng* or *hōng* 与人; and (iii) *khit* + *hō·* + NP 乞与. For the third pattern, he provides the following example:

Xiamen Southern Min:

(23) 走私货　　　曹　　乞　　与　　海关　　没收去

　　 chaú-su-hè　　*chiâu*　*khit* + *hō·*　*hái-koan*　*boȧt-siu-khì*

　　 smuggled: goods　all　　PASS　　　customs　confiscated-away

　　 'All the smuggled goods were confiscated by Customs.' [= Example (12) in Zhou (1993: 81)]

By way of contrast, the Quanzhou dialect shows a different set of patterns: (i) *tng*[35] 传; (ii) *thō*[2] ~ *hō*[2] (度) 与; and (iii) *khit* 乞. The marker *khit* can combine with the first three passive morphemes *tng*[35], *thō*[2] and *hō*[2] to form compound markers, which shows its productivity and wider use in this dialect.

It seems that the same description could be made for Taiwanese Southern Min as for the Xiamen and Zhangzhou dialects. In modern Taiwanese, the use of *khì* + *hō·* as a compound passive marker is also possible (see Bodman (1955) for the same phenomenon in Malaysian Hokkien) and can be substituted for *hō·* alone in example (21), or used as below. Often the character for the verb *khì* 'to go' is used as the written form for this marker, obscuring the relationship:

Taiwanese Southern Min:

(24) 去　　　与　　侬　　　　拍

　　 khì　　*hōng* (<*hō lâng*)　*phah*

　　 PASS　PASS:person　　beat

　　 'get beaten up by someone'

This compound passive marker appears to be related to *khit* + *hō·* + NP (乞 + 与 + NP) through lenition of the final consonant of *khit*, and is merely conveniently represented by the homonym *khì* 去 'go', for example, as in Bodman (1955). This would explain the remarkable functional and phonetic similarity between these two compound markers in the three dialects.[17] The passive marker *hō·* can also be used in a more restricted way in the

Quanzhou dialect as described in Zhou (1993) where, however, *khit* is the preferred form.

Cognates of *khit* 乞 in this passive function are scattered across other Southern Min dialects such as Yongchun, Quanzhou, Datian, Dongshan, Chaoyang, Shantou (Swatow) and Suixi, and generally in the Northeastern Min dialects of Fuzhou, Gutian, Ningde, Zhouning, Fuding and Fuqing (see Chen and Li 1991: 116; Yuan et al. [1960] 1989: 278–279, 305; Nakajima 1979: 285; Huang 1996: 530 on Shantou; Feng 1993 on Fuqing). Some dialects which use a cognate of *khit* 乞 as the verb 'to give' and in the dative function do not necessarily use it in the passive function; for example, the passive marker in the isolate Putian *kek⁵* does not appear be related to the verb 'to give'/dative marker *k'œʔ*. These data seem to suggest that *hō·* may be the innovative or revived form in modern Southern Min, specifically for the Xiamen, Zhangzhou and Taiwanese varieties, given the historical data available on *khit* 乞 as a passive. Relevant t·o this thesis is the fact that Yongchun (Southern Min), located northwest of Quanzhou, uses *hō·* as the verb 'to give' and the dative marker, and as a passive marker alongside *khit* 乞, as too for at least the verbal meaning 'give' in Shunchang, an outlier Southern Min dialect in Western Min territory whose speakers migrated from Yongchun and Anxi in the 19th century (Chen and Li 1991: 458).

Furthermore, observe that both passive markers have grammaticalized out of the same class of verbs, namely verbs of giving, which leads us to conjecture that grammatical renovation occurred in the central Southern Min dialects of Zhangzhou, Xiamen and Taiwanese involving a reinvigoration of an already existing form (see Peyraube (to appear) for similar phenomena). This process is most complete in Taiwanese but has progressed to a lesser extent for the sub dialect area of Zhangzhou and Xiamen and even less for the subdialect area of Quanzhou and Yongchun where *khit* is still highly productive.

If *khit* was the main form used for the passive in 17th century Southern Min dialects (as seen in the *Arte*, the *Doctrina Christiana* and the 16th century *Lìjìngjì*), then *hō·* has made very little headway in taking over from *khit* in neighboring Quanzhou, and is similarly a competing form in Yongchun as a passive marker. Moreover, most other Southern Min dialects, such as Dongshan and Datian in Fujian province, Chaoyang and Shantou in northeastern Guangdong province, Suixi on the Leizhou peninsula in Guangdong province, not to mention the dialects of Northeastern Min, such as Fuzhou, make use of cognates of *khit* in all these functions. Possibly the renovation of *khit* by *hō·* in the passive function in the

Zhangzhou dialect area postdated these early modern 17th century texts with the innovation slowly spreading to neighboring areas such as Xiamen and Quanzhou, then northwest to Yongchun, eventually being transported to Taiwan which was settled from the time of the early Qing dynasty (mid-17th century onwards) largely from Zhangzhou and Quanzhou, as is well known (see section 3).[18]

Cheng (1991, 2: 308) states that *yǔ* 与 'give' is the etymological source for Taiwanese *hō·* from which we can assume that both forms *khit* and *hō·* probably co-existed in the Min dialect group from its early formation period, given that the two verbs can be traced back to at least the Han and Wei dynasties (Zhang 1989: 382). I argue therefore that in some contemporary dialect groups, *hō·* is winning out and the compound passive marker *khit hō·* is an intermediate hybrid form and a telltale sign of a residue of an earlier stage. Taiwanese, Xiamen and Zhangzhou exemplify this outcome within Southern Min. In other dialect groups such as Northeastern Min, *khit* predominates while in still others, such as Quanzhou, both are in use in conjunction with other passive markers, but there is a preference for the use of *khit*. The Quanzhou dialect has not undergone the same extent of change as Xiamen, Zhangzhou and Taiwanese dialects, in the direction of functional replacement of *khit* by *hō·*. This appears to be an archetypal example of different outcomes for competing morphsyntactic forms (see Wang 1969; Lien 1994b, to appear).

It is curious however that *khit* and *hō·* developed a passive rather than a benefactive usage in preverbal position in modern Southern Min period. Other prepositions, such as *kāng ~ kā*, came instead to be employed in the benefactive function, which is discussed in the next section. The structure with *yǔ* 与 in preverbal position is a relatively late one according to Peyraube (1988), taking place in the latter half of the Tang dynasty (9th century), which means that this occurred after Southern Min dialects putatively split off from Northern Chinese. This gap in the range of functions of *khit* and *hō·* in comparison with Medieval Chinese or Northern Chinese *gěi* merits the further attention of scholars. Table 1 compares diachronic and synchronic data from Min dialects on these three types of construction formed with verbs of giving.[19]

Table 1: Dative Causative and Passive Markers in Min Dialects

Construction Type 句法结构	17th Hokkien Texts 十七世纪初的闽南话	Modern Min Dialects 现代闽语	
		Taiwanese Southern Min 台湾闽南语	Other Min Dialects 其他闽方言
Ditransitive Verb-[*Dative marker* + IO]-DO Verb complement/enclitic: 动补结构 / 动词后缀 + 间接宾语（+直宾）	乞 *kît, kir[khit]* 度 *tôu[tho·]*	与 *hō·*	乞 *k'øyʔʌ* Fuzhou 福州 乞 *k'œʔ* Putian 莆田 与 *t'ɔ↘* Quanzhou 泉州 与 *hō·* Xiamen 厦门 与 *hō·* Zhangzhou 漳州 与 *hō·* Yongchun 永春 乞 *k'əʔ^8* Dongshan 东山 乞 *k'iʔ^2* Chaoyang 潮阳 *k'i*ʌ Suixi 遂溪
DitransitiveVerb-DO-[*Dative marker* + IO] 双宾结构：VERB + 直宾 + *khit* + 间宾	乞 *kît, kir[khit]*	与 *hō·*	乞 *k'øyʔʌ* Fuzhou 福州 乞 *k'œʔ* Putian 莆田 与 *hō·* Xiamen 厦门 乞 *k'əʔ^8* Dongshan 东山 乞 *k'iʔ^2* Chaoyang 潮阳 *k'i*ʌ Suixi 遂溪
Causative 使动式	乞 *kît, kir[khit]*	与 *hō·*	乞 *k'əʔ^8* Dongshan 东山
Passive 被动式	乞 *kît, kir[khit]*	与 *hō·* and 乞与 *khit hō·*	乞 *k'øyʔʌ* Fuzhou 福州 乞 *k'it*¬ Quanzhou 泉州；also 传 *tnɔ^{35}*; *thɔ^{12}* 度 ~ *hɔ^{12}* 与 与 *hō·* Xiamen 厦门 and 乞与 *khit hō·* 与 *hō·* Zhangzhou 漳州 与 *hō·* ~ 乞 *k'it* Yongchun 永春 乞 *k'əʔ^8* Dongshan 东山 *k'iʔ^2* Chaoyang 潮阳 Shantou 汕头 *k'i*ʌ Suixi 遂溪 *puŋ*¬ 分 Chaozhou, also *xɐʔ*ʌ *боŋ*¬ 分 Hainan 海南

5. BENEFACTIVE, ABLATIVE AND COMITATIVE *câng* 共

The commitative 'with, and' meaning is expressed by the function word *câng* for which the *Doctrina Christiana* uses either the characters 共, 同 or 与, the first two representing vernacular Hokkien and the third, literary Chinese. In the *Arte*, *câng* (*kāng*) is described as having an ablative meaning (1620: 3) and combining with verbs of buying, selling, borrowing, lending and speaking (1620: 11–12). This is neatly echoed in the description given by Douglas (1873: 188) for the Amoy (Xiamen) comitative preposition *kā ~ kāng*, although it represents just a subset of the functions identified in Tsao (1991) for contemporary Taiwanese. Douglas further observes ([1873] 1899: 188) that, as a preposition, Xiamen *kā ~ kāng* can only be used with persons, with the meanings of ' 'to, from, for', and often with the converse meaning to *hō·*, the passive marker'.

Both these prepositional and connective uses of *câng* (*kāng*) can be found in the *Doctrina Christiana* which contains thirty-one examples of this morpheme. The primary meaning is the comitative one of 'and, with', comprising thirteen examples, while the ablative 'from' meaning has ten, the benefactive 'for' meaning six, and the goal sense 'to', two.

In its turn, the morpheme *câng* in the two 17th century texts can be related to the Medieval Chinese *gòng* 共. According to Liu and Peyraube (1994: 187-188), the use of *gòng* 共 as a preposition 'with' is attested from the Early Medieval period (2nd-6th centuries) onwards, while its use as a connective 'and' became common in the second half of the Late Medieval period, specifically from the Song dynasty onwards (10th-13th centuries). Its lexical source can be traced back to a verb 'to share (with)' as used in pre-Qin Classical Chinese. By the end of the Eastern Han (2nd century AD), this verb had developed a grammaticalized function as an adverb 'together', the semantic input to the later uses of 'with' and 'and'. This marker thus has a semantically similar source to the comitative in West African Benue-Kwa languages such as Yoruba and Engenni described in Lord (1993: 47-57) which are respectively 'be included among, be together with' and 'bring along with'. *Gòng* 共 continued to be used as both a preposition and conjunction until the end of the 16th century after which it was subject to the process of renovation, being replaced by *hé* in Northern Chinese (see Liu and Peyraube 1994 for details). The functions of *kā* in Taiwanese are briefly described next.

For contemporary Taiwanese, Tsao (1991) identifies five main constructions using the marker *kā*. These are: (i) its use with ditransitive verbs to mark Goal or (ii) to mark Source; (iii) its use with monotransitive verbs to mark the Patient with a similar, though broader, function to the Mandarin disposal construction with *bǎ*; (iv) a benefactive use; and (v) its use as a passive prefix on the verb. Adopting Tsao's analysis, I give an example of each of the first four categories, adding in a fifth, connective, use, and making comparisons with the usage of *câng* in the *Doctrina Christiana* and the *Arte*. The last use as a passive prefix is not relevant to the discussion of *câng* as found in the two 17th century texts. Apart from the passive prefix, all these different uses of *kā* have the structure: (NOUN$_{AGENT}$) + [共 *KA* + NOUN] + VERB.

5.1 Goal Marker with Ditransitive Verbs of Communication

Kā marks ditransitive verbs of communication such as 'teach', 'tell a story', 'ask a question' and 'make a phone call' which Tsao labels as 'outward verbs'. Tsao observes however that *kā* may not co-occur with 'inward verbs' with the sense of giving to mark the recipient. This is the exclusive province of the dative marker *hō·*:

Taiwanese Southern Min:

(25)　伊　　共　　我　　讲　　一　　项　　事志
　　　i　　*kā*　　*guá*　　*kóng*　　*chit*　　*hāng*　　*tāichì*
　　　3SG　KA　　1SG　　talk　　one　　CLF　　matter
　　　'S/he talked to me about a matter.'

In the *Arte*, there are examples of this use with the speech act verbs *ta^n* 'to talk' and *suè* 'to discuss':

Arte:

(26)　我　　共　　你　　说　　只　　件　　事
　　　guà　　*câng*　　*lù*　　*suè*　　*chǐ*　　*kia^n*　　*sû*
　　　1SG　　KANG　　2SG　　talk　　this　　CLF　　matter
　　　'I talk to you about this matter.'
　　　[*yo a ti digo este negocio*] [*Arte* 1620: 11]

In the *Doctrina Christiana* there are also two examples with verbs of communication where the Goal sense of 'to' could be interpreted:

Doctrina Christiana:

(27)　(a) 慰闷
　　　　　ui bun
　　　　　'console' [DC 26a, p.180]

(b) 报喜说

    po hi sue [DC 13b, p.164]

    'announce good news to Mary (saying)'

Mary consoles the apostles before her death (a rosary prayer):

(28)	汝	共	他	慰闷	毕
	lu	*cang*	*t'a*	*ui bun*	*pit*
	2SG	KANG	3SG	conscle	finish

'You gave consolation to them (*continues*: You were not in pain or suffering). [DC 26a, p.180]

5.2 Source Marker with Ditransitive Verbs of Taking Away

In this use, *kā* marks the source in. a similar manner to an ablative case marker with the category of verbs of taking away such as 'buy', 'fine', 'borrow from', 'mortgage', and 'cheat (of money)'. This is the sense of 'from' mentioned in the Carstairs Douglas dictionary (1873: 188):

(29) **Kā i chioh**, borrow from him.

    Kā i thó, demand frrm him.

    Kā i boé, buy from him.

It is also exemplified in the *Arte* (1620: 11) wherein it is however explained that *câng* is ambiguous between the ablative 'from' and 'help/for' senses:

(30)	汝	共	我	买	鱼
	lù	*câng*	*guà*	*bèi*	*hū*
	2SG	KANG	1SG	buy	fish

'You bought fish from/for me.'

    [*tu ayu da me a conprar pescado; conprame mi pescado*]

Barclay provides a similarly equivocal example in the supplement to Douglas (1873: 90). In the *Doctrina*, there were ten ablative examples of *câng*, five used with the verb *kei* 'to separate, deliver, remove' and five with the verb *kiu yǐn cheng* 求人情 'beseech mercy (from God)'. The first verb is used in the V-O compound *kei-chue* as in (31), which could either have a literal ablative interpretation in the text of 'take away our sins from us' or the extended benefactive meaning 'take away our sins for us':

Doctrina Christiana:

(31) 是　巴礼　共　　人　　解罪

　　　si　*Pale*　*cang*　*lang*　*kei chue*

　　　be　padre　KANG　person　absolve:sin

　　　'(Penitence) is when the father absoives us of our sins.' [DC 6b, p.1S3]

In such a case of polysemy, overlapping of interpretations is to be expected.

5.3 Benefactive Marker

When *kā* is used as the benefactive marker for, the noun it marks is not an argument of the verb:

(32) **kā i khui**, 'to open it for him, as a door' [Douglas 1873: 188]

Taiwanese Southern Min:

(33) 你　的　衫　伊　会　kā　你　洗

　　　lí　*ê*　*saⁿ*　*i*　*ē*　*kā*　*lí*　*soé*

　　　2SG　POSS　clothes　3SG　can　KA　2SG　wash

　　　'He can wash your clothes for you.' [Cheng & Tsao 1994: 23]

The following two examples from the *Doctrina Christiana* show this benefactive use of *câng* (*kāng*) 'for + Noun':

Doctrina Christiana:

(34) 与　人　净　水

　　　cang　*lang*　*cheng*　*sui*

　　　KANG　person　cleanse　water

　　　'(Christ commanded the disciples) to perform baptism for people.' [DC 24a, p.177]

This benefactive sense of *câng* is evident in six occurrences in the section on the Works of Mercy in the *Doctrina Christiana*, including (34) which shows how this interpretation could develop from the commitative meaning. Example (34) can of course be translated into contemporary Taiwanese (35) with the use of *kâ*:

Taiwanese Southern Min:

(35) 共　俍　行　　洗礼

　　　kā　*lāng*　*kiaⁿ*　*sóelé*

　　　KA　person　perform　baptism

'(Christ commanded the disciples) to perform baptism on/for people.'

A further semantic extension to marking the patient is suggested by such examples as (34) whereby an action performed for someone (Benefactive) can be reinterpreted as an action performed on someone (Patient). This interpretation is however only in a nascent stage for the six benefactive examples found in the *Doctrina Christiana*, whereas both case roles are possible for (35), which brings us to the next section on patient marking.

5.4 Patient Marker with Monotransitive Verbs

Kā in contemporary Taiwanese Southern Min has a function similar to the disposal construction with *bǎ* in Mandarin where it marks a preverbal and typically referential direct object and co-occurs with a transitive action verb. Its usage is however broader than Mandarin *bǎ* in forming two major types of construction with and without telic predicates (for details, see Tsao 1991).

Taiwanese Southern Min:

(36) 所以　　阮　　拢　　共　　裤　　　　褪　起　来

só-i　　gún　lóng　kā　khò　　thǹg-khì lai

therefore　1PL　all　KA　trousers　take: off-DIR

'So we all took off our trousers (to go swimming).' [Jesse's Story: 116-117][20]

The use of *kā* to unequivocally mark a patient was not found in either of the 17th century texts.[21] There were, however, two examples of literary *chiang* 将 in the second half of the *Doctrina* used in this function where it combines with other literary expressions, such as the following patient NP *t'a siu chioc* 'his hands and feet':

Doctrina Christiana:

(37) 将　　　他　　手　　足　　钉　　在　　居律　　上

chiang　t'a　siu　chioc　teng　tu　Culu　chio

PRETR　3SG　hand　foot　nail　at　Cross　on

' (They) nailed his hands and feet to the Cross.' [DC 22a, p.174]

Many Southern Min dialects use a cognate of this pretransitive patient marker *chiang* 将, which belongs to the literary stratum, alongside the use of a colloquial level marker, typically a cognate of *kā* (see Table 1). Hybrid forms, such as the fallowing kind of construction in Taiwanese, are quite common (see Chappell to appear (a)): [22]

Taiwanese Southern Min:

(38)　　将　　　门　　　kā　　关　　　起来

chiong　　mn̂g　　kā　　kuiⁿ　　khìlâi

PRETR　door　KA　close　INCHOATIVE

'Close the door.' [Cheng & Ts20 1994: 37]

Typologically, the pretransitive use represents an interesting development for Sinitic languages which typically make use of a verb of taking or holding in this function of object marker, as is the case in many West African Benue-Kwa languages (Lord 1993). Wu dialects such as Suzhou and Shanghai, some Xiang dialects in Hunan and some Hakka dialects, use cognates of Mandarin *ná* 拿 'to take, hold', while Meixian Hakka and Hong Kong Cantonese use cognate forms of *jiāng* 将, also 'to take, bring'. In fact *jiāng* 将 is the exponent of the pretransitive common at the end of the Early Medieval period during the Sui dynasty (6th century AD) which was replaced by *bǎ* 把 'to grasp, hold' during the Tang dynasty for Late Medieval Chinese (7th–13th centuries) (see Peyraube 1996; Sun 1996).[23]

5.5 Connective or Comitative Marker

This forms by far the largest category of examples in the *Doctrina* with thirteen occurrences of *câng* in this function in the text. Twelve instances are used to connect equal status nouns as exemplified by (39) while the remaining one is used with the verb *pien lun* 辩论 'to debate, argue with' (17b). Other comitative markers used in the *Doctrina* are *cab~hap* 合 and *peng* 并. These are explicitly defined in the *Arte* as meaning with (1620: 3a, 3b) as, for example, *câb lāng* 甲人 *con el honbre* 'with the man'.

Doctrina Christiana:

(39)　乃　　汝　　子　　西士氏　　援　　汝　　身　　与　　神魂　　同　　登

nai　lu　chia　Jesu　uan　lu　sin　**cang**　sinhun　tong　teng

then　2SG　son　Jesus　support　2SG　body　**and**　soul　together　ascend

天堂　　受　　福

t'iantong　siu　hoc

heaven　receive　blessing

'Then your son Jesus took your body and soul up to Heaven to be blessed.'

[*Doctrina* 26b, p.180]

This use is similar to that described by Cheng and Tsao (1994: 28-31) for Taiwanese Southern Min *kap* 合 or *kah*. In modern Taiwanese Southern Min, *kap ~ kah* is used as a conjunction

312

between two nouns of equal syntactic status in a similar way to these 17th century texts:

Taiwanese Southern Min:

(40) 伊　　合　　　　我　　拢　　有　　去

　　 i　　*kap~kah~kā*　*goá*　*lóng*　*ū*　*khì*

　　 3SG　with　　　　1SG　all　　have　go

'S/he and I have both gone.' [Cheng & Tsao 1994: 29]

A development relevant to this study is that Southern Min *kah* and *kap* are evidently merging into a form indistinguishable from *kā* when used in an unstressed context, reinforced by similarities in meaning and function (see Cheng and Tsao 1994: 28–31).[24] Note that Douglas (1873: 188, 196) specifically mentions that *kāng* 共 and *kap* 合 are the colloquial forms which can be grouped with *kā* as corresponding to the reading form *kiōng*. Diachronically, this tendency is augmented by the fact that the final phase in the development of the comitative markers in Chinese is to just such a conjunctive use (see Liu and Peyraube 1994 on *gòng*, *tóng* and *hé*). In other words, the pathway already exists upon which to analogize.

I conclude this section with a few observations comparing the phonetic form of the marker *câng*, reconstructed as *kang* (no tonal value) in the 17th century by van der Loon (1967: 140), with contemporary Southern Min dialects. Douglas (1873: 188, 196) explicitly describes *kāng* as Chinchew usage, that is, belonging to the Quanzhou dialect, and equates it with Amoy *kā*. This is confirmed for contemporary usage by Zhou (1991: 246) who explains that both 共 *kåʔ* and *kāŋ* can be used in the Xiamen or Amoy dialect while Lin (1993: 243) lists *kaŋ↓* as the marker in the contemporary Quanzhou dialect corresponding to the three meanings in Mandarin of *bǎ*, *gěi* and *xiàng*: 把 给 向, that is, a pretransitive, a benefactive and a goal marker according to the examples provided. Fuzhou (Northeastern Min) also makes use of *kaʔ˥* as an object marker in the disposal construction whiie the Chaozhou dialect (Southern Min) similarly uses *kaʔ³²* for the pretransitive (Huang 1996: 665). Many other Min dialects use cognates of *kā* in all or some of these five functions, most showing the loss of the final velar nasal (see Table 2).

Hence it appears that the form has atrophied in Taiwanese from *kāng* to *kā*, while both forms are maintained as allomorphs on the mainland in the case of the Xiamen dialect, or retained as the full form in the more conservative Quanzhou dialect: *kaŋ↓*. Therefore, the usage of *kā* in modern Southern Min dialects such as Taiwanese shows preservation of a feature of Medieval Chinese grammar in Southern Min. Its range of functions on the other hand has increased significantly to include the patient marker usage among other new functions. These comparisons are displayed in the following table.

Table 2: Comitative Markers and Their Semantic Extensions in Min Dialects

Construction Type 句法结构	17th Hokkien Texts 十七世纪初的闽南话	Modern Min Dialects 现代闽语	
		Taiwanese Southern Min 台湾闽南话	Other Min Dialects 其他闽方言
Comitative 伴随标志 'and', 'with'	共 *câng* [kang]	共 *kā*	*køyk*²³ ~ *køyŋ*↓ Fuzhou 福州 *kak*³ Putian 莆田 共 *kåʔ* ~ *kāŋ* Xiamen 厦门 *kaʔ*³² Dongshan 东山 *kaʔ*⁵ Chaoyang 潮阳 *kaŋ*↓ Suixi 遂溪
Goal 标的标志 'to' in preverbal position			*køyk*⁵ Fuzhou 福州 *kak*³ Putian 莆田 共 *kaŋ*↓ Quanzhou 泉州 共 *kåʔ* ~ *kāŋ* Xiamen 厦门 *kǎ*³ Dongshan 东山 *kai*³ Chaoyang 潮阳
Source 来源标志 'from' in preverbal position			共 *kåʔ* ~ *kāŋ* Xiamen 厦门 *kā*³ Dongshan 东山 *kai*³ Chaoyang 潮阳
Benefactive 受惠者标志 'for, in place of' in preverbal position			共 *kaŋ*↓ Quanzhou 泉州 *kåʔ* ~ *kāŋ* Xiamen 厦门 *kǎ*³ Dongshan 东山 *kai*³ Chaoyang 潮阳 But: 乞 *køyk*²³ Fuzhou 福州 *kek*³ Putian 莆田
Patient 受事者标志 in the disposal construction	Not attested		*kaʔ*┤ Fuzhou 福州 共 *kaŋ*↓ Quanzhou 泉州 *kaʔ* ~ -*kāŋ* Xiamen 厦门 *kǎ*³ Dongshan 东山 *kaʔ*³² Chaozhou 潮州 *kaʔ*↓ Hainan 海南
	将 *chiang*		*tsyoŋ*⁵⁵ ~ *tsiaŋ*┤ Fuzhou 福州 将 *tsyœŋ*⁵⁵ Putian 莆田 将 *tsyɔŋ*┤ Quanzhou 泉州 将 *tsyɔŋ*┤ Xiamen 厦门 将 *tsiaŋ*┤ Chaozhou 潮州 *tsaŋ*³³ Chaoyang 潮阳 将 *tsiaŋ*┤ Hainan 海南 *lia*┤ Suixi 遂溪

6. THE DIMINUTIVE

In Taiwanese, the diminutive of nouns is formed with the suffix -*á* 仔. Yang (1991) and Lien (1998) claim that its source morpheme is Southern Min *kiáⁿ* 'son'. In this section, I show that these early 17th century texts provide additional support for this claim.

In the early 17th century grammar of Southern Min, the *Arte*, the following description is given for the diminutive:

Arte:

(41) "The diminutive is formed with the final particle *ia* or *nia* or *guia*:

kéiguìa	圭仔	'little chicken' [pollito]
bôguìa	帽仔	'little hat' [sonbrerillo]
tóguìa	刀仔	'litte knife' [guedilito]." [1620: 6a]

In contemporary Taiwanese, these three words mean *ke-á* 'chicken, little chicken', *bō-á* 'hat' and *to-á* 'knife, small knife' respectively, indicating partial bleaching of the diminutive feature. Note that only one of the variants is illustrated by these three examples. I return to this after briefly discussing the etymology of the diminutive.[25]

In modern Taiwanese Southern Min, the morpheme -*á* is used not only as a diminutive, but also as an empty marker of the noun category, sometimes with a meaning-discriminating function (see Lien 1998). I reproduce an example of each of this kind:

Taiwanese Southern Min:

(42) (i) 狗	狗仔	(ii) 鴨	鴨仔	(iii) 糖	糖仔
kâu	*kâu-á*	*ah*	*ah-á*	*th'ⁿg*	*th'ⁿg-á*
'dog'	'ittle dog'	'duck'	'duck'	'sugar'	'candy'

Lien also describes the development of a pejorative meaning of -*á* when it is infixed between family and given names, and for certain occupations:

(43) 搬戏仔	牵猪哥仔
puaⁿ hì-á	*khan-ti-ko-á*
'actor'	'pigbreeder' (a man who leads about a boar)

This diminutive morpheme can be traced back to the lexeme for 'son', annotated as 子 *kĭaⁿ* in the *Arte* (1620: 2b, 11a, 12b), but with completely missing diacritics in the *Doctrina*

Christiana (for example, *kia* 'son' 1607: 15b). In the *Arte*, it is used in the first chapter to exemplify the tone category which has nasalization, but again the tone diacritic is omitted in later examples. The form *kĭaⁿ* clearly corresponds however to contemporary Taiwanese and Amoy *kiaⁿ* 'son' for which the character 囝 is often used. Furthermore, the lexeme *kiaⁿ* is still used as a kind of suffix to mark the young of the species for animals, postposed after the reduced diminutive form:

(44) 牛仔囝   狗仔囝

   gû-á-kiaⁿ   *káu-á-kiaⁿ*

   ox-DIMN-offspring   dog-DIMN-offspring

   'calf'   'puppy'

The diminutive suffix in contemporary Taiwanese Southern Min undergoes extensive morphophonemic alternation, described in detail in Lien (1998). This suggests that the three forms noted by the anonymous authors of the *Arte* are similarly allomorphs and that the initial illustration of this suffix with examples of only the one allomorph *-guia* is purely fortuitous. These gaps notwithstanding, the *Arte* and the *Bocabulario* [Lexicon] furnish us elsewhere with examples of all these written variants, if not allomorphs, of the diminutive suffix in *-kìa*, *-ìa* and *-nìa*.

In the *Doctrina Christiana*, only two real examples are to be found with a diminutive suffix and this involves a repetition in prayer form of one particular passage in the Mysteries of the Rosary, relating how Mary made an offering to God at the temple of a pair of white doves forty days after the birth of Jesus (see also Yue, 1999: 17). There are also transliterations of the Spanish words for 'person' and 'glory' which use this morpheme but without its function: *piersonya* 别孙仔 (e. g. 10b, p.159), reconstructed as *piat sun ìā* by van der Loon (1967: 142, f. 130), and *Goloria* 嗷啰哩仔:

Doctrina Christiana:

(45) 送   一   对   白   鸽   仔

   sang   *cheg* *tui*   *pe*   *kap*   —

   present one   pair   white dove

   '(She) offered a pair of white doves (to God).' [DC 16b, p.167]

As the example shows, the Spanish romanization is missing for precisely the diminutive particle as it is for the entire preceding passage in narrative form which contains the same story. Fortunately, in the list of classifiers given at the end of the *Arte*, this noun appears under the entry for *tuì* 对 'pair' (1620: 28):

Arte:

(46) 四　　对　　鸽　　仔
　　　sỳ　　*tuì*　　*câb*　　*guìa*
　　　four　　pair　　dove　　DIMN
　　　'four pairs of doves [quatro pares de palomas]'

An occurrence of a similar lexeme is also found in the *Bocabulario* [Lexicon], cited in van der Loon (1967: 142), but under a different form and glossed as a diminutive: *kap iā* 'young pigeon' (B. 43b).[26] It is interesting to note Douglas contradictory observation (1873: 196) of 250 years later wherein he states that the diminutive must not be used with *kap* 'pigeon' in order to avoid ambiguity with *kap-á* 'a small land frog'.

In the same list, there is also one serendipitous example for the lexeme 'window' with the second allomorph, which is rendered in this case as *-yà* (1620: 27), an alternative spelling to *-ià* (see van der Loon 1967: 110)

Arte:

(47) 四　　扇　　窗仔
　　　sỳ　　*sỳ*ⁿ　　*tángyà*
　　　four　　CLF　　window
　　　'four windows [*4 venianas*]'

These are nice examples since they show that even in the early 17th century, the diminutive suffix had developed a purely noun marking function: the head nouns do not mean 'little window' or 'little dove', as they are glossed neutrally as *ventanas* 'windows' and *palomas* 'doves' in the Spanish. There are also two further examples in the *Arte* which contain the word for 'child' 简仔 *kĭn nia*, furnishing us with the third variant of the diminutive (1620 15). This is *gín-á ~ gin-ná* 囝仔 in modern Taiwanese (see the example of the passive in (19) with this lexeme).

However, van der Loon (1967: 142) reconstructs the 'diminutival and familiarity suffix' with only two allomorphs and these are *ngia ~ iā* 仔, presupposing a development of the nature kiaⁿ > ŋia > iaⁿ, with only the nasal velar and zero initials in alternation. He lists the following additional examples from the *Bocabulario* [Lexicon]:[27]

(48) *kin iã* (others said *kan iã*): boy, slave (B. 50b, 126b); *huan iã*: Tagalogs (B. 25a); *kap iã*: young pigeon (B. 43b); *sã ngiã*: coat (B. 173b); *bo ngia/bo iã*: hat (B. 28b, 162b); *k'a tsing t'au ngia*: toe (B. 4la)

As can be seen, only one of these examples has a diminutive gloss, *kap iã* 'young pigeon', strengthening the claim that this morpheme had at least two functions of diminutive and noun marker in the early 17th century. It also had the function of a predicate modifier with the meaning of 'to Verb a little', as a final example from van der Loon shows. This usage is not found in contemporary Taiwanese Southern Min, though it may be readily understood:

(49) *lòh hou iã* 'it rains a little' (B. 109a)

Norman (1989, 1991) has claimed that the reconstructed form for 'son' -*kian*- is one piece of evidence for an Austroasiatic substrate in Min languages. Early references to this word can in fact be dated back to Medieval Chinese texts, cited by Yang (1991: 166), who proposes this same source for the diminutive suffix, based on evidence from the Tang poet Gù Kuàng 顾况 (725?–816?). Gù Kuàng annotates the character 囝 as meaning 'son' in colloquial Min, in section 13 of the poem 上古之什 *Shànggǔ zhī shí*. Gù Kuàng gives the pronunciation as 蹇 which is *jiǎn* in contemporary standard Mandarin:

(50) 囝   音   蹇,   闽   俗   呼   子   为   囝
      jiǎn   *yīn* *jiǎn,* mǐn   *sú*   *hū*   *zǐ*   *wéi* *jiǎn*
      (word) sound jiǎn   Min   common call   son   as   jiǎn

   "The sound of this character 囝 is *jiǎn*, the Min commonly use *jiǎn* for 'son'."

On the comparative dialectal front, Yang (1991) also points out that the diminutive suffix in Chaozhou dialect of Minnan retains the full form of *kiaⁿ*:

(51) 鼎仔

   Chaozhou: ***tiaⁿ kiaⁿ*** as opposed to Xiamen, Zhangzhou, Taiwanese: *tiaⁿ-á* 'a wok'

In the Fuzhou dialect, the diminutive suffix and nominalizer is the cognate *kiaŋ*ꜗ <'son' which, similar to Taiwanese and Xiamen, has various allomorphs (Yuan et al. 1989: 302), while it is *kia?*↘ in Hainan and *a*↑ ~ *a*↑ 仔 in Quanzhou. This semantic shift for the more general case of 'child' > 'diminutive exponent' is well-attested in other languages of the world, for example see Heine et al. (1993) and Jurafsky (1996). The *Arte* provides 'live' evidence of this more sex-specific change from 'son' to the diminutive and noun marking functions proposed in Yang (1991) and Lien (1998).

7. CONCLUSION

The findings of this analysis can be summarized in the following manner. Several different diachronic processes can be observed in these data from the two early modern Southern Min texts when compared with contemporary accounts of the grammar of Southern Min dialects such as Taiwanese and Xiamen (Amoy):

(i) *Grammatical renovation* appears to be the process which has affected the dative ~ passive ~ causative marker *khit* 乞, in particular for the central Southern Min dialects of Taiwanese, Xiamen and Zhangzhou where *hō·* 与 is the primary modern exponent. Both the forms *khit* 乞 and *hō·* 与 probably co-existed over many centuries since both can be separately traced back to the verbal uses of 'give, ask for' in Late Archaic Chinese. At some stage they became competing forms, when *hō·* 与 was grammatically reinvigorated and developed the passive function in preverbal position which its cognate in standard literary Northern Chinese, *yǔ* 与, never developed. The morpheme *qǐ* ~ *khit* 乞 certainly had an incipient passive use as a verb meaning 'to suffer' as early as the 9th century Dun Huang Bianwen 敦煌变文 (Buddhist transformation texts written in the vernacular style) (see Jiang 1989: 372; Zhang 1989: 380). This was the point of time by which *yǔ* 与 had developed its preverbal benefactive usage, as earlier noted in on 4.2. Renovation is a common and regular diachronic process. For example, the dative marker *yǔ* 与 was replaced by *gěi* 给 between the Modern Chinese and contemporary periods for Mandarin, circa 18th century (Jiang 1989; Zhang 1989; Peyraube 1996: 179). The same process probably affected the use of *tôu* [*tho·*] 度 as a verb complement and marker of a following recipient (indirect object). This verb of giving is also superseded by *hō·* 与 in contemporary Taiwanese, assuming for the moment it existed in an earlier stage of the language. A simpler explanation however for *tôu* [*tho·*] 度 is that it represents a Quanzhou element in the *Doctrina Christiana* that continues to be used in the contemporary dialect, where it has also developed this passive function in the preverbal position. Again, this would suggest a relatively recent development for both *hō·* 与 and *tôu* [*tho·*] 度 of their passive usage.

(ii) The comitative ~ benefactive ~ source ~ goal marker *càng* [*kāng*] 共 illustrates a case of phonological attrition on the one hand and broadening of functions on the other: in contemporary Taiwanese, this marker bas the form *kā* thereby showing loss of the final velar nasal. The full form, *kaŋ√*, has been retained in other Southern Min dialects such as the Quanzhou dialect while it is a possible allomorph in Amoy or Xiamen, allowing us to link it with *câng* [*kāng*] 共 and the Medieval Chinese comitative. The grammatical functions of *kā* as described in Tsao (1991) have increased to include its use as a pretransitive marker of the patient noun, similar in function to Mandarin *bā*, and a passive prefix on the verb. The morpheme *kā* also forms a hybrid structure with *chiong* 将 in contemporary Taiwanese, a patient marker which belongs to the literary stratum. There are just two examples of *chiang* 将 in this function in the *Doctrina Christiana*.[28]

It is possible that omission of the patient marking use of *câng* simply represents a gap in the translation of the *Doctrina Christiana* and the grammatical description given in the *Arte* by the missionaries. Typologically, this latter development into a patient marker represents a divergence within Sinitic, since most of its branches use an exponent which has grammaticalized from a verb of taking or holding.

(iii) For the diminutive marker, the *Arte* provides us with incontrovertible evidence that Taiwanese Southern Min *-á* evolved from the morpheme for 'son': it explicitly lists *ia* ~ *nia* ~ *guia* [*kia*] as the three variant forms that could be used as a diminutive suffix in this 17th century dialect. This shows us that a process of phonological atrophy was in train since nasalization or some kind of nasal ending appears to have been lost by this time for some of the variants, a process which conforms to that described in Lien (1998) for the Taiwanese Southern Min diminutive.

Furthermore, all three categories exemplify some kind of conceptual shift from (i) a fully lexical verb *khit* ~ *hō·* 'give' to a postverbal dative marker, then into a causative marker and finally into a passive marker; (ii) a preposition 'with' to a prepositional kind of case marker of Source, Goal, Benefactive and Patient in the case of *kā*, then finally into a connective use, which can be traced back to its Medieval Chinese usage as a commitative preposition 'with', and eventually to the verb *gòng* 'share (with)' in Archaic Chinese; and (iii) the noun for 'son' to a diminutive and noun marking suffix -á.

If it is true that the phonological system of the *Doctrina Christiana* represents the Haicheng subdialect of the Zhangzhou Southern Min group, as van der Loon (1967) argues, then the dative, causative and passive morphosyntax appears to be at variance with this, showing more grammatical features of the contemporary Quanzhou dialect than of Zhangzhou or Xiamen (and by inference, Taiwanese, where the Zhangzhou *qiāng* or 'accent' dominates).[29] This is reinforced by one piece of evidence from Yue's analysis of the same texts (1999). She observes that the *Doctrina Christiana* only employs the VP-NEG neutral question form, apart from two instances where the romanization is at variance with the character text, indicating the use of the particle *a* as in the form VP-*a*-NEG. The VP-NEG neutral question form is also the dominant form in Quanzhou as opposed to Xiamen where both are in free variation, according to Yue (1999: 31).

Conversely, it may be that the Quanzhou dialect is simply more conservative in its grammar than the Zhangzhou dialect and for this reason remains closer in its passive, dative, comitative and other constructions formed with *kaŋ↘* to the language of these 17th century texts. Further large scale dialect research is needed to reveal the precise diachronic and synchronic relationships more clearly than this present sketch could hope to achieve.

NOTES

[1] I use the term 'grammatical renovation' in preference to both 'renewal', which refers to 'the replacement of a dying form by a newer, usually periphrastic, form with a similar meaning' (Hopper and Traugott 1991: 164), and to 'lexical replacement' which, similarly, is not entirely accurate for describing this phenomenon of one grammatical function word being replaced by another. I thank Debra Ziegeler for insightful discussion on this and other principles involved in grammaticalization processes.

[2] According to van der Loon (1967:101, f.22), the term 'Sangley' used for the Chinese population living in and around the Manila district may have its etymology in either *cháng lái* 常来 'to come often' or *shāng lái* 商来 'to come for trading' given the fact that these immigrants first came to the Philippines as traders. Lien Chinfa (pers. comm.) suggests Southern Min *seŋlí* 生理 'trade, mercantile business' as a more apt etymology.

[3] The character and romanized versions of the Southern Min *Doctrina Christiana* have been collated in the appendix of van der Loon (1967) to the great benefit of subsequent researchers.

[4] See Yue (1999) and van der Loon (1966) for a more detailed description of the contents.

[5] Van der Loon (1967: I05) further observes that Franciscan missionaries must have made the copy now held in the British Museum since 'St Francis' is regularly substituted for 'St Dominic' in the text, apart from several oversights which neatly allow him to make this inference.

[6] I am grateful to Alain Peyraube for making the manuscript from the Barcelona University Library available to me. Note that the Barcelona copy is given a separate title in handwriting of *Grammatica China* on the frontispiece while the original title is somewhat obscure and illegible on the second page. This explains the delay for scholars to realize it was none other than the *Arte de la lengua Chiõ Chiu*. Prof. Peyraube is of the view that the Barcelona *Arte* predates the copy held in the British Museum (pers. comm.). During a visit to London in June 1998, I was unable to view the British Museum copy of the *Arte* due to an ongoing relocation of the rare manuscripts to a new building in St Pancras. For this reason, I have not yet compared it with the Barcelona copy.

[7] The SOAS Library in London holds a copy of this work. Comparing T. S. Bayer's Latin translation with the Barcelona copy of the *Arte* shows that the main section on the grammar is longer in the original Spanish version with an added appendix of cardinal numerals and classifiers. Otherwise, the data and grammatical description more or less correspond, given some rearrangement of the 9 chapters on the part of Bayer.

[8] See Ting (1983), You (1992), Chappell (to appear (b)) and Sagart (to appear) for further discussion of different views on the formation of the Min dialects.

[9] Norman (1999) divides Inland Min into three groups: the Jiàn dialects, Shàowǔ and Yǒng'ān.

[10] Many scholars also use 'Amoy' (the anglicization of *Ē-mn̂g* 厦门 or Xiàmén in Mandarin) as a cover term for this group of Southern Min dialects, including Taiwanese, for example, Williams (1874/1896: xxxiii) and Douglas (1873/1899: 609). Similarly, 'Hokkien' (from Fújiàn 福建 , the name of the province) commonly refers to Southern Min dialects as in Medhurst (1832), Bodman (1955) and van der Loon (1966, 1967) despite the fact that Northeastern Coastal Min and Inland, or Western, Min dialects all belong to this geographic area too.

[11] Little syntactic data is available for Inland (Western) Min apart from Chen and Li (1991).

[12] For other studies on Sinitic using a typological approach, see Chappell (in press, 1999) and Chappell (forthcoming).

[13] Thanks to Stella Norman for her perceptive remark in pointing out this more apt interpretation. All the citations from the *Doctrina Christiana* refer to the reproduction given in Appendix II to van der Loon's 1967 article on this topic. The characters and romanization follow the first two lines in the text provided by van der Loon (who reproduces the two sets of original transcriptions underneath the characters) while I have added in the interlinear glossing and translation into English. Most of the tone diacritics for the Spanish romanization have been omitted in the

available copies of these manuscripts. For some syllables, the romanization is missing, indicated by '-' as in example (1) above. I express my thanks to Chinfa Lien and Imogen Chen for sharing their native speaker intuitions with me for Taiwanese Southern Min. I remain solely responsible for any errors in interpretation.

[14] The Chinese characters given in the parentheses refer to those used in the *Arte* and do not necessarily reflect the true etymological source.

[15] Van der Loon (1967: 133) reconstructs this verb with an aspirated initial *t'ou*.

[16] Cheng and Tsao (1994) also discuss the use of *hō·* in a special pivot construction and an imperative construction with resultative verb compounds which, not being attested in the two 17th century texts, are not further discussed here.

[17] In informal fast speech, the pronunciation is not necessarily distinct for *khit* 乞 and *khì* 去 'go' since *khit* 乞 tends to be unstressed in this context. This would also exemplify a regular tone, change from 4th tone to 3th tone (*yīnrùshēng* to *yīnqùshēng*) (F. Tsao, pers. comm.). The use of *khì* 'go' in this passive function could nonetheless be seen as semantically appropriate for the expression of adversity which it strongly codes (Chu-Ren Huang, pers. comm.), which can be related to its use as a co-occurring directional verb in the *hō·* passive (Tsao 1988).

[18] This conjecture assumes for the present that Zhangzhou is the center of innovation, given van der Loon's attribution of the language of the 17th century *Doctrina Christiana* to this dialect area. The direction of change may however have commenced in Quanzhou, given certain grammatical features of these texts which reflect contemporary usage in this dialect (see conclusion). Quanzhou, the famed Zayton in Marco Polo's depiction of China in the 13th century, was also an important trading port in the Song, Yuan and early Ming dynasties before the harbor silted up and foreign trading was placed under an imperial ban.

[19] This table purports neither to be exhaustive in any way of all Min dialects nor to be complete in its details for the use of each marker in the dialects for which data was available in the form of published lexica, concordances and grammars. As can be immediately viewed from the table, there was a dearth of information particularly on causatives in Min dialects in the four main references consulted, namely Yuan et al. ([1960] 1989), Nakajima (1977, 1979) and Chen & Li (1991). Note that the phonetic form for each marker is faithful to the original source and the characters are reproduced from these texts when they are provided without any comment on their authenticity as to the etymological source.

Yuan et al. ([1960] 1989): Fuzhou, Chaozhou, Hainan, Xiamen

Nakajima (1977): Dongshan

Nakajima (1979): Fuzhou, Putian, Dongshan, Chaoyang

Yue-Hashimoto (1985): Suixi

Lin and Chen (1989): Yongchun

Chen and Li (1991): Fuzhou, Putian, Xiamen, Zhangzhou, Quanzhou, Yongchun (18 Min dialects are represented in this volume)

Zhou (1991): Xiamen

Lin (1993): Quanzhou

Note that unrelated markers are used for the passives and datives in three of the representative dialects for Western Min (classified as Northern and Central Min in this reference) listed in Chen and Li (1991).

[20] This title refers to a transcription of a spoken narrative in Taiwanese Southern Min.

[21] Lien (1995: 231) lists *kā* as having a patient-marking function in the Chuang Lin Taoist liturgical texts he examines from the Ming period. It certainly could be a contextual inference in some of the examples in the *Doctrina* but not a full-fledged component of meaning for the latter text in my view.

[22] In this use of *kā*, fusion and contraction with a following third person singular pronoun has occurred, a regular feature in Min dialects. Tsao views this form as the input to the development of the passive prefix use of *kā*.

[23] See Huang (1996: 656-665) for details on the pretransitive in these dialects. Some other dialect groups employ cognates of the verb *gěi* 给 'to give' or *bāng* 帮 'to help' as a patient marker which has typically developed a benefactive meaning 'for' in Northern Chinese, particularly for *bāng* 帮 'to help' in colloquial Taiwanese Mandarin.

[24] Tsao Feng-fu considers these morphemes as forming a word family (pers. comm.).

[25] Note that for the diminutive form *-guìa*, there is no nasalization marked while the tone diacritic is different from that for the lexeme for 'son', 子 *kǐaⁿ*, the former representing the traditional *shǎng-shēng* category, realized as a high falling tone in Amoy and Taiwanese and the latter representing the *yīnqù* low falling tone (see *Arte* and van der Loon 1967: 109-113). Furthermore, in the Spanish romanization *k-* is used interchangeably with *gu-* and *qu-* for the unaspirated voiceless velar plosive initial /k/. In the Church romanization, these suffixes would thus correspond to *-kiá, -niá* and *-iá* respectively.

[26] In the Barcelona copy of the *Arte*, nasalization is clearly not marked on the examples of the diminutive suffix which could of course be due to a number of factors. Since van der Loon (1967) presents a masterly reconstruction of the phonological system of the dialect represented by the *Doctrina Christiana*, I have no reason or basis to disagree and will leave this problem of the different allomorphs/forms occurring in the *Bocabulario* and the *Arte* and the stages of

grammaticalization these might evidence to phonologists to unravel.

I note also that van der Loon reconstructs only two forms for the diminutive *ngia ~ iã* on the basis of the data in both these texts and, presumably for this reason, a different form for 'hat' *bo ngia/bo iã* from that given in (41) above (see example (48) below). He claims (1967: 142, f.130) that *ngia* is mainly used after words ending in a vowel and *iã* only after those ending in consonants. See Lien (1998) for a discussion of this problem of the path of phonological attrition for this suffix concerning the issue of whether nasalization preceded consonantal loss or vice versa for the diminutive.

[27] I have had no access to this document for the same reason as given in Note 5.

[28] Note here that the two transliterations used here for the character refer to the representation of this morpheme in the Church romanization for contemporary Southern Min which is *chiong* versus *chiang* as used in the *Doctrina Christiana*.

[29] I am indebted to Chinfa Lien for this observation.

ACKNOWLEDGEMENTS

This analysis was carried out during research visits to the Centre de Recherches Linguistiques sur l'Asie Orientale, CNRS/EHESS, Paris, during June and July, 1998 and National Tsing-Hua University, Hsin Chu, from October 1998 to March 1999 with the findings being presented at the *Troisième Colloque International sur la Grammaire du Chinois Ancien* held in Paris in June 1998; and also at seminars in the Linguistics Institutes at Tsing-Hua University (December 1998) and Academia Sinica (January 1999) on the same topic. Funding for this research is provided by an Australian Research Council Large Grant "A semantic typology of complex syntactic constructions in Sinitic languages" (A59701190).

I would like to thank the following colleagues for their comments, ideas and criticisms: Ang Ui-jin, Christoph Harbsmeier, Chu-Ren Huang, Jiang Lansheng, Charles Li, Li Jen-kuei, Chinfa Lien, Jerry Norman, Alain Peyraube, Laurent Sagart, Stanley Starosta, Feng-fu Tsao, Anne Yue-Hashimoto and Debra Ziegeler. I have greatly profited from discussions with Chinfa Lien and Feng-fu Tsao while revising this paper at National Tsing-Hua University, Hsin Chu in early 1999.

I would also like to acknowledge Imogen Yu-chin Chen for her assistance in translating sections of the *Doctrina Christiana* and in providing modern Taiwanese equivalents for the relevant examples, as well as Catherine Travis for the translation of the Spanish in the *Arte*. Dr. Chen made use of *shengjing. Taiyu Hanziben* [The Holy Bible. Taiwanese Han Character] (1996) and *Sin Ku Iok ê Seng Keng* [Amoy Romanized Bible] (1995) to confirm biblical nomenclature for the translations into Taiwanese Southern Min, while I referred to Gasparri (1932) for the appropriate wording in the English translations of the catechisms. The regular caveat applies that the author remains solely responsible for any errors or misinterpretations contained in this article.

ABBREVIATIONS

CAUS causative verb or marker; CLF classifier; DAT dative marker; DIR directional verb complement; DIMN diminutive; DO direct object; IMP imperative; INC inclusive; IO indirect object; NEG negative; NP noun phrase; O object; PASS passive marker; PL plural; POSS possessive or genitive marker; PREP preposition; PRETR pretransitive or disposal marker of patient noun; S subject; SG singular; V verb; VP verb phrase; 1 2 3 for 1st, 2nd and 3rd person pronouns. The symbol ' is used to mark aspiration on a consonant.

REFERENCES

Arte de la lengua Chiõ Chiu (1620) Manuscript from Biblioteca Universitaria Provincial Barcelona (Handwritten title: Gramatica China). Anonymous author(s).

Bayer, Gottlieb Siegfried [Theopbili Sigefridi Bayeri] (1730) Grammatical Linguae Sinicae Popularis in provincia Chin Cheu. In *Museum Sinicum: in quo Sinicae Linguae et Literature Ratio Explicator*. Vol 1: 137-165. St Petersburg: Imperial Academy (ex typographia academiae imperatoriae).

Bielenstein, Hans (1959) The Chinese colonization of Fukien until the end of the T'ang. In Søren Egerod & Else Glahn (eds.), *Studia Serica Bernhard Karlgren Dedicata: Sinological Studies Dedicated to Bernhard Karlgren on His Seventieth Birthday*, 98–122. Copenhagen: Ejnar Munksgaard.

Bodman, Nicholas Cleaveland (1955) *Spoken Amoy Hokkien*. Kuala Lumpur: Government Federation of Malaya.

Chappell, Hilary (1986) Formal and colloquial adversity passives in standard Chinese. *Linguistics* 24. 6: 1025–1052.

Chappell, Hilary. Forthcoming. The grammaticalization of the verb *kóng* 'say' in Taiwanese Southern Min: A case of reanalysis. In Charles N. Li & Alain Peyraube (eds.), *Morphological Change in Chinese*. Studies in Language Companion Series. Amsterdam: John Benjamins.

Chappell, Hilary. In press, 1999. The double unaccusative construction in Sinitic languages. In Doris Payne & Immanuel Barshi (eds.), *External Possession and Related Noun Incorporation Constructions*. Typological Studies in Language Series 39, 197–232. Amsterdam: John Benjamins.

Chappell, Hilary. To appear (a). Language contact and areal diffusion in Sinitic languages: Problems for typology and genetic affiliation. In Alexandra Y. Aikhenvald & R. M. W. Dixon (eds.), *Areal Diffusion and Genetic Inheritance: Case Studies in Language Change.*

Chappell, Hilary. To appear (b). Synchrony and diachrony of Sinitic languages: A brief history of Chinese. In H. Chappell (ed.), *Synchronic and Diachronic Perspectives on the Grammar of Sinitic Languages.*

Chappell, Hilary. To appear (c). Causative structures in two early modern Southern Min texts with *khit* 乞 'give', *sù* 賜 'bestow' and *sú* 使 'cause, send'.

Chen, Zhangtai & Rulong Li (1991) *Mǐnyǔ Yánjiū* [Research on Min Dialects]. Beijing: Yuwen Press.

Cheng, Robert (1974) Causative constructions in Taiwanese. *Journal of Chinese Linguistics* 2. 3: 279–324. Reprinted in R. L. Cheng (ed.) 1997, 201–251.

Cheng, Robert (1991) Tóngyìyǔ xiànxiàng zài Tái Huá duìyì cíkù-li de chǔlǐ wèntí: tiáojiàn hé cùchéng jiégòu [The problem of processing synonymous expressions in Taiwanese Mandarin Lexicon—the case of conditional and causative constructions]. *Dì-èr Jiè Zhōngguó Jìngnèi Yǔyán Jí Yǔyánxué Guójì Yántǎohuì Lùnwénjí.* Nankang: Academia Sinica. Reprinted in R. L. Cheng (ed.), 1997, 279–319.

Cheng, Robert Liangwei (ed.) (1997) *Taiwanese and Mandarin Structures and Their Developmental Trends in Taiwan. II: Contacts Between Taiwanese and Mandarin and Restructuring Their Synonyms.* Taipei: Yuan-Liou Publishing Co.

Cheng, Ying & Feng-fu Tsao (1994) Mǐnnányǔ 'kā' yòngfǎ zhījiǎn de guānxī [Relationships between the uses of 'kā' in Southern Min]. In Tsao Feng-fu & Tsai Meihwei (eds.), *Papers from the 1994 Conference on Language Teaching and Linguistics in Taiwan.* I: 23–46. Taipei: The Crane Publishing Co.

Doctrina Christiana en letra y lengua china. n.d. Attributed to Miguel Benavides, Juan Cobo and their Chinese interpreters. Manila: Keng Yong. Blockprinted ca. 1607.

Douglas, Carstairs ([1873]1899) *Chinese-English Dictionary of the Vernacular Spoken Language of Amoy, with the Principal Variations of the Chang-Chew and Chin-Chew Dialects. Supplement by Thomas Barclay.* London: Trübner & Co. Reprinted by SMC Publishing Inc., Taipei, in 1990.

Feng, Aizhen (1993) *Fúqīng Fāngyán Yánjiū* [Research on the Fuqing Dialect]. Beijing: Zhongguo Shehui Kexue Press.

Gasparri, Peter Cardinal (1932) *The Catholic Catechism.* London: Sheed and Ward.

Hashimoto, Mantaro (1986) The Altaicization of Northern Chinese. In J. McCoy & T. Light (eds.) *Contribution to Sino-Tibetan Studies.* Leiden: E. J. Brill, 76–97.

Heine, Bernd, Tom Güldemann, Christa Kilian-Hatz, Donald A. Lessau, Heinz Roberg, Mathias Schladt & Thomas Stolz (1993) *Conceptual Shift: A Lexicon of Grammaticalization Processes in*

African Languages. [Afrikanistische Arbeitspapiere 34/35]. Cologne: Institüt fur Afrikanistik.

Hopper, Paul J. & Elisabeth Closs Traugott (1991) *Grammaticalization*. Cambridge: Cambridge University Press.

Huang Borong (1996) *Hànyǔ Fāngyán Yǔfǎ Lèibiān* [Concordance of Chinese dialect grammar]. Qingdao: Qingdao Press.

Huang, Shuan-fan (1995) *Yǔyán, Shèhuì Yǔ Zúqún Yìshī* [Language, Society and National Consciousness]. Taipei: The Crane Publishing Co.

Jiang, Lansheng (1989) Bèidòng guānxìcí 'chī' de láiyuán chūtàn [A preliminary investigation of the passive marker 'chi']. *Zhongguo Yuwen* 5: 370–377.

Jurafsky, Daniel (1996) Universal tendencies in the semantics of the diminutive. *Language* 72. 3: 533–578.

Lien, Chinfa (1994a) The order of Verb-Complement constructions in Taiwan Southern Min. *Tsinghua Journal of Chinese Studies* 24. 3: 345–369.

Lien, Chinfa (1994b) Lexical diffusion. In R. E. Asher (ed.), *Encyclopedia of Language and Linguistics*. Volume 4: 2141–2144. Oxford: Pergamon Press.

Lien, Chinfa (1995) Language adaptation in Taoist liturgical texts. In David Johnson (ed.), *Ritual and Scripture in Chinese Popular Religion. Five Studies*. Chinese Popular Culture Project Publications (CPCP3), 219–246. University of California at Berkeley.

Lien, Chinfa (1998) Táiwān Mǐnnányǔ cízhuì 'á' de yánjiù [Research on the Taiwanese Southern Min suffix á]. In *Dì-èr Jiè Táiwān Yǔyán Guójì Yántǎohuì Lùnwén Xuǎnjí* [Selected papers from the Second International Symposium on Languages in Taiwan], 465–483.

Lien, Chinfa. To appear. Competing morphological changes in Taiwanese Southern Min. In H. Chappell (ed.), *Synchronic and Diachronic Perspectives on the Grammar of Sinitic Languages*.

Lin, Liantong (1993) *Quánzhōu Fāngyánzhì* [A Record of the Quanzhou Dialect]. Beijing: Zhongguo Shehui Kexue Press.

Lin, Liantong & Chen Zhangtai (1989) *Yǒngchūn Fāngyánzhì* [A Record of the Yongchun Dialect]. Beijing: Yuwen Press.

Liu, Jian & Alain Peyraube (1994) History of some coordinative constructions in Chinese. *Journal of Chinese Linguistics* 22. 2: 179–201.

Lord, Carol (1993) *Historical Change in Serial Verb Constructions* (Typological Studies in Language 26). Amsterdam: John Benjamins.

Mcgregor, William B. In press, 1999. An early Rapist grammar of Nyulnyul (Dampier Land, Western Australia). In L. Jooken, P. Desmet, P. Schmitter & P. Swiggers (eds.), *The History of Grammatical and Linguistic Praxis*. Leuven, and Paris: Peeters.

Medhurst, W. H (1832) *A Dictionary of the Hok-këën Dialect of the Chinese Language According to the Reading and Colloquial Idioms: Containing about 12,000 characters*. Macao: East India Company.

Mei, Tsu-Lin (1998) The time of the formation into fusion words of the Southern Min plural personal pronouns. Paper presented at the International Workshop on Chinese dialects in memory of Li Fang-kuei, August 1998. Seattle: University of Washington.

Nakajima, Motoki (1977) *Mǐnyǔ Dōngshān Dǎo Fāngyán Jīchǔ Yǔhuìjí* [A Study of the Basic Vocabulary of the Min Dialect in the Tung Shan Island]. Tokyo: Institute for the Study of Languages and Cultures of Asia and Africa.

Nakajima, Motoki (1979) *Fújiàn Hànyǔ Fāngyán Jīchǔ Yǔhuìjí* [A Comparative Lexicon of Fukien Dialects]. Tokyo: Institute for the Study of Languages and Cultures of Asia and Africa.

Norman, Jerry (1982) Four notes on Chinese-Altaic linguistic contacts. *Tsinghua Journal of Chinese Studies* 14. 1-2: 243–247.

Norman, Jerry (1988) *Chinese*. Cambridge: Cambridge University Press.

Norman, Jerry (1991) The Min dialects in historical perspective. In William W-Y. Wang (ed.), *Languages and Dialects of China*. Journal of Chinese Linguistics Monograph Series 8: 325–360.

Norman, Jerry (1999) Voiced initials in the upper register of *Mǐnběi* dialects. Seminar presented at the Linguistics Institute, Academia Sinica, 25th January 1999.

Peyraube, Alain (1988) *Syntaxe diachronique du chinois: évolution des constructions datives du 14e siècle av. J.-C. au 18e siècle*. Paris: Collège de France, Institut des Hautes Etudes Chinoises.

Peyraube, Alain (1989) History of the passive construction in Chinese until the 10th century. *Journal of Chinese Linguistics* 17. 2: 335–372.

Peyraube, Alain (1996) Recent issues in Chinese historical syntax. In C.-T. James Huang & Y.-H. Audrey Li (eds.), *New Horizon in Chinese Linguistics*, 161–214. Dordrecht: Kluwer Academic Publishers.

Peyraube, Alain. To appear. On the europeanization of Chinese grammar.

Sagart, Laurent. To appear. Vestiges of Old Chinese derivational affixes in modern Chinese dialects. In H. Chappell (ed.), *Synchronic and Diachronic Perspectives on the Grammar of Sinitic Languages*.

Shengjing. Taiyu Hanziben [The Holy Bible. Taiwanese Han Character] (1996) Taipei: Shengjing Gonghui.

Shibatani, Masayoshi (1973) Semantics of Japanese causativization. *Foundations of Language* 9: 327–373.

Sin Ku Iok ê Seng Keng (1995) Amoy Romanized Bible. Taipei: The Bible Society in the R. O. C.

Sun, Chaofen (1996) *Word-order Change and Grammaticalization in the History of Chinese*. Stanford: Stanford University Press.

Talmy, Leonard (1976) Semantic causative types. *Syntax and Semantics* 6, 43–116.

Ting, Pang-Hsin (1980) *Táiwān Yǔyán Yuānliú* [The Origin and Development of Taiwan's Languages]. Taipei: Student Book Co.

Ting, Pang-Hsin (1983) Derivation time of colloquial Min from Archaic Chinese. *Bulletin of the Institute of History and Philology* 54. 4: 1–l4.

Tsao, Fengfu (1988) The functions of Mandarin *gěi* and Taiwanese *hōu* in the double object and passive constructions. In R. L. Cheng & S. F. Huang (eds.), *The Structure of Taiwanese: A Modern Synthesis*, 165–208. Taipei: The Crane Publishing Co.

Tsao, Fengfu (1991) On the mechanisms and constraints in syntactic change: Evidence from Chinese dialects. *International Symposium on Chinese Languages and Linguistics* 2: 370–388.

van der Loon, Piet (1966) The Manila incunabula and early Hokkien studies. Part I. *Asia Major. New Series* 12: l–43.

van der Loon, Piet (1967) The Manila incunabula and early Hokkien Studies. Part II. *Asia Major. New Series* 13: 95–186.

Wang, Li (1935/1980) *Hànyǔ Shǐgǎo* [*Draft History of the Chinese Language*]. Beijing: Zhonghua Shuju.

Wang, William S-Y. (1969) Competing change as a cause of residues. *Language* 45: 9–25.

Williams, S. Wells ([1874]1896) *A Syllabic Dictionary of the Chinese Language: arranged according to the Wu-fang Yuen Yin, with the pronunciation of the characters as heard in Peking, Canton, Amoy, and Shanghai*. Shanghai: American Presbyterian Mission Press.

Yang, Hsiu-fang (1991) *Táiwān Mǐnnányǔ Yǔfǎgǎo* [A grammar of Taiwanese Southern Min]. Taipei: Ta An Press.

You Rujie (1992) *Hànyǔ Fāngyánxué Dǎolùn* [Chinese Dialectology] Shanghai: Shanghai Jiaoyu Press.

Yuan Jiahua et al. ([1960]1989) *Hànyǔ Fāngyán Gàiyào* [An Outline of Chinese Dialects]. Beijing: Wenzi Gaige Press.

Yue, Anne O. (1999) *The Min translation of the Doctrina Christiana*. Journal of Chinese Linguistics Monograph Series 14: 42–76.

Yue-Hashimoto, Anne (1985) *The Suixi Dialect of Leizhou: A Study of Its Phonological, Lexical and Syntactic Structure*. Hong Kong: The Chinese University of Hong Kong.

Yue-Hashimoto, Anne (1991) Stratification in comparative dialectal grammar: a case in Southern Min. *Journal of Chinese Linguistics* 19. 2: 139–171.

Yue-Hashimoto, Anne (1993) *Comparative Chinese Dialectal Grammar: Handbook for Investigators* (*Collection des Cahiers de Linguistique d'Asie Orientale* 1). Paris: Ecoles des Hautes Etudes en Sciences Sociales.

ZHANG Huiying (1989) Shuō "gěi" hé "qǐ" [On *gěi* and *qǐ*]. *Zhongguo Yuwen* 5: 378–383, 401.

Zhou, Changji (1991) *Mǐnnánhuà Yǔ Pǔtōnghuà* [*The Southern Min Dialect and Standard Chinese*]. Beijing: Yuwen Press.

Zhou, Changji (1993) Xiàménhuà de bèidòngjù [Passive sentences in the Xiamen dialect]. *Zhongguo Yuwen* 80–85.

（本文发表于 *Journal of Chinese Linguistics*，Vol. 28.2，第 247—302 页，2000 年）

几个闽语虚词在文献上和方言中出现的年代

梅祖麟

1. 导言

最近几年我跟朋友之间有这样的对话。

客：近来在做什么研究？

主：在研究方言语法史，尤其是方言虚词史。

客：什么时候才有比较完整的方言记录？

主：明代。比方说，记录吴语的有冯梦龙的《山歌》，记录闽南话的有《荔镜记》，西班牙传教士在菲律宾转写的闽南话《基督教教义》(*Doctrina Christiana*)，都是明代的作品。

客：更早的方言记录可真没有了吗？

主：方言实词词汇的记录当然还有更早的，如扬雄《方言》以及《尔雅》《方言》的郭璞注。但是方言虚词的资料不多，方言语法结构的资料更是凤毛麟角。

客：那么你做的方言语法史研究，最早可以早到什么年代？

主：有些闽语虚词的来源可以追溯到五代、六朝，甚至于汉代。吴语的虚词"仔（著）"，大致可以追溯到六朝。

话说到这里，客摆出顾左右而言他的姿态。他心里怎样想我是知道的："你这个人简直是挂羊头卖狗肉。刚说比较完整的闽语的记录，最早能早到明代。转过身来又说有些闽语虚语的来源可以追到五代、六朝、汉代。难道你没有资料就能做研究？真是大言不惭，跟你这种人说话都是废气。"

这样的对话发生了几回以后，我觉得有替自己辩白的必要。我想借第三届汉学会议的机会来说明，我是挂羊头卖羊肉的。下面就要举例说明，并分析虚词来源的资料的性质。

第一，有些虚词本来是通语，后来在其他方言里不流行了，只保存在闽语里，于是变成闽语特有的方言虚词。如《世说》"坐著膝前"的方位介词"著"，台湾闽南话说 ti^6；"月既不解饮"（李白诗）的助动词"解"（胡买切，晓也），台湾话 ue^6。

第二，有些虚词很早就是闽地的特殊语词，碰巧在文献上记录下来了。如闽语人称代词复数词尾用"侬"，"汝侬"（你们）出现于《祖堂集》（952 年序）。闽语小称词尾用"囝",台湾话 a³。唐代顾况说:"囝音蹇,闽俗呼子为囝"。

以上推断虚词的年代,是靠文献上的记载。比方说,助动词"解"字最早的出处是南朝,如"晋明帝解占冢宅"(《世说·术解》),"即唤木匠而问言:解作彼家端正舍不?"(南齐,求那毗地译《百喻经》,《大正藏》卷四,544 中)。据此,台湾话助动词"解 ue⁶"(会)的来源可以追溯到南朝。

除了利用文献的著作年代以外,还有一种方法可以用来推断虚词进入闽地的年代。闽语有三个时间层次,分别属于秦汉、南朝、晚唐(罗杰瑞 1979)。因此:

第三,利用音韵层次的信息可以推断"坐著膝前"的"著","若夥"(多,多少)的"夥"是秦汉时期进入闽地的,第三人称代词"伊"字是南朝从吴地传入闽地的。

2. 从通语变来的闽语虚词:"著"和"解"

2.1 方位介词"著"字

"他坐在椅子上"这句话,台湾话说"伊坐 ti⁶ 椅囝顶"。ti⁶ 的本字是"著"。"著"是个知系声母鱼语御韵的字,这类的字还有在台湾话里变成 ti 音的,如"箸"ti⁶、"猪"ti¹。

方位介词"著"字的用例,有些出现于东吴南朝的文献,例如:

其身坐著殿上。(吴,康僧会译《六度集经》,《大正藏》III,6 下)|畏王制令,藏著瓶中。(刘宋,求那跋陀罗译《过去现在因果经》III,621 下)|长文尚小,载著车中……文若亦小,坐著膝前。(《世说·德行》)

以上是江东地区写成的文献。还有一些用例出现于北方写成的文献,例如:

若持枯草及燋牛屎,积著其上,手触足蹈,无所能烧而不成熟。(西晋,竺法护译《修行地道经》,《大正藏》XV,194 中)|譬如大官捕诸飞鸟,皆剪其翅,闭著笼中。(同上,XV,199 上)|作其百段,掷著江中。(《敦煌变文集》,《伍子胥变文》)|坐著我众蕃之上。(同上,《李陵变文》)|知远把瓦忭内羹饭都泼著洪信面上。(《刘知远诸宫调》)

竺法护世居敦煌,他的译场主要设在长安、洛阳。众所皆知,晚唐五代的敦煌变文以及金代的《刘知远诸宫调》都是在北方写成。

方位介词"著"的用例既然出现于南北两地的文献,我们认为它曾经是通语的虚词。

后来,方位介词"著"在晚唐五代的北方话里被"在"替代,如"似顽石安在水中"(《敦煌变文集》,《庐山远公话》),"抛在一边"(同上);在上海、苏州等吴方言里被 la² 替代，如"坐 la² 伊面"（坐在那边），la² 是促化的"来"字（郑张尚芳 1995：179）。这样，原来是通语的方位介词"著"字的流行地区逐渐缩小，终于变成闽语特有的方言虚词。

2.2 助动词"解（胡买切）"

漳腔台湾话的助动词 ue⁶（泉腔 e⁴），意思是"能、会"，来源是"解"，《广韵》上声蟹韵："解，胡买奶，晓也"（罗杰瑞 1989：337）。

助动词"解"的用例，南朝已经出现，如：

晋明帝解占冢宅，闻郭璞为人葬，帝微服往看。（《世说·术解》）| 即唤木匠而问言：解作彼家端正舍不？（南齐，求那毗地译《百喻经》，《大正藏》IV，544 中）| 风生解刺浪，水深能捉船。（萧纲《棹歌行》）

唐代北方诗人的诗里也有用例：

月既不解饮，影徒随我身。（李白《月下独酌》）| 世人解听不解赏，长飙空中自来往。（李颀《听安万善吹觱篥歌》）| 入春解作千般语，拂曙能先百鸟鸣。（王维《听百舌鸟》）| 隐士休歌紫芝曲，词人解撰河清颂。（杜甫《洗兵马》）

可见助动词"解"字在盛唐以前是通语。

从晚唐五代开始，助动词"解"在北方话里被"会"字替代，例如：

石门云"更会作什么？"（《祖堂集》2.140）| 除是法师会飞，才能到彼。（《大唐三藏取经诗话》，第十五）| 白虎精闻语，心生忿怒。被猴行者化一团大石，在肚内渐渐会大。（同上，第六）| 天地会坏否？（《朱子语类》4）

助动词"会"散播到吴语（苏州 uᴇ⁵）客家（梅县 voi⁵）粤语（广州 wui⁴）等大方言（《汉语方言词汇》473），以致助动词"解"变成了闽语特有的方言虚词。

3．从闽地或江东的方言词变来的虚词

3.1 人称代词复数词尾 -n

台湾话的人称代词，单数和复数差一个 -n 词尾：

	第一人称	第二人称	第三人称
单数	我 gua³	汝 li³	伊 i¹
复数	阮 guan³	恁 lin³	個 in¹

闽语有个表示"人"的"侬"字。"侬"字失落了韵母，就变成 -n 尾。下面是陈章太、李如龙（1991：114—115）的资料：

	我们	你们	他们
福鼎	我侬 $ue^3 nen^2$	汝侬 $ni^3 nen^2$	伊侬 $i^3 nen^2$
龙岩	我侬 $gua^3 lan^2$	汝侬 $li^3 lan^2$	伊侬 $i^3 lan^2$

福鼎是闽东方言。龙岩是闽南方言。跟台湾话比较，可知台湾话的复数词尾 -n 来自"侬"字的声母 *n-。

"汝侬"出现于《祖堂集》3.108.13：

又述示学偈曰：

瞎眼善解通，聋耳却获功。

一体归无性，六处本来同。

我今齐举唱，方便示汝侬。

祖传佛祖印，继续老胡宗。

太田辰夫先生《祖堂集口语语汇索引》（京都，1962，油印本）"汝侬"条下注"侬，原误浓"。"汝侬"的意思是"你们"。这首偈的作者是睡龙和尚，《祖堂集》3.106：

睡龙和尚嗣雪峰，在泉州。师号道溥，姓郑，福唐县人也。出家于宝林院，依年具戒，便参见雪峰，密契玄关，更无它住。

福唐县在今福建福清县东南。雪峰义存禅师（822—908）是九世纪的人，《祖掌集》序作于 952 年。书中只有"汝侬"，仅一见，没有"我侬"、"伊侬"，但我们有理由相信三身代词的复数词尾都用"侬"字。"汝侬"反映九、十世纪的闽语，可能是这个语词最早的记录。

指"人"的"侬"字出现于南朝乐府：

赫赫盛阳月，无侬不握扇。（《夏歌》，《乐府诗集》卷44，页7右）| 忆我怀中侬，单情何时双？（梁包明月《前溪歌》，45.5 右）| 诈我不出门，冥就他侬宿。（《读曲歌》，46.6 右）

据上所述，"侬"（人）是南朝江东地区的方言词，也就是说，长江以北没有这个语词。再参照《祖堂集》的"汝侬"，可知九、十世纪的闽地已经把"侬"字用作人称代词复数词尾。"侬"字的 *n- 声母，就是台湾话人称代词复数词尾 -n 的来源。

3.2 表示小称的名词词尾 a³（～儿，～子）

台湾话的小称词尾 a³，厦门话的 a³，来源是"囝"。例如北京话的"小刀儿"，福州话说"刀 iaŋ³（< kiaŋ³）"，潮州话说"刀 kiã³"，厦门、漳州、台湾说"刀 a³"，泉州话说"刀 kã³"。女婿泉州叫"囝婿 kã³ sai⁵"，潮州叫"囝婿 kiã³, sai⁵"，泉州、潮州的词尾 kã³、kiã³ 和本方言"囝婿"的"囝"同音。

《全唐诗》顾况诗《上古之什补亡训传十三章》有《囝》一章，自注："囝音蹇，闽俗呼子为囝"。《集韵》狝韵九件切亦曰："闽人呼儿曰囝"。再往上推，这个语词 *kian³ 借自南亚语（Norman & Mei 1976, Norman 1991：335—336），原因是"囝"在上古、中古汉语找不到语源，南亚语系却有不少同源词，例如越南语 con，高棉语 koun，孟语 kon，卡西语 khu:n，意思都是"孩子、子女"。

综上所述，*kian³（孩子、子女）这个语词在顾况诗自注"闽俗呼子为囝"这句话以前已经在长江以南的地区流行，汉化以后变成闽人呼儿的词语，写作"囝"，然后变成小称词尾。

小称词尾"～子"在魏晋南北朝兴起，"～儿"尾兴起在唐代以后。我们猜想闽地用"囝"为小称词尾是受了"～子"尾、"～儿"尾的影响。因此闽地"～囝"尾的兴起当在南北朝以后。

4. 用音韵层次来给虚词断代

4.1 闽南话方位介词"著 ti⁶"

罗杰瑞（1981：37）给"书、鼠、锯、箸"这四个鱼韵字列了比较闽语字表。本文又添上"猪、著在、汝、鱼、许那"这几个鱼韵字。

（1）	书	鼠	锯	箸	猪	著在	汝	鱼	许那
福安 i/øi	tsøi¹	tshi³	køi⁵	tøi⁶	tøi¹	—	ni³	—	—
福州 y/øi	tsy¹	tshy³	køi⁵	tøi⁶	ty¹	(tyɔ²⁸)	ny³	ny²	(xi³)
厦门 i, u	tsu¹	tshu³	ku⁵	ti⁶	ti¹	ti⁶	li³	hi²	hi³
揭阳 ɯ	tsɯ¹	tshɯ³	kɯ⁵	tɯ⁶	tɯ¹	(to⁶)	lɯ³	hɯ²	hɯ³
建瓯 y	sy¹	tshy³	ky⁵	ty⁶	—	—	—	ny⁵	—
建阳 y	sy¹	tshy³	ky⁵	ty⁶	—	—	—	ny²	—
永安 y	šy¹	tšhy³	ky⁵	ty⁵	—	—	—	ŋy⁵	—
将乐 y	šy¹	tšhy³	ky⁵	thy⁶	—	—	—	—	—

建瓯、建阳、永安、将乐指猪用"豬"不用"猪"，第二人称用"你"不用"汝"，远指词建瓯、建阳用 [u⁷]，永安用 [uɒ³]，本字都不是"许"（罗杰瑞 1991：350；陈章太、李如龙 1991：89，93，94），所以"猪"、"汝"、"许那"下面建瓯等四个方言点缺项。放在圆括号里的项目，音韵演变不合上列表里显示的规律，只是参考性质。

上面的表说明，厦门话"箸、猪、著在、汝、许那、鱼"等语词属于同一个时间层次，所列八个方言的语词也都属于这个层次。

这里就出了个问题。按照 2.1 节的论证，方位介词"著"字属于南朝层次。"箸、猪、汝、鱼"等鱼韵字在闽语里的音韵演变规律跟"著在"字相同，也应该属于南朝层次。我们知道秦始皇、汉武帝时代已经有汉人迁入闽地。这些汉人管猪、筷子、鱼、老鼠、锯子叫什么？第二人称代、远指词用什么语词？

罗杰瑞（1981：48）另外又列了个鱼韵的比较字表。

（2）		梳	疏	初	苎	箸	猪	著在	
福安	œ	sœ¹	søe¹	tshœ¹	tœ⁶	tøi⁶	tøi¹	—	i/øi
福州	ø	sø¹	sø¹	tshø¹	tø⁶	tøi⁶	ty¹	(tyɔ²⁸)	y/øi
厦门	ue	sue¹	sue¹	tshue¹	tue⁶	ti⁶	ti¹	ti⁶	i,u
揭阳	o	—	so¹	tsho¹	—	tuu⁶	tuu¹	(to⁶)	ɯ
建瓯	u, y	su¹	su¹	tshu¹	ty⁴	ty⁶	—	—	y
建阳	o	so¹	so¹	tho¹	—	ty⁶	—	—	y
永安	au	sau¹	sau¹	tshau¹	tau⁴	ty⁵	—	—	y
将乐	u, y	šu¹	šu¹	tšhu¹	thy⁹	ty⁶	—	—	y

"梳、疏、初、苎"是罗氏表里原有的字，我们又在旁边加上"箸、猪、著在"这三个字，以资比较。

"著"、"苎"都是澄母鱼语御韵的字，《切韵》声母相同，韵母相同，只是声调有别，"苎"字上声，"箸"字去声。它们的韵母在闽语里演变规律不同，说明"梳、疏、初、苎"属于一个时间层次，"书、鼠、锯、箸"等字属于另一个时间层次。现在的问题是孰先孰后。

有三个理由可以说明"梳、疏、初、苎"所代表的时间层次较晚，绝对年代在南朝；"书、鼠、锯、箸"所代表的层次较早，在秦汉时代已经传入闽地。

第一，"书、鼠、锯、箸、汝、鱼"都属最常用的基本词汇，"梳、疏、初、苎"不都属基本词汇。一般的情形是前者比后者早。比方说昔韵字里，厦门话的"尺" [tshio²⁷] 比"夕" [sia²⁸]、"锡" [sia²⁷]、"益" [ia²⁷]、"亦" [ia²⁸]、"赤" [tshia²⁷] 早。一个字如果有几个意义，一般是基本义比引申义早，例如厦门话"席囝"的"席"[tsio^{28}]比"筵席"的"席"[sia^{28}]早（参看罗杰瑞1979）。

第二，《切韵》和非闽语方言用擦音的地方，闽语往往用塞擦音。这是闽语特征之一，产生年代在《切韵》以前（参看罗杰瑞1991：343—344）。"鼠"、"书"都是书母字，书母《切韵》音ś-。"鼠"字闽语八个方言点声母都作tsʰ-或tśʰ-。"书"字闽东作ts-，闽西作s-；闽西的s-可能是受了非闽语方言的影响（罗杰瑞1991：344）。这两个字的塞擦音说明"鼠"、"书"进入闽语的年代是秦汉。

第三，南朝浙东盛产麻布、葛布。刘淑芬（1992：217）指出"山阴的葛布，诸暨、剡县的麻布，都是其中的精品"，而苎麻和葛分别是制造麻布、葛布的原料。南宋编纂的《嘉泰会稽志》（总页6487）："葛之细者，旧出葛山（原注：属会稽）"，又："苎之精者，本出苎罗山（原注：属诸暨）"。浙西新安郡（治所在浙江淳安以西的始新）也是苎麻产地。《梁书》卷五十三《良吏传》：伏暅为太守，"郡多苎麻，家人乃至无以为绳，其厉志如此"。

刘淑芬（1992：206—207）曾经按照《宋书》、《隋书》所记载浙东、福建的总户数作过一个比较表，今摘录其中的一部分：

（3）	浙东总户数	福建总户数
刘宋	90,519 户	5,884 户
隋（大业五年）	53,582 户	12,420 户

浙东地区是指西晋会稽、东阳、新安、临海四郡。临海在刘宋分为临海、永嘉两郡。新安在隋代分为新安、遂安两郡。福建地区是指西晋的建安、晋安两郡。上面的表显示从刘宋到隋代，浙东总户数减少40%，福建总户数增加一倍有余。至于其原因，刘淑芬（1992：209）说过：

> 梁朝末年，部分浙东沿海居民移往福建和广东，是大业五年浙东著籍户口数较刘宋锐减的原因。早在东晋时，就有浙东人民迁居广东，但这仅是少数避役百姓。浙东人民真正大批移民福建、广东，始于梁末。一因侯景之乱（548—552），战事扩及三吴、会稽，……二则伴随着侯景乱事而来的浙东大饥荒，以会稽郡最为严重，死者十之七八，存活者多逃往福建。陈文帝曾下诏书，允许梁末迁到福建的晋安、建安、义安诸郡的人还归本乡，但还归乡土者恐怕也很有限。隋代福建户数比刘宋时显著地增加。而这些避难移往福建、广东的人，多沿海道，这也可以解释此时濒海的会稽、临海二郡著籍户口的锐减。

浙东盛产苎麻和梁末浙东移民潮这两件事合起来说明，南朝的浙东移民给福建带来了苎麻，也带来了"苎"字。相反地，秦汉时代的移民已带来了"箸"字。这就是为什么这两个字在闽语里韵母演变不同。

据此，闽南话方位介词 [ti⁶] 字的传入年代是秦汉。

于是，我们的论证陷入自相矛盾的困境。按照音韵的尺度，方位介词"著 ti⁶"进入闽语的年代是秦汉，按照文献的标准，年代是南朝。因此，我们需要审查表示"在"义的"著"字的用例。

下面引的东汉翻译佛经出于两位译者，安世高公元后 148 年抵洛阳，译经时期在 150 到 170 年左右。支娄迦谶的译经时期在 170 到 190 年左右。

（4）"著"用作主要动词，意思是"在"。

（4甲）八十种虫生身中，二种发根生，三种著头，一种著脑，三种在额，二种著眼根，二种著耳根，二种著鼻根，二种著口门，二种在齿，二种在齿根，一种在舌，一种著舌根；一种著口中上颚，一种在咽，二种在膝下，二种著臂根，二种在手，二种著肘，二种著脾，一种著乳根，一种著脊根……如是八十种虫著身中，日夜食身……。（安世高译《地道经》，《大正藏》XV234 下—235 上）

（4乙）问第三止。何以故，止在鼻头。报用数息相随，止观还净。皆从鼻出入。意习故处为易识。以是故著鼻头也。（安世高译《大安般守意经》XV166 下）

例（4甲）"著"和"在"互文见意，"著"的意思就是"在"。例（4乙）问句说"何以故，止在鼻头"，答句说"以是故著鼻头"，"著"和"在"也是互文见意。

闽南话的 [ti⁶]，福州话的 [tyɔ²⁸]，意思是"在"，本字是"著"，都可以用作主要动词。

（5甲）闽南话　伊 [ti⁶] 台北。（他在台北）
（5乙）福州话　伊 [tyɔ²⁸] 福州。（他在福州）

此外东汉译经中的"著"字还有两种用法：

（6）V＋N＋著＋处所词
（6甲）心譬如怨家掷人著恶道中，无有期也。（支娄迦谶译《遗日摩尼宝经》XII 194 上）。
（6乙）其二儿则答言：亦无华香，当何以供？其一儿则脱著身白珠著手中，使报谓二儿：是犹可以供佛智者。（支娄迦谶译《阿阇世王经》XV 394 下）
（7）V＋著＋处所词
（7甲）譬如有黠人，拖张海边故坏船补治之，以推著水中，持财物置其中。（支娄迦谶译《道行般若经》VII452 上）
（7乙）至笃晷数数轻易及挝捶闭著牢狱。（支娄迦谶译《遗日摩尼宝经》XII189 下）

（6）、（7）这两种"著"字的用法在魏晋南北朝的文献中也有：

（8）V＋N＋著＋处所词

（8甲）辄含饭著两颊边，还吐与二儿。（《世说·德行》）

（8乙）埋玉树著土中。（《世说·伤逝》）

（9）V＋著＋处所词

（9甲）皆剪其翅，闭著笼中。（西晋，竺法护译《修行地道经》XV194中）

（9乙）文若亦小，坐著膝前。（《世说·德行》）

综上所述，可得两个结论。（一）"在"义"著"字在东汉的演变大概是：

（a）著＋N（"著"用作主要动词）
（b）V＋N＋著＋处所词
（c）V＋著＋处所词

（二）（a）、（c）两种用法台湾话都有：

	闽南话	东汉译经
（a）	伊 ti⁶ 台北。	八十种虫著身中。（XV235 上）
（b）	坐 ti⁶ 椅囝顶。	闭著牢狱。（XII189 下）

因此，从音韵演变和文献出处两方面来看，台湾话的"著在 ti⁶"字都是在秦汉时代传入闽地的。

4.2 闽南话第三人称代词 i¹

第三人称代词闽东一般用"伊"，如福州、福安、厦门、揭阳 i¹；闽西一般用"渠"，如建瓯 ky⁴、永安 ŋy¹、将乐 ky³。现在要讨论的是闽东方言"伊"字的时间层次。

"伊"字是影母脂韵。罗杰瑞《福建政和话的支脂之三韵》（1988）收录闽方言脂旨至韵比较字表，今转录若干。

（10）闽语脂旨至韵比较字表

	福安	福州	厦门	揭阳	建瓯	建阳	政和
*i	ei	i, ei	i	i	i	i,oi	i
1. 伊	ei¹	i¹	i¹	i¹	—	—	—
2. 姨	ei²	i²	i²	i²	i³	i⁹	i²
3. 餈	sei²	si²	tsi²	[tsi²]	tsi⁵	tsoi²	tsi²

4.	四	sei⁵	sei⁵	si⁵	si⁵	si⁵	soi⁵	si⁵
5.	尸	sei¹	si¹	si¹	si¹	tshi¹	tsi¹	-
	*əi	ai	ai	ai	ai	i	i	i
6.	屎	sai³	sai³	sai³	sai³	si³	i³	si³
7.	师	sai¹	sai¹	sai¹	sai¹	—	—	—
8.	指_手~	[tsai³]	tsai³	tsãi³	tsai³	i³	i³	i³

"尸"、"屎"都是书（审三）母脂韵的字。两相比较可见两个层次音韵演变不同。

"伊、姨、眷、四、尸"在共同闽语的韵母可以拟作 *i（参看罗杰瑞 1981：37）。脂韵开口中古音正是 *i。可见"伊、姨"等字属于南朝层次。"屎、师、指"都是来自脂部的脂韵字。脂部三等的音值是上古 -jid，西汉到魏晋 -jiəd，南北朝 -jiɛd（丁邦新 1975：240）。从音值的观点来看，"屎、师、指"的 *-iə 可以来自西汉到魏晋之间的任何一个阶段。但是我们认为闽语白读中较早的层次来自秦汉时期，所以暂且把"屎、师、指"的年代订在秦汉。

"伊"在先秦是个指示词，如"所谓伊人，在水一方"（《诗经·秦风·蒹葭》），西汉还是如此用法："伊年暮春，将瘗后土，礼灵祇"（《汉书·扬雄传·河东赋》），作为第三身代词出现于《世说新语》，如"羊郑是世婚，江家我顾伊，庾家伊顾我"（《方正》），"勿学汝兄，汝兄自不如伊"（《品藻》）（参看吕叔湘 1984：17；江蓝生 1988：247），也出现于其他南朝作品：

〔刘夫人唤诸女与周生语〕一人应曰："下仙未敢与高人语。"刘曰："高下未必可定，伊犹沉滞尘喧，共启悟之耳，何高之有！"（梁陶弘景《周氏冥通记》，《津逮秘书》本，3.5）

综上所述，"伊"字进入闽语的年代，按照音韵的标准是南朝，按照文献出处的标准也是南朝。这个例子跟方位介词"著 ti⁶"不同。方位介词"著"我们长久以来以为用文献的标准应该订在南朝（梅祖麟 1989；梅祖麟、杨秀芳 1995），是经过一番折腾才弄清楚时代当是秦汉。

4.3 闽语"若夥"的"夥"

台湾话询问程度、数量用 dzua⁶ 或 lua⁶，俗写作"偌"，意思相当于北京话"多么高？"的"多么"，"多高？"的"多"。例如"偌悬？"就是"多高？"，"偌重？"就是"有多么重？"。"偌"也可以用于陈述句，指某种程度，"有偌长就牵偌远"。下面打算说明（i）dzua⁶、lua⁶ 是"若夥"的合音词，（ii）按照音韵的标准，"若夥"的"夥"是秦汉时代进入闽语的。

罗杰瑞（1983：204）说明上古歌部字在闽语里的演变：

*uai	箩	麻	我	破	大	夥
福安	lo^2	mo^2	ŋo^3	pho^5	to^6	o^6
福州	lai^2	muai^2	ŋuai^3	phuai^5	tuai^6	uai^6
厦门	lua^2	muã^2	gua^3	phua^5	tua^6	ua^6
建瓯	suɛ^5	muɛ^5	uɛ^4	phuɛ^5	tuɛ^6	—
永安	suo^2	muo^2	ŋuo^1	phuo^5	—	—

这类在共同闽语的韵母可以拟作 *uai（罗杰瑞 1981：50）。歌部在先秦、西汉的音值是 *-ai（<*-al）或 *-al。到了东汉，*-ai 的 *-i 尾失落，就变成 *-a（丁邦新 1975：239）。由此可见共同闽语 *-uai 韵的字属于东汉以前的时间层次——因为东汉以后歌部的字就没有 *-ai、*-uai 这样的韵母。

《方言》"凡物盛多谓之寇，齐宋之郊，楚魏之际曰夥"。《广韵》"夥，胡果切，楚人云多也"。"夥"是歌部字，中古匣母果韵，匣母在闽语里往往变成零声母。闽方言表示"多"、"多少"的语词有些含有"夥"字（罗杰瑞 1983：204）：

福安 ni^{28} o^6（多少，how many，how much）"若夥"

福州 nio^{28} uai^6 "若夥"

厦门 bo^2 ua^6（不多，少许）"毛夥"

邵武 uai^3（多）"夥"

上面厦门话"毛夥"的"毛"，是借用"饥者毛食"（《后汉书·冯衍传》）的"毛"字。这个"毛"字意思是"无"，是"无有"的合音词（罗杰瑞 1995：32）。

厦门、漳州、泉州俗写的"偌"都是"若夥"的合音词：

	厦门	漳州	泉州
若夥	*lio^{28} ua^6	*dzio^{28} ua^6	*lio^{28} ua^4
（多__？）	lua^6	dzua^6	lua^4

"若"字日母。日母漳州话 dz- 音，所以漳腔台湾话"偌"字音 dzua^6。厦门、泉州日母 l-音，所以泉腔台湾话"偌"字音 lua^6。

文献记载中没有"若夥"这个语词。"若夥"的构词结构和"几多"相似。"几多"最早出现于南北朝隋代：

（11）几多

（11甲）复令悲此曲，红颜余几多？（《庾子山集》40）

（11乙）仁须几多金银珍宝，随意所须，从我索之。（隋，阇那崛多译《佛本行集经》，《大正藏》190：829下）

我们猜想"若夥"是受了"几多"的影响而产生的。果真如此，"若夥"在闽语里的产生时期当在隋代以后。至于"若夥"变成合音词的年代，目前一无所知，可能明代的闽语资料里有用例。另外有件事是很清楚的：无论是福安、福州"若夥"的"夥"字（o⁶，uai⁶），还是厦门 lua⁶、漳州 dzua⁶ 的后半截 -ua⁶，它们所反映的都是秦汉时代歌部"夥"字的 *-uai 韵。

5. 余论和结论

第二节用"著"、"解"这两个例子来说明，有些闽语的虚词，本来是通语，因此在文献里较早地、比较完整地记录下来了。所以虽然比较完整的闽语的记录只能追溯到明代，我们还是有足够的文献资料来研究这些词的历史，最早可以早到南朝，甚至于到秦汉。第三节用"汝侬"、小称词尾"囝"来说明，有些闽语虚词的来源，至晚在唐代已是方言词，正巧有文献把它们记录下来了。因此这些虚词的历史，不因资料的缺乏而被限制在明代或明代以后。可惜"汝侬"、"囝"字这类的资料极少。

第四节所讨论的问题其实是本文的核心部分。

人用两只眼睛去看，可以判断距离。一只眼睛瞎了，或者遮住了，只用一只眼睛去看，开车一定会撞车，打网球保管接不着球。同样地，用文献和音韵两个角度去看，才能超越文献资料的限制，才能把虚词或虚词来源进入闽地的时代订得更准。

举例而言，4.1节说明闽语的"汝"字属于秦汉层次，4.3节说明闽语的"我"字属于秦汉层次，4.2节《世说》"江家我顾伊，庾家伊顾我"等例说明闽语"伊"字属于南朝时代。这倒跟我们一般语法史的知识相符合：先秦第一人称主要用"吾、我"，第二人称主要用"汝、尔"，根本没有第三身代词——"其"是所有格代词，"之"是宾格代词。因此"渠、他、伊"等在现代方言中流行的第三身代词都是晚起的。不过有人可以质问："你所引的'伊人'（《诗经》），'伊年'（《汉书》）都是北方写成的文献。秦汉时期根本没有闽地语言的记载。焉知当时闽地没有第三人称代词'伊'字？"我们可以理直气壮地回答，按照4.2节的（10）闽语脂旨至韵比较字表，闽语脂旨至韵有两套音韵演变，分别属于两个时间层次。"伊"字属于较晚的、南朝的那个层次。

由此可知现在在闽语里流行的"伊"字是南朝时代进入闽语，并不是上古或秦汉时代遗留下来的。

上面的讨论还留下若干尚待解答的问题：（1）表示"人"义的"侬"字什么时候进入闽语？（2）4.1 节"梳、疏、初、苎"这四个字都是庄系知系声母，同层次其他声母的鱼语御韵字在闽语里怎样演变？这两个问题因为闽语的时间层次分析做得不到家，目前还不能回答。还有（3）闽南话远指词"许"（厦门 hi³，揭阳 hɯ³），按照音韵标准，应该属秦汉时代，但是"如许"和"许_那"字单用，可靠的用例似乎没有比《后汉书》、南朝乐府更早的，令人费解。

最后讨论一下，（1）汉语语法史的范围，（2）有什么资料可以利用，（3）为什么要用比较方法。

我们现在常见的近代汉语语法史——也就是用《敦煌变文集》、《祖堂集》、《朱子语类》等书写成的语法史——其实是早期官话的语法史。所谓上古汉语语法史、中古汉语语法史，也是某个时期的北方方言的语法史。原因很简单，南北朝以前，中国的政治文化中心一直在北方，所以《孟子》、《战国策》、《史记》、东汉南北朝译经所反映的是一种以北方方言为基础的通语。

但是理想的汉语语法史不应该只是北方方言的语法史。我们希望能有闽语语法史、粤语语法史、吴语语法史等等。这里就出现本文一开始就提到的问题。

众所皆知，汉语史的资料是用方块字写的。三千年连续不断的文字记载虽然让我们自傲，但也有先天不足之处。（i）方块字写的资料所包含的音韵信息太少，（ii）用方块字记录的方言语料，最早的不会早过明代。在这种情形下，想研究方言语法史就有巧妇难为无米之炊的感觉。

目前最大一宗没有充分利用的资料是各大方言的方言调查报告。尤其是闽语，在董同龢先生（1959）、罗杰瑞（1979，1981）、杨秀芳（1983）倡导下，闽语的时间层次分析已经有了相当不错的基础。换句话说，汉藏比较可以告诉我们甲骨文以前汉语的状况，比较闽语研究也可以告诉我们《荔镜记》、*Doctrina Christiana* 以前闽地语言状况。本文的目的之一是想把闽语时间层次研究和闽语虚词史研究联系起来。疏漏错误之处在所不免，敬希海内外方家不吝指教。

参考文献

Ting, Pang-hsin（丁邦新）（1975）*Chinese Phonology of the Wei-Chin Period*. Institute of History and Philology, Academia Sinica, Special Publications No.65. Taipei : Institute of History and Philology, Academia Sinica.

王育德（1969）福建语における"着"の语法について，《中国语学》总第 192 号。

太田辰夫（1962）《祖堂集口语语汇索引》（油印本）。

太田辰夫（1987）《中国语历史文法》，蒋绍愚、徐昌华译，北京：北京大学出版社。

北京大学中国语言学系语言学教研室编（1995）《汉语方言词汇》（第二版），北京：语文出版社。

江蓝生（1988）《魏晋南北朝小说词语汇释》，北京：语文出版社。

吕叔湘（1984）《近代汉语指代词》，上海：学林出版社。

施宿（1980）《嘉泰会稽志》，台北：大化书局。

梅祖麟（1989）汉语方言里"著"字三种用法的来源，《中国语育学报》第 3 期。

梅祖麟（1997）台湾闽南语几个常用虚词的来源，《训诂论丛》（第三辑），台北：中国训诂学会出版。

梅祖麟、杨秀芳（1995）几个闽语语法成分的时间层次，《"中研院"历史语言研究所集刊》66.1。

陈章太、李如龙（1991）《闽语研究》，北京：语文出版社。

董同龢（1959）四个闽南方言，《"中研院"历史语言研究所集刊》30.2。

杨秀芳（1983）《闽南语文白系统的研究》，台湾大学博士学位论文。

杨秀芳（1992）从历史语法的观点论闽南语"著"及持续貌，《汉学研究》10.1。

蔡俊明（1991）《潮州方言词汇》，香港：香港中文大学吴多泰中国语文研究中心。

刘淑芬（1992）《六朝的城市和社会》，台北：台湾学生书局。

郑张尚芳（1995）方言中舒声促化现象，《中国语言学报》第 5 期。

罗杰瑞（Norman, Jerry）（1979）Chronological strata in the Min dialects，《方言》第 4 期。梅祖麟译：闽语词汇的时代层次，《大陆杂志》第 2 期。

罗杰瑞（Norman, Jerry）（1981）The Proto-Min finals，《"中研院"国际汉学会议论文集》语言文字组，台北："中研院"。

罗杰瑞（Norman, Jerry）（1983）Some ancient Chinese dialect words in the Min dialects，《方言》第 3 期。

罗杰瑞（Norman, Jerry）（1988）福建政和话的支脂之三韵，《中国语文》第 1 期。

罗杰瑞(Norman, Jerry)(1989)What is a Kejia dialect？《"中研院"第二届国际汉学会议论文集》语言与文字组，台北："中研院"。

罗杰瑞（Norman, Jerry）（1991）The Min dialects in historical perspective. In William S-Y. Wang (ed.) *Languages and Dialects of China*, 325−360. Berkeley：Journal of Chinese Linguistics.

罗杰瑞（Norman, Jerry）（1995）建阳方言否定词探源，《方言》第 1 期。

Norman, Jerry（1991）*Chinese*. Cambridge and New York：Cambridge University Press.

Norman, Jerry, & Tsu-Lin Mei（1976）Austroasiatics in ancient South China：Some lexical evidence. *Monumenta Serica* 32：274−301.

Van der Loon, P.（1966-1967）The Manila incunabula and early Hokkien studies, Part I &II, *Asia Major*, New Series 12.1(1966): 1-43, 13.1-2(1967): 95-186.

Doctrina christiana: Primer libro impreso en Filipinas. Manila: Imprenta de la Real y Pontificia Universidad de Santo Tomas de Manila, 1951.

（本文发表于《南北是非：汉语方言的差异与变化》，第 1—21 页，台北："中研院"语言学研究所，2002 年）

《汕头话读本》所见潮州方言中性问句

施其生

壹 引言

余霭芹先生认为朱德熙先生论及的反复问句实际上包括两种不同的涵义：一种是狭义的，即 VP-neg-VP 句型；另一种是广义的，包括了 VP-neg-VP 和"可 VP"两种句型。由于反复问句在字面上不表示问话人的意见和态度，所以建议采用"中性问句"的提法。余先生提出还应该区分 VP-neg-VP 和 VP-neg（如现代方言中的"去不？"），并把 VP-neg、VP-neg-VP、"可 VP"看作中性问句的三种基本句型（余霭芹 1988，1992）。

本文采用余先生"中性问句"的提法。不过，汉语方言里的中性问句有多种不同的句型，不同类型的句型在分布上有一定的地域性，和方言的类属有密切的关系。我们认为，对于具有类型学意义的中性问句句型的分类，应该根据疑问语义的负载形式是用肯定否定相叠还是用疑问副词分不同的层次（施其生 2008）：

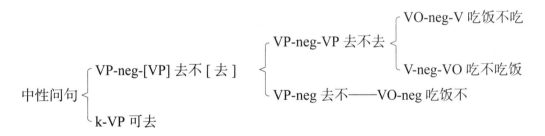

疑问句中，还有两种句式和上述句式有密不可分的关系，一种是选择问句，记为 VP₁-(or)-VP₂（or 代表选择连词，可省略），如"喝白酒还是喝红酒？"；另一种是带有疑问语气词的是非问句，记为 VP-m（m 代表疑问语气词），如"喝酒吗？"。学界普遍认为 VP-neg-VP 即所谓"正反问"或"反复问"，只是选择问 VP₁-(or)-VP₂ 的一种特殊形式；当 VP₂=negVP₁ 且省略 or 时，VP₁-(or)-VP₂ 便成了 VP-neg-VP。而 k-VP 则有学者指出和 VP-m 在许多方面相似。

关于潮汕方言以至闽南方言的中性问句，我们曾作过一些考察和探讨，提出过一些看法（施其生 1990，2000，2008），但是未尽之处尚多。1886 年出版的潮州话教材

A HANDBOOK OF THE SWATOW VERNACULAR（《汕头话读本》，以下简称《读本》）中有不少中性问句的语料，对继续探讨相关问题颇有价值，本文考察这些语料及其所能说明的问题。

《读本》1886 年出版于新加坡，由古友轩承印，是"专为英人学习潮语，潮人学习英语而发"（卷首出版说明），编著者林雄成，是英属海峡殖民地治安法庭翻译员。作者在前言中说："本书的编者懂英语，母语为汕头话，而不是学会了中文的欧洲人，因此，书中表达完全可以非常口语化。""本书属介绍性读本，不做任何修饰，使用的句子乃当地人日常用语"，"汕头地区有多种地方方言，虽然在新加坡，也可能在汕头，说澄海话更普遍，但本书选用的是潮州府方言。"[1] 从书中的注音和用词来看，作者所言不讹，本书当反映当时潮州方言的标准语 ——潮州府城话的口语，有相当高的语料价值。

全书共 33 课 169 页。内容包括词、短语和句子。各页分三栏，左栏为汉字书写的潮州方言词句；中栏为注音，采用罗马字拼音，声调只标本调的调类，不标调值和变调。右栏为对应的英文说法。

左栏用汉字表示的词句其实不是严格的潮州话，除用字大量采用训读，有些词语还用共同语书面语的词语代替，有些连音节数都和中栏的注音不同，但意义的对应是比较准确的。中栏用罗马字拼音注出的才是地道的潮州话口语的词句。本文取中栏的注音，将其转写为汉字例句，有必要注音的在汉字后再加注国际音标，无适当汉字可用的音节以方框"□"后加注音表示。例句编号为笔者所加，普通话翻译亦出自笔者；句后的数字是出现的页数和行数，如 6.1 是第 6 页第 1 行。

贰 《读本》所见中性问句及相关疑问格式

汕头方言的肯定、否定和疑问焦点常集中在情态的层面上（详下文），中性问句常常要加肯定否定词，否定词又常常和肯定词合音，归纳结构式，判别类型时常常碰到"难题"，本节先依具体结构分列书中所见的中性问句，以便下节具体分析和归类。结构式中的符号及其所代表的成分如下：

a	肯定助动词，如"有、会、好、爱、着……"
A	含肯定义的动词，如"有、会、好、爱、着……"
n	否定助动词或副词，如"无、袂、弄、嫒、免、唔……"
n'	否定副词"未"
N	含否定义的动词，如"无、袂、孬、嫒、免……"

V　　谓词

VP　谓词或谓词性短语

m　　语气词"咩 [me²]"

k　　疑问副词"□ [kha？₋]"

or　选择连词"阿 [₋a]、阿是 [₋a ˢsi]"

(一) a-VP-(or)-n

① 伊会死阿无他会不会死　45.6

② 潮州府会赢过汕头阿无潮州府是不是比汕头好　48.18

③ 昨夜月蚀汝有看阿无昨晚月蚀你看了没有　52.15

④ 汝个人会唔孬阿无你身体是不是不舒服　64.16

⑤ 人会食阿无人能不能吃饭　65.9

⑥ 会痒阿无痒不痒　162.13

⑦ 汝今暝会得来阿无你今晚能来吗　46.1

⑧ 伊昨日有来阿无你昨天来了没有　43.6

⑨ 门有关阿无门关了没有　56.13

⑩ 有洗阿无洗了没有　57.3

⑪ 汝礼拜日有去礼拜阿无你星期天去礼拜了没有　168.21

⑫ 汝个箱有锁定阿无你的箱子锁牢了没有　73.1

⑬ 汝个面有抹粉阿无你的脸搽粉了没有　73.15

⑭ 者买有阿无这东西买到没有　15.7

⑮ 咱□ [ma²] 起爱出门，食有够阿无咱们明天要出门，吃够了没有　88.19

(二) A-(or)-N

⑯ 汝有阿无你有没有　6.1

⑰ 厅有人客阿无厅里有没有客人　56.19

⑱ 洗浴房有水阿无洗澡间有没有水　57.8

⑲ 水罐有水阿无水罐有没有水　73.8

⑳ 有烧水阿无有热水没有　73.13

㉑ 恁个乡里有塔阿无你们村里有塔没有　59.19

㉒ 汕头埠有市阿无汕头有集市没有　59.22

㉓ 荷兰薯还了有阿无马铃薯还有没有　89.20

㉔ 合 [ka？₋] 荷兰西行吟，有交关阿无和法兰西行呢，有关系没有　163.22

㉕ 明起有人来阿无明天有人来没有　33.12

(三) a-VP-(or)-n'

㉖ 伊有来阿未他来了没有　44.10

㉗ 佃 [꜀in] 有来阿未他们来了没有　44.12

㉘ 我个□ [ut꜇] 房汝有扫阿未我的寝室扫了没有　57.1

㉙ 火炉有起火阿未火炉生了火没有　68.9

㉚ 茶花有开阿未茶花开了没有　83.4

㉛ 火船有□ [꜁pun] □ [꜀pi] 阿未轮船响了汽笛没有　160.17

㊃ VP-(or)-n'

㉜ 伊转来阿未他回来了没有　19.8

㉝ 日出阿未太阳出来了没有　29.10

㉞ 老爹坐堂阿未老爷坐堂了没有　165.1

㉟ 食床披床布阿未饭桌铺了台布了没有　73.16

㊄ VP-(or)-n-V

㊱ 汝知阿唔知你知不知道　33.13

㊲ □ [꜃la] 阿唔□ [꜃la] 够不够　90.1

㊳ 汝晓弹琴阿唔晓你会不会弹琴　67.19

㊴ 是阿唔是是不是　52.4

㊵ 是者阿唔是是不是这种　17.2

㊶ 汝是天主教阿唔是你是不是天主教　169.1

㊷ 汝是传道理个人阿唔是你是不是讲道理的人　169.3

㊸ 是分伊治阿唔是是不是让他杀　47.12

㊅ a-VP-m

㊹ 汝有去咩你去了吗　6.3

㊺ 汝有□ [tshue꜄] 咩你找了吗　19.11

㊻ 汝有记得我咩你记着我吗　19.1

㊼ 伊敢去咩你敢去吗　16.8

㊽ 伊会伤着咩他伤着了吗　17.7

㊾ 伊会死咩他会死吗　17.9

㊿ 我好去咩我能去吗　46.14

(51) 我好呾咩我能说吗　46.16

(52) 汝个房个门有锁咩你的房门锁了吗　56.17

(53) 汝爱食零须药咩你要吃点药吗　64.19

(54) 汝爱□ [thɯŋ꜄] 子咩你要打克拉棋吗　64.15

(55) 汝听我会见咩你听得见我吗　6.15

(56) 汝掠伊会着咩你抓得着他吗　15.13

(57) 汝会走赢伊咩你跑得赢他吗　49.5

(58) 汝有爱听零□ [ˆlo] 咩你想听一些吗　169.6

(59) 爱请先生咩要请医生吗　161.14

(60) 汝会泅咩你会游泳吗　161.4

㊆ A-m

(61) 有上大个咩有最大的吗　49.10

(62) 今年有闰月咩今年有闰月吗　52.13

(63) 海有涌咩海有浪吗　30.18

(64) 信皮爱咩信封要吗　69.7

(65) 许贱个是咩那个是吗　5.7

㊇ VP-m

(66) 师父个内在地块汝知咩师傅家在哪里你知道吗　55.1

(67) 汝晓读咩你会读吗　18.14

(68) 汝晓算咩你会算吗　16.5

(69) 汝昔八来□ [ˆtsie] 咩你以前来过这里吗　44.5

(70) 汝上食果子咩你喜欢吃水果吗　98.18

㊈ k-(a)-VP-m

(71) 被告个人□ [khaʔˌ] 有认咩被告那人认了吗　165.9

(72) 汝□ [khaʔˌ] 八去府城咩你去过府城吗　59.11

(73) 汝□ [khaʔˌ] 八食榴莲咩你吃过榴莲吗　98.15

㊉ VP_1-(or)-VP_2

(74) 只个月大阿是细这个月是大还是小　52.9

(75) 流□「ˆti」阿是洘 [ˆkho] 潮是涨还是退　30.16

叁　分类的讨论

第㊁类格式 A-(or)-N（有钱阿无）可看作第㊀类格式 a-VP-(or)-n（有来阿无）的特例。因为第㊁类格式中的肯定否定词都是兼类词，后面的宾语是谓词性成分时，这些词是助动词（a、n），构成的是第㊀类格式 a-VP-(or)-n。后面没有宾语，或宾语是名词性的，这些词就成了一般动词（A、N），形成第㊁类格式 A-(or)-N。比较：

有来阿无来了没有　a-VP-(or)-n

有钱阿无有钱没有　A-(or)-N

本质上，两类格式都是由肯定词和否定词对举构成的疑问格式。

第⊜类以"未"作 n' 的 a-VP-(or)-n'（伊有来阿未）和第⊖类的结构可说完全相同。不过这类句式也有其特殊之处：1）n' 限于"未"，是对 VP 的已然性的否定，不像第⊖类的 n 可用其他各种否定词，是对 VP 的各种情态（存在、可能、意愿、许可等等）的否定；2）a 只限于用"有"，而且可以省去；3）答语和第⊖类不同，肯定性的不用肯定词，而是要用"VP"的已然貌，比较：

第⊖类　有来阿无_{来了没有}——有。/ 无。

第⊜类　转来阿未_{回来了没有}——转来了。/ 未。

第⊝类格式 VP-(or)-n'（转来阿未）常常可以加上一个肯定词"有"而成为第⊜类：

伊有转来阿未。

日有出阿未。

老爹有坐堂阿未。

食床有披床布阿未。

但是也有不能加肯定词的，如"汝毕业未"不能说成"* 汝有毕业未"。从第⊜类的肯定词 a 很受限制，并且第⊜类均可省去肯定词变成第⊝类，而第⊝类却只有一部分可变成第⊜类来看，句末否定词为"未"的中性问句，强势句式是第⊝类。

从类型学的角度看前面四类，尽管格式不完全相同，但主导格式应是 a-VP-(or)-n。

潮州方言的 a-VP-(or)-n 格式和古代汉语以及现代粤语如开平方言中的 VP-neg 还是有所不同，不同之处在于否定词 n 不是针对 VP 而是针对肯定词 a 的，即闽语的中性问句是通过肯定词及其否定形式（否定词）的对举来表示疑问，虽然在类型上我们可以将它也归入 VP-neg 型，但是这个特点绝不可以掩盖。试比较现代普通话、广州话和汕头话、海康话的一些例子，其差异还是很重要的：

普通话	去不去？	香不香？
广州话	去唔去？	香唔香？
汕头话	爱去（阿）唔？	会芳（阿）峇?
海康话	有去无？	有芳无?

第⊞类格式 VP-(or)-n-V9（知阿唔知）是和前四类很不相同的一种类型，已经是 VP-neg-VP 而不是 VP-neg 了。但这类格式中的 V 在《读本》中只见到"知"、"晓"、"是"三个。据笔者调查所见，在闽南话的中心区域，如泉州、厦门、漳州、潮州，这种句式中的 V 仍然只限于"是"、"知"、"晓（懂）""八（也作捌，认识）"、"相信"、"好（[hāu²]，

肯）"、"敢"、"应承"、"口 [ʰla]（够）"、"堪值（值得）"等极少数动词，离闽南方言的中心地带泉州、厦门、漳州、潮州越远，这种句式的使用越自由，到雷州半岛和海南岛，才和 VP-neg 势均力敌。因此笔者认为闽南方言最具普遍性的主流格式还是 VP-neg，VP-neg-VP 估计是后起的变化。（参见施其生 2000）

第六、七、八类是一个大类，特点是句末用了语气词"咩"，类似是非问句。其中第七类其实是第六类的特例。第七类的 V 都是含肯定义的动词 A，这种动词在谓词性成分前是个助动词 a，构成第六类句式；在名词性成分前是一般动词 A，构成第七类句式，情形和第二类之于第一类相似。因此 3 种句式实际上只有两个小类，一类是有肯定词(a 或 A) 的，一类是没有肯定词的，即 a-VP-m/A-VP(汝有去咩 / 海有涌咩) 和 VP-m（汝知咩），而后者又大多可以加上肯定词而变成前者，如"汝知咩"也可以说成"汝会知咩"，情形又和第四类之于第三类相似。因此 3 种句式在类型学上看，其主导格式应是第六类 a-VP-m。

细加考察，这一大类带"咩"的句式，还不是典型的是非问格式，而是一种介于中性问和是非问之间的句式。"咩"也未成为典型的是非问语气词，而是介于否定词和是非问语气词中间的一个语气词。这类句式仍排斥否定性谓语，即 V 前不能有 n，V 也不能是否定词，如不说"*汝无去咩"、"*汝无咩"，倒可以有肯定词 a（如"汝有去咩"），其语气词的分布几乎和中性问句的否定词相同，即结构功能上类似一个通用的否定词，这些特点和中性问相同而和是非问不同；句中不用选择连词，句末不用否定词而用语气词，其语气词在语义上不含否定成分，这些又和是非问相同而和中性问不同；整个格式已有部分摆脱了主流中性问句中的肯定词 a，显示出一种从中性问句中脱胎出来的过渡状态；在疑问功能上，由答语可以看到两个小类一个和中性问相同，一个和是非问相同，这也说明其介于中性问句和是非问句之间，比较：

第六类	a-VP-m	汝有去咩——有。——无。
第七类	A-m	海有涌咩——有。——无
中性问	a-VP-n	汝有去无？——有。——无。
第八类	VP-m	汝知咩？——口 [eˀ²] / 知。——唔知。[2]
是非问	VP？	汝知啊？——口 [eˀ²] / 知。——唔知。

第九类 k-(a)-VP-m（汝口 [khaʔ₂] 去府城咩 ）是一种混合型的格式，兼有 k-VP 与 VP-m 的特点。当代潮汕方言的部分地区，k-VP 与 VP-neg 两大类型并存并用，而且有二者的混合型 k-VP-neg（见施其生 1990，2000），《读本》出现这类 k-VP-m，是一

个很耐人寻味的现象。《读本》虽然不见 k-VP 和 k-VP-neg，有可能是编者个人习惯于多说 VP-neg，或者记录时忽略并存的 k-VP，因为同时期出版的用潮州话翻译的《马太福音》(*MATTHEW* (Tie-chiu Dialect)) 便有 k-VP 的例子：

⑦⑥ 恁岂是唔捌读着圣经所呾你们是不是没读过圣经所说的？("岂" 为疑问副词□ [khaʔₑ] 的俗写)（102 页）

可见当时应该已经有 k-VP 型，笔者曾论证过潮州方言中性问句的固有类型是 VP-neg，k-VP 是后来从漳州传入的（施其生 2000），这里不妨推测，《读本》出现的 k-VP-m，正是疑问副词□ [khaʔₑ] 进入潮州方言，进而形成 k-VP-neg 以至 k-VP 的突破口，因为在语义功能上，□ [khaʔₑ] 与 "咩" 是最为相近的一对虚词，而南方方言中，副词与助词异曲同工的例子非常多。（参见施其生 1995）

第⑩类 VP₁-(or)-VP₂（大阿是细）是选择问格式，其 or 用 "阿是"，现在的口语完全可以说成 "阿"，而且 "大阿是细" 完全可以加一个肯定词说成 "是大阿是细"，其结构实质上是 a-VP₁-(or)-a-VP₂，其中的 or 其实只是 "阿"，这个 "阿" 和中性问句中的 "阿" 并无二致，可见潮州方言中性问句中的 "阿" 是个连词，不是个判断语气词，和近代白话以及现代晋语 "去也不" 中的 "也" 还是不太相同。通常认为选择问如果后项正好是前项的否定式就成了反复问（狭义中性问），这对于普通话之类的 VP-n-VP 无疑是对的，但是汕头方言的 a-VP₁-(or)-a-VP₂，如果 VP₂ 正好是和 VP₁ 相反的否定形式，譬如 "细" 说成 "荬大（不大）"，这句话只能说成 "是大阿是荬大"，和相应的中性问句 "是大阿�" 相差甚远。由此我们窥见潮州方言反复问的一正一反，不是 VP 与其否定式，而是肯定词与其否定式，这正是闽语反复问句的特点，上文已经说过。

综上所述，《读本》中所见的疑问句，若加以类型学的进一步概括，主要有 5 种：

中性问	a-VP-(or)-n	（有来阿无）（主流）
	VP-(or)-n-V	（知阿唔知）（非主流）
准是非问	a-VP-m	（汝有去咩）
中性问与准是非问混	k-(a)-VP-m	（汝□ [khaʔₑ] 去府城咩）
选择问	VP₁-(or)-VP₂	（只个月大阿是细）

肆 一些结论

对《读本》的语料考察，使我们得以发现或确认以下一些认识：

1. 潮州方言中性问句的固有结构是 a-VP-neg。这种结构是闽语的主流结构，可以归属 VP-neg 型，但是和一般的 VP-neg 有重要的不同，主要是通过肯定词和否定词的对举来表示疑问，其最主流的形式是 a-VP-(or)-n（有去阿无）。潮州方言反复问的一正一反，不是 VP 与其否定式，而是肯定词与其否定式，这正是闽语反复问句的特点。

2. 当时的潮州方言已出现一种"准是非问句"(a)-VP-m（汝知咩、汝有去咩），这种句型介于中性问句 a-VP-(or)-n 和是非问句 VP-m 之间，其语气词"咩"也介于否定词和是非问语气词之间，这说明汉语带疑问语气词的是非问句和 VP-neg 型中性问句有密切的关系，是非问语气词的确和句末否定词有密切关系。

3. 虽未见于《读本》，但可以确认百余年前的潮州方言已出现中性问句的另一类型 k-VP，具体形式为 k-a-VP(□ [khaʔ] 有认）。当时还有一种由 k-VP 中性问句(□ [khaʔ] 有认）和"准是非问句"(a)-VP-m（有认咩）混合而成的句型 k-(a)-VP-m（□ [khaʔ] 有认咩）已见诸《读本》，这种形式很可能是 k-VP 型进入潮州方言的突破口，而且 k 和 m 在疑问功能上很接近，说明 k-VP 和是非问句 VP-m 在疑问功能上的确十分接近。

4. 潮州方言中性问句 a-VP-(or)-n 中的"阿"和选择问句的"阿"一样，是个连词而不是语气词。

5. 百余年前的潮州话已出现少量 VP-neg -VP 中性问句，但此格式在潮州方言中的生成能力很有限，结合当今此格式在闽语各地的分布情况，可以看出是外来的后起格式，很可能是共同语影响的结果。

附 注

[1] 原文是英文："The present work differs in one respect from all other work on the Swatow language pre-viously published, as it has been compiled by one to whom it is a mother tongue and who has learned English, instead of by a European who has learned Chinese, so that it has been possible to confine the sentences strictly to the colloquial form." "This work makes no pretence of being more than introductory, and the sentences are such as may be heard from the lips of the natives in every day use", "From the various dialects in the Swatow region that of the department city known as Ch'ao-chow-foo (or Tie-chiu-hu in this dialect) has been chosen, although that of the department of Theng Hai is more extensively spoken in Singapore and perhaps in Swatow also."

[2] 口 [èʔ] 为表肯定的叹词。

参考文献

施其生（1990）汕头方言的反复问句，《中国语文》第 3 期。

施其生（1995）论广州方言虚成分的分类，《语言研究》第 1 期。

施其生（1996）论"有"字句，《语言研究》第 1 期。

施其生（2000）闽南方言中性问句的类型及其变化，《语言变化与汉语方言》，美国华盛顿
  大学、台北"中研院"语言学研究所筹备处。

施其生（2008）台中方言的中性问句，《语文研究》第 3 期。

项梦冰（1990）连城（新泉）话的反复问句，《方言》第 2 期。

游汝杰（1993）吴语里的反复问句，《中国语文》第 2 期。

余霭芹（1988）汉语方言语法的比较研究，《中研院史语所集刊》LIX—1。

余霭芹（1985）广东开平方言的中性问句，《中国语文》第 4 期。

朱德熙（1985）汉语方言里的两种反复问句，《中国语文》第 1 期。

朱德熙（1991）"V-neg-VO"与"VO-neg-V"两种反复问句在汉语方言里的分布，《中国语文》
  第 5 期。

（本文发表于《方言》2009 年第 2 期，第 126—133 页）

厦门方言词汇一百多年来的变化
——对三本教会厦门话语料的考察

李如龙　徐睿渊

一

厦门地处中国东南大门，作为郑成功的复台基地和闽南人旅居南洋的出入口，早在 17 世纪初，就已成为重要的商埠。1842 年"五口通商"后，西方传教士批量进入厦门。为了传教，他们用罗马字母创制了记录厦门方言的"白话字"，并以之翻译圣经、印书办报，在海内外闽南语使用地区组织推广，影响很大。周恩来总理在 1958 年《当前文字改革的任务》报告中曾经提到："鸦片战争以后，帝国主义国家派来中国的商人和传教士愈来愈多。他们为了学习汉语和传播宗教的需要，拟订了我国各地方言的拼音方案，其中如闽南的白话字（即厦门话的拉丁字母拼音方案）影响最大，曾经出版过许多书籍。据说至今厦门一带还有许多侨眷用这套拉丁字母跟海外的亲属通讯。"（许长安、李熙泰，1993：2）

闽南白话字的源头，可以追溯到 1815 年马礼逊在马六甲开办的英华学院所拟定的汉语罗马字方案。该方案本是为外国人学厦门话而设计的。传教士获得在厦传教权后，为了让信徒们阅读《圣经》、理解教义，便用罗马字翻译《圣经》，并于 1850 年在厦正式推行。（许长安、李熙泰，1993：65—68）在此后的 100 多年中，闽南白话字迅速传播。据黄典诚 1955 年的调查统计，当时海内外约有 11.5 万人使用闽南白话字。（许长安、李熙泰，1993：70—71）而在大陆地区发现的闽南白话字出版物约有 298 种，其中图书 120 多万册，报刊 110 多万份，内容涉及各种教会书籍和报刊、科学读物，以及中国古籍和闽南方言词典。（许长安、李熙泰，1993：76）在这些教会材料中，影响最大的是 19 世纪下半叶出版的三种：

1853 年（咸丰癸丑年）鹭门梓行所刊 *Anglo-Chinese Manual with Romanized Colloquial in the Amoy Dialect*（《翻译英华厦腔语汇》），美国归正教会 E. Doty（罗啻）著。

1873 年伦敦 Trüber & Co. 公司出版的 *Chinese-English Dictionary of the Vernacular of Spoken Language of Amoy with the Principle Variations of the Chang-chew and Chin-*

chew Dialects（《厦英大词典》），英国长老会 Carstairs Douglas（杜嘉德）著。

1892 年（光绪壬辰年）厦门萃经堂所印《英华口才集》，英国伦敦公会 John Macgowan（马约翰）著。下文分别简称《语汇》、《词典》和《口才集》。

罗啻是最早在厦门教会学校推广白话字的教会长老之一。他于 1844 年抵厦，在市区的新街、寮仔后、竹树脚和郊区禾山一带布道、建教堂、设教会，工作了 20 年，直至年老多病。（吴炳耀，1988）他在已故传教士 William J. Pohlman 自用的厦门方言词汇手册基础上修订了用字、注音符号和声调符号，增加了词条（特别新增商贸用语和货物名称两部分），写成《语汇》。《语汇》以厦门方言词汇为主，共分 26 个义类。每个词条以白话字记音，对应英文释义和汉字。

杜嘉德自幼学习古代和现代语言，熟悉希伯来语，善于速记法。他 1851 年毕业于格拉斯哥大学，1855 年在爱丁堡自由教会学院修完神学课程，同年抵厦门传教布道。（洪惟仁，1993）据记载，他也曾到泉州、安海、台湾等地拓展教会力量，到漳州访问太平天国革命军（Bowra，1983），对各地闽南方言都有所了解。从《词典》所记录的材料可以看出，杜嘉德辨音细致，对闽南各地的语音和用词差别十分敏感。他以 J. Lloyd 和 Alexander Stronach 两位传教士未出版的词汇手稿、罗啻的《语汇》、中国传统韵书《十五音》和 Medhurst（麦都思）的《福建方言词典》为参考基础，不断增加条目并重新编排，终于完成这部以收集口语词汇为主的闽南方言词典。《词典》用白话字记音，按词条的音序排列，配以英文释义但不注汉字。因为杜嘉德发现约有 1/4 到 1/3 的词条找不到相应的汉字，且当时在伦敦无法用汉字排版。主观上，杜嘉德认为厦门话应该是一种语言而不是方言。跳出汉字的束缚，厦门话可以得到更多重视和发展。《词典》出版之后，杜嘉德获得了格拉斯哥大学的博士学位。

马约翰 1863 年抵厦。关于他的记录所见不多，只有杜嘉德在《词典》的《前言》提到这本《口才集》时，认为此书对初学者很有帮助。《口才集》是教授外国人学习闽南话的课本。此书前 14 课按词性列举了一些口语常用词；中间 26 课按义类列举厦门方言词语，如鱼类、蔬菜、旅行、疾病、礼貌用语等，并用例句展示其用法；最后，作者提供了大量的情景对话以练习句型，内容涉及商贸、船务、文教、习俗等。书中所有的词条、例句和对话都用白话字记音，附英文释义和汉字。此外，还有对近义词的随文辨析和语法特点的简述。

这三本白话字语料都在前言里对厦门方言语音系统做了详细描述，内容包括声母、韵母、单字调和连读变调。从中可见三位作者对厦门话的记录相当翔实可靠。尽管对一些具体音值尚有争议，但正是这些争议真实地反映了当时厦门方言的语音面貌。

下面，我们拿这三本语料所记录的词汇和现今的厦门方言词汇作比较，考察 100 多年来厦门方言词汇发生的变化。[1]

二

综观三本词典的记录，厦门方言词汇中的常用基本词 100 多年来变化不大。

如《语汇》第 3 部分人体外部器官共收 76 条名词，其中 74 条至今沿用。[2] 如：

英文释义	汉字	厦门方言	英文释义	汉字	厦门方言
head	头壳	t'au2 k'ak7	eye	眼睛（目珠）	bak8 chiu1
ear	耳子（耳囝）	hi6 a3	face	面	bin6
nose	鼻	p'in6	mouth	嘴（喙）	ch'ui5
tongue	舌	chih8	teeth	牙齿（喙齿）	ch'ui5 k'i3
neck	颔颈	am6 kun3	throat	喉咙（咙喉）	na2 au2
shoulder	肩头	kieng1 t'au2	back	背脊（胛脊）	ka1 chiah7
hand	手	ch'iu3	finger nails	指甲（掌甲）	chng3 kah7
navel	肚脐	tò6 chai2	waist or loins	腰	io1
belly	腹（腹肚）	pak7 tò3	foot	脚（骹）	k'a1

发生变化的词只有 2 条，占 2.63%：tiong1 k'i3（门牙）今已失传；kha1 liam2（小腿胫骨的中段）是早期闽语的说法，至今仍见于福州话，现代厦门话称为 kha1 p'in6 liam2（脚鼻臁）。

第 23 部分时间和季节共收时间词 54 条，53 条沿用至今，唯有 tong1 kim1 chit8 tiap8（当今）今天失传，仅占 1.85%。如：

英文释义	汉字	厦门方言	英文释义	汉字	厦门方言
spring	春	ch'un1	autumn	秋	ch'iu1
eternity	永远	ieng3 oan3	future time	后来	au6 lai2
next year	明年	men2 nin2	last year	旧年	ku6 nin2
Monday	拜一	pai5 it7	1st month	正月	chian1 geh8
birth day	生日	sin1 jit8	1st day of month	初一	ch'oe1 it7
day light	天亮（天光）	t'in1 kng1	morning	早晨（早起）	cha3 k'i3
forenoon	上午（顶昼）	tieng3 tau5	noon	日午（日昼）	jit8 tau5

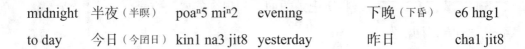

| midnight | 半夜（半暝） | poaⁿ5 miⁿ2 | evening | 下晚（下昏） | e6 hng1 |
| to day | 今日（今囝日） | kin1 na3 jit8 | yesterday | 昨日 | cha1 jit8 |

又如《口才集》里的人称代词、指示词等与今无异；第 32 部分前置词包含了方位词和介词 35 个，只有 bin6-tsiuⁿ6（面上）被 bin6-ting3（面顶）所替代，占 2.85%。而"面上"的用法至今仍见于泉属方言。这是方位词"上"和"顶"两个近义词竞争的体现（详见下文）。

<h1 style="text-align:center">三</h1>

至于一般词汇，我们考察了收词规模最大的《词典》按音序排列的前 3349 条词语，其中只有 1674 条和现今的厦门方言意义和用法相同，另一半发生了各种变化。词汇是否发生变化，首先和义类有关。就已经掌握的情况说，涉及文化、风俗、制度和生活习惯的词语变化比较大。

《词典》中收录了大量有关信仰和风俗习惯的词：道教的仪式"醮"有天公醮、平安醮、水醮、火醮、雨醮、虎醮、清醮、三朝醮等。和风俗习惯相关的仪式和器具名称繁复多样，有迎棺材进屋的仪式"接板"、棺材入土的仪式"进葬"、葬礼后的净身仪式"小净"、接灵位的仪式"接返主"、亲人去世后第七日的仪式"七日招魂"。葬礼上书写着被葬人名字的条幅称为"陵帧"，净身仪式上的薰香是"净香"，表明服丧身份的、挂在手腕上的铜钱称为"手尾钱"。这些特有的词语在今天只有老年人或郊区的母语者才能理解其中的一部分。

随着生活习惯的改变，服饰方面的名词也有不小变化。《语汇》第 8 部分的 57 条衣着名词（section8. of dress），有 8 条老派才懂但几乎不用、年轻人已经完全不解，约占 14%。如 ui1 su1 kun2（围私裙）受通语影响改称 ui2 kun2（围裙）；i1 chiuⁿ2（衣裳）改称 saⁿ1（衫），soh8（铘）改称 ch'iu3 k'oan2（手环），都是旧有的多种说法简化合并；siⁿ5 te6（扇袋）、bian3 liu2（冕旒）、t'au2 bin3（头抿）、mò2 tai6 siau3 beh8（毛大小袜）则是因旧有事物消失而淘汰。

有关文化和制度等上层建筑的名词变化更大：《语汇》第 14 部分有关文化的词有 15 条退出口语，约占 38.46%；第 15 部分有关科举考试的词除了"秀才"等保留于"博饼"的风俗中，其余 27 条都退出口语，约占 77.14%；第 16 部分涉及统治机构的官职，只有"候补、官员、委员"至今沿用，其余 54 条退出口语，约占 94.74%。

发生了变化的词语有哪些不同的演变类型呢？

（一）有些词语退出日常使用范围，成为历史词语。这类词大多和旧事物、旧制度、旧习惯有关。如上文提到的和上层建筑相关的词；又如《口才集》第 39 课列举了进出口商品 320 多条，其中 46 条已不为人们所熟知，约占 14.3%，如：良羌、母丁香、花剪绒、藤黄、晏息油、血竭、多罗呢等。第 40 课有关商业流通的专门术语 400 多条，其中约有 7.5% 成为历史词，如：出字白、手本、约字、九八行、饷关、保认、船口单等。

《词典》的收词也存在类似情况，如：O1-a1-leng2（乌鸦翎，官员装饰用品）；ang2-thO2（红涂，即土耳其鸦片）；tiau2-bo6（朝帽，上朝所戴礼帽）；kun1-ki1-bo6（军机帽，军官所戴之帽）；be3-khoai5（马快，衙门中勘查偷盗事件的走卒）；teng3-be3-koan1（顶马官，高层官员身边骑马的小官员）；heng2-meng2（行名，衙门中负责律法事务的师爷）。

（二）有些有特色的、活跃的方言词语精简合并了，原有的说法或消失或已被淡忘，逐渐退出日常口语。从这些精简合并的词语，我们可以看到词汇系统内部的竞争，如近义词的竞争，书面语和口语的竞争，通语词和方言词的竞争，以及上下位词的竞争：

近义词的竞争。方位词 chiun6（上）在《词典》中相当活跃，如：chiun6-bin6（上面）、ngn5-chiun6（向上）、lO6-chiun6（路上）、beh7-kang5 goa3-sin1-chiun6（卜降我身上）等。而同样表示"上"的方位词 teng3（顶）构词能力也很强，如 teng3-e6（顶下）、thn1-teng3（天顶）、soan1-teng3（山顶）、chhu5-teng3（厝顶）、teng3-thau2（顶头）、teng3-bin6（顶面）、bin6-teng3（面顶）等，但今天的厦门话，"上"作为方位词已完全被"顶"所取代，只保留着动词的用法，如 chiun6-soan1（上山）、peh7-chiun6-piah7（爬上壁）。

又如同样是书面语词，表"羡慕"义的"him1-bO6（欣慕）"和"loan2-bO6（□慕）"已经很陌生了，而"him1-soan6（欣羡）"的用法仍很普遍。

另外，还有"绳、索、线"，"赞、帮"，"嚷、喊、喝"，"木、柴"等几组近义词的竞争。这类竞争往往是单向的、缓慢的，都经过一段并行兼用时期。而竞争的结果则是词汇系统趋于简单。

书面语和口语的竞争。老派厦门人在表示"不一定"时，多用"bi6-pit7（未必）"或"bi6-pit7-lien2（未必然）"。后来这种说法为口语"bo2-tian6-tioh8（无定着）"和"bo2-it7-ting6（无一定）"所替代。"bO6-seng6（茂盛）"多是文人所用，口语里则说"ong6（旺）"。"bai2-tsong5（埋葬）"和"siu1-bai2（收埋）"现在口语中多说"tai2"。

通语词和方言词的竞争。关于通语词和方言词的竞争，前人在研究汉语词汇史已有阐述。汪维辉认为，"从某种意义上说，汉语常用词在历史上的新旧更替，就是方言词跟方言词或方言词跟通语词之间此消彼长的结果。"（汪维辉，2000：400—401）李如龙进一步指出："通语与方言的竞争贯穿了汉语词汇发展演变的整个过程，至今还在进行。"（李如龙，2004：194）通语词和方言词的竞争表现为双向的相互影响，这里说的主要是通语词对方言词的影响。厦门方言原称自然现象"雾"为"bO2（雺）"，"bu6（雾）"则指事物有污渍、斑点，黯淡无光泽。后因受共同语影响，自然现象"雾"及相关词（如起雾 ta5-bu6）也称 bu6；bO2（雺）的用法已很少见。这类例子比比皆是："不倒翁"由 a1-put7-to3（阿不倒）改称 put7-to3-ong1（不倒翁），"做生意的本钱"由 bu3-tsi^{n}2（母钱）改称 pun3-tsi^{n}2（本钱），"地毯"由 chi^{n}1 tiau2（氈条）改称 te6 t'an3（地毯），"发烧"由 jiet8-cheng5（热症）改称 hoat7-sio1（发烧），"天花"由 chia^{n}5-tsu1（正珠）改称 thien1-hoe1（天花）等。

通语词的影响不仅表现在词汇更替上，也表现在语素的构词能力上。"番"这个语素在厦门方言里多和舶来品有关，既可指人，也可指物。由于共同语的影响，不但新的外来事物大多遵从普通话的名称，连一些旧有的常用"番"类词也被普通话词逐渐取代，"番"的构词能力大大降低。如 hoan1-a3-han1-tsu2（番团番薯）改称 ma^{n}3-leng2-tsu2（马铃薯），hoan1-a3-pia^{n}3（番团饼）改称 pia^{n}3-koa^{n}1（饼干），hoan1-a3-he1（番团灰）改称 tsui3-ni^{n}2（水泥）等。

有些和通语词同形的厦门方言词在通语的影响下逐渐丢失固有词义，转而承载与通语词一致的词义：tong6-cheng6（动静），原指提起某个话题或问题，现指消息、情况；leng3-cheng6（冷静）原先有"孤独；孤立；环境沉寂冷清"三个义项，现在都为"平静、镇定"所取代；koan1-chio5（关照），原指书中所引用的文章或论著，现指关心、照看。

上下位词的竞争。原先厦门方言表示"看"的动作有一系列下位词：chiam1（瞻）：观望；bai6：拜访、有礼貌地询问；siam1：窥视、偷看；tshu3（鼠）：眯着眼睛看，多指视力差的人；lio3：快速看、浏览；koan1（观）：仔细看；tham5（探）：拜访；siong5（相）：久看。而现在的厦门方言有些已经几乎不用，如 chiam1 和 bai6，都被上位词"看"所替代；其余几个词偶尔可从老派口中听到，但构词能力降低，许多生动说法都被"看"及其构成的词组所替代。由于泛化而省简下位词也是方言词汇萎缩的一种方式，这使现代方言的表达变得单调了。

从总体上说，早期有特色的方言词多，后来趋于合并简化。有些特色词虽然还在使用，但活跃程度和构词能力已大不如前。这是方言萎缩的常见方式。

（三）一些常用词的义项发生变化。变化的情况大致有三类：义项增多、义项减少和义项转移。就多数的情况说，发生变化的义项多为比喻义和引申义。

义项增多。如：am5-kong1-chiau3（暗公鸟），本义是猫头鹰，现也喻指习惯熬夜、熬通宵的人；toa6-bong1（大摸），原指鸡冠花花冠大，现也指供人食用的禽类的翅、腿肥大；chiuⁿ6-toh7（上桌），原指宴会前把食物摆上饭桌，现也指宴会开始时各人就座；chha2-thhau（柴头），原指木块，现也形容人迟钝、应变能力差；tho3-tse5（讨债），原指要回债款，现也形容小孩挥霍，使父母重负有如付出欠债；seng5-chi3-chhui5（圣旨喙），原指讨价时不肯让步，现也用来形容那些不肯改变决定或对事态发展判断准确的人；chiah8-tiau2（食牢），原指人对鸦片上瘾，现泛指吃东西上瘾。

义项减少。如：beng2（明），《词典》记录有 6 个义项：clear，bright，plain，just (as mandarin)，Ming dynasty，ripe，as pine-apple。而最后一个义项"（菠萝）成熟"，在现代厦门话已丢失。《词典》举例 ong2-lai2 u6-beng2（王梨有明）和 ong2-lai2 put7-chi3-beng2（王梨不止明），释义均为 the pine-apple is yellow and ripe（菠萝黄了熟了）。现今都只说"熟"。又如 chhai5-thau2（菜头），原指白萝卜和饭馆等餐饮机构的总负责人，后一义项今已消失。

义项转移。如：ba6-hioh8，原指风筝，现指老鹰；ban2（蛮），原指做事拖拉懒散，现指顽固、难以说服；an1-thai1（安胎），原指用迷信的办法去除孕妇子宫的疼痛，现指用药物保胎；lu3-chiong5（女将），原来除了指女性将领，还指和男人交谈时过分大胆、外露的女人，后一义项现已消失，前一义项则引申指事业有成、有才干的女人。

四

从以上分析可以看出，100 多年来，厦门方言的词汇既有传承也有变化。传承既表现在那些与原有词汇保持一致的词上，也表现在旧词基础上产生的新词和新义项上。变化的表现丰富多样：首先，变化的程度不同。有些词完全消失；有些只保留在老派口中；有些成为历史词语，只在特定的场合出现；有些则保留在郊外农村。其次，变化的范围不同：有些词完全被近义词取代，有些只是义项增减。

词汇的传承是必要的。孙常叙认为："汉语基本词汇的古今传承，便是汉语延续发展的一个基本部分。"（孙常叙，2006：378）共同语如此，方言也如此。在没有遭受突然或特殊冲击的情况下，厦门方言词汇的发展变化总是持续而缓慢的，这是方言在社会生活中使老幼沟通、世代相传的需要。

词汇的变化也是必然的。社会生活不断演变，人的认知不断发展，为了适应社会生活的交际需要，词汇就必须不断调整。和语音、语法相比，词汇反映社会生活的变化最敏感、最快速。从这个意义上说，研究词汇的变化是了解社会生活变迁最直接、最便捷的途径。

透过厦门方言词汇100多年来的演变，我们不难看出厦门人物质生活、文化生活、语言生活和思维方式的演变。反过来说，正是这些社会生活的变迁，造成了厦门方言词汇百年来的变化。

（一）物质生活的变迁

基本的日用器物名称100多年来有不少保留原貌，如桌、椅、碗、盘等，而有些日用器具因其少用，分类趋于简单，相关名称也逐渐淘汰。如蜡烛在100多年前是重要的照明物，种类有油烛、蜡烛、花烛、通宵烛等；其中的各部分也有专门名称：蜡烛的芯称为烛芯，滴下的烛油称为烛泪，烛心燃烧时结成的花状物称为烛屎，蜡烛上装饰用的蜡制花朵称为烛花；与之相关的器具还有：烛台（蜡烛架）、烛芒（芦苇做的烛台）、鹤团烛台（鹤形烛台）、烛仓（烛台上插蜡烛的槽）、烛剪（剪烛心用的剪刀）、烛架（做蜡烛用的模具）、柴烛或柴烛鼓（木制的烛形油灯）。如今蜡烛只在停电或祭祀时偶尔用用，这些名词好些都不用了。

19世纪下半叶厦门是重要的贸易港口，税收是商品流通中不可忽视的环节。《词典》收录了一系列和税收相关的词：拍饷（收税）、纳饷（缴税）、饷银（税款）、税厘饷（所得税）、走饷（漏税）、饷单（税单）、饷关（海关）等。如今这些词都已经被普通话词语所替代。

生产行业的增减和兴衰也会带来词汇上的批量变动。百年来厦门行业的变化，可以从《语汇》中略见一斑。一些在当时颇为重要的行业现在已经消失，如做篾、拍索（做绳子）、烧灰（烧制石灰）、箍桶、脚夫；一些行业合并了，专有的称呼也发生了变化，如当时有专门买卖蜡烛的人，称为"卖烛的侬"。现在蜡烛只是日用杂货之一，这个称呼也就消失了。

交通工具的变化也很明显。当时最重要的交通工具是"船"，《语汇》中就有23种不同种类的船的名称。而现在最重要的交通工具"车"，在当时只有牛车、马车、货车和火薰车（火车）四种，驾驶的方式只有"赶"和"拖"两种。

（二）文化生活的变迁

科举教育在100多年前的文化生活中地位相当重要，相关的词语数量多，且大部分是共同语借词。《语汇》第15部分便收录了37条有关科举考试的词，如投考者的资格有童生、幼童、老童，考试后获取的"学历"有拔贡、岁贡、副榜贡、秀才、举人、解员、进士、会元、状元、榜眼、探花等，考试的类型有小试、乡试、会试、殿试，考官有学台、大主考、副主考、大总裁，考场有考棚、贡院等，可见考试等级明确、体系完整。如今科举制度消失了，这些词也成为历史词语。有关教育的有另外一些热点词语。

宗教信仰在旧时代的人民生活里也占有重要地位。《词典》不但收有基督教、佛教和道教用词，甚至民间信仰的各种神仙鬼怪、仪式、器具和信念都有详细记录。如民间崇拜的关帝爷、周仓爷、榕树爷、王爷、虎将、观将爷、井神、招财王、贤武大帝等；又如巫师跳神有一整套程序和专用词语：求巫师来跳神称为"找圣"，"童子"（男巫）跳神要"念咒"，若无效，则"催咒"；鬼神上身了称为"上身"或"上童"。这些词语如今只有郊区和市区的一些老年人知道。

关于群众文艺的词语，旧时有许多与地方戏有关的词语：演戏称为"搬戏"，演出开始称为"出戏"，演出前的排演称为"套戏"，当演员称为"妆戏"，挑选演出选段称为"择戏"，为剧团或演员捧场称为"跟戏"，把剧团请到家里演出称为"带戏"等。可见看戏是当时老百姓的主要娱乐活动，而今，文艺形式多样了，地方戏面临着衰落萎缩的尴尬局面，相关词语也逐渐萎缩了。

这三本书还收录了有关清王朝政府官职和统治机构的词语。《语汇》中此类名词70多条，反映了严格的等级和完整的体系。和科举教育词语一样，这些词现在大多已经成为历史词语。

（三）语言生活的变迁

在 20 世纪 50 年代推广普通话以前，共同语对厦门方言词汇的影响，主要表现在与上层建筑和意识形态相关的领域。但近几十年来，随着普通话的普及，通语词汇大量进入厦门方言，如学科专门用语、各种病症、流行时尚事物、新科技语等。许多年轻人甚至已无法用方言说出自己的姓名而直接用通语来指称。这是也是方言萎缩的表现之一。

书面语影响不断加大，在年轻人中表现尤为明显，如通语的关联词用惯了，便带进方言口语，如：

普通话	厦门方言旧有说法	厦门方言新派说法
如果……就……	若是……着……	若是……着……；如果……就……
如果不……就……	若是无 / 唔……着……	若是无 / 唔……着……；如果无 / 唔……就……

尽管	随时 / 虽然 / 虽罔	虽然
相反地	反转	相反
如果	若；设使	若；如果；假设
或者	抑是	抑是；或者
不过，但是	唔俗	唔俗；不过；但是

而文言词的影响则有所减弱。原先一些文人带到口语的文言词，如《口才集》对话中出现的旧时称谓"小女、小犬、拙内、尊驾"等，现在都很少使用了。

外来词的输入在 100 多年前的厦门话主要表现在马来语上，主要方式是音译（如 sap7-bun2：肥皂）或音译和意译相结合（如 sia6-kO1-bi3：西米）；这是厦门话直接从外语借入的，并不经过共通语做中介。这是厦门与东南亚频繁密切交往的表现之一。后来借入的外来词大多来自英语，先借入共通语再传入方言，如沙发、X 光、MP3、cool。

（四）思维方式的变迁

旧时厦门人认为血是不祥之兆，与血有关的病症都要有所避讳，如咳红（咳血）、呕红、啡红（吐血）、放红（便血）等。而今人们对病理常识了解增多，对"血"不再忌讳，称"血"为"红"的说法也逐渐消失了。

《词典》编纂时，电器和电的知识还未普及，带"电"的语素只有雷公电母等。后来，人们对"电"虽有所了解，但并不明确，误把热水瓶保温的功效和"电"相联系，称之为"电罐"、"电瓶"。如今家用电器普及，带"电"语素日渐增多，如电珠（灯泡）、电火（又称电灯）、电视、电脑、电话、电笔等等。这类语词的变化比比皆是，限于篇幅，不再列举。

附 注

[1] 本文考察的变化，单纯指词汇方面的变化。与词汇相关的语音和语法变化暂不反映。如"谜"在《词典》中读为 be6；今厦门音读为 be2。据《广韵》，谜，莫计切，隐言也，与《词典》中的读音相合。《集韵》除此反切，还收入与今普通话和厦门方言读音相符的"绵批切"。也就是说，100 多年前厦门方言"谜"字还保存着较古老的读音。但在词义方面，《词典》的释义与今无异。因此这只是语音的变化，不在我们的讨论范围内。然而，《词典》中"谜"有个近义词"猜"，其注解是"a riddle; to guess one"。在现代厦门话中，前一义项已经消失，在此义项上产生的合成词"灯猜"也为"灯谜"所替代。这就体现了词汇系统中近义词的竞争引起的变化，应是本文关注的内容之一。

[2] 虽然三本材料采用的白话字拼写系统和符号略有不同，但这些音值上的细微差别并不影响
读者对词汇的理解和判断。因此引用时我们尽量忠实原文的标音符号、英文释义和汉字注
释。为了便于输入和理解，我们把三本材料的声调符号统一改为调类标音法（阴平 1，阳
平 2，上声 3，阴去 5，阳去 6，阴入 7，阳入 8）。所注汉字先录原书所注，若不合本字则
在括号中注出本字；若本无汉字加注之。本字未明者用□表示。

参考文献

Bowra, C.A.V.（包罗）(1983) 厦门，余丰译，《厦门文史资料》第二辑，中国人民政治协商会议
福建省厦门市委员会文史资料研究委员会编（内部发行）。

Doty, E.（罗啻）(1853) *Anglo-Chinese Manual with Romanized Colloquial in the Amoy Dialect*（《翻
译英华厦腔语汇》), 厦门：鹭门梓行 .

Douglas, Carstairs（杜嘉德）(1873) *Chinese-English Dictionary of the Vernacular of Spoken Language
of Amoy with the Principle Variations of the Chang-chew and Chin-chew Dialects*（《厦英大词
典》), London: Trüber & Co. 台北：南天书局有限公司，1990.

Macgowan, John（马约翰）(1892)《英华口才集》，厦门：厦门萃经堂。

洪惟仁（1993）杜嘉德《厦英大辞典》简介，《闽南语经典辞书汇编》（第四册），洪惟仁编，
台北：武陵出版社。

李如龙（2004）词汇系统在竞争中发展，《汉语应用研究》，北京：中国传媒大学出版社。

孙常叙（2006）《汉语词汇》，北京：商务印书馆。

汪维辉（2000）《东汉—隋常用词演变研究》，南京：南京大学出版社。

吴炳耀（1988）百年来的闽南基督教会，《厦门文史资料》第十三辑，中国人民政治协商会议
福建省厦门市委员会文史资料研究委员会编（内部发行）。

许长安、李熙泰（1993）《厦门话文》，厦门：鹭江出版社。

（本文发表于《厦门大学学报（哲学社会科学版）》2007 年第 1 期，第 84—91 页）

Two Early Sources on the Shaowu Dialect

Jerry Norman (罗杰瑞)

1. INTRODUCTION

The city of Shàowǔ 邵武 is located in northwestern Fújiàn 福建 on the Fùtún 富屯 river only some thirty kilometers from the Jiāngxī 江西 border. Its dialect I earlier referred to as a "quasi-Mǐn" dialect (Norman 1973), but would now prefer to call it a Far Western Mǐn dialect. This group of Mǐn 闽 dialects differs from the commonly known Min dialects in one very important respect; in Shàowǔ and the other dialects of this group, the three series of Proto-Mǐn voiced stops have all become aspirates giving them, superficially at least, the appearance of being Kèjiā 客家 dialects. As I have shown elsewhere, however, there are compelling reasons for including them in the Mǐn group of dialects (Norman 1973, 1974).

I have recorded Shàowǔ data from two different native speakers who speak slightly differing varieties of the dialect. Speaker A (the late Mr. Zhāng Bó 张 博 of Táiběi 台 北) was from just south of the city; speaker B (Mr. Shā Huī 沙辉 of Táiběi 台北) was born and grew up in the city of Shàowǔ.[1] The most striking difference between the two varieties is that speaker A had <u>th</u> in words where speaker B has <u>tsh</u>. In addition there are a few differences in individual words; otherwise, the two varieties are almost identical. A concise description of the phonology of variety A can be found in an earlier article of mine (Norman 1974).

A few Shàowǔ forms are recorded in the brief survey report on the dialects of Fújiàn by Pān Màodǐng 潘茂鼎 et al. (1963). An interesting examination of problems relating to words in the Shàowǔ entering tone category has recently been published by Chén Zhāngtài 陈章 太 (1983). I recently discovered two much older sources for the Shàowǔ dialect, both quite short, but interesting when examined in the light of my field data. In this article I would like to examine these two sources. To put them into a proper context, I will begin by giving a sketch of the initials, finals and tones of the Shàowǔ city dialect (variety B).

368

2. SHAOWU INITIALS, FINALS AND TONES

The Shàowǔ initials are as follows:

p	ph	m			f	
t	th	n	l			
ts	tsh				s	
tš	tšh				š	
k	kh	ŋ			h	Ø (zero)

The finals are very similar to those reported for variety A (Norman 1969, 1974).

		a	e	o	ə	ɯ
	i	ia	ie	io		
	u	ua	ue	uo	uə	
	y		ye			yi
		ai	ei	oi	əi	
		au		ou	əu	iu
		iau		iou		
		uai	uei			
		an	en	on	ən	
	in		ien			
		uan		uon	uən	
	yin		yen			
	ŋ	aŋ		oŋ	uŋ	
		iaŋ		ioŋ	iuŋ	
				uoŋ		
		yaŋ				

The tonal values recorded for the two varieties of Shàowǔ were identical.[2]

1.	yīnpíng	very low, slightly falling, [21].
2.	yángpíng	low level, [22].
3.	shǎngshēng	high level, [55].
4.	yīnqù	low rising, [13]~[213].
5.	yángqù	high rising, [35].

6. yīnrù   high falling, [53].

In addition to these tones there are also atonic syllables very similar to those found in Standard Chinese. There is only one case of tone sandhi: shǎngshēng (high level) syllables generally take on a falling configuration when they occur before certain atonic syllables in the same word: tsou^{55} 'bird', but tsou^{53}ə 'id.'; this sandhi value is identical to that of the entering tone.

3. WALKER'S 1878 DESCRIPTION OF THE SHAOWU DIALECT

In an 1878 article in The Chinese Recorder and Missionary Journal called "Shao-wu in Fu-kien: a country station", the Reverend J. E. Walker gave a brief description of the Shàowǔ dialect of his time. Here I will compare Walker's data to my own recordings collected almost a century later.[3]

Walker recorded the Shàowǔ tones in the following way:

Shang' ₌p'ing, — low, easy and slightly falling

Shang' shang', — high, falling

Shang' k'ü', — low, rising

Shang' juh₌, — medium falling

Hia ₌p'ing, — medium even

Hia k'ü₌, — high, rising

Walker's "shang' ₌p'ing" (shàngpíng 上平) corresponds to my yīnpíng; the two descriptions (his and mine) are remarkably similar. The "shang' shang'" (shàngshǎng 上上) corresponds to my yīnshǎng. In Walker's day this was a high falling tone; both of my speakers had a high level tone except before atonic suffixes. It is quite clear that the sandhi variant here preserves an older tonal value; originally the shǎngshēng was undoubtedly high falling in all positions and subsequently became high level except where it preceded an atonic suffix; in this latter case it retained its original value. The two qù tones described by Walker (his "shang' k'ü'" and "hia k'ü'") both correspond exactly to my description. The same can be said for his "hia ₌p'ing" and my yángpíng if Walker's "even" can be interpreted as meaning 'level'. Walker describes the "shang² juh₂" as medium falling where I recorded a high falling tone. The explanation for this would seem to be that after the yīnshǎng tone became high level, the pitch of the yīnrù tone moved higher.[4] Walker's and my tonal values are compared in the table below.

Shàowǔ Tones in 1878 and Now

Tonal Category	Walker (1878)	Norman
1. yīppíng (shang² ₌p'ing)	low falling	very low, failing
2. yángpíng (hia ₌p'ing)	medium, even	low level
3. yīnshǎng (shang² shang²)	high falling	high level
4. yīnqù (shang² k'ü²)	low rising	low rising
5. yángrù (hia k'ü²)	high rising	high rising
6. yīngrù (shang² juh₂)	medium failing	high falling

Walker's description is notable both for its accuracy in identifying the tones with their correct etymological categories and for its clear description of the tonal values. He further remarks that "the missing Hia-juh has coalesced, not with the shang² juh₂, but with the Hia k'ü, and while words, belonging to the shang² juh₂ form a distinct tone class, the tone is not abrupt and the words often take on a final n or ng" (1878: 349-350). This statement is verified in all details by my own data. His last remark refers to the peculiar Shàowǔ treatment of Middle Chinese final p which, in words of popular origin, becomes n. In the nearby Guāngzé 光泽 dialect the development is to m (Xióng 1960). Walker illustrates this trait with the following examples:

	Mandarin	Cantonese	Shàowǔ	Foochow
目	muh₂	mok	mu²	muk₂
发	fah₂	fat	fai₂	hwak₂
合	hoh₂	hop	hon²	hak₂

For the three Shàowǔ words given by Walker, I have recorded mu⁶, fai⁷ and hon⁶ respectively.

Walker also comments on the lexicon of the dialect. His forms are listed below with comments based on my field notes. My Shàowǔ forms are designated A (from speaker A) or

B (from speaker B) unless both speakers agreed, in which case no designation is used.

1. ꜀hang 'I'. haŋ³. It should be noted that the Shàowǔ pronouns are an etymological puzzle—they bear no resemblance to those of any other known Chinese dialect. Walker suggested that Shàowǔ haŋ³ was related to Northern Chinese ǎn 俺 ; this seems rather doubtful in view of the initial Shàowǔ h̲.

2. ꜁hien (sic) 'thou'. hien³. Walker's tone is obviously erroneous since Shàowǔ has no yángshǎng category.

3. ꜁yen ꜁tai 'you and I'. A en¹ tai¹~ en¹ tai. This is the inclusive first person plural pronoun; tai¹ is the plural suffix for pronouns and is almost certainly simply the word 多, found also in the expression ki³ tai¹ 几多 'how many?'. Walker's suggestion that it represents 侪 is unfounded.[5] Speaker B apparently does not distinguish inclusive and exclusive first person plural pronouns; at any rate I was unable to elicit one from him. Note that Walker's form differs from mine in having an initial y̲ for the first syllable and in belonging to a different tonal class.

4. ꜁hu 'he, she'. hu³. For Walker's tonal error, see number 2 above.

5. ꜀hang ꜁tai 'we'. haŋ³ tai¹. This is the exclusive form of the first person pronoun; cf. number 3.

6. ꜀hang tai kai꜒ 'our'. haŋ³ tai¹ kai⁵. The possessive suffix kai⁵ is in origin the measure 个 and is probably a survival of an earlier stage when many Southern Chinese dialects employed measures with pronouns to indicate possession; several modern Yue 粤 dialects still form pronominal possessives in this way (Yue 1979: 266). Note that the plural suffix in Shàowǔ is frequently atonic: haŋ³ tai¹~ haŋ³ tai.

7. chong 'this'. tsoŋ⁷. The rù tone of this word appears anomalous; it is almost certainly to be explained as a fusion word of some sort, probably of an older *tši⁷ (cf. Xiàmén tsit⁷ 'this') and ioŋ⁶ 'kind, sort, type'.[6] Jiàn-ōu 建瓯, a Northwestern Mǐn dialect spoken in the same general region as Shàowǔ, has ioŋ⁷ for 'this' where its closely related sister dialect of Jiànyáng 建阳 has i⁷; the Jiàn-ōu is also best explained as a fusion of i⁷ and ioŋ⁶ 'kind, sort'.

8. ong꜂ 'that'. oŋ⁷. This form is likewise to be explained as a fusion of an earlier *u⁷ 'that' (cf. Jian-ou u⁷ 'id.') and ioŋ⁶.

9. chong꜂ ꜁tai 'these'. This is the same as form number 7 plus the plural suffix. I did not record such a form in my material. Walker's tone on the second syllable is

probably a mistake.

10. ₋nong 'where', ₋nong ₋e 'id.'. noŋ²ə. I did not record the unsuffixed form.

11. chong₋, k'wi 'here'. For 'here' I recorded tšoŋ⁷ə for both varieties of Shàowǔ. The origin of the syllable k'wi is unclear.

12. ꞈsha, sha ka 'what'. ša⁷kə. It is interesting that Walker has a yīnshǎng tone for this form; it shows that the modern form preserves the older phonetic tonal value (see above) but has as a result entered a new tonal category.

13. ng, m 'negative'. Shàowǔ has ŋ⁶ for the negative which generally corresponds to Peking bù.

14. mo or mao 'negative'. Shàowǔ has mau⁶ for the existential negative generally corresponding to Peking méi. I cannot explain why Walker gives two forms for each of the Shàowǔ negatives. Note that Walker assigned no tonal category to any of the negative forms he cites.

15. ꞈhie 'sign of the future', hie³. This corresponds to a widely distributed Mǐn auxiliary verb which corresponds semantically to Peking huì 会. Etymologically the Shàowǔ and other Mǐn forms are to be connected with 解 (广韵 , 蟹韵 , 胡买切 , 晓也).[7]

16. kin 'child'. kin⁷ə 'son, child'. This word belongs to the yīnshǎng category, so this is a case of the sandhi phenomenon mentioned above; kin³ is related to the common Mǐn word for 'son, child'; cf. Fúzhōu 福州 kiaŋ³, Jiàn-ōu kyen³ and Xiàmén 厦门 kiã³.

17. k'oꞋ 'to go'. kho⁵. Cf. Jiàn-ōu kho⁵, Fúzhōu kho⁵.

18. naꞋ 'only'. I recorded no such form, but the word is clearly cognate to Fúzhōu na⁶ 'only, if' (Maclay and Baldwin 1870: 568).

19. miang 'name'. miaŋ⁷. For an explanation of the tone (which Walker failed to give) see Norman 1973.

4. THE SHAOWU FUZHI OF 1901

The Shàowǔ fǔzhì compiled by Wáng Chēn 王琛 and published in 1901 contains a short section on the dialects of Shàowǔ prefecture which in addition to Shàowǔ county contained the counties of Guāngzé 光泽 , Jiàníng 建宁 and Tàiníng 泰宁 . The subsection called fāngyán 方言 in the fēngsú 风俗 section of the work (juàn 9, 9b-10b) contains 53 lexical items comprised of words which the compilers apparently thought peculiar to this region of Fujian. The glossing system is rather arbitrary; in some cases pronunciation is indicated by means of a homophonous character which is also supplemented by an ad hoc fǎnqiè reading here and there; in other cases merely the local writing of the word in question is given. It is doubtful that a meaningful interpretation of the material could be made without reference to a more exact phonological record of the forms. I have been able to identify the great majority of the Shàowǔ forms from my field notes. Below the forms which I have been able to interpret in this way are listed and discussed in order. I have made no attempt to interpret forms from any dialect other than that of Shàowǔ county.

1. 邵光泰三县人自称皆曰姎：杭上声．Reference here is to the Shàowǔ first person pronoun han^3 already discussed in section 3.1. above.

2. 称人曰贤：上声邵光语．This is the second person pronoun hien^3; cf. section 3.2.

3. 称他人曰俯：泰宁曰许建宁曰舍．The third Person pronoun hu^3; cf. section 3.4.

4. 呼男曰萨：平声．Reference here is to sa^2, a morpheme occurring in several words referring to male persons: sa^{2}nin^2 □人 'man, male person'; B lau^{3}sa^2 kai 老□人 'old man'. Comparable forms occur elsewhere in Western Fújiàn: Jiānglè 将乐 tion^1 phy^{1}sa^2 丈夫□ 'man, male person', Yǒng-ān 永安 tiam^4 pu^{1}sɔ^2 丈夫□ 'id.'. The etymology of these morphemes is obscure.

5. 老叟曰老萨．B lau^{3}sa^2 kai 'old man'.

6. 妇人曰娅娘：建宁曰夫娘．A a^{1}nion^2 'woman'.

7. 男子曰囝．kin^{7}ə, A kin^{7}tse 'son, child'.

8. 女子曰娅娘囝．A a^{1}nion^{2}kin^3 'daughter, girl'.

9. 呼酒曰走：邵光语建宁读皆本音．tsou^3 'liquor, wine'.

10. 饭曰盆去声，三县同建宁读本音．phən^6 'cooked rice'.

11. 菜曰茨去声．A the^5, B tshe^5 'vegetable'.

12. 诸稻皆曰禾．B uai^2 'rice plants'. In Pān (1963) this word is recorded as ᵻvæi.

13. 诸谷皆曰粟读如菽光泽读后本字．sy^7 'grain'.

14. 鸡曰陔．A kai^1, B kəi^1 'chicken'.

15. 牛曰愚．ny^2 'cow'.

16. 足曰屄．khau^1 'foot'. This word is common to all the Mǐn dialects: Fúzhōu kha^1, Xiàmén kha^1, Jiàn-ōu khau^1, Yǒng-ān kho^1. It is related to the Middle Chinese word 跤 (广韵, 肴韵, 口交切, 胫骨) 'shin bone'.

17. 筋曰卷：平声. B kyen¹ 'tendon'.

18. 耳朵曰忍头. nin³ khuei. The first syllable is etymologically related to 耳; the second syllable is probably 窟 'orifice'; it also occurs in phi⁵ khuei 'nose'. No such form as 耳头 for 'ear' was recorded in my own field work.

19. 露曰梭：去声邵光语. lu⁶. The word for 'dew' is one of those which has an initial s- in several Western Mǐn dialects: Jiàn-ōu su⁶, Jiànyáng so⁶, Yǒng-ān sau⁵. Although I failed to record a form with s-, it is possible that Shàowǔ had pronunciations with initial s- at the time the Shàowǔ fǔzhì was compiled. If regular, *su⁵ would be the expected Shàowǔ form.

20. 日午曰妒：邵武语. tu⁵ 'noon'. Compare the following: ha³tu 下昼 'afternoon'; A tu⁵kan¹ tsə 昼间子, B tu⁵thəu⁷ 昼头 'noon'; šoŋ⁶ tu 上昼 'morning'. The morpheme tu⁵ is etymologically to be connected with 昼 (广韵, 宥韵, 陟救切, 曰中). Its use in the sense of 'noon' is widespread in other Min dialects: Fúzhōu tau⁵, Jiàn-ōu te⁵, Jiànyáng to⁵, Xiàmén tau⁵, Yǒng-ān to⁵.

21. 二曰腻. ni⁶ 'two'.

22. 四曰细. si⁵ 'four'.

23. 六曰速. su⁷ 'six'. This form illustrates the typical Western Mǐn development of Proto-Min *lh > s (or š) (Norman 1973).

24. 九曰苟：建宁读本音. kou³ 'nine'.

25. 尺曰绰. tšho⁷ 'foot (measure)'.

26. 锅曰鼎：都讲切建宁读锅本音. tiaŋ³ 'cooking pot'. This is the word universally employed for 'cooking pot' in the Mǐn dialects: Fúzhōu tiaŋ³, Xiàmén tiã³, Jiàn-ōu tiaŋ³, Jiànyáng tiaŋ³, Yǒng-ān tiɔ̃³.

27. 桌曰盘. phon² 'table'. The use of 盘 for 'table' seems to be peculiar to the dialects of the Shàowǔ region.

28. 灶曰沮：去声. tsu⁵ 'stove'.

29. 臼曰去：上声. khy³tsə 'mortar'.

30. 冷曰清. A thən⁵, B tshən⁵ 'cold'. Comparable forms are widespread in Mǐn: Fúzhōu tsheiŋ⁵, Xiàmén tshin⁵, Jiàn-ōu tsheŋ⁵, Jiànyáng thoiŋ⁵.

31. 些须小物曰能子：能去声读如嫩. A kai nən² tsə~kai nən³ tsə. Note the tonal discrepancy between the gloss and the Shàowǔ A forms; Shàowǔ has lən⁶ fon 嫩 in my notes.

32. 去曰叮 : 去声 . $\underline{kho}^5$ 'go'. See section 3.17.

33. 来曰釐 .$\underline{li}^2$ 'come'. Cf. Fúzhōu $\underline{li}^2$.

34. 无曰毛 : 去声 . $\underline{mau}^6$. Related negatives are distributed throughout the Mǐn, Gàn 赣 , Xiāng 湘 and Yuè dialects. The Far Western Mǐn dialect forms agree tonally with the dialects of Jiāngxī and Húnán 湖南 rather than with the other Mǐn dialect. For example, most Mǐn dialects have a $\underline{yángpíng}$ tone for the existential negative: Fúzhōu $\underline{mo}^2$, Xiàmén $\underline{bo}^2$, Jiàn-ōu $\underline{mau}^3$, Jiànyáng $\underline{mau}^9$, Yǒng-ān $\underline{mau}^2$; cf. Nánchāng 南昌 (a Gàn dialect) $\underline{mau}^6$, Chángshā 长沙 (a Xiāng dialect) $\underline{mau}^6$ (Beijing Daxue 1964: 343).

35. 走曰祖 . $\underline{tsu}^3$ 'run'.

36. 跌曰胆 .$\underline{tan}^3$ 'trip and fall'. Cf. Jiàn-ōu $\underline{tueŋ}^3$, Jiànyáng $\underline{tueŋ}^3$.

37. 立曰跂 . $\underline{khi}^3$ 'stand'. Etymologically to be identified with (广韵 , 纸韵 , 渠绮切 , 立也). The use of this etymon for 'to stand' is common throughout most of Southeast China and can be found in the Wú 吴 , Gàn, Xiāng, Mǐn, Yuè and Kèjiā groups. Despite this widespread distribution, I have been unable to find reference to a single ancient textual example.

38. 看曰仰 : 去声 . $\underline{niaŋ}^5$ 'look'. The Shàowǔ word is probably related to Jiàn-ōu $\underline{iaŋ}^5$, Jiànyáng $\underline{iaŋ}^5$ and Yǒng-ān $\underline{iɔ̃}^5$ 'to look, to watch'. Possibly also related are Fúzhōu $\underline{auŋ}^5$ and Xiàmén $\underline{ŋ}^5$ 'id.'. The etymology of these forms is unclear.

The remaining glosses in the $\underline{Shàowǔ\ fǔzhì}$ are either not from the Shàowǔ dialect, or else I failed to record the corresponding Shàowǔ forms in my field work.

NOTES

[1] I recorded material from Mr. Zhāng in 1966 while a Fulbright fellow in Taiwan. Material supplied by Mr. Shā was collected in 1977; this latter work was supported in part by a grant from the Committee on Chinese Civilization of the American Council of Learned Societies.

[2] Tonal categories are numbered according to the following scheme: 1 $\underline{yīnpíng}$, 2 $\underline{yángpíng}$, 3 $\underline{yīnshǎng}$, 4 $\underline{yángshǎng}$, 5 $\underline{yīnqù}$, 6 $\underline{yángqù}$, 7 $\underline{yīnrù}$, 8 $\underline{yángrù}$. Any tonal category which cannot be conveniently placed in this scheme is numbered 9.

[3] Walker's article contains many obvious errors, especially in its use of the tonal symbols. I have cited the forms exactly as they occur in the article. The most common error is the omission of tone designations.

[4] This shift in tonal values seems to follow a general tendency which can be observed in Chinese dialects: if a dialect has only one falling tone, it is almost always a high falling tone. Thus, when the Shàowǔ shǎngshēng became high level except before atonic suffixes, the yīnrù, which was originally a low falling tone (perhaps something like [31]), according to this principle, took on a higher pitch. This resulted in the somewhat unusual situation in which the old unshifted shǎngshēng syllables occurring before atonic suffixes merged phonetically with yīnrù syllables.

[5] This etymology is impossible on phonological grounds. Middle Chinese 侪 dẓ'ai would have to have had a yángpíng tone; moreover, there are no cases of Middle Chinese dẓ' becoming t in Shàowǔ.

[6] The Xiàmén form is also a fusion of *tši 'this' (cf. Fúzhōu tsi³ 'id.') and *it 'one'.

[7] On the use of 解 as an auxiliary verb, see the very interesting comments and examples in Zhāng (1975:129-131). The form even survives in the Standard Language in the phrase xièbukāi 解不开 'can't understand' (Xīnhuá Zìdiǎn 1971: 472).

REFERENCES

Beijing Daxue (1964) *Hànyǔ fāngyán cíhuì*. Beijing: Wenzi Gaige Chubanshe.

Chen, Zhangtai (1983) Shàowǔ fāngyán de rùshēng. *ZGYW* 2. 109-111.

Maclay, R. S. & C. C. Baldwin (1970) *An Alphabetic Dictionary of the Chinese Language in the Foochow Dialect*. Foochow: Methodist Episcopal Mission Press.

Norman, Jerry (1969) *The Kienyang dialect of Fukien*. Ph.D. dissertation. University of California, Berkeley.

Norman, Jerry (1973) Tonal development in Min. *JCL*. 1. 222-238.

Norman, Jerry (1974) The Shaowu dialect. *Orbis*. 23. 238-334.

Pan, Maoding et al. (1963) Fújiàn hànyǔ fāngyán fēnqū lüèshuō. *ZGYW*. 6. 475-495.

Walker, J. E. (1878) Shao-wu in Fu-kien; a country station. *The Chinese Recorder and Missionary Journal*. 9. 343-352.

Wang, Chen et al. (1901) *Shàowǔ fǔzhì*. Reprint 1967. Taibei: Chengwen Chubanshe.

Xinhua Zidian (1971) Beijing: Shangwu Yinshuguan.

Xiong Zhenghui (1960) Guāngzé Shàowǔ huà li de gǔ rùshēngzì. *ZGYW*. 10. 310.

Yue, Anne O. (1979) The Tengxian dialect of Chinese. *Computational Analyses of Asian and African Languages*.

（本文发表于 *Journal of Chinese Linguistics*，Vol. 13. 2，第 331—342 页，1985 年）

一百多年来新界客家方言音系的演变 *

张双庆　　庄初升

一

　　新界是香港特别行政区地域最大的一个组成部分，包括深圳河以南、界限街以北的北九龙半岛及香港周围海面上的大小岛屿 235 个（以大屿山为最大，统称离岛），面积 984.74 平方公里，约占香港总面积的 92%。在 1898 年英国殖民者"租借"以前，新界属于广州府新安县辖地，历史上与深圳河以北的深圳、宝安、东莞一带一直有着非常紧密的地缘联系。

　　英国殖民者把 1898 年以前就居住在新界的乡村居民及其后代称为"原居民"，允许他们拥有耕地和建造小型楼房。新界的原居民主要有两大类，一类是自称为"本地人"或"围头人"的广府系居民，所操的"本地话"或"围头话"属于粤方言系统，与东莞的"本地话"（以莞城话为代表）非常接近；一类是客家人，所操的客家话与深圳沙头角、东莞清溪及惠阳淡水一带的客家话基本相同。新界的客家人多是清朝康熙八年（1669）迁海复界以后陆续从广东东部等客家地区迁移而来的，至今只有三百多年的历史。客家人虽然比本地人较迟入住新界，但由于规模大，人数多，大有后来居上之势。今天，新界的原居民中乃是以客家人为大宗，他们广泛分布在西贡、大埔、沙头角、沙田、荃湾、离岛各地，而即便是本地人相对集中的元朗、屯门等地，也有客家人入住其中。根据我们最近的调查，在新界六百多个村落中，客家村落约占了54%。但是，由于最近几十年来广州话的广泛普及，在这些客家村落中，掌握和使用客家话的客家人正越来越少。时至今天，四十岁以下的客家人已多数转用广州话了。

　　我们深入调查过西贡荔枝庄、沙头角麻雀岭、沙田赤泥坪和屯门杨小坑四个客家话方言点，它们分别位于新界地区的东部、北部、中部和西部，从地域上来说具有一定的代表性。根据实地调查的经验，我们认为上述四个客家话方言点的音系所反映出来的个别差异，与其说是地域上的差异，不如说是发音合作人由于年龄、文化程度和语感的不同所反映出来的个人差异。所以，就同一个年龄层次而言，我们认为新界客家话地区各个角落的口音都是基本相同的。下面以西贡荔枝庄作为新界客家话的代表，

---

* 本文是"新界方言调查研究"的成果之一，得到香港政府研究资助局的资助。巴色会客家方言圣经的影印件是柯理思（Christine Lamarre）教授和刘镇发博士提供的，谨此向他们致以诚挚的谢意。

[1] 全面归纳其语音系统，并简要分析其音韵特点。

1. 语音系统

（1）声母 17 个

p	布斧搬冰	pʰ 破抱扶病	ᵐb 马米尾棉	f 火法荒风	v 话位滑黄
t	多低短答	tʰ 腿头达糖	l 路梨南裂		
tʃ	祭猪捉周	tʃʰ 徐初池出		ʃ 书衫细色	ʒ 雨油县荣
k	家肝光脚	kʰ 旗跪牵裙	ᵑg 耳严月额	h 鞋口嫌糠	ø 哑鸭安轭牛~

（2）韵母 49 个

a	马挂	ɔ 河初	ɜ 婿洗			i 徐去	u 布字
ai	裁鞋	oi 袋灰		iɔi	kʰiɔi⁵³ 累		ui 配桂
au	高炒		ɜu 头口	iau 笑彪	iu 流酒	
				ia 写惹	ɔi 靴茄	
am	南凡		ɜm 森参人~	iam 验嫌	im 林深	
an	炭山	ɔn 肝碗	ɜn 田藤	iɔn 软	in 鳞情	
				iun 银裙		un 吞滚
aŋ	行~走钉			iaŋ 病平		
		ɔŋ 糖江		iɔŋ 粮凉		
				iuŋ 兄共		uŋ 葱龙
ap	答法		ɜp 笠粒	iap 接协	ip 十习	
at	发达	ɔt 割脱	ɜt 裂北		it 七直	ut 骨物
ak	石笛			iak 脊锡		
		ɔk 托壳		iɔk 脚雀		
m	唔不	ŋ 五吴		iuk 菊肉		uk 木绿

（3）声调 6 个

调类	调值	例字
阴平	34	坐野吹鳞毛近
阳平	21	牌池流田船龙
上声	31	果五跪酒碗滚

去声	53	路树怪问病共
阴入	2	鸭割郭额色目
阳入	5	十舌滑石贼毒

说明：① b、g 这两个浊塞音都带有同部位的鼻音，实际音值是 ^{m}b、^{ŋ}g。

②v 有时接近 w，ʒ 有时接近 j，都不是很典型的浊擦音。

③i 与 tʃ、tʃʰ、ʃ、ʒ 相拼时实际音值是 ɿi，如：椅 ʒɿi^{31}。

④阴平的实际调值是 334，阳平的实际调值是 211。

⑤例字下面加横线的是白读音。

2. 音韵特点

（1）古全浊声母今读塞音、塞擦音时一律为送气清音，如：婆 pʰɔ^{21}、茶 tʃʰa^{21}、簿 pʰu^{34}、扶 pʰu^{21}、词 tʃʰu^{21}、跪 kʰui^{31}、头 tʰɛu^{21}、酬 tʃʰiu^{21}、床 tʃʰŋ^{21}、白 pʰak^5。

（2）古精、庄、知、章组声母今读合流，如：将 tʃiɔŋ^{34}、庄 tʃɔŋ^{34}、张 tʃɔŋ^{34}、章 tʃɔŋ^{34}；徐 tʃʰi^{21}、初 tʃʰɔ^{34}、除 tʃʰu^{21}、处 tʃʰu^{53}（发音人李茂先生读为舌叶音 tʃ、tʃʰ、ʃ，另据调查，还有一些中、老年人塞擦音读 tʃ、tʃʰ，而擦音读 s，新派则一般读为舌尖前音 ts、tsʰ、s）。

（3）古非组的白读层还保留"古无轻唇音"的痕迹，如：符 pʰu^{21}、扶 pʰu^{21}、舞 ^{m}bu^{31}、雾 ^{m}bu^{53}、沸 pui^{53}、肺 pʰui^{53}、飞 pui^{34}、肥 pʰui^{21}、尾 ^{m}bui^{34}、味 ^{m}bui^{53}、发 pɔt^2、粪 pun^{53}、分 pin^{34}、网 ^{m}biɔŋ^{31}、望 ^{m}bɔŋ^{53}、伏 pʰuk^5。

（4）泥、来母今读逢洪音基本不分，如：怒＝路 lu^{53}、脑＝老 lau^{31}、南＝蓝 lam^{21}，但逢细音时则有别，如：女 ŋ^{31}\ŋgi^{31} ≠ 旅 li^{31}、娘 ^{ŋ}giɔŋ^{21} ≠ 良 liɔŋ^{21}、浓 ^{ŋ}giuŋ^{21} ≠ 龙 luŋ^{21}。

（5）有 ^{m}b、^{ŋ}g 两个带轻微同部位鼻音的浊塞音声母，^{m}b 来自明母和微母，^{ŋ}g 来自疑母、泥母和日母，如：马 ^{m}ba^{34}、雾 ^{m}bu^{53}、耳 ^{ŋ}gi^{31}、验 ^{ŋ}giam^{53}、娘 ^{ŋ}giɔŋ^{21}（有的发音人发的则是比较纯粹的浊塞音 b、g）。

（6）晓、匣母的一些字（主要是合口字）读 f，如：火 fɔ^{31}、贺 fɔ^{53}、花 fa^{34}、湖 fu^{21}、画 fa^{53}、欢 fɔn^{34}、荒 fɔŋ^{34}。

（7）溪母的口语字读 h 声母，这是 kʰ 的送气成分凸现而丢失塞音成分的结果，如：开 hɔi^{34}、去 hi^{53}、起 hi^{31}、口 hɛu^{31}、糠 hɔŋ^{34}、肯 hen^{31}、坑 haŋ^{34}、客 hak^2。有少数合口字进而演变成 f 声母，如：苦 fu^{31}、裤 fu^{53}。

（8）韵母比较完整保留 -m、-n、-ŋ、-p、-t、-k 六个中古时期的辅音韵尾，如：惨 tʃʰam³¹、杂 tʃʰap⁵、沉 tʃʰim²¹、急 kip²、安 ɔn³⁴、八 pat²、根 kin³⁴、笔 pit²、堂 tʰɔŋ²¹、脚 kiɔk²、巷 hɔŋ⁵³、壳 hɔk²、甥 ʃaŋ³⁴、摘 tʃak²、铜 tʰuŋ²¹、读 tʰuk⁵。曾摄字本来应该收 -ŋ\-k 尾，今天变成收 -n\-t 尾，如：等 tɛn³¹、色 ʃɛt²。

（9）没有撮口呼韵母，如：徐 tʃʰi²¹、鱼 ŋ²¹、雨 ʒi³¹、全 tʃʰɛn²¹、雪 ʃɛt²、群 kʰiun²¹、律 lut⁵、绿 luk⁵。

（10）止摄开口三等的精组和庄组字读 u，如：紫 tʃu³¹、私 ʃu³⁴、师 ʃu³⁴、子 tʃu³¹、事 ʃu⁵³，与读 ɿ 的梅县等地的客家话不同。但是，也有少数口语常用字读 i，如：刺 tʃʰi⁵³、死 ʃi³¹、四 ʃi⁵³。

（11）山摄三、四等梅县等地今读带有 -i- 介音的字，新界客家话丢失了 -i- 介音，读 ɛn/ɛt，混入了曾开一，如：田 = 藤 tʰɛn²¹、前 = 层 tʃʰɛn²¹、绝 = 贼 tʃʰɛt⁵、歇 = 黑 hɛt²。

（12）古合口一、二等韵的见系字今读多变成开口，如：果 kɔ³¹、瓜 ka³⁴、快 kʰai⁵³、挂 ka⁵³、管 kɔn³¹、关 kan³⁴、光 kɔŋ³⁴、镬 vɔk⁵、国 kɛt²\kɔk²、横 ₋直 vaŋ²¹，读合口的如：棍 kun⁵³、骨 kut²。

（13）部分浊音声母上声字读阴平调，这些字都是口语中的常用字。这类字如果有文、白异读，则白读音为阴平调，如：坐 tʃʰɔ³⁴、马 ᵐba³⁴、下 ₋底~ha³⁴、社 ʃa³⁴、惹 ᵑgia³⁴、野 ʒa³⁴\ʒa³¹、簿 pʰu³⁴、卤 lu³⁴、吕 li³⁴、苎 tʃʰu³⁴、语 ᵑgi³⁴、柱 tʃʰu³⁴、羽 ʒi³⁴、买 ᵐbai³⁴、弟 tʰai³⁴\tʰi⁵³、礼 li³⁴、被 ₋子pʰi³⁴、美 ᵐbui³⁴、你 li³⁴、理 li³⁴、以 ʒi³⁴、累 积~lui³⁴、尾 ᵐbui³⁴、咬 ᵑgau³⁴、某 ᵐbɛu³⁴、亩 ᵐbɛu³⁴、母 ᵐbu³⁴、藕 ᵑgɛu³⁴、后 前~heu³⁴\heu⁵³、舅 kʰiu³⁴、有 ʒiu³⁴、友 ʒiu³⁴、淡 tʰam³⁴、懒 lan³⁴、旱 hɔn³⁴、免 ᵐbɛn³⁴、演 ʒɛn³⁴、满 ᵐban³⁴、断 tʰɔn³⁴、暖 lɔn³⁴、软 ᵑgiɔn³⁴、晚 ᵐban³⁴、近 kʰiun³⁴\kʰiun⁵³、笨 厚pʰun³⁴、丈 tʃʰɔŋ³⁴\tʃʰɔŋ⁵³、上 ₋山ʃɔŋ³⁴、养 ʒɔŋ³⁴、痒 ʒɔŋ³⁴、蚌 pʰɔŋ³⁴、猛 ᵐbaŋ³⁴、动 tʰuŋ³⁴\tʰuŋ⁵³、重轻~tʃʰuŋ³⁴。

（14）次浊声母平声字在口语中读阴平调，如：魔 ᵐbɔ³⁴、毛 ᵐbau³⁴、谋 ᵐbɛu³⁴、鳞 lin³⁴、蚊 ᵐbun³⁴、笼 luŋ³⁴、聋 luŋ³⁴。

（15）古入声按照古声母的清、浊分化为阴入和阳入两个入声调，调值阴入低阳入高，与多数客家话相同。值得注意的是，有一部分次浊声母入声字读为阴入调，如：笠 lip²、粒 lip²、抹 ᵐbat²、袜 ᵐbat²、日 ᵑgit²、膜 ᵐbɔk²、劈 (花草)的刺儿lɛt²、脉 ᵐbak²、额 ᵑgiak²、木 ᵐbuk²、目 ᵐbuk²、六 luk²。

（16）文、白异读。主要有三类表现，一是表现在声母，如（"\"之前的是白读，之后的是文读）：扶 pʰu²¹\fu²¹、知 ti³⁴\tʃi³⁴、飞 pui³⁴\fui³⁴、肥 pʰui²¹\fui²¹；二是表现在韵母上，如：个 kai⁵³\kɔ⁵³、世 ʃɛ⁵³\ʃi⁵³、研 ŋgan²¹\ŋgen²¹；三是表现在声调上，如：野 ʒa³⁴\ʒa³¹、弟 tʰai³⁴\tʰi⁵³、后前~hɛu³⁴\hɛu⁵³、鳞 lin³⁴\lin²¹、近 kʰiun³⁴\kʰiun⁵³。

二

客家方言随着客家移民进入新界一带只有三百多年的历史，清朝嘉庆二十五年（1820）王崇熙编纂的《新安县志》虽然已经注意到把客籍村庄和本籍村庄区分开来，但并没有涉及客家方言。真正利用近代语言科学知识对新界一带的客家方言进行记录和研究的始于十九世纪中叶，开创者是巴色会的传教士。巴色会（The Basel Missionary Society）又称"巴色差会"或"巴色传道会"，是"福音教驻巴色的差会"（The Evangelical Missionary Society at Basle）的简称，属于基督教新教的信义宗，其总部位于瑞士北部的巴色城，与德国、法国交界。1846 年，巴色会派遣瑞典人韩山明牧师（Rev. Theodore Hamberg）和德国人黎力基牧师（Rev. Rudolph Lechler）前来中国传教，于翌年 3 月 19 日抵达香港。由于在 1860 年北京条约尚未签订之前清政府只允许基督教传教士在五口岸传教，一般不准他们深入到内地活动，所以，韩山明牧师被巴色会指定为专向香港一带的客家人传教，开始学习客家话；黎力基牧师被巴色会指定为专向潮汕人传教，开始学习潮州话。到了 1852 年 2 月，黎力基牧师被潮州府尹驱逐出境，并被限定日后不准再到潮汕地区传教，迫于无奈，他只好返回香港转而向客家人传教。所以，"自一八五二年十二月，他（按：指黎力基）和韩山明牧师及差会新派来的韦永福牧师经过三人会议，并已取得差会同意之后，便改换方针，开始三人合作，专向客籍民族传道。一八五三年春，他和韦永福牧师到沙头角工作，以后再迁入布吉李朗接替韩山明牧师的工作"。[2] 总之，巴色会在华早期的传教工作，实际上是以香港为基地，往北辐射到新界沙头角、新安布吉（今属深圳）、东莞李朗以至惠阳淡水等客家地区。

为了更加广泛和深入地在中国各地平民百姓中传播基督教教义，近代来华的西方基督教传教士通常是先学会说所到之地的方言口语，再着手编写和出版方言圣经等，供当地教徒使用。如前所述，巴色会是以香港作为基地专门向客家人传教的基督教教会组织。从十九世纪五十年代开始，巴色会传教士就以新界一带的客家话作为基础方言，编写和出版了大量的方言圣经和少数的方言字典、方言词汇、方言语法及方言启蒙课本。韩山明牧师在 1854 年 5 月 13 日逝世前撰有客家方言字典，可惜全书未能杀青，遗稿共 180 页，现在已经不容易看到了。黎力基牧师于 1860 年在柏林出版了罗马字拼音本的客家话圣经《马太传福音书》（*Das Evangelium des Matthaeus im Volksdialekte der Hakka-Chinesen*），于 1965 年在香港出版了罗马字拼音本的客家话圣经《路加传福音书》（*Das Evangelium des Lucas im Volksdialekte der Hakka-Chinesen*）。[3] 贾立言、冯雪冰在《汉文圣经译本小史》一文中指出，"《圣经》最初译成该种方言（按：指客家方言）的为《马太福音》，由黎力基（Rudolph Lechler）于一八六零年印于柏林，供巴色教会之用。"[4] 罗香林在《香港与中西文化之交流》一书中也指出，"黎牧师旋赴潮汕等地传教，既屡遭阻折，乃转而代韩山明牧师于宝安等地，发展教务，并着手以客家方言翻译圣经，初成马太福音，以罗马字拼音本，于一八六零年于柏林出版。是为客方言有圣经之始。"[5] 由此可见，这本罗马字拼音本的《马太传福音书》乃是第一部的客家方言圣经。此后巴色会传教士编写的汉字本圣经，有一部分就是以黎力基的罗马字拼音本作为底本的。汉字本的客家话圣经大概到了 1883 年左右才出版，香港中文大学图书馆馆藏的汉字本《马可福音传》的显微资料，扉页上注明是客话，光绪九年（1883）新镌。余伟雄在《崇真会一百四十年来之工作、影响与展望》一文中指出，"最先用汉字翻译客话圣经的，是毕安和露润滋两位牧师，这种汉字的客话圣经译本，初次出版的年代，大概于一八八三年间印行，至一九零四年，汉字圣经的改订本，也出版矣"。[6] 到了 1884 年，汉字和罗马字拼音对照竖排的《圣经书节择要》也出版了，全书共四卷，扉页上注明是光绪十年（1884）新刻，香港和盛印字馆活版。从内容来看，这是从当时业已出版的客家话圣经新、旧约的各篇中精选一些语句而编写成的一部"客家话圣经语录"，一共有 395 句。

要准确地了解一百多年前新界客家方言的语音系统，唯一可靠的文献数据就是上述巴色会传教士编写和出版的罗马字拼音本的圣经。当然，由黎力基牧师编写的于 1860 年在柏林出版的《马太传福音书》参考价值最高。另外，1884 年出版的《圣经书节择要》是目前我们所能看到的唯一一部汉字和罗马字拼音对照排版的客家话圣经，它对于我们的研究工作则具有独到的便利之处。关于方言圣经所使用的罗马字拼音，邹嘉彦、游汝杰在《汉语与华人社会》一书中指出，"Lepsius 是 19 世纪后半叶的著名语音学家，在语音学界创制国际音标之前，Lepsius 系统是权威的拼音系统，他曾出版专著用他设计的系统标记许多非印欧语，包括中国的官话和客家话。后来陆续出版的客家话罗马字圣经都是使用这个系统的。别种方言罗马字圣经的拼音方案也是在 Lepsius 系统的基础上制定的"。[7] 巴色会传教士在标写客家话时，如用 ts、tsh、s 表示舌尖前音 ts、tsʰ、s，用 tš、tš、š 表示舌叶音 tʃ、tʃʰ、ʃ，用 ń 表示舌根鼻音 ŋ，用 -y- 表示 -i- 介音等等，已经与后来的国际音标相当接近了。另外，客家方言有 6 个调类，分别是这样表示的：阴平、阳平、上声、去声、阴入、阳入。[8] 这些调类符号都一律标在罗马字拼音的右边，平声、入声标在右下方，上声、去声标在右上方。阴、阳分调的，如阴平与阳平，阴入与阳入，相比之下调值低的用下加一横的办法来区别，如阳平低阴平高，阴入低阳入高，所以阳平标为"˪"，阴入标为"˩"。总之，从最早的《马太传福音书》到后来的《圣经书节择要》，客家话罗马字圣经的整个拼写系统都显得非常缜密，除了少数地方明显属于排版错误的，我们基本上看不出有什么破绽。

三

1860 年罗马字拼音本的《马太传福音书》和 1884 年汉字、罗马字拼音对照本的《圣经书节择要》尽管相隔二十多年，但它们就使用的符号和所反映的音系来看都差别甚微，如 a 元音，前者使用 a，后者则使用 ɑ，实际上是印刷体与手写体的差别。下面就拿今天新界客家话的音系与《马太传福音书》和《圣经书节择要》所反映的音系作比较，考察其一百多年来的发展演变。两书所表现出来的细微差异，有必要时在下面随文注明。

一、客家话圣经有两套塞擦音、擦音声母，精组、庄组与知组二等合流，标为 ts、tsh、s，如：做 tso˩、千 tshen˩、前 tshen˪、新 sin˩、寻 tshim˪、争 tsań˩、初 tsho˩、衫 sam˩、床 tshoń˪、生 sań˩、拆 tshak˩、撞 tshoń˩；知组三等与章组合流，标为 tš、tšh、š，如智 tši˩、重 tšhuń 轻~\tšhuń˩ 贵~、治 tšhi˩、真 tšin˩、出 tšhut˩、串 tšhon˩、顺 šun˩、书 šu˩、十 šip˩。今天的长汀、兴宁、于都、乐昌等地的客家方言还保留着精、庄、知二与知三、章有别的格局。但是，今天的新界客家话精、庄、知、章组都已经合流，老派读舌叶音，新派读舌尖前音，还有一些中、老年人塞擦音读舌叶音，擦音读舌尖前音。新界客家话精、庄、知、章组一百多年来的演变可图示为：

精、庄、知二 ts [ts]、tsh [tsʰ]、s [s] ↘

                            tʃ、tʃʰ、ʃ → tʃ、tʃʰ、s → ts、tsʰ、s

知三、章 tš [tʃ]、tšh [tʃʰ]、š [ʃ] ↗

二、《马太传福音书》反映了古泥母字在洪音前读为 l，如：奴 lu˪、泥 lai˪、内 lui˩、宁 ~可 len˪、南 lam˪、难 苦~lan˩、能 len˪、农 luń˪，与来母不分；在细音前读 n 或者 ń[ŋ]，如：拈 nyam˩、娘 nyoń˪、你 ńi˪、女 ńi'\ń˩，则与来母有别。《圣经书节择要》则反映了泥、来母不论逢洪、细都基本有别的事实，如：内 nui˩≠类 lui˩、粘 nyam˩≠廉 lyam˪、怒 nu˩≠路 lu˩。但是，有些泥母字，如"拿"、"难 苦~"、"难 困~"、"能"有时读 n，有时读 l，说明已经开始混入来母。古泥、来母在洪音前"不分"显然是比"有别"更为晚近的语音现象。那么，为什么同样是以新界一带的客家话作为基础方言的方言圣经，比《圣经书节择要》早了二十几年的《马太传福音书》反而泥、来不分呢？我们推测，至少在从《马太传福音书》到《圣经书节择要》先后成书的二十多年间，新界一带客家话泥、来母的读音存在新、老派的差异，可能《马太传福音书》依据的是新派的口音，而《圣经书节择要》依据的则是老派的口音。今天新界的客家话泥、来母在洪音前基本不分，在细音前则还有别，泥母读 ᵑg 或者 g（混入疑母），来母读 l，其一百多年来的演变可图示为：

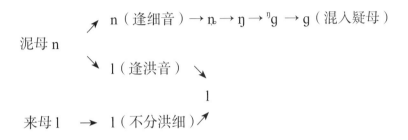

三、客家话圣经疑母字逢洪音及 i 韵母读 ń[ŋ]，如：饿 ńo˪、硬 ńan˪、眼 ńanˊ、误 ńu˪、外 ńoi˪、傲 ńau˪、义 ńi˪、遇 ńi˪、语 ńi˪、疑 ńi˪，读为声化韵时也是 ń，如：五 ń˘˘、鱼 ń˪；逢 i 之外细音读 n，如：验 nyam˪、业 nyap˪、月 nyet˪、愿 nyen˪、狱 nyuk˪、言 nyen˪（-y- 表示 -i- 介音）。今天新界客家话疑母字都读 ᵑg 或者 g，一百多年来的演变可图示为：

$$\begin{array}{l} \nearrow \quad \text{ŋ（逢洪音及 i 韵母）} \quad \longrightarrow \\ \text{疑母 ŋ} \qquad\qquad\qquad\qquad\qquad\qquad\qquad\qquad \text{ᵑg} \rightarrow \text{g} \\ \searrow \quad \text{n（逢 i 之外细音）} \rightarrow \text{n̠} \rightarrow \text{ŋ} \nearrow \end{array}$$

客家话圣经日母字逢 i 韵母读 ń[ŋ]，如：二 ńi˪、耳 ńiˊ；逢 i 之外细音则读 n，如：人 nyin˪、热 nyet˪、日 nyit˪、入 nyip˪、忍 nyun˪、让 nyoń˪、弱 nyok˪、肉 nyuk˪；少数口语中的非常用字则读零声母，如：然 yen˪、若 yok˪、容 yuń˪、辱 yuk˪。今新界客家话大部分日母字读 ᵑg 或者 g，混入了疑母，"然、若、容、辱"等少数字则读 j 或者 ʒ 声母，一百多年来的演变可图示为：

$$\begin{array}{l} \nearrow \quad \text{ŋ（逢 i 韵母）} \quad \longrightarrow \\ \text{日母} \rightarrow \text{n（逢 i 之外的细音）} \rightarrow \text{n̠} \rightarrow \text{ŋ} \rightarrow \text{ᵑg} \rightarrow \text{g} \\ \searrow \quad \text{n̠（少数口语非常用字）} \rightarrow \text{j(i)} \rightarrow \text{ʒ} \end{array}$$

上述泥母、疑母、日母今读逢细音（或 i 以外的细音）时要经历一个舌面化的 n̠ 的阶段，在今天的某些客家方言中还可以找到证据，如梅县话：尿 n̠iau²、娘 ₌n̠iɔŋ、月 n̠iat₌、业 n̠iap₌、二 n̠i²、入 n̠ip₌。

四、客家话圣经里的止摄开口及个别遇摄的 ts、tsʰ、s 声母字（都是精、庄组的字）只标出声母和调类，没有标出韵母，这是为什么呢？这是因为这类字在那个时候读的是 ɿ 韵母，而罗马字里正好没有 ɿ 这个符号，因此只好付阙。为了以示区别，《马太传福音书》的编者对这类字的声母作了一些改造，也就是把 tsɿ、tsʰɿ、sɿ 这三类音节分别标为 tz、thz、sz，如：祖 tz′、自 thz`、稣 sz﹐，很显然，tz、thz、sz 乃是从 ts、tsʰ、s 改造过来的。《圣经书节择要》则直接标为 ts、tsh、s，或者改造为 tʂ、ths、ʂ，不是很一致，如"子"，有时标为 ts′，有时标为 tʂ′；又如"慈"，有时标为 tsh﹐，有时标为 ths﹐；再如"事"，有时标为 s`，有时标为 ʂ`。上述这类字在今天梅县等地的客家话中仍然读 ɿ 韵母，保留了早期的面貌。今天新界客家话则读 u 韵母，详见上文"音韵特点"第（10）条，其演变可能经历了这样一个过程：ɿ → ʅ → u。

五、客家话圣经中流摄开口一等、三等的韵母是有严格区别的，与今天梅县等地的客家话相同，如：凑 tsheu ≠ 就 tshyu`。今天新界客家话老派的口音也有区别，开口一等有人读为 ɛu，有人读为 eu，都与三等 iu 有别。但是，新派的口音则开口一等混入了三等，如：楼 = 流 liu²¹、走 = 酒 tsiu³¹、狗 = 九 kiu³¹，体现了开口一等韵的演变，其过程：ɛu → eu → iu。据调查，在上述问题上老派与新派并没有绝对的年龄界限，西贡荔枝庄的李茂先生（1925 年生）属于老派的口音，比他年龄稍大的沙头角上禾坑的李满堂先生（1921 年生）则属于新派的口音。

六、客家话圣经中流摄开口三等的章组声母字读 u，如：周 tʃu﹐、兽 tʃhu`、手 ʃu′、守 ʃu′、收 ʃu﹐、受 ʃu`、仇 ʃu﹐，与今天梅县等地的客家话一样。但是，我们也同时注意到《圣经书节择要》中"咒"字除了有 tʃu`的读法，还至少有三个地方出现 tʃyu`的读法，体现这类字已经开始从 u 韵母向 iu 韵母演变了。上述各字在今天新界客家话老派的口音中还有 u 韵母的读法，如沙头角麻雀岭曾九先生（1934 年生）"周"读 tʃu³⁴，"兽"读 tʃhu⁵³，"手"读 ʃu³¹，但已经不容易听到了，绝大多数的发音人都读为 iu 韵母。

七、客家话圣经中古合口见系声母字（主要是一、二等字）读唇化的 kw（kv）、khw、w，与今天的广州话相同，如：寡 kwa′、关 kwan﹐（kvan﹐）、国 kwet﹗（kvet﹗）、贵 kwui`（kvui`）、归 kwui﹐、规 kwui﹐、鬼 kwui′、怪 kwai`、夸 khwa﹐、禾 wo﹐、王 woń﹐、位 wui`。同时我们也注意到有些同类的字有两读，以《圣经书节择要》为例，如：快 khwai`\khai`、话 wa`\va`、跪 khwui′\khui′、畏 wui`\vui`、万 wan`\van`、物

wut﹑\vut﹑，甚至有少数字已经没有唇化色彩，如：亏 khui﹑、葵 khui﹚、广 koń′、完 voń﹚、往 voń﹚，[9] 说明当时唇化声母已经开始消失了。与多数地方的客家话一样，今天新界的客家话已经完全没有唇化声母了，甚至连 -u- 介音也没有了，详见上文"音韵特点"第（12）条。

八、客家话圣经中还有少数字的读音与今天新界的客家话不同，如（前者是《圣经书节择要》的读音，后者是西贡荔枝庄的读音）：虾 ha﹚\ha³⁴阴平、阻 ts′\tʃɔ³¹、助 ths′\tʃʰɔ⁵³、产 san′\tʃʰan³¹、训 hyun﹚\fun⁵³、旷 khoń′\kʰɔŋ⁵³去声、狱 nyuk﹚\ʒuk⁵。显然，今天的这些读音都是广州话的影响造成的，但这种影响是零星的而不是成系统的。

四

邹嘉彦、游汝杰曾指出，"方言历时比较的前提，是最好有用同一方言记录下来的不同历史时期的内容或项目一致的数据。方言《圣经》是很理想的资料。通过同一种方言早期《圣经》和晚期《圣经》的比较，或与现代方言的比较，可以了解一百年来方言的历史演变"。[10] 如上所述，十九世纪中叶以后属于欧洲基督教教会组织之一的巴色会所编写、出版的罗马字拼音本的客家方言圣经，准确地记录和完整地保留了香港新界一带客家方言的语音面貌，是我们探讨一百多年来新界客家方言音系演变的唯一可靠的文献资料。通过历时的比较研究，我们发现在一百多年间新界客家方言的一些重要的音韵特点已经发生了重大的变化，但变化的规律也是非常清晰的，如分别来自精、庄、知二与章、知三的两套不同的塞擦音、擦音声母已经合并为一套塞擦音、擦音声母，这些演变规律对于研究客家方言史乃至于汉语语音史都具有重要的启发意义。

最近几十年来，由于城市化进程的加快和广州话作为香港区域共同语的广泛普及，新界客家方言的发展、演变空前剧烈，一方面表现为使用范围逐渐缩小和使用人口逐渐减少，另一方面表现为方言本身在语音、词汇、语法诸层面都发生了急剧的变化。我们通过对新派口音与老派口音的共时差异的比较，可以进一步体察方言音系历时演变的动态过程，也可以反过来对上述某些使用方言圣经数据进行历史比较所得出的成果进行检验。

附　注

[1] 西贡荔枝庄的发音合作人李茂先生，男，生于 1925 年，小时候曾读过旧式学堂，文化程度较高。我们谨此向李先生深表谢忱！

[2] 毕恩助（著）、曾荣辉（译）:《巴色传道会差遣韩黎二牧来吾客族地区传道简史》(1974 年),
载《香港崇真会立会一百四十周年纪念特刊》(香港 : 基督教香港崇真会编印，1987 年)，
页 87。

[3] 这两本罗马字拼音本的客家话圣经都没有出现汉字，书名使用德文和罗马字拼音对照，卷
首的体例说明使用德文，正文则一律是罗马字拼音。

[4] 贾立言、冯雪冰:《汉文圣经译本小史》，载 George Milligan（著），贾立言、冯雪冰（译）:
《新约圣经流传史》(上海 : 广学会，民国二十三年〔1934〕)，《附录一》，页 235。

[5] 罗香林:《香港与中西文化之交流》(香港 : 中国学社，民国五十年〔1961〕)，页 183。

[6] 余伟雄:《崇真会一百四十年来之工作、影响与展望》，载《香港崇真立会一百四十周年纪
念特刊》，页 67。

[7] 邹嘉彦、游汝杰:《汉语与华人社会》(上海 : 复旦大学出版社，香港 : 香港城市大学出版
社，2001 年)，页 203。

[8]《马太传福音书》在卷首的体例说明中分别把这六个调类称为上平、下平、上、去、上入
和下入。

[9] 从整个音位系统来看，w 和 v 是同一个音位的两个自由变体，早期以 w 为主，这是个摩擦
很轻的略带展唇的半元音；今天则以 v 为主，这是个唇齿浊擦音，摩擦也较轻。

[10] 邹嘉彦、游汝杰:《汉语与华人社会》，页 205。

（本文发表于《中国文化研究所学报》第十二期，第 441—450 页，2003 年）

客家方言及其他东南方言的唇化软腭音声母 *

庄初升

壹 引言

汉语语言学中称为"舌根音"或"舌面后音"的辅音 [k]、[kʰ]、[g]、[ŋ]、[x]、[ɣ] 等也通称为"软腭音"（Velar），后者是基于被动发音器官来命名的。多年来，我们在客家方言的田野调查中发现，部分客家方言点中古见组声母今读两组软腭音声母，一组是普通的 k、kʰ，来自古开口字（下文简称"k 组"）；一组是唇齿化的 kv、kʰv（少数方言点还有 ŋv），来自古合口字（下文简称"kv 组"）。kv 组与下文将要讨论的粤语中的 kw、kʰw 和吴语中的 kw、kʰw、gw、ŋw、hw（下文一律简称"kw 组"）具有很高的相关性，本文统称为唇化软腭音声母。换句话说，本文所理解的唇化软腭音声母包括唇齿化软腭音声母 kv 组和一般性唇化软腭音声母 kw 组。唇齿化软腭音 kv 组声母并非复辅音，而是舌根与软腭成阻的同时，上齿与下唇也轻微接触，实际上具有双发音部位。因为这类声母基本上来自古见组合口字，而且发展演变趋势是 k 组或 ku- 组，因此其本质上是一类带有唇齿化色彩的软腭音声母，唇齿音是形容性的，而软腭音才是根本性的。可能正是这样的缘故，很多学者在面对这类声母时常常处理为 ku- 组声母，即作为普通的 k 组声母带 -u- 介音，如"海陆丰历史文化丛书"（2013）编纂委员会对陆河（河田）的客家方言音系的处理。

我们认为把上述唇齿化软腭音 kv 组声母处理为 ku- 组声母，一方面不利于正确地解释某些客家方言中 k 组声母不与 -u- 介音相拼的成因，如五华话；一方面不利于正确地认识某些客家方言中 -u- 介音的来源，如梅县话。下面以我们实地调查的近 30 个客家方言点的材料为基本依据，再以 19 世纪中叶以来西方传教士、汉学家所编写的客家方言罗马字拼音文献作为旁证，证明在早期客家方言中构拟一套唇化软腭音声母对于客家方言语音史来说具有重大的必要性。本文第三部分还旁及粤语、赣语和吴语等东南方言的相关问题，认为早期东南方言中除闽语之外，可能普遍存在 kv 组或 kw

---

* 国家社科基金重大项目"海内外客家方言的语料库建设和综合比较研究"（14ZDB103）、国家社科基金重大项目"海外珍藏汉语文献与南方明清汉语研究"（12&ZD178）、国家社科基金一般项目"明末以来西方人创制的汉语罗马字拼音方案研究"（13BYY103）。

组的唇化软腭音声母，这在东南方言的语音史研究中要特别引起注意。

贰　客家方言的唇化软腭音声母

2.1　我们多年来所调查的粤、赣、闽、湘、桂、川及香港新界的近 30 个客家方言点中，古见组合口字今读 kv 组声母的有陆河（河田）、清新（鱼坝）、南雄（雄州）、连城（莲峰）、炎陵（沔渡）等，见表 1：

表 1　古见组合口字今读 kv 组声母的客家方言

	过	瓜	古	外	块	拐	挂	桂	跪
陆河	kvɔˀ	ˍkva	ˋkvu	ŋɔiˀ	kʰvaiˀ	ˋkvai	kvaˀ	kviˀ / kuiˀ	kʰviˀ / kʰuiˀ
清新	kvɔˀ	ˍkva	ˋku	ˍgɔiˀ	faiˀ	ˋkvai	kvaˀ	kvɐiˀ	ˍkʰvɐi
南雄	kɔˀ	ˍkva	ˋku	vɔaˀ	kʰvɔaˀ	ˋkvɑ	kvaˀ	kviˀ	kviˀ
连城	kuˀ	ˍko	ˋkviɛ	ŋvaˀ	kʰvaˀ	ˋkva	koˀ	kviˀ	kʰviˀ
炎陵	koˀ	ˍkva	ˋku	ŋoiˀ	kʰvaiˀ	ˋkvai	kvaˀ	kveiˀ	ˋkʰui
	葵	官	括 ₍包~₎	关	原	决	军	郭	琼
陆河	ˍkʰvi / ˍkʰui	ˍkvɔn	kvatˀ	ˍkvɔn	ȵiɔnˀ	kɛtˀ	ˍkiun	kvɔkˀ	ˍkʰiun
清新	ˍkʰvɐi	ˍkvɔn	kʰvɔtˀ	ˍkvan	ˍian	kʰyatˀ	ˍkvɐn	kvɔkˀ	ˍkʰin
南雄	ˍkvi	ˍkvõã	kʰɤˀ	ˍkvõã	ȵioŋˀ	tɕiɤˀ	ˍtɕiɤŋ	ˍkoˀ	ˍtsɤŋ
连城	ˍkʰvi	ˍkuo	kʰuˀ	ˍkva	ŋveˀ	kviˀ	ˍkvãi	kuˀ	ˍkʰvãi
炎陵	ˍkʰvei	ˍkon	kvæˀ	ˍkvan	ȵienˀ	tɕieˀ	ˍtɕin	koˀ	tɕʰiəŋˀ

　　表 1 的 18 个古见组合口字中，有一、二等字，也有三、四等字，三、四等的"原""决""军""琼"读 kv 组的方言点很少。另外，一等的"古"字韵母与一般的客家方言无异，都是单元音 u，声母是唇化的 kv，比较罕见。"块""拐""桂""葵""关"都读 kv 组（"块"清新读 faiˀ，显然与粤语后来的影响有关），比较一致。其他的例字或者多数方言点，或者少数方言点甚至个别方言点读 kv 组，有些参差，如一等的"过"字，南雄、连城、炎陵都读如开口一等字，表明 kv 组的唇化成分 v 已经率先丢失。kv 组的唇化成分 v 在不同的方言点中，甚至在同一个方言点的不同音韵条件下存留与否具有较大的差异性，体现语言发展演变的不平衡性。连城没有 u 韵母，唯有 uo、ue

两个合口呼韵母，"官"字读 ˳kuo 不读 ˳kvo 是一个例外，目前还找不到合理的解释。

2.2 在我们所调查的近 30 个客家方言点中，古见组合口字今读 k 组且不带 -u- 介音的有五华（横陂）、龙川（龙母）、惠州（惠城）、东莞（樟木头）、新界（荔枝庄）、龙南（汶龙）等 6 个，见表 2：

表 2 古见组合口字今读 k 组且不带 -u- 介音的客家方言

	过	瓜	古	外	块	拐	挂	桂	跪
五华	kɔ²	˳ka	ˉku	˳ŋoi²	kʰai²	ˉkai	ka²	kui²	ˉkʰui
龙川	kɔ²	˳ka	ˉku	˳ŋoi²	fai²	ˉkai	ka²	kɛi	ˉkʰui
惠州	kɔ²	˳ka	ˉku	ŋoi²	fai²	ˉkai²	ka²	kui²	kʰui²
东莞	kɔ²	˳ka	ˉku	˳goi²	kʰai²	ˉkai	ka²	kui²	ˉkʰui
新界	kɔ²	˳ka	ˉku	ˉⁿgoi²	kʰai²	ˉkai	ka²	kui²	ˉkʰui
龙南	ko²	˳ka	ˉko	ŋoi²	kʰəi²	ˉkai	ka²	kəi²	ˉkʰəi

	葵	官	括包~	关	原	决	军	郭	琼
五华	˳kʰui	˳kɔn	kat₎	˳kan	˳ȵiɛn	kɛt₎	˳kiun	kɔk₎	˳kʰiun
龙川	˳kʰui	˳kɔn	kat₎	˳kɔn	˳ȵiɔn	kʰiɔt₎	˳kiun	kɔk₎	˳kʰiun
惠州	˳kʰui	˳kɔn	kat₎	˳kan	˳ȵyɛn	kyɛt₎ / kʰyɛt₎	˳kun	kɔk₎	˳kʰən
东莞	˳kʰui	˳kɔn	kat₎	˳kan	˳gen	kʰɛt₎	˳kiun	kɔk₎	˳kʰiun
新界	˳kʰui	˳kɔn	kat₎	˳kan	˳ⁿgɛn	kʰɛt₎	˳kiun	kɔk₎	˳kʰin
龙南	˳kʰəi	˳kɔn	kɔt₎	˳kan	˳ȵyon	tɕye	˳tɕyin	kɔk₎	˳tɕʰiɤŋ

表 2 所开列的 6 个方言点的音系中尽管都有合口呼韵母，但 u 都是主元音，不存在带 -u- 介音的韵母，如五华的合口呼韵母是 u、ui、un、uŋ、ut、uk，龙南合口呼韵母甚至只有 u、un。因此，表 2 的 18 个古见组合口字都是今读 k 组且不带 -u- 介音。这 6 个方言点中，龙川、惠州、东莞和新界属于东江流域（珠江的三大支流之一），而五华毗邻龙川，龙南毗邻东江源头地区之一的定南县（同属江西省赣州市）。可见，古见组合口字今读 k 组且不带 -u- 介音的客家方言主要分布在东江流域及其邻近地区。

2.3 其他大部分的方言点中，古见组合口字今读 k 组的，或多或少带有 -u- 介音，见表 3：

表3 古见组合口字今读 k 组且或多或少带 -u- 介音的客家方言

	过	瓜	古	外	块	拐	挂	桂	跪
梅县	kuɔ³	₌kua	⁼ku	ŋɔi³	kʰuai³	⁼kuai	kua³	kui³	⁼kʰui
丰顺	⁼kuɔ	₌kua	⁼ku	⁼ŋuai	⁼kʰuai	⁼kuai	⁼kua	⁼kui	⁼kʰui
翁源	kou³	₌kua	⁼ku	₌ŋoi	kʰuai³	⁼kuai	kua³	kui³	⁼kʰui
仁化	kou³	₌kuo	⁼ku	ŋua	⁼kʰua	⁼kua	kua³	kui³	⁼kʰui
上犹	₌ko	₌kua	⁼ku	₌oe	₌kʰuæ	⁼kuæ	₌kua	tɕyi / kue	tɕʰyi
信丰	kʉ³	₌kua	⁼ku	ŋə³	kʰuæ³	⁼kuæ	kua³	kue³	kʰue
会昌	₍kou	₌kuɑ	⁼ku	ŋuɛ	₍kʰuei	⁼kuɛ	₌kuɑ	kuei	kʰuei
兴国	kɔ³	₌ka	⁼ku	ŋuæ³	kʰuæ³	⁼kuæ	ka³	kui³	kʰui
宁都	ko³	₌ka	⁼ku	ŋuai³	kʰui³	⁼kai	ka³	kui³	⁼kʰui
宁化	ko³	₌kɒ	⁼ku	ⁿga³	kʰuai³	⁼ka	kɒ³	ki³	⁼kʰi
长汀	ko³	₌kua	⁼ku	ŋue³	kʰue³	⁼kue	kua³	kui³	⁼kʰui
武平	ko³	₌kua	⁼ku	ŋoi³	kʰuai³	⁼kuai	kua³	kui³	⁼kʰui
永定	⁼kou	₌kua	⁼kə	⁼ⁿgai	⁼kʰuai	⁼kuai	⁼kua	⁼kuei	⁼kʰuei
来宾	ko³	₌kua	⁼ku	₌ŋoai	kʰuai³	⁼kuai	kua³	kuəi³	⁼kʰuəi
成都	ko³	₌kua	⁼ku	ⁿgɔi	kʰuai³	⁼kuai	kua³	kuei³	⁼kʰuei

	葵	官	括(包~)	关	原	决	军	郭	琼
梅县	₌kʰui	₌kuɔn	kuat₌	₌kuan	₌ȵian	kiat₌	₌kiun	kuok₌	₌kʰiun
丰顺	₌kʰui	₌kuan	kuat₌	₌kuan	₌ȵiɛn	kiɛt₌	₌kiun	kuok₌	₌kʰiun
翁源	₌kʰui	₌kuan	kuat₌	₌kuan	₌ȵien	kiet₌	₌kiun	kok₌	₌kʰiun
仁化	₌kʰui	₌kuaŋ	kʰuo³	₌kuaŋ	₌ȵiŋ	kʰiɛ³	₌kiŋ	kou³	₌kʰɛŋ
上犹	₌kʰue	₌koẽ	kua³	₌kuã / ⁼kʰuã	₌yẽ	tɕyɔt₌	₌tɕyiŋ	ko³	₌tɕʰiŋ
信丰	₌kʰue	₌kṁ	⁼ko / kʰuə	₌kuã / kʰã	₌ĩ	tɕie	₌tɕiŋ	kʉ³	₌tɕʰiŋ
会昌	₌kʰuei	₌koŋ	kua³	₌kua	₌ȵiɔŋ	kya³	₌kin	kɔ³	₌kin
兴国	₌kʰui	₌kuã	kua³	₌kuã	₌ŋyã	tʂua	₌tɕyiŋ	kɔ³	₌tʂʰuiŋ
宁都	₌kʰui	₌kuan	kuat₌	₌kan	₌nan	tʃat₌	₌tʃen	kɔk₌	₌tʃʰuŋ
宁化	₌kʰi	₌kaŋ	kaʔ₌	₌kaŋ	₌ȵien	kieʔ₌	₌kiŋ	koʔ₌	₌kʰiŋ

	过	瓜	古	外	块	拐	挂	桂	跪
长汀	ˌkʰue	ˌkŋ	ˌkua	ˌkuaŋ / ˌkŋ	ⁱŋ	ꜛtʃe	ꜛtʃeŋ	ˌko	ˌtʃʰeŋ
武平	ˌkʰi / ˌkʰui	ˌkon	kuat	ˌkuan	ȵan	tat	ˌtun	kok	ˌtʰuŋ
永定	ˌkʰuei	ˌkuãi	kuaiʔ	ꜛkuãi	ᵑgiẽ	kiɛʔ	ꜛkũi	kɔʔ	tsʰioŋ
来宾	ˌkʰuəi	ˌkoan	koat	ꜛkoan	ȵien	kiet	ˌkin	kok	ˌkʰiun
成都	ˌkʰuei	ˌkɔŋ	kæʔ	ꜛkuæ / ꜛkɔŋ	ⁱẽ / yẽ	tɕyeʔ	ˌtɕyn	kɔʔ / kueʔ	tɕʰin / tɕʰyn

表3中一共有15个方言点，可见这种类型在客家方言中较为常见。其中，宁化见组合口字今读 k 组且带 -u- 介音的字很少，表3中唯有"块"字，此外还有"恢 ˌkʰuai、遂 ˌkʰuai、阔 kʰuaiʔ、危 ᵑguai、魏 ᵑguaiꞋ、滚 ꜛkuaŋ、棍 kuaŋꞋ、昆坤 ˌkʰuaŋ、捆 ꜛkʰuaŋ、困 kʰuaŋꞋ"等。其实，宁化见组开口字今读也有带 -u- 介音者，混同于合口字，如：该 = 乖 ˌkuai、割 = 刮 kuaiʔ、干~部 = 棍 kuaŋꞋ。因此，宁化见组合口字今读 k 组所带的 -u- 介音，可能是开、合口混同之后新产生的，与我们这里所讨论的问题性质不同。另外值得注意的是，表3的 18 个例字中，几乎没有一个字在所有方言点中都读带 -u- 介音，可见 k 组之后的 -u- 介音存在与否甚为参差。特别是像兴国、宁都，k 组之后的 -u- 介音残缺不全，到底是刚刚产生还是一种遗存？还值得进一步研究。比较明确的是，梅县、丰顺、翁源、武平、来宾等方言点中 -u- 介音只能与 k 组相拼，-u- 介音显然是从 kv 组的唇化成分 v 元音化、圆唇化而来的，详见下文分析。

2.4 根据巴色会传教士所编写的客家方言圣经、课本等罗马字拼音文献，一百多年前香港新界的客家方言有一套唇化软腭音声母，但时至今天已经完全消失，如上面表2所示。庄初升、黄婷婷（2014：64）指出："罗马字圣经中古合口见系声母字（主要是一、二等字）读唇化的 kw（kv）、khw、w，与今天的广州话相同，如：寡 kwa³、关 kwan¹（kvan¹）、国 kwet⁶（kvet⁶）、贵 kwui⁴（kvui⁴）、归 kwui¹、规 kwui¹、鬼 kwui³、怪 kwai⁴、夸 khwa¹、禾 wo²、王 woŋ²、位 wui⁴。同时我们也注意到有些同类的字有两读，以《圣经书节择要》为例，如：快 khwai⁴/khai⁴、话 wa⁴/va⁴、跪 khwui³/khui³、畏 wui⁴/vui⁴、万 wan⁴/van⁴、物 wut⁵/vut⁵，甚至有少数字已经没有唇化色彩，如：亏 khui¹、葵 khui²、广 koŋ³、完 voŋ²、往 voŋ³，说明当时唇化声母已经开始消失了。《启蒙浅学》中大多读 kw、khw、w，也存在一字两读的情形，如：跪 khwui³/khui³，但不常见，另外如'亏 khui¹、葵 khui²、捆 khun³、光 koŋ¹'也不常见。与多数地方的客家方言一样，今天新界的客家方言已经完全没有唇化声母了，甚至连 -u- 介音也没有了……"

荷兰汉学家范德斯达特（P. A. van de Stadt）编写的《客家词典》(*Hakka-woorden-boek*) 于 1912 年在巴达维亚（今雅加达）出版，这是一部记录印尼梅县腔客家方言的词典。根据庄初升、陈英纳（2013）的归纳，该词典所记录的印尼梅县腔客家方言有 24 个声母，即 p[p]、ph[pʰ]、m[m]、f[f]、w[v]、t[t]、th[tʰ]、n[n]、l[l]、k[k]、kh[kʰ]、ng[ŋ]、h[h]、kw[kw]、kwh[kʰw]、ts[ts]、tsh[tsʰ]、s[s]、tsj[tʃ]、tsjh[tʃʰ]、ny[ɲ]、sj[ʃ]、y[j]、[ø]（中括号内是我们用国际音标的转写），其中 kw[kw]、kwh[kʰw] 就是上面我们所说的唇化软腭音舌面声母。庄初升、陈英纳（2013：132）指出："相比之下，今天梅县的客家方言少了 tsj[tʃ]、tsjh[tʃʰ]、sj[ʃ]、y[j] 和 kw[kw]、kwh[kʰw] 这两套声母，乃是近百年来发展演变的结果。"今天的梅县话属于上面表 3 所示的古见组合口字今读 k 组且带 -u- 介音的类型，特别需要强调的是今天梅县话的 -u- 介音都只与 k 组相拼而不与其他声母相拼，ua 的例字如"瓜挂"，cɔ 韵的例字如"果过"，uai 韵的例字如"乖快"，uan 韵的例字如"关惯"，uɛn 韵的例字如"耿"，ucn 韵的例字如"官棺"，uaŋ 韵的例字"矿梗₋ᵣ"，ucŋ 韵的例字如"光广"，uat 韵的例字如"括刮"，uet 韵的例字如"国"，uak 韵的例字如"礦"，uɔk 韵的例字如"郭"。

综合上面所列举的语言事实，我们有理由相信早期的客家方言中存在一组唇化软腭音声母，这组声母在陆河等少数地方的客家方言中保留至今，在更多地方的客家方言中沿着两个方向发展，一是像五华话一样 kv 组的唇化成分消失，一是像梅县话一样 kv 组的唇化成分元音化、圆唇化为一般的介音 -u-。结合广州方言等其他东南方言来看，上述两种或许都共同经历过从 kv 组到 kw 组的过程，图示如下：

$$kv、k^hv \rightarrow kw、k^hw \begin{array}{l} \nearrow k、k^h（五华话等）\\ \searrow ku-、k^hu-（梅县话等）\end{array}$$

叁　其他东南方言的唇化软腭音声母

我们进一步比较发现，东南方言中除了客家方言之外至少还有粤语、赣语和吴语存在唇化软腭音声母[1]。下面分别论述。

3.1　粤语

早期的罗马字粤语文献中广州话的占据绝大多数。1828 年英国传教士马礼逊

（R. Morrison）的《广东省土话字汇》（*A Vocabulary of the Canton Dialect*）制定了第一个粤语罗马字拼音系统，设有 kw 组声母，如：过 kwo、鬼 kwei、卦 kwa、惯 kwan、君 kwǎn、群 kwǎn、国 kwok（不表现送气）。此后，美国人裨治文（E. C. Bridgman）的《粤语文选》（*A Chinese Chrestomathy in the Canton Dialect*，1841），美国人卫三畏（S. W. Williams）的《拾级大成》（*Easy Lessons in Chinese*，1842），英国人湛约翰（John Chalmers）的《英粤字典》（*An English and Cantonese Pocket-Dictionary for the Use of Those Who Wish to Learn the Spoken Language of Canton Province*，1862），德国人罗存德（W. Lobscheid）的《广州方言习语选录及阅读》（*Select Phrases and Reading Lessons in the Canton Dialect*，1864），英国人德呢克（N. B. Dennys）的《初学阶》（*A Handbook of the Canton Vernacular of the Chinese Language*，1874），德国人欧德理（E. J. Eitel）的《粤语中文字典》（*A Chinese Dictionary in the Cantonese Dialect*，1877），英国人波乃耶（James Dyer Ball）的《粤语易通》（*Cantonese Made Easy*，1883）等等，都设有 kw 组声母。

李新魁（1987：68）指出，清代学者王炳耀编写《拼音字谱》，"他把舌根音声母分为 k 和 kw 两套，对后者称为'满口音'，表明其为圆唇化舌根声母。这与现代学者的分析是一致的。"彭小川（1990）考证了清代粤语韵书《分韵撮要》所反映的声母系统，认为"归"类、"葵"类的音值分别是 kw、k'w，说明两百多年前粤语已有圆唇化的舌根音。

一般认为今天广州话还有 kw 组声母，以前研究粤语的学者普遍称为"圆唇化舌根声母"（李新魁 1987、彭小川 1990）、"圆唇化声母"（李新魁 1990）、"圆唇声母"（施其生 1991），"圆唇舌根声母"（片冈新、李燕萍 2009），现在看来需要商榷。发这类音，双唇略展，双唇不圆才是其主要特征，李新魁等（1995）称为"唇化音"，麦耘（1999）称为"唇-舌根音"。本文称为"唇化软腭音"，是基于这类音本质上还是软腭音（演变路向也是一般的软腭音），只不过多了唇化的形容性成分。

但伍巍、王媛媛（2006：126）认为，广州话音系中 kw-ku 与 k'w-ku 两组音之间并不存在对立，毫无别义功能，"既然如此，以牺牲音系结构的完整来屈就个别音的发音特征，这显然是不可取的方法。因此，我们还是赞同广州音系的'一分法'，还广州话舌根声母音节中合口韵母 -u- 介音的本来身份，这既是客观的语音事实，也是科学处理广州音系的需要。"我们认为，k 组与 kw 的分立，不但不影响"音系结构的完整"，而且把 kw 组与 k 组带 -u- 介音视为两种不同性质的读音和两种不同序列的层次，可以更好地解释粤语内部和某些东南方言之间相关语音现象的共时差异和历时演变。k 组与 kw 的分立才是科学处理广州音系的需要。

根据李新魁等（1995：110），广州市原近郊的文冲方言，"kw、kw'、w 声母带唇齿浊擦音色彩，在与 u 韵母相拼时尤为明显，如'孤'念作 kvu⁴⁴，'乌'念作 vu⁴⁴ 等。"

根据张双庆、庄初升（2003），香港新界地区蚝涌的"围头话"和三门仔的"疍家话"（均属于粤语）既没有 kw 组声母，也没有 -u- 介音，如"果"都读 ˏkɔ，"瓜"都读 ˏka，"拐"都读 ˏkai，"龟"都读 ˏkei，"关"分别读 ˏkan、ˏkaŋ，"广"分别读 ˏkœŋ、ˏkɔŋ。与五华等地的客家方言一样，新界的这两个粤语方言点都是 kw 组声母的唇化成分已经彻底消失。反之，如果认为早期的粤语是 k 组带 -u- 介音，就很难解释 -u- 介音何以会消失。

3.2 赣语

根据笔者和万波教授 2007 年的实地调查，赣语邵武话有 22 个声母，包括 k 组和 kv 组，下面是这两组的声母例字，见表 4：

表 4　邵武话 k 组和 kv 组声母的例字

k 哥姑斤建	kʰ 柯茄苦哭	ŋ 鹅牙咬雁	x 拖河解晓也寒
kv 果寡官郭	kvʰ 课扩窟矿		

根据笔者 2007 年的实地调查，与邵武毗邻的赣语光泽话也有 22 个声母，也包括 k 组和 kv 组（比邵武多了 ŋv），下面是这两组的声母例字，见表 5：

表 5　光泽话 k 组和 kv 组声母的例字

k 歌家缸公	kʰ 茄旗虎穷	ŋ 鹅岸元硬	h 驼柱含胸
kv 贵桂光梗	kvʰ 亏跪权群	ŋv 瓦危月外	

邵武和光泽处于福建省西北部，与江西省接壤。邵武和光泽的语音系统中虽然四呼都有，但是合口呼只有一个 u 韵母，也就是说没有带 -u- 介音的合口呼韵母。

我们注意到南昌话的音系，13 个带 -u- 介音的韵母 ua、uo、ue、uai、uan、uat、uon、uot、uɛt、uaŋ、uaʔ、uɔŋ、uɔʔ，与梅县话一样都只能与 k 组声母相拼（熊正辉 1995）。我们推测，这些韵母的介音 -u- 都是由 kv 组的唇化成分元音化、圆唇化而来的。

现在能看到的早期赣语罗马字文献唯有邵武话的几种。张双庆、庄初升（2007：3）指出："1873 年秋天，美国美部会传教士和约瑟（J. E. Walker）、吴思明（S. F. Woodin）、柯为梁（D. W. Osgood）等从福州出发，沿闽江到达邵武。……和约瑟是美部会闽北传教事业的开拓者，也是最早使用罗马字拼音来记录邵武方言的传教士。"和约瑟发表了 Shao-wu in Fu-kien: a country station（1878）一文并编写了一份叫 *Shaowu K'iong Loma T'se*（《邵武腔罗马字》，1887）的邵武话字表。另外，和约瑟的妻子 Ada E. Walker 与一位叫 Mr. Chang 的人还合编了一份只有 4 页的 *Alphabet of Romanized Shaowu*（《邵武罗马字母》），差不多同一时期由福州 M. E. Mission Press 出版。不过，上述文献中并没有见到 kw 组声母，相应地都拼写为 ku- 组，如：果 kuo²、科 k'uo¹、瓜 kua¹、乖 kuai¹、快 k'uai³。我们推测早期的邵武话应该也有唇化软腭音声母，上述文献之所以拼写为 ku- 组，可能是受到福州话怀特拼音方案的影响，这套方案如实地反映了福州方言没有唇化软腭音的特点。1847 年，美国美以美会传教士怀特（Moses Clark White，1819—1900）到达福州，他采用琼斯（William Jones）音标系统来记录福州话，撰写的《福州的中国话》（The Chinese Language Spoken at Fuh Chau）一文于 1856 年发表。美部会的传教士最早也于 1847 年抵达福州，1865 年决定向地处福建内地的闽北山区展开传教工作。同样是美国的传教士，美部会的传教士在福州期间受到怀特拼音方案的影响或许有可能。

3.3 吴语

早期的罗马字吴语文献中上海话最多，其他的还有杭州、苏州、宁波、绍兴、台州、温州等。除了杭州之外，其他方言点的罗马字文献中都有 kw 组声母。下面分别介绍。

（1）上海话

英国传教士艾约瑟（J. Edkins）于 1853 年著有《上海方言口语语法》（*A Grammar of Colloquial Chinese as Exhibited in the Shanghai Dialect*），这是西方人的第一部描写非官话的汉语方言语法著作。从该书的罗马字拼音来看，当时的上海话应该存在 kw 组声母，包括 kw、k'w、gw、ngw、hw 等，如：瓜 kwó、寡 kwó、花 hwó、华 hwó、化 hwó、淮 hwái、快 k'wá、规 kwé、贵 kwé、馈 gwé、跪 kwè、危 ngwé、汇 hwei、欢 hwén、官 kwén、管 kwén、阔 k'weh、昏 hwun、滚 kwun、骨 kweh。此外，英国人詹姆斯·萨默斯（James Summers）的《上海方言约翰福音书》（*The Gospel of Saint John in the Chinese Language, According to the Dialect of Shanghai*，1853），英国人麦嘉湖（J. MacGowan）的《上海方言短语集》（*A Collection of Phrases in the Shanghai Dialect*，1862），美国人晏玛太（M. T. Yates）的《中西译语妙法》（*First Lessons in*

Chinese，1871），美国人戴维斯（D. H. Davis）、薛思培（J. A. Silsby）的《汉英上海方言词典》（*Shanghai Vernacular Chinese-English Dictionary*，1900），美国人金多士（G. McIntosh）的《上海方言通用短语》（*Useful Phrases in the Shanghai Dialect: with Index Vocabulary and Other Helps*，1908），美国人卜舫济（F. L. Hawks Pott）的《上海方言教程》（*Lessons in the Shanghai Dialect*，1913）等等所反映的早期上海话音系中，也应该存在 kw 组声母。特别需要指出的是，晏玛太《中西译语妙法》（1871）在声母表中分别列出了 k 组和 kw 组声母。

但是我们注意到，周同春（1988）、陈忠敏（1995）根据艾约瑟的《上海方言口语语法》（1853）所归纳的 19 世纪中叶上海话的音系中，把 w 都处理为 -u- 介音，相应的声母部分只有 k 组而没有 kw 组。徐奕（2010）根据晏玛太《中西译语妙法》（1871）所归纳的上海话音系中，亦如是处理。根据许宝华、陶寰（1997），今天上海话 "[-u-] 介音的实际音值是 [ʋ-]"（见引论第 9 页），而且所有带 -u- 介音的韵母 uɑ、uɛ、ue、uã、uɑ̃、uəŋ、uaʔ、uɑʔ、uəʔ、uɔ 都只能与 k 组声母相拼，这就使我们更加坚信早期的上海话存在唇化软腭音声母 kw 组。

（2）苏州话

1891 年大美国圣经会托印的《马可传福音书（苏州土白）》（1891）是唯一的苏州话罗马字圣经译本，可以看到 kw 组声母。1892 年苏州文学会 (A Committee of the Soochow Literary Association) 编写的《苏州方言字音表》（*A Syllabary of the Soochow Dialect*），实际上是按照音序排列的苏州话同音字汇，也有成系列的 kw 组声母，包括 kw、kwʻ、gw、ngw、hw，如：瓜 kwo、乖 kwa、快 kw‘a、歪 hwa、恢 kw‘ae、葵 gwæ、危 ngwae、豁 hwah、欢 hwön、刮 kwah、官 kwön、窟 kw‘eh、骨 kweh、忽 hweh、坤 kw‘en、狂 gwang、光 kwông（原书声调标在汉字的四角上，这里省略）。

蔡佞（2010）根据 1892 年的《苏州方言字音表》，归纳出 19 世纪末苏州话的音系，其中声母部分只有 k 组而没有 kw 组，韵母部分则有 12 个带 -u- 介音的韵母。丁邦新（2003）实际上是根据陆基民国二十四年（1935）写定的《注音符号·苏州同音常用字汇》整理而成的苏州话同音字汇。从陆基的注音字母及丁邦新的国际音标转写来看，那个时候的苏州话 kw 声母已经演变成 k 组带 -u- 介音了。根据北大中文系语言学教研室（2003），今天的苏州话带 -u- 介音的韵母 uɒ、uE、uø、uən、uɒŋ、uaŋ、uaʔ、uɤʔ 都只能与 k 组声母相拼。

（3）宁波话

美国人睦礼逊（W. T. Morrison）的《宁波方言字语汇解》（*An Angle-Chinese Vocabulary of the Ningpo Dialect*，1876），美国人蓝亨利（H. Rankin）的《宁波土话初

学》（1896 年再版），德国人穆麟德（P. G. von Möllendorff）的《宁波方言便览》（*The Ningbo Colloquial Handbook*，1899/1910）和《宁波方言音节》（*The Ningpo Syllabary*，1901），英国人高富、戴德生（J. H. Taylor）、慕稼谷（G. E. Moule）翻译的《新约书》（1868），英国人庄延龄（Edward Harper Parker）的《宁波方言》（*The Ningpo Dialect*，1884）等，应该都存在 kw 组声母，包括 kw、kw'、gw、ngw、hw 等，以睦礼逊（W. T. Morrison）《宁波方言字语汇解》为例，如：化 hwô、呼 hwu、吾 ngwu、怪 kwæ、危 ngwe、葵 gwe、灰 hwe、括 kwah、关 kwæn、阔 kw'eh、宽 kw'un、玩 ngwun、昏 hweng、光 kwông、狂 gwông。

胡方（2001）根据穆麟德《宁波方言音节》（1901）整理出百年前宁波方言的声母系统（用国际音标转写），当中唯有 k 组而没有 kw 组声母，可见作者也是把唇化成分 w 理解为合口呼介音 -u-。根据汤珍珠、陈忠敏、吴新贤（1997），宁波方言所有带 -u- 介音的韵母 ua、uo、uɛ、uɐɪ、uã、uɔ̃、uəŋ、uæʔ 都只能与 k 组声母相拼。

（4）绍兴话

穆麟德《宁波方言音节》的后面附有宁波、绍兴、台州三地的字音对照表，由此我们可以看到百年前的绍兴话也有 kw 组声母，包括 kw、kw'（k'w）、gw、ngw、hw 等，如：化 hwô、古 kwu、乖 kwa、剑 kwæ、冠 kwön、刮 kwæh、唤 hwön、兀 ngweh、匡 kw'ông、况 hwông、国 kwoh、公 kwoŋ、共 gwong、哭 k'woh。

王福堂（2008a）根据上述《宁波方言音节》的附录整理了百年前绍兴方言的声母和韵母，其中声母部分只有 k 组而没有 kw 组，韵母部分则有 15 个带 -u- 介音的韵母。根据王福堂（2008b），现代绍兴话所有带 -u- 介音的韵母 ua、uɛ、uo、uæ、uẽ、uõ、uaŋ、uɒŋ、uoŋ、uaʔ、uæʔ、ueʔ、uøʔ、uoʔ 都只能与 k 组声母相拼，与上海、苏州、宁波相同。

（5）台州话

目前我们能看到的台州话罗马字拼音文献还有大英圣书会（British & Foreign Bible Society）1897 年编印的《新约书》（SING-IAH SHÜ）。从这部罗马字圣经和上述《宁波方言音节》的附录来看，早期的台州话也有 kw 组声母，包括 kw、kw'、gw、ngw、hw 等，以《宁波方言音节》的附录为例，如：瓜 kwa、伙 hwu、化 hwa、乖 kwa、外 ngwe、奎 kwe、官 kwön、冠 kwön、宦 ngwæn、宽 kw'e、刮 kweh、甩 gwan、坤 kw'eng、婚 hweng、兀 ngwæh、光 kwong、广 kwong。另外，我们注意到《宁波方言音节》的附录中古遇摄合口一等见系字宁波、绍兴读 kw 组（这很容易令人想起表 1 陆河的"古"字读 'kvu 的类型），而台州读 k 组（包括零声母），可见这两组声母在编者看来是有所不同的，否则没必要在同一部书中使用两套拼写法，如：

表6 穆麟德所记古遇摄合口一等见系字宁波、绍兴、台州的读音

	古	雇	枯	戽	户	互
宁波	kwu	kwu	kwʻu	hwu	wu	ngwu
绍兴	kwu	kwu	kwʻu	hwu	wu	wu
台州	ku	ku	kʻu	u	u	u

根据林晓晓（2012），台州路桥方言除了 uəŋ、uəʔ 之外，其他带 -u- 介音的韵母 uA、uɛ、ue、uã、uõ、uAʔ、uoʔ 都只能与 k 组声母相拼。

（6）温州话

目前我们能看到的温州话罗马字拼音文献有大英圣书会编印的《新约圣书》(1894) 和《马可福音书》(*The Gospel of mark in Wenchow Colloquial*，1902) 等，应该都有 kw 组声母。秋谷裕幸、王莉（2008）对《马可福音书》(1902) 的音系进行细致的整理、归纳，声母部分就有 kw 组，作者构拟为 kʋ、kʋʰ、gʋ、hʋ、fiʋ 等；韵母部分相应地没有带 -u- 介音的合口呼。

其实，早在 1995 年郑张尚芳就根据 9 种的地方韵书和早期记音材料，敏锐地指出早期的温州话中有 kw 组声母。他认为："kw 组六母的实际读法更早应是 [ᵏw] 等，w 是形容性圆唇成分（不像元音那样可以延长），现郊县永嘉、乐清、文成都读作唇齿性的，所以标作 [kʋ] 等。"（郑张尚芳 1995：347）他后来进一步指出："早期音有一套唇化喉牙音声母，如'关'kwa，'灰'hwai。其中 w 只是声母的唇化成分，不能像 u 那样延长。今老派虽然没有了，但指明其祖辈或父辈确是如此读，还有人能保持 hw、ʔw 两母的又音。永嘉、乐清、文成等邻县方言也仍有保持这套声母的，多读成齿唇 kv 系。所以早期音应读 kv 系（严式是 kʋv 系）。"（郑张尚芳 2008：72—73）

根据北大中文系语言学教研室（2003），今天的温州话中只有 ua、uɛ、uɔ、uai、uaŋ 等 5 个带 -u- 的合口呼韵母，而且辖字很少。实际上，早期温州话罗马字拼音文献中所记录的 kw 组声母字，都已经演变成 k 组且不带 -u- 介音，正像表 2 的五华话等客家方言一样。

肆 余论

如上所述，我们有足够的证据表明早期吴语中普遍存在唇化声母 kw、kʰw、gw、ŋw、hw（温州还有 fiw），不但有古见组合口字读 kw、kʰw、gw、ŋw，还有古晓组合

口字读 hw、ɦw。严格来说，因为 h、ɦ 是喉音，hw、ɦw 只能称为唇化喉音声母。相比之下，粤、客、赣语的唇化声母只限于来自古见组合口字的软腭音，古晓组合口字经过 hw、ɦw 的阶段已经演变成 f、v（w）声母和零声母 -u- 介音了。吴语中这种演变还在进行，王福堂（2008a）指出 20 世纪 50 年代绍兴东头埭口音中晓组合口呼字声母已经开始与非组声母相混。温州话的这种演变甚至已经基本完成，如"悔"由 hwai 变成了今天的 fai，"外"由 wha[*ɦʋɑ] 变成了今天的 va。以上事实告诉我们，东南方言中的古晓组合口字唇齿化的动因，不是一般所理解的合口介音 -u-，而是唇化成分 v 或者 w。我们若把晓、匣母的早期形式构拟为 *xv、*ɣv，它们唇化的过程可图示为：

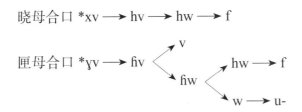

关于这个问题，我们将另外撰文讨论。东南方言中，我们在闽语的田野调查和文献整理过程中未曾发现 kw 组声母。这样就不难理解闽语中的 hu- 为何没有变成 f 的道理了。

李新魁（1996：77）指出："粤语的舌根音声母有普通的 [k k']与唇化的 [kw kw']之分。许多音韵学家，如陆志韦、李方桂等，都指出在汉魏或更早以前，汉语具有唇化音声母。粤语的这一套声母可能是古音的遗留。"现在看来，早期东南方言中除了闽语之外都有这套唇化声母，有的遗存至今，有的已经丢失唇化成分，有的演变为 k 组带 -u- 介音。以前学界对这个问题的认识存在误区，以后在东南方言的语音史研究中要特别加以注意。

附 注

[1] 湘语的调查报告中没有见到相关的描写记录，但是我们注意到长沙（北京大学中文系语言学教研室 2003）、益阳（崔振华 1998）、新化（罗昕如 1998）、汨罗（陈山青 2006）等地湘语带 -u- 介音的合口呼韵母都只能跟 k 组声母相拼，我们推断早期湘语中也存在唇化软腭音声母。据北京大学中文系语言学教研室（2003：22），长沙方言"韵头（介音）i、u、y 发音较短促，带辅音性"。另外据罗昕如教授告知，新化方言的 -u- 介音唇形略展，但不带摩擦；据陈山青教授告知，汨罗(长乐)方言的 -u- 介音展唇且带轻微的唇齿摩擦。土话方面，据麦耘（2008）所记录的广西八步鹅塘"八都话"音系，有 kʷ、kʷh、ŋʷ 组声母；张双庆主编（2004：11），粤北连州市连州镇土话"所有合口呼韵母的 u 介音唇形都微展，并带有

轻微的摩擦"，该土话带 -u- 介音的合口呼韵母也只能与 k 组声母相拼。另据麦耘教授告知，连州沙坊土话也有这套唇化软腭音声母。

参考文献

北京大学中文系语言学教研室（2003）《汉语方音字汇（第二版重排本）》，北京：语文出版社。

蔡佞（2010）19 世纪末的苏州话，《吴语研究——第五届国际吴方言学术研讨会论文集》，上海：上海教育出版社。

陈山青（2006）《汨罗长乐方言研究》，长沙：湖南教育出版社。

陈忠敏（1995）上海市区话语音一百多年来的演变，《吴语和闽语的比较研究》，上海：上海教育出版社。

崔振华（1998）《益阳方言研究》，长沙：湖南教育出版社。

丁邦新（2003《一百年前的苏州话》，上海：上海教育出版社。

"海陆丰历史文化丛书"编纂委员会（2013）《语言》，广州：广东人民出版社。

胡方（2001）试论百年来宁波方言声母系统的演变，《语言研究》第 3 期。

李新魁（1987）一百年前的广州音，《广州研究》第 10 期。

李新魁（1990）数百年来粤方言韵母的发展，《学术研究》第 4 期。

李新魁（1996）粤音与古音，《学术研究》第 8 期。

李新魁、黄家教、施其生、麦耘、陈定方（1995）《广州方言研究》，广州：广东人民出版社。

林晓晓（2012）浙江台州路桥方言同音字汇，《方言》第 2 期。

罗昕如（1998）《新化方言研究》，长沙：湖南教育出版社。

麦耘（1999）广州话介音问题商榷，《中山大学学报》第 4 期。

麦耘（2008）广西八步鹅塘"八都话"音系，《方言》第 1 期。

彭小川（1990）粤语韵书《分韵撮要》的声母系统，《第二届国际粤方言研讨会论文集》，广州：暨南大学出版社。

片冈新、李燕萍（2009）十九世纪末一个承先启后的粤语罗马拼音系统：标准罗马方案，《粤语跨学科研究：第十三届国际粤方言研讨会论文集》，香港：香港城市大学语言资讯科学研究中心。

秋谷裕幸、王莉（2008）温州方言《马可福音书》的音系，《中国语言学集刊》第二卷第二期，北京：中华书局。

施其生（1991）广州方言的介音，《方言》第 2 期。

汤珍珠、陈忠敏、吴新贤（1997）《宁波方言词典》，南京：江苏教育出版社。

王福堂（2008a）绍兴方言百年来的语音变化，《吴语研究——第四届国际吴方言学术研讨会论文集》，上海：上海教育出版社。

王福堂（2008b）绍兴方言同音字汇，《方言》第 1 期。

伍巍、王媛媛（2006）广州音系舌根声母 kw、k'w 讨论，《暨南学报》第 4 期。

熊正辉（1994）《南昌方言词典》，南京：江苏教育出版社。

徐奕（2010）晏玛太《中西译语妙法》所反映的 19 世纪上海话语音，《吴语研究第五届国际吴方言学术研讨会论文集》，上海：上海教育出版社。

许宝华、陶寰（1997）《上海方言词典》，南京：江苏教育出版社。

张双庆主编（2004）《连州土话研究》，厦门：厦门大学出版社。

张双庆、庄初升（2003）《香港新界方言》，香港：商务印书馆。

张双庆、庄初升（2007）19 世纪美部会、圣公会传教士与闽北方言研究，《中国语文研究》第 2 期。

郑张尚芳（1995）温州方言近百年来的语音变化，《吴语研究》，香港：香港中文大学新亚书院。

郑张尚芳（2008）《温州方言志》，北京：中华书局。

周同春（1988）十九世纪的上海语音，《吴语论丛》，上海：上海教育出版社。

庄初升、陈英纳（2013）早期荷兰人编印的两种印尼客家方言文献，《文化遗产》第 2 期。

庄初升、黄婷婷（2014）《19 世纪香港新界的客家方言》，广州：广东人民出版社。

A Committee of the Soochow Literary Association (1892) *A Syllabary of the Soochow Dialect*（《苏州方言字音表》）.

Edkins, J. (1853) *A Grammar of Colloquial Chinese as Exhibited in the Shanghai Dialect*. Shanghai Presbyterian Mission Press.

Möllendorff, P. G. Von (1901) *The Ningpo Syllabary*（《宁波方言音节》）.

Morrison, R. (1828) *A Vocabulary of the Canton Dialect* （《广东省土话字汇》）. Macao: The Honorable India Company's Press.

Morrison, W. T. (1876) *An Angle-Chinese Vocabulary of the Ningpo Dialect*（《宁波方言字语汇解》）.

（本文发表于《方言》2016 年第 2 期，第 158—168 页，收入本书时有修改）

论十九世纪客家话文献《启蒙浅学》中所见的趋向补语 *

柯理思

1. 引论

1.1 《启蒙浅学》简介

巴色会（Basel Mission，或称 Basel Evangelical Missionary Society）的客家话出版物除了《圣经》之外还包括当时在所办的各所学校里使用的种种课本，《启蒙浅学》一书是其中之一。我们十年前访问巴色会图书馆时发现，除了巴色会的正式记录所提到的罗马字本 Khi^3 $mung^2$ $tshen^3$ hok^5 以外（使用 Lepsius 式的标音符号），书架上还藏着一本没有封面的小书，正是与 Lepsius 本对应的汉字本《启蒙浅学》。

在巴色传道会的各样记录中能找到有关这个罗马字本的简单记载，德语简称为 Lesebuch（读本），英文全名为 *First Book of Reading in the Romanised Colloquial of the Hakka-Chinese in the Province of Canton*，在瑞士巴色排版印刷，但没有涉及作者的姓名，而且找不到有关汉字本的记载。至今为止唯一的线索是《巴色传道会史》一书中的一段记录（Schlatter 1916：391），说当时负责教育事业的 Jakob Lörcher 在十九世纪八〇年代初为了出版一部小读本（Lesebuch），造了 60 多个新的方言字。[1]《启蒙浅学》的汉字本也使用大量独特的客家方言字（有的字还加上注释如"X，YZ 切"）。不管从出版时期还是从方言字这一点来看，这个"读本"很可能就是《启蒙浅学》。罗马字本的第一版在 1879 年出版，而汉字本完全依据罗马字本的排版，每一页每一行一一对应，因此汉字本每行的字数参差不齐。我们凭这个特点推测，汉字本大概晚于罗马字本。《启蒙浅学》一书为上下两段，每段还分成上下两卷，汉字本字数大约五万二千字。内容如下：

---

* 本文原发表于"第二届汉语方言小型研讨会——客家语研究"（"中研院"语言学研究所，2004 年 12 月），发表后作过不少改动，在修改过程中参考了各位同行在研讨会讨论时提出的意见，在此特别想向魏培泉、连金发、赖惠玲、严修鸿、钟荣富诸位，以及以客话为母语的各位与会者致谢。我们还参考了二位匿名审稿人的建议。本研究得到日本教育科学部的科研项目 B(1)13410129 以及 B(2)14310221 的资助。

表 1 《启蒙浅学》的分段与内容（揓 lau¹ ＝和）

段・卷	标题	课文号	汉字本的页码	罗马字本的页码
上段　上卷	讲论各样生物揓死物	1—120	一—三十三	1~66
上段　下卷	讲论生物揓死物箇性情	121—162	三十四—五十七	67~114
下段　上卷	比喻劝人	163—179	五十八—六十三	115~126
下段　下卷	报应篇	180—238	六十四—九十九	127~198

1.2 举例说明

本文举例只标课文号和课文标题，不标页码。汉字本原来没有标点符号，我们是依照 Lepsius 本附上的。标音基本上依据罗马字本的 Lepsius 式符号，只做了以下几个改动：后鼻音 [ŋ] 原来由 n 上附加一点来标注，本文写成 ng；成音节 s 和 m 原来在 s、m 下边附加圆圈，圆圈在本文中省略。声调符号一律改成数字：1 ＝阴平（上平），2 ＝阳平（下平），3 ＝上声，4 ＝去声，5 ＝阳入（上入），6 ＝阴入（下入）。汉字本和罗马字本基本上一一对应，只有个别的字不对应，或许是刻错的字。例句中出现不对应的字句时用 [ ] 括号和注释加以说明。方言字无法造字时用"□"来代替。

2. 考察对象

汉语有专门表达空间位移的语法范畴：趋向补语。从历史演变来看，趋向补语与结果补语范畴一样，形成、成熟得比较晚，所以方言之间的出入相当大。趋向补语构成一个封闭的类，这一点与结果补语不同。《启蒙浅学》中的趋向补语范畴的主要成员如下，与巴色会的语法书（1909 年）所举的趋向词相吻合（Chappell & Lamarre, 2005: 111—115）：

客观参照 D_{nd}	šong¹ 上	ha¹ 下	lok⁵ 落（落，进）	tšhut⁶ 出	tšon³ 转（回）	ko⁴ 过	hi³ 起
主观参照 D_d	loi² 来	hi⁴ 去					
〔记号〕主观参照略称 D_d，D=directional，d=deictic；客观参照略称 D_{nd}，nd=nondeictic							

本文讨论"一般动词＋趋向动词"所构成的句法组合，简称为"VD 格式"。我们用记号"D"来总括由"D_d"、"D_{nd}"和"$D_{nd}D_d$"构成的各类趋向成分。经过对《启蒙浅学》一书中所见的趋向补语的全面考察，我们企图解决以下两个问题：

（一）汉语有不少方言在一般动词和趋向动词之间可以或者必须加入某一个助词，其性质和功能至今还不十分明确，因为其具体句法分布等按方言而有不同（柯理思、刘淑学 2001；柯理思 2002）。某一些南方方言，如湖南的新化方言或者香港粤语，在前项动词 V 和趋向动词 D 之间可以插入几种不同的助词，和体貌助词同形。这些助词所起的句法作用和其表示体貌意义时的功能似乎有密切关系。巴色会的出版物中也能见到类似的语法格式。比如，例句 (1)—(4) 引自巴色会出版的客家话语法书。[2] "tau^{3}倒"是附在动词后表示动作的达成和实现的一个常见的体标记：

（1）佢　行　紧　路　当　时，有　人　<u>走　倒　来</u>。
　　　Ki^2　hang^2　kin^3　lu^4　tong^1　ši^2, yu^1　nyin^2　<u>tseu^3　tau^3　loi^2</u>.
　　　'When he was walking on the road, there came a man.'

（2）喏　张　脚　锄　在　箇　里　<u>捡　倒　来</u>，
　　　Nya^3　tšong^1　kyok^6　tsho^2　tshoi^1　kai^4　li^1　<u>kyam^3　tau^3　loi^2</u>,
　　　就　爱　放　转　箇　里　去。
　　　tshyu^4　oi^4　fong^4　tšon^3　kai^4　li^1　hi^4.
　　　'You must put this hoe back where you took it from.'

"ha^{4}下"（大概来源于动量词"一下"）表示尝试、短时、瞬时等体貌意义，也出现在动词和趋向补语之间，下面的例句都是祈使句，例句的德语翻译没有表达任何"从上往下"的具体趋向意义：

（3）捡　下　去。
　　　Kyam^3　ha^4　hi^4.
　　　'Just take it away.'

（4）书　桌　做　正，就　搬　下　来。
　　　Šu^1　tsok^6　tso^4　tšang^4　tshyu^4　pan^1　ha^4　loi^2.
　　　'If (or when) the desk is finished, bring it here.'

但是那些助词也可以不出现，并不是强制性成分。趋向补语就紧接在动词后，如：tšha^1 loi^2 㧡　来，tai^4 loi^2 带　来 "to bring over（towards speaker）"（Chappell & Lamarre 2005：112）。

动趋式（本文所说的 VD 格式）一般认为是由连动式（或者并列式）发展而来的格式（太田 1958：210；吴福祥 1996：395—396；梁银峰 2005）。在汉语诸方言中使用的"一般动词＋趋向动词"组合在句法结构上不一定是均匀的句法组合。比如说前项（一般动词）和后项（趋向动词）也可能是同等的，或者可能是前项对后项起修饰性作用，类似于现代共同语的"走着来"一类组合。[3] 我们认为，插入在 V 和 D 之间的种种语法成分是作为解决 V 和 D 的句法关系问题的一个重要线索。本文的记号 D 指的是"位于另一个动词后的趋向动词"，其句法性质不一定是北方话里一般所说的"补语"。

（二）有不少汉语方言不用"V+ 趋向补语 + 处所词"格式（下面简称为"VDL"格式），只用"V 到 + 处所词"或者类似的格式（"到"可以由其他成分来取代）。比如北部吴语（见刘丹青 2003：274—275）、湖南的娄底方言（见刘丽华 2001：268）、西安方言（见王军虎 1997）：

（5）a.【共同语】走进屋里来 / 跳下水去 / 送回北京来 / 拿出图书馆去

　　　b.【娄底话】行到只肚里_{里面}来 / 钻到只水肚里去 / 送到北京来 / 拿到图书馆前_{外面}去

（6）a.【西安话】* 搬进楼去 /* 跑上山来 /* 拿回屋里_{家里}去 /* 走出城来

　　　b.【西安话】搬到楼里去 / 跑到山上来 / 拿到屋里_{家里}去 / 从城里走出来

除此之外，笔者亲自调查的河北、陕西、山西的几种冀鲁官话、关中方言、晋方言也如此。[4] 比如在这些方言里，在共同语里常用的格式（7a）和（8a）不能成立，为了表示同样的意义则应该改成格式 b（处所名词不出现），或者用其他格式，比如把趋向动词换成引进终结点的"到"（格式 c）。如果趋向动词原来引进位移的起点，就可以使用前置的介词结构（格式 d）。比如：

（7）a.* 把钱包搁进书包（里）。　　b. 把钱包搁进去。

　　　　　　　　　　　　　　　　　c. 把钱包搁到书包里（去）。

（8）a.* 把椅子搬出楼来。　　　　　b. 把椅子搬出来。

　　　　　　　　　　　　　　　　　d. 把椅子从楼里搬出来。

与此相反，共同语（普通话、国语）在书面语里经常使用"V+ 趋向补语 + 处所词"一类格式，如"走上讲台"、"跑进屋"等。而且趋向补语为"出"和"下"时，其后的处所词 L 可以引进位移的起点，如"搬出楼来"、"跳下舞台"（见刘月华 1998）。香港粤语和共同语一样，使用"VDL"格式，如例句（9）—（11）（引自张洪年 1972：112—117）。D 由"出"担任时，L 可以表达位移的起点（例句（9）和（11a））或者终点（例句（11b））：

（9）我一行出大会堂，就即刻搭计程车翻屋企。

　　　〔共同语：我一走出大会堂，就⋯⋯〕

（10）行入酒楼 〔共同语：走进酒家〕

（11）行出花园 →〔共同语 (a)：走出花园〕处所词 L 表示位移的起点。

　　　　　　　→〔共同语 (b)：走到花园里去/来〕处所词 L 表示位移的终点。

巴色会文献所反映的客家话经常用"落、出、上、下、转"等趋向补语来引进处所词，如上文的例句（2）中的"fong⁴ tšon³ kai⁴ li¹ hi⁴ 放转箇里去"（放回那个地方去）。趋向动词原来可以带处所宾语，如"上台、进屋"等。但是以上所介绍的北方、吴等方言中，趋向动词出现在另一个动词后作补语时就失去带处所宾语的能力，这表示其论元结构（argument structure）已经发生变化了，可以看作趋向动词语法化为趋向词（directional）的一个形式表现。而客语、粤语的趋向动词出现在一般动词后仍然可以带处所宾语，说明其保留动词更多的句法特点。

可见，本文针对的这两个问题均涉及 VD 格式中的趋向动词 D 的句法性质问题。我们准备在下面的第 3 节和第 4 节里分别讨论这两个问题，第 5 节专门讨论"ha⁴ 吓"的语法化问题。

3．动词和趋向补语之间所出现的体貌成分（"V Asp D"格式）

经常出现在这个句法环境中的成分有三个："ha⁴ 吓"、"kin³ 竟"和"tau³ 倒"。可以按照趋向成分的类型（表示非指示趋向的动词 D_{nd} 还是表示指示趋向的 D_d）分成两类格式。

3.1 "V-ha⁴-D$_{nd}$"(V 吓 D$_{nd}$) 和 "V-ha⁴-loi²"、"V-ha⁴-hi⁴"(V 吓 D$_d$)(吓 =ha⁴)

3.1.1

"V-ha⁴-D$_{nd}$"：10 例（"V 吓落" 4 例；"V 吓落 L" 1 例；"V 吓过" 3 例；"V 吓出" 1 例；"V 吓转" 1 例）。

先要说明《启蒙浅学》汉字本在用字上的一些原则。该书对白读音的字往往采取加上口字旁的办法，比如 tshoi¹ 写成"啛"，而"在"念 tshai⁴, voi⁴ 写成"哙"等。"下"字也按其读音写成不同的汉字，一律把 ha¹ 写成"下"，把 ha⁴ 写成"吓"（例外极少，大概属于刻错的字）。

在《启蒙浅学》中，"吓"ha⁴ 有时插在一般动词和趋向动词之间。比如例句 (12) 的"V 吓起"[5] 作为两个连续的动作的前项，强调"刚拿起的时候"就有一只老鼠跑出来把她吓坏，她就把装鸡蛋的篮子掉到地上：

（12）后来主人婆喊佢上棚顶，捡下箇只张鸡□箇篮来。佢捡吓 [起] 箇时，就有

只老鼠猋出来吓倒佢，……〔223 好手势箇妹子〕（kai⁴ 箇＝那；pyau¹ 猋＝跑；tšong¹ 张＝装）

Heu⁴-loi² tšu³-nyin²-pho² ham⁴ ki šong¹ phang²-tang³, kyam³-ha¹ kai⁴ tšak⁶ tšong¹ kai¹-tšhun¹ kai⁴ lam⁵ loi². Ki² <u>kyam³-ha⁴-hi⁵</u> kai⁴ ši², tshyu⁴ yu¹ tšak⁶ lao⁴-tšhu³ pyau¹-tšhut⁶-loi² hak⁶-tau³ ki²,...

"V-ha⁴-D$_{nd}$" 还可以表达两个连续动作的后续事件，同样强调两个事件在时间上的紧接和动作的瞬时体，在某些句子里和"一……就"或者副词"粘势"（nyam²-ši⁴＝马上）共现。例句 (13) 描写一个小偷想要偷一条刚刚做好的铁链，一拿起来就烫手，铁链就掉下来：

（13）啱啱有人就快快□起箇铁链来。就大声暗一句痛，铁链也跌吓落，因为铁链还好烧，热吓嘌五只手指都燥开。〔217 铁链〕（□ ya³ ＝拿；lat⁶-ha⁴ 热吓 ＝热得；kya¹ 嘌＝他的）

Ngam¹-ngam¹ mau² nyin² tshyu⁴ fai⁴-fai⁴ ya³-hi³ kai⁴ thet⁶-len⁴ loi². Tshyu⁴ thai⁴ šang¹ hem¹ yit⁶ ki¹ thung⁴, thet⁶-len⁴ ya¹ <u>tet⁶-ha⁴-lok⁵</u>, yin¹-wui⁴ thet⁶-len⁴ han² hau³ šau¹, lat⁶-ha⁴ kya¹ ng³ tšak⁶ šu³-tši³ tu¹ tsau¹-hoi¹.

"V 吓 D$_{nd}$" 有时仅仅强调动作的瞬时完毕，比如例句（14）的老鹰猛扑小猫（šok⁶ 相当于英语的 'swoop down'，"lok⁵ 落"在这儿保留原义），完全是一个"突发"事件：

（14）忽然间有只鹞婆□吓落，吊开一只猫仔。〔129 猫乸有死胆〕（hoi¹ 开 ＝掉）

Fut⁶-yen²-kan¹ yu¹ tšak⁶ yau⁴-pho² <u>šok⁶-ha⁴-lok⁵</u>, tyau⁴-hoi¹ yit⁶ tšak⁶ myau⁴-tsai³.

梅县客家话有一个语法格式与本节所介绍的"V 吓 D"相似："V 阿 D"格式。林立芳 (1996) 和侯复生 (2002) 都提到梅县方言的这个格式，其中的"阿"音 a⁵²，念去声，用法、调类和韵母均与巴色会文献的"吓"ha⁴ 相应，a 和 ha（去声）很可能是同源词。梅县话的"V 阿 D$_{nd}$"与"V＋阿＋结果补语 R"平行，相当于共同语的"一 VR（或 VD）就 VP₂"（见例句（15）（17）（18）（20）），或者"刚 VR（刚 VD）"（例句（16）（19））。上述几个客家方言的 a 所表达的体意义和共同语的"一 V"相近，表示瞬时体（见陈光 2003）。比如：

（15）新娘子<u>行阿</u>入门就端茶端饭（新娘一走进家门就送茶送饭）（林立芳 1996:3）

（16）这係倻才从书店<u>买阿</u>转个书。（这是我刚从书店买回来的书）（侯复生 2002：333）

朱炳玉 (1998) 所描写的五华客家话的助词"啊"（读轻声），也具有类似的用法。在巴色会的文献里也能见到与林文、侯文所描写的"V+ 阿 + 体貌标记"相对应的格式，比如巴色会出版的语法书里[6]有这样的例句（"hoi¹ 开"表示完成）：

（17）Kong³　ha⁴　hoi¹　tshyu⁴　tseu³.

　　　讲　　吓　　开　　就　　　走。

　　　'As soon as he'd said that, he went away.'

Charles Rey 的《客法辞典》(1926) 也提到一个助词"阿"a⁴（去声），可以出现在动词和表示动作达成的"倒"，或者表示动作完成的"帛 phet"之间（phet 相当于巴色会文献的"开 hoi¹"），也可以插在一般动词和趋向动词之间。据《客法辞典》，这种 a⁴ 表示"动作刚刚结束"，例如：

（18）食阿帛就来 'Viens dès que tu auras mangé' "你一吃完就过来"（Rey 1926:3，以下同）

（19）种阿倒个菜 'les légumes qui viennent d'être plantés' "刚刚种上的蔬菜"

（20）行阿转就去睡目 'il s'est mis au lit dès son retour' "他一回来就马上去睡了"

3.1.2

"V-ha⁴-loi²"（V 吓来）：2 例；"V-ha⁴-hi⁴"（V 吓去）：4 例。

林立芳 (1996) 和侯复生 (2002) 讨论"阿"插在动词和补语之间的用法时都没有举"V 阿来"或"V 阿去"的例句，但从巴色会文献的"V 吓来"、"V 吓去"的用例来看，其中的 ha⁴"吓"的功能与上述"V 吓 / 阿 + 趋向补语"里的"吓 / 阿"相似。我们有两方面的根据：

（一）"V 吓来 / 去"的例句并不表示从上往下的运动。比如例句 (21) 的公羊看见镜子中的自己就斗起来，从故事的上下文来看，动作都发生在楼上，公羊并没有"往下"跑，后来是佣人回来，一进门听见镜子被打碎的声音，上楼发现羊把镜子打烂了。"斗吓来"和"猋吓去"并不等于"斗下来"、"跑下去"，但其后的"跌下来"就是"掉下来"的意思。请注意后者的读音为 ha¹：

（21）镜肚箇只也斗吓来摙佢打。箇真羊牯猋吓去，斗一吓，箇玻璃镜俾佢斗烂里，箇兜玻璃碎玲玲铃铃跌下来。箇使婆啱啱撇竟水转，一落大门听倒玲玲铃铃响就快快走上楼里去，看倒……〔206 羊牯〕（tu³ 肚 = 里；lau¹ 摙 = 同；teu¹ 兜 = 些；pin¹ 俾 = 给；kin³ 竟 = 着）

Kyang⁴-tu³ kai⁴ tšak⁶ ya¹ <u>teu⁴-ha⁴-loi²</u> lau¹ ki² ta³. Kai⁴ tšin¹ yong²-ku¹ <u>pyau¹-ha⁴ -hi⁴</u>, teu⁴ yit⁶ ha⁴, kai⁴ po¹-li²-kyang⁴ pin¹ ki² teu⁴-lan⁴ li¹, kai⁴ teu¹ po¹-li²-sui⁴ lin¹- lin¹-lang¹-lang¹ tet⁶-ha¹-loi². Kai⁴ s³-pho² ngam¹-ngam¹ tshau¹-kin³ šui³ tšon³, yit⁶ lok⁵ thai⁴ mun¹ thang⁴-tau³ lin¹-lin¹-lang¹-lang¹ hyang³ tshyu⁴ khwai⁴-khwai⁴ tseu³- šong¹ leu² li¹ hi⁴, khon⁴-tau³...

可见"V 吓 D_d"与"V 吓 D_nd"表示瞬时完毕等体貌意义。比如例句（22）的"吓"强调"一刀斩去"的突然性。例句（23）强调两个事件在时间上的紧接：阿新上街去了，很晚才回来，一回来就进屋。

（22）佢拔出喈刀，等竟箇蛇来，就一刀<u>斩吓去</u>，好彩斩中喈颈背箇只骨……〔132 人摸蛇打交〕

Ki² phat⁵-tšhut⁶ kya¹ tau¹, ten³-kin³ kai⁴ ša² loi², tshyu⁴ yit⁶ tau¹ <u>tsam³-ha⁴-hi⁴</u>, hau³-tshoi³ tsam³-tšung⁴ kya¹ kyang³-poi⁴ kai⁴ tšak⁶ kwut⁶...

（23）佢就出街，好暗正转。<u>转吓来</u>就落房间，因为好瘰就坐吓箇凳里去。〔192 黄牛泡〕

Ki² tshyu⁴ tšhut⁶ kai¹, hau³ am⁴ tšang⁴ tšon³. <u>Tšon³-ha⁴-loi²</u> tshyu⁴ lok⁵ fong²-kan¹, yin¹-wui⁴ hau³ khoi⁴ tshyu⁴ tsho¹-ha⁴ kai⁴ ten¹ li¹ hi⁴.

（二）表示从上往下的位移时（即与共同语的"V 下去 / 来"相应时），在《启蒙浅学》中用"V 下来 / 去"，其中的"下"读 ha¹（阴平），罗马字本标音不同，汉字本用字也不同。上文的例句（21）的"跌下来"和例句（12）的"捡下 + 宾语 + 来"就是这种"VD（O）来"结构。请再看两例。例句（24）的龙眼是从龙眼树上掉下来的，例句（25）是讲一个放牛的孩子爬到树顶上以后发现牛进了花园，把蔬菜吃掉，孩子就从树上跳下来。

（24）忽然间有只龙眼<u>跌下来</u>，喈喈口中喈鼻孔，……〔167 论人唔知造化主箇智慧〕

Fut⁶-yen²-kan¹ yu¹ tšak⁶ lyung²-ngan³ <u>tet⁶-ha¹-loi²</u>, ngam¹-ngam¹ tep⁶-tšung⁴ kya¹ phi⁴-kung¹,...

（25）后来箇只亚僬在树顶看倒牛食菜就好唧，在树里<u>跳下来</u>，捉箇条牛打好粗擦。〔189 掌牛亚僬〕（a¹-tsyau² 亚僬 = 孩子；at⁶ = 生气；tshoi¹ 在 = 从）

Heu⁴-loi² kai⁴ tšak⁶ a¹-tsyau² tshoi¹ šu⁴ tang³ khon⁴-tau³ nyu² šit⁵ tshoi⁴ tshyu⁴ hau³ at⁶, tshoi¹ šu⁴-li¹ <u>thyau²-ha¹-loi²</u>, tsuk⁶ kai⁴ nyu² ta³ hau³ ths¹-tshat⁶.

"跌下来 tet⁶-ha¹-loi²" 有 4 例（146，167，181，206），"跌下 O 来"（158）、"落下水来"（146）、"tem¹ 下来"（tem¹ = 'touch, come down to'，223）、"跳下来"（189）、"揞下 O 来"（223）各 1 例，就是说"V 下（O）来"格式总共 9 例，音均作为 ha¹，有明显的"从上往下"的空间趋向意义，因此有充分的根据判断《启蒙浅学》中的"V-ha¹-D$_d$"和"V-ha⁴-D$_d$"有别。前者的 ha¹ 是趋向动词，后者的 ha⁴ 来源于表示时间短暂等意义的体貌标记，这个体貌标记本身来源于动量词 ha⁴。

3.2 "V-kin³-D$_{nd}$"（V 竟 D$_{nd}$）、"V-kin³-loi²"（V 竟来）、"V-kin³-hi⁴"（V 竟去）（竟 =kin³）

"kin³"是持续体标记，在其他出版得晚一些的巴色会文献中一般写成"紧"，在《启蒙浅学》和早期的圣经中作为"竟"，功能相当于梅县客家话的"等"。

3.2.1

"V-kin³-D$_{nd}$"（V 竟 D$_{nd}$）6 例，D 为"落"4 例，"上"、"下"各 1 例。例 (26) 的"落"引进处所词。主语是一只老鼠的尸体。

（26）箇老鼠竟久竟蹲竟落地坭，……〔145 推车仔〕"V 竟落 L"（tshun² = 在地里陷下去）

Kai⁴ lau⁴-tšhu³ kin³ kyu³ kin³ tshun²-kin³-lok⁵ thi⁴-nai²,...

（27）……故此上帝使箇水一点完一点跌竟落，好似过里米筛唻匀。〔146 讲论水〕

...Ku⁴-ths³ Šong⁴-ti⁴ s³ kai⁴ šui³ yit⁶ tyam³ wan² yit⁶ tyam³ tet⁶-kin³-lok⁵, hau³ s⁴ ko⁴-li¹ mi³-si¹ kan⁴ yun².

（28）看倒凳头箇黄牛泡俾佢坐烂净里，箇兜汁唉箇凳头流流溜溜流竟下。〔192 黄牛泡〕（pin¹ 俾 = 被；li¹ 里 = 了；teu¹ 兜 = 些）

Khon⁴-tau³ ten⁴-theu² kai⁴ wong²-nyu²-phau² pin¹ ki² tsho¹-lan⁴-tshyang⁴-li¹, kai⁴ teu¹ tšip⁶ tshoi¹ kai⁴ ten⁴-theu² lyu²-lyu²-lyu⁴-lyu⁴ lyu²-kin³-ha¹.

这个格式在共同语里不存在，从语境和共现的副词来看（比如例句（26）的副词"竟久竟"、（27）的"一点完一点"等），"V 竟 D$_{nd}$"似乎强调动作往某个方向逐渐进行。"V 竟 D"所出现的句子是描写眼前的位移，而不是叙述某个变化或事件。

3.2.2

"V-kin³-loi²"（V 竟来）：9 例；"V-kin³-hi⁴"（V 竟去）：8 例。

"V 竟 D$_d$"一共 17 例，其中的动词 V 表示位移方式如"pyau¹ 猋"（= 跳，快跑，124，207，129，211）、"pui¹ 喺"（145x2）、"hang² 行"（= 走，227，128）、"yu² 泅"（=

游，132 ）、"tseu³ 走"（ = 跑，193，195，222 ）、"翻"（ 229 ）、"hem¹ 喊"（ = 大声叫，232 ），及物动词有 "tšok⁶ 着"（ = 穿，214 ）、"tšha¹ 撒"（ 198 ）、"tšui¹ 追"（ 185 ）。

和共同语的 "V 着来 / 去" 一样，"V 竟来 / 去" 强调位移 "来 / 去" 时位移体的姿势或者伴随动作，其中的趋向动词可以理解为表示施事的位移。例句（30）的位移体是一匹马，马同情路上碰到的乞丐，一定要等到主人给他们钱才肯行走，共同语翻成 "走着去" 不太自然。例句（29）和（31）是共同语经常用 "跑来"、"游来" 的语境。

（29）有嚹喀象俾人吓惊里，就放势猋竟走，人看倒佢<u>猋竟来</u>，侪侪都走命。

〔124 象唔忘恩〕（有嚹 = 有一次；nya³ 喀 = 这；li¹ 里 = 了；sa²-sa² 侪侪 = 人人）

Yu¹ pai³ nya³ tšak⁶ syong⁴ pin¹ nyin² hak⁶-kyang¹ li¹, tshyu⁴ fong⁴-ši⁴ pyau¹-kin³-tseu³, nyin² khon⁴-tau³ ki <u>pyau¹-kin³-loi²</u>, sa²-sa² tu¹ tseu³ myang⁴.

（30）唉路中唔知几多攞食佬，只只都奉顶帽来攞钱，倕骑箇条马看倒就唔行，爱等到箇攞食佬攞倒里正行 [……] 跟尾遇倒有攞食箇就诈得□钱俾佢，咁样箇马正肯<u>行竟去</u>。〔128 马有记才〕（攞食佬 = 讨饭的；跟尾 = 然后；kan⁴-yong⁴ 咁样 = 这样；正 = 才）

Tshoi¹ lu⁴ tšung¹ m¹ ti¹ ki³ to¹ lo¹-šit⁵-lau³, tšak⁶ tšak⁶ tu¹ pung³ tang³ mao⁴ loi² lo¹ tshen², ngai¹ khi² kai⁴ thyau² ma¹ khon⁴-tau³ tshyu⁴ m¹ hang², oi⁴ ten³-tau³ kai⁴ lo¹-šit⁵-lau³ lo¹-tau³-li¹ tšang⁴ hang² [...] ken¹-mui¹ ngi²-tau³ yu¹ lo¹-šit⁵ kai⁴ tshyu⁴ tsa⁴ tet⁶ tang¹ tshen² pin¹ ki², kan⁴-yong⁴ kai⁴ ma¹ tšang⁴ hen³ <u>hang²-kin³-hi⁴</u>.

（31）谁不知箇条蛇向竟喀只艇<u>泅竟来</u>……〔132 人接蛇打交〕

Šui²-put⁶-ti¹ kai⁴ thyau² ša² hyong⁴-kin³ kya¹ tšak⁶ thyang⁴ <u>yu²-kin³-loi²</u>,...

还有 4 例动词带受事宾语，为 "V 竟 O 去"（缴竟水去（123）；揽竟只猫去（141）；揽竟喀只猫去（141）；担竟箇箩□去（218））。再举两例稍显特殊一点的伴随动作："tšok⁶ 著" 和 "hem¹ 喊"（大声叫 ）。

（32）箇只打工箇人衫唔够著，想摸喀主人借件马褂<u>著竟去</u>。〔214 马褂〕（sam¹ 衫 = 衣服；tšok⁶ 着 = 穿；lau¹ 搂 = 跟 ）

Kai⁴ tšak⁶ ta³-kung¹ kai⁴ nyin² sam¹ m¹ keu⁴ tšok⁶, syong³ lau¹ kya¹ tšu³-nyin² tsya⁴ khen⁴ ma¹-kwa⁴ <u>tšok⁶-kin³-hi⁴</u>.

（33）……随路喊<u>竟去</u>咁样话："唉耶！你兜看吓番人箇智慧，有几大；……"〔231 写字〕

...Tshui² lu⁴ <u>hem¹-kin³-hi⁴</u> kan²-yong⁴ wa⁴: "Ai¹-ya¹! Ngi²-teu¹ khon⁴-ha⁴ fan¹-nyin² kai⁴ tši⁴-fui⁴, yu¹ ki³ thai⁴;..."

3.3 "V-tau³-loi²"（V 倒来）15 例、"V-tau³-O-loi²"（V 倒 O 来）4 例

进入"V 倒来"格式的动词有"tseu³ 走"（209x2, 218, 222）、"pui¹ 飞"（145x2, 153）、"kyam³ 捡"（133，205）、"lot⁵ 捋"（'gather'，147）、"kyu⁴ 救"（129）、"tai⁴ 带"（231，232）、"□ lam³"（= 掏，198）、"tsuk⁶ 捉"（200）、"sau⁴ 扫"（63）一共 14 例，大部分动词表示使动意义，引起受事的位移，除了表示施事和受事同时移动的"拿"类之外，还有表示受事位移的前提动作，如"救、捉、捡"。没有"V 倒去"的例子，大概与"倒"所表达的达成意义有关，一般如果表示负面意义的（或不如意的）动作的完成就用"开"（比如"死开"、"卖开"），"倒"含"得到"的意思（如"养倒"（生孩子）、"买倒"），所以和"来"结合比较自然。我们尚未发现"V 倒 D_{nd}"的例句。出现在"V 倒来"的动词是及物动词时，其中的"倒"的达成意义更明显：

（34）噶邻舍不过係俾兜烟你，佢唔知头揽只银子都□倒来。〔198 有良心箇西印度人〕（他原来给你的是烟，并不知道里边连银子也采来了。lam³ = 'grasp, seize'）

Nya³ lin²-ša⁴ put⁶-ko⁴ he⁴ pin¹ teu¹ yen¹ ngi², ki² m¹ ti¹ theu² lau¹ tšak⁶ nyun²-tsai³ tu¹ <u>lam³-tau³-loi²</u>.

（35）"牧师娘你嚇边知牧师啱啱爱你搭噶件东西去俾佢?"嚟家眷对佢话："正先你带倒来箇块刨口话催知。"〔231 写字〕（nyong⁴-pen¹ 嚇边 = 怎么; nya³ 噶 = 这; 正先 = 刚才）

"Muk⁵-s¹-nyong² ngi² nyong⁴-pen¹ ti¹ muk⁵-s¹ ngam¹-ngam¹ oi⁴ ngi² tap⁶ nya³ khen⁴ tung¹-si¹ hi⁴ pin¹ ki²?" Nga¹ ka¹-ken¹ tui⁴ ki² wa⁴: "Tšang⁴-sen¹ ngi² <u>tai⁴-tau³-loi²</u> kai⁴ khwai⁴ phau²-heu³ wa⁴ ngai² ti¹."

进入"V 倒 O 来"格式的动词有"tsya⁴ 借"（223）、"tai⁴ 带"（127）、"tšha¹ 搽"（230）、"tseu¹ 撒"（227）各 1 例。比如下边的例句里先出现"带来"，然后出现"带倒条来添"。狗把受伤的伙伴带到曾经治过它的兽医那里，让兽医给自己的朋友看病：

（36）早时大法国箇京城，有只人有只狗仔拗断脚骨就带来俾医生医。医好里箇条狗仔就走。过开几日佢来撅医生箇门。医生打开门来，看倒箇条狗仔带倒条来添，也係断开脚骨箇，跳吓跳里来。〔127 狗晓顾狗〕（khet⁵ = 'scratch'; thyam¹ 添：用在句末表示"还、再"）

Tsau³-ši² thai⁴ Fap⁶ kwet⁶ kai⁴ kin¹-šang², yu¹ tšak⁶ nyin² yu¹ tšak⁶ keu³-tsai³ au³-thon¹ kyok⁶-kwut⁶ tshyu⁴ tai⁴-loi² pin¹ yi¹-sang¹ yi¹. Yi¹-hau³-li¹ kai⁴ thyau² keu³-

tsai³ tshyu⁴ tseu³. Ko⁴-hoi¹ ki³ nyit⁶ ki² loi² khet⁵ yi¹-sang¹ kai⁴ mun². Yi¹-sang¹ ta³-hoi¹ mun² loi², khon⁴-tau³ kai⁴ thyau² keu³-tsai³ <u>tai⁴-tau³ thyau² loi²</u> thyam¹, ya¹ he⁴ thon⁴-hoi¹ kyok⁶-kwut⁶ kai⁴, thyau⁴ ha⁴ thyau⁴ li¹ loi².

3.4 "V 倒来"、"V 竟来" 和 "V 来" 的对比

"V 竟来"相当于共同语的"V 著来"，按道理是强调位移时的姿势或者伴随动作，而"V 倒来"的"倒"则保持其表示动作达成（实现）的体貌意义。动词为"飞、走"等表示位移方式的动词时，"V 倒来"在意义上与"V 竟来"似乎比较接近。但是如果仔细观察上文举的"V 竟来 / 去"的例句 (29)—(33)，就能发现位移还没完成，而"V 倒来"(34)—(36) 大多用在位移已经完成的语境里。请比较下边的"走竟来"和"走倒来"：

（37）冇几久有只兵总头昂昂里大大步<u>行竟来</u>，行到噯只石嗜，……〔227 本分爱做箇事唔好推过别人〕（ten¹ 嗜 = 那儿；li¹ 里 = 地）

Mau² ki³ kyu³ yu¹ tšak⁶ pin¹-tsung³-theu² ngong⁴-ngong⁴ li¹ thai⁴-thai⁴ phu⁴ <u>hang²-kin³-loi²</u>, <u>hang²-tau³</u> nya¹ tšak⁶ šak⁵ ten¹, ...

（38）就听倒喀妹子喑好凄凉，佢就快快<u>走倒来</u>，看倒喀妹子满眼都係眼汁，对喀娾话，"有条蛇走倒来上下啮倒佢。"〔209 草龙〕（妹子 = 女儿；眼汁 = 眼泪；娾 mi¹ = 母亲）

Tshyu⁴ thang¹-tau³ kya¹ moi⁴-ts³ hem¹ hau³ tshi¹-lyong², ki² tshyu⁴ khwai⁴-khwai⁴ <u>tseu³-tau³-loi²</u>, khon⁴-tau³ kya¹ moi⁴-ts³ man¹ ngan³ tu¹ he⁴ ngan³-tšip⁶, tui⁴ kya¹ mi¹ wa⁴: "Yu¹ thyau² ša² <u>tseu³-tau³-loi²</u> šong⁴-ha⁴ ngat⁶-tau³ ngai²."

在例句（37）的谓语"行竟来"前有描写施事走过来时的姿势的修饰语"昂昂里大大步"，位移"来"没完成，所以后面需要说明他们"走到"那块大石头。而在例句（38）中，母亲听到女儿大声叫就赶快"跑来"才能看见女儿的眼泪，蛇也要先"跑到"姑娘身边才能咬到她。请再比较"飞竟来"和"飞倒来"的例句：

（39）有死尸在一笪嗜就周围箇虫都<u>咻竟来</u>寻箇死尸，寻倒就埋落箇地坭里去。〔145 推车仔〕（yit⁶ tat⁶ thang⁴ 一笪嗜 = 一个地方；寻倒 = 找到）

Yu¹ si³-ši¹ tshoi¹ yit⁶ tat⁶ thang⁴ tshyu⁴ tšu¹-wui² kai⁴ tšhung² tu¹ <u>pui¹-kin³-loi²</u> tshim² kai⁴ si³-ši¹, tshim²-tau³ tshyu⁴ mai²-lok⁵ kai⁴ thi⁴-nai¹ li¹ hi⁴.

（40）人家供鸡供鸭佢也<u>咻倒来</u>同吓食。〔153 禾鸠仔〕（thung²-ha⁴ 同吓 = 一起）

Nyin²-ka¹ kyung⁴ kai¹ kyung⁴ ap⁶ ki² ya¹ <u>pui¹-tau³-loi²</u> thung²-ha⁴ šit⁵.

例句（39）的虫可以一边飞一边找老鼠的尸体，但（40）的鸟为了"一块吃"一定要先结束"飞行"的运动。下边例句的"V 倒来"前有表示意愿"想"或者表示使动的"喊"（＝叫），突显位移的达成。例句（41）讲一个孩子想要捉住逃出来的鸟，放回盒子，不让他母亲知道他打开了盒子：

（41）亚欢想<u>捉倒来</u>，张转箇盒里去，唔俾喀媄知佢打开盖。〔200 白燕雕〕（张＝放）

A^1-fon^1 syong^3 <u>tsuk^6-tau^3-loi^2</u>, tšong^1-tšon^3 kai^4 hap^5 li^1 hi^4, m^1 pin^1 kya^1 mi^1 ti^1 ki^2 ta^3-hoi^1 koi^4.

（42）路上看倒只马脚铁就喊喀穦子<u>捡倒来</u>。〔205 马脚铁〕（lai^4-ts^3 穦子＝儿子）

Lu^4-šong^4 khon^4-tau^3 tšak^6 ma^1-kyok^6-thet^6 tshyu^4 ham^4 kya^1 lai^4-ts^3 <u>kyam^3-tau^3-loi^2</u>.

（43）忽然间有只鹞婆□吓落，吊开一只猫仔。猫嫲十分呷，焱竟去想<u>救倒来</u>。〔129 猫嫲有死胆〕（at^6 呷＝生气）

Fut^6-yen^2-kan^1 yu^1 tšak^6 yau^4-pho^2 šok^6-ha^4-lok^5, tyau^4-hoi^1 yit^6 tšak^6 myau^4-tsai^3. Myau^4-ma^2 šip^5-fun^1 at^6, pyau^1-kin^3-hi^4 syong^3 <u>kyu^4-tau^3-loi^2</u>.

从以上例句可以推测，"V 竟来"也许保持相当明显的连动式的特点，从句子的体貌特点来看，其中的"来"不像共同语的趋向补语，"V-kin^3 来"中的动词 V 和位移"来"是同时进行的动作。与此相反，"V 倒来"所表示的位移是已经完成的，因此可以说，两者还保持原来的体貌意义：未完成和完成，并没有虚化成"结构助词"或者"趋向补语标记"。我们在 3.5 节继续讨论这个问题。

3.5 讨论："动词 + 体标记 + 趋向动词"格式？

在湖南新化方言里"倒"表示持续体，也可以连接趋向补语，充当"中补结构助词"（罗昕如 1998：284 的用语），如：

（44）行倒去 / 拿倒来 / 抬倒进来 / 取倒落来（普通话：'走去、拿来、抬进来、取下来'）

新化方言也可以把完成体标记"咖"[.ka] 插在"VD"之间（罗昕如 1998：252）：

（45）部摩托车逗小王骑咖去哩。（普通话：'摩托车被小王骑走了'）

（46）粒人咸副走咖出去哩。（普通话：'人都跑出去了'）

张洪年（1972：116—118）把香港粤语的类似结构叫做"第二种复合方向补语"，书中举"V 翻 D"、"V 咗落"（N.B. "落"与"上"对立，客家话的"落"往往与"出"对立）、"V 咗去"、"V 紧 D"等例子。"翻"、"咗"、"紧"都是粤语常用的体标记，其中的"紧"属于未完成体。

这种句法分布和功能与北方话的"VXD"、"VX 来 / 去"格式的 X 成分有所不同（柯理思、刘淑学 2001，柯理思 2002）。对各方言中的"VXD"、"VX 来"等格式的 X 成分的性质，我们暂时还不敢下结论，但是我们相信，这些格式的句法意义在汉语诸方言里不会是同等的。南方方言的"V+ 体标记 + 趋向动词"格式允许几种不同的体标记出现在一般动词 V 和趋向动词 D 之间，对这个语言事实可以采取两种不同的分析方法。或者其中有一部分的 V 和 D 的组合在句法性质上与北方方言的"动趋式"有别（比如可以把"V kin^3 D"看作连动式），或者我们把"VD"、"V kin^3 D"、"V ha^4 D"和"V tau^3 D"都看作同类的语法格式（这是张 1972 对粤语的处理方法）。如果选择后一种分析法，即使我们把这种趋向动词 D 叫做"趋向补语"，应该承认其构成的 VD 组合与北方话的动趋式不同。趋向补语从语义上看是一种趋向词 (directional)，和动作的有界性 (boundedness) 没有直接关系。但是北方话的动趋式是一种结果句式，倾向于表示有界的事件（见沈 1995；Kang 2001），这与上述的"V-kin^3-D$_{nd}$"格式的语法意义冲突。这个问题恐怕要进一步考察活的语言才能得到答案，文献的例句给我们提供一些线索而已。描写各地方言的"VXD"格式的语义特点和句法特点，可以帮助我们对动趋式和动结式的发展有更全面的认识。

下边的表 2 介绍《启蒙浅学》中出现的趋向动词和体貌标记的结合情况。可见，不插入任何成分的"V+D$_{nd}$D$_d$"格式非常普遍（一共出现 59 次，请看表 2 的右下角），但如果我们看"V 来"和"V 去"一类组合，就发现其使用频率远远低于插入体貌标记的"VX 来 / 去"格式。如果排除带宾语的格式，前者仅出现 5 例（"带来、捡来、带去（x2）、送来"），而"V 吓来 / 去"、"V 竟来 / 去"和"V 倒来"加起来却有 38 例。

《启蒙浅学》中没有发现"V 吓 D$_{nd}$+D$_d$"的用例，我们在同时期的《新约圣经使徒行传》中也没有见到。但是朱炳玉（1998）在描写五华客家话的述补式的文章里举了好几个"V-a-D$_{nd}$ 来 / 去"的例句（五华客家话的"a 啊"轻读），从共同语的翻译来看，其功能和以上讨论的"V-ha^4- 来 / 去"和"V-ha^4-D$_{nd}$"中的 ha^4 非常近。因此，我们推测，本文献里没有出现"V-ha^4-D$_{nd}$"格式并不意味这个格式不存在。同样，该文献中没有发现"V-kin^3-D$_{nd}$D$_d$"和"V-tau^3-D$_{nd}$D$_d$"的用例。

原来体标记和结果补语的界限不一定很清楚，比如在巴色会文献中，"hoi^1 开"和

"tau³ 倒"可以进入可能式。共同语的趋向补语格式有一个与本节讨论的"V + 体标记 + D"接近："走了过来"、"拿了下来"等（主要用在书面语里）。巴色会的客语文献中还经常使用一个完成貌标记"li¹ 里"，相当于共同语的"了"，可以放在"hoi¹ 开"和"tau³ 倒"后，也没有可能式，没有补语的特点。但《启蒙浅学》中没有出现"V 里 D"的用例。

表 2　插在动趋式"VD$_{nd}$""VD$_d$"中间的体貌标记 ha⁴, kin³, tau³

	来	去	D$_d$总数	落	出	上	下	转	过	起	D$_{nd}$总数	D$_{nd}$+D$_d$ (D$_{nd}$来/D$_{nd}$去)
V 吓 ~	2	4	6	4	1	/	/	1	3	1	10	/
V 吓 ~ L	/	/	/	1	/	/	/	/	/	/	1	/
V 竟 ~	9	8	17	6	/	1	1	/	/	/	8	/
V 竟 O ~	/	4	4	/	/	/	/	/	/	/	/	/
V 竟 ~ L	/	/	/	1	/	/	/	/	/	/	1	/
V 倒 ~	15	/	15	/	/	/	/	/	/	/	/	/
V 倒 O ~	4	/	4	/	/	/	/	/	/	/	/	/
V+Asp ~	26	12	38	10	1	1	1	1	3	1	18	0
VØ ~	3	2	5	/	/	/	/	/	1	/	/	59(43/16)

4．引进处所词的趋向补语："VD$_{nd}$L"中的 D 成分

4.1《启蒙浅学》中的动趋式：趋向动词带处所宾语和不带处所宾语两种格式的比例

动趋式后不一定出现处所词，请先看看《启蒙浅学》中的动趋式的整个面貌：表 3 前三行的格式在 D 成分后不带处所词，后四行的格式带处所词。我们先对表 3 作简单的补充说明：

（一）表里的统计数字只包括表示空间位移的谓语句。

（二）"O"代表宾语，受事宾语占多数，偶尔也能见到几个存现宾语，统计上没有区分开来。

（三）因为本文的重点放在"VD$_{nd}$L"格式上，就排除了"起"和"开"的例句。

（四）"来、去"后往往出现另一个谓词，有时可以解释为第一个动词的目的。如果从上下文看动作没有表示位移就排除，如果整个谓语句有明显的位移意义或者可以解释为空间位移，就包括进来。

（五）"下"一般与 ha¹ 对应，"吓"与 ha⁴ 对应。如果汉字本和 Lepsius 本之间有出入就依据 Lepsius 本（见下文 4.5 节）。"爬下山来"的 ha¹ 引进的处所是位移路径，另一例引进终点。"V ha⁴ L"相当于共同语的"V 到 L"，我们另外处理（见下文的表 4）。

（六）"V 出 L"的处所词 L 都表示位移终点。

表3　动趋式"VD$_{nd}$(D$_d$)"和受事宾语、处所词的组合

	落 lok⁵	出 tšhut⁶	上 šong¹	下 ha¹	转 tšon³	过 ko⁴	D$_{nd}$ 总数（来 / 去）
V ~ 来 / 去	2/9	29/2	0/1	6/0	4/4	2/0	59(43/16)
V ~ O	/	8	/	/	2	/	10
V ~ O 来 / 去	1/0	21/1	/	3/0	5/1		32(30/2)
V ~ L	2	/	/	/	3	/	5
V ~ L 来 / 去	**2/43**	**0/3**	**5/7**	**1/1**	**2/8**	**1/1**	**74(11/63)**
V ~ OL 来 / 去	0/4	/	/	/	/		4(0/4)
V ~ 来 / 去 L		0/1	1/0				

表3的统计说明，《启蒙浅学》的 VD 格式的趋向动词经常连接处所词，如果我们拿不带受事宾语的双音节的趋向动词为例，后边连接处所词的格式占 55% 左右，即占多数。在同时期出版的小说《小额》（反映清末北京话）中，这个比例为 6%。下边在 4.2 至 4.7 节顺着表3的顺序分别讨论每个趋向动词（落、出、上、下、转、过）的情况，然后在 4.8 节和 4.9 节中再举使用趋向补语以外的形式（"到"、"ha⁴" 等）引进处所词的各种格式。

4.2 "V-lok⁵-L-loi²"（V 落 L 来）2 例、"V-lok⁵-L-hi⁴"（V 落 L 去）43 例

"lok⁵ 落"在巴色会文献里往往有"进"的意思，与"出"成对。巴色会文献中很少用"入"。"lok⁵ 落"作趋向动词带处所宾语，也往往有"进入"的意思，如："落寡妇婆箇屋家"（199）、"落噱房里"（200）、"落大门"（206）、"落船"（＝上船，141）等。可是"落"也没有完全失去其原来"掉落"的意义，大概是一种语义扩张现象。在本文所考察的"V 落 L"的大部分用例中，"落"有明显的"进入"意义（即位移的参照

是三维的），可是有时也碰到可疑的例句，比如（47）的"地下"和（48）的老鼠掉在"狮背"上，大概是二维的平面，"落"在这儿保留"掉落"的意义（该文献的方位词"里"兼有"上"的功能，可见客家话对三维和二维的区别不太敏感）：

（47）𠉂家眷读开就□落地下，……〔231 写字〕（nga¹ 𠉂＝我的；读开＝读完；fit⁶ ＝扔）

Nga¹ ka¹-ken⁴ thuk⁵-hoi¹ tshyu⁴ fit⁶-lok⁵ thi⁴-ha¹,...

（48）有只失吓脚，跌落狮背里来吓吓箇条狮跳起来好唧气，……〔130 老鼠都晓报恩〕

Yu¹ tšak⁶ šit⁶-ha⁴ kyok⁶, tet⁶-lok⁵ s¹-poi⁴ li¹ loi² hak⁶-ha⁴ kai⁴ thyau² s¹ thyau²-hi³-loi² hau³ at⁶-hi⁴, ...

因为现在缺乏明确的标准来判断"落"的意义，我们暂时把全部的"V 落 L"都包括进来作统计。[7]

"落"用在动词后引进位移的终点处所的用例频率很高，先举表示自移（autonomous motion）的例句。动词由"tet⁶ 跌"（130，132，158，169，185，223）、"tseu³ 走"（137，143，148，189，212）、"tson¹ 钻"（145，147，149，158，185，202）、"suk⁶ 缩"（155）、"mi⁴ 微"（148）、"sok⁵ □"'to suck up liquid'（146，155）、"piau¹ 㵘"（171x2）、"sip⁵ 寂"（180x2）、"wat⁶ 挖"（145）、"pha² 爬"（145）充当，一共 30 例，其中还有 2 例不带"去／来"（146，177）。

（49）到暗晡就好瘿，走落箇大树山里去，咗一窬树头下睡。〔137 乌蝇〕（暗晡＝晚上）

Tau⁴ am⁴-pu¹ tshyu⁴ hau³ khoi⁴, tseu³-lok⁵ kai⁴ thai⁴ šu⁴-san¹ li¹ hi⁴, tshoi¹ yit⁶ pho¹ šu⁴ theu²-ha¹ šoi⁴.

（50）唝吓都钻落箇死老鼠底下去，□竟箇死老鼠去箇地坊里。〔145 推车仔〕（tung¹＝carry）

Won²-ha⁴ tu¹ tson¹-lok⁵ kai⁴ si³ lau⁴-tšhu³ tai³-ha¹ hi⁴, tung¹-kin³ kai⁴ si³ lau⁴-tšu³ hi⁴ kai⁴ thi⁴-lak⁵ li¹.

表示动作者使某物位移的"致移"（caused motion）动词有"fong⁴ 放"（165，201，205，207，211，212，215）、"sem³ 掺"（91）、"wun⁴ 韫"（142）、"mai² 埋"（145）、"pok⁶ 博"（'to graft a tree'，154）、"thoi⁴ 袋"（184）、"thun² 沌"（'bury in the water'，158）、"len¹ 拎"（218）、"ap⁶ 押"（＝押犯人，185）、"fit⁶ □"（'throw'，231），一共 15 例。

（51）故此转嗲睡房撵倒一包金仔轻轻<u>袋落箇只孝子箇袋里去</u>，正到转去睡。

〔184 好心待爷娘〕（tšha¹ 撵 = carry, bring；thoi⁴ 袋 = 装在口袋里）

Ku⁴-ths³ tšon³ kya¹ šoi²-fong² tšha¹-tau³ yit⁶ pau¹ kim¹-tsai³ khyang¹-khyang¹ <u>thoi⁴</u> <u>-lok⁵ kai⁴ tšak⁶ hau²-ts³ kai⁴ thoi⁴ li¹ hi⁴</u>, tšang⁴ tau⁴-tšon³-hi⁴ šoi⁴.

（52）有只富贵人俾嗲仇敌捉倒<u>押落一间好暗箇监牢里去</u>。〔185 坐监侪〕

Yu¹ tšak⁶ fu⁴-kwui⁴ nyin² pin¹ kya¹ šu²-thit⁵ tsuk⁶-tau³ <u>ap⁶-lok⁵ yit⁶ kan¹ hau³ am⁴</u> <u>kai⁴ kam¹-lau² li¹ hi⁴</u>.

（53）嗲亚嬭卖开蜜糖，后来买倒老蟹<u>放落箇罌里去</u>养竟。〔212 蜜糖罌〕

Kya¹ a¹-mi¹ mai⁴-hoi¹ mit⁵-thong², heu⁴-loi² mai⁴-tau³ lao⁴-hai³ <u>fong⁴-lok⁵ kai¹ ang¹</u> <u>li¹ hi⁴</u> yong¹ kin³.

"V 落 OL 去" 4 例（没有 "V 落 OL 来"）。例句 (54) 还包括 "V 落 L 去" 的用例。

（54）……<u>又擂落头嗢水底里去</u>捋东西食，还之又唍只<u>微落水底里去</u>。〔148 鸭〕

（lui² 擂 = to pound、theu²-na¹ 头嗢 = 头、lot⁶ 捋 = gather、mi⁴ 微 = dive）

...<u>Yu⁴ lui²-lok⁵ theu²-na¹ šui³-tai³ li¹ hi⁴</u> lot⁶ tung¹-si² šit⁵, han²-tši¹ yu⁴ won² tšak⁶ <u>mi⁴-lok⁵ šui³-tai³-li¹ hi⁴</u>.

（55）每日爱<u>放落只石仔嗑酒罌里去</u>，唔爱捡出佢来……〔210 石仔〕

Mui¹ nyit⁶ oi⁴ <u>fong⁴-lok⁵ tšak⁶ šak⁵-tsai³ nya¹ tsyu³-ang¹ li¹ hi⁴</u>, m¹ oi⁴ kyam³-tšhut⁶ ki² loi², ...

4.3 "V-tšhut⁶-L-hi⁴"（V 出 L 去）3 例

趋向动词 "tšhut⁶ 出" 可以带表示位移终点的处所宾语，如 "出街"（= 上街，164），也可以带表示位移起点的处所宾语（Chappell and Lamarre 2005：90）。"V 出 L" 的 3 例中 L 都表示位移的终结点。三例都表示致使位移："tho¹ 拖"、"fit⁶ □"（= 扔）、"kyuk⁵ □"（= 赶、追）。

（56）有只耕菜园箇人咘嗲坆菜里锄倒五条牛筋草<u>□出园篱背里去</u>。〔152 牛筋草〕

（fit⁶ = 扔）

Yu¹ tšak⁶ kang¹ tshoi⁴-yen² kai⁴ nyin² tshoi¹ kya¹ tshoi⁴-lak⁵ li¹ tsho²-tau³ ng³ thyau² nyu²-kin¹-tshau³ <u>fit⁶-tšhut⁶ yen²-li¹ poi¹ li¹ hi⁴</u>.

（57）撵条棍来打箇羊牯，<u>□出门外去</u>。〔206 羊牯〕"kyuk⁵ = 追、赶"

Tšha¹ thyau² kwun⁴ loi² ta³ kai⁴ yong²-ku¹, <u>kyuk⁵-tšhut⁶ mun²-ngoi⁴ hi⁴</u>.

4.4 "V-šong^1-L-loi^2"（V 上 L 来）5 例、"V-šong^1-L-hi^4"（V 上 L 去）7 例

趋向动词"šong^1 上"可以带处所词如"上山"（209）、"上棚顶"（223）等。进入"V 上 L（来 / 去）"格式的动词有"liap^5 蹽"（122）、"pui^1 嘥"（125x2）、"pyau^1 猋"（132）、"thyau^2 跳"（134）、"tap^6 搭"（138）、"ta^3 打"（141）、"khi^1 企"（站，179）、"tseu^3 走"（181，206）、"pan^1 攀"（189）、"khet^5 撅"（203）。其中只有一句（60）是被动句，表示致移。

（58）夏天，就肯嘥上树顶里去，还之嘥上瓦背里来 。〔125 孔雀〕

Ha^4-then^1, tshyu^4 hen^3 pui^1-šong^1 šu^4-tang^3 li^1 hi^4, han^2-tši^1 pui^1-šong^1 nga^3-poi^4 li^1 loi^2 pu^1.

（59）箇条蛇就猋上艇里来，……〔132 人接蛇打交〕

Kai^4 thyau^2 ša^2 tshyu^4 pyau^1-šong^1 thyang^4 li^1 loi^2, ...

（60）后来箇条船到里印度海边就俾风打上岸来，……〔141 猫使人发财〕

Heu^4-loi^2 kai^4 thyau^2 šon^2 tau^4-li^1 Yin^4-thu^4 hoi^3-pen^1 tshyu^4 pin^1 fung^1 ta^3-šong^1 ngan^4 loi^2, ...

（61）……佢就走上一只大楼棚顶里去唡命。〔181 救命箇鸡 tšhun^1〕（唡命 pyang^4 myang^4 = hide for one's life）

...Ki^2 tshyu^4 tseu^3-šong^1 yit^6 tšak^6 thai^4 leu^2-phang^2 tang^3 li^1 hi^4 pyang^4 myang^4.

4.5 "V-ha^1-L-loi^2"（V 下 L 来）1 例、"V-ha^1-L-hi^4"（V 下 L 去）1 例

上文已指出，"下"有几个读音。动词"下"按照 Rey（1926）以及谢永昌（1994：224）的叙述，念阴平 ha^1 时表示非致使的用法，如"下马、下轿、下棚（＝下楼）"，念上声 ha^3 时有致使的用法"使某物下去 / 下来"。谢永昌举的动词读音还有 ha^4，但是那不见得是固有的口语层次的读音。

1909 年出版的客家话语法书和辞典举不少动词和趋向补语 ha^1 的例句（"放下"fong^4 ha^1 'put down'，见 Chappell & Lamarre 2005：114）。据 Rey（1926）和巴色会的语法书，"下"念去声 ha^4 时除了作动量词之外还用来修饰名词，如"下卷、下入、下平"，还出现在"天下"等词语中。但方位词一般读阴平 ha^1，如"脚下、底下、地下"等。《启蒙浅学》里的趋向动词作主要动词带处所宾语时念阴平 ha^1，比如"你系出街还之下花园都爱锁竟门"（206，罗马字本作〔ha^1 fa^1-yen^2〕），符合 Rey（1926）、MacIver（1926）和语法书的记载。我们在上文（3.1.2 节）讨论过"V ha^4 来 / 去"中的 ha^4，主张其来源于动量词"（一）吓"，还认为"V 下来 / 去"的 ha^1 来源于趋向动词"下"（"V 下（O）来"一共 8 例，见上文）。出现在"V ~ L 来"、"V ~ L 去"的

句法环境中的 ha 也有两种读音 ha¹ 和 ha⁴，ha¹ 只有 2 例，均表示从上到下的运动，应该是趋向动词 "ha¹ 下"：

（62）走左走右焱竟上滩，还之微下水底里去。〔150 鱼〕（mi⁴ = 'to dive'）
Tseu³ tso³ tseu³ yu⁴ pyau¹-kin³ šong¹ than¹, han²-tši¹ mi⁴-ha¹ šui³ tai³ li¹ hi⁴.

（63）漫漫爬下山来转到屋家，……〔186 讲石榴花〕（ = 从山上爬下来回家）
Man⁴-man⁴ pha²-ha¹ san¹ loi² tšon³ tau⁴ wuk⁶-ka¹, ...

与之相反，"V ha⁴ L 来 / 去" 的 18 个用例不一定表示从上到下的运动。Lepsius 本的 ha⁴ 在汉字本里一般写成 "吓"，只有两个例外，可能是汉字本刻错的字，Lepsius 本作 ha⁴ 而汉字本写成 "下"，表示的位移趋向都不是 "从上到下"。[8] 因此，我们决定把 "V 吓 L 来" 的 1 例和 "V 吓 L 去" 的 17 例处理为另一个语法格式，把其中的 ha⁴ 和趋向动词（补语）的 ha¹ 区别开来，前者在 4.9 节里讨论。

4.6 "V-tšon³-L-loi²"（V 转 L 来）2 例、"V-tšon³-L-hi⁴"（V 转 L 去）8 例

趋向动词 "tšon³ 转" 可以带处所宾语，如 "转屋家"（140）。出现在 "V 转 L 来 / 去" 格式里的动词有 "tseu³ 走"（136x2，141）、"tam¹ 担"（218）、"pu¹ 嘣"（'stay'，122）、"thoi² 抬"（133）、"tau⁴ 到"（80，135）、"tai² 带"（190）、"khai¹ 搣"（'bring'，199）、"tšong¹ 张"（ = 装，200）、"tšhong⁴ 撞"（176）。另外 "转" 经常与表示 "给予" 之类的动词搭配，空间位移意义淡薄一点，那时不带 "去 / 来"（198，219）。上文举的例句（41）里出现 "张转箇盒里去"（放回笼子里去），下边再举表示致使位移的例句。

（64）另取年年耶稣生日箇哺，人就寻倒偃，抬转屋家去，……〔133 耶稣生日箇松树〕
Lang⁴-tshi⁴ nyen²-nyen² Ya²-s¹ sang¹-nyit⁶ kai⁴ pu¹, nyin² tshyu⁴ tshim²-tau³ ngai², thoi²-tšon³ wuk⁶-kha¹ hi⁴, ...

4.7 "V-ko⁴-L-loi²"（V 过 L 来）1 例、"V-ko⁴-L-hi⁴"（V 过 L 去）1 例

趋向动词 "ko⁴ 过" 可以带处所宾语："佢过一只打铁厂"（217）。"V 过 L 来 / 去" 出现 2 次，处所词都带方位词，不表示位移的路径，表达位移的终点：

（65）松鼠仔生来好快滑，……时常都哇嗑畲树跳过箇畲树去，……〔138 松鼠〕
Sung¹-tšhu³-tsai³ sang¹-loi² hau³ khwai⁴-wat⁵, ... ši²-šong² tu¹ tshoi¹ nya³ pho¹ šu⁴ thyau⁴-ko⁴ kai¹ pho¹ šu⁴ hi⁴, ...

（66）有日恩憐箇白鸽有一对嘅过亚福箇白鸽笼里来作薮。〔201 白鸽〕

Yu¹ nyit⁶ En¹-lin² kai⁴ phak⁵-kap⁶ yu¹ yit⁶ tui⁴ pui¹-ko⁴ a¹-fuk⁶ kai⁴ phak⁵-kap⁶ lung² li¹ loi² tsok⁶ teu⁴.

4.8 "V-tau⁴-L-hi⁴"（V 到 L 去）、"V-tau⁴-L-loi²"（V 到 L 来）

在汉语不少方言中，"VDL"的 D 成分限于"到"或者意义相似的成分，"里外上下"等信息依靠方位词来表达，不用"V 进 L"、"V 出 L"等格式（见上文第 2 节）。《启蒙浅学》虽然能看到"V 到 L"，但是频率不高（"透"2 例、"走"3 例、"行"1 例、"上"1 例）。如果拿后边带主观方向词"来 / 去"的格式"V ～ L 去"、"V ～ L 来"来对比，"tau⁴ 到"出现 4 次，其他成分 D（落、出、上、下、转、过）出现 74 次（见上文的表 3 以及下文的表 4）。

（67）……随渐箇兜水竟上竟上，上到樽喙里来，咁样佢就食得箇水倒。〔165 讲论雕雀都有坚心〕（tšoi⁴ 喙 = 嘴；kan²-yong⁴ 咁样 = 这样；šit⁵-tet⁶ kai⁴ šui³ tau³ 食得箇水倒 = 喝得到那水）

...Tshui²-tshyam⁴ kai⁴-teu⁴ šui³ kin³ šong¹ kin³ šong¹, šong¹ tau⁴ tsun¹-tšoi⁴ li¹ loi², kan²-yong⁴ ki² tshyu⁴ šit⁵-tet⁶ kai⁴ šui³ tau³.

（68）也有只狐狸走到树头下来咁样话……〔166 讲论鸡公七狐狸使计〕

Ya¹ yu¹ tšak⁶ fu²-li² tseu³ tau⁴ šu⁴-theu² ha¹ loi² kan²-yong⁴ wa⁴...

"到"有时和指示动词结合作为"去到"、"来到"，前者在共同语里不用。"到"还出现在动词和"来 / 去"之间，如"V 到去 /V 到来"（4 例），与共同语不同，有必要进一步研究，因为这种句法环境靠近趋向动词 D 所出现的环境：

（69）箇 [只] 后生送到去就转，转来就对将军话……〔128 马有记才〕

Kai⁴-tšak⁶ heu⁴-sang¹ sung⁴-tau⁴-hi⁴ tshyu⁴ tšon³, tšon³-loi² tshyu⁴ tui⁴ tsyong¹-kyun¹ wa⁴...

4.9 "V-ha⁴-L-loi²"（V 吓 L 来）1 例、"V-ha⁴-L-hi⁴"（V 吓 L 去）17 例

进入"V 吓 L 来 / 去"格式的动词有自移动词如"tseu³"（141，128，134，135，153）、"pui¹ 飞"（131）、"yen² 延"（155）、"tsho¹ 坐"（192）、"ken³ 卷"（144），还有一半是表示致移的动词："fong⁴ 放"（192，197）、"sang¹ 生"（~tšhun¹，144，155）、"thui¹ 推"（145）、"tsuk⁶ 捉"（220）、"phan¹ 拚"（176）、"kai⁴ 解"（～犯人，141）、"tam¹ 担"（218）。

（70）……唔知佢走吓嗦里去，就寻佢唔倒。〔135 山兔〕

...M¹ ti¹ ki² tseu³-ha⁴ nai¹-li¹ hi⁴, tshyu⁴ tshim² ki² m¹ tau³.

（71）……唍吓人都俾箇兜本土人捉倒，鲜吓王帝噔去。〔141 猫使人发财〕（ten¹ ＝那儿）

...Won²-ha⁴ nyin² tu¹ pin¹ kai⁴-teu¹ pun³-thu³-nyin² tsuk⁶-tau³, kai⁴-ha⁴ wong²-ti⁴ ten¹ hi⁴.

（72）王帝查问箇时有好多老鼠在箇里作□捸来捸去，都敢走吓王帝噔来。〔141 猫使人发财〕

Wong²-ti⁴ tsha²mun⁴ kai⁴ ši², yu¹ hau³ to¹ lau⁴-tšhu³ tshoi¹ kai⁴ li¹ tsok⁶-hyak⁶ lot⁵-loi² lot⁵-hi⁴, tu¹ kam³ tseu³-ha⁴ wong²-ti⁴ ten¹ hi⁴.

（73）……想将箇老鼠推吓箇地坊里去。〔145 推车仔〕

...Syong³ tsyong¹ kai⁴ lau⁴-tšhu³ thui¹-ha⁴ kai⁴ thi⁴-lak⁵ li¹ hi⁴.

（74）亚新看倒冇噇好放，就接倒放吓箇凳里去。〔192 黄牛泡〕（tang⁴ 噇＝地方）

A¹-sin¹ khon⁴-tau³ mau² tang⁴ hau³ fong⁴, tshyu⁴ tsyap⁶-tau³ fong⁴-ha⁴ kai⁴ ten⁴ li¹ hi⁴.

（75）转吓来就落房间，因为好瘭就坐吓箇凳里去，……〔192 黄牛泡〕

Tšon³-ha⁴-loi² tshyu⁴ lok⁵ fong²-kan¹, yin¹-wui⁴ hau³ khoi⁴ tshyu⁴ tsho¹-ha⁴ kai⁴ ten⁴ li¹ hi⁴, ...

（76）跟尾听倒喀爸俾人捉吓土耳其国去卖俾只人做奴仆，……〔220 好薑子〕（pin¹ 俾＝给）

Ken¹-mui¹ thang⁴-tau³ kya¹ pa¹ pin¹ nyin² tsuk⁶-ha⁴ Thu³-ngi³-khi² kwet⁶ hi⁴ mai⁴ pin¹ tšak⁶ nyin² tso⁴ nu²-phuk⁵,...

可见，在"V 吓 L 去"的大部分例句里，"吓"相当于共同语的"到"，引进位移的终结点；虽然有一部分可以理解为"下"（74，75），其他只表达终点。我们暂时假设，出现在"V~L"格式中引进处所词的"ha¹ 下"和"ha⁴ 吓"是不同的语法成分。上文提出过"V-ha⁴ 来/去"格式中的"ha⁴ 吓"还保留体貌意义，但是从我们所观察的 18 个"V-ha⁴-L"的用例来看，其体貌意义和引进位移终点的语法功能之间的语义演变还不十分明确。这个问题准备在第 5 节继续讨论。

4.10 其他零碎的格式

（一）"V O L 去"："故此日日放只石仔喀酒罂里去"（210）、"射兜药水喀耳朵里去"

（224）等。

（二）"V倒（O）在L"："漏倒好多核桃壳在箇坪里"（180）、"唔曾 tshau⁴倒在箇嚛"（181）、"na⁴-ha² 抬倒在喀里 tsha⁴ 路"（227）。

（三）"VO在L"："催放只盒仔在棹面里"（200）、"正放箇铁链在箇门边里来嚛冷佢"（217）。

巴色会文献里没出现"V在L"格式，本文对这几个句法格式不准备作更深入的讨论。

4.11 几个相关的问题

4.11.1 方位词的问题

共同语的书面语的"进、上、下"等趋向补语带处所词时往往不带方位词。巴色会文献所反映的客家话并不如此。比如"V落（O）L来/去"的49例中有40个处所词带方位词，大部分是"里"。在"V上L来/去"的12例中，有10个处所词带方位词"里"，可见共同语的"上"和"里"的区别不存在。连"V出L"的3例都含方位词（"外"或"里"）。客家话的方位词包括 ten¹，相当于共同语的"我这儿"、"国王那儿"的"这儿"、"那儿"。共同语不能说"跑上楼上去"，只能说"跑上楼去"，而《启蒙浅学》就有"走上楼里去"的说法（206羊牯，见上文例句（21））。

方位词的附加影响到处所词和趋向动词的句法关系和语义关系。不带方位词的处所词和趋向补语构成动宾关系，在语义上也存在着多种多样的关系，处所词可以表示位移的路径（过桥、下山、出门）和起点（下床、出牢）等。带方位词的处所词一般作为位移的终结点。

4.11.2 "V (D) 去 / 来 +L"

部分例句的处所词 L 放在 D_{nd} 和"来/去"之间，这个词序和共同语一样。但是还能见到处所词出现在"来/去"之后的格式。后一种格式"V（D_{nd}）去/来 +L"在闽南语和粤语中普遍存在。

（77）冷天箇时好多嘛去别嚛较暖箇地方，……〔142 唸唱箇雕〕

　　　Lang¹ then¹ kai⁴ ši² hau³ to¹ pui¹-hi⁴ phet⁵ thang⁴ kau⁴ non¹ kai⁴ thi⁴-fong¹, ...

（78）有只亚僬咛县城走出去树山里，……〔183 天乌地暗〕

　　　Yu¹ tšak⁶ a¹-tsyau² tshoi¹ yen⁴-šang² tseu³-tšhut⁶-hi⁴ šu⁴-san¹ li¹, ...

在趋向动词做主要动词的句子里也能找到这个词序，如"佢落去喀媄房间"（212）、"落去喀店里"（225）、"佢都落去水里衔起来"（134）、"就话喀妹子转去房间"（212）等。

4.12 引进处所词的形式：总结

和吴语、北方官话等相反，客家话大量使用"VDL"格式，即用动词后的趋向动词来引进处所词。值得注意的是，"VDL 来 / 去"格式中的大部分处所词带方位词，表达位移的终点。除了趋向补语之外，还有一个专门引进位移终点的功能的形式："ha^4"，与动量词和短时貌标记同音，意思相当于共同语的"到"。"到"引进位移的终结点的用例并不多见。

表 4　引进处所词 L 的形式

	D 总数	到 tau^4	吓 ha^4
V ~ L 来 / 去	74 (11/63) [77%]	4 (3/1) [4%]	18 (1/17) [19%]

5. "ha^4 吓"的语法化途径的问题

5.1 重新讨论 "V+ha^4+L（来 / 去）"中的成分 ha^4

上文 4.5 节已指出，"V 吓 L 去"的大部分例句的"ha^4 吓"相当于共同语的"到"，引进位移的终结点。这相当于侯复生（2002）所说的"介词"用法的"阿"。在"V ~ 来 / 去"的格式中，ha^1 和 ha^4 有明显的对立，ha^1 和趋向动词"下 ha^1"有关，表示从上至下的位移，而 ha^4 与这种趋向意义无关，却和动量词"下 ha^4"所表达的短暂体貌意义有明显的关系。可是"V ~ L（去 / 来）"中的 ha^1 和 ha^4 的关系似乎不那么简单。语法书没有提到这个格式。

为了得到更充分的判断材料，我们又考察了另一种巴色会文献：新约圣经的《使徒行传》部分。该文献与《启蒙浅学》成书年代相同（1883 年），有一定的篇幅（28,000 字），也有与汉字本完全对应的罗马字本（*The New Testament in the Colloquial of the Hakka Dialect*, 2nd revised edition. Basel, 1992），还有两个重要的好处：一是圣经比《启蒙浅学》会话部分多，因此命令句等句式更丰富，二是有对应的原文（我们参考了英文和官话翻译本）。[9]《使徒行传》中有 12 例"V + ha^4 + 处所"，分别为"V + ha^4 + L"5 例、"V + ha^4 + L + 来"1 例、"V + ha^4 + L + 去"5 例、"V + ha^4 + O + L + 去"1 例。还有十几个例句用"V + ha^1 + 来 / 去",以及 2 例用"V + ha^1 + L + 来"的句子。下面先举用 ha^4 来引进位移的终结点的几例(圣经与《启蒙浅学》不同,ha^4 有时写成"下",有时用"吓")。

(79)保罗揽一揽柴,<u>放下火里去</u>,……〔二十八章 3〕

Pau^3 lo^2 lam^3 yit^6 lam^3 tshai^2, <u>fong^4 ha^4 fo^3 li^1 hi^4</u>, ...

保罗拾了一捆柴,放在火上

and when Paul had gathered a bundle of sticks, and laid them *on* the fire

(80)将 [……] 嘅轭,来尚<u>吓门徒嘅颈里</u>。〔十五章 10〕

Tsyong^1 [...] kai^4 ak^6, loi^2 šong^3 <u>ha^4 mun^2 thu^2 kai^4 kyang^3 li^1</u>.

要把……的轭、放在门徒的颈项上

...to put [a yoke] *upon* the neck of the disciples

(81)……日日都奔人<u>抬下圣堂里安做美门嘅门口里</u>放竟。〔三章 2〕

...Nyit^6 nyit^6 tu^1 pin^1 nyin^2 <u>thoi^2 ha^4 šin^4 thong^2 li^1 on^1 tso^4 mui^1 mun^2 kai^4 mun^2 heu^3 li^1</u> fong^4 kin^3.

天天被人抬来,放在殿的一个门口,那门名叫美门

...whom they laid daily *at* the gate of the Temple which is called Beautiful, [to ask alms...]

(82)奔恶鬼迷倒嘅人,就<u>跳吓佢兜身上</u>,……〔十九章 16〕

Pin^1 ok^6 kwui^3 mi^2 tau^3 kai^4 nyin^2, tshyu^4 <u>thyau^4 ha^4 ki^2 teu^1 šin^1 šong^4</u>, ...

恶鬼所附的人、就跳在他们身上

the man in whom the evil spirit was leaped *on* them, ...

以上几个句子的原文也好,语境也好,都不包含"从上至下"的趋向意义。官话的译文也证明这一点。但是 ha 念阴平的时候,就有明显的"从上至下"意义了:

(83)就在木架里<u>取下来</u>埋。〔十三章 29〕

Tshyu^4 tshai^4 muk^6 ka^4 li^1 <u>tshi^3 ha^1 loi^2</u> mai^2.

就将他从木头上取下来,放在坟墓里

they took him *down* from the tree, and laid him in a sepulchre

(84)在城墙里,奔篮<u>缒下</u>佢去走。〔九章 25〕

Tshai^4 šang^2 syong^2 li^1, pin^1 lam^2 <u>tšhui^4 ha^1</u> ki^2 hi^4 tseu^3 .

用筐把他从城墙上缒下去

let him *down* by the wall in a basket

（85）请千总明日爱<u>带下</u>佢嗹嚛来。〔二十三章 15〕

Tshyang¹ tshen¹ tsung³ min² nyit⁶ oi⁴ <u>tai⁴ ha¹</u> ki² nya¹ ten¹ loi².

叫他带下保罗到你们这里来

that he bring him *down unto* you tomorrow

能不能把例句（79）—（82）中的 ha⁴ 看作来源于动量词"ha⁴ 吓"呢？在现阶段，一个标记从表示短暂等语法意义转到表示位移的终结点，似乎还有相当大的距离。圣经的"V+ha⁴+终结点（来/去）"格式与《启蒙浅学》（例句（70）—（76））一样，经常出现在一般的叙述句中，没有体貌助词 ha⁴ 固有的时间/语气意义。语法书指出命令句的动词往往带"词尾"ha⁴（Chappell & Lamarre 2005：110）。为了进一步阐明动词后的 ha⁴ 的基本功能，我们再举圣经的几个例句。"V-ha⁴（O）"经常用在命令句，或者意愿句（即 hortative sentences）：

（86）佢兜就<u>爱嚇</u>吓佢兜。〔四章 17〕

Ngai² teu¹ tshyu⁴ oi⁴ hak⁶ ha⁴ ki² teu¹.

我们必须恐吓他们

let us straitly *threaten* them

（87）另日再<u>爱听</u>禹讲吓佢。〔十七章 32〕

Lang⁴ nyit⁶ tsai⁴ oi⁴ thang⁴ ngi² kong³ ha⁴ ki².

我们再听你讲这个罢

we *will hear* thee again of this matter

（88）佢兜分付佢两侪<u>爱出</u>吓公会正〔四章 15〕

Ki² teu¹ fun¹ fu⁴ ki² lyong³ sa² oi⁴ tšhut⁶ ha⁴ kung¹ fui⁴ tšang⁴

分付他们从工会出去

when they had commanded them *to go aside out* of the council, ...

以上 3 个例句的"V-ha⁴"前都出现能愿动词"爱"（要）。与之相反，在很多方言里，引进位移终结点的标记往往和表示完成貌的体标记有关。两者的共同点可能是"有界化功能"，但是我们在现阶段还无法解释为什么 ha⁴ 会变成引进位移终点的标记。同时，我们也没法解释为什么趋向动词 ha¹ 出现在动词后作趋向补语时，有时会保留"从上至下"的意义而念 ha¹，有时会念成去声 ha⁴。

5.2 引进程度补语、状态补语的补语标记 ha⁴

在上节 5.1 讨论的问题还涉及引进描写／程度补语的标记"ha⁴"的来源问题。侯复生 (2002) 提到梅县客家话的"阿"a⁵² 还有一个引进结果补语和状态补语的功能。严修鸿 (2001) 曾描写过广东平远客家话的状态补语标记，认为这个助词（念 a，去声）来源于"下"。

（89）佢秋晡夜肚痛，痛阿满头大汗。（他昨天晚上肚子痛，痛得满头大汗）（侯 2002：340）

（90）我当昼食下饱 ku⁴ ku⁴ 尔唻。（我中午吃得饱饱的）（严 2001：45）

在巴色会文献里，"吓 ha⁴"也担任这个功能，而且使用频率较高，例如：

（91）佢就呷起来搋竞嚓只罂，拚吓箇石壁里去，<u>拚吓□碎</u>，……〔176 讲论气係有喙里来〕

Ki² tshyu⁴ at⁶-hi³ loi² tšha¹-kin³ kya¹ tšak⁶ ang¹, <u>phan¹-ha⁴ kai⁴ šak⁵-pyak⁶ li¹ hi⁴</u>, phan¹-ha⁴ sap⁶-sui⁴, ...

（92）在箇嚦□竟箇只牧师冇干粮带倒，<u>饿吓软嚦嚦里</u>。〔181 救命箇鸡□〕

Tshoi¹ kai⁴-thang⁴ pyang⁴-kin³ kai⁴ tšak⁶ muk⁵-s¹ mau² kon¹-lyong² tai⁴-tau³, <u>ngo⁴-ha⁴ nyon¹-nai¹-nai¹ li¹</u>.

（93）箇亚僬俾嚓爸<u>话吓面红面绿</u>，唔敢担起头看嚓爸。〔189 掌牛亚僬〕

Kai⁴ a¹-tsyau² pin¹ kya¹ pa⁴ <u>wa⁴-ha⁴ men⁴ fung² men⁴ lyuk⁵</u>, m¹ kam³ tam¹-hi³ theu² khon⁴ kya¹ pa⁴.

在巴色会文献里引进程度、状态补语的助词还有"去"、"得"和"倒"（这几个助词在平远客家话也用，见严修鸿 2001）。我们认为补语标记 ha⁴ 是从引进位移终点的标记发展而来的，从"V 吓 L"到"V 吓 + 结果／程度"的语法化途径非常自然。所以，在"吓 ha⁴"发展引进程度／状态补语的功能之前，应该先经过表示动作的终结点（即动作者或受动者因为动作而达到的位置）的一个阶段。

5.3 引进位移终结点和动作所达成的结果状态的标记 ha⁴ 的来源问题

下图显示出我们对"ha⁴"的语法化的两种假设，1 > 2 和 4 > 5 的两个演变是不成问题的，至于第 3 阶段发生什么，是假设甲还是假设乙成立，就需要进一步考证。假设甲对语义上的具体演变过程在现阶段缺乏根据和说服力，而假设乙缺乏能够解释语音变化的合理说明。我们在其他方言以及有关客家话的二手材料中都找不到很美满的答案。[10]

	1	2	3	4	5

假设甲　V-ha^4 　　　＞　　V-ha^4 来 / 去
　　　　动量词　　　＞　　V-ha^{4}O　　　＞　　　？
　　　　　　　　　　　　　体貌标记　　　　　　　　　V-ha^4-L 来 / 去　　＞　　V-ha^4-VP$_2$
　　　　　　　　　　　　　　　　　　　　　　　　　　引进动作的　　　　　　引进程度或结果状态
　　　　　　　　　　　　　　　　　　　　　　　　　　终结点

假设乙　下 ha^1 　　　＞　　V-ha^1 来 / 去　　＞　　ha^1 ＞ ha^4?
　　　　趋向动词　　　　　趋向补语

6. 结论

6.1《启蒙浅学》的"VD$_{nd}$"和"VD$_d$"两种组合中都可以插入体标记"ha^4 吓"、"kin^3 竟"和"tau^3 倒"。这些成分的语法功能和其作为体标记时的语法意义有密切的关系，因而不能把这些成分看作一种"趋向补语标记"或者"结构助词"，应该作为体标记的句法功能和分布之一来描述。如果客家话的 VD 组合是动结式的一个下位类，在体貌特点上也应该表示一个有界的事件，在一般动词和趋向动词之间插入持续标记 kin^3 的 VD 格式则只能看作一种连谓结构。但是还有一种可能，就是整个"动词＋趋向动词"格式在句法上和北方话不同，本身没有体貌特点，凭附加成分获得实现、持续等体貌特征，体标记的插入现象就是这个差异的一个具体表现而已。这个问题涉及动趋式和动结式的异同，需要继续研究。

6.2"VD$_{nd}$D$_d$"格式非常普遍，可是如果我们看"V 来"和"V 去"一类组合，就发现它使用频率低于"VX 来 / 去"（见表 1 和表 2）。如果排除带宾语的格式，前者有 5 例（"带来、捡来、带去 (x2)、送来"，"V 吓来 / 去"），"V 竟来 / 去"和"V 倒来"加起来却有 38 例，说明在趋向补语作为指示趋向词"来 / 去"时，我们观察的客语语料偏于使用加入体标记的格式"V+Asp+D$_d$"。

6.3"VD$_{nd}$L（来 / 去）"中的趋向补语 D$_{nd}$ 是引进位移终点的常用形式（77%），在这一点上客家话与北方话、吴方言等不同。可是巴色会文献中还有一个经常用来引进位移终结点的形式（17%），和动量词、短暂貌标记 ha^4 同音。这个成分的来源问题虽然在现阶段还不能下结论，但其功能与梅县客家话的 a^{52} 平行，很可能是同源词。其中的 ha^4 也用来引进程度 / 状态补语。

附 注

[1] 详看 Chappell & Lamarre (2005：331) 的有关考察。

[2] *Kleine Hakka-Grammatik*，原书为德语，例句只有 Lepsius 式标音和德语翻译。例句 (1)—(4) 引自 Chappell & Lamarre（2005：103，137，110，138），作者凭据罗马字标记构拟客家话的汉字标记，再将例句的德文翻译成英文。

[3] 这种情况在共同语中也会存在。柯理思 (2005) 对现代汉语（普通话）的"走去"一类组合进行考察，主张不是典型的动趋式（但是该格式属于书面语）。

[4] 具体有陕西合阳、富平、延川，山西万荣、大同、蒲县、长治，河北冀州。Lamarre（2003b）描写河北冀州方言。

[5] 这个句子在汉字本里作"捡吓去"，我们凭 Lepsius 本的标音 kam³-ha⁴-hi³ 和语境改作"捡吓起"。

[6] *Kleine Hakka-Grammatik*，1909 年，见 Chappell & Lamarre(2005：98)。

[7] 如果把这些例句的"跌落"看作已词汇化的双音节动词，从句法格式的角度就说不通，因为后边的处所词都带方位词，不像一般的动宾关系。

[8] "摘转来放下嗱高楲顶高里去。"（197）、"就 [嘀 wo³] 嗱薀子担下对面箭条村去。"（218）。我们依据 Lepsius 本的标音和语境分到"V 吓 L 去"里。其中前者的动作甚至有"从下到上"的趋向。

[9] 官话圣经译文引自《官话新旧约圣书》，圣书工会 (British and Foreign Bible Society) 印发，1913 年。

[10] 我们感谢审稿人的建议，即可以考虑客家话借来了闽语的 ka（原来有"到"的意思）。这个可能性不能完全排斥，但巴色会文献中还能见到"tau⁴ 到"引进程度补语，意思和闽语的 ka 接近，为什么还要借用呢？另外平远客家话也好，巴色会的文献所反映的客家话也好，还有其他南方方言，引进补语的标记往往来源于趋向词（"来、去"等）。这些补语标记的功能是从引进位移终结点的功能产生的，还是这些趋向动词先获得了某种实现体词尾的意义再变成补语标记呢？进一步考察这些方言的助词的语法化过程也一定可以给我们提供一些线索。

参考文献

Chappell, Hilary & Christine Lamarre (2005) *A Grammar and Lexicon of Hakka: Historical Materials from the Basel Mission Library.* Paris: Ecole des Hautes Etudes en Sciences Sociales.

Kang, Jian (2001) Perfective aspect particles or telic aktionsart markers? Studies of the directional compounds. *Journal of Chinese Linguistics* 29.2: 281–339.

Lamarre, Christine (2001) Verb complement constructions in Chinese dialects: types and markers. *Sinitic Grammar: Synchronic and Diachronic Perspectives*, ed. by Hilary Chappell, 85–120. Oxford:

Oxford University Press.

Lamarre, Christine (2002) Early Hakka corpora held by the Basel Mission Library: an introduction. *Cahiers de Linguistique - Asie orientale* 31.1:71–104.

MacIver, Donald (1926[1991]) *A Chinese-English Dictionary Hakka-Dialect as Spoken in Kwang-Tung Province*, 2nd edition. Revised by M. C. MacKenzie. Shanghai: Presbyterian Mission Press. Reprinted by Southern Materials Center, Taipei.

Rey, Charles (1926[1988]). *Dictionnaire Chinois-Français, dialecte hac-ka*. Imprimerie de la Société des Missions Etrangères. Reprinted by Southern Materials Center, Taipei.

Schlatter, Wilhelm (1916) *Geschichte der Basler Mission, 1815–1915. II. Band: Die Geschichte der Basler Mission in Indien und China*. Basel: Verlag der Basler Missionsbuchhandlung.

陈光（2003）准形态词"一"和现代汉语的瞬时体，《语言教学与研究》第 5 期。

侯复生（2002）梅县方言谓词后面的"啊"，《客家方言研究：第四届客方言研讨会论文集》，谢栋元主编，广州：暨南大学出版社。

柯理思（2002）汉语方言里连接趋向成分的形式，《中国语文研究》第 1 期。

柯理思（2003a）汉语空间位移事件的语言表达——兼论述趋式的几个问题，《现代中国语研究》第 5 期。

柯理思（2003b）从河北冀州方言对现代汉语"V 在 + 处所词"格式的再探讨，《汉语方言语法研究和探索》，戴昭铭主编，哈尔滨：黑龙江人民出版社。

柯理思（2005）讨论一个非典型的述趋式："走去"类组合，《语法化与语法研究》（二），沈家煊、吴福祥、马贝加主编，北京：商务印书馆。

柯理思、刘淑学（2001）河北冀州方言里"拿不了走"一类格式，《中国语文》第 5 期。

梁银峰（2005）论汉语趋向补语产生的句法动因——从东汉魏晋南北朝出现的三种句法格式谈起，《汉语史学报》第 5 期。

林立芳（1996）梅县方言动词的体，《动词的体》，张双庆主编，香港：香港中文大学中国文化研究所吴多泰中国语文研究中心。

林立芳（1997）梅县方言口语单音动词汇释，《梅县方言语法论稿》，北京：中华工商联合出版社。

刘丹青（2003）《语序类型学与介词理论》，北京：商务印书馆。

刘丽华（2001）《娄底方言研究》，长沙：中南大学出版社。

刘月华（1998）《趋向补语通释》，北京：北京语言文化大学出版社。

罗昕如（1998）《新化方言研究》，长沙：湖南教育出版社。

沈家煊（1995）"有界"与"无界"，《中国语文》第 5 期。

太田辰夫（1958）《中国历史文法》，东京：江南书院。

王军虎（1997）《西安话音档》，上海：上海教育出版社。

吴福祥（1996）《敦煌变文语法研究》，长沙：岳麓书社。

谢永昌（1994）《梅县客家方言志》，广州：暨南大学出版社。

严修鸿（2001）平远客家话的结构助词，《语言研究》第 2 期。

张洪年（1972）《香港粤语语法的研究》，香港：香港中文大学出版社。

朱炳玉（1998）五华客家话的述补结构，《深圳教育学院学报》第 3 期。

（本文发表于《语言暨语言学》第七卷第二期，第 261—295 页，2006 年）

早期客话文献《客话读本》中的双标式差比句及其相关问题 *

石佩璇　李　炜

差比，是指两个对象在程度、数量或形状等属性上存在差异的语义范畴，通过句法手段表达这种语义关系的句子类型称为差比句。差比句一般由以下四个成分组成：1. 比较主体 X；2. 基准 Y；3. 比较标记 M；4. 比较结果 A，比较结果可以是动词性成分 VP，也可以是形容词性成分 AP。汉语常见的差比句类型主要有两种：一是"比 A 式"，即：比较结果在基准之后 / 比较标记在比较结果之前，如"X＋比 / 强 / 赶＋Y＋A"（比较标记以"比"为代表，简称"比 A 式"）。二是"A 过式"，即：比较结果在基准之前 / 比较标记在比较结果之后，且 A 不限于单音节形容词，还可以是双音节形容词或形容词短语、动宾短语及特定形容词的有标记项 [1]（吴福祥 2010：239），如"X＋A＋过 / 起＋Y 式"（比较标记以"过"为代表，简称"A 过式"）。

在反映广东中、东部客家方言早期面貌的《客话读本》（1936）[2] 出现不同于以上两种类型的差比句，如："阿來比四妹過會阿来比四妹懂事 | 中國比日本過大中国比日本大"。这类差比句比较结果在基准之后，但句中同时采用两个比较标记"比"和"过"。我们将句中强制出现两个比较标记（比较标记可以是动词、介词、副词或其他成分）的差比句称为双标式差比句 [3]，差比句中左边的比较标记称为"前标"，右边的比较标记称为"后标"。本文主要考察该书（以下简称《读》）以及现代客家方言中的双标式差比句。

壹　《客话读本》中的双标式差比句

《读》的差比句有三种形式：双标式、A 过式和比 A 式。我们以《读》前四册（共 20.9 万字）为样本进行统计，三种句式分别出现了 31 例、15 例和 6 例，双标式差比

* 本项研究受国家社科基金重大项目"海外珍藏汉语文献与南方明清汉语研究"（项目号：12&ZD178）及广东省哲学社会科学规划项目"海外珍藏汉语文献与清代官话语法研究"（项目号：GD13CZW15）的资助。本文曾在第二届全国中文学科博士生论坛宣读，修改中吸取了施其生、庄初升、刘街生、林华勇、陆烁的宝贵意见，谨此致谢。

句在数量上占优势。

《读》中双标式差比句的具体形式为"X＋比＋Y＋過＋A"。两个标记"比"和"過"必须强制出现，但是各有分工："比"标记基准，"過"标记比较结果。"過"所标记的比较结果 A 可以是形容词性成分 AP，也可以是动词性成分 VP。如：

① 中國比日本過大 中国比日本大｜日本比中國過小 日本比中国小。（《读》第 15 课）

② 但係也有東西比舊年過貴介 但是也有东西比去年贵的。（《读》第 88 课）

③ 吾等今日還有這等米，都算比佢等過好 我们现在还有这些米，也算比他们好。（《读》第 280 课）

以上例句的比较结果是 AP。

④ 吾等現下所讀介白話文聖經，……比起以前譯倒介過有進步 我们现在读的白话文圣经，……比以前翻译的进步。（《读》第 401 课）

⑤ 轉到屋家，將寶貝拿來變賣，變倒好多錢，比先行還過發財 回到家里，把宝贝拿去变卖，卖了很多钱，比以前还有钱。（《读》第 667 课）

以上例句的比较结果为 VP。

此外，句中还可以出现程度副词、数量成分，如：

⑥ 所以在街上買東西介人，比平時**格外**過多 所以在街上买东西的人，比平时格外多。（《读》第 44 课）

⑦ 樂善家裏好貧窮，但係佢有一隻鄰舍比佢**又**過窮 乐善家里很穷，但是他有一个邻居比他还穷。（《读》第 280 课）

⑧ 矮仔話：你雖然係唔知，比吾總過近**等**哩 矮子说：你虽然不知道，总是比我们更近些啊！（《读》第 328 课）

如果这些量化成分出现在比较结果的补语位置，一般是程度略高的量化成分，如例⑧的"等（一些）"。[4]

出现后标"過"是双标式差比句的特点，后标"過"究竟是什么呢？为了说明后标"過"的性质问题，我们先考察"過"在《读》中的其他相关用法。

"過"在《读》的非差比句中，也可以用在形容词或动词前作程度副词，表示程度略高。如：

⑨ 吾想到你怕過歡喜在尔貴國住 我想你可能更喜欢住在自己国家？（《读》第 67 课）

⑩ 佢行介路，係係山路過多 他走的路，山路多一些。（《读》第 180 课）

⑪ 吾唔使咁好介，拿過便宜等子介來 我不用那么好的，拿便宜些的！（《读》第 583 课）

形容词后还可以带程度或数量成分，如例 ⑪ "等子（一些）"，但一般不能是表示量大的成分，如 "*过便宜好多"。

"过" 前还可加其他表示程度的副词 "还、太、忒、更" 等，如：

⑫ 人人都用錢，件件都用錢，**還**過方便人人都用钱，每件物品都用钱，更方便。（《读》第 42 课）

⑬ 做春天介衫褲，吾狂**太**過薄做春天的衣服，我担心太薄了！（《读》第 160 课）

⑭ 這頂**忒**過大，戴唔着这顶太大，戴着不合适。（《读》第 252 课）

⑮ 改開幾尺深，看倒下背有一塊大石板，就**更**過歡喜挖了几尺深，看到下面有一块大石块，就更高兴了。（《读》第 168 课）

另外，"過" 可以出现在表示反向对比的差比关系复句中[5]，如：

⑯ 兩條路都去得着，不過這條路過近，該條路過遠两条路都到得了，不过这条路近一些，那条远一些。（《读》第 97 课）

⑰ 好介就過貴，毛咁好介就過便宜好的就贵一些，没那么好的就便宜一些。（《读》第 118 课）

⑱ 因為種佢就過難，捫佢就過容易因为种树难，绑着树压制它生长就容易。（《读》第 299 课）

⑲ 又拿出四隻鐵球來，兩隻過大，兩隻過細又拿出四个铁球，两个大一些，两个小一些。（《读》第 514 课）

值得注意的是，"過" 在差比复句中，主要用于突显比较基准和比较主体在程度上的对立，因而差比复句的比较结果都只能是相对的，如 "远—近"、"贵—便宜"、"难—容易"、"大—细"。"过" 没有出现在表示程度差别的比较句中，比如："* 这条路近，该条路过近这条路近，那条路更近"。如果要表示比较双方在表达程度上的差别，在 "過" 前必须加上表示程度的副词 "还、更、又" 等。例如：

⑳ 王："咁**早**起身啊！" 龍："你還過**早**了！"王："那么早起床啊！"龙："您更早！"（《读》第 306 课）

㉑ 人唔單止愛追求物質介**進步**，**更**過愛追求靈性介**進步**人不但要追求物质上的进步，更要追求灵性上的进步。（《读》第 258 课）

㉒ 人介肉身咁多病痛，儕儕都知**冤枉**，但係還有一樣心靈介罪病**又還過凶**肉身那么多病痛，人人都知道很惨，但是心灵上的病更惨。（《读》第 543 课）

㉓ 吾平素**唔歡喜**多講多話介，**更**過**唔肯**講別人秘密介事介我向来不喜欢多嘴，更不会说别人的秘密。（《读》第 582 课）

由此可见，在差比复句中，"過" 并不能独立表示程度加深，必须借助其他程度副词如 "还、又、更" 来表达。在这种情况下，"過" 的程度义已经减损，而用于强调比较双方的 "对立"，显示出与程度副词不一样的功能，"比较" 功能逐步突显。

根据以上例子"過"的语义差别，我们将《读》中"過"的用法分为"$過_1$"和"$過_2$"：强调程度义、用作程度副词的"過"记为"$過_1$"；强调差异对比的"過"记作"$過_2$"。我们发现，双标式差比句中的后标"過"和差比复句中的"過"都是"$過_2$"，在句中突显的是"对比"，而不表示程度增加，我们首先感受到的是"差比义"，而非"程度义"。和差比复句一样，双标式差比句如果要强调差别的程度，也必须借助其他程度副词"还、更"表示。如：

㉔（谜面）天高不算高，比天**更過**高天高不算高，比天还要高。（谜底）夫。（《读》第 403 课）

㉕ 這等石頭比海水**還過**重，吾等就埋在深坭肚裏，與世界隔絕这些石头比海水更重，我们就埋在深土里，与世界隔开。（《读》第 480 课）

由此再次证明，《读》双标式差比句的"過"已经没有了程度义，不是程度副词"$過_1$"，而是强调比较功能的"$過_2$"。

根据《读》中"過"的用法，我们可以构拟出双标式差比句后标"$過_2$"的语法化路径："$過_2$"从"$過_1$"发展而来，在与程度副词"太、过、忒"连用的语境中，程度义减损；进入双标式这个结构后，"程度略高"语义被消解，而突显出"比较"的语义特征，语法化为"$過_2$"。因而，《读》中双标式差比句的准确表达式应该是"X + 比 + Y + $過_2$ + A"。

贰 双标式差比句在当今客家方言中的分布

双标式差比句不仅在反映广东中、东部地区早期客话情况的《读》是优势句式，在现今的粤中、东、北地区的客家话也是优势句式，普遍存在于各地客家方言中。列举如下：

粤东、粤中、粤北客话[6]：

㉖ a 梅县：西瓜比哈密瓜过大一滴西瓜比哈密瓜大一些 | 张三比李四过有钱张三比李四有钱。

b 五华：偃比你过高滴把哩我比你高一些 | 张三开车开啊比李四过好张三比李四会开车。

c 梅州大埔：今日比昨晡日较冷今天比昨天冷。（黄婷婷 2009：359）

d 梅州丰顺：今天做个乜事都比成日手脚较猛今天做什么事都比平时动作快 | 佢比你较细十岁 / 有兜呢他比你小十岁 / 很多！（黄婷婷 2009：354）

e 河源紫金：阿叔比阿哥过有钱叔叔比哥哥有钱。

f 河源龙川：西瓜比哈密瓜较大（一）滴西瓜比哈密瓜大一些 | 张三比李四较叻开车张三比李四会开车。

g 河源连平：西瓜比哈密瓜过大滴子西瓜比哈密瓜大一些 | 你比佢过有钱你比他有钱。

h 韶关新丰：佢比你较大我比你大。（周日健 1990：174）

以上客话，双标式的前标都是"比"，后标的形式有"过"和"较"。我们发现，在这类客话区中，后标的语法化程度较高，所标记的比较结果可以是形容词或动词性成分，也可出现表程度的量化成分，有些地区（如丰顺客话）的量化成分还可以是高程度的。

刘纶鑫（2001）对江西赣州、吉安、九江地区等 37 个方言点的客家方言进行考察，认为江西客话的语法特点是比较句用"比……过"的形式，且可在比较结果后加上数量补语，如：

㉗ a 渠比你较 / 过高他比你高。

　　b 你比渠较 / 过能干你比他能干。

　　c 今日个字写得比昨日个较 / 过好今天写的字比昨天写的好。

　　d 你个纸比渠个较 / 过大一粒你的纸比他的厚。

广西客话也用双标式表达差比：

㉘ a 广西来宾：佢比你过大他比你大。[7]

　　b 广西贺州：张三比李四较会开车张三比李四会开车。

台湾四县客话 (罗肇锦 1984：282) 也采用双标式：

㉙ a 今年比旧年较 [kʰaˀ] 冷今年比去年冷。

　　b 他做事比佢较 [kʰaˀ] 细心他做事情比我细心。

闽西和闽南客话中也普遍存在双标式：

㉚ a 宁化：佢老伯比佢较纳得苦他哥哥比他更能吃苦。（张桃 2004：260）

　　b 连城：今晡比昨晡（较）冷今天比昨天冷。（项梦冰 1997：425）[8]

　　c 上杭：的个比介个较好这个比那个好。（邱锡凤 2007：164）

　　d 武平：禾刀子比磨镰□ [kɔˀ] 好用禾刀比镰刀好用。（林清书 2004：181)

　　e 平和：今日比昨日较寒今天比昨天冷。（福建省地方志编纂委员会 1998：339）

湖南客话（黄伯荣 1996）也主要用双标式：

㉛ a 酃县：你比佢较高你比我高 | 糖比梨较甜糖比梨甜。

　　b 汝城：我比你哽 [koŋˀ] 壮我比你胖些 | 今晡日比昨晡日哽冷今天比昨天冷些 | 打輾脚比走较快㤦跑比走快些。

据兰玉英（2005，2007），四川成都东山客话也使用双标式[9]：

㉜ a 龙泉洛带：样个比该个过好这个比那个好。

    b 新都泰兴：样个比该个过好这个比那个好。

广东、福建、广西、四川、台湾等不同地区的客家方言，差比句在后标"过"、"较"的具体选择上虽有不同，但都是同时采用了前标"比"和后标"过/较"两个比较标记。由此可见，双标式差比句是客家方言的常见句式。

双标式差比句不仅是客家方言的常见句式，而且在同时存在多种差比句类型的客话地区，双标式差比句也是优势句式。据黄婷婷（2009：358）的考察，粤东、闽西、赣南的客家方言中最普遍的句式是双标式差比句。刘纶鑫（1999，2001）也指出，存在双标式差比句是江西客方言区别于赣方言的语法特征。在客家人聚居的粤中和粤东北地区，双标式更是占绝对优势。从分布和使用频率的角度，我们可以说，双标式差比句是客家方言的语法特征之一。

这些采用双标式差比句的客家方言，后标"过/较"的语义虚化程度是不同的。鄞县客话、连城客话中后标"较"词汇义比较实在，连城客话的"较"和比较结果后的数量词不能共现（项梦冰 1997：425），这一类后标属于程度义明显的"过₁/较₁"；湖南汝城和广东梅县、紫金、新丰的客话中"过/较"虽有程度加深的意义，但比较结果可以加表示相差程度小的量化成分，后标"过/较"更倾向表"比较"而非"程度"，但仍有"程度略高"的语义残留，介于"过₁/较₁"和"过₂/较₂"之间；江西、丰顺客家话的"较"程度义更虚，功能上也进一步泛化，可以带表示量大的程度补语和数量词，这类客家话的后标属于"过₂/较₂"，程度义在这个结构中已经被消解。

从以上的考察可以看出，当今不同地区的客话，双标式差比句后标"过/较"的语法化程度是不同的。这也在共时层面体现出后标"过/较"从"过₁/较₁"到"过₂/较₂"的语法化过程。"过/较"的语法化程度越高，比较的语义特征就越明显，双标式也越典型。当后标"过/较"为"过₂/较₂"时，"X+比+Y+较/过+A"是最典型的双标式差比句。

叁　不使用双标式差比句的客话情况

双标式差比句是《读》的优势句式，但我们也注意到，《读》（第1至4册）有15例"A过式"，如：

㉝ 中國大過日本中国比日本大。(《读》第 15 课)

㉞ 這裏件件東西都差過北京介，總係北京打人就毛咁會这里每件东西都比北京的差，但北京打人没有那么厉害。(《读》第 232 课)

㉟ 交結朋友，愛交結倒贏過自己介來结交朋友，要结交那些比自己好的朋友。(《读》第 366 课)

以上差比句中比较结果 A 仅限于单音节形容词，其中"赢过"就占 5 例，根据我们对"A 过式"差比句类型的界定标准，只能说《读》具有"A 过式"的表达式，尚不能构成一个成熟的差比句类型。《读》的差比句类型仍是双标式差比句为主。

然而，在反映香港新界客家方言的早期文献《启蒙浅学》(1880，以下简称《启》)中，没有出现一例双标式差比句，而采用"A 过式"。如：

㊱ 幾唔多揀食，摸豬一樣，但係伶俐過豬它不太挑食，和猪一样，但是比猪干净。(《启》第 148 课)

㊲ 獨獨係食菜虱，噲食多過圓龜仔只吃菜虱，比圆龟仔更能吃。(《启》第 144 课)

㊳ 今下因爲你唔聽倕話，故此倕送俾姪子，佢係好過你好多现在因为你不听我的话，所以我送给侄子，他比你好多了。(《启》第 200 课)

㊴ 今下倕哋知佢愛，也愛愛佢過父親现在我们知道他的爱，也要比爱父亲更爱他。(《启》第 236 课)

以上差比句中，比较结果 A 可以是形容词 (不限于单音节)，如例 ㊱；也可以是动词短语，如例 ㊲；形容词可受副词修饰，格式后可以加上程度副词，如例 ㊳；而且比较主体可以作句子的宾语，如例 ㊴。由此可见，《启》的差比句是典型的"A 过式"。

同为客话，为何差比句的类型完全不同？我们认为，《读》的双标式差比句式是客话的固有句式，而早期香港新界客话《启》采用"A 过式"是与粤语接触过程中，受粤语影响的结果。在当今与粤语密切接触的珠三角客家方言中，也多采用与粤方言一致的"A 过式"差比句。比如中山客话采用的是"A 过式"，与粤方言同，没有双标式差比句 (甘甲才 2003)。另据本人考察，在广东惠阳、增城、信宜思贺 (细倕)[10]等粤客杂居、双方言交流频繁的地方，客话的差比句也不采用双标式，而采用"A 过式"，如：

惠阳：张三开车会过李四张三比李四会开车 | 倕肥过佢我比他胖。

增城：西瓜大过哈密瓜啲仔西瓜比哈密瓜大一些 | 张三有钱过李四张三比李四有钱。

信宜思贺 (细倕)：□ [ti˩] 只大过个只这个比那个大。(李如龙 1999：212)

粤方言作为强势方言，对珠三角地区其他方言的影响作用不能忽视。根据周柏胜、刘镇发（1998：231）的调查，香港新界十岁以下的小孩几乎没有人会讲客家话了，客家人转移到说粤语的过程即将完成，粤语的势力也在香港及邻近的深圳、东莞、惠阳等客家话区扩张。《启蒙浅学》的客话以及中山、增城、惠阳、信宜客话所处的地理环境有个共同之处，就是与粤方言密切接触。新界、中山、惠阳、增城、信宜等地的客家人与粤方言的居民杂处，客话处于粤语的包围中。我们不排除这些地区的客话采用与粤方言相同的"A过式"，是客家方言受粤方言影响的结果，而这种影响早在一百年前的早期客话文献中就存在。客方言固有的双标式差比句只有在客家腹地以及客家意识较为强烈的地区被保留下来。

另外，《读》（第1至4册）还出现了6例的"比A式"差比句，这6例"比A式"的比较结果A后均出现表示高程度补语。如：

⑩ 吾骑驢，比該隻推車介還赢**得多**我骑驴，比那推车的好多了。（《读》第83课）

⑪ 人介智慧比鵰子大**得多**，都不能夠加先知得吉凶，莫話烏鴉，佢樣般知得呢人的智慧比鸟大多了，尚且不能事先知道吉凶，更不用说乌鸦，它怎么能事先知道呢？（《读》第105课）

⑫ 這個唔算光，比北京介月光還爭**好遠**这个不算亮，比北京的月亮差多了！（《读》第232课）

如上文所述，《读》双标式中比较结果如果出现量化成分，多是量小程度低的成分，高程度补语只出现一例。在具体程度差别的表达上，《读》中"比A式"和双标式形成互补。

根据我们在梅县、五华、龙川、连平等地区的调研，在比较结果出现程度高的量化成分时，一般也不使用双标式而用"比A式"。但与《读》不同的是，"比A式"和双标式的使用情况在比较结果出现低程度的量化成分时，存在年龄上的差别：年长者倾向使用双标式差比句，年轻人则同时使用"比A式"和双标式，部分甚至更倾向使用"比A式"。这是否预示着，这些客话地区的双标式在后标"过/较"完全虚化为"过$_2$/较$_2$"之前，将被"比A式"取代？在双标式语义完全可以用"比A式"表达的前提下，双标式采用了两个比较标记，与语言的经济原则相悖，再加上普通话的强势影响，客话地区双标式被"比A式"取代是完全有可能的。

四、余论

双标式差比句有两个比较标记，在形式上又分别与"A过式"和"比A式"的比较标记"比"、"过"重合，因而有学者推测这是汉语从古代差比句"A于/如/过式"向现代差比句"比A式"发展的过渡阶段在方言中的表现，称之为"混合式差比句"。

我们认为，这种推测是值得商榷的。首先，双标式差比句的"过"和"A过式"的"过"只是同形词，而无语义或语法上的关联，前者的"过"是程度副词发展而来，后者的"过"从经过义动词虚化而来。其次，如果存在"X+A+过+Y"向"X+比+Y+A"过渡阶段的中间状态，用"比"将前者的宾语Y提至A前，"过"应该仍然是在A之后，合理的中间形态应该是"X+比+Y+A+过"而非"X+比+Y+过+A"。事实上，黄晓惠（1992）对差比句进行历时考察后，否定了"A过式"发展至"比A式"这一路径的可能，因为在汉语史上并没有过渡形态。可见，双标式差比句不可能是"A过式"向"比A式"发展的中间状态，并非两个语序类型的"混合体"。

只是这种差比句为何同时采用两个比较标记？在福建闽语中，存在"我较高伊"的差比句类型，比较标记"较"直接加于比较结果前。更早期的客话是否是以"我较高伊"为蓝本，后起的"比"将比较基准提前，而成为双标式？历史上，福建曾是客家人入粤的重要中转站，客家话与福建闽南语有接触历史，也不排除这种可能。对双标式的来源问题，我们将进一步研究。

附：主要调查合作人情况

广西贺州客话，叶建华，男，62岁，教师，长年在贺州市生活。广东紫金客话，廖映新，女，31岁，教师，长年在河源生活。广东梅城客话，李惠萍，女，23岁，学生，在梅城出生长大，19岁后外出读书。广东梅县客话，叶辉丽，女，31岁，政府职员，在梅县出生长大，19岁后外出读书。广东五华客话，张嘉炜，男，20岁，学生，在五华出生长大，19岁后外出读书。广东龙川客话，张戈，男，20岁，学生，在龙川出生长大，19岁后外出读书。广东增城客话，蒋玉婷，女，26岁，教师，在增城出生长大，19岁后外出读书。广东惠阳客话，黄女士，女，40岁，文员，长期在惠州生活。

附 注

[1] 吴福祥（2010：239）认为，存在"A过式"表达式不等于存在"A过式"差比句类型，判断一个方言是否存在"A过式"差比句，必须同时满足以下参数：A可以是双音节形容词或形容词短语、动宾短语及特定形容词的有标记项，A前可以添加否定词构成否定式，格式后可以出现量化成分。并指出，按照这个标准，只有粤方言才存在"A过式"差比句类型。

[2]《客话读本》是瑞士巴色会传教士经缇福（C. G. Kilpper）在1911—1936年间，用客家方言编写的用于客家话教学和传教工作的阅读课本，1936年在老隆出版。《客话读本》一共八册840篇共约40万字，全部用汉字写成。内容以中国民俗故事、日常生活对话、基督教道理、客家风俗介绍为主，口语程度较高，较好地保留了当时广东中、东部客家话的实际情况。现藏于瑞士巴色会图书馆。笔者所有的《客话读本》是微缩照相机拍摄的图片，由

香港中文大学人类学朱大成教授、中山大学中文系庄初升教授提供。谨向两位教授表示感谢！为最大程度呈现早期文献《客话读本》原貌，本文援引《客话读本》例子时保留了繁体字和自造字。下文《启蒙浅学》的引例亦如是。

[3] 刘丹青（2008：203）将同时出现级标记和比较基准上前置词的差比句看作"双重标记的差比句"。本文借用"双重标记"的说法，但对"标记"的定义与刘先生不尽相同，详见下文。

[4] 比较结果带高程度补语仅见一例：该等月餅店裏介生理，比往年就更過鬧熱得多。（《读》第 674 课）

[5] 差比关系除了可以通过语法手段即差比句实现，也可以通过语用推理的手段实现。差比复句就是通过语用推理手段实现的其中一种形式。

[6] 广东地区的客话调研主要着眼于较为纯正的客家话。参考《广东统计年鉴》（2010）及各县县志，选择客家人口占当地总人口 80% 以上的地区所使用的客话作为调查对象。除注明外，文中例句为笔者调研所得，调查合作人简况附于文后。

[7] 广西来宾客话情况由柳州师专郑盛锦老师提供。

[8] 连城客话的双标式差比句后标"较"加括号，是因为连城客话的"较"和数量词只能二者择一，见项梦冰（1997：425）。

[9] 四川和台湾客话转引自吴福祥（2010：242）。

[10] 据李如龙先生（1999）考察，粤西的粤方言和客方言居民都自发将当地客家话分为"大倕"和"细倕"两种，在粤客居民穿插杂居的地带，受粤语影响较大的客家话被称为"细倕"。

参考文献

福建省地方志编纂委员会（1998）《福建省志·方言志》，北京：方志出版社。

甘甲才（2003）《中山客家话研究》，汕头：汕头大学出版社。

黄伯荣（1996）《汉语方言语法类编》，青岛：青岛出版社。

黄婷婷（2009）广东丰顺客家方言的差比句，《方言》第 4 期。

黄晓惠（1992）现代汉语差比格式的来源及演变，《中国语文》第 3 期。

李蓝（2003）现代汉语方言差比句的语序类型，《方言》第 3 期。

李如龙（1999）《粤西客家方言调查报告》，广州：暨南大学出版社。

李如龙、张双庆（1992）《客赣方言调查报告》，厦门：厦门大学出版社。

李炜（1999）京 x 话——一级京兰话、京广话语法问题例析，《双语双方言》（二），香港：彩虹出版社。

刘丹青（2008）《语法调查研究手册》，上海：上海教育出版社。

刘纶鑫等（1999）《客赣方言比较研究》，北京：中国社会科学出版社。

刘纶鑫（2001）《江西客家方言概况》，南昌：江西人民出版社。

吕叔湘（1991）《现代汉语八百词》，北京：商务印书馆。

施其生（2012）闽南方言的比较句,《方言》第 1 期。

温宪元等（2011）《广东客家》, 桂林: 广西师范大学出版社。

吴福祥（2010）粤语差比式 "X+A+ 过 +Y" 的类型学地位——比较方言学和区域类型学的视角,《中国语文》第 3 期。

项梦冰（1997）《连城客家话语法研究》, 北京: 语文出版社。

张赪（2004）明代差比句,《语言暨语言学》第 5 期。

张双庆、郭必之（2005）香港粤语两种差比句的交替,《中国语文》第 3 期。

张双庆、庄初升（2003）《香港新界方言》, 香港: 商务印书馆。

张桃（2004）《宁化客家方言语法研究》, 厦门大学博士学位论文。

赵金铭（2002）汉语差比句的南北差异及其历史嬗变,《语言研究》第 3 期。

中国社会科学院、澳大利亚人文科学院（1987）《中国语言地图集》, 香港: 香港朗文（远东）出版公司。

周柏胜、刘镇发（1998）香港客家话向粤语转移的因素和趋势,《方言》第 3 期。

周日健（1990）《新丰方言志》, 广州: 广东高等教育出版社。

庄初升（2010）清末民初西洋人编写的客家方言文献,《语言研究》第 1 期。

庄初升、黄婷婷（2014）《19 世纪香港新界的客家方言》, 广州: 广东人民出版社。

（本文发表于《方言》2014 年第 3 期，第 253—260 页）

英国传教士 J. Edkins
在吴语语言学上的重要贡献
——《上海方言口语语法》评述

钱乃荣

Joseph Edkins（1823—1905），中文名字为艾约瑟，英国人，传教士，汉学家。毕业于伦敦大学，1848 年被伦敦布道会派来中国，9 月 2 日到上海，任伦敦教会驻上海代理人，先协助墨海书馆麦都思工作。1856 年麦都思离任回国后，他继任监理，主持该馆的编辑出版工作。1852—1860 年间，编译《中西通书》（原名《华洋和合通书》），年出一册（其中有三年由庞台物、伟烈亚力编）。与李善兰等合译《格致西学提要》《光论》、《重学》三卷本等。1858 年 3 月回国休假，翌年 9 月携新婚夫人返沪。1860 年赴烟台。又与杨笃信等传教士 5 人应太平天国李秀成之邀，去苏州见李秀成、洪仁玕。1861 年，又赴天京（南京）上书洪秀全，被驳；移居天津，并在天津设立教会。1863 年迁至北京传教。1872 年在北京与丁韪良创办《中西闻见录》月刊。1875 年获英国爱丁堡大学神学博士学位。1880 年被中国海关总税务司赫德聘为海关翻译，起初在北京任职，后迁上海，1905 年在沪逝世。

艾氏对中国宗教、文学和历史有广泛的知识。编译《欧洲史略》、《希腊志略》、《罗马志略》、《富国养民策》、《西学启蒙》等书，由上海总税务司出版，在当时中国知识界有一定影响。主要译著还有《中国在语言学方面的成就》（1871）、《中国的宗教》（1878）、《中国的佛教》（1893）、《中国的罂粟》（1898）、《北京记》（1898）、《访问苏州的太平军》等书。在语言学方面，除了本文所述《上海方言口语语法》外，艾氏还出版了《中国官话口语文法》（1857 年初版，1864 年二版）和一部词典《上海方言词汇集》（1869）。

《上海方言口语语法》是第一部描写汉语方言白话的语法著作，英文书名为 *A Grammar of Colloquial Chinese, as Exhibited in the Shanghai Dialect*。第一版是 1853 年由伦敦布道团出版的，共 248 页；上海长老会于 1868 年再版，共 225 页。笔者所持的是 1868 年的第二版。该书用英文编写，全书共三部分：语音、词类、句法。

该书系统地记录了开埠 10 年时上海县城方言的语音和语法。尽管它是一本语法书，然其语音、语法并重，并提供了当时丰富的语言、社会和文化背景知识。在描写和论述的基础上，艾氏还将上海话同官话、闽语及上海周边地区的方言进行了一些共时性的比较。

下文分语音和语法两部分评述艾约瑟此书对吴语语言学的贡献。

一、对吴语语音学的贡献

艾约瑟以他高超的语音学修养，对 19 世纪中叶开埠不久的上海方言语音状况进行了准确的全面的描写和分析。

此书既用西方的辅音、元音系统的分析方法记录了上海方言语音，同时又用汉语传统方法对上海话的韵母和声调进行了梳理归纳。

1. 辅音和声母方面

作者首次提出了上海方言中的所谓"浊声母"与"清不送气声母"的对立是清辅音中的"宽（broad）音"和"窄（thin）音"的区别。（p.5）全书用斜体 p、t、k 记写单音节和多音节开头音节上的宽音声母，用正体 p、t、k 记写窄音声母。他还正确记出了在连读词的后音节高层调中，哪些宽音才改读真浊音 [b]、[d]、[g]，记为 b、d、g。（p.8，p.46）

这在过了 130 年后才有学者在语音实验做出的语图上重新发现证实。曹剑芬（1982）指出了吴语常阴沙话的浊音声母实际上是清音，在连读前字低声调中为清音和连读后字上高声调中是浊音的实验结果。艾约瑟在 19 世纪就凭自己的优异的听力正确地辨认出这个历来的难题，确实是不易的。后来在 1995 年，沈钟伟、王士元（1995）进一步以具体的实验数据证明了上海话的浊塞音是"松辅音"而与"紧辅音"（不送气清音）相对立。笔者（1992）也认为吴语的浊辅音是松清辅音。

艾约瑟的听音十分仔细，他还说"在高层调中的擦音 v、z，在低层调时读作 f、s，即使在前边没有字时，也常常听成 v、z"。（p.46）声母 dz 和 z 可以互换，口语中为 z，书面词为 dz，如"豺狼"的"豺"的声母读 dz。（p.47）

作者还发现了上海方言单字音的"端、短、断、对"等字的声母是真浊音 [d]，他说这是高层调的例外。（p.40）这是他首次发现上海语音中端母发音上读阴调浊音，即后来大家称呼的缩气浊音。

作者还指出上海方言中缺乏 sh[ɕ], ch[tɕʻ] 和弱 j[tɕ] 的发音，而在官话和苏州话中却存在。（p.4）这是作者比别人对上海话的见组声母观察更为细致的结果，他说："还要提到的是声母 k 的发音趋势，当在 i 前面时，在高层调系列中读音常像 t[t]，在低层调系列中像 d[d] 或 dj[dz]。"（p.58）这说明了当时的上海城里见组声母在细音前的读音不是用舌面塞擦音发音的。笔者在现今的松江、奉贤等上海郊区语音变化迟缓的地方，依然听到了这样的音，是用舌面中塞音来读的，听起来接近舌尖塞音或舌面前塞音。

他说，dj（"序"的声母）"这个音接近英语 june 中的 j 发音，也可读成 z，在当地有两读现象"。（p.2）这说明在 19 世纪中叶，精组字 z 母在撮口呼里已先开始与见组字合并（即开始不分尖团）。书中仅举此一例，且是两读。从上海话在 20 世纪中叶尖团音大规模合并的情况和上海郊区现今尖团音合并情况来看，都是从撮口呼字先开始的。

作者认为，送气的塞擦音，送气音应介于两个辅音之间。他说："在复声母中，送气音是在 t 和 s 或 t 和 sh[ɕ] 之间的。"（p.45）这种描写是符合发音实际情形的。现今公布的《国际音标》（修订至 1993 年）中都不列像 ts 一类的"塞擦音"，显然认为它们是复辅音，而擦音 [s]、[ɕ] 不可能送气，这样只能有 [tʻ] 和 [s]、[ɕ] 复合的 [tʻs]、[tʻɕ] 了。

作者还说明了 "ng n m v l 和 j" 这些鼻音边音和零声母字，"除少数例外外，都属低层声调"，（p.48）即属阳调类字。

2. 元音和韵母方面

作者归纳了上海方言的 15 个元音，（p.5）并从元音的发音长短来区分了长音、短音和其他元音。他又首次按中国人的理解方式排列了上海口语音和文读音的韵母表，（p.51—54）归纳了 63 个韵母及其 20 个文读形式。

凭着敏锐细致的听力，艾氏记录了在 19 世纪中叶，上海话中的中古咸山摄字带有弱鼻音，用斜体 n 表示，指出在 an[æ̃]，en[ẽ]，ûn[ỹ] 三个韵上。这第三个韵从当时的其他文献看只有他记下来了。他还指出："当后面有字时，听得更清楚。"（p.2）他详细说明道："韵尾 n 也受到前面元音的影响，在 a[æ]，e[e]，ö[ø]，û[ʏ] 之后，当后面没有字时，它几乎听不到的，但若后面有字时，一个明确的辅音会使 n 得到注意，它作为一个轻鼻音，仍旧可以听到。"（p.56）

作者还说："元音 i[ɪ]，o[ɔ] 是不与 n 相连的，当前边是 u[ʌ] 时，常常用 ng[ŋ] 来取代 n[n] 的位置。在官话中，n 常放在 ü[y] 之后。"（p.56—57）这里他说明的是在上海话其他的带鼻音韵母，实际都读后鼻音韵。不过他仍在韵母表中记录了 5 个或用的前后鼻韵。

他引用《李氏音鉴》的记音，使我们看到上海话前后鼻音合并中最后阶段的面貌:"上海话语音的规律是这样的。在官话中保留的那些以 NG 结尾的字,凡以 IN 结尾的那些字,变 N 为 NG,而以 UN 结尾的可以随意地用 N 或 NG 来取代 N。这样上面的字(即银盈,勤檠,神绳,林灵,贫平,金京)就分别读为 niun(g) yung,*k*iun(g) *k*iung,zun(g) zung,ling ling,*p*ing *p*ing,kiun(g) kiung。"(p.55)在艾氏的记音中,也按实际读音分别记录此时还残留着的 [ʌn] 或 [ʌŋ] 的差异。前后鼻音韵的系统整齐区分,笔者在 2003 年调查一名青年的浙江新昌方言中仍有发现。在上海方言区的川沙镇上,石汝杰先生在调查中还发现了一派有 in、ing 的区别。(石汝杰 1983)

他还指出如 úng[uŋ] 韵如果在后字上读为 óng[oŋ]。"当某个字单独发音,或在复合词中位于最后时,常为 ó;而位于首位时,常为 ú。如:松江 Súng-kong;吴淞 *Ng sóng*;中国人 tsúng kóh niun;勿拉当中 veh 'lá tong tsóng。"(p.54)这些细微的差异都是其他上海方言著作中所没有记到的。

作者首次发现并准确细致地记录了上海话中的两个入声韵尾 h[ʔ]、k[k],中古 k 韵尾字,仍读 k 韵尾;中古 t、p 韵尾,在上海话中读 h[ʔ] 韵尾。他还提及"在低层调字的前面的 k 听为 g"。(p.55)他还按发音原貌记下了 k 尾入声韵在音变中的词汇扩散面貌。这是这本书最精彩的语音实录之一。

书中首次开创用正体和斜体字母区别零声母字的阴阳声调分属。对阴调类齐齿、合口零声母字音,分别用正体 y、w 表示开头,阳调类零声母字则用斜体 *y*、*w* 表示开头。(p.4)书中阳调零声母开口呼字也用斜体字母表示。

作者将"而"字读音记为 rh。这是准确的,2005 年平悦铃用动态腭位仪实验证明了上海话"而"的发音是接触在腭上的发音,更近于 [r] 而非艾氏以后一般语言学家均描写的 [l]。(平悦铃 2005)

作者首次认识到汉语中有舌尖元音,虽在注音中用 z 记,但他建议用 i 上加两点来表示这个舌尖元音。(p.5)这种标示法沿用至今。

他还首次用 ü(u 加两点)表示 [y],还指出这个音在上海话里可变换读为 [ɿ]。"书 sú,在松江及黄浦东面发音为 sü[sy],在宝山地区变成 sz[sɿ]。"(p.4)

3. 声调和重音方面

作者明确划分了吴语中的两层调类。他指出"南音"("存在于江苏部分地区,即扬子江以南,浙江及江西部分地区。"p.6)声调分高层(上层系列,Upper Series)调类和低层(下层系列,Lower Series)调类。此即吴语中的阴调类在高层,阳调类在低层。

他概括了高层调和低层调系列具体落实在什么字上，认为"声母是一个鉴别方法。即所有宽音、塞音和擦音，弱送气音，以及流音和鼻音都是低层调。包括强送气音的其他辅音为高层调系列"。（p.40）

作者首次提出 8 个区别性的特征（u，upper 高；l，lower 低；r，rising 升；f，falling 降；q，quick 急；s，slow 缓；e，even 平；sh，short 短），区分了上海话的 8 个声调，每个声调准确地用了其中的 2—3 个特征。（p.11）还记录了其他几个方言的声调。这是很科学的声调分类法。当时系统性的"区别性特征"的理论还远远没有诞生。

他又提出了可以用类似音乐音阶的 5 度来描写声调。实际上首次推出了用源自音乐的五度音高来描写声调的方法。书中的第 57 节专门讨论了"声调与音乐的关系"。（p.41）在这段话中，他说："仅仅在均匀的时候，音乐的记谱法才能充分地、恰当地描绘声调。在偏斜曲折方面，记出来是必要的。但音乐中却不容许有，因为这样就破坏了和谐性。然而短音和急音可能被描述为音乐中的断奏符号，小提琴可以被做成从一个音符到另一个音符通过而产生连续的声音，这声音已经被引用为'汉语就是如此'，以此阐明声调的偏斜曲折。就时间而论，在音乐上是那么连续不断地细分，但没有比急促的和舒缓的两种声调的层次出现更多。Kircher 认为五个声调是在一个音阶八度音中的前五个音符 do，re，mi，fa，sol；但是实际上，对于一个方言来说，高度的差异通常不比两个更多。音程在两个连续系列之间变化，比江南更好的例子是在中国北方的部分地区，在江南，大约是一个八度音的一半。"

作者首用在字母注音上划圈形式记录上海话声调，上声在注音的左上角用"'"表示，去声在右上角用"'"表示，入声（因有韵尾）和平声（缺省）不用符号。

作者指出低层第一声调（即阳平声调）是低长声调（即 22），这是黄浦江的东部和上海城里的发音，而在黄浦江向西，很快为急低声调所取代（即 31）。（p.27）此项区别，笔者认为实际上是区分上海方言区和松江方言区以及将浦东与浦西合为一区的主要根据和标志。（钱乃荣 2003）他还说明了两个相近的声调阳平与阳上调形的不同，在于阳平是真正自然的慢吞吞，即是长音。（p.31）他指出了"音长"也是区别声调的要素，上海话阳平、阳上这两个声调的主要差异是在"音长"上，这是很正确的。

他还指出低层第二声调（即阳上）不稳定，有时读成第三声调（即阳去）。次浊声母字的声调"全部保持其自然状态，除了 m、ng、n、r 声母和没有声母出现的元音的词，原在这个声调中的塞音、擦音开头的字，目前正处于向低层第三声调转变过程中"。"声母 v 由官话中的 w 而来，故仍保留在第二声调中。"（p.31）这种情形与笔者现今在上海郊区有些地方调查所得次浊阳上字仍留在上声中而全浊声母并入阳去（如80 年代的南桥镇老派音）或渐渐并入阳去（如 80 年代松江镇老派音）的走向和次序相同。

作者以他出色的才能首次以单字声调为纲排列字组，讨论吴语中最复杂难辨的连读变调，并同时讨论重音位置和重音与声调的关系。（p.15—40）以后这方面的研究长期处于停顿状态，直到 1964 年郑张尚芳才又开启连读变调的研究（郑张尚芳 1964），到 20 世纪末才又见到有的论文重新探讨起连读声调和重音关系问题。

这里只能举一些例子说明连调和重音问题：

作者指出在连读的后字上，下降或平调不会把声母由清辅音改变为浊辅音。他说：在 p.p. 组、s.p. 组和 *p.p.* 组中（即"阴平＋阴平、阴上＋阴平、阳平＋阴平"组里），最后一个字的声调下降或变为平坦。在这种情况下，首辅音保持不变。这样，"工夫 kúng fú"不会变为 kúng vú，尽管 fú 的调子已为降调。

作者讨论到阴去字开头和阴上开头的连读变调，其开头的变调正好与阴去单字调和阴上单字调调形相反。他说："在高层第二声调和第三声调之间有交替现象发生，当二者位于相同的字前，前面一个音节会变为对方（即上上—去上，去去—上去）。"（p.27）这为笔者在 20 世纪 80 年代调查的上海老派连调所证实。这可能就是后来阴上、阴去声调合并的语音内在原因之一。

作者指出阳平声调在后字位置时往往在高调层上成为高平调。"当独自发音时，第二声并不平，除非以高调形式发音。当位于最后一个字时，它经常上升为高层第二声，这样听上去就显得平了。"（p.32）

他观察到连读后的一些在高位上的声母发生了变化。其中有"弱送气音（即 ɦ），在连读组后字中会消失"。这个现象的观察是正确的，是连读后产生的变化。直到 1978 年叶祥苓在《方言》发表《苏州方言的连读变调》时重新指出这一现象，如"清华（原有 ɦ）＝青蛙（原无 ɦ）"。

在说明重音与声调关系方面，作者说："入声字声调短促，不适于在其位置上读重音。"（p.24）

他指出："高层调连读主重音通常在最后一个音节上。但常有例外，重音最易为平声和去声吸引。"（p.27）

"在三音节词中，会出现次重音，是在最重要的字上有所停顿，或者是第一和第二个字在声调上自然地需要重读。"（p.27）

他说到去声以外的声调加阴平，变为去声之外声调加阳平。他说："高层第一声调位于后字时，如前边的字是重音，它就变为低层第一声调，既低又平，在末尾又有上升；如是位于高层第三声调之后，无论是高层还是低层第三声调，高层第一声调都不会变化。"（p.27）这个观察是正确的。

作者还讨论到不是一个语音词的字组如"造屋、街市头上、动咾动、重来死、看重"等的连读规律，认为："从这些例子中可以看到，急声或第三声，和较长的声调几乎一样多。总的说来用法是，在连读字组里的平衡是支持较快形式的。当单独使用时，几乎全部读原调。文读中变化的数量与口语用法中大致相同。在连读字组中，通常最后一个字声调较急，倒数第二个字声调较长。但也并非总是如此。"（p.36）这里实际上是谈到了我们所谓的"窄用式"连读字组的情况。（许宝华等 1981）

作者还谈到了声韵相同的字组，可以通过重音和变调的不同来区分。如"'情理'和'尽礼'，可能认为由于重音的差异而把二者区分开的，在当地人的发音中，是完全靠声调的方式区分二者。在许多这样的例子中，最后一个字会上升变为平声，变为高层第二声调。这样，'瞎眼'的'眼'和'情理'的'理'都变为高而平（即 44）了（即后字阳上因连读而变读为阴上，于是与不连读的'尽礼'能够区分）"。（p.33）这里他实际谈到了利用现在所谓的"广用式"连调与"窄用式"连调可以分别两个声韵调均相同的字组读音。

又如，他谈到连读多个字组的重音，"一个例子中（'听过歇拉者'），第一个重音在'听'上，第二个重音在'拉'上，因为'拉'是长音，所以吸引了重音"。（p.26）

这些都是作者在上海方言连读变调以及重音分布与连读调之间关系问题上的研究成果。

4. 严式的忠实的记音

该书用描写性的记音方法记录上海方言，记录的是上海口语的实际读音，对上海话正在发生变化的读音不是按音位方式来记音，因此为后代保存了 19 世纪中叶上海话语音的严式读音记录以及当时的音变实际面貌。同时书中经常关注到邻近地方的语音变读差异。

作者用严式记音符号记写实际语音，如实地记录当时在上海城里正在词汇扩散的几组音位。1. 入声韵 k 尾向 h 尾的扩散合并；2. 声母 dz 母向 z 母扩散合并；3. 全浊阳上声调向阳去声调的扩散合并；4. 中古疑母字疑母脱落向零声母合并。

他描写得很细致："在第四声调（即入声）结尾处的辅音，在有些方言中是这样三个 k，t，p，相应于其他声调字最后的 ng，n，m。在上海话语音中仅能听得见第一种情况。它出现在 á[æ]，ó[o]，o[ɔ]，u[ʌ] 后。在高层调系列的辅音前面听上去为 k，尤其是 s，t 前；在低层调系列前听上去为 g，尤其是 z，d 前。"（p.39）"如在 ih[ɪʔ] 中，若以 k[k] 结尾的话，经常会插入一个短 u[ʌ]。如：'力'，听上去为 lik[lik] 或 liuk[liʌk]。当

在 úh[ʌʔ] 和 óh[oʔ] 里的一些字韵尾不读 k 时，它们就变 úh[ʌʔ] 和 óh[oʔ] 为 eh[eʔ]。这样，'末 móh' 就会变成 meh[meʔ]，许多字都遵循这一规则，在韵母中变化它们的位置。"（p.56）

在此书全文中记到的入声韵中，他都按实际读法记下它们的读音，我们已经统计出来 k 韵向 ʔ 韵扩散"不变、两读、已变"的具体情况。（游汝杰 1998；钱乃荣 2003）

dz 母变 z 母的情形也如实记录，如："茶、从、全、尽"等读 dz，"坐、直、情、齐"等读 z，"在、造、城、前"等两读。（详见钱乃荣 2003: 22）

关于中古阳上字，笔者统计了该书第二、三单元中自由运用中的全浊阳上字，其中有 18 个字未变，11 个字有时读阳上有时读阳去，18 个字已归入阳去。（详见钱乃荣 2003: 29—32）

作者还记录了一个"溪"母常用字"去"在当时的实际语音变化情形。他说："当某个本地人被问及，kʻiʻ[kʻi] 与 cʻhiʻ[tɕʻi] 哪个是'去'的正确发音时，他会回答是前者。然而对于外国人来讲，用 cʻhiʻ 来表示的拼读法似乎更确切些。实际上，这个读音正处于由 kʻi 向 cʻhi 转变的过渡阶段。"（p.2）这样的描写方法真实可靠，今崇明方言的"去"仍读 [kʻi]。

这里顺便提及的是，艾氏这种语言发展观使他在观察语言现象时经常注意其变化的两可现象，记录并了解它们的转变情况。留下的这些资料十分珍贵。再举个语法方面的例子。他说到上海话补语标记的"得"当时正从"来"向"得"改变，如"写来好看——写得好看"。他说："受过教育的人常避免使用'来'，而用'得'来代替，但在稍低的阶层中用'来'却极为普遍。"（p.188）到现今上海郊区还多用"来"，城区用"得"或"得来"。

艾氏还记录了上海话文读音（p.51—54）和一些不规则常见读音，这些都为后代保存了研究的有用资料。

作者在叙述中经常随记相关的重要资料。如他记到通摄字"v 在黄浦以东发音成了 ɦ"，如"冯、服"的声母（说明当时浦西已经先变，浦东还未变）。"鼻化 e 的发音越过黄渡、朱家阁就为 œ 了。"（p.54）"'船、满'等字苏州都为 œ 韵，而在上海是鼻化 e 韵。"（p.4）（这是松江上海音与苏州平江府太仓州方言的分界）又如入声 k 尾"在上海稍偏西的地方和宁波的地方都没有"。（p.55）"阳上的发音仍存在于至少是中国的中心地区的白话口语中。"（p.34）但全浊阳上声调"在苏州与杭州之间的嘉兴地区已经没有了"。（p.35）从这些记录中可见作者敏锐的观察力和对我国东南部方言的了解程度。

在辨认声调时，该书还介绍了比字法，如三个阳调用同声韵的字比较："良，两，亮；埋，买，卖；泥，你，义；人，忍，认；油，有，佑；题，弟，地；随，罪，睿。"

他比较了上海话与官话的音节总数，上海话是 570 个，官话是 411 个。认为"其差异源于宽声母 b，g，d，v，z 的存在"。（p.57）

二、对吴语语法学的贡献

1. 语法和韵律问题

艾约瑟在研究汉语的基础上，创造性地提出了研究汉语要分语法和韵律（即节奏）两个方面，并要将两方面结合起来观察的精辟观点。他在分析词语的组合和使用规律时，常常谈到上海话口语中韵律的制约作用。他说："汉语口语句法可以分成两个题目：语法的（或'句法的'）和韵律的（或'节奏的'），彼此独立又互相联系。前一个标题下面可以包括支配、陈述和一部分的词组系统内容，在后者下面应该包括正确地建立重叠、对偶以及词组系统的剩下部分内容。后者可以称之为韵律，这个词更适合应用在对诗歌的规则上。在现代的著作中，在一个共同的题目下面把句法和韵律的分配掺和起来已经被认为是更方便的。"（p.212）

冯胜利（2000）在他的《汉语韵律句法学》的前言中说道："最早发现韵律制约句法现象的，当首推马建忠。"（p.2）"值得回味的是，马氏虽然惊人地发现了韵律的作用，但他却说：'排偶声律说，等之自郐以下耳。'——将韵律的研究排斥在句法之外。"（p.3）冯先生尚未注意到在《马氏文通》诞生的 45 年前，艾约瑟的著作上便已开始了对上海方言的韵律和句法结合的研究。

艾约瑟专门用了独立的一节，研究汉语口语句法的韵律。他认为："词语的习性可以这样阐明：词组的黏合受字数制约，并成为构成所有新句子的基础，而且不知不觉地有条理地控制着本地的说话的人。人们会完全像很可能越过词类中间的互相支配的规则那样，未注意到他的词语的韵律。"（p.214）他在语音、词类、句法三章里都谈及韵律。

作者注意到上海话句子结构中的四字短语节奏及其重音情形："汉语说话或书写的句子都对称排列着。像历史小说的著作那样，存在于日常生活口语中的那些不太精心制作的形式中，同样用韵律可以愉悦和帮助读者。在一个可以流畅地说汉语的人的文体中，你会发现四词分句要比任何其他长句多得多和频繁出现。这种方式可以称之为上海方言的'偶式抑扬格'，重音要落在二字词组的后一个音节上；如'财主人家有丧事要请和尚道士做做功德'这句话里有三组四字短语。"还指出在入声字碰巧为后附

词时，如"大关节目"的"目"，会有明显的重音。（p.212）

他认为："方言中重音落在倒数第二个音节上，这样的四字方式可以称之为一个偶式长短格音步。"

在"读起来看"中，重音落在第一个和最后一个字上，这些句子中，中间的词是重读词的后附词。

他讨论了上海话中三字组、二字组的韵律："三字韵脚，如果它是由两个非重读、一个重读音节构成的话，可以称其为'抑抑扬格'，如'壁立直'、'敲敲鼓'、'梁惠王'。如果重音落在三字组中第一个字上的话，可以称其韵脚为'扬抑抑格'，如'做末者'。扬抑抑的例子很少，并主要是局限于句子中，包括后附词，它是不会有重音的。在某些情况下，重音落在中间那个字上，如'放飘子'（放风筝），'子'是后附词，就将重音移到前一个字上了。""两个字的复合词举不胜举，可以称其为'抑扬格'，如'上山'。"（p.213）作者对上海话三字格的基本韵律为"抑抑扬格"的分析直到如今看来也是正确的，甚至像上海人的姓名三字组里，用的也是"抑抑扬格"。

对于大于四字组的词，上海话的读法是分拆为两字、三字来读的。这一点作者也谈到。"众所周知，一般词组的数量要多于四字对偶的词，而四字词组不是很多的。一般词的组合可以很容易地处理为更短小的两字、三字或四字词的韵脚，注意这种分隔停顿，我们经常能发现它们；如'喜怒哀惧爱恶欲'这个七字词组中的界线记号出现在第四个字之后，五字词组的界线是出现于第二个字之后的；其他的可以划分为每两个字或三个字为一组。"（p.213）这些韵律的规律总结是符合实际的。

他又说："好的诗歌以及街头民歌中，七字或五字诗体的分隔符，一般都在第四个字和第二个字之后，不过会按照作者的感受和文章的即兴状态而出现变化。"（p.213）

"通过分隔停顿标记，四字词组可以分成更小一点的二字词，而那些三字词组会分成一字和二字词。这样，次重音可以在词组的第一个部分中听到。"（p.213）

"在有些四字词组中，重音落在第一个和第四个字上，如'乡下百姓'。但最常见的是落在第二个和第四个字上，如'富贵贫贱'、'去邪归正'。当转移到第一个或第三个字上去时，是因为这个字在应该是一个重读词的后附词或有一个轻的声调上面。"（p.214）

作者得出结论说："从这样的分析中可以得出结论，大部分汉语散文句子，都自发本能地降为二字、三字和四字词组，并有位置上的重音来标记它们；后附词通常不带重音，常常不能算作它附加上去的那个词组的独立成分。"（p.214）

作者认为上海话中的有些构词法也是考虑到用词时遵循韵律关系而产生的。他认为后缀"子"、"头"在古典文献中从未使用过，它们形成了汉语口语的主要特征。"子"

和"头"给予它们所限定的名词个性和限定性。"它们也有助于凑足句子的韵律节奏。某些词附加上它们之后，就可与那些在语音上相似于它们的名词区分开来了。语缀'儿rh'，在官话省份中很常见，在杭州方言也有，但在本地已被'子'取代了。'日子'有别于'日头'，是根据后接语缀区分的。"（p.69）汉语的构词后缀只有少数有区别意义的作用，确实如艾氏所述，不少是为了增加一个音节成为双音节词，如"老虎"之于"虎"、"老鹰"之于"鹰"起韵律上的和谐作用。艾氏首次提出这一现象。

他还谈到韵律节奏的作用有时破坏了语法上的结构关系。如："'全、秃'，后置于名词，在陈述句中通常充当判断成分中的第一个字。如：米咾肉秃有；人全拉看戏。"他说明道："语音使得这些辅助词与后面的词更靠近，而不是与它们自己的名词靠近。韵律还通常引起两组成分合为一句。如：男女秃有；官府全好。"（p.75）

他认为"序数词往往靠基数来表达，当在有韵律场合，句中没有空位置放语助词。如：今朝念一（今天第21号）、咸丰二年（咸丰第二年）。"（p.98）

在谈到授受类双宾语句时，他认为"在 da mihi 和 give it to me 中，与格的标记被省略了。谐音的助词'拉''lá'，被用来凑足韵律。如：拨我一篓；拨饭拉我；拨饭我吃。"（p.76）

他还说到在句子中，"在许多场合，一个名词要跟在动词之后，而在英语中是不必要的。如：走路、织布、射箭、纺纱、活命。"又如"'话说话'，就意思来讲，'说话'一词是多余的"。"当名词位于一个动词支配之下时，相搭配的另一个动词通常也要附加上，如'寻饭吃'，其中'吃'是多余的。""当意思中不需要有名词时，引入它的原因只能从句子的韵律结构上来寻找，这对于汉语来讲是特别的，基本的。"（p.116）

艾氏认为"对偶"也是一种韵律。他专辟一节讨论了三种对偶形式。"（a）词组形式中的对偶词；（b）在肯定和否定分句中并列出现的疑问形式；（c）在语音或意思上相对照的句子。"（p.210）

"意思上相反的名词，当它们组合成词组时，像是一个并列的词。如：昼夜、山海。形容词和动词，当它们形成对偶的词组时，经常失去它们作为修饰语的特性，而变为名词了。如：酸甜苦咸；第条路多少远近？""疑问句的对偶形式有重要的语法作用。比如，连续地用肯定和否定形式，可表示提问。如：遭蹋字纸倻想罪过勿罪过？""在对偶陈述句的例子中，许多句子简单地由意思上的重复来构成，通过加上否定语助词来表示性质或行为上的相反。如：有铜钱就做，吭没铜钱勿要做；各人要心平勿要做怨恨。""对偶的陈述句一些最好的修饰语，是由一个众所周知的词组构成那些词语，使分句延长。如：上有天理下含人情；先有风后有雨；远水救勿得近火；前世无仇今世无冤；东耳听进西耳听出；推勿转头拎勿转脑。"作者认为，这是修饰"文章"的主要手段，为写出有文采的作品，受教育的阶层要在此花费相当多的时间与精力。"另一类对偶的陈述句，是由彼此间在结构和相关意思上都对应的词构成的。许多谚语就属这一类：债有主冤有头。"（p.210—212）这些话讨论了以后较少有人关注的汉语语句的独特的对称成句现象。

2. 词法方面

在艾约瑟之前中国的语言著作中刘汉语词类划分是很落后的，用的是"实字眼"（动词或名词）、"虚字眼"（其他词，形容词称为"呆虚词"）或"活字眼"（动词）、"死字眼"（名词）等模糊概念。艾约瑟的语法运用西方语言学的构词法和造句法系统地划分和解释了上海方言的词类。

作者论述上海话构词法时，具体讨论到单纯词和复合词的构词细节。虽然当时没有"语素"的概念，但他实际上讨论到了上海方言中的不成词的黏着语素。他说："另一类词的结构是，没有附接成分就不能使用。例如'衣'，不能单独使用，只能出现在复合词中，如下：衣裳、布衣；再如'猪、日、房、礼'，也只能出现在复合词中：猪驴、过房、江猪、礼物、日食。在结构上，除非是韵律上的需要，否则附接成分不可省：着衣裳、杀猪驴个、日头落山、租房子、送礼物。"（p.67）可见，他已看到了相反的现象，即汉语中由于韵律的需要，黏着语素是可以有条件单用的。这在现代汉语中确实常见，比如在"注意钱物"中的"物"便是。

在谈到复合词时，他指出汉语的规律是："如果其配置关系是由种类和种属构成，前者在先。如：柏树、茶壶、鸡蛋、牡丹花、宰相船、阶沿石、红纬帽子。"谈到词缀，他说："如果没有特定的词作前缀的话，'石'字就需要'头'字作为附加成分。当形成复合词时，辅助词是可省略的。如：阶沿石、磨刀石、红纬帽子。在最后一个例子中，'子'是作为辅助词保留的，如果乐意的话，也可省掉。"（p.67—68）

谈到汉语构词语序，他说："当复合名词以并列形式出现时，由整体和部分构成，或者是由实体和意外因素或属性构成，前者在先。如：手心、手套、树根、树叶、头发、首饰。""两个或两个以上的名词，在意义同源，或者有逻辑关联时，可以并列，其顺序依据本地的使用习惯。如：亲眷、信息、街路、货色、财帛、福禄寿、酒色财气。"（p.68）在偏正式中，"文章中谈及由竹子产生的东西，第一个词是'竹'，凭借第二个词把'竹牌'、'竹帘'、'竹纸'区别开来，每种形式所表示的都是外部形状，而第一个词表示质地材料。""在所遵循的规则中，生来的内在本质的名词应位于前面，而附加的辅助词'头、子、处、法'等放在后面；如：饭吭寻处；写法总个。""两个字的名词中，其中一个字是动词，作为种类来讲的动词位于首位；如：算盘、印板、话柄。""许多不可分离的双音节名词中，实质与形式的表示在日常使用中并不明显，如从词源学的角度注意可发现它们有相同的顺序；如：文章、地方。表示实质的字位于前面。"（p.184—185）他说："这些词的使用顺序的最初原因，可能是出于意思上现实的或是想象的顺序，发音的方便，韵律或是任意的；但无论是什么原因，它们都被严格地保持下来，或许采用另一种顺序，但意思不会改变。至于这些以及其他的固定复合词，在各种词类中都可找到，必须在很大方面归因于像汉语这样的一种简易的单音节和声调语言使用为一种会话的手段。""在这一类中，也包括反义名词，其中有些常用的词，组词之间不用虚词。如：姊妹、禽兽、天地、山水人物、铜钱银子。这类短语并不是可即兴创造的。它们是旧有的形式，现代汉语并不允许它们自身造出新的词。每种方言都有其自己因袭的词语配列，既有它的独特的声调发音模式，又有它的字母的变化。但在所有的方言中，绝大多数短语和词一样，在中国的其他地区也是常见的，甚至在福建，语言的一致性是没有地区限制的，没有被这些差异带来问题。"（p.68）

他还谈到由名词与量词合成的名词："在接下来的部分中要谈及许多辅助名词，其位置是位于数词和名词之间，它们并通常跟在名词之后，省略数词。这样就可构成一个复合词，其中表示类别的意义的虚词常被保留下来。A piece of 由‘块’表示，a bar of 由‘条’表示，如：冰块、钢条、船只、人头、书本、纸张。"（p.70）

他还归纳了上海话名词中的类后缀，如表示代理商、行业和职业："夫（脚夫）、手（凶手）、作（木作）、匠（泥水匠）、司务（裁缝司务）、家（店家）、人（捉鱼人）。"（p.70）特别提到吴语特色的"个"。他说："附加上‘个’，它跟在动词或名词后，表示某类职业者。如：吃粮个、撑船个、管账个、卖花个、摆渡个。"（p.71）

"‘阿’这个词，可加在用于亲属和专门的人名称呼上，只不过表示声音和谐。这样，‘哥哥’在上海话中就称作‘阿哥’ah（文读为啊 á），还有‘阿爹’或‘爹爹’。在称呼小孩子的名字和其他生活卑微的人时，它也会附加在适合的名字上。"（P.71）

他在"词组中字的关系"的一段中，注意到词的含义与组成成分在含义上和功能上的不同："在最接近复合词的一类中，当不同的词类的词组成双音节词时，它们中的一个词会失去其本来的语法上的确切性，而变成对于另一个音节的一个附加成分。如‘交’在名词‘交界’中，是没有支配名词功用的，在‘相交朋友总要实际’中也是如此。""当词与词结合起来形成一个新的复合词语时，它们在意思上会不同于来源词的双方的意思，它们在语法上的确切性会失去，而组成的新短语会被清楚地认识到是一个总体，按照它的意义，作为一个名词、动词等。这样‘引（to lead）’和‘线（thread）’，能组成复合词‘引线（a needle）’，‘方’和‘便’组成‘方便’，‘裁’和‘缝’

组成'裁缝'。"

对汉语和上海话中的特殊词类的认识，作者也有许多创见。如对封闭类词的分析。

该书记录了19世纪中期上海话的各类代词。认为代词主要是单纯词，但频繁地容许有双音节形式。还有些代词或语助词，其本身并无意义（如：是、个），是加上前缀或附加成分。

1. 人称代词：单数第一人称代词是"我"，第二人称代词是"侬"，第三人称代词是"伊"或"其"。复数形式是"你 ní"（后人写作"伲"——笔者注）或"我你 'ngú 'ní"，表示"我们"；"倷 ná'"或"侬倷 nóng' ná'"表示"你们"；"伊 í"表示"他们"。当代词仅仅由一个字组成时，空缺的位置常由"是"来填补，如"是我（我）"，"是伊、是其（他）"，"是倷众人（你们所有人）"。2. 反身代词："自"用在复合词中。3. 指示代词：指示代词有"第个（这个）"、"个个"和"伊个（那个）"。4. 疑问代词："啥"、"几（什么，多少）"不可单独使用，还有"何"、"那（发音 'á）"不单独使用。5. 关系代词。没有可单独使用的关系代词，其位置由"个"、"所"来填补，不可单独使用，并且使用很受限制。6. 物主代词，没有。它们的位置是由"个"来填补的，跟在人称代词之后。7. 个体代词："各"，"每"，"逐"。8. 相互代词，没有。所借用的形式"大家"是代用词。9. 不定代词："某"，"啥"，"几"，"多"。10. 关联的或修饰性的代词"秃"、"全"、"别"可单独使用，还有"凡"不可单用。（p.101—103）

在人称代词后，当前面是动作介词时，需要有一个地点名词"喊头"，如"到我喊头来"。

艾氏把上海话中的"量词（这是后来采取的称呼）"区分并命名为"数助词（numeral particles）"和"辅助名词（auxiliary substantives）"两种。第一种数助词是与称谓性名词或全称名词一起使用的，以"个"、"只"最常用，列举了"根、管"等31个；第二种助名词是保留其自身意义的，在翻译成英语时须译成名词。（p.83）其中限定数量和形状有意义的语助词"间、块"等43个，限定书、笔画的助名词"句、点"等20个，表示容器的助名词"碗、盘"等12个，表示度量的助名词（包括时间度量），列举了"亩、尺"等44个，限定集体名词的助名词"双、套"等15个，此外还有表示次数的量词"趟、记"等5个。对量词这样划分是条件明确的，书中为我们保存了大量具有旧上海话特色的量词。（p.81—89）

通过量词的不同使用，他把名词分类为："1. 称谓性的或全称的名词，或者个体存在的种类名称，如：人、山、树、房、衣。状态和物质都包括在内，并且所有情况下都要把不定冠词作为前缀。2. 物质名词，如：谷、金、水。这里所包含的物质，需要有其他的词来限制其形式，如'一蒲式耳（bushel）谷'，'一把金子'，'一杯水'，'一根铁'。……3. 集体名词，或者形式上为单数，却也能表示复数的名词。4. 抽象名词或属性名字或存在方式，由所结合的物质中抽象出来的。数词以及度量、形状名词也在这类中，尽管它们由此与大量精神、道德术语相关，但并不常见。抽象名词可以有两类，即有物质与精神的区别。5. 亲属名词，如：父亲、国王。由于第二类物质名词，诸如'蒲式耳'、'把'、'杯'等提供了形式，或许应该称这类辅助词为正式名词，从而形成第六类。"（p.81—82）这样分类无疑是科学的。

艾氏把上海方言中的介词分为两种：前置介词（preposition）和后置介词（postposition）。他说："前置介词位于名词之前，末尾音节和词根构成一个词，一起用在古代语言中表示格；而且单独的后缀很常见。在现代欧洲语言中，后缀形式很少使用，前置介词执行了格助词的功能。在 Tartar 语里，被其他语言称为介词的语助词，却出现在名词之后，因此称其为后置介词。在满语中，间接格共有 4 个，从语助词族中挑选出来的后缀构成词。在书写时，它们随意与名词相连，也可不连，都可以作单独成分词使用。汉语在使用不相连的格助词时，会出现这样的情况，有些附属于名词之前，有些附属于名词之后，并不违背其他民族的通常的习惯用法。"（p.78）

他分别解释了上海话前置介词"打、对、从、到、拉、替、搭、试、勒拉（是一个表示方位的语助词，也放在名词之前。在官话中它是'在'）"的意义，同时解释了用作方位格的后置介词"里、前、外、后、上 long'（文读：'zong）、下"，复合词"里向"等。而且他指出："英语中的某些介词，很容易地从动词或名词减弱而来。"（p.135）说明英语与汉语的介词从来源来说也是相同的。

刘丹青（2003）再次肯定和全面论述了汉语中前置介词和后置介词的并存，并提出"框式介词结构"的理论。笔者（2001）主编的《现代汉语》已将起引介从属成分给核心成分作用的前置词、后置词，包括所谓的结构助词"的"、"地"、"得"都归入介词类。

艾氏还详细对比了与英语同义的上海话介词，像：of，领属格语助词可以通过并列形式或加语助词"个"字来表达，如"中国个规矩"、"别人个事体"。with（工具格的）、by，可以用"担"、"拨拉"、"拨"来表达，如"担篙子撑"。except 可以用动词"除脱"来表达，还经常在该分句句末加上"以外"、"外头"，如"除脱之侬个外头就是我"。besides 可用"勿算"表示，放在分句句尾，如"小末勿算共总有一百"。beyond 可用"过去"或"外头"表示，如"广东过去"。through 或 pass 可用"经过"或单用"过"来表示，如"路上经过杭州"。towards 可用动词"朝、望、对"表示，如"朝第边走"。（p.135—136）

他在当时就运用动词的"格 case"的理论方法分析了上海话中动词所带的各种"格"。

"主格"和"宾格"是没有助词标记的。通常的句子的语序是"及物动词后面带宾语，并且前面加上主格词，如：官府刻薄百姓。当动词'送、给'后接两个宾语时，近一些的靠近动词，远一些的位于最后，常与'拉'连用。如：送礼物拉侬 present you with gifts；拨饭拉侬吃 give you rice。"其他的格：所有格或领属格是靠"个"kú'来表达的，如"伊个声气，花个蕊头"。当领属格助词省却时，一个复合名词形成了，如"花蕊头"。"to a place"是用"到"表示的，通常后接名词，并与一个行动动词连用；from 或 by（离格）是用"自"zz'，"从"zóng，"由"yeu 或"打"'táng 表示的。其中最后的"打"字最常用；"for"、"instead of"（替代格）的意思可以由下面这几个词表示："替、代、代替、忒、为"。它们是都在使用中的；"in"和"at"（方位格），可用"勒拉"leh 'lá 和"拉"'lá 表示，前置于名词，"里"或"里向"后置于名词；"with"、"of"（工具格）用动词"担"tan（上海西边是"拿"nan）或 nó 表示，放于名词之前，后面再跟动词。还可用后缀"个"表示，动词通常放在它和名词之间；表示"by"（手段格）的辅助动词是"拨"peh，放于工具名词之前，主要动词受或不受它的支配；"along with"（与格）是由"忒、替、同"来表示的。受支配的名词后再加上"一淘"，当使用"同"时，这个附加词（一淘）可省。（p.76—78）

作者简明归纳了上海话中语助词"拨"的四种用法：表主动：拨三两各铜钱拉伊。表被动：拨拉父母责备；我个帽子拨拉人偷之去者。表原因：拨拉伊死；伊拨拉我吃亏者。表许可：啥人肯拨拉别人欺负呢；拨拉别人哄骗侬。（p.127）

他说到了及物双音词动词的及物用法："有些双音节动词是及物的，词中的一个成分是名词。如：回头、弄神、到手、算计。这些词可以看作是及物的，例如在下面的句子中'勿好弄神朋友'、'就来回头我（马上回来告诉我）'。"（p.117）

不及物动词的语序一般是位于句子最后："当后面没有介词或其他动词时，不及物动词常位于最后。如：此地坐、几时来、我船上来。""当有介词来连接不及物动词与名词时，动词的位置可前可后。如'到此地来'等同于'来到此地'。同样，'坐拉第搭'与'拉第搭坐'同义。"（p.126）

作者还关注讨论了上海话中动词后的辅助词，即刘丹青（1994）所称的"唯补词"。他说："在双音节动词中，出现了许多辅助性的词，它们几乎或完全失去了作为独立动词的本来的意义。从下面的例子可以注意到，这些前接成分或前置词，正如被描述的那样，对于主要动词来讲常常没有附加什么东西。如：得 tuh（听得），脱 t'eh（断脱），见 kíen'（望见），着 záh（捉着），住 dzû'（锁住），杀 sah（话杀），到 tau'（用到）。"

（p.114—115）这类封闭类词现在还为不少语法书所忽视，未专列出来讨论其语法功能。

他列举了派生动词的几种惯常用法："表开始：提起笔来；表反身：自怨自；表集合：合拢来；表分开：拆开来；表完成：造完；表阻碍：挡住；表抛弃：丢脱。"

艾氏讨论到汉语中的动补结构问题。

"这里许多短语的顺序，也有可能是根据时间上的先后次序来安排的。就是说，两个动作的表达是连续的。如：打败、敲开、咬破、请坐、写完、吊死。"（p.113—114）

"下面的复合动词是由及物动词和形容词并列构成的：加长、亲近、掘深、减轻、填高。'好'这个词，可加在许多动词之后，有'完成'的意思，如'做好'。"（p.116）

他与英语相对比："这些例子显示在汉语中，语言里表达结果目的系统的那类派生词，它们的补偿形式是如何构成的。替代结构，像 prolongare，to lengthen，是从拉丁语 longus 或 long 而来的，或者说 lengthen 是从英语 length 而来的，我们有一个分离出来的形容词前缀'长'。许多英语短语是以同样的方式组合的，如 rub smooth，rub dry，意义和语法结构相同于汉语形式：磨光，揩干。"（p.116）

他详细讨论了动词带趋向词、能愿词等的三字组所表达的语法意义。

动词可与"来"、"去"相结合，表示动作行为的方向。如："敲进去、担上来、走下来、杀前去"。"开始"与"结束"的动作是靠附加成分"起来"和"成工"表示的，动词"起"也可单用。还有"完、停、好"都可用来表示"完成"，如：写起来、做成工、画成工、今朝做起、几时做完。靠肯定和否定的语助词的帮助来形成的词组是相当多的，正因如此，它们的形式成为语言的一大特征。汉语口语用语很大程度上靠它们来表达，在力度与精确度方面，它需要把握。

在这些词组中，"得"tuh 与"勿"veh（官：不 púh），位置居中，某些辅助词和一些形容词和动词位置在后。主要动词的意思就这样以各种方式限制和修改了。"得"与"勿"在意思上是相反的，它们修改后所产生的动词意义也应该是相反的。它们可以简化成下列各组形式。第一，表示施事，他能做或是知道如何实现某动作，可以说"做得来"；否定式如"做勿来"。第二，表示施事，周边环境允许他实现某种行为，可以说"当得起"；否定形式如"读勿起"，"拖勿起"。第三，表示动作能够成功，如"寻得着"；否定式如"打勿着"。这些复合词中出现几个形容词，如："全、直、多、好、满、完、全、通、明、白"等。如：读勿全、伸勿直、差勿多、话得好、补得满。

艾氏讨论了上海话动词的时态形式。（p.130—132）他认为"现在时"的表示形式，不必有辅助词。如：我勿做啥；来呢勿来；懂勿懂；怕冷否。其他的时态用的语助词有：a."歇"，一会儿，这个语助词在它出现的短语中表示"过去"的意思，并可能最确切地表示一种"不定过去时"。如：看歇戏否；去歇两回。b."者，哩"，这些语助词表示已完成或已决定的行为。英语语法中与其相当的往往是过去分词，并与助动词 to be 相连接。如：买好拉者 they are bought；卖脱者 it is sold；我去者 I am going。c."过"，这个语助词有"过去时态"的意义。如：到过两回；花种过多少。d."歇者"或"歇拉者"，表示"过去时"（perfect time）。如：认得过歇者；忒伊话歇者；钟敲歇拉者；托拨歇者。e."过歇"，所指的过去时间比上面提到的过去要更远些。如：来过歇者；勿曾去过歇；学过歇拉者。f."要"，表示将来时；有时前面加上"将"。如：要落雨者；明朝要去。g."将"，经常用于将来时。如：将有闹事。h."之"，这个字附加在动词之后，形成一个过去分词的时态。英语中的辅助分词为 having。如：看之书末晓得者；懂之末好讲；做之兵咾打仗去者。在此他还说到"之"的作用："作为一个表示关系时态的语助词，这个词可以用在过去时或将来时中。在前面的例子中，它是叙事体的分词的标记，如：看见之山高咾走上去者。在后面的例子中，它还成为将来时的标志，正如英语中的 when 引导的句子，如：写好之拨拉我看。When you have written it，let me see it. 条件语助词'末'经常用在第一个分句的句末。"（p.132）i."曾"，肯定句中的过去时用"之"，否定句中的过去时用"曾"。如：勿曾看歇；勿曾来。采用这个语助词，而在英语中是用现在时态的，如：勿曾去 He is not gone。

他说到汉语表达时态时的一个重要特点，到如今一直为许多研究者所忽视，笔者认为这是汉语表示时态功能的一个重要特点。他说："如果有时间状语的话，上面这些语助词不必要用了。如：昨日去个 He went yesterday；我后日去 I shall go on the day after tomorrow."笔者补充说得完整一些，是动词前的时间词制约后边的时态词，如："我看电影了。"后边的"了"表示"现在时"的当下状态，但"我昨天看电影了。""我晚上看电影了。""了"就退而表示"昨天"或"晚上"的"当时"。

在讨论将来时句子时他指出："表示将来时的那些语助词不用在否定句中，如：我勿去 I shall not go."（p.132）"如果要用在将来时的否定句中，其意思就是'希望'或'必须'，如'我勿要去'（我不想去）。当有'将'出现时，必定位于前面，这样当句子中使用'勿'时，将'就不能形成它的一部分了。""勿见得"（不可能），常用在将来时的否定句中。如"勿见得落雨"（It is not likely to rain. 或 It will not rain.）。（p.132—133）

作者在叙述形容词时说："在复合词中，名词会把它前面的其他名词变成形容词。如：洋刀、石路、牛奶。""动词与虚词'个'或'拉个'合用时，就会变为后面名词的形容词。如：种拉个稻、死个人多、爱拉个小囡、活个物事。"（p.93）

艾氏注意到上海话中相当发达的三音节的状态形容词。如：瞎搭搭、硬邦邦、软

滋滋、滑汰汰、闹嚷嚷、毛萋萋、暖筒筒、直条条、矮矬矬、短悠悠、白雪雪、黑搨搨。（p.92）

该书详细地列举了形容事物的各种"比较级的表达方法"。a."再"，again，位于形容词前面修饰。如：再强有否（你有更便宜点儿的吗）？b."点"，a little，放在形容词之后修饰。如：第本书好点。c."一眼"，a little。如：倒好一眼。d."还"，still，further，与"要"结合，使后面的形容词变成比较级。如：工夫还要细。e."比"，compare，使后面的形容词变成比较级。当"比"用在否定形式中时，形容词可以省略。如：上海勿比苏州；勿算比我好。f."更"，better，有时后面跟着"加"字。如：勿去更好。g."越"，重叠使用，在句中带两个成分，以加强对比；有时后面加上"发"字。如：越多越好；越发穷越发要生病。h."又"，again，十分常见的形式。常用"比"字放在句子的开头。如：落雨又大。i."又加"，still more，前面经常用上"比"。如：比我又加明白。k."加，添，放大"，add 之义，increase 之义。如：今朝风加大；鞋子要放大。（按：原文序号从 i 跳到 k。）l."得多"，可以加在形容词之后以加强比较。如：第二只鸡重得多。m. 与比较级形式相比，这种形式是通过首位的肯定形式来表达的，指出了要对比的宾语的差异。如：高六寸。（p.94—96）

"在所给的例子中可有三类辅助词。1. 名词性的语助词（particle），跟在所修饰的形容词之后，表示仅有轻微的变化。这种变化可能是增加或是减少，根据比较形容词的意义而定。2. 动词。其中动词'比'最常用，可与其他词合用，也可不合用。它保留了作为一个动词的语法，不因在形容词比较级中充当辅助词而有所影响。其他动词的使用表示了附加意义。它们的反义词用在类似的形式中，例如'减少'，'减脱'。3. 连词和副词。它们表达了一种差别，然而没有具体指明是多一些或是少一些，所以它们可以对应于英语中的后缀 er，而不是 more 这个词。'越　越'的重叠形式，正好对应于 the 这个语助词，如 the sooner the better（越早越好）。这类英语形式常常认为是可以省略的，在解释的时候，所省略的成分需要补充出来。在相应的汉语习惯用语中，是不依靠这种省略法假说的。"（p.96）

艾氏又列出全部形容词最高级的表示法。"头三个词（顶、最、极）放在所修饰的形容词之前。其余的放在后面。"可见当时上海话程度副词的后置情形。a."顶"，highest，top，如：天狼星顶亮。b."最"，exceedingly，the most，如：鸢鸟当中凤凰最好看。c."极"，extremely，这个词可用在所修饰的形容词之前或之后。如：聪明得极；极深奥。d."野"，very，前面需要有辅助性动词"来"或"得"。如：黄浦里险得野。e."死"，这个词在它与形容词之间有个辅助性动词"来"。如：米行情贵来死。f."吪做"，there is nothing that can be done，这个表达形式也需要"来"。如：风大来吪做。g."煞"，

very，如：强盗多煞。h."头一",the first in importance，最重要的。如：头一要紧。i."了勿得"，remarkably，exceedingly，如：好来了勿得。j. "了反勿得"，意思同上。如：重来了反勿得。k. "话勿得"，或是"话勿来"，very，unspeakable，或是"勿了事"，endlessly，如：大来话勿得。l."得利害",severe，如：重得利害。此外，还有"完"，如：容貌黄完；"十分，十二分"，如：物事十分好。（p.96—98）

艾氏还首次研究了上海方言的语气和语气词。这里的语气是指广义的。

他认为："在许多情况下，语气完全是由意义来决定的，没有特别的标记：'我去买。'（陈述语气）'是侬去还便当。'（假设语气）'侬去买。'（祈使语气）'买是容易。'（不定语气）在拉丁语法中，这四个主要语气，也是没有明显标志的。"（p.127—128）

他关注到了标示词。"位于分句句末的'者'和'末'，分别标志着在陈述句中的陈述和条件。如：现在落雨末年世好者；年纪大末勿要者。""在许多情况下，这些词是省略的，并不影响句义。如：勿落雨百姓要苦恼。""而在两个相连的分句中，无论前面的分句是否是条件句，这些辅助词都要用上。如：看见之讨饭个末就打起来者。这些分句都是过去时的。""陈述分句独立存在，常加'者'字，如'来者、去者'。"即"者（哉）"是成句词。

"可能语气的词组已经列举了许多。其能力的类别有：绝对的或自然的，有限的或心理上的，前者的例子有：写勿来，讲究得来，弯勿转。""会"加在动词前可以表示一种可能性，"念勿来"相当于"勿会念"。限定的可能语气是靠"起"来表达的，如：当勿起，牵勿起，吃勿起。"允许"和"禁止"语气可通过如下词表示：a."得"。如：看得，看勿得。b."好"、"可以"，也能表示"许可"的意思，如：好进去否，可以吃得。表示祈愿语气的动词是由"巴勿得"、"恨勿得"表达的（"恨"*h*ng‘ 在上海的西边读 *h*ung‘），如：我巴勿得快点到；恨勿得做好。

祈使语气：（1）它的否定形式中有"要"字，加上常用的否定词"勿"，如：勿要闹。（2）祈使语气的肯定形式，单用动词来表示，或者是在某些动词后附加上"末者"或"罢"，如：走末者，去罢。所有的单个动词或动词词组，除了那些加肯定词或否定词的以外，都可以用作祈使语气。如"走过来"的意思可以是 I am passing you（我正经过你），或 pass over to me（走向我）。（p.128—129）

"疑问形式有两种：a.用疑问词'曼'*man*'和'否''*vá* 来表达。如：饭好曼？去否？ b.把问题并排地放在肯定和否定形式中。中间常有个语助词'呢'*ní*。如：肯去勿肯去？晓得勿晓得？买呢勿买？在'呢'后，第二个分句有时候加上'啥'*sá* 来补充。如：要打呢啥？"（p.130）

"个，它除了用作数助词和领属格，以及用在关系代词的句子中以外，还可用在陈述相关的动词、形容词的最后，表示陈述语气。如：好个，好拉个，勿能做个。""之，是过去式或过去分词的标志，但可以发现，它常常是动词的陈述语气形式。如：前年做之宰相者，本地白也会话之，明朝要写好之末者。""者，是动作已完成或正在进行的标志，不管它由动词还是由形容词表达；它也可以是祈使词。如：做拉者 it is done；好者 it is right；去拉个者 he is gone；吾拉做者 I am doing it。"

作者还收集了当时在上海方言中存在的一些特殊的表示方式的副词，其形式是在重叠形容词后加上"然，乎，能，里"，如"隐隐然、兴兴然、约约乎、几几乎、稀稀能、险险能、快快里、慢慢教"等。（p.136）这些词大多在现今已不用了。

上海话中的大量拟声词，艾氏也注意并记载到，还注意到它们的声调特征。他说："模仿自然声音的重叠形式是经常用到的。如：丁冬丁冬（鼓的声音）、鏾锒鏾锒（鼓、马铃的声音）、帖塌帖塌（鞋的声音）、结怪结怪（鸡鸣声）、刮腊刮腊（风吹芦苇之声）、兵兵浜浜（敲冰的吵声）、以列以列（嘶叫声）、以挨以挨（门辗轧声）、胡庐胡庐（吹笛声）、煇爆煇爆（爆竹点燃声）。"他说明："这类词在口语对话中经常出现，在某种程度上，被认为是太随意了而不被收入到这里提到过的那些正式的书里。在这些拟声词中，不大出现第二、第三声调。其他方言中所使用的形式与此不同。"（p.137）

3. 句法方面

艾约瑟十分重视语序问题。一开始就全面叙述上海话的语序。他从构词的语序一直讲到词组组合的语序。

他说："一个名词支配另一个名词，作一个领属格的定语，总是位于那个名词之前，中间要插入语助词'个'。如：牛个角比之鹿个角短。""形容词前置于所修饰的名词，可以有'个'，也可以或没有'个'。如：大地方；利害个物事。"（p.163）"数词带上辅助词，可以修饰名词，前置于名词。""副词大多放在所修饰的形容词和动词前面。如：忒认真。""副词可跟在形容词之后，如：近煞；好极。""在介词结构中，某些方位格跟在所修饰的词之后；其余的包括'在，勒拉，勒里'，意思是 being at 或 in，放在所修饰的名词之前。如：勿在乡下。"（p.164）

他讨论了汉语中复杂的词性转化情形。如："形容词当跟在带'个'的名词之后时，这个形容词是解释为名词的。如：心里向个勿好，总要改正。""形容词常用作及物动词的宾语，结果必然是在此情况下解释作名词。如：学好；讲和。""一些组合形式，组成及物动词带着一个支配词。也包括动词和它带的宾语在内。如：第条河开多少阔？"（p.165）"当一个形容词被另一个所修饰时，它会变成名词；英语中的用法也是如此，下面就是某些颜色词的例子：浓黑；淡红。"（p.166）

艾氏指出："在许多语言中，把动词认作名词是很常见的。出于这种目的，使用了不定式和动名词形式，也用现在分词形式。在汉语中，这些都是完全相同的，用的是词根自身。"（p.166）他在当时就指出了汉语的动词不必通过形态可直接转为名词用，实际上是指出了许多语言中开放类词与句子成分都是不一一对应的，只是汉语中没有形态表现而已。朱德熙先生（1985）在《语法答问》中把词类与句子成分是否一一对应作为英语、汉语的主要特点差别的论点是值得商榷的。笔者（1996）有专文陈述，其中还说到英语、汉语的封闭类词都是与句子成分一一对应的。

艾氏分别举例上海话中有："a. 动词作为陈述的主语，后面跟谓语（英语用不定式和现在分词）。如：活命难；会得胜总好个；国度乱做生意勿便当个。b. 动词作主语，后接作为属性的名词（在拉丁语语法中，是动名词的领属格）。如：种田个家生有锄头铁搭咾还有多许；教书个本事勿有。c. 动词可以前置或后置于表示格的语助词。如：我现在拉做 I am now doing it；勒拉吃茶 drinking tea（inter biberdum. 在喝中。按：前者是拉丁语。下同）；勒里打算 he is considering（inter putandum. 在打算中）；做官里向也有辛苦（in magistrate gerendo. 在实施地方行政官职务中）。d. 动词支配另一个动词。如：断绝往来；勿曾有啥争论。e. 动词可以作为实现某行为的手段。如：问之咾晓得；勿留心咾忘记脱者。拉丁语中被动态的动名词与形容词相连，如同主动态的动名词与名词相连。在我们方言中相应的形式是，复合词可以翻译成形容词或被动态的动名词：可恶 to be hated，或 hateful；好笑，laughable, fit to be laughed at。"（p.167—168）

他还讨论了"副词用作形容词"情况。如："派生副词像纯粹的形容词一样，成为一个陈述语的谓语。如：人是好好能个。它们还可修饰名词。如：做私底下个事体。"相反，"形容词用作副词"："有些形容词前置于动词，在这种情况下必须看作副词。如：多话两句；酒要少吃。""后置介词用作形容词"："当表示位置格的语助词'外、上、下、前、后'放在所修饰的词之前时，它们就是形容词。当放在后面时为后置介词。如：外国—城外；下手—手下，手底下。"（p.169）

艾氏谈到汉语中的对等词的语法表现："对等的词有相同的语法功能，词组的排列形式有两个到五个，甚至更多的字，形成许多种类。关于位置的规则，整个词组可根据具体情况定为一个单独的名词、动词或形容词。如：伊个行事，全是仁义道德；勿能用之器皿像生，测量伊个长阔高深。"（p.171—172）"一组词是由两个对等的词组成的，每个词都可接纳修饰或支配成分。如：飞禽走兽；欢天喜地。"（p.174）

艾氏专门讨论了词的"重叠"的各种表现。他说："词的重叠经常会影响到重叠词的语法意义。在另些时候采取同义反复，是只不过出于韵律上的原因，或是为了强调语势，如同英语一样。格在一个在重叠的词中是有语法价值的，要被首先考虑到。"

（p.176）"重叠的形容词放在动词之前来修饰动词，很像副词。如：拢拢总总有一百。原始的副词并不重叠。""当动词重叠时，是出于韵律的原因，或双声的需要。下面的例子将展示这些看似是同义反复的用法。a. 有或没有支配词的单个动词重叠。如：要买点饭吃吃；我不过浇浇花咾，修修丫枝。b. 在两个字的动词词组中，第二个字经常重叠。如：孛相相；笑嘻嘻。c. 四个字的动词词组中，容纳一个单个重叠的动词。如：打败之咾纷纷各散；打赢之咾归来得意扬扬；星光闪闪。d. 许多二字动词词组，是通过重叠每个词来扩展的。如：事体定定当当；勿必疑疑惑惑；牙齿活活落落。e. 动词交替重叠，并带两个宾格。如：总要劳心劳力；年成好者谢天谢地。"（p.179—180）

句子的语序的时间顺序是艾氏首先关注到的。他说："在复合动词中，如果要表示逐步性的行为，在时间上先发生的词放在前面。表示结束性动作的词放在后面。如：担来销化；灯点完者；拨拉贼匪打输。""表示'能力'的助动词，形成一种可能语气的模式，前置于动词。如：勿会白话；勿能去。"（p.185）"当动词的宾语是个动作时，在汉语中是用动词表示的，而不用动词性的派生词、不定式或动名词形式，语言中的这种用法是有复合语法规则的形式的。如：勿免死；勿想吃。"还有"将来时态，以及祈使句和可能语气中的辅助词前置于动词。如：总要去；勿能来。""表示方向和动作，开始和结束等的助动词，跟在主要动词之后。如：买进来；抱进抱出。在时间上优先的词常常决定了动词的顺序。如：我去送；要来相帮；打杀别人。"（p.186—187）这就是后来戴浩一先生说的汉语句子排列的时间顺序。

艾约瑟论述"简单陈述句"也很精彩。

他一开头就说到汉语有"独词句"和形容词谓语句："最简单的句子中只有一个词，其中一个字形成主语，另一个构成谓语。主语常在前面。如：马来；天热。""谓语偶然会放在前面。如：出会；落水。这些形式也可以解释为无人称动词带个宾语。"他又说："一个形容词其本身完全可以构成谓语，并且与前面的主格词是没有系词来连接的。如：桃子熟者。"（p.187）

他讨论到汉语的主语可以由各类词和词组充当。他说："主语可以由名词或名词词组，代词，动词或动词词组，或看作名词的地点副词、时间副词构成。如：日头勿出来；庵堂寺院秃有烧香；第个是好点个；买是勿能；挑咾扛勿会个；此地有雪；明朝初六。""主语有时因含义自明而省略的。如：总要立定主意。""形容词有时也能带一个谓语。如：善咾恶总要辨出来。"他提及汉语句子主、宾语可以系词为核心的转动位置："任何修饰名词的词，其位置如果并排移动的话，可以变为谓语，如'第座房子是拉个'可以转换成'是第座房子'。"（p.188）"当使用系词时，其形式有'是，得，来得，来'，前置于形容词性的谓语，而'做'以及某些词组中的'为'、'作'前置于名词。如：道理是勿差个；心里来得笨；我勿做兵；我勿为官府；写来好看；写得勿好。"
他说："可以做谓语的有：名词，形容词，动词，副词，或是它们的词组，如：比我大
个是阿哥；赦免小过失好个；戏咾戏法咾啥勿看；价钱最大个是珍珠八宝；伊勿能办事
体。"（p.189）

他在当时已经具体归纳了句子的种种"扩展"方式。他说："很多变化会引入句子
中，无外乎是将适用的修饰性的词和词组补充到分离的分句中。……主语可以这样扩
展：a.通过加上一个形容词前缀。如：穷苦个人多。b.通过名词的并列，有或没有'个'
都可，之间的关系是种类与属类，或者是主语与定语。如：乡下人告荒去者；上辈个
好处要讲拉子孙听。c.通过及物的不定式带宾语的形式。如：吃牛肉真罪过。d.通过
为格助词支配的名词或动词附加成分。如：屋里向呒没人；勒拉睏个辰光有贼偷之去
者。e.通过在名词前加上数词和数助词。如：两个女人投井者。f.通过在名词前加上
指示词、领属词或其他修饰性的代词。如：第部牛车了脱者。g.通过前面附加上地点
副词、时间副词，可以带领属的标志，或不插入语助词。也可以这么说，这里的副词
都被当作了名词。如：此地个水清个；荡搭个人掉皮个；间壁房子火灼；什盖能个谣言
拉城里。"（p.190—191）

"谓语可以以类似的方式进行扩展。可以采取下面几种形式。a.名词带上其形容词。
如：是其勿是正派人。b.名词并列，其关系是种类和属类，主题和属性，有或没有'个'
都可。如：伊话个勿是上海话。c.动词并列。英语中的动词是靠 and、to、of 来连接的，
翻译成两个相应的动词并列。如：我要走前去做；我勿来打侬。d.动词带上宾语。如：
别人恨伊拉。e.动词、名词或地点副词、时间副词，放在带'拉'或'在'的结构中。如：
东家勿拉屋里。f.修饰性的代词和数词，带上相当于在主语中的名词占用的语助词。如：
银子有一百两；第把雨伞是吾个。g.动词由各种副词来修饰，可以在并列中位于前面，
或是带上作为附属性的系词'得'、'来'，就放在后面。如：件件事体秃是做得正经个；
菩萨一定晓得。h.动作的原因、方式、工具、地点或时间，可由前置于动词的名词表
示。如：黄衣裳是皇帝送个；从小到大是爷娘照应。j.表示原因、方式等的相同情况，
也由格助词来表示，附加在名词后面。如：张举人到苏州去者。（按：原文序号从 h 跳
到 j。）k.形容词带上修饰性的副词。如：是倻飘流个人试多。"（p.191—193）

他还注意到"省略"和"补充"现象。如上海话中常见的介词的省略现象："在相
似的例子中，省略介词的现象是很多的。其中有几个是必不可少的，故不能省。然而
汉语书写和会话中的简明扼要，很大程度上要归功于这里所提到的介词省略问题。相
对于简明扼要来讲，在许多情况下出于文字或华丽的目的，要进行尽量的补充，加些
措辞或修饰词组。"

艾氏接着系统讨论"从句"和"并列句"。

他用在世界语言类型学具有普遍意义的"从句"句法概念概括地分析归纳了上海话中7种从句形式。

他逐项分说从句,从"宾语从句"始:"表示一个行为的宾语的分句,通常跟在包含行为的句子之后。如:领伊到学堂读书;请和尚拜忏。末尾的 that 或 to 常用助动词'要'、'叫'来表示。如:横劝竖劝叫伊学好;关鸟拉笼里要伊叫个。末尾的 that 常省略,或用动词来表示,这种方法常用于两个分句以外的句子,如此以便于增强句子的整体韵律感。下面就是这种用法的常见句子:送勒依看;话拨俫听;拨饭伊吃;斟酌起来看。表示动词宾语的分句中,单个动词常常重叠,不重叠也可。如:舍点物事拉我吃吃;要到店里去买。包含行为的分句常由名词或名词词组构成,并加上表示原因或方式的助动词,还有运动动词'来',或用'去'收尾分句。如:叫瞎子来拜斗;挪石灰浆来刷壁;担马来骑到海滩去。"(p.196—198)

"关系从句":"关系分句与语助词'个'字一起,作为一个修饰语可前置于被修饰的词。如:做惯拉个生活勿吃力个;行方便个人家子孙要多者。""表示原因、方式、手段等形式,以同样的方式放在所从属的词之前。如:祖宗传下来个派头勿好改换;山上泉眼出个水清个。"(p.199)

"主语从句":"有些助动词和介词形式可用来引导主语,是出现在一个从句形式中的。如:话到死过以后个事体难讲;造到发大财是勿能个。""这些词对于引导作为从句的主语来讲,并不是不可缺少的,如'大是大个(as to size it is large)'。"(p.200)

"与此相似的是放在疑问代词之前的动词形式的结构,由此成为关系词。如:随便那里一样事体要做差个;勿论啥官总要得贿个。"

"由一个动词和名词构成的主语,常带着一个引导性的从句形式。如:待别人要有礼貌;存心要存得好。""许多从属的根据情况的从句是靠动词来引导的,并放在主要陈述语之前。如:落大雨个辰光去者;照之我个想头要换朝代者;读之七年书咾考之秀才;得胜之多回咾末脚死拉战场上。""当前面有否定语助词时,从句中的动词有时放在末尾。如:兵丁勿算武官死有五十干。""表示按照情况的从属性陈述常放在主语和谓语之间。如:贪官已经受之姓张箇银子就拿姓李箇放拉监牢里。"(p.200—201)

"时地从句":"表示时间和地点的从句放在主句之前。如:住拉啥地方勿肯话;清明节气几时黄历上有;到明朝我又到伊墙头去。"(p.200)

"原因从句":"许多从句是表原因的,通过语助词'咾'来与主句连接,或者用'因为'来引导,插入到主句之中。如:做事情勿勤谨咾勿成功者;上司参之伊咾革脱之官者;勿要因为事体多咾勿尽心。连词可以放在引导性从句之前。如:因为三代前

头过第个名字勿可再题。"（P.201）

"条件从句"："表示条件的引导性从句可以由某些语助词的意思形成，或者从它们的位置，或者根据句子的自然特性，来理解成条件从句。a. 没有任何语助词的条件句的例子：勿教训个儿子伊总要人下流。b. 条件分句的末尾有'末'字的例子：家里穷末勿要怨恨爷娘勿发财；要做好官末，只要念头动，舌头动，笔头动，造出多许善事体。c. 条件分句作为一种假设情况，由条件性连词来引导的例子：若使考过秀才要伊去乡试；倘有婚丧喜庆应该请伊吃酒。d. 条件从句作为一种事实，由'既然'或'末'来引导的例子：既然望雨落勿要惹厌日头；既然要末再去买末者。e. 条件分句被引入到主句中间的例子：但是娘子虽然聪明勿好拨伊办外头个事务。"（p.202—204）

后来汉语语法书中都用"偏正复句"、"主谓、动宾词组作定语、宾语"等汉语独特的分析方法解释汉语，实际上是不利于很多语法规律的揭示和解释的。最近刘丹青（2005）主张汉语的句法研究要重新回到世界共性的"从句"概念上来。

谈到省略，艾氏还说到汉语语序位置的重要性，可以引起介词或连词的省略。"就前面数页中所出现的几个例子来说，位置规则常使某些语助词成为多余的。如表示连续性的副词短语中，and、by等是省略的，如'一个一个'one by one；'一日大一日'greater and greater every day。所以，在表示原因、方式、支配等从句中，常省略前置介词。因为它们放在主语之前，很容易被理解的。同样的理由，连词的省略也不影响条件分句（如a组的例句）。"（p.204）

"如果带'得、勿、来'的动词和形容词词组，直接地被认为是原始地构成主体的陈述部分，包括在主语及其谓语本身内，在许多情况下，它们必须被认作从句。a. 这些词组可以形成一个修饰性的分句，或主语的一个谓语。如：做勿来个事体多；礼体好得极。b. 对于一个前边句子的谓语来说，词组可以构成解释性的分句。如：勿好话弄勿来。"（p.204）

下面来看"并列句"。

"可以看到，并列的句子通常出现在没有任何语助词的并列形式中。a. 对一个谓语来讲可以有几个主语。如：文武百官乡绅士庶秃出来求雨。b. 对一个主语来讲可以有几个谓语，或对一个陈述句来讲，可以有几个解释的分句。如：多请朋友勿免浪用钱财废事失业。"（p.205—206）

"连词'咾'是很常见的，用在词组之间；通过中间插入这个语助词'咾'，并列的词的任何词组的结构可以被分开，成为独立的主语、谓语或宾语。如：坟墓周围种个树木咾筑个篱笆；一家里向有爷咾娘咾小团咾差团咾丫头；知县要管个一县里个漕白犯法咾词讼咾验尸个事体。""当要连续地表达两个并列的意思时，可以用'而且’、‘也’和‘又’，相当于 both...and...。如：也要加长也要加阔。”“通过表示反义的语助词 only（仅）、but（但）、yet（仍）等来引导的陈述句，可形成另一类并列句。如：小道理圣人贤人勿屑为，但是平常人全要晓得个；好人该当亲近个倒要远开伊。”（p.206—208）

“推论句和原因句形成了并列句的另一类。如：故此呒没出头个日子；半个身体三个时辰浸拉水里所以怪勿得有点勿自在。”“在原因句中，可用表原因的连词，或在句末用表示原因的词语；有时二者同时使用。如：勿能得胜兵丁勿好个缘故；文理为啥勿好因为读书少。”（p.208）

“句子中用成对的连接形式，有时短的词组可以取代连词。a. 例如 not only...even，可用‘勿要话’和‘就是’表示，用在补充句中：勿要话爷娘教训伊勿转，勿要话亲友劝诫伊勿转，就是菩萨也点化伊勿转。b. 英语中句首的几个短语，例如 I suppose that、probably 可以用‘只怕’、‘恐怕’或‘我想’来表示：打杀之雄鸳雌鸳独干子躲拉恐怕要气杀。”（p.208—209）

从上可见，艾约瑟十分细致地记录了上海方言中的句子的类型及其表达法，我们在现今许多语法书中尚不能看到如此有条理的归纳。

当然，由于 19 世纪中叶的语言学理论和实践的条件限制，艾约瑟在本书中的有些论述也存在可以进一步推敲的地方。比如对非常复杂难辨的上海话复杂型连读变调、重音以及语音词的切割方面的规律，作者的分辨难免有粗疏之处。由于当时没有“语素”一说和汉语“词”一级单位的难以划分，他对汉语的语素、词和词组之间的区分及其与汉字的关系仅用 word、group 的概念分析，因此在使用上有相混之处。他对上海话句子的时态方面的理解和论述也比较粗。但是他毕竟开始了对当时在吴方言中地位和影响还不高的上海方言的系统研究。

本文对于艾氏书中涉及中国东南部其他方言的论述未作评述。

艾约瑟不愧为 19 世纪的一位语言学家，他观察语言的方法和运用的语言学理论在当时都是领先的。他又在不太长的时间内悉心调查和准确观察到了上海话及其周边的许多重要特点，有不少精辟的论述和独到的见解。他的这部著作不论从当时来说还是现今来看，都堪称第一流的语言学著作，为我们保存了上海话语音语法方面最早的相当全面的文献。这是研究中国方言语法的第一部语言学著作，对上海方言和吴语以及中国语言的语法学的创建作出了杰出的贡献，在准确记录和分析研究方言语料方面作出了示范，使上海方言和吴语的语言学研究从一开始就走上了一定的科学高度，迈出了可圈可点的第一步，因此具有开创性的意义。

参考文献

曹剑芬（1982）常阴沙话古全浊声母的发音特点——吴语清浊音辨析之一,《中国语文》第 4 期。

冯胜利（2000）《汉语韵律句法学》, 上海：上海教育出版社。

刘丹青（1994）唯补词初探,《汉语学习》第 3 期。

刘丹青（2003）《语序类型学与介词理论》, 北京：商务印书馆。

刘丹青（2005）语法调查与研究中的从属小句问题,《当代语言学》第 3 期。

平悦铃（2005）《上海方言语音动态腭位研究》, 香港：香港文汇出版社。

钱乃荣（1992）《当代吴语研究》, 上海：上海教育出版社。

钱乃荣（1996）词类与句子成分的对应关系,《汉语拼音小报》6 月 19 日。

钱乃荣（2001）《现代汉语》（修订本）, 南京：江苏教育出版社。

钱乃荣（2003）《上海语言发展史》, 上海人民出版社。

沈钟伟、王士元（1995）吴语浊塞音的研究——统计上的分析和理论上的考虑,《吴语研究》,
　　香港：香港中文大学新亚书院。

石汝杰（1983）《川沙音系》, 复旦大学硕士论文。

游汝杰（1998）西洋传教士著作所见上海话的塞音韵尾,《中国语文》第 2 期。

许宝华、汤珍珠、钱乃荣（1981）新派上海方言的连读变调,《方言》第 2 期。

郑张尚芳（1964）温州方言的连读变调,《中国语文》第 2 期。

朱德熙（1985）《语法答问》, 北京：商务印书馆。

（本文发表于《语言研究集刊》第三辑, 上海辞书出版社, 2006 年, 第 13—44 页）

西洋传教士著作所见上海话的塞音韵尾

游汝杰

西洋传教士艾约瑟 Joseph Edkins（1823—1905）所著 *A Grammar of Colloquial Chinese, as Exhibited in Shanghai Dialect*（《上海话口语语法》，Presbyterian Mission Press，1853 年初版，1868 年第 2 版，共 225 页）是第一部汉语方言语法学著作。此书第一章第四节末尾论及当时上海话的塞音韵尾，此段文字不长，但对吴语塞音韵尾的历史研究很重要。先译述如下：

从韵母表中看到的一个最奇妙的事实，即是带 k（在阳调的字前变为 g）韵尾的促声韵，它们的元音相类似。这个特点在上海西南方向的稍远一点地方就消失了，在宁波话里也没有人提到过。

兹将官话里的促声字（元音）的主要形式，按几种通用的正字法列表如下：

Morrison 和 Medhurst	ă	ě	eě	eïh ih	uě	ĭh	ŭh	ǒ
Prémare	ă	ě	ié	ǐ	ue	ě	uh	ǒ
Williams	áh	eh	ieh	ih	ueh	eh	uh	óh
本书	áh	eh	ieh	ih	iöh	uh	úh	óh

大多数以 k 收尾的促声字的元音是表中最后三个元音：u ú ó。别的促声字，例如包含 ih 的字，如果以 k 收尾，常常指人一个短的 u。例如"力"字听起来是 lik 或 liuk。情况相同的是：包含 uh 或 oh 的字，如果不以 k 收尾，那么 úh 或 óh 就变为 eh。所以"末"móh 就变为 meh。许多符合这一规律的字，韵尾皆如此变化，当避开 k 的时候就用 ah 和 e 配置；如果恢复以 k 结尾韵母则相应地变为 u ú ó。然而应该看到官话的 a 在促声调里变为 a，长的 a 只用作 u 的白读形式。例如"百"，白读为 pák，文读为 puk。因此在上海话里在促声调中 á u ó o 配 k 尾，a e ö 不配辅音韵尾，i 则是普通的（即可配可不配——译注）。

相对于福建话和南方其他方言而言，这条规律比较简单。在那些方言里，据韵书记载，有 p t k 三个韵尾，也能找出它们跟元音的关系。在福建话里三个韵尾除了都可以跟 a 相配外，各自只能跟某些元音相配。

促声调里的 k t p 跟（阳声调的）韵尾 ng n m 相配，这一条南方方言原有的规则不适用于上海以北的方言。就韵尾系统而言，确实有这种限制，但是也不是很严格的。有些以 t 收尾的字既列在以 ng 结尾的字之后，又列在以 n 结尾的字之后。另有些以 k 收尾的字列在以元音收尾的字之后。不过符合的字比例外字要多得多，所以这条规则还是不容置疑的。既然在上海话里只有韵尾 k 仍在使用，那么这条见于韵书的古老的语音规则在现代使用的中心地带一定是更远的南方。实际上使用范围包括从上海到广州的沿海省份以及江西和湖南。兹从韵类的角度来分析见于该书的 k 尾和 h 尾字。

从上述译文中可以看出：第一，艾约瑟对切韵音系的韵尾系统及其与当时方言的关系有相当的了解。第二，当时的上海话里仍有 k 韵尾。作者对它的描写和分析是十分仔细的。作者记录的入声字从韵尾来看分为两类，一类是以 h 收尾的，如"法" fah、"瞎" hah、"月" nioh、"热" nyih；另一类则是以 k 收尾的。k 韵尾的存在应该是可信的。第三，当时上海话的 k 韵尾与元音的关系密切，它只跟某些元音相配。

艾约瑟未将它跟韵类的关系作分析。

见于此书的韵母表及其他部分以 k 收尾的字及读音和所属摄见表 1：

表 1

字	若	略	郭	削	乐	作	霍	脚	虐	格	逆
音	zak	liak	kwok	siak	lok	tsok	hok	kiak	ngok	kak	niuk
韵	药	药	铎	药	铎	铎	铎	铎	药	陌	陌
摄	宕	宕	宕	宕	宕	宕	宕	宕	宕	梗	梗

字	百	划	射	额	革	毒	筑	熟	狱	屋	直	刻
音	pak	vuak	zok	ngak	kak	dok	tsok	zok	niok	ok	dzuk	k'uk
韵	陌	麦	昔	陌	麦	沃	屋	屋	烛	屋	职	德
摄	梗	梗	梗	梗	梗	通	通	通	通	通	曾	曾

"木"字在韵母表里有两读：mok 和 moh；"石"字在韵母表里记为 zak，但是在第 20 页"宝石"一词中记为 zah。此类韵尾有 k 和 h 两读的字及其读音和所属韵摄见表 2：

表 2

字	角	落	国	目	木	吃	读	薄	各	脚	缩	约	独	学	石
音	kok	lok	kok	mok	mok	k'iuk	dok	bok	kok	kiak	sok	yak	dok	hok	zak
	koh	loh	koh/kwoh	moh	moh	k'iuh	doh	boh	koh	kiah	soh	yah	doh	hoh	zak
韵	觉	铎	德	屋	屋	锡	屋	铎	铎	铎	药	屋	觉	昔	
摄	江	宕	曾	通	通	梗	通	宕	宕	宕	宕	屋	通	江	梗

从表 1 和表 2 来看，此书的 k 尾韵有七个：ak，ok，uk，iuk，iak，iok，uak。

见于全书的以 k 收尾的入声字一共有 37 个，包括 15 个收 k 和收 h 两可的入声字。其中"射"字较特殊，"射"字在《广韵》里属假摄祃韵或梗摄昔韵，在今吴语里也有入声一读。其余 36 个字在切韵音系里分别属江摄、宕摄、曾摄、通摄、梗摄。属这几个摄的入声字在中古汉语里都是收 k 尾的。艾约瑟所记的韵尾 h 的实际音值应该就是喉塞音 ʔ，也即今吴语入声韵尾的读音。从"词汇扩散理论"来考察，这 15 个韵尾两可的字，可以认为是正处于变化之中的字，而另 22 个字则是已经完成变化的字，收 h 尾的字则是未变化的字。收 h 尾的字元音是 i、ɿ、ə、e、ø、æ；收 k 尾的元音是 ɔ 和 a。ɔ 和 a 是后低元音。后低元音发音时口腔和喉部展开较大，发音结束后接上一个舌根塞音较方便。从音理上来看，艾约瑟的记录是可信的。

差不多同时艾约瑟还出版了《上海方言词汇》，即，J. Edkins, *A Vocabulary of the Shanghai Dialect*，Shanghai: Presbyterian Mission Press. 151p., 1869。这是最早的上海方言词典。作者为配合所著《上海口语语法》而撰此词典。此书塞音韵尾也分为 -h 和 -k 两套。-h 前的元音短，如 -ih 必；-k 前元音长，如 ok 屋。

见于此书以 k 收尾的字（共 9 个）及读音和所属韵摄见表 3：

表 3

字	托	虐	若	宅	陌	学	录	熟	肉
音	tʻok	ngok	zak	dzak	mak	ok	lok	zok	niok
韵	铎	药	药	陌	陌	觉	烛	屋	屋
摄	宕	宕	宕	梗	梗	江	通	通	通

此书中韵尾有 k 和 h 两读的字（共 12 个）及其读音和所属韵摄见表 4：

表 4

字	恶	着	格	革	陌	隔	百	剥	读	独	毒	醒
音	ok	dazk	kak	kok	mok	kak	pak	pok	dok	dok	dok	ok
	oh	dzah	kah	kah	moh	kah	pah	poh	doh	doh	doh	oh
韵	铎	药	麦	陌	陌	陌	陌	觉	屋	屋	沃	烛
摄	宕	宕	梗	梗	梗	梗	梗	江	通	通	通	通

从艾约瑟的记录来看在当时的上海话里塞音韵尾 k 和 ʔ 并存。在现代的某些汉语方言里也可以发现这两个塞音韵尾并存的现象。例如现代海南文昌方言有四种塞音韵

尾:"纳、力、六、腊"分别收 -p/-t/-k/-ʔ;现代的福州话塞音韵尾大多数人只有一种 -ʔ,但是也有一部分老年人和中年人是 -ʔ 和 -k 并存的,大致是 ɛ、æ 和 ɔ 韵读 -ʔ 尾,其他韵母读 -k 尾。不过 -k 尾韵正在逐渐减少。所以从方言比较的角度来看,艾约瑟的记录也是可信的。

同时代的其他传教士有关上海话的著作也分塞音韵尾为 k 和 h 两类,就我所见,还有以下数种。

第一种

J. MacGowan, *A Collection of Phrases in the Shanghai Dialect*, Shanghai: Presbyterian Mission Press, 193p, 1862.

作者中文名为麦考文。此书是为初学者所写的上海话课本。也是最早的用西文写的上海话课本。全一书按话题分为 29 课,如家长、数目、商业等。课文前有罗马字母标音说明,如 h 前的 a 很像 mat 中的 a,主要说明元音,对辅音只是简略交待,很像英语,除 j 像法语外。每课先出中文,后出罗马字。不标声调。入声韵尾分为 -h 和 -k 两套。

见于此书的以 k 收尾的字(共 33 个)及读音和所属韵摄见表 5:

表 5

字	搁	落	恶	烙	络	作	霍	索	各	凿	酌
音	kok	zak	ok	lok	lok	tsok	hok	sok	kok	zok	tsak
韵	铎	铎	铎	铎	铎	铎	铎	铎	铎	铎	铎
摄	宕	宕	宕	宕	宕	宕	宕	宕	宕	宕	宕
字	略	着	约	觉	乐	戳	浊	角	龌	学	捉
音	leak	tsak	yak	kok	ngok	tsok	dzok	kok	ok	ok	tsok
韵	药	药	药	觉	觉	觉	觉	觉	觉	觉	觉
摄	宕	宕	宕	江	江	江	江	江	江	江	江
字	逆	射	石	麦	划	速	簏	读	屋	祝	烛
音	niuk	sok	sak	mak	vak	sok	lok	tok	wuk	tsok	tsok
韵	陌	昔	昔	麦	麦	屋	屋	屋	屋	屋	烛
摄	梗	梗	梗	梗	梗	通	通	通	通	通	通

韵尾有 -k 和 -h 两读的字(共 11 个)及其读音和所属韵摄见表 6:

表 6

字	药	筑	剥	国	直	测	木	六	福	督	玉
音	yak	tsok	pok	kok	tsuk	t'sak	mok	lok	fok	tok	niok
	yah	tsoh	poh	koh	tsuh	t'sah	moh	loh	foh	toh	nioh
韵	药	屋	觉	德	职	职	屋	屋	屋	沃	烛
摄	宕	通	江	曾	曾	曾	通	通	通	通	通

从表 5 和表 6 可知，此书的 k 尾韵有六个：ok，ak，uk，iuk，eak，iok。从韵类来看麦考文的 k 尾韵比艾约瑟少了一个 uak，而且在字音分布上也有所不同，例如"学、各"两字，麦考文只收 -k 尾，艾约瑟则是 -k 尾和 -h 尾两可。

第二种

上海土白《马太福音》（罗马字本），1895 年。

此书收 -k 尾入声字共 61 个，在各摄的分布如下：

宕摄 15 字：约着博药若脚却摸弱雀缚薄膊削酌

梗摄 15 字：伯百石麦役白拍掰吓客隔拆只责赤

通摄 24 字：督牧束秃独伏服福狱蓄木屋读族卜哭嘱祝渎六覆复仆录

江摄 1 字：剥

曾摄 3 字：国或惑

臻摄 1 字：实

山摄 1 字：活

其余入声字一律收 -h 尾。同一个入声字只用一种韵尾，没有有时收 -k 尾，有时收 -h 尾的两可现象。

第三种

Gilbert McIntosh, *Useful Phrases in the Shanghai Dialect, with Index, Vocabulary and Other Helps*, Shanghai: American Presbyterian Mission Press, 109p, 1906; 2nd ed., 113p, 19cm, 1908; 5th ed., 121p, 1922; 7th ed., 1927.

全书分 22 课，每课有若干英、中、罗马字对照的句子。书前有罗马字拼音说明。书末有英文和罗马字对照的词汇索引。从第四版（作者序于 1921 年）开始增加一课《新词语》（有轨电车和无轨电车）。增加的一课是 R. P. Montgomery 所定。不标声调。据二版（1908 年）序言，罗马字系统是参用 J. A. Silsby 创制的系统。此系统最初用于上海市政委员会出版的警察守则，于 1899 年为沪语社（the Shanghai Vernacular Society）所采用。初版时所写的罗马字拼音系统说明将入声分为 -h 和 -k 两套。-k 尾韵有三个：

ak ok iak，比艾约瑟的记录少了两个，即 uak 和 uok。用例如下：邮政局 Yeu-tsung-jok（p43）；英国 Iung-kok（p5）；著之（外罩衣装）tsak-ts（p51）；脚 kyak（p28）；iak 韵未见用例。同一个入声字只用一种韵尾，没有有时收 -k 尾，有时收 -h 尾的两可现象。

第四种

Hawks Pott, D. D., *Lessons in the Shanghai: Dialect*, Shanghai Presbyterian Mission Press, 99p, 1907; 151p, rev. ed., 1913; 174p, rev. ed., MeiHua Press, Shanghai, 1939. (French Translation, Imprimerie de la Misson Catholique, Shanghai, 1922; 1939)

此书入声韵分为收 -h 和收 -k 两套，即 ah，eh，ih，auh，oeh，uh 和 ak，ok，iak。同一个入声字只用一种韵尾，没有有时收 -k 尾，有时收 -h 尾的两可现象。从 1907 年序刊的《前言》可知，此书拼写法采用上海传教士所用的罗马字系统（the Shanghai System of Romanization）。这个系统最初可能是 J. A. Silsby 牧师制定的。他曾于 1897年出版上海话音节表，即 J. A. Silsby, *Shanghai Syllabary, Arranged in phonetic order*, 42p, Shanghai: American Presbyterian Mission Press, 1897。

第五种

D. H. Davis, D. D., *Shanghai Dialect Exercises, in romanized and character, with key to pronunciation and English index*, 278p，上海徐家汇土山湾印书馆 1910 年。

此书将入声韵分为收 -h 和收 -k 两套，即 ah，eh，ih，auh，oeh，uh 和 ak，ok，iak。与上述 Pott 课本一样。同一个入声只用一种韵尾，没有有时收 -k 尾，有时收 -h 尾的两可现象。此书《前言》指出："应该出现韵尾 k 的地方有时却用 h"。

第六种

R. A. Parker, *Lessons in the Shanghai Dialect*, Shanghai: Shanghai Municipal Council, Kwang Hsueh Publishing House（广学书局），1923.

书前《标音说明》将入声韵分为收 -h 和收 -k 两套，即 ah，eh，ih，auh，oeh，uh 和 ak，ok，iak。与上述 Pott 课本一样。同一个入声字只用一种韵尾，没有有时收 -k 尾，有时收 -h 的两可现象。作者并指出 h 也用于指示它前面的元音。ah 的发音好像英语 at 中的 a；ak 发音好像英语 what 中的 a。

从以上八种文献，可以发现下述基本事实：

第一，西洋传教士的著作将上海话的入声韵分为收 -k 尾和收 -h 尾两套。

第二，收 -k 尾的入声韵属宕摄、江摄、通摄、梗摄、曾摄。属这几个摄的入声字在中古汉语里都是收 -k 尾的。

第三，宕摄、江摄、通摄、梗摄、曾摄字的韵尾分为三类，第一类只收 -k 尾，第二类只收 -h 尾，第三类收 -k 尾或收 -h 尾两可。

第四，将上海话的入声韵分为收 -k 尾和收 -h 尾两套，最初见于艾约瑟著作，也见于差不多同时代的麦考文的著作，但两者在韵类和字音分布上不甚相同。入声韵分为收 -k 尾和收 -h 尾两套的这一标音原则为后出的英美传教士所采用，并曾于 1899 年为沪语社所公认。

通过对上述八种文献的分析，可以得出几点结论。

第一，十九世纪上海话的塞音韵尾分为收 -k 尾和收 -h 尾两套。前者相当于今粤语的 -k 韵尾，后者相当今吴语的喉塞音韵尾 -ʔ。

第二，带 -k 尾的入声韵主元音大多是低元音 a 或后元音 o。

第三，-k 尾正处于演变为 -ʔ 尾的过程中。

第四，艾约瑟和麦考文的记录比较可靠，二十世纪初年的文献可能是因袭 J. A. Silsby 牧师制定的拼音系统。

第五，上海话的塞音韵尾 -k 并入喉塞音韵尾 -ʔ 的年代下限是十九世纪末至二十世纪初。

参考文献

周同春（1988）十九世纪的上海语音，《吴语论丛》，上海：上海教育出版社。

（本文发表于《中国语文》1998 年第 2 期，第 108—112 页）

论 160 年前上海话声母 [dz]/[z] 变异

——兼论北部吴语从邪澄崇船禅等母读音变异现象*

陈忠敏

壹 引言

赵元任在（1928/2011: 39—40）谈到吴语声母时说："'j'系里所以不一定加'dj'，是因为古音的床禅跟今音的'dj''zh'都是一笔糊涂账，能分辨的如常熟、常州、宁波等地，它们辨类的法子，又是一处一个样子，所以只拼为一个'zh'类。同样，从邪母也一律用'z'代表，不另加'dz'。这一笔糊涂账并不是不值得算，是因为一时不容易算出来，等算出来了关于古今方言的异同上可以有一种有趣的比较。"他所说的声母实际上包括古从、邪、澄、崇、船、禅六母。本文分析 160 年前传教士的上海话记音中 [dz]/[z] 声母变异，并比较今北部吴语相关情况，来讨论和解答赵先生所说的"糊涂账"。

英国传教士 Joseph Edkins（艾约瑟，1823—1905）1853 年编写的 *A Grammar of Colloquial Chinese, as Exhibited in the Shanghai Dialect*（《上海方言口语语法》）是一部记录开埠初期上海县城的方言面貌的专著，对当时的上海县城方言的语音、词汇、句法等所作的描写十分精当、仔细。经总结，Edkins 记录的当时上海县城话的声母共有 29 个（陈忠敏 1995），见表 1。

表 1

p [ʔb] 比	p' [pʰ] 批	*p*, b [b] 皮	m [m] 米	f [f] 飞	*f*, v [v] 微
d, t [ʔd] 多	t [tʰ] 拖	*t*, d [d] 杜	n [n] 怒		l [l] 路
ts [ts] 精	ts' [tsʰ] 清	*ts*, dz [dz] 尽		s [s] 心	*s*, z [z] 寻
ki [c] 鸡	k'i [cʰ] 去	*ki*, gi [ɟ] 其	nj [ɲ] 拟	hi [ç] 希	dj [j] 序
k [k] 公	k' [kʰ] 空	*k*, g [g] 共	ng [ŋ] 我	h [h] 火	*h*, y, w [ɦ] 河
ø [ʔ] 爱					

* 本研究受国家社科基金重点项目"上海市方言地图集"（批准号 15AYY005）、国家社科基金重大项目"汉语方言自然口语变异有声数据库建设"（批准号 12&ZD177）子课题"上海方言自然口语变异有声数据库建设"资助，特此鸣谢。

表 1 中方括号内是拟音（据陈忠敏 1995 略作改动），方括号外是 Edkins 的标写，以下同。中古全浊声母原书用两套字母标写，处于词首或句首的，用一套斜写的清音字母，即 *p*，*t*，*ts*，*ki*，*k*，*f*，*s*，*h*；处于连读音节中或者句末、词末的，则用一套浊音字母标写，b，d，dz，gi，g，z，dj（y，w）；不过也有例外，处于词首 / 句首有时也用浊音字母标写。本文为清晰计，统一都用浊音字母。双唇、舌尖塞音有先喉塞音（pre-glottalized stop），又可称为内爆音（implosive）；古见组、晓匣组声母在细音（i[i]、ü[y]）前腭化，不过舌面收紧点较靠后，是舌面中音；阳调类零声母字合口的（不包括 u 韵）用小写的 w 表示，如"划"wáh [ɦuaʔ]，u 韵跟开口呼同，用斜体 *h* 表示，如"河"*h*u[ɦu]，齐齿呼的（不包括 i 韵）用小写的 y 表示，如"药"yáh[ɦiaʔ]，i 韵跟开口呼同，用斜体 *h* 表示，如"移"*h*i[ɦii]，撮口呼 ü[y] 韵无特殊标记，如"雨"ü[y]。

今上海市区方言多数派声母有 28 个，见表 2。

表 2

[p] 比	[pʰ] 批	[b] 皮	[m] 米	[f] 飞	[v] 微
[t] 多	[tʰ] 拖	[d] 杜	[n] 怒		[l] 路
[ts] 真	[tsʰ] 村			[s] 生	[z] 存
[tɕ] 鸡	[tɕʰ] 去	[dʑ] 其	[n̠] 拟	[ɕ] 希	[ʑ] 序
[k] 公	[kʰ] 空	[g] 共	[ŋ] 我	[h] 火	[ɦ] 河
ø [ʔ] 爱					

比较表 1 和表 2 可知，今天上海市区方言多数派声母系统与 160 年前的上海县城话声母系统唯一的不同就是后者多了个舌尖浊塞擦音 [dz] 声母。

贰 对传教士记录的分析

从中古音来源来看，160 年前上海话 [dz] 声母的字涵盖从、邪、澄、崇、船、禅六母。Edkins 书里能收集到的读 [dz] 声母的汉字有（黑体字有 [dz]/[z] 异读）：[从] **齐在罪造聚就裁**瞧**财钱**前**存贱从全泉**暂**尽情墙樯牂贼杂昨**秦；[邪] 随辞**绪序**袖寻循席；[澄] 池住茶除**朝**轴**沉**站场长肠丈**重撞**阵**传**篆**着**直逐俦浊；[崇] **柴豺**助查乍；[船] **剩射**；[禅] **辰城**成常。

这六母涉及中古精、知、庄、章的浊塞擦、擦音。这个 [dz] 声母可以跟细音、洪音相配，也可以跟阴声韵、阳声韵、促声韵相配（拟音见陈忠敏 1995，下同）。如：情 dzing[dziŋ]，聚 dzü[dzy]，财 dzé[dze]，重 dzóng[dzoŋ]，射 dzák[dzaʔ]。这六母中也有许多只读浊擦音 [z] 的字。如在 Edkim 书里下列这些字只有 [z] 声母一种读法：[从] 自慈字坐座才瓷曹漕蚕绝匠曾层静净；[邪] 徐邪斜谢旋详象像习俗寺词；[澄] 厨迟潮赵绸陈虫；[崇] 闸事；[船] 船神顺绳舌实食；[禅] 树仇受寿善上臣甚裳尚石十什拾熟折时是市竖。

能读 [dz] 声母的字，很多都有 [z] 声母的异读。如：在 dzé[dze]（242 节，"现在"），zé[ze]（53 节，"实在"）；罪 dzûi[dzɤe]（45 节，"罪"），zûe[zɤe]（40 节，"罪"）；前 dzien[dziẽ]（36 节，"前世"），zien[ziẽ]（177 节，"前日子"）；随 dzûi[dzɤe]（49 节，"随便"），zûe[zɤe]（40 节，"随"）；寻 dzing[dziŋ]（54 节，"寻"），zing[ziŋ]（227 节，"寻得着"）；传 dzén[dzẽ]（68 节，"传下来"），zén[zẽ]（383 节，"传下来"）；朝 dzau[dzɔ]（404 节，"朝代"），zau[zɔ]（258 节，"朝西转弯"）；豺 dzé[dze]（68 节，"豺狼虎豹"），za[za]（68 节，"豺狼虎豹"）；柴 dzé[dze]（68 节，"柴门"），za[za]（68 节，"稻柴"）；射 dzák[dzaʔ]（283 节，"射角 obliquely"），zok[zoʔ]（218 节，"射箭"）；城 dzung[dzʌŋ]（37 节，"城头"），zung[zʌŋ]（37 节，"京城"）；辰 dzun(g)[dzʌŋ]（55 节，"日月星辰"），zun(g)[zʌŋ]（404 节，"辰光"）。

John MacGowan（麦高温）1862 年著有 *A Collection of Phrases in Shanghai Dialect*，所记的上海方言也有 [dz]/[z] 声母异读，也涵盖从、邪、澄、崇、船、禅六母。不过，哪些字读 [dz] 声母，哪些字 [z] 读声母，哪些字有异读，跟 Edkins 所记录的不尽相同（据钱乃荣 2013 总结）：从母 [dz] 在座藏情尽罪绝钱财，[z] 就净匠蚕前皂贼造静坐杂墙截族；邪母 [dz] 随俗，[z] 席旋涎斜像象；澄母 [dz] 茶厨肠长潮阵沉绸赚场直值朝重著宅传侄，[z] 直场尘；崇母 [dz] 煤；船母 [dz] 剩乘，[z] 绳神船顺实赎才食；禅母 [dz] 常，[z] 上市寿时裳熟是城尚辰善。

从古音来源看，读 [dz] 还是 [z] 显得毫无规律。钱乃荣（2013）认为这反映了上海话 [dz] 到 [z] 的音变现象，某些字的 [dz]/[z] 异读是 [dz] 到 [z] 音变中间环节中的词汇扩散现象。

笔者认为这并不是音变问题，而是文白异读相互竞争、相互替代现象，其中读 [dz] 声母是文读层，读 [z] 的是白读层。理由如下：

第一，Edkins 在书中 68 节有一段说明，文内 R. 表示文读（reading form），C. 表示白读（colloquial form）："The d is in some words retained in reading, when dropped in the colloquial form." 原书举例：豺狼虎豹 zá (R. dzé) long 'hú pau' [za R. (dze) lã hu pɔ]；稻柴 *t*au zá (C.) [dɔ za]；柴门 dzé (R.) mun [dze mʌŋ]；造完 'zau (R. dzau) wén [zɔ (R.

dzɔ) uɛ̃]。

今苏州话音系没有 [dz] 声母，不过，苏州话在十九世纪末也是有 [dz] 声母的。苏州传教协会（The Soochow Missionary Association）在 1891 年编著的《苏州方言字音表》（*A Syllabary of the Soochow Dialect*）就列有 [dz] 声母，并有特别的说明："The initial is usually pronounced as z, by the common people. Scholars, however, prefer dz." 这跟上述 Edkins 的说明有异曲同工之处，更加证明上海、苏州两地方言的 [dz]/[z] 的变异是文白异读。

第二，文白异读一般在词汇上具有语体色彩的通俗与文雅之分，一般来说文读音出现在比较文雅的词语中，而白读音出现在常用的口语词语中。从 Edkins 所收集的词语的语体色彩来看也符合 [z] 声母字口语化、[dz] 声母字文言化的趋势。如："罪"在 46 节口语词"罪过"中的记音是 zé [ze]，同节"定罪"中的"罪"记音是 dzûe [dzɥe]；"辰"在 55 节"日月星辰"中记音为 dzun(g) [dzʌŋ]，在 404 节"辰光"这一口语词中记音为 zun(g) [zʌŋ]；"柴"在 68 节口语词"稻柴"一词中记音为 zá [za]，在同节"柴门"一词中记 dzé [dze]。上述各词 [dz] 声母与文言词语对应，[z] 声母与土白色彩词语对应非常明显，[dz] 文读，[z] 白读的关系一目了然。

第三，北部吴语里，声母系统中有 [dz] 和 [z] 对立的，且字有 [dz]/[z] 异读的，往往也是读 [dz] 声母的是文读音，读 [z] 声母的是白读音。如江苏海门话精、庄、章组全浊声母三四等字读塞擦音 [dz(dʑ)] 声母的是文读，读擦音 [ɕz] 声母的是白读（王洪钟 2011：82—83）：钱 ɕzie^2 | dʑie^2 || 净 ɕzin^6 | dʑin^6 || 坐座 szu^4 | dzu^4 || 造 szɔ^4 | dzɔ^4 || 唇辰晨 szən^2 | dzən^2。

浙江临安、湖州等地方言从、邪、澄、崇、船、禅等六母也多混，今声母读浊塞擦音 [dz dʑ] 的多为文读层声母，读对应的浊擦音 [z ʑ] 则为白读层声母（徐越 2007：61，79）。如临安话：词 zɿ^2 | dzɿ^2 || 治 / 社 zue^6/zuo^6 | dze^6 || 谁 zue^2/zuo^2 | dze^2。

北部吴语各点从、邪、澄、崇、船、禅六母浊塞擦音 / 擦音差异构成一致的文白异读系统差异，也可证明 160 年前上海话 [dz]/[z] 的变异也是文白异读的差异，而不是 [dz]>[z] 的音变。

叁　北部吴语相关现象的分析

江南一带方言从邪、船禅不分由来已久。《颜氏家训·音辞篇》就说"南人以钱（从）为涎（邪），以石（禅）为射（船），以溅（从）为羡（邪），以是（禅）为舐（船）"。日本空海所著《篆书万象名义》更多保留原本《玉篇》的反切。今本《玉篇》从邪母有分，而《篆书万象名义》反切里以邪母字切从母字者很多，也反映了当时江南吴语从邪母不分（周祖谟 1966）。陆德明《经典释文》中也指出当时的江南方言的这一现象：聚，似主反，又俗裕反，"聚"是从母字，"似"是邪母字，以"似"为"聚"的反切上字，也说明当时江南方言从邪不分的现象。周祖谟（1966）认为："广韵'钱''贱'为从母字，'涎''羡'为邪母字，南人以钱为涎、以贱为羡者谓读涎为钱，读羡为贱，是江东语音邪母读为从母，音 dz，不音 z。"

其实《颜氏家训》并不能说明当时江南从邪两母到底是读浊擦音还是浊塞擦音。唐《可洪音义》倒是能证明当时的吴语从邪两母都是读浊擦音。其卷二五说："渍，疾赐反……，又似赐反者吴音也。""渍疾"从母，"似"邪母。联系今北部吴语，读擦音为白读，读塞擦音为文读，更能判断当时江南一带从邪、船禅不分的读音应该是浊擦音，而不是浊塞擦音。

今杭州话从、邪、澄、崇、船、禅等六母基本上只有塞擦音一读，所以郑张尚芳认为从邪母读塞擦音这种文读层是以杭州话为中心向周边吴语扩散开去的（郑张尚芳 2007）。现在看来在北部吴语作为文读的 [dz] 或 [dʑ] 声母不仅包括从邪母，还应包括澄母、船母、崇母、禅母等，而它们对应的白读层读音是浊擦音 [z] 或 [ʑ] 声母。我们认为北部吴语从、邪、澄、崇、船、禅等六母读浊塞擦音这种文读的来源是早期的杭州话。

南宋以后，杭州话的影响力在整个江南地区式微，从、邪、澄、崇、船、禅等六母读塞擦音的文读层读音在跟读擦音的白读层读音竞争中也逐渐退出历史舞台。不过，文读层消失的过程和程度在各地吴语是不一的，有的消失得快，有的消失得慢；有的一部分字里消失，有的则是大部分字里消失，以至于此六母在今北部吴语对应复杂、混乱。表3是浙北杭嘉湖吴语和上海话从、邪、澄、崇、船、禅等六母读音对照（杭嘉湖各点材料取自徐越 2007 第八章"字音对照"；Edkins 的是拟音；高本汉上海记音据《中国音韵学研究》第四卷"方言字汇"）。

表3

	罪	象	随	袖	重	直	柴	虫	船	涉
杭州	dzɥei⁶	dʑiaŋ⁶	dzɥei²	dʑiɣ⁶	dzoŋ⁶	dzəʔ⁸	dzɛ²	dzoŋ²	dzuɐ²	dzəʔ⁸
余杭	dze⁶	dʑiã⁶	zɛ²	dʑiɯ⁶	dzoŋ⁶	dzəʔ⁸	dza²	dzoŋ²	zuo	dzəʔ⁸
临安	dze⁶	ziã⁶	ze²	zɣ⁶	dzoŋ⁶	dzɛʔ⁸	za²	dzoŋ²	zœ²	dzɛʔ⁸
昌化	zei⁶	ziã⁶	zei²	zi⁶	zəŋ⁶	dzieʔ⁸	za²	zəŋ²	zyɛ̃²	dzyʔ⁸
富阳	dze⁶	ziã⁶	ze²	ziɥ⁶	dʑyoŋ⁶	dzɛʔ⁸	za²	dʑyoŋ²	zyɛ̃¹	dzɛʔ⁸

（续表）

嘉兴	zue⁴	dziã⁴	zue²	dziu⁶	zoŋ⁶	zɤʔ⁸	za²	zoŋ²	zɤ²	zɤʔ⁸
嘉善	zɛ⁶	ziɛ̃⁶	zɛ²	ziə⁶	zoŋ⁶	zəʔ⁸	za²	zoŋ²	zø²	zøʔ⁸
平湖	zue⁶	ziã⁶	zue²	ziou⁶	zoŋ⁶	zəʔ⁸	za²	zoŋ²	zø²	zɤʔ⁸
海盐	zue⁴	dziã⁴	ze²	ze⁶	zoŋ⁶	zəʔ⁸	za²	zoŋ²	zɤ²	zəʔ⁸
海宁	zɛ⁴	ziaŋ4	zɛ²	zɤɯ⁶	zoŋ⁶	zɤʔ⁶	za²	zoŋ²	zɤ̃²	zyɤʔ⁸
桐乡	dzi⁴	zia⁴	zi²	zɯ⁶	dzoŋ⁴	dzəʔ⁸	za²	dzoŋ²	zɛ̃²	zɛʔ⁸
湖州	ze⁴	ziã⁴	dze²	ziʉ⁶	dzoŋ⁴	dzəʔ⁸	za²	dzoŋ²	zɛ²	dzeʔ⁸
德清	zɛ⁴	ziã⁴	ze²	zø⁶	zoŋ⁶	zəʔ⁸	za²	zoŋ²	zø²	zəʔ⁸
安吉	zei⁴	zia⁴	dzei²	ziʉ⁶	dzoŋ⁴	dzəʔ⁸	za²	dzoŋ²	zɛ²	dzəʔ⁸
长兴	zei⁴	ziã⁴	dzei²	zi⁶	dzoŋ⁴	dzəʔ⁸	za²	dzoŋ²	zɤ²	dzəʔ⁸
Edkins	dz/zɥe⁴	ziã⁴	dz/zɥe²	ziɤ⁶	dz/zoŋ⁴	dzʌʔ⁸	dze²/ za²	zoŋ²	zẽ²	dzʌʔ⁸
高本汉	dzœ		dzœ	ziə	dzoŋ	dzəʔ	za	dzoŋ	ze	dzəʔ

从表 3 可以看出杭州话所有字声母都读塞擦音，其他各点每个字读擦音还是塞擦音并不一致。其中"柴""船"是江南一带十分重要的生活材料和交通工具，两个字只有杭州话读塞擦音，其他各点都是擦音，也就是说其他各点都用白读层的读音，这符合文白异读在词语中的惯例。苏南吴语从邪母读塞擦音还是擦音各点的对应也不十分整齐（王轶之 2011）。我认为由于杭州话权威地位的消退，在北部吴语里这一文读层的标记正逐渐退出历史舞台。换句话说，语言接触（文白读竞争）产生不同语言层次的逐词（字）替代，才会出现这种混乱的状态。

肆　上海话 [dz] 声母消失的年代

上海话这一层文读音的消失大概在上世纪初期。1900 年 Davis & Silsby 的 *Shanghai Vernacular Chinese-English Dictionary* 中的汉字记音从、邪、澄、崇、船、禅等六母虽然也有记为 [dz] 的，但是词典的前言说 [dz] 母在大多数上海出生的人中已经归为 [z] 母了，有的还有 [dz]/[z] 异读。如从母字"情"，他标写了两个读音：dziŋ/ziŋ，从母字"昨"他标写了六种读音：dzo/dzoʔ/dzɔʔ/zo/zɔ/zɔʔ，三种是浊塞擦音，另三种则是浊擦音。

高本汉（1915—1926）的上海话记音也保留 [dz] 声母。以从母字为例，高氏收从母字共 47 个，其中 31 个从母字读浊塞擦音 [dz]："慈材在齐罪惭錾潜渐残贱全秦尽存曾赠情藏囚聚丛从杂捷集截绝疾籍寂"；16 个字记浊擦音 [z]："座自字蚕前静墙匠曹皂就袖贼昨嚼族"。

不过所记 31 个读 [dz-] 的从母字里，有一部分有浊擦音 [z-] 的异读，高氏把这些音放在附注里。它们是（高氏著作原文入声韵没有 [-ʔ] 韵尾，今按上海话读音加入韵尾 [-ʔ]）："齐" 578 页记 [dzi]，附注说还有 [zi] 另读；"鉴" 588 页记 [dzɛ]，附注说还有 [ze] 另读；"潜" 592 页记 [dzie]，附注说还有 [zie] 另读；"全" 612 页记 [dzie]，附注说还有 [ze/dze] 另读；"曾" 627 页记 [dzəŋ]，附注说还有 [zəŋ] 另读；"情" 632 页记 [dziŋ]，631 页附注说还有 [ziŋ] 另读；"聚" 680 页记 [dzy]，679 页附注说还有 [zʯ] 另读；"杂" 690 页记 [dzeʔ]，附注说还有 [zeʔ] 另读；"截" 700 页记 [dziʔ]，附注说还有 [ziʔ] 另读；"席" 715 页记 [dziʔ]，附注说还有 [ziʔ] 另读。

可见高氏更看重方言读音跟中古音类的对应，所以他的记音是选择读书音或规范读音。古从、澄、崇、船四母如果有读 [dz/z] 异读的，就主记浊塞擦音，浊擦音只在附注里交待。

赵元任（1928）记录上海话分为三派：旧、混、新，三派都没有 [dz] 声母，从、邪、澄、崇、船、禅六母统统记为 [z]。他的调查略晚于高本汉，相信应该跟高本汉记音不会差距很大，上海话 [dz] 声母不至于在短短十几年内一下子消失殆尽，这也是我们怀疑高本汉记音具有选择性的一个理由。大概到了上世纪初，随着杭州话在吴语里的权威地位逐渐消失，此六母的文读层读音 [dz] 也从上海话里消失。在北部吴语里，这一文读层总的趋势是在不断的消亡过程中，不过各地消亡的程度不一，哪些字先消失，哪些字还保留 [dz] 声母也有参差。

伍　结语

语音变化除了语言内部自身的变化外，还有由语言接触激发的变化。新语法学派强调的规则音变是指语言内部的音变，把语言接触激发的音变排除在外。其实两种音变都会产生不规则的音变现象，即我们所讲的语音变异。不过两种变异性质不同，表现形式也会不一样。由语言内部造成的语音变异是一个音变链上的前后阶段，表现为词汇扩散式（lexicon diffusion）的音变（王士元 1988）。160 年前上海话的 [dz]/[z] 变异并不是音变链中前后两个阶段，上海话里不存在浊塞擦音变为浊擦音的平行音变，比如没有 [dz] 变为 [z] 的音变。由语言接触，特别是文白异读，引起的变异往往跟词或字的语体色彩有关，这也是我们判断 160 年前上海话的 [dz]/[z] 变异是语言接触造成的变异的一个理由。由于杭州话权威性在各吴语点消退的程度不一，所以各地从、

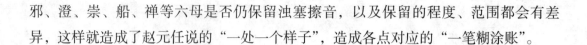

邪、澄、崇、船、禅等六母是否仍保留浊塞擦音，以及保留的程度、范围都会有差异，这样就造成了赵元任说的"一处一个样子"，造成各点对应的"一笔糊涂账"。

参考文献

陈忠敏（1995）上海市区话语音一百多年来的演变，载《吴语和闽语的比较研究》，上海：上海教育出版社。

高本汉（1915—1926/1940）《中国音韵学研究》（中译本），长沙：商务印书馆。

钱乃荣（2013）从 19 世纪英国传教士上海方言著作中的五项音变看词汇扩散，《大江东去——王士元教授八十岁贺寿文集》，石锋、彭刚主编，香港：香港城市大学出版社。

王洪钟（2011）《海门方言研究》，北京：中华书局。

王士元（1988）语言的演变，《语言学论丛》第十一辑，北京：商务印书馆。

王轶之（2011）从邪母在北吴中的演变初探，《中国语言学集刊》第五卷第一期，北京：中华书局。

徐越（2007）《浙北杭嘉湖方言语音研究》，北京：中国社会科学出版社。

赵元任（1928/2011）《现代吴语的研究》，北京：商务印书馆。

郑张尚芳（2007）吴语中官话层次分析的方言史价值，《历史层次与方言研究》，丁邦新主编，上海：上海教育出版社。

周祖谟（1966）万象名义中之原本玉篇音系，《问学集》（上），北京：中华书局。

Edkins, Joseph (1853) *A Grammar of Colloquial Chinese, as Exhibited in the Shanghai Dialect.* Shanghai: Shanghai Presbyterian Mission Press.

Davis, D. H. & J. A. Silsby (1900) *Shanghai Vernacular Chinese-English Dictionary.* Shanghai: The American Presbyterian Mission Press.

MacGowan, John (1862) *A Collection of Phrases in Shanghai Dialect.* Shanghai: Shanghai Presbyterian Mission Press.

Soochow Literary Association (1892) *A Syllabary of the Soochow Dialect.* Shanghai: Shanghai Presbyterian Mission Press.

（本文发表于《方言》2015 年第 4 期，第 340—345 页）

一个语法层次演变的实例
——上海方言 160 年中现在完成时态的消失过程

钱乃荣

在时态中间，现在完成时态是最为常用的一个时态，在上海城区方言（通称上海话）里，"时"和"体"结合的现在完成时态是最后一个消失的时态形式。此形态消失后，北方方言的体形态、时范畴用词汇形式表达的方式终于完全覆盖了上海话的时体表达形式。但在旧松江府（原包括松江方言区和上海方言区）的大片农村中，现在完成时态至今仍然存在。

一　老上海话中时体结合的现在完成时态

1843 年上海开埠后，西方传教士和日本学者从 1853 年起写了大量的上海方言著作，他们都记录了上海方言里的"现在完成时态"句式，如 1853 年艾约瑟的《上海口语语法》，1862 年麦高温的《上海方言习惯用语集》，1892 年御幡雅文的《沪语便商》，直到 1939 年蒲君南的《上海方言课本》等。

上海话的现在完成时态的肯定形式是"V 拉哉"，疑问形式是"V 拉蛮"，否定形式是"勿曾 V"。这个时态的句子与上海话其他时态的句子一样是用"SOV"或"TSV"的语序表达的。[1] "V 拉"本是上海话存续体的形式，表示动作行为发生或完成后所产生的状态在延续着，如："我坐拉。"大致是普通话"我坐在那儿"或"我坐着"的意思。"哉 [tsɛ]"（或写作"者"），原来是在上海话某些句子末尾表示"当下状态"的语气助词，大致相当于普通话的"了₂"，如"我吃仔饭哉。"是普通话"我吃了饭了"的意思。表示完成后延续的"拉 [lɑ]"与表示当下状态的"哉"结合，即构成"现在完成时态"，表示到现在为止事件行为已完成的语法意义。"蛮"音"[mɛ̃]"，笔者认为是"勿曾"的合音词。[2] "蛮"后来随着 19 世纪末上海话中咸山摄字的鼻化音消失元音高化促音化，而读作"[meʔ]"，写作"末"或"没"。

150 年前，上海话的"现在完成时态"，与英语的"现在完成时"相对应，例句如下。英国传教士多以英语的"现在完成时态"的形式来翻译这些句子。

（1）一百块洋钱我已经收拉哉。（麦 51 页。I have already received one hundred dollars. 英语翻译是书中原文，"麦"为麦高温（1862）的简称，下同）

（2）小囡睏起拉哉。（麦 52 页。The child has gone to sleep.）

（3）奶婶婶已经有一个拉哉。（麦 51 页。I have already obtained a wet nurse.）

（4）辛俸付过拉侬拉哉。（麦 53 页。Your wages have been given to you.）

（5）就是上回老爷教我去寻个几部书，寻着之咾，担来拉者。就是上次老爷叫我去找的几部书，找到后已经拿来了。[3]（土 47 页。"土"为师中董（1908）的简称，下同）

（6）大个妹妹末，出嫁拉者。大的妹妹，已经出嫁了。（松 141 页。"松"为 Morrison（1883）的简称，下同）

（7）侬话拉几样小物事，现在做末做拉者，还勿曾烧。你说到的几件小东西，现在已经做了，还没有烧。（土 22 页）

（8）账还清拉没？——还清拉者。账还清了没有？——还清了。（土 25 页）

1862 年麦高温书中共有 29 个上海话现在完成时态形式的句子，英语的对照文有 58.6% 译成英语的"have V-ed"现在完成时态句子，没有译成英语现在完成时态的句子，笔者从语感上体会也全部都有现在完成的语义。例如以下四句：

（9）饭好吃拉哉。（麦 50 页。The dinner is all ready.）

（10）房子收作好拉哉。（麦 50 页。The house is already put in order.）

（11）一个礼拜堂造好拉哉。（麦 50 页。The chapel is built.）

（12）第位学生读啥书拉哉？（麦 122 页。What book is this scholar reading?）

按上海话原文，（9）句的语义是"到现在的时候已经可以吃饭了。"（10）句的语义是"到现在为止房子已经收拾好了。"（11）句的语义是"一个礼拜堂到现在已经造好了。"（12）句的语义是"这个学生一直到现在读什么书？"英语的译文没用现在完成时态句，只是英国人的语言使用习惯与我们不同而已。但是，普通话"V 了"的"完成体"句子适合译成英语完成时态句子只有 24.2% 的比率，（赵世开、沈家煊，1984）而且很大一部分句子的语义确实不是"完成"义，如："我当了营业员。""喝了那杯药！"

二 现在完成时态发生变化的背景

上海话的"现在完成时态"句子在 19 世纪中叶及现今上海郊区是十分常见和普遍使用的句子。在它发生较大变化之前，有下面两个情况值得注意。

1. 自身产生的一些变体

变体之一是与邻近体的混用。它有时与上海话经历体"V过"、"V过歇"合用，例如：

（13）日头里晒过歇拉哉。已经晒过太阳了。（麦51页）

（14）拨先生骂过拉者。已经被先生骂过了。（黄58页。"黄"为黄在江（1942）的简称，下同）

（13）、（14）句的意思可看作站在说话者当时的立场去看过去已发生到现在来看已经完成的事件，所以麦高温仍把（13）句译成现在完成时态句子："It has been aired in this sun."这种情形与普通话中"V了"和"V过"由于有时都可表示"完成"义，因此可以互换的情况相似。如："我看了那个电影。""我看过那个电影。""我看过了那个电影。"

变体之二是"拉哉"自身使用范围的扩展。"V拉哉"在20世纪30年代仍在用，不过那时已经扩用到形容词后，动宾、动补结构后。例如：

（15）侬勿要实介能样子难过，侬个令堂也已经交关难过拉哉。你别这样难过，令堂也已经很难过了。（蒲72页。"蒲"为蒲君南（1939）的简称，下同）

（16）只可以拉陆路上来，因为拉江阴咾镇江侪封江拉哉。只能从陆路上来，因为江阴和镇江到现在都已经封江了。（蒲105页）

（17）今朝堂门上头一只门灯，拨拉学生子踢高球咾，踢坏拉哉。今天堂门上面的一个门灯，因被学生踢高球踢坏了。（蒲202页）

（18）铜钿付清拉哉。钱到现在付清了。（黄57页）

"拉哉"扩用至形容词后和动补、动宾结构后以后，"拉哉"原来表达的明确的"现在完成时态"的语义开始扩大化，扩大化的结果就是意义虚化、淡化，慢慢成为表达"现状"语气。这是"拉哉"继续语法化的趋势。[4] 如现今上海郊区说"篮球打得蛮紧张拉哉。""紧张"前已可加程度副词，还可以在动词前加表示"进行体"的"正"："篮球正打得紧张拉哉"。"拉哉"继续虚化，甚至到后来还能用于虚拟的将来可能发生的行为，如："我要明朝去上海拉哉。"这是"拉哉"继续语法化成为语气助词的结果。

2. "实现体"与"现在完成时态"的并存

北京话是没有"现在完成时态"形式的，它有不同于上海话的"完成体"（又称"实现体"），是用"SVO"语序的"SV了O了"形式表示的，如"我吃了饭了。"这个形式在19世纪中叶以前的历史上，就已经在北部吴语中形成了一个相应的用"SVO"语序表示的"V仔O哉"形式（"仔[tsɿ]"又写作"之"）。这个形式在苏州方言中最为稳定，成为其表达实现、完成义的唯一形式。上海方言原来受吴语区权威方言苏州话的影响很大，在上海方言中也另外叠加进去一种新的完成体表达形式："V仔O哉"。例如：

（19）前年做之宰相者。前年做了宰相了。（艾161页。"艾"为艾约瑟（1868）的简称，下同）

（20）买之大斤者。买了好多斤了。（艾75页）

（21）一只船遇着仔风浪哉。一条船遇到了风浪了。（麦50页）

（22）嘴唇发之白者。嘴唇发白了。（土77页）

在发展相对滞后的上海话中，"V仔O哉"和"OV拉哉"两种语序不同的形式并存，表示外延不尽相同内涵相近的完成体意义，有相当长的一段时间。直到20世纪末21世纪初那一轮普通话大潮席卷下的上海话大变化时代，才趋于合一。

三 现在完成时态的逐渐消亡

造成上海话现在完成时态开始发生覆盖性演变的原因，是20世纪20年代以后推行的国语对北部吴语的第一次强大的辐射，它在五方杂处的、经济文化方面已成为中心的上海最早发生了影响，松江话系统的旧上海话就在当时发生了一系列的变化，变成新上海话。这次大变化就发生在20世纪二、三十年代，现在完成时态的变化只是其中之一。

让我们来看看20世纪30年代以后，上海话原有的现在完成时态是如何渐渐消亡的。

1. 时间副词开始替代"体"形式

"拉哉"的时态意义在混用和扩用中渐渐发生含混和异化的同时，北方话的影响开始南下。第一个改变是用时间副词代替体形态，比如（15）句"侬个令堂也已经交关难过拉哉"已经是"拉哉"和"已经"叠用的句子，"拉哉"原有的意义被叠用上去的副词"已经"大致表达了，"拉哉"承担的语义也就相应淡化，如果说成"侬个令堂也已经交关难过"也可以，语义几近。

在当时的国语中，实际上已经发生了时间名词表示"时"形式后的、以时间副词替代"体"形式的变化，这种过渡在现今普通话中也可看出来，如："我参加了运动队。>我已经参加了运动队。>我已经参加运动队。""V了"渐渐被"已经V"替代。这种情况在20世纪30年代已开始影响上海话，这时的上海话课本上已有不用"拉哉"只用表示当下状态的"哉"的句子，其中，副词"已经"代替了"拉"。例如：

（23）我到之贵国已经十五年哉。我到了贵国已经 15 年了。（蒲语 97 页。"蒲语"为蒲君南
　　　（1941）的简称，下同）

（24）已经来勿及者。已经来不及了。（黄 57 页）

（25）伊已经乡下去者。他已经去乡下了。（影山巍 45 页）

（26）地个是已经过时货者。这个已经是过时货了。（影山巍 64 页）

这是"拉哉"形态失落的开始。用副词替代形态，是受北方话影响的一种演变方式。[5] 由时间名词替代"时"形态，由时间副词替代"体"形态，这是汉语继续向孤立语进化的表现。它对上海方言时态的影响，使"拉哉"发生了动摇，"拉"从"哉"前失去。

2. 现在完成时态否定式的转变

上海话现在完成时态的否定式变得最快，它原是"勿曾 V"，有时音变为"勿能 V"。例如：

（27）现在寄来伊买个货色还勿曾到。（麦 28 页。The goods which I entrusted to him to buy
　　　have not yet arrived.）

（28）价钱勿曾讲落。价钱还没谈下来。（麦 29 页）

（29）现在十点半勿能满哩。现在十点半还没到呢。（麦 162 页）

现今上海郊区农村多读成"勿能"。但是由于国语的影响，在 1928 年赵元任记录的上海话中，"呒没"和"勿曾"两种形式已经处于并用的过渡状态。（赵元任 1928:103）黄在江在 1942 年也记录了两种形式的并用。例如：

（30）还既呒没转来。还没有回来。（黄 87 页）

（31）还勿曾寻着。还没有找到。（黄 87 页）

到 70 年代以后，只有 60 岁以上的老年人"呒没"和"勿曾"并用，绝大多数的上海人已只用"呒没"。1988 年出版的《上海市区方言志》（简称"上"，下同）中说："'勿曾'新派已不用，新派用'呒没'替换'勿曾'。"（上 452 页）例如：

（32）我呒没吃夜饭。我没有吃晚饭。（上 349 员）

（33）伊来勒哦？——伊还呒没来。他来了吗？——他还没来。（当 1044 页。"当"为《当代吴语研究》（1992）的简称，下同）

到 20 世纪末，上海话中只有"呒没"一种形式了。由此可见，共同语层次对上海话的覆盖是经过 A > A/B > B 过程进行的。

3. 现在完成时态疑问式的转变

1）"拉蛮" > "拉末" > "末"

现在完成时态的疑问形式原用"拉蛮"，如："我叫侬买个物事买拉蛮？"（麦53页。I told you to buy some articles, have you bought them？）但是就在19世纪中叶已经发生了掉"拉"的现象，疑问句的掉"拉"变化比肯定句快。例如：

（34）饭用蛮？（艾162页。Have you dined?）

（35）饭吃曼？吃饭了没有？（艾47页）

这可能与"蛮"这个合音词的标志独特鲜明有关，"蛮"在上海话中只出现在一种用法里，用了"蛮"省了"拉"其原来意义同样可标志。另外，这时还有混用"过蛮"或"个蛮"的现象，对"拉蛮"也是一个冲击。"过"在上海话中也表示"完成"，"过蛮"与"拉蛮"在这儿语义相近，"个"更是表示"近过去"义的，"个蛮"代替"拉蛮"更容易地发生了。例如：

（36）侬早饭吃过蛮？（麦52页。Have you breakfasted?）

（37）关税还个蛮？（麦33页。Have you paid in the duties yet?）

在普通活中，"你吃过饭了没有？"和"你吃了饭了没有？"也是可以换用的，语义相似。

20世纪初"蛮"失去鼻音韵尾成为"没[meʔ]"，或"末"（又写作"味"），"拉蛮"就变为"拉末"。例如：

（38）格味现在已经离任拉没？——已经离任拉者。那么现在已经离任了没有？——已经离任了。（土55页）

（39）三刻到快者，小菜齐好拉末？好快者。三刻快到了，菜都齐了没有？快好了。（松236页）

（40）我个说话侬懂拉末？我的话你现在懂了没有？（御幡雅文5页）

（41）侬八字出拉末？——勿曾出。你到现在出了八字了没有？——没出。（蒲58页）

虽然，如（41）句那样，在30年代末"拉末"还普遍使用，但是，从20年代起，"拉末"形态已经开始萎缩，开始失去"拉"，简化为"V末"，这是"拉末"舍前留后的用法，与前述的"拉蛮"变为"蛮"也是对应的。例如：

（42）苹果买好末？——买勿着。苹果买好没有？——买不到。（卜25页。"卜"为卜舫济（1920）的简称，下同）

（43）去看看医生来末？去看医生了没有？（卜25页）

（44）周浦到末？——也有半里把路。周浦到了没有？——还有半里左右路。（蒲 31 页）

（45）迪只台子揩过末？这个桌子擦了没有？（黄 62 页）

当然，单用"没"，前无"拉"，事件"直到现在"的含义便失去了。

唯补词（参看刘丹青 1994）"好"、"完"的加入也可成为"拉"失落的填补词，它们又加重了完成的意味。例如：

（46）枕头衣咾被单净好拉蛮？枕巾、被单洗好了没有？（麦 42 页）

（47）房子收作好拉哉。房间收拾好了。（麦 50 页）

（48）第件长衫破完拉者，勿好着个者。这件衬衫完全破了，不能穿了。（松 107 页）

例（47）、（48）经简化就变成"房子收作好哉。""长衫破完者。"有了"好"、"完"后，失去"拉"，这在韵律上有时更便于构成双音结构，不过语义也偏重于"好"、"完"而失落"延续至现在"的含义。例如：

（49）做完末？做完没有？（卜 33 页）

（50）饭烧好末？烧好哉。饭做好吗？做好了。（卜 30 页）

（51）衣裳做好末？勿曾，要歇两日做好。衣服做好没有？没有，要等两天做好。（卜 30 页）

"末"在 40 年代语音变为"[məʔ]"，与普通话的"吗（么＋啊）"已经十分接近，这为语义上过渡到与普通话"吗"相对应的上海活的"否"埋下了伏笔。

2）"拉否"的产生

在"拉末"变为"末"的同时，与普通话完成体问句句尾"没有"变"吗"相似的变化（如："他吃饭了没有？"简为"他吃饭了吗？"）在上海话中也发生了，这就是另一种退化形式"拉否"的产生。"拉否"是"拉末"舍后留前的简化。完成时态的"没"（末）变成了一般时态是非问句（如：我回去好否？）用的疑问语气助词"否 [vɑ]"（或写作"哦"，语义相当于普通话的"吗"）问句开始简化为对"现状"的一般提问形式，变化从形容词谓语句开始，到动词谓语句。例如：

（52）身体爽快拉唔？身体到现在舒服了吗？（麦 13 页）

（53）侬一只表开准作垃唔？你的一个手表拨准了吗？（麦 103 页）

（54）侬今朝好拉否？——好拉。你今天好吗？——好。（松 29 页）

（55）有人教侬来否？——弗曾有歇。有人叫你吗？——没有过。（松 29 页）

（56）对面房子里有人拉否？——无没啥人拉。对面房子里有人在吗？——没有谁在。（丁卓 98 页）

到了 30 年代"拉否"用得更多。这类句子，虽已不用"勿曾"来问，但从其肯定和否定的回答来看，还留在"现在完成时态"中。

3）"拉"、"了"读音相混

"侬饭吃拉蛮？"变成了"侬饭吃拉否？"以后，到20世纪后期，上海人便普遍说作"侬饭吃了否？"如："枕头衣㖸被单净好拉蛮？"变成"枕巾帮单被汏好了哦？"（钱乃荣2003：379）其原因是这时上海话中的"垃拉[leʔ lɑ]"（麦5页），后字早已变为入声，赵元任在1928年就改写作"辣辣[lʌʔ lʌʔ]"（赵元任1928：104）。"辣[lʌʔ]"、"了（或写作'勒'[ləʔ]）"语音相近。到了80年代青少年人中，上海话语音发生了"/ʌʔ/音位"和"/əʔ/音位"合并为"/ɐʔ/音位"的音变。于是"辣"、"了"完全同音，读为"[lɐʔ]"，"侬饭吃拉否？"就成了"侬饭吃了否？"，与普通话"你吃饭了吗？"相比较，只剩下OV变为VO的语序问题了。

4. 现在完成时态肯定式的被取代

上海话现在完成时态肯定式的转变，是由两处出发的。

其一是直接被替代。上海话中早已存在的"SV仔O哉"实现体形式，在20世纪60年代以后，又发生了普通话带来的重大变化，即作为北部吴语特征词的体助词"仔"和语气助词"哉"在上海话里都变作"了[ləʔ]"，相当于普通话的"了$_1$"和"了$_2$"，"SV仔O哉"便变读为"SV了O了"，"我吃仔饭哉"就变成了"我吃了饭了"。（57）、（58）两例可以说明这个变化。

其二是从原来的"现在完成时态"变来。"SOV拉哉"变为"SOV了了"。两个"了"像普通话的"了$_1$"、"了$_2$"合为一个"了"一样，形成了"SOV了"或"TSV了"的模式，如（61）例。前述的"V拉哉"变成"已经V哉"，现今又变为"已经V了"，也加快了这个过渡，如（62）例。（60）例透露了这两处出发的变化的中间态的信息，"VO"与"OV"并存于一句话中。

（57）水位低勒两米。/ 水位低仔两米。水位低了两米。（宫田等104页）

（58）就要落雨勒。/ 就要落雨哉。就要下雨了。（宫田等106页）

（59）我吃勒饭再去。我吃了饭再去。（当1020页）

（60）我吃饭吃好了。我吃了饭了。（当1018页）

（61）搿门题目我会算勒。这道题目我会算了。（上354页）

（62）伊已经讲勒两趟勒。他已经讲了两次了。（上437页）

在1984年出版的宫田一郎等著的《上海语苏州语学习と研究》中有这样一段话，说明了20世纪80年代初"哉"比"仔"先为"了"所取代的具体情况："上海话中，语气助词'哉'现在只在部分老年人中使用，是比较旧的用法，多数人都用'勒'。

时态助词'仔'（又读 zl）使用也不如'勒'普遍。"（宫田等 1984：106）笔者在 2003 年继续说到"仔"的问题："五六十年代以后，……'仔'渐被'了[ləʔ]'（又写作'勒'）替代，现在新派已都用'了'。如：'风吹了一夜天。''六岁起，连今年读了五年了。'只有老年人和少数滞后的中年人还有用'仔'的。郊区仍用'仔'。"（钱乃荣 2003：269）

5. 语序的转变

"蛮（＞否）"、"拉（＞了）"、"仔（＞了）"、"哉（＞了）"和"勿曾（＞吪没）"的改变为上海话现在完成时态和实现体的合并铺平了道路，它使上海话的现在完成时态变成了：肯定式为"SOV 了"（我饭吃了），疑同式为"SOV 了否"（侬饭吃了否？），否定式为"SO 吪没 V"（我饭院没吃）。

造成上海话中现在完成时态最后消失的，是 20 世纪 70 年代以后普通话在上海新的一次大普及，此时上海话又处于演变的高潮期。到 80 年代的青年一代（现今已成为 45 岁以下的大多数上海人），在他们的新上海话中，"SVO"和"SOV"两种语序开始并行出现在时体表现中。其肯定式是"SV 了 O 了"或"SOV 了"，疑问式是"SVO 了否"或"SOV 了否"，否定式是"S 吪没 VO"或"SO 吪没 V"。于是，在他们的上海话中，向"SVO"转化的与普通话"实现体"相似的形式都形成了："我吃了饭了。""侬吃饭了否？""我还吪没吃饭。"与"SOV"语序的句式自由的变换已使用在他们的对话中。

90 年代以后，"SOV"向"SVO"语序的转化，成为当代青少年在普通话传媒大普及背景下将上海话继续推进的一个重要标志，当代年轻人在会话中"SVO"语序所占比率急速提高。[6] 至此，原来上海话中"SOV 拉哉"最终被抛弃，普通话的"实现体"层次完全覆盖了上海话。具体来说：

疑问式：

"侬饭吃拉蛮？" ＞ "侬饭吃辣否？" ＞ "侬饭吃了否？" ＞ "侬吃了饭了否？"

肯定式：

"我饭吃拉哉。" ＞ "我饭吃了。" ＞ "我吃了饭了。"

否定式：

"我饭勿曾吃。" ＞ "我饭院没吃。" ＞ "我既没吃饭。"

综上所述，上海话在 160 年里完成了完全采用与普通话相同的形式来表示完成与实现的过程，从而丢失了"现在完成时态"的表现手段。不过，用"实现体"形式并不能表达出"到现在为止已完成或刚完成"的语法意义，必要时，其缺憾可在动词前

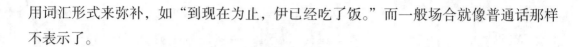
用词汇形式来弥补，如"到现在为止，伊已经吃了饭。"而一般场合就像普通话那样不表示了。

四　余论

岂止如此？上海话与普通话一样，将来时是有标记的（动词前用"要"等表示），一般过去时和现在时都无标记。但老上海话在表示"完成"和"进行"意义时，有"现在完成时态"、"过去完成时态"、"现在进行时态"、"过去进行时态"4 种形态区别。过去完成时态（用"V 拉个"）句子如："学堂就拉过面曲湾里，门口头，贴一张纸条拉个。学校就在那边曲湾里，以前门口已经贴着一张纸条的地方。"（土 6 页）"伊个人脚那能跷拉个？毛病呢还是生成功拉个？那个人脚怎么病的？以前生的病还是生出来时已经那样的？"（御幡雅文 43—44 页）现在进行时态（用"拉 V 哉"、"拉里 V（哉）"）句子如："吾拉做哉。我现在正在做呢。"（艾 161 页，I am doing it.）"相公请上，小人拉里叩头哉！相公请上，小人在叩头呢！"（《翡翠园》6 出 21 页）"勒里打算。正在打算。"（艾 167 页。He is considering.）过去进行时态（用"垃拉 V"）句子如："我垃拉吃。当时我在吃。"（卜 13 页，I was eating.）除了"过去进行时态"在 19 世纪中叶随上海话中"拉里（近指）"、"垃拉（远指）"对立的[7] 消失而消失外，"过去完成时态"、"现在进行时态"和"现在完成时态"一样，在 20 世纪以来受到普通话至少 100 年的层次覆盖和磨合，在 21 世纪初中青年的新上海话里消失。[8] 上海话彻底告别了动词谓语句中时体结合的时态形式，走上仅有体形态、时用词汇形式表示的不归路。

在汉语方言发展的历史上，不仅有一种方言的语音对另一种方言进行层次性的覆盖，在语法上，同样也有层次覆叠的现象。上海方言在共同语的强大辐射下，某些重要的语法形式在近现代可以渐渐被普通话语法形式覆盖改变，形成上海方言发展史上过去和现在的两个不同层次，19—20 世纪里 4 个时体结合的时态被普通话的两个体形式覆盖，就是一个生动的实例。可喜的是，我们在老中青几代的上海人中还能看到演变的轨迹，并在郊区可以得到早期语料的验证。从时体范畴来看，上海话在普通话的带动下，向孤立语又迈进了一步。

附　注

[1] 这儿 T 指做话题的受事类成分。如上海话经历体句子："侬外国人家住过歇唔？你住过外国人家吗？"（麦 41 页）存续体句子："伊现在乡下去拉。他现在去乡下留在那儿。"（丁卓 133 页）

[2] 比较常州话的疑问式"V 文"即"V 勿曾",否定式"分 V"是"勿曾 V","文（声母 v）"、"分（声母 f）"皆为"勿曾"的合音。上海话的"蛮"也是"勿曾"（读作 [məʔ zən]）的合音，韵母鼻化，"勿"的声母古老一点，像上海话"物事东西"的"物"一样，读 [m]。又如，《金瓶梅》里完成体疑问句用"V 了不曾"形式。

[3] 用普通话翻译上海话现在完成时态的句子，多会感到缺少"到现在为止"这样的含义。以下例句同。

[4] 这种由动词开始变为介词又变为体助词再变为语气助词的连续语法化过程在上海方言的"拉在"字结构中普遍存在。如"垃拉"："我垃拉屋里。我在家里。"（动词）|"我垃拉屋里看书。我在家里看书。"（介词）|"我垃拉唱歌。我在唱歌。"（进行体助词）|"辩点饭留垃拉。这点饭留着。"（存续体助词）|"足球踢得正好紧张垃拉。足球踢得正紧张呢。"（语气助词）

[5] 词汇形式替代形态表达，在上海话 160 年的变迁中多见。上海话许多形态的混用、简化和失落起自 20 世纪三四十年代。比如，上海话原用"V 过"表示完成。像："侬早饭吃过否？你吃过早饭吗？"用"V 歇"表示经历，像："侬大黄蛇吃歇否？你曾经吃过大黄蛇吗？"后来"过"、"歇"叠用为"V 过歇"，用法向普通话靠近，再用"V 过"代替"V 过歇"，如要明确表示经历，便须在"V"前加上副词"曾经"。上海话原用"过"表示虚拟将来的"重新再来一遍"的意思，如："菜勿熟。——烧过！菜不熟。——重新煮！""烧过"即"再烧一次"的意思。160 年里经历了"V 过" > "重新 V 过" > "重新 V"的过渡，现今中老年用"重新 V 过"，而青年只用"重新 V"了。

[6] 不仅是完成体，原来用 SOV 语序的经历体句、意愿句、是非问句等，他们都多用 SVO 语序。如："我辩部电影看过了。我看过这个电影。" > "我看过辩只电影了。""侬面饼要带否？你要带上面饼吗？" > "侬要带面饼否？""种花末，侬空地有否？如果种花的话，你有空地吗？" > "要是种花，侬有空地否？"

[7] 卜舫济《上海方言教程》中说过上海话"垃里"是"here"，"垃拉"是"there"。（卜 13 页）在早期的上海话著作句子中，"垃里"的近指含义是可以明显体会到的。所以上海话"过去进行"用远指的"垃拉"，"现在进行"用近指的"垃里"以及"哉"。

[8] 在当代青年的新上海话中，过去、现在都用时间词表示，或随上下文看出；完成用"V 了"，进行用"辣 V"或"辣盖 V/ 辣海 V"。但是在六十岁左右的上海人的上海话里，现在进行时态还存在着，而且是常说的，用"辣辣 V 了（<辣里 V 哉）"表达。如："我饭辣辣吃了。我现在正在吃饭。""侬看，伊辣辣来了。你看，他现在正在过来。"过去完成时态用"V 辣个（< V 拉个）"，现在完成时态用"V 辣了（< V 拉哉）"，都偶尔会说到，如："侬勿要调皮，我对侬有数辣个。你别调皮，我过去对你一直是有数的。""我文章写好辣了。文章到现在我已经写好了。"

参考文献

丁卓（1936）《中日会话集》，上海：三通书局。

黄在江（1942）《ポケット上海语》，上海：现代出版社。

宫田一郎、许宝华、钱乃荣（1984）《上海语苏州语学习と研究》，东京：光生馆。

刘丹青（1994）唯补词初探，《汉语学习》第 3 期。

钱乃荣（1992）《当代吴语研究》，上海：上海教育出版社。

钱乃荣（2003）《上海语言发展史》，上海：上海人民出版社。

许宝华、汤珍珠（主编）（1988）《上海市区方言志》，上海：上海教育出版社。

影山巍（1936）《详注现代上海语》，东京：文求堂。

御幡雅文（1924）《沪语便商，一名上海语》，上海：日本堂书店（初版：1892 年）。

赵世开、沈家煊（1984）汉语"了"字跟英语相应的说法，《语言研究》第 1 期。

赵元任（1928）《现代吴语的研究》，北京：清华学校研究院。

（清）朱素臣《翡翠园》，北京：中华书局，1988 重版。

Anonymous（师中董）（1908）《土话指南》，上海：土山湾慈母堂（初版：1889 年）。

Bourgeois, Albert（蒲君南）（1939）*Leçons Sur le Dialecte de Changhai.* Cour Moyen, Imprimerie de T'ou-sè-wè.

Bourgeois, Albert（蒲君南）（1941）*Grammaire du Dialecte de Changhai.* Cour Moyen, Imprimerie de T'ou-sè-wè.

Edkins, Joseph（艾约瑟）（1868）*A Grammar of Colloquial Chinese, as Exhibited in the Shanghai Dialect.* Shanghai: Presbyterian Mission Press.（初版：1853）

MacGowan, John（麦高温）（1862）*A Collection of Phrases in Shanghai Dialect.* Shanghai: Presbyterian Mission Press.

Morrison, George Emest（1883）*Leçons ou Exercices de Langue Chinoise Dialecte de Pott.* Song-Ki-ang, Zi-Ka-Wei, a L'orphelinat de Tou-Sè-Ve.

Pott, F. L. Hawks（卜舫济）（1920）*Lessons in the Shanghai Dialect.* Shanghai: Presbyterian Mission Press.（初版：1907）

（本文发表于《中国语文》2004 年第 3 期，第 232—240 页）

吴语早期文献所见的"等"字句 *

一 引言

据《现代汉语八百词》（增订本，166—167 页），现代汉语的"等"字主要有两类用法：

（1）用作动词：（a）表示等候、等待，如：他正等着你呢 | 你等等我；（b）用在"等 + 动 / 小句 [+ 的时候（之后、以后）]"的结构中，如：等下了雨就追肥 | 等吃过饭再去。

（2）表示列举未尽或用在列举之后煞尾，如：唐代著名诗人李白、杜甫、白居易等 | 中国有长江、黄河、黑龙江、珠江等四大河流。

"等"在汉语史上还可以用在指称词后面，如：公之等《史记·日者列传》| 此等怏怏，素不服官《南史·恩幸传》；或者表示类似的同动词常用与之相呼应的助词，比如：皆如编发等《维摩诘经·上》（参看吕叔湘 1982：159；太田辰夫 2003：102，182）。

本文旨在讨论吴语早期文献所见的一类特殊语法现象。吴语完整的文献数据，最早可以上推至明代晚期，其中较为著名的有明末冯梦龙（1574—1646）所辑《山歌》，以及《六十种曲》中若干南戏的宾白（梅祖麟 1998：69）。此外，还有一些吴语区的文人用官话写成的白话小说，由于作者的方言背景，这些小说带有不同程度的吴语成分。著名的有冯梦龙的"三言"、凌濛初（1580—1644）的"二拍"、韩邦庆（1856—1894）的《海上花列传》等等。[1] 其中还包括一些文人所作的丽情小说（部分作品作者已不甚可考），例如钱乃荣先生（1994）介绍的《肉蒲团》、《绣榻野史》和《浪史奇观》，写作时代为晚明至清初。本文就将以《绣榻野史》（以下简称《绣》）中所见材料为主，探讨早期吴语里"等"的几种语法功能。[2]

《绣》书题为情颠主人著，实为明代浙江余姚人吕天成（1580—1618）所作 [3]，有万历年间刻本，作者于万历二十三年（1595）开始创作此书 [4]。从钱乃荣先生（1994）

---

* 本文初稿完成后，曾蒙刘丹青、游汝杰、张谊生等先生赐阅并提出修改意见，谨此致谢。文中尚存错漏，则由作者负责。

的研究以及我们的考察来看，《绣》大致反映了北部吴语某个方言的早期面貌，故而《绣》作为早期吴语的文献资料是可信的。

二 《绣榻野史》中"等"的三种用法

《绣》一书篇幅不大，但却记录了丰富的吴语词汇。其中有个非常突出的语法现象，就是有大量的"等"字句，这些"等"字句可分为三类："等$_1$"（表给予）、"等$_2$"（表使役）、"等$_3$"（表被动）。下面分别加以讨论。

2.1 表示给予义的动词或介词（等$_1$），《绣》共 4 见。例如：

a. 把 +N1+ 等 + N2 +V

① 你肯再把阿秀等我弄一弄罢。（44 页；把阿秀给我弄一弄）

② 后头要把母猪等你杀完了，我们两个骡子要等你骑了，才算报得完哩。（97 页）

从句式看，上面两例均为处置式。吴福祥先生将近代汉语的广义处置式"把 + N1 + V + N2"（此类处置式的述语动词所表示的动作涉及两个论元，语义上处置性较弱）分成几个小类，其中有一类属于"处置（给）：把 N1 给与 N2"的结构（参阅蒋绍愚、曹广顺 2005：354）。例如：

（1）善知识将佛法菩提与人，亦不为人安心。（神会和尚语录，南阳和上顿教解脱禅门直了性坛语）

（2）莫将天人（女）施沙门，休把娇姿与菩萨（敦煌变文集，维摩诘经讲经文）

这两例中的"与"用作表给予的动词。下面几例属于"处置（给）：把 + N1 + 与 + N2 + V"的句式，其中的"与"可以理解为介词"给"：

（3）我将马王与圣子乘。（佛本行集经；把马王给圣子骑）

（4）师曰：将饭与阇梨吃底人，还有眼也无？（祖堂集，卷 4，丹霞和尚）

（5）将饭与人吃，感恩则有分，为什摩却成不具眼去？（同上）

（6）我而今穷乏，你那鹿肉将与我，我把这儿子与你去。（元朝秘史，卷一；把儿子给你拿去）

（7）次日因见女婿家中全无活计，养赡不起，把十五贯钱与女婿作本，开店养身。（醒世恒言，卷 33；把钱给女婿作本）

冯春田先生（1991：19）认为，例（4）、（5）即"将饭给阇梨吃"、"将饭给人吃"的意思，此处"与"可由介词"给"替代。关于两句中"将"的句法性质，梅祖麟先生（2005：168）是把例（4）看作"V（NP$_2$）与 NP$_1$V"的句式，认为"将"作动词。

如果"将"作动词（相当于动词"拿"），就和下文所举的"与"字句（兼语句）同属一类。从句式和语义上说，把这两例的"将"看作介词也并无不可。

上引《绣》中的两例处置句也是"处置（给）：把 +N1+ 与 +N2+V"的句式，"等"相当于"给"。其中例②是两个并列分句，从句式和语义看，前一分句当然应理解为处置句；后一分句其实是省略了"把"字，完整的句子应该是"要（把）我们两个骡子等你骑了"，此时"等"也相当于"给"。

b. 兼语句式：

③ 你如今只是来了等我吃还便罢。（31 页；给我吃倒还罢了）

④ 我怕你病，安排药等你吃，你倒要自死。（49 页；安排药来给你吃）

试比较下面几例"与"的用法：

（1） 可耐伊家忒恁村，冷饭拿来与我吞。（清平山堂话本，快嘴李翠莲记；冷饭拿来给我吞）

（2） 你可将一坛酒来，与我吃了，做我不著，捉他去见大尹。（警世通言，卷 28；拿一坛酒来，给我喝了）

（3） 既是他们疑心，且卖一桶与我们吃。（水浒传，16 回；就卖一桶给我们吃）

2.2 表示使役义（等₂），"等₂"在《绣》中共出现 20 多次。

a. 表示"使、让"：

① 少不要搁在大里肩头上，等他看看也动情。（11 页；使他看着也动情）

② 且拍开等我看一看。（28 页；让我看）

b. 表示"容许、听任"：

③ 狗忘八，你倒等他骂我么。（94 页；容许他骂）

④ 又把自家腿压在两只脚上，不等他动。（60—61 页；不许他动）

⑤ 原来是大嫂捉弄我，快些等我拿出来罢。（62 页；容许我拿出来）

例③说的是金氏、麻氏二人争醋，东门生对麻氏谩骂其妻金氏无动于衷，于是金氏怒斥东门生，说"你倒等他骂我么"，此处"等"无疑表示的是"容许、听任"；例④是说金氏将自己的腿压在麻氏的脚上，"不等他动"的意思只能是不允许她动，而非"不等着她动"；例⑤说的是麻氏请求金氏允许自己将缅铃取出，这里的"等"也只能理解为容许。

2.3 表示被动义的介词（等₃），此类"等"用例最多，在《绣》中共有近30例。下面略举数例讨论：

① 你去见他，笑他怎么这等没用东西，直等我安排的讨饶。（21页；被我安排得讨饶）

② 阿弟差了，阿嫂等你戏了，就是你的老婆一般的了。（56页；被你戏）

③ 奴家恨他，因此骗上了你来，等我丈夫戏还哩。（79页；骗了你来，被我丈夫戏还）

④ 我有个道理，只不等麻氏晓得了。（80页；只是不能被麻氏知道了）

前三例为"N1+ 等 +N2+VP"的句式，从语义关系看，N2是VP的施事：若N1是VP的受事，就是典型的被动句式，"等"则为被动标记；若"等"是等待义的动词，此句便是连动句式，这时VP的所指必定是未然的，因为是N1等待VP的发生。就例①至例③在《绣》中的上下文来看，这三例的VP都表示已然。例①说的是金氏怂恿东门生去当面取笑赵大里，笑他反被金氏戏弄。"戏弄"已经成事实了，动作已经结束，"等"当然无法表示等待；例②是东门生的话，他对赵大里说，既然"阿嫂（指金氏）等你戏了"，那么"（阿嫂）就是你的老婆一般的了"，这里"戏"的动作已发生，所以"等"也只能是个被动标记；例③从上下文看，同样也是在麻氏被东门生"戏还"之后，金氏对麻氏说的话，"等"也是"被"的意思；例④也不能理解成"道理（办法 N1）不能等着麻氏（N2）知道"，而是"办法不能被麻氏知道"。

下面几例《绣》中的"等"，同样当作"被"理解：

⑤ 等他拖出做了一根尾耙也好。（43页；被他拖出）

⑥ 若等他有些龊龊带出，就倒兴了。（25页；被他带出）

⑦ 这样小官人，等我一口水吞了他才好哩。（3页；被我吞了）

三　其他历史文献里的"等"

《明清吴语词典》（石汝杰、宫田一郎2005：127）的"等"字条下列有"让、使"义项：

① 月公道："我徒弟自有，徒孙没有，等他做我徒孙吧。"就留在寺中。（型世言，30回）

② 如此说，相公请坐了，等我一头斟酒，一头说便了。（党人碑，9出）

③ 我今日呦勿要开啥牢店哉，且等耳朵里静办勾日把介。（报恩缘，15出）

④ 明朝要到上海去住格两日，……等倪散散心看，勿然是坐勒屋里向，倪头脑子也涨格哉。（九尾龟，24回）

《词典》所谓的"吴语"主要是指苏南、上海及浙北地区的方言，即为广大的北部吴语方言（石汝杰、宫田一郎 2005：前言 5），但因《词典》未收《绣》一书，我们就无法从《词典》了解到"等"在四百年前的吴语中的完整用法。《绣》的刊行稍早于《型世言》（初刻于崇祯年间），《绣》的材料除了提供了"等₂"更早的文献用例，更说明了"等"在晚明吴语里还可以兼表给予和被动。

再举个一百多年前苏州话的"等₂"的例子：

⑤ 就来仔末，等俚哚亭子间里吃。（海上花列传，21 回；让他们在亭子间里吃）

下面一些元代以后文献中所见"等"，一般认为都是表使役的"让"：[5]

① 则著他背狗皮号令在长街市，也等那一辈儿狗党狐朋做样子。（杀狗劝夫，四，尾煞）
② 梅香，休要吵闹，等他歇息，我且回去咱。（倩女离魂，三，斗鹌鹑；让他歇息）
③ 我不要半星热血红尘洒，都只在八尺旗枪素练悬，等他四下里皆瞧见。（窦娥冤，三；让他瞧见）
④ 你不晓的意思，等我解与你听。（渔樵闲话，一；让我讲解给你听）
⑤ 老夫一生辛勤，挣这铜斗儿家计，等他这般废败，便死在九泉下也不瞑目！（东堂老，楔子；家当让他如此废败）
⑥ 还要分付后槽，将这厮收的好者，不要等他溜了。（生金阁，一；让他溜了）
⑦ 两位姐姐，看得高兴啊，也等我每看看。（长生殿，窥浴；也让我们看看）

其中例⑤可理解成"（家当）任由他废败"，这时"等₂"表示"让"；但也可以说成"（家当）被他废败"，那"等"就相当于"被"了，"他"是"废败"的施事，"家当"是受事。这点颇类似于"与"、"给"由表使役向表被动转化的重新分析（可参看江蓝生 2000、蒋绍愚 2002、梅祖麟 2005 等先生的论述）。

再看几个宋元（明）以来江南白话小说中"等₂"例子，如：

① 秀才不嫌家间澹薄，搬到家下，与老汉同住几日，随常茶饭，等老汉也不寂寞，过了岁朝再处。（二刻拍案惊奇，11 回；使老汉不寂寞）
② 塔下必有寺院，院内必有僧家，且等人走走。（西游记，28 回；让人走）
③ 莫嚷，莫嚷！等他抬！（西游记，84 回；让他抬）[6]

例①、②顾之川（2000：42）曾引过。顾先生认为，"'等'在'等待'义的基础上虚化出'使'、'让'义"。例③的上下文是当时三藏、孙行者等人都已经在被人抬着走，孙行者说"等他抬"，意思就是"任由他抬"，当然也就无法理解成一般意义的"等"。这应该是《西游记》中吴语成分的反映。[7]

四 《绣榻野史》中"待"的语法功能

《绣》中除了可见"等"表给予、使役、被动的用例以外，同样表示等待义的"待"也有和"等"平行的三种用例。比如：

4.1 表示给予义

① 今夜晚他来待你伴伴，做过刨婆婆用。（71页；给你作伴）

此句的上下文是说，金氏将其夫东门生收藏的几幅春意图摆出，供麻氏观赏，这句话是金氏对麻氏所说。这里的"他"实指那些图画儿，此句当理解为"今天晚上（这些图）给你作伴"。

4.2 表示使役义

a. 使、让：

② 你便说说我听，待我发一发兴。（6页；让我发一发兴）

b. 容许：

③ 今晚你不待我出去，我定要去了。（23页；不容许我出去）

④ 如今待我自家记数。（21页；容许我自己数）

例③是金氏对东门生所说的话，意思是无论丈夫容许与否，她也一定要出门。此处"待"明显相当于表容许的"让"；例④的"待"同样是要求允许的意思，而非等待义。

4.3 表示被动义

⑤ 不想今日待我解了裹脚，在此捏弄。（14页；被我解了裹脚）

⑥ 我的心肝，待我咬落了才快活。（21页；（球儿）被我咬落）

从上下文看，例⑤所说"解裹脚"的动作已经完成，而不能是"等着我解了裹脚"，因此"待"不是等待义，只能看成被动标记；例⑥的意思当然不能是"等着我咬落"，而应该理解为"被我咬落"。

《明清吴语词典》（115页）也列了早期吴语表"让、使"义的"待"：

① 到叫我是踱头！也罢，站定了，待我踱一个与你看看。（缀白裘，3集2卷）

② 舒大少，吱吱吱吱可不像是老虫叫么，待我去捉只猫来。（续海上繁华梦，2集14回）

同样，受材料的限制，《词典》也并没有给出早期吴语的"待"表给予、被动的例子。

《绣》及其他吴语文献出现和"等"字语法功能平行的"待",有两种可能:一、在《绣》作者的方言里,"待"和"等"一样,的确有给予、使役和被动三种用法。二、"待"、"等"之间只是简单的词汇替代,后者是当时的口语词,而前者则略带书面语的意味。我们知道,从汉语史看,"待"表示等待义要比"等"早,而且自中古以后直到现在,两者间文言和口语的对比色彩还较明显。现代方言中"待"不常用,也似乎未见和"等"相平行的特殊用法,其语法功能的演变自然也就无从谈起。所以,我们倾向于第二种解释,即认为"待"字句的产生只是"等"字句模拟的结果。

五 现代南方方言里的"等"

既然《绣》反映的是早期吴语,那么上述"等"的用法自然会在今天的南方方言里有所表现。下面分类举例。[8]

5.1 表给予义的"等₁"

黎川(赣语):我个车子坏了,汝等 [tɛŋ⁴⁴] 我整一下好么你给我修一下好吗(引介受益对象"我",相当于"替、为")

高安老屋周家(赣语):你等 [tɛŋ⁴²] 替我写封信 | 我俚娘等替我买个一双鞋子

萍乡(赣语):这件事等 [tẽ³⁵] 给你做(连动句式)| 我等嘎渠一本书我给了他一本书(双宾语结构)

石城(客家话):街上个屋税等 [tɔu³¹] 粮管所呃街上的房子租给粮管所了(用作后助动词) | 到来广州呃时打个电话等僙到了广州的话打个电话给我(与格句式)| 拿杆笔等渠拿支笔给我(与格句式)

5.2 表使役义的"等₂"

常州(吴语):东西你放勒过头吧,等 [tǝŋ⁵⁵] 我来做你把东西放那儿吧,让我来做

常熟(吴语):能㑚□ lɛ²⁴ 哉,等 [tǝŋ⁴⁴] 渠去 lɛ²⁴ 你别弄了,让他去弄

汤溪(吴语):等 [nai⁵³⁴⁻⁵²] 渠归去让他回去

娄底(湘语):他不听话啊,等 [tẽ⁵¹] 我来啰 | 先生起介身哩啊,等我到只讲台桌子高里坐一下唧哒老师走了,让我到讲台上坐坐。此外,还见于湖南长沙等湘语。

萍乡(赣语):等他去哭,不要齿答理他。另外还见于江西莲花、高安老屋周家、宜春等赣语。

贵阳(西南官话):等 [tǝn⁵³] 我看下让我看看 | 等他先学到让他先学着,以后再……

成都（西南官话）：不听劝告的人，等 [təŋ⁵³] 他去碰壁 | 不免将我玉姐喊来，等他
　　去看看可救得活否（川剧传统剧目汇编，第四集）

广州（粤语）：等 [teŋ³⁵] 我睇下让我看看 | 打开窗口，等啲新鲜空气入嚟让新鲜空气进来

5.3 表被动义的"等₃"

汤溪（吴语）：个碗等渠打打破那个碗被他打碎了 | 些酥饼等渠个农买买了那些酥饼被他一
　　个人买光了 | 等大水头桥冲冲走那座桥被大水冲走了 [9]

衢州（吴语）：其等 [tən⁴⁵] 我敲勒两记他被我打了两下

株洲（湘语）（参看伍云姬 1998：3，缺例句）

南昌（赣语）：碗等 [tɛn²¹³] 我搭摔碎了 | 脚踏车等人家偷泼了

萍乡（赣语）：我等渠打嘎一餐我被他打了一顿 [10]

平江（赣语）：他等 [ten³²⁴] 狗咬了一口。另外还见于江西永修赣语。

江西石城（客家话）：水牛等贼牯偷走水牛被贼偷了 | 水缸等大细□ [tə] 打烂□ [tʰəu]
　　水缸被小孩打破了 | 买电视机个票 tə 等偓跌□ [tʰəu] 那座桥被大水冲走了

江西上犹（杜溪）[tẽ⁴²]、福建武平（武东）[tẽ³¹]（客家话）：佢等癫狗咬哩一口
　　他被疯狗咬了一口

　　可见，三种用法的"等"在吴、湘、西南官话、客赣、粤语等南方话里有着不同
程度的分布。

　　如果能注意到更多的早期吴语的文献资料，对方言虚词的探源工作也会有所帮
助。如戴昭铭先生（2003：91—92）曾提出：吴语区诸暨、嵊县（崇仁）的"得"、
嵊县（太平）的"带"、衢州的"等"这几个被动标记都来自于动词"代"，"得"是
"代"的促化，"等"由韵尾 [n] 在例句"等我"的 [ŋ] 声母逆同化而来（"代"如何能
变成嵊县太平话的"带"，戴先生未作解释），理由是浙江天台话里的"代"有"替、
给"的意思。诚然，虚词作为一个封闭类系统，其音韵变化往往会比较特别，就吴语
而言，的确有众多弱化、促化之类的音变，然而正是由于虚词系统音变复杂、容易产
生例外，我们在虚词探源时就要慎用所谓"音变规则"。说"等"由"代我"的韵尾
变化而来，无法用系统内的音变规则去验证；"等"出现的环境很多，故而不能单凭
一点作此推测，况且"代→等"也不只是韵尾的演变，它涉及整个韵母的音变。我们
认为，既然早期吴语有"等"表示被动的明确用例，还是应该将衢州话被动标记 [tən⁴⁵]
的本字定为"等"。[11]

六　余论

6.1《绣榻野史》作为晚明吴语的一项共时资料，它反映的是 400 多年前某个吴语方言的语法现象，即早期吴语的"等"可以有表示给予、使役和被动三种用法。

从《绣》显示的方言背景和现代汉语方言的分布看，"等"三种用法的出现也许最早在南方开始，兴起于江浙、江西一带 [12]。上文所引的元杂剧各例，均来自赵琦美脉望馆《古今杂剧》的明抄本，或是明代臧晋叔的《元曲选》（序作于 1616 年），缺乏可信的元刊本，故而这些"等"字句的形成年代只能大致定在明代，说它们和晚明吴语的"等"有关，应该没有问题 [13]。梅祖麟先生（1988，1998）曾讨论过完成貌助词"著"在白话文献和现代方言的分布，认为"著"萌芽于江浙地带，而后散播到吴、湘、闽语及西南官话当中；南、北方言在完成貌助词的发展史上有所不同，北方话的"动 + 了 + 宾"作为完成式的标准句型的年代，和《大慧书》中"著"字作为完成助词出现的年代密切衔接。"等"表给予、使役、被动的三种用法可能和完成貌助词"著"一样，至迟在明代出现于江南，然后向其他方言区传播。

受材料的限制，《绣》中未见"等₁"在处置、兼语等句式以外的结构中出现，但就客赣方言的数据来看，我们或可推测早期吴语的"等₁"也可用于与格、双宾等其他句式 [14]。早期吴语"等"的语法功能，应和晚唐五代的"与"字相类似（梅祖麟 2005：167—168）。

"等"的三种语法功能之所以能在南部吴语、客赣、湘语里保存较完整，大概是因为古江西在地理上有"吴头楚尾"之称，而湘、赣、浙地区的方言在古代又有密切联系（游汝杰 2000：107；Norman 1988, 1995：174—200）；另外，也可能跟该地区受官话成分冲击相对较小有关。至于北部吴语、西南官话、粤语的"等"只能表示使役，是原本就无其他用法的"等"，还是受官话的影响而后来消失了？现在还不容易断定。

6.2 不少研究汉语语法史的学者已经谈到"与、给、乞、教"等动词的语法化问题 [15]，而"等"字的特殊用法学界似乎还未及注意。这一方面是由于目前所见历史文献，大多只能反映官话的语法史；另一方面也因为对各方言早期数据的发掘尚显不足，方言语法史（尤其是吴语语法史）的探讨还有待深入展开。就吴语的文献资料而言，诸如《山歌》之类的早期苏州话的材料大家比较关注，而同时代（甚至更早）的、其他吴语地区的基本数据也还亟待利用。本文的工作，主要是从《绣榻野史》所见材料出发，分析早期吴语里"等"的特殊用法，将现代南方话的相关语法现象追溯至四百多年前的明代。至于等待义的动词"等"在早期吴语为何会有类似于"给"的语法演变，背后的演变机制如何，本文没有涉及。给予义动词的典型用法是带两个名词性论元，一

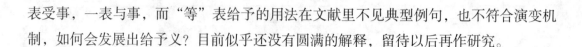

表受事，一表与事，而"等"表给予的用法在文献里不见典型例句，也不符合演变机制，如何会发展出给予义？目前似乎还没有圆满的解释，留待以后再作研究。

附 注

[1] 石汝杰、宫田一郎（2005：824—847）附有吴语早期文献资料的详细书目。

[2] 我们见到的《绣榻野史》，是台湾经联出版事业公司出版的民国四年上海图书馆排印本，本文所引的例句后括号内的数字表示所在页码。明显讹误之处，我们随文校改，恕不一一注出。由于《绣》记录的是某种早期吴语，方言词较多，故下文在讨论"等"字句时，必要时会对有些典型例句的上下文及句义作些说明。

[3] 据明人王骥德《曲律》卷四："勤之(按：吕天成字勤之)童年便有声律之嗜，既为诸生，有名，兼工古文词。与余称文字交二十年，……勤之制作甚富，至摹写丽情亵语，尤称绝技。世所传《绣榻野史》、《闲情别传》，皆其少年游戏之笔。"

[4] 参看《〈曲品〉校注》（吕天成撰、吴书荫校注，中华书局 1990 版）附录三"吕天成和他的作品考"。

[5] 例句引自李崇兴等（1999：74）、王锳（2005：77）及许宝华、宫田一郎（1999：6186）。

[6] "三言"、"二拍"是明末冯梦龙（苏州人）根据宋元以来的话本小说编定而成的，吕叔湘先生认为"话本系文献大致可信其依据汴京与临安之口语"（《汉语语法论文集》增订本，70 页），故应带有江南白话的成分。《西游记》、《金瓶梅》等几部小说也都多少带有吴语和江淮官话的成分（可参阅蒋绍愚 2005：327—336 的评述）。近来颇有学者从音韵演变、词汇、语法结构诸多方面讨论吴语与江淮官话之密切关系，可参看李小凡、陈宝贤（2002），鲁国尧（2002、2003），袁毓林、王健（2005）等学者的相关论文。

[7] 参阅章培恒《百回本〈西游记〉是否吴承恩所作》，《社会科学战线》1983 年第 4 期,300 页。

[8] 以下所引方言材料，主要来自《现代汉语方言大词典》（李荣先生主编，江苏教育出版社）各分卷本，许宝华、宫田一郎（1999），伍云姬（1998），李如龙、张双庆（2000）及钱乃荣（1992），其余来自作者自己的调查。

[9] 上引"等"字句在曹志耘（2000：67）用的都是介词"约"（同音字）。据曹志耘先生的描述，在汤溪话里，这些"约"字句都可换成"等"。

[10] 《萍乡方言词典》（江苏教育出版社 1998 版）只列了表使役的"等"，但根据我们的调查，"等"在萍乡话实际上还有表给予和被动的用法。

[11] 戴先生（2003:92）认为吴语表"替、给"义的介词"搭 / 脱 / 得"（吴语的"得"和"等"有相似的语法功能，"得"的用法在湘语里也能见到）也是从"代"演变来的，这些虚词的来源如何，还应作进一步考察。

[12] 现代北方话罕有此类的"等"，但也有例外，如河南话有"等₂"的用法（顾之川 2000：42）。

[13] 我们现在见到晚明吴语文献中的"等"有三种语法功能，而语法演变实际发生的年代又要早于文献著录的年代，因此，吴语的三类"等"至少在晚明以前就出现了。

[14] 最近读到林素娥（2007），根据该文的报导，湘语邵东话中的"等"不仅可以表示给予，如"我等本书等你"（我给本书给你），还可以充当处置句标记，如"我等古本书等你"（我把这本书给你）。

[15] 如江蓝生（2000）、蒋绍愚（2002）、洪波（2004）、梅祖麟（2005）等，《近代汉语语法史研究综述》（蒋绍愚、曹广顺 2005：379—418）对相关研究作了较全面的总结，可参看。

参考文献

曹志耘（2000）汤溪方言的介词，《介词》，李如龙、张双庆主编，广州：暨南大学出版社。

戴昭铭（2003）弱化、促化、虚化和语法化——吴方言中的一种重要的演变现象，《汉语方言语法研究和探索——首届国际方言语法学术研讨会论文集》，哈尔滨：黑龙江人民出版社。

冯春田（1991）《近代汉语语法问题研究》，济南：山东教育出版社。

顾之川（2000）《明代汉语词汇研究》，开封：河南大学出版社。

洪波（2004）"给"字的语法化，《南开语言学刊》第四辑，天津：南开大学出版社。

江蓝生（1999/2000）汉语使役与被动兼用探源，《近代汉语探源》，北京：商务印书馆。

蒋绍愚（2002）"给"字句、"教"字句表被动的来源——兼谈语法化、类推与功能扩展，《语言学论丛》第二十六辑，北京：商务印书馆。

蒋绍愚（2005）《近代汉语研究概要》，北京：北京大学出版社。

蒋绍愚、曹广顺（2005）《近代汉语语法史研究综述》，北京：商务印书馆。

李崇兴等（1999）《元语言词典》，上海：上海教育出版社。

李如龙、张双庆（主编）（2000）《介词》，广州：暨南大学出版社。

李小凡、陈宝贤（2002）从"港"的词义分布和地域分布看古吴语的北界，《方言》第 3 期。

林素娥（2007）北京话"给"表处置的来源之我见，《汉语学报》第 4 期。

鲁国尧（2002/2003）"颜之推谜题"及其半解，《中国语文》2002 年第 6 期、2003 年第 2 期。

吕叔湘（1982）《中国文法要略》，北京：商务印书馆。

梅祖麟（1988/2000）汉语方言虚词"著"字三种用法的来源，《梅祖麟语言学论文集》，北京：商务印书馆。

梅祖麟（1998）《朱子语类》和休宁话的完成态"著"字，《语言学论丛》第二十辑，北京：商务印书馆。

梅祖麟（2005）闽南话 hɔ˧ "给予"的本字及其语法功能的来源，《永远的 POLA——王士元先生七秩寿庆论文集》，台北："中研院"语言学研究所。

钱乃荣（1992）《当代吴语研究》，上海：上海教育出版社。

钱乃荣（1994）《肉蒲团》、《绣榻野史》、《浪史奇观》三书中的吴语，《语言研究》第 1 期。

石汝杰、宫田一郎（2005）《明清吴语词典》，北京：中华书局。

太田辰夫（2003）《中国话历史文法（修订译本）》，蒋绍愚、徐昌华译，北京：北京大学出版社。

王锳（2005）《诗词曲语词例释（第二次增订本）》，北京：中华书局。

伍云姬（主编）（1998）《湖南方言的介词》，长沙：湖南师范大学出版社。

许宝华、宫田一郎（主编）（1999）《汉语方言大词典》，北京：中华书局。

游汝杰（2000）《汉语方言学导论（修订本）》，上海：上海教育出版社。

袁毓林、王健（2005）吴语的动词重叠式及相关的类型学参项——从几种语法格式的分布地域看古吴语的北界，《吴语研究》，上海：上海教育出版社。

Alain, Peyraube（贝罗贝）(1991/2005) Syntactic Change in Chinese: Grammaticalization, *BIHP* 59.3: 617–652. 中译本：汉语的语法演变——论语法化，吴福祥、孙梅清译，《汉语语法化研究》，北京：商务印书馆。

Hopper, Paul & Elizabeth Traugott (2003) *Grammaticalization* (2nd edition). Cambridge: Cambridge University Press.

Norman, Jerry (1988/1995) *Chinese*. Cambridge: Cambridge University Press. 中译本：《汉语概说》，张惠英译，北京：语文出版社。

（本文发表于《中国语文研究》2007 年第 2 期，第 33—42 页）

早期吴语的句法类型特征

——见于西方传教士上海话、宁波话、温州话课本*

林素娥

前　言

从功能角度来说，方言是方言区人们进行交际的重要工具，它一般只有口头形式，没有书面形式（除粤语外）。在这种自然口语中，句子的基本结构受语用因素支配，以话题–说明来组织句子十分明显。如：

> 拉现在春末，乡下种田人要一日忙一日哉 S_1；起初末，耕田 S_2；后来末，散种咾插秧 S_3；是望歇两日有好收成也 S_4。（*Shanghai dialect exercise*, 1910，Lesson 10）

上例为复句，共四个分句（S_1—S_4），前三个分句，都以时间词"现在春"、"起初"、"后来"为叙述的出发点，为后面的说明部分提供时间范畴，它们也是说听者已知的或通过语境可推测的，即话题，而说明部分则是说者要表达的目标，也是听者未知而需要特别留意的部分；上海话"末"黏附在话题上，标注话题的句法性质。

话题一般都出现，但主语却可以不出现，如上例中 S_2—S_4 主语"乡下种田人"都承前省略，S_2、S_3，若没有话题，则影响表达。可见，话题在上海话句法中的重要性。

话题是汉语语法研究中的重要课题。自 Chao（1968）提出以话题–说明代替主语–谓语分析汉语句子结构的观点之后，Li & Thompson（1976）更明确地提出话题属句子成分，是具有类型学意义的重要参数，世界语言可分为注重主语型（英语）、注重话题型（汉语）、主语和话题都注重型（日语）、主语和话题都不注重型（菲律宾语）等四类。他们的研究突出了话题在语言类型学中的重要地位，也使话题成为国际、国内语言学界讨论的热点问题。尽管对汉语话题性质仍有不同看法，但汉语为话题优先语言观在语言学界得到普遍认同 [1]，汉语话题属于语法成分，它是分析汉语等话题优先语言句子的必有成分。

---

* 该研究获国家社科基金项目"吴语、粤语与湘语语序类型比较研究"（批准号：07CYY007）与上海大学创新项目"一百年间上海话句法类型特征之研究"（A.10-0102-09-004）资助，特此致谢！并感谢游汝杰先生提供传教士方言学课本。

话题特征在汉语方言内部具有不同的典型度，徐烈炯、刘丹青（1998）运用吴语上海话语料，得出吴语是比官话话题优先更典型的汉语方言。他们着眼于话题特征本身的经验描写，提出上海等地吴语属于 STV 型发达的语言，也是一种最弱的 SVO 而 SOV 倾向最明显的方言。这与桥本（1985）的研究有些出入，桥本从地理类型学角度得出：吴语像闽、粤、客等南方方言一样，是一种 SVO 强于北方官话的方言。那么这种不同，到底是因为吴语历时演变造成，还是研究者观察的理论视角不同造成的呢？结合吴语早期语料文献，可以帮助我们解答这个疑问。

十九世纪下半期至二十世纪上半期来华的西方传教士及日本商人，编写了不少吴方言课本、语法书等，这些著作是进行方言一百多年历时演变研究的宝贵资料（游汝杰 2002）。本文选取上海话课本（5 本）、宁波话（1 本）、温州话（1 本）观察得出：一百年前的吴语就是一种话题优先典型的汉语方言。所选课本分别为：

Benjamin Jenkins, *Lessons in the Shanghai dialect,* 1850.（记作"BE1850"）

F. L. Hawks Pott, D. D.（卜舫济）, *Lessons in the Shanghai Dialect*, Shanghai Presbyterian Mission Press, 1907.（记作"F.L. 1907"）

D. H. Davis, D. D., *Shanghai Dialect Exercises, in Romanized and Character, with Key to Pronunciation and English Index*, 上海：徐家汇土山湾（Tu se wei Press）印书馆。1910.（记作"D.H.1910"）

DR. R. A. Parker, *Lessons in the Shanghai Dialect, in Romanized and Character, with Key to Pronunciation*, Shanghai: Shanghai Municipal Council, Kwang Hsueh Publishing House, 1923.（记作"DR.1923"）

王廷珏《增补实用上海话》，上海：美术工艺制版社出版部，民国二十九年（1940）。（记作"王 1940"）

P. G. von Mollendorff, *The Ningbo Colloquial Handbook*（《宁波方言便览》）, Shanghai: American Presbyterian Mission Press, 1910. 此书实际写于十九世纪末期。（记作"P.G.1910"）

P. H. S. Montgomery, *Introduction to the Wenchow dialect*, Shanghai: Kelly & Walsh, 1893.（记作"P.H.1893"）

一 吴语受事话题句分布广

及物结构（transitive structure）中受事优先充当哪种句法成分，由语序类型决定。普通话是话题优先的语言，受事成分往往受语用因素影响，可选择作话题或次话题。

如"这碗饭我吃完了"，肯定陈述句中及物动词"吃"的受事"这碗饭"是确指的对象，是已知信息，易于在句首作话题，"我吃完了"则用来说明话题，这种"受事话题–说明"的结构，体现了汉语话题优先特征。

吴语上海等方言中，这种受事话题句使用更常见。普通话常用的见面问候语"吃（饭）了吗"，上海话最自然的表达是"（侬）饭吃好哦？"。刘丹青（2001）指出，上海话受事话题句高达 1/3 强，一般多分布在是否问句（如"侬钢笔有哦"）、反复问句和否定陈述句中，而特指疑问句、反意疑问句、肯定陈述句等大多使用 VO 语序。钱乃荣（1997）也分别指出吴语上海话 SOV（即本文的受事话题句）分布的八种句法环境。不过，早期吴语上海话受事话题句分布的句类更丰富。在句法位置上，受事成分不仅可以在主谓之间做次话题，也可以在主语前，做主话题。

1.1 是非问句和正反问句

是非问句和正反问句中受事成分充当话题的倾向在上海话、宁波话和温州话中都非常强烈。如：

上海话：

（1）A：馒头侬担拉否？

　　　B：担哩。

（2）铜钱侬还有得多否？　　　　　　　　　　　　　　　　　　（BE1850）

（3）A：侬帽子有吪？

　　　B：吪没。

（4）伊个先生饭吃末？

（5）中国桃子侬吃过歇末？

（6）我个衣裳裁缝做好末？　　　　　　　　　　　　　　　　　（F.L.1907）

（7）（甲）布机有否？

　　　（乙）布机有一千部。

（8）（甲）我伲行里，东洋货，西洋货，随便甚杂货，都办个。

　　　（乙）出口货做否？　　　　　　　　　　　　　　　　　（王 1940）

宁波话：

（9）蚊虫英国有弗？

（10）葛个小人豆有种过弗？

（11）葛件衣裳明朝做拉好弗？

（12）你天亮饭吃过弗？

（13）上海个道台看见过弗？

（14）A：饭吃得落弗？

　　　　B：吃弗落。

（15）葛种介個货色你拉地方有弗有？

（16）糙米饭先生吃弗吃？ （P.G.1910）

温州话：

（17）A：你灯点起罢未？

　　　　B：我点起罢，渠吹炎。

（18）A：你饭吃罢未？

　　　　B：我还未吃。

（19）A：该本书你读完罢未？

　　　　B：十分我□ [ts'z²] 过八分罢。（"□"表本字未明）

（20）A：该个字你识弗识？

　　　　B：该个字我还未□ [ts'z²] 过。

（21）A：佢土话懂弗懂。

　　　　B：我听见讲佢不懂。 （P.H.1893）

　　上海话、宁波话、温州话虽构成是非问句的语气词不同，但句中若带受事，则都采取话题句表达。BE1850第一到三册共19课中带受事的是非问句共67例，全都采用受事话题句。

　　宁波话若受事为指人的名词，也可以出现在句首做话题，如例（13）。这种高生命度的名词极易与施事主语相混，但宁波话仍出现在句首作话题，这表明话题在宁波话中有固有的句法位置，所以无须担心高生命度名词充当话题时与主语混淆。

　　在是否问句中，还有一类偏离话题句的结构。如：

上海话：

（22）一把刀伊担拉否？

（23）一只篮侬肯借拉我否？

（24）A：一只鸟侬要拨伊否？

　　　　B：是要拨伊。

（25）两匹布侬辫拉？ （BE1850）

（26）一只狗要买吓？ （F.L.1907）

　　以上用例中句首数量结构所指无定，是新信息，也是焦点信息，其语义属性偏离了话题表确指或类指义，也不符合话题为旧信息的语用特征，但早期上海话却可以出现在主语前，例（22）—（25）在主语前，例（26）施事主语省略，数量结构"一只狗"出现在话题位置上。这与是否问句中受事的话题倾向强烈有关，由于受事倾向于前置，当它偏离了话题的语义语用属性时，也被前置，就出现了 OV 语序的迹象。

1.2 否定句

否定句也是早期吴语受事话题结构分布的主要句类。如：

上海话：

（27）<u>馒头</u>我勿担。

（28）<u>榔头</u>末勿担，担之钉来。

（29）<u>背心</u>伊吭没。

（30）<u>洋钱</u>末吭没个者，铜钱有两千拉哩。　　　　　　　　　　　　（F.L.1907）

（31）现在<u>东西</u>勿曾偷着，倒返而吃之素个布丁，终要求先生救救我一条命。（DR.1923）

（32）（甲）我<u>酒</u>勿大会吃个，吃杯麦茶罢。

（33）（主）格末依看，屋里向醒醒来，<u>窗上个玻璃</u>也勿揩，<u>蓬尘</u>也勿撢，<u>地板</u>也勿拖，
　　　　像甚样式呢？　　　　　　　　　　　　　　　　　　　　　　（王 1940）

上海话否定副词"勿"、"勿曾"与动词"吭没"构成否定句，若带受事成分，也都优先充当话题或次话题，例（30）、（32）句首名词与后一分句中名词构成对比性话题，并用"末"来突出话题的性质。

宁波话：

（34）<u>阿拉茶</u>嘸呐。

（35）<u>现银子</u>我身边弗带，请你上来帐上。

（36）<u>葛一桶水</u>掣弗起来。　　　　　　　　　　　　　　　　　　　（P.G.1910）

宁波话"嘸呐"表示"没有"的意思，作否定动词，"弗"为否定副词，表示"没"、"不"的意思，它们构成的否定句也用受事话题句来表达，如例（34）—（36）。

温州话：

（37）<u>许本书</u>识得个字还未数。

（38）其<u>铜钱</u>弗舍得用。　　　　　　　　　　　　　　　　　　　　（P.H.1893）

温州话"未"构成已然动作的否定句，"弗"用来否定未然或习惯性动作句，这些句子也采取受事话题句，如（37）、（38）。

是否问句、反复问句以及否定陈述句是早期上海、宁波、温州等方言话题句分布

的主要句类，这与当代上海话受事话题句的分布是一致的，表明 100 多年来吴语话题句就广泛地分布在这些句类中，但实际上，肯定句也是话题句分布的重要句类，特别是当句子表达某种主观意愿或祈使、命令等语气时，受事话题句几近成为唯一合法的表达。

1.3 肯定句类中的话题句

1.3.1 表示意愿或祈使的肯定句

这类句子在上海话中常用表示必须的情态助词"要"、加强语气的"脱我"（"帮我"、"给我"的意思）。如，例（39）—（44）；句中谓词，一般都带结果补语，或者用表示反复义的重叠式。如：

上海话：

（39）馒头要侬切开来。

（40）羊肉要侬割脱一颜。

（41）羊肉要烧来熟点。

（42）第只袋要侬背一背。

（43）第颜羊肉脱我割脱之。

（44）第个鸡汤脱我烧一烧热。 （BE1850）

宁波话：

（45）东西量量看。

（46）豌要强拉干净。

（47）地毯上灰尘担点掉。

（48）客间收作好起来。

（49）衣裳折好放来衣橱里。

（50）出来之，门锁锁好。

（51）地板扫扫其。

（52）葛票货色我贱贱贵贵要卖掉。 （P.G.1910）

温州话：

（53）字典撬起。

（54）衣裳□ [t'aih] 落。（脱下衣服）

（55）许本书□ [tso¹] 来丏我。（拿那本书来给我）

（56）该日天色冷，你衣裳著著一件添。 （P.H.1893）

以上各例用来表达说者的主观意愿或对听者的一种要求、命令，句中受事成分都前置做话题，话题句也是表达意愿句或祈使句的基本句式，很少用处置结构表达。

1.3.2 动补结构做谓词的受事话题句

动补结构或动词带体标记做谓词，不表达意愿或祈使时，若带受事成分，也有很强的话题化倾向，尤其是宁波话，这类陈述句的受事话题化倾向十分强烈。如例（57）—（65），其中例（65）为无定数量名短语充当受事话题；温州话则虽多用话题结构，但这些话题多作处置介词宾语（下文展开），上海话不如宁波、温州两方言强烈。如：

宁波话：

（57）葛个道理我前头听过兑。

（58）一百部书都印好兑。

（59）衣裳濯好兑。

（60）律法皇帝已经定当兑。

（61）屋拢总拆掉兑。

（62）一票银子我付完兑。

（63）前礼拜雨 落拉大大。

（64）葛档生意铜钱可以稳赚。

（65）一百块洋钱我已经收到兑。（P.G.1910）

温州话：

（66）火烛 烧起。（P.H.1893）

上海话：

（67）侬看，第个窗帘侬弄坏者。

（68）若然第件案子能够破脱末，我要大大里赏赐倻。（DR.1923）

（69）伊就大大里动气咾话，我是中国人，只会教中国个圣贤书，外国书是外国人读个，就是杀脱我个头末，我也勿情愿教个。

（70）我有一个朋友拉苏州做教习个，伊话，要弃脱蝇苍，勿是拉伊拉已经出来个后首。

以上上海话例（67）、（68）都用话题结构，但例（69）—（70）虽用动补结构做谓语，但受事仍做动词宾语。

从受事话题所分布的两类肯定句来看，影响话题化的因素有两个，其一是表示祈使、意愿的语气，这对三地方言受事话题化的制约是一致的，其次是句法上谓语必须带补语、体标记或其他成分，这个句法条件对宁波话受事话题化的影响最明显。

此外，受事话题句也分布在特殊疑问句中。如：

上海话：

（71）袜侬要买几双？

（72）<u>第封信</u>侬要拨拉啥人？

（73）<u>手</u>侬为啥净来勿干净？　　　　　　　　　　　　　　　　　　　（BE1850）

温州话：

（74）你<u>铜钱银</u>肯多少帮我否？　　　　　　　　　　　　　　　　　　（P.H.1893）

综上所述，吴语上海、温州、宁波话受事话题化十分活跃，受事可分布在各句类中（是非问、正反问、特殊疑问句、否定陈述句、祈使句、意愿句等）作主话题和次话题。这表明，在吴语这种话题优先典型的汉语方言中，受事易于在某种特定的句法或语用因素的驱使下，实现话题化，甚至表示无定数量名结构的受事也可以出现在动词前，形成 OV 结构。

二　吴语处置句发达

处置式并非 SOV 语序的句法表现，而与汉语话题化倾向有关。虽不少学者（Tai 1973；Li & Thompson 1974；桥本 1985）将处置式看做汉语 SOV 语序的表现，但处置式在普通话中出现率很低（Sun & Givón 1985），在结构上与 OV 语序的关系也并不密切，却与受事话题句关系密切（朱德熙 1982），"处置介词 -NP"结构表示有定的对象或类属义，它和动词可以没有选择关系，它控制着代词复指和同指 NP 成分的删除等（Tsao 1979，1990；Mei 1979），功能、形式、语用的研究都表明处置结构具有话题结构的特征，所以处置式的发达也是反映方言话题化程度的句法现象。如：

上海话：

（75）答应之末第个老板日夜赶紧个做，拿₁多化个火药放拉一只研钵里叫徒弟拼命个磨，研之长远药力忽然爆起来，"砰"个一响，拿₂房子全轰脱咾烧杀之七个人，看见之真正是凄惨。

（DR.1923）

例（75）中"拿₁"引介"多化个火药"作话题，述题部分"研之长远药力忽然爆起来，'砰'个一响，"进行说明，并推进到新的话语阶段，用"拿₂"来引进具有相关性的话题"房子"。

早期吴语上海、温州、宁波等方言处置结构都很活跃，成为实现受事话题化的重要句法手段。

早期上海话用"拿 [nau]"字处置句十分常见。如：

（76）有一只内河个小火轮行过咾激起浪头来拿第只小船冲翻之。

（77）拉第个时候第两个佣人就趁此机会拿伊拉捉牢之，哙送到官府地方去。

（78）必过伊个头有点蓬松伊个嘴里衔一粒大珍珠哙第粒珍珠个直径大约有一寸多，后首拨掘坟个小工拿珍珠从嘴里挖之出来，难末尸首立刻变颜色哙渐渐能腐料者，到末脚来变成功一摊水。

（79）后来巡捕来者就拿车夫打之一顿，车夫既然受之铜钱上个损失，又遭着肉身上个痛苦，实在是悔气。

（80）吃西瓜顶算省，吃完之拿西瓜皮盐之当粥菜，西瓜子抄熟之当小吃。

（81）我虽然勿懂化学，但是听见人家话碎玻璃再可以放拉炉里烧哙做东西个，实盖想起来我侬应该拿碎玻璃聚拢来放拉一处，一末可以免脱散拉地上触伤苦恼人个脚，二末再可以拿碎玻璃卖拨拉玻璃店里哙赚几个铜钱。

（82）伊连忙拿₁珍珠放拉伊个身边之哙，独方步走出去者，嘴里话"多谢，多谢"，难末第个伙计就跑上去拉住伊，第个女人就拿₂伊个伙计打两记耳光，后来第片店里个东家晓得事体勿对者，就出来讨饶哙认错，第个女人才肯拿₃珍珠拿出来，伊并且话俫勿肯卖可以话勿实，为啥要实盖吭规矩哙吨人呢，我现在打侬就是要教训。

（DR.1923）

上举用例（75）—（82）中"拿"表示处置，处置宾语是上文已经谈及的，也是说明部分叙述的对象，处置宾语具有话题的特点；"拿"表处置很常见，一段话中，随着话题推进，多次使用处置介词来引进新的话题，如例（82）"拿₁"、"拿₂"分别引进新话题"珍珠"和"伊个伙计"，"拿₃"则激活有话语间隔的话题"珍珠"，并将话语不断推进。从功能角度来看，早期吴语"拿"字处置句发达并不奇怪，因为在吴语这样的话题优先语言中，话语的推进往往是以话题来展开，话题是重要的句法成分，除了表示话题句法成分性质的形态标记即话题标记在发展之外，具有介引话题功能的其他句法成分也得到发展，如处置标记"拿"。

温州话、宁波话处置结构也是常见的句式。如：

（83）我把三板划岸边去。

（84）把该两张纸□ [pah] 起。

（85）把箱收拾起。

（86）造反咯人把男女老少□ [oh] 杀爻。

（87）有个人放枪，把其个小□ [si] 儿伤着重□ [shie¹]。

（88）你两个□ [si] 儿，一个面貌顶生好，一个面貌丑甚，许个面貌好个耻笑许个面貌生土□ [le] 个，许个人就生气，把茶碗□ [choa] 破爻末碎。有个人讲其两句，其慌爻就讲茶碗是宕落爻个，其大家把其个辫儿揪牢，要把其拔去，其□ [lai²] 倒地下把手倒着。

（P.H.1893）

例（83）—（88）温州话用"把"[2] [po¹]字引介新话题，如例（88）"茶碗"、"其个辫儿"、"其"、"手"，将话语层层推进。温州话"把"可做量词、动词，但做处置介词是其主要功能，温州话（1893）中搜集 74 例"把"字句及短语，处置介词用法有 56 例。

宁波话也用"把 [pô][3]"表处置。如：

（89）<u>把</u>我个裕袄放来皮箱里。

（90）<u>把</u>葛星碗盏碟子拁去园来橱里。

（91）好<u>把</u>火炉放来外头。

（92）偌去<u>把</u>帐子挂子。

（93）昨日落拉一阵大雨<u>把</u>我隔开来河葛边。

（94）我<u>将</u>葛件事干告诉偌，偌勿要扬开。

（95）走到一塔地方，叫拉骷髅，来葛头<u>把</u>耶稣等两犯人钉来十字架，一人来顺手边，一个来左手边。

（96）其拉带其去时候，拿一个吉利奈人西门，从田阪晨介来，<u>把</u>十字架放来其身上，拨其背来耶稣后背。　　　　　　　　　　　　　　　　　　　　　（P.G.1910）

尽管处置句形成较晚，但上海话、温州话、宁波话并不少用，这种句式的发展和活跃与其整体句法类型特征相关。从话语功能来看，处置介词不仅表达处置意义，它还具有引介话题的功能，处置句发达是吴语话题优先句法特征的重要内容。

三　"基准＋比较结果"的差比句

语序类型学中差比句存在两种不同的线性序列，一为"形容词（比较结果 adjective）– 比较标记（marker）– 基准（standard）"，如"taller than John"、"我高过你"，这种词序的差比句往往与 VO 语序和谐；二为"基准 – 比较标记 – 形容词"式，它与 OV 语序和谐（Greenberg 1963）。Dryer（1992）考察 625 种语言中形容词（adjective）和基准（standard）的词序分布，也得出 OV 语言以"基准＋形容词（StAdj）"为差比句式，而 VO 语言差比句则用"形容词＋基准（AdjSt）"的语序，不过汉语则成了唯一的例外。

实际上，汉语差比句中基准与形容词常常并没有语义上的选择关系。如"房子我比你大"，属性主体"房子"与形容词"大"具有语义上的选择关系，而基准"你"并不是形容词"大"的必有论元，它与形容词语义关联松散；其次，从语用信息角度来看，"基准"一般多为有定的已知信息，具有话题的特征，而"形容词"为比较的结果，是未知的信息，所以"基准＋形容词"的词序，遵循着"旧信息＋新信息"信息组织原则，与"话题－述题"的表达是一致的，这种语序体现了话题优先语言的句法特点。这样，在话题倾向越强的方言或语言中，"基准"前置为话题的要求越高，也更倾向于采用"基准＋形容词"的结构。

早期吴语具有话题优先典型的句法特征，这也反映在差比句整齐划一地使用"基准＋形容词"的词序上。上海话使用"比／比之＋基准＋结果"的差比句，宁波话、温州话与上海话差比句词序一样，但一般只用"比"作比较标记。

（97）A：侬第个小囝比之个个大点否？

　　　B：大点。

（98）A：侬第只箱子比之个只轻点否？

　　　B：倒重点。

（99）A：侬第件背心比之个件长点否？

　　　B：长点。

（100）A：侬个银子搭我个一样数目否？

　　　 B：侬比我多。

（101）A：第个人个马比我多呢少？

　　　 B：马末比侬少点，驴子呢比侬多点。　　　　　　　　　（BE1850）

（102）现在拉租界里造房子，比之从前是大两样哉。

（103）讲到救火个家生，现在是比从前更加好咾灵巧。

（104）我想第日上，坐电气车个人，比之闲常日脚，要加添多倍拉。

（105）印度国里，老鼠个数目，比之人个数目来得多。

（106）因为人个性命，比之铜钱，是更加宝贝也。　　　　　　　（D.H.1910）

BE1850 与 D.H.1910 中用"比之"比"比"更常见，但"基准＋结果"的词序是一致的。不过，在 DR.1923 中则"比"字差比句比较常见。如：

（107）台湾是福建对面个一个小岛，天气本来是比上海热，但是今年夏天热得更加利害。

（108）从杭州有黄包车到现在，伊个生意是十分发达，车夫拉车子比上海个车夫要好得

　　　　多。

（109）讲到穿耳朵眼吃个苦头确实比缠脚多得多者。

（110）我看杭州个包车比之上海个汽车还要出风头。

（111）伊个两只眼睛虽然瞎，但是分辩物品个本事，比之亮子还要来得利害，我有空个

　　　　工夫末，我终要到伊个店里去坐坐咾勃相相。

（112）莫干山是浙江西南个一个有名声个地方，山青水秀比之江西个牯岭还要好。

（DR.1923）

早期宁波话、温州话则一律用"比"字差比句。如：

（113）葛个东西比其好两倍。

（114）其女人个气力比其大。

（115）中国字比外国字难写。

（116）塘头个说话，比葛头个说话好讲。

（117）俉拉葛头个规矩，比阿拉塘头好。

（118）柴比煤炭贱点。

（119）塘头个田稻比阿拉葛头个迟点。 （P.G.1910）

（120）该比许个还好呐。

（121）该俫个屋宕比旁搭高呐。

（122）该个屋宕比许个屋宕好多。

（123）其字眼比我识多来个。

（124）菜油比麻油贱呐。 （P.H.1893）

早期上海话、宁波话、温州话都采用"基准＋比较结构"的词序，这种词序与其语序类型并不相悖，吴语并不是典型的 VO 语言，但却是一种话题优先典型的汉语方言，差比句采取"形容词＋基准＋比较结果"的结构，"基准"是有定成分，有些基准与句子谓语没有句法语义上的联系，它们之间的关系得靠语境（上下文）关联，如例（104）"闲常日脚"与谓语"添"，（109）"缠脚"与谓语"多"等，语义关系非常松散，只有联系比较前项（上文）才能明确这些基准与谓语之间的语义关系，例（104）应该是"闲常日脚坐电气车个人"，是谓语"添"的论元成分，例（109）联系比较前项，得出"缠脚"应该是"缠脚吃个苦"，与"多"构成论元关系。"基准"与谓语间松散的句法语义关系符合汉语话题–述题关系，所以基准就是话题，比较结果构成述题。早期吴语采取"基准＋比较结构"的差比句与它话题优先的句法类型特征相吻合。

四　处所题元的前置

处所题元是指由处所词充当的处所宾语或状语。普通话中"我去北京"中"北京"作"去"的宾语，表示终点，也可以做状语，如"到北京去／来"，广州话处所题元则只能作宾语，如"佢去／来北京"，这种句法分布的差异，与方言语序类型有着密切关系。广州话 SVO 语序比普通话典型，采用"去 / 来 + 终点"结构也不足奇怪，而普通话 SVO 语序并不典型，处所题元状语化的结构与这种语序类型特征相和谐。处所题元是汉语方言类型比较研究的重要参项。

刘丹青（2004）比较粤语、吴语、官话等方言"来 / 去"句处所题元句法位置，得出粤语（方所后置倾向）–官话（介于两者之间）–吴语（方所前置倾向）的类型差异。这种类型差异，与粤语、官话、吴语的语序类型是相和谐的。今吴语上海等方言优先选择"处所题元 + 来 / 去"的结构，特别是绍兴、宁波等地采取"终点 + 来 / 去"结构的前置式，这种句法表现与其受事次话题化而引起的 SOV 萌芽是和谐的。

传教士方言课本中，上海话、温州话等处所题元则以"到 + 终点 + 来 / 去"为常，偶尔也见用"终点 + 来 / 去"的前置式，宁波话则大量使用"终点 + 来 / 去"，但是三方言都没有"来 / 去 + 终点"的用法。

（125）我要到花旗国去。

（126）到伊爷墙头去。

（127）我勿到啥人场化去。

（128）俫爷是要到侬阿哥场化去否?

（129）侬可以到我场化来一淘去看戏否?

（130）A：侬啥场化去买个?

　　　B：苏州去买个。　　　　　　　　　　　　　　　　　　　　（BE1850）

例（125）、（126）肯定陈述句，都采用"到 + 终点 + 去"的结构；例（127）特殊疑问词用作任指，例（128）、（129）用"否"构成是非问句，也都采用"到 + 终点 + 去 / 来"结构，不过，例（130）特殊疑问句则采用"啥场化 + 去"结构提问，并用"苏州 + 去"作答，从句子信息结构来看，"苏州"显然是句子的自然焦点，应该在谓语动词后，但答句却采取了"苏州 + 去"的句式，这类结构在王1940中较常见。如：

（131）黄包车，虹口小菜场去否?

（132）送侬巡捕房里去。

（133）城里独怕勿曾去。

（134）（乙）还好侬忙呀，我伲长远勿见者，阿里来?

　　　（甲）屋里来，我出门去之一趟，昨日刻转来。

（135）（甲）老兄阿里来?

　　　（乙）我从茶会上来，侬今朝勿曾出去?　　　　　　　　　（王 1940）

例（131）—（134）中处所题元在谓语动词"去 / 来"前，从句类来看，例（131）

为是非问句，例（132）肯定陈述句，例（133）为否定句，例（134）是特殊疑问句，"处所题元＋去／来"的结构分布不受句类限制。不过，例（135）的问答形式与例（134）同，而例（135）则用"从＋源点＋来"作答，且这种结构更为普遍，"源点＋来"、"从＋源点＋来"结构对比表明，前者很可能是从后者隐去前置词"从"而来，因为前置词往往在谓词和后置词表义完备时可以省去。

温州话表处所的疑问词也常用在"来／走"前，如：

（136）你老人家<u>若宕</u>来？

（137）你老人家末<u>若宕</u>走？　　　　　　　　　　　　　　　　　　　（P.H.1893）

不过，优势结构仍然是"到／走＋终点＋去"。如：

（138）到<u>若宕</u>去？

（139）A：其走<u>若宕</u>去罢，你晓得弗晓得？

　　　　B：其走<u>街□</u> [de] 去罢。　　　　　　　　　　　　　　　　　（P.H.1893）

尽管上海话、温州话课本中，以"到／走＋处所题元＋去／来"为优势结构，不过，宁波话普遍可见的是"处所题元＋去／来／到"的结构。如：

（140）<u>塘头</u>来过弗？

（141）我想<u>扬子江上头</u>去。

（142）<u>北京</u>到过弗？

（143）<u>城里头</u>到过么？

（144）倷<u>阿里</u>去？

（145）其<u>船里</u>来，快弗？　　　　　　　　　　　　　　　　　　　　（P.G.1910）

例（140）—（144）都采用"终点＋来／去／到"的词序，例（145）"船里"很特殊，处所短语"船里"表示"乘船"的意思，处所短语表示方式，宁波话一般用"趁 [ts'ing]"作介词，接"船 [jün]"作宾语，但此例隐去前置介词"趁"，用"船里"和"来"使语义完备，这也表明宁波话是一种前置词功能很弱而后置词功能强的方言。

五　处所后置词活跃

类型学中的 Adposition[4] 是指语言中黏附在名词性短语上，表示该名词与句中动词的语法或语义关系的词，比如英语 "The cat sleeps on the sofa" 中 "on" 在名词短语 "the sofa" 前，引进前置性短语 "on the sofa"，"on" 为附置词中的前置词（preposition）；

汉语"放桌子上"中"上"则在名词短语"桌子"后，引介后置性短语，"上"则为后置词（postposition）。所以根据它与名词短语的位置关系，附置词可分为前置词和后置词。

附置词与语序基本类型相关（correlation），是语序类型学研究的重要参项，具有很强的预测力。如果一种语言是 OV 语言，则常使用后置词，若是 VO 语言，则常使用前置词，前置词、后置词的使用与语序类型相关。

早期吴语虽属于前置词和后置词并存的方言，但表示处所的后置词十分丰富。如：

宁波话：

（146）茶壶，按<u>来</u>茶几<u>上</u>。 （P.G.1910）

温州话：

（147）我坐<u>是</u>楼<u>上</u>，其坐<u>是</u>下转。 （P.H.1893）

上海话：

（148）难末伲回<u>到</u>房子<u>里</u>去，担之伲个行李就到船上吃之夜饭咾困个。 （DR.1923）

例（146）"来"表所在，为宁波话前置词，"上"则黏附在"茶几"上，表示方向，为宁波话后置词；例（147）温州话表示场所"是"与表示方向的后置词"上"构成框式结构，不过，这种组合是句法的，不是词汇的，所以不宜看作框式附置词；例（148）上海话表示终点的前置词"到"与后置词"里"共现。可见，早期吴语也是前置词和后置词并存的汉语方言，表示所在、终点等意义的前置词，与表示方向的"上、里"等后置词共现。不过，早期吴语表处所的后置词比较发达。

"地方"可黏附在普通名词和专有名词后，并不附加实在的处所意义，表义很虚，标明所黏附名词的处所性质。如：

（149）伊（骆驼）走拉沙漠<u>地方</u>有大功劳拉人个，伊走拉沙漠<u>地方</u>可以忍耐七日勿吃啥。（126 课）

（150）拉夏天热个辰光拉上海有多化外国人到乡下<u>地方</u>去避暑。

（151）今年上海<u>地方</u>，从湖北来个难民实在多，因为拉湖北河阳泉<u>地方</u>有水荒，田里无没出产。（133 课）

（152）中国<u>地方</u>马个用头，做手脚及别国个多，因为拉内地里少开阔个路咾，就是乡下人家耕田，都勿用马，全是用牛。

（153）酒钱末，拉中国各处<u>地方</u>勿论做啥大小个事体，终有人要讨酒钱。

（154）拉烟台<u>地方</u>顶好勃相，好拉海洋里向游水。

（155）拉山东<u>地方</u>，有一个人姓赵，伊有两个儿子。

（156）船上个客人，也勿敢进第个口子。拉口子里向个人，也勿许出去到别块<u>地方</u>，恐怕病要传染开也，拉香港<u>地方</u>从前有实盖个事体。　　　　　　　　（D.H.1910）

上海话"地方"可以做普通名词"沙漠"、名词短语"乡下"的处所后置词，如例（149）、（150），也可以接在地名、国名上，如（151）—（156），成为高频使用的处所后置词。

宁波话也用"地方"或"地面"作处所后置词。如：

（157）收票来我<u>地方</u>。

（158）山东<u>地面</u>周围转方大约七十二万里。

（159）广西<u>地方</u>出好树木。　　　　　　　　　　　　　　　（P.G.1910）

宁波话"地方"表处所时，不仅可用在专有名词后，也可用在人称代词后。如：

（160）<u>丝</u>不是你大家<u>地方</u>出个呢？　　　　　　　　　　　（P.G.1910）

不过，温州话仅有例（160），"地方"用在复数人称代词后。

此外，"场化"、"块"、"墙头"等名词也都可以在人称代词或指人名词后表处所，有些也可以用在处所名词后。如：

（161）垃拉我<u>场化</u>　垃拉伊<u>场化</u>　垃拉伲<u>场化</u>

（162）垃拉俉<u>场化</u>　垃拉伊拉<u>场化</u>

（163）勿垃拉到伊兄弟<u>场化</u>去者。

（164）侬是要差人担物事到皮匠<u>场化</u>否？

（165）几点钟侬到外国人<u>场化</u>去。

（166）看地方起，像江湾，杨树浦咾甚，近来完，不过鸟少点，像苏州，杭州<u>场化</u>末，山多，格咾野鸡野鸭，伊套野货美多个，倒是路远点，一日天转来勿。（王1940）

（167）到伊爷<u>墙头</u>去。

（168）郎中先生几时到俉阿哥<u>墙头</u>去。　　　　　　　　　　（BE1850）

（169）我拉前年个夏天避暑，拉伊<u>块</u>个辰光我看见之多条大蛇。　　（DR.1923）

（170）而且拉每条桥<u>块</u>下，扎之柏子个牌楼咾，装之各奇，各式个金丝灯。（D.H.1910）

上举用例中"场化"的使用很普遍，可用在人称代词、指人名词、专有地名等上，表示处所或标记词语的处所性质；"墙头"、"块"的使用不及"场化"常见，如例（168）—（171）都用作处所的后置词。

处所后置词活跃也是现代吴语的一大特点，比如温州话"拉 [la⁰]"可以在代词或指人名词后，如"蓝水笔是我拉（钢笔在我这儿）"，"票走老王拉（票子到老王那儿拿）"，例中"拉"读轻声，它主要表示所黏附的名词或代词的处所性，与处所词不同，它与早期吴语各方言"地方""场化"一样，都是吴语中的处所后置词。这些处所后置词与普通话处所指示代词"这里/那里"不同，"这里/那里"虽也常用在其他体词后表示处所，但带有较实在的处所意义，若与表示处所的名词组合，则形成叠床架屋的现象，造成语义冗余，表达不经济，所以处所名词后一般都不用"这里/那里"，而吴语"地方""场化"等则可以黏附在处所名词上，它是一个表义虚化的功能词，即后置词，尽管在语音形式上还没有弱读迹象。

六　小结

根据一百多年前西方传教士的方言学课本，本文从句法类型学角度初步探讨了早期吴语上海、宁波和温州话的相关句法表现，概括如下：

（1）早期上海话、宁波话和温州话受事话题化的倾向强烈，是非问句、正反问句、否定陈述句、表示意愿或祈使的肯定句等句类都成为受事话题句分布的句类，这种受事话题化也与句法结构自身的调整不可分割，尤其是宁波话，谓语动词重叠或附加其他成分，都倾向于用受事话题句表达。

（2）处置介词虽仍表达某种处置意义，但其语用功能与话题标记相似，处置介词带受事宾语也是实现吴语受事话题句的重要手段，"拿"、"把"做处置介词，具有引进新话题、激活有间隔的话题等功能，处置结构在三地吴语中发达，是吴语话题优先典型的句法表现。

（3）早期吴语都采取"基准－形容词"的词序，"比"字差比句是吴语最基本的差比句式。这种结构中基准与形容词的语义关系松散，"基准－形容词"与"话题－说明"结构相似，所以吴语采取"基准－形容词"的差比句词序，也与其话题优先典型的句法特征有关。

（4）处所题元的句法分布也与语序类型有着密切关系。早期吴语上海话、温州话等处所题元以"到/走＋终点＋来/去"为常，偶尔也见用"终点＋来/去"的前置式，宁波话则大量使用"终点＋来/去"，但是三方言都没有"来/去＋终点"的用法。

（5）处所后置词是一类黏附在体词性成分上，表示体词处所性质的词，早期吴语"地方""场化"等可黏附于人称代词、普通名词、专有名词上表示处所，是功能活跃的处所后置词。

基于以上五个方面的句法特征，从类型学角度来看，我们相信早期吴语（一百多年前）就是一种话题优先典型而 SVO 语序较弱的汉语方言。

附 注

[1] Trask（1993）《标准英语语言学词典》收录 topic prominence（Li & Thompson）。Trask, R. L. (1993) *A Dictionary of Grammatical Terms in Linguistics*. USA: Routledge.

[2] 当代温州话用"逮"做处置介词，如"你逮地下扫两扫爻。（你把地扫一扫）"（游汝杰 2003：222）；该书记作"把"字，应借用了官话形式，不过，我们相信，在处置句式的使用上，该书应反映了温州方言的实际情况。

[3] 此处宁波话"把"，当代宁波方言一般记作"拨"字。

[4] 沈家煊（2000）《现代语言学词典》（北京：商务印书馆）译为附置词，刘丹青（2003）《语序类型学与介词理论》（北京：商务印书馆）中称为介词。为避免与传统语法中的"介词"概念混淆，本文采用附置词的说法。

参考文献

曹逢甫（1979/1995）《主题在汉语中的功能研究》，谢天蔚译，北京：语文出版社。

刘丹青（2001）吴语的句法类型学特点，《方言》第 4 期。

刘丹青（2004）方所题元的若干类型学参项，《中国语文研究》总 9 期。

钱乃荣（1997）吴语中的 NPS 句和 SOV 句，《语言研究》第 2 期。

桥本万太郎（1985）《语言地理类型学》，余志鸿译，北京：北京大学出版社。

徐烈炯、刘丹青（1998）《话题的结构与功能》，上海：上海教育出版社。

游汝杰（1981）温州方言的语法特点及其历史渊源，《复旦学报（社会科学版）》语言文字专辑。

游汝杰（2002）《西洋传教士方言学著作书目考述》，黑龙江：黑龙江教育出版社。

朱德熙（1982）《语法讲义》，北京：商务印书馆。

Chao, Yuanren (1968) *A Grammar of Spoken Chinese*. Berkeley: University of California Press.

Dryer, Matthew S. (1992) The Greenbergian word order correlations. *Language* 68: 81–138.

Dryer, Matthew S. (2005) Order of adposition and noun phrase. *WALS*, 346–349.

Greenberg, Joseph H. (1963) Some universals of grammar with particular reference to the order of meaningful elements. In Joseph H. Greenberg (ed.) *Universals of grammar*, 73–113. Cambridge MA: MIT Press.

Li, Charles N. & Sandra Thompson (1974) An explanation of word order change: SVO SOV. *Foundations of Language* 12: 201–214.

Li, Charles N. & Sandra Thompson (1976) Subject and topic: A new typology of language. In. C. Li (ed.), *Subject and Topic*. New York: Academic Press.

Mei, Kung (1980) Is Modern Chinese really a SOV language? In Ting-chi Tang, Feng-fu Tsao & Ing Li (eds.) *Papers from the 1979 Asian and Pacific Conference on Linguistics and Language Teaching*: 261–273. Taipei: Taiwan Student Book Co.

Sun, Chao-fen & Givón Talmy (1985) On the so-called SOV word order in Mandarin Chinese: A quantified text study and its implications. *Language* 61(2): 329−351.

Tai, James (1973) On two functions of place adverbials in Mandarin. *Journal of Chinese Linguistics* 3.2/3: 154−179.

Tsao, feng-fu (1990) *Sentence and Clause Structure in Chinese: A Functional Perspective* (《国语的句子与子句结构》). Taipei: Taiwan Student Book Co.

（本文发表于《中国语文研究》2010 年第 1 期，第 1—15 页）

罗明坚、利马窦《葡汉辞典》
所记录的明代官话

杨福绵

一、《葡汉辞典》手稿的发现

天主教耶稣会史学家德礼贤（Pasquale D'Elia, S. J., 1890—1963）于 1934 年，在罗马耶稣会档案馆中发现了一组手稿，编号是 Jap.—Sin, I, 198。手稿共 189 页，是写在中国纸上的。长 23 公分，宽 16.5 公分。这组手稿的内容并不一致，只是因为纸张和墨迹相同，档案保管人（年代姓名未详）把它们编为一组。手稿第 32 页至 165 页是一部葡萄牙语和汉语对照的辞典。我们称它为《葡汉辞典》（以后简称《辞典》）。《辞典》前后的附页内容零散不一。包括学习汉语用的笔记，词汇，天干地支，十五省名称，天文知识及天主教教义，简介等杂项。其中最值得注意的是第 3a 页至 7a 页，用罗马字标题的 Pin ciù ven tà ssì gnì（见附图一）。德礼贤把它译成《平常问答词意》。[1]不过据笔者最近研究的结果应该译为《宾主问答辞义》。德氏把 Pin 误读为 Pim（平），把 ciù 误读为 ciã（常），把 gnì（义）误认为 yi（意）。原来这是一本会话小册子，是帮助新到中国的传教士学习会话用的。在对话各句子前面都标有 ciu gin iuo（主人曰），chè iuo（客曰），tũ iuo（童曰），ven yuo（问曰），ta yuo（答曰）等字样。"主人"是指传教士；"客"（人）是指来访的中国文人或官员；"童"是指传教士雇用的童仆。全文用罗马字拼写，因为没有汉字，所以有许多词句不易辨认。从笔迹来看，我们可以断定这篇对话是罗明坚写的。其罗马字系统大致和《辞典》中用的相同。其余杂组笔记，是利玛窦或他的汉语教师写的。

二、《葡汉辞典》的编者和年代

根据手稿的纸张、笔迹，以及内容，我们可以证明这部《辞典》的主编者是罗明坚（Michele Ruggieri, S. J., 1543—1607），合编者是利玛窦（Matteo Ricci, S. J., 1552—1610）。编纂年代当是罗利二氏初入中国广东肇庆传教的时期。他们两人于 1583 年秋天抵达肇庆，而罗氏则于 1588 年冬离开中国返回罗马。因此这部书稿当在 1584——

1588 年间完成。也很可能是罗氏亲自带回罗马去的。除了笔迹以外，我们还可以根据《辞典》前的附页，得到更确切的结论。上面提到的《宾主问答辞义》里 5a 页有下面一段宾主对话：

Che iuo: si fu tau cie li yi chi nien liau

[kʻəʔ yoʔ: sɿ fu tau tʃɛ li i ki niɛn liau]

客曰：师父到这里已几年了？

Ta iuo: zai yeu liã nien

[taʔ yoʔ: tsʻai iəu liaŋ niɛn]

答曰：才有两年。

Che iuo: giu chin ni schiau te' ngo mun cie piẽ cuõ cua po schiau te'

[kʻəʔ yoʔ: ʒu kin ni xiau təʔ ŋo mun tʃɛ piɛn kuɔn xua poʔ xiau təʔ]

客曰：如今你晓得我们这边官话不晓得？

Ta iuo: ye schiau te' chi chiu

[taʔ yoʔ: iɛ xiau təʔ ki ky]

答曰：也晓得几句。

Che iuo: ye chian te

[kʻəʔ yoʔ: iɛ kiaŋ təʔ]

客曰：也讲得？

Ta iuo: lio schio kiã chi chiu

[taʔ yoʔ: lioʔ xioʔ kiaŋ ki ky]

答曰：略学讲几句。

附页中（自 12a 页至 16b 页）还有用中文写的天主教教义介绍。文中有"僧（罗、利二氏初到中国时自称为'僧'）……三年前到广东肇庆"。罗利二氏于 1583 年秋天到肇庆开始学习汉语并建堂传教。因此"才有两年"和"三年前"，应该是 1585 至 1586 年间。也正是这个时期，他们二人在加紧学习汉语，感到双语辞典的需要，才着手编写了这部《葡汉辞典》。以葡语为原语是因为葡语是当时欧洲及亚洲葡萄牙殖民地的共同交际语。到印度、中国及日本等地来传教或经商的人士都通晓葡语。

三、《辞典》的内容

手稿没有封面，也没有书名和编者的姓名。德礼贤称它为 *Dizionario portoghese-cinese*（《葡汉辞典》），并撰文介绍过。[2]《辞典》编排的方式分三栏：第一栏是葡语词条，依拉丁字母 ABC 次序排列，不过有时次序不太严格。词条始自 Aba da vestidura "裙子"，终于 Zunir a orelha "耳朵响"。德氏以为始自 Abitar "居住"，[3] 这是因为他把《辞典》的第一页（手稿第 32a 页，见附图二，三）遗漏了。这一栏不但收葡语单词，有时也兼收词组和短句。例如葡语 Aguoa "水" 条下收了十七条词组：

葡语词	罗马字	汉语词
Aguoa	scioj	水
Aguoa de frol	zen sciã scioj	甑香水
Aguoa de poso	çin scioj	井水
Aguoa de fonte	yuõ [sic!] scioj	泉水（案 yuõ 为 çiuõ 之误）
Aguoa do rio	ho scioj	河水
Aguoa da chuva	yu scioj	雨水
Aguoa salguada	yen scioj	盐水
Aguoa salobra, cozida	chiu [sic!] guo scioj	煮过水（案 chiu 为 ciu 之误）
Aguoa …		（有六条葡语词组未填汉语对应词语）
Aguoa clara	çin scioj	清水
Aguoa da fazer	tau scioj	挑水（案 tau 为 tiau 之误）
Aguoar	（无罗马字）	灌水（案当为 cuon scioj）
Aguoar o vinho	zã scioj	渗水（酒中掺水；"渗" 为 "掺" 之误）

第二栏是罗马字注音，是罗明坚的笔迹。这是罗氏在肇庆学习汉语汉文时所创制的最早的罗马字注音，不过系统尚不完备。例如，无送气音和声调符号；声母和韵母的拼法尚未完全一致，不免有模棱含混的地方。我们可以称它为罗氏方案。利玛窦晚年（1606 年）在北京时，赠给了程大约（字幼博，1541—1616？）四篇罗马字注音文章。程氏把这四篇文章收入了他编的《程氏墨苑》里而刊行于世。[4] 利氏还写了一部《西字奇迹》，但是久已失传。最近顾保鹄教授发现了这部书的孤本，现存于罗马梵蒂冈图书馆（全书共六页，编号是 Racc. G. Orientale 231. 12）。顾教授并撰文介绍证实了《西字奇迹》的内容只是三篇罗马字注音文章，而且这三篇文章和《程氏墨苑》

所收的四篇罗马字注音文章中的前三篇完全相同。更指出这六页的书边上清楚地刻着《西字奇迹》的书名，是 1605 年利氏在北京刻印的原本，次年利氏在这三篇文章后面又加写了一篇《述文赠幼博程子》，连同四幅木刻宗教画，赠给了程氏（见附图五）。[5]这两种罗马字拼音文章中的音韵系统，是根据罗氏方案修订而成的。我们可以称它为利氏方案。后来金尼阁（Nicolas Trigault, S. J., 1577—1628）于 1626 年在杭州刊行的《西儒耳目资》就是根据利氏方案增订而成的。罗常培先生对利氏及金氏的方案做过详细的研究介绍。[6]《辞典》中并不是每个汉字、每个汉语词或词组都有罗马字注音。一般来说，在一个词条中，只有第一个词或主要的词有注音，它后面的同义词或文言词则没有注音（见下面论第三栏中所举的例子）。

第三栏是汉字汉语词条。是中国人的笔迹。大概是罗利二氏的汉语教师或其他文人书写的。汉语词条中包括单音节词、双音节词、词组和短句，这些词语以口语为主，兼附同义词和文言词，可以代表明代的口语，是明末官话的珍贵语言资料。一条葡语词可能有好几个汉语对应词。一般先列口语词，然后再列同义或近义词及文言词，例如：

葡语词	罗马字	汉语词
Bom parecer	piau ci	嫖致，美貌，嘉（"嫖"为"标"之别字）
Escarnar	co gio	割肉，切肉，剖肉
Espantadigo	chijn pa	惊怕，骇然，惊骇
Esperar, confiar	van, cau, sin	望，靠，信
Estudar	to sciu	读书，看书，观书
Fallar	chiã cua, sciuo cua	讲话，说话
Fallar Mãdarin	cuõ cua, cin yin	官话，正音（案 Mãdarin 即 Mandarin）
Falecer	ssi, uan, cu	死，亡，故，殁

自 32a 页至 34a 页第三栏后附加了意大利语词条，从笔迹上看似乎是利玛窦添加的。这部《辞典》手稿尚未完成。据初步统计，葡语词汇约收 6000 余条，而与之对应的汉语字词只有 5460 多条，有 540 多条葡语词汇未填汉语的对应词。这并不足为奇，因为这部《辞典》可能是中国第一部葡汉双语辞典，[7] 当时根本没有类似的辞书可以参考，有许多西方的词语，汉语里还没有合适的对应译法。例如在葡语"水"的词条中有一条是 Aguoa benta，是天主教的主教或神父祝圣过的水，简称"圣水"（英语叫 Holy water），当时罗利二氏刚到中国，这个宗教名词尚未翻译，所以只好付诸阙如。

　　这部《辞典》是否有副本，后来是否完成出版，我们不得而知。在利氏晚年所著的《中国传教史》（何高济等译为《利玛窦中国札记》，刘后余、王玉川译为《利玛窦中国传教史》）第四卷第三章最后一段记述传教士们编字典的事，编纂工作是利氏及其他传教士于 1598 年，由北京返回南京的途中开始的。他说："神父们租了一艘很好的船，价钱非常便宜，因为回程的船多半是空的，租金都不贵。但舵手很穷，没有别的助手，也没有仪器设备。因此航行了一个月才到临清。为了避免荒废旅途中的时光，早来（中国）的会士们，便利用这段时间编写了一部优美的字典。钟鸣仁修士（Sebastiano Hernandez, S. J., 1563?—1621?）精通中国语言，给予了很大的帮助。他们把汉语的字和词按照一定的规律和次序编成了一套表格，这对（后来传教士）学习汉语有很大的帮助。他们发现，这个语言（即汉语）都是由单音节的字或词组成；中国人发音时，必须注意每个字的声调和送气音，要注意用哪一类的发音来区别词义，否则每个词或字听起来好像都没有区别一样。这是中国语言最难学的地方。对于仔细分辨送气音和不同的声调方面，郭居静神父（Lazzaro Cattanco, S. J., 1560—1640）贡献很大。因为他是一位优秀的音乐家，善于分辨各种细微的声韵变化，精确地辨明声调的高低。于是他们拟定了五个符号来区别声调，一个符号来表示送气。利玛窦神父命令全体耶稣会士都一律采用这几个符号，不得擅自增减更改，以免造成混乱。会士们将统一的标音法用于已编好的字典，及将来要编的其他字典，这样都可以彼此传阅，一目了然，使我们全体会士在这门学问上，获得更大的效果与用途。"[8]

　　德礼贤以为利氏上面所述的字典就是《葡汉辞典》。他说："我也找到了欧洲人编写的第一部欧汉字典。这是罗明坚和利玛窦合编的第一部汉学著作。毫无疑义地，这便是季尔赫尔（Athanasius Kircher）在 1667 年所提到的，他说：'我有一部为我们（耶稣会传教士）使用的汉语词典手稿，如能获得印刷费，我很想把它付印成书。'"[9] 但是事实恐怕并非如此。十七世纪耶稣会史学家巴尔多里（Daniello Bartoli, S. J., 1608—1685）在他的《耶稣会史》中称这部字典为 *Vocabulario Sinicoeoruopeo*（《汉欧字汇》或《汉欧字典》）。[10] 上述季尔赫尔称它为《汉语字典》，而且是可以付梓的定稿，就是说，其中罗马字系统声调及送气音符号都已定型。这一切都表示这部字典的原语是汉语，是一部《汉欧（葡）字典》，它与《葡汉辞典》并非一书。那么《汉欧（葡）字典》是否已经出版？这问题很难回答，因为现在我们尚未发现和这部手稿相同的辞典。不过还有一个探究的线索，那就是费赖之（Louis Pfister, S. J., 1833—1891）的《入华耶稣会士列传》1934 年法文增订版的卷末参考书中（996 页）附了一条 *Catalogue Ms de Pékin*（《北京手抄（耶稣会士人名）目录》）。在该条脚注中谓这份目录是裴化行（Henri Bernard, S. J.）和范德本（Fr. Van den Brandt, C. M.）两位神父在一部《汉葡字典》手稿附录里发现的。而这部字典是他二人于 1933 年在北京图书馆发现的。该手稿编号是 22.658，共 8 + 624 + 34 页，32 开本。字典未标明编著者姓名、成书年月及地址。费氏书增订人在括弧里注有"或许是 1660—1661？（年间完成的）"。[11] 这部字典很可能是根据利玛窦等的《汉欧（葡）字典》编成的。不过要解答这个问题，必须查阅该稿本，并与《葡汉辞典》的罗马拼音方案以及词汇作一番比较和考证的工作，才能得到结论。

四、罗明坚汉语拼音早期方案的系统

上一节已经提过，《辞典》中所用的罗马字拼音系统恐怕是中国最早的一套汉语拼音方案。不过因为它属于初创，在声母和韵母拼写法上，尚未完全定型，甚至有些模棱混淆的地方。下面就把这方案的拼写特点摘要地介绍一下。

4.1 根据十六世纪意大利语及葡萄牙语字母的拼音

（1）根据意大利语的拼法：

（a）c=[tʃ] 或 [tʃʻ]：在 i,e 元音前。例如：战 cen [tʃɛn]，丈 ciam [tʃɛŋ]；臭 ceu [tʃʻəu]，出 cio [tʃʻoʔ]。利氏方案中改用 ch 和 chʻ。

（b）c=[k] 或 [kʻ]：在 a,o,u 元音前。例如：该 cai [kai]，官 cuon [kuɔn]；看 can [kʻan]，可 co [kʻɔ]，苦 cu [kʻu]。利氏方案中改用 k，kʻ，q（u），qʻ（u）。

（c）c=[x]：有时在 u 元音前。例如：花 cua [xua]，火 cuo [xuɔ]，欢 cuon [xuɔn]。意大利中西部托斯卡纳（Toscana）区方言中，c 在两个元音之间读如 [x]。罗氏用 c 代表 [x]，大概是借用了这个方言的读法。不过这样一来，（b）和（c）便混淆了。因此利氏方案中把 c 改为 h。

（d）ch=[k] 或 [kʻ]：在 i,e 元音前。例如：家 chia [kia]，狗 cheu [kəu]；巧 chiau [kʻiau]，口 cheu [kʻəu]。利氏方案中改用 k 及 kʻ。

（e）q=[k] 或 [kʻ]：在 u 元音前。例如：怪 quai [kuai]，广 quan [kuaŋ]；快 quai [kʻuai]，旷 quam [kʻuaŋ]。

（f）sch=[x]：在 i 元音前。例如：喜 schi [xi]，下 schia [xia]，学 schio [xiɑʔ]。利氏方案中改用 h。

（g）sc=[ʃ]：在 i 元音前。例如：是 sci [ʃʅ]，水 scioi [ʃui]，善 scien [ʃɛn]。利氏方案中用葡语字母 x。

（h）z=[ts] 或 [tsʻ]：在 i（ʅ），a，e，u 元音前。例如：自 zi [tsʅ]，在 zai [tsai]，助 zu [tsu]；菜 zai [tsʻai]，粗 zu [tsʻu]。利氏方案中改用 ç 及 çʻ。

（i）gn=[ŋ]：例如：业 gnie' [ŋieʔ]，砚 gnien [ŋiɛn]，源 gniuon [ŋyɔn]。利氏方案中改用葡语字母 nh。

（2）根据葡萄牙语的拼法：

（a）ç（或 çc）=[ts] 或 [ts']：在 i 元音前。例如：自 çi [tsɿ]，节 cie' [tsieʔ]，酒 çiu [tsiəu]；慈 çci [ts'ɿ]，前 çien [ts'iɛn]。

（b）g=[ʒ]：在 e，i 元音前。例如：入 ge' [ʒəʔ]，人 gin [ʒin]，肉 gio [ʒoʔ]。利氏方案中在其他元音（指 a，o，u）前改用法语字母 j。

（c）-m=[-ŋ]：例如：当 tam [taŋ]，像 siam [siaŋ]，中 cium [tʃuŋ]。

（d）-ṽ=[-n] 或 [-ŋ]：例如：天 tien 或 tiẽ [tiɛn]，看 can 或 cã [k'an]；当 tam 或 tã [taŋ]；窗 zam 或 zã [ts'aŋ]；想 siam 或 siã，siáo [siaŋ]；顿 tun 或 tũ [tun]；东 tun 或 tũ [tuŋ]。从上面的几个例子可以看出，用这个鼻化音符号代表 -n 和 -ŋ 很容易把 an～aŋ 和 un～uŋ 两对韵相混。因此利氏方案中把它取消了（见下 4.3（2））。

4.2 声母拼法特点

（1）无送气音符号。这并不证明罗氏当时未注意到送气音的存在，而只是还没有找到适当的符号。原来罗曼语族语言中没有送气音与不送气音的区别，因而在用罗马字拼写汉语音节，包括拼写人名地名时，都不加送气音符号。利氏方案中采用了 /'/ 号附在辅音后面上端表示送气音，例如：怕 p'a [p'a]，他 t'a [t'a]，开 c'ai [k'ai]，以别于罢 pa [pa]，大 ta [ta]，该 [kai] 等。后来拟制汉语拼音方案的人大多沿用了利氏的方法。

（2）用同一音标拼写不同的声母

（a）以 c 拼 [k]，[k']，[x]。上面 4.1（1）（b），（c）已举过数例，这种模棱两可的拼音，大多出现在合口韵前面，偶尔也出现在开口韵前面。例如看和僕（汉）都拼作 can，但为数甚少。一般在开口韵前罗氏用 h [x]，例如：海 hai [xai]，好 hau [xau]，后 heu [xəu]，黑 hə' [xəʔ]。

（b）以 g 拼写 [x] 及 [ʔ] 声母。例如：湖 gu [xu]，滑 gua [xua]，灰 guei [xuei]；瓦 gua [ʔua]，卧 guo [ʔuɔ]，为 guei [ʔuei]。关于瓦、卧、为等字声母 g 字的音值，我们还不甚清楚，它可能代表一种喉塞音或喉擦音。罗常培把它拟为浊喉擦音 [ɣ]。我们把它拟为喉塞音 [ʔ]。因为瓦、卧、为等字，在现代江淮方言中，没有读擦音的，绝大多数读零声母。再者，从喉塞音变为零声母，更合乎音变的规律。

（3）用同部位的辅音拼写同一个声母。例如以 c 及 g 拼 [x]：红 [xuŋ] 有 cum 及 gum 两种拼法；以 ch 及 gh 拼 [k(i)]：紧 [kin] 有 chin 及 ghin 两种拼法，起 [k'i] 有 chi

及 ghi 两种拼法。不过第二种拼法（gh）比较少见。

（4）同一个字的声母（及韵母）拼法不同。有一些字的拼法声母（和韵母）不同，有时音标相同，有时音标完全不同。例如花字有 cua [xua]，fa [fa] 两种拼法，还字有 cuan，guan [xuan]，fau [fau] 三种拼法。cua 及 cuan 是罗氏方案的官话音拼法；fa，fau 是当时某种方音的拼法。我们把《辞典》中声母有两种不同拼法的一些字和几个现代方言读法比较如下，见表 1：

表 1

例字	罗氏记音		现 代 方 音						
	官话音	方音	扬州	南京	北京	长沙	南昌	梅县	广州
花	cua [xua]	fa [fa]	₋xuɑ	₋xuɑ	₋xua	₋fa	₋ɸa	₋fa	₋fa
火	cuo [xuo]	fo [fɔ]	ˊxo	ˊxo	ˊxuo	ˊxo	ˊɸo	ˊfɔ	ˊfɔ
户	cu [xu]	fu [fu]	xu²	xu²	xu²	fu²	ɸu²	fu²	wu²
婚	cun [xun]	fun [fun]	₋xuɐn	₋xuɐn	₋xun	₋fən	₋ɸun	₋fun	₋fɐn
还	cuan [xuan]	fan [fan]	₋xuɛ̃	₋xuã	₋xuan	₋fan	₋ɸan	₋fan	₋wan

从表 1 我们可以看出，罗氏的官话音与现代官话方言音（南京、扬州、北京）音大致相同。而他拼的方音则与现代（客家）梅县相同。

和上面的例子正相反，有一些字的官话音声母是 f，方音声母是 c [x]，见表 2：

表 2

例字	罗氏记音		现 代 方 音					
	官话音	方音	南京	扬州	北京	厦门	潮州	福州
法	fa [faʔ]	cua [xuaʔ]	faʔˋ	fæ˔	ˊfa	huat˔	huap˔	xuaʔ˔
费	fi [fi]	cuei [xuei]	fəi²	fəi²	fei²	hui²	hui²	xie²
伏	fu [fuʔ]	cuo [xuoʔ]	fuʔˋ	fɔ˔	₋fu	hɔk₌	hok₌	xuʔ₌
服	fu [fuʔ]	cuo [xuoʔ]	fuʔˋ	fɔ˔	₋fu	hɔk₌	hok₌	xuʔ₌

表 2 里面的罗氏的官话音除"费"字的韵母外，其他都和现代北京音相同。而他拼的方音声母和韵母却和厦门与潮州方音相同或相近。

读者不禁要问：罗氏既然学习的是当时的官话标准音，怎么会有南方方音出现呢？这个问题并不难解答。罗明坚和利玛窦到中国后的第一站是广东省的肇庆。他们二人在那里开始学习官话，一定请了一两位中国文人做语言教师，这一点利氏在他致上峰的信中也提到过的。这些教师大概都不是北方人，而是南方人，其中一定有操客家话或闽方言的广东人或福建人。他们当然会说官话，不过在教罗利二氏官话时，有时不小心偶尔会把自己的方音土话流露出来。罗明坚当时刚开始学汉语，读汉字，也分不清哪个是标准音，哪个是方音，听见老师怎么读便怎么记，把听到的方音也记了下来。而手稿未经修改便送到罗马去了，一直保存到今天。这对研究明代方音的人，倒是一批很珍贵的资料。《辞典》中方音异读的出现，可以证明罗氏的拼写和记音相当客观正确。

（5）同一个声母有时用单辅音，有时用复辅音拼写。例如，用 ç 或 çc 拼写 [ts] 或 [ts'] : 则 çe' [tsəʔ]，姊 çci [tsɿ]，窃 çe' [ts'əʔ]，慈 çci [ts'ɿ]；用 s 或 ss 拼 [s] : 色 se' 或 sse' [səʔ]；用 c 或 cc 拼 [tʃ] 或 [tʃ'] : 知 ci 或 cci [tʃɿ]，迟 ci，齿 cci [tʃ'ɿ] 等。

（6）同一个字拼写时，有时有声母，有时无声母。这种情形只出现在古"疑"母齐齿呼的字里。例如，义有 gni [ŋi] ~ yi [i] 两种拼法，业有 gnie' [ŋieʔ] ~ ie' [ieʔ] 两种拼法。利氏方案中仍保存两种拼法，只是把 gn 改为 nh，例如业 nhiě ~ iě。金尼阁的《西儒耳目资》中也有两种拼法，即 niě' ~ iě'。这暗示在明末清初期间"疑"声母在高元音 i 前，处在逐渐消失的过程中。

4.3 韵母拼法特点

（1）同一韵母拼法不同

（a）韵母 i [i] 拼作 i，j，y，ij，iy。例如：悲 pi、py，起 chi、chij、chiy，基 chij，计 chi。做韵头时，例如：羊 iam、jam、yam，曰 iuo、yuo。这是因为当时意大利语中的 i，j，y 三个字母可以通用。

（b）韵母 ui [ui] 拼作 ui，uj，oi，oj。例如：吹 ciui [tʃ'ui]，睡 sciuj [ʃui]，水 scioi、scioj、sciuj [ʃui]，乳 giuj、gioj [ʒui]。

（c）合口韵 uo [uɔ] 有时拼做开口韵 o [ɔ]。例如：过 cuo [kuɔ]、co [kɔ]；货 cuo [xuɔ]、co [xɔ]。

（d）合口韵 uon [uɔn] 有时拼作开口韵 on [ɔn]。例如：乱 luon [luɔn]，lon [lɔn]；船 ciuon [tʃ'uɔn]，cion [tʃ'ɔn]；捲 chiuon [kyɔn]，chion [kiɔn]。

以上（c）和（d）两种拼法暗示出，罗氏的汉语教师在发音时，有时把合口韵说成开口韵，这大概是受了自己方言的影响。现代有些方言如江淮方言及某些南方方言，中古合口韵字有读开口韵的，见表 3：

表 3

例字	罗氏记音		现 代 方 音					
	官话音	又音	北京	扬州	南昌	梅县	广州	厦门
过	cuo [kuɔ]	co [kɔ]	kuoꜜ	koꜜ	kuoꜜ	kuoꜜ	kwoꜜ	<u>koꜜ</u>
货	cuo [xuɔ]	co [xɔ]	xuoꜜ	xoꜜ	xoꜜ	foꜜ	foꜜ	<u>hoꜜ</u>
乱	luon [luɔn]	lon [lɔn]	luanꜜ	luõꜜ	lɔnꜜ	lɔnꜜ	lynꜜ	luanꜜ
船	ciuon [tʃʼuɔn]	cion [tʃʼɔn]	ˌtʂʼuan	ˌtsʼuō	ˌtsʼɔn	ˌsɔn	ˌtʃʼyn	<u>ˌsuan</u> <u>ˌtsun</u>

从表 3 看来，罗氏的开口韵又音介于扬州、南昌、梅县等方音之间。他的老师之一很可能是客家人。

（2）鼻音韵尾 -m，-n，-ṽ 的混用

前面讨论拼写法时已经指出，按照葡语的拼写法，罗氏用了两个韵尾辅音，即 -m [-ŋ] 及 -n [-n]。不过除此以外，他又兼用鼻化元音符号 ṽ，这个符号可以代表 -m 及 -n，甚至于有时用 -n 代 -m。这一来，鼻音韵尾 [-ŋ] ~ [-n] 便发生了混淆的现象。例如 zəm [tsʼəŋ]，又拼做 zan，zã；单 tan [tan] 又拼做 tã；当 tam [taŋ] 又拼做 tan，tã；东 tum [tuŋ] 又拼做 tun，tũ 等。不过单 tan 从来也不拼做 tam；山 san 从来也不拼做 sam；顿 tun 从来也不拼做 tum。由此可见当、东等字的标准拼法是 tam，tum，而 tan，tã，tun，tũ 只是 tam，tum 的省略拼法。利氏方案中的拼法则完全标准化了。

（3）同一个字韵母拼法不同。例如猫 mau [mau] 又拼做 meau，miau [miau]；筛 sai [sai] 又拼做 ssi [sʅ]；子 zi，çi [tsʅ] 又拼做 zai [tsai]（今作"崽"）；该盖 cai [kai]，coi [koi]；海 hai [xai]，hoi [xoi]；在 zai [tsai]，zoi [tsoi]。猫字的 mau 是官话音；meau，miau 是方音。今梅县音 miauꜜ，厦门音 miauꜜ，南昌音 miɛuꜜ。该、海等字的又音大概是受了客家或广东话的影响，今把各字官话音和方音列表比较如下，见表 4：

表 4

例字	罗氏记音		现代方音		
	官话音	方音	北京	梅县	广州
该	cai [kai]	coi [koi]	ˌkai	ˌkɔi	ˌkɔi
盖	cai [kai]	coi [koi]	kaiꜜ	kɔiꜜ	kɔiꜜ
海	hai [xai]	hoi [xoi]	ˊxai	ˊhɔi	ˊhɔi
在	zai [tsai]	zoi [tsoi]	tsaiꜜ	tsʼaiꜜ	tsɔiꜜ

（4）同一个字声母和韵母拼法不同。例如：耍 scia [ʃa]，so [sɔ]；手 sciou [ʃəu]，siu [sy]；书 sciu [ʃu]，ssi [sᴢ̩]；序 su [su] 或 [sy]（？），ssi，si [sᴢ̩] 或 [sʐ̩]（？），sciu [ʃu]。"序"字的标准拼法是 siu [sy]，罗氏的拼法杂乱不一，可能是因为教师发音不太正确所致。现代方音中序字梅县音 si²，广州音 tsœy²，厦门音 su²。

（5）因文白异读而韵母不同者。下面的例子，第一个读法是白话音，第二个读法是文言音：白，百 pa [paʔ]，po [poʔ]；去 chij [kʻi]，chiu [kʻy]；锯 chi [ki]，chiu [ky]；行 schin [xin]，ham [xaŋ]；隔 chie' [kieʔ]，che' [kəʔ]；食 cie' [tʃˋəʔ]，scie' [ʃəʔ]；生 sen [sɛn]，sin [sin]；灯 ten [tɛn]，tin [tin]。

（6）入声韵 e' [əʔ]

上面已经提到罗氏方案中没有标声调的符号。但是遇有古入声收 e 元音时，罗氏便在 e 后面加上一个 " ' " 号，例如得 te'，墨 me'，色 se'，裂 lie'，七，节 çie' 等，而在其他元音后则不加此号，例如拉 la，不 po，国 cuo 等。这个符号可能代表元音的短促及喉塞音韵尾 [ʔ]。因为早期的 e'，ie' 在利氏方案中写作 ĕ，iĕ。其他入声韵也加 "˘" 号，如 ǎ，iǎ，ǒ，iǒ 等。这个 "˘" 符号是代表入声的，下面还要讨论他们所学的口语，是以当时（明末）南京一代的方言为标准的。现代的江淮方言中绝大多数还保存着入声及喉塞音韵尾。

五、《葡汉辞典》里所反映的音韵系统及其特点

下面的声母及韵母表（表 5、表 6），包括拟音、罗氏方案、利氏方案及例字。拟音是参照意大利语及葡萄牙语语音拼法及罗常培的拟音而成的。罗氏方案是根据《辞典》里的汉字注音，利氏方案是根据利氏赠给程大约的四篇注音文章归纳出来的。罗氏方案里未标送气音符号，拟音里的符号是参照利氏方案添进去的。表中的例字也是从《辞典》中选出的。每个例字后面的注音是罗氏方案的拼法。括弧里是利氏方案的拼法。但是因为四篇注音文章里的字数有限，有时找不到和早期对应的字例，便用《西儒耳目资》里的字和拼法补缺，注音用斜体字母以示区别。《西儒耳目资》的方案虽源于利氏方案，但也有不同之处，有关这两个方案的异同，可参阅罗常培著《耶稣会士在音韵学上的贡献》一文。[12]

表 5 声母表

拟音	罗氏	利氏	例　　字
[p]	p	p	邦 pam (pām), 不 po (pǒ·), 抱 pau (páu)
[p']	p	p'	怕 pa (p'á), 破 po (p'o), 僻 pie' (p'iě)
[m]	m	m	玛 ma (mà), 门 men (mên), 明 min (mīm)
[f]	f	f	方 fam (fām), 非 fi (fī), 法 fa (fǎ)
[v]	v, u	v	万 van (ván), 无 uu (vû), 味 ui, vi (ví)
[t]	t	t	大 ta (tá), 道 tau (táo), 东 tum (tūm)
[t']	t	t'	他 ta (t'ā), 桃 tau (t'âo), 通 tum (t'ūm)
[n]	n	n	难 nan (nân), 能 nen (nêm), 内 nui (núi)
[l]	l	l	赖 lai (lái), 流 leu (liêu), 雷 lui (lûi)
[ts]	c, ç, çc	ç (e, i)	则 çe (çě), 自 ci (çú), 姊 çci (çù), 即 çie (çiě·)
	z	ç (a, o, u)	子 zi (çù), 早 zau (çào), 哉 zai (çāi), 助 zu (çú)
[ts']	c, ç, çc	ç' (e, i)	窃 ce ('çiě), 慈 çci ('çû̂), 前 çien (çiên)
	z	ç' (a, o, u)	草 zau (ç'ào), 愁 zeu (ch'êu), 粗 zu (ç'ū)
[s]	s, ss	s	死 si (sù), 事 ssi (sú), 三 san (sān), 山 san (xān), 小 siau (siào)
[tʃ]	c, cc (e, i)	ch	战 cen (chén), 知 ci, ccy (chī), 正 cin (chím)
[tʃ']	c, cc (e, i)	ch'	臭 ceu (ch'éu), 齿 ci, ccy (c'hì), 城 cin (ch'îm)
[ʃ]	sc (i)	x	是 sci (xí), 手 scieu (xèu), 辰 scin (xîn)
[ʒ]	g (e, i)	g (e, i)	入 ge' (jǒ), 然 gen (gên), 人 gin (gin)
		j (o, u)	肉 gio (jǒ), 如 giu (jû), 宂 gium (jùm)
		lh	儿 gi (lh̀), 耳 gi (lh̀), 二 gi (lh̀)
[k]	c (a, o, u)	c (a, o, u)	改 cai (cài), 过 co (cúo), 故 cu (cú)
	ch (e, i)	k (i)	狗 cheu (kèu), 家 chia (kiā), 锯 chiu (kiú)
	q (u)	q (u)	怪 quai (quái), 鬼 quei (quèi), 广 quam (quàm)
[k']	c (a, o, u)	c' (a, o, u)	开 cāi (c'āi), 可 co (c'ò), 堪 can (c'ān)
	ch (e, i)	k' (i)	口 cheu ('kèu), 巧 chiau (k'iào), 去 chiu ('kiú)
	q (u)	q' (u)	快 quai ('kuái), 葵 quei (q'uēi), 旷 quam (q'uám)
[ŋ]	ng (a, o, u)	ng	爱 ngai (ngái), 碍 ngai (ngái), 我 ngo (ngò)
	ngh (e)		额 nghe (gě), 恩 nghen (gēn), 硬 nghen (gém)

[ŋ]	gn	nh (i)	义 gni (*nî*), 业 gnie' (*nhiě*), 浓 gnium (*nûm*)
[x]	h (a, e, o)	h	好 hau (hào), 后 heu (hèu), 何 ho (hô)
	c (u)		花 cua (hōa), 火 cuo (huò), 玩 cuon (*uôn*)
	g (u)		湖 gu (hû), 滑 gua (*hoǎ*), 灰 guei (hōei)
	sch (i)		喜 schi (*hì*), 下 schia (*hiá*), 学 schio (hiǒ)
[ʔ]	g (u)	g, ø	瓦 gua (*uà*), 卧 guo (guó), 为 guei (guéi), 艾 gai (gái), 吾 gu (gû), 王 guam (*uâm*), 外 guai (vái)
[o]	i, j, y	i, j, y	以 i, y (ì, j, ỳ), 因 in, yn (īn, ȳn), 羊 iam, jam, yam (yâm), ~ie', ye' (yě), 吕 (厕)o (ō), 五 u (*ù*), 恶 u (*ú*)

表 6 韵母表

拟音	罗氏	利氏	例 字
[ɿ]	i	ụ	思 ssi (sū), 死 si (sù), 四 si (sú)
[ʃ]	i, y	i, y	之 ci (chȳ), 时 sci (xî), 是 sci (xí), 齿 cí, ccy (ch'î)
[ər]	i	lh	而 gi (lĥ), 耳 gi (lh̀), 二 gi (lh̀)
[i]	i, ij, y	i, y	欺 chij (k'ī), 其 chi (k'î), 肥 fi (fi), 利 li (lý), 医 y (í)
[u]	u	u	都 tu (tū), 徒 tu (t'û), 主 ciu (chù), 树 sciu (xú)
[y]	u	iu, yu	女 nu, gnu (niù), 驴 lu (liû), 序 su (siú), 鱼 yu (yû)
	iu	iu	居 chiu (kiū), 鱼 iu (iû), 举 chiu (hiù)
[a]	a	a	怕 pa (p'á), 马 ma (mà), 他 ta (t'ā), 拿 na (nâ)
[ia]	ia	ia, ya	家 chia (kiā), 下 schia (hiá), 牙 ia (yâ), 雅 ia (yà)
[ua]	ua	oa	瓜 cua (*koā*), 花 cua (hoā), 化 cua (hoá)
[ɔ]	o	o	破 po (p'ó), 多 to (tō), 我 ngò (ngò), 何 ho (hô)
[io]	io	iue (?)	瘸 chio (*'kiue*), 靴 schio (*hiue*)
[uɔ]	uo	uo, oo	火 cuo (huò), 卧 guo (guó), 座 zuo (çóo)
[ɛ]	e	e	者 cie (chè), 这 cie (ché), 车 cie (ch'ē)
[iɛ]	ie, ie'	ie, ye	些 sie' (siē), 邪 sie (siê), 也 ie (yè), 夜 ie (yé)
[ai]	ai, ay	ai	来 lai, lay (lâi), 开 cai (k'āi), 海 hai (hài)
[iai]	iai, yai	iai	解 chiai (kiài), 街 chiai (*kiāi*), 鞋 schiai (hiâi)

[uai]	uai	oai, uai	乖 quai (*kuāi*), 快 quai ('*kuái*), 淮 guai (hoâi)
[uei]	uei, uej	oei, uei, uey	鬼 nuei (kuèi), 窥 quey ('*kuéi*), 灰 guei (hoei), 为 guei (guêy)
	oi	oei	贝 poi (*poéi*), 陪 poi (*poêi*), 妹 moi (*moéi, múi*)
	ui		衰 soi (*sūi*), 碎 soi (*súi*), 水 scioi (*xùi*)
[ui]	ui, uj	ui	对 tui (*túi*), 内 núi (*núi*), 泪 lui (*lúi*), 锥 ciui (*chūi*), 吹 ciui (*c'hūi*), 睡 sciui (*xúi*)
		ụ (?)	乳 giuj (*jù*)
[au]	au	ao	包 pau (*pāo*), 好 hau (hào), 少 sciau (xào)
[iau]	iau	eao, iao	燎 liau (leâo), 了 liau (leáo), 小 siau (siào)
[əu]	eu	eu	州 ceu (chēu), 臭 ceu (ch'eu), 手 scieu (xèu)
		ieu	流 leu (*liêu*), 硫 leu (*liêu*)
[iəu]	ieu	eu	求 chieu ('kiê*u*), 九 chieu (kièu), 救 chieu (kiéu)
[an]	an	an	谈 tan (t'ân), 感 can (càn), 山 san (xān)
[iɛn]	ian	ien	间 chian (kiēn), 闲 schian (hiên), 眼 yan (*ièn*)
	ien	ien	点 tien (tièn), 天 tien (t'iēn), 焉 ien (iên)
[uan]	uan, uoan	uan, uon	关 cuan (kuan), 宽 quoan (k'uon), 玩 guan (*uán*)
[ɔn]	on	uon	半 pon (puón), 团 ton ('tuón), 短 ton (tuòn)
[uɔn]	uon	uon	乱 luon (*luón*), 观 cuon (quōn), 欢 cuon (huōn)
	uon	un	饨 tuon (*tún*), 吞 tuon ('*tūn*), 顺 sciuon (*xún*)
		uen	滚 cuon (kuèn), 困 cuon ('kuen)
[yɔn]	iuon	iuen	捲 chiuon (kiuèn), 全 çiuon (ç'iuên), 冤 yuon (*iuēn*)
		un	尊 çiuon (*çūn*), 村 çiuon (ç'ūn)
[ɛn]	en	en	根 chen (kēn), 恩 nghen (gēn), 珍 cen (chēn), 善 scien (xén), 然 gen (gên)
[əŋ]		em	灯 ten (tēm), 曾 çen ('çêm), 生 sen (sém)
[uɛn]	uen	uen	分 fuen (fuēn), 问 vuen (vuén), 瘟 guen (*uēn*)
[in]	in	in	林 lin (lîn), 谨 chin (kìn), 沉 cin (ch'în), 身 scin (xīn) 人 gin (gîn), 尽 çin (çín), 心 sin (sīn)

[iŋ]	in	im, ym	命 min (mín), 鼎 tin (tìm), 经 chin (kīm), 形 schin (hîm), 整 cin (chìm), 证 cin (chým), 城 cin (ch'îm), 净 çin (çím), 请 çin ('çim)
[un]	un	un, uen	粪 fun (fuén), 顿 tun (tún)
[yn]	iun	iun	君 chiun (kiūn), 裙 chiun ('kiûn), 云 iun (iûn)
[aŋ]	am	am	方 fam (fām), 倘 tam (t'àm), 浪 lam (lám), 上 sciam (xám), 藏 zam (ç'âm), 往 uam (vàm)
[iaŋ]	iam	iam, eam	量 liam (leâm), 降 chiam (kiam), 将 çiam (çiām), 想 siam (siàm), 像 siam (siám)
[uaŋ]	uam	uam, oam	广 quam (quàm), 旷 quam (k'uám), 黄 guam (hôam)
[uŋ]	um	um, om	风 fum (fūm), 同 tum (t'ûm), 工 cum (cūm, cōm), 众 cium (chúm)
[yŋ]	ium	ium	穷 chium (k'iûm), 熊 schium (hiûm), 兄 schium (hiūm), 容 yum (yûm), 用 yum (yúm)
[aʔ]	a	ǎ	法 fa (fǎ), 拉 la (lǎ), 杀 sa (xǎ)
[iaʔ]	ia	iǎ	甲 chia (kiǎ), 瞎 schia (hiǎ), 压 ia (iǎ)
[uaʔ]	ua	oǎ, uǎ	刮 cua (kuǎ), 滑 gua (hoǎ), 刷 sciua (xoǎ)
[əʔ]	e'	ě	墨 me' (mě), 得 te' (tě), 肋 le' (lě), 色 se' (sě)
[iəʔ]	ie'	iě·, yě·	笔 pie' (piě·), 力 lie' (lyě·), 释 scie' (xiě·)
[ieʔ]	ie'	iě	别 pie' (piě), 裂 lie' (liě), 节 cie' (çiě)
[yeʔ]	iue	iuě	雪 siue (siuě)
[ɔʔ]	o	ǒ	博 po (pǒ), 落 lo (lǒ), 索 so (sǒ)
[iɔʔ]	io	iǒ	略 lio (liǒ), 学 schio (hiǒ), 雀 çio (çiǒ)
[oʔ]	o	ǒ·	不 po (pǒ·), 逐 cio (chǒ·), 肉 gio (jǒ·)
[ioʔ]	io	iǒ·, yǒ·	曲 chio ('kiǒ·), 蓄 hio (hiǒ·), 欲 io (yǒ·)
[uoʔ]	uo	oě	国 cuo (quoě), 忽 cuo (hoě), 说 sciuo (xoě)
[yo]	iuo	iuě	绝 z (i)uo (çiue), 月 iuo (iuě)
[uʔ]	u	ǔ	没 mu (mǔ), 祝 ciu (chǔ)

从上面的声母和韵母表，我们对罗氏方案的音韵系统可以得到一个概括的认识，也可以发现罗氏方案与利氏方案在音韵方面的一些差异。而罗氏方案更代表了罗利二氏当时学习的官话音韵系统。下面我们举出一些重要的声韵特点。

5.1 声母

（1）古见晓二组字声母 k，k'，x 及古精组声母字 ts，ts'，s 在齐齿呼及撮口呼韵母前尚未腭化。例如：叫 chiau [kiau]，欠 chien [k'iɛn]，晓 schiau [xiau]，去 chiu [k'y]；蕉 giau [tsiau]，前 çien [ts'iɛn]，小 siau [siau]，取 çiu [ts'y]。

（2）古疑母字在开口韵前一部分读 ŋ，例如：我 ngo [ŋo]，傲 ngau [ŋau]，额 nghe [ŋɤʔ]。一部分属于古影母的字也读 ŋ，例如：爱 ngai [ŋai]，恩 nghen [ŋɛn]。古疑母字在齐齿及撮口韵前一部分读 ɲ，例如：疑、义 gni [ɲi]，业 gnie' [ɲieʔ]，源 gniuon [ɲyɔn]；在合口韵前读 [ʔ]，例如：瓦 gua [ʔua]，吾 gu [ʔu]，外 guai [ʔuai]。

（3）古知、庄、章三组字声母有一部分读 ts、ts'、s，而在利氏方案及《西儒耳目资》中，则改为 tʃ、tʃ'、ʃ 了。表 7 中除罗氏利氏方案及现代方音外又加上了《西儒耳目资》（简称《耳目资》）及《中原音韵》拟音。[13]

表七

例字	罗氏	利氏（耳目资）	中原音韵	扬州	南京	北京	梅县	广州	厦门
渣	za	chā	₌tʃa	₌tsa	₌tʂɑ	₌tʂa	₌tsa	₌tsa	₌tsa
诈	za	chá	tʃaˀ	ˀtsa	tʂɑˀ	tʂaˀ	tsaˀ	tsaˀ	tsaˀ
站	zan	chán	tʃanˀ	tsɛ̃ˀ	tʂɑ̃ˀ	tʂanˀ	tsanˀ	tsamˀ	tsamˀ
状	zan (zam)	chóam	tʃuaŋˀ	tsuaŋˀ	tʂũˀ	tʂuaŋˀ	tsɔŋˀ	tsɔŋˀ	<u>tsɔŋˀ</u>, tsn̩ˀ
柴	zai	c'hâi	₌tʃ'ai	₃tsɛ	₌tʂ'aa	₌tʂ'ai	₌tʂ'ai	₌tʂ'ai	₌tʂ'ai
抄	zau	c'hāo	₌tʃ'au	₌ts'ɔ	₌tʂ'ɔu	₌tʂ'au	₌ts'au	₌ts'au	₌us'au
巢	zau	c'hâo	₌tʃ'au	₌ts'ɔ	₌tʂ'au	₌tʂ'au	₌ts'au	₌ts'au	
愁	zeu	'cêu	₌tʃ'ou	₌ts'əu	₌ts'əu	₌tʂ'ou	₌seu	₌sau	₌siu
窗	zan (zam)	choām	₌tʃ'uaŋ	₌ts'uaŋ	₌tʂuã	₌tʂ'uaŋ	₌ts'uŋ	₌ts'œŋ	<u>ts'ɔŋ</u>, ts'n̩
施	ssi	xī	₌ʃi	₌sɿ	₌ʂʅ	₌ʂʅ	₌sɿ	₌si	₌si
狮	ssi	sū, xī	₌ʃi	₌sɿ	₌ʂʅ	₌ʂʅ	₌sɿ	siˀ	<u>su</u>, ₌sai
事	ssi	sú, xí	ʃiˀ	sɿˀ	ʂʅˀ	ʂʅˀ	sɿˀ	siˀ	suˀ (tai)
杀	sa	xǎ	₌ʃa	saʔˀ	₌ʂa	₌ʂa	satˀ	satˀ	satˀ

（续表）

例字	罗氏	利氏 （耳目资）	中原 音韵	扬州	南京	北京	梅县	广州	厦门
晒	sai	*xái*	ʃaiˀ	sɛˀ	ʂɐeˀ	ʂaiˀ	saiˀ	saiˀ	saiˀ
山	san	xān	ʃan	˳sɛ̃	˳ʂɑ̃	˳ʂan	˳san	˳san	<u>˳san</u>, ˳suã
生	sen	sēm	˳ʃəŋ	˳sɛŋ	˳səŋ	˳ʂəŋ	˳seŋ	˳saŋ	<u>˳siŋ</u>, ˳sĩ

按，文中的南京音据《江苏省和上海市方言概况》，江苏人民出版社 1960 年。该书未列的字只得阙如。

　　除表 7 中所列字外，尚有师 ssi，si，使 sy，双 san（=sam），筛 sai，寨 zai，庄 zan（=zam），拆 za' 等字。

　　利氏方案的声母读法除愁、狮、事、生等字外和《中原音韵》及北京音大致相同，而罗氏方案的声母读法则和扬州、梅县及厦门等方音相同。这可能代表早期官话的特点，但也可能是受了南方汉语教师方音的影响。

　　（4）古知系禅母字声母一部分读清擦音 ʃ（sci）。例如：臣、辰、晨、禅、尝、丞等。今列表比较如下，见表 8：

表 8

例字	罗氏	利氏 （耳目资）	中原 音韵	北京	扬州	南京	成都	梅县	广州	厦门
臣、辰、晨	scin	*xīn*	˳tʃˀən	˳tʃʂˀən	˳tsˀəŋ	˳ʂʐˀəŋ	˳sən	˳sən	˳ʂɐŋ	˳sin
尝	sciam	xâm, c'hâm	˳tʃˀaŋ	˳tʂˀaŋ	˳tsˀaŋ	˳tʂˀã	˳saŋ	soŋ	˳sœŋ	˳ʂioŋ
禅	scien	c'hen	˳tʃˀien	˳tʂˀan	˳tɕˀĩ	（蝉）˳san	san²,˳sam	sin²,˳sim	˳sian	
丞	s(c)in	c'him	˳tʃˀiəŋ	˳tʂəŋ	˳tsˀəŋ	˳tʂˀəŋ	（乘）˳sən	tsˀən	seŋ	˳siŋ

　　表 8 里的禅母字，《中原音韵》、北京、扬州分别读塞擦送气音 tʃ、tɕ‘、ts‘（或 tɕ‘）。利氏方案中禅、丞二字读塞擦送气音 tʃ；晨尝等字仍读擦音 ʃ，尝字又读 tʃ。成都、梅县、广州、厦门都读擦音 s。罗氏方案的读法很可能是早期江淮官话的特点。利氏方案的塞擦音，大概是受了北方官话的影响。成都及四川话绝大多数地区是擦音 s 或 ʂ。它很可能也是早期江淮官话声母的遗迹（理由见 5.3 及 6.2）。

　　（5）古见系匣母字"完"及疑母字"玩"的声母读 x。这种读法，在现代方言中很少见，见表9：

表9

例字	罗氏	利氏（耳目资）	中原音韵	北京	扬州	南京	成都	长沙	顺德	广州	梅县	厦门
完	cuon	*huôn*	₌on	₌uan	₌uõ	₌uã	₌xuan	₌xõ	₌hyn	₌jyn	₌van	₌uan
玩	cuon, cuoã, guan	*uón*	₌on	₌uan	₌uẽ	₌uã	₌uan	₌õ	wun⁼	₌wan	₌ŋuan	₌guan

表9中"完"字在罗氏及利氏（《西儒耳目资》）方案中的声母都是 x（c 或 h）；现代方言中成都及长沙是 x，顺德和南海是 h（₌hyn）[14]。《中原音韵》、北京、扬州、梅县、广州和厦门等都不是擦音 x 或 h。罗氏及利氏方案和成都及长沙的 x 声母，是保存了古匣母遗留下来的擦音，也可能是早期江淮官话特点之一。"玩"字只有罗氏方案中读 cuon [xuɔn] 或 cuoã, guan [xuan]；利氏方案、《中原音韵》以及现代方言都不是擦音 x 声母。擦音的读法大概是"完"字类化作用的结果。

5.2 韵母

（1）没有卷舌韵儿 ər。罗氏方案中只有 i（[ɿ] 或 [ʅ]）韵。而、耳、二等字都读 gi [ʒʅ]，跟《中原音韵》的读法 [ʒʅ] 相同。利氏方案中才改为 lh [ər]。

（2）撮口韵 y 的标准拼写法是 iu，但是罗氏方案中有时只写作 u，与 u [u] 韵相混。例如女 nu，序 su 等。晚期方案中都改为 iu。

（3）古果摄合口三等戈韵见系字读 iuo，有时写成 io。例如瘸（瘸）chiuo，靴 schio，利氏方案中改为 iue。

（4）古蟹摄开口二等蟹、佳两韵见系字是 iai。例如解 chiai，鞋 schiai，矮 yai 与《中原音韵》相同。下面表中列出几个现代方言的读法和罗氏的方案比较，见表10：

表10

例字	罗氏	利氏（耳目资）	中原音韵	扬州	南京	北京	梅县	广州
街	chiai	kiāi	₌kiai	₌tɕiɛ	₌tɕiɐ	₌tɕiɛ	₌kiai	₌kai
鞋	schiai	*hiâi*	₌xiai	₌xɛ	₌ɕiɐ	₌ɕiɛ	₌hai	₌hai
矮	yai	*iài*	⸢iai	⸢iɛ	⸢ɐ	⸢ai	⸢ai	⸢ai

（5）古蟹摄合口一、三等及止摄合口三等韵字有三种拼法，即 oi, ui, uei。oi 经常出现在帮组、精组、知系生母和书母字后。例如背 poi，妹 moi，碎 soi，水 scioi 等。ui 经常出现在端系字和知系字后。例如对 tui，泪 lui，吹 ciui，睡 sciui 等。uei 经常出现在见系字后。例如鬼 quei，灰 guei，为 guei 等。利氏方案中仍有三种写法，即 oei，ui, uei。罗常培把这三个韵分别拟为 uɛi, ui 和 uɛi，[15] 我们则是 ui（oi, ui）及 uei（uei）。从现代音位论的观点来看，这三个韵可以归并成一个 uei 或 ui 韵。罗氏把遇摄合口三等韵日母"乳"字也写作 ui 韵，读 giuj [ʒui]。这个字在《中原音韵》及大多数现代方言里，都读 u 韵。《西儒耳目资》里读 u [ʮ] 韵。梅县读 ji˚，广州读 ˚jy，厦门读 ˚lu。广东的东莞、深圳（沙头角）、中山（南蓢合水）读 ˚zui，宝安读 ˚jui。[16] 罗氏的读法很可能是受了广东东莞一带出生的汉语教师的影响。

（6）古蟹摄合口三等非组字，止摄开口及合口三等帮系字读 i。例如：悲 pi，被 pi，美 mi，肺 fi，味 vi 等。止摄开口三等帮组字在《西儒耳目资》里又读 oei。例如：悲 pi，poēi；披 ‘pī，‘poēi；美 mì，moèi。

（7）古流摄开口三等尤韵字读 ieu [iəu]，只有来母字读 eu [əu]。例如：流、浏、硫等：leu。这可能是受了广东方音 ˛leu 的影响。有时 ieu 韵也写作 iu，与 y（鱼）韵相混。例如：修 siu，须 siu，就 çiu，取 çiu 等。

（8）古山摄一、二等帮组字及见系合口字韵读法不同；一等字读 on, uon，二等字读 an, uan。例如：搬 pon [po]，班 pan [pan]，官 cuon [kuɔn]，关 cuan [kuan]。这是早期官话和江淮方言音韵上的突出特点之一。表 11 把罗氏方案和几个主要江淮方言做一比较。

表 11

例字	罗氏	利氏（耳目资）	中原音韵	北京	南京	安庆	扬州	合肥	泰州
搬	pon	puōn	˛pon	˛pan	˛pã	˛pon	˛põ	˛põ	˛pũ
班	pan	pān	˛pan	˛pan	˛pã	˛pan	˛pæ̃	˛pæ̃	˛pɛ̃
官	cuon	kuōn	˛kon	˛kuan	˛kuã	˛kon	˛kõ	˛kõ	˛kũ
关	cuan	kuān	˛kuan	˛kuan	˛kuã	˛kuan	˛kuæ̃	˛kuæ̃	˛kuɛ̃

值得注意的是这两对字在北京（和北方）已合并为一个 an 韵。罗氏的两个方案，《中原音韵》以及现代江淮方言大部分还保存着区别，只有南京和北京一样合并为一个 ã 韵。这是因为南京在过去四百年中，人口迁移，居民中北方人大量增加，南京话

已显著地向北方话靠拢了（参看后面第七节）。

（9）古山摄合口韵与古臻摄合口韵的混淆。罗氏方案中这两个韵（即 uon [uɔn] 和 un [un]，iuon [yɔn] 和 iun [yn]）的写法有时呈现混淆现象。例如裙、群二字有时写作 chiun [kʻyn]，有时写作 chiuon [kʻyɔn]。有的字应写 un 的也写作 uon，例如寸 çuon，笋 suon，滚 cuon 等。利氏方案（《西儒耳目资》）中则分成了 uon，un，iuo，iuen 四个韵。见表12：

表12

例字	罗氏	利氏（耳目资）
官	cuon [kuɔn]	quõn [kuɔn]
劝	chiuon [kʻyɔn]	kʻiuén [kʻyɛn]
远	yuon [yɔn]	yuèn [yɛn]
裙	chiuon [kʻyɔn] chiun [kʻyn]	kʻiûn [kʻyn]
寸	çuon [tsʻuon]	çʻún [tsʻun]
笋	suon [suon]	siùn [syn]
云	yuon [yɔn] iun [yn]	iûn [yn]

这种混淆，可能是罗氏的汉语教师分不清这两个韵所致。值得注意的是，晚期的山摄合口三等韵及远字的韵母已由 yn 变为 yɛn，而向北方话靠拢了。

（10）古山摄开口三等韵章日两组的字读 ɛn（en）；与古臻摄字相同，例如战 cen [tʃɛn]，善 scien [ʃɛn]，然 gen [ʒɛn]，珍 cen [tʃɛn] 等。

（11）古深、臻两摄开口一等见溪二母字及三等知系字读 in，例如根、跟 chin [kin]，肯 chin [kʻin]；镇 cin [tʃin]，晨、身 scin [ʃin]，人 gin [ʒin] 等。古曾摄开口一等，及梗摄开口二等见溪母字读 in，例如灯、等 tin [tin]，冷 lin [lin]，升 scin [ʃin]，生 sin [sin]，更 chin [kin]，坑 chin [kʻin] 等。不过有些字有两种读法，例如根又读 chen [kɛn]，灯、等又读 ten [ten]，冷又读 len [lɛn]，生又读 sen [sɛn]，-en 是白话音（见前4.3（5）例）。

镇、晨、身、人等字的韵母和《中原音韵》的 iən 韵相同，政、成、升等字的韵母在利氏方案中改为 im [iŋ]，也和《中原音韵》的 iəŋ 韵相同。这些字在现代方言里绝大多数失去了介音 i。保留元音 i 的有广州、厦门等少数方言。相反地，灯、冷、更、坑等字，罗氏方案读 in，利氏方案改为 em [ɛŋ]，这些字在《中原音韵》中读 əŋ，现代方言中读 iŋ 或 in 的只有双峰等少数湘方言和厦门。例字比较表见表十三。

（12）古深—臻两摄和曾、梗两摄开口韵字韵尾相混，即所谓 -n/-ŋ 不分，一律收 -n。利氏方案中把 -n 和 -ŋ 分成了两个韵。罗氏方案可能反映了当时南方（南京）官话的特点，利氏方案则显示受了北方官话的影响，下面将其方案和现代方言列表比较，见表 13：

表 13

例字	罗氏	利氏（耳目资）	中原音韵	北京	南京	扬州	梅县	厦门
宾	pin	pīn	꜀piən	꜀pin	꜀piŋ	꜀piŋ	꜀pin	꜀pin
兵	pin	pīm	꜀piən	꜀piŋ	꜀piŋ	꜀piŋ	꜀pin	꜀piŋ
等	tin	tèm	꜂təŋ	꜂təŋ	꜂təŋ	꜂təŋ	꜂ten	꜂tin
能	nen	nêm	꜁neŋ	꜁nəŋ	꜁ləŋ	꜁ləŋ	꜁nən	꜁liŋ
冷	lin	lèm	꜂ləŋ	꜂ləŋ	꜂ləŋ	꜂ləŋ	꜂ləŋ	꜂liŋ
林	lin	lìn	꜁liəm	꜁lin	꜁lin	꜁liŋ	꜁lim	꜁lim
灵	lin	lîm	꜁liəŋ	꜁liŋ	꜁liŋ	꜁liŋ	꜁lin	꜁liŋ
增	çen	çēm	꜀tsəŋ	꜀tsəŋ	꜀tsəŋ	꜀tsəŋ	꜀tsən	꜀tsiŋ
亲	çin	ç'īn	꜀tsʻiən	꜀tɕʻin	꜀tɕʻiŋ	꜀tɕʻiŋ	꜀tsʻin	꜀tsʻin
清	çin	ç'īm	꜀tsʻiəŋ	꜀tɕʻiŋ	꜀tɕʻiŋ	꜀tɕʻiŋ	꜀tsʻin	꜀tsʻiŋ
镇	cin	chín	tʃiən꜄	tʂən꜄	tʂəŋ꜄	tsəŋ꜄	tsən꜄	tin꜄
政	cin	chím	tʃiən꜄	tʂən꜄	tʂəŋ꜄	tsəŋ꜄	tsən꜄	tsiŋ꜄
身	scin	xīn	꜀ʃiən	꜀ʂən	꜀ʂəŋ	꜀səŋ	꜀sən	꜀sin
升	scin	xīm	꜀ʃiəŋ	꜀ʂəŋ	꜀ʂəŋ	꜀səŋ	꜀sən	꜀siŋ
根	chin	kēn	꜀kən	꜀kən	꜀kən	꜀kən	꜀ken	꜀kun
更	chin	kēm	꜀kəŋ	꜀kəŋ	꜀kən	꜀kəŋ	꜀ken	꜀kiŋ
今	chin	kīn	꜀kiəm	꜀tɕin	꜀tɕiŋ	꜀tɕiŋ	꜀kim	꜀kim
经	chin	kīm	꜀kiəŋ	꜀tɕiŋ	꜀tɕiŋ	꜀tɕiŋ	꜀kin	꜀kiŋ
因	in	īn	꜀iən	꜀in	꜀iŋ	꜀iŋ	꜀in	꜀in
英	in	īm	꜀iəŋ	꜀iŋ	꜀iŋ	꜀iŋ	꜀in	꜀iŋ

现代江淮方言中如江苏省的句容、南京、扬州等大多数方言不分 ən/əŋ 和 in/iŋ；安徽省沿淮河的部分市、县及皖中、皖南各地也不分 ən/əŋ。蚌埠市、合肥市、芜湖市、安庆市等地的读音倾向于 ən/in，滁县、泾县等地的读音倾向于 ən/iŋ。[17] 因此我们可以肯定它是明代和现代江淮方言的特点之一。

（13）古宕、江两摄开口二三等庄组字仍读开口，而《中原音韵》、北京及大多数现代方言读合口，例见表 14：

表 14

例字	罗氏	利氏（耳目资）	中原音韵	北京	扬州	南京	梅县	广州
撞	zam [tsaŋ]	c'hoam, choám, c'huām	ʧuaŋ˃	tʂuaŋ˃	tsuaŋ˃	tʂuā˃	tsɔŋ˃	tsɔŋ˃
状	ciam [ʧaŋ]	choám, chuám	ʧuaŋ˃	tʂuaŋ˃	tsuaŋ˃	tʂuā˃	tsɔŋ˃	tsɔŋ˃
疮	zam [ts'aŋ]	c'hoām, c'huām, c'hām, c'ām	˛ʧ'uaŋ	˛tʂ'uaŋ	˛ts'uaŋ	˛tʂuã	˛tʂ'ɔŋ	˛tʂ'ɔŋ
窗	zam [ts'aŋ]	c'hoām, c'huām	˛ʧ'uaŋ	˛tʂ'uaŋ	˛ts'uaŋ	˛tʂuã	˛ts'uŋ	˛ts'œŋ
双	sam [saŋ]	xoām, xuām	˛ʃuaŋ	˛ʂuaŋ	˛suaŋ	˛suã	˛suŋ	˛sœŋ

罗氏方案的 aŋ 不一定是当时官话的特点，因为现代江淮方言中反映这个特点的，可以说绝无仅有。现代客粤方言大多是 ɔŋ 或 œŋ/uŋ（来自古江摄），大多数吴语也是 aŋ 或 ã。不过我们不能证明罗氏方案是受了说吴语的教师的影响，却可以说是受了说广东或客家方言教师的影响。

5.3 声调

罗氏拼音方案中，虽然未标声调符号，但是我们可以肯定他当时并不是不知道声调的存在和重要，而是还没有找到适当的标调符号。因为他和利氏在澳门学汉语时，利氏于 1583 年 2 月 13 日自澳门给富尔纳里神父（Martino de Fornari, S. J.）的信中说："在海中航行了一个多月。上主曾让我患重病……一下船，身体便康复了。我立刻开始学习中文。您要知道中国话比希腊语和德国话都难；在发音上有很多同音异义的字，许多话有近千个（按，原文如此）的意义。除此以外，尚有以声音的高低来区别的四个声调。"[18] 利氏所说的四个声调就是平、上、去、入。平声又分清（阴），浊（阳），所以实际上有五个。利氏方案中的五个声调符号是 ˉ ˆ ˋ ˊ ˇ，代表清平、浊平、上声、去声和入声。这是他和郭居静神父于 1598 年编《汉欧字典》时制定的。这五个符号 ˉ

ˇ 是借自拉丁语，ˋ ˊ 是借自法语。后来金尼阁在他的《西儒耳目资》中也采用了这五个符号，并且在首卷的《译引首谱》中，以问答对话的方式，解释了声调的高低。不过他只提出了某调的高低，而没有指出声调的升降。

《西儒耳目资》出版以后五十六年，有一位多明我会会士范芳济神父（Francisco Varo, O. P., 1627—1687），在福州用西班牙语编写了一部《官话技术》（*Arte de la Lengua Mandarina*）。技术即语法，稿本于 1682 年完成，范氏把它带到广州。他逝世后由芳济格会会士毕伯多神父（Pedro Piñuela, O. F. M.）加以修订，于 1703 年在广州刊行（见附图六）。范氏照拉丁语词类的模式，描述当时官话的词类和句法，全书的词汇和例句只用罗马字拼音，而未加汉字。这部书可能是外国人所著的汉语语法中最早的一部。作者用西班牙语口语中常用的叹词 a, ai 及否定词 no 在口语中出现时的语调，来描写官话中五个声调的调值。自然这种方法也很难精确地把实际调值描写出来，不过至少能给读者一个大概的轮廓。我们根据郭、利二氏的符号短线的来源，和金氏及范氏的描述，再参照现代江淮方言的各地调值，把这五个调号的调值构拟如下（x 代表任何一个音节）。

（1）清平（阴平）：x̄（33：˧）。郭氏用短平线来标清平调，暗示它是一个平调。金氏在《西儒耳目资》里描写声调的原文简短而紧凑，不便拆开。因此我们先把全文录下，以后再分开引用。他说："问曰：高低何似？答曰：平声有二，曰清曰浊；仄声有三，曰上，曰去，曰入。五者有上下之别。清平无低无昂，在四声之中。其上其下每有二，最高曰去，次高曰入，最低曰浊，次低曰上。"[19] 稍后又说："问曰：便哉，但平声一曰清，一曰浊，何也？答曰：清平不高不低，如钟声清远。浊平则如革鼓冬冬之音。……中国即未绘诸笔，然用不高不低之清平，极高之去声，次下之上声，次高之入声，极低之浊平……。问曰：先生所定若此，毋乃颠倒次第否？答曰：中国五音之序曰清、浊、上、去、入。但极高与次高相对，极低与次低相对，辨在针芒，耳鼓易愦。余之所定，曰清，曰去，曰上，曰入，曰浊。不高不低在其中，两高与两低相形，如泰山与丘垤之悬绝。凡有耳者，谁不哲之乎？"[20]

金氏谓"清平无低无昂……不高不低，如钟声清远"，这表示它是一个平调；"在四声之中"，表示它是一个中平调。范氏说："发这个声调时，声音要平，不可升，也不可降，就好像我们说（叹词）ai! 字一样。"[21] 从上面的三种描写，我们可以有把握地把它拟作中平调 33。现代江淮方言中江苏的兴化是中平调 33；高邮和安徽的贵池是半高平调 44。

（2）浊平（阳平）：x̂（21：˨）。郭氏用法语的长音符号 ˆ 来标阳平调，暗示它是一个低调。因为法语长音符号表示低长元音，例如 âme 读 [ɑ:m]，tête 读 [tɛ:t]。金氏谓"最低为浊"，又谓"极低之浊平"。范氏说："发这个声调时，要把第二音节稍微降低。如果只有一个音节如 ŷ，当把声音拉长，好像有两个音节一样。就好像我们卡斯提尔人（catillians）向某人说 No（不）字一样。假设有一个人对我说约翰偷了人家的东西。我不以为然，便向他说：No diga esso，pucs Juan avia de hazer tal cosa（你不可说：约翰做了那样的事！）。这样向那个人说 No（不）字，并且把语音把持着而降低些，便成了第二个声调。"范氏所谓"音节"，是指带复合元音的音节或单元音音节在发音时，因为声调的下降，听起来好像两个元音一样。我们把阳平调拟成半低、微降调 21，很符合郭、金、范三氏的描写。现代江淮方言中安徽无为方言是半低降调 21，庐江是低平调 11；江苏的盐城、射阳、高邮是低降升调 213。

（3）上声 x̀（42：˩）。郭氏用法语开音符号 ` 来标上声，暗示它是一个降调，因为法语开音符号 ` 只加在 e 元音上，使它读成较低的 [ɛ]，例如 père [pɛ:r]，après [aprɛ]。金氏谓"次低曰上"或"次下之上声"。范氏说；"第三个声调发音时，先在元音上把握住一点，然后把声音降低三分之一，好像一个人在厌烦或生气时说 No!（不！）一样……。这是一个高调，发音时要响亮。"[22] 我们把它拟作中降调 42，似乎符合郭、金、范三氏的描写。现代江淮方言中江苏的新海连和扬州是中降调 42；安徽的天长是中降调 41。

（4）去声 x́（45：˩）。郭氏用法语闭口音符号 ´ 来标去声，暗示它是一个高调。因为闭口音符号 ´ 只加在 e 元音上，使它读成高元音 [e]，例如 été [ete]，blé [ble]，金氏谓"最高曰上"或"极高之上声"。范氏说："第四个声调，发音时，先在第一音节上把握住一点，然后把声音提高三分之一……要用肯定的口气发音，就好像当我决意做某事时，有人从中阻碍我说：你不可做！我用果断的口气回答他说：Como no?（怎么不可以？）用这种口气发音，并把 no 字的音拉长些，就是第四声了。"金氏的"最高"和"极高"表示它是一个高调 5。范氏的"把握住这一点……把声音提高三分之一"表示从半高升到最高。因此我们把它拟做高微升调 45。现代江淮方言中江苏的射阳是高微升调 45。

（5）入声 x̃（45：˩）。郭氏用拉丁语短元音符号来标入声，暗示它是一个短促的声调。金氏谓"次高曰入"或"次高之入声"。范氏说："第五个声调事实上和第四个相同，只是在发音的结尾，胸部要用力，就好像我们中间，有人要吓唬别人。他乘人不防的时候喊一声 'a'。这样把尾音缩短，便成了第五声。"郭氏的短元音符号和范氏的"胸部要用力……把尾音缩短"，无疑是表示入声是一个带喉塞音 [ʔ] 韵尾的促声。金氏的"次高"可以释为由半高上升的声调，和范氏的"提高三分之一"相吻合。因此我们把它拟成高微升调 45。现代江淮方言中入声大多数带喉塞音尾。这是江淮方言的特点之一。安徽的芜湖和贵池是高升调35；江苏的南京、句容、盐城、泰兴，安徽的天长、无为等地是短高平调5；其他地区大多是短半高平调4。今把利氏晚期的调类、符号、起讫点、调号及例字列表如下，见表15：

表15

调类	利氏调号	起讫点	调号	例字	
清平	x̄	33	˧	天 t'iěn	声 xīm
浊平	x̂	21	˩	人 gîn	言 yên
上声	x̀	42	˥˩	雨 yù	水 xùi
去声	x́	45	˧˥	万 ván	岁 súi
入声	x̌	45	˧˥	百 pě	业 nhiě

金尼阁在解释声调的高低时，也注意到了五个调值之间的对比性差别（contrastive difference）以及差别的细微难辨，因此他才用对比的方法把五个声调分为极高次高，极低次低及不高不低三种类型来辨认。他说："中国五音之序曰清、浊、上、去、入。但极高与次高相对，极低与次低相对，辨在针芒，耳鼓易惛。余之所定，曰清，曰去，曰上，曰入，曰浊。不高不低在其中，两高与两低相形，如泰山与丘垤之悬绝，凡有耳者，谁不哲之乎？"他这种对比的方法是合乎现代描写语言学原则的。

近年来，中外学者对早期江淮方言声调的调值，也进行了一些构拟工作。鲁国尧把金氏的五个声调符号所代表的调值拟为：清平33，浊平131或121，上声31，去声35，入声535或424。[23] 他的构拟法是把金氏符号短线的平、斜、曲折的形状，解释为调值的高低、升降、曲折的变化，换句话说，就好像现代汉语里用的五度标记法一样。因此他把浊平拟为131或121，把入声拟为535或424。不过这种说法不完全可靠。因为他不了解金氏用的符号是借自法语和拉丁语的重音符号。其中有曲折的符号如 ̂ 和 ̌，并不代表调值的曲折，而只是代表长音（ ̂ ）或短音（ ̌ ）。

平山久雄用比较语言学的办法，构拟了江淮方言的"祖调"。他所拟的阴平是 *42，阳平是 *11，上声是 *'435，去声是 *35，入声未拟。[24] 他拟的阳平和去声的调值和利氏的调值相近；他拟的上声调值 *'435 是一个"紧喉作用的曲折高升调"，和利氏的不曲折的高升调也很近似。平山氏没有构拟入声的祖调，大概是因为资料不足，或问题复杂。但是现代江淮方言的入声大多数是短高调4或5。我们不妨把它拟为短高升调 *45。这样一来，平山所拟的江淮方言的祖调，和利氏方案的调值就更接近了。

以上我们把所拟的利氏晚期五个声调，和几个现在江淮方言的调值分别做了一些各别的比较。其中有的相同，有的相近。出乎意料之外，在查阅四川省各地方言声调时，发现了有不少方言点和利氏的调类和调值相同或相似。四川方言点中有入声的地区大多数在四川的西部，即岷江流域、金沙江下游及青衣江下游的四十八个县市。[25]其中以青衣江下游的峨眉、南溪、峨边、马边等地的调值和利氏的最近似。今列表比较如下，见表 16：

表 16

调值 ＼ 调类	阴平	阳平	上声	去声	入声
利氏	33	21	42	45	<u>45</u>
峨眉	44	21	42	13	55
南溪	55	21	53	13	45
夹江	44	31	42	24	55
峨边	55	31	42	13	25
马边	55	21	42	24	34

从表 16 可以看出，峨眉及其他四点的调类及调值和利氏的基本上相同：阴平都是平调，利氏的中平和峨眉及夹江的半高平，相差不甚远。阳平都是低降调。上声都是中降调；南溪的中降调 53 也可以写作 42。去声都是升调：峨眉、南溪、峨边是低升调，夹江、马边是中升调，和利氏的高微升调很接近。入声都是高调：南溪和利氏的相同；峨边、马边的中升调和利氏的高升调也很近似；峨眉和夹江的高平调也和利氏的高微升调仡点相同。

四川这几处以及其他不少方言点的调类及调值和利氏的相同，是否偶合，抑或是有语言亲属关系？答案是：并非偶合，而是由于四川方言和安徽的江淮方言有亲属关系。根据最近崔荣昌的研究，[26] 在元末明初，有许多湖广（即今湖北、湖南）及安徽军民移居四川的合川、重庆、南溪、广安等处。其中也有不少是迁自现代江淮官话区的湖北省黄（岗）孝（感）片的麻城和孝感一带方言区的。无疑地，这几处（及其他多处）的方言保存了一些明代江淮官话的音韵特点。四川方言与江淮方言内部详细的关系，值得我们作进一步的考查和探究。

六、《葡汉辞典》里所记录的词汇及语法特点

根据初步研究比较的结果，我们可以肯定，《辞典》中所收的词汇和例句，除掉一小部分是受了闽粤方言的影响之外，基本上代表当时（明末）的官话，是非常珍贵的语言资料，有待全面详细的研究和探讨。下面只把有代表性的及一些特殊的词汇和语法例句分类列出。遇有和现代某处方言相同的词汇或例句时，便把方言地名附在括弧里。遇到原文只有汉字没有拼音时，括弧里的拼音是我加的。

6.1 词汇举例

（1）不带后缀的名词

1. 主人娘 ciu gin niã [tʃu ʒin niaŋ] 女主人（厦门）

2. 乳母 giui mi [ʒui mu] 奶妈，婢女

3. 村夫 çiuon fu [ts'yɔn fu]（梅县）

4. 村婆 çinon po [ts'yɔn p'ɔ] 村妇

5. 人客 gin chie' [ʒin k'ieʔ] 客人（广州、梅县）

6. 后生家 heu sin chia [xəu sin kia]（广州、梅县、潮州：后生）；少年（sciau nien）[ʃau niɛn]

7. 口涎 cheu yen [k'əu iɛn]；口液（cheu ye）[k'əu iɛ]；口水（cheu scioi）[k'əu ʃui]（成都、广州）

8. 腋下 shcie schia [xieʔ xia] 胳肢窝（梅县）

9. 跫脚 chio chio [k'io kioʔ] 瘸子

10. 龟背 quei poi [kuei pui] 驼背（梅县）

11. 火房 cuo fam [xuɔ faŋ] 厨房（洛阳、灵宝、寿阳、蓝山）

12. 厕坑 ci chin [ts'ʅ k'in] 厕所（广州）

13. 家火 chia cuo [kia xuɔ] 家伙（南京）

14. 尿碗 niau guan [ŋiau ʔuan]（扬州：尿壶）；夜壶 ye gu [iɛ xu]（北方）

15. 手袜 scieu va [ʃəu vaʔ]（广州）

16. 锁匙 so ti [sɔ t'i] 钥匙（南昌、梅县、广州、厦门）。按 ti [t'i] 疑为 sci [ʃ] 之误。

17. 所在 so zai [sɔ tsai] 地方，处所（厦门）

18. 窟堀 cu lũ [k'oʔ luŋ] 窟窿（北方、南京）

19. 马架 ma chia [ma kia] 马鞍，驮鞍

20. 猪寮 ciu liau [tʃu liau] 猪圈（厦门：寮 liau 小屋）

21. 鸽寮 co liau [koʔ liau] 鸽舍

22. 壁蛇 pie' scie [piəʔ ʃɛ]（南昌）；四脚蛇 si chio scie [sɿ kioʔ ʃɛ]（成都、南京、句容）

23. 田鸡 tien chi [tʻiɛn ki]（北方）；水鸡 scioi chi [ʃui ki]（扬州、高邮、泰州）；水蛙 scioi ua [ʃui va]

24. 蜘蛛 ci ciu [tʃʅ tʃu]（北方）；八脚 pa chio [paʔ kioʔ]

25. 蚜蟖 chia cie' [kia tsieʔ] 蟑螂（广州：甲由 katˌ tsatˌ；厦门：ˌka tsuaʔˌ）

（2）带后缀的名词

26. 矮子 yaj zi [iai tsɿ]（成都、扬州、衡阳、钟祥）

27. 伴子 gua zai [ʔua tsai]（成都：女娃子；庐江、砀山、临泉：小娃儿 [小孩子]）；丫头 ya teu [ia tʻəu]

28. 贩子 fan zi [fan tsɿ]（南京）

29. 痴子 ci zi [tʃʻʅ tsɿ] 傻子（南通、钟祥）

30. 索子 so zi [soʔ tsɿ] 绳子（成都、昆明、厦门；梅县：索）

31. 纽子 niu zi [niu tsɿ]（成都、新海连、盐城、泰州、南通）

32. 衫子 san zi [san tsɿ] 上衣（西安、合肥；梅县、广州：衫）

33. 桃子 tau zi [tʻau tsɿ]（成都、昆明、扬州、合肥、苏州）

34. 梨子 li zi [li tsɿ]（南京、扬州、泰州、南通、合肥）

35. 枣子 zau zi [tsau tsɿ]（扬州、合肥、长沙、南昌、苏州）

36. 柑子 kon zi [kɔn tsɿ] 橘子（成都、梅县；潮州：柑）

37. 驴子 lu zi [lu tsɿ]（成都、扬州、合肥）

38. 柱头 ciu teu [tʃu tʻəu]

39. 锄头 zu teu [tsʻu tʻəu]（南京、扬州、南昌、广州、厦门）

40. 锅头 cuo teu [kuo tʻəu]（梅县：镬头）

41. 斧头 fu teu [fu tʻəu]（成都，扬州，合肥，梅县，广州）

42. 和头 ho teu [xɔ tʻəu] 和解者

43. 兆头 ciau teu [tʃau tʻəu] 预兆（厦门）；先兆（sien ciau）[siɛn tʃau]

44. 牛牯 ngieu cu [ŋiəu ku] 公牛（合肥：牯牛；南昌、梅县、广州）

45. 驴母 lu mu [lu(ly) mu] 母驴（厦门、潮州）

46. 狗母 cheu mu [kəu mu] 母狗（厦门、潮州）

（3）形容词

47. 闹热 nau ge’ [nau ʒəʔ] 热闹（南京、扬州、梅县、厦门）

48. 嫖致 piau ci [piau ʧʅ] 美丽，好看（庐江、桐城、澧县、江华、桂东）；生得好 sen te’ hau [sɛn təʔ xau]（北方）；美貌（mi mau）[mi mau]（北方）

49. 利 li [li] 快，锋利（梅县、广州、厦门）

50. 牢固 lau cu [lau ku]（南通、句容、盐城：牢；长沙、南昌）；坚实（chien scie’）[kiɛn ʃəʔ]；罕固（han cu）[xan ku]

51. 滛浊 u cio [uʔ tʃoʔ]（扬州：污糟；淮阴、南通、安庆、贵池、定远：龌龊）

52. 艰计 can chi [kan ki] 困难，不可能

53. 不得闲 po te’ schian [poʔ təʔ xian] 忙（南京、广州）；有事干 yeu ssi con [iəu sɿ kɔn]；不暇（po schia）[poʔ xia]

（4）副词

54. 几久 chi chiu [ki kiəu] 多久（南昌、梅县）

55. 几多 chi to [ki tɔ] 多少（南昌、梅县、广州）

56. 如今 siu chin [ʒu kin] 现在（南京；合肥：而今；长沙、南昌、梅县）；此时（çi sci）[ts‘ɿ ʃʅ]

57. 不曾 po çen [poʔ ts‘ɛn] 没有（南京、泰州、梅县）

58. 还不曾 guan po cen [xuan poʔ ts‘ɛn] 还没有；尚未（sciam vi）[ʃaŋ vi]

（5）动词

59. 讲话 chiam cua [kiaŋ xua] 说话（南京、长沙、南昌、梅县、广州）

60. 晓得 ciau te’ [xiau təʔ] 知道（南京、扬州、梅县）

61. 欢喜 cuon sci [xuɔn xi] 喜欢（南京、南昌、梅县、厦门）

62. 食酒 cie’ ciu [tʃ‘əʔ tsiu]（南京、扬州、盐城、如皋、南通、安庆）

63. 逆气 gnie’ chi [ȵiəʔ k‘i] 打嗝（梅县）

64. 屙（屙）尿 o niau [ɔ niau]（扬州、铜陵、梅县、临川、广州）

65. 挝痒 cuo iam [xuɔ iaŋ]

66. 打价 ta chia [ta kia] 还价

67. 讲笑 chiã siau [kiaŋ siau] 开玩笑（厦门）

68. 弄把戏 lun pa schi [luŋ pa xi]

69. 整干净 cin con çin [tʃin kɔn tsin] 弄干净（广州）

70. 迺鳞 ccy lin [tʃʅ lin] 刮去鱼鳞（泰州）

71. 洗口 si cheu [si kʻəu]（厦门）；素（漱）口（su cheu）[su kʻəu]（北方、泰州）

72. 下雨 schia iu [xia y]（北方、泰州）

73. 下雷 schia lui [xia lui] 打霹雳

74. 下屎 schia sci [xia ʃʅ] 拉屎，大便

75. 备办 pi pan [pi pan] 预备（厦门）

76. 起房子 chi fam zi [kʻi taŋ tsʅ] 盖房子（南京；泰州、广州：起屋）

77. 发性 fa sin [faʔ sin] 发怒

78. 榔埋 lũ mai [luŋ mai] 聚集，集合

6.2 词汇特点

从上面所举的词汇，可以归纳出下列的特点：

1. 名词

a）和现代江淮方言相同的，不带后缀的有 13. 家火，18. 窟埆，22. 四脚蛇，23. 水鸡等。带后缀的有 26. 矮子，28. 贩子，29. 痴子，31. 纽子，32. 衫子，33. 桃子，34. 梨子，35. 枣子，37. 驴子，39. 锄头，41. 斧头等。江淮方言的后缀和北方官话有所不同。例如江淮方言"纽子"北方是"扣子"，"衫子"北方是"褂子"，"桃子"、"枣子"北方是"桃儿"、"枣儿"，"梨子"、"驴子"北方是"梨"、"驴"，"斧头"北方是"斧子"，"锄头"北方是"锄"。

b）和其他方言相同的：和成都话相同的有 7. 口水，22. 四脚蛇，26. 矮子，27. 伴子，30. 索子，33. 桃子，37. 驴子，41. 斧头等。成都话词汇和江淮方言相同的原因，大概跟移民有密切的关系。上面已经提过，元末明初有许多湖广及安徽军民移居四川，其中不少是从现代江淮方言区黄孝片的麻城、孝感等处移入的，因而他们保存了一些江淮方言的特点。和梅县相同的有 3. 村夫，8. 胲下，10. 龟背，40. 锅头等。和广州相同的有 7. 口水，12. 厕坑，15. 手袜，25. 蜘蟟等。和梅县、广州相同的有 5. 人客，6. 后生家。和厦门相同的有 1. 主人娘，17. 所在，20. 猪寮，21. 鸽寮，43. 兆头，45. 驴母，46. 狗母等。和多种（南方）方言相同的有 11. 火房，16. 锁匙，30. 索子，32. 衫子，35. 枣子，36. 柑子，39. 锄头，41. 斧头，44. 牛牯等。

2. 形容词和副词

a）和江淮方言相同的有 47. 闹热，48. 嫖（标）致，51. 溔浊，53. 不得闲，56. 如今，57. 不曾等。

b）和南昌、梅县、广州相同的有 49. 利，54. 几久，55. 几多等。《宾主问答辞义》

中（36，66 页）也有"几久"、"几多"和"不曾"的疑问句。例如："主人曰：相公到此有几久了？答曰：有许久。问曰：贵处到这里有几多日程？答曰：有几多。""客曰：这几时……（字迹不易辨认）不知师傅定了银子不曾？"可见这几个副词是明代江淮官话中常用的。

3. 动词

a）和江淮方言相同的有 59. 讲话，60. 晓得，61. 欢喜，62. 食酒，64. 屙尿，66. 打价等。"食"字即现代汉语的"吃"字。这几个动词都是有代表性的江淮和南方方言词汇。

b）和其他方言相同的：和广州相同的有 69. 整干净。和厦门相同的有 67. 讲笑，71. 洗口，75. 备办等。78. 榔埋的"榔"字是现代的"拢"字；"埋"字可能是借自广州话的"埋"（mɑi˩），用在动词后作补语，表示趋向或成为某种样子。

4. 名词、形容词和动词构词词素次序和北方官话不同的有 5. 人客（客人），47. 闹热（热闹），61. 欢喜（喜欢）。这种词素次序颠倒的结构，也是江淮和南方方言的共同特点之一。

6.3. 语法特点

1. 比较句

79. 大过他 ta co ta [ta kɔ tʻa] 比他大（广州：大过佢）

80. 近过他 chin co ta [kin kɔ tʻa]

81. 做强过他 zo chiam co ta [tsɔ kʻiaŋ kɔ tʻa]

这几个比较句例的语法，显然是受了广州话的影响。

2. "把"字句

a）表示"指使"，"容许"或"听任"的

82. 把他进来 pa ta çin lai [pa tʻa tsin lai] 让他进来

83. 不把进来 po pa cin lai [poʔ pa tsin lai] 不让进来

84. 把他欢喜 pa ta cuon schi [pa tʻa xuɔn xi] 让他喜欢；把欢喜他 pa cuon schi ta [pa xuɔn xi tʻa]

85. 把他憔懆 pa ta ziau zau [pa tʻa tsiau tsau] 让他着急

b）表示"给"、"与"的

86. 把他食 pa ta cie' [pa tʻa tʃʻə] 给他吃

87. 把草他食 pa zau ta cie' [pa tʻa tsʻau tʃʻə] 给他草吃，牧放

c）使成式（？）表示"感受"的

88. 把工夫 pa cum fu [pa kuŋ fu] 用工夫，忙（于）

89. 把辛苦 pa sin cu [pa sin k'u]（受）辛苦

90. 把愁事 pa ceu ssi [pa ts'ɘu sʅ] 发愁

91. 把烦恼 pa fan nau [pa fan nau] 烦恼

84. 把他欢喜，又作"把欢喜他"，主语被移到谓语后面去了，这个句型和广州话的"动词＋直接宾语＋间接宾语"相同，例如"畀本书我"。所不同的，这里的直接宾语不是名词而是动词（谓语）。87. "把草他食"和下面 111. "送酒他食"的结构词序相同。

3. "得"字句

92. 背得 poi te' [pui təʔ] 能背诵，背得出；念得 niē te' [niɛɘ təʔ] 能念，会念

93. 讲得 chiam te' [kiaŋ təʔ] 会讲，会说

94. 字读得 zi to te' [tsʅ toʔ təʔ] 会读（这个）字，认得（这个）字

95. 说不得 sciuo po te' [ʃuoʔ poʔ təʔ]；讲不来（chiam po lai）[kiaŋ poʔ lai]

96. 抵不得 ti po te' [ti poʔ təʔ] 受不了，受不住；难当（nan tam）[nɑn tɑŋ]

97. 抵不得羞 ti po te' siu [ti poʔ toʔ siɘu]（案 siu 为 sieu 之误）；怕羞（pa siu）[p'a sieu]

98. 舍不得（scie po te'）[ʃɛ poʔ təʔ]

99. 看不得远（can po te' yuon）[k'an poʔ təʔ yɔn]

92. 背得，93. 讲得等例句，是江淮方言中表示"可能"（"会"）的句法，是江淮方言语法特点之一。本文前面《宾主问答辞义》对话中的例句，可以代表明代江淮官话的句法。99. 看不得远，北方官话说"看不远"或"看得不远"。动补结构中插进"不得"，也许是明代官话的语法。现在江淮方言中是否还有这类的句型，尚待调查。

4. "紧"字句

100. 好得紧 hau te' chin [xau təʔ kin]；
　　甚妙（scin miau）[ʃin miau]；
　　甚好（scin hau）[ʃin xau]

101. 惊得紧 chin te' chin [kin təʔ kin]；
　　甚怕（scin pa）[ʃin p'a]

102. 要财得紧 iau zai te' chin [iau ts'ai təʔ kin] 很贪财，很贪婪

"紧"在形容词后面，借"得"字的帮助，做补语，语势更重，表示程度更高。它相当于现代汉语的"很"。元曲中已出现这类的句子，例如"灵验得紧"。[27]《宾主问答辞义》里也有"紧"字句："客曰：好得紧。"范芳济的《官话精髓》里也有"紧"字。

他称它为表示"最高级的"（super lativo）虚词，并列出它的同义词"得极"，"到极"，"不过"。他在"好不过"hào pǒ kuó [xau poʔ kuo] 例句的后面加了"上好"xáng hào [ʃaŋ xau]，"好得紧"hào tě kìn [xau təʔ kin]，"好得很"hào tě hèn [xau təʔ xen]，"极好"kiě hào [kiəʔ xau]。[28] 可见明末清初"紧"和"很"两者并用，到后来"很"才渐渐取代了"紧"。

5. 其他词句

103. 甚么东西 scin mo tŭ si [ʃin mo tuŋ si]；
    甚么子 scin mo zi [ʃin mo tsɿ]

104. 甚么所在 scin mo so zai [ʃin mo sɔ tsai]；
    何处 ho ciu [xo tʃʽu]

105. 这等 cie tin [tʃɛ tin] 这样，这么；
    这等样大 cie tin jam ta [tʃɛ tin iaŋ ta] 这样（么）大

106. 欢喜不胜 cuon schi po scin [xuɔn xi poʔ ʃin]；
    甚喜（scin schi）[ʃin xi]

107. 饿险死 guo schiě si [ʔuo xiɛn sɿ] 几乎饿死，险些饿死；
    饿馁几死（guo nui（?）chi si）[ʔuo nui ki sɿ]

108. 弄他睡 lŭ ta sciui [luŋ tʽa ʃui] 使他睡

109. 弄他发性 lŭ ta fa sin [luŋ tʽa faʔ sin] 使（让）他生气
    激发他怒（chie' fa ta nu）[kiəʔ fa tʽa nu]

110. 去别所在 chiu pie' so zai [kʽy pieʔ sɔ tsai] 到别处去

111. 送酒他食 su çiu ta cie' [suŋ tsiu tʽa tʃʽəʔ] 送酒给他喝

解释：

103. 甚么子：河南灵宝是"什么子"[ʂɿ˩ moˋ tsɿˊ]，安徽宿县、阜南等处是"啥子"。"啥"（sha）字是"甚么"或"什么"shi-ma 的合音。[29]

104. 甚么所在：和现代闽南（厦门）的"甚物所在"(ˌsim miʔ˳ ˋsɔ tsaiˋ) 相同。大概是受了闽方言的影响。

105. 这等：已见于元曲《玉镜台》二折白："腕平著，笔直著。小姐，不是这等？"明代的《李善长狱词》："若是这等，事业也不久远！"[30] 此外明末葡籍天主教耶稣会士罗儒望（João da Rocha, S. J., 1565—1623）在他用白话译的《天主圣启蒙》（于 1609 年前后出版）中也有许多用"这等"的句子，例如："这等我们先前做过被虏人么？"（6a 页）"为什么这等常常用他？"（10a 页）由此可见"这等"在明末还是常用的指示代词。

106. 欢喜不胜：是"不胜欢喜"的倒装句。"不胜"是补语副词，即"欢喜得不得了"。

107. 饿险死：即"险些饿死"或"差一点没饿死"。"险"字插在动补动词"饿死"二字的中间，比较特殊。但"病几死"之类的说法是早已有之的。

108. 弄他睡和 109. 弄他发性是使成式的例句。

110. 去别所在：这个例句，大概是受了闽南方言的影响。因为北方方言普遍说"到别处去"。台湾通行的国语（即普通话）里像"我去台北"，"我去学校"一类的句子非常普遍。近年来北京话受了方言的影响，也有人说"我去北京"，"我去学校"等。

111. 送酒他食：是双宾语句，和粤方言的句式相同，即指物宾语在前，指人宾语在后，且后宾语为补语性质，例如"佢畀三本书我（他给我三本书）"，无疑地是受了粤方言的影响。

七、《葡汉辞典》的官话基础方言

从上面列举的音韵及词汇特点，我们可以肯定罗明坚和利玛窦所学习和记录的语言，是当时通用的官话。这官话和现代的江淮方言基本上相同。它的基础方言不是以北京话为基础的北方官话，而是以当时的南京话为基础的南方（江淮）官话。下面我们分别讨论。

7.1 罗利二氏所学习的口语是当时的官话

这一点可以用文献来证明。当时（自 1573 至 1606）任东印度区耶稣会监会（Visitor）的范礼安神父（Alessandro Valignano, S. J., 1539—1606）曾于 1577 年至澳门视察，居留了几个月，研究中国的文化和习俗，是他指派了罗明坚和利玛窦到中国来传教。在他著的《耶稣会东印度发展史》一书里称传教士所学习的中国话为官吏或法庭的语言。他说："中国各省有各省彼此不能了解的语言。中国人还有另外一种语言，是官吏和宫廷通用的官方语言（el proprio lenguaje de los mandarines y de la corte）。这种语言就好像我们的拉丁语一样。我们的两位神父（指罗明坚和利玛窦）正在那里（即澳门）学习这种语言，并且已取得了很大的进步。"[31]

罗明坚于 1583 年 2 月 7 日，从肇庆给罗马耶稣会总会长阿瓜委瓦神父（Claudio Acquaviva, S. J., 1543—1615）写信报告他到中国后的传教工作，信中提到有关学习语言的情形，他说："葡萄牙人在这个港口（案指澳门）和中国人通商，并借一些中国仆役担任翻译。因此，起初为找一位能教我中国宫廷式的语言（da lingua della corte）的老师非常困难。但是为了传教，我必须学习这种语言和文字。如果老师只会说中国话，而不谙葡萄牙语，也是无济于事，因为我听不懂。"稍后，他又说："只可惜，目前对中国话，我还不能运用自如。再者，我学的是宫廷的语言（lingua cortegiona），中国人称为官话（lingua mandarina）。但是在澳门没有学习的机会，只有到中国内陆，和中国人一起，才学得好。"[32]

利玛窦于 1592 年 11 月 12 日从韶州给住在罗马的法比神父（Fabio de' Fabj, S. J.）写信说："中国十五省都使用同样的文字。但是各省的语言不同。还有一种通用的语言，我们可以称它为宫廷和法庭的语言（la lingua della corte e forense），因为它通用于各省法庭和官场。我们目前学习的，正是这种语言。"[33]

后来利氏在《中国传教史》里，首次把"官话"的名称介绍给西方的读者，他说："在这些不同的语言中，有一种叫做'官话'（cuonhoa [kuɔn xua]）的语言，就是法庭的语言，通用于各省的官庭和法庭。学会了官话，可以在各省使用，就连妇孺都能用官话跟外省人交谈。"[34]

本文前面提到的《宾主问答辞义》中的对话中也提到传教士学习官话：客曰："如今你晓得我们这边官话不晓得？"答曰："也晓得几句。"客曰："也讲得？"答曰："略学讲几句。"[35]

以上文献记载可以证明罗、利二氏及当时的其他传教士学习的口语是官话，不是方言。

7.2 明末清初官话的基础方言不是北京话而是南京话

从本文所举的音韵、词汇及语法的例子，可以很清楚地看出，明末清初的官话的基础方言不是北京话，因为它有的许多特点在北京话里没有或不常见。音韵方面，如"班、搬"和"关、官"韵母的不同；"镇、政"和"根、更"韵母的合拼，入声的保存等。词汇方面，如四脚蛇，水鸡，桃子，枣子，斧头，闹热，欢喜，嫖（标）致，牢固，讲，晓得，食（吃）酒；屙（屙）尿，如今，不曾等；语法方面如背得，讲得等，都和现代的北京话不同，而和现代的江淮方言相同。这证明它属于南方（江淮）官话，而不属于北方官话。

我们主张明末清初的官话基础方言是当时的南京方言，可以从两方面来证明：第一，南京曾为明朝的首都。明代初年，太祖朱元璋，建文帝朱允炆及成祖朱棣早期，都以南京为首都。从洪武元年（1368 年）至永乐十九年（1421 年）成祖迁都北京，长达五十三年之久，迁都后又以南京为行在多年。徐达攻取大都，朱棣坐镇北京及后来迁都北京时，都曾带了大批南京人及其他江淮方言区的人士北上，南京话在明代占据了一个颇为重要的地位。[36] 迁都后，它在北京大概也沿用了将近二百年。因为利玛窦自 1601 年至 1610 年（万历二十九年至三十八年）一直住在北京，而他说的官话似乎还是他在南方（肇庆，韶州，南昌和南京）所学的南方官话，因为在他 1606 年赠给程大约的四篇罗马字注音文章里的音韵系统，和他在肇庆时所编《辞典》里的系统，基本上相同。虽然当时北京话里入声早已消失（与利氏同时的徐孝《司马温公等韵图经》可以证明），但是利氏的音系中仍然存在。可见当时以南京话为基础方言的官话，在北京还甚通行，否则利氏为适应宫廷官吏、文人，以及北京居民的语言，一定会把以南京音为主的官话音系改为以北京音为主的官话音系了。

第二，最有力的证明是明末清初官话的音韵词汇和语法特点跟现代江淮方言区相同。那么明代官话的基础方言也必定在江淮方言区内。而当时最占优势的方言，自然是首都南京话。因此我们说明代官话的基础方言为南京话，是合情合理的。

有一件历史记事，也可以暗示南京话是当时官话的基础方言。利玛窦在他的《中国传教史》第四卷第十一章里，记载了一位太监赠送书童教神父中国话的事。事情发生在 1600 年利玛窦再次由南京去北京时。新到中国的庞迪我神父（Diego de Pantoja, S. J., 1571—1618）是他的助手。他们乘坐由刘步惜（原文 leupusie）太监率领的马船船队，沿运河北上，到了山东省西北的临清，太监因故先行。临别前，为报答神父们的善待，"把他在南京买的一个书童，当作礼物，留给了神父们。他说他送给他们这个男童，是因为他口齿清楚。可以教庞迪我神父纯粹的南京话。"[37] 值得我们注意的是上面这一段记事是译自由金尼阁改订出版的《利玛窦中国传教史》，而不是译自利氏意大利原文。这一段记事的原文是："太监刘步惜很高兴地把他在南京买的一个书童，送给神父们，当做礼物。因为这个男童会讲地道的中国话（che parlava molto bene [la] lingua cina），可以教正要学中国话的庞迪我神父。"[38] 金尼阁把利玛窦原文的"地道的中国话"改成了"纯粹的南京话"，可见当时的南京话就是地道的中国话，换言之，就是当时官话的基础方言，是明末标准官话的代表，否则庞迪我就没有必要去学纯粹的南京话，而应该等到抵达北京后，学纯粹的北京话了。鲁国尧据何高济的中译本看出了这一点，今以利氏意大利文原本证明之。

有一点我们应注意：就是现在的南京话和四百多年以前的南京话，在音韵、词汇、语法等方面都发生了相当大的差异。有一些早期江淮方言的特点已经消失了。例如上面提过的古山摄开口及合口一、二等韵的字，在现代江淮方言里保持着区别，即"搬"和"班"及"官"和"关"的韵母不同，而在南京话里这两个韵母已合并为一，没有分别了。这是因为从明末到现在四百多年中，因为战乱及多次的迁移聚散，南京的人口发生了巨大的变动。现在南京的居民大半已不是四百多年前南京人的后裔，而是外来户的子孙。他们的语言跟明代的江淮官话有相当的距离。因为这些外来户，绝大多数是皖北和苏北人，其中也包括不少清代迁来的回族和一些满族贵族。他们大都是从北方来的，原来都说北方话，因而南京话的北方话成分逐渐增加，对向北方话转变起了很大的推动作用，使南京话北方话化了。抗日战争胜利后到现在，南京话更进一步向普通话靠拢了。[39] 现在我们如要追寻现代江淮官话的后裔，必须在南京以外的毗邻县市，例如扬州、泰州及安徽省的合肥、安庆等地去找。[40]

八、结语

1986 年在台湾第二届国际汉学会议上，笔者用英文发表了《利玛窦的葡汉辞典：一个历史和语言学的介绍》。近数年又继续研究，用中文写成此文。1989 年夏我又赴罗马耶稣会档案馆查阅原件，发现是罗明坚的笔迹。所以，《葡汉辞典》当是罗利二氏共同的作品。

《葡汉辞典》可能是学习中国官话的第一部双语辞典。明代虽已有《华夷译语》一类的番汉对照分类词汇，但是还不能称为狭义的双语辞典。其非汉语只包括中国少数民族及邻国的语言，如蒙古、西藏、女真、朝鲜、安南等译语，并没有包括欧洲语言。罗氏的《葡汉辞典》按拉丁字母 ABC 顺序排列，先列葡语词条，后列罗马字汉语拼音，最后列汉语对应词。这种双语辞典的排列法，当时在中国尚属首创。

《辞典》中的罗马字注汉字音，是汉语最早的拉丁字母拼音方案。是利氏及《西儒耳目资》拼音系统的前身，也是后世一切汉语拼音方案的鼻祖。编写这部辞典时，罗明坚因为到中国时间不久，初学汉语，记音时，有些汉字的拼写法尚不一致，甚至有模棱含混的地方。不过从拼音资料整体来说，已可使我们归纳出一个大致的官话音韵系统。罗氏记录的方音，反映他的汉语教师不是北方北京人，而是南方闽粤人，其中有说广东（广州）话的，有说客家话的，有说闽南话的。这些方音的记录，给我们留下了一些明代粤、闽、客方音的珍贵资料。

在比较罗氏所记录的明代官话和现代江淮方言时，发现了四川西部方言，在音韵、声调和词汇方面和明代官话及现代江淮方言有许多共同特点。这是因为元末明初，有大批说江淮官话的安徽和湖北人移居四川所致。这是一个非常重要的发现。值得方言学者作进一步的比较研究。

《辞典》中所收录的词汇和短句，除去一小部分是受了粤、闽、客方言影响之外，绝大部分都能代表明代以南京话为基础方言的官话，是研究明代官话和早期江淮方言珍贵的资料。本文所举出的例子，只是其中的一小部分。资料整体，尚待更进一步的整理和研究。在比较明代官话和现代江淮方言词和语法时，因为现代方言词汇和语法资料的不足，比较的结果还不够深入详尽。作者希望国内外的同好，加以补充，并对本文提出意见。

附录一：《葡汉辞典》声韵表

一、声母（23）：

p	八边抱	p'	怕骗破	m	马面母	f	法飞房	v	袜万味
t	大店道	t'	他天同	n	那年内			l	来舰辇
ts	在酒诈	ts'	才钱愁			s	三先生		
tʃ	知战竹	tʃ'	常城出			ʃ	是善辰	ʒ	日然如
				ɲ	义业浓				
k	高见过	k'	开欠哭	ŋ	爱硬额	x	好晓玩		
ø	以牙五					ʔ	瓦卧为		

二、韵母（52）：

ɿ	子辞死	i	悲地儿	u	布都奴驴	y	居许鱼
ʅ	知齿是						
a	把打拿	ia	家下牙	ua	瓜化瓦		
ɛ	这车惹	iɛ	借邪夜				
o	破么我	io	痂靴	uo	过火卧		
ai	买带菜	iai	街鞋矮	uai	快坏外		
				uei	贝妹鬼		
				ui	对雷乳		
au	包刀少	iau	嫖鸟小				
əu	头手流	iəu	九修有				
an	谈三汉	iɛn	边棉仙	uan	关还换		
ɛn	恩生然	in	宾明星	uɛn	分问瘟		
				un	粪顿顺	yn	君裙云
ɔn	搬短团安			uɔn	官乱滚	yon	捲全村
aŋ	方当藏	iaŋ	讲想羊	uaŋ	光黄往		
uŋ	风公中					yŋ	穷兄用
aʔ	八拉杀	iaʔ	甲瞎压	uaʔ	刮滑刷		
əʔ	墨得色	iəʔ	笔力一				
		ieʔ	别裂节			yeʔ	雪
ɔʔ	博落索	iɔʔ	略学雀				
oʔ	不逐肉	ioʔ	曲蓄欲	uoʔ	国忽说	yoʔ	蹶月绝
uʔ	没祝						

附 注

[1] D'Elia，1942—1949，I：23，脚注 1. 利玛窦 1983：336 译注①："即《平常问答词意》"，误。

[2] D'Elia，1938 及 1938a。

[3] D'Elia，1938：173 及 1942—1949，I：23，脚注 1。

[4] 程大约，1609 及利玛窦，1957。

[5] 顾保鹄，1983；尹斌庸，1986：7，其结论与顾氏不谋而合，只是晚了三年。

[6] 罗常培，1930。

[7] 明代的《华夷译语》是番汉对照的分类词汇，不是狭义的双语辞典。

[8] D'Elia，1942—1949，I：31—33，利玛窦，1983：336，译者注①谓 "即《平常问答词意》"，误；利玛窦，1986：286—287。

[9] D'Elia，1938a：695。

[10] Bartoli，1665，16：196—200。

[11] Pfister, 1932—1934，II：996。

[12] 罗常培，1930。

[13] 根据董同龢，1968：57—71；参考周德清，1969 及 1970。

[14] 詹伯慧、张日昇，1987：238。

[15] 罗常培，1930：271。

[16] 詹伯慧、张日昇，1987：52。

[17] 合肥师范学院，1962：199。

[18] Tacchi-Venturi，1911—1913，II：27；利玛窦，1986a：31。

[19] 金尼阁，1957：50b。

[20] 同上，51a—52a。

[21] Varo，1703：5a—5b，第一声（清平）及第二声（浊平）。

[22] Varo，1703：5b—6a，第三声（上）、第四声（去）及第五声（入）。

[23] 鲁国尧，1985：49。

[24] 平山久雄，1984：192—193。

[2S] 梁德曼，1982：25—28；杨时逢，1984：1019—1066；1117—1132。夹江的去声，梁氏写作 213，杨氏写作 24。今从杨氏。

[26] 崔荣昌，1985：6—10，14。崔氏所引的资料是根据《四川大学学报》1960：3 所载《四川方言音系》。

[27] 龙潜庵，1985：735，田宗尧，1985：1208。

[28] Varo，1703：16b。

[29] 杨时逢、荆允敬，1971：135；合肥师范学院，1962：162—163。

[30] 刘坚，1985：346，注 [14]；田宗尧，1985：945。

[31] Valignano，1944：254—256。

[32] Tacchi-Venturi，1911—1913，II：411—412；利玛窦，1986a：446—447。

[33] 同上，II：91 利玛窦，1986a：109。

[34] D'Elia，1942、1949，I：38，利玛窦；1983：30，利玛窦 1986：23。

[35] 除此以外，尚有上面论《辞典》第三栏时所举的例子：Fallar Mãndarin 官话，正音。

[36] 鲁国尧，1985：50—51。

[37] Ricci，193：362；利玛窦，1983：391。

[38] D'Elia，1942—1949，II：111；利玛窦，1986a：337。

[39] 鲍明炜，1980，1986；林焘，1987。

[40] 贺巍 1985：165—170；颜逸明，1987：65。

参考文献

鲍明炜（1980）六十年来南京方音向普通话靠拢情况的考察，《中国语文》第 4 期。

鲍明炜（1986）南京方言历史演变初探，《语言研究论集》第一辑，南京：江苏教育出版社。

鲍明炜、颜景常（1985）苏北江淮官话与北方话的分界，《方言》第 2 期。

北京大学中文系语言教研室（1962）《汉语方音字汇》，北京：文字改革出版社。

北京大学中文系语言教研室（1964）《汉语方言同汇》，北京：文字改革出版社。

董同龢（1968）《双语音韵学》，台北：广文书局。

顾保鹄（1983）喜见利玛窦神父的《西字奇迹》孤本，《教友生活周刊》11 月 10 日。

合肥师范学院方言调查工作组（1962）《安徽方言概况》（内部发行）。

贺巍（1985）河南山东皖北苏北的官话，《方言》第 3 期。

湖南师范学院中文系汉语方言普查组（1960）《湖南省汉语方言普查总结报告（初稿）》，湖南
　　师范学院中文系。

江苏省和上海市方言调查指导组（1960）《江苏省和上海市方言概况》，南京：江苏人民出版社。

金尼阁（1957）《西儒耳目资》，北京：文字改革出版社。

利玛窦（1605）《西字奇迹》，北京。

利玛窦（1927）《明季之欧化美术及罗马注音》，北平：辅仁大学。

利玛窦（1957）《明末罗马字注音文章》，北京：文字改革出版社。

利玛窦（1983）《利玛窦札记》，何高济等译，北京：中华书局。

利玛窦（1986a）《利玛窦中国传教史》，刘后余、王玉川译，台北：光启出版社，辅仁大学
　　出版社。

利玛窦（1986b）《利玛窦书信集》，罗渔译，台北：光启出版社，辅仁大学出版社。

梁德曼（1982）《四川方言与普通话》，成都：四川人民出版社。

林焘（1987）北京话溯源，《中国语文》第 3 期。

刘坚（1985）《近代汉语读本》，上海：上海教育出版社。

龙潜庵（1985）《宋元语言辞典》，上海：上海辞书出版社。

鲁国尧（1985）明代官话及其基础方言问题，《南京大学学报》第 4 期。

罗常培（1930）耶稣会士在音韵学上的贡献，《历史语言研究所集刊》第一本第三分。

罗明坚（1585？）《宾主问答辞义》（手稿）。

罗儒望（译）（1609？）《天主圣教启蒙》（出版者不详）。

罗韵希等（1987）《成都方言词典》，成都：四川社会科学院出版社。

平山久雄（1984）江淮方言祖调值构拟和北方方言祖调值初探，《语言研究》第 1 期。

饶秉才等（1981）《广州话方言词典》，香港：商务印书馆。

日下恒夫（1974）清代南京话方言の一斑，《关西大学中国文学纪要》5。

田宗尧（1985）《中国古典小说用语辞典》，台北：联经出版事业公司。

厦门大学中国语言文字研究所汉语方言研究室（1982）《普通话闽南方言词典》，福州：福建人
民出版社，香港：三联书店。

杨福绵（1983）利玛窦对中国语言学的贡献，（香港）《公教报》1 月 7 日、14 日。

杨联升（1957）老乞大朴通事里的语法语，《历史语言研究所集刊》第二十九本上。

杨耐思（1981）《中原音韵音系》，北京：中国社会科学出版社。

杨时逢（1984）《四川方言调查报告》，台北："中研院"历史语言研究所。

杨时逢、荆允敬（1971）灵宝方言，《清华学报》第 1、2 期（合刊）。

颜逸明（1987）八十年代汉方言的分区，《华东师范大学学报》第 4 期。

尹斌庸（1986）《西字奇迹》考，《中国语文天地》第 2 期。

詹伯慧、张日昇（主编）（1987）《珠江三角洲方言字音对照》，香港：新世纪出版社。

周德清（1970）《中原音韵》，台北：艺文印书馆。

Aubazac, Louis (1909) *Dictionnaire français-cantonnais.* Hong Kong: Nazareth, rev. ed.

Bartóli, Daniello, S. J. (1665) *Dell'historia della Compagnia di, Giesù. La Cina.* Torino, 1825, repr.

D'Elia, Pasquale, S. J. (1938) Il primo dizionario Europeo-Cinese e la fonetizzazione Italiana del
Cinese. *Atti del XIX Congresso Internazionale degli Orienalisti.* Rome, 172–178.

D'Elia, Pasquale, S. J. (1938a) Découverte de nombreux et importants documents relatifs a l'histoire
des missions catholiques en Chine de 1580 à 1610. *Atti del XIX Congresso Internazionale degli
Orientalisti.* Rome, 693–698.

D'Elia, Pasquale M., S. J. (1942–1949) *Fonti Ricciane.* Rome: La Libreria dello Stato.

Douglas, Castairs (1899) *Chinese-English dictionary of the vernacular or spoken language of
Amoy, with the principal variations of the Chang-chew and Chin-chew dialects.* London: The
Presbyterian Church of England.

Eitel, Ernest John (1877) *A Chinese-English dictionary in the Cantonese dialect.* Hong Kong: Kelly &

Walsh.

Hemeling, Karl, E. G. (1902?) *The Nanking Kuan Hua.* Shanghai: Statistical Dept. of the Inspectorate General.

Kühnerst, Franz (1894) *Die Chinesische sprache zu Nanking.* Vienna: F. Tempsy.

Kühnerst, Franz (1893) Einige bemerkungen über die Sheng im Cinesischen und den Nanking-dialect. *Wiener Zeitschrift für de Kunde des Morgenlandes* 7, 302–310.

MacIver, Donald (1926) *A Chinese-English dictionary, Hakka dialect as spoken in Kwang-tung province.* Shanghai: American Presbyterian Mission Press.

Mello, A. H, de, et al. (1962) *Dicionário Chinês-Português.* Macao: Imprensa National. / *Cantonese-Portuguese* (《中 [粤] 葡字典》).

Pfister, Louis, S. J. (1932–1934) *Notices biographiques et bibliographiques sur les Jésuites de l'ancienne mission de Chine. 1552-1773.* 2 vols. *Variétés Sinologiques*, 59. Shanghai: Imprimerie de la Mission Catholique.

Rey, Charies (1926) *Dictionnoire Chinois-français Dialecte Hac-ka.* Hong Kong: Nazareth. Rev.ed.

Ricci, Matteo, S. J. & Nicolas Trigault S. J. (1953) *China in the Sixtenth Century: The Journals of Matthew Ricci, 1583-1610.* Tr. by Louis Gallagher J. S. J. New York: Random House.

Tacchi-Venturi, Pietro, S. J. (1911–1913) *Opere storiche del P. Matteo Ricci, S. J.* 2 vols. I. *Commentarj della Cina* (1911); II. *Le lettere dalla Cina* (1913).

Valignano, Alessandro, S. J. (1944) Ed. by Joseph Wicki, S. J. *Historia del Principio y Progresso de la Compañia de Jesus en las Indias orientales (1542-1564).* Roma: Institutum Historicum Societatis Jesu.

Varo, Francisco, O. P. (1703) *Arte de la lengua Mandarina.* Ed. by Pedro Piñuela, O. F. M. Canton.

Weingartner, Fredric F. (1975) EI primero diccionario Europeo-Chino. *Boletin de la Associación Española de Orientalistas* 11, 223–227.

（本文发表于《中国语言学报》第 5 期，第 35—81 页，1995 年）

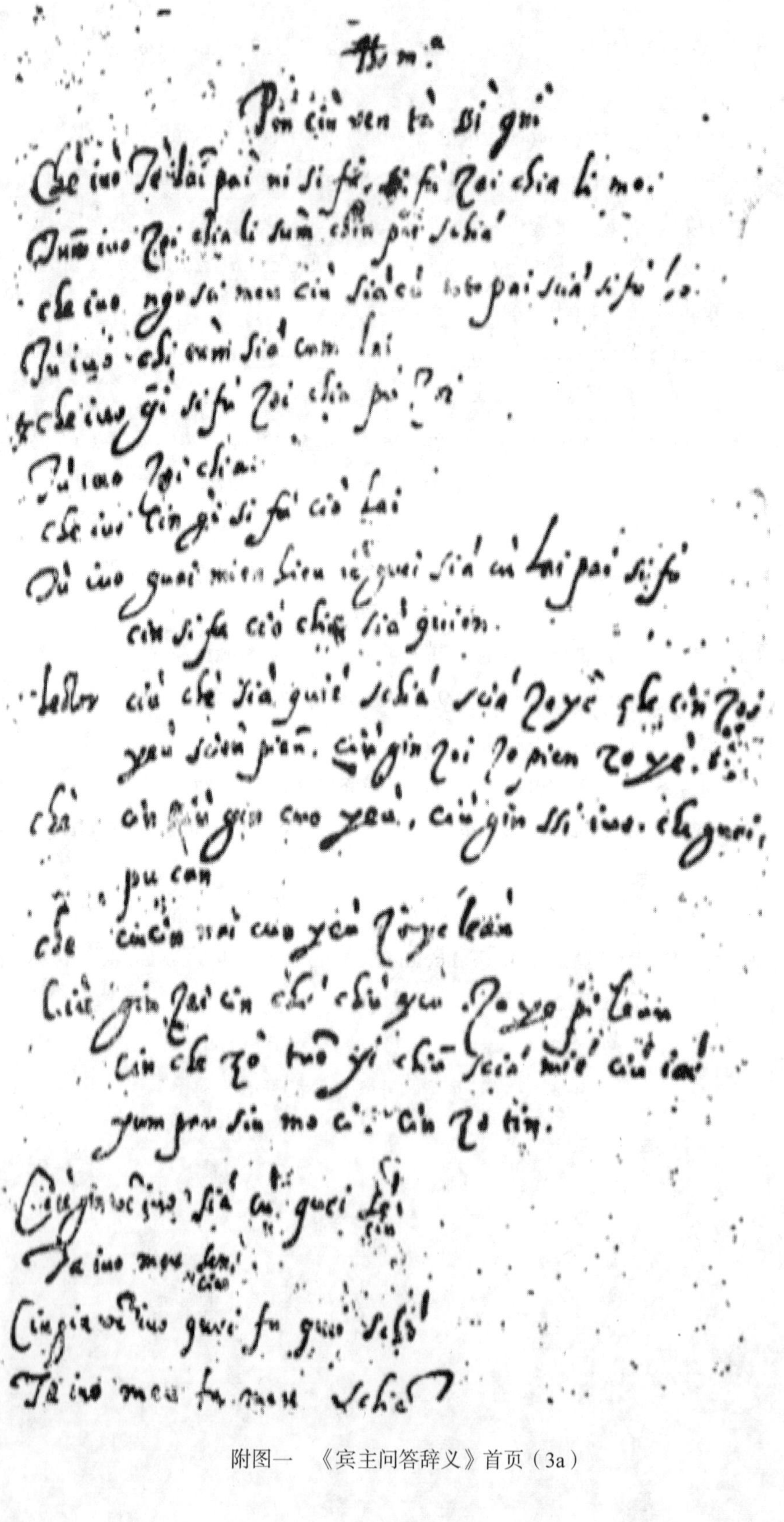

附图一　《宾主问答辞义》首页（3a）

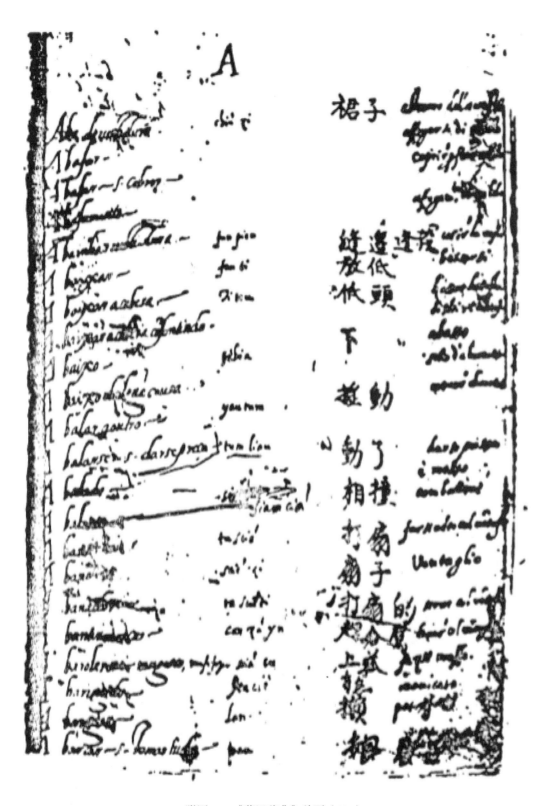

附图二　《葡汉辞典》首页（32a）

附图三　《葡汉辞典》第二页（33a）

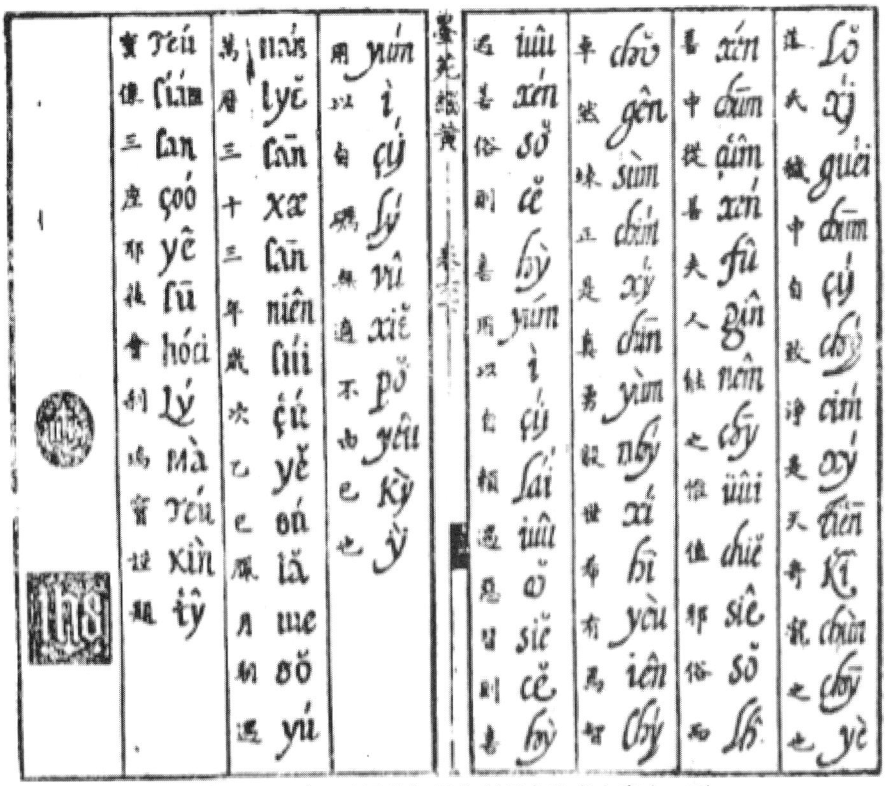

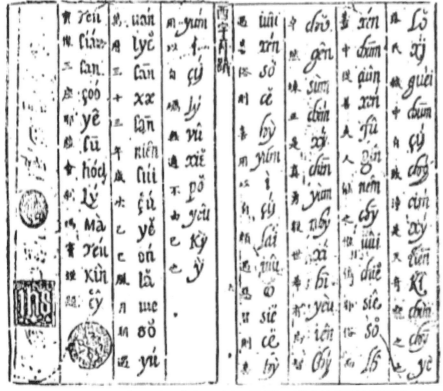

附图四　《程氏墨苑》所收利玛窦注音文章之一页

附图五　利玛窦《西字奇迹》之一页（"谨题"下盖有梵蒂冈图书馆印）

附图六　范芳济的《官话技术》封面

《西儒耳目资》的调值拟测 *

曾晓渝

明代来华传教士金尼阁（Nicolas Trigault）著的《西儒耳目资》（1626）[1]，记录了当时官话的五个声调：清、浊、上、去、入。它们与中古音及今普通话的调类对应关系是：

中古音　　　金氏调类　　　普通话

平 —— 清 —— 阴
　　 —— 浊 —— 阳
上 —— 上 —— 上
去 —— 去 —— 去
入 —— 入 —— 阴阳上去

金氏的"清、浊、上、去"四声很整齐地与普通话的四声相对应，例外的字只有百分之三。金氏音系中的"入声"与中古《切韵》音系的相对应，无一例外。就调类而言，金氏的声调系统一目了解，但这个系统的调值如何，则有必要着重探讨。

过去，对《西儒耳目资》音系进行过研究的主要有罗常培、陆志韦、李新魁三位先生[2]，但他们都没谈及调值问题。汉语语音史研究中的调值构拟，的确难度较大。不过，近年来中外学者已陆续有这方面的论文发表，其中有的直接论及明代官话声调的调值[3]，在此基础上，我们尝试对《西儒耳目资》音系中的五个声调进行调值的拟测。

一

我们确定金氏音系声调的高低升降的实际读法，主要依据金尼阁《西儒耳目资》中关于"清、浊、上、去、入"五声的描写。另外，还着重参考了基本与金尼阁同时代来华的传教士万济谷（Francisco Varo）（1627—1687）著的《官话方言语法》（1703年版）中关于明末官话五个声调的描述。[4] 我们认为，金尼阁和万济谷所记述的是同一种官话，理由是：1.《利玛窦中国札记》（利玛窦、金尼阁著，何高济、王遵仲、李

* 本文为作者硕士学位论文《〈西儒耳目资〉音系研究》中的一节。写作过程中，承蒙导师刘又辛、林序达教授指教，并经鲁国尧教授、尹斌庸研究员审阅斧正，谨此深表谢意。

申译，中华书局 1983 年出版，以下简称《札记》）中指出，明代来华传教士们所学的汉语是一种"整个帝国通用的口语"，"懂得这种通用的语言，我们耶稣会的会友就的确没有必要再去学他们工作所在的那个省份的方言了。"（p.30）可见，利玛窦、金尼阁以及万济谷，他们所学的不是传教所在地的方言，而是当时全国通用的那一种官话。2. 为了帮助传教士们掌握汉语声调，利玛窦与另一位较早来华的传教士郭居静神父合编了《音韵字典》。[5] 利氏在《札记》中记述道："他们采用五种记号来区别所用的声韵，使学者可以决定特别的声韵而赋予它各种意义，因为他们共有五声。郭居静神父对这个工作做了很大的贡献。他是一个优秀的音乐家，善于分辨各种细微的声韵变化，能很快辨明声调的不同。……这种以音韵书写的方法，是由我们两个最早的耶稣会传教士所创作的，现在仍被步他们后尘的人们所使用。"（p.336）利玛窦、郭居静创造的五种标调记号，由金尼阁、万济谷原原本本地沿用了下来。这套符号便是：

阴　阳　上　去　入

-　^　ˋ　ˊ　ˇ

金尼阁在《西儒耳目资》中说："平仄清浊甚次，敝友利西泰（按：即利玛窦）首至贵国，每以为苦，惟郭仰凤（按：即郭居静）精于乐法，颇能觉之，因而发我之蒙耳。"（上册 p.144—145）无疑，金尼阁所学汉语与利氏、郭氏一致，故采用的标调符号也与之相同；而万济谷亦采用完全相同的标调符号，由此可以设想万济谷所学汉语无异于金尼阁所学的。3. 将万济谷的声韵调注音与金尼阁的相比较，可以看出两者音系基本一致。例如（金氏的 -m 即 -ng）：

	万济谷	金尼阁
阴平	威风 goēi fūng	goēi fūm
	西瓜 sī kuā	sī kuā
阳平	缘由 iuên iêu	iuên iêu
	鹅翎 gô lîng	gô lîm
上声	诱感 ièu kàn	ièu kàn
	米粉 mì fuèn	mì fuèn
去声	厉害 lí hái	lí hái
	辩论 pién lún	pién lún
入声	博学 pǒ hiǒ	pǒ hiǒ
	黑墨 hě mě	hě mě

如果说金尼阁、万济谷所学的不是同一汉语官话方言，那么，他们的注音就不可能如

此相似。所以，鉴于以上几种理由，我们认为金尼阁、万济谷记述的是同一种官话方言。既然如此，我们将金尼阁《西儒耳目资》和万济谷《官话方言语法》两部书中关于当时汉语声调的描写材料相互参照使用，就基本消除疑虑了。

我们先来看金尼阁的描述：

> 清平无低无昂，在四声之中。其上其下每有二，最高曰去，次高曰入，最低曰浊，次低曰上。（上册 p.148）

> 清平不高不低，如钟声清远；浊平则如革鼓冬冬之音，旅人所知如是，恐于五方，未免有一二不相合耳。……正音如是，或有不合，土音而已。（上册 p.149—150）

> 不高不低之清平，极高之去声，次下之上声，次高之入声，极低之浊平，……曰 ā á à ǎ â。……中国五音之序曰清、浊、上、去、入，但极高与次高相对，极低与次低相对，辨在针芒，耳鼓易悟。余之所定，曰清，曰去，曰上，曰入，曰浊。不高不低在其中，两高与两低相形，如泰山与丘垤之悬绝，凡有耳者，谁不晰乎？（上册 p.151）

> 清平不低不昂，去、入皆昂，上、浊皆低。读法：清、去、上、入、浊，一低一昂，易分故耳。盖低昂相对，如皂白之易别，故一低一昂，对之愈近，辨之愈易明也。（上册 p.14）

我们可以将以上金尼阁的描述精简如下：

清平 ˉ 无低无昂，不高不低，在四声之中。

浊平 ˆ 上浊皆低，最低曰浊。

上声 ˋ 上浊皆低，次低曰上。

去声 ˊ 去入皆昂，最高曰去。

入声 ˇ 去入皆昂，次高曰入。

此外，我们再来看看万济谷《官话方言语法》中关于当时五个声调的描述：

> 第一声发成平稳的延长音，没有升降或别的变化，像一个人有点儿痛苦地呻吟一声：唉（ai）！不过发音是平稳的。例如：goēi fūng[威风]、sī kuā [西瓜]。中国人称这一声调为"平清"，意思是平而清楚；他们还叫这声为上平。（Varo 1703：3a）

> 第二声的发音，如果一个词是两个音节（按：实际是两个元音音素组成的复合元音音节），那么第二个音节的音调稍稍往下降；如果只有一个音节（按：指单元音音节），如像 ŷ（按：音值是 [ɿ]），人们将延长这个音节的读音，好像它是两个音节。这声调就像我们 Castile（按：以前西班牙北部的一个王国）人对一个告诉自己约翰犯了偷窃的人说"不（no）"一样，因为不同意他的说法，便答道："不，不要说约翰已经干了这样的事！"（西班牙文：No diga esso, Pues Juan avia de hazer lal cosa!）在这种情况下，人们向那人所说的

"不（no）"的声调有些阻塞和下降；这就是中国人所发的第二声。例如：iuên iêu [缘由]、gô lîng[鹅翎]。中国人称这一声调为平浊，平的意思是平而浑浊；他们也称这个调为下平。（ Varo 1703：3a ）

第三声的发音，从元音的一点开始，然后以稍微烦躁和生气的语气将声音下降三分之一，就像我已命令一个人做某些事，而他做得很糟或不令人满意，这时，我就对他说："不，我不喜欢你做的事。"（西班牙文：No, no quiero que hagas.）第三声的声调就像在这种情况下所说的"不（no）"。例如：iêu kàn[诱感]、mì fuèn[米粉]。中国人称这声为上声，上声的意思就是高声或大声发音。（ Varo 1703：5a ）

第四声的发音，从第一音节的一点开始，然后上升三分之一。如果这个调是单音节的，那么它将被延长发音。当我们发出肯定语气的反问句时，末尾的语调就是这个声调。譬如，当我被指使做什么事，一个人对我来说（好像他要阻止我）："你不应该做这事。"我以一种不容置疑的语气回答："为什么不？！"（西班牙文：Como no?!）那么，将这时我发的"不（no）"音末尾延长，就是第四声的声调。比如：lí hái[厉害]、pién lún[辩论]。中国人称这声为去声，去就是去或跑的意思。（ Varo 1703：5a ）

第五声实际上与第四声相同，只是在 [发音的] 末尾要作一种胸腔的努力；就好像我们中有一个不安分的人想要与别人打架，发出一种要打架的声音：啊（a）。不过，"啊"的末尾是短促的；用这样的方法发出的声调就是第五声。例如 pǒ hiǒ[博学]、hě mě [黑墨]。中国人称这一声为入声，其意思是进入的声音或在里面发出的声音。（ Varo 1703：5a—b ）

以上万济谷对汉语声调的描写，虽然显得有些外行，但对于我们真切了解当时官话的声调调值，有很大的帮助。这里，我们亦将万济谷的描述精简如下：

第一声 ˉ 平稳的延长音，没有升降变化，像病人呻吟声"ai"的语调。

第二声 ^ 音调稍往下降，有些阻塞，像制止人说坏消息时说的"不（no）"的语调。

第三声 ` 音调下降三分之一，像烦躁生气时说的"不（no）"的语调。

第四声 ´ 音调上升三分之一，将反问句末的"不（no）"音调延长，就是这一声调的读法。

第五声 ˇ 第五声音高与去声一样，但发音短促，像打架前发出的"啊"的语调。

还有一点应该弄清楚，万济谷用了西班牙语的各种语调来比喻描绘汉语的各个声调，那么，印欧语的语调概貌如何呢？罗常培、王均先生通过对印欧语系诸语言的语调进行综合研究，得出结论："大概一般的陈述句、命令句、感叹句和含特殊疑问词的问句等，多用降调的口气语调。一般的问句，未完的句子，或句子的前一些部分，或有些含蓄的句子，多升调。"[6] 这与汉藏语系诸语言的语调基本一样。现在，我们就来对金氏、万氏的声调描述进行具体分析，进而拟测出各个声调的调值。

为了便于简明地比较分析，有必要列下表：

调类名称	二者描述要点
阴平	金氏：无低无昂，不高不低
	万氏：平稳的延长音，无升降变化
阳平	金氏：最低曰浊，上浊皆低
	万氏：音调稍往下降
上声	金氏：次低曰上，上浊皆低
	万氏：音调下降三分之一
去声	金氏：最高曰去，去入皆昂
	万氏：声调上升三分之一
入声	金氏：次高曰入，去入皆昂
	万氏：音高与去声同，发音短促

根据上表，我们可以作出这样的理解：金氏所说的"高"，是就声调音高而言的高音；金氏所说的"昂"，是就声调调型而言的上升调；金氏所说的"低"，则有两种含义，当与"高"并提时，是指低音；当与"昂"并提时，是指下降调。于是，我们就能够确定《西儒耳目资》声调系统的调值了：

清平	浊平	上声	去声	入声
ˉ	^	ˋ	ˊ	ˇ
33	21	42	35	34

我们仍然采用五度标记法。王士元先生曾肯定此法说："一些语言的声调有人用九个之多的音高语音等级来标写，但是我们还没有发现任何语言有五个以上不同的音高等级，而五级音高正是高明的赵氏符号法所考虑到的音高等级的最大数值。"[7]

二

鲁国尧、杨福绵先生曾分别于1985、1986年拟测出了利玛窦、金尼阁音系的声调调值[8]，这里，有必要将两位先生的拟测结果与我们的拟测作一下比较：

	阴平	阳平	上声	去声	入声
鲁	33	131/121	31	35	534/424
杨	55	21	42	35	5
本文	33	21	42	35	34

鲁先生将阳平和入声拟作两个双向调，我们的拟测与之相异，主要基于以下考

虑。郑锦全先生在《汉语方言亲疏关系的计量研究》（载《中国语文》1988 年 2 期 p.87—102）一文中谈道：

在 737 个方言点全部 3,433 个声调里，不同调型的声调数量上的分布如下：

降调 1,125　　　　　　降升调 352

平调 1,086　　　　　　升降调 80

升调 790

降调出现次数最高，而双向调（指降升调和升降调）比较稀少。这些发现证实了早先提出的一些观点，也为其后关于声调的自然性和共性的讨论提供了数据。

调型的相互关系和同现现象在当时就显然值得深入研究。起初发现，如果一种方言出现升降调，同时也会出现升调，这使我们对系统内部声调的相互关系有了更深刻的了解。随后，又对不同调型间的相关程度作了计算。下面的表摘自 Cheng（1977）文，概括了这样一些关系（相关系数的范围在 -1 到 +1 之间）：

	平调	升调	降调	升降调
升调	.8359			
降调	.8504	.8078		
升降调	-.0953	.1229	-.0531	
降升调	.5386	.4841	.4412	-.0552

频率和相关度，除了表明汉语方言的数量模式，还有助于我们对声调历史拟构的合理性加以评价和确定（参看 Mei 1977 文）。

郑先生的研究告诉我们，双向调在汉语声调中很少，出现频率约 10% 左右；而且，在同一声调系统中，升降调与降升调的相关系数极小；更主要的还在于，金氏、万氏描述的阳平、入声两调都不像是双向调，所以，我们把金尼阁音系的阳平拟作 21 调，把入声拟作短促的 34 调。

杨福绵先生把阴平调拟作 55 调，理由是："根据万济谷的描写，我们确信第一声为平声，但是不能确定它是高平、中平还是低平。然而，因为现在大多数官话方言阴平调都是高平调，所以我们可以有理由地推测它是高平调 55。"（1986）我们觉得，确定三百年前的阴平调值，不能仅仅以现代部分官话方言的阴平调值为依据。事实上，现代汉语官话区方言的阴平调有相当一部分不是高平调，据郑锦全先生的统计，汉语阴平的平均调值为 3.47（五度制量表上的调高）。况且，金尼阁已讲得很明白："清平无低无昂，在四声之中。……清平不高不低。"所以，我们认为金氏音系的阴平调值以中平的 33 调为宜。

另外，杨先生把入声拟作短促的 5 调，我们拟作短促的 34 调。金尼阁说"去入皆昂"，昂即升调；万济谷也说："第五声实际与第四声相同，只是在 [发音的] 末尾要作一种胸腔的努力；……这 a 的末尾是短促的。"显然，去声与入声在调高、调型上都十分相似，区别在韵母元音的长短上。从今天汉语方言看，较短促的入声调可以是升调，例如：[9]

吴方言：绍兴　　　阴入 45　　阳入 12

苏州　　　阴入 14　　阳入 23

温州　　　阴入 23　　阳入 12

湘方言：长沙　　　　入 24

闽方言：福州　　　阴入 23

粤方言：阳江　　　阴入 45

合浦　　　阴入 13

西南官话四川地区的长宁、珙县、高县、江安、古蔺等地的入声为 34

鉴于以上的理由，我们把入声调拟作了 34 调。其余几调的拟测结果大致相同，不赘述。

三

利玛窦、金尼阁等使用的五个标调符号" ˉ ^ ˇ ` ´ "，是不是调型符号呢？对此，我们找不到充足的理由予以肯定的答复。

在拉丁文中，为了读音方便，往往在一个词的不同元音上加"‒"（长音符号）和" ˇ "（短音符号）；而在意大利文中，"`"表示元音的开口音，"´"表示元音的闭口音。例如：

拉丁文：ăbundē 丰盛　　　abūsīvē 冒用

ăbŭ-tor 浪费　　　cŭnĕātīm 三角形

意大利文：é [e]　　　ó [o]

è [ɛ]　　　ò [o]

发明汉语罗马字注音的" ˉ （阴）、^ （阳）、` （上）、´ （去）、ˇ （入）"五个声调符号的是利玛窦、郭居静，他俩都是意大利人，既精通意大利语，也必定懂拉丁语，因为拉丁语是中世纪欧洲各国宗教、文化、科学研究等方面的共同书面语。可以说，意大利文、拉丁文的各种附加符号会对利玛窦、郭居静为汉字标音产生一定的作用。道理很简单，既然他们能够发明用罗马字母为汉语的辅音、元音注音，那么，也完全可能借用罗马文的语音附加符号为汉语声调注音。值得注意的是，"‾"符号，拉丁文中表长音，汉语中表可以延长的阴平调；"˘"，拉丁文中表短音，汉语中表短促的入声调。也许，这不是巧合。另一方面，如果说"‾ˆ ` ´"是汉语五声的调型标号（横标记时间，纵标记音高），这又不大符合金氏、万氏对声调发音的描述，亦不符合汉语声调系统内部调型间相互关系的一般模式，这在前面已作论述。所以，我们以为，利氏、金氏音系中的五个声调符号不大可能是调型符号，而是受拉丁文、意大利文的语音附加符号的启发而创造出的汉语调类标记符号。

结语：根据金尼阁《西儒耳目资》、万济谷《官话方言语法》中对明末官话五个声调的生动描述，并参照汉语声调系统内部调型间相互关系的一般模式，我们测拟出了《西儒耳目资》所记录的明末官话五个声调的调值，它们是：阴33、阳21、上42、去35、入34。

附 注

[1] 本文所依据的《西儒耳目资》是文字改革出版社1957年影印本，共上、中、下三册。

[2] 罗常培《耶稣会士在音韵学上的贡献》，《史语所集刊》一本三分（1930）；陆志韦《金尼阁西儒耳目资所记的音》，《燕京学报》第33期（1948）；李新魁《记表现山西方音的〈西儒耳目资〉》，《语文研究》1982年1期。

[3] 参见鲁国尧《明代官话及其基础方言问题》，《南京大学学报》（哲社）1985年4期；远藤光晓《〈翻译老乞大·朴通事〉里的汉语声调》，《语言学论丛》第十三辑；Fu-mien Yang（杨福绵），The Portuguese-Chinese Dictionary of Matteo Ricci: A Historical and Linguistic Introduction（第二届国际汉语学会论文，1986年12月，台北）。

[4] 转引自杨福绵先生论文第八章，为了引文及讨论方便，这里我们将原英文译为汉语。

[5] 参见尹斌庸《〈西字奇迹〉考》，《中国语文天地》1986年2期。

[6] 罗常培、王均《普通话音学纲要》第144页，商务印书馆，1981年。

[7] 王士元《声调的音系特征》，《国外语言学》1987年第1期。

[8] 同[4]。

[9] 参见袁家骅《汉语方言概要》，文字改革出版社1960年；梁德曼《四川方言与普通话》第28页，四川人民出版社1982年。

（本文发表于《语言研究》1992年第2期，第132—136页）

试论琉球官话课本的音系特点

陈泽平

壹

古琉球王国与中国明清两朝政府有良好的交往。洪武年间，明太祖遣闽人船工三十六姓移民琉球那霸久米町。也是从那时起，琉球国不断向南京、北京的国子监及福州的琉球馆派遣留学生。两国人员往来多半也都经由福州。在福州琉球馆学习的琉球留学生称为"勤学人"，他们学习语言、文化和各种生产技艺，再回国传授他人。当时学习汉语官话在琉球受到政府鼓励，蔚为风气。琉球民间使用过多种手抄的汉语课本。日本学者十分重视收集这样的汉语课本，并加以研究。

濑户口律子教授是研究琉球官话课本的专家，所著《琉球官话课本研究》一书，正如李新魁教授在序言中指出的那样，引录了各种难得的资料，相当详尽地论述了琉球与中国建立良好的政治关系和睦邻关系以及派遣官生来华学习文化和语言等情况。作者还对《官话问答便语》、《学官话》和《白姓官话》等三种课本的内容做了相当详细的介绍和初步分析。

《官话问答便语》、《学官话》两书作者和年代都不可考。《白姓官话》从序文推测，可能是在乾隆十四年到十八年（1749—1753）之间编写的。以下本文将这三种教材合称为"琉球课本"。

这三种教材都只有问答形式的课文，用现在的说法即所谓"情景会话"，既没有19世纪西洋人编教材所用的语音描写或字母标音方法，也没有用中国传统的韵图或射标法等来说明音系。可以推想，当时的这种"对外汉语教学"的教学手段十分朴素，语音就靠师徒相授受，老师带着念课文，学生跟着模仿罢了。

据日本学者六角恒广的介绍，直到明治三年（1870）日本外务省创办汉语学所培养汉语人才，使用的教学方法还是如此："当时是既没有科学的方法也没有辞典和语法书的时代，除了完全把唐通事时代的东西照搬进汉语学所进行中国语教学外，没有其他道路。学生亦把教师的讲述作为唯一的依据，以其为基准反复进行练习、掌握，之外没有别的方法。教师的讲述，好也罢，坏也罢，都像口传的一样被尊重。"（六角恒广 1992：33）

这样学习一门外语当然是很困难的，特别是语音即发即逝，学生只能依赖传统的方法在课本上做一些简单的标注来帮助记忆。琉球的官话教材上这样的标注有两类：

其一，课文上的每一个汉字都用发圈法标明调类，平上去入分别标在左下、左上、右上、右下四角，阴平阳平用圈号和点号区别，共有 5 个调。这个现象说明汉语的声调特性在教学中受到特别的重视。琉球学生学习汉语，声调既是重点，也是难点，这符合我们一般的经验。很明显，这些调号都是使用者后加的。

其二，有些字在书眉上"直音法"注音，例如：庵音安、俭音见、餐音参、钳音乾、奠音店。有些同音字直接夹注在行间，紧挨着被注字。有的注一个同声韵不同调的字，再说明应读的调类，例如：盆音烹下平、坦音堂上声、鸳音元上平；但有时用不同调的字注音也不加说明，因为正文的每一个字已经都标上调号了。可以看出，一般规律是用比较常用的字来注不那么常用的字，显然是用已掌握的字来给生字注音。这些标注大约是先生在备课过程中记写的，或者是学生在听课时根据先生的发音记录的。既然当时还没有发明更好的注音工具，这是最方便的手段。这样注出的同音字在《官话问答便语》中最多，《学官话》次之，《白姓官话》中最少。

这些同音字的选择看来只是反映了中国人教师的口音，并没有任何权威工具书的依据。如果以《中原音韵》、《音韵阐微》或《新华字典》为标准来对照，其中很多同音字的选择是错的。用现在的话说，这个（或这些）从事对外汉语教学的教师资质颇有问题，多有误人子弟之处。而他们的无心"失误"，却留给我们一个有趣的课题：当时的琉球人学说的中国官话究竟是什么样的？由于琉球的官话是从福州传过去的，是福州的先生教的，因此，研究这些课本，我们还可以探知，明清时期福州人说的官话是怎么回事。更进一步，也许我们可以从这个具体的例子约略估摸出当时东南方言区的官话使用的一般情况。

贰

很多学者都认为明清官话分为南北两派。大致说来，南方官话区别于北方官话之处主要是：第一，保留入声，有 5 个声调。第二，见系细音字的声母不腭化；或见系虽腭化，精组不腭化，构成尖团对立。第三，保留疑母，或者还有微母。一般认为，北京话是北方官话的代表，而南方官话的代表就是南京话。这里所谓的"南方官话"仍是个地域方言的概念，大致等于今天的江淮官话区。明清两代也是官话方言上升为全国范围的共通语的主要时期。那么，在更远的南方，作为一种权威社会方言来接受的，究竟是北方官话还是南方官话呢？这个问题众说纷纭，一直没有确切的答案。通过剖析"琉球课本",我们至少可以比较确切地了解"琉球官话"的真相。

六角恒广(1992)主要根据史料认为,在中国的明清时期,日本的"实用唐语"教学有两个中心。一个是长崎的"唐通事"。唐通事的工作是负责接待管理来自中国东南沿海以及南洋一代的商船,他们使用的唐语分别为"南京口"、"福州口"和"漳州口"。"口"即方言口语,所谓"南京口"指下江官话,是应用面最广的。另一个就是琉球王国的唐通事。"在琉球学习的是北京官话,或是'以北京官话为中心'的北方官话,这一点与只限于与南方唐船进行贸易的长崎唐通事的唐话大不相同。"(六角恒广1992:283)但六角氏没有从语言学的角度对这个判断做出论证说明。

濑户口(1994a)认为,"琉球课本"除了明显的闽语影响,主要反映了南方官话的特征。她的这个判断主要是根据声调特征做出的。课本中的标调反映出有5个调,平分阴阳,浊上归去,保留入声。把这个声调格局与现代汉语各重要方言的调类进行对比,作者发现只有代表江淮官话的南京方言相符合。李新魁先生在序言中表示赞同,认为这个结论"是相当有道理的"。

叶宝奎(2001)认为:"濑户口律子的分析是可信的,但她的结论还值得商榷。根据声调的分析,证明《白姓官话》音系不是当时的北京话,也不是北方方言的其它次方言,更不是吴、闽、粤、客家方言的音系,这是正确的。但是仅仅根据声调来证明《白姓官话》是根据南京话来写的,理由是不充分的。……作为琉球人学习汉语官话的课本,他所依据的应当是通行全国的汉民族共同语的标准音,而不是一地方言。"(叶宝奎2001:262—263)[1]

据叶宝奎(2001)详细的考察,明清时期的官话音应该指一种较为保守的读书音系统,也就是他所说的"通行全国的汉民族共同语的标准音"。叶先生说的这个读书音系统是以莎彝尊《正音咀华》、潘冯禧《正音通俗表》以及《罗马字官话新约全书》为代表的,与以北京音为代表的"北音"以及以南京音为代表的"南音"都有区别。

我们认为,这里所谓的"读书音"跟南方方言区中实际存在"文读音"不同,其内涵应该是像《切韵》音系"一样,只是"书面语音系统"的另一种说法。它只是理论上存在,并不诉诸唇吻,以南方方言为母语的人无法根据当时相当粗糙的语音学描述自己琢磨出该怎么发音。所以,即使当时的教学者心目中真有一个"正音"的观念,也未必能够付诸语言实践。方言区人士学官话,终究还是要靠对非南即北的现实语音系统的模仿。

我们还认为光靠调类特征来下判断是不可靠的。诚然,声调特征是判断一种地域方言系属的最重要指标之一,但这里要讨论的不是一种从古到今自然演进的地域方言,而是作为第二语言习得的共通语变体,不能不考虑母语方言对这个共通语变体的影响。"平分阴阳、浊上归去"是大多数官话方言以及南方方言的共同特征，从中不能得到什么定性的依据。至于入声调的存在，我们认为也不足以证明琉球官话是学了南京音或"标准音"。入声既是一种调类，也是一种韵类。喉塞韵尾的顽固存在使原入声字摆脱不掉短促的调值。吴闽客粤方言区的人说普通话难改入声短促的毛病，是大家在"推普"工作中共同的经验。这样的"普通话"实际上都多出了这个短促的入声调，而且不能认为是学了南京话或遵从传统正音观念的缘故。

叁

对"琉球课本"的音系下判断，更重要的是考察同音字组反映出来的声母韵母特征。这一方面，濑户口做了很多工作。同音字组并不直接显示音值，只能从中观察音类的分混。根据她的分析，"琉球课本"反映官话特征的主要有如下几点（濑户口1994a：25—30。原分 10 条，今概括为 7 条）：

1. 全浊声母消失，变与清声母同音。

2. 微、云、以、疑四纽相混，并混同于影纽。

3. 知章两组混同。

4. 在细音韵母之前，见系声母与知组章组已经合流。

5. 止摄蟹摄的三等韵并为一类。

6. 三四等韵大面积合并。一些摄的一二等与三等合并。

7. 鱼虞韵合流。

从以上对声母韵母的特征分析上，看不出哪一点是属于南方官话而不是北方官话的。相反，见系细音字腭化，一般认为是北方官话的特点。推断"琉球课本"的见系细音字声母腭化的证据是如下一些同音字组（括号中是书中旁注的同音字）：

　　　警（整）、饥（知）、鞋（舌）、兮（诗）、治（记）、针（金）、朝（交）、
　　　占（见）、希（诗）、曦（诗）、绸（求）、降（胀）、险（善）

我们从"琉球课本"中发现同类的例子还有：

　　　钳（缠）、闪（闲）、针（今）、禁（正）

这些同音字组的存在说明了见系细音字已经腭化到位，变成舌面音了。

濑户口（1994a）大概已经意识到对同音字组分析的结果尚不足支持她的结论，所以在强调声调特征对判断音系属性的重要性之后，又在"结语"中谨慎地提到"琉球课本"中的一些词汇语法现象："我们之所以认为这三种官话有反映'南方地区官话'的可能，主要是从所使用的词语和一些语法特点着眼。并且，这三种课本所加的声调

符号，表明其有入声的存在，这就使我们更加倾向于认为它们所表现的官话，可能是流行于广大南方地区的官话。"（濑户口 1994a：86）但用词汇语法现象来区分南北官话体系是一项更加困难的工作。到目前为止，相关学科的研究水平还不能提供足够的支持。从她的举例中看，这些课本除了一些可以认定的福州方言词语以外，并没有哪些词汇语法现象可以作为区分南北官话的鉴定标准。

日本学者长泽规矩也编的《唐话辞书类集》中有一本很特殊的长崎"唐通事"的工具书《粗幼略记》。原书是手写本，作者小寺玉晁，年代未详。据编者推测，可能是明和期间的（1764—1771）的作品，也就是"琉球课本"同时期的文献。《粗幼略记》的内容主要是当时中日贸易的货物名称等。每条词目的左右两侧都用日文假名注音，该书开头处写有"右注南京音左注福州音"。从这些假名对音可以清楚看出，当时的南京话见系细音声母都用キ、ヒ注音，与精照系的细音チ、シ丝毫不混。略举数例如下（假名转写为日语罗马字）：

锦绸 kin chiu 京青布 kin chin pu 交枝花 kiau chu hua 杭线 han shien 朽 hiu

机巧 ki kiau 沉香 chin hian 鞘皮 shiau pi

南京浦口人胡垣的《古今中外音韵通例》作于光绪十二年（1866），比"琉球课本"和《粗幼略记》晚了一个世纪，仍然说"金陵读'坚、沾、尖'分为喉齿牙三音"，依叶宝奎（2000：278—280）的考订，此时见系细音字的声母还没有腭化。直至更晚的劳乃宣《增订合声简字谱》（1905）才见到见系分出的腭化音，而精组尚未腭化，尖团仍然有别。

既然南京话要到 20 世纪初才腭化，就不可能是"琉球课本"描写的对象。而闽语的见系细音字不腭化。所以"琉球课本"中的这种腭化音只能是从官话学来的。所谓"官话正音"的可能性也可以因此排除。可以推断，"琉球课本"学习模仿的是演进更早的北方官话。

肆

从"琉球课本"中的同音字组可以看到一些特点，这里指出与见系细音字有关的两点：

第一，前面所列说明见系细音腭化的同音字组用现代普通话读起来并不同音。这些同音字组有一个共同的特点，与见系字同音的都是知组、章组的三等字，没有精组字，也没有庄组字。这样的分布格局说明，这些知章组三等字的韵母仍然带有 [-i-] 介音，尚未转化为开口呼，可见声母也还没有卷舌化，与庄组合流。因此可以推定，知章组的声母还是与舌面前音很相近的舌叶音。见系细音字与知章组细音字互相注音只是因为它们十分相近，但并不完全相同，因为如果完全相同了，稍后知章组再离开见组、进入庄组就不可能了。当然，这只是被学习模仿的官话音系的情况，在学习者这一方面，可能并没有舌面舌叶的区别。

第二，尽管见系细音字的声母已经腭化到位了，但与精组细音字仍判然有别。在全部三种教材中，除了上文的举例，我们另外还收集到见系细音字作为被注字共37例，其中36例以见系字注音；与此同时，精组细音字有29例，其中28例以精组字注音。可见"琉球课本"音系尖团音泾渭分明，唯一的例外分别是"欠（前去声）"、"簪（讲上平）"，应该可以看作偶然的误读。以下罗列这些同音字组：

见系字

具（句）、忌（记）、效（孝）、歧（其）、骑（其）、寄（记）、祁（其）、器（气）、期（鸡）、车（拘）、驱（去平声）、健（见）、献（现）、姜（江）、刑（行）、钳（乾）、减（拣）、拑（乾）、遣（谦上声）、鉴（见）、妗（近）、牵（谦）、俭（见）、险（显）、咸（贤）、竞（近）、仅（景）、协（歇）、具（句）、减（间）、巾（今）、捡（见）、颈（今）、兼（间）、拣（减）、经（今）

精组字

捷（接）、萧（消）、鲜（先）、线（先去声）、煎（尖）、寝（进上声）、潜（前）、浸（静）、腥（心）、婶（醒）、井（进）、亲（井）、疾（集）、袭（习）、蓆（什）、迹（集）、积（集）、靖（进）、抢（详）、携（喜）、新（心）、嗄（青）、星（心）、靖（进）、井（尽）、寂（集）、遂（岁）、碎（岁）

上述两点也许可以丰富我们对北方官话语音史的认识。李汝珍的《李氏音鉴》（1810）的成书时间比"琉球课本"晚了约半个世纪，他清楚地表明，当时的北音已经不辨"香厢、姜将、羌枪"了。也许18世纪后半叶正是北京音系精组腭化、导致尖团合流的时期。

伍

从"琉球课本"的同音字组观察其语音特点，最突出之处其实并不在于它与北京音或是南京音相似，而是它与福州方言音系的血缘关系。濑户口（1994a：87）对此有很好的分析，她指出了以下几点：

1. 中古晓匣纽字与清唇音相混。例如：

灰（非）、滑（法）、荤（分）、互（付）、焚（红）、粪（混）、肥（回）、慌（方）

2. 齿头音声母与正齿音声母不分。例如：

斋（栽）、债（在）、舍（色去声）、稍（嫂）、祀（事）、嗣（士）、寸（春去声）、找（早）

3. 中古的日母字变读为零声母。例如：

乳（雨）、儒（予）、嚷（养）、演（染）、赢（仁）、样（襄）、软（远）、饶（摇）

4. 三种鼻音韵尾混而为一。例如：

零（林）、惭（藏）、腥（新）、鳗（忙）、贫（平）、尘（成）、坛（堂）、范（放）

5. 三种入声韵尾也没有分别。例如：

协（歇）、察（插）、积（集）、历（立）、折（则）、屋（物）、癖（匹）、寂（集）

从这些强烈的语音特征来看，"琉球课本"使用者实际上学到的只是一种"福州的官话"。这与琉球"勤学人"在福州的琉球馆学习官话的史实是吻合的。清代以来从琉球来中国学习的留学生大多数是久米町的闽人舟工后裔。根据方言调查的经验，闽语方言岛在一个聚居的村落保持两三百年是十分正常的，这些从琉球来福州的"勤学人"很可能仍会说闽语。《白姓官话》所附的《林先生校正序》作者林守超自称"闽县老儒"。他在序言中谈道："……天下言语，各有不同，俱系土音，难以通行。惟有正音官话，所以通行天下。学习者唇喉齿舌，须当辨别清明，方得正音官话"，这只是泛泛而论。实际他自己所说的官话，我们已经从"琉球课本"的读音附注中看到，就发音而言，学北方官话学得十分勉强，大体上就是在福州方言音系的基本框架里纳入了官话。在这个方枘圆凿的纳入过程中，福州方言中存在而官话没有的成分可以舍弃，如疑纽 [ŋ-]；而官话有、福州方言中不存在的音素却学不来，如日纽 [zˌ/ʒ-] 和轻唇音 [f-][2]。福州方言能分而官话不分的音类可以按对应规律合并，例如去声的阴阳两类；但官话中区分而福州方言不能区分的音类仍然相混，例如平翘舌声母和前后鼻韵母 [-n]、[-ŋ]。"琉球课本"不能分卷平舌声母却能够清楚地区分尖团音声母，显然是因为后者存在可以利用的语音对应规律。除了这一点外，这个音系的声韵调系统跟当时的福州话韵书《戚林八音》十分接近：声母包括零声母共 17 个，多了一套舌面音 [tɕ-、tɕh-、ɕ-]，少了一个 [ŋ-]；韵母系统阴阳入三分，只有一种鼻音韵尾 [-ŋ] 和一种入声韵尾 [-ʔ]；两类去声调和两类入声调分别合并。

至于存在入声调的问题，我们同意叶宝奎（2001）的看法，承认传统的"正音"观念起了作用。尽管《等韵图经》、《李氏音鉴》都清楚表明北京音系中入声已经不存在了，由于区分平仄的需要，国语正音应该有入声的观念一直持续到 20 世纪初的"读音统一会"时期。南方人士肯定乐于接受这种观念并且毫无困难地付诸实践。

陆

作为社会共通语的"官话"是个十分模糊的概念，它是在统一帝国的行政系统运作和各地经济往来中自然出现的社会语言现象，也一直处在这种自然而不自觉的状态中，不像现在的普通话一样具有明确的内涵和法律地位。明清两朝也是一个音韵蜂出的时代，各种大同小异的官话韵书并存于世，何为"正音"的讨论不绝于耳，也从另一方面说明了事实上并不存在明确的、实体意义上的标准音。耿振生（1992）、丁锋（1995）各自对反映明代官话音系的各种主要文献做了一个梳理，最终都得到相同的结论："官话的核心部分是比较稳固的，是人们共同承认的官话成分；官话的非核心部分有些游移不定，可以因时、因地、因人的观念有些变化。……不规范性、游移性是近代官话语言有别于现代普通话的主要特点。"（耿振生 1992：121—122）南方方言区的一般人士学说官话只是为了应付交际需要，并不刻意寻求标准音。京城是全国政治、经济、文化中心，其基础方言有更大的影响，自然而然地成为模仿的对象；而模仿的结果必然是糅进各地方音的特点，产生出种种范围更加广泛的官话变体。不管语言学家如何看待这些变体，它们不同于作为母语的当地方言，可以与外地人大致沟通，老百姓就认为是"官话"。

综上所述，我们认为明清时期，福州人学说的官话是对北方官话的模仿。这与永乐十八年（1420）明成祖迁都以后，北京稳定地作为两朝首都的历史事实相符。由于历史文化条件的限制，当时福州人学习官话在语音方面难以摆脱方言母语的强烈影响，画鹄不成而类鹜，也形成了一套相对固定的音系特征。体现在"琉球课本"附注上的音系从整体上说，既不是南京音，也不是北京音，更不是"通行全国的汉民族共同语的标准音"，它仅仅属于"福州的官话"。

附 注

[1] 叶先生的一个论据是《白姓官话》的作者籍贯山东，既不说北京话，也不说南京话；而且是知识分子，因而必然懂得要用标准音来教外国人。然而，《白姓官话》本是漂流到琉球的中国商人向琉球的唐通事提交的口语体报告书，内容是叙述自己滞留在琉球期间的经历，对当地政府和人民的协助表示感谢，并没有编写课本的意图。乾隆十八年（1753）由琉球的"勤学人"将这个文本带到福州，经他的先生"闽县老儒林启升守超氏"校正，才被采用做课本的。文本固然是山东人的作品，教书的却是福州人，书上加注的读音记号自然也是依据这位闽县老儒的口音。

[2] 参考前文所述知章组的情况，推断日纽字很可能仍有 [-i-] 介音，因此发音部位可能也在舌叶或舌面上，容易与喻纽等相混，变成零声母。福州方言没有轻唇音，非敷奉的文读音都并入晓匣。

参考文献

长泽规矩也（1970）《唐话辞书类集》，东京：古典研究会，汲古书院。

丁锋（1995）《琉球汉对音与明代官话音研究》，北京：中国社会科学出版社。

丁锋（1998）《球雅集》，东京：好文出版。

傅力（1991）元明清三代的"推普"工作，《语文建设》第 9 期。

耿振生（1992）《明清等韵学通论》，北京：语文出版社。

黄绍武（1919）《闽音正读表》，上海：宏文阁。

濑户口律子（1994a）《琉球官话课本研究》，香港：香港中文大学中国文化研究所。

濑户口律子（1994b）《白姓官话全译》，东京：明治书院。

濑户口律子、左藤晴彦（1997）《琉球官话课本语汇索引》，东京：大东文化大学东洋研究所。

黎新第（1995）明清时期的南方系官话方言及其语音特点，《重庆师院学报》第 4 期。

六角恒广（1992）《日本中国语教育史研究》，王顺洪译，北京：北京语言学院出版社。

鲁国尧（1985）明代官话及基础方言问题，《南京大学学报》第 4 期。

徐恭生（1987）琉球国在华留学生，福州：《福建师范大学学报》第 4 期。

叶宝奎（2001）《明清官话音系》，厦门：厦门大学出版社。

张升余（1998）《日本唐音与明清官话研究》，西安：世界图书出版公司。

（本文发表于《方言》2004 年第 1 期，第 47—53 页，2006 年）

明末官话调值小考

高田时雄

　　金尼阁的《西儒耳目资》（1626）不仅是中国历史上第一部采用完整的罗马字标音汉字的字典，也是明末官话的一件重要材料。过去有些学者主张《西儒耳目资》所反映的语音是山西或西北的方言，但根据当时天主教传教士有关中国语言的记述，它的基础方言为通行于全国的官话是不容置疑的。[1]

　　罗明坚、利玛窦等早期耶稣会士于16世纪80年代开始在广东传教，当时为了学习汉语的方便起见已采用罗马字母拼写汉字。藏在罗马耶稣会档案馆的《葡汉辞典》[2]中，能看到他们的早期罗马字标音方式。这个标音方式基于意大利语的正字法，而不像后来结晶于《西儒耳目资》的葡萄牙式的罗马字。罗、利在肇庆时，肇庆知府王泮送给他们的教堂两块匾额，一块写着"迁花寺"，另一块写着"西来净土"。[3]罗明坚把这些匾额的字抄录下来而且附上罗马字注音。这个材料今天还藏在耶稣会档案馆中。[4]其注音是 sien cua si（迁花寺）、sci lai cin tu（西来净土）。这跟他与利玛窦合著《葡汉辞典》的注音基本一致。不仅如此，利玛窦晚年写成的《中国传教史》意大利文稿本也是采用类似的意大利式标音法。

　　《西儒耳目资》的罗马字母标音法已于1605年利玛窦在北京刊刻的《西字奇迹》[5]中使用，所以目前一般认为《西儒耳目资》的标音法不是金尼阁的创始而是沿袭利氏之旧的。那么，利玛窦从何时开始创制而使用这个标音法呢？关于这一点，利玛窦在《中国传教史》上有所交代。1598年，利玛窦等第一次赴北京，但形格势禁，先回南京，途中船上讨论语言问题。

　　　　（利玛窦等）神父们已经是传教团中最老练的人物而精通汉语的钟鸣仁修士也在，编纂了一部很好的词汇（un bello vocabulario），并给这个语言的诸多问题加以整理。因此，其后能够两倍容易地学会汉语。他们提醒，这个语言由单音节的语音或文字构成，而每个语音带声调或气音时，发音上极其重要区别这些特点。用此发音的区别才可以分别而听懂多种文字与语音；否则，它们无法区别。学习这个语言的困难，正由于这个原因。他们一面准确区别带气音，一面也注意到五种不同的声调。对此，郭居静神父的贡献非常大。他有音乐的知识，用以非常正确地观察而进行区别。由此他们制定了五种声调（符号）与一种气音（符号）。[6]

此时，利玛窦与郭居静等讨论描写汉语的细致语音特点的符号问题，创制出一套新的标音符号系统。郭居静对音乐的造诣很深，特别是在声调的分析和声调符号的创制方面扮演了最重要的角色。如果没有郭居静的协助，新符号就必定不会实现。[7] 我们可以想象这个新标音法已试用于这时所编的"词汇"。很遗憾，这个"词汇"至今尚未发现。[8] 但毫无疑问，它是金尼阁编《西儒耳目资》时的基本材料之一。金尼阁于1610 年来华，翌年与郭居静一起被李之藻邀请到杭州开教。[9] 我们可以想象此时郭居静将他的标音符号传授给金尼阁。

现在只对声调符号而说，《西儒耳目资》的五声符号，即清平（ˉ）、浊平（ˆ）、上声（ˋ）、去声（ˊ）与入声（ˇ）等，每一个符号很可能来自西方古典语言的补助符号，但其高低升降的形状也应该是模拟实际调值的。郭居静利用这些符号来记录汉语声调时，他的头脑里也许浮现了乐谱。如果现在能够看到这样的乐谱，那就对拟测明末官话调值很有价值。郭居静的乐谱当然已不存在，但天主教传教士材料中并非没有。小文介绍此材料而期望对明末官话调值的研究有所小补。

梵蒂冈教廷图书馆藏有一部手抄汉拉字典（Borgia Cinese 475），是意大利汉学家蒙突奇（Antonio Montucci，1762—1829）旧藏书之一。[10] 这部字典原来是拿玻里传信部红衣主教安得捏里（Cardinal Antonelli）收藏，后归英国著名外交家斯当东（Sir George Leonard Staunton，1737—1801）之手，蒙突奇购得此书是 1811 年。字典是从"一"至"钥"的部首排列，写在用红色刻印的格纸上 [11]，每页横排 10 行，行分 3 栏，左为汉字字头与其拉丁字母标音，中栏最宽，留给拉丁文注解，右栏横竖两分计作 4 栏填进同义字。后有附录几种。书前有导论称作《著作目的与使用法》（Operis ratio et usus）。其中谈到官话声韵，而特别对于声调调值加以很明确的说明，即用乐谱来描述五声。[12] "音乐（＝乐谱）可以大约记录这些声调如下（musica possit aliqualiter describere hos tonas sic）"。

清平与浊平都用全音符来表现，而上去声则用连接四个十六分音符的，然则音长似有很大的差别。但按理说，除了短促的入声字以外，每个字的音长基本是平衡的，所以此处不应该照样理解。因为上去声有高低升降，所以为了表现平滑的音高推移，就采用十六分音符的连音符。至于入声用两个十六音符，明显地表示其为短促的声调。总之，这可以说是一种易懂而令人信服的方法。如用五度标调法，五声各个调值可以定为：清平 33、浊平 11、上声 42、去声 24、入声 12 或 23。这部字典的导论何时由何人所写是无法得知，可能稍晚一点，但出于在华天主教传教士之手是不容置疑的。那么，即使不是一无所改地继承郭居静的乐谱，肯定是一脉相承有所根据的。

过去，研究明末官话调值[13]，使用的材料仅限于《西儒耳目资》与万济国《官话语法》[14]而不及其他。现在，不妨介绍另外一种材料。这也是一部手抄汉拉字典的附录。[15]其注记之四亦有官话声调符号的说明，如下。

（一）符号（‐）表示单纯第一声，所以（带此符号的字）应该将声音提高，而保持其音高稍微拉长。正如病人由于其痛苦发 aÿ 音扬其语调而拉长之。

（二）符号（＾）是为第二声设而降低音高而发的。例如以平静的声音庄重地回答时发出 oui。

（三）第三声用符号（ˋ）来表现。快速将声音降低而发音。例如生气的人不高兴地回答 non。

（四）第四声的符号是（ˊ）。表示此声调的字应该以相等于第三声的下降程度提高声音。如用乐谱而言，可以音阶的第四、第五、第六音（fa、sol、la）相当准确地表现。同样，第三声随着第六、第五、第四音而渐低就可以巧妙表现。

（五）符号（ˇ）表示第五声，短促而一口气地发音。接近于非常轻微地发音我们音乐中所用的第四音（fa）。

这个说明明显地受了万济国《官话语法》的影响，有的地方甚至于只抄了万济国的文本。但利用音阶说明的部分却是崭新的方案，也许是遵守传教士用音乐记录汉字音传统。即第三声（上声）为 la、sol、fa，而第四声（去声）为 fa、sol、la。上引之梵蒂冈音谱，如果假定第一线为 do，上声便为 si ra sol fa，而去声为 mi fa sol la，与此距离不大，也可以说是基本一致。至于第五声，此材料说音高是 fa 音，然则梵蒂冈的 re mi 稍微低一点，上面假定的 12 或 23，似为后者更合适。以往诸家拟测入声调值，分歧比较大，如鲁国尧 535/424，杨福绵 45，曾晓渝 34，王松木 24/35。一般拟测得高一点，想必是被《西儒耳目资》的描述"最高曰去，次高曰入"所迷惑的。但这边《西儒耳目资》的说明全文如此："平声有二，曰清，曰浊。仄声有三，曰上，曰去，曰入。五者有上下之别，清平无低无昂。在四声之中，其上其下每有二。最高曰去，次高曰入。最低曰浊，次低曰上。"高低与升降稍有混乱，而先将浊平与上归属于"下"，去入归属于"上"。然则入声之次高是只对去声而言，并非对其他全部声调而言的。然则即使有"次高曰入"的说明，不用给入声过高的音高。

另外，浊平的调值，除鲁国尧外，各家一致拟测为 21，是以万济国的描写为根据的。万济国《官话语法》对浊平的说明是："第二声，如一个词具有两个音节，就稍微下降第二音节发音，而只有一个音节，例如 y，就应该稍微拉长声音，使其好像是两个音节。"这个说明容易受误解，"一个词具有两个音节"实际上意味着两个单元音组成的复元音音节，比如说 ai 是由 a 与 i 两个音组成的。据万济国的说明，复元音的第二音，就是说 ai 的 i 应该稍微下降。这正是各家将浊平调值拟测为 21 的原因。但是，万济国也说单元音的时候只有拉长声音而没有音高变化。既然是一个声调，这样的分歧是不会存在的。复元音的第二个音很容易就力尽而难以保持低音，所以万济国特别注意有意识地将第二音的音高保持其最低位置而稍有夸张地给予指示的。所以，浊平的调值还是以 11 为妥当。

各家对明末官话调值的拟测本来没有很大的差别，本文的意图只是介绍天主教传教士的零星材料而对已往的研究稍微有所补充。

附 注

[1] 参看鲁国尧《明代官话及其基础方言问题》，《南京大学学报（哲学社会科学）》1985 年第 4 期，47—52 页。

[2] 罗马耶稣会档案馆 ARSI, Jap.-Sin., I, 198, ff. 32r-169r。

[3] 这是 1584 年的事件。德礼贤《中国传教史》（*Fonti Ricciane*）第 1 卷，第 199 页。

[4] 参看《中国传教史》图版 12。原图为 ARSI, Jap.-Sin., I, 9, ff. 263-264。

[5] 梵蒂冈图书馆藏本（Raccolta Generale Oriente III 231-12）是《西字奇迹》唯一现存的本子。利玛窦在北京与程大约结识，似给他送过此书板片，而程氏将其收录在他的《程氏墨苑》中。参看王重民《罗马访书记》，载《冷庐文薮》，上海古籍出版社，1992，第 801 页。

[6]《中国传教史》第 2 卷，第 32 页。

[7]《西儒耳目资》译引首谱·问答云："敝友利西泰，首至贵国，每以为苦，惟郭仰风精于乐法，颇能觉之，因而发我之蒙耳。"

[8] 中译本《利玛窦中国札记》的译者将此"中国词汇"误认为《平常问答词意》。这是由于误读德礼贤《利玛窦史料》（即本文的《中国传教史》）所致，应该纠正。《平常问答词意》是罗明坚、利玛窦合著《葡汉词典》草稿中放在词典正文之前的罗马字注音对话录，不是词汇。而且，根据杨福绵神父的意见，此 Pin ciù ven tà ssì gnì 注音应是《宾主问答辞义》，而并非如德礼贤所想象的《平常问答词意》。这个纠正是有说服力的。参看魏若望所编《葡汉辞典》（2001，澳门·里斯本）所附之"罗明坚和利玛窦的《葡汉辞典》（历史语言导论）"106—107 页。

[9] 丁至麟《杨淇园先生超性事迹》云："岁辛亥（1611）我存公（李之藻）官南都，与利先生同会郭仰凤（居静）、金四表（尼阁）交善，比告归，遂延郭金二先生入越。"（钟鸣旦等

编《徐家汇藏书楼明清天主教文献》第 1 册，第 218 页，台北，辅仁大学神学院，1996）
又参看方豪《中国天主教史人物传》上册，第 118 页，北京，中华书局，1988；方豪《李
之藻研究》，第 33—36 页，台北，商务印书馆，1966。

[10] 蒙突奇于 1829 年将其全部藏书卖给罗马传信部（Propaganda Fide），现藏梵蒂冈图书馆。
其全貌可见伯希和原著、高田时雄新编《梵蒂冈图书馆汉籍目录》（*Inventaire sommaire
des manuscripts et imprimés chinois de la Bibliothèque Vaticane*），京都，1995。

[11] 格纸尺寸为 17.2cm×11.9cm。

[12] 举例采用 ia 音，可能是由《西儒耳目资》而来的。译引首谱·问答云"五声之殊，总本一音，
如鸦、牙、雅、亚、鸭，此五字，总本乎一音，用西字可书，曰 ia。欲分平仄，五声各有
本号，则分之矣。"

[13] 讨论明末官话调值的文章，除了上引鲁国尧《明代官话及其基础方言问题》和杨福绵《罗
明坚和利玛窦的〈葡汉辞典〉（历史语言导论）》（此文初稿发表在"中研院"于 1989 年出
版的《第二届国际汉学研讨会论文集》中）以外，尚有曾晓渝《〈西儒耳目资〉的调值拟测》，
《语言研究》1992 年第 2 期（总第 23 期），第 132—136 页；王松木《〈西儒耳目资〉所反
映的明末官话音系》（中正大学中国文学研究所硕士学位论文），1994 年 12 月。

[14] 最近出现英译本，很有参考价值。柯蔚南与烈维《万济国的官话语法》（ W. South Coblin
and Joseph A. Levi, *Francisco Varo's Grammaer of the Mandarin Language*, 2000, Amsterdam/
Philadelphia, John Benjamin Publishing Company ）。

[15] 大英图书馆 Add. 23620, pp.978ff. Annotationes quaedam gallicae cerca usum dictionarii hujusce
duplicis, id est Sinico-latini, & mere sinici.

（本文发表于《语言学论丛》第二十九辑，第 145—150 页，商务印书馆，2004 年）

《人中画》琉球写本的"自家"

——兼论汉语南北双方反身代词发展轨迹*

李丹丹

日本天理图书馆藏琉球官话课本五种,包括《白姓官话》与《人中画》琉球写本等。《人中画》琉球写本(简称琉本)约改编于 18 世纪中叶(鱼返 1957:69;佐藤 1978:71;李炜、李丹丹 2007:75),与北京官话作品《红楼梦》庚辰本[1](简称《红》)的年代相近。虽然如此,二者的语言特点却有较大的区别。仅举二者的反身代词形式为例:琉本的反身代词主要形式为"自家",出现 84 例;"自己"仅出现 13 例。《红》的反身代词主要形式为"自己",出现 478 例;"自家"仅出现 3 例,这 3 例为:

(1)那宝玉是个丈八的灯台——照见人家,照不见<u>自家</u>[2] 的。(红 19、409·5 [3])

(2)如今连他正紧(经)婆婆大太太都嫌了他,说他"雀儿拣着旺处飞,黑母鸡一窝儿,<u>自家</u>的事不管,倒替人家去瞎张罗"。(红 65、1534·5)

(3)虽然还有辐余的,但他们既辛苦闹一年,也要叫他们剩些,粘补粘补<u>自家</u>。(红 56、1315·5)

其中例(1)(2)的"自家"出现在熟语中,不一定代表当时的实际语言现象;例(3)的"自家"有两解,一为反身代词,一为"自己家",从其所在句子的整体意义来看,似乎更接近于后者。即使为前者,《红》中的反身代词"自家"与"自己"相比,也数量极少。这与琉本的情况正好相反,琉本"自家"大大超过"自己",是反身代词的主要形式。

现存《人中画》各版本中,琉本与编写于清初顺治年间(1644—1661)的《人中画》

---

* 本文为笔者中国中山大学博士学位论文《清琉球官话课本〈人中画〉语法研究》的部分内容,是笔者在京都大学人文科学研究所担任外国人共同研究者时写成,得到中国国家社科基金项目(07BYY046)、国家留学基金(留金出【2007】3020 号)、广东省哲学社会科学"十五"规划 2005 年度项目(05J-01)的资助,特此致谢。文中使用的《官话问答便语》赤木本《启蒙浅学》、《广东土语字汇》、《二荷》分别由木津祐子、李炜、池田巧、关瑾华诸先生提供;近代汉语文献所用版本蒙佐藤晴彦先生教正;本文承导师李炜先生审阅,并曾在日本中国近世语学会 2007 年秋季集会上报告(大东文化大学,2007-12-16),会上得到佐藤晴彦、木津祐子、盐山正纯、竹越孝等先生的指教,深表谢忱。

啸花轩刻本（李炜、李丹丹 2007：72，简称"啸本"）关系最为密切[4]，为了研究琉本反身代词主要形式为何与《红》截然不同，先来看看啸本的情况。

1．啸本反身代词形式在琉本中的演变

啸本的反身代词有"自""自家""自己"三种形式，其在琉本中的演变模式可用表格表示如下，见表1[5]：

表 1

		琉本				
		自	自家[6]	自己[6]	零形式	总计
啸本	自	4	40	4	10	58
	自家	/	28	2	/	30
	自己	/	2	1	1	4
	零形式	/	14	4	/	18
总 计		4	84	11	11	110

下面分别说明。

1.1 啸本"自"共出现 58 例，在琉本仍为"自"4 例、替换为"自家"40 例、替换为"自己"4 例、替换为零形式 10 例（即不出现反身代词，如 7b，下不赘举）。[8] 如：

（4a）要相公自来也是小事，但路远日子短，……（啸/风/三[9]、264·17）

（4b）要相公自来，也是小事。总是路远，日子又短……（琉/风/三、6·a·8）

（5a）花小姐自心有病，恐怕新郎看出。（啸/终/四、355·2）

（5b）花小姐自家心上有毛病，恐怕新郎看出来。（琉/终/四、2·b·3）

（6a）不期过了许多时，商春荫只是自读，并不提起。（啸/寒/一、369·17）

（6b）不想过了好久，商春荫总是自己读书，并不提起拜先生。（琉/寒/一、12·b·6）

（7a）报到下处，黄舆自不中到不在心，见汪费中了，到以为奇事，替他欢喜。（啸/自/一、282·11）

（7b）报到下处，黄舆不中，也不在心上，见汪费中了，到是奇事，替他欢喜。（琉/自/一、6·b·5）

1.2 啸本"自家"共出现 30 例,在琉本仍为"自家"23 例、替换为"人称代词 +自家"5 例、替换为"自己"1 例、替换为"人称代词 + 自己"1 例,如:

（8a）傅老因渡江路远,日午就打发女儿上轿,<u>自家</u>也坐一乘轿子亲自送来。（啸 / 狭 / 三、320・17）

（8b）傅老人家,因渡江路远,上午时候,就打发女儿上轿,<u>自家</u>也坐一乘轿子,亲自送来。（琉 / 狭 / 三、5・a・5）

（9a）见问道<u>自家</u>身世,不觉感动于内,蹙了双眉道……（啸 / 自 / 一、286・15）

（9b）后来见问到<u>他自家</u>身上,就眉毛愁起来说……（琉 / 自 / 一、14・a・8）

（10a）柳春荫认得是<u>自家</u>人,便大哭起来。（啸 / 寒 / 一、363・12）[10]

（10b）柳春荫认得是<u>自己</u>家人,就大哭起来。（琉 / 寒 / 一、2・a・3）

（11a）李天造听见说儿子死了,打动<u>自家</u>心事,不觉掉下泪来。（啸 / 狭 / 一、309・1）

（11b）李天造听见说儿子死了,打动<u>他自己</u>的心事,吊下眼泪来。（琉 / 狭 / 一、15・a・3）

1.3 啸本"自己"共出现 4 例,琉本仍为"自己"1 例、替换为"自家"2 例、替换为零形式 1 例,如:

（12a）舍<u>自己</u>之功名,成就吕柯之夫妇。（啸 / 风 / 四、278・21）

（12b）舍吊<u>自己</u>的功名,成就吕柯的夫妻。（琉 / 风 / 四、15・a・2）

（13a）又叫船家点起灯来,方才<u>自己</u>换去湿衣。（啸 / 狭 / 二、312・18）

（13b）又叫船家点起灯来,才把<u>自家</u>衣裳换了。（琉 / 狭 / 二、5・a・3）

1.4 啸本原无反身代词,琉本补出"自家"13 例、补出"人称代词 + 自家"1 例、补出"自己"4 例,不赘。

可见,啸本的反身代词形式主要为"自",其次为"自家",再次为"自己";琉本的反身代词形式主要为"自家",其次为"自己","自"已濒临消失。啸本的三种反身代词形式,在琉本中总是优先替换为"自家",尤其值得注意的是有 2 例"自己"替换成"自家"。从近代汉语发展的历史看,"自家"在宋代就开始淡出反身代词领域,"自己"成为主要的反身代词形式（参见吴福祥 1994：36）,也即是说,年代越后"自家"在反身代词领域的比例应该越小。琉本的成立年代约比啸本迟一百年,琉本对啸本反身代词的替换似乎是违反近代汉语发展的规律的。

无独有偶,同样编写于 18 世纪中叶的另一种琉球官话课本《白姓官话》天理本（濑户口、李炜 2004：84；木津 2004b：51）,其反身代词"自家 / 自己"分别出现 6/3 例,"自家"是"自己"的两倍。可见,反身代词主要形式为"自家"而不是"自己",不是琉本的特殊用法,在同时期的其他琉球官话课本中也有类似的情况。反身代词在琉本等材料所代表的官话系统与《红》所代表的官话系统中的发展是不同步的。

2."自家／自己"在南北文献中的分布差异

吴福祥（1994：36）对唐宋文献中的"自家""自己"进行了功能分类，据其提供的数据，唐宋文献中的"自家""自己"还没有显示出明显的地域分布差别，本文对宋后期及以后的文献进行了调查，调查的结果恰能以作者的籍贯分为两类，详见表2。

北人作品从《元刊杂剧三十种》开始，"自家"的数量就被"自己"超过，到了17世纪中叶的《醒世姻缘传》中，"自己"已数倍于"自家"；南人作品直至17世纪前半期的《二刻拍案惊奇》，"自家"的数量还多于"自己"。如果将《红》与琉本的资料续入该表，可以发现其各自延续的正是北方与南方文献中"自家／自己"的分布格局:《红》的"自家"比《醒世姻缘传》更少，而琉本的"自家"还是大大超过"自己"。

表2

	年代	文献	作者	籍贯	自家	自己
北人作品	12 世纪后期—13 世纪初	明嘉靖本董解元西厢记	董解元[11]		8	1
	13 世纪末—14 世纪中叶	元刊杂剧三十种之24 种	关汉卿等 16 位北方籍作者	大都等地	3	6
	15 世纪初	元代汉语本老乞大			1	5
	17 世纪中叶	同德堂本醒世姻缘传	西周生		156	946
南人作品	14 世纪中叶	新刊元本蔡伯喈琵琶记	高明	浙江温州	2	1[12]
	16 世纪初—17 世纪初	盛明杂剧之 11 种	徐渭等 6 位南方籍作者	浙江江苏等地	17	4
	17 世纪前半期	尚友堂本二刻拍案惊奇	凌濛初	浙江吴兴	136	99

3."自家"在北京官话中的消失和在南方方言中的保存

3.1《红》之后的北京官话作品中，"自家"逐渐减少，"自己"逐渐成为反身代词的唯一形式，表 3 是本文调查的数据:

表 3

编写时代	作品	自家	自己
19 世纪中期	儿女英雄传	8	588
19 世纪后半期	语言自迩集	2	43
19 世纪末	官话指南	0	29

3.2 南方文献中"自己"的比例也随时代发展逐渐增加，并取代"自家"成为反身代词的主要形式。但是"自家"并没有消失，直至 20 世纪初，广东佛山人、长期在上海生活的吴趼人的作品《二十年目睹之怪现状》中还存在 26 例"自家"（"自己"479 例）。

3.3 现代南方方言中吴语和客语的反身代词形式也为"自家"，这与清代材料的表现是一致的：

（14）吴语：大家勿许代，我自家吃。（海上花列传 4、23·b·8）

译文：大家不许代，我自己喝

（15）客语：自从唔曾听过智慧个人怨自家读得书多。（启蒙浅学 188 课）

译文：从来不曾听过有智慧的人怨自己书读得多

3.4 闽语的情况比较复杂，各个次方言保存了汉语不同历史时期的反身代词形式。现代闽北方言说"自"，这是汉语较早的反身代词形式。现代闽东方言说"自家"，这与清代材料的表现是一致的：

（16）祭司长就扯破自家衣裳讲。（马可福音·福州土白 14、97·5）

译文：祭司长就扯破自己的衣服说

现代闽南方言区各地的说法如下（李如龙 1999：266）：

	泉州	漳州	厦门	汕头	海康	海口
家自	kai^4ki^6	ka^1ti^6	ka^4ki^6	ka^1ki^0	ka^1ki^1	ka^1ki^6

李如龙认为闽南各地说法"首音节应是'家'……，末音节可能是从'自'变来的，声调都是阳去本调（末音节不变调），声母是类化而成的"。[13] 也即为"家自"，是"自家"的一个语音/词序变体。

3.5 现代粤语的反身代词为"自己"，这与《广东土语字汇》（辞典）、*Cantonese Made Easy*（课本）、《马可福音·广东话》（圣经）等几种清代粤语材料的表现是一致的。但在木鱼书《新批绣像第九才子二荷》中我们发现了 6 例 "自家"，如：

（17）重有啯种想折花枝难入手，好过佢<u>自家</u>长抱恨绵绵。（二荷 3 卷·被哄遇生）

　　译文：还有想折花枝却又无从下手的那种，比他自己长怀着遗憾要好

而该书中的 "自己" 只出现了 4 例，"自家" 仍比 "自己" 多。[14]

3.6 可见，琉本等琉球官话课本的反身代词形式与南方方言的情况较为相似，保存着早期的反身代词形式。本文 1.3 中提到啸本有 2 例 "自己" 在琉本中被替换成 "自家"，这表面上似乎违背近代汉语发展的主流规律，但在琉本所处的年代，南方多种方言都以 "自家" 为反身代词的主要形式，替换成 "自家" 是合乎当时的语言事实的。啸本的反身代词形式在琉本中的演变反映的正是近代汉语内部发展的一种路线，近代汉语在南北双方的发展进度和演变模式并不完全相同。

4. 南北双方反身代词形式反展差异之成因

文章至此，需要解决的另一个问题是，究竟何种因素导致了元以后反身代词形式在汉语南北双方的发展差异。从语言事实看来，本文试图做出一种假设：南北双方的反身代词形式是等速发展的，但北方第一人称复数排除式和包括式（简称 "排除式" 和 "包括式"）对立的出现和发展，大大推进了北方反身代词主要形式从 "自家" 演变为 "自己" 的进程。

4.1 在排除式和包括式的对立出现之前，据吴福祥（1994:33），晚唐五代以前 "自家" 仅见零星用例，而 "自己" 则未见一例，晚唐五代以后两者才渐多起来。此时 "自家" 多作反身代词，但是也有少数称代第一身（单数）。到了宋代，"自家" 作第一人称的用法更加成熟，还能够表示第一人称复数。而 "自己" 则一直都只作反身代词。

4.2 据刘一之（1988：110），排除式和包括式的对立在文献上始出现于 12 世纪初《三朝北盟会编》中的《燕云奉使录》和《茅斋自序》。但《燕云奉使录》和《茅斋自序》都用 "某等" 表示排除式；前者用 "自家、自家濮、自家们"[15]、后者用 "吾曹" 表示包括式。"自家" 在《三朝北盟会编》中还可以作第一人称单数（吴福祥 1994：35；刁晏斌 2003：9）。

12 至 13 世纪初的《刘知远诸宫调》中出现了 "咱"，表示包括式（刘一之 1988：106，如 18），但 "咱" 还可作反身代词（如 19）。

（18）独自一身尚漂蓬，向咱家中拮力受雇。（刘知远诸宫调 6·b·10）

（19）<u>您咱</u>两口儿夫妻侣水如鱼，这壁四口儿心生很劣。（刘知远诸宫调10·a·9）

稍后的《董解元西厢记》（简称《董》），"咱"除作包括式（如20）外，还能作反身代词（如21）、第一人称单数（如22）；同时"自家"也能作反身代词（如23）、第一人称单数（如24）；此外"自己"也能作反身代词（如25）。

（20）自心思忖，怕<u>咱</u>做夫妻后不好。（董卷四4·b·4）

（21）恁时节是<u>俺咱</u>可怜见你那里。（董卷五6·a·6）

（22）<u>咱</u>不曾胡来，俏倬是生涯。（董卷一1·a·5）

（23）夫人休出口，怕旁人知道，到头赢得<u>自家</u>羞。（董卷六3·a·1）

（24）相国夫人怕伊不信<u>自家</u>说，请宽尊抱。（董卷三2·a·1）

（25）对景伤怀恨<u>自己</u>，病里逢春，四海无家一身客寄。（董卷一14·a·7）

也即是说，在北方出现包括式和排除式的对立的初期，能作包括式的有"自家"和"咱"，能作第一人称单数的有"自家"和"咱"，能作反身代词的有"自家""咱"和"自己"。[16]词汇系统有着经济性的特点，要求最大限度地避免重复（Zipf 1949：19），"自家""咱""自己"的功能的交叉重合，是与这种特点相悖的。从语法化的角度来看，能表达同一语法功能的多种并存形式经过筛选和淘汰，最终会缩减到一二种（Hopper 1991），因此"自家""咱""自己"的功能必将进行整合。

4.3 从表2可知，《董》到《元刊杂剧三十种》的北人作品（简称《元》）之间，是北方反身代词主要形式从"自家"演变为"自己"的关键时期，我们的调查发现，在《董》至《元》之间，也是"自家""咱""自己"进行功能整合的关键时期，详见表4。

表4

	包括式	第一人称单数		反身代词		
	咱	自家	咱	自家	咱	自己
董	13	21	6	8	13	1
元	49	12	66	3	3	6

语言演变有变化和竞争两种方式（徐通锵1991：348）。"咱"具有"自家"的所有意义（早期的包括式、后来的第一人称单数和反身代词），又在语音上符合时代的主流（当时"你们""我们"的合音形式"您""俺"也流行开来），在与"自家"的

竞争中全面处于优势。

① 在汉语出现的新意义"包括式"方面,"咱"在字形上符合充当表示新语法意义的汉字标记的优胜原则[17],既不是常用字[18],又不是难写字,因此迅速战胜了"自家"。《董》以后,"自家"很少再表示包括式,"咱"成为表示包括式的主要形式[19],就是这种竞争结果的体现。

② 在第一人称单数领域,"咱"也侵占了"自家"原来的地盘。表第一人称单数,《董》"自家"21例,"咱"仅6例;《元》"自家"12例,"咱"66例,显示了"咱"在此领域也击败了"自家"[20]。

③ 在反身代词领域,《董》"咱"的数量(13例)也超过"自家"(8例)。②③都是汉语原有的旧意义,"咱"在此两领域的胜利意味着"自家"已成为一个过时的旧形式,开始走向式微。

但是"咱"在反身代词领域的竞争对手还有"自己"。与"自己"相较,作反身代词的"咱"只能跟在人称代词后面,独立性弱(试比较例21和例25),在《元》中数量回落。"自己"超过了"自家"成为反身代词的主要形式。

因此,北方的反身代词主要形式从"自家"演变为"自己",除了反身代词内部自身的演变外,还因为排除式与包括式对立的出现大大推动了"自家"走向式微的过程。

4.4 南方方言中闽语有排除式和包括式的对立,据梅祖麟(1988:143):

	厦门	潮州	福州
排除式	ᶜgun, ᶜguan	ᶜuŋ, ᶜo	ŋuai kɔʔnøyŋ
包括式	ᶜlan	ᶜnaŋ	naŋ ŋa kaʔnøyŋ

闽语表示包括式的词汇形式与"咱"的音韵差别很大,来源与北方明显不同,属于底层的语法现象[21]。包括式也没有像"咱"一样发展出反身代词、第一人称代词等意义,因此也没有对"自家"形成冲击。因此"自家"及其语音/词序变体"家自"在闽语中保存了下来。

4.5 赵元任(1927:95)、刘一之(1988:109)、梅祖麟(1988:144)都认为吴语中的温州话也有排除式和包括式的对立。刘丹青(1999:106)、曹志耘(1999:131)、万波(1999:145)报告,江苏吴江、浙江严州、江西安义方言也都有包括式,现将各地报告整理如下:

	温州	吴江		严州			安义
		同里/松陵	黎里/芦墟	淳安	遂安	建德	
包括式	卬你	吾它	吾咖	歪搭	□滴	尔夏	俺
	$\eta u\mathrm{ɔ}^2\dot{\eta}i^{4\text{-}5}$	$\dot{\eta}t\mathrm{h}o$	$\dot{\eta}t\mathrm{h}o$	$ua^{224}ta\mathrm{ʔ}^5$	$ka^{33}ti^{24}$	$n^{213}ho^{55}$	ηon^{213}

郑张尚芳（2003：356）认为温州话"第一身复数还有包括式'卬你'，相当官话的'咱们'，不过那其实是'我伉你'的合音。"实际上，温州等地的包括式来源都是"第一人称单数＋连词＋第二人称单数（即：我和你）"的合音或减省说法（刘丹青 1999：121；曹志耘 1999：134；万波 1999：154），与"自家"在意义上并无交涉，也从未有过竞争。因此"自家"在这些方言中也都保存了下来。

4.6 其他南方方言本身缺乏排除式和包括式的对立，没有来自外部的压力、反身代词内部的演变速度缓慢，投射到南方方言区的人所讲的南方官话里，"自己"取代"自家"成为反身代词主要形式的时间也就较北方迟缓。

5．小结及余论

北方包括式的来源与闽语、温州话等都不同，是汉语与阿尔泰民族的语言接触引发的。[22] 表达新意义包括式的新形式"咱"出现后，触发了一系列后续性演变，最后导致"自家"成为一个走向式微的旧形式。现在，我们可以回过头来回答本文开头提出的问题：琉本与《红》的反身代词主要形式的差异，是由南北双方反身代词的发展进程不同造成的，而从更深层的原因来看，这种差异是由语言接触引发的。[23]

本文对琉本"自家"的考察到此为止，但由"自家"引发的思考尚未结束。据刘一之（1988：109）《元本琵琶记校注》中有排除式和包括式的区别，刘氏认为作者是温州人，温州话中也有排除式和包括式的对立，"虽然从语音上看和'咱每'没有关系，但是语义是相同的，高明可能因此一下子就掌握了'咱每'的用法"。如果这个说法成立的话，琉本和其他琉球官话课本都没有排除式和包括式的对立，但福州话却有着严格的排除式和包括式的对立，琉本及其他琉球官话课本反映的"官话"是否为福州的官话，尚需进一步讨论。

附 注

[1] 本文所用材料版本如下：《人中画》琉球写本、《白姓官话》，日本天理大学图书馆藏本。《人中画》啸花轩写刻本，见《古本平话小说集》（上），路工、谭天合编，人民文学出版社1984年。《红楼梦》甲戌本、己卯本、庚辰本、戚序本，见《古本小说集成》，上海古籍出

版社 1994 年。《红楼梦》甲辰本，书目文献出版社 1989 年。《刘知远诸宫调》，文物出版社 1958 年。《明嘉靖本董解元西厢记》，中华书局 1963 年。《元刊杂剧三十种》《新刊元本蔡伯喈琵琶记》，见《古本戏曲丛刊》，商务印书馆 1958 年。《元代汉语本〈老乞大〉》，庆北大学校出版社 2000 年。《盛明杂剧》戊午春仲诵芬室 1918 年（仿明本），京都大学文学部藏本。《二刻拍案惊奇》《醒世姻缘传》《儿女英雄传》《海上花列传》，见《古本小说集成》，上海古籍出版社 1994 年。《足本二十年目睹之怪现状》，世界书局 1935 年。*Yü-yen tzǔ-erh chi*，a progressive course designed to assist the student of colloquial Chinese, as spoken in the capital and the metropolitan department, in eight parts, Secretary to H. B. M. Legation at Peking，京都大学文学部藏本。《官话指南》，文求堂 1903 年，京都大学文学部藏本。《马可福音·福州土白》，British & Foreign Bible Society，1912，东洋文库藏本。《马可福音·广东话》，British & Foreign Bible Society，1916，东洋文库藏本。*Cantonese Made Easy*, 3rd ed. Kelly & Walsh, 1904，京都大学文学部藏本。《广东省土语字汇》，the Honobable East India Company's Press, 1828。《新批绣像第九才子二荷》，清光绪壬辰年莞城萃英楼藏板。《启蒙浅学》，The Basel Missionary Society，1879，东京大学柯理思教授藏本。

[2] 吕叔湘（1985：90）记此例为"自己"，其所据版本为亚东图书馆程乙本。《红楼梦》八十回本现存 5 种，其中甲戌本（1754 年）19、56、65 回俱缺；己卯本（1759 年）与庚辰本（1760 年）同，此 3 例皆为"自家"；甲辰本（1784 年）19 回为"自己"，后两回皆为"自家"；戚序本 19 回为"自家"，后两回皆为"自己"。年代越后的版本，"自家"改为"自己"的比例越高。

[3] 表示"回数、页数·行数"，页数与行数之间若出现 a 表示页表，b 表示页里，以下类推。

[4] 我们对《人中画》各个版本进行了调查，目前《人中画》发现的版本中写刻本除①啸本外，另有②乾隆四十五年刊泉州尚志堂本（4 篇 4 卷）、③哈佛燕京大学哈佛燕京学社汉和图书馆本（残存《自作孽》第一回与《寒彻骨》第三回）。抄本除④天理图书馆琉球写本外，另有⑤大连图书馆藏之乾隆十年刊"植桂楼藏板"抄本（3 卷），又有⑥日本京都大学文学部藏之琉球写本（16 卷存 13 卷，缺《狭路逢》3 卷）、⑦日本东京大学总合图书馆藏之琉球写本（16 卷存 14 卷，缺《自作孽》2 卷）、⑧石垣市立八重山博物馆藏之琉球写本（16卷存《自作孽》2 卷）、⑨天理图书馆藏之另一琉球写本（16 卷存《狭路逢》3 卷）。此外还有⑩以《世途镜》之名收编了《人中画》八卷八回（《狭路逢》3 卷、《自作孽》3 卷、《寒彻骨》3 卷）的"本衙藏板"，和⑪以《姻缘扇》之名收编了《人中画》不分卷八回《风流配》的琴韵书舍刊本，共计 11 种版本。其中⑦大塚（1984：26）记作"抄本？ 15 卷？（风流配、狭路逢、终有报、寒彻骨）"，后大塚（1987：30）又改为"抄本 16 回"，都没有确定其为琉球写本。笔者从大塚（1984）所记的内容，排除⑦为尚志堂本的抄本，由怀疑并证实其应为琉球写本，该书系由武藤长平先生在琉球所访得，但其图书馆卡片上有"风月主人撰"的错误记录，故一直没有引起学界的注意。最近，笔者又发现了⑫关西大学总合图书馆长

泽文库藏有《人中画》之《终有报》四回，初步研究，也应为《人中画》琉球写本之残本。笔者对④⑥⑦⑫四种琉球写本进行了比较，虽然它们在总目录、回目名、回数、个别用字上存在一些差异，但是内容完全对应，语言大致相同，应该是同一版本的不同抄本。在这4种写本中，天理本与啸本是对应最为整齐的包括"风流配""自作孽""狭路逢""终有报""寒彻骨"五个故事的16回本。赵伯陶（1993：前言）提出，《寒彻骨》位于啸本全书之末，其最后一叶字迹草率，笔划单弱，与全书刻工风格明显不同，疑是该本刷印时，其藏板中最后一、二块或有损坏遗失情况，而重新雕版一块。"也即是说，除了最后一两块板外，其他各处啸本都保持了其"祖本"的实际面貌。在没有发现比啸本更早的版本之前，我们认为，剔除掉《寒彻骨》最后一页的内容后，用啸本来代表《人中画》琉球写本的母本系统，是比较合理的。具体的论述详见李丹丹（2008）。以上版本⑦和⑫研究资料的获得，分别得到木津祐子先生与内田庆市先生的帮助，深表谢忱。

[5] 啸本的"自"能作状语、定语；"自家"能作主语、定语、状语，与人称代词/指人名词联合作主语、状语；"自己"能作状语、定语。琉本的"自家"可以作主语、定语、状语，与人称代词联合作主语、定语、状语；"自己"可以作主语、宾语、定语、状语，与人称代词联合作定语。琉本的"自家"和"自己"并无明显的功能上的分工。

[6] 包括"指人名词/人称代词＋自家"的情况在内。

[7] 包括"人称代词＋自己"的情况在内。

[8] 本文讨论的啸、琉两本不包括题目、拟话本开头结尾处的诗词、公文等文言部分。

[9] 表示出自"啸花轩本/风流配/第一回"，下类推。啸本目前尚无影印本面世，本文所据为《古本平话小说集》。

[10] 但两句意义稍异，(10a)"自家人"意为"自己人"，(10b)"自己家人"意为"自己的家人"。

[11] 本表文献的年代、作者及籍贯主要根据刘一之（1988），需要说明的如下：董解元的生平事迹不可考，学界的主流意见认为其为12世纪后期至13世纪初人。《董解元西厢记》中有许多西北方言，所以确定它是属于北方话系统的，大概没有问题"（刘一之 1988：105）。《元刊杂剧三十种》的北人作者及籍贯如下：关汉卿（大都）、高文秀（山东）、郑廷玉（河南彰德）、马致远（大都）、武汉臣（济南）、尚仲贤（河北）、纪君祥（大都）、石君宝（山西平阳）、张国宾（大都）、孟汉卿（安徽）、王伯成（涿州）、岳伯川（济南）、狄君厚（平阳）、孔文卿（平阳）、宫天挺（河北大名）、郑光祖（平阳）（刘一之 1988：102）。《醒世姻缘传》的作者西周生的生平事迹亦不可考，但该书是用山东方言写成的，也是没有争议的（罗福腾 1996：229）。《盛明杂剧》中的南人作者及籍贯如下：徐渭（浙江山阴）、陈与郊（浙江海宁）、叶宪祖（浙江余姚）、孟称舜（浙江山阴）、王衡（江苏太仓）、竹痴居士（浙江余姚）（刘一之 1988：96）。

[12] 此例为：(26) 黄允休了自己媳妇，去取那袁氏。（卷下、23·b·6）但"自己"之"己"被涂掉，改作"的"字。如果原作非"自己"，乃抄者笔误所致，后被校正，可能《元本

琵琶记》原作中"自己"尚未滥觞；如果原作为"自己"，后被改掉，可能用"自己"不符合当时一般的表达习惯。无论如何，都说明当时南人作品中，"自己"还不是常见用法。

[13] 施其生（1993：186）记汕头方言的"自己"为"家己"，李如龙（1999：266）认为声调不合，漳州声母也不合。钱奠香（1999：339）也提到，海南屯昌方言相同于共同语"自己"的代词应为"家自"，而非"家己"，因为在屯昌方言中声调不合，"己"不能读阴平调。"家自"的"自"念 k-，是由于"家"字声母同化的结果。

[14] 木鱼书因为其说唱文学的体裁，可能夹杂着书面语或有着仿古趋雅的成分，因此不能据此说明当时粤语反身代词的主要形式为"自家"。要确定粤语早期的反身代词形式，必须等待时代更早、口语性质更纯粹的粤语材料的发现。但《二荷》的事实至少提醒我们，粤语的反身代词形式可能也由"自家"转化为"自己"，只不过相比于其他南方方言，更早地完成了这个转化过程。

[15] 此处据刘一之（1988：106），但实际上"们"应作"门"（又见于太田 1987：106）。另刁晏斌（2003：9）认为《三朝北盟会编》中的"'自家'多表复数，义同'我们'"，与刘一之（1988）、吴福祥（1994）的观点不同。我们认为《三朝北盟会编》表示复数之"自家"应表示包括式，义同后世之"咱们"。

[16] 实际上，共同构成这种混乱局面的还有"咱家"。吕叔湘（1985：97）认为"咱"似为"自家"的切音，从"自家"转化而来。太田（1987：107）也提到，"由'自家'合成的'咱'，从宋代就有，它和'自家'有相同的三种意义和用法"。也即"咱"＝"自家"。但"咱"受当时"人称代词＋家"的类化还出现了一个"咱家"（＝自家＋家）的形式。"咱家"也能作第一人称单数和包括式，如：

（27）不是咱家口大，略使权术，立退干戈。（董卷二 15·b·7）

（28）谁指望是他劣相的心肠先改，想咱家不枉了为他害。（董卷五 8·b·2）

"咱家"受"你家""我家"等形式的产生而类化产生，"咱"附上"家"之后并没有产生新意义，可视为"咱"的一个变体。后又同"你家""我家"形式在汉语共同语中的消失而类化消失，所以虽然其与"自家""咱"在第一人称单数和包括式这两种功能上重合，但不直接参与"自家""咱""自己"的竞争。其作第一人称单数/包括式的次数为：《董》4/1，《元刊杂剧三十种》之北人作品 1/1，在《老乞大》中已不见。《盛明杂剧》中《郁轮袍》有 1 例"咱家"：（29）诸王来与咱家庆寿（8·b·5），作第一人称单数，当为仿元杂剧的用法。

[17] 江蓝生（1995：189）提出："由于语法成分的汉字标记一般只记音，因而在早期往往因人因地因时而异，很不固定。随着时间的推移，经过筛选淘汰，逐渐趋于统一。淘汰的原则是：1. 避免常用字，如采用常用字，往往增加偏旁以示区别；2. 避免难写字。如果既常用，笔话又繁多（如'灋'），十之八九会被淘汰。"

[18] "不是常用字"此条相对于"咱"有两义：一、在《刘》之前"咱"字少见；二、不是原

来常用的汉字标记"自家"。

[19] "自家"表第一人称单数的用法在《老乞大》中已经消失,但"登场报名之自家尤为后世道白所袭用"(吕叔湘 1984:23),故在戏剧中尚能见到。但用"自家"登场报名只限于生、末、丑等,且用"奴家"(《元本琵琶记》《盛明杂剧》)、"妾身"(《盛明杂剧》)等。

[20] "迄乎我咱、你咱已成熟语,'自家'之本义遂减杀至于不复可辨"(吕叔湘 1984:22),其意义也逐渐消亡,我们的调查发现,在《老乞大》中此用法已经消失。

[21] 据梅祖麟(1988:143),古代闽粤一带的非汉语可能有三种,台语、南岛语、奥亚语,它们都有包括式和排除式的区别。

[22] 吕叔湘(1984:32)提出"包容排除二式之分……颇疑缘于北方外族语言之影响"。后梅祖麟(1988:142)根据刘一之(1988)所作的工作,认为在 12 世纪"阿尔泰诸民族中和汉族接触最密切的是契丹和女真,因此我们认为北方系官话是受了女真或契丹语的影响而引进包括式和排除式的对立。"吴福祥(2007:5)提及由语言接触引发的演变的具体现象时提到"宋金时期汉语在阿尔泰语影响下获得第一人称复数包括式和排除式的区别"。李作南等(1993:59)认为"通过两种语言的互相翻译,大大促进了蒙汉两种语言的互相影响。汉语中第一人称代词复数包括式和排除式的区别,就是从蒙汉语的翻译中形成和发展起来。"考虑排除式和包括式对立出现的时间,梅祖麟的意见是较为具体而恰当的。

[23] 很多语言学家主张,语言演变有"内部因素促动的演变"(internally motivated change)和"接触引发的演变"(contact-induced change)两种类别,接触引发的演变也包括语言接触的各种间接后果(吴福祥 2007:4)。

参考文献

魚返善雄(1957)人中画と琉球人,《人间味の文学》,东京:明德出版社。

太田辰夫(1958)《中国语历史文法》,东京:江南书院。中译本:《中国语历史文法》(修订译本),蒋绍愚、徐昌华译,1987,北京:北京大学出版社。

太田辰夫(1998)《(新订)中国历代口语文》,京都:朋友书店。

大塚秀高(1984)《中国通俗小说书目改定稿(初稿)》,东京:汲古书院。

大塚秀高(1987)《增补中国通俗小说书目》,东京:汲古书院。

木津祐子(2004a)赤木文库藏《官话问答便语》校,《冲绳文化研究》总第 31 号,东京:法政大学冲绳文化研究所。

木津祐子(2004b)琉球编纂の官话课本に见る"未曾""不曾""没有"—その课本间差异が意味すること—,《中国语学》总第 251 号。

木津祐子(2004c)清代福建的官话——以琉球官话课本的语法特点为例,《第五届国际古汉语语法研讨会暨第四届海峡两岸语法史研讨会论文集》(Ⅱ),台北:"中研院"语言学研究所。

佐藤晴彦(1978)琉球官話课本研究序说——写本《人中画》のことば(1),《人文研究》第 2

期，大阪：大阪市立大学文学会。

佐藤晴彦（1980）琉球官話課本研究序説——写本《人中画》のことば（2），《人文研究》第 4 期，大阪：大阪市立大学文学会。

陈泽平（2004）试论琉球官话课本的音系特点，《方言》第 1 期。

曹志耘（1999）严州方言的代词系统，《代词》，李如龙、张双庆主编，广州：暨南大学出版社。

刁晏斌（2003）《〈三朝北盟会编〉语法研究》，开封：河南大学出版社。

江蓝生（1995）说"么"与"们"同源，《中国语文》第 3 期。

江蓝生（1999）从语言渗透看汉语比拟式的发展，《中国社会科学》第 4 期。

濑户口律子、李炜（2004）琉球官话课本编写年代考证，《中国语文》第 1 期。

李丹丹（2008）《清琉球官话课本〈人中画〉语法研究》，中山大学博士学位论文。

李如龙（1999）闽南方言的代词，《代词》，李如龙、张双庆主编，广州：暨南大学出版社。

李炜、李丹丹（2007）从版本、语言特点考察《人中画》琉球写本的来源和改写年代，《中山大学学报（社会科学）》第 6 期。

李作南、李仁孝（1993）论汉语第一人称代词的发展和蒙语对它的影响，《内蒙古大学学报（社会科学版）》第 4 期。

刘丹青（1999）吴江方言的代词系统及内部差异，《代词》，李如龙、张双庆主编，广州：暨南大学出版社。

刘一之（1988）关于北方方言中第一人称代词复数包括式和排除式对立的产生年代，《语言学论丛》第十五辑，北京：商务印书馆。

路工（1985）古本小说新见，《访书见闻录》，上海：上海古籍出版社。

罗福腾（1992）山东方言比较句的类型及其分布，《中国语文》第 3 期。

吕叔湘（1984）释您，俺，咱，喒，附论们字，《汉语语法论文集》（增订本），北京：商务印书馆。

吕叔湘（1985）们和家，《近代汉语指代词》，北京：商务印书馆。

梅祖麟（1988）北方方言中第一人称代词复数包括式和排除式对立的来源，《语言学论丛》第十五辑，北京：商务印书馆。

钱奠香（1999）屯昌方言的代词，《代词》，李如龙、张双庆主编，广州：暨南大学出版社。

施其生（1993）汕头方言的人称代词，《方言》第 3 期。

孙楷第（1957）《中国通俗小说书目》，北京：作家出版社。

万波（1999）赣语安义方言的人称代词和指示代词，《代词》，李如龙、张双庆主编，广州：暨南大学出版社。

吴福祥（1994）敦煌变文的人称代词"自己""自家"，《古汉语研究》第 4 期。

吴福祥（2005）汉语历史语法研究的目标，《古汉语研究》第 2 期。

吴福祥（2007）关于语言接触引发的演变，《民族语文》第 2 期。

徐通锵（1991）《历史语言学》，北京：商务印书馆。

赵伯陶（1993）《人中画》前言，《中国话本大系》，南京：江苏古籍出版社。

赵元任（1928）《现代吴语的研究》，北京：清华学校研究院。

郑张尚芳（2003）温州话指代词系统及强式变化并近指变音，《汉语方言研究和探索（首届国际汉语方言语法学术研讨会论文集）》，哈尔滨：黑龙江人民出版社。

Hopper, P. J. (1991) On some principles of grammaticalization, In Traugott & Heine *Approaches to Grammaticalization*, Vol. 1: 17–36.

Zipf, G. K. (1949) *Human Behavior and the Principle of Least Effort*. Cambridge: Addison-Wesley Press.

（本文发表于《中国语学》总第 255 号，第 78—93 页，2008 年）

琉球官话课本中表使役、被动义的"给"*

琉球官话课本语法研究价值较高的有 3 种:《官话问答便语》(以下简称《官》),《白姓官话》(以下简称《白》),《学官话》(以下简称《学》)。据我们考证,《官》作于 1703 年或 1705 年,《白》作于 1750 年,《学》作于 1797 年, 恰好在 18 世纪初、中、末 3 个时段上。[1] 为了称述方便起见, 我们把琉球官话课本所反映的官话系统简称为"琉球官话"。琉球官话的主要特色之一就是用"给"来表达使役义和被动义。

1. 琉球官话表使役、被动义的"给"

"给"的基本用法是表给予义, 在这一点上《官》、《白》、《学》与《红楼梦》等北京官话作品无异, 不赘。"给"表使役、被动义才是琉球官话的特色, 其出现次数见表 1:

表 1

	"给"总数	使役义"给"	被动义"给"
官	16	6	0
白	36	6	4
学	33	8	5

兹列举用例如下:

(1) 船头上把锦标插着, 给这些爬龙船(的)去抢。(《官》)

(2) 至于有病时候, 也不去投神保安, 也不去请医吃药, 死能(宁)可给他死, 想要用钱这万万不能的。(《官》)

(3) 若是略略有些力量也要轻轻铺序, 家中给妻儿欢喜, 外面给亲友敬重。所以勉强备办, 不肯令人取笑。(《官》)

（4）这边人多炒（吵）闹，恐怕病人不安，所以另盖这一间小房，给他住在里头养病。（《白》）

（5）你兄们都是大邦人物，礼义之乡言动举止，那（哪）一件不是给人可学的。（《白》）

（6）若有便人，烦劳通事寄个口信去，给他知道，若得闲请他来这里玩玩。（《白》）

（7）这个人原生杨梅疮，如今变做疯毒了。好怕人，一身希臭的。他当日才生的时节为什么请医生调治，给他烂到这个样呢？（《学》）

（8）你把头儿朝过来笑一笑，给我亲个嘴儿就罢了。（《学》）

（9）要买这些东西么，给我讲就不买他（它），这个年过得过不得呢？（《学》）

（10）寡剩几担豆子，没有丢吊（掉）也给海水打滥上霉了。（《白》）

（11）那豆子原是草包包的，要打开包晒晒才好，里头原是给雨打湿了的。（《白》）

（12）这里地方毒蛇狠（很）多，若是给他（它）咬了立刻就死，有药也不会救得来。各位小心要紧。（《白》）

（13）你们在大清是哨船还是做买卖的船，怎么样给风飘到这里来呢？我们是载某样东西要到某地方去做买卖的船，使（驶）到某地方被风打到这块来的。（《学》）

（14）你还敢争嘴？你做事件件都给人看破了，如今不敢用你了。（《学》）

（15）这个东西给雨淋湿了，拿去晒晒。（《学》）

例（1）—（9）是使役句，例（10）—（15）是被动句。琉球官话的"给"字使役句和"给"字被动句的区别主要表现在两个方面：一是主语。在"给"字被动句中主语常常出现，没出现也可明确补出，而且这个主语一定是受事主语。而在"给"字使役句中主语则常常不出现，而且往往无法明确补出。[2] 二是主要动词。"给"字被动句中的主要动词都是及物动词（例（13）的"飘"作及物动词用），其后不带宾语；主要动词区域不是一个光杆动词，其后一定有动态助词"了"等（或补语）出现以表示动作业已实现，而且这个"业已实现"在语义上是指向受事主语的。"给"字使役句其主要动词可以不是及物动词（如例（2）、（3）、（7）），可以是光杆动词（如例（1）、（2）、（3）、（6）、（9）），可以带宾语（如例（8））。例（7）的"（烂）到这个样"也表示动作业已实现，但在语义上是指向"给"后的兼语"他"的。

2．清代北京官话表使役、表被动义的"给"和"叫、让、教"

我们对四种清代北京官话作品中出现的"给"进行了统计和分析，这四种作品是：《红楼梦》（作于18世纪中期，以下简称《红》）、《儿女英雄传》（作于19世纪中期，以下简称《儿》)、《语言自迩集》(作于 19 世纪下半期，以下简称《语》)、《小额》(作于 19 世纪末，以下简称《小》)。在这四种作品中我们发现了 5 个表使役、被动义的"给"，仅出现在《红》、《儿》两个作品中。现将 5 例全部列举如下：

（16）我的梯己两件，收到如今，没给宝玉看见过，若经了他的眼，也没了。(《红》40 回)

（17）千万别给老太太、太太知道。[3] (《红》52 回)

（18）我不象你这等怕死贪生，甘心卑污苟贱，给那恶僧支使，亏你还有脸说来劝我！(《儿》7 回)

（19）我原是给你们取笑的——拿我比戏子取笑。(《红》22 回)

（20）就是天也是给气运使唤着，定数所关，天也无从为力。(《儿》3 回)

例（17）是使役句。例（18）—（20）是被动句，因为句中的"我"和"天"是受事主语，"原是……VP 的"和"是……VP 着"也可以看作是动作业已实现。例（16）有歧义，可做两种理解：

A 我的梯己两件，收到如今，（我）没给宝玉看见过……

B 我的梯己两件，收到如今，（这两件梯己）没给宝玉看见过……

如果是 A 就是使役句，如果 B 就是被动句。我们倾向于前者，我们认为表实现义的"见过"在语义上是指向整句所体现的动作行为本身，不是指向"梯己"，换句话说"梯己"并不是"看（见过）"的受事主语。

《红》、《儿》中共出现了约 2097 个"给"，其中 3 个表使役义，2 个表被动义；《官》、《白》、《学》中共出现 85 个"给"，其中 20 个表使役义，9 个表被动义。见表 2：

表 2

	"给"总数	使役、被动义"给"	出现频率比
《红》、《儿》	2097	5	0.24%
《官》、《白》、《学》	85	29	34%

清代北京官话表使役、被动义动词的口语形式主要用"叫"，到了清末则主要用"让"。近代汉语常用的"教"，在清代北京官话中已渐趋消亡。现将它们在清代四种北京官话作品中的出现情况列表如下。见表 3：

表3

	叫		让		教	
	使役义	被动义	使役义	被动义	使役义	被动义
《红》	1477	47	151	0	37	2
《儿》	594	25	145	0	31	1
《语》	194	45	6	0	5	0
《小》	16	2	107	24	0	2

下举几个"叫、让"表使役、被动义的用例：

（21）不回去也罢了，只叫金荣赔不是便罢。（《红》9 回）

（22）索性让我一不作二不休，见一个杀一个，见两个杀一双，杀个爽快！（《儿》6 回）

（23）昨儿我叫他们买一百个鸡子儿送上山来。（《语》第 3 章）

（24）刚才他们那一党找我克啦，打算明儿给您赔不是来，让我先央求央求您。（《小》16 页）

（25）下作小娼妇，好好的爷们，都叫你教坏了。（《红》30 回）

（26）公子断然没想到从城里头憋了这么个好灯虎儿来，一进门就叫人家给[4]揭了。（《儿》38 回）

（27）我的帽子叫风刮下去了。（《语》第 3 章）

（28）王妈你可给我瞧着点儿狗，上回我就让他给咬了一下子。（《小》15 页）

例（21）—（24）是使役句，例（25）—（28）是被动句。琉球官话中也有表使役义的"叫"（见附注 [2]），但没有表被动义的"叫"；也没有出现表使役、被动义的"让"和"教"。因此，我们可以得出这样的结论：表使役义的词兼表被动义，是清代北京官话的特征；表给予义的词兼表使役义和被动义，则是琉球官话的特征。

3. 南方方言的"拨、乞、畀、分"与琉球官话的"给"

汉语南方方言大都用表给予义的词兼表使役义和被动义。比如苏州话用"拨（拨来）"，福州话用"乞"，广州话用"畀"，梅县话用"分"。清末苏州话小说《海上花列传》就是用表给予义的"拨（拨来）"兼表使役义和被动义，"拨（拨来）"在《海上花列传》中共出现 244 个，其中表给予义的有 140 个，表使役义和被动义的共有 104 个，下面分别列举使役义和被动义的用例如下：

（29）拨俚吃点末哉，我来筛。（8回）

　　　　[让他喝点（酒）吧，我来筛]

（30）拨耐做姨太太阿好？（8回）

　　　　[让你做姨太太好不好]

（31）耐看玉甫近日来神气常有点呆缎缎，拨来俚哚圈牢仔，一步也走勿开哉。（7回）

　　　　[你看玉甫这几天神情有点儿发呆，被她们圈牢了，一步也走不开了]

（32）最好笑有一转拍小照去，说是眼睛光也拨俚哚拍仔去哉。（7回）

　　　　[最可笑有一回去照相，说是眼睛光也被他们拍了去了]

现代苏州话的"拨（拨来）"与《海上花列传》中的情况无异，参看石汝杰（2000），不赘。

福州话"乞"分别表使役义和被动义，例如（引自陈泽平，2000）：

（33）乞伊多歇几日（让她多休息几天）

（34）衣裳乞雨沃滥咯（衣服被雨淋湿了）

广州话"畀"分别表使役义和被动义，例如（笔者调查）：

（35）我唔畀你去！（我不让你去）

（36）我畀老豆闹咗一餐（我被老爸骂了一顿）

梅县话"分"分别表使役义和被动义，例如（笔者调查）：

（37）分阿七讲两句（让阿七说两句）

（38）贼古分警察捉走□[e]（小偷被警察抓走了）

琉球官话的"给"与苏州话的"拨（拨来）"、福州话的"乞"、广州话的"畀"、梅县话的"分"在功能上是一致的。换言之，给予动词兼表使役义和被动义是汉语南方方言和琉球官话的共同特征。所以，仅从"给"的角度看，琉球官话具有鲜明的汉语南方方言色彩。

4．一点推论

清代北京官话"叫"的使役义出现频率远远高于被动义："让"的使役义用例在18世纪中期就已大量出现，其被动义用例则到19世纪末才出现，这说明了一个事实:"叫、让"先有使役义,后有被动义。正如太田辰夫(1958:247)所说:叫、让的"使役义是本义,被动义是从使役义转化而来的"。琉球官话课本《官》中的"给"只出现了给予义和使役义两类用例,没有出现被动义的用例;而晚于《官》半个世纪和近一个世纪的《白》和《学》中的"给"则出现了被动义的用例。据此,我们认为:清代北京官话用使役动词兼表被动义,汉语南方方言和琉球官话用给予动词兼表使役义和被动义,这是它们的差异;而在先有使役义、后有被动义这一点上,三者是一致的。

附 注

[1] 见濑户口律子、李炜《琉球官话课本编写年代考证》,《中国语文》2004年第1期。

[2]《官》、《白》、《学》中已出现不少表使役义的"叫"(但没有出现表被动义的"叫"),出现次数分别为《官》13、《白》18、《学》22,出现数量超过了表使役义的"给"且呈递增趋势。但我们发现琉球官话的"叫"和"给"表使役义的侧重有所不同:"叫"大多表支使(吩咐)义(如下例(1)、(2)、(3));少数表容许义和致使义(如下例(4)、(5));相反,"给"不表支使(吩咐)义,只表容许义和致使义(如正文例(1)—(9)),其中有些句子的容许义中还混合着些许给予(如正文例(4)、(5))。表支使(吩咐)义时句前主语常常出现,而且这个主语一定是施事主语(如下例(1)、(2)、(3));表容许义和致使义时句前主语常常不出现,而且往往无法明确补出(如正文例(1)、(2)、(3)、(6)、(7)、(9)及下例(5))。下面是琉球官话"叫"表使役义的几个用例:

    (1)担子我先叫他挑在船上等候。(《官》)

    (2)弟们是二月二十一日收到奇界岛,蒙那里老爷叫小船拉进港里。(《白》)

    (3)等我明日替你们叫两个泥水匠来修拾罢。(《学》)

    (4)天地间要生他,你如何叫他不生。(《官》)

    (5)就是做花子,千山万水路途遥远奔走艰难,想来总是他乡饿鬼,叫人怎不心伤。(《白》)

[3] 由"知道"充当主要动词的"给/叫/让"字句都是使役句,如果在"知道"后面加上"了"则变为被动句。这在否定祈使句中表现得尤为明显,因为会有重音分布上的对立。我们以现代北京话为例:

    A. 别给/叫/让老太太、太太知道!(使役)
    　　　　　　　　　　　　．

    B. 别给/叫/让老太太、太太知道了!(被动)
    　　　　　　　　　　　　　．．

加"."的为重音所在。使役句的"别"语义上指向后面整个儿动作行为。被动句的"别"仅指向"知道",这个"了"在北京话里往往读作[・lou],表示对虚拟的实现的一种担心。

[4] 这里的"给"是助词，用于加强被动语势，但其本身并不表达被动义。参看李炜《加强处
置/被动语势的助词"给"》，《语言教学与研究》2004年第1期。

引用书目

《官话问答便语》、《白姓官话》、《学官话》，日本天理大学附属图书馆藏本。《红楼梦》，
曹雪芹著，人民文学出版社1996年。《儿女英雄传》，文康著，松颐校注，人民文学出版社
1986年。《语言自迩集——19世纪中期的北京话》，威妥玛著，张卫东译，北京大学出版社
2002年。（本文依据《语言自迩集》中的北京口语片段，不包括作者的叙述语。）《小额（社会
小说）》，松龄（松友梅）著，太田辰夫、竹内诚编，日本汲古书院1992年。《海上花列传》韩
邦庆著，典耀整理，人民文学出版社1986年。

参考文献

陈泽平（2000）福州方言的介词，《介词》，李如龙、张双庆主编，广州：暨南大学出版社。

陈泽平（2004）试论琉球官话课本的音系特点，《方言》第1期。

江蓝生（2000）汉语使役与被动兼用探源，《近代汉语探源》，北京：商务印书馆。

蒋绍愚（1994）《近代汉语研究概况》，北京：北京大学出版社。

李炜（2004）北京话表达使役、被动义的历史与现状，（日本）《外国语学研究》总第5号。

桥本万太郎（1987）汉语被动式的历史·区域发展，《中国语文》第1期。

泉敏弘（1985）北方"给"使役、被动用法の来源，（日本）《中国语学》总第232号。

石汝杰（2000）苏州方言的介词体系，《介词》，李如龙、张双庆主编，广州：暨南大学出版社。

太田辰夫（1958）《中国语历史文法》，东京：江南书院。

唐钰明（1988）唐至清的"被"字句，《中国语文》第4期。

杨敬宇、李炜（2002）南宁平话的"乞"及其相关句式，《汉语学报》第4期。

张惠英（1989）说"给"和"乞"，《中国语文》第5期。

张振兴（1999）从汉语方言的被动式谈起，《汉语语法特点面面观》，邢福义主编，北京：北京
语言文化大学出版社。

（本文发表于《中国语文》2007年第2期，第144—148页）

琉球写本《人中画》的与事介词及其相关问题

——兼论南北与事介词的类型差异*

李 炜 王 琳

1. 琉球写本《人中画》中介词"替"的用法

琉球写本《人中画》（以下简称"琉本《人》"）是清代琉球官话系列课本（18 世纪教琉球人学汉语的课本）中的阅读本，其母本是早于它一个世纪的啸花轩写刻本《人中画》（以下简称"啸本《人》"），琉本《人》于 18 世纪中叶编写而成，和其他琉球官话课本一样，呈现出鲜明的汉语南方方言语法特征（李炜、李丹丹，2007）。

琉本《人》共出现 462 例"替"，除了 67 例连词用法、2 例动词用法，其余的 393 例均用作介词，大部分用法是现代汉语所没有的。我们将这些介词分为以下三类，分别进行考察。

第一类：

（1）他才去见县官、学官，到不替黄舆讲，反替那财主说得稳稳当当的了。（琉本·自作孽，第一回）

（2）若不好说，定有暧昧的情了，替我捞起来！（琉本·终有报，第四回）

第一类的"替"介引受益对象，表示受益关系。例（1）中的"替"表示服务义，在现代汉语中相当于"给、为、替"，但现代汉语的"给、为、替"分别只能有琉本《人》"替"的一部分用法，较之后者，其使用范围要窄得多，某些在琉本《人》中成立的句子在现代汉语中是不成立的。而且琉本《人》中所有的"给"均不表服务义[1]，"替"几乎是表达服务义的唯一介词。例（2）中的"替"表示"顺某人之意而为之"（吕叔湘，1982）的意志义。意志义在现代汉语中很常见，但在这里仅此 1 例，说明还

---

* 本项研究受到国家社会科学基金项目"清代琉球官话系列课本语法研究"（项目号：07BYY046）、广东省哲学社会科学"十五"规划项目"现代汉语与事介词的演变研究"（项目号：05J-01）和"中山大学优秀研究生导师逸仙创新人才培养计划"（项目号：11100-3126200）的资助。本文曾于 2009 年 12 月在潮州韩山师院召开的广东省中国语言学会 2008—2009 学术年会暨语言接触国际研讨会上宣读。《中国语文》审稿专家提出了宝贵的修改意见，谨致谢忱！

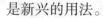

是新兴的用法。

第二类：

（3）张媒婆笑说："唐相公这样拣精拣肥的主顾，就有正经的大好亲事，我也没有这些气力替你缠了……"（琉本·终有报，第二回）

（4）这时候汪费手里很好，不要讲黄舆为他许多的好情，只说替他同来一番，听见他要回去，也该送些盘缠才是，就像替他不相干的事一般，都不提起。（琉本·自作孽，第一回）

（5）柳春荫听了，恰又取名叫春荫，替旧名一样，就满心欢喜说："春荫最好！"（琉本·寒彻骨，第一回）

（6）就是当日不看风信就开船，这是我李天造的罪，替我儿子李春荣何干？（琉本·狭路逢，第三回）

第二类的"替"介引相与对象，表示相与关系。具体来说：例（3）的"替"表示交互义；例（4）的"替"表示协同义；例（5）的"替"表示等比义；例（6）的"替"表示关联义。这些"替"在现代汉语中相当于"和、跟、同"。琉本《人》中"和"、"跟"还是动词；"同"没有表示交互义的用例，表示协同义的数量也不多。[2]

第三类：

（7）刘恩听了，忙忙进去替柳春荫说知。（琉本·寒彻骨，第一回）

（8）老头子说："就是才先说的那个青年的相公，原要买花，因看见了扇子，连花都不买，拿着扇子读来读去，就象癫子一般，定要替我买……"（琉本·风流配，第二回）

第三类的"替"介引指涉对象，表示指涉关系。例（7）的"替"表示顺指义，即动作的方向从主语指向介词宾语，是一种顺向的指涉，在现代汉语中相当于"给、跟、对、向、和、同"；例（8）的"替"表示逆指义，即动作的方向从介词宾语指向主语，是一种逆向的指涉，在现代汉语中相当于"跟、向"等。琉本《人》中"同"无顺指义的用法[3]，"向"也无逆指义的用法，"对"则仅有一例[4]。

以上三类"替"分别表达与事范畴的受益、相与、指涉三种关系，为了称述方便，我们权且将能够表达这三种关系的介词称为"与事介词"，并将其内部系统分为两个层级。[5] 第一层级由三大类——受益关系、相与关系和指涉关系构成；[6] 第二层级则由三大类下位的八小类构成。如下图。

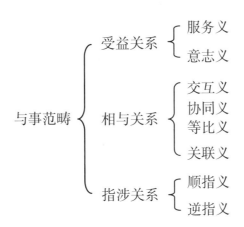

琉本《人》中"替"是可以通表以上三大类八小类用法的强势介词，其他介词虽可表达与事范畴的其中一类或两类关系，但没有一个可以像"替"一样通表的。那么其母本与事介词的使用情况又是怎样的呢？我们对照了啸本《人》，上述八例相应地分别为：

（1a）他再去见县官、学官，到不替黄舆讲，反与那财主说得稳稳的了。（啸本·自作孽，第一回）

（2a）若不好说，定有暧昧之情，与我拚起来！（啸版·终有报，第四回）

（3a）张媒婆笑道："唐相公这等拣精拣肥的主顾，就有正经的好大亲事，我也没这些气力与你缠了……"（啸本·终有报，第二回）

（4a）此时汪费手中有余，且莫说黄舆为他许多好情，只说与他同来一番，听见要回去，也该送些盘缠才是，却像不关他事一般，全不提起。（啸本·自作孽，第一回）

（5a）柳春荫听了恰又取名春荫，与旧名相同，便满心欢喜道："春荫最好！"自此，柳春荫改为商春荫了。（啸本·寒彻骨，第一回）

（6a）况当日匆忙开船，皆我李天造之罪，与幼子李春荣何干？大王到反宽我之死，而夺幼子之生？（啸本·狭路逢，第三回）

（7a）刘恩听了，忙进去与春荫说知。（啸本·寒彻骨，第一回）

（8a）张老儿道："就是方才说的那位少年相公，原要买花，因看见了扇子，连花都不买，拿着扇子读来读去，就像疯了的一般，定要与我买……"（啸本·风流配，第二回）

啸本《人》的"与"是和琉本《人》的"替"相平行的表达与事范畴三种关系的"强势介词"，即除了"与"、"替"，虽然有其他相关介词表达与事范畴，但是在各自版本中均不存在其他通表与事关系的介词，且无论在功能还是数量上均无法和"与"、"替"相比，例略。啸本《人》的与事介词"与"除个别一两例，整体被改写为琉本《人》的"替"（见表1）。[7]

表 1　两种版本《人》与事介词 "与"、"替" 比较

分类		啸本 "与"	琉本 "替"
受益关系	服务义	30	114
	意志义	1	1
相与关系	交互义	81	84
	协同义	40	54
	等比义	11	15
	关联义	16	17
指涉关系	顺向指涉义	53	101
	逆向指涉义	3	7
共计		235	393

　　由表 1 我们可以看出，琉本《人》与事介词 "替" 与啸本《人》与事介词 "与" 是一脉相承的，只是前者的数量比后者多。经过对比发现，多出的近 160 例有从零形式改写的，也有从表与事范畴的其他介词改写而来的。这说明在通表受益、相与、指涉三种关系方面，琉本《人》"替" 的 "强势" 度高于啸本《人》的 "与"。其他四种琉球官话课本 [8] 中的与事介词 "替" 也可通表整个与事范畴并兼做连词，不赘（李炜，2006）。顺便说一句，与近代汉语一样，啸本中的 "与" 除了做与事介词和连词，还做给予动词，而琉本中的 "替" 则不能做给予动词。

2.《红楼梦》、《儿女英雄传》中的与事介词

　　琉本《人》由一个与事介词 "替" 通表受益、相与、指涉三种关系是特殊现象，还是同时期语料的共同现象呢？

　　我们考察了清代中后期以北京官话为主要特征的《红楼梦》（以下简称《红》）和《儿女英雄传》（以下简称《儿》）中与事介词的使用情况，发现二者中除了 "与"，均不存在由一个强势介词通表这三大类八小类的用法，它们的与事介词呈多样化、专职化的态势。在这两部作品中，"与" 虽可通表三大类关系，但已非强势介词。《红》、《儿》中与事介词 "与" 和其他与事介词的出现比例依次分别为 416（与）：1886 和 99（与）：2270。我们将《红》、《儿》中所有相关与事介词的整理结果简述

如下，并附表 2。

1. 受益关系介词。《红》中主要使用"给"和"替"，且二者势均力敌；到《儿》中，"给"的数量远远超过"替"，成为受益介词的代表。举例如下：

（9）宝玉道："酸疼事小，睡出来的病大。我替你解闷儿，混过困去就好了。"（《红》第 19 回，264 页）

（10）一会儿又用手指头给他理理头发，一会儿又用小手巾儿给他沾沾脸上的眼泪……（《儿》第 20 回，278 页）

2. 相与关系介词。《红》中使用"与"、"和"、"同"，虽然三者均可表交互义、协同义、等比义、关联义，但它们在使用时有主次分工：交互义主要使用"和"，协同义主要使用"同"，关联义主要使用"与"，等比义主要使用"和"、"与"。《儿》与《红》的情形大体相同：交互义主要使用"合"，协同义主要使用"同"，等比义、关联义主要使用"合"。举例如下：

（11）原来宝玉急于要和秦钟相遇，却顾不得别的，遂择了后日一定上学。（《红》第 9 回，130 页）

（12）尹先生说："你们女子有同母亲共得的事，同父亲共不得；有合母亲说得的话，合父亲说不得……"（《儿》第 17 回，241 页）

（13）没甚说的便罢，若有话，只管回二奶奶，是和太太一样的。（《红》第 6 回，99 页）

（14）他虽合咱们满洲汉军隔旗，却是我第一个得意门生，他待我也实在亲热。（《儿》第 2 回，18 页）

3. 指涉关系介词。《红》《儿》中均主要使用"和"／"合"、"向"。不同的是在两部作品中"与"、"给"虽均可表指涉，但在《红》中二者的比例为 62:85，在《儿》中二者的比例则为 1:120。举例如下：

（15）等我去到东府瞧瞧我们珍大奶奶，再向秦钟他姐姐说说，叫他评评这个理。（《红》第 10 回，142 页）

（16）这年正是你的周岁，我去给你父母道喜。（《儿》第 19 回，270 页）

表2 《红》/《儿》与事介词用例统计

分类		与	给	替	和/合	同	向	对
受益关系	服务义	44/2	232/593	272/123	0/0	0/0	0/0	0/0
	意志义	2/0	9/11	0/0	0/0	0/0	0/0	0/0
相与关系	交互义	93/7	0/0	0/0	165/239	13/19	0/0	0/0
	协同义	50/12	0/0	0/0	80/74	197/248	0/0	0/0
	等比义	41/36	0/0	0/0	55/42	13/23	0/0	0/0
	关联义	123/41	0/0	0/0	74/73	5/4	0/0	0/0
指涉关系	顺向指涉义	62/1	85/120	8/2	292/345	8/4	288/275	24/42
	逆向指涉义	2/0	0/0	0/0	61/20	0/0	5/13	0/0
共计		416/99	326/724	280/125	727/793	236/298	293/288	24/42

由以上统计，我们可以直观地看到，清代中后期《红》、《儿》中的与事介词系统比起琉本《人》要复杂得多。在《红》和《儿》中，与琉本《人》中"替"同时代层次的强势介词的表达形式呈多样化的态势，主要分两大类：一类是与给予动词同形表受益关系兼表指涉关系顺指义的"给"[9]，另一类是可表相与关系和指涉关系逆指义并兼做连词的"和/合、同"类介词。

3. 南北方言与事介词的选择对立

典型南方方言吴语苏州话的"搭"[10]、闽语福州话的"共"、粤语广州话和客家梅县话的"同"均可在本方言系统内部通表与事范畴的受益、相与、指涉，并兼做连词（连词例略）。见表3。

表3 典型南方方言与事介词用例

分类		苏州话	福州话[11]	广州话	梅县话	普通话译句
受益关系	服务义	我搭俚烧饭。	我共伊煮饭。	我同佢煮饭。	𠊎同佢煮饭。	我给他煮饭。
	意志义	耐还勿搭我滚出去！	汝故伓共我滚出去！	你仲唔同我躙出去！	你还不同𠊎滚出去！	你还不给我滚出去！

（续表）

分类		苏州话	福州话[11]	广州话	梅县话	普通话译句
相与关系	交互义	搭耐商量商量。	共汝商量商量。	同你商量下。	同你商量商量。	跟你商量商量。
	协同义	搭俚经常勒海一道。	共伊经常着一堆。	经常同佢喺埋一齐。	同佢经常在一起。	和他经常在一起。
	等比义	我搭耐一样高。	我共伊平平悬。	我同佢一样高。	倨同佢一样高。	我跟他一样高。
	关联义	搭我搭啥界阶？	共我有什乇干过？	同我有乜嘢关系？	同倨有嘛解关系？	和我有什么关系？
指涉关系	顺指义	搭先生鞠仔个躬。	共先生鞠躬一下。	同老师鞠咗个躬。	同老师鞠了个躬。	给老师鞠了个躬。
	逆指义	俚要搭我借50块洋钿。	伊卜共我借50块钱。	佢要同我借50蚊。	佢要同倨借50块钱。	他要跟我借50块钱。

除了表3所举四种典型南方方言，还有其他南方方言如：福建平和话的"合"、南宁平话的"凑"和"共"、赣南石城客话的"赢"[12]都可通表与事范畴的三大类关系八小类意义（例略）。

以上南方方言的与事介词虽然选择各异，但它们有一个共同点：在本方言系统内部，均可以由一个兼做连词的介词通表与事范畴的三大类八小类意义，各种语义功能在分布上是完全平行的，与琉本《人》中"替"的情形也相平行，但与《红》《儿》中与事介词的选择情况相对立。需要强调的是，琉本《人》中的"替"并非方言用法，而是与其功能相同的"搭、共、同"等介词、连词的官话表达形式（李炜，2006）。另外，南方方言中"搭、共、同"等介词、连词与"替"一样，都不能做给予动词，在以上四种典型南方方言中，给予动词分别为"拨、乞、畀、分"，而这些词又都不能够做与事介词用，它们与琉球官话课本中"给"的功能一样：做动词表示给予、使役，做介词引进施事表被动（李炜、濑户口律子，2007）。

北方方言又如何呢？我们首先选取了北方方言的代表语北京话为考察对象，统计了自清末以来的七部北京话作品——《小额》《骆驼祥子》（对话部分）《四世同堂》（对话部分）、《龙须沟》《茶馆》《评书聊斋志异》和《京味小说八家》（对话部分），发现这些作品中的与事范畴均由多个介词来表达：受益关系用"给、为、替"等，其中意志义只用"给";相与关系用"跟、[13] 和、同";指涉关系顺指义用"跟、给、对"等，逆指义用"跟、向、和"。如：

（17）回头叫到我这儿，不论那位，给我拿上去过一过得啦。（《小额》，278 页）

（18）吃完，都给我滚，我好招待亲友。（《骆驼祥子·十三》，70 页）

（19）这就是我要和你商量商量的呀！（《四世同堂·九》，79 页）

（20）老三！我想啊，你可以同他一路走。（《四世同堂·十二》，109 页）

（21）我们孩子他妈笑着对我说："赶明儿你戴上帽子写东西吧，好看，跟堂·吉诃德的仆人桑科一样。"（《京味小说八家·傻二舅》，490 页）

（22）小丁宝，听着，这跟你有密切关系！甚至于跟王掌柜也有关系！（《老舍剧作·茶馆》，333 页）

（23）……老师父，您多慈悲，我这给您叩头啦！（《评书聊斋志异》第 1 集，4 页）

（24）真一个钱也不跟咱们要？（《老舍剧作·龙须沟》第 2 幕，268 页）

以上八例中的与事介词依次表示与事范畴中八小类意义：服务义、意志义、交互义、协同义、等比义、关联义、顺指义、逆指义。

此外，我们还调查了西北四种方言——西宁话、兰州话、银川话、西安话，发现四者在与事介词的选择上与北京话基本一致。见表 4。

表 4　西北方言与事介词用例

分类		西宁话	兰州话	银川话	西安话
受益关系	服务义	我给我阿爷拿药去哩。	我给我爷取药去哩。	我给我爷取药去哩。	我给俺爷取药去。
	意志义	———	———[14]	你给我滚出去！	你给我滚出去！
相与关系	交互义	你阿哥跟我打了一顿。	你哥跟 / 连我打了一仗。	你哥跟我打了一仗。	你哥跟我干咧一仗。
	协同义	老文跟尕李一搭去了深圳了。	老文跟 / 连尕李一搭里去了深圳了。	老文跟小李一搭里去了深圳了。	老文跟小李一块儿去咧深圳咧。
	等比义	青海的花儿跟甘肃的花儿一样，都是回民唱的。	青海的花儿跟 / 连甘肃的花儿一样，都是回民唱的。	青海的花儿跟甘肃的花儿一样，都是回民唱的。	青海的花儿跟甘肃的花儿一样，都是回民唱的。
	关联义	这个事跟我俩没啥关系。	这个事跟 / 连我没啥关系。	这个事跟我没啥关系。	这个事跟我没啥关系。

（续表）

分类		西宁话	兰州话	银川话	西安话
指涉关系	顺指义	老师给我点了个头。	老师给我点了个头。	老师给我点了下头。	老师给我点咧下头。
	逆指义	尕王跟老李借了点钱。	尕王跟／连老李借了些钱儿。	小王跟老李借了些钱。	小王跟老李借咧些钱。

无论是二百多年以来的北京话，还是如今的西北方言，与事介词大体都分为两大类：一类是与给予动词同形表受益关系兼表指涉关系顺指义的"给"，另一类是表相与关系和指涉关系并兼做连词的"跟、和、同"类介词[15]。普通话与事介词的情形亦如此（例见李炜，2006）。

4. 结论

有关介词"替"表达相与、指涉关系的现象，前人已有关注，如李崇兴（1994）曾举出《元曲选》宾白部分"替"用作相与关系和指涉关系的用例各一个：

（25）刘唐哥，我也曾替你同在衙门中来，直这般狠也！（1620）

（26）你要替我唱喏，你叫一声："老人家，我唱喏哩！"我们便知道了。（1729）

这里，我们再补充一例"替"表指涉关系的：

（27）你如今和夫人两个孩儿牵羊担酒，一径的来替你陪话。可是我不是了。左右，将酒来，你满饮此一杯。（346）

据我们的统计，《元曲选》宾白中出现了九十多个与事介词"替"（例略），表相与关系和指涉关系的也不过以上三例，其余均表受益关系。值得注意的是，李崇兴（1994）还同时指出介词"和"表达受益关系的用法，例如：

（28）虽然和俺两个孩儿分另了家私（替两个孩儿跟另外一个人分家）（456）

（29）既然如此，就劳你和金哥妹子添妆则个。（1228）

（30）争奈有老婆在家，和我生了一儿一女。（1327）

在《元曲选》宾白部分，表相与关系和指涉关系的强势介词"和"有数百用例（例略），但表达受益关系的介词"和"也仅此三例。李先生认为这类特殊用法的"替"、"和"

均是以吴语为背景的，他的观察有一定的道理。其实，从本质上说，不管是哪个介词，只要能通表受益、相与、指涉三种关系，就应该是典型南方方言共有的特征。通过以上事实我们看到，以一个与事介词通表受益、相与、指涉三种关系在《元曲选》宾白中属于"罕见"用法，正常情况是"替"主要用于表达受益关系，而"和"主要用于表相与关系和指涉关系并兼做连词（例略），这恰恰说明《元曲选》宾白是以北方话为主要特征的，与琉本《人》的南方方言特征形成对立。

如果撇开"给"不管，只看一个介词是否能通表相与、指涉两类关系并兼做连词的话，那么无论是古代汉语中的"与"、《元曲选》中的"和"、琉本《人》中的"替"、典型南方方言中的"搭、共、同"，还是现代北京话、西北方言和普通话的"跟"，七者在这一点上都是共同的。

从共同语层面看，可以认为是现代汉语的动词兼介词"给"和介词兼连词"跟"等，最终取代了古代汉语的"与"，但在这个渐变过程中，介词"替"曾经试图取代"与"的大部分功能（除了不做动词），遗憾的是，这一"南支"官话现象，最终未能在现代汉民族共同语中留下位置。

附 注

[1] 在琉球官话中，"给"有表给予义和使役义的动词及表被动义的介词用法，没有表受益义的介词用法（李炜、濑户口律子，2007）。"为"虽可表受益义，但仅有两例。

[2] "同"作"协同义"介词有 10 例。

[3] 另有"对、向"，虽出现的次数不算少，分别为 21 例和 3 例，但"对"所选择的动词范围很窄，仅限于"说"和"笑"。

[4] 这 1 例为：我是对奶奶（太太）当面明公正气求的，又不是私情暗昧，老爷问太太就知道，怎么说个送官呢？（琉本·终有报，第三回）

[5] 我们对汉语与事范畴的界定参照了李如龙先生（2000）的说法，他在谈到闽南方言中有关"与事"的介词时所举的实例与我们这里所谈的三大类八小类关系完全一致。

[6] 相与介词和指涉介词有介词宾语跟主语之间关系方向的不同：相与介词是一种双向关系，指涉介词是一种单向关系。

[7] 啸本《人》的"与"有三种用法：给予动词、与事介词和连词，琉本《人》的"替"则只有与事介词和连词的用法。

[8] 其他四种分别为：《官话问答便语》（1703 年或 1705 年）、《白姓官话》（1750 年）、《学官话》（1797 年）和《广应官话》（1797 年到 1820 年之间），这些琉球官话课本均为日本天理大学附属图书馆藏本（濑户口律子、李炜，2004）。

[9] "向"和"对"是书面语体的表达。

[10] 我们还考察了对话部分为吴语的《海上花列传》（清光绪年间），全书的 403 例介词"搭"也是可以通表受益（111 例）、相与（71 例）、指涉（221 例）三种关系。

[11] 福州话的材料由陈泽平先生提供，谨致谢忱。

[12] 平和方言的材料可参考庄初升（2000），南宁平话的材料可参看覃远雄（2000），石城方言的材料可参看曾毅平（2000）。

[13] 从我们所掌握的北京话语料看，直到清末民初"跟"才在北京话里发展为成熟且强势的与事介词，用于表相与关系和指涉关系（包括顺指义和逆指义）并兼做连词。

[14] 在今天新派兰州话里也可以听到"你给我滚出去！"的说法，但是老派的兰州话的"给"不能表达意志义，要说也只能说"滚着出去！"。

[15] 本文在 2009 年 12 月潮州会议上宣读后，江蓝生先生在与我们私下讨论时，希望我们在探讨南北方言类型对立的基础上进一步关注"中部方言"的相关情况。江先生的指教我们完全接受。如上所述，汉语在与事介词的选择上，存在着典型的南方方言与北京话及西北方言之间的鲜明对立，而中部的相关情况却复杂得多，例如我们正在调查的中原官话河南禹州方言中的"□ [kɯ²⁴]"，它疑似可做给予动词同时通表与事范畴三类关系并兼做连词（例略），但它至少存在以下两个问题：1. 假定"□ [kɯ²⁴]"为"给"，则其语法功能和古汉语的"与"就完全一致了，也即是说它整体替代了"与"，但替代后又没有发生语法功能的变化或产生新的语法功能，那么这个替代的意义又何在？ 2."□ [kɯ²⁴]"的本字尚未考定，不能排除是来源不同的字。这类现象不单河南话中有，湖南、湖北等地方言中也存在。我们认为首先应对汉语南北两端的相关情况进行正确的描写与解释，其结论才将有助于我们最终解决"中部方言"的相关问题，对此江先生表示赞同。

引用书目

琉球写本《人中画》，日本天理大学附属图书馆藏本。《红楼梦》，曹雪芹著，人民文学出版社 1996 年。《儿女英雄传》，文康著，知识出版社 2001 年。《海上花列传》，韩邦庆著，人民文学出版社 1982 年。《小额》，松友梅著，广东人民出版社 1985 年。《骆驼祥子》，老舍著，北京燕山出版社 2009 年。《四世同堂》，老舍著，人民文学出版社 1998 年。《老舍剧作》，老舍著，傅光明选编，浙江文艺出版社 2007 年。《评书聊斋志异》（一、二集），陈士和讲述，百花文艺出版社 1980 年。《京味小说八家》，刘颖南、许自强编，文化艺术出版社 1989 年。《元曲选》，臧晋叔编，中华书局 1958 年。

参考文献

濑户口律子、李炜（2004）琉球官话课本编写年代考证，《中国语文》第 1 期。

李崇兴（1994）《元曲选》宾白中的介词"和""与""替"，《中国语文》第 2 期。

李如龙（2000）闽南方言的介词，《介词》，李如龙、张双庆主编，广州：暨南大学出版社。

李炜（1989）兰州话、河州话两种混合语及其关系——兼谈西北话的阿尔泰化,《双语双方言》（一）, 陈恩泉主编, 广州: 中山大学出版社。

李炜（2006）琉球官话课本中的与事介词"替",《中山人文学术论丛》（七）, 澳门: 澳门出版社。

李炜、濑户口律子（2007）琉球官话课本中表使役、被动义的"给",《中国语文》第 2 期。

李炜、李丹丹（2007）从版本、语言特点考察《人中画》琉球写本的来源和改写年代,《中山大学学报（社科版）》第 6 期。

吕叔湘（1982）《中国文法要略》, 北京: 商务印书馆。

覃远雄（2000）南宁平话的介词,《介词》, 李如龙、张双庆主编, 广州: 暨南大学出版社。

曾毅平（2000）石城（龙岗）方言的介词,《介词》, 李如龙、张双庆主编, 广州: 暨南大学出版社。

庄初升（2000）闽语平和方言的介词,《介词》, 李如龙、张双庆主编, 广州: 暨南大学出版社。

（本文发表于《中国语文》2011 年第 5 期, 第 419—426 页）

琉球官话课本的使役标记"叫"、"给"及其相关问题*

王　琳　李　炜

有关使役的问题，已有不少学者做出很多相关的研究。但前期多数学者将使役等同于使令、致使，或者将使令与致使等同，如：谭景春（1995）、彭利贞（1996）、范晓（2000）、何元建、王玲玲（2002）等，他们持一种较为狭义的使役观。江蓝生（2000）指出，"所谓使役，是指动词有使令、致使、容许、任凭等意义"。洪波、赵茗（2005）按照使役度把"使役"分成了三个等级：命令（高强度使役）、致使（中强度使役）和容让（低强度使役）。从全面性来说，江先生给使役下的定义更为科学，也更为广泛，我们采取江先生对使役的看法，把任凭义从容让义中剥离出来，然后将使役形式所表达的意义称为使役范畴。使役作为一种范畴，其内部系统可以根据使役者对被使役者的控制强弱度分为两个下位范畴：一个是由使令和致使构成的、使役者对被使役者控制度较强的使役，简称"令致类"使役；另一个是由容许和任凭构成的使役者对被使役者控制度较弱的使役，简称"容任类"使役。本文所谈的两个使役标记是与被动范畴有密切关系的"叫、给"，其余暂不讨论。

一、琉球官话课本中使役标记"叫"、"给"的使用情况

琉球官话系列课本[1]中的使役标记"叫"、"给"在表达使役范畴时语义分工明确，没有交叉。

1.1 令致类使役

关于使令和致使的语义特征，吕叔湘（1982）《中国文法要略》第七章"致使句"

---

* 本项研究受到国家社会科学基金重大项目"海外珍藏汉语文献与南方明清汉语研究"（项目号：12&D178）、国家社会科学基金项目"清代琉球官话系列课本语法研究"（项目号：07BYY046）和"中山大学优秀研究生导师逸仙创新人才培养计划"（项目号：11100-3126200）的资助。《中国语文》审稿专家提出了宝贵的修改意见，在此谨致谢忱！

一节早有论述。刘永耕（2000）对使令类动词的表述是："施事者以一定的行为支配受事者，意欲促使受事者发出某行为或接受某变化。"对致使的表述是"由于主体的作用而使客体产生一种状态"。同时指出"使令类动词和致使词是汉语动词中两个既相联系又相区别而易混淆的次范畴"。

琉球官话系列课本中共出现 257 例使役标记"叫"[2]，其中琉本《人》、《官》、《白》、《学》各出现 203 例、13 例、18 例、23 例，这些使役标记"叫"均表示使役范畴中的令致类使役，不表容任类使役。我们将琉本《人》与早于它一个世纪的母本啸花轩写刻本《人中画》（简称啸本《人》）进行了对照，发现了不少琉本的使役标记"叫"由啸本的"使、令、命"改写而来。如：

（1）知县判完，<u>叫</u>书办读给众人听，众人都磕头叩谢。（《琉 / 狭 / 二》）

（1'）知县判毕，<u>令</u>值堂吏读与众人听，众人俱各磕头感谢。（《啸 / 狭 / 二》）

（2）知县就<u>叫</u>鼓手、彩旗，各人迎去公馆。（《琉 / 狭 / 三》）

（2'）县尊就<u>命</u>鼓乐、彩旗个个迎归寓所。（《啸 / 狭 / 三》）

（3）就<u>叫</u>跟随的童子，又拿两个钟子、两双快子同吃。（《琉 / 终 / 一》）

（3'）因<u>命</u>跟随童子，又取了两付钟箸，送酒同饮。（《啸 / 终 / 一》）

（4）我们吃几杯酒，我自然<u>叫</u>他出来相见。（《琉 / 风 / 四》）

（4'）容杯斝少伸，当<u>令</u>拜谒。（《啸 / 风 / 四》）

（5）那好<u>叫</u>我女儿有不交杯的公婆？又那好<u>叫</u>我女婿有不同床的父母？（《琉 / 狭 / 三》）

（5'）岂可<u>使</u>小女有不合卺之公、姑，又岂可<u>使</u>小婿有不同床之父母？（《啸 / 狭 / 三》）

（6）怎么会<u>叫</u>得他来呢？（《琉 / 风 / 四》）

（6'）而不能<u>致</u>之以来（《啸 / 风 / 四》）

（7）若久汤冷了，将冷汤倒吊，<u>叫</u>他再放热汤进来，重新再洗，你想快活不快活呢？（《官》）

（8）就是做花子，千山万水，路途遥远，奔走艰难，想来总是他乡饿鬼，<u>叫</u>人怎不心伤？（《白》）

（9）如今借重列位，替弟们对他们父兄说一声，<u>叫</u>他下次不要这样了。（《学》）

例（1）—（4）的"叫"对应啸本中（1'）—（4'）的"命、令"，表示施事者有意识地支使、要求受事者做某事，是令致类使役的使令义。施事者和受事者大多指人，"叫"后的 V 一般是自主动词（马庆株，1989）。

例（5）、（6）的"叫"对应啸本中（5'）、（6'）的"使、致"，表示施事者不是有意识地，只是客观上引起或导致受事者出现某种结果或状态，是令致类使役的致使义。施事者常常是一个事件，而非人，受事者可以是人也可以是物，"叫"后的 V

多数是非自主动词或形容词。

《官》、《白》、《学》虽然没有对应例句，但从上下文语义上，我们可以判断例（7）和例（9）表示的是令致类使役的使令义，例（8）表示的是令致类使役的致使义。

1.2 容任类使役

容任类使役的下位意义是容许义和听任义。琏球官话系列课本中共出现 44 例使役标记 "给"，其中琏本《人》、《官》、《白》、《学》各出现 24 例、6 例、6 例、8 例。这些使役标记 "给" 均表示使役范畴中的容任类使役，不表令致类使役。我们将琏本《人》与啸本《人》进行了对照，发现了不少琏本的使役标记 "给" 由啸本的 "容、能、与" 改写而来。如：

（10）花满好，寡是老爷仔细，不当肯<u>给</u>人看。（《琏/终/一》）

（10'）花虽好，只是老爷性癖，不甚肯<u>容</u>人看。（《啸/终/一》）

（11）大王果有灵感，明明指示我儿子李春荣的骨殖所在，<u>给</u>我捡回去埋葬，就是神明可怜。（《琏/狭/三》）

（11'）如果大王有灵，明明指示孩儿李春荣骸骨所在，<u>得能</u>归葬，便是神圣可怜。（《啸/狭/三》）

（12）本司不是舍不得一个知县，不<u>给</u>你去做。（《琏/自/一》）

（12'）本司不是吝惜一知县，不<u>与</u>黄兄选去。（《啸/自/一》）

（13）请大人端坐，<u>给</u>我磕头。（《琏/寒/一》）

（13'）请大人尊坐，<u>容</u>不肖子拜于膝下！（《啸/寒/一》）

（14）年间这地方所出粮米，皆多少缴纳王府，还剩多少，<u>给</u>做官的收去，这就是俸禄了。（《官》）

（15）因为这边人多炒闹，恐怕病人不安，所以另盖这一间小房子，<u>给</u>他住在里头养病。（《白》）

（16）你把头儿朝过来笑一笑，<u>给</u>我亲个嘴儿就罢了。（《学》）

（17）至于有病，也不去投神保病，也不去请医吃药，死宁可<u>给</u>他死，想要用钱，这万万不能的。（《官》）

（18）他当日才生的时节，为什么不请医生调治，<u>给</u>他烂到这个样呢？（《学》）

例（10）—（16）表示的是容任类使役的容许义，即事理条件或人为因素的许可，"给" 后的 V 多是自主动词，如 "看、捡、磕头、亲" 等；例（17）、（18）表示的是容任类使役的任凭义，"给" 后的 V 多是非自主、非可控动词，如 "死、烂" 等。从琏本《人》与其母本啸本的对照来看，琏本《人》的 "给" 字使役句均由啸本表示容许义的句子改写而来，且均用于对话体中，《官》《白》《学》中的用例也表明，使役标记"给"仅表达容任类使役；使役范畴的另一类——令致类使役在琉球官话系列课本中的表达则使用的是使役标记"叫"。

琉球官话系列课本中使役标记"叫"和"给"的语义分布情况如表 1 所示：

表 1 琉球官话系列课本中使役标记"叫"和"给"的语义分布情况

语料	使役标记"叫"		使役标记"给"		总计
	令类致使役	容任类使役	令类致使役	容任类使役	
《官》	13	0	0	6	19
《白》	18	0	0	6	24
琉本《人》	203	0	0	24	227
《学》	23	0	0	8	31
总计	257	0	0	44	301

由以上考察和统计分析，我们可以看出，使役标记"叫"与使役标记"给"在琉球官话系列课本中呈现出互补分布的态势：前者表达令致类使役，后者表达容任类使役。二者在琉球官话课本中分工明确，没有混用的情况。

二、清中叶以降语料中使役标记"叫"和"给"的使用情况

2.1 与琉球官话课本同时期的语料中使役标记"叫"和"给"的使用情况

琉球官话课本中这种表达使役两分的现象是同时期语言的共同现象还是个别现象？我们考察了分别代表清中叶北京官话、北方官话、中原官话、江淮官话的《红楼梦》（简称《红》）《老乞大新释》（简称《老新》）和《重刊老乞大谚解》（简称《重老》）、《歧路灯》（简称《歧》）、《儒林外史》（简称《儒》）和以山东方言为背景的《聊斋俚曲集》（简称《聊》）中使役范畴的表达情况，发现《红》《歧》《聊》中的"叫（教）"既可以表示令致类使役，也可以表示容任类使役；《儒》的"叫"既可表达令致类使役，也可表达容任类使役；"给"则只表达容任类使役，不表达令致类使役。如：

（19）凤姐笑道："这话没的叫人恶心。不过托赖着祖父的虚名，作个穷官儿罢咧，谁家有什么？不过也是个空架子。"（《红》第 6 回）

（20）今日侄子还去，带人收拾院子，盘锅垒灶，安置床铺。总要事事妥当，万不叫伯母挂心。（《歧》第 67 回）

（21）因着合他常相处，该钱也无个账目存，这一来叫人心不愤。（《聊·墙头记》第 3 回）

（22）杜少卿叫小厮拿出一个金杯来，又是四个玉杯，坛子里舀出酒来吃。（《儒》第 31 回）

（23）今儿你既老远的来了，又是头一次见我张口，怎好叫你空回去呢。（《红》第 6 回）

（24）耘轩道："到底是什么事央他，你也叫我知道。"（《歧》第 1 回）

（25）我那儿你死活捱着，有我在不叫你抱瓢！（《聊·翻魔殃》第 3 回）

（26）若不肯给我知道，我倒反焦心。（《儒》第 45 回）

例（19）—（22）表达令致类使役，例（23）—（26）表达容任类使役。有江淮官话特征的《儒》中出现的 12 例使役标记"给"表达的均是容任类使役，不表令致类使役，这与琉球官话课本的情况是平行一致的，而与北方方言作品《红》《歧》《聊》的使役标记"叫"兼表令致类、容任类使役，"给"不表令致类使役的情况形成对立。

我们将考察的结果整理如表 2 所示：

表 2　清中叶使役标记"叫"和"给"的语义分布情况

语料		使役标记"叫"		使役标记"给"	
		令类致使役	容任类使役	令类致使役	容任类使役
北京官话	《红》前 80 回 [3]	581	105	2[4]	0
	《红》后 40 回 [5]	676	83	0	0
北方官话	《老新》[6]	22	11	0	0
	《重老》[7]	26	13	0	0
中原官话	《歧》[8]	915	132	0	0
山东方言	《聊》	693	94	0	0
江淮官话	《儒》	430	11	0	12
琉球官话	琉球官话课本	249	0	0	37

2.2 清中叶后语料中使役标记"叫"和"给"的使用情况

我们还考察了年代稍后的北京官话作品《儿女英雄传》（简称《儿》）、《语言自迩集》（简称《语》）、以东北官话为语言基础的《华音启蒙谚解》（刊行于 1883 年，简称《华》）（岳辉，2006）、以地道北京话写成的《小额》（简称《小》）、《官话指南》（简称《官'》）、现代北京话语料《骆驼祥子》和《四世同堂》的对话部分（分别简称《骆》、《四》）。这些作品中的"叫（教）"、"让"可表令致类使役和容任类使役 [9]，"给"几乎没有表示容任类使役的用例。如：

（27）一来答谢上天**叫**咱们父子婆媳完聚的天恩；二来祝赞着那十三妹姑娘增福延寿，将来得个好婆婆、好女婿。我还打算另设张桌儿，望空遥拜他一拜，心里才过的去呢。（《儿》第 12 回）

（28）老兄，话虽是这样儿说，现在他既落到这步田地上，可当真的瞧着**叫**他死么？（《语》）

（29）**教**底下们叫那个厨房的，预备各样点心荤素酒菜来罢。（《华》）

（30）我在顺治门外，大街路东礼部做官的宅里，恼半天的口，一半候儿不**教**回来，所以在那里耽误的咧。（《华》）

（31）善全因为刚才让票子联拍了一顿，听见说他奶奶**叫**他拿钱，心里很不愿意。（《小》）

（32）很好，很好，不用让他忙，**叫**他接着我的得啦。（《小》）

（33）可是你还得把那根绳子，拴到屋里来，**叫**他们透透风是要紧的。（《官'》）

（34）向阳儿的那一间闲屋子，**叫**他住怎么样？（《官'》）

（35）都不可靠，我不愿意**教**他们吊儿啷当的瞎起哄。（《骆》）

（36）我要有你这么个儿子，少**教**我活几岁也是好的！（《骆》）

（37）哥！踢破了鞋，不又**教**妈妈生气吗？（《四》）

（38）老命不要了，我不能**教**你在这儿撒野！（《四》）

而在有南方方言色彩的作品，如：用晚清苏州话写成的《海上花列传》（简称《海》）的对话部分、清末粤语课本《粤语全书》（简称《粤》）以及 20 世纪初有南方方言色彩的《文明小史》（简称《文》）、《孽海花》（简称《孽》）中，其令致类使役使用"叫"、"让"、"令"等，不用与给予动词同形的使役标记；其容任类使役使用"让"、"给"或与给予动词同形的使役标记（如《海》中的"拨"、《粤》中的"俾"等），不用"叫"。例如：

（39）耐说仔末**让**阿姐先走，我末多坐歇，阿是蛮好？（《海》第 19 回）

（40）耐放心，我也勿**拨**俚多吃末哉。（《海》第 5 回）

（41）又有一种蚊，咬人个阵时，就竖起个身，呢的蚊係**令**人发热嘅，好多热症都係嘅得嚟。（《粤》第 63 课）

（42）若然**俾**佢传开就好费事咯。（《粤》第 63 课）

（43）只有那个通事，说是昨日骑马，受了伤，身上发烧，头里昏晕，不能行动，现在卑职衙门里，另外收拾了一间书房，**让**他在那里养病。[10]（《文》第 4 回）

（44）这个事情，我总得同你商量**叫**他们同我回去，我情愿收拾房子给他们住，供给他们，决不难为于他，你可放心的了。（《文》第 10 回）

（45）听说还有拚着脑袋给朝里的老大们砍掉，讨着娘娘的快活哩！（《孽》第 9 回）

（46）况且没有把柄的事儿，<u>给</u>一个低三下四的奴才含血喷人，自己倒站着听风凉话儿！

（《孽》第18回）

（47）难道我们听她<u>给</u>这些暴君污吏宰杀吗？（《孽》第17回）

我们将清中叶后使役标记"叫"和与给予动词同形的使役标记的使用情况整理作表3。

表3　清中叶后使役标记"叫"和与给予动词同形的使役标记使用情况

语料	使役标记"叫"		与给予动词同形的使役标记	
	令类致使役	容任类使役	令类致使役	容任类使役
《儿》[11]	522	122	0	1
《语》[12]	156	29	0	0
《华》[13]	29	4	0	0
《小》[14]	9	2	0	0
《官'》	99	11	0	0
《骆》	24	3	0	0
《四》[15]	209	14	0	0
《海》[16]	15	0	0	52（拨）
《粤》	17	0	0	26（俾）
《文》	438	0	0	22（给）
《孽》	208	0	0	11（给）

从表3可见，这种对立的情况不仅在清中叶，在清末也存在，同时我们也从南方历时文献中看出与给予动词同形的词可以作为使役标记表容任类使役。

三、现代南北方言中使役表达的类型差异

琉球官话课本中表达使役二分的现象与清中叶以降的南方文献中表现一致，而与北方文献中的表现存在差异。那么在现代南北方言中的情况又是怎样的呢？先看表4：

表 4　典型南方方言使役标记用例

典型南方方言	叫喊类 / 使令类使役标记	与给予动词同形的使役标记
	令类致使役	容任类使役
吴语上海话	叫伊早点回去。（李荣，2002：942） 侬想叫我出洋相啊？（钱乃荣，2000）	勿拨伊先走。（不要让他先走） 总算拨我逃脱哉。（总算让我逃走了）
闽语福州话	底侬谁叫汝做其？（谁叫你做的）（李荣 2002：942） 叫伊快伙滴行。（让他快点走）	汝想参加，就乞汝参加。（你想参加，就让你参加吧） 乞伊多歇几日。（让他多休息几天）（陈泽平，2000）
粤语广州话	仝你唔开心，唔好意思。（让你不高兴，对不起） 叫佢快啲走。（让他快点走） 叫佢冇（唔好）走。（让他别走）	你想参加，就畀你参加啦。（你想参加，就让你参加吧） 冇（唔好）畀佢走。（别让他走）
客家梅县话	话佢嫒去。（让他别去） 话佢快点行。（让他快点走） 喊佢下楼来。（让他下楼来）	嫒分佢去。（别让他去） 分阿七讲两句。（让阿七说两句）（李炜、濑户口律子，2007）
南宁平话	渠□ [tsep³³] 眼乞我，吆我冇出声。（他眨眼给我，叫我别出声）（杨敬宇、李炜，2004）	渠有个伯爷，冇乞渠住亚间屋。（他有个大伯，不给他住这间房）（杨敬宇、李炜，2004）

　　表 4 是我们搜集、调查吴、闽、粤、客等典型南方方言中令致类和容任类使役的表达情况，发现典型南方方言中使役的表达要分为两块：表令致类使役时使用"叫"（吴语、闽语、粤语）、"令"（粤语）、"话"（客家话）、"喊"（吴语、客家话）、"吆"（平话）等叫喊类 / 使令类动词，暂且称为叫喊类 / 使令类使役标记；表容任类使役时使用与给予动词同形的"拨"（吴语）、"度、护（互）、传、乞"（闽语）、"畀"（粤语）、"分"（客家话）、"乞"（平话）等。

　　在闽语中，表令致类使役的动词多用"叫"，表容任类使役则用与给予动词同形的使役标记。据李如龙（1997，2000），"护、度、传、乞"均可表给予、使役、被动，"护"是同音字，多见于厦门、漳州一带，"度"多用于泉州一带，厦门也用，"传"是泉州专用，"乞"是闽南地区通用。我们经过调查核实，它们在表使役时仅表容任类使役，不表令致类使役。另据林寒生（2002）的调查，闽东福州、长乐、福清、永泰、古田、福安、宁德、寿宁、周宁、福鼎，闽南的厦门和泉州，广东潮州、汕头、澄海等地的"乞"可以表示使役，我们对这些方言点也进行了进一步的调查，发现这些方言点的

"乞"均有容任类使役的用法，而没有令致类使役的用法，如例（48）；令致类使役多用"教"、"叫"，如例（49）、（50）：

（48）闽语厦门话：要去抑或是怀去，<u>互</u>我佫想一下。（李荣，2002：544）

（49）闽语泉州话：<u>教</u>恁小弟莫用去。（叫你弟弟别去）

（50）闽语屯昌话：我<u>叫</u>伊来去了［lɔu³⁵］。（我叫他来了）（钱奠香，2002：169）

而现代北方方言表令致类使役和容任类使役时，一般均使用"叫"或"让"，即令致类、容任类使役是同一个词，如：内蒙古呼和浩特、山西忻州、阳曲，甘肃敦煌，山东烟台、博山、枣庄，河北昌黎，河南洛阳（李炜，2002）、安阳等方言（例略），基本上不使用"给"，且令致类使役和容任类使役没有形式上的区分。据《普通话基础方言基本词汇集》、《汉语方言词汇》、《现代汉语方言大词典》，大部分北方地区均以使用"叫、让"为常。不过，"整个山东方言基本都是把用'叫'表示被动意义的格式作为一种常用说法。"（钱曾怡，2001：304）而据我们的调查，使役亦然。具有晋语色彩的小说《李家庄的变迁》中表令致类和容任类的使役都用"叫"，据我们的调查，晋语以使用"叫"为主。[16] 属于中原官话的陕西关中话、西北方言也多用"叫"，不用"让"。东北官话、北京官话则以"让"多见。

四、结语

琉球官话课本中使役的表达正好与南方文献、现代南方方言的表达相平行：表容任类使役时使用与给予动词同形的使役标记——"给"（琉球官话课本、南方文献）、"拨"（吴语）、"度、护（互）、传、乞"（闽语）、"畀"（粤语）、"分"（客家话）等，表令致类使役时使用叫喊类或使令类使役标记——"叫"、"话"、"喊"、"令"等。这种表达使役二分的平行现象，再一次证明了琉球官话课本的南方方言色彩，同时也证明有必要区分使役范畴的两种下位范畴。而北方文献、现代北方方言表令致类和容任类使役时主要使用"叫"或"让"，即令致类与容任类使役是同一个词，因此，南北方言在使役范畴的表达上存在着类型上的差异。

附 注

[1] 琉球官话课本即清中叶琉球国人学习汉语官话的课本，主要作于18世纪，其中语料价值较高的有：日本天理大学藏本《官话问答便语》（简称《官》）、《白姓官话》（简称《白》）、琉球写本《人中画》（简称琉本《人》）、《学官话》（简称《学》）。其中琉本《人》由五个故事组成，包括：《风流配》《自作孽》《狭路逢》《终有报》《寒彻骨》，为行文方便，均以

首字简称，数字表示每个故事的回目。

[2] 李炜、濑户口律子（2007）发现《官》、《白》、《学》中的"叫"大多表示支使（吩咐）义，我们考察琉球官话系列课本的结果与之相近，但还发现不少表致使的用例。

[3] 有 25 例"教"表令致，8 例"教"表容任，其余都是"叫"。

[4] "给"在《红》中出现的这两例分别为：1. 麝月瞧时，果见有指顶大的烧眼……说："赶天亮就有才好。千万别给老太太，太太知道。"（第 52 回）2. 我的梯己两件，收到如今，没给宝玉看见过，若经了他的眼，也没了。（第 40 回）第 2 句是老太太说的，老太太是金陵人氏，不免会带有江淮官话的方言特点。

[5] 有 6 例"教"表令致，其余都是"叫"。

[6] 有 1 例"叫"表令致，其余都是"教"。

[7] 有 3 例"叫"表令致，其余都是"教"。

[8] 有 16 例"教"表令致，6 例"教"表容任，其余都是"叫"。

[9] 关于"让"的问题，我们将另文讨论。

[10] 此例与例（15）"给他住在里头养病"表义一致，证明琉球官话中的这例"给"是表容任类使役的。

[11] 有 20 例"教"表令致，18 例"教"表容任，其余都是"叫"。

[12] 该书中有 3 例"教"表令致，2 例"教"表容任，其余都是"叫"。

[13] 有 10 例"叫"表令致，其余都是"教"。

[14] 有 1 例"教"表容任，其余都是"叫"。

[15] 有 21 例"叫"表令致，其余都是"教"。

[16] 并非"叫"、"让"都用（李荣主编，2002）。

引用书目

《官话问答便语》、《白姓官话》、琉球写本《人中画》、《学官话》，日本天理大学附属图书馆藏本。啸花轩写刻本《人中画》，《古本平话小说集》（上），路工、谭天合编，人民文学出版社 1984 年。《红楼梦》，人民文学出版社 1996 年。《儿女英雄传》，文康著，知识出版社 2001 年。《小额》，松友梅著，广东人民出版社 1985 年。《骆驼祥子》，老舍著，北京燕山出版社 2009 年。《四世同堂》，老舍著，人民文学出版社 1998 年。《语言自迩集——19 世纪中期的北京话》，威妥玛著，张卫东译，北京大学出版社 2002 年。《华音启蒙谚解》，汪维辉主编《朝鲜时代汉语教科书丛刊》，中华书局 2005 年。《老乞大新释》（影印本），韩国奎章阁藏书 4871 号。《重刊老乞大谚解》（影印本），韩国弘文阁 1984 年。《歧路灯》，李绿园著，栾星校注，中州书画社 1980 年。《儒林外史》（影印本），人民文学出版社 1974 年。《聊斋俚曲集》，蒲松龄著，《蒲松龄全集·聊》，盛伟编，学林出版社 1998 年。《官话指南》，《改订 官话指南》，郑永邦、吴启太合著，金国璞改订，东京文求堂藏版，明治 39 年（1906 年）三刊于东京，日本京都大学文学部藏本。《海上花列传》，韩邦庆（清），人民文学出版社 1982 年。《粤语全书》，悟民氏编，上海石印书局／上海图书局 1921/1932—1933 年。《文明小史》，李伯元著，中华书局 1959 年。《孽海花》，曾朴著，韩秋白点校，中华书局 2002 年。《李家庄的变迁》，赵树理著，人民文学出版社 1980 年。

参考文献

北京大学中国语言文学系语言学教研室（1995）《汉语方言词汇》，北京：语文出版社。

陈章太、李行健（主编）（1996）《普通话基础方言基本词汇》，北京：语文出版社。

陈泽平（2000）福州方言的介词，《介词》，李如龙、张双庆主编，广州：暨南大学出版社。

范晓（2000）论"致使"结构，《语言研究和探索》（十），北京：商务印书馆。

何元建、王玲玲（2002）论汉语使役句，《汉语学习》第 4 期。

洪波、赵茗（2005）汉语给予动词的使役化及使役动词的被动介词化，《语法化与语法研究》（二），北京：商务印书馆。

江蓝生（2000）汉语使役与被动兼用探源，《近代汉语探源》，北京：商务印书馆。

李荣（主编）（2002）《现代汉语方言大词典》，南京：江苏教育出版社。

李如龙（1997）泉州方言的动词谓语句，《动词谓语句》，李如龙、张双庆主编，广州：暨南大学出版社。

李如龙（2000）闽南方言的介词，《介词》，李如龙、张双庆主编，广州：暨南大学出版社。

李炜（2002）清中叶以来使役"给"的历时考察与分析，《中山大学学报（社会科学版）》第 3 期。

李炜、濑户口律子（2007）琉球官话课本中表使役、被动义的"给"，《中国语文》第 2 期。

林寒生（2002）《闽东方言词汇语法研究》，昆明：云南大学出版社。

刘永耕（2000）使令类动词和致使词，《新疆大学学报（社会科学版）》第 1 期。

吕叔湘（1982）《中国文法要略》，北京：商务印书馆。

马庆株（1989）自主动词与非自主动词，《中国语言学报》第 3 期。

彭利贞（1996）论使役语义的语法表现层次，《杭州大学学报》第 4 期。

钱奠香（2002）《海南屯昌闽语语法研究》，昆明：云南大学出版社。

钱乃荣（2000）上海方言中的介词，《介词》，李如龙、张双庆主编，广州：暨南大学出版社。

钱曾怡（2001）《山东方言研究》，济南：齐鲁书社。

谭景春（1995）使令动词和使令句，《语言研究和探索》（七），北京：商务印书馆。

汪维辉（2005）《朝鲜时代汉语教科书丛刊》，北京：中华书局。

杨敬宇、李炜（2004）南宁平话的"乞"及相关句式，《汉语学报》第 4 期。

岳辉（2006）《华音启蒙谚解》和《你呢贵姓》的语言基础，《吉林大学社会科学学报》第 4 期。

（本文发表于《中国语文》2013 年第 2 期，第 155—162 页）

西南官话的"跟"

——从《华西官话汉法词典》说起*

李 炜　　刘亚男

　　李炜、王琳（2011）根据琉球官话课本中介词"替"和吴语、闽语、粤语、客家话等典型南方方言与事介词的语义功能，整理出汉语的与事系统"受益—相与—指涉"，但该系统并未充分考虑各下位语义功能之间的内在联系及其语法化的合理演进路径。李炜、石佩璇（2015）从历时的角度，以北京话"给"和"跟"的语法化路径为切入点，根据汉语与事系统各语义关系的演进情况，将汉语的与事系统修订为"受物—受益—指涉—相与—并列"。而这一与事系统恰好跟古代汉语"与"的多功能模式相对应。

　　在古代汉语中，"与"是既做给予动词又做与事介词并兼做并列连词的多功能词，但在当今的北京话及西北方言、典型南方方言中，都不存在由一个多功能词承担以上三种功能的现象，呈现出"多对一"的关系。比如北京话和西北方言是用给予动词、与事介词"给"以及与事介词和并列连词"和、跟"等来对应古代汉语的"与"，而典型南方方言是用给予动词"拨、乞、畀、分"和与事介词、并列连词"搭、共、同"等来对应古代汉语的"与"（李炜、王琳 2011）。

　　那么，汉语在进入现代语法阶段后，是否都是这种"多对一"的情况呢？有没有"一对一"的情况——只是在词汇上实现了对"与"的更替而语法功能却基本保持不变呢？回答是肯定的。

1. 《华西官话汉法词典》中的"跟"

　　出版于 1893 的《华西官话汉法词典》(*Dictionnaire Chinois-Français de la Langue*

---

* 本项研究受到 2012 年度国家社科基金重大项目"海外珍藏汉语文献与南方明清汉语研究"（项目号：12&ZD178）、广东省哲学社会科学"十二五"规划 2013 年度项目"海外珍藏汉语文献与清代官话语法研究"（项目号：GD13CZW15）的资助。本文曾于 2013 年 12 月在中山大学召开的"广东省中国语言学会 2012—2013 学术年会暨语言共时与历时交叉研究国际研讨会"上宣读。承蒙唐钰明先生审阅，谨致谢忱。感谢审稿专家提出的宝贵意见。

Mandarine Parlée Dans L'ouest de la Chine）是"由在四川生活了数年的传教士们和当地的教士们合作编写的，它收纳了生活在四川、云南和贵州的农村人和城市人的日常口语"，[1] 为我们展现了 100 多年前西南官话的语音、词汇和语法面貌。

值得注意的是，《华西官话汉法词典》（以下简称《华西》）中的"跟"（kēn，原书注音）除了做跟随义动词外，主要的语法功能与古代汉语的"与"相一致，分别做表给予的动词、表与事关系的介词以及表并列的连词。例如：

（1）要等新的上坎才有钱跟你。要等有了新的收入才有钱给你。（《华西·坎》193 页）

（2）买东西不跟钱。买东西不给钱。（《华西·跟》206 页）

（3）跟他几棒棒。给他几棍子。（《华西·棒》402 页）

（4）这股地方我照买价让跟你。这个地方我按照买价让给你。（《华西·价》228 页）

（5）断十吊钱跟他，断得公道。判十吊钱给他，判得公道。（《华西·断》603 页）

（6）跟他脱衣服。替他脱衣服。（《华西·脱》592 页）

（7）好好歹歹要跟我做完。好好歹歹要给我做完。（《华西·好》83 页）

（8）这个事（这句话）你要跟我讲清楚。这件事（这句话）你要和我讲清楚。（《华西·讲》233 页）

（9）我的牛是跟人家令的。我的牛是向人家借的。（《华西·令》334 页）

（10）你跟我打伙开店子。你跟我合伙开店。（《华西·伙》113 页）

（11）不要跟他两个顽。不要和他们两个玩儿。（《华西·顽》379 页）

（12）跟雪一样白。和雪一样白。（《华西·雪》477 页）

（13）这个老婆婆跟他的媳妇长行有一点口舌。这位老婆婆和她的儿媳妇经常发生口角。（《华西·舌》17 页）

（14）差人跟强盗是通的。衙役和强盗是串通好的。（《华西·通》593 页）

我们根据"跟"的语法功能，将"跟"分为"跟₁、跟₂、跟₃、跟₄"。例（1）—（3）的"跟"为"跟₁"，是句中的主要动词，表给予义。例（4）、（5）的"跟"为"跟₂"，位于主要动词之后，动词性较"跟₁"弱，表达弱给予义。例（6）—（13）的"跟"为"跟₃"，做表与事关系的介词。鉴于"跟₃"所表达的与事关系下位义不同，我们将"跟₃"分为"跟₃ₐ、跟₃ᵦ、跟₃𝒸"。例（6）—（7）的"跟"为"跟₃ₐ"，表受益关系，其中例（6）的"跟₃ₐ"表服务义，例（7）的"跟₃ₐ"表意志义。例（8）、（9）的"跟"为"跟₃ᵦ"，表指涉关系，其中例（8）的"跟₃ᵦ"表顺指义，例（9）的"跟₃ᵦ"表逆指义。例（10）—（13）的"跟"为"跟₃𝒸"，表相与关系，依次表协同义、交互义、等比义和关联义。例（14）的"跟"为"跟₄"，在句中做连词，表并列关系。

以上例（1）—（7）中的"跟"（即"跟₁、跟₂、跟₃ₐ"）按照普通话的语感来理解是比较费解的，但如果换成古代汉语的"与"就顺畅了。需要说明的是，虽然"与"

和这种"跟"在功能上相对应，但"与"是汉语古代、近代语法层次的多功能词，而"跟"是汉语现代语法层次的多功能词。那么，这种多功能词"跟"在当今西南官话中还存在吗？带着这个问题，我们对当今西南官话进行了田野调查。

2. 当今西南官话中的多功能词"跟"

《华西》中用"跟"做给予动词、与事介词和并列连词的现象在当今西南官话中仍然存在。例如：

（15）我同学跟了我一本书。我同学给了我一本书。

这个苹果跟你，那个苹果跟他。这个苹果给你，那个苹果给他。

跟一个苹果。给一个苹果。（四川泸州、四川宜宾江安、贵州毕节）

（16）把盐拿跟我哈。把盐递给我一下。

我送几本书跟你。我送几本书给你。（四川泸州、四川宜宾江安、贵州毕节、贵州遵义、湖北恩施建始）

（17）跟叔叔倒茶。给叔叔倒茶。

还不快点跟我站倒！还不快点给我站住！（四川泸州、四川宜宾江安、贵州毕节、贵州遵义、湖北恩施建始、湖北宜昌、湖北荆州石首、湖北武汉汉口）

例（15）、（16）、（17）中的"跟"分别为"跟$_1$、跟$_2$、跟$_{3a}$"。至于"跟$_{3b}$、跟$_{3c}$、跟$_4$"的用法与普通话基本一致，不赘。需要说明的是，根据我们的调查，如今"跟$_1$、跟$_2$、跟$_{3a}$"从分布区域上看，主要集中在城市郊区和乡镇；从使用群体的年龄上看，中老年人常用，而年轻人不常用。

从历时和共时两方面来看，我们可以肯定，"跟"做给予动词、与事介词并兼做并列连词应当是西南官话本有的。

本文开头提到，古代汉语"与"的主要语法功能，北京话及西北方言是用动词兼介词的"给"和介词兼连词的"和、跟"等来对应，而典型南方方言是用给予动词"拨、乞、畀、分"等和介词"搭、共、同"等来对应。显然，在这个问题上，西南官话与南北方言的表现均不同。我们可以从下面的语义分布图来看西南官话、北方方言、典型南方方言三者之间的这种差异。

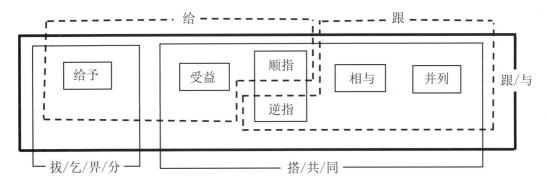

由上图我们看到，西南官话的"跟"和古代汉语的"与"语义区域是重合的。

我们说这种多功能词"跟"是西南官话本有的，但这并不意味着当今所有西南官话的情况都是如此。

3. 现代西南官话"跟"多功能的萎缩

由于受普通话的影响，现代西南官话多功能词"跟"的用法出现了不同程度的萎缩，"跟₁、跟₂、跟₃、跟₄"都有的方言点并不是普遍存在的。我们调查了30多个方言点，发现只有9个方言点不同程度地保留了"跟₁、跟₂、跟₃ₐ"的用法，大多数方言点中的"跟"只有"跟₃ᵦ、跟₃ᵪ、跟₄"的用法，其他用法已经逐渐被"给"所取代，即已呈现出与普通话趋同的情形。详见表1。

表1　现代西南官话中"跟"的语法功能分布表[2]

方言点	跟					
	跟₁	跟₂	跟₃			跟₄
			跟₃ₐ	跟₃ᵦ	跟₃ᵪ	
泸州	+	+	+	+	+	+
宜宾江安	+	+	+	+	+	+
宜宾长宁	+	+	+	+	+	+
毕节	+	+	+	+	+	+
遵义	−	+	+	+	+	+

（续表）

方言点	跟					
	跟$_1$	跟$_2$	跟$_3$			跟$_4$
			跟$_{3a}$	跟$_{3b}$	跟$_{3c}$	
恩施建始	−	+	+	+	+	+
宜昌	−	±	+	+	+	+
荆州石首	−	±	+	+	+	+
武汉汉口	−	−	±	+	+	+
成都	−	−	−	+	+	+
达州	−	−	−	+	+	+
绵阳	−	−	−	+	+	+
德阳	−	−	−	+	+	+
资中	−	−	−	+	+	+
襄阳	−	−	−	+	+	+
自贡	−	−	−	+	+	+
内江	−	−	−	+	+	+
荆州	−	−	−	+	+	+
仙桃	−	−	−	+	+	+
贵阳	−	−	−	+	+	+
重庆	−	−	−	+	+	+

从表 1 我们可以看出，"跟$_1$、跟$_2$、跟$_{3a}$"的萎缩不是同时发生的，而是渐进性的。首先作为给予义动词的"跟$_1$"率先消失（如遵义方言），其次是位于主要动词之后动词性较弱的"跟$_2$"（如武汉汉口方言），再次是与事范畴中表受益关系的介词"跟$_{3a}$"（如成都方言）。

从表 1 的矩阵中我们得出两条蕴含共性：

A. 如果该方言存在"跟$_1$"，那么也一定存在"跟$_2$、跟$_{3a/b/c}$、跟$_4$"，反之不然；

B. 如果该方言存在"跟$_2$"，那么也一定存在"跟$_{3a/b/c}$、跟$_4$"，反之不然。

也可以反过来说：

A'. 如果该方言不存在"跟$_2$"，那么也一定不存在"跟$_1$"，反之不然；

B'. 如果该方言不存在"跟$_{3a}$"，那么也一定不存在"跟$_2$、跟$_1$"，反之不然。

我们所调查的 30 余个西南官话方言点皆然。也就是说，现代西南官话多功能词"跟"的萎缩是按照"跟 $_1$—跟 $_2$—跟 $_{3a}$"的顺序从实到虚依次消失的，消失至"跟 $_{3a}$"即止，即保留与普通话用法基本一致的"跟 $_{3b}$、跟 $_{3c}$、跟 $_4$"。

无独有偶，我们曾经考察清中叶以来"给"对"与"的取代（李炜 2002），发现北京话历时材料中"给"也是按照"与 $_1$—与 $_2$—与 $_{3a}$"的顺序取代"与"的。详见表 2。

表 2 清中叶以来"与"的功能萎缩情况统计[3]

历时语料	与					
	与 $_1$	与 $_2$	与 $_3$			与 $_4$
			与 $_{3a}$	与 $_{3b}$	与 $_{3c}$	
《红楼梦》（前八十回）（约 80 万字）	29	186	42	34	230	343
《红楼梦》（后四十回）（约 34 万字）	0	18	4	30	77	160
《儿女英雄传》（约 61 万字）	0	0	1	1	96	147
《骆驼祥子》（约 14 万字）	0	0	0	0	0	258

从表 2 我们看到，从《红楼梦》前八十回到后四十回，"与 $_1$"已经消失，"与 $_2$"由 186 例锐减为 18 例；到了《儿女英雄传》，"与 $_2$"也消失了，"与 $_{3a}$"只有 1 例[4]；到了《骆驼祥子》，"与 $_{3a}$、与 $_{3b}$、与 $_{3c}$"都消失了，"与"只保留了"与 $_4$"（并列连词）的用法，且只存在于高语体[5]中，这跟普通话的情形相一致。

4．结论

对于古代汉语"与"的主要语法功能（给予动词、与事介词、并列连词），北京话及西北方言、典型南方方言都呈现出"多对一"的对应关系，而位于中部的西南官话则存在"一对一"的对应关系。看来，汉语方言类型的差异并非"南北"差异这么简单，"中部方言"[6]的情况很值得我们关注。可以预见的是，受普通话越来越强大的影响，西南官话中一个多功能词做给予动词和通表三种与事关系的介词以及并列连词的现象终将消失。

我们知道，多功能词的演化路径（即语法化路径）一般遵循着从实到虚的单向性原则。本文所反映出的西南官话多能词"跟"的部分功能萎缩的过程（即"跟 $_1$、跟 $_2$、

跟 $_{3a}$"被"给"取代的过程），也循着由实而虚的路径；古代汉语多能词"与"的部分功能（即"与 $_1$、与 $_2$、与 $_{3a}$"）萎缩的过程也同样如此。

附 注

[1] 引自该词典前言，原文前言为法语。该词典为当时活跃在西南地区的巴黎外方传教士所编，书中没有提及编者姓名。全书近 6 万字，基本按音序排列，词条和词条下的例句先用汉语书写，再分别用法语的拼写法来注音，最后词条和例句都配有法语的翻译（或直译，或意译）；虽然是一部词典，但每个词条下面都提供了大量口语性的例句，语料价值很高。

[2] 表 1 中"＋"表示可用。"－"表示不可用。"±"表示"跟"正在被"给"取代，这包括"给"在使用频率上已明显高于"跟"或年轻人只用"给"不用"跟"、只有一些老年人使用"跟"等情况。此外，根据我们的调查，当今绝大多数西南官话中"跟"的用法与普通话完全一致，除表格中所列举之外，还有四川内江、眉山、乐山，广西桂林、柳州，湖北利川，贵州黔南，重庆云阳等地区。篇幅所限我们没有在表格中一一列举。总之，"跟 $_1$、跟 $_2$、跟 $_{3a}$"应当属于方言中的濒危现象。可以肯定，这种濒危现象会在不久的将来变为彻底消失。

[3] "与"功能的萎缩是在汉语进入现代语法阶段以后"给"（跟"与 $_1$、与 $_2$、与 $_{3a}$"对应）与"和、跟"等（跟"与 $_{3b}$、与 $_{3c}$、与 $_4$"对应）对其分别取代的结果。这里，我们只说明了"给"对"与 $_1$、与 $_2$、与 $_{3a}$"的取代过程，不涉及"跟"等对"与 $_{3b}$、与 $_{3c}$、与 $_4$"的取代过程。

[4] 此例为：我合你三载相依，多承你与我掌持这小小门庭⋯⋯（《儿》十八回，250 页）

[5] 这里"高语体"指风格古雅的书面叙述语体。

[6] 2009 年 12 月在潮州韩山师院召开的广东省中国语言学会 2008—2009 学术年会暨语言接触国际研讨会上，我们曾提出，汉语在与事介词的选择上存在着典型的南方方言与北京话及西北方言之间的鲜明对立。江蓝生先生在与我们私下讨论时希望我们在探讨南北方言类型差异的基础上进一步关注"中部方言"的相关情况，当时我们认为应该把南北两端的问题搞清楚再考虑"中部方言"的问题，但江先生这一问题的提出对我们有很大的启发，我们对西南官话以上问题的思考也源于此。

引用书目

《华西官话汉法词典》（ *Dictionnaire Chinois-Français de La Langue Mandarine Parlée Dans L'Ouest de La Chine* ），Imprimerie de Société des missions Étrangères（外方传教会印书局），1893 年香港出版。

参考文献

李炜（2002）从《红楼梦》《儿女英雄传》看"给"对"与"的取代，《兰州大学学报（社科版）》第 4 期。

李炜、王琳（2011）琉球写本《人中画》的与事介词及相关问题——兼论南北与事介词的类型差异，《中国语文》第 5 期。

李炜、石佩璇（2015）北京话与事介词"给""跟"的语法化及汉语与事系统，《语言研究》第 1 期。

附录：西南官话方言调查发音人相关信息

方言点	调查总人数	性别、人数	年龄区间（老人指 60 岁及以上）
泸州	21 人	男 12 人，女 9 人	20 岁—75 岁，其中老人 9 人
宜宾江安	6 人	男 3 人，女 3 人	25 岁—65 岁，其中老人 2 人
宜宾长宁	6 人	男 3 人，女 3 人	25 岁—70 岁，其中老人 2 人
毕节	9 人	男 4 人，女 5 人	20 岁—70 岁，其中老人 3 人
遵义	8 人	男 5 人，女 3 人	20 岁—70 岁，其中老人 3 人
恩施建始	6 人	男 2 人，女 4 人	25 岁—65 岁，其中老人 2 人
宜昌	4 人	男 2 人，女 2 人	25 岁—65 岁，其中老人 1 人
荆州石首	5 人	男 2 人，女 3 人	25 岁—70 岁，其中老人 2 人
武汉汉口	5 人	男 3 人，女 2 人	25 岁—65 岁，其中老人 2 人
成都	5 人	男 2 人，女 3 人	20 岁—65 岁，其中老人 1 人
达州	4 人	男 2 人，女 2 人	25 岁—65 岁，其中老人 1 人
绵阳	3 人	男 1 人，女 2 人	25 岁—65 岁，其中老人 0 人
德阳	4 人	男 1 人，女 3 人	20 岁—65 岁，其中老人 1 人
资中	5 人	男 2 人，女 3 人	25 岁—65 岁，其中老人 2 人
襄阳	5 人	男 3 人，女 2 人	25 岁—65 岁，其中老人 1 人
自贡	3 人	男 2 人，女 1 人	25 岁—65 岁，其中老人 0 人
内江	3 人	男 1 人，女 2 人	25 岁—65 岁，其中老人 1 人
荆州	5 人	男 3 人，女 2 人	20 岁—65 岁，其中老人 1 人
仙桃	6 人	男 3 人，女 3 人	25 岁—65 岁，其中老人 2 人
贵阳	6 人	男 4 人，女 2 人	25 岁—65 岁，其中老人 2 人
重庆	4 人	男 3 人，女 1 人	25 岁—65 岁，其中老人 1 人

（本文发表于《中国语文》2015 年第 4 期，第 358—363 页）

从给予句 S_2、S_3 的选择看汉语语法地域类型差异*

李　炜　石佩璇

朱德熙（1979）把与"给"相关的给予义句式分为以下四种：

S_1：N_1+V+ 给 $+N_2+N_3$　　　　我送给他一本书。

S_2：N_1+V+N_3+ 给 $+N_2$　　　　我送一本书给他。

S_3：N_1+ 给 $+N_2+V+N_3$　　　　我给他打件毛衣。

S_4：$N_1+V+N_2+N_3$　　　　　　我送他一本书。

以上四种句式，S_1 和 S_4 为双宾句 [1]，S_2 和 S_3 是非双宾句。S_2 和 S_3 最明显的区别在于"给 N_2"的位置：S_2 的"给 N_2"在主要动词 V 之后，S_3 的"给 N_2"出现在主要动词 V 之前。[2] 朱德熙（1979）认为，S_2 可容纳的动词包括给予义动词 V_a、取得类动词 V_b 和制作义动词 V_c；S_3 在表达给予义时，只能容纳 V_b 和 V_c 两类动词，一般不能为 V_a。[3] 而根据我们的调查，在实际使用中，S_3 可以容纳 V_a、V_b、V_c 三类动词，表达给予义；且 S_3 的主要动词为 V_a 时，给予义最强（详见下文）。下面结合历时文献和共时田野调查，考察 S_2 和 S_3 在汉语官话和相关方言中的分布情况及成因。

1. 清中叶以来官话文献中给予句 S_2、S_3 的分布

根据目前掌握的官话文献，含"给"的给予句最早见于清中叶（李炜 2002）。具有鲜明南方地域特征的琉球官话课本 [4]《官话问答便语》《白姓官话》、琉本《人中画》以及《学官话》（以下简称《官话》《白》《琉》《学》）不用 S_3，只用 S_2。S_2 的主要动词涵盖了 V_a、V_b 和 V_c，如：

（1）老爷还问，他死了，穿的衣裳有没有？好<u>做些衣服给他</u>。（《白》）[5]

---

* 本项研究受到国家社科基金重大项目"海外珍藏汉语文献与南方明清汉语研究"（项目号：12&ZD178）及广东省哲学社会科学规划项目"海外珍藏汉语文献与清代官话语法研究"（项目号：GD13CZW15）的资助。本文曾在"第八届现代汉语语法国际研讨会暨 30 周年庆典"（杭州，2015 年 10 月）和"历史语言学研究高端论坛"（兰州，2017 年 6 月）上宣读。

（2）他不当打紧，<u>娶一个瞎眼的小姐给他</u>。（《琉/寒/三》）

（3）难道肯把这银子<u>分些给我</u>不成？（《琉/狭/二》）

（4）那好的人，玉帝就赐他福祥，那不好的人，玉帝就<u>降下灾祸给他</u>，却不是更要紧的？（《学》）

年代稍后的《孽海花》（1905年）、《文明小史》（1903—1906年）、《鲁迅小说集》（19世纪10年代—30年代）（以下简称《孽》《文》《鲁》）也只用S₂，不用S₃。S₂用例如：

（5）筱亭非常快活，就靠着窗槛，当书桌儿，<u>写了一封求救的信给丈人傅容</u>。（《孽》第14回，119页）

（6）当下冲天炮<u>掏了一张西文片子给他</u>，他也<u>掏张西文片子给冲天炮</u>。（《文》第56回，326页）

（7）但在前几天，却有学生总会<u>上一个呈文给政府</u>。（《鲁·端午节》，95页）

《孽》《文》《鲁》的作者均为南方人[6]，和琉球官话课本一样，他们的作品都具有南方地域特征，我们称之为"南部官话文献"。

北京官话文献却有不同的选择。我们选取了以下7部清中叶以来的北京官话文献为研究语料，考察S₂、S₃的使用情况。这7部文献分别是：《红楼梦》（前80回，18世纪50年代；后40回，18世纪90年代），《儿女英雄传》（19世纪40年代），《语言自迩集——19世纪中期的北京话》（19世纪40年代—80年代），《官话指南》（1881年），《小额》（19世纪90年代），《燕京妇语》（1906年），《评书聊斋志异》（一、二集）（1954年）[7]，分别简称为：《红》《儿》《语》《官》《小》《燕》《评》。

《红》同时出现S₂、S₃。在前80回，S₂占主要优势，S₃数量少，两者用例分别为25例和4例；后40回中S₂仍占优势，但S₃的比例逐渐增大，两者用例分别为7例和4例。S₂用例如：

（8）我有一件事，用些冰片麝香使用，好歹舅舅每样<u>赊四两给我</u>，八月里按数送了银子来。（《红》第24回，322页）

（9）不管<u>拿些什么给他们</u>，他们那里看得出来？（《红》第60回，840页）

（10）咱们商量了<u>写封书给琏二叔</u>，便卸了我们的干系了。（《红》第117回，1603页）

S₃的用例如：

（11）这是二十两银子，暂且<u>给这孩子做件冬衣</u>罢。（《红》第6回，105页）

（12）我们姑娘叫<u>给姑娘送了一瓶儿蜜饯荔枝</u>来。（《红》第82回，1181页）

《红》主要使用 S_2，S_3 还是一个新兴句式，但在《儿》中，S_3 大量出现并占据优势地位（30例），S_2 则迅速萎缩（6例，例略）。S_3 的用例如：

（13）我除了<u>给他送些薪水</u>之外，凭你送他甚么，一概不收。（《儿》第16回，259页）

（14）我本说到了京<u>给张姑娘添补些簪环衣饰</u>。（《儿》第23回，415页）

（15）有这项钱，你倒是<u>给他作几件上路素色衣裳</u>，如此事事从实，他也无从辞起。（《儿》第20回，351页）

自《儿》之后的北京官话文献，S_3 延续了其优势地位；S_2 迅速萎缩，直至消失。这些文献的 S_3 用例如：

（16）我<u>给你买一张纸，一管笔</u>，可以不可以？（《语》第三章，80页）

（17）他就叫我们伙计，<u>给他雇了俩小车子</u>。（《官》第1卷第21章）

（18）这才知道一切的事情，赶紧又<u>给文紫山写了一封信</u>，是求他跟王爷说说，专治小额，害不着别人的事情。（《小》，31页）

（19）你<u>给我送两枝儿</u>来罢。（《燕》第二十课22乙，107页）

（20）回头我再<u>给您沏上一壶好茶叶，勤续两趟开水</u>，算我孝敬您。（《评》第1集，248页）

全部使用情况见表1。

表1　北京官话文献中 S_2 和 S_3 的使用情况

语料	S_2 用例	S_3 用例	S_2 : S_3 比值 [8]
《红》（前80回）	25	4	6.25
《红》（后40回）	7	4	1.75
《儿》	6	30	0.2
《语》	8	13	0.615
《官》	0	14	0
《小》	0	17	0
《燕》	0	7	0
《评》	0	63	0

可见，S_3 是清中叶才发展起来的新兴句式，但自19世纪中期的《儿》开始，S_3 已反转成为表达给予义的强势非双宾给予句式。[9] 也就是说，自清晚期始，北京官话文献在表达给予义时主要使用 S_3，S_2 逐渐消失。

我们在关注 S_2、S_3 在南部官话文献和北京官话文献中存在对立情况的同时，又发现了和前两者情况都不相同的第三种官话文献——西南官话文献。清末西方传教士编写的西南官话文献——《华西官话汉法词典》（1893 年）《西蜀方言》（1900 年）和《华西初级汉语初阶》（1917 年）（以下简称《汉法》《西蜀》《华西》）[10] 同时使用 S_2 和 S_3。在这些文献中，与"给"等值的还有"跟"（李炜、刘亚男，2015）。S_2 用例如（21）—（23），S_3 的用例如（24）—（26）。

（21）多少要**拿点跟他**。多少要拿点给他。（《汉法》，9 页）

（22）**分点给我**。（《西蜀》，45 页）

（23）你就**端一盘给人家**。《华西》18 课，193 页）

（24）要**跟你发一百钱**。要给你拨一百钱。（《汉法》，435 页）

（25）**给我写个来帐**。（《西蜀》，19 页）

（26）我们**给他多买一点**。（《华西》27 课，231 页）

全部使用情况见表 2。

表 2　西南官话文献中 S_2、S_3 的使用情况

语料	S_2	S_3
《汉法》	7	13
《西蜀》	3	6
《华西》	2	2

从以上的考察发现，南部官话文献和北京官话文献在 S_2、S_3 的使用上形成鲜明对立，南部官话文献只用 S_2，不用 S_3；北京官话文献自清晚期起主要使用 S_3，逐渐弃用 S_2；而西南官话文献则同时使用 S_2 和 S_3。

值得注意的是，以上三类文献均是具有共同语特征的官话。同是官话文献，为何会呈现出如此大的差异？我们认为这与这些官话文献相关的方言语法特征有关。

2. 当今方言中 S_2、S_3 的分布情况

当今典型南方方言如粤语、客家话、闽语和吴语（主要是南部吴语），在给予句 S_2、S_3 的选择上，只用 S_2，不用 S_3。例如：

（27）你<u>赔翻二十蚊畀我</u>。你赔我二十块钱。（广州话）

（28）我<u>买咗三本书畀细佬</u>。我买了三本书给弟弟。（阳江粤语）

（29）佢借欸五块钱分佢。他借了五块钱给我。（梅县客家话）

（30）<u>织一件毛衣分 / 拿佢</u>。织一件毛衣给他。（连城客家话）[11]

（31）姨姨<u>送蜀合花瓶乞我</u>。阿姨送了一对花瓶给我。（福州话）

（32）我<u>写一张批护伊</u>。我写一封信给他。（福建平和闽语）

（33）君牧个毛病，亏得我<u>荐仔个医生拨俚</u>，吃仔两贴药，难好点哉。君牧的病，幸亏我给他推荐了个大夫，吃了两帖药，现在好些了。（苏州话）

（34）买拨辣我一根项链，今年又<u>送一只戒子拨我</u>。他买给我一条项链，今年又送给我一个戒指。（上海话）

以上方言表示给予义的动词分别是"畀"（粤语）、"分、拿"（客家话）、"乞、护"（闽语）、"拨"（吴语），他们与 N_2 组合后，均分布在主要动词之后。

当今北京话以使用 S_3 居多，如：

（35）旅行社<u>给大伙儿送了份纪念品</u>。

（36）<u>给他取了五千块钱</u>。

（37）春儿<u>给老爷子沏了壶龙井</u>。

西北方言基本使用 S_3[12]，例如：

（38）你<u>给尕娃拿个馍馍</u>。你给孩子拿个馒头。（西宁话）

（39）楼上老回回<u>给我炸了一袋子油香</u>。楼上的老回民给我炸了一袋油香。（银川话）

（40）他<u>给我发给了一个证明</u>。他给我发了一个证明。（兰州话）

（41）你<u>娃娃哈小人书哈买给</u>。你给孩子买本小人书。（河州话）[13]

（42）哥<u>给她拿了个勺勺子</u>。哥哥给她拿了个勺子。（新疆乌鲁木齐回族方言，简称"乌回话"）

西宁话、银川话、兰州话、河州话、乌回话等西北方言只用 S_3，不用 S_2，在 S_2、S_3 的选择上，比北京话更纯粹。

我们对泸州等 18 个西南官话区的方言点进行调查，发现这些方言同时使用 S_2 和 S_3，只是使用频率有所不同：有些地区较常使用 S_3，如四川泸州、德阳、资中、贵州毕节、黔南、重庆云阳、渝北、武汉汉口、襄阳、荆州、荆州石首、宜昌、宜昌五峰、恩施建始、利川忠路等；而贵阳更倾向使用 S_2；有些地区则没有明显倾向，如达州大竹、绵阳江油。略举三例如下：

（43）我跟 / 给你送几本书。| 我送几本书跟 / 给你。我送几本书给你。

（44）跟/给他拿个苹果。| 拿个苹果跟/给他。给他拿一个苹果。

（45）跟/给叔叔倒杯水。| 倒杯水跟/给叔叔。给叔叔倒杯水。

由此可见，当今汉语方言在S_2和S_3的使用上存在地域差异，粤语、客家话、闽语、吴语等典型的南方方言（以下简称"南部方言"）多用S_2，不用S_3；北京话及西北方言（以下简称"北部方言"）主要使用S_3，有些甚至只使用S_3；西南官话区诸方言（以下简称"西南方言"）则同时使用S_2和S_3。这三类方言对S_2和S_3的选择，与南部官话、北京官话、西南官话三种文献的S_2和S_3分布情况是相对应的。

我们认为，官话文献中S_2和S_3的分布差异应当看作方言类型差异在共同语层面上的投射。不同地域方言背景的作家在写作时，不自觉地将各自母语的语法特点迁移到作品中，在官话文献中体现出了S_2和S_3的地域差异，形成了琉球官话课本等南部官话文献和《红》等北京官话文献中S_2和S_3分布对立的现象。西南地区的传教士编写文献时，主观上就追求最大程度地保留云、贵、川地区方言的语法特征，他们编写的西南官话文献同时使用S_2和S_3，也就十分自然了。

3．普通话实际使用中S_2、S_3分布情况及产生原因

事实上，S_2、S_3在共同语层面的分布差异不仅存在于文献中，在当今汉民族共同语——普通话的实际使用中也存在着相应的差异。

2012年10月，我们在广东中山大学不同专业新生中调查普通话S_2和S_3的使用情况。问卷分别列出由动词V_a、V_b、V_c组成的S_2和S_3两组句子，调查被访者在说普通话时这两组句子的使用情况。我们向新生随机发放326份问卷，回收有效问卷293份。在有效问卷中，母语为南部方言的120位，母语为北部方言的35位，母语为西南方言的53人。[14] 结果表明，120位南部方言背景的被访者中有97位选择"更倾向使用S_2"（约为80.8%，包括只使用S_2及更常用S_2两种情况），35位北部方言背景的被访者中有30位选择"更倾向使用S_3"（约占85.7%，包括只使用S_3及更常用S_3两种情况），53位西南方言背景的被访者中选择"更倾向使用S_2""更倾向使用S_3"各有23位（均约为43.4%）。也就是说，在说普通话时，以不同方言为母语的被访者对S_2和S_3做出了不同的选择：南部方言区的被访者主要使用S_2，北部方言区的被访者主要使用S_3，西南方言区的被访者的S_2和S_3使用频率相当。也就是说，普通话在实际使用中受到使用者母语方言的影响产生不同的"变体"。使用者将各自母语方言的语法特征迁移

至普通话中，使得其普通话也呈现出相对应的地域特征。这种地域特征与三种官话文献中 S_2 和 S_3 的分布差异基本一致。

为何不同地域会对 S_2 和 S_3 存在不同选择？我们认为，这与"给"（及等值的给予动词）在不同地域方言中的语法化路径及语义范围不同有关。S_2 中的"给"是弱化动词，带受物对象，表给予；S_3 中的"给"是表服务义的与事介词，介引受益者（李炜、石佩璇 2015），两者性质不同。南部方言与给予动词同形的词如"畀、分、乞、护、拿、拨"等在动词前只能兼表使役义和被动义（李炜、濑户口律子 2007），一般没有表示受益的与事介词用法[15]，其受益义是用另一个与给予动词无关的介词如"同"（粤语、客家话）、"共"（闽语）、"搭"（吴语）等表达的（李炜、王琳 2011）。也就是说，南部方言不接受"* 畀 / 分 / 乞 / 护 / 拿 / 拨你送一本书"（给你送一本书），而接受"同 / 共 / 搭你送一本书"（为你送一本书）的说法，但后者并不表给予义。[16] 南部方言中与给予动词同形的词大多没有发展出受益义的介词，这是南部官话文献、南部方言不使用 S_3，以及受南部方言负迁移影响的普通话不接受 S_3 的原因。[17] 北部方言和西南方言的给予动词发展出表示受益的与事介词用法（李炜、石佩璇 2015；李炜、刘亚男 2015），是给予句 S_3 产生的基础。不同的是，西南官话文献及西南方言的"给 / 跟"和近代汉语的"与"主要功能是"一对一"的对应关系，仅实现了词汇上的更替（李炜、刘亚男 2015）；北京官话文献及北部方言的"给"则不是对近代汉语"与"功能的完全继承，而与北方阿尔泰语的与位格呈现出平行的现象（李炜、石佩璇 2015）。我们认为，北京官话文献和北部方言主要使用 S_3，不能排除是与阿尔泰语接触的结果。[18]

从 S_2 和 S_3 选择差异的角度看，汉语官话和相关方言在语法层面至少存在三种类型：南部型、北部型和中部型。"南部型"，包括以琉球官话为代表的南部官话及相关南部方言（粤、客、闽、南部吴语）；"北部型"，以北京官话为代表的北部官话及其他阿尔泰化程度较深的方言（如西宁话、银川话、兰州话、河州话、乌回话等西北方言）；"中部型"至少包括西南官话及西南方言。事实上，除了给予句，在与事范畴、使役、被动范畴等语法项目上，汉语官话和相关方言的语法层面也存在南、北、中三种类型。对此，我们将继续研究。

附录：方言调查合作人信息

广州话，李健慈，女，33 岁，在广州出生长大、学习、工作、生活。

阳江粤语，刘敏玲，女，25 岁，在阳江出生长大、学习，18 岁后外出。

梅县客家话，叶辉丽，女，35 岁，在梅县出生长大，18 岁后外出。

北京话，王健，男，33 岁，在北京出生长大，18 岁后外出。

西宁话，文祯亚，男，57 岁，在西宁出生长大、学习、工作，40 岁后外出。

银川话，段超，男，30 岁，在银川出生长大，18 岁后外出。

兰州话，第一作者母语，在兰州出生长大，25 岁后外出。

河州话，陈元龙，男，46 岁，在甘肃临夏（古城河州所在地）出生长大、学习、工作。

乌回话，苏健，女，55 岁，在乌鲁木齐市出生长大、学习、工作。

附 注

[1] 胡裕树（1995）认为，"给"等可以直接附着在动词或其他词语后边，构成一个整体，相当于一个动词。据此，我们可以将 S_1 定性为双宾给予句式。

[2] 张敏（2011）将这两者分别称为介宾补语式和介宾状语式。

[3] 朱德熙先生（1979）认为，V_a 分两类：一类是给予义具有不确定性的 V_{a1}，如"写"类、"寄"类动词；一类是含固有给予义的 V_{a2}，如"卖"类动词。V_{a1} 具有不确定性，当它不表给予义时，句中给予义由"给"承担，S_3 句式成立。当主要动词是固有给予义的 V_{a2}，句中的"给"只表服务义，不表给予义。

[4] 琉球官话课本即清中叶琉球国人学习汉语官话的课本，主要作于 18 世纪，其中语料价值较高的有：日本天理大学藏本《官话问答便语》（1703 或 1705）、《白姓官话》（1750）、琉球写本《人中画》（18 世纪中期）、《学官话》（1797）。其中琉本《人中画》由五个故事组成，包括：《风流配》《自作孽》《狭路逢》《终有报》《寒彻骨》，为行文方便，《人中画》的五个故事语料均以首字简称，数字表示每个故事的回数。根据李炜和濑户口律子（2007、2011）、王琳和李炜（2013）、李丹丹（2013）等的考察，琉球官话课本在与事、使役、被动、反身代词等重要语法范畴上具有鲜明的南方地域特征。

[5]《官话》的编写年代较早，语言面貌主要体现汉语近代语法特征（濑户口律子、李炜，2004），主要用"与"表给予。《官话》只有含"与"的 S_2，没有含"与"的 S_3，如：有小孩子奉大人命来拜年，<u>分些果子与他</u>，又<u>分些铜钱与他</u>。

[6]《孽海花》作者曾朴，江苏常熟人，主要在上海、江苏等地活动。《文明小史》作者李宝嘉，江苏常州人，主要在常熟、上海等地活动。鲁迅，浙江绍兴人，少时在南京求学，主要在上海工作、生活。

[7] 改革开放后，北京作为全国政治经济文化中心，社会交流频繁，北京话的面貌有了较大的变化，一些原先"京味"特征鲜明的作家如王朔等也受到了影响（详见李炜，2004）。为保险起见，我们只选取了 20 世纪 60 年代之前的北京官话文献作为研究语料。

[8] 此列数据是 S_2/S_3 的结果。数值大于 1，表示 S_2 用例多于 S_3；数值小于 1，表示 S_2 用例少于 S_3。数值越大，表示 S_2 优势越明显。

[9] S_3 从新兴句式发展到强势句式，除了数量上日益占据优势，功能上也日趋成熟。主要体现

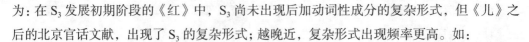

为：在 S₃ 发展初期阶段的《红》中，S₃ 尚未出现后加动词性成分的复杂形式，但《儿》之后的北京官话文献，出现了 S₃ 的复杂形式；越晚近，复杂形式出现频率更高。如：

（1）舅太太便叫人在下首<u>给他铺了个大红坐褥坐下</u>。（《儿》第 27 回，509 页）

（2）我去<u>给您弄碗汤喝</u>，热热地一赶汗，就好啦！（《评》第 1 集，85 页）

S₃ 复杂形式的出现，是 S₃ 给予句成熟的标记之一。有关给予义句式复杂形式拟另文讨论。

[10] 这三种文献均由在我国云、贵、川地区传教的传教士编写。传教士认为这是"华西"地区（the west）的官话（Mandarin）。虽然《西蜀方言》的中文书名为"方言"，但外文使用"官话"（Mandarin）表述。《华西官话汉法词典》（*Dictionnaire Chinois-Français de la Langue Mandarine Parlée Dans L'ouest de la Chine*）是由在四川生活了数年的外国传教士和当地传教士合作编写的，它收纳了生活在四川、云南和贵州的农村人和城市人的日常口语，展现了 100 多年前西南官话的语音、词汇和语法面貌。《西蜀方言》（*West Mandarin, or the Spoken Language of Western China, with Syllabic and English Indexes*）由中国（基督教）内地会（China Inland Mission）传教士 Adam Grainger 编写，该书比较全面地反映了 19 世纪末期西蜀地区的口语读音、词汇、语法及当地的习俗和价值观。《华西初级汉语初阶》（*Chinese Lessons for First Year Students in West China*）由加拿大基督教卫斯理会的启尔德编写，体现了 20 世纪初四川地区西南官话的情况。

[11] 以下连城客家话及译句转引自项梦冰（1997）；福州话及译句转引自陈泽平（2000）；平和闽语及译句转引自庄初升（2000）；苏州话及译句转引自石汝杰（2000）；上海话及译句转引自钱乃荣（2000）。文中调查例句，除标明出处外，均为作者调查所得。

[12] 西北方言在与事系统、使役等多个重要语法项上与北京话相平行；而且，相对于汉语其他方言，西北方言和北京话在历史上和阿尔泰语有过长期而密切的接触（李炜、石佩璇，2015；李炜、王琳，2011；王琳、李炜，2013）。因而在此一并考察。

[13] 兰州话的"给 N₂"和河州话的"N₂ 哈"都位于句子 VP 前，句中的主要动词是且只能是"Vₐ、V_b、V_c"，都是给予句 S₃。主要动词后跟起终点标记作用的"给"，以彰显句子的给予义（李炜，1987）。不同的是，兰州话和北京话、西宁话等一样，用表受益义的与事介词"给"引进 N₂，河州话用表与位格的后置词"哈"来标记。顺便说一下，河州话标记宾格的后置词也用"哈"，标记和同格的后置词用"啦"（例见李炜，1993）。

[14] 在有效问卷中，我们只选取了母语为本文涉及的三类方言的被访者作为调查对象进行统计考察，母语为其他方言的（如华北官话、中原官话、东北官话、江淮官话、赣方言、湘方言等），暂不列入统计。

[15] 个别南部方言点的给予动词也有发展为表示受益的与事介词的情况，如惠来鳌江（闽语）、福清城头（闽语）、温州（吴语）等。但是，这些南部方言中由给予动词发展出来的表受益的介词均纯粹表示受益，并非本文所说的动词为 Vₐ、V_b、V_c 三类，且宾语为有界的可供转移的名词的表给予义的 S₃，如惠来鳌江话中可以说"乞汝捶腰（给你捶背）"，但是

不能说"乞汝倒杯茶（给你倒杯茶）"，也就是说，这些南部方言在非双宾给予句 S_2、S_3 的选择上，依然选择 S_2。

[16] S_3 能表给予义，其中一个重要因素是选取了"给"作为与事介词。"给"的给予动词实义滞留在语法化过程中，因而可以在表受益义的前提下表示给予义（李炜、石佩璇，2015）。南部方言"同/共/搭你送一本书"的与事介词"同、共、搭"等与给予动词无关，不表给予义。

[17] 朱德熙认为，当主要动词为 V_{a2} 时，S_3 不能表给予义。我们也注意到，不少以南部方言为母语的学者也不大接受由 V_a 构成的给予句 S_3，但我们对随机选取的 50 位使用 S_3 的被访者（包括北部方言区和西南方言区）的进一步调研发现，当主要动词为 V_a 时，无论从"只表达""优先表达"还是"可表达"给予义的角度，都以由 V_a 为主要动词的 S_3（V_a）所占的比例最大，给予义最突显。见表3。

表3　普通话实际使用中 S_3 "给予义" 表达情况

	S_3（V_a）	S_3（V_b）	S_3（V_c）
可表"给予义"	26人	19人	16人
优先表"给予义"	15人	10人	7人
只表"给予义"	9人	6人	4人
选择率	100%	70%	54%

[18] 张敏（2011）也注意到北方介宾状语式（即 S_3）的非汉语来源现象。当然，我们也不排除这是北部汉语自身发展的结果。

引用书目

《白姓官话》、琉球写本《人中画》、《学官话》，日本天理大学附属图书馆藏本。《孽海花》，曾朴著，上海古籍出版社，1980。《文明小史》，李宝嘉著，上海古籍出版社，1997。《鲁迅小说集》，鲁迅著，人民文学出版社，2000。《红楼梦》，曹雪芹著，人民文学出版社，1982。《儿女英雄传》，文康著，人民文学出版社，1983。《语言自迩集——19世纪中期的北京话》，威妥玛著，张卫东译，北京大学出版社，2002。《官话指南》，吴启太、郑永邦著，金璞国改订，东京文求堂藏版，1906 年三刊于东京，日本京都大学文学部藏本。《小额》，松友梅著，刘一之标点注释，世界图书出版公司，2011。《燕京妇语》，好文出版社，1992。《评书聊斋志异》（一、二集），陈士和讲述，百花文艺出版社，1980。《华西官话汉法词典》（*Dictionnaire Chinois-Français de la Langue Mandarine Parlée Dans l'ouest de la Chine*），Imprimerie de la Société des Missions Étrangères（外方传教会印书局），香港，1893。《西蜀方言》（*West Mandarin, or the Spoken Language of Western China, with Syllabic and English Indexes*），Adam Grainger, Shanghai:

American Presbyterian Mission Press（上海美华书馆），1900。《华西初级汉语初阶》（*Chinese Lessons for First Year Students in West China*），Omar L. Kilborn, M. A., M. D.（启尔德），the Union University（联合大学），1917。

参考文献

陈泽平（2000）福州方言的介词，《介词》，李如龙、张双庆主编，广州：暨南大学出版社。

胡裕树主编（1995）《现代汉语》（重订本），上海：上海教育出版社。

濑户口律子、李炜（2004）琉球官话课本编写年代考证，《中国语文》第 1 期。

李丹丹（2013）《清琉球官话课本〈人中画〉语法研究》，北京：北京大学出版社。

李炜（1987）兰州方言给予句中的"给"——兼谈句子给予义的表达，《兰州大学学报（社会科学版）》第 3 期。

李炜（1993）甘肃临夏一带方言的后置词"哈""啦"，《中国语文》第 6 期。

李炜（2002）从《红楼梦》、《儿女英雄传》看"给"对"与"的取代，《兰州大学学报（社会科学版）》第 4 期。

李炜（2004）清中叶以来北京话的被动"给"及其相关问题——兼及"南方官话"的被动"给"，《中山大学学报（社会科学版）》第 3 期。

李炜、濑户口律子（2007）琉球官话课本中表使役、被动义的"给"，《中国语文》第 2 期。

李炜、王琳（2011）琉球写本《人中画》的与事介词及其相关问题，《中国语文》第 2 期。

李炜、石佩璇（2015）北京话与事介词"给""跟"的语法化及汉语与事系统，《语言研究》第 1 期。

李炜、刘亚男（2015）西南官话的"跟"——从《华西官话汉法词典》说起，《中国语文》第 4 期。

李炜等（2015）《琉球官话课本语法研究》，北京：北京大学出版社。

钱乃荣（2000）上海方言中的介词，《介词》，李如龙、张双庆主编，广州：暨南大学出版社。

沈家煊（1995）"有界"与"无界"，《中国语文》第 5 期。

石汝杰（2000）苏州方言的介词体系，《介词》，李如龙、张双庆主编，广州：暨南大学出版社。

王琳、李炜（2013）琉球官话课本的使役标记"叫"、"给"及其相关问题，《中国语文》第 2 期。

项梦冰（1997）《连城客家话语法研究》，北京：语文出版社。

张敏（2011）汉语方言双及物结构南北差异的成因：类型学研究引发的新问题，《中国语言学集刊》第四卷第二期，北京：中华书局。

庄初升（2000）闽语平和方言的介词，《介词》，李如龙、张双庆主编，广州：暨南大学出版社。

朱德熙（1979）与动词"给"相关的句法问题，《方言》第 2 期。

朱德熙（1983）包含动词"给"的复杂句式，《中国语文》第 3 期。

（本文发表于《中国语文》2017 年第 6 期，第 662—669 页）